Psychology

Pierre-Auguste Renoir   *The Luncheon of the Boating Party*, 1881   Oil on canvas

More than 100 years after Renoir painted this convivial moment at a riverside restaurant in France, the scene's charm and mystery remain. What, for instance, is going through the mind of the woman facing us, leaning on the railing? The same curiosity that lends added interest to this painting prompts us to want to know more about all aspects of human motivation and behavior. This book describes what the science of psychology has so far revealed about why we think, feel, and act as we do.

Third Edition

Psychology

David G. Myers

Hope College
Holland, Michigan

Worth Publishers

Psychology, *Third Edition*

Copyright © 1986, 1989, 1992 by Worth Publishers, Inc.

All rights reserved

Manufactured in the United States of America

Library of Congress Catalog Card Number: 91-72014

ISBN: 0-87901-506-3

Printing: 2 3 4 5 — 96 95 94 93 92

Development editor: Christine Brune

Design: Malcolm Grear Designers

Art director: George Touloumes

Production editor: Karen Landovitz

Production supervisor: Barbara Anne Seixas

Layout: Patricia Lawson

Picture editor: June Lundborg Whitworth

Line art: Bruce P. Maddocks, Warren Budd, and Demetrios Zangos

Composition and separations: TSI Graphics, Inc.

Printing and binding: Von Hoffmann Press, Inc.

Cover: Pierre-Auguste Renoir, *The Luncheon of the Boating Party* (detail), 1881
Oil on canvas, 51" × 68", © The Phillips Collection, Washington, DC.
(Fine art consultant: Steven Diamond)

Illustration credits begin on page IC-1, and constitute an extension
of the copyright page.

Worth Publishers

33 Irving Place

New York, New York 10003

To Laura

Contents in Brief

Contents

Part One

Foundations of Psychology 1

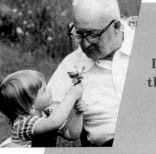

Part Two

Development Over the Life Span 59

Part Three

Experiencing the
World 129

Part Four

Learning and
Thinking 225

Part Five
Motivation and
Emotion 349

Part Six
Personality, Disorder,
and Well-Being 409

Part Seven
Social Behavior   **549**

Preface

The more things change, the more they stay the same. My vision for this third edition of **Psychology** remains the same: *to merge rigorous science with a broad human perspective in a book that engages both the mind and the heart.* I want to set forth clearly the principles and processes of psychology, and to be sensitive to students' needs and interests. My aim is a book that helps students to gain insight into important phenomena of their everyday lives, to feel a sense of wonder about seemingly ordinary human processes, and to see how psychology addresses issues that cross disciplines. I also want to produce a book that conveys to its readers the inquisitive, compassionate, and sometimes playful spirit in which psychology can be approached. Believing with Thoreau that "Anything living is easily and naturally expressed in popular language," I seek to communicate scholarship with crisp narrative and vivid storytelling.

To achieve these goals, I have steadfastly tried to follow eight principles:

1. *To exemplify the process of inquiry.* I strive to show students not just the outcome of research, but how the research process works. Throughout, the book tries to excite the reader's curiosity. It invites readers to imagine themselves as participants in classic experiments. Several chapters introduce research stories as mysteries that progressively unravel as one clue after another is put into place.

2. *To teach critical thinking.* By presenting research as intellectual detective work, I exemplify an inquiring, analytical mindset. Whether they are studying development, cognition, or statistics, students will become involved in, and see the rewards of, critical reasoning. Moreover, they will discover how an empirical approach can help them to evaluate competing ideas and claims for highly publicized phenomena—ranging from subliminal persuasion, ESP, and mother-infant bonding to astrology, basketball streak-shooting, and hypnotic age regression.

3. *To put facts in the service of concepts.* My intention has been not to fill students' intellectual file drawers with facts, but to reveal psychology's major concepts—to teach students how to think, and to offer psychological ideas worth thinking about. In each chapter I place emphasis on those concepts I hope students will carry with them long after they complete the course.

4. *To be as up-to-date as possible.* Few things dampen students' interests as quickly as the sense that they are reading stale news. While retaining psychology's classic studies and concepts, I also present the discipline's most important recent developments. Fifteen percent of the references in this edition are from the 1990s.

5. *To integrate principles and applications.* Throughout—by means of anecdotes, case histories, and the posing of hypothetical situations—I relate the findings of basic research to their applications and implications. Where psychology can illuminate pressing human issues—be they racism and sexism, health and happiness, or violence and war—I have not hesitated to shine its light.

6. *To enhance comprehension by providing continuity.* Many chapters have a significant issue or theme that links the subtopics, forming a thread that ties the chapter together. The Learning chapter conveys the idea that bold thinkers can serve as intellectual pioneers. The Thinking and Language chapter raises the issue of human rationality and irrationality. The Psychological Disorders chapter conveys empathy for, and understanding of, troubled lives. "The uniformity of a work," observed Edward Gibbon, "denotes the hand of a single artist." Because the book has a single author, other threads, such as nature-nurture interaction, weave throughout the *whole* book, and students hear a consistent voice.

7. *To reinforce learning at every step.* Everyday examples and rhetorical questions encourage students to process the material actively. Concepts presented earlier are frequently applied, and thereby reinforced, in later chapters. Pedagogical aids in the margins, such as those found on pages 17, 241, and 552, augment learning without interrupting the text narrative. Each chapter concludes with a narrative summary, defined key terms, and suggested readings attuned to students' interests and abilities.

8. *To convey respect for human unity and diversity.* Time and again, readers will see evidence of our human kinship—our shared biological heritage, our common mechanisms of seeing and learning, hungering and feeling, loving and hating. They will also better understand the dimensions of our diversity— our *individual* diversity in development and aptitudes, temperament and personality, and disorder and health; and our *cultural* diversity in attitudes and expressive styles, child-rearing and care for the elderly, and life priorities.

Third Edition Features

This new edition retains much of the voice, organization, and content of its predecessors. I have, however, thoroughly updated and added to the book (38 percent of the references are new) and revised nearly every paragraph. Following Albert Einstein's dictum that "Everything should be made as simple as possible, but not simpler," my aim has been to make this the most engaging, informative, and pedagogically effective book possible.

The major organizational innovation is a new concluding Chapter 19 on Social Diversity. Recognizing the reality of multicultural life in our shrinking global village, this capstone chapter explores cultural, ethnic, and gender diversity, and shows how people can and do respond when confronting social diversity.

In dealing with topics such as culture and gender, textbook authors usually pursue one of two strategies—to isolate the topics in single compartments, or to have them seep in wherever appropriate. After wrestling with this question, I concluded that both ways are best. The focused coverage of culture and gender in Chapter 19 enables the sort of depth one finds in a distinct presentation of any important topic, such as is given the biological, developmental, or learning perspectives earlier in the book. Yet, as each of these perspectives also pops up everywhere in the book, so do culture and gender. A cross-reference guide to the integrated coverage of culture and gender throughout the book is at the end of Chapter 19. Similar guides are provided for the integrated biological perspective (at the end of Chapter 2), for the coverage of drugs (at the end of Chapter 7), for industrial/organizational psychology (at the end of Chapter 12), and for psychological disorders (at the end of Chapter 15).

Supplements

Psychology is accompanied by a comprehensive and widely acclaimed teaching and learning package. For students, there is *Discovering Psychology*, by Richard Straub (University of Michigan, Dearborn). Students have found this study guide enormously helpful in directing their study and enhancing their learning. Using the SQ3R (survey, question, read, rehearse, review) method, each chapter contains overviews, guided study and review questions, progress tests consisting of factual questions, and "challenge" tests consisting of conceptual and applied questions. Answers to test questions are explained—enabling students to know why each possible answer is right or wrong—and page-referenced to the textbook. *Discovering Psychology* is available as a paperback and on disks, entitled *Diskcovering Psychology*, for use on IBM PC or Macintosh.

The award-winning computer software developed by Thomas Ludwig (Hope College) brings some of psychology's most important concepts and methods to life. *PsychSim: Interactive Graphic Simulations for Psychology* contains 16 programs for use on the IBM PC or Macintosh. Some simulations engage the student as experimenter—conditioning a rat or electrically probing the hypothalamus. Others engage the student as subject—responding to tests of memory or visual illusions. Still others provide a dynamic tutorial/demonstration of, say, hemispheric processing or cognitive development principles. Student worksheets are provided. The new PsychSim programs are significantly enhanced over the previous PsychSim edition, which received the 1990 Educom/NCRIPTAL Higher Education Software Award for "Best Psychology Software"—marking the first time that software specifically designed for introductory psychology has been so honored.

The *Instructor's Resources*, created by Martin Bolt (Calvin College), have been acclaimed by users everywhere. The resources include ideas for organizing the course, chapter objectives, lecture/discussion topics, classroom exercises, student projects, film and video suggestions, and the popular ready-to-use handouts for student participation. The third edition resources package is 30 percent new and 10 percent bigger. It now includes many more color acetate transparencies, and it offers many new demonstration handouts. Worth Publishers has supported Frank Vattano (Colorado State University), in collaboration with the Annenberg/CPB Office and WNET/New York, in making available apt, brief video clips from the PBS series *The Brain* and *The Mind*. Most recently, Frank Vattano, with the consultation of Charles Brewer (Furman University) and myself, edited 38 modules from *The Mind*. Although Worth Publishers makes them available to anyone who teaches psychology or who wishes to purchase a set for other uses, the modules are ordered to correspond to this book.

The **Test Bank** and **Alternate Test Bank**, by John Brink (Calvin College), include factual/definitional questions, conceptual questions, and essay questions. Each question is keyed to a learning objective, page-referenced to the textbook, and rated "easy," "medium," or "difficult." These questions are available on disks in several versions for computerized test generation on IBM PC, Macintosh, or Apple II.

In Appreciation

Aided by more than 200 consultants and reviewers over the last eight years, this has become a far better, more accurate book than one author alone (this author, at least) could have written. My indebtedness continues to each of the teacher-scholars whose influence I acknowledged in the two previous editions.

It gives me pleasure to thank the 74 esteemed colleagues who contributed criticisms, corrections, and creative ideas to this new edition. A first important group of expert psychologists and educators critiqued all or parts of the second edition, offering page-by-page comments and suggestions. For the resulting hundreds of improvements I am indebted to:

Richard Bowen, *Loyola University of Chicago*

John Conklin, *Camosun College*

Bill Davis, *Texas Southmost College*

Gil Einstein, *Furman University*

Steve Fox, *Morehead State University*

Erna Furman, *Cleveland Center for Research in Child Development*

Ross Hartsough, *University of Manitoba*

Brian Healy, *Behavioral and Developmental Pediatrics, Evanston Hospital*

Myra Heinrich, *Mesa State College*

Ann Johnson, *University of St. Thomas*

Harold Kassel, *Richard J. Daley College*

Robert M. Levy, *Indiana State University*

Donald T. Lysle, *University of North Carolina—Chapel Hill*

Salvador Macias III, *University of South Carolina, Sumter*

Robert R. McCrae, *National Institute on Aging*

Deborah R. McDonald, *New Mexico State University—Las Cruces*

Rick Mitchell, *Harford Community College*

Paul Moes, *Dordt College*

Joan Piroch, *University of South Carolina, Coastal Carolina*

Jeanne Riddell, *Grossmont College*

Toby Silverman-Dresner, *William Paterson College of New Jersey*

Nicholas Spanos, *Carleton University*

Michael E. Tirrell, *Stonehill College*

Elliot Valenstein, *University of Michigan—Ann Arbor*

Paul Whitney, *Washington State University*

A second group of reviewers critiqued third edition chapters at various draft stages. For their expertise and many creative suggestions I thank:

Lela Jean Alvers, *Johnson County Community College*

Johnston Beach, *U.S. Military Academy, West Point*

Frank Bernieri, *Oregon State University*

Richard Brislin, *East-West Center: Institute on Culture and Communication*

Robert C. Brown, Jr., *Georgia State University*

David Buss, *University of Michigan—Ann Arbor*

James F. Calhoun, *University of Georgia*

J. Craig Clarke, *Salisbury State University*

Roberta A. Eveslage, *Johnson County Community College*

Howard S. Friedman, *University of California—Riverside*

Lou Fusilli, *Monroe Community College*

Richard M. Gist, *Johnson County Community College*

Irving I. Gottesman, *University of Virginia*

John Governale, *Portland State University*

Rolf Holtz, *Lamar University*

C. Harry Hui, *University of Hong Kong*

Irene Hulicka, *State University of New York College at Buffalo*

Patricia A. Jarvis, *Illinois State University*

Ellen Kimmel, *University of South Florida*

Ken Kotovsky, *Carnegie-Mellon University*

Bruce Landon, *Douglas College*

Phillip Langer, *University of Colorado, Boulder*

Darrell Anthony Luzzo, *Johnson County Community College*

Terry Mason, *Niagara Community College*

Frederick R. Maxwell, *Southwest Missouri State University*

Donald McBurney, *University of Pittsburgh*

Steven E. Meier, *University of Idaho*

Douglas Mook, *University of Virginia*

Joel Morgovsky, *Brookdale Community College*

David Perkins, *Ball State University*

Jean Phinney, *California State University, Los Angeles*

Peter Platenius, *Queen's University*

Michael Poteat, *East Carolina University*

Barbara Quigley, *Morehead State University*

Howard Rachlin, *State University of New York—Stony Brook*

Bradley Redburn, *Johnson County Community College*

Linda Rubin, *Johnson County Community College*

Dave Schroeder, *University of Arkansas, Fayetteville*

Gary Seabaugh, *Johnson County Community College*

John J. Shaughnessy, *Hope College*

James M. Thomas, *University of Nebraska—Omaha*

Tova Vitiello, *Kirkwood Community College*

Frank Vitro, *Texas Women's University*

Scott Vrana, *Purdue University*

Benjamin Wallace, *Cleveland State University*

Gordon Wood, *Michigan State University*

Kaye Young, *North Iowa Area Community College*

Mary Lou Zanich, *Indiana University of Pennsylvania*

Through all three editions, I have benefited from the meticulous critiques, probing questions, and heart-warming encouragement of Charles Brewer (Furman University).

At Worth Publishers—a company whose entire staff is devoted to the highest quality in everything they do—a host of people played key supportive roles. Alison Meersschaert commissioned this book, envisioned its goals and a process to fulfill them, and nurtured the book nearly to the end of the draft first edition. Managing editor Anne Vinnicombe brought the first two editions to fulfillment while meticulously scrutinizing the accuracy, logical flow, and clarity of every page.

I developed this third edition guided by editor Christine Brune. Her warm encouragement, gentle admonitions, and meticulous attention to countless details—while orchestrating with timely precision a whole team of reviewers and editors—made my work as pleasure-filled and pain-free as bookmaking can possibly be. Editor Barbara Brooks repeatedly amazed me with her sensitivity and insightful suggestions on every chapter. Copyeditor Debbie Posner once again displayed her good humor and creativity in helping me apply the finishing touches. Production editor Karen Landovitz displayed impressive competence in guiding the transformation of manuscript into book.

I extend thanks again to Worth's artistic and production team, led by George Touloumes and Barbara Seixas, for crafting a final product that exceeds my expectations.

At Hope College, the supporting team members for this edition included Melissa Johnson and Kim Bundy, who researched, checked, and proofed countless items, and Kathy Adamski, who typed my extensive correspondence to other researchers and teachers without ever losing her good cheer. Working with determined speed and infectious joy, Phyllis and Richard Vandervelde put every word of this book into the word processor, then saw each of these words several more times (along with many new words), before finally coding them all for electronic delivery.

Again, I gratefully acknowledge my writing coach, poet Jack Ridl, whose influence continues to be evident in the voice you will be hearing in the pages that follow.

After hearing many dozens of people say that this book's supportive supplements are the best available, I must again thank Martin Bolt, John Brink, Thomas Ludwig, and Richard Straub for their abundant talents, dedication, and friendship.

Finally, my gratitude goes to the many students and instructors who have used the first two editions and written to offer suggestions or just an encouraging pat on the back. It is for them, and for those students who are about to begin their study of psychology, that I have done my best to introduce as effectively, accurately, and joyfully as I can the field I love.

When the people who paint the Golden Gate Bridge finish, it is time to start over again. So it seems with an introductory textbook in a dynamic field. The ink is barely dry before one begins envisioning the next edition. By the time you read this, information gathering for the fourth edition will be under way. Letters and suggestions from instructors and students will again influence our decisions about what to change and what to keep the same. So, please, do share your thoughts.

David Myers

Department of Psychology
Hope College
Holland, Michigan 49423

To Students

The investment you are about to make in studying psychology has the potential to enrich your life and enlarge your vision. Although many of life's significant questions are beyond psychology, some mighty important ones are illuminated by even a brief course in psychology. Through painstaking research, psychologists have gained insights into brain and mind, depression and joy, dreams and memories. Even the unanswered questions can enrich us, by renewing our sense of mystery about "things too wonderful" for us yet to understand. What is more, your study of psychology can help teach you *how to ask important questions*—how to think critically as you evaluate competing ideas and pop psychology's claims.

Having your life enriched and your vision enlarged (and getting a decent grade, too) requires effective study. These hints may help:

1. *To increase your comprehension and retention, process information actively.* This book is structured to help you process information actively and thus to remember it better. Study each chapter using the SQ3R study method: First *survey* a chapter using the outline found at the beginning of the chapter. As you prepare to read each section, use its heading to form a *question* that you should be able to answer after you've finished the section. Then *read*, actively searching for the answer. Having read a section, *rehearse* in your own words what you read. After completing a chapter, spend time with the *review* found at the end of the chapter to reinforce your understanding of the chapter's organization and main points. Taking time not only to read, but also to survey, question, rehearse, and review, will boost both your understanding and your memory of the material.

2. *Distribute your study time.* One of psychology's oldest findings is that "spaced practice" promotes better retention than "massed practice." You'll remember material better if you space your time over several study periods rather than cram it into one long study blitz. Better to give your study of this text one hour a day, with one day off a week, than six hours at a time. Doing this requires a disciplined approach to managing your time. (Richard Straub explains time management in ***Discovering Psychology***, the study guide that accompanies

this text.) For example, rather than trying to read all of a chapter in a single sitting, read just one of the chapter's sections, and then turn to something else.

3. *In class, listen actively.* As psychologist William James urged nearly 100 years ago, *"No reception without reaction, no impression without . . . expression."* Listen for the main and sub-ideas of a lecture. *Write them down.* Ask questions during and after class. In class, as in your private study, process the information actively and you will understand and retain it better.

4. *Overlearn.* Psychology tells us that "overlearning improves retention." Most of us are prone to overestimating how much we know. You may understand a chapter as you read it, but by devoting extra study time to testing yourself and reviewing what you think you know, you will retain your new knowledge long into the future.

5. *Be a smart test-taker.* If a test contains both multiple-choice questions and an essay question, turn first to the essay. Read the question carefully, noting exactly what the instructor is asking. On the back of a page, pencil in a list of points you'd like to make, and then organize them. Before writing, put aside the essay and work through the multiple-choice questions. (As you do so, your mind may continue to mull over the essay question. Sometimes the objective questions will bring pertinent thoughts to mind.) Then reread the essay question, rethink your answer, and start writing. When finished, proofread to eliminate spelling and grammatical errors that make you look less competent than you are. When reading multiple-choice questions, don't confuse yourself by trying to imagine how each of the alternatives might be right. Try instead to recall the answer *before* reading the alternatives given. Answer the question as if it were a fill-in-the-blank; first cover the answers and complete the sentence in your mind, and then find the alternative that best matches your own answer.

While exploring psychology, you will learn a lot more than techniques for effective study. If you gain a deepened appreciation of how we humans perceive, think, feel, and act, then you may indeed find your life enriched and your vision enlarged. I hope this book will guide you toward that end, and in such fashion as imagined by educator Charles Eliot a century ago: "Books are the quietest and most constant of friends, and the most patient of teachers."

David Myers

Psychology

Part One

Foundations of Psychology

We begin by laying a foundation for our exploration

of psychology. In Chapter 1, I introduce psychology

and its methods and consider what psychology is and

how we do it. Understanding how psychologists ask

questions will prepare us to understand their research

findings and to think critically about everyday events.

In Chapter 2, we consider the biological foundations

of our behavior. We will see how our nervous system,

body chemistry, and brain play a vital role in virtual-

ly everything else this book describes—our develop-

ment as individuals, our abilities to perceive, learn,

and think, and our normal and sometimes disordered

behavior and emotions.

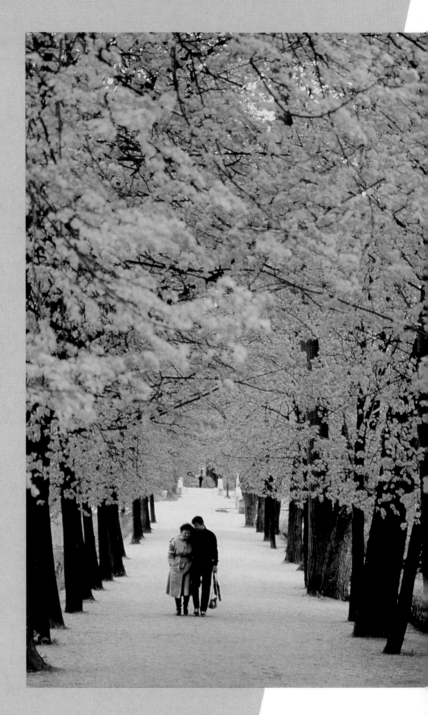

Introducing Psychology

I was relaxing in the barber's black leather chair, enjoying my last haircut before leaving Seattle, when the barber struck up a conversation:

"What do you do?"

"Next week I'll be moving to Iowa to begin graduate school," I replied.

"What are you studying?"

"Psychology."

The haircutting ceased as the friendly barber took a step back, and timidly wondered aloud:

"So what do you think of me?"

For my barber, as for many people whose exposure to psychology comes mostly from popular books, magazines, and TV, psychologists analyze personality, practice psychotherapy, and dispense child-rearing advice.

Do they? Yes, and much more. Consider some of psychology's questions, questions that from time to time you may wonder about:

Have you ever found yourself reacting to something just as one of your parents would—perhaps in a way you vowed you never would—and then wondered how much of your personality you inherited? To what degree are you really like your mother or your father? *To what extent is your parents' influence transmitted through their genes? To what extent through the environment they gave you?*

Have you ever played peekaboo with a 6-month-old infant and wondered why the baby finds the game so delightful? The baby reacts as if, when you momentarily move behind a door, you actually disappear—only to reappear later out of thin air. *What do babies actually perceive and think?*

Have you ever awakened from a nightmare and, with a wave of relief, wondered why we have such crazy dreams? *How often do we dream? Why do we dream?*

Have you ever been to a circus and wondered how someone trained the poodles to dance, the lions to jump through hoops, the chimps to ride bikes? *What are the limits on what we can train animals to do?*

Do you ever get depressed or anxious and wonder whether you'll ever feel "normal"? *What triggers our moods? Can we control our state of mind?*

Why is this child so thrilled with a game of peekaboo with his grandmother?

As this scene in Glasgow, Scotland, makes clear, all of the world's countries are becoming multicultural.

Have you ever worried about how to act among people of a different culture, race, or sex? In what ways are we alike as members of the human family? How do we differ? And, as citizens of multicultural countries and a shrinking global village, *how can we replace mistrust with understanding and cooperation?*

Such questions provide grist for psychology's mill, for psychology is a science that seeks to answer all sorts of questions about us all: how we think, feel, and act.

What Is Psychology?

What are psychology's roots? From what perspectives do psychologists operate? What do they do?

Psychology's Roots

Psychology is a young science with roots in many disciplines, from physiology to philosophy. Wilhelm Wundt, who founded the first psychology laboratory in 1879 at Germany's University of Leipzig, was both a physiologist and a philosopher. Ivan Pavlov, who pioneered the study of learning, was a Russian physiologist. Sigmund Freud, renowned personality theorist, was an Austrian physician. Jean Piaget, this century's most influential observer of children, was a Swiss biologist. William James, author of an important 1890 psychology textbook, was an American philosopher (Figure 1–1).

This list of pioneering psychologists illustrates that psychology has its origins not only in many disciplines, but also in many countries. Today, psychology's researchers and students, like its historic pioneers, are citizens of many lands. In the last few decades, psychology has flourished more in North America, where there are now about 200,000 psychologists, than in Third World countries such as China (2000 psychologists), Nicaragua (500 psychologists), or Nigeria (fewer than 100 psychologists) (Akin-Ogundeji, 1991; Antaki, 1989; DeAngelis, 1988; Vetter, 1989). Worldwide, however, the field is thriving, from Australia and New Zealand to Western Europe to the developing nations.

"I'm a social scientist, Michael. That means I can't explain electricity or anything like that, but if you ever want to know about people I'm your man."

Drawing by Handelsman; © 1986 The New Yorker Magazine, Inc.

From 1984 to 1989, the number of psychological periodicals doubled, from 535 to 1061 (APS Observer, 1989).

Hermann Ebbinghaus *in Germany reports the first experiments on memory (1885).*

Alfred Binet *(shown) and* **Theodore Simon** *devise the first intelligence test for use with Parisian schoolchildren (1905).*

Wilhelm Wundt establishes the first psychology laboratory at the University of Leipzig, Germany (1879).

Margaret Floy Washburn, *the first woman to receive a Ph.D. in psychology, synthesizes research on animal behavior in* The Animal Mind *(1908).*

Edward L. Thorndike *in the United States conducts the first experiments on animal learning (1898).*

American Psychological Association is founded (1892).

1875   1880   1885   1890   1895   1900   1905   1910   1915

G. Stanley Hall, *a student of Wundt's, establishes the first American psychology laboratory at Johns Hopkins University (1883).*

Sigmund Freud *in Austria introduces his psychoanalytic theory in* The Interpretation of Dreams *(1900).*

John B. Watson *in the United States champions psychology as the science of behavior (1913).*

William James *publishes the widely used* Principles of Psychology *in the United States (1890).*

Mary Whiton Calkins *creates paired-associates technique for studying memory; becomes president of American Psychological Association (1905).*

Ivan Pavlov *in Russia begins to publish his classic studies of animal learning (1906).*

Figure 1–1 A timeline of psychology's pioneers, 1879–1913.

With research ranging from recording nerve cell activity to studying the effectiveness of psychotherapy, psychology is difficult to define. Psychology began as the science of mental life. Just over a century ago, Wilhelm Wundt's basic research tool was introspection (self-examination) of one's own emotional states and mental processes. Wundt focused on *inner* sensations, feelings, and thoughts. Thus, until the 1920s, psychology was defined as "the science of mental life."

From the 1920s into the 1960s, American psychologists led by John Watson redefined psychology as "the science of observable behavior." After all, they said, science is rooted in observation. You cannot observe a sensation, a feeling, or a thought, but you *can* observe people's *outer* behavior in reaction to external stimulation.

In the 1960s, psychology began to recapture its initial interest in conscious and unconscious mental processes. Many psychologists now study how our minds process and retain information. To encompass psychology's concern both with overt behavior and covert thoughts and feelings, we define **psychology** as *the science of behavior and mental processes.*

During its short history, psychology has wrestled with a few big issues that will reappear throughout this book. One of the biggest is this: Are we humans affected more by *internal* or *external* influences? Is your eating and sexual behavior mostly "pushed" by internal pressures or "pulled" by external incentives? Is your social behavior better explained by the presence of enduring inner traits or by the temporary demands of external situations? Are your personality and intelligence influenced more by your genes or by your experience? Is your humanness a product of your biology or your culture?

This controversy over the relative contributions of genes and experience, called the **nature-nurture issue**, will reappear throughout this book. Clearly, the influences on us are both internal and external. The issue is their relative importance and how they interact.

This debate is longstanding. The ancient Greek philosophers Plato and Aristotle took opposite sides. Plato assumed that character and intelligence are largely inherited and that ideas are inborn. But Aristotle argued that there is nothing in the mind that does not first come in from the external world through the senses. In the 1600s, philosophers John Locke and René Descartes took up the debate. Locke believed that the mind is a blank slate at birth and that most knowledge comes in through the senses. Descartes believed that knowledge is not dependent on sense experience. In our own time the nature-nurture debate continues. Thus, the question of internal and external influences weaves a thread from the ancient past to our time. Psychology is a young science but an old subject.

Perspectives on Behavior and Mental Processes

Whether psychologists emphasize nature or nurture depends on their theoretical perspective. Each of psychology's major perspectives influences the questions psychologists ask and the kinds of information they consider important. Consider the six perspectives highlighted in Table 1–1.

Throughout this book, important concepts are set in boldface type. As a study aid, you can find these terms with their definitions both at the end of each chapter and at the end of the book.

Table 1-1	*Psychology's Perspectives*	
Perspective	**Focus**	**Emphases**
Biological	How the body and brain create emotions, memories, and sensory experiences	How evolution and heredity influence behavior; how messages are transmitted within the body; how blood chemistry is linked with moods and motives
Psychoanalytic	How behavior springs from unconscious drives and conflicts	Analysis of personality traits and disorders in terms of sexual and aggressive drives or as the disguised effects of unfulfilled wishes and childhood traumas
Behavioral	How observable responses are acquired and changed	How we learn to fear particular objects or situations; how we can most effectively alter our behavior, say, to lose weight or stop smoking
Humanistic	Our capacity to choose our life patterns and not just be driven by unconscious forces or shaped by environment	How we seek maturity and fulfillment; how people experience and understand their own lives
Cognitive	How we process, store, and retrieve information	How we use information in remembering, reasoning, and solving problems
Social-cultural	How behavior and thinking vary across situations and cultures	How as, say, Africans, Asians, Australians, or North Americans, we are alike as members of one human family; how we are different, as products of different environments

Consider how from each perspective we might view an emotion such as anger.

Someone working from a **biological perspective** might study the brain circuits that trigger the physical state of being "red in the face" and "hot under the collar."

Someone working from a **psychoanalytic perspective** might view an outburst as an outlet for unconscious hostility.

Someone working from a **behavioral perspective** might study the facial expressions and body gestures that accompany anger, or determine which external stimuli result in angry responses or aggressive acts.

Someone working from a **humanistic perspective** might want to understand what it means to experience and express anger—from the person's own point of view.

Someone working from a **cognitive perspective** might study how the ways we perceive a frustrating situation affect the intensity of our anger, and how an angry mood affects our thinking.

Someone working from a **social-cultural perspective** might explore how anger and its expression vary across cultural groups.

It's obvious that the biological, psychoanalytic, behavioral, humanistic, cognitive, and social-cultural perspectives describe and explain anger very differently. This need not mean that they contradict one another. Rather, they are six useful ways of looking at the same psychological state. By using all six, we gain a fuller understanding of anger than any single perspective can provide.

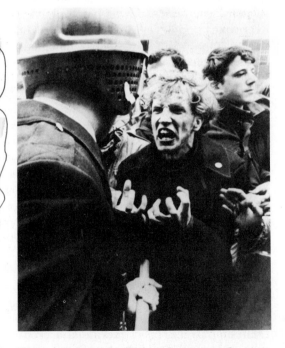

We can study an emotion such as anger from several perspectives, each of which explores different aspects. Taken together, these studies provide a fuller understanding of the emotion.

It's like explaining why polar bears hibernate—because their inner physiology drives them to do so? Because cold environments hinder food gathering during winter? Both perspectives are useful, and complementary.

This important point—that different perspectives can complement one another—is true of all the academic disciplines, each of which provides a different perspective on nature and our place in it. The basic sciences investigate nature's building blocks—atoms, energy forces, living cells—seeking principles based on objective observation. The humanities (literature, philosophy, and the like) address questions of life's meaning and value and use more subjective methods. Psychology lies near the middle of this continuum; it uses scientific methods to explore our thoughts and actions.

Each perspective has its questions and its limits. Differing perspectives are like different two-dimensional views of a three-dimensional object (Figure 1–2).

Each two-dimensional perspective is helpful and can be compatible with the others, but none by itself reveals the whole picture. If you ignore psychology's limits you will be disappointed. Don't expect psychology to answer the ultimate questions posed by Russian novelist Leo Tolstoy (1904): "Why should I live? Why should I do anything? Is there in life any purpose which the inevitable death that awaits me does not undo and destroy?" Instead, expect that psychology will help you better understand why people feel, think, and act as they do. Then you should find the study of psychology both fascinating and useful.

Psychology's Subfields

To many people, psychology is a mental health profession devoted to such practical issues as how to have a happy marriage, how to overcome anxiety or depression, and how to raise children. For **clinical psychologists**—psychologists who study, assess, and treat troubled people—such ideas are apt. They administer and interpret tests, provide psychotherapy, manage mental health programs, and conduct research. By contrast, **psychiatrists** are medical doctors who are licensed to prescribe drugs and otherwise treat physical causes of psychological disorders along with the psychotherapy they often provide.

Many psychologists work outside the mental health professions. Some conduct **basic research** that builds psychology's knowledge base. In the pages to follow we will meet a wide variety of researchers: *biological psychologists* exploring the links between brain and mind; *developmental psychologists* studying our changing abilities from womb to tomb; *personality psychologists* investigating our inner traits.

Other psychologists conduct **applied research** that tackles practical problems. For example, *industrial/organizational psychologists* study and advise on behavior in the workplace. They use psychology's concepts and methods to help organizations select and train employees, boost morale and productivity, and design products and assess people's responses to them.

With perspectives ranging from the biological to the cultural, and with settings from the clinic to the laboratory, psychology has become the meeting place for different disciplines. More and more,

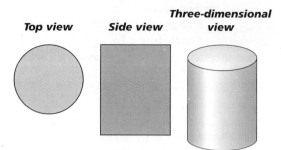

Top view **Side view** **Three-dimensional view**

Figure 1–2 What is this object? One person, looking down from the top, says it is a disk. Another, looking at it from the side, says it is a rectangle. Their differing perspectives seem contradictory. In fact, they are complementary, for we can assemble their respective images into a complete three-dimensional view of the object, a cylinder. The views of behavior and mental processes offered by psychology's different perspectives are often like this: A lot depends on your point of view.

Aided by a sound-analyzing computer, a developmental psychologist studies the acoustical qualities of a baby's cry. An infant's healthy, normal cries signal a healthy brain.

psychology connects with fields ranging from mathematics and biology to sociology and philosophy. And more and more, psychology's methods and findings aid other disciplines. Psychologists teach in medical schools, law schools, and theological seminaries; they work in hospitals, factories, and corporate offices; they engage in interdisciplinary studies such as psychohistory, the psychological analysis of historical characters, and psycholinguistics, the study of the relation between language and the cognitive or behavioral characteristics of its users.

After some of the events of the last decade, one is tempted to propose a new interdisciplinary field: psychoceramics, the study of crackpots.

The Scientific Approach

With its diverse perspectives and wide-ranging subfields, what unifies psychology? It's the *attitudes* and the *methods* with which psychologists approach the unknown.

The Scientific Attitude

Science is much more than a collection of facts. Science is an attitude, a way of thinking about the world. As a scientist, a psychologist aims to approach the world objectively, with an attitude of *open-minded skepticism*— an openness to new ideas along with skeptical scrutiny of all ideas, new and old.

Consider some familiar claims. Can a theater owner make you hungry by flashing on the screen an imperceptibly brief message— EAT POPCORN? Do lie detectors tell the truth? Can astrologers analyze your character and predict your future based on the position of the planets at the moment of your birth? As you will see in the chapters to follow, we can test all such claims objectively. In the arena of competing ideas, we can discover which ones match the facts.

Putting a scientific attitude into practice requires a good measure of *humility*, because it means that we may have to reject our own ideas. In the last analysis, what matters is not my opinion, or yours, but whatever truths nature reveals. If animals or people don't behave as our ideas lead us to expect, then so much the worse for our ideas. This is the humble attitude expressed in one of psychology's early mottos: "The rat is always right."

Historians of science tell us that these attitudes of open-minded skepticism and humility helped make modern science possible. Many of its founders were people whose religious convictions made them humble before nature yet skeptical of any human authority (Hooykaas, 1972; Merton, 1938). Of course, scientists, like anyone else, can have big egos and may cling stubbornly to their preconceptions. None of us can resist viewing nature through the spectacles of our preconceived ideas. Still, the ideal that unifies psychologists with all scientists is the skeptical yet humble and open-minded scrutiny of competing ideas.

"Truth is arrived at by the painstaking process of eliminating the untrue."
Arthur Conan Doyle's Sherlock Holmes

"My deeply held belief is that if a god anything like the traditional sort exists, our curiosity and intelligence are provided by such a god. We would be unappreciative of those gifts . . . if we suppressed our passion to explore the universe and ourselves."
Carl Sagan (1979a)

The Scientific Method

Psychologists apply this scientific ideal as they make observations, form theories, and then refine their theories in the light of new observations.

In everyday conversation, we sometimes use "theory" to mean "mere hunch." In science, a **theory** *explains*; it does so through an integrated set of principles that *organize* and *predict* observable behaviors or events. By organizing isolated facts, a theory simplifies things. There are now so many known facts about behavior—Nobel-laureate psychologist Allen Newell (1988) estimates 3000, including 29 that govern behavior while typing at a keyboard—that we could never hope to remember them all. A theory, however, offers a useful summary.

A good theory of depression, for example, will first organize countless observations concerning depression into a much shorter list of coherent principles. Say we observe over and over that depressed people recall their past, describe their present, and predict their future in gloomy terms. We might therefore theorize that low self-esteem is a prime cause of depression. So far so good: Our self-esteem principle neatly summarizes a long list of facts about depressed people.

Yet no matter how reasonable a theory may sound—and low self-esteem certainly seems a reasonable explanation of depression—we cannot consider it "true" or "valid" until we test it. A good theory implies *testable predictions*, called **hypotheses**. Such predictions give direction to research by enabling us to test and revise the theory. To test our self-esteem theory of depression we might assess people's self-esteem and see whether, as we hypothesized, people who have poorer self-images are indeed more depressed.

In doing so, we should be aware that our theory itself can bias our observations. For example, once we've theorized that depression springs from low self-esteem, we may be tempted to perceive depressed people's comments as self-disparaging. As one check on our biases, we can report our research precisely enough to allow others to **replicate** (repeat) our observations. If other researchers recreate the essence of our study and get similar results, then our confidence in the reliability of our finding grows.

In the end, our theory will be useful if it powerfully organizes and predicts—if it (1) effectively organizes a wide range of observations and (2) implies clear predictions that anyone can use to check the theory or to derive practical applications. (If we boost people's self-esteem, will their depression lift?) Eventually, our theory will probably give way to a revised theory (such as the one on pages 462–464) that better organizes and predicts what we know about depression.

Good theories explain by:
1. *organizing observed facts*
2. *making testable and practical predictions*

A theory implies hypotheses, which predict observations, which in turn we use to refine the theory.

Psychology's Methods

If you want to grasp the essence of psychology and to become a smart consumer of popularized psychology, you must first understand how psychologists ask questions. Figure 1–3 sums up the alternative methods. The research *setting* may be a laboratory or the "real world" (the *field*). The *assessment technique* also varies. In some studies, researchers *observe* and record behavior; in other studies, people *self-report* on their thoughts and behavior. The crucial distinction, though, is among the *research methods*—descriptive, correlational, and experimental. To think critically about claimed psychology findings we need to recognize these designs and to know what conclusions we can rightly draw from each.

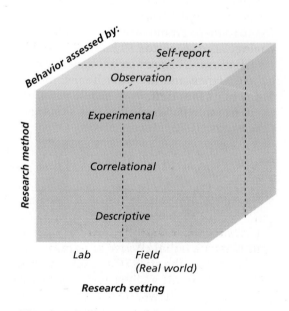

Figure 1–3 The varieties of psychological research. (Adapted from Hendricks & others, 1990.)

Description

The starting point of any science is description. In everyday life, all of us observe and describe people, often forming hunches about why they behave as they do. Professional psychologists are doing much the same, only more objectively and systematically.

The Case Study Among the oldest research methods is the **case study**, in which psychologists study one or more individuals in great depth in the hope of revealing things true of us all. Much of our early knowledge about the brain came from case studies of individuals who suffered a particular impairment after damage to a particular brain region. Sigmund Freud constructed his theory of personality from a handful of case studies. Developmental psychologist Jean Piaget taught us about children's thinking after carefully observing and questioning his own three children. Case studies can, however, be time-consuming. Moreover, any given individual may be atypical, making the case misleading.

The Survey The **survey** method looks at many cases in less depth. A survey asks people to report their behavior or opinions. Questions about everything from sexual practices to opinions about policies and politicians have been put to the public. It's hard to think of a significant question that survey researchers have not asked: Louis Harris (1987) reports that 89 percent of Americans say that they have high stress, 95 percent believe in God, 70 percent favor hand gun registration, and 96 percent say there is something about their appearance they would like to change. Yet surveys have limitations. They are valid only if the questions are clear and unbiased, the respondents are representative of the total group being studied, and their answers are honest.

Wording Effects Asking questions is tricky, because even subtle changes in the order or wording of questions can have big effects. For example, 8 in 10 Americans agree that "Women with young children should be able to work outside the home." But 7 in 10 also agree that "Women should stay home if they have young preschool children" (*Public Opinion*, 1984, 1985). Asked, "Which in your opinion is more to blame for crime and lawlessness in this country—individuals or social conditions?" 6 in 10 blame social conditions. But when asked to agree or disagree that *"Individuals* are more to blame than *social conditions* for crime and lawlessness in this country," more than half agree (Krosnick & Schuman, 1988).

   The moral: Wording survey questions is a delicate matter.

Sampling Like the Harris polls, most surveys sample a target group. If you wished to survey the students at your college you could question them all, but probably there are too many. Instead, you survey a representative sample of the total student **population—** the whole group you want to study and describe. How can you make your sample representative of the population under study? By making it a **random sample**, one in which every person in the entire group has an equal chance of participating.

   To sample the students at your institution randomly, you would *not* send them all a questionnaire, because the conscientious people who return it would not represent a random sample. Rather, you would aim for a representative sample by starting at a random point and selecting, say, every tenth or twentieth person from an

" 'Well my dear,' said Miss Marple, 'human nature is very much the same everywhere, and of course, one has opportunities of observing it at closer quarters in a village.' "
Agatha Christie
The Tuesday Club Murders, 1933

"One final question: Do you own or have you ever owned a fur coat?"

alphabetical listing and then making sure you get responses from virtually all. Better to have a small, representative sample of 100 than a haphazard, unrepresentative sample of 500.

The random-sampling principle also works in national surveys. Imagine that you had a giant barrel containing 60 million white beans thoroughly mixed with 40 million green beans. A scoop that randomly sampled 1500 of them would contain about 60 percent white and 40 percent green beans, give or take 2 or 3 percent. Sampling voters in a national election survey is like sampling the beans; 1500 randomly sampled people provide a remarkably accurate snapshot of the opinions of a nation.

But getting a random sample can be a huge task. Some people will not be home. Others—often 30 percent or more in urban areas—may refuse to cooperate. Worse, some survey takers make little effort to gather a representative (random) sample. Shere Hite's book *Women and Love* reported survey findings based only on a 4.5 percent response rate from mailings to an unrepresentative sample of 100,000 American women. The response was doubly unrepresentative, because not only did she have a modest, self-selected return, but the women initially contacted were members of women's organizations. Nonetheless, "It's 4500 people. That's enough for me," reported Hite. And it was apparently enough for *Time* magazine, which made a cover story of her findings—that 70 percent of women married 5 years or more were having affairs, and that 95 percent of women feel emotionally harassed by the men they love (Wallis, 1987). Evidently it didn't matter that on less publicized surveys, *randomly* sampled American women express much higher levels of satisfaction: Half or more report feeling "very happy" or "completely satisfied" with their marriage; only 3 percent say they are "not at all happy" (Peplau & Gordon, 1985). And only 1 in 10 reports having had an affair during their current marriage (Greeley, 1991).

The moral: Before believing survey findings, consider the sample.

Naturalistic Observation Watching and recording the behavior of organisms in their natural environment is known as **naturalistic observation.** Naturalistic observations range from watching chimpanzee societies in the jungle to observing parent-child interactions in different cultures to recording students' self-seating patterns in the lunchrooms of desegregated schools.

Like the case study and survey methods, naturalistic observation does not *explain* behavior. It simply *describes* it. Nevertheless, description can be revealing. We once thought, for example, that only humans use tools. Then naturalistic observation revealed that chimpanzees sometimes insert a stick in a termite mound and withdraw it, eating the stick's load of termites. Chimps and baboons also use deception (a tool of sorts) to achieve their aims. Psychologists Andrew Whiten and Richard Byrne (1988) repeatedly saw one young baboon pretending to have been attacked by another as a tactic to get its mother to drive the other baboon away from its food.

Through naturalistic observations we have also learned that culture shapes child-rearing. In the Soviet Union, children learn to "get along" and "go along" with their group. American child-rearing more often emphasizes individual achievement and rewards assertiveness. Naturalistic observation also reveals that at school,

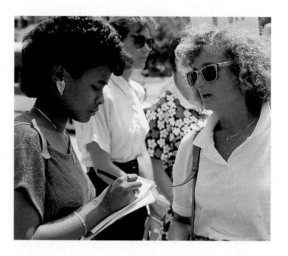

Psychologists use the survey method to gain information about specific groups of people. Well-done surveys use random sampling to gather information representative of the entire population being studied.

"You can see a lot by just looking."
    Yogi Berra

Naturalistic observation can involve activities as different as watching children at play or in the classroom or, as here, studying nesting birds in their natural habitat.

students of different races often shun each other outside the classroom (page 616). This suggests that special efforts to engage students in cooperative play and work may be needed to foster social integration.

Correlation

Describing behavior through case studies, surveys, and naturalistic observation is a first step toward predicting it. When we notice that one trait or behavior accompanies another, we say the two correlate. A **correlation** is a statistical measure of relationship: It reveals how closely two things vary together and thus how well one *predicts* the other. A *positive* correlation indicates a *direct* relationship, meaning that two things increase together or decrease together. If amount of violence viewed on television correlates positively with aggressive social behavior (which it does), then people's TV viewing habits will predict their aggressiveness. A *negative* correlation—equally predictive—indicates an *inverse* relationship: As one thing increases, the other decreases. Our findings on self-esteem and depression illustrate a negative correlation: People who score *low* on self-esteem tend to score *high* on depression.

So, *correlation enables prediction.* But does TV violence *cause* aggression? Does low self-esteem *cause* depression? If, based on the correlational evidence, you assume that they do, you have much company. Perhaps the most irresistible thinking error made both by lay people and by professional psychologists is assuming that correlation proves causation. It does not! If watching TV violence correlates positively with aggressiveness, does this mean that watching TV violence influences aggressive behavior? It may. But might not aggressive people prefer violent programs?

And what about the negative correlation between self-esteem and depression? Perhaps low self-esteem does cause depression. But perhaps instead depression causes people to be down on themselves. Or perhaps self-esteem and depression are causally unrelated. As Figure 1–4 suggests, *both* low self-esteem and depression might be caused by some underlying third factor, such as distressing events or a biological predisposition. Among men, length of marriage correlates positively with hair loss—because both are associated with a third factor, age.

The moral: Although correlation enables prediction, it does not provide explanation. Knowing that two events are correlated need not tell us anything about causation. *Correlation does not imply causation.* Remember this principle and you will be the wiser as you see reports of scientific studies in the news and in this book.

The Appendix describes psychology's statistical tools more fully.

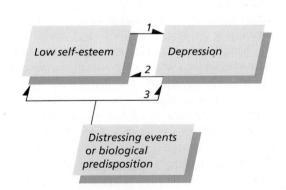

Figure 1–4 People low in self-esteem tend to be more depressed than those high in self-esteem. One possible explanation of this negative correlation is that a bad self-image causes depressed feelings. But, as the diagram indicates, other combinations of cause-effect relationships among these factors are possible.

Experimentation

To isolate cause and effect—to *explain* what helps cause, say, depression—psychologists conduct **experiments**. Experiments enable a researcher to focus on the possible effects of a single factor or two *by holding constant other factors and testing the one or two by manipulating them.* If behavior changes predictably when we vary an experimental factor, then it's having an effect. Note that unlike correlation studies, which uncover naturally occurring relationships, experiments manipulate something to see its effect. To illustrate, let's consider two experiments.

Do Black Sports Uniforms Affect Perceptions? Cornell University psychologists Mark Frank and Thomas Gilovich (1988) noticed that in virtually all cultures from the Orient to Western Europe to central Africa, the color black connotes evil. In movies, the bad guys wear black. It's a "black day" when we get "blackballed" or "blackmailed." Iran's Ayatollah Khomeini reportedly referred to the residence of the U.S. president as the "Black House."

Summarizing these varied observations, Frank and Gilovich proposed a simple, small-scale theory: Black garb suggests evil, cuing us to *perceive* people dressed in black as evil and cuing those who wear black to *act out* their evil image. Frank and Gilovich knew that a useful theory must offer testable predictions. So they derived several hypotheses. First, they predicted that people unfamiliar with football and hockey would rate the black uniforms of National Football League and National Hockey League teams as seeming more evil than nonblack uniforms. Indeed, for both sports, people rated black uniforms as bad, mean, and aggressive.

Second, Frank and Gilovich hypothesized, and found, a positive correlation between black team uniforms and total penalties for aggressive play. In all but 1 of the 17 seasons between 1970 and 1986, the football teams with black uniforms were penalized a disproportionate number of yards. Likewise, in all 16 hockey seasons between 1970–1971 and 1985–1986, the teams wearing black uniforms spent more time in the penalty box. Moreover, when the Pittsburgh Penguins switched to black uniforms during the middle of the 1979–1980 season, their penalties increased from an average of 8 minutes per game to 12 minutes. So, in these two sports at least, there definitely has been a correlation between black uniforms and penalized play.

Remember, a correlation is simply a relationship between two factors—in this case, uniform color and penalties. Correlation cannot prove a cause-effect relationship. Maybe there is no cause-effect connection; maybe organizations wanting an aggressive image simply choose black outfits and hire aggressive players. (For the Hell's Angels, white outfits just won't do.) But can you imagine *possible* causes of this correlation? Frank and Gilovich suggested two: The correlation occurs because referees *perceive* acts by players in black as more violent than similar acts by players not wearing black. Or, players who wear black uniforms *enact* the expected tough image.

In experimenting to evaluate these two possibilities, Frank and Gilovich found, first, that uniform color did indeed affect perceptions. They videotaped two staged football plays in which black- or white-clad defenders drove the ball carrier back several yards and then threw him to the ground, or hit the ball carrier violently in

In traditional westerns you can always tell the good guys from the bad guys by the color of their outfits.

midair. For comparison, the experimenters took the color out of the picture to create a **control condition**— a condition lacking the experimental treatment. When all the players' jerseys appeared dull gray, raters judged the tackles of the white- and black-clad defenders as equally aggressive. In the **experimental conditions**, raters saw the same videotape in full color. With the color on, the raters (knowledgeable fans and professional referees) were more likely to judge the tackles as illegal when committed by players wearing black (Figure 1–5). Thus, the control condition of an experiment provides a baseline against which we can compare the effect of the treatment found in the experimental condition.

In a second experiment, Cornell students came to an experiment on "the psychology of competition." Frank and Gilovich randomly assigned them to wear either black or white jerseys and then invited them to choose some games. When the students donned black rather than white jerseys, they preferred more aggressive games. So, *on average* (such findings tell us only about group trends), wearing black affected not only perceptions but behavior as well.

The Frank and Gilovich experiments were fairly simple. They manipulated just one factor, jersey color. We call this experimental factor the **independent variable** because we can vary it independently of the other factors, such as the age or size of the players. Experimenters examine the effect of one or more independent variables on some measurable behavior, called the **dependent variable** because it can vary depending on what takes place during the experiment. In Frank and Gilovich's first experiment, the dependent variable was the subjects' perceptions of illegal aggression in response to (a) the control condition (videotape with dull gray jerseys) and to (b) the experimental conditions (videotape showing the black vs. white jerseys). Table 1–2 shows the independent and dependent variables in their second experiment.

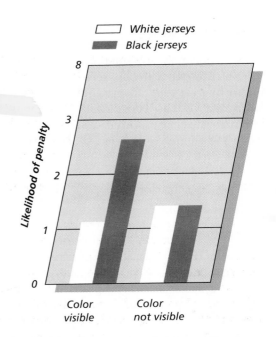

Figure legend: ☐ White jerseys ■ Black jerseys

Figure 1–5 Perceptions of violence. People judged videotaped midair tackles as more likely illegal when enacted by a player wearing black—but only when the color of the jersey was visible. (From Frank & Gilovich, 1988.)

Table 1-2	*The Design of the Second Frank and Gilovich Experiment*

	Condition	Independent variable	Dependent variable
Random assignment of subjects	Experimental condition	Black jerseys	Aggressiveness
	Control condition	White jerseys	Aggressiveness

Remember: An experiment has at least two different conditions, a comparison or *control* condition and an *experimental* condition. In this way it tests the effect of at least one *independent* variable (the experimental factor) on at least one *dependent* variable (the response that is measured).

Note that a key feature of experiments is **random assignment**. If enough individuals of different ages and opinions are randomly assigned to two groups, the random assignment will roughly equalize the two groups in age, opinion, and every other characteristic that could possibly affect the results. With random

Summary of Experimental Design:

Independent variable
The experimental factor you manipulate; the treatment itself.

Dependent variable
The behavior observed; the factor that might be affected by changes in the independent variable.

Experimental condition
The condition that exposes subjects to the independent variable.

Control condition
A condition identical to the experimental one, except subjects are not exposed to the independent variable.

assignment, we can therefore say that if the two groups behave or feel differently at the end of the experiment, it very probably is due to the experiment's independent variable.

Note, too, that in this series of studies a very simple *theory*, inspired by everyday observations, generated *hypotheses* that were confirmed by the *correlation* between uniforms and penalties, which in turn stimulated *experiments* that examined causation. Table 1–3 compares the features of psychology's research methods.

Table 1-3	*Comparing Research Methods*			
Research method	Basic purpose	How conducted	What is manipulated	Where (mostly) conducted
Description	To observe and record behavior	Case studies, surveys, and naturalistic observations	Nothing	Field
Correlation	To detect naturally occurring relationships; to assess how well one variable predicts another	Computing statistical association	Nothing	Field (and lab)
Experimentation	To explore cause and effect	Manipulating a factor and using random assignment to eliminate preexisting differences among subjects	The independent variable	Lab (and field)

How freely can we generalize Frank and Gilovich's findings? Surely we don't perceive Catholic clergy and Hassidic Jews as aggressive, nor does wearing black cause them to act more aggressively. Frank and Gilovich suspect—but can't know without further research—that the effects occur only in situations involving competition and aggressive confrontation.

As so often happens, the answering of one question has led to the asking of another. Scientific inquiry is a voyage of discovery toward a horizon, beyond which yet another horizon beckons.

These concepts—experimental and control condition, independent and dependent variable, random assignment—are important and powerful, yet easily confused. So let's put them to work with another intriguing set of experiments.

"In solving one discovery we never fail to get an imperfect knowledge of others of which we had no idea before, so that we cannot solve one doubt without creating several new ones."
Joseph Priestly
Experiments and Observations on Different Kinds of Air, 1775–1786

Can Subliminal Tapes Improve Your Life? A new generation of entrepreneurs would have you believe so. Mail order catalogs, cable television ads, and bookstores offer tapes with imperceptibly faint messages that will "reprogram your unconscious mind for success and happiness." While underachieving students listen to soothing music, subliminal messages (below one's threshold for hearing) persuade the unconscious that "I am a good student. I love learning." Procrastinators can be similarly reprogrammed to think "I set my priorities. I get things done ahead of time!"

Is there *anything* to these wild and sometimes wacky claims? Might positive subliminal messages help us, even a little? In Chapter 5, Sensation, we will see that subliminal sensation is for real. We do process much information without conscious awareness. And under certain conditions, a stimulus too weak to recognize can subtly affect us.

But does this subtle, fleeting effect extend to the powerful, enduring effects claimed by the subliminal tape merchants? Anthony Greenwald, Eric Spangenberg, Anthony Pratkanis, and Jay Eskenazi (1991) decided to find out. They randomly assigned eager university students to listen daily for 5 weeks to commercial subliminal tapes designed to improve either self-esteem or memory. Then the researchers manipulated an experimental factor. On half the tapes the researchers switched the labels. People given these tapes *thought* they were receiving affirmations of self-esteem, when, actually, they heard the memory enhancement tape. Or they got the memory tape but *thought* their self-esteem was being recharged.

In this experiment, what was the independent variable? The dependent variable? (See page 18.)

Were the tapes effective? Scores on both self-esteem and memory tests, taken before and after the 5 weeks, revealed no effects. Zilch. Nevertheless, those who *thought* they had a memory tape *believed* their memories had improved. Same for those who thought they had a self-esteem tape. Although the tapes had no effects, people *perceived* themselves receiving the benefits they expected. Reading this research, we can hear echoes of the testimonies that adorn the mail order tape catalogs: "I really know that your tapes were invaluable in reprogramming my mind," wrote one thankful customer.

Our natural tendencies to try new remedies when we are in an emotional down can further distort a testimony. When our emotions rebound to normal, we attribute the rebound to something we have done. If 3 days into a cold we start taking vitamin C tablets and find our cold symptoms lessening, the pills may seem more potent than they are. If, after doing exceptionally poorly on the first exam, we listen to a "peak learning" subliminal tape and find our next exam score improved, we may be deceived into crediting the tape. Whether or not a remedy is effective, enthusiastic users will probably endorse it. To find out whether it actually is effective we must experiment.

And that is precisely how we evaluate new drug treatments and new methods of psychological therapy (see Chapter 16, Therapy). In many of these studies, the subjects are "blind" (uninformed) about what treatment, if any, they are receiving. One group might receive the treatment (say, a particular subliminal message or a new drug), while others receive a pseudotreatment—an inert **placebo** (a tape without the expected message, a pill with no drug in it). Often both the subject and the research assistant who collects the data will not know which condition the subject is in. This **double-blind procedure** allows researchers to check the actual effects of a treatment apart from their subjects' and their own enthusiasm for it.

Commonly Asked Questions About Psychology

We have discussed psychology's historical roots, its current perspectives, and its research methods. We have seen how case studies, surveys, and naturalistic observations allow us to describe behavior. We have noted that correlational studies assess the extent of relationship between two factors, indicating how well we can predict one thing, knowing another. And we have examined the logic that underlies experiments, which use control conditions and random assignment of subjects to isolate the effects of an independent variable on a dependent variable.

This is reasonable preparation for understanding what lies ahead. Yet, knowing this much, students often approach psychology with a mixture of curiosity and apprehension. So before we plunge in, let's address some typical questions and concerns.

Aren't Laboratory Experiments Artificial? When you see or hear a report of psychological research, do you ever wonder whether people's behavior in the laboratory has anything to do with their behavior in real life? Does detecting the blink of a faint red light in a dark room have anything useful to say about flying a plane at night? Does our tendency to remember best the first and last items in a list of unrelated words tell us anything about how we remember the names of people we meet at a party? After viewing a violent, sexually explicit film, does an angered man's increased willingness to push buttons he thinks electrically shock a woman really say anything about whether violent pornography makes men more likely to abuse women? Where on earth but a psychological laboratory does someone squint at red lights in a dark room, watch unrelated words flash on a video screen, or push buttons that supposedly deliver electric shock?

Before you answer, consider the intent of laboratory experiments. Far from considering artificiality a problem, the experimenter *intends* the laboratory environment to be a simplified reality—one where important features of everyday life can be simulated and controlled. Like an aeronautical wind tunnel that recreates atmospheric forces under controlled conditions, an experiment enables a psychologist to recreate psychological forces under controlled conditions.

Obviously, deciding whether to push a button that delivers shock is not literally the same as slapping someone in the face. But the principle is the same. The experiment's purpose is not to recreate the exact behaviors of everyday life but to test theoretical principles (Mook, 1983). *It is the resulting principles—not the specific findings—that help explain everyday behaviors.* When psychologists apply laboratory research on aggression to actual violence, they are applying theoretical *principles* of aggressive behavior, principles refined through many experiments. Similarly, it is the *principles* of the visual system, developed from experiments in artificial settings (such as looking at red lights in the dark), that we apply to more complex behaviors such as night flying.

The point to remember: As psychologists, our concerns lie less with particular behaviors than with general principles that help explain many behaviors.

Doesn't Everything Depend on One's Culture? If culture shapes behavior, what can psychological studies done with North Americans—often with White North Americans—really tell us about people in general? As we will see time and again, our cultural diversity greatly affects our specific behaviors and attitudes. Our culture influences our standards of promptness and frankness, our attitudes toward premarital sex and differing body shapes, our tendencies to be casual or formal, and much more. Being aware of such differences can restrain our assuming that others will, or should, think and act as we do. Given the growth in cultural diversity, the need for such awareness becomes urgent.

Answer to question on page 17: In the subliminal tapes experiment, the primary independent variable was the type of subliminal message (self-esteem vs. memory). (This experiment actually had a second independent variable as well: people's beliefs about which tape they received.) The primary dependent variable was improvement on the self-esteem and memory measures.

Yet our shared biological heritage unites us as members of a universal family. The same underlying processes guide humans everywhere. A Western woman who wears cologne may not understand a Masai woman who grooms her hair with animal excrement, but both are responding to cultural standards of beauty. Varying languages—verbal and nonverbal—may impede communication across cultures. Yet all languages share deep principles of grammar, and people from opposite sides of the globe can communicate with a smile or a frown. People in different cultures vary in loneliness, yet across cultures shyness and low self-esteem magnify loneliness (Jones & others, 1985). Japanese prefer their fish raw while North Americans prefer theirs cooked, but the same principles of hunger and taste influence both. It is truly said that we are each in certain respects like all others, like some others, and like no other. Studying people of all races, sexes, and cultures helps us sort these out.

The point to remember: Even when specific attitudes and behaviors vary across cultures, as they often do, the underlying processes are much the same.

What Do Animal Experiments Tell Us About People? Many psychologists study animals because, like animal lovers everywhere, they find them fascinating. Psychologists also study animals to learn about people. Human physiology resembles that of many other animals. That is why animal experiments have led to treatments for human diseases—insulin for diabetes, vaccines to prevent polio and rabies, transplants to replace defective organs.

Likewise, the processes by which humans see, exhibit emotion, and become obese operate in rats and monkeys. To discover more about the basics of human learning, researchers are even studying sea slugs. To understand how a combustion engine works you'd do better to study a lawn mower's engine than a Cadillac's. Humans, like Cadillacs, are more complex. But it is precisely the simplicity of the sea slug's nervous system that makes it so revealing.

Is It Ethical to Experiment on Animals? During the 1980s, a growing animal protection movement protested the use of animals in psychological, biological, and medical research—some 20 million animals annually, according to the National Research Council (1988). Mobilization for Animals, a network of some 400 animal protection organizations, has declared that in psychological experiments animals are shocked "until they lose the ability to even scream in pain, . . . deprived of food and water to suffer and die slowly from hunger and thirst, . . . put in total isolation chambers until they are driven insane or even die from despair and terror," and made "the victims of extreme pain and stress, inflicted upon them out of idle curiosity." Psychologists Caroline Coile and Neal Miller (1984) analyzed every animal research article published in the American Psychological Association journals during the preceding 5 years. They found not one study in which any of these allegations was true. Even when researchers used shock, it usually was of a mild intensity that humans can easily endure on their fingers. During the 1980s, standards of animal care improved further. About 7 percent of psychology's studies have involved animals, 95 percent of which are rats, mice, rabbits, or birds. About 10 percent of these animal studies involved electric shock (Coile & Miller, 1984; Gallup & Suarez, 1985). In British psychology departments, where

One's culture decrees appropriate social behaviors for different situations. This Japanese schoolgirl is simply greeting her teacher, but her behavior would seem unnaturally formal to someone from a Western society.

Is it right that researchers use animals to advance our understanding of how humans function? For animal rights activists, no purpose justifies hurting, frightening, or (as here) manipulating an animal. However, most psychologists and medical researchers believe that animal research is both necessary and ethically justified so long as researchers observe strict standards for animal care and inflict no unnecessary pain.

animal use has dropped by two-thirds since 1977, electric shock is used in but 4 percent of animal studies — all involving rats (Thomas & Blackman, 1991).

Moreover, say researchers, this is not the morality of good versus evil but of compassion for animals versus compassion for people. How many of us would have attacked Pasteur's experiments with rabies, which in causing some dogs to suffer led to a vaccine that spared millions of people, and dogs, from agonizing death? And would we really wish to have deprived ourselves of the animal research that led to effective methods of training retarded children; of relieving fears and depression; and of controlling obesity, alcoholism, and stress-related pain and disease?

Out of the heated debate on this subject, two issues emerge. The basic one is whether it is right to place the well-being of humans above that of animals. In experiments on stress and cancer, is it right that mice get tumors so that people might not? Defenders of research on animals argue that anyone who has eaten a hamburger, worn leather shoes, tolerated hunting and fishing, or supported the extermination of crop-destroying or plague-carrying pests has already agreed that, yes, it is sometimes permissible to sacrifice animals for the sake of human well-being. After all, the most fundamental of rights is the right not to be eaten.

If we give human life first priority, the second issue is the priority given the well-being of animals. So, what safeguards should protect animals? Most researchers today feel ethically obligated to enhance the well-being of captive animals and protect them from needless suffering. They welcomed national animal protection legislation updated by the United States in 1985 and Britain in 1986 and the accompanying regulations and laboratory inspections (Cherfas, 1990; Johnson, 1990).

Ironically, animals have themselves benefitted from animal research. Studies have helped improve their care in laboratories and zoos. By revealing our behavioral kinship with animals, experiments have also increased our empathy with them. At its best, a psychology that is concerned for humans and sensitive to animals can serve the welfare of both.

Is It Ethical to Experiment on People? If the image of people receiving supposed electric shocks troubles you, you may find it reassuring that most psychological research involves no such stress. Blinking lights, flashing words, and pleasant social interactions are the rule.

Occasionally, though, researchers temporarily stress or deceive people. This is done only when judged essential to a justifiable end, such as understanding and controlling violent behavior or studying mood swings. Such experiments wouldn't work if the participants knew all there was to know about the experiment beforehand. Either the procedures would be ineffective or the participants, wanting to be helpful, might try to confirm the researchers' predictions.

Ethical principles developed by the American Psychological Association and the British Psychological Society urge investigators to (1) obtain the informed consent of potential participants, (2) protect them from harm and discomfort, (3) treat information about individual participants confidentially, and (4) fully explain the research afterward. Moreover, most universities today screen research proposals through an ethics committee that safeguards participants' well-being.

"I believe that to prevent, cripple, or needlessly complicate the research that can relieve animal and human suffering is profoundly inhuman, cruel, and immoral."
Psychologist Neal Miller (1983)

"Please do not forget those of us who suffer from incurable diseases or disabilities who hope for a cure through research that requires the use of animals."
Paraplegic psychologist Dennis Feeney (1987)

"'The greatness of a nation can be judged by the way its animals are treated."
Mahatma Gandhi, 1869–1948

Is Psychology Free of Value Judgments? Psychology is definitely not value-free. Researchers' values influence their choice of research topics—whether to study worker productivity or worker morale, sex discrimination or sex differences, conformity or independence. Values can also color "the facts." Our preconceptions can bias our observations and interpretations; sometimes we see what we are predisposed to see. Even the words we use to describe a phenomenon can reflect our values. Whether we label sex acts we do not practice as "perversions" or as "sexual variations" conveys a value judgment. The same holds true in everyday speech, as when one person's "terrorists" are another's "freedom fighters." Both in and out of psychology, labels describe and labels evaluate.

Popular applications of psychology also contain hidden values. When people defer to "professional" guidance about how to live—how to raise children, how to achieve self-fulfillment, what to do with sexual feelings, how to get ahead at work—they are accepting value-laden advice. A science of behavior and mental processes can help us reach our goals, but it cannot decide them.

Aren't Psychology's Theories Mere Common Sense? Perhaps the most common criticism of psychology is that it merely documents the obvious by dressing in jargon what people already know: "So what else is new—you get paid for this?"

In several experiments, psychologist Baruch Fischhoff and others (Slovic & Fischhoff, 1977; Wood, 1979) found that events seem far less obvious and predictable beforehand than in hindsight. Once people learn the outcome of an experiment or an historical episode, it suddenly seems less surprising to them than to people asked to guess the outcome. Finding out that something has happened makes it seem inevitable. So things appear to political columnist George Will (1989), who chides social scientists for "stumbling upon the obvious with a sense of discovery." Psychologists call this 20/20 hindsight vision the **hindsight bias**, also known as the *I-knew-it-all-along phenomenon.*

The phenomenon is easy to demonstrate. Give half the members of a group some purported psychological finding and the other half an opposite result. For example, imagine reading, "Psychologists have found that separation weakens romantic attraction. As the adage says, 'Out of sight, out of mind.'" Could you imagine why this might be? Most people can, and nearly all will then report that the finding is unsurprising.

But what if you had read the opposite: "Psychologists have found that separation strengthens romantic attraction. As the adage says, 'Absence makes the heart grow fonder.'" People given this result can also easily explain it and overwhelmingly see *it* as unsurprising common sense. Obviously, when both a statement and its opposite seem like common sense, there is a problem.

Nevertheless, it would be surprising if many of psychology's findings had *not* been foreseen. As the English philosopher Alfred North Whitehead (1861–1947) once remarked, "Everything important has been said before." Regardless of whether psychological studies reveal that "you're never too old to learn" or "you can't teach an old dog new tricks," the findings will have been anticipated. Should a psychologist discover that we are attracted to people whose traits are different from our own, someone is sure to chortle, "Of course! My grandmother could have told you that 'opposites attract.'" Should it instead turn out that we are attracted to people

People interpret ambiguous information to fit their preconceptions. A duck or a rabbit? (From Shepard, 1990.)

"It is doubtless impossible to approach any human problem with a mind free from bias."
Simone de Beauvoir
The Second Sex, 1953

whose traits are similar to our own, the same person may remind the psychologist, "Everyone knows that 'birds of a feather flock together.'" It's not that common sense is always wrong, but that it so often is a judgment we make *after* we know the results.

You may have noticed this hindsight phenomenon after reading a mystery: The solution, once revealed, appears obvious. We also experience hindsight bias while looking back on history. In contrast to their preelection uncertainty, people *after* a presidential election exude confidence that they could have told you how it would turn out (Powell, 1988). To doctors given case information plus an autopsy report, a cause of death may seem obvious—something they easily could have foreseen, knowing the symptoms. But it is not so obvious to doctors told the same symptoms without the autopsy report (Dawson & others, 1988). From our 1990s vantage point, it may in hindsight seem obvious that Eastern European countries would exchange communism for democracy. But it wasn't obvious to United Nations ambassador Jeanne Kirkpatrick when in 1980 she warned, "The history of this century provides no grounds for expecting that radical totalitarian regimes will transform themselves."

But then again, sometimes psychological findings *do* jolt our common sense. Throughout this book we will see how research has both inspired and overturned popular ideas—about aging, about sleep and dreams, about personality assessment—and how it has surprised us with discoveries about how the brain's chemical messengers control our moods and memories, about animal abilities, about the effects of stress on our body's capacity to fight disease. If some people see psychology as mere common sense, others have an opposite concern—that it is becoming dangerously powerful.

Isn't Psychology Potentially Dangerous? Is it an accident, someone once wondered, that astronomy is the oldest science and psychology the youngest? Exploring the external universe is one thing, but exploring our own inner universe is even more dangerous and threatening. Might psychology be used to manipulate people? Might it become the tool of someone seeking to create a totalitarian *Brave New World* or *Nineteen Eighty-Four*?

Knowledge is a power that, like all powers, we can use for good or evil. Nuclear power has been used to light up cities—and to destroy them. Persuasive power has been used to educate people—and to deceive them. The power of mind-altering drugs has been used to restore sanity—and to destroy it.

Although it has the power to deceive, psychology strives to enlighten. Psychologists are exploring ways to enhance moral development, perceptual accuracy, learning, creativity, and compassion. And psychology speaks to many of the world's great problems—war, overpopulation, prejudice, and crime—all of which are problems of attitudes and behavior. Psychology also speaks to humanity's deepest longings—for love, for happiness, even for food and water. Psychology cannot address all the great questions of life, but it speaks to some mighty important ones.

How to Study This Book

As we will see in Chapter 9, Memory, to master any subject you must *actively process* it. Your mind is not like your stomach, something to be filled passively; it is more like a muscle, which grows

"Life is lived forwards, but understood backwards."
Søren Kierkegaard, 1813–1855

"It is easy to be wise after the event."
Sherlock Holmes, in Arthur Conan Doyle's *"The Problem of Thor Bridge"*

stronger with exercise. Countless experiments reveal that people learn and remember material best when they put it in their own words, rehearse it, and then review and rehearse it again.

The famous **SQ3R** study method incorporates these principles (Robinson, 1970). SQ3R is an acronym for its five steps: *S*urvey, *Q*uestion, *R*ead, *R*ehearse, *R*eview.

To study a chapter, first *survey*, taking a bird's-eye view as you note its headings. Notice how the chapter is organized.

As you prepare to read each section, use its heading to form a *question* that you should answer. For this section, you might have asked, "How can I most effectively and efficiently master this book?"

Then *read*, actively searching for the answer. At each sitting, read only as much of the chapter as you can absorb without tiring. Usually, a single main chapter section will do—the "Commonly Asked Questions" section you just finished, for example.

Having read a section, *rehearse* in your own words what you read. Test yourself by trying to answer your question, rehearsing what you can recall, then glancing back over what you can't recall.

Finally, *review*: Read over any notes you have taken, again with an eye on the chapter's organization, and quickly review the whole chapter.

Survey, question, read, rehearse, review. This book's chapters are organized to facilitate your use of the SQ3R study system. Each chapter begins with a chapter outline that aids your *survey*. Chapter headings and subheadings suggest *questions* you might be asking as you *read*. The material is organized into sections of readable length, and the end of a section is the time to *rehearse* what you have learned. The chapter summaries *review* the chapter's essentials and list key terms to help you check your mastery of important concepts. Survey, question, read. . . .

As you read psychology, you will learn much more than effective study techniques. Psychology teaches us how to ask important questions—how to think critically as we evaluate competing ideas and popular claims. It deepens our appreciation for how we humans perceive, think, feel, and act. By so doing it can enrich our lives and enlarge our vision. Through this book I hope to help guide you toward that end. As educator Charles Eliot said a century ago: "Books are the quietest and most constant of friends, and the most patient of teachers."

Summing Up

What Is Psychology?

Psychology's Roots Beginning with the first psychological laboratory, founded in 1879 by German philosopher and physiologist Wilhelm Wundt, psychology's modern roots can be found in many disciplines and countries. Psychology's basic issues and research activities lead us to define the field as the science of behavior and mental processes.

Perspectives on Behavior and Mental Processes There are many perspectives on human nature. Within psychology, the biological, behavioral, psychoanalytic, humanistic, cognitive, and social-cultural perspectives are complementary. Each has its own purposes, questions, and limits. Together they provide a fuller understanding of mind and behavior.

Psychology's Subfields Psychologists' activities are widely varied, ranging from the diagnoses and therapies of clinical psychologists to the basic research conducted by biological, developmental, or personality psychologists to the applied research of industrial/organizational psychologists.

The Scientific Approach

The Scientific Attitude Scientific inquiry requires a mixture of skeptical scrutiny of competing ideas and open-minded humility before nature.

The Scientific Method Observations stimulate the construction of theories, which organize the observations and imply predictive hypotheses. These hypotheses (predictions) are then tested to validate and refine the theory and to suggest practical applications.

Psychology's Methods

To describe, predict, and explain behavior and mental processes, psychologists use three basic research methods: description, correlation, and experimentation.

Description Through case studies, surveys, and naturalistic observations, psychologists observe and describe behavior and mental processes.

Correlation The strength of relationship between one factor and another is expressed in their correlation. Knowing how closely two things are correlated tells us how much one predicts the other. But correlation is only a measure of relationship; it does not reveal cause and effect.

Experimentation To discover cause-and-effect relationships, psychologists conduct experiments. By constructing a controlled reality, experimenters can manipulate one or two factors and discover how these independent variables affect a particular behavior, the dependent variable. In many experiments, control is achieved by randomly assigning people either to be experimental subjects, who are exposed to the treatment, or control subjects, who are not exposed.

Commonly Asked Questions About Psychology

Aren't Laboratory Experiments Artificial? By intentionally creating a controlled, artificial environment, researchers aim to test theoretical principles. These principles help us to understand, describe, explain, and predict everyday behaviors.

Doesn't Everything Depend on One's Culture? Although attitudes and behaviors vary across cultures, the principles that underlie them vary much less. Cross-cultural psychology explores both our cultural differences and the universal similarities that define our human kinship.

What Do Animal Experiments Tell Us About People? Some psychologists study animals out of an interest in animal behavior. Others do so because knowledge of the physiological and psychological processes of animals enables them to better understand the similar processes that operate in humans.

Is It Ethical to Experiment on Animals? Only about 7 percent of all psychological experiments involve animals, mostly rats, mice, rabbits, and birds. Rarely in these experiments do animals experience pain. Nevertheless, opposition to animal experimentation by animal rights groups has raised two important issues: Is the temporary suffering of even a few animals in medical and psychological research justified if it leads to the relief of human suffering? And if human well-being is indeed given first priority, what safeguards should protect animal well-being?

Is It Ethical to Experiment on People? Occasionally researchers temporarily stress or deceive people in order to learn something important. Professional ethical standards provide guidelines concerning the treatment of human participants.

Is Psychology Free of Value Judgments? Psychology is not value-free. Psychologists' own values can influence their choice of research topics, their theories and observations, their labels for behavior, and their professional advice.

Aren't Psychology's Theories Mere Common Sense? Experiments reveal a hindsight bias also called the I-knew-it-all-along phenomenon: Learning the outcome of a study can make it seem like obvious common sense. But things seldom seem so obvious before the results are known.

Isn't Psychology Potentially Dangerous? Knowledge is power that can be used for good or evil. Applications of psychology's principles have so far been mostly for the good, and psychology addresses some of humanity's greatest problems and deepest longings.

Terms and Concepts to Remember

psychology The science of behavior and mental processes.

nature-nurture issue The longstanding controversy over the relative contributions of genes and experience to the development of psychological traits and behaviors.

biological perspective Emphasizes the influences of heredity and physiology upon our behaviors, emotions, memories, and sensory experiences.

psychoanalytic perspective Emphasizes unconscious drives and conflicts, many of which may stem from childhood experiences.

behavioral perspective Emphasizes environmental influences on observable behaviors.

humanistic perspective Emphasizes people's capacities for choice and growth—studies people's subjective experiences.

cognitive perspective Emphasizes how we process, store, and retrieve information and how we use it to reason and solve problems.

social-cultural perspective Emphasizes the differences and similarities of thinking and behavior in different social situations and cultures.

clinical psychology A branch of psychology involving the assessment and treatment of those who suffer psychological disorders.

①**psychiatry** A branch of medicine dealing with psychological disorders; practiced by physicians and sometimes involving medical (for example, drug) treatments as well as psychological therapy.

②**basic research** Pure science; aims to increase the scientific knowledge base.

③**applied research** Scientific study that aims to solve practical problems.

④**theory** An explanation via an integrated set of principles that organizes and predicts observations.

⑤**hypothesis** A testable prediction, often implied by a theory.

⑥**replication** Repeating the essence of a research study, usually with different subjects in different situations, to see whether the basic finding generalizes to other subjects and circumstances.

case study An observation technique in which one person is studied in depth in the hopes of revealing universal principles.

survey A technique for ascertaining the self-reported attitudes or behaviors of people by questioning a representative, random sample of them.

population All the cases or members in a group from which samples may be drawn for study.

⑦**random sample** A sample that fairly represents a population because each member has an equal chance of inclusion.

⑧**naturalistic observation** Observing and recording behavior in naturally occurring situations without trying to manipulate and control the situation.

★**correlation** A statistical measure that indicates the extent to which two factors vary together and thus how well either factor predicts the other.

experiment A research method in which the investigator manipulates one or more factors (independent variables) to observe their effect on some behavior or mental process (the dependent variable) while controlling other relevant factors.

control condition The condition of an experiment in which the experimental treatment is absent; serves as a comparison for evaluating the effect of the treatment.

Ⓕ**experimental condition** The condition of an experiment that exposes subjects to the treatment, that is, to the independent variable.

Ⓤ**independent variable** The experimental factor that is manipulated; the variable whose effect is being studied.

Ⓗ**dependent variable** The variable that is being measured; in an experiment, the variable that may change in response to manipulations of the independent variable.

random assignment Assigning subjects to experimental and control conditions by chance, thus minimizing preexisting differences between those assigned to the different groups.

Ⓘ**placebo** [pluh-SEE-bo] An inert substance that may be administered instead of a presumed active agent, such as a drug; may trigger the effects believed to characterize the active agent.

Ⓕ**double-blind procedure** An experimental procedure in which both the subject and the staff are ignorant (blind) about whether the subject has received the treatment or a placebo. Commonly used in drug evaluation studies.

hindsight bias The tendency to believe one would have foreseen how something turned out, *after* learning the outcome. (Also known as the *I-knew-it-all-along phenomenon.*)

SQ3R An acronym for *S*urvey, *Q*uestion, *R*ead, *R*ehearse, *R*eview—a method of study.

For Further Reading

The best effect of any book is that it excites the reader to self-activity.
Thomas Carlyle, 1795–1881

At the conclusion of each chapter I suggest several books or articles you could explore for further information.

For many students, the most helpful supplementary source will be *Discovering Psychology* by Richard Straub, the innovative study guide that accompanies this text. It begins with a guide to managing your time and improving the productivity of your study. For each text chapter, *Discovering Psychology* provides learning objectives; a programmed review of the chapter; multiple-choice practice quizzes (with answers—including explanations of what is wrong with the incorrect choices); and a discussion of key terms. My students who have trouble with exams find it a valuable study aid—almost like a tutor.

For an informative free booklet that describes psychology's fields and careers, you can write the American Psychological Association, 1200 Seventeenth Street N.W., Washington, D.C. 20036, and request "Careers in Psychology."

Biological Roots of Behavior

On the time scale of human existence, the last 150 years are only a few ticks of the clock. But that's how recently a scientific understanding of the biological roots of our behavior began to emerge. We have come far since the early 1800s, when a German physician named Franz Gall invented *phrenology,* an ill-fated theory which held that bumps on the skull could reveal our mental abilities and character traits.

Despite its wrong-headedness, phrenology focused attention on the idea that various brain regions have specific functions. In little more than a century, we have also realized that the body is composed of cells; that among these are nerve cells that conduct electricity and "talk" to one another by sending chemical messages across a tiny gap that separates them; and that specific areas of the brain serve specific functions (though not the functions that Gall supposed). You and I are privileged to be living at a time when scientific discoveries about the most basic aspects of our biology and behavior are occurring at an exhilarating pace.

Throughout this book you will find examples of how our biology underlies our behavior and mental processes. Every idea, every mood, every memory, every urge that you or I have ever experienced is fundamentally a biological phenomenon. Our thoughts, emotions, and behaviors are all biological events. By studying the links between biology and psychology, **biological psychologists** are gaining new clues to sleep and dreams, depression and schizophrenia, hunger and sex, stress and disease. We therefore begin our study of psychology with a look at its biological roots.

In his theory called phrenology, Gall speculated that the brain's functions were linked with various bumps on the skull.

"The living body and its brain, on the one hand, and behavior and the mind, on the other, are indissoluble. Therefore, studying and learning about one necessarily implies studying and learning about the other."
Mortimer Mishkin (1986)

The Nervous System

Our **nervous system** is an electrochemical communication system that enables us to think, feel, and act. For scientists, it is a happy fact of nature that the nervous systems of humans and other animals operate similarly. All animal nervous systems are constructed of building blocks called **neurons**, or nerve cells. The neurons of various animals are organized in remarkably similar ways. So similar, in fact, that small samples of brain tissue from a person and a monkey are indistinguishable. This similarity allows researchers to study simple animals, such as squids and sea slugs, to discover how neurons operate and communicate, and to study mammals' brains to understand the organization of our own. Human brains are more complex, but our nervous systems operate according to the same principles that govern the rest of the animal world.

Neurons and Their Messages

Neural Pathways Information travels in the nervous system through three types of neurons. The **sensory** or *afferent* (meaning "inward") **neurons** send information from the body's tissues and sensory organs inward to the brain and spinal cord, which process the information. This processing usually involves a second class of neurons, the **interneurons** of the brain and spinal cord. The central nervous system then sends instructions out to the body's tissues via the **motor** or *efferent* (meaning "outward") **neurons.**

[handwritten: Not Synonomus]

Let's catch our breath with an example. The simplest of neural pathways are those that govern our **reflexes,** our automatic responses to stimuli. A simple reflex pathway is composed of a single sensory neuron and a single motor neuron, which often communicate through an interneuron. One such pathway enables the pain reflex (Figure 2–1). When your fingers touch a hot stove, neural activity excited by the heat travels via sensory neurons to interneurons in your spinal cord. These interneurons respond by activating motor neurons to the muscles in your arm, causing you to jerk your hand away.

To the brain

Sensory neuron
(incoming information)

Interneuron

Spinal cord

Motor neuron
(outgoing information)

Muscle

Skin receptors

Figure 2–1 In this simple reflex, information from the skin receptors travels inward via a sensory neuron to an interneuron in the spinal cord, which sends a signal outward to the muscles in the arm via a motor neuron. Because this reflex involves only the spinal cord, you jerk your hand away from the candle flame *before* your brain responds to the information that caused you to experience pain.

Because the simple pain reflex pathway runs through the spinal cord and out, you jerk your hand from the hot stove *before* your brain receives and responds to the information that causes you to feel pain. Information travels to and from the brain mostly by way of the spinal cord's interneurons. Were the top of your spinal cord severed, you would not feel such pain. Or pleasure. If your spinal cord were severed, your brain would literally be out of touch with your body. Thus, you would lose all sensation and voluntary movement in body regions whose sensory and motor neurons connect with the spinal cord below its point of injury. Male paraplegics (whose legs are paralyzed) are usually capable of an erection (a simple reflex)

"If the nervous system be cut off between the brain and other parts, the experiences of those other parts are nonexistent for the mind. The eye is blind, the ear deaf, the hand insensible and motionless."
    William James
    Principles of Psychology, 1890

if their genitals are stimulated. But, depending on where and how completely the spinal cord is severed, they may have no genital feeling and be genitally unresponsive to erotic images (Kennedy & Over, 1990). To feel bodily pain or pleasure, the sensory information must reach the brain.

Generating a Neural Impulse Each neuron consists of a cell body and one or more branching fibers (Figure 2–2). The fibers are of two types: The **dendrites** receive information from sensory receptors or other neurons, and the **axons** pass it along to other neurons. Unlike the short dendrites, axons may be short or may project through the body up to several feet. The cell body and axon of a motor neuron are roughly on the scale of a basketball attached to a rope 4 miles long. A layer of fatty cells, called the **myelin sheath**, insulates the fibers of some neurons. The sheath helps speed their impulses.

"Dendrite" is derived from the Greek word dendron, *meaning tree.*

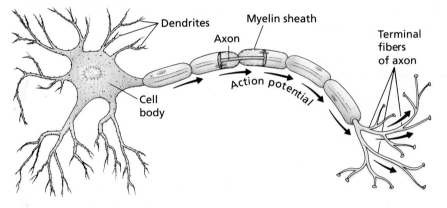

Figure 2–2 A simplified diagram of a motor neuron. Each neuron consists of a cell body and one or more branching extensions or fibers. The dendrites and cell body receive information from sensory receptors or other neurons. If this input exceeds a threshold, the neuron fires an electrical impulse (the action potential) down its axon, whose terminal fibers send this outgoing information to other neurons or to the body's muscles or glands.

A neural impulse fires when the neuron is stimulated by pressure, heat, light, or chemical messages from adjacent neurons. The impulse, called the *action potential*, is a brief electrical change that travels down the neuron, rather like a spark traveling down a firework fuse. The neuron, a miniature decision-making device, receives signals on its dendrites and cell body from hundreds or even thousands of other neurons. The combined signals trigger an impulse if their sum exceeds a minimum intensity, called the **threshold**. If the threshold is reached, the neuron transmits an electrical impulse down its axon, which branches into junctions with hundreds or thousands of other neurons and with the body's muscles and glands.

"I sing the body electric."
  Walt Whitman
  Children of Adam, 1855

Increasing the stimulus above the threshold, however, will not increase the impulse's intensity. (The neuron's reaction is an *all-or-none response*; neurons, like guns, either fire or they don't.) Nor does the strength of the stimulus affect the impulse's speed. Depending on the type of fiber, the impulse travels at speeds ranging from a sluggish 2 miles per hour to a breakneck 200 miles or more per hour. But even this top speed is 3 million times slower than the speed of electricity through a wire. That helps to explain why, unlike the nearly instantaneous reactions of a high-speed computer, it may take a quarter-second or more for you to react to a sudden event, such as a child darting in front of your car.

You can remember the dendrite-axon sequence as DA—District Attorney.

How then do we detect the intensity of a stimulus? How do we distinguish between a gentle touch and a firm hug? Although a strong stimulus cannot trigger a stronger or faster impulse in a neuron, it can trigger more neurons to fire, and to fire more often.

How Do Nerve Cells Communicate? Neurons interweave so intricately that even with a microscope it is hard to see where one neuron ends and another begins. A hundred years ago many scientists believed that the branching axons of one cell fused with the dendrites of another in an uninterrupted fabric. But then British physiologist Sir Charles Sherrington (1857–1952) noticed that neural impulses were taking more time to travel a reflex pathway than they should. Sherrington inferred there must be a brief interruption in the transmission.

We now know that the axon terminal of one neuron is indeed separated from the receiving neuron by a tiny gap less than a millionth of an inch wide. This junction Sherrington called the **synapse,** and the gap is called the synaptic gap or cleft. To the Nobel laureate, Spanish neuroanatomist Santiago Ramón y Cajal (1832–1934), these near-unions of neurons—"protoplasmic kisses," he called them—were one of nature's marvels. How does the nerve impulse execute the protoplasmic kiss? How does it cross the tiny synaptic gap? The answer is one of the important scientific discoveries of our age.

By an elegant mechanism, the axon's knoblike terminals release chemical messengers, called **neurotransmitters**, into the synaptic gap (Figure 2–3). Within 1/10,000th of a second, the neurotransmitter molecules cross the gap and bind to receptor sites on the receiving neuron—as precisely as a key fits a lock. For an instant, the neurotransmitter unlocks tiny "gates" at the receiving site. This allows ions (electrically charged atoms) to enter the receiving neuron, thereby either exciting or inhibiting its readiness to fire.

"All information processing in the brain involves neurons 'talking to' each other at synapses."
Solomon H. Snyder (1984)

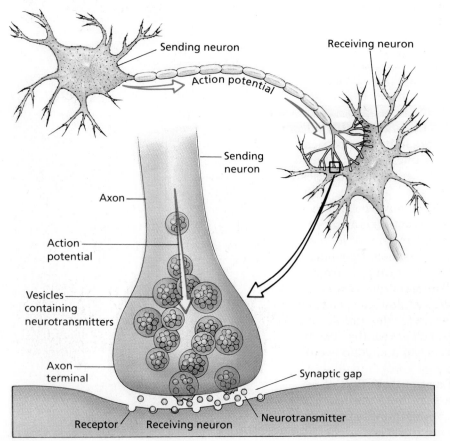

Figure 2–3 Electrical impulses (action potentials) travel from one neuron to another across a junction known as the synaptic gap. When a signal reaches the axon terminal, it stimulates the release of neurotransmitter molecules from the sacs, or vesicles, containing them. These molecules cross the synaptic gap and bind to receptor sites on the receiving neuron. This allows ions—electrically charged atoms (not pictured here)—to enter the receiving neuron, thereby influencing its rate of firing.

Most neurons have a resting rate of random firing that increases or decreases with input from other neurons and from chemicals that affect their sensitivity. Roughly speaking, the neuron is democratic: If it receives more excitatory than inhibitory messages, the cell fires more easily and often. More electrical impulses flash down the axon, releasing more packets of neurotransmitters, which zip across their synaptic gaps to other neurons.

How Do Neurotransmitters Influence Us? The discovery of dozens of different neurotransmitters has created a neuroscience revolution. Why are there so many neural messengers? Are certain neurotransmitters found only in specific places? What are their effects? Can we boost or diminish these effects through drugs or nutritional changes? Could such changes affect our moods, memories, or mental abilities? These are questions that intrigue neuroscience researchers and fascinate those of us who are their spectators.

We now know that a particular neural pathway in the brain may use only one or two neurotransmitters, and that particular neurotransmitters may have particular effects on behavior and emotions. One of the best understood neurotransmitters, **acetylcholine (ACh)**, is the messenger at every junction between a motor neuron and muscle. With powerful electron microscopes, neurobiologists can magnify thinly sliced specimens of tissue enough to see the sacs that store and release ACh molecules. When ACh is released to the muscle cells, the muscle contracts.

If the transmission of ACh is blocked, muscles cannot contract. Curare, a poison that certain South American Indians put on the tips of their hunting darts, occupies and blocks ACh receptor sites, leaving the neurotransmitter unable to affect the muscles. The result is total paralysis. Botulin, a poison that can form in improperly canned food, causes paralysis by blocking the release of ACh. Some nerve gases and insecticides interfere with ACh transmission; this too causes paralysis. By contrast, the venom of the black widow spider causes a flood of ACh. The result? Violent muscle contractions, convulsions, and possible death.

The Endorphins An exciting discovery about neurotransmitters occurred when Candace Pert and Solomon Snyder (1973) attached a radioactive tracer to morphine, allowing them to see exactly where in an animal's brain it was taken up. (Morphine, an opiate drug, elevates mood and eases pain.) Pert and Snyder discovered that the morphine was taken up by receptors in areas linked with mood and pain sensations.

It was hard to imagine why the brain would contain these "opiate receptors" unless it had its own naturally occurring opiates. Why would the brain have a chemical lock, unless it also had a key that would fit it? Researchers soon confirmed that the brain indeed contains several types of neurotransmitter molecules similar to morphine. Named **endorphins** (short for *end*ogenous [produced within] m*orphine*), these natural opiates are released in response to pain and vigorous exercise (Farrell & others, 1982; Lagerweij & others, 1984). They may therefore help explain all sorts of good feelings, such as the "runner's high," the pain-killing effects of acupuncture, and the indifference to pain in some injured people, such as David Livingstone reported in his 1857 *Missionary Travels*:

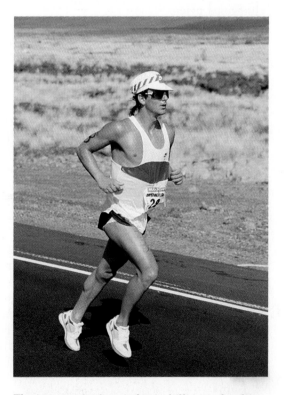

The increased release of pain-killing endorphins contributes to "runner's high," that feeling of increased emotional well-being that sometimes comes to those engaging in endurance sports, such as this triathlon contestant.

I heard a shout. Starting, and looking half round, I saw the lion just in the act of springing upon me. I was upon a little height, he caught my shoulder as he sprang, and we both came to the ground below together. Growling horribly close to my ear, he shook me as a terrier does a rat. The shock produced a stupor similar to that which seems to be felt by a mouse after the first shake of the cat. It caused a sort of dreaminess in which there was no sense of pain nor feeling of terror, though [I was] quite conscious of all that was happening. . . . This peculiar state is probably produced in all animals killed by the carnivora; and if so, is a merciful provision by our benevolent creator for lessening the pain of death.

Drugs and Neurotransmitters If indeed the endorphins lessen pain and boost mood, why not flood the brain with artificial opiates, thereby intensifying the brain's own "feel good" chemistry? One problem is that when flooded with opiate drugs such as heroin and morphine, the brain may stop producing its own natural opiates. When the drug is withdrawn, the brain may therefore be deprived of any form of opiate. For a drug addict, the result is pain and agony that persists either until the brain resumes production of its natural opiates or receives more of the drug.

Cocaine, for instance, floods the brain with substitute excitatory neurotransmitters, producing a "rush." This suppresses the brain's production of its own excitatory neurotransmitters, resulting in a crash of depression when the drug wears off. As we will see in later chapters, mood-altering drugs, from alcohol to cocaine, share a common effect: They trigger lingering aftereffects. For suppressing the body's own neurotransmitter production, nature charges a price.

Such are the risks inherent in trying to improve our mental state by altering our brain's chemistry. Alert to these dangers, researchers try to understand the effects of specific neurotransmitters by experimenting first with animals and only then verifying the results on people. In this way they are discovering how neurotransmitter abnormalities influence depression and schizophrenia.

The good news is that such knowledge is enabling the creation of new therapeutic drugs, such as those used to alleviate schizophrenia. Some do so by mimicking or blocking a particular neurotransmitter (Figure 2–4). Others work by hampering the neurotransmitter's breakdown or its reabsorption. But designing a drug can be harder than it sounds, because some chemicals don't have the right shape to slither through the blood-brain barrier by which the brain fences off unwanted chemicals circulating in the blood. For example, scientists knew that the tremors of Parkinson's disease result from the death of nerve cells that produce a neurotransmitter called dopamine. Giving the patient dopamine as a drug didn't help, though, because dopamine couldn't cross the blood-brain barrier. But L-dopa, a raw material for making dopamine, could sneak through. When patients were injected with L-dopa, their healthy, dopamine-making neurons produced extra dopamine, helping them regain control over their muscles.

Divisions of the Nervous System

The nervous system's building blocks, the neurons, function through several subsystems (Figure 2–5). The **central nervous system (CNS)** includes all the neurons in the brain and spinal cord. But first we will look at the **peripheral nervous system (PNS)**,

Physician Lewis Thomas on the endorphins: *"There it is, a biologically universal act of mercy. I cannot explain it, except to say that I would have put it in had I been around at the very beginning, sitting as a member of a planning committee."*
    The Youngest Science, 1983

Figure 2–4 Drugs that mimic or block natural neurotransmitters. Part (a) shows a neurotransmitter molecule stimulating a receptor. Part (b) shows a drug molecule (an "agonist") that is similar enough to the neurotransmitter to mimic its effects. This may, for example, produce a temporary "high" by amplifying normal sensations of arousal or pleasure (as with opiate drugs and cocaine). Part (c) shows a drug molecule (an "antagonist") enough like the natural neurotransmitter to occupy its receptor site and block its effect, but not similar enough to stimulate the receptor. Some poison and snake venoms paralyze by blocking acetylcholine receptors that produce muscle movement.

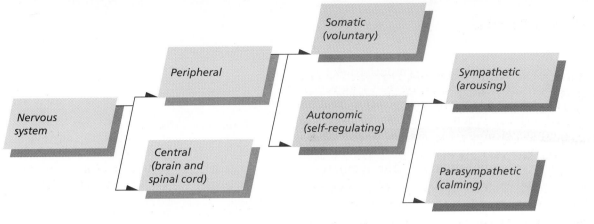

Figure 2–5 The functional divisions of the human nervous system.

which links the central nervous system with the body's sense receptors, muscles, and glands.

Our peripheral nervous system has two components—somatic and autonomic. The **somatic nervous system** transmits *sensory input* (touch and taste, for example) to the CNS from the outside world and directs *motor output*, the voluntary movements of our skeletal muscles. As you reach the bottom of this page, the somatic nervous system will report to your brain the current state of your skeletal muscles and carry instructions back, triggering your hand to turn the page.

Our **autonomic nervous system** influences the glands and the muscles of our internal organs. Like an automatic pilot, it can be consciously overridden. But usually it operates on its own (autonomously) to influence our internal functioning, including our heartbeat, digestion, and glandular activity.

The autonomic nervous system is a dual system (Figure 2–6). The **sympathetic nervous system** arouses us for defensive ac-

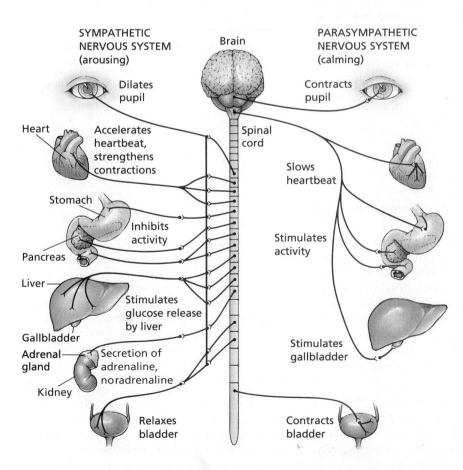

Figure 2–6 The autonomic nervous system controls the more autonomous (or self-regulating) internal functions, including those shown here. Its sympathetic division arouses and its parasympathetic division calms, allowing routine maintenance activity. Most organs are affected by both divisions. For example, sympathetic stimulation accelerates heartbeat while parasympathetic stimulation slows it.

tion. If something alarms or enrages you, the sympathetic system will accelerate your heartbeat, slow your digestion, raise your blood sugar, dilate your arteries, and cool you with perspiration, making you alert and ready for action. When the stress is over, the **parasympathetic nervous system** produces the opposite effects. It calms you down by decreasing your heartbeat, lowering your blood sugar, and so forth. In everyday situations, the sympathetic and parasympathetic nervous systems work together to keep us in a steady internal state.

The Brain

In a jar on a display shelf in Cornell University's psychology department resides the well-preserved brain of Edward Bradford Titchener, a great turn-of-the-century experimental psychologist and proponent of the study of consciousness. Imagine yourself gazing at that wrinkled mass of grayish tissue. Is there any sense in which Titchener is still in there?[1]

You might answer that without the living whir of electrochemical activity there could be nothing of Titchener in his preserved brain. Consider then an experiment about which the inquisitive Titchener himself might have daydreamed. Imagine that just moments before his death, someone removed Titchener's brain from his body and kept it alive by pumping enriched blood through it as it floated in a tank of cerebral fluid. Would Titchener now still be in there? Further imagine, to carry our fantasy to its limit, that someone transplanted the still-living brain into the body of a badly brain-damaged person. To whose home should the recovered patient return?

That we can imagine such questions illustrates how convinced we are that we live in our heads. And for good reason: As Woody Allen has said, the brain is a very important organ. The brain makes possible the functions we attribute to the mind: seeing, hearing, remembering, thinking, feeling, speaking, dreaming. But precisely where and how are such mind functions tied to the brain? Let us first see how scientists explore such questions.

The Tools of Discovery

It is exciting to consider how fast and far the neurosciences have progressed within a lifetime. For centuries, the human brain lay largely beyond the reach of science. The neuron is too small to study with the naked eye, its impulses too faint to record with ordinary electrodes. We were able to feel bumps on the skull, dissect and analyze lifeless brains, and observe the effects of specific brain diseases and injuries. But there were no tools high-powered yet gentle enough to explore the living brain. Now, that has all changed. Whether in the interests of science or medicine, we can selectively destroy tiny clusters of normal or defective brain cells, leaving their surroundings unharmed. We can probe the brain with tiny electrical pulses. We can snoop on the messages of individual neurons and on the mass action of billions. We can see color representations of the brain's energy-consuming activity. These new tools and techniques have made possible a neuroscientific revolution.

The human brain. Unlike other neural fibers, made white by a fatty covering called the myelin sheath, unmyelinated brain tissue is gray.

"I am a brain, Watson. The rest of me is a mere appendix."
    Sherlock Holmes, in Arthur Conan Doyle's
    "The Adventure of the Mazarin Stone"

---

[1] Carl Sagan's *Broca's Brain* (1979a) inspired this question.

Clinical Observations The oldest method of studying brain-mind connections is to observe the effects of brain diseases and injuries. Such observations were first recorded some 5000 years ago. But it was not until the last two centuries that physicians began systematically to record the results of damage to specific brain areas. Some noted that damage to one side of the brain often caused numbness or paralysis on the body's opposite side. Others noticed that damage to the back of the brain disrupted vision, and that damage to the left front part of the brain produced speech difficulties. Gradually, crudely, the brain was being mapped.

Manipulating the Brain Now, however, scientists need not wait for brain injuries to occur randomly. They can electrically stimulate the brain. Or they can surgically produce a brain **lesion** (destruction of tissue) in specific brain areas in animals. For example, a lesion in one well-defined region of a rat's brain reduces eating, causing the rat to starve unless force-fed. Conversely, a lesion in a nearby area produces overeating.

Recording the Brain's Electrical Activity Modern researchers have also learned to eavesdrop on the brain. Modern microelectrodes have tips so small they can detect the electrical activity in a single neuron, making possible some astonishingly precise findings. For example, we can now detect exactly where the information goes after someone strokes a cat's whisker.

This electrical activity in the brain's billions of neurons sweeps in regular waves across its surface. The **electroencephalogram (EEG)** is an amplified tracing of such waves by an instrument called an electroencephalograph. Studying an EEG of the gross activity of the whole brain is like studying the activity of a car engine by listening to the hum of its motor. However, by presenting a stimulus repeatedly and having a computer filter out electrical activity unrelated to the stimulus, one can identify the electrical wave evoked by the stimulus (Figure 2–7). Observing abnormalities in such brain-wave responses is an easy, painless way to diagnose certain forms of brain damage.

Brain Scans Other new windows into the brain give us a Supermanlike ability to see inside the brain without lesioning it. For example, the **CAT (computerized axial tomograph) scan** examines the brain by taking x-ray photographs that can reveal brain

Figure 2–7 An electroencephalograph provides amplified tracings of waves of electrical activity in the brain. Here it is detecting brain response to sound, making possible an early evaluation of what may be a hearing impairment.

damage (Figure 2–8). Even more dramatic is the **PET (positron emission tomograph) scan**. A PET scan depicts the activity of different brain areas by showing each area's consumption of its chemical fuel, the sugar glucose (see illustration, page 46). Active neurons burn more glucose. When a person is given a temporarily radioactive form of glucose, the PET scan measures and locates the radioactivity, thereby detecting where this "food for thought" goes. In this way, researchers can see which brain areas are most active as the person performs mathematical calculations, listens to music, or daydreams.

A new way of looking into the living brain exploits the fact that the centers of atoms, including those in our brains, spin like tops. In **MRI (magnetic resonance imaging)** the head is put in a strong magnetic field, which aligns the spinning atoms. Then a brief pulse of radio waves disorients the atoms momentarily. When the atoms return to their normal spin they release detectable signals, which are processed into computer-generated images of the concentrations of these atoms. The result is a detailed picture of the brain's soft tissues. For example, MRI scans reveal enlarged fluid-filled brain areas in some patients suffering from schizophrenia, a disabling psychological disorder (Figure 2–9).

These new tools have indeed triggered a scientific revolution, most of whose pioneers are still active. To be learning about the neurosciences now is like studying world geography while Magellan was exploring the seas. Every year the explorers announce new discoveries, which also generate new interpretations of old discoveries. Such times can be unsettling, but they are never dull.

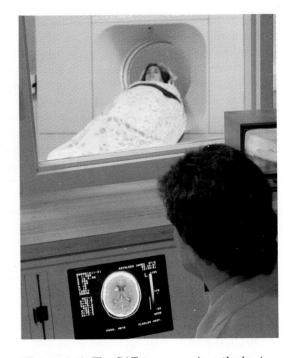

Figure 2–8 The CAT scan examines the brain by taking a series of x-rays from different positions. A computer analyzes the data and arranges them into an image representing a slice through the brain at whatever angle the operator requests.

Figure 2–9 MRI scan of a normal person (left) and a schizophrenia patient (right). Note the enlarged fluid-filled brain ventricles in the brain on the right.

How the Brain Governs Behavior

Brain tool kit in hand, we are ready to explore. Opening the skull, the first thing we might notice is the brain's size. In dinosaurs the brain represents 1/100,000th of the body's weight, in whales 1/10,000th, in elephants 1/600th, in humans 1/45th. It looks like a principle is emerging. But keep on. In mice the brain is 1/40th the body's weight and in marmosets 1/25th. So there are exceptions to the rule of thumb that the ratio of brain to body weight provides a clue to a species' intelligence.

More useful clues to an animal's capacities come from the brain's structures. In primitive vertebrate (backboned) animals, such as sharks, the brain primarily regulates basic survival functions: breathing, resting, and feeding. In lower mammals, such as rodents, a more complex brain enables emotion and greater memory. In advanced mammals, such as humans, the brain processes more information, enabling us to act with foresight.

Right hemisphere

Left hemisphere

Corpus callosum: axon fibers connecting two cerebral hemispheres

Thalamus: relays messages between lower brain centers and cerebral cortex

Hypothalamus: controls maintenance functions such as eating; helps govern endocrine system; linked to emotion and reward

Cerebral cortex: ultimate control and information-processing center

Eye

Optic nerve

Pituitary: an endocrine gland

Reticular formation: arousal system that activates cerebral cortex

Medulla: controls heartbeat and breathing

Spinal cord: pathway for neural fibers traveling to and from brain; controls simple reflexes

Amygdala: neural centers in the limbic system linked to emotion

Hippocampus: a structure in the limbic system linked to memory

Cerebellum: coordinates voluntary movement and balance

Cerebral cortex   Limbic system   Brainstem

Figure 2–10 The structures of the human brain with a simplified view of its three principal regions—the brainstem (spinal cord, medulla, reticular formation), the limbic system (hypothalamus, amygdala, hippocampus), and the cerebral cortex. The brainstem region controls automatic survival functions. The limbic system enables memory, emotion, and behaviors that meet basic needs. The cerebral cortex receives, processes, and retrieves information; makes decisions; and directs voluntary actions.

Roughly corresponding to these three stages of brain evolution are three of the vertebrate brain's principal layers—the brainstem, the limbic system, and the cerebral cortex (Figure 2–10). With the elaboration of each succeeding layer, tight genetic controls relax and the organism's adaptability increases. Thus, amphibians, such as frogs, have a small cortex and operate extensively on prepro-grammed genetic instructions; the larger cortex of mammals offers increased capacities for learning and thinking, enabling them to be more adaptable.

Brain evolution has not greatly altered the basic mechanisms for survival. Rather, as the English neurologist John Hughlings Jackson recognized a century ago, evolution has added new brain systems on top of the old, much as the earth's landscape covers the old with the new. Digging down, one discovers the fossil remnants of the past—brainstem components still performing much as they did for our distant ancestors.

The Brainstem and Basic Survival The **brainstem** is the brain's oldest and innermost region. It is therefore also called the "old brain" or "central core." The brainstem begins where the spinal cord enters the skull and swells slightly, forming the **medulla**. Here lie the controls for your heartbeat and breathing. Here also is the crossover point, where most nerves to and from each side of the brain connect with the opposite side of the body. This peculiar cross-wiring is but one of many surprises the brain has to offer.

"No one has the remotest idea why there should be this amazing tendency for nervous system pathways to cross."
David H. Hubel and Torsten N. Wiesel (1979)

Extending from the rear of the brainstem is the **cerebellum**, with its two wrinkled hemispheres. The cerebellum influences learning and memory, but its most obvious function is muscular control. On orders from the cortex, the cerebellum coordinates voluntary movement. If you injured your cerebellum, you would probably have difficulty walking, keeping your balance, or shaking hands. Your movements would be jerky and exaggerated.

Atop the brainstem sits a joined pair of egg-shaped structures called the **thalamus**. This is the brain's sensory switchboard: It receives information from the sensory neurons and routes it to the higher brain regions that deal with seeing, hearing, tasting, and touching. We can think of the thalamus as being to neural traffic what London is to England's train traffic: Sensory input passes through it en route to various destinations. The thalamus also receives some of the higher brain's replies, which it directs to the cerebellum and medulla.

Inside the brainstem, the **reticular formation** (also known as the *reticular activating system*) extends from the spinal cord right up to the thalamus. This finger-shaped network of neurons helps control arousal and attention. As the spinal cord's sensory input travels up to the thalamus, some of it branches off to the reticular formation, which filters incoming stimuli and relays important information to other areas of the brain (Figure 2–11).

The people who first dissected and labeled the brain used the language of scholars, Latin and Greek. Their words are actually attempts at graphic description: For example, "cortex" means bark, "cerebellum" is little brain, and "thalamus" is inner chamber.

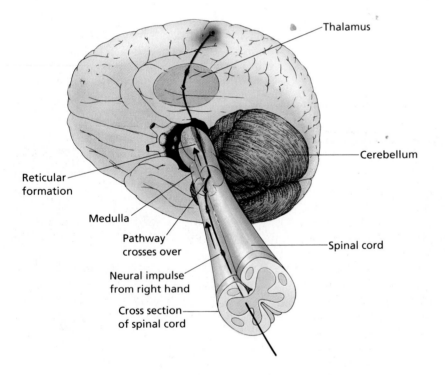

Thalamus

Cerebellum

Reticular formation

Medulla

Pathway crosses over

Spinal cord

Neural impulse from right hand

Cross section of spinal cord

Figure 2–11 We can imagine looking up at the brain from the bottom. First, we see the spinal cord, which then swells to form a tube (the medulla), on which rests a pair of egg-shaped structures (the thalamus), surrounding which, as we will see, are additional layers. Hanging at the back is the baseball-sized cerebellum. Sensory information, say, from your right hand, travels up the spinal cord, crosses over to the left side at the medulla, and is routed to higher brain regions through the thalamus.

In 1949, Giuseppe Moruzzi and Horace Magoun discovered that electrically stimulating the reticular formation of a sleeping cat almost instantly produced an awake, alert animal. Magoun also severed a cat's reticular formation from higher brain regions without damaging the nearby sensory pathways. The effect? The cat lapsed into a coma from which it never awakened. Magoun could clap his hands in the cat's ear, even pinch it; still, no response.

Under the influence of the cerebral cortex, the reticular formation controls not only arousal but also attention. While you are concentrating on this paragraph (or for that matter when you are asleep), you are, thanks to your reticular formation, less sensitive to the sound of someone talking nearby. In the same way, a sleeping cat's brain sorts through countless noises, blocking out the irrelevant ones and arousing the animal if it detects a significant sound. This illustrates one of the recurring themes of this book: our brain's capacity to process information without conscious awareness. Remarkably, our brainstem manages these life-sustaining functions with little or no conscious effort. Whether you are asleep or awake, life functions go on, freeing the higher brain regions to dream, to think, to talk, to savor a memory.

The Limbic System: Emotion, Motivation, and Memory At the border (or "limbus") of the brainstem and the cerebral hemispheres is a doughnut-shaped neural system called the **limbic system**. As we will see in Chapter 9, two limbic system components, the amygdala and the hippocampus, enable memory. For now, let's look at the limbic system's links to emotions, such as fear and anger, and to basic motives, such as those for food and sex. As we will see, the limbic system's influence on emotions and motives occurs partly through its control of the body's hormones.

The Amygdala Two almond-shaped neural clusters in the limbic system, called the **amygdala**, influence aggression and fear. In 1939, psychologist Heinrich Klüver and neurosurgeon Paul Bucy surgically lesioned part of a rhesus monkey's brain that included the amygdala. The operation transformed the normally ill-tempered monkey into the most mellow of creatures. Poke it, pinch it, do virtually anything that normally would trigger a ferocious response, and still the animal remained placid. In later studies with other wild animals, including the lynx, wolverine, and wild rat, researchers noted the same effect. What then might happen if we electrically stimulated the amygdala in a normally placid domestic animal, like a cat? Do so in one spot and the cat prepares to attack, hissing with its back arched, its pupils dilated, its hair on end. Move the electrode only slightly within the amygdala and the cat cowers in terror when caged with a small mouse.

These experiments testify to the amygdala's role in such emotions as rage and fear. Still, we must be careful not to think of the amygdala as *the* control center for aggression and fear. The brain is *not* neatly organized into structures that correspond to our categories of behavior. Aggressive and fearful behavior involve neural activity in all levels of the brain—brainstem, limbic system, and cerebral cortex. Even within the limbic system, stimulating neural structures other than the amygdala can evoke such behavior. Similarly, if you manipulate your car's carburetor, you can affect how the car runs; but that doesn't mean that the carburetor by itself runs the car. It is merely one link in an integrated system.

✦ Given that amygdala lesions change violent monkeys into mellow ones, might such lesions do the same in violent humans? Such "psychosurgery" has produced varied results (Mark & Ervin, 1970; Valenstein, 1986). In a few cases involving patients who suffered brain abnormalities, it reduced fits of rage, though sometimes with devastating side effects on the patient's ability to function in everyday life. For ethical reasons, and because of the uncertainties

You can check your understanding of the essential functions of each of these four brainstem areas by answering these questions: Within what brain region would damage most likely disrupt your ability to skip rope? Your ability to sense tastes or sounds? In what brain region would damage perhaps leave you in a coma? Without the very breath and heartbeat of life? (See page 40.)

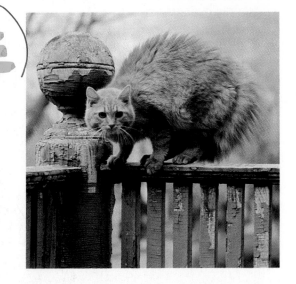

Electrical stimulation of the amygdala provokes physical reactions such as the ones shown by this cat. Such stimulation activates which division of the autonomic nervous system—sympathetic or parasympathetic? (See page 40.)

involved, drastic psychosurgery is highly controversial and seldom used. Perhaps, though, as we learn more about how the brain controls behavior, we will learn to alleviate brain disorders without creating new ones.

The Hypothalamus Another of the limbic system's fascinating structures lies just below *(hypo)* the thalamus, and so is called the **hypothalamus**. By lesioning or stimulating different areas in the hypothalamus, neuroscientists have isolated groups of neurons within it that perform amazingly specific bodily maintenance duties. Some of these neural clusters influence hunger; still others regulate thirst, body temperature, and sexual behavior.

The story of a remarkable discovery about the hypothalamus illustrates how progress in scientific research often occurs—when curious, open-minded investigators make an unexpected observation. Two young McGill University neuropsychologists, James Olds and Peter Milner (1954), were trying to implant electrodes in the reticular systems of white rats. One day they made a magnificent mistake. In one rat, they incorrectly placed an electrode in what was later discovered to be a region of the hypothalamus (Olds, 1975). Curiously, the rat kept returning to the place on its tabletop enclosure where it had been stimulated by this misplaced electrode, as if it were seeking more stimulation. Upon discovering their mistake, the alert investigators recognized that they had stumbled upon a brain center that provides a pleasurable reward.

In a meticulous series of experiments, Olds (1958) then went on to locate other "pleasure centers," as he called them. (What the rats actually experience only they know, and they aren't telling.) When Olds allowed rats to trigger their own stimulation in these areas by pressing a pedal, they would sometimes do so at a feverish pace—up to 7000 times per hour—until they dropped from exhaustion. Moreover, they would do anything to get this stimulation, even cross an electrified floor that a starving rat would not cross to reach food (Figure 2–12).

Answers to questions at top of page 39: the cerebellum, the thalamus, the reticular formation, and the medulla.

The cat on page 39 is aroused via its sympathetic nervous system.

Figure 2–12 A rat readily crosses an electrified grid, accepting the painful shocks, to press a lever that sends electrical impulses to its "pleasure centers." (Adapted from Gazzaniga, Steen, & Volpe, 1979.)

Similar pleasure centers in or near the hypothalamus were later discovered in many other species, including goldfish, dolphins, and monkeys. In fact, animal research reveals both a general reward system that triggers the release of the neurotransmitter dopamine, and specific centers associated with the pleasures of eating, drinking, and sex. Animals, it seems, come equipped with built-in reward systems for activities essential to survival.

"If you were designing a robot vehicle to walk into the future and survive, . . . you'd wire it up so that behavior that ensured the survival of the self or the species —like sex and eating —would be naturally reinforcing."
Candace Pert (1986)

These dramatic findings made people wonder whether humans, too, might have limbic centers for pleasure. Indeed they do. One neurosurgeon has used electrodes to calm violent patients. Stimulated patients report mild pleasure; unlike rats, they are not driven to a frenzy by it (Deutsch, 1972; Hooper & Teresi, 1986).

The hypothalamus and the endocrine system   The hypothalamus exerts its control in two ways: electrochemically, by triggering activity in the autonomic nervous system; and chemically, by secreting **hormones**. Hormones are chemical messengers produced in one tissue that travel through the bloodstream and affect other body tissues. Sometimes the affected tissue is the brain: Hormones acting on the brain influence our interest in sex, food, aggression, and nurturance.

Hormones are secreted by the glands of the **endocrine system** (Figure 2–13), the second of the body's communication systems. Unlike the speedy nervous system, which zips messages from eyes to brain to hand in a fraction of a second, endocrine messages use the slow lane. Several seconds or more may elapse before the bloodstream carries a hormone from an endocrine gland to its target tissue. But these endocrine messages are often worth waiting for, because their effects are usually longer-lasting than the effects of a neural message.

The endocrine system's hormones influence many aspects of our lives, from growth to reproduction, from metabolism to mood, keeping everything in balance while responding to stress, exertion, and internal thoughts. In a moment of danger, for example, the autonomic nervous system will order the **adrenal glands** on top of the kidneys to release *epinephrine* and *norepinephrine* (also called *adrenaline* and *noradrenaline*). These hormones increase heart rate, blood pressure, and blood sugar, providing us with a surge of energy. When the emergency passes, the hormones—and the feelings of excitement—linger awhile.

The most influential gland in our endocrine system is the **pituitary gland**, a pea-sized structure at the base of the brain. One of its hormones has the important task of regulating body growth. Too little of this hormone will produce a midget; too much, a giant. Since 1985, genetic engineering has made possible the commercial production of pituitary growth hormone, making it available to children who suffer pituitary dwarfism. One recent experiment with older adults who had stopped producing growth hormone suggests that injections of this synthetic hormone may have a rejuvenating effect, reversing the normal pattern of muscle loss and fat gain (Rudman & others, 1990).

Besides releasing its own hormones, the secretions of the pituitary influence the release of hormones by other endocrine glands. This makes the pituitary a sort of master gland. Actually, though, its master is the hypothalamus, a key neural system that lies just above it. The hypothalamus, in turn, monitors blood chemistry and takes orders from the whole brain. Thinking about sex (in your brain cortex) can stimulate your hypothalamus to influence your pituitary gland. The pituitary triggers your sex glands to release more sex hormones, which may in turn influence your brain and behavior.

This feedback system (brain → pituitary → other glands → hormones → brain) illustrates the intimate connection of the nervous and endocrine systems. The nervous system directs endocrine se-

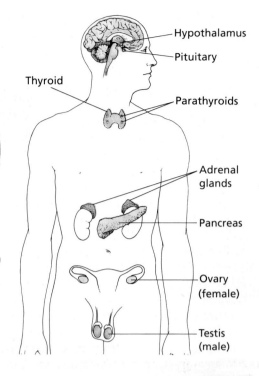

Figure 2–13 The body's major endocrine glands. The pituitary releases hormones that, in turn, regulate the hormone secretions of other glands. The pituitary's master is the hypothalamus, a key neural system. Thus, the hypothalamus is a major link between the nervous and endocrine systems.

Imagine a synthetic pituitary growth hormone that had no harmful side effects. Knowing that taller people tend to be more successful in business, politics, and sports, would you give this drug to your children?

cretions, which affect the nervous system. Conducting and coordinating this electrochemical orchestra is that maestro we call the brain.

Or should we say the mind? Note how fruitless it is to argue whether our brains or our minds are in charge. In the sex example, the mind influences the brain, which influences the body, which influences the mind. Asking whether brain or mind is in control is like asking whether a computer's output is produced by its hardware or its software. The answer is both, acting together as one whole mind-brain system.

The Cerebral Cortex and Information Processing To review, our brainstems are organized much like those of other vertebrates, and our limbic systems are similar to other mammals'. Most of what makes us distinctively human arises from the complex functions of our highly developed cerebral cortex. When the cortex ceases to function, a person vegetates without voluntary movement, without the experiences of sight, sound, and touch, without consciousness.

Structure of the Cortex Opening a human skull and exposing the brain, we would see a wrinkled organ, shaped rather like the meat of an oversized walnut. Covering the brain is the **cerebral cortex**, a ⅛-inch sheet of cells composed of billions of nerve cells and their countless interconnections. To get a feel for the complexity of these interconnections, consider that you could join 2 8-studded Lego bricks 24 ways and 6 bricks nearly 103 million ways. With some 10^{10} neurons, each having roughly 10^4 contacts with other neurons, we end up with something like 10^{14} (100 trillion) cortical synaptic connections. Being human takes a lot of nerve.

The first thing you would notice about the cerebral cortex is its wrinkled appearance. These folds greatly increase the brain's surface area. In rats and other lower mammals, the surface of the cortex is much smoother, which means there is less of this neural fabric.

The cortex is only the thin outer layer of the ballooning left and right cerebral hemispheres. The hemispheres, which account for 80 percent of the brain's weight, are filled with axons that interconnect the neurons of the cortex with those of other brain regions.

We can view each brain hemisphere as divided into four regions, or *lobes*. Starting at the front of your brain and going around over the top, these are: the **frontal lobes** (behind your forehead), the **parietal lobes** (at the top and to the rear), the **occipital lobes** (at the back of your head), and the **temporal lobes** (just above your ears). These lobes are convenient geographic subdivisions separated by *fissures*, or grooves (Figure 2–14). As we will see, the lobes are not distinct operating units. Each lobe carries out many functions, and some functions require the interplay of several lobes.

Functions of the Cortex More than a century ago, autopsies of partially paralyzed or speechless people revealed damage to specific areas of the cortex. But this rather crude evidence did not convince everyone that specific parts of the cortex perform specific functions. After all, if control of speech and movement were diffused across the entire cortex, damage to almost any area might produce the same effect. Likewise, a television would go dead with its power cord cut, but we would be deluding ourselves if we were to think we had "localized" the source of the picture in the cord. This analogy suggests how easy it is to err when trying to localize brain functions.

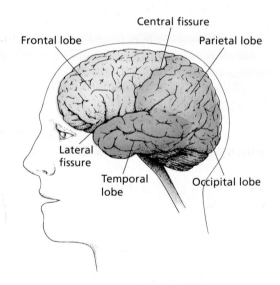

Figure 2–14 The basic subdivisions of the cortex. We can view the cortex as divided into four lobes in each hemisphere, separated by fissures, or grooves.

Motor functions In 1870, German physicians Gustav Fritsch and Eduard Hitzig applied mild electrical stimulation to the cortexes of dogs and made an important discovery: They could make different body parts move. The effects were selective: Stimulation caused movement only when applied to an arch-shaped region at the back of the frontal lobe, running roughly from ear to ear across the top of the brain. This arch we now call the **motor cortex** (Figure 2–15). Moreover, when the researchers stimulated specific parts of this region in the left or right hemisphere, specific body parts moved on the *opposite* side of the body.

A half century ago, neurosurgeons Otfrid Foerster in Germany and Wilder Penfield in Montreal mapped the motor cortex in hundreds of wide-awake patients. The surgeons needed to know the possible side effects of removing different parts of the cortex. So, before putting the knife to the brain, they would painlessly (the brain has no sensory receptors) stimulate different cortical areas and note body responses. Like Fritsch and Hitzig, they found that when they stimulated different areas of the motor cortex at the back of the frontal lobe, different body parts moved. They were therefore able to map the motor cortex according to the body parts it controlled (Figure 2–16). Interestingly, those areas of the body requiring precise control, such as the fingers and mouth, occupied the greatest amount of cortical space.

Neuroscientist José Delgado demonstrated the mechanics of motor behavior. In one monkey, he evoked a smiling response over 400,000 times. In a human patient, stimulation of a certain spot on the left motor cortex triggered the right hand to make a fist. Asked to keep the fingers open during the next stimulation, the patient, whose fingers closed despite his best efforts, remarked, "I guess,

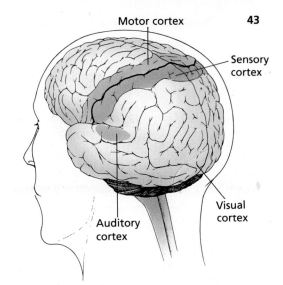

Figure 2–15 The motor cortex, in front of the central fissure, controls voluntary muscle movements. The sensory cortex, to the rear of the central fissure, receives input from the skin and muscles. The occipital lobes at the rear receive input from the eyes. An auditory area of the temporal lobes receives information from the ears.

Figure 2–16 A depiction of the proportion of left hemisphere tissue devoted to each body part in (a) the motor cortex and (b) the sensory cortex. As you can see, the amount of cortex devoted to a body part is *not* proportional to that part's size. Rather, the brain devotes more tissue to sensitive areas and to areas requiring precise control. For example, the fingers have a greater representation in the cortex than does the upper arm.

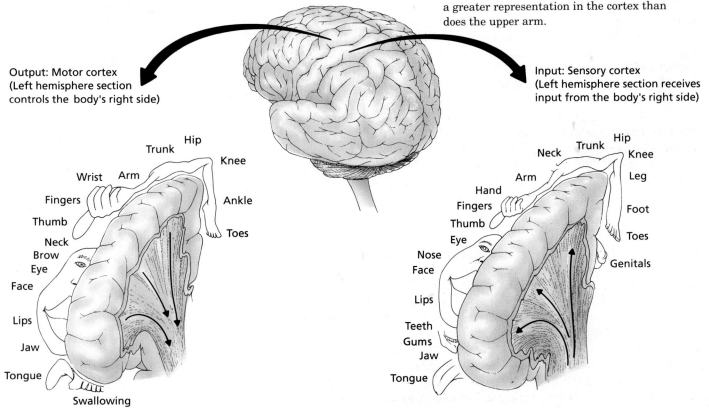

Output: Motor cortex
(Left hemisphere section controls the body's right side)

Input: Sensory cortex
(Left hemisphere section receives input from the body's right side)

Doctor, that your electricity is stronger than my will" (Delgado, 1969, p. 114).

Sensory functions If the motor cortex sends messages out to the body, where do *incoming* messages reach the cortex? Penfield identified a cortical area that specializes in receiving information from the skin senses and from the movement of body parts. This area, parallel to the motor cortex and just behind it at the front of the parietal lobes, we now call the **sensory cortex** (Figure 2–15). Stimulate a point on the top of this band of tissue, and the person may report being touched on the shoulder; stimulate some point on the side, and perhaps the person will feel something on the face.

The more sensitive a body region, the greater the area of the sensory cortex devoted to it; your supersensitive lips project to a larger brain area than do your toes (Figure 2–16). Similarly, rats have a large area of the brain devoted to whisker sensation, owls to hearing sensations, and so forth. If a monkey or a human loses a finger, the region of the sensory cortex devoted to receiving input from that finger branches to receive sensory input from the adjacent fingers, which now become more sensitive (Fox, 1984). As this illustrates, the brain is sculpted not only by our genes but also by our experience.

Further exploration identified where the cortex first receives messages from the other senses (Figure 2–15). At this moment you are receiving visual information in the occipital lobes at the very back of your brain. Stimulated there, you might see flashes of light or dashes of color. So, in a sense, we *do* have eyes in the back of our head. From there the visual information you are now processing goes to other brain areas that specialize in tasks such as identifying words, detecting emotions, and recognizing faces.

Any sound you are hearing right now is processed by the auditory areas in your temporal lobes. Most of this auditory information travels a circuitous route from one ear to the auditory receiving area above your opposite ear. Stimulated there, you might hear a sound.

Association areas So far we have pointed out small areas of the cortex that either receive sensory information or direct muscular responses. In humans, that leaves some three-fourths of the thin wrinkled layer, the cerebral cortex, uncommitted. Neurons in these **association areas** (the gray areas in Figure 2–17) communicate mainly with one another and with the cortical neurons of the sensory and motor areas.

The visual and auditory cortex areas also receive sensory input. Thus, the sensory cortex is sometimes called the somatosensory cortex *to emphasize that its input comes from body (somatic) stimulation.*

Figure 2–17 As animals increase in complexity, there is an increase in the "uncommitted" or association areas of the cortex. These vast areas of the brain are responsible for integrating and acting on information received and processed by sensory areas. (From Rose, 1983.)

Motor areas

Sensory areas

Association areas

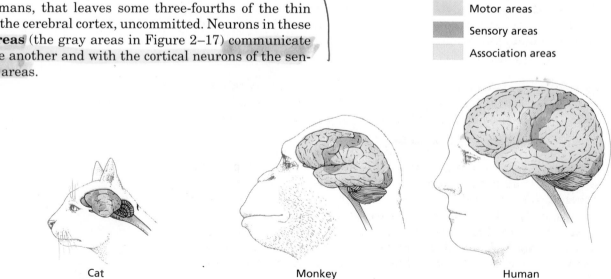

Rat   Cat   Monkey   Human

Electrically probing the association areas doesn't trigger any response. So, unlike the sensory and motor areas, we can't so neatly specify the functions of the association areas. Their silence seems to be what someone had in mind when formulating one of pop psychology's most widespread myths: that we ordinarily use only 10 percent of our brains. The myth implies that if we could activate our whole brain, we would be far smarter than those who drudge along on 10 percent brain power. But from observing surgically lesioned animals and brain-damaged humans, we know that the association areas are not dormant. Rather, they interpret, integrate, and act on information processed by the sensory areas.

Association areas in the frontal lobe enable judging and planning. People with damaged frontal lobes may have intact memories, score high on intelligence tests, and be well able to bake a cake—yet they may be unable to plan ahead to *begin* baking the cake for a birthday party.

Frontal lobe damage can also alter personality, leaving a person uninhibited, coarse, and even promiscuous. The classic case is Phineas Gage, a railroad worker. One afternoon in 1848, 25-year-old Gage was packing gunpowder into a rock with a tamping iron. A spark ignited the gunpowder, shooting the rod up through his left cheek and out the top of his skull, leaving his left frontal lobe massively damaged. To everyone's amazement, Gage was still able to sit up and speak, and after the wound healed he returned to work. Although his mental abilities and memories were intact, his personality was not. The affable, soft-spoken Phineas Gage was now an irritable, profane, capricious person who lost his job and ended up earning his living as a fairground exhibit. This person, said his friends, was "no longer Gage."

The association areas of the other lobes also perform mental functions. For example, an area on the underside of the right temporal lobe enables us to recognize faces. If a stroke or head injury destroyed this area of your brain, you would still be able to describe facial features and to recognize someone's sex and approximate age, yet be strangely unable to identify the person as, say, Mikhail Gorbachev, your next-door neighbor, or even your spouse. But by and large, complex mental functions such as learning and memory don't reside in any one place. There is no one spot in a rat's (admittedly small) association cortex that, when damaged, will obliterate its ability to learn or remember a maze. Such functions seem spread throughout much of the cortex.

Language Complex human abilities, such as language, result from the intricate coordination of many brain areas. For example, consider the curious finding that damage to any one of several cortical areas can cause **aphasia**, an impaired use of language. It is even more curious that some aphasic people can speak fluently but are unable to read (despite good vision), while others can comprehend what they read but are unable to speak. Still others can write but not read, read but not write, read numbers but not letters, or sing but not speak. These observations are puzzling because we think of speaking and reading, or writing and reading, or singing and speaking, as merely different examples of the same general ability. Consider the clues that helped lead to the solving of this mystery of language:

Phineas Gage's skull pierced by a tamping rod.

Clue 1: In 1865, French physician Paul Broca reported that damage to a specific area of the left frontal lobe, later called **Broca's area**, left a person struggling to form words, yet able to sing familiar songs and comprehend speech.

Clue 2: In 1874, German investigator Carl Wernicke discovered that damage to a specific area of the left temporal lobe **(Wernicke's area)** left people able to speak words but in a meaningless way. Asked to describe a picture that showed two boys stealing cookies behind a woman's back, one patient responded: "Mother is away her working her work to get her better, but when she's looking the two boys looking the other part. She's working another time" (Geschwind, 1979).

Clue 3: It was later discovered that reading aloud involves a third brain area. The *angular gyrus* receives the visual information from the visual area and recodes it into the auditory form from which Wernicke's area derives its meaning.

Clue 4: Nerve fibers interconnect these brain areas.

Norman Geschwind assembled these clues into an explanation of how we use language. When you read aloud, the words (1) register in the visual area, (2) are relayed to the angular gyrus, which then transforms the words into an auditory code that is (3) received and understood in the nearby Wernicke's area, and (4) sent to Broca's area, which (5) controls the motor cortex, creating the pronounced word (Figure 2–18). Depending on which link in this chain is damaged, a different form of aphasia occurs. Damage to the angular gyrus leaves the person able to speak and understand but unable to read. Damage to Wernicke's area disrupts understanding. Damage to Broca's area disrupts speaking. The general principle bears repeating: Complex abilities result from the intricate coordination of many brain areas.

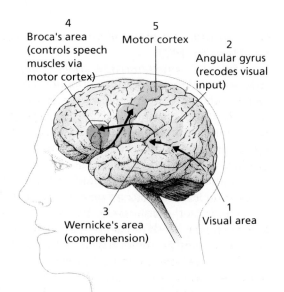

Figure 2–18 Reading aloud requires the coordination of several brain areas. The arrows show the movement of information in the brain from the time a word is read until it is spoken. (Adapted from "Specialization of the human brain" by N. Geschwind. Copyright © 1979 Scientific American, Inc. All rights reserved.)

Question: If your Broca's area were damaged, could you write a letter? (See page 48.)

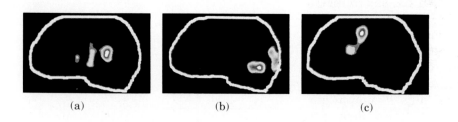

(a)   (b)   (c)

Brain Reorganization

If injury or illness destroys brain tissue, are its special functions forever lost? If you scrape your knee, new cells will generate to repair the damage. Not so with the neurons of the central nervous system. If the spinal cord is severed or if brain tissue is destroyed, the injured neurons normally will not regenerate.

That's the bad news. The good news is the brain's **plasticity**. Earlier we noted the plasticity of the sensory cortex. In one experiment, neuroscientists surgically cut the neural pathways for incoming information from a monkey's arm. The area of the sensory cortex that formerly received this input gradually shifted its func-

PET scans, such as these, detect the activity of different areas of the brain by measuring their relative consumption of a temporarily radioactive form of the brain's normal fuel, glucose. This series of side-view PET scans of left-facing patients shows levels of increased brain activity in specific areas: (a) when hearing a word—auditory cortex and Wernicke's area; (b) when seeing a word—visual cortex and angular gyrus; and (c) when repeating a word—Broca's area and the motor cortex. The red blotches show where the brain is rapidly consuming glucose.

tion and began to respond when researchers touched the animal's face (Barnes, 1990).

Moreover, when one brain area is damaged, other areas may in time reorganize and take over some of its functions. If neurons are destroyed, nearby neurons may partly compensate for the damage by making new connections that replace the lost ones. These new connections are one way the brain struggles to recover from, say, a minor stroke. They are also the brain's way of compensating for the gradual loss of neurons with age.

Our brains are most plastic when we are young children—before cortical regions' functions become fixed (Kolb, 1989). If the speech areas of an infant's left hemisphere are damaged, the right hemisphere will take over much of its language function. After age 5, left hemisphere damage permanently and severely disrupts language.

As an extreme example of plasticity, consider a 5-year-old boy whose severe seizures, caused by a deteriorating left hemisphere, required removing the *entire* hemisphere. What hope for the future would such a child have? Is there any chance he might attend school and lead a normal life, or would he suffer permanent retardation?

This is an actual case, and, astonishingly, the individual was at last report an executive. Half his skull is filled with nothing but cerebrospinal fluid—functionally it might as well be sawdust—yet he has scored well above average on intelligence tests, completed college, and attended graduate school part-time (Smith & Sugar, 1975; A. Smith, 1987). Although paralyzed on the right side, this man (along with other such cases of "hemispherectomy") testifies to the brain's extraordinary powers of reorganization when damaged before it is fully developed.

Could we enhance the brain's self-repair by transplanting brain tissue? Even in this era of heart transplants and skin grafts, transplanting neural tissue still sounds like science fiction. But in experiments with animals, neuroscientists are now trying, with some success, to mend the brain by replacing destroyed nerve cells with healthy ones (Gash & others, 1986; Dunnett, 1989). In one dramatic experiment, Randy Labbe and her colleagues (1983) removed a portion of the frontal lobes from a group of rats and replaced it with tissue from the frontal lobes of rat fetuses. (Fetal neurons have a remarkable ability to grow and make connections with the host brain.) Later, compared to rats who had similar portions removed but had not received the transplanted fetal cortical tissue, these rats learned a maze twice as fast. Thus, transplants of appropriate brain tissue may in some cases partially replace lost or damaged tissue.

Might transplants of brain tissue someday enable neurosurgeons to repair the human brain? The tremors of Parkinson's disease and the progressive deterioration of Alzheimer's disease, for example, involve a degeneration of brain tissue that normally produces vital neurotransmitters—dopamine in Parkinson's disease, acetylcholine in Alzheimer's. If we transplanted dopamine-producing tissue into the brains of Parkinson's patients, would the tissue survive and release the needed neurotransmitters? Using such tissue from patients' own adrenal glands or, better yet, from miscarried fetuses, experimental surgery on dozens of patients in Sweden, Mexico, the United States, and elsewhere has raised hopes that it might (Kimble, 1990; Office of Technology Assessment, 1990).

If transplanted brain tissue indeed alleviates Parkinson's disease, would you favor or oppose the use of brain tissue from aborted fetuses?

Our Divided Brains

We have seen that while certain attributes of mind are localized in particular brain regions, the brain nevertheless acts as a unified whole. Moving your hand, hearing, recognizing faces, even perceiving color, motion, and depth, depend on specific brain centers. Yet complex functions such as language, learning, and loving involve the coordination of many brain areas. Both principles of brain functioning—specialization and integration—are apparent in research on the two brain hemispheres.

For more than a century, clinical evidence has shown that the brain's two sides serve differing functions. Accidents, strokes, and tumors in the left hemisphere generally impair reading, writing, speaking, arithmetic reasoning, and understanding. Similar lesions in the right hemisphere do not have such dramatic effects. Brain-damaged Vietnam veterans were also less likely to suffer prolonged unconsciousness if injured in the right hemisphere (Fischman, 1986). Small wonder, then, that the left hemisphere became known as the "dominant" or "major" hemisphere, and its silent companion to the right as the "subordinate" or "minor" hemisphere. (With some left-handers, this is reversed—see page 52.)

By 1960, the assumption of left hemisphere superiority was well accepted. But then the "minor" right hemisphere was found to be not so limited after all. The story of this discovery is a fascinating chapter in psychology's history.

Splitting the Brain In 1961, two Los Angeles neurosurgeons, Philip Vogel and Joseph Bogen, were considering surgery for several patients who suffered from epilepsy. The surgeons speculated that major epileptic seizures were caused by an amplification of abnormal brain activity that reverberated back and forth between the two hemispheres. If so, they wondered whether they might control severe epilepsy by cutting communication between the hemispheres. In order to do so, the surgeons would have to sever the **corpus callosum**, the wide band of axon fibers connecting the two hemispheres (Figure 2–19).

They had reason to believe that such an operation would not be seriously incapacitating. Psychologists Roger Sperry, Ronald Myers, and Michael Gazzaniga had divided the brains of cats and monkeys in this manner, without serious ill effects. So Vogel and Bogen operated. The result? Seizures were nearly eliminated and the patients were surprisingly normal, their personalities and intellect hardly affected. Waking from the surgery, one patient even managed to quip that he had a "splitting headache" (Gazzaniga, 1967).

Answer to question on page 46: Yes. Broca's area produces a program for controlling the muscles of speech. If damaged, a victim can still understand speech and communicate through gestures or writing.

— Corpus callosum

Figure 2–19 The corpus callosum is a large band of neural fibers that connects the two brain hemispheres. To photograph the half brain shown here, the hemispheres were separated by cutting through the corpus callosum and lower brain regions.

If you chatted with one of these **split-brain** patients you probably would not notice anything unusual. You could understand why only a decade earlier neuropsychologist Karl Lashley jested that maybe the corpus callosum served only "to keep the hemispheres from sagging." But surely a broad band of 200 million nerve fibers capable of transferring more than a billion bits of information per second between the hemispheres must have a more significant purpose. It does, and the ingenious experiments of Sperry and Gazzaniga revealed its purpose and provided a key to understanding the two hemispheres' special functions.

Shortly after one of the split-brain operations, the researchers noted that when they placed an unseen object in a patient's left hand, he denied it was there. This came as no surprise to Sperry and Gazzaniga. They knew that information from the left hand went to the right hemisphere, and their animal experiments suggested that the right hemisphere would be unable to send this information to the speech-controlling areas of the left hemisphere. More extraordinary results came when Sperry and Gazzaniga conducted some perceptual tests.

Our eyes connect to our brains in such a way that, when we look straight ahead, the left half of our field of vision transmits through both eyes to our right hemisphere (Figure 2–20). Likewise, the right side of our field of vision transmits only to our left hemisphere. One woman, having lost a vision-related part of her *right* hemisphere to a massive stroke, sometimes complained that nurses had not put dessert or coffee on her tray. When her head was turned, so that the tray came into view in the right half of her field of vision (where her *left* visual cortex could detect it), she would say, "Oh, there it is— it wasn't there before" (Sacks, 1985, p. 73).

Left
visual field

Right
visual field

Left
hemisphere

Right
hemisphere

Corpus callosum

Figure 2–20 Information from the left half of your field of vision is received only by your right hemisphere, and information from the right half of your visual field is received only by your left hemisphere. (Note, however, that each eye receives sensory information from *both* the right and left visual fields.) The data received by either hemisphere is quickly transmitted to the other across the corpus callosum. In a split-brain patient, with a severed corpus callosum, this information sharing does not take place.

In those of us with healthy, intact brains, information presented only to our right hemisphere quickly gets sent to our left hemisphere, which names it. But what happens in an otherwise healthy person whose corpus callosum has been severed? To find out, experimenters ask a split-brain patient to look at a designated spot. Then they send information to either the left or right hemisphere (by flashing it to the right or left visual field). Finally, they quiz each hemisphere separately.

See if you can guess the results of an experiment using this procedure (Gazzaniga, 1967). While the patients stared at a dot, the word HEART was flashed across the visual field with HE in the left visual field and ART in the right. First, what did the patients *say* they saw? Second, asked to identify with their *left* hands what they had seen, HE or ART, what did they *point* to?

As Figure 2–21 shows, the patients *said* they saw ART, and so were startled when their left hands *pointed* to HE. When given an opportunity to express itself, each hemisphere reported only what *it* had seen.

Similarly, when a picture of a spoon was flashed to the right hemisphere, the patients could not say what they saw; but when asked to identify what they had seen by feeling with their left hands an assortment of objects hidden behind a screen, they readily selected the spoon (Figure 2–22). If the experimenter said, "Right!" the patient might reply, "What? Right? How could I possibly pick out the right object when I don't know what I saw?" It is, of course, the left hemisphere doing the talking here, bewildered by what its other half knows. It was as if the patients had "two separate inner visual worlds," noted Sperry (1968).

The left hemisphere, which acts as the brain's press agent, does mental gymnastics to rationalize reactions it does not understand (Figure 2–23). If the patient followed an order sent to the right

Figure 2–21 Testing the divided brain. When an experimenter flashes the word HEART across the visual field, the split-brain patient reports seeing the portion of the word transmitted to her left hemisphere. However, if asked to indicate with her left hand what she saw, she points to the portion of the word transmitted to her right hemisphere. (From Gazzaniga, 1983.)

Figure 2–22 The nonverbal right hemisphere sees the spoon flashed on the screen and directs the left hand to locate it among the objects hidden behind the screen. But the split-brain patient cannot say what he has seen. (From Gazzaniga, 1983.)

Figure 2–23 When an experimenter flashes simple commands to the right hemisphere of split-brain patients, they comply. Asked about their response, their left hemisphere, which controls speech and is unaware of what the right hemisphere has seen, invents—and seemingly believes—plausible explanations for what it does not comprehend. Thus, Michael Gazzaniga (1988) concludes that the left hemisphere is an "interpreter" that instantly constructs theories to explain our behavior. (From Gazzaniga, 1985.)

hemisphere ("Walk"), the interpretive left hemisphere would offer a ready explanation ("I'm going into the house to get a Coke").

These experiments demonstrate that the right hemisphere understands simple requests and easily perceives objects. In fact, the right hemisphere is superior to the left at copying drawings, recognizing faces, and reading emotions. Its perceptual superiority is apparent in one of Sperry's films. A split-brain patient's left hand (directed by the right hemisphere) easily rearranges some blocks to match a drawing. When the right hand (directed by the left hemisphere) tries to perform the same perceptual task, it makes many errors. The bumbling performance frustrates the right hemisphere, which is observing all this. So it triggers the left hand to interrupt the bumbling right hand; but the persistent right hand pushes the left hand away. Outside the laboratory, a few split-brain patients have been bothered by the unruly independence of their left hand, which may unbutton a shirt while the right hand buttons it. Split-brain surgery, said Sperry (1964), leaves people "with two separate minds."

To summarize, split-brain patients reveal the special functions of each hemisphere. The left hemisphere is more logical, verbal, and able to deal with things in sequence. The right is more emotionally intuitive, skilled at spatial relations, and able to deal with things all at once. But neuropsychologists advise us to beware the fad of locating complex human capacities, such as abilities in science or art, in either hemisphere. Imaginative writers have had a field day with the left-right dichotomy. Traditional schooling fails to educate the right side of the brain, some have told us. "The left-right dichotomy in cognitive mode is an idea with which it is very easy to run wild," observes Sperry (1982). Complex activities such as practicing science, studying psychology, or creating art emerge from the *integrated* activity of both hemispheres. Even when simply reading a story, both hemispheres are at work—the left understanding the words and finding meaning, the right appreciating humor, imagery, and emotional content (Levy, 1985).

Studying the Normal Brain What about the 99.99+ percent of us with undivided brains? Have scientists found our hemispheres similarly specialized? They have indeed, by evidence from several different types of studies. For example, when a person performs a *perceptual* task, brain waves, blood flow, and glucose consumption reveal increased activity in the *right* hemisphere; when a person speaks or calculates, activity increases in the left hemisphere.

Innocent and carefree, Stuart's left hand didn't know what the right was doing.

Close-Up   **Left-Handedness—Is Being a Lefty All Right?**

Judging by our everyday conversation, left-handedness is not all right. To be "coming from left field," or to offer a "left-handed compliment" is hardly more complimentary than to be "sinister" or "gauche" (words derived from the Latin and French for left). On the other hand, right-handedness is "right on," which any "righteous" "right-hand man" "in his right mind" usually is.

How Many People Are Left-Handed?

About 10 percent (somewhat more among males, somewhat less among females) of the human population is left-handed. Judging from cave drawings and the tools of prehistoric humans, this veer to the right occurred long ago in the development of our species. Thus, right-handedness prevails today in all human cultures (Corballis, 1989). Moreover, it appears prior to culture's impact: Ultrasound observations of fetal thumb-sucking reveal that more than 9 in 10 fetuses suck the right hand's thumb (Hepper & others, 1990). This right-hand bias is uniquely human; other primates are more ambidextrous.

Is Handedness Inherited?

Observing 150 babies during the first 2 days after birth, George Michel (1981) found that two-thirds consistently preferred to lie with their heads turned to the right. When he restudied a sample of these babies at age 5 months, almost all of the "head right" babies reached for things with their right hands, and almost all of the "head left" babies reached with their left hands. Such findings, along with the universal prevalence of right-handers, hint that genes influence handedness.

Is the Brain Organization of Left-Handers Opposite That of Right-Handers?

Tests reveal that about 95 percent of right-handers process speech primarily in the left hemisphere (Springer & Deutsch, 1985). Left-handers are more diverse. More than half process speech in the left hemisphere, as right-handers do. About one-quarter process language in the right hemisphere; the other quarter use both hemispheres more or less equally. Such left-handers may therefore require better communication between the hemispheres. This might explain the discovery that the corpus callosum averages 11 percent larger in left-handers (Witelson, 1985).

So, Is It All Right to Be Left-Handed?

Left-handers are more numerous among people with reading disabilities, allergies, and migraine headaches (Geschwind & Behan, 1984). Lefties also have shorter life expectancies due in part to left-handedness sometimes being associated with birth stress or deficiencies in the body's disease-fighting immune system (Coren & Halpern, 1991). But left-handedness is also more common among musicians, mathematicians, professional baseball and cricket players, architects, and artists, including such luminaries as Michelangelo, Leonardo da Vinci, and Picasso. Although left-handers must tolerate elbow-jostling at dinner parties, right-handed desks, and awkward scissors, it seems the pros and cons of being a lefty are roughly equal.

On occasion, hemispheric specialization has been even more dramatically shown by briefly sedating an entire hemisphere. To check for the locus of language before surgery, a physician may inject a sedative into the neck artery that feeds blood to the hemisphere on its side of the body. Before the drug is injected, the patient is lying down, arms in the air, conversing easily. Can you predict what happens when the drug flows into the artery going to the left hemisphere? Within seconds, the right arm falls limp, and, assuming the person's left hemisphere controls language, the subject becomes speechless until the drug wears off. When the drug goes into the artery to the right hemisphere, the *left* arm falls limp, but speech is still possible.

In sports, strategic factors explain the higher-than-normal percentage of lefties. For example, it helps a soccer team to have left-footed players play the left side of the field (Wood & Aggleton, 1989).

These PET scans show how active the right hemisphere becomes when the subject is listening to music (right) compared to resting (left). Red signifies the most activity, blue the least.

Other tests confirm hemispheric specialization. Most people recognize pictures faster and more accurately when flashed to the right hemisphere, but recognize words faster and more accurately when flashed to the left hemisphere. If a word is flashed to your right hemisphere, perception takes a fraction of a second longer—the length of time it takes to send the information through the corpus callosum to the more verbal left hemisphere.

Finally, which hemisphere would you suppose enables sign language among the deaf? Is it the right hemisphere, because of its visual-spatial superiority? Or the left, because of its preparedness to process language? Studies reveal that just as hearing people use the left hemisphere to process speech, hearing-impaired people use the left hemisphere to read signs (Bellugi & others, 1989). A stroke in the left hemisphere therefore disrupts a deaf person's ability to sign much as it would disrupt a hearing person's use of spoken language.

So, a variety of observations—of people with "split" brains and people with "normal" brains—converge beautifully. There is now little doubt that we have unified brains with specialized parts, and that infants are born with their brains "prewired" accordingly (Hahn, 1987). From looking at the two hemispheres, which look alike to the naked eye, who would suppose that they contribute so uniquely to the harmony of the whole?

From nineteenth-century phrenology to today's neuroscience we have come a long way. Yet what is unknown still dwarfs what is known. We can describe the brain. We can learn the functions of its parts. We can study how the parts communicate. But how does this electrochemical whir give rise to a feeling of elation, a creative idea, or a memory of Grandmother's freshly baked cookies?

To judge from one series of interviews with leading brain scientists, feelings of wonder are commonplace, and sometimes lead to mystical and spiritual inspirations. In the words of Candace Pert (1986, p. 390), "I see in the brain all the beauty of the universe and its order—constant signs of God's presence." Others ponder philosophical mysteries: How does the material brain give rise to consciousness? And to what extent can a thing understand itself? The mind seeking to understand the brain—that is the ultimate scientific challenge.

"If the human brain were so simple that we could understand it, we would be so simple that we couldn't."
Emerson M. Pugh, quoted by George E. Pugh
The Biological Origin of Human Values, 1977

Summing Up

As the first step in understanding our behavior and mental processes, we have examined the biological roots of how we think, feel, and act.

The Nervous System

Neurons and Their Messages The body's circuitry, the nervous system, consists of billions of individual cells, called neurons. Neurons usually receive signals from other neurons through their branching dendrites and cell body, then combine these signals in the cell body and transmit electrical impulses, the action potential, down their axon. When these signals reach the end of the axon, they stimulate the release of chemical messengers, called neurotransmitters. These molecules traverse the tiny synaptic gap between neurons and combine with receptor sites on neighboring neurons, thus passing on their excitatory or inhibitory messages. Neurotransmitters are now being studied to discern their importance for human thought and emotion.

Divisions of the Nervous System The central nervous system's (CNS) neurons in the brain and spinal cord communicate with the peripheral nervous system's (PNS) sensory and motor neurons. The PNS consists of the somatic nervous system, which directs voluntary movements and reflexes, and the autonomic nervous system, whose sympathetic and parasympathetic divisions control our involuntary muscles and our glands.

The Brain

The Tools of Discovery Clinical observations have long revealed the general effects of damage to various brain areas. But powerful new technologies now reveal brain structures and activities in the living brain. By surgically lesioning or electrically stimulating specific brain areas, by recording the brain's surface electrical activity, and by displaying neural activity with computer-aided brain scans, neuroscientists explore the connections between brain, mind, and behavior.

How the Brain Governs Behavior Each of the brain's three basic regions—the brainstem, the limbic system, and the cerebral cortex—represents a stage of brain evolution.

The brainstem begins where the spinal cord swells to form the medulla, which controls heartbeat and breathing. The cerebellum, attached to the rear of the brainstem, coordinates muscle movement. Within the brainstem, the reticular formation controls arousal and attention. On top of the brainstem is the thalamus, the brain's sensory switchboard.

Between the brainstem and cerebral cortex is the limbic system, which has been linked primarily to memory, emotions, and drives. For example, one of its neural centers, the amygdala, is involved in aggressive and fearful responses.

Also in the limbic system, the hypothalamus has been linked to various bodily maintenance functions, to pleasurable rewards, and to the control of the endocrine system. The endocrine system releases hormones, which travel through the bloodstream to target organs and tissues, where they affect emotional states, growth, and other body functions.

Each hemisphere of the cerebral cortex has four geographical areas: the frontal, parietal, occipital, and temporal lobes. Small, well-defined regions within these lobes control muscle movement and receive information from the body senses. However, most of the cortex—its association areas—is uncommitted to such functions and is therefore free to process other information.

Some brain regions are known to serve specific functions. In general, however, human emotions, thoughts, and behaviors result from the intricate coordination of many brain areas. Language, for example, depends on a chain of events in several brain regions.

Brain Reorganization If one hemisphere is damaged early in life, the other will pick up many of its functions, thus demonstrating the brain's plasticity. The brain becomes less plastic later in life. Frequently, however, nearby neurons can partially compensate for damaged ones, as when a person recovers from a stroke or brain injury.

Our Divided Brains Clinical observations long ago revealed that the left cerebral hemisphere is crucial for language. More recent experiments on split-brain patients have refined our knowledge of each hemisphere's special functions. By testing the two hemispheres separately, researchers have confirmed that for most people the left hemisphere is the more verbal, and that the right hemisphere excels in visual perception and the recognition of emotion. Studies of normal people with intact brains confirm that each hemisphere makes unique contributions to the integrated functioning of the brain.

Terms and Concepts to Remember

biological psychology A branch of psychology concerned with the links between biology and behavior. (Some biological psychologists call themselves *behavioral neuroscientists, neuropsychologists, physiological psychologists,* or *biopsychologists.*)

nervous system The body's speedy, electrochemical communication system, consisting of all the nerve cells of the peripheral and central nervous systems.

neuron A nerve cell; the basic building block of the nervous system.

sensory neurons Neurons that carry incoming information from the sense receptors to the central nervous system.

interneurons Central nervous system neurons that intervene directly between the sensory inputs and motor outputs.

motor neurons The neurons that carry outgoing information from the central nervous system to the muscles and glands.

reflex A simple, automatic, inborn response to a sensory stimulus, such as the knee-jerk response.

dendrite The bushy, branching extensions of a neuron that receive messages and conduct impulses toward the cell body.

axon The extension of a neuron ending in branching terminal fibers through which messages are sent to other neurons or to muscles or glands.

myelin [MY-uh-lin] **sheath** A layer of fatty cells segmentally encasing the fibers of many neurons; makes possible vast-ly greater transmission speed of neural impulses.

threshold The level of stimulation required to trigger a neural impulse.

synapse [SIN-aps] The junction between the axon tip of the sending neuron and the dendrite or cell body of the receiving neuron. The tiny gap at this junction is called the *synaptic gap* or *cleft.*

neurotransmitters Chemical messengers that traverse the synaptic gaps between neurons. When released by the sending neuron, neurotransmitters travel across the synapse and bind to receptor sites on the receiving neuron, thereby influencing whether it will generate a neural impulse.

acetylcholine [ah-seat-el-KO-leen] **(ACh)** A neurotransmitter that, among its functions, triggers muscle contraction.

endorphins [en-DOR-fins] "Morphine within"—natural, opiatelike neurotransmitters linked to pain control and to pleasure.

central nervous system (CNS) The brain and spinal cord.

peripheral nervous system (PNS) The neurons that connect the central nervous system to the rest of the body. It consists of the sensory neurons, which carry messages to the central nervous system from the body's sense receptors, and the motor neurons, which carry messages from the central nervous system to the muscles and glands.

somatic [so-MAT-ik] **nervous system** The division of the peripheral nervous system that receives information from various sense receptors and controls the skeletal muscles of the body.

autonomic [aw-tuh-NAHM-ik] **nervous system** The part of the peripheral nervous system that controls the glands and the muscles of the internal organs (such as the heart). Its sympathetic division arouses; its parasympathetic division calms.

sympathetic nervous system The division of the autonomic nervous system that arouses the body, mobilizing its energy in stressful situations.

parasympathetic nervous system The division of the autonomic nervous system that calms the body, conserving its energy.

lesion [LEE-zhuhn] Tissue destruction. A brain lesion is a naturally or experimentally caused destruction of brain tissue.

electroencephalogram (EEG) An amplified recording of the waves of electrical activity that sweep across the brain's surface. These waves are measured by placing electrodes on the scalp.

CAT (computerized axial tomograph) scan A series of x-ray photographs taken from different angles and combined by computer into a composite three-dimensional representation of a slice through the body.

PET (positron emission tomograph) scan A visual display of brain activity that detects where a radioactive form of glucose goes while the brain performs a given task.

MRI (magnetic resonance imaging) A technique that uses magnetic fields and radio waves to produce computer-generated images that distinguish among different types of soft tissue; allows us to see structures within the brain.

brainstem The central core of the brain, beginning where the spinal cord swells as it enters the skull; it is the oldest part of the brain and is responsible for automatic survival functions.

medulla [muh-DUL-uh] The base of the brainstem; controls heartbeat and breathing.

cerebellum [sehr-uh-BELL-um] The "little brain" attached to the rear of the brainstem; it helps coordinate voluntary movement and balance.

thalamus [THAL-uh-muss] The brain's sensory switchboard, located on top of the brainstem; directs messages to the sensory receiving areas in the cortex and transmits replies to the cerebellum and medulla.

reticular formation A nerve network (also called the *reticular activating system*) in the brainstem that plays an important role in controlling arousal and attention.

limbic system A doughnut-shaped system of neural structures at the border of the brainstem and cerebral hemispheres; associated with emotions such as fear and aggression and drives such as those for food and sex.

amygdala [ah-MIG-dah-la] Two almond-shaped neural centers in the limbic system that are linked to emotion.

hypothalamus [hi-po-THAL-uh-muss] A neural structure lying below *(hypo)* the thalamus; it directs several maintenance activities (eating, drinking, body temperature), helps govern the endocrine system via the pituitary gland, and is linked to emotion and reward.

hormones Chemical messengers, such as those manufactured by the endocrine glands, that are produced in one tissue and affect another.

endocrine [EN-duh-krin] **system** The body's "slow," chemical communication system; a set of glands that secretes hormones into the bloodstream.

adrenal [ah-DREEN-el] **glands** A pair of endocrine glands just above the kidneys. The adrenals secrete the hormones epinephrine (adrenaline) and norepinephrine (noradrenaline), which help to arouse the body in times of stress.

pituitary gland The endocrine system's most influential gland. Under the influence of the hypothalamus, the pituitary regulates growth and controls other endocrine glands.

cerebral [seh-REE-bruhl] **cortex** The intricate fabric of interconnected neural cells that covers the cerebral hemispheres; the body's ultimate control and information-processing center.

frontal lobes The portion of the cerebral cortex lying just behind the forehead; involved in speaking and muscle movements and in making plans and judgments.

parietal [puh-RYE-uh-tuhl] **lobes** The portion of the cerebral cortex lying at the top of the head and toward the rear; includes the sensory cortex.

occipital [ahk-SIP-uh-tuhl] **lobes** The portion of the cerebral cortex lying at the back of the head; includes the visual areas, each of which receives visual information from the opposite visual field.

temporal lobes The portion of the cerebral cortex lying roughly above the ears; includes the auditory areas, each of which receives auditory information primarily from the opposite ear.

motor cortex An area at the rear of the frontal lobes that controls voluntary movements.

sensory cortex The area at the front of the parietal lobes that registers and processes body sensations.

association areas Areas of the cerebral cortex that are not involved in primary motor or sensory functions; rather, they are involved in higher mental functions such as learning, remembering, thinking, and speaking.

aphasia Impairment of language, usually caused by left hemisphere damage either to Broca's area (impairing speaking) or to Wernicke's area (impairing understanding).

Broca's area An area of the left frontal lobe that directs the muscle movements involved in speech.

Wernicke's area An area of the left temporal lobe involved in language comprehension.

plasticity The brain's capacity for modification, as evident in brain reorganization following damage (especially in children) and in experiments on the effects of experience on brain development.

corpus callosum [KOR-pus kah-LOW-sum] The largest bundle of neural fibers connecting and carrying messages between the two brain hemispheres.

split-brain A condition in which the two hemispheres of the brain are isolated by cutting the connecting fibers between them (mainly those of the corpus callosum).

For Further Information

You can find more information regarding the biology of behavior on the following text pages:

For Further Reading

Bloom, F. E., Lazerson, A., & Hofstadter, L. (1988). *Brain, mind, and behavior* (2nd ed.). New York: Freeman.

A lavishly illustrated summary of recent brain research written to accompany the 1984 PBS television series "The Brain."

Hooper, J., & Teresi, D. (1986). *The three-pound universe.* New York: Macmillan.

Science journalists Hooper and Teresi queried dozens of brain researchers. The result is a personalized picture of how the neurosciences are revealing new insights into emotion, memory, madness, and even spirituality.

Ornstein, R., & Thompson, R. F. (1984). *The amazing brain.* Boston: Houghton Mifflin.

An excellent introduction to recent brain research, written by two psychologists involved in it.

Sacks, O. (1985). *The man who mistook his wife for a hat.* New York: Summit Books.

Fascinating case studies of people whose disorders reveal the brain's workings.

Springer, S. P., & Deutsch, G. (1989). *Left brain, right brain* (3rd ed.). New York: Freeman.

An award-winning description of research on the two hemispheres of brain-damaged, split-brain, and normal subjects. Discusses handedness, gender differences, learning disabilities, and theories of consciousness.

Part Two

Development Over the Life Span

How, over time, do we come to be the persons we are,

and how might we expect to change in the future? In

the next two chapters we consider how we develop—

physically, cognitively, and socially—during infancy

and childhood (Chapter 3) and during adolescence,

adulthood, and later life (Chapter 4).

The Developing Child   *Chapter 3*

In mid-1978, the newest astonishment in medicine, covering all the front pages, was the birth of an English baby nine months after conception in a dish. The older surprise, which should still be fazing us all, is that a solitary sperm and a single egg can fuse and become a human being under any circumstance, and that, however implanted, [this multiplied] cell affixed to the uterine wall will grow and differentiate into eight pounds of baby; this has been going on under our eyes for so long a time that we've gotten used to it; hence the outcries of amazement at this really minor technical modification of the general procedure—nothing much, really, beyond relocating the beginning of the process from the fallopian tube to a plastic container.

Lewis Thomas
The Medusa and Snail, 1979

The developing person is no less a wonder after birth than in the womb. Physically, mentally, socially, we are always in the process of becoming. As we journey through life from womb to tomb, when and how do we change?

Usually we notice how we differ. To developmental psychologists our commonalities are just as important. Virtually all of us—Confucius, Queen Elizabeth, Martin Luther King, Jr., you, and I—began walking around age 1 and talking by age 2. As children we all engaged in social play in preparation for life's serious work. We all smile and cry, love and hate, and occasionally ponder the fact that someday we will die.

Developmental Issues

Unlike most other chapters in this book, this one and the next focus not so much on a topic—the brain, learning, thinking, personality, social behavior—as on a *perspective*. The developmental perspective examines how all such things *change* over the life span. **Developmental psychologists** study physical, mental, and social changes occurring throughout the life cycle. Much of their work centers on three major issues:

1. *Nature or nurture:* How much is our development influenced by our genetic inheritance and how much by our experience?

2. *Continuity or stages:* Is development a gradual, continuous process? Or does it proceed through a sequence of separate stages?

3. *Stability or change:* Do our individual traits persist? Or do we become different persons as we age?

Nature or Nurture?

Our **genes** are the biochemical units of heredity that make each of us a distinctive human being. The genes we share are what make us people rather than dogs or tulips. Do our individual genetic makeups also explain why one person is outgoing, another shy? Why one person is slow-witted and another smart? Are human traits, like eye color, pretty much fixed? Or are they changeable?

Our answers affect how we view certain social policies. Suppose you presume that people are the way they are "by nature." You probably will not have much faith in programs that try to compensate for educational disadvantage or rehabilitate prisoners. And you will probably agree with developmental psychologists who emphasize the influence of our genes. As a flower unfolds in accord with its genetic blueprint, so our genes design an orderly sequence of biological growth processes called **maturation**. Maturation decrees many of our commonalities: standing before walking, using nouns before adjectives. Although extreme deprivation or abuse will retard development, the genetic growth tendencies are inborn. Maturation sets the basic course of development and experience adjusts it.

If you take the nurture side of the debate, you probably agree with the developmentalists who emphasize external influences. As a potter shapes a lump of clay, our experiences shape us. In reality, almost everyone agrees that our behaviors are a product of the *interaction* of our genes and our past and present experiences. If an attractive, athletic teenage boy is treated as a leader and sought out by girls, shall we say his positive self-image is due to his genes or to his environment? It's both, because his environment is reacting to his genetic endowment. Asking which factor is more important is like asking whether the area of a soccer field is due more to its length or to its width.

More than 98 percent of our genes are identical to those of chimpanzees. Not surprisingly, the physiological systems and even the brain organizations of humans and chimpanzees are quite similar.

Nature or nurture? Stability or change? How much is this outgoing baby's disposition due to her heredity and how much to her upbringing? How likely is it that she will be an outgoing adult? These questions illustrate two basic issues of developmental psychology.

Continuity or Stages?

Adults are vastly different from infants. But do they differ as a giant redwood differs from its seedling—a difference created by gradual, cumulative growth? Or do they differ as a butterfly differs from a caterpillar—a difference of distinct stages?

Generally speaking, researchers who emphasize experience and learning see development as a slow, continuous shaping process. Those who emphasize biological maturation tend to see development as a sequence of genetically predetermined stages or steps; although progress through the various stages may be quick or slow, everyone passes through the stages in the same order.

Stability or Change?

For much of this century, psychologists took the position that once a person's personality forms, it hardens like clay and remains set for life. Researchers who have followed lives through time are now debating the extent to which our past reaches into our future. Is development characterized more by *stability* over time or by *change?* Are the effects of early experience enduring or temporary? Will the cranky infant grow up to be an irritable adult? Or is such a child as likely to become a placid, patient person? Do differences among classmates in, say, aggressiveness, aptitude, or strivings for achievement persist throughout the life span? In short, to what degree do we grow to be merely older versions of our early selves, and to what degree do we become new persons?

Most developmentalists now believe that for certain traits, such as emotional intensity, there is an underlying continuity, especially in the years following early childhood. Yet as we age we also change—physically, mentally, socially. Thus, we have today's life-span view: Human development is a lifelong process.

At the end of this chapter and the next we will reflect on these three developmental issues. But first, our main agenda: to examine human development across the life span, beginning where life begins and ending where life ends.

Prenatal Development and the Newborn

From Life Comes Life

Nothing is more natural than a species reproducing itself. Yet nothing is more wondrous. Consider human reproduction. The process starts when a woman's ovary releases a mature **ovum** (egg), a cell roughly the size of the period at the end of this sentence, and the nearly 300 million sperm deposited during intercourse begin their race upstream toward it. A girl is born with all the ova she will ever have, although only a few will ever mature and be released. A boy, in contrast, begins producing sperm cells at puberty. The manufacturing process continues 24 hours a day for the rest of his life, although the rate of production—more than 1000 sperm during the second it takes to read this phrase—does slow down with age.

Like space voyagers approaching a huge planet, the sperm approach a cell 85,000 times their own size. The relatively few sperm that make it to the egg release digestive enzymes that eat away the egg's protective coating, allowing a sperm to penetrate (Figure 3–1). As it does so, an electric charge shoots across the ovum's surface, blocking out all other sperm during the minute or so that it takes the egg to form a barrier. Meanwhile, fingerlike projections sprout around the successful sperm and pull it inward. The egg nucleus and the sperm move toward each other and, before half a day elapses, fuse. The two have become one.

Consider it your luckiest of moments. The one sperm among 300 million needed to make you, in combination with that one particular egg, won the race. A 7-year-old boy was overheard explaining the idea to a friend: "Robbie, do you know how many sperm were trying to be you? (Robbie shook his head.) Well, there were millions. I saw it on *Nova.* They were all racing against you, but *you* won. Anybody who is alive won. So you're a winner and I'm a winner; everybody's a winner" (Mahoney, 1989).

When egg and sperm unite, the 23 **chromosomes** carried in the egg pair up with the 23 chromosomes brought to it by the sperm. These 46 chromosomes contain the master plan for your body. Each chromosome is composed of long threads of a molecule called

Figure 3–1 Development begins when sperm and egg unite. The result is a single cell that, if all goes well, will become a 100-trillion-cell human being.

"From the very moment that the sperm hits the egg, a precarious trip on the thin edge of biological extinction has begun."
Ralph Blair
Nevertheless Joy!, 1989

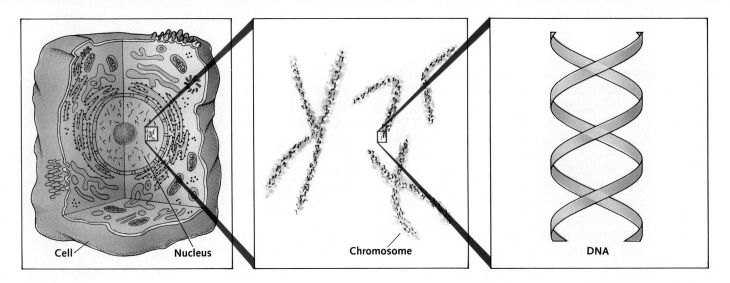

Figure 3–2 The genes: their location and composition. Contained in the nucleus of each of the trillions of cells in your body are chromosomes. Each chromosome is composed in part of the molecule DNA. Genes are segments of DNA that form templates for the production of proteins. By directing the manufacture of proteins, the genes determine our individual biological development.

DNA (deoxyribonucleic acid). DNA in turn is made of thousands of genes, functional segments capable of synthesizing specific *proteins* (the biochemical building blocks of life) (Figure 3–2).

Your sex is determined by your twenty-third pair of chromosomes, the sex chromosomes. The member of the pair that came from your mother was an **X chromosome.** From your father, you received either an *X* chromosome, making you a girl, or a **Y chromosome,** making you a boy. The *Y* chromosome contains a single gene that throws a master switch triggering the testes to develop and produce the principal male hormone, **testosterone,** which in turn triggers the development of external male sex organs. Inject this gene fragment of the *Y* chromosome into female mice embryos carrying a normal pair of *X* chromosomes and they may grow up as males (Koopman & others, 1991).

Prenatal Development

Even at your fortunate moment when one lucky sperm won the race, your destiny was not assured. Fewer than half of fertilized eggs, called **zygotes,** survive beyond the first week (Grobstein, 1979). If human life begins at conception, then most people die without being born.

But for you and me good fortune prevailed. Beginning as one cell, each of us became two cells, then four—each cell just like the first. Then, within the first week, when this cell division had produced a zygote of some 100 cells, the cells began to *differentiate*—to specialize in structure and function. Within 2 weeks, the increasingly diverse cells became attached to the mother's uterine wall, beginning approximately 37 weeks of the closest human relationship (Figure 3–3).

The zygote's outer part attaches to the uterine wall and becomes the placenta, through which nourishment passes. The inner cells become the **embryo**. During the next 6 weeks, the embryo's body organs begin to form and function. The heart begins to beat and the liver begins to make red blood cells. Embryos carrying a *Y* chromosome begin to secrete testosterone, diverting them down the road to maleness.

By 9 weeks after conception, the embryo has become unmistakably human and is now a **fetus.** By the end of the sixth month, internal organs such as the stomach have become sufficiently formed and functional to allow a prematurely born fetus a chance of survival.

Prenatal development
zygote: *conception to 2 weeks*
embryo: *2 weeks through 8 weeks*
fetus: *9 weeks to birth*

(a)

(b)

(c)

(d)

At each prenatal stage, genetic *and* environmental factors affect development. The placenta screens out many potentially harmful substances, while allowing nutrients and oxygen to pass through. But along with nourishment, some damaging agents called **teratogens** pass through with potentially tragic effects. Pregnant women never drink or smoke alone. When the mother takes a drink, alcohol enters her bloodstream — and her fetus's — and depresses activity in both their central nervous systems. When she puffs on a cigarette, she and her fetus both experience reduced blood oxygen and a shot of nicotine. If she is a heavy smoker, her newborn will probably be underweight, sometimes dangerously so. If she is a heroin addict, her baby is born a heroin addict. If she carries the AIDS virus, her baby often does, too.

If the mother drinks heavily, her baby will be at risk for birth defects and mental retardation. For some infants, the effects are visible as **fetal alcohol syndrome,** which involves small, misproportioned heads and lifelong brain abnormalities, often resulting in mental retardation. If the mother uses crack, her baby, having been deprived of nutrients and oxygen while in the womb, may suffer deformities and growth impairment. In the early 1990s, as the first wave of a new "crack baby" generation began school, urban special education programs braced for a surge in the numbers of withdrawn, impulsive, hyperactive children.

The Competent Newborn

Newborns come equipped with reflexes ideally suited for survival. Infants will withdraw a limb to escape pain. Put a cloth over their faces, interfering with their breathing, and they will turn their heads from side to side and swipe at it. New parents are often awed by the coordinated sequence of reflexes by which babies get food. The **rooting reflex** illustrates this: When something touches their cheeks, babies will open their mouths and vigorously "root" for a nipple. Finding one, they will automatically close on it and begin sucking — which itself requires a coordinated sequence of tonguing, swallowing, and breathing. Failing to find satisfaction, the hungry baby may cry — a behavior that parents are predisposed to find highly unpleasant to hear and very rewarding to relieve.

The pioneering American psychologist William James (who once said, "The first lecture on psychology I ever heard was the first

Figure 3–3 Prenatal development. (a) The embryo grows and develops rapidly. At 40 days, the spine is visible and the arms and legs are beginning to grow. (b) Five days later the inch-long embryo's proportions have begun to change. The rest of the body is now bigger than the head, and the arms and legs have grown noticeably. (c) By the end of the second month, when the fetal period begins, facial features, hands, and feet have formed. (d) As the fetus enters the fourth month, it weighs about 3 ounces.

Tera literally means "monster"; teratogens are "monster-producing" agents, such as chemicals and viruses, that may harm the fetus.

This boy displays the small, misproportioned head that is characteristic of fetal alcohol syndrome. He will probably also suffer impaired physical and mental growth.

I ever gave") presumed that the newborn experiences a "blooming, buzzing confusion." Until the 1960s, few people disagreed. It was said that, apart from a blur of meaningless light and dark shades, newborns could not see. Then, just as the development of new technology led to progress in the neurosciences, so too did new investigative techniques enhance the study of infants. Scientists discovered that babies can tell you a lot—if you know how to ask. To ask, you must capitalize on what the baby can do—gaze, suck, turn the head. So, equipped with eye-tracking machines, pacifiers wired to electronic gear, and other such devices, researchers set out to answer parents' age-old question: What can my baby see, hear, smell, and think?

They discovered that a baby's sensory equipment is "wired" to facilitate social responsiveness. Newborns turn their heads in the direction of human voices, but not in response to artificial sounds. They gaze more at a drawing of a human face than at a bull's-eye pattern; yet they gaze more at a bull's-eye pattern—which has contrasts much like that of the human eye—than at a solid disk (Fantz, 1961). They prefer to look at objects 8 to 12 inches away, which, wonder of wonders, just happens to be the approximate distance between a nursing infant's eyes and the mother's (Maurer & Maurer, 1988). Newborns, it seems, arrive perfectly designed to see their mothers' eyes.

Babies' perceptual abilities are continuously developing during the first months of life. Within days of birth, babies can distinguish their mothers' facial expression, odor, and voice. A week-old nursing baby, placed between a gauze pad from its mother's bra and one from another nursing mother, will usually turn toward the smell of its own mother's pad (MacFarlane, 1978). At 3 weeks of age, an infant who sucks on a pacifier that sometimes turns on recordings of its mother's voice and sometimes that of a female stranger will suck more vigorously when it hears its mother's voice (Mills & Melhuish, 1974). So not only can infants see what they need to see, and smell and hear well, but they are already using their sensory equipment to learn.

Two teams of investigators reported the astonishing and controversial finding that, in the second week—or even the first hour of life—infants can imitate facial expressions such as tongue protrusions (Field & others, 1982; Meltzoff & Moore, 1983, 1985, 1989). Follow-up studies revealed that some newborns are consistently more expressive and imitative than others (Field, 1989). Nevertheless, studies of babies in Scotland, Japan, and Nepal suggest that newborns' ability to imitate may be a universal human trait (Bower, 1989).

If so, this is a remarkable feat. How do newborn babies relate their own facial movements to those of an adult? And how can they coordinate the movements involved? The findings are controversial because they contradict the presumption that the newborn's sensory and motor abilities are minimal.

Researcher Tiffany Field (1987) notes, "Our knowledge of infancy was in its infancy 20 years ago, but what we have learned since then has dramatically changed the way we perceive and treat infants." More and more, she goes on to say, psychologists see the baby as "a very sophisticated perceiver of the world, with very sensitive social and emotional qualities and impressive intellectual abilities." The "helpless infant" of a generation ago has become today's "amazing newborn."

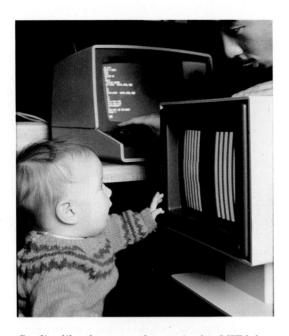

Studies like the one underway in this MIT lab are exploring infants' abilities to perceive, think, and remember. Experiments show that even very young infants are capable of sophisticated visual discrimination and will look much longer at an unfamiliar pattern. Such tests have changed psychologists' ideas of what the world looks like to a baby.

Imitation? When Andrew Meltzoff shows his tongue, an 18-day-old boy responds similarly. "As our experimental techniques have become more and more sophisticated," reports Meltzoff (1987), "the infants themselves have appeared more and more clever."

Infancy and Childhood

During infancy, a baby grows from newborn to toddler, and during childhood from toddler to teenager. Beginning in this chapter with infancy and childhood and continuing in the next chapter with adolescence through old age, we will see how people of all ages develop—physically, cognitively, and socially.

Physical Development

Brain Development While you resided in your mother's womb, your body was forming nerve cells at the rate of about one-quarter million per *minute*. On the day you were born you had essentially all the brain cells you will ever have. However, at birth the human nervous system is immature: The neural networks that enable us to walk, talk, and remember are still forming (Figure 3–4).

Maturation and Infant Memory   The lack of neural connections helps explain why our earliest memories do not predate our third or fourth birthdays (Kihlstrom & Harachkiewicz, 1982). For parents, this "infantile amnesia," as Freud called it, can be disconcerting. After all the hours we spend with our babies—after all the frolicking on the rug, all the diapering, feeding, and rocking to sleep—what would they consciously remember of us if we died? Nothing!

But if nothing is consciously recalled, something has still been gained. From birth (and even before), infants can learn (Blass, 1987; Bower, 1977; Lancioni, 1980). Newborns can learn to turn their heads to the left or right to receive a sugar solution when their forehead is stroked. Given occasional reminders, 3-month-old infants who learn that moving their leg propels a mobile will remember the association for at least a month (Figure 3–5).

Such learning tends not to persist unless reactivated. Nevertheless, early learning may prepare our brains for those later experiences that we *do* remember. For example, children who become deaf at age 2, after having been exposed to speech, are later more easily trained in sign language than those deaf from birth (Lenneberg, 1967). This suggests the first 2 years are critical for learning language.

Animals such as guinea pigs, whose brains are mature at birth, more readily form permanent memories from infancy than do animals with immature brains, such as rats (Campbell & Coulter, 1976). Because human brains are also immature at birth, these findings cast doubt on the idea that people subconsciously remember their prenatal life or the trauma of their birth.

Experience and Brain Development   Experience, as well as biological maturation, helps develop the brain's neural connections. Although "forgotten," early learning is not erased. Rather, it helps prepare our brains for thought and language, and also for later experiences.

How do early experiences leave their "marks" in the brain? Working at the University of California, Berkeley, Mark Rosenzweig and David Krech caged some rats in solitary confinement and others in a communal playground (Figure 3–6, page 68). Rats living in the deprived environment usually developed a lighter and

At birth   3 months   15 months

Figure 3–4 In humans, the brain is immature at birth. These drawings of sections of brain tissue from the cerebral cortex illustrate the increasing complexity of the neural networks in the maturing human brain. (From Conel, 1939–1963.)

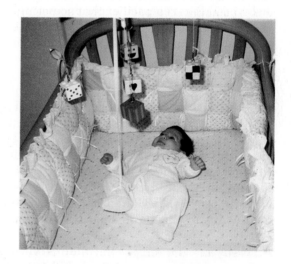

Figure 3–5 Babies only 3 months old can learn that kicking moves a mobile—and can retain the learning for a month. (From Rovee-Collier, 1989.)

Impoverished
environment

Enriched
environment

Figure 3-6 Experience affects the brain's development. In pioneering experiments, Mark Rosenzweig and David Krech reared rats either alone in an environment without playthings or with others in an environment enriched with playthings that were changed daily. In 14 out of 16 repetitions of this basic experiment, the rats placed in the enriched environment developed significantly more cerebral cortex (relative to the rest of the brain's tissue) than those in the impoverished environment. (From "Brain changes in response to experience" by M. R. Rosenzweig, E. L. Bennett, and M. C. Diamond. Copyright © 1972 Scientific American, Inc. All rights reserved.)

thinner brain cortex with smaller nerve cell bodies, as well as fewer glial cells (the "glue cells" that support and nourish the brain's neurons). Rosenzweig (1984; Renner & Rosenzweig, 1987) reported being so surprised by these effects of experience on brain tissue that he repeated the experiment several times before publishing his findings—findings that have led to improvements in the environments provided for laboratory, farm, and zoo animals—and for institutionalized children.

Recent studies extend these findings. Several research teams have found that infant rats and premature babies benefit from the stimulation of being touched or massaged (Field & others, 1986; Meaney & others, 1988). "Handled" infants of both species gain weight more rapidly and develop faster neurologically. William Greenough and his University of Illinois colleagues (1987) further discovered that repeated experiences sculpt a rat's neural tissue—at the very spot in the brain that processes the experience. This sculpting preserves activated neural connections while allowing unused connections to degenerate.

Throughout life our neural tissue is changing. Sights and smells, touches and tugs activate and strengthen some neural pathways, while others weaken from disuse. It's like paths through a forest: Less traveled paths are abandoned, popular paths are broadened. Our genes dictate our overall brain architecture, but experience directs the details. If a monkey is trained to push a lever with a finger several thousand times a day, the brain tissue that controls the finger changes to reflect the experience. The wiring of basketball star Michael Jordan's brain reflects the thousands of hours he has spent shooting baskets. Experience nurtures nature.

Motor Development As the infant's muscles and neural networks mature, ever more complicated skills emerge. Although the age at which infants sit, stand, and walk varies from child to child, the sequence in which babies pass these developmental milestones is universal (Figure 3-7).

Can experience retard or speed up the maturation of physical skills? For example, do babies bound to a cradleboard for much of their first year—a traditional practice among Hopi and Navajo Indians—walk later than do unbound infants? Or, if allowed to spend an hour a day in a walker chair after age 4 months, will babies walk earlier? Amazingly, in view of what we now know about the effects experience has on the brain, the answer seems to be no (Dennis, 1940; Ridenour, 1982).

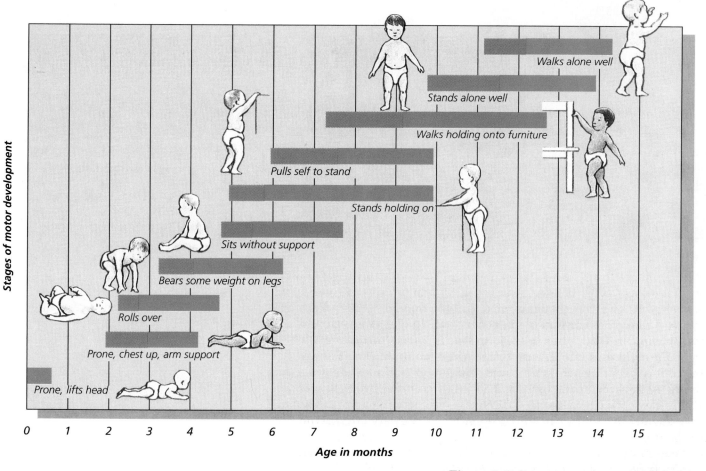

Stages of motor development

Walks alone well

Stands alone well

Walks holding onto furniture

Pulls self to stand

Stands holding on

Sits without support

Bears some weight on legs

Rolls over

Prone, chest up, arm support

Prone, lifts head

| 0 | 1 | 2 | 3 | 4 | 5 | 6 | 7 | 8 | 9 | 10 | 11 | 12 | 13 | 14 | 15 |

Age in months

Biological maturation—including the rapid development of the cerebellum at the rear of the brain—creates a readiness to learn walking at about 1 year of age. Experience before that time has no more than a small effect. This is true for other physical skills, including bowel and bladder control. Until the necessary muscular and neural maturation has occurred, no amount of pleading, harassment, or punishment can lead to successful toilet training.

After a spurt during the first 2 years, growth slows to a steady 2 to 3 inches per year through childhood. With all of the neurons and most of their interconnections in place, brain development after age 2 similarly proceeds at a slower pace. The sensory and motor cortex areas continue to mature, enabling fine motor skills to develop further (R. Wilson, 1978). The association areas of the cortex—those linked with thinking, memory, and language—are the last brain areas to develop.

Figure 3–7 Some stages of motor development in infants. Although some infants reach each milestone ahead of others, the order of the stages is the same for all infants. The colored bars show developmental norms. The far left and right sides of the bar indicate the ages by which 25 percent and 90 percent have mastered this movement. Where the colors meet shows the point at which half the infants have mastered the movement. (Adapted from Frankenburg & Dodds, 1967.)

To predict a girl's adult height, double her height at 18 months. To predict a boy's adult height, double his height at 2 years.

Cognitive Development

When the association areas develop, the child's mental abilities surge ahead (Chugani & Phelps, 1986; Thatcher & others, 1987). Brain and mind develop together. **Cognition** refers to all the mental activities associated with thinking, knowing, and remembering. Few questions intrigue developmental psychologists more than these: When and how do children begin to see things from another's point of view? Reason logically? Think symbolically? Simply put, how does a child's mind grow? Such were the questions posed by **developmental psychologist Jean Piaget** (pronounced Pee-ah-ZHAY).

Jean Piaget (1930): "If we examine the intellectual development of the individual or of the whole of humanity, we shall find that the human spirit goes through a certain number of stages, each different from the other."

"Who knows the thoughts of a child?" wondered poet Nora Perry. As much as anyone of his generation, Piaget knew. His interest began in 1920, when he was working in Paris to develop questions for children's intelligence tests. While administering tests to find out at what age children could answer certain questions correctly, Piaget became intrigued by children's *wrong* answers. Where others saw childish mistakes, Piaget saw intelligence at work. The errors made by children of a given age, he noted, were often strikingly similar.

The more than 50 years Piaget spent with children convinced him that *the child's mind is not a miniature model of the adult's.* Young children actively construct their understandings of the world in radically different ways than adults do, a fact that we sometimes overlook when teaching children. Piaget further believed that the child's mind develops through a series of stages, in an upward march from the newborn's simple reflexes to the adult's abstract reasoning power. An 8-year-old child therefore comprehends things that a 3-year-old cannot. An 8-year-old might grasp the analogy "getting an idea is like having a light turn on in your head," but trying to teach the same analogy to a 3-year-old would be fruitless.

"For everything there is a season, and a time for every matter under heaven."
Ecclesiastes 3:1

How the Mind of a Child Grows The driving force behind this intellectual progression is our unceasing struggle to make sense of the world. To this end, the maturing brain builds concepts, which Piaget called **schemas**. Schemas are ways of looking at the world that organize our past experiences and provide a framework for understanding our future experiences. We start life with simple schemas—those involving sense-driven reflexes such as sucking and grasping. By adulthood we have built countless schemas that range from knowing how to tie a knot to knowing what it means to be in love.

Piaget proposed two concepts to explain how we use and adjust our schemas. First, we interpret our experience in terms of our current understandings. In Piaget's terms, we incorporate, or **assimilate**, new experiences into our existing schemas. Given a simple schema for *dog*, a toddler may call all four-legged animals *doggies*. But we also adjust, or **accommodate**, our schemas to fit the particulars of new experiences. The child soon learns that the original *doggie* schema is too broad, and accommodates by refining the category.

Look carefully at the "devil's tuning fork" above. Now look away—no, better first study it some more—and then look away and draw it. Not so easy, is it? Because this tuning fork is an impossible object, you have no schema into which you can assimilate what you see.

When we can't assimilate new experiences because they just won't fit our old schemas, our schemas may change to accommodate the experiences. For example, when people of one race view those of another race through their preconceived ideas ("He looks threatening . . .") they are assimilating. When their experiences in integrated school or work settings modify their schemas (". . . but he's a really nice guy"), they are accommodating.

Piaget's Theory and Current Thinking on Cognitive Stages

Science itself is a process of assimilation and accommodation. Scientists use their preconceived theories (for example, that newborns are passive, incompetent creatures) to assimilate (incorporate) observations. Then, as new observations collide with these theories, the theories change to accommodate (adjust to) the findings. Thus, the new concept of the newborn as competent replaces the old schema. That, Piaget believed, is how children (and adults) construct reality. What we know is not reality exactly as it is, but our constructions of it. And that is how Piaget's own concepts have functioned—first by helping us understand children's behavior and then by changing to accommodate new findings.

Piaget described cognitive development as occurring in four major stages (Table 3–1).

We more easily assimilate this photo of Picasso's wife, Françoise Gillot, than his abstract drawing of her. We readily assimilate realistic art and photos because they better fit our available schemas.

Table 3–1	*Piaget's Stages of Cognitive Development*	
Age range	**Description of stage**	**Developmental milestones**
Birth to nearly 2 years	*Sensorimotor* Experiencing the world through senses and actions (looking, touching, mouthing)	• Object permanence • Stranger anxiety
About 2 to 6 years	*Preoperational* Representing things with words and images but lacking logical reasoning	• Ability to pretend • Egocentrism
About 7 to 11 years	*Concrete operational* Thinking logically about concrete events; grasping concrete analogies and performing arithmetical operations	• Conservation • Mathematical transformations
About 12 through adulthood	*Formal operational* Abstract reasoning	• Scientific reasoning • Potential for mature moral reasoning

The developing child, he believed, moves from one age-related plateau to the next. Each plateau has distinctive characteristics that permit specific kinds of thinking. To appreciate how the mind of a child grows, let's look at each of Piaget's stages in light of current thinking about cognitive development.

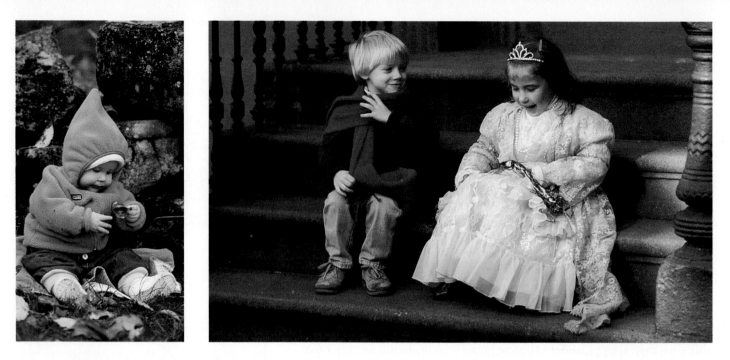

Sensorimotor Stage During the **sensorimotor stage**, from birth to nearly age 2, babies understand the world through their sensory and motor interactions with objects—through looking, touching, mouthing, and grasping. At first they seem unaware that things continue to exist apart from their perceptions.

In one of his tests, Piaget would show an infant an appealing toy and then flop his beret over it to see whether the infant searched for the toy. Much before the age of 8 months, they did not. They lacked **object permanence**—the awareness that objects continue to exist when not perceived. The infant lives in the present. What is out of sight is out of mind. By 8 months, infants begin to develop what psychologists now believe is a memory for things no longer seen. Hide the toy and the infant will momentarily look for it. Within another month or two, the infant will look for it even after being restrained for several seconds.

Object permanence emerges simultaneously with a fear of strangers, called **stranger anxiety**. Watch how infants of different ages react when handed over to a stranger and you will notice

In the sensorimotor stage of development, from infancy until nearly age 2, children explore the world through their senses. They enjoy the smell, feel, and taste of almost anything they can get their hands on. As the child moves into the preoperational stage, after about 18 months, pretending becomes possible.

"Children think not of what is past, nor what is to come, but enjoy the present time, which few of us do."
   La Bruyère, 1645–1696
   Les caractères: De l'homme

Object permanence. Younger children are still developing the sense that things continue to exist when not in sight; but for this 8-month-old child, out of sight is not out of mind.

that, beginning at 8 or 9 months, they often will cry and reach for their familiar caregivers. Is it a mere coincidence that object permanence and stranger anxiety develop together? Probably not. After about 8 months of age, children have schemas for familiar faces; when they can't assimilate a new face into these remembered schemas, they become distressed (Kagan, 1984). This illustrates an important principle: The brain, the mind, and social-emotional behavior develop together.

But today's researchers wonder: Do children's cognitive abilities really grow through distinct *stages*? Does object permanence in fact appear rather abruptly, much as a tulip blossoms in spring? Today's researchers see development as more continuous than did Piaget. For example, they now view object permanence as unfolding gradually, beginning with young infants looking for a toy where they saw it hidden a second before.

Researchers such as Jean Mandler (1990) also believe that Piaget and his followers underestimated young children's competence. Before age 2, Piaget assumed, infants cannot think. They can recognize things, smile at them, crawl to them, manipulate them. But they have no concepts or ideas. Theirs is a life not thought about, only lived.

Consider, however, a simple experiment. Andrew Meltzoff and Richard Borton (1979) gave 1-month-old babies one of two pacifiers to suck on without letting them see the objects (Figure 3–8). When later shown both pacifiers, the infants *looked* mostly at the nipple they had *felt* in their mouth. As 9-month-olds, infants can also imitate actions witnessed 24 hours earlier (Meltzoff, 1988). Clearly, they are more capable of conceptual thinking than Piaget believed.

Figure 3–8 Infants *can* think. After sucking on one of these two pacifiers, babies looked longer at the nipple they had felt in their mouth. (From Meltzoff & Borton, 1979.)

Preoperational Stage Seen through the eyes of Piaget, preschool children are still far from being short grownups. Although aware of themselves, of time, and of the permanence of objects, they are, he said, **egocentric**: They cannot perceive things from another's point of view. Children's conversations may reveal their egocentrism (Phillips, 1969, p. 61):

"Do you have a brother?"
"Yes."
"What's his name?"
"Jim."
"Does Jim have a brother?"
"No."

The preschooler who blocks your view of the television while trying to see it herself and the one who asks a question while you are on the phone both assume that you see and hear what they see and hear. When relating to a young child, it may help to remember that such behaviors reflect a cognitive limitation: The egocentric preschooler is not intentionally "selfish" or "inconsiderate," but rather has difficulty taking another's viewpoint.

Preschoolers also find it easier to follow positive instructions ("Hold the puppy gently") than negative ones ("Don't squeeze the puppy"). Parents who abuse their children generally have no understanding of these limits. They see their children as junior adults who are in control of their behavior (Larrance & Twentyman, 1983). Thus they perceive children who stand in the way, spill food, disobey negative instructions, or cry as willfully malicious.

Although Piaget's concept of egocentrism is important, preschoolers are *not* purely egocentric. Given very simple tasks, 4-year-olds will adjust their explanations to make them clearer to a blindfolded listener and will show a toy or picture with the front side facing the viewer (Gelman, 1979; Siegel & Hodkin, 1982).

Between the ages of 2 and 3, children do, however, become more capable of thinking symbolically. Judy DeLoache (1987) discovered this when she showed a group of 2-year-olds a model of a room and hid a model toy in it (say, a miniature stuffed dog behind a miniature couch). The children could easily remember where to find the miniature toy. But they could not readily locate the actual stuffed dog behind the couch in the real room. Only 6 months older, 3-year-olds, however, usually went right to the actual stuffed animal in the real room, showing that they could think of the model as a symbol for the room.

Piaget believed that during this preschool period and up to about age 7, children are in what he called the **preoperational stage**—unable to perform mental operations. For a 5-year-old, the quantity of milk that is "too much" in a tall, narrow glass may become an acceptable amount if poured into a short, wide glass. This is because the child focuses only on the height dimension and is incapable of performing the *operation* of mentally pouring it back. The child lacks the concept of **conservation**—the principle that the quantity of a substance is *conserved* (remains the same) despite changes in its shape.

Once again, however, researchers have spotted the rudiments of Piaget's cognitive stages at an earlier age than he supposed. If questioned in a way that makes sense to them, 5- and 6-year-olds will exhibit some understanding of conservation (Donaldson, 1979). Thus, the abilities to take another's perspective and to perform mental operations are not utterly absent in the preoperational stage—and then suddenly present. Rather, these abilities begin earlier and develop more gradually than Piaget believed.

Concrete Operational Stage By about 7 years of age, children enter the **concrete operational stage**. They begin to grasp that a given quantity remains the same no matter how its shape changes.

The preoperational child cannot perform the mental operations essential to understanding conservation. Closed beakers with identical volumes seem suddenly to hold different amounts after one is merely inverted.

By age 11, children can mentally pour the milk back and forth between different-shaped glasses, so they realize that change in shape does not mean change in quantity. They also enjoy jokes that allow them to use their new concepts, such as conservation:

> Mr. Jones went into a restaurant and ordered a whole pizza for his dinner. When the waiter asked if he wanted it cut into 6 or 8 pieces, Mr. Jones said, "Oh, you'd better make it 6, I could never eat 8 pieces!" (McGhee, 1976).

During the concrete operational stage, said Piaget, children fully gain the mental abilities needed to comprehend mathematical transformations and conservation. When my daughter Laura was 6, I was astonished at her inability to reverse arithmetic operations—until considering Piaget. Asked, "What is eight plus four?" she required 5 seconds to compute "twelve," and another 5 seconds to then compute twelve minus four. By age 8, she could reverse the process and answer the second question instantly.

If Piaget was correct—if children construct their understandings and think differently than adults—what are the implications for preschool and elementary school teachers? Piaget contended that teachers should build on what children already know, give them concrete demonstrations, and stimulate them to think for themselves. Future teachers, remember: Young children are incapable of adult logic. Understand how children think, and realize that what is simple and obvious to you—that, say, subtraction is the reverse of addition—may be incomprehensible to a 6-year-old.

Formal Operational Stage By age 12, reasoning expands from the purely concrete to encompass abstract thinking. As they approach adolescence, said Piaget, children become capable of solving hypothetical propositions and deducing consequences: *If* this, *then* that. Systematic reasoning, which Piaget called **formal operational** thinking, is now within their grasp.

But are younger children incapable of abstract logic? Consider this simple problem:

> If John is in school, then Mary is in school. John is in school. What can you say about Mary?

Many 7-year-olds have no trouble answering correctly (Suppes, 1982). This illustrates why, once again, critics say the rudiments of Piaget's cognitive stages begin earlier than he realized.

Reflections on Piaget's Theory Piaget's stage theory is controversial. In some ways it gets high marks. Despite cultural variations in the *rate* at which children progress down the developmental highway, Piaget's ideas find support. Studies around the globe, from aboriginal Australia to Algeria to North America, reveal that human cognition everywhere unfolds basically as he proposed (Segall & others, 1990). Today's researchers do, however, see development as more continuous than did Piaget. By detecting the beginnings of each stage at earlier ages, they have revealed conceptual abilities that Piaget missed.

What remains of Piaget's ideas about the child's mind? Plenty. Piaget identified important cognitive milestones and stimulated interest in how the mind develops. That we today are adapting his ideas to accommodate new findings surely would not have surprised him.

Piaget's writings have influenced many educators to provide children with situations and encouragement that will prompt them to do their own exploring and discovering. For younger children, especially, direct observation has proved an effective learning tool.

For more information on formal operational reasoning, see Chapter 4, Adolescence and Adulthood.

Social Development

Babies are social creatures from birth. Almost from the start, parent and baby communicate through eye contact, touch, smiles, and voice. The resulting social behavior promotes infants' emerging sense of self and their survival, so they, too, eventually may bear and nurture a new generation.

In all cultures, infants develop an intense bond with those who care for them. Beginning with newborns' attraction to humans in general, infants soon come to prefer familiar faces and voices and then to coo and gurgle when given their mothers' or fathers' attention. By 8 months, when object permanence and stranger anxiety fully emerge, infants will crawl wherever the mother or father goes and may become distressed when separated from them. At 12 months, many infants cling tightly to a parent when frightened or expecting separation and, when reunited, shower the parent with smiles and hugs. No social behavior is more striking than this intense infant love, called **attachment,** a powerful survival impulse that keeps infants close to their caregivers. Among the early social responses—love, fear, aggression—the first and greatest is this bond of love.

Origins of Attachment   A number of elements work to create the parent-infant bond.

Body Contact   For many years, developmental psychologists reasoned that infants became attached to those who satisfied their need for nourishment. It makes perfect sense. But an accidental finding revealed that this explanation of attachment is incomplete. During the 1950s, University of Wisconsin psychologist Harry Harlow bred monkeys for his learning studies. To equalize the infant monkeys' experiences and to prevent the spread of disease, he separated the monkeys from their mothers shortly after birth and raised them in sanitary, individual cages, each containing a cheese-cloth baby blanket (Harlow & others, 1971). Surprisingly, the infants became intensely attached to their blankets: When the blankets were taken to be laundered, the monkeys became distressed.

Harlow soon recognized that this attachment to the blanket contradicted the idea that attachment derives from the association with nourishment. But could he show this more convincingly? To pit the drawing power of a food source against the contact comfort of the blanket, Harlow created two artificial mothers. One was a bare wire cylinder with a wooden head, the other a cylinder wrapped with foam rubber and terry cloth. He could associate either with nourishment by attaching a bottle.

When reared with both a nourishing wire mother *and* a non-nourishing cloth mother, the monkeys overwhelmingly preferred the cloth mother (Figure 3–9). Like human infants clinging to their mothers, the monkeys would cling to their cloth mothers when anxious. They also used her as a secure base from which to venture into the environment, as if attached to the mother by an invisible elastic band that stretches so far and then pulls the infant back. Further studies with Margaret Harlow and others revealed that other qualities—rocking, warmth, and feeding—could make the cloth mother even more appealing.

In human infants, too, attachment usually grows from body contact with parents who are soft and warm and who rock, feed, and

Figure 3–9 Harry Harlow reared monkeys with two artificial mothers—one a bare wire cylinder with a wooden head and an attached feeding bottle, the other a cylinder covered with foam rubber and wrapped with terry cloth but without a feeding bottle. Harlow surprised many psychologists when he reported that the monkeys much preferred contact with the comfortable cloth mother even while feeding from the nourishing wire mother.

SKiP

pat. All this should reassure the fathers of breast-fed infants: Attachment does not depend on feeding alone.

Familiarity Another key to attachment is familiarity (Rheingold, 1985). In many animals, attachments based on familiarity form during a sensitive, **critical period**—an optimal period shortly after birth when certain events must take place if proper development is to occur (Bornstein, 1989). The first moving object that a gosling, duckling, or chick sees during the hours shortly after hatching is normally its mother. Thereafter the young fowl trails after her, and her alone.

Konrad Lorenz (1937) explored this rigid attachment process, called **imprinting.** He wondered what ducklings would do if he was the first moving creature they observed. What they did was follow him around: Everywhere that Konrad went, the ducks were sure to go. Further tests revealed that some species of baby birds would imprint to a variety of moving objects—an animal of another species, a box on wheels, a bouncing ball—and that, once formed, this attachment was often difficult to reverse (Colombo, 1982).

Parents reciprocate their infants' attachment. Most mammals lick and groom their newborns during the first hours after birth and, if prevented from doing so, may later reject their offspring. Proponents of "bonding" maintain that body contact during the first hours after birth similarly boosts parent-infant attachment in humans (Kennell & Klaus, 1982). But developmental psychologists who have scrutinized the research on mother-infant bonding are unconvinced (Goldberg, 1983; Lamb, 1982; Myers, 1987). Although human infants prefer faces and objects with which they are familiar, they *don't* have a precise critical period for becoming attached. We can welcome the trend toward involving parents in the childbirth process. But mothers who have had cesarean deliveries and parents who have adopted children need not worry that their attachment to their children is deficient.

Likewise, there is little evidence that breast-feeding gives mother and child a psychological advantage. Bottle-fed infants usually enjoy nearly the same cuddling, eye contact, and sensory experience as nursing infants. To be sure, breast-feeding is recommended as ideal as an intimate and pleasurable source of perfect nutrition—as perfect as any mammal's milk is for its own offspring. But, psychologically speaking, to have been bottle-fed is not to be handicapped (Fergusson & others, 1987).

Temperament and Parenting The quality of parent-child attachment depends not only on comfortable contact and a growing familiarity but also on inborn traits that the child brings into the relationship. The infant's **temperament** includes the inborn rudiments of personality and especially refers to the child's emotional excitability—whether reactive, intense, and fidgety or easygoing, quiet, and placid. From the first weeks of life, "easy" babies are cheerful, relaxed, and predictable in feeding and sleeping. "Difficult" babies are more irritable, intense, and unpredictable (Chess & Thomas, 1987).

The most emotionally reactive newborns tend also to be the most reactive 9-month-olds (Wilson & Matheny, 1986; Worobey & Blajda, 1989). And 4-month-olds who react to changing scenes with arched back, pumping legs, and crying are usually fearful and inhibited in their second year. Those who react with relaxed smiles

When imprinting studies go awry . . .

"The Far Side" cartoon is reprinted by permission of Chronicle Features, San Francisco.

are usually fearless and sociable in their second year (Kagan, 1990). The most inhibited and fearful 2-year-olds often are still relatively shy as 7-year-olds (Kagan, 1989). And the most emotionally intense preschoolers tend to be relatively intense as young adults (Larsen & Diener, 1987). With age, many shy, inhibited infants relax, but few fearless, spontaneous infants become shy.

Physiological tests reveal that high-strung infants have high and variable heart rates and a reactive nervous system (Kagan, 1989). Infant monkeys also vary in temperament. Some are timid and fearful, others more relaxed (Suomi, 1983). And in monkeys as in humans, the timid, anxious ones become more physiologically aroused when facing new or strange situations.

How are children's temperaments linked with parental behavior? Placed in a strange situation (usually a laboratory playroom), some infants show *secure attachment*. In their mother's presence they play comfortably, happily exploring their new environment. When she leaves, they are distressed; when she returns, they seek contact with her. Other infants show *insecure attachment*. They are less likely to explore their surroundings and may even cling to their mother. When she leaves, they cry loudly; when she returns, they may be indifferent or even hostile toward her (Ainsworth, 1973, 1989; Van IJzendoorn & Kroonenberg, 1988). What accounts for these differences?

In studies the world over, some babies seem more disposed to forming a secure attachment—just as, from birth, some babies are easier to hold, cuddle, and comfort. But there is more to infant differences than temperament. Another possible influence on attachment is the mother's behavior. Mary Ainsworth (1979) observed mother-infant pairs at home during the first 6 months and then later observed the 1-year-old infants in a strange situation without their mothers. Sensitive, responsive mothers—mothers who continually noticed what their babies were doing and responded appropriately—had infants who usually became securely attached. Insensitive, unresponsive mothers—mothers who attended to their babies when they felt like doing so but ignored them at other times—had infants who often became insecurely attached. The Harlows' monkey studies, in which the artificial mothers were the ultimate in unresponsiveness, produced even more striking effects. When put in strange situations without their artificial mothers, the deprived infants were more than distressed—they were terrified (Figure 3–10).

The attachments of early childhood eventually relax. Whether raised entirely at home or also in a day care center, whether living in North America, Guatemala, or the Kalahari Desert, anxiety over being separated from parents peaks at around 13 months and then gradually declines (Kagan, 1976) (see Figure 3–11). With time, children become familiar with a wider range of situations and communicate with strangers more freely.

Does this mean that, as we develop, our need for and love of others fades away? Hardly. In other ways our capacity for love grows, and our pleasure in touching and holding those we love never ceases. The power of early attachment nonetheless gradually relaxes, allowing children to move out into the world. One might even say that much of the life cycle story boils down to a poignant rhythm of attachment and separation—from the attachment of fetal life to the separation of birth, from infant attachment to adolescent separation, from the attachment of marriage and parenthood to the separation of death.

Figure 3–10 Monkeys raised by artificial mothers were terror-stricken when placed in strange situations without their surrogate mothers.

Figure 3–11 Infants' anxiety over separation from parents. In an experiment, groups of infants who had and had not experienced day care were left alone by their mothers in an unfamiliar room. In both groups, the percentage who cried when the mother left peaked at about 13 months. (From Kagan, 1976.)

Close-Up *Father Care*

Michael Lamb (1979): "Mothers and fathers can be equally effective as parents. They just have different styles."

Perhaps you are wondering why mothers are the focus of so much developmental research. Why not fathers, too? The common assumption, long seen in child-custody decisions, has been that fathers are less interested and less competent in child care than mothers. In both subtle and not-so-subtle ways, psychologists have accepted this assumption. Infants who lack mother care are said to suffer "maternal deprivation"; those lacking father care are said merely to experience "father absence."

Across the world mothers do assume more responsibility for infant care, and young children more quickly turn to their mothers for comfort and support (Hartup, 1989). Moreover, a breast-feeding mother and nursing infant have wonderfully coordinated biological systems that predispose their responsiveness to one another. Nevertheless, many modern fathers are becoming more involved in infant care, and researchers are becoming more interested in fathers.

One of the leading father-watchers, Ross Parke (1981), reports that fathers can be as interested in, sensitive to, and affectionate toward their infants as mothers typically are. Although mothers usually do most of the infant care, fathers are as capable (at least when researchers are watching). Although most infants prefer their mothers when anxious, when left alone they are as distressed by their father's departure as by their mother's. Moreover, infants whose fathers have shared in their diapering, bathing, and feeding are more secure when left with a stranger. Preschoolers with involved fathers tend to become adults who are especially concerned with being kind, sensitive, and warmhearted (Koestner & others, 1990).

Looking for differences, research psychologists have also uncovered several distinctive ways in which fathers and mothers interact with their infants. Fathers smile less at their babies (males smile less at everyone). They spend more of their interaction in play rather than caregiving (especially with sons). And they play with more physical excitement (Parke, 1981).

However, fathers who are the primary caregivers interact with their babies more, as mothers typically do. This suggests that father-mother differences are not biologically fixed, but have social roots as well. Animal research confirms this. When the Harlows caged monkey mothers and fathers with their infants, the fathers, too, were protective and affectionate toward their infants.

Within two-parent families, both parents have yet another gift to offer: their support of one another. Mothers and fathers who support one another and who sense this mutual support and agreement in child-rearing are more responsive to their infants and feel more competent as parents (Dickie, 1987).

Thanks partly to such research, "fathering" is shifting meaning. "Fathering a child" once meant impregnating, "mothering" meant nurturing. More and more these days, fathering and mothering both mean parenting.

Effects of Attachment Does a trusting, secure attachment have lasting benefits? Does the quality of an infant's attachment predict the child's social competence in the years that follow? As adults, our romantic love styles still exhibit childlike secure, trusting attachment or insecure, anxious attachment (Feeney & Noller, 1990; Hazan & Shaver, 1990; Simpson, 1991). But do our early attachment patterns actually predict our later social behavior?

Secure Attachment Promotes Social Competence   At the University of Minnesota, Alan Sroufe and his colleagues (1983) identified infants who were securely attached at 12 to 18 months of age—those who used their mother as a base for comfortably exploring the world and as a haven when distressed. When Sroufe restudied these infants as 2- to 3-year-olds, he saw them functioning more confidently than other toddlers. Given challenging tasks, they were more enthusiastic and persistent. With other children they were more outgoing and responsive.

Some psychologists believe these children's social competence reflects not their early parenting but the continued responsive parenting that these children were *still* receiving (Lamb, 1987). What is more, competent parents and their competent children share common genes that may predispose similar temperaments.

Regardless, developmental theorist Erik Erikson says that securely attached children approach life with a sense of **basic trust**—a sense that the world is predictable and reliable. A child who will let parents leave is a child who trusts they will return. Erikson attributed basic trust not to one's continuing positive environment or to one's inborn temperament, but to early parenting. He theorized that infants blessed with sensitive, loving caregivers form a lifelong attitude of trust rather than fear.

Deprivation of Attachment   If secure attachment nurtures social competence, what are the results of parental deprivation? In all of psychology, no research literature is more saddening. Children reared in institutions without the stimulation and attention of a regular caregiver, or locked away at home under conditions of extreme neglect, are often withdrawn, frightened, even speechless. Adopted into a loving home, they usually progress rapidly, especially in their cognitive development. Nevertheless, they frequently bear scars from their early neglect (Rutter, 1979).

So, too, did the Harlows' monkeys if reared in total isolation, without even an artificial mother. As adults they either cowered in fright or lashed out in aggression when placed with other monkeys their age. Upon reaching sexual maturity, most were incapable of mating. Artificially impregnated females often were neglectful, sadistically cruel, or even murderous toward their firstborn offspring. The unloved had become the unloving.

Most abusive human parents, too, report they were battered or neglected as children (Kempe & Kempe, 1978). Many condemned murderers report the same. One study of fourteen young men awaiting execution for juvenile crimes found that "twelve had been brutally physically abused" (Lewis & others, 1988).

So, do most victims of child abuse become abusive? Is today's victim predictably tomorrow's predator? No. Most abused children do *not* later become violent criminals or abusive parents. But 30 percent do abuse their children—a rate four times higher than the national rate of child abuse (Kaufman & Zigler, 1987; Widom, 1989a,b). Moreover, young children terrorized through sexual abuse or wartime atrocities (being beaten, witnessing torture, and living in constant fear) also suffer scars—often nightmares, depression, and a troubled adolescence (Browne & Finkelhor, 1986; Goleman, 1987).

Disruption of Attachment   Judges who must decide custody in cases of child neglect or abuse often wonder: Does uprooting children, even from neglectful or abusive parents, predispose them to

"Out of the conflict between trust and mistrust, the infant develops hope, which is the earliest form of what gradually becomes faith in adults."
Erik Erikson (1983)

Monkeys raised in total isolation from the sight or sound of other monkeys for more than 6 months were terrified of other monkeys and either lashed out aggressively or cowered in fright.

In both the monkey experiments (which would not be conducted in today's climate of concern for animals) and in many cases of child abuse, the infants of abusive mothers cling to the only mother they know, as if all were forgiven.

In a 1989 Gallup poll of Americans, 8 percent of adults said, yes, they had been "a victim" of child abuse.

Close-Up **Children of Divorce**

Nearly half of North American marriages end in divorce (page 118). That sad fact makes people wonder and worry: Are children casualties of divorce? Does the stress of divorce and its aftermath erode children's well-being?

Mavis Hetherington and her colleagues (1989, 1992) summarize the available research: Divorce places "children at increased risk for developing social, psychological, behavioral and academic problems." Yet, they report, children's responses are diverse. Whether children cope well or develop behavior problems after divorce depends on such factors as the intensity of parental conflict, the child's temperament, and whether the child is uprooted from familiar friends and classmates in the process.

Following divorce, 9 in 10 children live primarily with their mothers. Although few studies compare children living with single fathers and single mothers, adolescent boys living with a single mother show a higher rate of aggression and other problem behaviors than do boys living with nondivorced parents or with their father (Hetherington & others, 1989; Stevenson & Black, 1988).

One recent study had British parents and teachers rate the behavior of 12,000 children as 7-year-olds and again 4 years later (Cherlin & others, 1991). At the second rating, boys whose parents had divorced during the 4 years had about one-fourth more behavior problems than those whose families remained intact. But the apparent effect of divorce on boys was nearly halved when allowance was made for predivorce behavior differences between the two groups. (For girls, adjusting for preexisting behavior problems did not reduce the apparent divorce effect.) For boys, it seems, family troubles begin taking a toll in advance of divorce.

Typically, divorce provides children with a double dose of stress. Immediately following their parents' divorce, many children feel angry, resentful, and depressed. Young children may blame themselves. Older children may exhibit heightened aggression and noncompliance. Within 2 or 3 years, life typically settles back to a more comfortable equilibrium. Then, often 3 to 5 years after the divorce, there may come a second dose of stress: the custodial parent's remarriage. Because 75 percent of divorced mothers and 80 percent of divorced fathers remarry, most children of divorce will gain a stepparent. Especially for girls, the new stepfather's intrusion into the home may at first be an unwelcome event, disrupting the single mother-daughter relationship and necessitating another period of readjustment.

Data amassed from eight national surveys suggest that this double stress does leave its mark on some children (Booth & Edwards, 1989; Glenn & Weaver, 1985). Compared to those who grew up in intact families, children of divorce grow up with a diminished feeling of well-being. As adults they are more likely to divorce and less likely to say they are "very happy." There is wisdom, it seems, to society's ages-old idea that a loving, stable home life offers the best hope for nurturing children.

But sometimes a stable partnership is not to be. If divorce is stressful for children, so is a conflict-laden marriage, report Hetherington and her associates (1989). Moreover, they say, easygoing children usually cope well with the challenge of divorce and remarriage, and may even emerge better prepared to cope with later challenges.

---

later emotional difficulties? What happens to an infant when attachment is disrupted?

Separated from their families, both monkey and human infants become upset and, before long, withdrawn and even despairing (Bowlby, 1973; Mineka & Suomi, 1978). Fearing that such extreme stress might cause lasting damage (and when in doubt acting to protect parents' rights), courts are usually reluctant to remove children from their homes.

However, if placed in a more positive and stable environment, infants generally recover from the distress of separation. In studies of adopted children, Leon Yarrow and his co-workers (1973) found that when children over 6 months of age were removed from their foster mothers, they initially had difficulties eating, sleeping, and relating to their new mothers. But by 10 years of age there was little visible effect. Children placed before the age of 6 months (with

"We can hazard a tentative conclusion: The child's later adjustment will be primarily determined by the quality of the relationship with the new caretakers, not by the experience of separation."

Eleanor Maccoby (1980)

little accompanying distress) were similar to those who had been adopted between the ages of 6 and 16 months (with much more distress). Although adoptions at later ages might more often be permanently disruptive, most year-old infants form new attachments without permanent emotional scars. Foster care that moves a child through a series of foster families and thereby prevents attachment can be very disruptive, however. So can repeated removal from a mother and then reunion with her.

Does Day Care Disrupt Attachment? In 1950, when some 15 percent of North American mothers worked outside the home, society's Perfect Mom was at the door with cookies, milk, and a sympathetic ear when her children arrived home from school. Today, with slightly over half of North American mothers of preschoolers employed, society's Supermom pursues a successful career while sharing parental duties with Dad. Where are the children of full-time working parents? About 40 percent are cared for in someone else's home. The rest are divided between day care centers and being cared for in their own homes (Bureau of the Census, 1990).

During the fifties and sixties, when Perfect Mom was the social norm, the research questions were, "Is day care bad for children? Does it disrupt children's attachments to their parents?" For the high-quality day care programs usually studied, the answers were no (Belsky, 1990). In *Mother Care/Other Care*, developmental psychologist Sandra Scarr (1986) explained that children are "biologically sturdy individuals . . . who can thrive in a wide variety of life situations." Scarr speaks for many developmental psychologists, whose research has uncovered no major impact of maternal employment on children's development (Gottfried & Gottfried, 1988; Hoffman, 1989).

That issue settled, the research questions have shifted to the effects of different forms of day care on different types and ages of children. We now know enough to distinguish good from poor day care. Scarr and Richard Weinberg (1986) explain: "Good care means three or four infants and toddlers per caregiver and six to eight preschoolers. . . . Good care also means a cheerful, stimulating, and safe physical environment. . . ." The ideal, then, is a verbally stim-

Drawing by Chast; ©1987 The New Yorker Magazine, Inc.

High-quality day care provides a safe, stimulating environment and a caregiver for every three to four toddlers.

ulating environment in which any child frequently talks with an adult caregiver. In this regard, quality day care offers a child more than does neglectful home care.

Parents of children 2 years and older may gain some relief from knowing that day care *can* mean high-quality child care. But the scientific jury is still debating infant day care. Developmental psychologists Jay Belsky (1988) and Edward Zigler (1986) express concern. In Belsky's words, "Children growing up in families using more than 20 hours per week of non-parental care in their first year of life are at heightened risk of seeming insecure as 1-year-olds and of being disobedient and aggressive at older ages." Believing that parent-infant emotional "attunement" requires a great commitment, Zigler advocates having the United States join nearly all other industrialized nations in establishing a national parental leave policy (Zigler & Frank, 1988).

Many developmentalists, including Sandra Scarr, believe that *quality* infant day care does not hinder secure attachment. For example, Alison Clarke-Stewart (1989) notes that the slightly greater disobedience of day care infants signifies greater independence and self-confidence. She wouldn't be surprised by two new studies of enriched infant day care in the United States and Sweden (Andersson, 1989; Field, 1990). In both, school children who had experienced quality day care during their first 6 months were *more* outgoing, popular, and academically successful than those who hadn't.

One striking outcome of research on parent care and day care is how *little* quality time children receive from parents, employed or not. One national survey revealed that employed mothers average only 11 minutes and fathers only 8 minutes per weekday in child-centered activities such as reading, conversing, and playing with their children. Homemaker mothers devote not much more to such activities—only about 30 minutes per day (Timmer & others, 1985–1986).

There is little disagreement that the half million preschool children actually left *alone* for part of the time their parents are at work deserve better. So do those children who merely exist for 9 hours a day in minimally equipped, understaffed centers with untrained and poorly paid caregivers. What all children need is a consistent, warm relationship with people whom they can learn to trust. What they often get in a society that places a much lower value on workers who care for its future citizens than for its leaky pipes is an annual staff turnover rate approaching 50 percent (Wingert & Kantrowitz, 1990).

"There is near consensus among developmental psychologists and early childhood experts that child care per se does not constitute a risk factor in children's lives; rather, poor quality care and poor family environments can conspire to produce poor developmental outcomes."
Sandra Scarr, Deborah Phillips, and Kathleen McCartney (1990)

The United States lags behind other industrialized nations in parental leave and child care policies. High-quality child care is a long-time standard elsewhere, as with these children: Out hiking in Sweden (left) and pausing for a steam bath in Germany (right).

Self-Concept Infancy's number one social achievement is attachment. Childhood's major social achievement is a positive sense of self. By the end of childhood, at about age 12, most children have developed a self-concept— a sense of their own personal worth and social identity. When and how does this sense of self develop? And how can parents foster a child's self-esteem?

"Is my baby aware of herself—does she know that she is a person distinct from others?" The baby cannot talk, so we cannot ask her. Perhaps, however, the infant's *behavior* can provide clues to the beginnings of her self-awareness. In 1877, biologist Charles Darwin offered one idea: Self-awareness begins when a child recognizes herself in a mirror. By this indicator, self-recognition emerges gradually over about a year, starting in roughly the sixth month, when the child reaches toward the mirror to touch her image as if it were another child (Damon & Hart, 1982, 1988).

How can we know when the child recognizes that the girl in the mirror is indeed herself and not just an agreeable playmate? In a simple variation of the mirror procedure, researchers sneakily dabbed rouge on children's noses before placing them in front of the mirror. Beginning by 15 to 18 months, children, upon seeing the red spot, will touch their own noses (Gallup & Suarez, 1986). Apparently, 18-month-olds have a schema of how their faces should look. It's as if they wonder, "What is that spot doing on *my* face?"

Beginning with this simple self-awareness, the child's self-concept gradually becomes stronger. By school age, children begin to describe themselves in terms of their gender, their group memberships, and their psychological traits. They come to see themselves as good and skillful in some ways but not others. They form a concept of which traits, ideally, they would like to have. By age 8 or 10, their self-images have become quite stable.

Children's views of themselves affect their actions. Children who form a positive self-concept are more confident, independent, optimistic, assertive, and sociable (Maccoby, 1980). This raises an important question: How can parents encourage a positive self-concept? How does their parenting style affect their children?

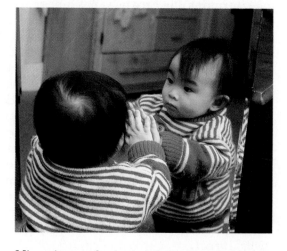

Mirror images fascinate infants from the age of about 6 months, but the recognition that the child in the mirror is "me" does not occur until about 18 months.

Child-Rearing Practices Parenting styles vary. Some parents spank, some reason. Some parents are strict, some are lax. Some parents seem indifferent to their children, some liberally hug and kiss them. Do such differences affect children?

The most heavily researched aspect of parenting has been how, and to what extent, parents seek to control their children. Several investigators have identified four parenting styles: (1) authoritarian, (2) authoritative, (3) permissive, and (4) rejecting-neglecting.

Authoritarian parents impose rules and expect obedience: "Don't interrupt." "Don't leave your room a mess." "Don't stay out late or you'll be grounded." "Why? Because I said so."

Authoritative parents are both demanding and responsive. They exert control by setting rules and consistently enforcing them, but also by explaining the reasons and, especially with older children, encouraging open discussion when making the rules.

Permissive parents submit to their children's desires, make few demands, and use little punishment.

Rejecting-neglecting parents are disengaged. They expect little and invest little.

Studies by Stanley Coopersmith (1967), Diana Baumrind (1983, 1991), and John Buri and others (1988) reveal that children with the highest self-esteem, self-reliance, and social competence usually have warm, concerned, authoritative parents. Although in most studies the subjects have been middle-class White families, studies with families of other races confirm the social and academic benefits of authoritative parenting (Baumrind, 1991).

What might account for this finding? As later chapters will explain, people given control over their lives become motivated and self-confident. Those who experience little control more often see themselves as helpless and incompetent. Likewise, children who sense enough control to attribute their behaviors to their choices ("I obey because I am good") internalize their behaviors. Coerced children ("I obey or I get in bad trouble") tend not to internalize their actions.

Of the four parenting styles, authoritative parenting provides children with the greatest sense of control, for two reasons. First, authoritative parents openly discuss family rules, by explaining them to younger children and reasoning about them with older children. When rules seem more negotiated than imposed, older children feel more self-control (Baumrind, 1983; Lewis, 1981). Second, when parents enforce rules with consistent, predictable consequences, the child controls the outcome. Recall that infants become more attached to parents who sensitively and predictably respond to their behaviors. Such infants experience control.

Before jumping to conclusions about the results of different parenting styles, we must heed a caution. The evidence is correlational. It tells us that certain parenting styles (say, being firm but open) are associated with certain childhood outcomes (say, social competence). But remember: Correlation need not reveal cause and effect. There may be other possible explanations (Figure 3–12). Perhaps socially mature, agreeable children *elicit* greater trust and more reasonable treatment from their parents than do less competent and less cooperative children.

Or consider this: Authoritative parents are more often well educated and less often enduring the stresses of poverty or recent divorce—factors that can affect children's competence (Hetherington, 1979). Or maybe competent parents and their competent children share genes that predispose social competence. Knowing that parents' behavior relates to their children's behavior does not prove cause and effect.

When considering "expert" child-rearing advice we should also remember that the advice given reflects the advice-giver's values. Should the chief end of childhood be unquestioning obedience? Then an authoritarian style is recommended. Are sociability and self-reliance a higher end? Then firm but open authoritative parenting is advisable. Different experts have different values, which helps explain their disagreements.

Parents struggle with conflicting advice and with the stresses of child-rearing. Indeed, the tens of thousands of dollars it costs to raise a child buy 20 years of not only joy and love but worry and irritation. Yet for most parents, a child is one's biological and social legacy—one's personal investment in the human future. To paraphrase psychiatrist Carl Jung, we reach backward into our parents and forward into our children, and through their children into a future we will never see, but about which we must therefore care.

Studies suggest that consistency in enforcing rules, combined with calm discussion and explanation, helps children achieve self-control.

Figure 3–12 Three possible explanations of the correlation between authoritative parenting and social competence in children.

Culture and Child-Rearing Social values differ not only from expert to expert, but also from one time and place to another. Do you prefer children who are independent or who respect authority?

If you live in Western Europe or North America, the odds are you prefer the former. Most parents in Western societies want their children to think for themselves. "You are responsible for yourself," our families and schools tell us. "Follow your conscience. Be true to yourself. Define your gifts. Satisfy your personal needs." But cultural values change over time. A half century ago, Western parents preferred obedience, respect, and sensitivity to others (Alwin, 1990; Remley, 1988). "Be true to your traditions," they taught their children. "Be loyal to your heritage and country. Show respect toward your parents and superiors."

Cultures also differ from place to place. Unlike most Westerners, who now raise their children to be independent, many Asian and African cultures focus on cultivating emotional closeness. Rather than being given their own bedrooms and sent off to day care or nursery school, infants typically sleep with their mothers and spend their days close to a family member (Roland, 1988; Whiting & Edwards, 1988). Children of communal cultures grow up with a stronger sense of "family self"—a feeling that what shames the child shames the family. Compared to Westerners, people in Japanese and Chinese cultures, for example, exhibit greater shyness toward strangers and greater concern for social harmony and loyalty (Bond, 1988; Cheek & Melchior, 1990; Triandis & others, 1988). "My parents will be disappointed in me" is a concern of 7 percent of American and Italian teenagers, 14 percent of Australian teens, but nearly 25 percent of teens in Taiwan and Japan (Atkinson, 1988).

After people immigrate to a contrasting culture, such differences often diminish, but seldom disappear. For example, Mary Stopes-Roe and Raymond Cochrane (1990) invited British parents to rate the importance of 13 character traits in children. Two-thirds of West Asian immigrant parents, but only one-fifth of native White parents, rated "obedience" among the three most important qualities. Among younger people, the culture difference was somewhat less, but still substantial. Such social diversity can challenge those of us in any culture to rethink the benefits and costs of our own assumed values.

Reflections on the Nature-Nurture Issue

Everyone agrees: We are all influenced by genes *and* experience. The question is, how important is each? For physical attributes such as hair color, the genetic factor predominates. For psychological attributes, the answer is less obvious. In Chapter 11, Intelligence, we will examine the thorny debate over genetic and environmental determinants of intelligence. Here we will consider some provocative findings on how nature and nurture influence the developing personality.

Infants and young children cannot take personality tests, so investigators observe their actual behavior and infer their temperament. As we have seen, children come with differing temperaments. Are such temperamental differences hereditary? They seem to be. Animal breeders selectively mate dogs, horses, and other animals to be either high-strung or easygoing. In one selective breeding study, Finnish psychologist Kirsti Lagerspetz (1979) took normal albino mice and bred the most aggressive ones with one another and the least aggressive ones with one another. After repeating this for 26 generations, she had one set of fierce mice, one of placid mice.

When researcher Stephen Suomi (1987) placed genetically predisposed "uptight" versus "easygoing" infant monkeys with foster mothers who were themselves uptight or easygoing, heredity overrode rearing. Compared to the naturally easygoing monkeys, the uptight monkeys reacted more anxiously to the stress of separation from their mother, even when raised by easygoing, nurturant foster mothers.

To judge from twin studies (see below), genes influence human temperament, too (Matheny, 1989). Moreover, newborns of different races exhibit differing average temperaments. Babies of Caucasian and African descent tend to be more reactive and irritable than Chinese and Native American babies (who share a common Asian descent). For example, if restrained, undressed, or covered with a cloth, Caucasian babies typically respond more intensely than Navajo infants (Freedman, 1979).

Studies of Twins

Selective breeding varies heredity but not environment, thereby revealing an effect of heredity. Could we do the reverse—vary environment but not heredity—to also see an effect of environment? Happily for our purposes, nature has given us ready-made subjects for this experiment: twins. **Identical twins**, who develop from a single fertilized egg that splits into two, are genetically identical (Figure 3–13). **Fraternal twins,** who develop from separate eggs, are genetically no more similar than ordinary brothers and sisters.

Do identical twins, being genetic replicas of one another, develop more personality similarities than fraternal twins? To find out, Birgitta Floderus-Myrhed and her colleagues (1980) gave tests of extraversion (outgoingness) and neuroticism (emotional instability) to nearly 13,000 pairs of Swedish identical and fraternal twins, as did Richard Rose and his colleagues (1988) to 7000 Finnish twin pairs, and A. C. Heath and colleagues (1989) to 3810 Australian twin pairs. Their consistent findings: On both extraversion and neuroticism, identical twins were much more similar than fraternal twins, suggesting a substantial genetic influence on both traits.

Most Navajo babies calmly accept the cradleboard; Caucasian babies protest vigorously. Findings like this suggest that the rudiments of personality are genetically influenced.

Curiously, twinning rates vary by race. Caucasians have twins roughly twice as often as Asians, and half as often as Africans (Diamond, 1986).

Figure 3–13 Identical twins develop from a single fertilized egg, fraternal twins from two.

Other dimensions of personality also reflect genetic influences. John Loehlin and Robert Nichols (1976) gave a battery of questionnaires to 850 U.S. twin pairs. Once again, identical twins were much more similar, and in a variety of ways—in abilities, personality, even interests. However, most of the identical twins also reported being treated more alike than fraternal twins, raising the possibility that their experience rather than their genes accounts for their similarity. Not so, said Loehlin and Nichols. Identical twins whose parents treated them alike were *not* psychologically more alike than identical twins who were treated less similarly.

Separated Twins   Imagine a science fiction experiment in which someone, driven by curiosity, decides to separate identical twins at birth and rear them in differing environments. Would such twins differ more from one another than do twins reared together? If so, our mad scientist reasons, one could only credit their differing environments. In reality, circumstances occasionally set up just these conditions.

Thus, in 1979 when University of Minnesota psychologist Thomas Bouchard read a newspaper account of the reuniting of 39-year-old twins who had been separated from infancy, he seized the opportunity and flew them to Minneapolis for extensive tests. Bouchard was looking for differences. What "the Jim twins," Jim Lewis and Jim Springer, presented were amazing similarities (Holden, 1980a,b). Both had married women named Linda, divorced, and married women named Betty. One had a son James Alan, the other a son James Allan. Both had dogs named Toy, chain-smoked Salems, served as sheriff's deputies, drove Chevrolets, chewed their fingernails to the nub, enjoyed stock car racing, had basement workshops, and had built circular white benches around trees in their yards. They also had similar medical histories: Both gained 10 pounds at about the same time and then lost it; both suffered what they mistakenly believed were heart attacks, and both began having late-afternoon headaches at age 18.

Identical twins Oskar Stohr and Jack Yufe presented equally striking similarities. One was raised by his grandmother in Germany as a Catholic and a Nazi, while the other was raised by his father in the Caribbean as a Jew. Nevertheless, they share traits and habits galore. They like spicy foods and sweet liqueurs, have a habit of falling asleep in front of the television, flush the toilet before using it, store rubber bands on their wrists, and dip buttered toast in their coffee. Stohr is domineering toward women and yells at his wife, as did Yufe before he was separated.

Aided by publicity in magazine and newspaper stories, Bouchard and his colleagues (1990) have now located and studied some five dozen pairs of identical twins reared apart. They continue to be impressed by the similarities not only of tastes and physical attributes but also of personality, abilities, and even fears. In Sweden, which has a national registry of 25,000 pairs of adult twins, Nancy Pedersen and her co-workers (1988) identified 99 separated identical twin pairs and more than 200 separated fraternal twin pairs. Compared with equivalent samples of identical twins reared together, the separated identical twins had more dissimilar personalities. Still, separated twins were more alike when genetically identical rather than fraternal. And separation shortly after birth (rather than, say, at age 8) didn't amplify their personality differences.

Identical twins Gerald Levey and Mark Newman were separated at birth, 9 months after sharing the same fertilized egg. When reunited at age 31, they discovered that they had chosen the same vocation.

The more bizarre similarities—such as flushing the toilet before using it—exist not because we have genes for specific behaviors, contends Bouchard. Rather, presented with a similar range of options, similarly disposed people often make similar choices. Even on traits for which heredity strongly influences personality (such as "social potency"—having an assertive, take-charge nature), it does so not through a single gene but through a complex combination of genes. To influence a complex trait it takes a very large number of genes each having very small effects (Plomin, 1990a).

The cute stories do not impress Bouchard's critics. They contend that if any two strangers of the same sex and age were to spend hours comparing their behaviors and life histories, they would probably discover many coincidental similarities. Even the more impressive data from the personality assessments are clouded by the reunion of many of the separated twins for some years before being tested. Moreover, adoption agencies tend to place separated twins in similar homes. When environments are similar, the impact of environment looks smaller relative to heredity. As twins age, differing experiences often make their personality differences more noticeable (McCartney & others, 1990). Nevertheless, the twin studies illustrate why scientific opinion has shifted toward a greater appreciation of genetic influences.

Adoption Studies

Adoption studies offer additional clues. For any given trait we can ask whether adopted children are more like their adoptive parents, who contribute a home environment, or their biological parents, who contributed their genes. The stunning finding from studying hundreds of adoptive families in Minnesota, Texas, and Colorado is that people who grow up together do *not* much resemble one another in personality, whether biologically related or not (Rowe, 1990). And in many studies of families without twins, the personalities of parents have been astonishingly unrelated to the personalities of their children. Sandra Scarr and her colleagues (1981) summarized the findings vividly:

> It would have to be concluded that upper-middle class brothers who attended the same school and whose parents took them to the same plays, sporting events, music lessons, and therapists and used similar child-rearing practices on them would be found to be only slightly more similar to each other in personality measures than to working-class or farm boys, whose lives would be totally different.

What we have here is developmental psychology's newest and one of its biggest puzzles: Why are children in the same family so different? Why do the shared genes and the shared family environment (the family's social class, the parents' personalities and marital status, day care versus home care, the neighborhood) have so little discernible effect on children's personalities? Is it because even though siblings share half their genes, each sibling has a very different combination of genes? Is it because each sibling experiences a different environment (differing peer influences, birth orders, life events)?

Twin and adoption studies reveal that genetic influences account for nearly 50 percent of person-to-person differences in traits

"In some domains it looks as though our identical twins reared apart are...just as similar as identical twins reared together. Now that's an amazing finding and I can assure you none of us would have expected that degree of similarity."
Thomas Bouchard (1981)

Coincidences are not unique to twins. Patricia Kern of Colorado was born March 13, 1941, and named Patricia Ann Campbell. Patricia DiBiasi of Oregon also was born March 13, 1941, and named Patricia Ann Campbell. Both had fathers named Robert, worked as bookkeepers, and have children ages 21 and 19. Both studied cosmetology, enjoy oil painting as a hobby, and married military men, within 11 days of each other. They are not genetically related. (From an AP report, May 2, 1983.)

"Two children in the same family [are on average] as different from one another as are pairs of children selected randomly from the population."
Robert Plomin and Denise Daniels (1987)

such as outgoingness and emotional instability. What accounts for the other 50 percent? Because siblings are *not* appreciably influenced by their shared home environment (shocking as that may sound), researchers assume they *are* influenced by their *non*shared experiences—their own unique experiences. Apparently what affects each child is not so much the parents per se as how the child interacts with and experiences them, plus other peer and cultural influences. The pendulum having recently swung strongly toward genetic determinism, Robert Plomin (1990b) and other researchers now remind people that "it's not all genetic."

Adoption studies, for example, show that, although the personalities of adopted children do not much resemble those of their adoptive parents, adoption has many effects. First, the home environment influences adopted children's values, beliefs, and social attitudes. Second, in adoptive homes, child neglect and abuse are rare. (Adoptive parents are carefully screened; natural parents are not.) So it is not surprising that nearly all adopted children thrive. They score higher than their biological parents on intelligence tests, and many become happier and more stable people than they would have in a stressed or neglectful environment. Children need not resemble their adoptive parents to have benefitted from adoption.

Studies of adoptive families have provided new clues to hereditary and environmental influences on development. How similar would you expect adopted children to be to their adoptive parents? To their biological parents?

How Much Credit (or Blame) Do Parents Deserve?

Parents typically feel enormous pride in their children's successes, and guilt or shame over their failures. They beam when folks offer congratulations for the child who wins an award. They wonder where they went wrong with the child who repeatedly is called into the principal's office. Psychiatry and Freudian psychology have at times been the source of such ideas, by blaming problems from asthma to schizophrenia on "bad mothering." Society reinforces such parent-blaming: Believing that parents shape their children as a potter molds clay, people readily praise parents for their children's virtues and blame them for their children's vices. Even among chimpanzees, when one infant is hurt by another, the victim's mother will often attack the offender's mother (Goodall, 1968).

This chapter has provided some confirmation of the power of parenting. The extremes provide the sharpest examples—the abused who become abusive, the loved but firmly handled children who become self-confident and socially competent. Moreover, parents noticeably influence their children's attitudes, values, faith, and politics.

Given our readiness to praise or blame, and to feel pride or shame, we do well also to remember a simple principle: Within the normal range of environments, children's genetically predisposed tendencies will assert themselves. Children are not so easily molded as clay. Moreover, as the next chapter illustrates, lives also are formed by environmental influences beyond parents' control—by peer influences, by chance events, by all sorts of life experiences.

It may be scary to realize how risky is the business of having and raising children. In procreation a woman and a man shuffle their gene decks and deal a life-forming hand to their child-to-be, who is then subject to countless influences beyond their control. Keeping in mind that lives are formed by influences both under *and* beyond parents' control, we should be slow to credit parents for their children's achievements and slower still to blame them for their children's problems.

"It's a mistake to look at a child and say, 'I'm going to make this child X or Y.' I say . . . let's see what that child does well at and enjoys. Then let's reinforce those kinds of things . . . what people in the past have called gifts."
Thomas Bouchard (1990)

To say that genes and experience are *both* important is true, but oversimplified. More precisely, their effects intertwine. Imagine two babies, one genetically predisposed to be attractive, sociable, and easygoing, the other less so. Assume further that the first baby attracts more affectionate and stimulating care than the second, and so develops into a warmer and more outgoing person. As the two children grow older, the more naturally outgoing one seeks activities and friends that encourage further social confidence.

What has caused their resulting personality difference? We cannot say that their personalities are *x* percent due to genes and *y* percent to experience, for the gene-experience effect is combined. In fact, genes *direct* experience (Scarr & McCartney, 1983). As we grow older we *select* environments well suited to our natures. Moreover, as in our imaginary example, our genetically influenced traits *evoke* significant responses in others. This helps explain why identical twins reared in different families recall their parents' warmth as remarkably similar—almost as similar as if they had the same parents (Plomin & others, 1988). Fraternal twins recall their early family life more differently—even if reared in the same family! Thus, "children experience us as different parents, depending on their own qualities," notes Scarr (1990).

The moral: Our genes influence the experiences that shape us. The correct view, say behavior genetics researchers, is not nature *versus* nurture, but nature *via* nurture.

"Heredity deals the cards; environment plays the hand."
　Charles L. Brewer (1990)

Summing Up

By studying the human life span from conception to death, developmental psychologists examine how we develop physically, cognitively, and socially.

Developmental Issues

Three issues pervade developmental psychology. First, to what extent are human differences influenced by our genes and to what extent by our experience? Second, is development a smooth, continuous process, or do we develop through distinct stages? Third, are our lives characterized more by stability of traits or by change?

Prenatal Development and the Newborn

From Life Comes Life The life cycle begins when one sperm cell out of the nearly 300 million ejaculated unites with an ovum to form a zygote.

Prenatal Development Attached to the uterine wall, the developing embryo begins to form body organs. By 9 weeks, the fetus becomes recognizably human. Along with nutrients, teratogens ingested by the mother can reach the developing child and place it at risk.

The Competent Newborn With the aid of new methods for studying babies, researchers have discovered that newborns are surprisingly competent. They are born with sensory equipment and reflexes that facilitate their interacting with adults and securing nourishment; they quickly learn to discriminate the smell and sound of their mothers; and they may even be capable of imitating simple gestures.

Infancy and Childhood

Physical Development Within the brain, nerve cells form before birth. Sculpted by experience, their interconnections continue to multiply after birth. Infants' more complex physical skills—sitting, standing, walking—develop in a predictable sequence whose actual timing is a function of individual maturation rate. Childhood—from toddlerhood to the teen years—is a period of slow, steady physical development.

Cognitive Development Jean Piaget's observations of children convinced him—and almost everyone else—that the mind of the child is not that of a miniature adult. Piaget theorized that the mind develops by forming schemas that help us assimilate our experiences and that must occasionally be altered to accommodate new information. In this way, children progress from the sensorimotor simplicity of the infant to more complex stages of thinking. For example, by about 8 months, an infant becomes aware that things still exist even when out of sight. This sense of object permanence coincides with the development of stranger anxiety, which requires the ability to remember who is familiar and who is not.

Piaget believed that preschool children are egocentric and unable to perform simple logical operations. However, he thought that at about age 7 children become capable of performing concrete operations, such as those required to comprehend the principle of conservation. Recent research shows that young children are more capable than Piaget believed. The cognitive abilities that emerge at each stage have begun developing in a rudimentary form in the previous stage.

Social Development Although the experiences of infancy are not consciously remembered for long and their effects may be reversed by later experiences, they can nevertheless have a lasting influence on social development.

Attachment style in infancy predicts later social development. Infants become attached to their mothers and fathers not simply because mothers and fathers gratify biological needs but, more important, because they are comfortable, familiar, and responsive. If denied such care, both monkey and human infants may become pathetically withdrawn, anxious, and eventually abusive. Once an attachment forms, infants who are separated from their caregivers will, for a time, be distressed. Human infants who display secure attachment to their mothers generally become socially competent preschoolers.

As with cognitive abilities, self-concept develops gradually. By 18 months, infants will recognize themselves in a mirror. By age 12, children's self-images are quite stable and are linked with their independence, optimism, and sociability. Children who develop a positive self-image and a happy, self-reliant manner tend to have been reared by parents who are neither permissive nor authoritarian, but authoritative without depriving their children of a sense of control over their own lives. Decisions about child-rearing involve value judgments about what traits to encourage in children. Cultural differences, such as between the communalism of Asian families and the individualism of Euro-American families, illustrate the impact of parental values.

Reflections on the Nature-Nurture Issue

Studies of the inheritance of temperament, and of twins and adopted children, provide scientific support for the idea that nature *and* nurture influence one's developing personality. Developmentalists generally agree that genes *and* environment, biological *and* social factors, direct our life courses, and that their effects intertwine.

Terms and Concepts to Remember

developmental psychology A branch of psychology that studies physical, cognitive, and social change throughout the life span.

genes The biochemical units of heredity that make up the chromosomes; a segment of DNA capable of synthesizing a protein.

maturation Biological growth processes that enable orderly changes in behavior, relatively uninfluenced by experience.

ovum The female reproductive cell, or egg.

chromosomes Threadlike structures made of DNA molecules that contain the genes.

DNA (deoxyribonucleic acid) A complex molecule containing genetic information that makes up the chromosomes.

X chromosome The sex chromosome found in both men and women. Females have two *X* chromosomes; males have one. An *X* chromosome from each parent produces a female.

Y chromosome The sex chromosome found only in males. When paired with an *X* sex chromosome from the mother, the result is a male child.

testosterone The most important of the male sex hormones. Both males and females have it, but the additional testosterone in males stimulates the growth of the male sex organs in the fetus and the development of the male sex characteristics during puberty.

zygote The fertilized egg; it enters a 2-week period of rapid cell division and develops into an embryo.

embryo The developing human organism from about 2 weeks after fertilization through the second month.

fetus The developing human organism from 9 weeks after conception to birth.

teratogens Agents, such as chemicals and viruses, that can reach the embryo or fetus during prenatal development and cause harm.

fetal alcohol syndrome Physical and cognitive abnormalities in children caused by a pregnant woman's heavy drinking. In severe cases, symptoms include noticeable facial misproportions.

rooting reflex A baby's tendency, when touched on the cheek, to open the mouth and search for the nipple.

cognition All the mental activities associated with thinking, knowing, and remembering.

schema A concept or framework that organizes and interprets information.

assimilation Interpreting one's new experience in terms of one's existing schemas.

accommodation Adapting one's current understandings (schemas) to incorporate new information.

sensorimotor stage In Piaget's theory, the stage (from birth to about 2 years of age) during which infants know the world mostly in terms of their sensory impressions and motor activities.

object permanence The awareness that things continue to exist even when not perceived.

stranger anxiety The fear of strangers that infants commonly display beginning by about 8 months of age.

egocentrism In Piaget's theory, the inability of the preoperational child to take another's point of view.

preoperational stage In Piaget's theory, the stage (from about 2 to 6 or 7 years of age) during which a child learns to use language but does not yet comprehend the mental operations of concrete logic.

conservation The principle (which Piaget believed to be a part of concrete operational reasoning) that properties such as mass, volume, and number remain the same despite changes in the forms of objects.

concrete operational stage In Piaget's theory, the stage of cognitive development (from about 6 or 7 to 11 years of age) during which children gain the mental operations that enable them to think logically about concrete events.

formal operational stage In Piaget's theory, the stage of cognitive development (normally beginning about age 12) during which people begin to think logically about abstract concepts.

attachment An emotional tie with another person; shown in young children by their seeking closeness to the caregiver and showing distress on separation.

critical period An optimal period during which an organism's exposure to certain influences or experiences will produce proper development.

imprinting The process by which certain animals form attachments during a critical period very early in life.

temperament A person's characteristic emotional reactivity and intensity.

basic trust According to Erik Erikson, a sense that the world is predictable and trustworthy; said to be formed during infancy by appropriate experiences with responsive caregivers.

identical twins Twins who develop from a single zygote that splits in two, creating two genetic replicas.

fraternal twins Twins who develop from separate zygotes (fertilized eggs); genetically no closer than brothers and sisters, but who have shared the fetal environment.

For Further Reading

Berger, K. (1991). *The developing person through childhood and adolescence* (3rd ed.). New York: Worth.

A comprehensive and readable textbook summarizing what we know about infancy, childhood, and adolescence.

Chess, S., & Thomas, A. (1987). *Know your child.* New York: Basic Books.

A respected wife-and-husband child psychiatrist team discuss how effective child-rearing adjusts to the temperamental traits of the individual child.

Dunn, J., & Plomin, R. (1990). *Separate lives: Why siblings are so different.* New York: Basic Books.

Examines sibling differences by interweaving research with the life stories of famous authors and their siblings.

Maurer, D., & Maurer, C. (1988). *The world of the newborn.* New York: Basic Books.

An award-winning look at how the world looks, sounds, smells, and feels to a newborn.

Plomin, R., DeFries, J. C., & McClearn, G. E. (1989). *Behavioral genetics: A primer (2nd ed.).* New York: Freeman.

Three leading researchers provide a state-of-the-art overview of genetics and how they influence personality, intelligence, psychological disorders, and social behavior.

Scarr, S. (1986). *Mother care/Other care.* New York: Basic Books.

An award-winning guide to child care by a leading developmental researcher.

Adolescence and Adulthood

Chapter 4

For much of this century, psychologists echoed poet Alexander Pope's sentiment that "as the twig is bent the tree's inclined." Developmental experts focused on the "critical" early years, reasoning that by the end of childhood our traits have nearly set, like clay. Life experiences will smooth the rough edges, but the pliable period is over. The legacy of infancy and childhood will reach decades into the future, for our characteristic personality traits are set in place.

Now, among a new generation of developmental psychologists, the once-popular belief that no important changes in personality occur after childhood has given way to a sense that development is *lifelong*. As today's life-span perspective emerged, psychologists began to look at how nature and nurture shape us in infancy and childhood, *and* in adolescence and beyond. At a 5-year high school reunion, friends may be surprised at the divergence of their paths. A decade after college, two former soul mates may have trouble keeping a conversation going. The old belief that development plateaus after childhood has given way to a realization that as long as we live, we develop.

Adolescence

Adolescence is life between childhood and adulthood. It extends from the physical beginnings of sexual maturity to the social achievement of independent adult status.

Adolescence is a time of transition. At earlier times in Western societies (and in some developing countries today), adolescence was but a brief interlude between the dependence of childhood and the responsibilities of adulthood (Baumeister & Tice, 1986). Adult status and responsibilities were bestowed shortly after sexual maturity, often marked by an elaborate initiation. The new adult worked, married, and had children.

Then, thanks to improved nutrition, sexual maturity began occurring earlier. And thanks to compulsory schooling, adult independence began occurring later. The resulting gulf between biological maturity and social independence is adolescence.

What are the teen years like? To St. Augustine, these years were a time of fiery passions involving

> the hot imagination of puberty.... Both love and lust boiled within me and swept my youthful immaturity over the precipice.

In Leo Tolstoy's *Anna Karenina*, the teen years were, rather,

> that blissful time when childhood is just coming to an end, and out of that vast circle, happy and gay, a path takes shape.

In her diary, written as she and her family hid from the Nazis, teenager Anne Frank observed,

> My treatment varies so much. One day Anne is so sensible and is allowed to know everything; and the next day I hear that Anne is just a silly little goat who doesn't know anything at all and imagines that she's learned a wonderful lot from books. . . . Oh, so many things bubble up inside me as I lie in bed, having to put up with people I'm fed up with, who always misinterpret my intentions.

To G. Stanley Hall (1904), the first American psychologist to describe adolescence, the tension between biological maturity and social dependence created a period of "storm and stress." Indeed, after age 30, many people look back on their teenage years as a time they would not like to relive, a time when the social approval of peers was imperative, one's sense of direction in life was in flux, and alienation from parents was deepest (Macfarlane, 1964).

Other psychologists note that, for many, adolescence is often as Tolstoy described it—a time of vitality without the cares of adulthood, a time of rewarding friendships, a time of heightened idealism and a growing sense of life's exciting possibilities (Coleman, 1980). These psychologists would not be surprised that 9 of 10 high school seniors agree with the statement, "On the whole, I'm satisfied with myself" (*Public Opinion,* 1987).

Have you any idea how you will look back on your life 10 years from now? Are you doing the things and making the choices that someday you will recollect with satisfaction?

Physical Development

Adolescence begins at **puberty**, the time of rapid growth and sexual maturation. Puberty starts with a surge of hormones, which trigger a 2-year period of rapid development that usually begins in girls at about age 11 and in boys at about age 13. Boys grow as much as 5 in-ches a year, compared with about 3 inches for girls—propelling the average male, for the first time in his life, to become distinctly taller than the average female (Figure 4–1). During this growth spurt, the reproductive organs, or **primary sex characteristics**, develop dramatically. So do the **secondary sex characteristics**, the nonreproductive traits of females and males, such as enlarged breasts and hips in girls, facial hair and a deepened voice in boys, pubic and underarm hair in both sexes (Figure 4–2).

The landmarks of puberty are the first ejaculation in boys, which usually occurs by about age 14, and the first menstrual period in girls, by about age 13. (These events need not signify fertility; it may be another year or more before ejaculations contain sufficient live sperm and the menstrual cycle includes ovulation [Tanner, 1978].)

The first menstrual period, called **menarche** (meh-NAR-key), is a memorable event, one that is recalled by nearly all adult women. Most experience and later recall a mixture of feelings—pride,

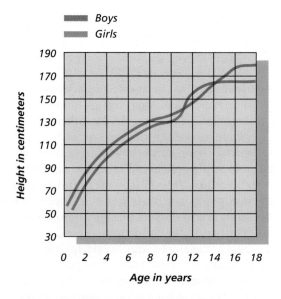

Figure 4–1 Throughout childhood, boys and girls are similar in height. At puberty, girls surge ahead briefly, but then boys overtake them at about age 14. (From Tanner, 1978.)

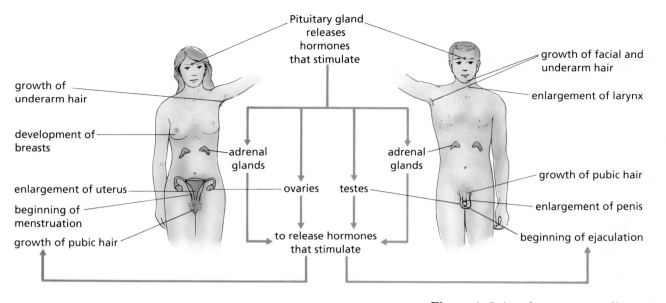

Pituitary gland releases hormones that stimulate

growth of underarm hair

development of breasts

enlargement of uterus

beginning of menstruation

growth of pubic hair

adrenal glands

ovaries

testes

adrenal glands

to release hormones that stimulate

growth of facial and underarm hair

enlargement of larynx

growth of pubic hair

enlargement of penis

beginning of ejaculation

Figure 4–2 At puberty, a surge of hormones triggers a variety of physical changes.

excitement, embarrassment, and apprehension (Greif & Ulman, 1982; Woods & others, 1983). For the first few months many keep it a secret from friends, and very few discuss it with their fathers (Brooks-Gunn, 1989). Girls well prepared for menarche usually experience it as a positive life transition. And a transition it is. Regardless of their age, girls afterward increasingly see and present themselves as different from boys and function more independently of their parents (Golub, 1983). Most men similarly recall their first ejaculation, which usually occurs as a nocturnal emission (Fuller & Downs, 1990).

As in the earlier life stages, the *sequence* of physical changes (for example, breast buds before visible pubic hair before menarche) is far more predictable than their *timing*. Some girls start their growth spurt at 9, some boys as late as age 16. Such variations have little effect on height at maturity, but they may have psychological consequences. Studies performed in the 1950s by Mary Cover Jones and her colleagues revealed that early maturation pays dividends for boys. Early-maturing boys, being stronger and more athletic during their early teen years and seemingly less childlike, tend to be more popular, self-assured, and independent.

For girls, early maturation can be stressful. In Sweden, North America, and New Zealand, studies of girls whose menarche comes either early (before age 12) or late (at age 14 or after) reveal that early maturation can amplify preexisting problems (Caspi & Moffitt, 1991; Simmons & Blyth, 1987; Stattin & Magnusson, 1990). If a young girl's body is out of sync with her emotional maturity and with what her friends are experiencing, she may begin associating with older friends and doing things considered out-of-bounds for girls her age. Moreover, the 11-year-old who towers over her classmates and becomes the object of sexual attention may temporarily suffer embarrassment and be the object of teasing (Petersen, 1987). But as her peers catch up, in junior and senior high school, her postpubertal experience may help her to enjoy greater prestige and self-confidence.

For smooth adjustment it's not only when we mature that counts, but also how people around us react to our physical development. Remember: *Heredity and environment interact.* In this case, how the environment responds to the youngster depends on the timing of maturation, as programmed by heredity.

Both early- and late-blooming adolescents tend to experience social embarrassment.

Cognitive Development

Adolescents' developing ability to reason gives them a new level of social awareness and moral judgment. As young teenagers become capable of thinking about their own thinking, and thinking about what other people are thinking, they begin imagining what other people are thinking about *them*. As their cognitive abilities continue to grow, many adolescents begin to think about what is ideally possible and become quite critical of their society, their parents, and even their own shortcomings.

Developing Reasoning Power Like physical maturity, cognitive maturity develops over time. Mature reasoning does not suddenly appear full-blown, which helps explain why many adolescents feel immune to the consequences of drug and alcohol use or sexual promiscuity. During the early teen years, reasoning is also egocentric. Adolescents often think that their private experiences are unique, and that their parents or friends (who have suffered the same experiences) just can't understand what it feels like to be dating or to hate school. The adolescent in love for the first time may sigh, "But, Mother, *you* don't really know how it feels to be in love" (Elkind, 1978).

Eventually, though, most achieve the intellectual summit that Piaget called <u>*formal operations*</u>. As we saw in Chapter 3, preadolescents reason concretely, but adolescents become capable of abstract, logical thinking. They can reason hypothetically and deduce consequences: *If* this, *then* that. Unlike children, adolescents can deduce that when someone hides a poker chip and says, "Either this chip is green or it is not green," the statement logically must be true (Osherson & Markman, 1974–1975). These abstract reasoning skills define Piaget's final stage of cognitive growth.

Older children may already have enough command of formal operations to learn algebra. But their capacity to reason systematically, as a scientist might in testing hypotheses and deducing conclusions, usually awaits the full development of their adolescent ability for formal reasoning (Inhelder & Piaget, 1958). We can see this new reasoning power in adolescents' pondering and debating such abstract topics as human nature, good and evil, truth and justice. Having perhaps envisioned God as a person in the clouds when

"The principal novelty of this period is the capacity to reason in terms of verbally stated hypotheses and no longer merely in terms of concrete objects and their manipulation."
   Jean Piaget (1972)

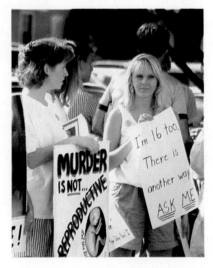

These adolescents demonstrating for and against abortion rights are illustrating their newfound ability to think logically about abstract topics—in this case, about whose rights are paramount, the mother's or the fetus's. According to Piaget, they are in the final stage of cognitive growth, formal operations.

first capable of symbolic thinking in early childhood, they may now seek a deeper conception of God and existence (Elkind, 1970; Worthington, 1989). Adolescents' logical thinking also enables them to detect inconsistencies in others' reasoning and between their ideals and actions. Indeed, their newfound ability to spot hypocrisy can lead to heated debates with parents, and silent vows never to lose sight of their own ideals (Peterson & others, 1986).

We did, however, note in Chapter 3 that today's developmental psychologists believe the rudiments of logic begin earlier than Piaget believed. Critics say that Piaget (1972) overestimated the number of people who attain formal logic. If uneducated in the logic of science and mathematics, some adolescents and adults don't achieve formal operational reasoning. Consider this conversation between researcher Sylvia Scribner (1977) and an illiterate Kpelle farmer in a Liberian village:

> **Sylvia Scribner:** *All Kpelle men are rice farmers. Mr. Smith is not a rice farmer. Is he a Kpelle man?*
>
> **Kpelle farmer:** *I don't know the man. I have not laid eyes on the man myself.*

Kpelle villagers who did have formal schooling could respond in kind to Scribner's formal logic.

Developing Morality A crucial task of childhood is learning right from wrong. To be a moral person is to *think* morally and *act* accordingly. Although as the French essayist Montaigne said, "It is a delightful harmony when doing and saying go together," such harmony often eludes us. "To put one's thoughts into action," noted the German poet Goethe, is "the most difficult thing in the world."

Moral Thinking   Piaget (1932) believed that children's moral judgments build on their cognitive development. Accordingly, Lawrence Kohlberg (1981, 1984) sought to identify cognitive stages through which moral thinking matures. To study moral thinking, Kohlberg posed stories to children, adolescents, and adults in which the characters face a moral dilemma. Ponder for a moment his best known dilemma:

> In Europe, a woman was near death from a very bad disease, a special kind of cancer. There was one drug that the doctors thought might save her. It was a form of radium that a druggist in the same town had recently discovered. The drug was expensive to make, but the druggist was charging ten times what the drug cost him to make. He paid $200 for the radium and charged $2,000 for a small dose of the drug. The sick woman's husband, Heinz, went to everyone he knew to borrow the money, but he could get together only about $1,000, which was half of what it cost. He told the druggist that his wife was dying and asked him to sell it cheaper or let him pay later. But the druggist said, "No, I discovered the drug and I'm going to make money from it." Heinz got desperate and broke into the man's store to steal the drug for his wife.

What do you think: Should Heinz have stolen the drug? Why was what he did right or wrong? Kohlberg would not have been interested in whether you judged Heinz's behavior as right or wrong—either answer could be justified—but rather in the *reasoning process* by which you arrived at your judgment. We all are moral philosophers, Kohlberg proposed, and our moral reasoning helps guide our judgments and behavior.

Kohlberg argued that as we develop intellectually we pass through as many as six stages of moral thinking, moving from the simplistic and concrete toward more abstract and principled reasoning. He clustered these six stages into three basic levels: preconventional, conventional, and postconventional.

Before age 9, most children have a *preconventional* morality of self-interest: They obey either to avoid punishment or to gain concrete rewards. (An example from children's responses to the above moral dilemma: "If you let your wife die, you will get in trouble.")

By early adolescence, morality usually evolves to a more *conventional* level that upholds laws and social rules simply because they are the laws and rules. Being able to take others' perspectives, adolescents may approve actions that will gain social approval or that will help maintain the social order. (An example from adolescents' responses: "If you steal the drug, everyone will think you are a criminal.")

Those who develop the abstract reasoning of formal operational thought may come to a third level. *Postconventional* morality affirms people's agreed-upon rights ("People have a right to live") or follows what one personally perceives as basic ethical principles ("If you steal the drug, you won't have lived up to your own ideals").

Kohlberg's controversial claim was that these levels form a moral ladder (Figure 4–3). The rungs extend from a young child's immature, preconventional morality at the bottom to, at the top, an adult's self-defined ethical principles. As with all stage theories, the sequence of levels does not vary. We begin on the bottom rung and ascend to varying heights.

Those who conform to society's rules often do not take kindly to those who seek to change those rules. Kohlberg contends that postconventional moral thinking, embodied here by Martin Luther King, Jr., may be rejected by those who, not comprehending, feel threatened by it.

Postconventional level
(may develop from adolescence on)

Morality of abstract principles: to affirm agreed-upon rights and personal ethical principles

Conventional level *(develops during late childhood and early adolescence)*

Morality of law and social rules: to gain approval or avoid disapproval

Preconventional level
(develops during early childhood)

Morality of self-interest: to avoid punishment or gain concrete rewards

Figure 4–3 Kohlberg's moral ladder.

Research confirms that children in various cultures do progress sequentially from the level Kohlberg called preconventional into the stages of his conventional level (Edwards, 1981, 1982; Snarey, 1985, 1987). However, the postconventional level appears mostly in the educated middle class of countries that value individualism, as in Europe and North America. And that is why critics contend the theory is biased against the moral reasoning of those in communal societies such as China and Papua New Guinea.

Carol Gilligan (1982; Gilligan & Attanucci, 1988) also notes a gender bias in Kohlberg's moral concepts, based as they initially were on the responses of male subjects. She contends that for women, moral maturity is less a matter of abstract, impersonal justice and more an ethic of caring relationships. For many women (and some men), morality derives more from personal emotional experience than from abstract principles. Measured by Kohlberg's yardstick, women's moral differences might seem like moral deficits.

Although studies haven't detected much difference between men's and women's moral reasoning (Blake & Cohen, 1985; Friedman & others, 1987; Thoma, 1986), women do in some ways display more of what Gilligan calls "an ethic of care." In the United States, polls continue to find that women more than men favor the Democratic party platform, which promotes programs for the disadvantaged. Women more often than men enter helping professions such as child care and social work. And daughters more than sons take primary responsibility for aging parents (Troll, 1987). In a 1989 Gallup poll, adult women were twice as likely as men to report talking daily with their parents.

Moral Action Our moral reasoning surely influences our moral talk, but talk is cheap. Morality is also doing the right thing, and what we do depends not only on our thinking but on social influences.

During World War II, many Nazi concentration camp guards were ordinary "moral" people who got corrupted by a powerfully evil situation (Arendt, 1963). Because of social influences, people's willingness to cheat, to discriminate racially, and to smoke marijuana are not neatly determined by their attitudes toward cheating, race, and drugs. The best predictor of whether a high school student smokes marijuana, for instance, is simply how many of the student's friends smoke it (Oetting & Beauvais, 1987).

Given the loose link between thinking and acting, effective moral education must focus on both. We can stimulate children's moral development through discussions of moral issues and their implications. We can also teach children to restrain their impulses, to delay small gratifications now for the sake of bigger gratifications later. Those who learn to do so become more socially responsible, academically successful, and productive (Funder & Block, 1989; Mischel & others, 1988, 1989).

And we can focus directly on just and caring moral commitments by both teaching and modeling such behaviors. When parents set high moral standards and practice what they preach, moral principles of justice and caring become forceful. Such was true of the parents of those morally courageous people who protected Jews in Nazi Europe (Oliner & Oliner, 1988).

Moral ideas grow stronger when acted on. As we will see in Chapter 18, Social Psychology, our actions feed our attitudes. We are as likely to act ourselves into a way of thinking as to think ourselves into action. To develop deeper moral principles, people can act on the ones they have. To stand up and be counted, to commit money and energy, to explain and defend our convictions is to believe them more strongly.

Should we agree that Kohlberg's postconventional, Western morality is indeed the "highest" and most "mature" level? Would society benefit if we all disregarded conventions and followed our own perceptions of universal ethical principles?

"It is obvious that the values of women differ very often from the values which have been made by the other sex."
Virginia Woolf
A Room of One's Own, 1929

"This might not be ethical. Is that a problem for anybody?"

Drawing by Vietor; ©1987 The New Yorker Magazine, Inc.

Social Development

Theorist Erik Erikson (1963) contends that each stage of life has its own "psychosocial" task. Young children wrestle with issues of *trust* (page 80), then *autonomy* (independence), then *initiative* (Table 4–1). School-age children develop *competence*, the sense that they are able and productive human beings. In adolescence, the task is to synthesize past, present, and future possibilities into a clearer sense of self. Adolescents wonder: "Who am I as an individual? What do I want to do with my life? What values should I live by? What do I believe in?" Erikson calls this quest to more deeply define one's sense of self the adolescent's "search for identity."

Forming an Identity To refine their sense of identity, adolescents usually try out different "selves" in different situations—perhaps acting out one self at home, another with friends, and still another at school and work. If two of these situations overlap—as when a teenager brings home friends with whom he is Joe Cool—the discomfort can be considerable. The teen asks, "Which self should I be? Which is the real me?" Often, this role confusion gets resolved by the gradual reshaping of a self-definition that unifies the various selves into a consistent and comfortable sense of who one is—an **identity.**

But not always. Erikson believes that some adolescents forge their identity early, simply by taking on their parents' values and expectations. Others may adopt a negative identity that defines it-

Table 4–1	*Erikson's Stages of Psychosocial Development*
Approximate age	**Description of task**
Infancy (1st year)	*Trust vs. mistrust* If needs are met, infant develops a sense of basic trust.
Toddler (2nd year)	*Autonomy vs. shame and doubt* Toddler strives to learn independence and self-confidence.
Preschooler (3-5 years)	*Initiative vs. guilt* Preschooler learns to initiate tasks and grapples with self-control.
Elementary school (6 years to puberty)	*Competence vs. inferiority* Child learns either to feel effective or inadequate.
Adolescence (teen years into 20s)	*Identity vs. role confusion* Teenager works at refining a sense of self by testing roles, then integrating them to form a single identity.
Young adulthood (20s to early 40s)	*Intimacy vs. isolation* Young adult struggles to form close relationships and to gain the capacity for intimate love.
Middle adulthood (40s to 60s)	*Generativity vs. stagnation* Middle-aged person seeks a sense of contributing to the world, such as through family and work.
Late adulthood (late 60s and up)	*Integrity vs. despair* When reflecting on his or her life, the elderly person may feel a sense of satisfaction or failure.

By trying out different roles, adolescents try out different "selves." Although some of their roles are uncomfortable for both the adolescents and their parents, most teenagers eventually forge a consistent and comfortable identity.

self in opposition to parents and society but in conformity with a particular peer group—complete, perhaps, with shaved head or multicolored, spiked hair. Still others never quite seem to find themselves or to develop strong commitments. For most, the struggle for identity continues past the teen years and reappears at turning points during adult life.

The late teen years, when many people begin attending college or working full-time, provide new opportunities for trying out possible roles. As college seniors, many students have achieved a clearer identity than they had as first-year students (Waterman, 1988). Their identity typically incorporates an increasingly positive self-concept. In several nationwide studies, researchers have given young Americans tests of self-esteem (sample item: "I am able to do things as well as most other people"). Between ages 13 and 23, the self-concept usually becomes more positive (O'Malley & Bachman, 1983). A clearer, more self-affirming identity is forming. With it comes a greater sense of control over one's future (Baumgardner, 1990).

During the teen years, identity also becomes more personalized. Daniel Hart (1988) asked youths of various ages to imagine a machine that would clone either (a) what you think and feel, (b) your exact appearance, or (c) your relationships with friends and family. He then asked them (and you might pause to ask yourself) which of these clones "is closest to being you?" Among seventh graders, three-fourths chose (c), the one with the same social network. Among ninth graders, three-fourths chose (a), the clone with their individual thoughts and feelings.

Developing Intimacy Erikson contended that the adolescent identity stage is followed in young adulthood by a developing capacity for **intimacy**, the ability to form emotionally close relationships. Once you have a clear and comfortable sense of who you are, said Erikson, you are ready for close relationships. But to Carol Gilligan and her colleagues (1982, 1990), the "normal" struggle to create one's separate identity describes individualist males more than relationship-oriented females. Gilligan believes females are less concerned than males with viewing themselves as separate individuals and more concerned with "making connections." Thus, females are less likely to exhibit Erikson's identity-before-intimacy sequence (Kahn & others, 1985).

"I am becoming still more independent of my parents; young as I am, I face life with more courage than Mummy; my feeling for justice is immovable, and truer than hers. I know what I want, I have a goal, an opinion, I have a religion, and love. Let me be myself and then I am satisfied. I know that I'm a woman, a woman with inward strength and plenty of courage."
Anne Frank
Diary of a Young Girl, 1947

As adolescents seek to form their own identities, they begin to separate themselves from their parents. What their friends are—what "everybody's doing"—they often become. In Western cultures, adolescence is typically a time of growing peer influence and diminishing parental influence, especially on matters of personal taste and life-style. When teen experiences are sampled by beeping them with electronic pagers at random times, most report feeling more free and open with friends than family (Larson & Bradney, 1988).

For a small minority, this means that parents and their adolescents are estranged. But for most, disagreement at the level of bickering is not destructive. One study of 6000 adolescents in 10 countries, from Australia to Bangladesh to Turkey, found that most liked their parents (Offer & others, 1988). "We usually get along but . . . ," adolescents often report (Steinberg, 1987). Positive relations with parents actually support positive peer relations. Although parent-adolescent conflict is most common between mothers and daughters (Tesser & others, 1989), high school girls who have the most affectionate relationships with their mothers tend also to enjoy the most intimate friendships with girlfriends (Gold & Yanof, 1985).

Moreover, most families easily bridge the generation gap, because it is rather narrow. Only 5 percent of U.S. teens report not getting on with their parents at all (Gallup Organization, 1988). Indeed, most adolescents closely reflect the social, political, and religious views of their parents (Gallatin, 1980). As often as not, "generation gaps" on such issues merely involve differences in the strength with which adolescents and their parents hold their shared opinions and values (Figure 4–4).

As identity and intimacy mature during the twenties, emotional ties between parents and children continue to loosen. During their early twenties, many still lean heavily on their parents. By their late twenties, most feel more comfortably independent of their parents and better able to empathize with them as fellow adults

Most teenagers say they generally have a good relationship with their parents. Only a small minority of teens report feeling estranged from their parents.

"When I was a boy of 14 my father was so ignorant I could hardly stand to have the old man around. But when I got to be 21, I was astonished at how much he had learnt in seven years."
    Mark Twain, 1835–1910

Figure 4–4 High school seniors' attitudes appear to be in much closer agreement with their parents' than many suppose. Agreement is greater, however, on basic values than on life-style choices. (From Bachman & others, 1987.)

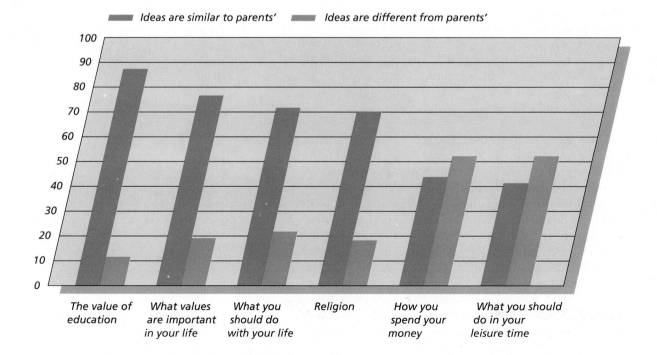

Ideas are similar to parents'   Ideas are different from parents'

The value of education | What values are important in your life | What you should do with your life | Religion | How you spend your money | What you should do in your leisure time

(Frank, 1988; White, 1983). As the twentieth century winds down, this graduation from adolescence to adulthood seems to be taking longer. Adolescents in Europe and North America are taking longer to finish college, to leave the nest, to establish their careers. From 1960 to 1990, Americans' average age at first marriage increased nearly 4 years (to 26 for men, 24 for women).

By some measures, the late twentieth century is a great time to be an adolescent. Between 1960 and the late 1980s, America's teens enjoyed the benefits of declining family poverty, smaller families, increased parental education, doubled per-pupil school expenditures (in constant dollars), double the number of teachers with advanced degrees, and an 11 percent drop in class size. By other measures, it's not so great. Simultaneously, their delinquency rate rose 110 percent, their suicide rate rose 136 percent, their homicide rate rose 194 percent, and their single parent birthrate rose 245 percent (Myers, 1992; Uhlenberg & Eggebeen, 1986). These are, it seems, the best of times and the worst of times.

Adolescent Sexuality and Pregnancy Adolescents' development obviously affects their interests and behavior. In U.S. government-sponsored surveys, the percentage of 15- to 19-year-old women reporting premarital sex rose from 29 percent in 1970 to 52 percent in 1988 (Centers for Disease Control, 1991). Those who begin having sex at a relatively young age tend to have more sex partners over time and to be more vulnerable to sexually transmitted diseases. Although teen sexual activity occurs with all classes and cultures, it is higher among teens who earn low grades, whose parents are not college graduates, who seldom attend religious services, and who use alcohol or marijuana (Harris & Associates, 1986; Orr & others, 1991).

Sexual behavior patterns vary across place as well as time: In Western Europe, the rates of adolescent sexual activity are higher than in the United States. In Japan, the reported rate has been lower—fewer than one-fourth of high school senior boys and one-tenth of girls say they have had intercourse (Tifft, 1985). Likewise, in Hong Kong a survey at the Chinese University found that 85 percent of the women believe virginity at marriage is essential (Wheeler, 1986). Premarital sex meets with greater approval in China (Burton, 1990). Yet, in general, premarital chastity is more highly valued in Asian and Arab countries (Buss, 1989).

Because most sexually active American teenagers use contraception inconsistently, if at all, the U.S. rate of teen pregnancy has surged (Figures 4–5 and 4–6). "Regardless of one's political philos-

Figure 4–5 In the United States, births to unwed mothers have risen sharply since 1960. (Data from National Center for Health Statistics.)

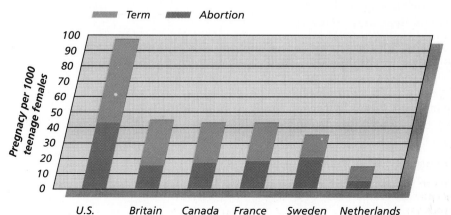

Figure 4–6 American teenagers become pregnant more often than their counterparts in other industrialized countries in the Western Hemisphere, apparently because they are less likely to use contraceptives. (Data adapted with permission from Jones & others, 1985.)

ophy or moral perspective, the basic facts are disturbing," reported the National Research Council (1987, p. 1): "More than 1 million teenage girls in the United States become pregnant each year, just over 400,000 teenagers obtain abortions, and nearly 470,000 give birth." (The rest miscarry.)

The increased adolescent pregnancy rate and the often impoverished futures of teenage mothers and their children have triggered new research on adolescents' use of contraceptives. Short of "just saying no," contraceptives are the surest strategy of preventing pregnancy. Yet 27 percent of sexually active 12- to 17-year-old Americans never use birth control and another 34 percent do so only occasionally (Harris, 1986). Why? Among the contributing factors are these:

1. *Ignorance:* In eight surveys, fewer than half the adolescents could correctly identify the safe and risky times of the menstrual cycle (Morrison, 1985). For example, in a national survey only 40 percent of 12- to 17-year-olds answered "true" to "The time when a girl is most likely to become pregnant is about two weeks after her menstrual period begins" (Harris, 1986). Ignorance becomes blind optimism in the minds of the many adolescents who report feeling virtually immune to pregnancy. Thus, most unwed teen mothers report surprise at finding themselves pregnant (Brooks-Gunn & Furstenberg, 1989). Most don't choose to become pregnant; rather, they and their partners fail to prevent pregnancy.

2. *High sex guilt:* Although sexual inhibitions reduce sexual activity, they also inhibit the planning of birth control for those who do engage in sex (Gerrard, 1987a,b; Mosher & Vonderheide, 1985; Whitley & Schofield, 1986). To begin taking birth control pills or to carry a condom is to decide to have intercourse, which sexually conservative teenagers are unlikely to do. When, as sometimes happens, passion overwhelms intentions, the result may be conception. For that matter, any teen wanting to appear "swept away" rather than deliberately sexual or promiscuous may hesitate to carry and produce a condom.

3. *Minimal communication about birth control:* Many teenagers are not comfortable discussing contraception with parents, partners, and peers (Kotva & Schneider, 1990; Milan & Kilmann, 1987). Teens are more likely to use contraceptives if they talk freely with friends or parents and are in an exclusive relationship with a partner with whom they communicate openly. Although traditional sex education courses might seem an ideal way to reduce ignorance and improve communication, studies indicate that such courses have given only a small boost to teenagers' use of contraceptives (National Research Council, 1987).

4. *Alcohol use*: Sexually active teens are typically alcohol-using teens (National Research Council, 1987). By depressing brain centers that control judgment, inhibition, and self-awareness, alcohol tends to break down normal restraints. Sexually coercive males commonly exploit this effect by trying to get their dates under alcohol's influence (page 211).

5. *Mass media norms of unprotected promiscuity*: The Planned Parenthood Federation (1986) has complained that television helps define sexual norms, which today are "Go for it *now. . . .*

"Will your child learn to multiply before she learns to subtract?"
Anti-teen-pregnancy poster for the Children's Defense Fund

Don't worry about anything." As noted elsewhere in this book (pages 248 and 570), social behaviors modeled on television can indeed have an influence. To find out what sexual behaviors television actually models, Louis Harris and Associates (1988) monitored American prime time network programs. Per hour, they counted 10 sexual innuendos, 5 embraces, and 1.8 implied acts of intercourse, exposing the average viewer to 14,000 sexual events during the 1987–1988 study year. Soap operas, especially, model behavior that produces unwanted pregnancies. Promiscuity is commonplace. In 1987, unmarried partners outnumbered married partners 24 to 1—with rarely any concern for birth control or sexually transmitted disease (Lowry & Towles, 1989). Planned Parenthood contends that repeated portrayals of unsafe sex, without consequence, amounts to a campaign of sex *dis*information.

"Students are aware that there have been changes over time in sexual attitudes, but they seem, at least many of them, to believe that history reached its final destination somewhere around 1975. They do not generally view themselves as part of an ongoing story."
Carole Wade (1990)

They did it 20,000 times on television last year.

*T*eenage pregnancy in the U.S. has reached epidemic proportions, shattering hundreds of thousands of lives and costing taxpayers $16 billion per year. Instead of helping to solve this problem, the TV networks have virtually banned any mention of birth control in programs and advertising. We need to turn this policy around. You can help.

I. On television, sex is good, contraception is taboo.

There's a lot of sex on television. We all know that. What most people don't realize is that while the networks have been hyping sex, they've banned all mention of birth control in advertising, and censor information about it in programming. (It is permitted in the news) Millions of dollars in sexually alluring ads are okay. Ads for vaginal sprays and hemorrhoidal products are okay. So are the ads which use nudity here and there to sell products. And characters like J.R. Ewing have been seducing women a few times an hour for eight years.

In 1978, researchers counted 20,000 sexual scenes on prime-time network television (which does not even include soap operas), with nary a mention of consequences or protection. It's even higher today. The only sexual mystery left seems to be how all these people keep doing it without contraception while nobody gets pregnant.

With all that worry-free hot action on television, it's no wonder American youngsters are having sex earlier and more often.

Finally, after long negotiations, the three networks agreed to let the spots run. But only after the dreaded "C-word" – "contraception" – was censored. Instead, the networks substituted this dynamic phrase: "There are many ways to prevent unintended pregnancy."

As for network policies censoring "birth control" within programs? No change. As for the rejection of commercials for contraceptive products like condoms, foams, the pill? No change. As for the reduction of irresponsible sexual imagery? No change. As for a sense of balance between sexual hype and realistic useful information? No change.

III. Blaming the public tastes

Network executives argue that they've a responsibility to uphold high standards of public taste. The mention of birth control (except in the news) would somehow violate that. Is that true? Does the public really want uneducated pregnant teenagers? And a tax bill for $16 billion?

A recent Louis Harris Poll showed exactly what the public wants. Most Americans believe that television portrays an unrealistic and irresponsible view of sex. And 78% would like to see messages about contraception on TV. A similar percentage wants more sex education in schools. So it's not the public which resists more responsible sexual imagery. It's the television executives who resist it. Why? Maybe it's just a creative problem for them. We think they can solve it. Right now they don't even mention birth control when it's exactly appropriate. Why can't J.R. ask his latest conquest if she is prepared?

How come nobody got pregnant?

Births to U.S. single mothers have quintupled since 1960, due partly to television's modeling of sexuality, suggests Planned Parenthood.

Adulthood

At one time, psychologists viewed adulthood, especially the center-of-life years between adolescence and old age, as one long plateau. No longer. Those who follow the unfolding of people's adult lives now believe development continues. Physically, cognitively, and especially socially, people at age 50 are different from their 25-year-old selves.

Recognizing that adults do change, developmental theorists have proposed various stages of adult development, complete with transition periods. When people become independent of their parents and assume work roles, a transition from adolescence to *early adulthood* occurs. This extends from the twenties (or earlier, depending on the culture and the individual) into the forties, when *middle adulthood* begins. Some developmentalists now distinguish the "young-old" years (age 65 to 75) of *later adulthood* from the "old-old" years (after age 75) of more rapid physical decline.

Labeling life's phases is a convenient way to organize the adult years. But the labels are arbitrary, and the transition points are fuzzy. Moreover, by itself age causes nothing. People do not get wiser with age, they get wiser with experience. People do not die of old age, they die of the physical deterioration that accompanies aging. And during adulthood, age only modestly predicts people's traits. If you know only that Maria is a 1-year-old and Meredith is a 10-year-old, you could say a great deal about each. Not so with adults who differ by a similar number of years. The boss may be 30 or 60; the marathon runner may be 20 or 50; your classmates may be teenagers or grandparents. Likewise, a 19-year-old can be a parent who supports a child or a student who still gets an allowance.

It's harder to generalize about adulthood than about life's early years. During the first months of life, biological maturation narrowly restricts our life course. The infant who is strapped on a cradleboard and the one who moves freely will both walk and talk at about the same age. But as the years pass, we sail a widening channel, allowing the winds of individual experience to diverge our courses more and more. Yet our life courses are in some ways similar. Our bodies, our minds, and our relationships undergo some changes in common with childhood friends, who in other ways now seem so very different.

Physical Changes

Although few of us are aware of it at the time, our physical abilities peak in early adulthood. Muscular strength, reaction time, sensory acuity, and cardiac output all crest by the mid-twenties. Like the declining daylight after the summer solstice, the decline in physical prowess begins imperceptibly. Athletes are often the first to notice. World-class sprinters and swimmers peak in their teens or early twenties. Women, who mature earlier, peak earlier than men. But most people—especially those whose daily lives do not require peak physical performance—hardly perceive the early signs of decline.

Physical Changes in Middle Adulthood   As middle-aged athletes know well, physical decline gradually accelerates (Figure 4–7). "I feel like a 15-year-old trapped in an aging 47-year-old body," said one middle-aged basketball player. But even diminished vigor is sufficient for normal activities. Moreover, during early and middle adulthood physical vigor has less to do with age than with a person's health and exercise habits. Many of today's physically fit 50-year-olds can run for miles with ease, while sedentary 25-year-olds find themselves huffing and puffing on a jog around the block.

As in adolescence, the physical changes of adult life may trigger psychological responses, which vary depending on how one views growing older. In some Eastern cultures, where respect and power come with age, outward signs of advancing years are accepted, even welcomed. In Western cultures, where the perceived ideal is smooth skin and a slim torso, the wrinkles and bulges that frequently accompany middle age can threaten self-esteem — something to try to avoid. But nature will not be denied; inevitably the lines appear, the youthful form begins to change its shape.

"I am still learning."
   Michelangelo's motto, 1560, at age 85

Figure 4–7 The body's physical capacities decline slowly during adulthood. (Adapted from Insel & Roth, 1976.)

For women, the foremost biological change related to aging is **menopause**, the ending of the menstrual cycle, usually beginning within a few years of age 50. Menopause and its occasional physical symptoms, such as hot flashes in some women, accompany a reduction in the hormone estrogen. Like the stereotype of adolescent storm and stress, the image of menopausal emotionality and depression clashes with reality: Menopause usually does *not* create psychological problems for women. One survey of 2500 middle-aged Massachusetts women found them no more or less depressed if experiencing menopause (McKinlay & others, 1987a,b). Apart from occasional stiff shoulders and headaches, Japanese women, too, report few symptoms of menopause (Lock & others, 1988).

What determines the emotional impact of menopause is the woman's attitude toward it. Does she see menopause as a sign that she is losing her femininity and sexual attractiveness and beginning to grow old? Or does she look on it as liberation from contraceptives, menstrual periods, fears of pregnancy, and the demands of children?

To learn women's attitudes toward menopause, Bernice Neugarten and her colleagues (1963) did what, amazingly, no one had bothered to do: They asked questions of women whose experience of menopause had not led them to seek treatment. When asked whether it is true that after menopause "women generally feel better than they have for years," only one-fourth of the premenopausal women under age 45 guessed yes. Of the older women who had experienced menopause, two-thirds said yes. As one woman said, "I can remember my mother saying that after her menopause she really got her vigor, and I can say the same thing myself." Social psychologist Jacqueline Goodchilds (1987) quips: "If the truth were known, we'd have to diagnose [older women] as having P.M.F.—Post-Menstrual Freedom."

Men experience no equivalent to the menopause—no cessation of fertility, no sharp drop in sex hormones. But they do experience a more gradual decline in sperm count, testosterone level, and speed of erection and ejaculation. Some may also experience psychological distress related to their perception of decreased virility and declining physical capacities. Nevertheless, after middle age most men and women remain capable of satisfying sexual activity.

Physical Changes in Later Life   Is old age "more to be feared than death" (Juvenal, *Satires*)? Or is life "most delightful when it is on the downward slope" (Seneca, *Epistulae ad Lucilium*)? What have we to look forward to? What is it like to grow old? To gauge your own understanding, take the following true/false quiz:

1. By the year 2030, 1 in 10 Americans will be 65 or older (see page 110).

2. Older people become more susceptible to short-term illnesses (see page 111).

3. The average life expectancy for a 65-year-old is 10 more years (see page 111).

4. About one-fourth of people aged 65 and older live in nursing homes, hospitals, homes for the aged, or other institutions (see page 111).

5. During old age many of the brain's neurons die (see page 111).

During middle adulthood, physical vigor depends more on exercise than on age. At age 44, Nolan Ryan pitched his seventh no-hit game.

[Handwritten margin note: Freedom — not have to worry about getting pregnant — not have to worry about menstrual cycle.]

6. If they live to be 90 or older, most elderly people eventually become senile (see page 112).

7. Recognition memory—the ability to identify things previously experienced—declines with age (see page 113).

8. Life satisfaction peaks in the fifties and then gradually declines after age 65 (see page 121).

9. Among the elderly, there are twice as many widows as widowers (see pages 121–122).

10. A fear of death preoccupies many older people (see page 123).

Life Expectancy The above statements—all false—are among the myths about aging exploded by recent research on North America's most rapidly growing population group. The post-65-year-old population in the United States rose from 1 in 25 in 1900 to 1 in 8 in 1990, en route to 1 in 5 by 2030 when baby boomers born in the 1950s and early 1960s will reach 65 (Figure 4–8). In developing countries, the proportionately small elderly population is growing even faster—and will double between 1980 and 2000. The number of childless adults also is rising. In China, where there were five children per elderly person in 1955, there will be but two children per elderly person in 2040 (Hugo, 1987). Clearly, countries that depend on children to care for the aged are destined for major social changes.

Sensory Abilities As we have seen, physical decline begins in early adulthood, but not until later life do people become acutely aware of it. As visual acuity diminishes and adaptation to changes in light level slows, older people have more accidents. Most stairway falls taken by older persons occur on the top step, precisely where the person typically descends from a window-lit hallway into the darker stairwell (Fozard & Popkin, 1978). By using what we know about aging when designing environments, we could reduce such accidents (National Research Council, 1990). Muscle strength, hearing, distance perception, reaction time, and stamina also diminish noticeably. In later life, the stairs get steeper, the newsprint smaller, and people seem to mumble more. After age 70, car accident rates per mile increase, reaching the relatively high teenage level by age 75 (National Research Council, 1990).

With age, the eye's pupil shrinks and its lens becomes less transparent, reducing the amount of light reaching the retina. In fact, a 65-year-old retina receives only about one-third as much light as its 20-year-old counterpart (Kline & Schieber, 1985). Thus, to see

Age	1960	1990	2030
65 and older	9.3 %	12.7 %	20.7 %
55–64	8.6	8.4	8.4
45–54	11.4	10.2	
35–44	13.4	15.2	12.1
25–34	12.7	17.4	13.0
18–24	8.9	10.3	12.3
Under 18	35.7	25.8	11.6
			21.9

Figure 4–8 The aging population. These U.S. Census data are paralleled by similar trends in many other nations.

The senses of sight, smell, and hearing all decline in later life. (From Doty & others, 1984.)

as well as a 20-year-old when reading, a 65-year-old needs three times as much light. That explains why older people sometimes ask younger people, "Don't you need better light for reading?"

Health For those growing older, there is both bad and good news about health. The bad news: The body's disease-fighting immune system weakens, making the elderly more susceptible to life-threatening ailments such as cancer and pneumonia. It's as if the very old have a very mild case of AIDS—the immune deficiency that hampers the body's ability to fight infections.

The good news: Thanks to a lifetime's accumulation of antibodies, older people *less* often suffer short-term ailments, such as common flu and cold viruses. For example, those over 65 are half as likely as 20-year-olds and one-fifth as likely as preschoolers to suffer upper respiratory flu each year (U.S. National Center for Health Statistics, 1990). This is one reason why older workers have lower absenteeism rates (Rhodes, 1983).

Although at birth the average American, Canadian, and Australian had roughly a 75-year life expectancy, current statistics show that those who survive to age 65 can on average expect to live until they are 83—or even longer if they are women; if they have parents who have lived past 80; or if they maintain a healthy way of life with regular exercise, proper nutrition, and no smoking. One survey revealed that most elderly people believe the majority of their peers suffer serious health problems. But when asked about their own health, fewer than one in four reported that *they* have such a problem (National Council on the Aging, 1976). So it shouldn't surprise us that only 5 percent of all those over 65 live in institutions such as nursing homes.

Bear in mind that age-linked changes need not be age-determined. For example, age per se does not affect blood pressure and blood cholesterol as much as do age-linked differences in nutrition and exercise, and the accumulated effects of smoking and drinking (Rowe & Kahn, 1987). Even hearing loss, taste loss, and lost lung capacity stem not from age alone; what we've subjected our ears, tongue, and lungs to also matters. If consumption and activity patterns rather than age itself determine "usual aging," then we age in good health.

Aging does, however, slow neural processes. During the early years of life, up to the teen years, we process information more and more speedily (Kail, 1991). But compared to teens and young adults, older people take a bit more time to react, to solve perceptual puzzles, even to remember names (Bashore & others, 1989; Schaie, 1989). Speed slows especially when the task becomes complex (Cerella, 1985; Poon, 1987). At video games, most 70-year olds are no match for a 20-year-old. (Nor, as I have discovered in play with my daughter, is a 48-year-old a match for a 14-year-old at Nintendo's perceptual speed game, Tetris.)

Beginning in young adulthood, there is also a small, gradual loss of brain cells, contributing to a 5 percent or so reduction of brain weight by age 80. But the proliferation of neural connections, especially in people who remain active, helps compensate for the cell loss (Coleman & Flood, 1986). This helps explain the common finding that adults who remain active—physically, sexually, and mentally—retain more of their capacity for such activities in later years (Jarvik, 1975; Pfeiffer, 1977). "Use it or lose it" is sound advice. We are more likely to rust from disuse than wear out from overuse.

"Everything I've got is 93. You don't see as well. You can't kick the back of your head. Your mind doesn't get old—your body does."
Actor George Burns, 1990

During this century, medical and nutritional advances have enabled a near doubling in life expectancies of those in industrialized countries (though not in Third World countries such as Nigeria, where life expectancy is 50 years). But there seems to be a biological age limit. Mathematical projections from death rate tables show that even if no one died before age 50 and heart disease and cancer were eliminated, life expectancy would increase only to 85 (Olshansky & others, 1990).

Most older people are in good enough health to maintain an active life. And the more active they remain, the more vigor they retain.

Senility and Alzheimer's Disease Some adults do, unfortunately, suffer a tragic loss of brain cells. A series of small strokes, a brain tumor, or alcoholism can result in progressive brain damage causing that mental erosion that we call senility. The most feared of all brain ailments, **Alzheimer's disease**, strikes 3 percent of the world's population by age 75. Up to age 95, the incidence doubles every 5 years (Figure 4–9). Alzheimer's symptoms are *not* the same as normal aging. (Occasionally forgetting where you laid the car keys or losing someone's name is no cause for alarm.) Nevertheless, the U.S. National Institute on Aging projects that the quadrupling of the over-85 age group by the year 2050 will produce 14 million Alzheimer's victims (Gelman, 1989).

Alzheimer's destroys even the brightest of minds. First memory, then reasoning and language deteriorate. As the disease runs its course, after 5 to 20 years, the patient becomes disoriented, then incontinent, finally mentally vacant—a sort of living death, preceding actual death, a mere body stripped of its humanity.

In its early stages, Alzheimer's disease is easily mistaken for mental laziness. Robert Sayre (1979) recalls his father shouting at his afflicted mother to "think harder" when she could not remember where she had put something, while his mother, confused, embarrassed, on the verge of tears, randomly searched the house. Caregiving family members of increasingly confused and helpless sufferers themselves often become the disease's exasperated and exhausted hidden victims.

Underlying the symptoms is a deterioration of neurons that produce the neurotransmitter acetylcholine. Deprived of this vital chemical messenger, memory and thinking suffer. An autopsy reveals two telltale abnormalities in these acetylcholine-producing neurons: shriveled protein filaments in the cell body and placques (globs of degenerating tissue) at the tips of neuron branches. At least two forms of Alzheimer's disease are hereditary, one linked with a gene defect on the twenty-first chromosome, the other apparently linked to the nineteenth chromosome (Marx, 1991). With continuing advances in our understanding of the chemical, neural, and genetic roots of Alzheimer's, hopes for eventual control of this dread disease grow.

Cognitive Changes

One of the most controversial questions in the study of the human life span is whether adult cognitive abilities, such as memory, creativity, and intelligence, parallel the gradually accelerating decline of physical abilities. Employers may wonder about their older workers. Should they encourage senior workers to retire—or capitalize on their experience? In general, people perceive the elderly as mentally less sharp (Kite & Johnson, 1988). Is this stereotype accurate?

Aging and Memory Early adulthood is the peak time for some types of learning and remembering. In one experiment, David Schonfield and Betty-Anne Robertson (1966) asked adults of various ages to learn a list of 24 words. Without giving any clues, the researchers asked some to *recall* as many words as they could from the list. As Figure 4–10 shows, younger adults had better recall—a finding that parallels the greater ease with which younger adults recall new names and process complicated information (Zacks &

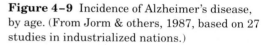

Figure 4–9 Incidence of Alzheimer's disease, by age. (From Jorm & others, 1987, based on 27 studies in industrialized nations.)

Figure 4–10 In this experiment of recall and recognition in adulthood, the ability to *recall* new information declined during early and middle adulthood but the ability to *recognize* new information showed little decline. (From Schonfield & Robertson, 1966.)

Hasher, 1988). Others, given multiple-choice questions that asked them simply to *recognize* which words they had seen, exhibited no memory decline with age. So, how well older people remember depends: Are they being asked simply to *recognize* what they have tried to memorize (minimal decline) or to *recall* it without clues (greater decline)?

Thomas Crook and Robin West (1990) confirmed the recall decline when they invited 1205 people to learn some names. Fourteen videotaped people said his or her name using a common format: "Hi, I'm Larry." Then the 14 individuals reappeared saying, for example, "I'm from Philadelphia"—providing a visual and voice cue to remember the person's name. As Figure 4–11 shows, people remembered more of the names after a second and third replay of the introductions. But regardless, younger adults' recall for the names surpassed that of older adults.

Part of the memory difficulty the elderly complain of may be normal forgetfulness. When a 20-year-old mislays her car keys, she gets frustrated; when her grandfather mislays his, he gets frustrated and blames his age. But the truth is more complicated. If asked to recall meaningless information—remembering nonsense syllables or unimportant events—then the older you are, the more errors you are likely to make. But the elderly's rich web of existing knowledge helps them catch meaningful information. Thus, their capacity to learn and remember skills and *meaningful* material shows less decline (Graf, 1990; Labouvie-Vief & Schell, 1982; Perlmutter, 1983). There also seems to be little decline with age in people's "prospective" memory—a type of memory involved in remembering *to do* something, such as taking a pill with meals or picking up bread on the way home (Einstein & McDaniel, 1990).

One other important complication: Right through their later years, people continue to diverge. If you think 20-year-olds differ widely in their abilities to learn and remember, consider this: 70-year-olds differ much more. Some 70-year-olds perform below nearly all 20-year-olds; other 70-year-olds match or outdo the average 20-year-old. Neuropsychologist Michela Gallagher (1990) has found that aging rats, too, vary much more than do young rats. Some old rats are as quick-witted as the smartest of young rats; others, for some reason, show their age.

To study this variability in aging, Gallagher taught young and old rats to swim to a platform just under the surface of a pool of cloudy water. The young rats all quickly learned where to find the platform, as did some of the old rats. When she later examined the rats' brain tissue, she found that, compared with the able rats (both young and old), slow-to-learn old rats had deteriorating brains. For example, they had fewer receptors in a part of the brain responsible for forming memories.

The moral: Because some brains age faster than others (for reasons not yet understood), we shouldn't lump all older rats (or people) together. But that's what the U.S. Federal Aviation Administration does in prohibiting pilots from flying airliners during their more accident-prone years, after age 60. Granting that it would be nice to discriminate accident-prone senior pilots from those showing no decline, the FAA in 1989 agreed to fund new research into pilot screening.

Adults' learning skills can also be seen in classrooms. In recent years, more and more adults have returned to school and turned to

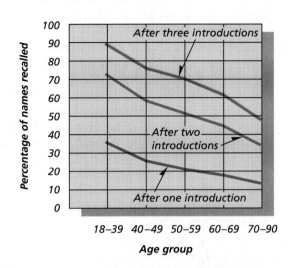

Figure 4–11 Recalling new names introduced once, twice or three times is easier for younger than older adults. (Data from Crook & West, 1990.)

"I don't recall."
  79-year-old Ronald Reagan's repeated answer when testifying at the trial of his adviser, John Poindexter

leisure education programs. By 1990, 43 percent of college students were age 25 and older (Bureau of the Census, 1990). Despite occasional difficulties in adjusting to the demands of coursework and testing, most older students do better than the typical 18-year-old, perhaps because they have clearer goals (Badenhoop & Johansen, 1980).

Aging and Intelligence What happens to our broader intellectual powers as we age? Do they gradually decline, like our ability to recall nonsense material? Or do they remain constant, like our ability to recognize meaningful material? The evolving answer to this question makes an interesting research story that illustrates psychology's self-correcting process. At any stage of scientific inquiry, we may reach conclusions that seem sound, that people readily accept, and that shape social policy. But then, with a growing awareness of shortcomings in the old research, we undertake new studies, which modify our understanding. Through its several stages, this particular research story illustrates the process (Woodruff-Pak, 1989).

Phase I: Cross-Sectional Evidence for Intellectual Decline   In **cross-sectional studies**, researchers test people of various ages at the same time. When giving intelligence tests to representative samples of people, researchers consistently find that older adults give fewer correct answers than younger adults (Figure 4–12). David Wechsler (1972), creator of the most widely used adult intelligence test, therefore concluded that "the decline of mental ability with age is part of the general [aging] process of the organism as a whole."

Until the 1950s, this rather dismal view of mental decline remained essentially unchallenged. Many executives established mandatory retirement policies assuming that their companies would benefit by replacing aging workers with younger, presumably more capable, employees. As everyone "knew," you couldn't teach an old dog new tricks.

Phase II: Longitudinal Evidence for Intellectual Stability   Colleges began giving intelligence tests to entering students about 1920, making it possible to retest older people who had taken an intelligence test years earlier. Several psychologists saw their chance to study intelligence **longitudinally**, by retesting the same people over a period of years. What they expected to find was the usual decrease in intelligence after about age 30 (Schaie & Geiwitz, 1982). What they actually found was a surprise: Until very late in life, intelligence remained stable, and on some tests it even increased (Figure 4–13).

How then are we to account for the findings from the cross-sectional studies? In retrospect, researchers saw the problem. When a cross-sectional study compares 70- and 30-year-olds, it compares not only people of two different ages, but of two different eras. It compares generally less educated people (born, say, in the early 1900s) with more educated people (born after 1950), people raised in large families with people raised in smaller families, people growing up in less affluent families with people raised in more affluent families.

According to this more optimistic view, the myth that intelligence sharply declines with age is laid to rest. As everyone "knows," given good health you're never too old to learn. At age 70, John Rock

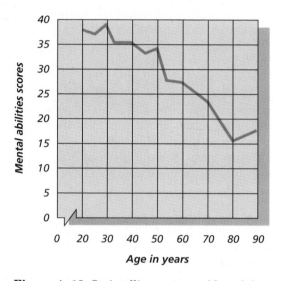

Figure 4–12 On intelligence tests older adults get fewer questions correct than younger adults. But see Figure 4–13. (From Geiwitz, 1980.)

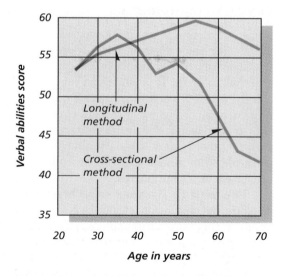

Figure 4–13 In this test of verbal intelligence, the cross-sectional method produced declining scores with age. The longitudinal method (in which the same people were retested over a period of years) produced *rising* scores well into adulthood. (From Schaie & Strother, 1968.)

developed the birth control pill. At age 78, Grandma Moses took up painting and was still painting after age 100. At age 81—17 years from the end of his college football coaching career—Amos Alozo Stagg was named coach of the year. At age 89, architect Frank Lloyd Wright designed New York City's Guggenheim Museum. Moreover, when people have kept alive their expertise—typing, playing chess, playing the piano—their abilities often remain intact well into their eighties (Schaie, 1987). As psychologist David Krech (1978) said, "He who lives by his wits, dies with his wits."

Phase III: It All Depends But the controversy is still not over. For one thing, longitudinal studies have their own pitfalls. Those who survive to the end of longitudinal studies may be bright, healthy people whose intelligence is least likely to decline. If so, such studies underestimate the average decline in intelligence.

Research is further complicated by the finding that intelligence is not a single trait (see Chapter 11, Intelligence). Intelligence tests that assess speed of thinking may place older adults at a disadvantage because of their slower neural mechanisms for processing information. But slower need not mean less intelligent. Given other tests that assess general vocabulary, knowledge, and ability to integrate information, older adults generally hold their own. Older Canadians surpass younger Canadians at answering questions such as, "Which province was once called New Caledonia?" (Told the right answer on missed questions, younger Canadians, though, have the edge a week later at recalling these answers [Craik, 1986].) German researchers Paul Baltes and Jacqui Smith (1990) are developing "wisdom" tests that assess traits such as expertise and sound judgment in life planning. Their results suggest that older adults more than hold their own on such tests. Other researchers note that with age there often comes the wisdom to reflect with greater detachment about the limits of one's knowing and the unpredictability of life (Birren & Fisher, 1990).

So, whether intelligence increases or decreases with age depends on what type of intellectual performance we measure. **Crystallized intelligence**—one's accumulated knowledge as reflected in vocabulary tests—*increases* up to old age. **Fluid intelligence**—one's ability to reason abstractly as when solving logic problems—*decreases* with age (Cattell, 1963; Horn, 1982). We can see this pattern on the intelligence scores of a national sample of adults. After adjusting for education, verbal intelligence held relatively steady from ages 20 to 74, while nonverbal, puzzle-solving intelligence declined (Figure 4–14).

"In youth we learn, in age we understand."
Marie von Ebner-Eschenbach
Aphorisms, 1883

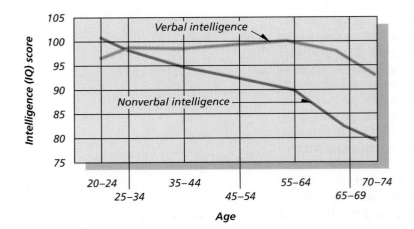

Figure 4–14 After adjustments for education, verbal intelligence holds steady with age, while nonverbal intelligence scores decline. (IQ scores from standardization sample of the Wechsler Adult Intelligence Scale, based on norms for 25- to 34-year-olds.) (Adapted from Kaufman & others, 1989.)

This helps explain why mathematicians and scientists produce much of their notable work during their late twenties or early thirties, while those in literature, history, and philosophy tend to produce their best work later—in their forties, fifties, and beyond, after accumulating more knowledge (Simonton, 1988). History bears out this finding. For example, poets reach their peak output earlier than prose authors—a finding observed in every major literary tradition, for both living and dead languages. So, whether intellectual performance increases or decreases with age depends on how we assess it.

Just as we cannot generalize that older adults are more or less intellectually competent, we can't say that they are more or less productive at work. That's the conclusion drawn by Glenn McEvoy and Wayne Cascio (1989) after assembling data gathered on nearly 40,000 workers in 96 studies. Apart from the inexperience of very young employees, age does not predict job performance.

Social Changes

Many differences between younger and older adults are created not by the physical and cognitive changes that accompany aging but by life events associated with family relationships and work. A new job means new relationships, new expectations, and new demands. Marriage brings the joy of intimacy and the stress of merging your life with another's. The birth of a child introduces responsibilities and significantly alters your life focus. The death of a loved one creates a sense of irreplaceable loss and a need to reaffirm your own life. Do these normal events of adult life shape a predictable sequence of life changes?

Adulthood's Ages and Stages Some psychologists describe the human journey through adulthood by intensively studying small samples of people. Daniel Levinson and others (1978, 1986) conducted lengthy interviews with 85 successful, middle-aged men and women. Based partly on their recollections, Levinson concluded that adults progress through periods of stability punctuated by times of upheaval and change. For example, he believes that as people enter their forties, they undergo a "midlife transition" to middle adulthood, which for many is a crisis, a time of great struggle or even of feeling struck down by life. They give up their dreams of fame and fortune (or the illusion that such bring happiness) and question their work and family commitments. The result, says Levinson, is often turmoil and despair. Fortyish people realize that they are no longer starting out, but rather drawing closer to the end. When this painful growth period concludes at about age 45, they again settle into new or deepened attachments, set about completing their careers, and become more compassionate and reflective.

Many researchers are skeptical about such efforts to define adult life as a series of neatly packaged stages, especially stages based merely on interviews with a select few people. To generalize from their career-oriented lives or to use their "midlife crises" to explain or justify the renouncing of old relationships is both misleading and dangerous (Gilligan, 1982). The fact—from large samples of people—is that job dissatisfaction, marital dissatisfaction, divorce, anxiety, and suicide do *not* surge during the early forties (Hunter & Sundel, 1989). Divorce, for example, is most common

Erik and Joan Erikson have focused their attention on the end of the life cycle as they themselves have aged. Shown here in their eighties, the Eriksons maintain that wisdom has little to do with formal learning: "What is real wisdom? It comes from life experience, well digested. It's not what comes from reading great books. When it comes to understanding life, experiential learning is the only worthwhile kind; everything else is hearsay."

"Midway in the journey of our life I found myself in a dark wood, for the straight way was lost."
Dante
The Divine Comedy, 1300–1321

among those in their twenties, suicide among those in their seventies and eighties.

Are these markers of crisis too crude to detect a more subtle midlife turmoil? National Institute of Aging researchers Robert McCrae and Paul Costa (1990) gave a "Midlife Crisis Scale" assessing sense of meaninglessness and mortality, job and family dissatisfaction, and inner turmoil and confusion to 350 30- to 60-year-old men. They could find "no evidence at all" that such concerns peak at midlife. Surprised, they gave their scale to a new group of 300 men, and a measure of emotional instability to nearly 10,000 men and women. "The results were an exact reconfirmation: There was not the slightest evidence" that distress peaks anywhere in the midlife age range (Figure 4–15).

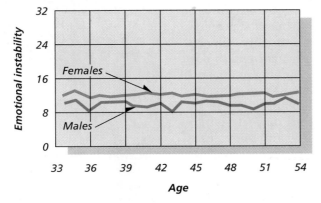

Moreover, the **social clock**—the cultural prescription of "the right age" to leave home, get a job, marry, have children, and retire—varies from culture to culture and era to era. In Jordan, 44 percent of brides are in their teens; in Hong Kong, only 3 percent are (United Nations, 1990). In contemporary Western nations, women increasingly enter the workplace and college classroom as adults. In earlier times, such ventures outside the home were unusual. Given variations in the social clock and individual experience, the stage theory critics suspect that any proposed timetable of adult ages and stages will have limited applicability.

Life Events and Chance Encounters More important than one's chronological age are life events. Marriage, parenthood, vocational changes, divorce, nest-emptying, relocation, and retirement mark transitions to new life stages whenever they occur—and increasingly they are occurring at unpredictable ages. The social clock is still ticking, but people feel freer to be out of sync with it.

Even chance encounters and events can have lasting significance, deflecting us down one road rather than another (Bandura, 1982). In the 1950s, actress Nancy Davis might never have met her future husband had she not, through a mix-up, begun to receive Communist Party mailings intended for another woman of the same name. During those early Cold War days of Hollywood blacklisting, Davis feared her career might be jeopardized by this mistaken identity. She went to see the president of the Screen Actors Guild, Ronald Reagan, and the rest is history (Reagan & Libby, 1980). Given the impact of chance encounters, it is small wonder that researcher Bernice Neugarten (1979, 1980) concludes that "adults change far more, and far less predictably, than the oversimplified stage theories suggest."

Figure 4–15 Early forties midlife crises? Among 10,000 people responding to a national health survey, there was not even a blip on the trend line of emotional instability ("neuroticism") scores. (From McCrae & Costa, 1990.)

Transitions in adult lives are often work- or family-related. As marriage at age 25, 45, or 65 heralds significant changes, so does the attainment of a college degree.

Adulthood's Commitments Two basic aspects of our lives do, however, dominate adulthood. Erik Erikson called them *intimacy* (forming close relationships) and *generativity* (being productive and supporting future generations). Researchers have chosen various terms—affiliation and achievement, attachment and productivity, commitment and competence. But Sigmund Freud (1935) put it most simply: The healthy adult, he said, is one who can love and work. For most adults, *love* centers on family commitments toward spouse, parents, and children. *Work* encompasses our productive activities, whether for pay or not.

Love "Traditional" families—father, mother, and children under 18—comprise only 27 percent of U.S. households. Who are the other 73 percent? They are older couples with an empty nest, single parents and their children, the widowed, singles, cohabiting men and women, and childless or voluntarily child-free married people. To judge from the North American divorce rate—roughly 40 percent of Canadian marriages and half of U.S. marriages end in divorce—marriage has become a union that often defies management. In Europe, too, divorce is nearly as common, after increasing 400 percent between 1960 and 1985 (Inglehart, 1990).

So, if we are freer to end miserable marriages, are surviving marriages happier? Are marriages no more often unhappy, just more likely to terminate when destructive? If you think so, consider this: Compared to back when divorce was less common, those in today's surviving marriages are actually *less* likely to describe their marriage as "very happy." For example, compared to younger married people surveyed in the mid-1970s, the number of "very happy" younger marrieds surveyed in the mid- to late 1980s was almost 10 percent lower.

In fact, among Americans married in the early 1970s, only a third in 1986 were still married *and* proclaiming their marriages very happy (Glenn, 1989). Newlyweds beware: Don't take a successful marriage for granted. Under normal circumstances, the odds are—despite what you think—that you will *not* live happily ever after. All things considered—rising divorce, declining marital happiness, rising rates of cohabitation (page 370) and births to single women (page 105)—researcher Norval Glenn (1989) declares the institution of marriage "not well."

Still, there is brighter news about marriage. More than 9 in 10 adults marry. Of those who divorce, 75 percent remarry—and their second marriages are virtually as happy as the average first marriage (Vemer & others, 1989). Although the relatively few people who feel trapped in an unhappy marriage typically feel miserable, married Europeans and North Americans are generally happier, especially when compared with those separated and divorced (Inglehart, 1990). In the United States, for example, fewer than 25 percent of unmarried adults, but nearly 40 percent of married adults, report being "very happy" with life (Glenn & Weaver, 1988).

Often, love bears children. The most enduring of life changes, having a child, is for most people a happy event. Even before their child's birth, people eagerly seek information and change their identities to incorporate parenthood (Deutsch & others, 1988). As children begin to absorb time, money, and emotional energy, however, satisfaction with the marriage itself often declines. This is especially so among those employed women who bear the traditional burden of increased chores at home (Belsky & others, 1986).

"One can live magnificently in this world if one knows how to work and how to love."
Leo Tolstoy, 1856

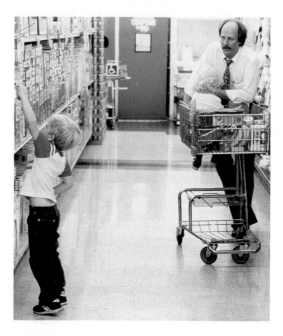

The growing number of single-parent households has altered the picture of the North American family. Single parents must find new social supports and, in many cases, learn new skills.

"Marry, and with luck it may go well. But when a marriage fails, then those who marry live at home in hell."
Euripides
Orestes, 408 B.C.

Another significant event in family life happens when children leave home. If you have left home, consider your parents' experience: Did they suffer an "empty nest syndrome"—was either of them distressed by a loss of purpose and relationship? Or did your parents discover renewed freedom, relaxation, and satisfaction with their own relationship?

Seven national surveys reveal that the empty nest is for most people a happy place (Adelmann & others, 1989; Glenn, 1975). Compared to middle-aged women who still have children at home, those whose nest has emptied report greater happiness and greater enjoyment of their marriage. Many parents therefore experience what sociologists Lynn White and John Edwards (1990) call a "post-launch honeymoon," especially if they maintain close relationships with their children. One such mother, 50-year-old Phoebe, explains: "Our family is very close. When my two sons come home I can't wait till they get here, I stay excited throughout their stay, and I'm in tears after they leave. Yet within a day or two we're back to enjoying our freedom—none of the aggravations of kids in the house, and our time is ours!" Bernice Neugarten (1974) would say that Phoebe speaks for many:

> Just as the major problem of middle-aged women is not the menopause, it is also not the empty nest. Most women are glad to see their children grow up, leave home, marry, and have their careers. The notion that they mourn the loss of their reproductive ability and their mother role does not seem to fit modern reality. No matter what the stereotypes tell us, it is not the way women talk when you listen.

Work For adults, a large part of the answer to "Who are you?" is the answer to "What do you do?" For most, to feel productive and competent is to raise children and to undertake a career.

Because it frequently takes time for people to settle into an occupation and because of the impact of chance encounters, career choices are hard to predict. During the first 2 years of college, most students cannot accurately predict their later career path. Most shift from their initially intended majors while in college, many find their postcollege employment in fields not directly related to their majors, and most will change careers (Rothstein, 1980). To many career counselors, this unpredictability means that the best edu-

"Appearances notwithstanding, for women, at least, midlife is not a stage tied to chronological age. Rather, it belongs to that point in the life cycle of the family when the children are grown and gone, or nearly so—when, perhaps for the first time in her adult life, a woman can attend to her own needs, her own desires, her own development as a separate and autonomous being."
Sociologist Lillian B. Rubin (1979)

For many, a satisfying and interesting occupation enhances happiness.

cation is not a narrow vocational training, but rather a broad liberal education, an education that fosters "the critical qualities of mind and the durable qualities of character that will serve [people] in circumstances we cannot now even predict" (Gardner, 1984).

Does work, including a career, indeed contribute to fulfillment, as Freud supposed? During the 1970s and 1980s, one approach to answering this question compared self-reported happiness among the roughly equal numbers of North American women who have or have not been employed. Their happiness difference—which slightly favors women who are employed—has always been far smaller than the person-to-person differences within each group (Adelmann, 1988; Campbell, 1981).

One reason for the roughly equal happiness of women who do and don't work for pay is that each role has its benefits—a freer life enriched by avocations for those not employed, and career-related identity and social support for those employed. Each role also has its costs. To some, housework is boring and socially isolating. But let's not romanticize punching a cash register; employed women often have low-paying, unrewarding jobs, from which they come home to a "second shift" of housework and child care. (For most women, work is never done. Today's average American husband does but one-third of the household tasks, though that's up from 15 percent in 1965 [Robinson, 1988].)

For some women and some men, the combined stresses of employment and work at home can overload the circuits (McClanahan & Adams, 1989). For many others, reports Patricia Linville (1987), there are emotional benefits to having multiple roles and identities—as parent, spouse, worker, amateur athlete, community leader, and so forth. When problems arise in any one area, one's whole sense of self feels less threatened. A difficult marriage, say, will be less devastating to the one who can think, "Despite my marital problems, I am a good parent" (or an effective worker).

From their studies at the Wellesley College Center for Research on Women, Grace Baruch and Rosaline Barnett (1986) conclude that what matters is not which roles a woman occupies—as paid worker, wife, and/or mother—but the quality of her experience in that role. Happiness is having work that fits your interests and provides a sense of competence and accomplishment; having a partner who is a close, supportive companion and who sees you as special; having loving children whom you like and feel proud of.

Well-Being Across the Life Span Researchers have also compared the sense of well-being among young and old. Who do you suppose are the happiest? The carefree youth? The up-and-coming young adults? The successful and secure middle aged? Or those enjoying the leisure of retired life?

To live is to grow older, which means that all of us can look backward with satisfaction or sorrow and forward with hope or dread. Adolescents are buffeted by mood swings and insecurity, parental power and peer pressures, identity confusion and career worries. In later life, we presume, income shrinks, work is taken away, the body deteriorates, recall fades, energy wanes, family members and friends die or move away, and the great enemy, death, looms ever closer. Small wonder that we presume the teen and over-65 years to be the worst of times (Freedman, 1978).

Drawing by M. Stevens; ©1989 The New Yorker Magazine, Inc.

"How many of us older persons have really been . . . prepared for the second half of life, for old age, death and eternity?"
Carl Jung
Modern Man in Search of a Soul, 1933

Surprisingly, they are not. People of all ages report similar feelings of happiness and satisfaction with life. Individuals vary, but more than 100 studies reveal that less than 1 percent of their variation in well-being relates to age (Stock & others, 1983). Ronald Inglehart (1990) confirmed this when he amassed interviews conducted during the 1980s with representative samples of nearly 170,000 people in 16 nations, including 10 Western European countries. As Figure 4–16 illustrates, age differences in life satisfaction were trivial.

Figure 4–16 Does well-being align itself with any particular age? Multinational surveys reveal that age differences in life satisfaction (and happiness) are trivial. (Data from Inglehart, 1990.)

Whatever the explanation—reduced stress, lowered aspirations, satisfaction over accomplishments, newfound sources of pleasure—the bottom line from hundreds of thousands of interviews with people of all ages in many countries is this: Older people report as much happiness and satisfaction with life as younger people do. Given that growing older is one sure consequence of living, an outcome that most of us prefer to its alternative, we can all take comfort in this finding.

The astonishing stability of well-being across the life span obscures some interesting age-related emotional differences. As the years go by, feelings mellow (Costa & others, 1987; Diener & others, 1986). Highs become less high, lows less low. Thus, although the *average* feeling level may remain stable, with age we find ourselves less often feeling excited, intensely proud, and on top of the world, but also less often depressed. Compliments provoke less elation and criticisms less despair as both become merely additional feedback atop a mountain of accumulated praise and blame. Psychologists Mihaly Csikszentmihalyi and Reed Larson (1984) mapped people's emotional terrain by periodically signaling them with electronic beepers to report their current activities and feelings. They found that teenagers typically come down from elation or up from gloom in less than an hour. Adult moods are less extreme but more enduring. For most people, old age offers less intense joy but greater contentment. As we age, life's emotional roller coaster provides a smoother ride.

Death and Dying Most of us will suffer and cope with the deaths of relatives and friends. Usually, the most difficult separation is from one's spouse—a loss suffered by five times more women than

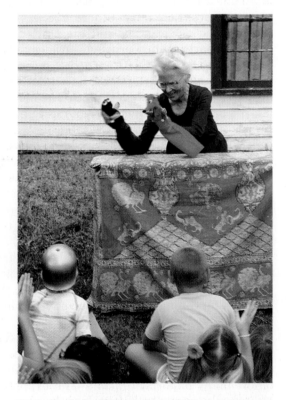

With the tasks of the earlier adult years behind them, many older adults have more time to enjoy pursuing their personal interests. No wonder their satisfaction with life usually remains high, especially if they are healthy and active.

Grief is intense when a loved one's death comes before its expected time on the social clock, whether it be due to war, illness, or accident. The family of Marine Reserve Captain Jonathan Edwards, an investment counselor who became the first Persian Gulf War casualty buried at Arlington National Cemetery, grieves during his burial.

men. Grief is especially severe when the death of a loved one comes before its expected time on the social clock. The accidental death of a child or the sudden illness that claims a 45-year-old spouse may trigger a year or more of mourning flooded with memories, eventually subsiding to a mild depression that sometimes continues for several years (Lehman & others, 1987).

Studies in Germany and the United States show that, with time, bereavement normally subsides (McCrae & Costa, 1988; Stroebe & others, 1988). Contrary to a popular myth, those who express the strongest grief immediately do not resolve their grief more quickly (Wortman & Silver, 1989). The normal range of reactions to a loved one's death is wider than most people suppose. Severe distress is common, but not inevitable.

Those who suffer a terminal illness live with the awareness of their impending death. In analyzing how people cope with the prospect of death, the stage theorists have once again arrived ahead of us. From her interviews with dying patients, Elisabeth Kübler-Ross (1969) proposed that the terminally ill pass through a sequence of five stages: *denial* of the terminal condition; *anger* and resentment ("Why me?"); *bargaining* with God (or physicians) for more time; *depression* stemming from the impending loss of everything and everyone; and, finally, peaceful *acceptance* of one's fate. Others propose similar stages—disbelief, protest, depression, recovery—for coping with a sudden physical impairment (Fitzgerald, 1970).

Critics question the generality of all such stages, stressing that each person's experience is unique. Real people, they say, don't fit into these neat boxes. Moreover, they argue, the simplified stages ignore many important factors—for example, that people who are old usually view death with less expressed fear and resentment (Wass & others, 1978–1979). Critics also express concern about the eagerness with which the death-and-dying formula has been popularized in courses and books. The danger, they fear, is that rather than having their feelings respected, dying people may be analyzed or manipulated in terms of the stereotyped stages: "She's just going through the anger stage."

"Do not go gentle into that good night,
Old age should burn and rave at close of day;
Rage, rage against the dying of the light."
  Dylan Thomas
  Do Not Go Gentle into That Good
  Night, 1952, a poem written to his
  father as he lay dying peacefully

Nevertheless, the death-education movement has enabled us to deal more openly and humanely with death and grief. A growing number of individuals are aided by **hospice** organizations, whose staff and volunteers work in special facilities and in people's homes to support and comfort the terminally ill and their families, to help make this a meaningful time "when good-byes can be said, when broken relationships can be healed, when forgiveness can be given or received" (Magno, 1989).

We can be grateful for the waning of death-denying attitudes. Facing death with dignity and openness helps people complete the life cycle with a sense of life's meaningfulness and unity—the sense that their existence has been good and that life and death are parts of an ongoing cycle. Although death may be unwelcome, life itself can be affirmed even at death. This is especially so for people who review their lives not with despair but with what Erik Erikson calls a sense of *integrity*—a feeling that one's life has been meaningful and worthwhile.

Reflections on Life-Span Development

Our survey of developmental psychology began in Chapter 3 by identifying three pervasive issues: (1) whether development is steered more by genes or experience; (2) whether development is a gradual, continuous process or a discrete series of stages; and (3) whether development is characterized more by stability over time or by change. We noted there how heredity and environment jointly affect human development. Let's now take stock of current thinking on the latter two issues.

Continuity and Stages

We have considered several stage theorists: Jean Piaget on cognitive development, Lawrence Kohlberg on moral development, and Erik Erikson and Daniel Levinson on psychosocial development. And we have seen their stage theories vigorously criticized. Piaget failed to recognize the early rudiments of later abilities. Kohlberg appeared biased by a worldview characteristic of educated males in individualistic cultures. The ideas of Erikson and Levinson are contradicted by research showing that adult life does not progress through a fixed, predictable series of steps.

Although research casts doubt on the idea that life proceeds through neatly defined, age-linked stages, the concept of stage remains useful. There are spurts of brain growth during childhood and puberty that correspond roughly to Piaget's stages (Thatcher & others, 1987). And stage theories contribute a developmental perspective on the whole life span, by suggesting how people of one age think and act differently when they arrive at a later age.

Stability and Change

This leads us to the final question: Over time, are people's personalities consistent, or do they change? If reunited with a long-lost grade school friend, would you instantly recognize that "it's the same old Andy"? Or is a person during one period of life likely to seem like a different person at a later period?

Obviously, either extreme is false: If there were no stability, we could not hope that the person we marry today would be the same person a decade later, or that the promising management trainee would remain suited for management. If there were no change, all juvenile delinquents would become career criminals; all alcoholics would drink themselves into the grave; life would be one long rut.

Still, the issue is real: Do infants' traits predict their childhood characteristics? Is the troubled adolescent likely to have a rocky adulthood? Will the assertive young woman still be noticeably assertive at age 60? Researchers who follow lives through time are debating the extent to which our past reaches into our future.

A generation ago, most psychologists and lay people assumed that once genes and early experience form our personalities, they remain set for life. Then, during the 1960s and 1970s, new findings suggested that throughout much of life personality evolves. For example, Jean Macfarlane (1964) followed 166 people from babyhood to age 30 and discovered that "many of our most mature and competent adults had severely troubled and confusing childhoods and adolescences." Often, the unhappy, rebellious adolescent became a stable, successful, happy adult. Alexander Thomas and Stella Chess (1986) similarly followed 133 people from infancy to early adulthood and found that the troubled children among them usually became stable adults.

Some researchers have found that even adults frequently undergo surprising and unpredictable changes. Reflecting on her studies of such changes during the life cycle, Bernice Neugarten (1980) reported that "the primary consistency we have found is a lack of consistency."

So, shall we conclude that later experience copies over early experience, erasing the voices of the past? If so, we can counsel parents of difficult babies and teenagers to be patient and hopeful. We can reassure the depressed, lonely young adult that development never ends: The struggles of the present may lay the base for a happier future.

On the other hand, much recent research reveals a consistency to personality. After painstakingly comparing people in their forties with ratings of the same people as junior high students, Jack Block (1981) concluded that there is an underlying stability to our basic social and emotional style. The troubled adolescent often turned out better than we would have guessed but, on the whole, it was the cheerful teenager who became the most cheerful 40-year-old.

Similarly, Avshalom Caspi and his colleagues (1987) found that, compared to milder-mannered boys, 9-year-old boys with explosive temper tantrums are more likely as adults to have trouble keeping good jobs and are twice as likely to have divorced by age 40. Leonard Eron (1987) and others found that the most physically aggressive 8-year-olds often became the most aggressive (and potentially violent) 30-year-olds (Figure 4–17). And David Magnusson and L. R. Bergman (1990) found that hyperaggressive Swedish 13-year-olds often developed adult records of crime and alcohol abuse.

Once people reach adulthood, their dispositions become even more stable. From their periodic retesting of Boston and Baltimore area adults, Robert McCrae and Paul Costa (1982) concluded, "For the great majority of people, the self-concept at age 30 is a good guide to personality at age 80." During the adult years, people's outgoingness, emotional stability, openness, agreeableness, and conscientiousness are persistent (Conley, 1985; Costa & McCrae, 1988;

"In most of us, by the age of thirty, the character has set like plaster, and will never soften again."
William James
Principles of Psychology, 1890

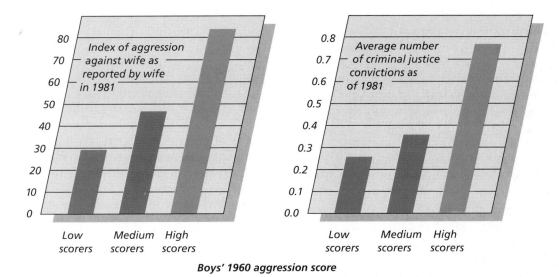

Boys' 1960 aggression score

Finn, 1986). Part of our consistency comes from our selecting environments and marrying people who help sustain our traits (Caspi & Herbener, 1990). Outgoing people, for instance, are more likely to seek social encounters that nourish their outgoingness and to marry sociable people.

So, should we conclude that throughout life we change, but our basic social and emotional styles become more stable as we grow older? Whatever their apparent disagreements, researchers do agree that:

1. The first 2 years of life provide a poor basis for predicting a person's eventual traits. As people grow older, predictability increases. There is less stability from age 14 to 18 than from 18 to 22 (Stein & others, 1986) and less stability from 20 to 30 than from 30 to 40 (Costa & McCrae, 1989).

2. The greater the span of years between assessments, the greater the likelihood that personality will have changed. From assessments of the traits of 25-year-olds, psychologists can better predict their personalities as 26-year-olds than as 40-year-olds (Schuerger & others, 1989).

3. Some characteristics, such as temperament, are more stable than others, such as social attitudes (Moss & Susman, 1980). But attitudes, too, become more stable with age (Krosnick & Alwin, 1989).

4. In some ways, we all change with age. Most shy, fearful toddlers begin opening up by age 4, and during adulthood most of us mellow. In the years after college, most people become calmer and quieter (Costa & McCrae, 1989). Such changes can occur without changing a person's position *relative* to others of the same age. The hard-driving young adult may mellow by later life yet still be a relatively hard-driving senior citizen.

Finally, we should remember that life contains *both* stability and change. Stability enables us to depend on others, motivates our concern for the healthy development of children, and provides our identity. Change motivates our concerns about present influences, sustains our hope for a brighter future, and enables us to adapt and grow with experience.

Figure 4–17 The stability of aggressiveness. Leonard Eron and Rowell Huesmann (1984) found that the aggressiveness displayed by 8-year-old boys (low, medium, or high—as shown by the colored bars) helped predict their aggressiveness 2 decades later, as revealed by their wives' reports and by their criminal convictions.

Throughout her 100 years, Iva Blake has adapted to her changing environment. However, she retains a strong personal identity—still gardening from her wheelchair.

"At 70, I would say the advantage is that you take life more calmly. You know that 'this, too, shall pass!'"

Eleanor Roosevelt, 1954

Summing Up

Today's developmental psychology assumes that development is lifelong. We grow and change and adapt during infancy and childhood, *and* during adolescence and adulthood.

Adolescence

Adolescence—the transition years between biological maturity and social independence—has lengthened in many countries, due to earlier maturation and prolonged education.

Physical Development Adolescence typically begins at puberty with the onset of rapid growth and developing sexual maturity. Depending on how other people react, early or late maturation can influence adjustment; this illustrates how genes and environment interact in shaping us.

Cognitive Development Piaget theorized that adolescents develop the capacity for formal operations, which enables them to reason abstractly. However, some developmentalists believe that the development of formal logic depends on schooling as well, and that the rudiments of logic appear earlier than Piaget believed.

Following Piaget's lead, Lawrence Kohlberg contended that moral thinking likewise proceeds through a sequence of stages, from a preconventional morality of self-interest, to a conventional morality concerned with gaining others' approval or doing one's duty, to (in some people) a postconventional morality of agreed-upon rights or universal ethical principles. But morality also lies in actions, which are influenced by the social situation and inner attitudes as well as by moral reasoning. Moreover, say Kohlberg's critics, the postconventional level represents morality from the perspective of individualist, liberal-minded males.

Social Development Erik Erikson theorized that a chief task of adolescence is to solidify one's sense of self—one's identity. For many people, this struggle continues into the adult years as new relationships emerge and new roles are assumed. Although adolescence has traditionally been viewed as a time of storm and stress, researchers have found that most teenagers relate to their parents reasonably well and generally affirm their parents' beliefs and attitudes.

Adulthood

During early life, we sail a narrow channel, constrained by biological maturation. As the years pass, the channel widens, allowing us to diverge more and more. By adulthood, age no longer neatly predicts a person's life experience and traits. Yet in some ways our bodies, minds, and relationships still undergo predictable changes. As long as we live, we adapt.

Physical Changes The barely perceptible physical declines of early adulthood begin to accelerate during middle adulthood. For women, a significant physical change of adult life is menopause, which generally seems to be a smooth rather than rough transition. After 65, declining perceptual acuity, strength, and stamina are evident, but short-term ailments are fewer. Neural processes slow, but the brain remains healthy, except for those who suffer brain disease, such as the progressive deterioration of Alzheimer's disease.

Cognitive Changes As the years pass, recognition memory remains strong, although recall begins to decline, especially for meaningless information. Research on how intelligence changes with age has progressed through several phases: cross-sectional studies suggesting a steady intellectual decline after early adulthood; longitudinal studies suggesting intellectual stability until very late in life; and today's view that fluid intelligence declines in later life, but crystallized intelligence does not.

Social Changes From close study of small samples of individuals, some theorists maintain that adults pass through an orderly sequence of life stages. Daniel Levinson contends that moving from one stage to the next entails recurring times of crisis, such as the early-forties time of transition to midlife. But people are not so predictable; life events involving love and work, and even chance occurrences, influence adult life in unanticipated ways.

Although few people grow old gratefully, most age gracefully, retaining a sense of well-being throughout life. Those who live to old age must, however, cope with the deaths of friends and family members and with the prospect of their own deaths.

Reflections on Life-Span Development

Chapters 3 and 4 touch on three pervasive issues in developmental psychology: nature and nurture, continuity and discrete stages, and stability and change in personality. Although the stage theories of Piaget, Kohlberg, and Erikson have been modified in light of later research, each theory usefully alerts us to differences among people of different ages and helps us keep the life-span perspective in view. Research findings that people's traits continue to change in later life have helped create a new emphasis on lifelong development. Nevertheless, there is also an underlying consistency to most people's temperaments and personality traits, especially after age 30.

Terms and Concepts to Remember

adolescence The transition period from childhood to adulthood, extending from puberty to independence.

puberty The early adolescent period of rapid growth and sexual maturation.

primary sex characteristics The body structures (ovaries and testes) that make sexual reproduction possible.

secondary sex characteristics Nonreproductive sexual characteristics such as female breasts and hips, male voice quality, and body hair.

menarche [meh-NAR-key] The first menstrual period.

identity One's sense of self; according to Erikson, the adolescent's task is to solidify a sense of self by testing and integrating various roles.

intimacy In Erikson's theory, the ability to form close, loving relationships; a primary developmental task in late adolescence and early adulthood.

menopause The time of natural cessation of menstruation; also refers to the biological and psychological changes experienced during a woman's years of declining ability to reproduce.

Alzheimer's disease A progressive and irreversible brain disorder characterized by gradual deterioration of memory, reasoning, language, and, finally, physical functioning.

cross-sectional study A study in which people of different ages are tested or observed at one point in time.

longitudinal study Research in which the same people are restudied over a long time period.

crystallized intelligence One's accumulated knowledge and verbal skills; tends to increase with age.

fluid intelligence One's ability to reason abstractly; tends to decrease during late adulthood.

social clock The culturally preferred timing of social events such as marriage, parenthood, and retirement.

hospice An organization whose largely volunteer staff provides support for dying people and their families either in special facilities or in people's own homes.

For Further Reading

Berger, K. (1988). *The developing person through the life span* (2nd ed.). New York: Worth.

A comprehensive, current, and readable textbook summary of what we know about infancy, childhood, adolescence, and adulthood.

Coles, R. (1990). *The spiritual life of children.* Boston: Houghton-Mifflin.

The eighth and final volume in psychiatrist Coles's exploration of children's lives. Using a case study approach, Coles's books record and reflect upon his extended conversations with children and their families.

Damon, W. (1988). *The moral child: Nurturing children's natural moral growth.* New York: Free Press.

Drawing on recent research, a developmental psychologist charts the course of moral development, stressing the value of authoritative rather than authoritarian parenting.

Silverstone, B., & Hyman, H. K. (1981). *You and your aging parent: The modern family's guide to emotional, physical, and financial problems* (2nd ed.). New York: Pantheon.

A useful book that provides information and practical advice on how to care responsibly for one's aging parents without feeling trapped.

Part Three

Experiencing the World

To experience the world around us, we must take in, process, and selectively interpret a myriad of messages. We first receive various stimuli that strike our bodies and transform them into neural messages that reach the brain—a process we investigate in Chapter 5, Sensation. We then organize and interpret these messages in meaningful ways that we consider in Chapter 6, Perception. Conscious experience can also occur in altered states—states induced by sleep, hypnosis, and drugs, the topics of Chapter 7, States of Consciousness. As we examine how we experience the world, we will touch on such controversial issues as: Can we be affected by stimuli that are too faint to be consciously perceived? What happens when we are deprived of sensory input? Is there extrasensory perception? Do some people have out-of-body experiences near death?

Sensation

Chapter 5

In a silent, cushioned, inner world of utter darkness floats your brain. From the outer world, myriad stimuli bombard your body. These facts raise a fundamental question that predates psychology by thousands of years and helped inspire its beginnings some 100 years ago: *How does the world out there get in?*

To modernize the question: How do we construct our representations of the external world? How do we manage to experience the world's form and texture, its motion and temperature, its aroma and beauty? To grasp how the world out there gets represented inside our heads, three computer concepts are useful: input, processing, and output. As Figure 5–1 illustrates, physical objects emit or reflect energy. Our sensory organs detect this energy (input) and encode it into neural signals that our brains organize and interpret (processing) as conscious experiences (output). The resulting perceptions affect our reactions, which may in turn modify our perceptions. The inexperienced softball outfielder who runs in too far to catch fly balls soon learns to judge them better.

Figure 5–1 How we process sensory input.

Environmental objects emit or reflect stimulus energy.

Light

Sound waves

Sensory receptors detect stimuli and encode them into neural information, which is passed on to the brain.

The brain organizes and interprets this information.

SENSATION

PERCEPTION

The distinction between sensation and perception is hazy, and growing hazier. In general, **sensation** refers to how our sense receptors and nervous system physically represent our external environment. This chapter's focus on sensation is therefore a "bottom-up" perspective on how we experience the world: It starts with receptors and works up to higher levels of processing. **Perception** refers to how we mentally organize and interpret this information. In the next chapter, we'll take a more "top-down" perspective on how, using our experience, expectations, and other higher-level factors, our minds construct what we see and hear. Although sensation and perception are actually one continuous process, we will look at perception as awareness, a mental process that takes up where sensation, its physiological base, leaves off. To recognize, say, an ⊓ and an ⌃ as *A*s and not *H*s or *R*s, we must be capable of sensing (detecting, encoding) and perceiving (organizing, interpreting) information. Sensation provides the raw information that perception constructs into our experiences.

Detail "The Forest Has Eyes" by Bev Doolittle © The Greenwich Workshop, Inc., Trumbull, CT.

Top-down processing: It takes most people a while to construct mentally (to perceive) all of the meaningful images in this Bev Doolittle painting, "The Forest Has Eyes."

Sensing the World: Some Basic Principles

Sensory systems enable organisms to obtain the information they need to function and survive. A frog, which feeds on flying insects, has eyes with receptor cells that fire only in response to small, dark, moving objects. A frog could starve to death, knee-deep in motionless flies, but let one zoom by and the frog's "bug detector" cells snap awake. A male silkworm moth has receptors so sensitive to the odor of the female sex-attractant that a single female silkworm moth need release only a billionth of an ounce per second to attract every male silkworm moth within a mile. Which is why there continue to be silkworms. We humans are similarly designed to detect what are, for us, the important features of our environments. Nature's sensory gifts suit the needs of each particular recipient.

Thresholds

We exist in a sea of energy. At this moment, you and I are being struck by x-rays and radio waves, ultraviolet and infrared light, very high and very low frequency sound waves. But to all of them we are blind and deaf. The shades on our senses, our windows on the world, are open just a crack, allowing us only a restricted awareness of this vast sea.

(a)

(b)

These two photographs show a flower as it appears (a) to the human eye and (b) to the eye of a bee. The bee's ability to perceive ultraviolet wavelengths enables it to see the "landing field" invisible to the human eye, and makes possible more efficient food gathering.

Absolute Thresholds To some kinds of stimuli we are exquisitely sensitive. Standing at the top of a mountain on an utterly dark, clear night, we can, given normal senses, see a candle flame atop another mountain 30 miles away. In a silent room, we can hear a watch ticking 20 feet away. We can feel the wing of a bee falling on our cheek and smell a single drop of perfume in a three-room apartment (Galanter, 1962).

Our awareness of these faint stimuli illustrates our **absolute thresholds**—the minimum stimulation necessary to detect a particular stimulus (light, sound, pressure, taste, odor). Psychologists usually measure absolute threshold by recording the stimulation needed for detection 50 percent of the time. For example, to test your absolute threshold for sounds, a hearing specialist exposes each ear to varying sound levels. For each pitch, the hearing test defines where half the time you correctly detect the sound and half the time you do not. For each of the senses, that 50–50 point defines your absolute threshold.

Signal Detection Detecting a weak stimulus, or signal, depends not only on the signal strength (such as the tone on a hearing test), but also on our psychological state—our experience, expectations, motivation, and fatigue. Thus, those who study **signal detection** report that there is no single absolute threshold. Exhausted parents of a newborn will notice the faintest whimper from the cradle, while louder, unimportant sounds go unnoticed. In a horror-filled wartime situation, failure to detect an intruder may mean death. Thus, a sentry standing guard alone at night may notice—and fire at—an almost imperceptible noise. In peacetime, when survival is not threatened, the same sentry requires a stronger signal before sensing danger.

Signal detection theorists seek to understand why people respond differently to the same stimuli, and why the same person's reactions vary as circumstances change. Such variations in signal detection can have life-or-death consequences when people are responsible for detecting blips on a radar screen, weapons at an airport security checkpoint, or critical signals on the monitoring equipment at a hospital nursing station. Studies of signal detection, in which people must judge whether a faint stimulus is present, have shown, for example, that after about 30 minutes of performing such tasks, people's vigilance diminishes. But this depends on the task, on the time of day, and even on whether the subjects are given a chance to exercise (Warm & Dember, 1986).

Subliminal Stimulation In 1956, controversy erupted over a report that New Jersey movie audiences were unwittingly being influenced by imperceptible flashed messages to DRINK COCA-COLA and EAT POPCORN. More than 35 years later, the controversy has erupted anew. Advertisers are said to manipulate consumers by imperceptibly printing the word *sex* on crackers and embedding erotic images in liquor ads. Rock recordings are said to contain "satanic messages" that can be heard if the recordings are played backward and that can unconsciously persuade the unwitting listener, even when played normally. Entrepreneurs offer to help us lose weight, stop smoking, or improve our memories with audiotapes of soothing ocean sounds that contain unheard messages such as, "I am thin," "Smoke tastes bad," and "I do well on tests. I have total recall of information." These claims make two assumptions: that unconsciously we can sense **subliminal** (literally, "below threshold") stimuli; and that, without our awareness, these stimuli have extraordinary suggestive powers. Can we? Do they?

Can we sense stimuli that are below our absolute thresholds? In one sense, the answer is clearly yes. Remember that the "absolute" threshold is merely the point at which we detect a stimulus half the time (Figure 5–2). At or slightly below this threshold we will still detect the stimulus some of the time. The answer is yes in another sense, too. People who plead total ignorance when asked to make some perceptual judgment—for example, when deciding which of two very similar weights is heavier—usually beat chance. Sometimes we know more than we think.

Can we be affected by stimuli too weak for us *ever* to notice? Recent experiments hint that, under certain conditions, the answer may again be yes. In one experiment, students were repeatedly shown a series of geometric figures, each for less than 0.01 second—long enough to perceive only a flash of light (Kunst-Wilson & Zajonc, 1980). Later, the students reported liking the presented figures more than figures that had not been flashed, even though they had no idea which were which. Moreover, invisible words can "prime" your response to a later question. If the word *bread* were flashed so quickly that you could detect only the flash, you might then detect a related word such as *butter* faster than unrelated words such as *bottle* or *bubble* (Carr & others, 1987; Marcel, 1983; Merikle & Reingold, 1990). Sometimes we feel what we do not know and cannot describe.

So, we *can* process information without being aware of it. A weak stimulus evidently triggers a weak response within us—a response that may reach our brain where it evokes a feeling, though not conscious awareness of the stimulus. What the conscious mind can't recognize, the heart may know.

But does the fact of subliminal *sensation* verify entrepreneurial claims of subliminal *persuasion?* Can advertisers or diabolical rock groups really manipulate us with "hidden persuasion"? The near-consensus among research psychologists is no. Their verdict is like that of astronomers who say that, yes, astrologers are right that stars and planets are out there, but no, they don't directly affect us. Similarly, those who study subliminal information processing say yes to subliminal sensation, but no to the possibility of "reprogramming your unconscious mind."

But let's overlook this gulf between laboratory research (which reveals an intriguing, but subtle and fleeting effect on cognition) and entrepreneurial claims of powerful, enduring effects on behavior. Let's simply ask, do commercial subliminal tapes work? Do they have compelling force?

In Chapter 1, we considered a typical experiment showing that

Figure 5–2 The absolute threshold is arbitrarily measured as the intensity at which we perceive a stimulus 50 percent of the time. As you can see from the graph, to be a subliminal stimulus merely means that we perceive it *less* than 50 percent of the time.

Sprinkled throughout the next several chapters you will find evidence that we process enormous amounts of information automatically, unintentionally, without awareness.

"The heart has its reasons which reason does not know."
     Pascal
     Pensees, 1670

"Finding the occasional straw of truth awash in a great ocean of confusion and bamboozle requires intelligence, vigilance, dedication and courage. But if we don't practice these tough habits of thought, we cannot hope to solve the truly serious problems that face us—and we risk becoming a nation of suckers, up for grabs by the next charlatan who comes along."
     Carl Sagan (1987)

they do not work. Earlier studies produced similar results (Moore, 1988). Shortly after news of the supposed EAT POPCORN effect swept North America, the Canadian Broadcasting Corporation used a popular Sunday night TV show to flash a subliminal message 352 times (*Advertising Age*, 1958). Asked to guess the message, none of the almost 500 letter-writers did so. Nearly half, however, did report feeling strangely hungry or thirsty during the show. But this was merely an effect of expectations. The actual message was TELEPHONE NOW. The effect of these 352 subliminal messages on Canadian telephone usage? Zilch, according to Canadian phone company records. All the evidence considered, say researchers Anthony Pratkanis and Anthony Greenwald (1988), "Subliminal procedures offer little or nothing of value to the marketing practitioner."

Difference Thresholds To function effectively, we need absolute thresholds low enough to allow us to detect important sights, sounds, textures, tastes, and smells. We also need to detect small differences among stimuli. A musician must detect minute discrepancies in an instrument's tuning. A wine taster must detect the slight flavor difference between two vintage wines.

The **difference threshold** (also called the **just noticeable difference,** or **jnd**) is the minimum difference a person can detect between any two stimuli 50 percent of the time. The difference threshold increases with the magnitude of the stimulus. Add 1 ounce to a 10-ounce weight and you will detect the difference; add 1 ounce to a 10-pound weight and you will not, because the difference threshold has increased. More than a century ago, Ernst Weber noted that regardless of their magnitude, two stimuli must differ by a constant proportion for their difference to be perceptible. This principle—that the difference threshold is not a constant amount but some constant proportion of the stimulus—is so simple and so widely applicable that we still refer to it as **Weber's law.** The exact proportion varies, depending on the stimulus. For the average person to perceive their differences, two lights must differ in intensity by 8 percent, two objects must differ in weight by 2 percent, and two tones must differ in frequency by only 0.3 percent.

Weber's law is a rough approximation that works well for nonextreme sensory stimuli. It also parallels some of our life experiences. If the price of a 50-cent candy bar goes up by a nickel, shoppers might notice the change; similarly, it might take a $5,000 price hike in a $50,000 Mercedes-Benz to raise the eyebrows of its potential buyers. In both cases, the price went up by 10 percent. Weber's principle: Sensory thresholds for detecting differences (measured as increased stimulation) are a roughly constant proportion of the size of the original stimulus.

Sensory Adaptation

Entering your neighbor's living room, you smell an unpleasant odor. You wonder how she tolerates it, but within minutes you no longer notice it. Jumping into a swimming pool, you shiver and complain how cold it is; a short while later a friend arrives and you exclaim, "C'mon in. Water's lovely!" These examples illustrate **sensory adaptation**—our diminishing sensitivity to an unchanging stimulus. (To experience this phenomenon, move your watch up your

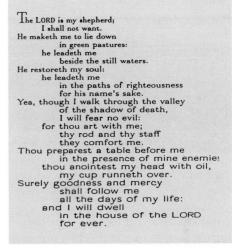

The difference threshold. In this computer-generated copy of Psalm 23, each line of the type face changes imperceptibly. How many lines are required for you to experience a just noticeable difference?

This tea taster must distinguish minuscule variations in flavor and aroma.

"We need above all to know about changes; no one wants or needs to be reminded 16 hours a day that his shoes are on."
Neuroscientist David Hubel (1979)

The body's capacity for sensory adaptation enables this swimmer to tolerate icy water.

wrist an inch: You will feel it—but only for a few moments.) After constant exposure to a stimulus, our nerve cells begin to fire less frequently.

Why, then, if we stare at an object without flinching, does it not vanish from sight? Because, unnoticed by us, our eyes are always moving, quivering just enough to guarantee that the retinal image continually changes. (For 9 in 10 people—-but, curiously, only 1 in 3 schizophrenia patients—this eye flutter turns off when the eye is following a moving target [Holzman & Matthysse, 1990].)

What if we could stop our eyes from moving? Would sights seem to vanish, as odors do? To find out, psychologists have devised ingenious instruments for maintaining a constant image on the retina. Imagine that we fitted a subject, Mary, with one of these instruments—a miniature projector mounted on a contact lens (Figure 5–3a). When Mary's eye moves, the image from the projector moves as well. Thus, everywhere that Mary looks the scene is sure to go.

If we project the profile of a face through such an instrument, what will Mary see? At first she will see the complete profile. But within a few seconds, as her sense receptors begin to fatigue, a strange phenomenon occurs. Bit by bit, the image will vanish, only later to reappear and then disappear—in recognizable fragments or as a whole (Figure 5–3b). Interestingly, the disappearance and reappearance of an image occurs in meaningful units. If a person is shown a word, it will disappear, and new words made up of parts of that word will appear and then vanish. This phenomenon anticipates the next chapter's major conclusion: Our perceptions are organized by the meanings that our minds impose.

Although sensory adaptation reduces our sensitivity, it offers an important benefit: It enables us to focus our attention on *informative* changes in our environment without being distracted by the uninformative, constant stimulation of garments, odors, and street noise. Our sense receptors are alert to novelty; bore them with repetition and they free our attention for things more interesting. This reinforces a fundamental lesson: We perceive the world not exactly as it is, but as it is useful for us to perceive.

(a)

BEER   PEER   PEEP   BEE   BE

(b)

Figure 5–3 A stabilized image. (a) A projector mounted on a contact lens makes the projected image move with the eye. (b) When first projected, the stabilized image is clear, but soon fragments fade and reappear. (From "Stabilized images on the retina" by R. M. Pritchard. Copyright © 1961 Scientific American, Inc. All rights reserved.)

Skip

Sensory thresholds and adaptation are not the only commonalities among the senses. All the senses receive sensory stimulation, transform it into neural information, and deliver that information to the brain. How do the senses work? Let us find out by beginning with vision, the most thoroughly studied of our windows on the world.

Vision

Part of your taken-for-granted genius is your body's ability to convert one sort of energy to another. Sensory **transduction** is the process by which our sensory systems convert stimulus energy into neural messages. Your eye, for example, receives light energy and transduces (transforms) it into neural electrochemistry. The study of any sensory system begins by analyzing how we transduce its triggering stimuli into neural messages.

The Stimulus Input: Light Energy

Scientifically speaking, what strikes our eyes is not color but pulses of electromagnetic energy that our visual system experiences as color. What we see as visible light is but a thin slice of the whole spectrum of electromagnetic radiation. As Figure 5–4 illustrates, the electromagnetic spectrum ranges from the long pulses or waves of radio transmission to the narrow band of the spectrum that we see as visible light to the imperceptibly short waves of cosmic rays. Other organisms are sensitive to differing portions of the spectrum. As we noted earlier, bees cannot see red, but can see ultraviolet light, the part of the spectrum that causes sunburn in humans.

Two physical characteristics of light help determine our sensory experience of it. Its **wavelength**—the distance from one wave peak to the next (Figure 5–5a, page 138)—determines its **hue** (the color that we experience, such as blue or green). **Intensity,** the amount of energy in light waves (determined by their *amplitude*),

Figure 5–4 The spectrum of electromagnetic energy ranges from radio waves over a mile long to gamma rays as short as the diameter of an atom. The narrow band of wavelengths visible to the human eye (shown enlarged) extends from the longer waves of red light to the shorter waves of blue-violet light.

Radiation used in communications   Infrared radiation   X-ray radiation   Cosmic ray radiation

800nm   400nm

Light

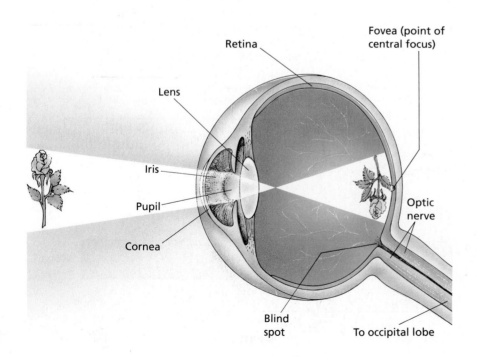

Figure 5-5 The physical properties of waves. (a) Waves vary in wavelength, the distance between successive peaks. Frequency, the number of complete wavelengths that can pass a point in a given time, depends on the wavelength. The shorter the wavelength, the higher the frequency. (b) Waves also vary in amplitude, the height from peak to trough. Wave amplitude determines the intensity of colors and sounds.

influences brightness (Figure 5–5b). Although the spectrum of visible light is a continuum of wavelengths, we humans tend to see four basic colors in it: red, yellow, green, and blue-violet. To understand *how* we transform physical energy into a sensation of color, we first need to understand our visual system's structure.

The Eye

In some ways, the eye functions like a camera (or, more exactly, the camera functions like the nineteenth-century understanding of the eye). In both eye and camera, light enters through a small opening, behind which a lens focuses the incoming rays into an image on a light-sensitive surface (Figure 5–6). The eye's small opening is the **pupil**. Its size, and therefore the amount of light entering the eye, is regulated by the **iris**, a colored muscle that surrounds and dilates or constricts the pupil. The **lens** focuses the incoming rays by changing its curvature, a process called **accommodation**. The light-sensitive surface on which the rays focus is the **retina**, the multilayered tissue that lines the inside of the back of the eyeball.

Figure 5-6 The eye. Light rays reflected from the rose pass through the cornea, pupil, and lens. The curvature and thickness of the lens change to bring either nearby or distant objects into focus on the retina. Light rays travel in straight lines. So rays from the top of the rose strike the bottom of the retina and those from the left side of the rose strike the right side of the retina. The rose's retinal image is thus upside-down and reversed.

For centuries, scientists have known that when the image of a candle passed through a small opening, its mirror image appeared inverted on a dark wall behind. This fact had scholars baffled. If the retina receives an upside-down image as shown in Figure 5–6, how can we see the world right side up? One idea was that the eye's sensing device is the lens. Realizing this wasn't so, the ever curious Leonardo da Vinci had another idea. Perhaps the eye's watery fluids bent the light rays, reinverting the image to the upright position as it reached the retina. But in 1604, the astronomer and optics expert Johannes Kepler showed that the retina did receive upside-down images of the world (Crombie, 1964). And how could we understand such a world? "I leave it," said the befuddled Kepler, "to natural philosophers."

The "natural philosophers," who eventually included research psychologists, discovered that the retina doesn't read the image as a whole. Rather, its millions of receptor cells convert light energy into neural impulses. These impulses are sent to the brain and assembled *there* to create a perceived, upright-seeming image.

The Retina If we were to follow a single particle of light energy into the eye, we would see that it first makes its way through the retina's outer layer of cells to its buried receptor cells, the **rods** and **cones** (Figure 5–7). When struck by light energy, the rods and cones generate neural signals that activate the neighboring *bipolar cells,* which in turn activate their neighboring *ganglion cells.* The axons from the network of ganglion cells converge like the strands of a rope to form an **optic nerve** that carries information to the brain.

Figure 5–7 The path of light through the eye. Before signals from the retina reach the brain, they pass through a switchboard of neural cells. A ray of light entering the eye triggers a photochemical reaction in the rods and cones (1) at the back of the retina behind the other neural layers. This chemical reaction in turn triggers the bipolar cells (2). The bipolar cells then activate the ganglion cells (3), which converge to form the optic nerve. The optic nerve transmits information to the brain's occipital lobe.

●

Figure 5–8 The blind spot. Where the optic nerve leaves the eye (Figure 5–7, page 139), there are no receptor cells. This creates a blind spot in our vision. To demonstrate, close your left eye, look at the spot, and move the page to a distance from your face (about 9 inches) at which the oncoming car disappears. In everyday vision the blind spot doesn't impair your vision because your eyes are moving and because one eye covers what the other misses.

Nearly a million messages can be sent by the optic nerve at once, through nearly 1 million ganglion fibers. Where the optic nerve leaves the eye there are no receptor cells—creating a **blind spot** (Figure 5–8).

Most cones are clustered around the **fovea,** the retina's area of central focus (Figure 5–7). In fact, the fovea contains only cones, no rods. Unlike rods, many cones have their own bipolar cells to help relay their individual messages to the cortex. This preserves their precise information, making them better able to detect fine detail. (Rods have no such hotline to the brain; they share bipolar cells with other rods, so their individual messages get combined.) To illustrate, if you pick a word in this sentence and stare directly at it, thereby focusing its image on the cones in your fovea, you will see that words a few inches off to the side appear blurred. This is because their image strikes the more peripheral region of your retina, where the rods predominate.

Only cones enable you to see color. As illumination diminishes, the cones adjust quickly, the rods more slowly. However, the rods remain sensitive in dim light, to which the cones do not respond. That is why you don't see colors in dim light. So when we enter a darkened theater or turn off the light at night, the pupils dilate to allow more light to reach the rods in the retina's periphery. Typically it takes 20 minutes or more before our eyes fully adapt. You can demonstrate dark adaptation by closing one eye for up to 20 minutes, then making the room light not quite bright enough to read this book with your open eye. Now open the dark-adapted eye, and read. This period of dark adaptation is yet another instance of the remarkable adaptiveness of our sensory systems, for it parallels the natural twilight transition between the sun's setting and darkness.

Knowing just this much about the eye, can you imagine why a cat sees so much better at night than you do? There are two reasons: A cat's pupils can open much wider than yours, letting in more light; and a cat has a higher proportion of light-sensitive rods (Moser, 1987). But there is a trade-off: With its fewer cones, a cat can't see details or color as well as you do.

Rod-shaped rods and cone-shaped cones as shown by a scanning electron microscope. Rods are more light-sensitive than the color-sensitive cones, which is why the world looks colorless at night. Some nocturnal animals, such as toads, mice, rats, and bats, have retinas made up almost entirely of rods. Others, such as chickens, have only cones; thus the phrase "to go to bed and get up with the chickens."

Table 5–1	*The Human Eye*	
	Cones	**Rods**
Number	6 million	120 million
Location in retina	Center	Periphery
Sensitivity in dim light	Low	High
Color sensitive?	Yes	No

Figure 5-9 How the brain's visual cortex receives images detected by the eye. Light rays reflected from the television screen strike the retina's millions of receptor nerve cells, triggering nerve impulses. These signals travel along a nerve pathway to the visual cortex at the back of the brain. The visual cortex receives not literal images, as shown here to illustrate the neural destinations, but formless neural information. (Adapted from Frisby, 1980.)

Visual Information Processing

We process visual information at progressively more abstract levels. At the entry level, the retina—which is actually a piece of the brain that migrates to the eye during early fetal development—processes information before routing it to the cortex. The retina's neural layers are not just passing along electrical impulses; they also help to encode and analyze the sensory information. Indeed, much of the important processing of visual information takes place in the retina's neural tissues. The third neural layer in a frog's eye, for example, contains the "bug detector" cells that fire only in response to flylike stimuli.

In human eyes, the information from the retina's nearly 130 million receptor rods and cones is received and transmitted by the million or so ganglion cells, whose fibers make up the optic nerve. A typical ganglion cell responds to light/dark contrasts revealed by its receptor cells. This helps the brain detect edges and other important features of the visual world. But most information processing occurs in the brain. Any given area of the retina relays its information to a corresponding location in the occipital lobe—the visual cortex at the back of the brain (Figure 5-9).

The sensitivity that enables retinal cells to fire messages can lead them to misfire as well. Turn your eyes to the left, close them, and then gently rub the right side of your right eyelid with your fingertip. Note the patch of light to the left, moving as your finger moves. Why do you see light? Why at the left?

Your retinal cells are so responsive that even pressure triggers them. But your brain interprets their firing as light. Moreover, it interprets the light as coming from the left—which is where light normally comes from when it activates the right side of the retina.

When trying to make sense of unusual neural discharges, the interpretive brain may conjure up illusions or hallucinations. When disease or drugs disturb our neural functioning, crazy but seemingly real experiences can result.

Feature Detection When individual ganglion cells register information in their region of the visual field, they send signals to the visual cortex. Nobelists David Hubel and Torsten Wiesel (1979) believe that when certain cortical neurons, called **feature detectors**, receive this information, they respond only to specific features of a scene—to particular bars, edges, and lines. From these elements the brain assembles the perceived image.

For example, Hubel and Wiesel report that a given brain cell might respond maximally to a line flashed at a particular tilt. If the line is tilted further—say, from a 2 o'clock to a 3 o'clock or 1 o'clock position—the cell quiets down (Figure 5–10). Thus, the feature detector cells record amazingly specific features that are abstracted from the visual information taken in by the eye. Feature detector cells pass this information to other cells that respond only to a more complex pattern, such as a particular angle formed by two lines. The basic idea is that complex perceptions arise from the interaction of many neurons, each performing a simple task.

Some higher-level brain cells respond selectively to specific visual stimuli, such as a face or an arm movement in a particular direction. Psychologist David Perrett and his colleagues (1988) report that for biologically important objects and events, monkey brains (and surely ours as well) have a "vast visual encyclopedia" distributed throughout their individual cells. Researchers also have identified nerve cells that may fire or not, depending on how a monkey *perceives* an image, even when physical input is constant. Special goggles give the monkey's two eyes contradictory information about an object that can be perceived as moving either up or down. If the image appears to be moving up (as "reported" by the monkey's eye movements), certain cells become active; if, a moment later, it seems to be moving down, other cells become active (Logothetis & Schall, 1989).

Researchers debate the precise nature of the features and patterns that brain cells detect. New research suggests that any image, such as a face, can be broken down into elementary patterns of changing light intensity. These component light waves can be described mathematically. Thus, in seeing, the brain may actually process mathematical-like codes that represent a perceived image (Kosslyn, 1987; Marr, 1982).

Parallel Processing Neural impulses travel a million times slower than a computer's internal messages, yet the brain humbles any computer by recognizing a familiar face instantly. It does so by processing the visual components simultaneously—a procedure called **parallel processing**. For example, the brain breaks vision down into subdimensions such as color, depth, movement, and form and works on each aspect simultaneously (Livingston & Hubel, 1988).

The distribution of subfunctions to different neural work teams explains a strange phenomenon. After a stroke, people may lose just one aspect of vision. For example, a person may perceive color but not movement. If something moves, it disappears until it stops. Other brain-damaged victims can tell you all about the subdimensions of an object—the size and color of a rose, for instance, or the features of a family member's face—without recognizing the object or the person. Still others have lost a neural area involved in consciously perceiving some aspect of their field of vision. One such woman was shown two drawings of a house, in one of which the left side was on fire. Asked to select which house she would prefer to

Figure 5–10 Electrodes record how individual cells in this monkey's visual cortex respond to different visual stimuli. Hubel and Wiesel won the Nobel prize for their discovery that most cells in the visual cortex respond only to particular features—for example, to the edge of a surface, or to a line at a 30-degree angle in the upper right part of the field of vision. More complex features trigger higher-level detector cells, which integrate information from these simpler ones.

live in, she thought the question silly, "because they're the same." Yet she consistently chose the house that was not burning (Marshall & Halligan, 1988). This uncanny ability to respond to something not consciously perceived, called *blindsight*, reminds us once again of the startling truth: Our brains are doing many things at once, automatically and without our awareness.

The other senses process information with similar speed and intricacy. Opening the back door, you recognize the aroma wafting from the kitchen even before stepping inside. Answering the phone, you recognize the friend calling from the moment she says "hi." Within a fraction of a second after such events stimulate the senses, millions of neurons have simultaneously coordinated in extracting the essential features, comparing them with past experience, and identifying the stimulus (Freeman, 1991).

This emerging scientific understanding of the senses illustrates that neuropsychologist Roger Sperry's (1985) comment still holds true: The "insights of science give added, not lessened, reasons for awe, respect, and reverence." Think about it: As you look at someone, the visual information is sent to your brain as millions of neural impulses, then reassembled into its component features, and finally, in some as yet mysterious way, composed into a consciously perceived image, which is then compared with previously stored images and recognized as, for example, your grandmother. The whole process (Figure 5–11) is as complex as taking a car apart, piece by piece, transporting it to a different location, then having specialized workers reconstruct it. That all of this happens instantly, effortlessly, and continuously is indeed awesome.

Color Vision Not on test

In the study of vision, one of the most basic and intriguing mysteries is how we see the world in color—and in such a multitude of colors. Our difference threshold for colors is so low that we can discriminate some 7 million different shades (Geldard, 1972).

At least most of us can. For about 1 in 50 people, vision is color-deficient—and that person is probably male, because the defect is genetically sex-linked. To understand why some people have color-deficient vision we must first understand how normal color vision works.

Modern detective work on the mystery of color vision began in the nineteenth century when Hermann von Helmholtz built on the insights of an English physicist, Thomas Young. They recognized a clue in the fact that any color can be created by combining the light waves of three primary colors—red, green, and blue. Young and Helmholtz inferred that the eye must have three types of receptors, one for each primary color (Figure 5–12).

A century later, researchers measured the response of various cones to different color stimuli and confirmed the **Young-Helmholtz trichromatic (three-color) theory**, which simply states that the retina has three types of color receptors, each especially sensitive to one of three colors. And surprise! Those colors are, indeed, red, green, or blue. When we stimulate combinations of these cones, we see other colors. For example, there are no receptors especially sensitive to yellow. Yet when both red- and green-sensitive cones are stimulated, we see yellow. Most color-deficient people are not actually "color blind." Rather, they simply lack functioning red- or green-sensitive cones. Their vision is dichromatic in-

Scene

Retinal processing: Receptor rods and cones → bipolar cells → ganglion cells

Feature detection: Brain's detector cells respond to elementary features—bars, edges, or gradients of light

Abstraction: Brain's higher-level cells respond to combined information from feature-detector cells

Recognition: Brain matches the constructed image with stored images

Figure 5–11 A simplified summary of visual information processing.

Figure 5–12 The three primary colors of light mix to create other colors. For example, red and green combine to create yellow. All three—red, green, and blue—combine to create white.

stead of trichromatic, making it difficult to distinguish red and green, as in Figure 5–13 (Boynton, 1979). Dogs, too, lack receptors for the wavelengths of red, giving them only limited, dichromatic color vision (Neitz & others, 1989).

Soon after Young and von Helmholtz proposed the trichromatic theory, physiologist Ewald Hering pointed out that other parts of the color vision mystery remained unsolved. For example, we see yellow when stimulating both red- and green-sensitive receptors. But how is it that people blind to red and green can often still see yellow? And why does yellow appear to be a pure color and not a mixture of red and green, as purple does of red and blue?

Hering found his clue to the answers in the well-known occurrence of *afterimages*. When you stare at a green square for a while and then look at a white sheet of paper, you will see red, green's "opponent color." Stare at a yellow square and you will later see its opponent color, blue, on the white paper (as in the flag demonstration in Figure 5–14). Hering surmised that there were two additional color processes, one responsible for red versus green perception, and one for yellow versus blue.

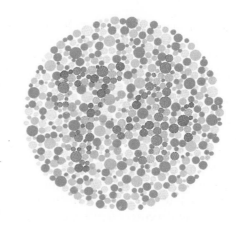

Figure 5–13 Color-deficient vision. People who suffer red-green blindness have trouble perceiving the number within the design above. (From Richmond Products, Boca Raton, FL.)

Figure 5–14 Afterimage effect. Stare at the center of the flag for a minute and then shift your eyes to the dot in the white space beside it. What do you see?

A century later, researchers confirmed Hering's **opponent-process theory**. *After* leaving the receptor cells, visual information is analyzed in terms of the opponent colors red and green, blue and yellow, and also black and white. Psychologist Russell DeValois (DeValois & DeValois, 1975) discovered that in the thalamus (where impulses from the retina are relayed en route to the visual cortex) some neurons are turned "on" by red, but turned "off" by green. Others are turned on by green, but off by red. So if you detect one of these colors at a particular point on the retina, you cannot simultaneously detect the opposing color at the same point; you therefore cannot see a greenish red.

Opponent processes explain afterimages, such as in the flag demonstration, in which we tire our green receptors by staring at green. When we then stare at white (which contains all colors), only the red part of the green/red pairing will fire normally.

The present solution to the mystery of color vision is therefore roughly this: Color processing occurs in two stages. The retina's red, green, and blue cones respond in varying degrees to different color stimuli, as the Young-Helmholtz trichromatic theory suggested. Their signals are then processed by the nervous system's opponent-process cells, en route to the visual cortex.

"Is it not stirring to understand how the world actually works—that white light is made of colors, that color measures light waves, that transparent air reflects light. . . ? It does no harm to the romance of the sunset to know a little about it."
Carl Sagan
"Skies of Other Worlds," 1988

Color Constancy People talk as if objects *possess* color. We say, "The tomato is red." Perhaps you have pondered the old question, "If a tree falls in the forest and no one hears it, does it make a sound?" We can ask the same of color: If no one sees the tomato, is it red?

The answer is no. First, the tomato is everything *but* red, because it *rejects* (reflects) the long wavelengths of red. Second, the tomato's color is our mental construction. As Isaac Newton (1704) noted, "The [light] rays are not coloured." Color, like all aspects of vision, resides not in the object but in the theater of our brains. Even with our eyes closed, while dreaming, we can see things in vivid color. Clearly, our experience of color depends on something more than the wavelength information received by our trichromatic cones and transmitted through the opponent-process cells of the thalamus.

That something more is the surrounding *context*. If you view only part of a tomato, without knowing what it is, its color will seem to change as the light changes. But if you see the whole tomato as one item in a bowl of fresh vegetables, its color will remain roughly constant as the lighting shifts—a phenomenon known as **color constancy**. Dorothea Jameson (1985) notes that a blue chip under indoor (tungsten) lighting matches the wavelengths reflected by a gold chip in the sunlight; yet bring a bluebird indoors and it won't look like a goldfinch. Likewise, a green leaf hanging from a brown branch may, when the illumination changes, now reflect the same light energy that formerly came from the brown branch. Yet to us the leaf stays greenish and the branch stays brownish.

We take this color constancy for granted, but the phenomenon is remarkable. It demonstrates that our experience of color comes not just from the object—the color is not in the isolated leaf—but from everything around it as well. You and I see color thanks to our brains' computations of the light reflected by any object *relative to its surrounding objects*.

In an unvarying context, we maintain color constancy. But what if we change the context? Because the brain computes the color of an object relative to its context, the perceived color changes (as is dramatically apparent in Figure 5–15). This principle—that we perceive objects not in isolation but in their environmental context—is especially significant for artists, interior decorators, and clothing designers. The color of a wall or of a swatch of paint on a canvas is determined not just by the paint in the can but by the surrounding colors. The color resides not in the paint, but in our heads.

"Only mind has sight and hearing; all things else are deaf and blind."
Epicharmus
Fragments, 550 B.C.

Figure 5–15 Color depends on context. In this painting by Joseph Albers (1975), the unchanging line *seems* to vary from gray to yellow as its surrounding context changes.

Hearing

Like our other senses, our hearing, or **audition**, is highly adaptive. We hear a wide range of sounds, but we best hear sounds having frequencies within a range that corresponds to the range of the human voice. We also are remarkably sensitive to faint sounds, an obvious boon to our ancestors' survival when hunting or being hunted. (If our ears were much more sensitive, we would hear a constant hiss from the movement of air molecules.) Moreover, we are acutely sensitive to differences in sounds. We can easily detect differences among thousands of human voices, which helps us instantly recognize the voice of almost anyone we know.

For hearing as for seeing, the fundamental question is: How do we do it? How do we transduce sound energy into neural messages that the brain interprets as a particular sound coming from a particular place?

The Stimulus Input: Sound Waves

The stimulus energy for hearing is sound waves—jostling molecules of air, each bumping into the next, like a shove being transmitted through the crowded exit tunnel of a football stadium. The resulting waves of compressed and expanded air are like the ripples on a pond circling out from where a tossed stone has broken the surface of the water. The strength, or amplitude, of sound waves determines their *loudness*. For sound as for light, we can tolerate stimulus intensities a trillion times more intense than the faintest detectable stimulus. The length and therefore the **frequency** of these waves determines their **pitch**: The longer the waves (thus, the lower their frequency), the lower the pitch; the shorter the waves (thus, the higher their frequency), the higher the pitch. A piccolo produces much shorter sound waves than a kettledrum.

The Ear

To hear, we must somehow convert sound waves into neural activity. The human ear accomplishes this feat through an intricate mechanical chain reaction (Figure 5–16). First, the visible outer ear channels sound waves through the auditory canal to the *eardrum*, a tight membrane that vibrates with the waves. The **middle ear** transmits the eardrum's vibrations through a piston made of three tiny bones (the *hammer, anvil,* and *stirrup*) to a snail-shaped tube in the **inner ear** called the **cochlea** (KOHK-lee-uh). The incoming vibrations cause the cochlea's membrane (the *oval window*) to vibrate the fluid that fills this tube. This motion causes ripples in the *basilar membrane,* which is lined with hair cells, so named because of their tiny hairlike projections. At the end of this sequence, the rippling of the basilar membrane bends these hair cells, triggering impulses in the adjacent nerve fibers. Through this mechanical

The remarkable details of this photo of the middle ear (see Figure 5–16) include the eardrum (at left, curving in a bit), the round window (black spot at far right), the stirrup (just left of round window), and the oval window (covered by stirrup). The actual distance from eardrum to oval window is less than 1 centimeter.

Figure 5–16 How we transform sound waves into nerve impulses that our brain interprets. (a) The outer ear funnels sound waves to the eardrum. The bones of the middle ear amplify and relay the eardrum's vibrations through the oval window into the fluid-filled cochlea. (b) The resulting pressure changes in the cochlear fluid cause the basilar membrane to ripple, bending the hair cells on its surface. Hair cell movements trigger impulses in the nerve cells at their bases, whose fibers converge to form the auditory nerve. (For clarity, the cochlea is shown partially uncoiled.)

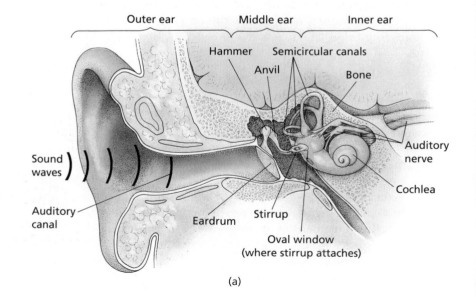

(a)

chain of events, sound waves cause the hair cells of the inner ear to send neural messages up to the temporal lobe's auditory cortex. From vibrating air to moving piston to fluid waves to electrical impulses to the brain: We hear.

How Do We Perceive Pitch? How do we know whether a sound is the high-pitched chirp of a bird or the low-pitched roar of a truck? Current thinking on how we discriminate pitch, like current thinking on how we discriminate color, combines two theories.

Place theory presumes that we hear different pitches because different sound waves trigger activity at different places along the cochlea's basilar membrane. Thus, the brain can determine a sound's pitch by recognizing the place on the membrane from which it receives neural signals. When Georg von Békésy (1957) cut holes in the cochleas of guinea pigs and human cadavers and looked inside with a microscope, he discovered that high-frequency waves triggered activity mostly near the beginning of the cochlea's membrane, a discovery that contributed to his 1961 Nobel prize.

Although place theory explains how we hear high-pitched sounds, it doesn't explain how we hear low-pitched sounds, because the neural signals they generate are not so neatly localized on the basilar membrane. **Frequency theory** suggests an alternative solution to the pitch-discrimination mystery. The basilar membrane vibrates with the incoming sound wave. This triggers neural impulses to the brain at the same rate as the sound wave. If the sound wave has a frequency of 100 waves per second, then 100 pulses per second travel up the auditory nerve. Thus, the brain can read pitch from the frequency of neural impulses.

Frequency theory can explain how we perceive low-pitched sounds. But individual neurons cannot fire faster than 1000 times per second, so how can it explain our sensing sounds with frequencies above 1000 waves per second (roughly the upper third of a piano keyboard and above)? Enter the *volley principle*: Like soldiers who alternate firing so that some can shoot while others reload, neural cells can alternate firing and thereby achieve a combined frequency well above 1000 times per second.

Place theory best explains how we sense the high pitches and frequency theory the lower pitches. Some combination of the two processes seems to handle the intermediate-range pitches.

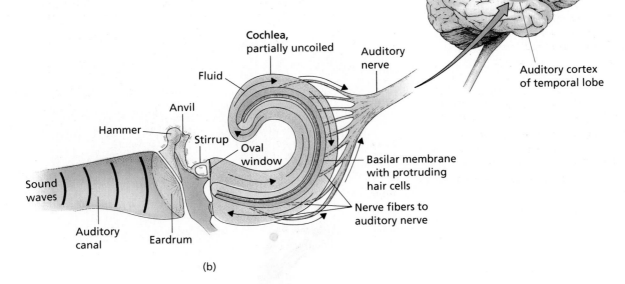

Cochlea, partially uncoiled

Auditory nerve

Auditory cortex of temporal lobe

Fluid

Anvil

Hammer

Stirrup

Oval window

Basilar membrane with protruding hair cells

Sound waves

Nerve fibers to auditory nerve

Auditory canal

Eardrum

(b)

Close-Up   *Noise*

Years between the speakers as lead guitarist of The Who caused serious hearing loss for Pete Townshend. He has publicized his ailment to warn others of the dangers of loud music.

Urban life is noisy. Traffic roars. Factory machines clatter. Jackhammers tear up pavement. Escaping to more pleasant sounds, runners stride to the beat of intense music on their headsets.

But the intensity of that sound may cause a problem. Brief exposure to extremely intense sounds, such as gunfire near one's ear, and prolonged exposure to intense sounds, such as amplified music, can damage receptor cells and auditory nerves (Backus, 1977; West & Evans, 1990). Although rock and roll may be here to stay, the sad truth for some rock musicians is that their hearing may not be. Prolonged exposure to sounds above 85 decibels produces hearing loss. (*Decibels* are the measuring unit for sound energy. The absolute threshold for hearing is arbitrarily defined as 0 decibels—see Figure 5–17.)

Noise affects not only our hearing but also our behavior. On tasks requiring alert performance, people in noisy surroundings work less efficiently and make more errors (Broadbent, 1978). People who live with continual noise in factories, in homes near airports, and in apartments next to trains and highways suffer elevated rates of stress-related disorders; high blood pressure,

anxiety, and feelings of helplessness are common (Cohen & others, 1986).

But is it the noise that causes the stress? Laboratory experiments on the psychological effects of noise suggest an answer. In one such experiment, David Glass and Jerome Singer (1972) recreated the noise of city life by tape recording the chattering of office machines and of people speaking various languages. While working at various tasks, people heard this noise, played either loudly or softly, either at predictable or unpredictable intervals. Regardless of the conditions, the people soon adapted to the noise and performed well on most tasks. However, having coped with the noise, those exposed to the *unpredictable* loud noise later made more errors on a proofreading task and reacted more quickly to frustration.

The conclusion: Noise is especially stressful when unanticipated or uncontrollable. That explains why the unpredictable and uncontrollable blaring of someone else's stereo can be so much more upsetting than the same decibels from your own. At such times we may wish that, as our eyes have eyelids, so our ears had earlids.

Figure 5–17 The intensity of some common sounds, measured in decibels.

How Do We Locate Sounds? The slightly different messages sensed by the two microphones used in creating a stereophonic recording mimic the slightly different sound messages received by our two ears. As the placement of our eyes allows us to sense depth visually (page 168), the placement of our two ears allows us to enjoy stereophonic ("three-dimensional") hearing. For example, if a car to the right honks, your right ear receives a more intense sound slightly sooner than your left ear. Because sound travels 750 miles per hour and our ears are but 6 inches apart, the loudness difference and time lag are extremely small. But our auditory system is so sensitive that our two ears can detect such minute differences (Brown & Deffenbacher, 1979; Middlebrooks & Green, 1991). A just noticeable difference in the direction from which two sounds come corresponds to a time difference of just 0.000027 second!

So how well do you suppose we do at locating a sound that is equidistant from our two ears, such as those that come from directly ahead, behind, overhead, or beneath us? Not very well, because such sounds strike the two ears simultaneously. You can experience this by sitting with closed eyes while a friend snaps fingers at various locations around your head. You will easily point to the sound when it comes from either side, but will probably make mistakes when it comes from directly ahead, behind, above, or below. That is why, when trying to pinpoint a sound, you cock your head, so that your two ears receive slightly different messages.

Hearing Loss

The ear's intricate and delicate structure makes it vulnerable to damage. Problems with the mechanical system that conducts sound waves to the cochlea cause **conduction deafness**. If the eardrum is punctured or if the tiny bones of the middle ear lose their ability to vibrate, the ear's ability to conduct vibrations diminishes. A hearing aid may restore hearing by amplifying the vibrations.

Damage to the cochlea's hair cell receptors or their associated nerves can cause **nerve deafness**. Once destroyed, these tissues remain dead, though a hearing aid may amplify sound to stimulate other hair cells. Nerve deafness has three causes—disease, biological changes linked with aging (Figure 5–18), and prolonged exposure to ear-splitting noise or music. Hearing losses with age are greatest in the higher frequencies. To older adults, birds seem to chirp more softly and whispered conversation becomes frustratingly unintelligible.

The barn owl hardly has to cock its head to ensure that each ear receives a different message. The right ear and its opening are directed slightly upward; the left ear and its opening, slightly downward. This built-in asymmetry enables the barn owl to pinpoint location of sound not only horizontally but vertically as well, making this species the successful nighttime hunter that it is. Even the faint sound of a field mouse scurrying through the grass provides enough information to allow the owl to locate its prey with deadly accuracy.

Figure 5–18 Elderly people tend to hear low frequencies well but suffer hearing loss for high frequencies. This high-frequency loss results from nerve degeneration near the beginning of the basilar membrane. Which explanation of hearing does this confirm, place or frequency theory? (From Wever, 1949.)

Close-Up *Living in a Silent World*

With the help of a computer at the Lexington Center in New York, this profoundly deaf boy is learning to speak. The computer screen displays for him the position of his teacher's tongue, the vibration of her nose, and the intensity of her voice. By matching her speech patterns, this boy will be able to speak more clearly.

Nonhearing and hearing-impaired people are a diverse group. Some are profoundly deaf, others partially impaired. Some were deaf "prelingually" (before developing language); others have known the hearing world. Some communicate with sign language and identify with the language-based culture of deafness; others, especially those postlingually deaf, are "oral" and converse with the hearing world by reading lips; some move between the deaf and hearing cultures. Among deaf children, about one-fourth attend residential schools, half attend special education programs in public schools, and the remaining fourth are partially or wholly mainstreamed into regular classrooms, sometimes aided by sign language interpreters (Kirk & Gallagher, 1989). Among the hearing-impaired as among the hearing, some of these students are slow learners, others are brilliant. Essentially all children, whether deaf or hearing, whether signers or speakers, display a remarkable ability to learn language (Meier, 1991).

Still, all hearing-impaired people face challenges. Because academic subjects are rooted in spoken languages, academic achievement may suffer. The social challenges are even greater. Unable to communicate in customary ways, deaf children and their playmates struggle to coordinate their play. Adolescents may suffer social exclusion and resulting low self-confidence. Even those who become hearing-impaired as adults may find the difficulties of social interaction producing a sort of shyness. "It's almost universal among the deaf to want to cause hearing people as little fuss as possi-

ble," reports Henry Kisor (1990, p. 244), a Chicago newspaper editor and columnist who lost his hearing at age 3. "We can be self-effacing and diffident to the point of invisibility. Sometimes this tendency can be crippling. I must fight it all the time. . . ."

I know. My 82-year-old mother, with whom we communicate by writing notes on an erasable "magic pad," lives in a silent world, long ago having withdrawn from the stress and strain of trying to interact with people outside a small circle of family and old friends. With my own hearing now declining on a trajectory toward hers, I find myself sitting front and center at plays and meetings, seeking quiet corners in restaurants, asking my wife to make necessary calls to friends whose accents differ from ours, using amplification devices for TV and telephone sounds. But the greatest frustration comes when, with or without a hearing aid, I can't hear the joke that everyone else is guffawing over; when, after repeated tries, I just can't catch that exasperated person's question and can't fake my way around it; when I can't hear the low frequencies of the bass that my son is playing in the school orchestra; when family members give up and say, "Oh, never mind" after trying three times to tell me something unimportant.

As my mother aged, she came to feel that seeking social interaction was just not worth the effort. But for newspaper columnist Kisor, communication *is* worth the effort: "So, for the most part, I will grit my teeth and plunge ahead" (p. 246). To reach out, to connect, to communicate with others, even across a chasm of silence, is to affirm our humanity as social creatures.

The Other Senses

For humans, seeing and hearing are the major senses. We depend on them, particularly for communication. Our brains give these two senses priority in the allocation of cortical tissue. For other animals, the priorities differ. Sharks and dogs rely on their extraordinary senses of smell, aided by the large segment of their cortexes devoted to it. Nevertheless, without our sense of touch, our senses of taste and smell, and our senses of body motion and position, we humans would be seriously handicapped, and our capacities for enjoying the world would be devastatingly diminished.

Touch

If you had to give up one sense, which would it be? If you could retain only one sense, which would it be?

Touch would be a good candidate for retention. Right from the start, touch is strangely essential to our development. As we noted in Chapter 3, The Developing Child, premature babies gain weight faster and go home sooner if stimulated by hand massage. Infant rats deprived of their mothers' grooming touch produce less growth hormone and have a lower metabolic rate—a good way to keep alive until the mother returns, but resulting in stunted growth if she's delayed. Infant monkeys allowed to see, hear, and smell their mothers, but not touch them, are desperately unhappy; much less so are those separated by a screen with holes, allowing touch. As lovers, we yearn to touch—to kiss, to stroke, to snuggle like spoons.

Our "sense of touch" is actually a mix of at least four distinct skin senses—pressure, warmth, cold, and pain. Touching various spots on the skin with a soft hair, a warm or cool wire, and the point of a pin reveals that some spots are especially sensitive to pressure, others to warmth, others to cold, still others to pain. Within the skin there are different types of specialized nerve endings. Does that mean that each type is a receptor for one of the basic skin senses, much as the eye's cone receptors correspond to light's basic colors?

Surprisingly, there is no simple relationship between what we feel at a given spot and the type of specialized nerve ending found there. Except for pressure, which does have identifiable receptors, the relationship between warmth, cold, and pain and the receptors that respond to them remains a mystery. Other skin sensations are variations of the basic ones:

Stroking adjacent pressure spots creates a tickle.

Repeated gentle stroking of a pain spot will create an itching sensation.

Touching adjacent cold and pressure spots triggers a sense of wetness, which you can experience by touching dry, cold metal.

Stimulating nearby cold and warmth spots produces a feeling of "hot." Cold spots respond either to very low or very high temperatures. We sense hot when a high temperature activates both warm and cold spots (Figure 5–19).

Pain Pain is the body's way of telling us that something has gone wrong. It draws our attention to a burn, a break, or a rupture, and tells us to change our behavior immediately. The few people who are born without the ability to feel pain may experience severe injury without ever being alerted by pain's danger signals. More nu-

William James (*Principles of Psychology*, 1890): "Touch is both the alpha and omega of affection."

Figure 5–19 Warm + cold = hot. When ice-cold water passes through one coil and comfortably warm water through another, we perceive the combined sensation as burning hot.

merous are those who endure chronic pain. The suffering of people with persistent or recurring backaches, arthritis, headaches, and cancer-related pain prompts two questions: What is pain? How might it be controlled?

What Is Pain? Pain is not only a property of the senses—of the region where we feel it—but of the brain as well. As the dreamer sees with eyes closed and the listener hears a ringing during utter silence, so amputees may feel pain in their nonexistent limbs. These "phantom limb sensations" indicate that with pain, as with sights and sounds, the brain can misinterpret neural activity.

Unlike vision, however, the pain system is not located in a simple neural cord running from a sensing device to a definable spot in the brain. Moreover, there is no one type of stimulus that triggers pains (as light triggers vision), and there are no special receptors (like the retina's rods and cones) for pain. At low intensities, the stimuli that produce pain cause other sensations, including warmth or coolness, smoothness or roughness.

Although no theory of pain explains all the available findings, psychologist Ronald Melzack and biologist Patrick Wall's (1965, 1983) **gate-control theory** provides a useful model. Melzack and Wall believe that the spinal cord contains a sort of neurological "gate" that either blocks or allows pain signals to pass on to the brain. The spinal cord contains small nerve fibers that conduct most pain signals, and larger fibers that conduct most other sensory signals. When tissue is injured, the small fibers activate and open the neural gate, and you feel pain. Large-fiber activity closes the pain gate, turning pain off.

Thus, one way to treat chronic pain is to stimulate (electrically, by massage, or even by acupuncture) "gate-closing" activity in the large neural fibers. Rub the area around your stubbed toe, and the competing stimulation will block some of the pain messages. Ice on a bruise serves not only to control swelling but also to trigger cold messages that close the gate on the pain signals. An arthritic patient, for example, may wear a small portable electrical stimulation unit next to a painful area. When the unit stimulates nerves in the area, the patient feels a vibrating sensation rather than pain (T. Murphy, 1982).

Melzack and Wall believe that the pain gate can also be closed by information from the brain. These brain-to-spinal cord messages help explain some striking psychological influences on pain. When distracted from pain signals (and soothed by the release of endorphins—see page 31), our experience of pain may be greatly diminished. Football injuries may be unnoticed, until taking the after-game shower. A mere paper cut while doing a dull job may hurt more. Clearly, there is more to pain than meets the sense receptors.

Pain Control If pain is indeed a physical and a psychological phenomenon, then it should be treatable both physically and psychologically. Depending on the type of symptoms, pain control clinics select one or more therapies from a list that includes drugs, surgery, acupuncture, electrical stimulation, massage, exercise, hypnosis, relaxation training, and thought distraction.

The widely practiced Lamaze method of prepared childbirth combines several of these pain control techniques. These include relaxation (through deep breathing and muscle relaxation), counter stimulation (through gentle massage), and distraction (through focusing attention on, say, a pleasant photograph). After Everett

"When belly with bad pains doth swell, It matters naught what else goes well."
Sadi
The Gulistan, 1258

"Pain is increased by attending to it."
Charles Darwin
Expression of Emotions in Man and Animals, 1872

needles placed somewhere in the body; will control pain.

Close-Up *Matter Over Mind*

At a New Zealand skeptics meeting, University of Canterbury physicist John Campbell explained heat diffusion principles that enable firewalking, then put his feet where his mouth was by leading 80 people across 12 feet of hot coals.

The phenomenon of firewalking has become a hot topic in the popular media. For $60 or so we can take a "mind over matter" class that supposedly enables us to alter our body's chemistry. The "proof": walking on red-hot coals without feeling pain or being burned. The psychological result: a newfound capacity to conquer one's fears. "If I can do something that's supposed to be impossible," says the elated firewalker, "I can do almost anything."

Skeptical scientists have taken a cool look at firewalking (Leikind & McCarthy, 1985, 1988). The secret, they report, lies not in any mental power to alter the senses but in the poor heat conductivity of the wood coals. Think of a cake baking in a 350° oven. Touch the aluminum cake tin and you'll get burned; touch the cake—like wood, a poor heat conductor—and you'll be okay. Cakes and coals do conduct some heat, so you'd better not stay in touch with them too long or you will get burned. Some have learned the hard way that he (or she) who hesitates is lost. But the 2 seconds or less that it takes to quick-step across hot embers puts each foot in contact with the coals for only a fraction of a second, and less than a second total time per foot. Wetting the feet on damp grass or on water before the firewalk provides further insulation (a phenomenon familiar to anyone who has used wet fingers to snuff a candle or test a hot iron). Confident of these facts, skeptical scientists have themselves performed the feat without the "mind over matter" training.

Worthington and his colleagues (1983) trained women in the use of such techniques, the women could more easily tolerate the pain of having their hand in ice water. The women's pain tolerance was even greater when a trusted "coach" encouraged them, as husbands or an intimate friend encourage Lamaze-trained women during childbirth.

Distracting people with pleasant images ("Think of a warm, comfortable environment") or drawing their attention away from the painful stimulation ("Count backward by 3's") is an especially effective way to increase pain tolerance (Fernandez & Turk, 1989; McCaul & Malott, 1984). The principle works in health care situations. A nurse will distract needle-shy patients with chatter and may ask them to look away when inserting the needle. For hospitalized patients, a pleasing window view of natural vegetation may have a similarly relaxing and distracting effect. In examining the records of one Pennsylvania hospital, Roger Ulrich (1984) discovered that surgery patients assigned to rooms that looked out on trees required less pain medication and had shorter stays than did those assigned to identical rooms that overlooked a brick wall.

Although Lamaze training reduces labor pain, most Lamaze patients request a local anesthetic during labor. Some—having expected a "natural, painless birth"—feel needless guilt and failure (Melzack, 1984). Melzack therefore advocates—as does the Lamaze program itself—childbirth training that prepares a woman "to cope with an event which is often extremely painful and, at the same time, one of the most fulfilling peak experiences in her life."

Taste

Like our sense of touch, our sense of taste involves four basic sensations—sweet, sour, salty, and bitter (McBurney & Gent, 1979). All other tastes are mixtures of these. Investigators have been frustrated in their search for specialized nerve fibers for each of the four basic taste sensations, but they have found areas of the tongue that have special sensitivities—the tip of the tongue for sweet tastes, the back of the tongue for bitter (Figure 5–20).

Taste is a chemical sense. Inside the little bumps on the top and sides of your tongue are 200 or more taste buds. Each contains a pore that catches food chemicals. These molecules are sensed by 50 taste receptor cells that project antennalike hairs into the pore. Some of these receptors respond mostly to sweet-tasting molecules, others to salty-, sour-, or bitter-tasting ones. It doesn't take much to trigger a response. When a stream of water is pumped across the tongue, the addition of a concentrated salty or sweet taste for but one-tenth of a second gets noticed (Kelling & Halpern, 1983). When a friend asks for "just a taste" of your soft drink, you can squeeze off the straw after a mere fraction of a second.

Taste receptors reproduce themselves every week, so if you burn your tongue with hot food it matters little. However, as you grow older, the number of taste buds decreases, as does taste sensitivity (Cowart, 1981). (No wonder adults enjoy strong-tasting foods that children resist.) Heavy smoking and alcohol use accelerate the decline in taste buds and sensitivities.

Although taste buds are essential for taste, there is more to taste than meets the tongue. Hold your nose, close your eyes, and have someone feed you various foods. A piece of apple may then be indistinguishable from a piece of raw potato; a piece of steak may taste like cardboard. To savor a taste, we normally breathe the aroma through our nose—which is why eating is not much fun when you have a bad cold. This is **sensory interaction** at work—the principle that one sense may influence another. Smell influences taste. Similarly, we correctly perceive the location of the voice directly in front of us partly because we also *see* that the person is in front of us, not behind, above, or beneath us.

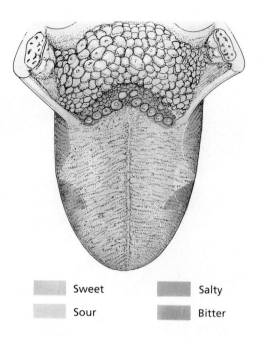

	Sweet		Salty
	Sour		Bitter

Figure 5–20 Different regions of the tongue have extra sensitivity to one or more of the four basic taste sensations—sweet, sour, salty, and bitter.

Smell

Breaths come in pairs—inhale, exhale—except at two moments: birth and death. Each day, as you inhale and exhale nearly 20,000 breaths of life-sustaining air, you bathe your nostrils in a stream of scent-laden molecules. More than you may realize, your resulting experiences of smell (olfaction) are intimate ones. To smell someone we must inhale something of the person. Like taste, smell is a chemical sense. We smell something when air-carried molecules of a substance reach a tiny cluster of 5 million receptor cells at the top of each of our nasal cavities (Figure 5–21). These olfactory receptor cells, waving like sea anemones on a reef, respond selectively to the aroma of brownies baking, to a whisp of smoke, to a friend's fragrance, and instantly alert the brain. Even nursing infants and mothers quickly learn to recognize each others' scents (McCarthy, 1986). A mother fur seal returning to a beach crowded with pups will find her own, aided by smell.

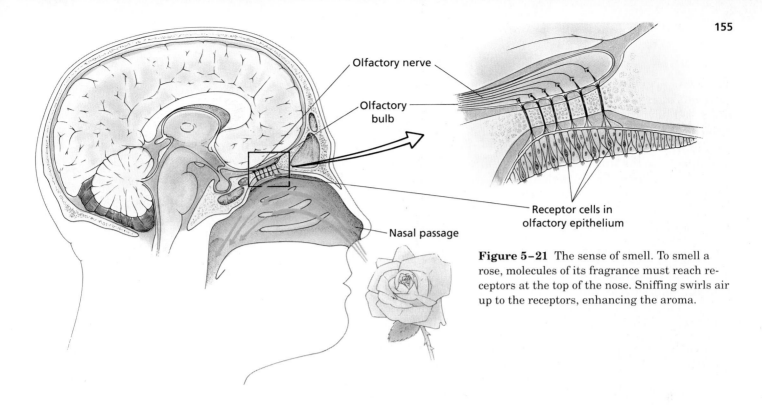

Olfactory nerve

Olfactory bulb

Receptor cells in olfactory epithelium

Nasal passage

Figure 5-21 The sense of smell. To smell a rose, molecules of its fragrance must reach receptors at the top of the nose. Sniffing swirls air up to the receptors, enhancing the aroma.

Precisely how olfactory receptors work is a mystery. Unlike light, which can be separated into its spectral colors, an odor cannot be separated into more elemental odors. Thus, unlike the retina, which detects myriad colors with sensory cells dedicated to red, green, or blue, olfactory receptors recognize odors individually. They do so thanks to a large family of genes that specify receptor proteins which recognize particular odor molecules (Buck & Axel, 1991).

The ability to identify scents peaks in early adulthood and gradually declines thereafter (see Figure 5-22). Despite our skill at discriminating scents, we aren't nearly so good at describing them. Words more readily portray the sound of a piccolo than the aroma of coffee. Compared to how we experience and remember sights and sounds, smells seem more primitive and harder to describe (Richardson & Zucco, 1989).

As any dog or cat with a good nose could tell us, we each have our own identifiable chemical signature. (One noteworthy exception: A dog will follow the tracks of one identical twin as though they had been made by the other [Thomas, 1974].) Animals that have many times more olfactory receptors than we do also use their sense of smell to communicate and navigate. Long before the shark can see its prey, or the moth its mate, odors direct the way.

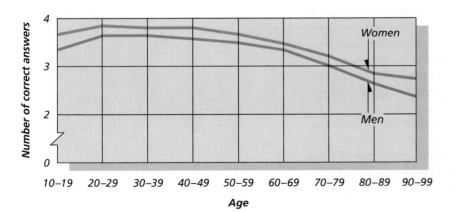

Figure 5-22 Age, sex, and sense of smell. Among the 1.2 million people who responded to a *National Geographic* scratch and sniff survey, women and younger adults most successfully identified six sample odors. (From Wysocki & Gilbert, 1989.)

Odors also have the power to evoke memories and feelings. In *Remembrance of Things Past,* the French novelist Marcel Proust described how the aroma and flavor of a bit of cake soaked in tea resurrected long-forgotten memories of his aunt's bedroom in the old family house. "The smell and taste of things," he noted, "bears unfaltering, in the tiny and almost impalpable drop of their essence, the vast structure of recollection."

Laboratory studies confirm that, though it's difficult to recall odors by name, we do indeed have a remarkable capacity to recognize long-forgotten odors and their associated personal episodes (Engen, 1987; Schab, 1991). Students who do a word exercise while smelling the aroma of chocolate remember the words better the next day if the chocolate aroma is again present (Schab, 1990). And pleasant odors evoke pleasant memories (Ehrlichman & Halpern, 1988). Compared to foul odors, the smell of the sea, the scent of a perfume, or an aroma like the floorwax smell in Grandma's kitchen bring to mind happier memories.

Pleasant moods produced by pleasant scents may also give a boost to workers' performance. That's what Robert Baron (1990) surmised after having students work in rooms with or without pleasant air scents. Pleasant scents boosted the subjects' moods and self-confidence, leading them to set slightly higher work goals on a clerical task and to negotiate more aggressively on a bargaining task. Such is the power of odors to switch on memories and to retrieve associated emotions.

Body Position and Movement

With only the five familiar senses we have so far considered, we would be helpless. We could not put food in our mouths, stand up, or reach out and touch someone. To know just how to move your arms to grasp someone's hand, you first need to know the current position of your arms and hands and then be aware of their changing positions as you move them. To take just one step requires feedback from and instructions to some 200 muscles.

Humans come equipped with millions of such position and motion sensors. They are all over our bodies—in the muscles, tendons, and joints—and they are continually providing our brains with information. If we twist our wrists 1 degree, the sensors immediately report it. This sense of the position and movement of body parts is **kinesthesis** (kin-ehs-THEE-sehs).

Have you ever considered life without kinesthesis, without, say, being able to sense the positions of your limbs when awakening during the night? Such is the experience of Christina, whose nerve fibers carrying information from muscles, tendons, and joints were destroyed by disease, leaving her floppy as a rag doll (Sachs, 1985). What does it feel like? Like she is disembodied, her body dead, not-real, not-hers. Against all odds, Christina has, however, learned to walk and eat—by visually attending to her limbs and directing them accordingly.

A companion sense called **equilibrium** monitors the position and movement of the whole body. The biological gyroscopes for our sense of equilibrium are in the inner ear. The *semicircular canals,* which look like a three-dimensional pretzel (Figure 5–16a, page 146), and the *vestibular sacs,* which connect the canals with the cochlea, contain substances that move when the head rotates or tilts. This movement stimulates hairlike receptors in these organs

Information from the taste buds (brown arrow) travels to an area of the temporal lobe not far from that where olfactory information is received. The brain's circuitry for smell (magenta arrow) also connects with areas involved in memory storage, which helps explain why a smell can trigger an explosion of memories.

Each of these flying trapeze artists must have a highly developed equilibrium and kinesthetic sense.

of the inner ear, which send messages to the brain that enable us continually to sense our body position and thereby maintain our balance.

If you've been twirling around and come to an abrupt halt, the fluid in your semicircular canals and your kinesthetic receptors does not immediately return to its neutral state. The aftereffect fools your dizzy brain with the sensation that you're still spinning. This illustrates a principle that underlies the next chapter's discussion of perceptual illusions. Mechanisms that normally give us an accurate experience of the world can, under special conditions, fool us. Understanding how we are fooled provides clues to how our perceptual system works.

Sensory Restriction

Imagine that one of your sensory windows on the world snapped shut. Would your other senses partially make up for the loss? People with sensory deficits show us the rich potential of each sense. Blind people cope by making greater use of their hearing—for example, by locating obstacles while attending to echoes bouncing off them. Helen Keller, blind *and* deaf, vividly experienced life's aromas, tastes, and touches.

Close your eyes and immediately you, too, will notice your attention being drawn to your other senses. When kissing, lovers minimize distraction and increase their touch sensitivity by closing their eyes. People who suffer aphasia—having lost the ability to comprehend language—typically become acutely sensitive to nonlanguage cues. You and I might miss the meaning conveyed by someone's intonation and gestures, but the aphasic reads these messages readily.

The loss of a sense is but one type of sensory restriction. Another is sensory monotony—the relatively unchanging sensory input experienced by prisoners in solitary confinement, nighttime truck drivers and airline pilots, and animals in barren zoos.

To investigate how sensory restriction affects us, experimenters have put thousands of people through controlled, temporary simulations of such conditions. Some have spent several days in monotonous environments—small rooms in which light and sound are unchanging. Others have passed time in dark, silent rooms, deprived of normal sensory input. Initial "sensory deprivation" experiments produced bizarre and widely publicized findings (Heron, 1957). The subjects, lying on beds and wearing translucent goggles to diffuse the light, typically began the experiment in good spirits. Here was a chance to make some easy money while enjoying a time for relaxation and creative thinking. Before long, however, they be-

"Ears are eyes to the blind," wrote Sophocles. So is touch. Those who lose one means of sensory input become more attentive to input from their other senses. This blind woman appreciates art through her sense of touch.

came disoriented. Many experienced hallucinations, and some became susceptible to piped-in messages arguing for the reality of ghosts.

As often happens in science, manipulating one factor simultaneously changes other factors. Are the effects of spending time in a monotonous environment caused by the sensory restriction or by the social isolation or stress of confinement? The dramatic reports from early experiments prompted many more investigations, most of which produced less newsworthy results (Suedfeld & Kristeller, 1982).

In fact, researchers have found sensory restriction does not disturb most people. More often, the experience reduces stress and helps people become more open to positive influence. In experiments with smokers and overweight people at the University of British Columbia, Peter Suedfeld (1980) found that restricted sensory input helps people modify their behavior. People wanting to alter their behavior were often able to increase their self-control after 24 hours of what he aptly calls REST—Restricted Environmental Stimulation Therapy.

In one such experiment conducted by Allan Best and Suedfeld (1982), smokers listened to antismoking messages while spending 24 hours lying on beds in quiet, dark rooms (rising only to drink a liquid diet available through tubes or to use toilets next to the beds). In the week that followed, none relapsed to smoking. A year later, two-thirds were still abstaining—double the number of abstainers who had received the instruction without the day of REST.

Shorter REST periods can also pay dividends. In one experiment, heavy-drinking college students spent 2½ hours in REST. After 1½ hours, a 5-minute message gave factual information about alcohol's negative effects. Unlike those in control conditions, the REST-plus-message group decreased their alcohol consumption by 55 percent during the ensuing 6 months (Cooper & others, 1988).

In other times and places, periods of solitude and sensory restriction have fostered human fulfillment. Sensory restriction is a traditional component of the "quiet therapies" of Japan (Reynolds, 1982, 1986). For example, Morita therapy for depressed or anxious people sometimes begins with a week of bed rest and meditation and then progresses to assigned light tasks. The religious visions of Moses, Mohammed, and Buddha reportedly occurred during times of solitude and contemplation. As living creatures we require sensory stimulation, but there are also times when we benefit from the peace and relaxation of restricted stimulation.

"It is in silence and not in commotion, in solitude and not in crowds that God best likes to reveal Himself."
Thomas Merton
The Silent Life, 1957

In this chapter we have taken a "bottom-up" look at how we experience the world, starting with how our ingenious sense receptors transduce physical energy into neural messages sent to our brain. But we've also glimpsed a need for the next chapter's "top-down" look at how our mind, too, shapes our experiences. Pain, for example, is a response to information coming both up the spinal cord's small nerves and down from what our mind is paying attention to. Our experiences are in the brain—so much so that the brain can choose how to interpret incoming neural activity, or may even conjure up perceived sights, sounds, and pains without external stimulation. Sensation (how we physically represent the environment) and perception (how we mentally organize and interpret it) are different aspects of one whole fabric—how we experience the world around us.

Summing Up

To study sensation is to study an ageless question: How does the world out there get represented inside our heads? Put another way, how are the external stimuli that strike our bodies transformed into messages that our brains comprehend?

Sensing the World: Some Basic Principles

Thresholds Each species comes equipped with sensitivities that enable it to survive and thrive. We sense only a portion of the sea of energy that surrounds us, but to this portion we are exquisitely sensitive. Our absolute threshold for any stimulus is the minimum stimulation necessary for us to detect it. Signal detection researchers report that our individual absolute thresholds vary with our psychological state.

Can we react to stimuli that are not only subthreshold (subliminal), but so weak that we could never consciously perceive them? Recent experiments reveal that we *can* process some information from stimuli too weak to recognize. But the restricted conditions under which this occurs would not enable unscrupulous opportunists to exploit us with subliminal messages. Nor is there any evidence or plausible theory that we can effortlessly "reprogram" our minds with subliminal tapes.

To survive and thrive, an organism must also have difference thresholds low enough to detect minute changes in important stimuli. In humans, difference thresholds (also called just noticeable differences, or jnd's) increase in proportion to the size of the stimulus—a principle known as Weber's Law.

Sensory Adaptation The phenomenon of sensory adaptation focuses our attention on changing stimulation by diminishing our sensitivity to constant or routine odors, sounds, and touches.

Vision

The task of our visual sense, as of each of our senses, is to receive stimulation, transduce it into neural signals, and send these neural messages to the brain.

The Stimulus Input: Light Energy The energies we experience as visible light are a thin slice from the broad spectrum of electromagnetic radiation.

The Eye After entering the eye through a cameralike lens, light waves strike the retina. The retina's rods and cones convert the light energy into neural impulses, which are coded by the retina before traveling up the optic nerve to the brain.

Visual Information Processing In the cortex, individual neurons respond to specific features of a visual stimulus, and their information is pooled by higher-level brain cells for interpretation. Subdimensions of vision (color, movement, depth, and form) are processed separately and simultaneously, illustrating our brain's capacity for parallel processing.

Color Vision Research on how we see color supports two nineteenth-century theories. First, as the Young-Helmholtz three-color theory suggests, the retina contains three types of cones. Each is most sensitive to the wavelengths of one of the three primary colors (red, green, or blue). Second, as opponent-process theory maintains, the nervous system codes the color-related information from the cones into pairs of opponent colors, as demonstrated by the phenomenon of afterimages and as confirmed by measuring opponent processes within visual neurons of the thalamus. As illustrated by the phenomenon of color constancy under varying illumination, our brains construct our experience of color.

Hearing

The Stimulus Input: Sound Waves The pressure waves we experience as sound vary in frequency and amplitude, and correspondingly in perceived pitch and loudness.

The Ear Through a mechanical chain of events, sound waves traveling through the auditory canal cause minuscule vibrations in the eardrum. Transmitted via the bones of the middle ear to the fluid-filled cochlea, these vibrations create movement in tiny hair cells, triggering neural messages to the brain.

Research on how we hear pitch supports both the place theory, which best explains the sensation of high-pitched sounds, and frequency theory, which best explains the sensation of low-pitched sounds. We localize sound by detecting minute differences in the loudness and timing of the sounds received by each ear.

Hearing Loss Hearing losses linked to conduction and nerve disorders can be caused by prolonged exposure to loud noise and by diseases and age-related disorders.

The Other Senses

Touch Our sense of touch is actually four senses—pressure, warmth, cold, and pain—that combine to produce other sensations, such as "hot." One theory of pain is that a "gate" in the spinal cord either opens to permit pain signals traveling up small nerve fibers to reach the brain or closes to prevent their passage. Because pain is both a physiological and psychological phenomenon, it often can be controlled through a combination of medical and psychological treatments.

Taste Taste, a chemical sense, is likewise a composite of four basic sensations—sweet, sour, salty, and bitter—and of the aromas that interact with information from the taste buds.

Smell Like taste, smell is a chemical sense, but there are no basic sensations for smell, as there are for touch and taste. Like other stimuli, odors can spontaneously evoke memories and feelings.

Body Position and Movement Finally, our effective functioning requires a kinesthetic sense, which notifies the brain of the position and movement of body parts, and a sense of equilibrium, which monitors the position and movement of the whole body.

Sensory Restriction

People temporarily or permanently deprived of one of their senses typically compensate by becoming more acutely aware of information from the other senses. Temporary experiences of sensory restriction often evoke a heightened awareness of all forms of sensation. Under supervision, sensory restriction may provide a therapeutic boost for those seeking control over problems such as smoking.

Terms and Concepts to Remember

sensation The process by which our sense receptors and nervous system receive and represent stimulus energies from our environment.

perception The process of organizing and interpreting sensory information, enabling us to recognize meaningful objects and events.

absolute threshold The minimum stimulation needed to detect a particular stimulus.

signal detection The task of judging the presence of a faint stimulus ("signal"). Signal detection researchers assume there is no single absolute threshold, because the detection of a weak signal depends partly on a person's experience, expectation, motivation, and level of fatigue.

subliminal Below one's absolute threshold for conscious awareness.

difference threshold The minimum difference in stimulation that a subject can detect 50 percent of the time. We experience the difference threshold as a just noticeable difference (jnd).

just noticeable difference (jnd) See *difference threshold*.

Weber's law The principle that, to perceive their difference, two stimuli must differ by a constant minimum percentage (rather than a constant amount).

sensory adaptation Diminished sensitivity that is a consequence of constant stimulation.

transduction Conversion of one form of energy into another. In sensation, the transforming of stimulus energies into neural impulses.

wavelength The distance from the peak of one light or sound wave to the peak of the next. Electromagnetic wavelengths vary from the long pulses of radio transmission to the short blips of cosmic rays.

hue The dimension of color that is determined by the wavelength of light; what we know as the color names (blue, green, and so forth).

intensity The amount of energy in a light or sound wave, which we perceive as brightness or loudness, as determined by the wave's amplitude.

pupil The adjustable opening in the center of the eye through which light enters.

iris A ring of muscle tissue that forms the colored portion of the eye around the pupil and controls the size of the pupil opening.

lens The transparent structure behind the pupil that changes shape to focus images on the retina.

accommodation The process by which the eye's lens changes shape to focus the image of near objects on the retina.

retina The light-sensitive inner surface of the eye, containing the receptor rods and cones plus layers of neurons that begin the processing of visual information.

rods Retinal receptors that detect black, white, and gray; necessary for peripheral and twilight vision, when cones don't respond.

cones Receptor cells concentrated near the center of the retina that function in daylight or in well-lit conditions. The cones detect fine detail and give rise to color sensations.

optic nerve The nerve that carries neural impulses from the eye to the brain.

blind spot The point at which the optic nerve leaves the eye, creating a "blind" spot because no receptor cells are located there.

fovea The central focal point in the retina, around which the eye's cones cluster.

feature detectors Nerve cells in the brain that respond to specific features of the stimulus, such as movement, angle, or shape.

parallel processing Information processing in which several aspects of a problem are processed simultaneously. The brain's natural mode of information processing for many functions, including vision; contrasts with the step-by-step (serial) processing of most computers and of conscious problem solving.

Young-Helmholtz trichromatic (three-color) theory The theory that the retina contains three different color receptors—one most sensitive to red, one to green, one to blue—which combined can produce the perception of any color.

opponent-process theory The theory that opposing retinal processes (red-green, yellow-blue, white-black) enable color vision. For example, some cells are stimulated by green and inhibited by red; others are stimulated by red and inhibited by green.

color constancy Perceiving familiar objects as having consistent color, even if changing illumination alters the wavelengths reflected by the object.

audition The sense of hearing.

frequency The number of complete wavelengths that pass a point in a given time (for example, per second).

pitch A tone's highness or lowness; depends on frequency.

middle ear The chamber between the eardrum and cochlea containing three tiny bones (hammer, anvil, and stirrup) that concentrate the vibrations of the eardrum on the cochlea's oval window.

inner ear The innermost part of the ear, containing the cochlea, semicircular canals, and vestibular sacs.

cochlea [KOHK-lee-uh] A coiled, bony, fluid-filled tube in the inner ear through which sound waves trigger nerve impulses.

place theory In hearing, the theory that links the pitch we hear with the place where the cochlea's membrane is stimulated.

frequency theory In hearing, the theory that the rate of nerve impulses traveling up the auditory nerve matches the frequency of a tone, thus enabling us to sense its pitch.

conduction deafness Hearing loss caused by damage to the mechanical system that conducts sound waves to the cochlea.

nerve deafness Hearing loss caused by damage to the cochlea's receptor cells or to the auditory nerves.

gate-control theory Melzack and Wall's theory that the spinal cord contains a neurological "gate" that blocks or allows pain signals to pass on to the brain. The "gate" is opened by the activity of pain signals traveling up small nerve fibers and closed by activity in larger fibers or by information coming from the brain.

sensory interaction The principle that one sense may influence another, as when the smell of food influences its taste.

kinesthesis [kin-ehs-THEE-sehs] The system for sensing the position and movement of individual body parts.

equilibrium The sense of body movement and position, including the sense of balance.

For Further Reading

Ackerman, D. (1990). *A natural history of the senses.* New York: Random House.

A sensuous book about how, and especially what, we can sense.

Frisby, J. P. (1980). *Seeing: Illusion, brain and mind.* Oxford: Oxford University Press.

A wonderfully illustrated introduction to the visual system.

Hubel, D. H. (1988). *Eye, brain, and vision.* New York: Scientific American Library.

A careful look at how we see the world.

Kisor, H. (1990). *What's that pig outdoors: A memoir of deafness.* New York: Hill and Wang.

A Chicago newspaper columnist provides a fascinating perspective on the worlds of the deaf and the hearing as he recalls the ups and downs of growing up deaf in a hearing culture.

Perception

Chapter 6

9/25/94 10:43pm.

I love you.

Hi, the B.P.

? Will you MARRY me. PLEASE.

yes / no

P.S. Just so that I'll know. (You know)

Some 2400 years ago, the philosopher Plato rightly discerned that we perceive objects through the senses, with the mind. But *how* does the mind work to create our perceptions? Through Chapter 5's bottom-up perspective we examined how we sense sights and sounds, tastes and smells. Now, taking a top-down perspective, we will see how, aided by our knowledge and expectations, we analyze sensory information. How do we see not just shapes and colors, but a rose in bloom, a familiar face, a sunset? How do we hear not just a mix of pitches and rhythms, but a child's cry of pain, the hum of distant traffic, a symphony? In short, how do we transform meaningless sensations into meaningful perceptions?

In the classic version of the now familiar nature-nurture debate, philosophers argued about how these perceptual processes originate. Is it through biological maturation or through experience? On one side, the German philosopher Immanuel Kant (1724–1804) maintained that knowledge comes from our *innate* (inborn) ways of organizing sensory experiences. On the other side, the British philosopher John Locke (1632–1704) argued that we *learn* how to perceive the world through our experiences of it. As we will see, it's now clear that different aspects of perception depend more or less on *both* nature's endowments and the experiences that influence what we make of our sensations.

Perceptual Illusions

During the late 1800s, when psychology was emerging as a distinct discipline, perceptual illusions fascinated scientists — and they still do. Illusions mislead us by playing on the ways we organize and interpret our sensations. Understanding illusions provides valuable clues to the ordinary mechanisms of perception. Consider five such perceptual puzzles:

Puzzle 1 At right is a classic illusion created in 1889 by Franz Müller-Lyer. Does either line segment, *AB* or *BC*, appear longer?

To most people the two segments appear the same length. Surprise! They are not. As your ruler can verify, line *AB* is a full one-third longer than line *BC*. Why do our eyes deceive us? (On page 172 we will discover one explanation.)

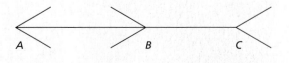

A ⟨———————⟩ B ⟨————— C

Puzzle 2 Above we have two unretouched photos of the same two girls, in the same room. The camera shows you these scenes much as you would see them if you were looking at each room through a single peephole. Why do the girls seem to change size? (Page 173 will reveal why.)

Puzzle 3 Is Gateway Arch in St. Louis taller than it is wide? Or vice versa? To most it appears taller. In truth, its height and width are equal. Once again, seeing is deceiving. Why? (On page 169 we will meet this phenomenon again.)

Puzzle 4 Aircraft pilots, ship captains, and car drivers perceive their surroundings under varying conditions of visibility. When their perceptions or reactions err—as happens in most commercial airplane accidents (Adler, 1989)—the results can be devastating. To simulate distance judgments, psychologist Helen Ross (1975) asked passersby to estimate the distances of white disks she had placed on the lawn at Britain's Hull University. Those who judged the distance in the thick morning fog perceived the disks to be farther away than did those who made their estimates in the midday sunshine. What does this suggest about how we normally judge distances? (Pages 167–170 explain distance perception.)

Morning fog

Midday sunshine

Puzzle 5 Illusions occur with the other senses, too. More than a century ago, the psychologist Wilhelm Wundt was puzzled by people's hearing the steady beat of a metronome or clock as if it were a repeating rhythm of two, three, or four beats—not as an unaccented click-click-click-click, which it is, but as, say, CLICK-click CLICK-click CLICK-click. From the steady beat that strikes the ear, each listener unconsciously shapes an auditory pattern. What perceptual principle is at work here? (See page 174 to find out.)

The emphasis on visual illusions in these puzzles reflects vision's preeminence among our senses. When there is conflict between vision and other sensations, vision usually dominates. We often experience this phenomenon of **visual capture**. When the sound of a movie comes from a projector behind us, we nevertheless perceive it as coming from the screen, where we *see* the actors talking. While viewing a roller coaster ride on a wraparound movie screen, we may brace ourselves, though our other senses tell us we're not moving. In both cases, vision *captures* the other senses.

Perceptual Organization

Early in this century, a group of German psychologists became intrigued with how the mind organizes sensations into perceptions. Given a cluster of sensations, the human perceiver organizes them into a **gestalt**, a German word meaning a "form" or a "whole." The Gestalt psychologists provided many compelling demonstrations of this ability. Look at Figure 6–1. Note that the individual elements of the figure are really nothing but eight blue circles, each containing three white lines. But when we view them all together, we see a *whole* form, a "Necker cube." Note, too, that the figure evokes more than one perception. Because the circles can be organized into several coherent images, each equally plausible, the mind switches back and forth from one to the next.

As the Gestalt psychologists were fond of saying, in perception the whole may differ from the sum of its parts. Combine sodium, a corrosive metal, with chlorine, a poison gas, and something very different emerges—table salt. Likewise, perceived form is an emergent property not inherent in an object's components (Rock & Palmer, 1990). There is far more to perception than meets the senses.

Such demonstrations led the Gestalt psychologists to describe principles by which we organize our sensations into perceptions. As you read about these organizational principles, keep in mind the fundamental truth they illustrate: Our brains do more than merely register information about the world. Perception is not just opening a shutter and letting a picture print itself on the brain. Always, we are filtering sensory information and inferring perceptions in ways that make sense to us.

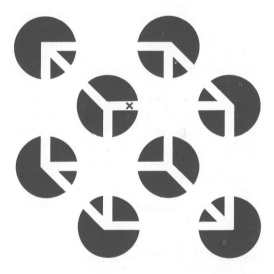

Figure 6–1 What do you see: circles with white lines, or a cube? If you stare at the cube, you may notice that it reverses location, moving the tiny X in the center from the front edge to the back. At times the cube may also seem to float in front of the page, with circles behind it; at other times the circles may become holes in the page through which the cube appears, as though it were floating behind the page. (From Bradley & others, 1976.)

Form Perception

Imagine that you wanted to design a video/computer system that, like your eye/brain system, could read handwritten addresses or recognize faces. What abilities would it need?

Figure and Ground To start with, the system would need to recognize the addresses and faces as distinct from their backgrounds. Likewise, our first task in perception is to perceive any object, called the *figure*, as distinct from its surroundings, called the *ground*. Among the voices you hear at a party, the one you attend to becomes the figure, all others part of the ground. As you read, the words are the figure; the white paper, the ground. In Figure 6–2, the **figure-ground** relationship continually reverses—but always we organize the stimulus into a figure seen against a ground. (Is there a candlestick in front of one face, or is that the background between two faces?) Reversible figure and ground demonstrates again that the same stimulus can trigger more than one perception.

Grouping Having discriminated figure from ground, we (and our video/computer system) must then organize the figure into a meaningful form. Some basic features of a scene, such as color, movement, and light-dark contrast we process instantly and automatically (Treisman, 1987). To bring order and form to these basic sensations, our minds follow certain rules for **grouping** stimuli together. These rules, identified by the Gestalt psychologists, illustrate their idea that the perceived whole differs from the mere sum of its parts (Rock & Palmer, 1990):

Proximity We group nearby figures together. We see below not six separate lines, but three sets of two lines.

Similarity If figures are similar to each other, we group them together. We see the triangles and circles as vertical columns of similar shapes, not as horizontal rows of dissimilar shapes.

Figure 6–2 Reversible figure and ground: One face or two? (From Shepard, 1990.)

Proximity   Similarity

Continuity We perceive smooth, continuous patterns rather than discontinuous ones. This pattern could be a series of alternating semicircles, but we perceive it as a wavy line and a straight line.

Closure If a figure has gaps, we complete it, filling in the gaps to create a complete, whole object. By filling the gaps in the shell's outline here, we see a whole seashell.

Connectedness We perceive spots, lines, or areas as a single unit when uniform and linked.

Continuity   Closure   Connectedness

The grouping principles usually help us perceive reality, but sometimes they lead us astray, as when viewing the doghouse in Figure 6–3.

Depth Perception

From the two-dimensional images that fall on our retinas we somehow organize three-dimensional perceptions. Seeing objects in three dimensions, called **depth perception**, allows us to estimate their distance from us. At a glance, we estimate the distance of an oncoming car or the height of a cliff. This ability is partly innate. Eleanor Gibson and Richard Walk (1960) discovered this using a miniature cliff with a drop-off covered by sturdy glass. The inspiration for these experiments occurred to Gibson as she was eating a picnic lunch on the rim of the Grand Canyon. She wondered: Would a toddler peering over the rim perceive the dangerous drop-off and draw back?

Back in their Cornell University laboratory, Gibson and Walk placed 6- to 14-month-old infants on the edge of a **visual cliff** (Figure 6–4). Their mothers then coaxed them to crawl out on the glass. Most refused to do so, preferring to crawl on the "shallow" side, thereby indicating that they could perceive depth. Newborn animals with virtually no visual experience—including young kittens, a day-old goat, and newly hatched chicks—respond similarly. What is more, during the first month of life, human infants turn to avoid objects coming directly at them but are unbothered by objects approaching at an angle that would not hit them (Ball & Tronick, 1971). Thus, our ability to perceive depth seems innate.

Figure 6–3 You probably perceive this doghouse as a gestalt—a whole (though impossible) structure. As the photo on page 183 shows, Gestalt grouping principles are at work here.

Figure 6–4 Eleanor Gibson and Richard Walk devised this miniature cliff with a glass-covered drop-off to determine whether human infants and newborn animals can perceive depth. Even when coaxed, infants are reluctant to venture onto the glass over the cliff, indicating that even the very young can perceive depth.

How do we do it? How do we transform two-dimensional retinal images into three-dimensional perceptions? Some of the cues we use require both eyes (**binocular cues**). Others are available to each eye separately (**monocular cues**).

Binocular Cues Because our eyes are about 2½ inches apart, our retinas receive slightly different images of the world. When the brain compares these two images, their **retinal disparity** (the difference in the two images) provides an important cue to distance. When you hold your finger directly in front of your nose, your retinas receive quite different views. (You can see this if you close one eye and then the other.) At greater distance—say, when you hold your finger at arm's length—the disparity is smaller.

The creators of 3-D movies and "Viewmaster" 3-D scenes simulate retinal disparity by photographing a scene with two cameras placed a few inches apart (a feature we might want to build into our seeing computer). When viewed through spectacles or a device that allows the left eye to see only the image from the left camera and the right eye the image from the right camera, the 3-D effect mimics normal retinal disparity.

Another binocular cue to distance is **convergence**, a muscular cue that indicates the extent to which the eyes turn inward when we look at an object. By noting the angle of convergence, the brain determines whether you are focusing just past your nose, or on this printed page, or on the person across the room.

Monocular Cues With both eyes open, we can readily and precisely touch the tip of a pen held in front of us; with one eye closed, the task becomes noticeably more difficult. This demonstrates the importance of binocular cues in judging the distance of nearby objects. How then do we judge whether a person is 100 feet or 100 yards away? In both cases, the retinal disparity while looking straight ahead is slight. At such distances we depend on monocular cues such as the following:

> **Relative size** If we assume that two objects are similar in size, we perceive the one that casts the smaller image on the retina as farther away.

> **Overlap** If one object partially covers another, we perceive it as closer. We perceive the young deer as closer than its partially obscured mother.

Relative size

Overlap

> **Aerial perspective** We perceive hazy objects as farther away than sharp, clear objects. (Recall from Puzzle 4, page 164, the effects of fog on judging distance.)

Texture gradient

Texture gradient We perceive a gradual change from a coarse, distinct texture to a fine, indistinct texture as a sign of increasing distance. Our visual system automatically reads the receding surface as distance.

Relative height We perceive objects higher in our field of vision as farther away. This may contribute to the illusion that vertical dimensions are longer than identical horizontal dimensions (as we saw in Puzzle 3, the St. Louis Gateway). Is the vertical line here longer, shorter, or equal in length to the horizontal line? Measure and see.

Relative motion As our heads move, stable objects in our environment appear to move relative to us. If while riding in a train you fix your gaze on some object—say, a tree—you see that the objects closer to you than the tree (the fixation point) appear to move backward. The nearer an object is, the faster it seems to move. Objects beyond the fixation point appear to move with you at a speed that decreases as the object gets farther away. Your brain uses these speed and direction clues to determine the objects' relative distances.

Relative height

Direction of
passenger's motion

Relative motion

Linear perspective

Linear perspective We interpret the apparent convergence of parallel lines as a clue to distance. The more they converge, the greater the perceived distance. Linear perspective can contribute to rail-crossing accidents, by leading people to overestimate a train's distance (Leibowitz, 1985). (A train's massive size also makes it appear to be moving more slowly than it is.)

Relative brightness Nearby objects reflect more light to our eyes. Thus, given two identical objects, the dimmer one seems farther away. This illusion also can contribute to accidents, as when a fog-shrouded vehicle, or one with only its parking lights on, seems farther away than it is. Shading, too, produces a sense of depth consistent with the assumed light source. Invert the illustration at right and the hollow becomes a hill, because we assume that light comes from above.

To convey depth on a flat canvas (Figure 6–5), artists use these monocular cues, as do people who must gauge depth with but one eye. In 1960, the University of Washington football team won the Rose Bowl, thanks partly to the superb passing of quarterback Bob Schloredt. Schloredt, who is obviously skilled at judging the distance of his receivers, must be super sensitive to monocular cues for distance, because he is blind in his left eye.

Relative brightness

Figure 6–5 By the time that "Bristol, Broad Quay" was painted (c. 1730, Anonymous), the techniques for showing perspective were well established. Note the effective use of distance cues such as texture gradient, overlap, and relative size and height.

Perceptual Constancy

So far we have seen that our video/computer system must first perceive objects as we do—as having a distinct form and location. Its next task is even more challenging: to recognize the object, without being deceived by changes in its size, shape, brightness, or color. Our **perceptual constancy** allows us to perceive an object as unchanging while the stimuli from it change—that is, we can identify things regardless of viewing angle, distance, and illumination. You glance at someone ahead of you on the sidewalk and instantly recognize a classmate. In less time than it takes to draw a breath, information reaching your eyes has been sent to the brain, where millions of neurons have extracted the essential features, compared them with stored images, and identified the person. Replicating this human perceptual feat, which has intrigued perception researchers for decades, provides a monumental challenge for our seeing computer.

Shape and Size Constancies   Thanks to *shape constancy* we perceive familiar objects as having a constant form, even while our retinal images of them change. When a door opens, it casts a changing shape on our retinas, yet we manage to perceive the door as having a constant doorlike shape (Figure 6–6).

   Size constancy—perceiving objects as having a constant size—allows us to perceive a car as big enough to carry people, even when we see it from two blocks away. This illustrates the close connection between an object's perceived *distance* and perceived *size*. Perceiving an object's distance cues us to its size. Likewise, knowing its general size—that the object is, say, a car—provides us with cues to its distance.

Figure 6–6 Shape constancy. A door casts an increasingly trapezoidal image on our retinas as it opens, yet we still perceive it as rectangular.

Box A   Box B

Perceiving shape. Do the tops of boxes *A* and *B* have different dimensions? They appear to. But if you measure, you will see they are identical. With both boxes we adjust our perceptions relative to our viewing angle. (From Shepard, 1981.)

Size-Distance Relationship   The marvel of size perception is how effortlessly it occurs. Given the perceived distance of an object and the size of its image on our retinas, we instantly and unconsciously infer the object's size. Although the monsters in Figure 6–7a (on page 172) cast the same retinal images, their context (linear perspective) cues us that the monster in pursuit is farther away. We therefore perceive it as larger.

   This interplay between perceived size and perceived distance helps explain several well-known illusions. For example, can you imagine why the moon looks larger—up to 50 percent larger—near the horizon than when high in the sky? For at least 22 centuries, scholars have wondered, and argued (Hershenson, 1989). A partial reason for the "moon illusion" is that cues to objects' distances at the horizon make the moon behind them seem farther away

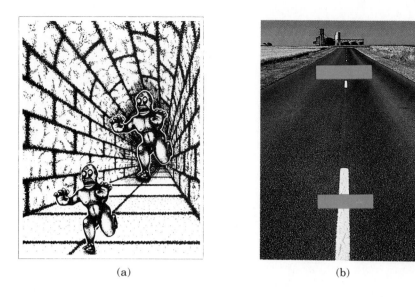

(a)   (b)

Figure 6–7 The interplay between perceived size and distance. (a) The monocular cues for distance make the pursuing monster look larger than the pursued. It isn't. (From Shepard, 1990.) (b) The Ponzo illusion. The two identical orange bars cast identical images on our retinas. But we believe that a more distant object can only create the same-sized image if it is larger. Thus, we perceive the bar that seems more distant as larger.

(Kaufman & Rock, 1962). Thus, the moon on the horizon seems larger (like the distant monster in Figure 6–7a and the distant bar in Figure 6–7b). Take away these distance cues—by looking at the horizon moon (or the monsters) through a paper tube—and it immediately shrinks.

The size-distance relationship helps us understand two illusions demonstrated at the start of this chapter. Puzzle 1, the Müller-Lyer illusion concerning the lengths of straight lines between arrow tips, has been the subject of more than 1250 scientific publications, but psychologists still debate its explanation. One is that our experience with the corners of rooms or buildings prompts us to interpret the vertical line on the ticket booth in Figure 6–8a as closer to us and therefore shorter, and the vertical line by the door as farther away and therefore longer.

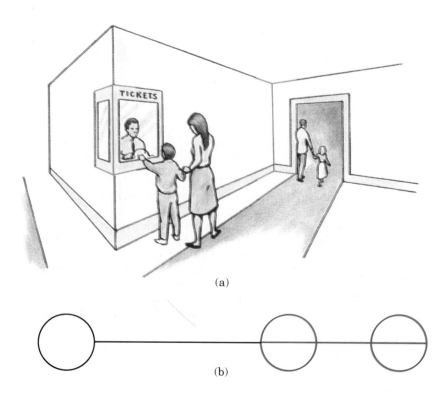

(a)

(b)

Figure 6–8 The Müller-Lyer illusion. (a) Richard L. Gregory (1968) suggests that the corners in our rectangularly carpentered world teach us to interpret "outward" or "inward" pointing arrowheads at the ends of a line as a cue to the line's distance from us and so to its length. The line defined by the corner at the ticket windows looks shorter than the line defined by the corner to the right. But if you measure them, you will see that both are the same length. (b) There is more to the Müller-Lyer illusion than size constancy, however, for if we replace the arrowheads with circles and judge whether the black or blue line segment seems longer, we still get much the same effect. Here the two line segments are equal. Most people judge the black line as longer, apparently because they perceptually adjust the lengths of the lines toward the distance separating the figures (From Day, 1984).

Supporting this theory, people are more susceptible to the Müller-Lyer illusion if, unlike many rural Africans, they have lived in a carpentered world of rectangular shapes (Segall & others, 1990). The phenomenon reflects cultural experience, not race, for the same study showed that Africans who live in carpentered cities are more vulnerable to the illusion than Africans in uncarpentered environments. Our experience in architectural contexts helps us construct our perceptions, top-down.

Anthropologist Colin Turnbull (1961, p. 252) noted another effect of experience on perception when he took an African Pygmy guide, Kenge, on his first trip out of the dense forest. As they were crossing a wide plain, buffalo loomed several miles away. Kenge, unaccustomed to judging size over unbroken distances, wondered, "What insects are those?" "When I told Kenge that the insects were buffalo, he roared with laughter and told me not to tell such stupid lies." As they drove on, the mystified Kenge became frightened as the buffalo grew bigger and bigger.

Size-distance relationships also explain Puzzle 2, the shrinking girls. As Figure 6–9 reveals, the room is distorted. But viewed with one eye through a peephole, its trapezoidal walls produce the same images as those of a normal rectangular room viewed with both eyes. Presented with the camera's one-eyed view, the brain makes the reasonable assumption that the room *is* normal, and perceives the girls as changing in size.

Figure 6–9 The illusion of the shrinking and growing girls. When viewed through a peephole with one eye, this distorted room, designed by lawyer-turned-scientist Adelbert Ames, appears to have a normal rectangular shape with both corners being the same distance away. Thus, anything in the near corner appears disproportionately large compared to anything in the far corner, because we judge their size based on the false assumption that they are the same distance away.

Our occasional misperceptions demonstrate the workings of our normally effective perceptual processes. The perceived relationship between distance and size is generally valid, but under special circumstances can lead us astray—as when helping to create the moon illusion, the Müller-Lyer illusion, and the distorted room illusion. Using distance cues to assess perceived size triggers illusions only if we aren't familiar with the object or if the distance cues are misleading. When we correctly interpret the distance cues — which we normally do—we perceive the size of objects correctly.

Brightness Constancy White paper reflects 90 percent of the light falling on it; black paper, only 10 percent. In sunlight the black paper may reflect 100 times more light than does the white paper indoors (McBurney & Collings, 1984), but it still looks black. This illustrates *brightness constancy*, our perceiving an object as having a constant amount of brightness even while its illumination varies. Perceived brightness depends on *relative luminance*—how much light an object reflects relative to its surroundings. If you view sunlit black paper through a narrow tube so nothing else is visible, it may look gray, because in bright sunshine it reflects a fair amount of light. View it without the tube and it is again black, because it reflects much less light than the objects around it. The phenomenon is similar to that of color constancy (page 145). A red apple in a fruit bowl retains its redness as the light changes, because our brain computes the light reflected by any object relative to its surrounding objects.

If perceived brightness stays roughly constant, given an unchanging context, what happens when the surrounding context changes? The same principle—that the brain computes brightness and color relative to surrounding objects—implies that brightness will change with context. As Figure 6–10 shows, that is precisely what happens.

Form perception, depth perception, and perceptual constancy illustrate how we organize our visual experiences. Perceptual organization applies to other senses, too. It explains why we group the clock's steady clicks into patterns (Puzzle 5, page 165). Listening to an unfamiliar language, we have trouble hearing where one word stops and the next one begins. Listening to our own language, we automatically hear distinct words. This, too, is a form of perceptual organization. But it is more, for we even organize a string of letters—THEDOGATEMEAT—into words that make an intelligible phrase, more likely "The dog ate meat" than "The do gate me at" (McBurney & Collings, 1984). This process involves not only organization but *interpretation*—finding meaning in what we perceive.

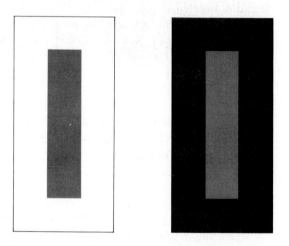

Figure 6–10 Brightness contrast. Although they are in fact identical, the perceived brightness of the interior rectangles differs depending on their surroundings. Like color constancy (page 145), this phenomenon has great significance for artists and interior designers.

Interpretation

So far we have seen that in some ways Immanuel Kant was correct (for example, that depth perception is innate) and in other ways John Locke was correct (for example, that through experience we learn to link the distance of an object to its perceived size). But just how important is experience? How radically does it shape our perceptual interpretations?

Sensory Restriction and Restored Vision

Writing to John Locke (1690), William Molyneux wondered whether "a man *born* blind, and now adult, taught by his *touch* to distinguish between a cube and a sphere," could, if made to see, visually distinguish the two. Locke's answer was no, because the man would never have *learned* to see.

Molyneux's hypothetical case has since been put to the test with dozens of adults who, though blind from birth, have gained sight (Gregory, 1978; Senden, 1932). Most were patients with catar-

"Let us then suppose the mind to be, as we say, white paper void of all characters, without any ideas: How comes it to be furnished? . . . To this I answer, in one word, from EXPERIENCE."
John Locke
An Essay Concerning Human Understanding, 1690

These blind children are learning to recognize goats by touch. If blind since birth, they probably would be unable to recognize goats by *sight* if their vision were restored.

acts—clouded lenses that enabled them to see only diffused light, rather as you or I might see the world through a Ping-Pong ball sliced in half. When their cataracts were surgically removed, the patients could distinguish figure from ground and could sense colors—suggesting that these aspects of perception are innate. But much as Locke supposed, the formerly blind patients often could not visually recognize objects that were familiar by touch.

Perhaps in these cases the surgery didn't completely restore the patients' visual equipment. Seeking to gain more control than provided by clinical cases, researchers have conducted Molyneux's imaginary experiment with animals. To discover whether altering a young animal's normal visual experience would permanently alter its perceptual abilities, they stitched closed the eyelids of infant kittens and monkeys or outfitted them with goggles through which the animals could see only diffuse, unpatterned light (Wiesel, 1982). After infancy, when their visual impairments were removed, these animals exhibited perceptual limitations much like those of human cataract patients. They could distinguish color and brightness, but not the form of a circle from that of a square. Their eyes had not degenerated; their retinas still relayed signals to their visual cortex. But the animals remained functionally blind to shape.

In both humans and animals, a similar period of sensory restriction that occurs later in life is not permanently disruptive. Cover the eye of an animal for several months during adulthood, and vision will be unaffected after removing the eye patch. Remove cataracts that develop after early childhood, and a human, too, will enjoy normal vision. The effects of visual experiences during infancy in cats, monkeys, and humans suggest there is a *critical period* (page 77) for normal perceptual development. Experience guides the organization of the brain's neural connections.

We can also see the profound effects of early visual experience in experiments with young animals who were reared with severely restricted visual input. Cambridge University researchers Colin Blakemore and Grahame Cooper (1970) reared kittens in darkness, except for 5 hours each day during which they were placed in a horizontally or vertically striped environment (as in Figure 6–11). Remarkably, kittens raised without exposure to horizontal lines later had difficulty perceiving horizontal bars, and those raised without vertical lines had difficulty seeing vertical bars. While two of these kittens played, a researcher playfully shook a long black rod. The kitten reared in a world of vertical lines would play with the rod only when it was held upright. When the rod was held flat, that kitten ignored it while its companion reared in a world of horizontal lines ran to play with it. Eventually, their selective blindness diminished, but the kittens never regained normal sensitivity. By sampling the activity of the kittens' feature-detecting brain cells, Blakemore and Cooper found that whether such cells responded mostly to horizontal or vertical lines depended on the kittens' early visual experience.

This research provides a partial answer to a question debated in Chapter 4, Adolescence and Adulthood: Does the effect of early experience last a lifetime? For some aspects of visual perception, the answer is clearly yes: We retain the imprint of early visual experiences far into the future.

Perceptual Adaptation

Given a new pair of glasses, we may feel slightly disoriented and dizzy. Within a day or two we adjust. Our **perceptual adaptation** to changed visual input makes the world seem normal again. Now imagine a far more dramatic new pair of glasses—one that shifts the apparent location of objects 40 degrees to the left. When you first put them on and toss a ball to a friend, it sails off to the left. Walking forward to shake hands with the person, you veer to the left.

Could you adapt to this distorted world? Chicks cannot. When fitted with such lenses, they continue to peck where food grains *seem* to be (Hess, 1956; Rossi, 1968). But humans adapt to distorting lenses quickly. Within a few minutes your throws would again be accurate, your stride on target. Remove the lenses and you would experience an aftereffect: At first your throws would err in the *opposite* direction, sailing off to the right; but again, within minutes you would readapt.

Now imagine an even more radical pair of glasses—one that literally turns the world upside down. The ground is up, the sky is down. Could you adapt? Fish, frogs, and salamanders cannot. When Roger Sperry (1956) surgically turned their eyes upside down, they thereafter reacted to objects by moving in the wrong direction. But, believe it or not, kittens, monkeys, and humans can adapt to an inverted world. Turn-of-the-century psychologist George Stratton (1896) experienced this when he invented and wore for 8 days optical headgear that flipped left to right *and* up to down, making him the first person to experience a right-side-up retinal image while standing upright.

At first, Stratton was disoriented. When he wanted to walk, he had to search for his feet, which were now "up." Eating was nearly impossible. He became nauseated and depressed. But Stratton persisted, and by the eighth day he could comfortably reach for something in the right direction and walk without bumping into things. When Stratton finally removed the headgear, he readapted quickly.

Figure 6–11 The experimental apparatus for the Blakemore and Cooper studies. From the time their eyes first opened up to age 5 months, these kittens were removed from darkness each day to spend 5 hours alone in a black-and-white striped cylinder with a clear glass floor. A stiff collar prevented the kittens from seeing anything else, even their own bodies. Afterward, these kittens were less sensitive to horizontal forms. (From Blakemore & Cooper, 1970.)

Dr. Hubert Dolezal views the world through inverted lenses. Remarkably, people can learn to adapt to an upside-down visual world.

Later experiments replicated Stratton's experience (Dolezal, 1982; Kohler, 1962). After a period of adjustment, people wearing the optical gear have even been able to ride a motorcycle, ski the Alps, and fly an airplane. Is this because through experience they perceptually reinvert their upside-down world to an upright position? No, the street, ski slopes, and runway still seem above their heads. But by actively moving about in this topsy-turvy world, they adapt to the context and learn to coordinate their movements.

Perceptual Set

As everyone knows, to see is to believe. As many people also know, but do not fully appreciate, to believe is to see. Our experiences, assumptions, and expectations may give us a **perceptual set**, or mental predisposition, that greatly influences what we perceive. Is the person in the center picture of Figure 6–12 a man playing the saxophone or a woman? What we see in such a drawing can be influenced by first viewing either of two unambiguous versions (Boring, 1930).

[handwritten note: do you see woman or man w/ sax?]

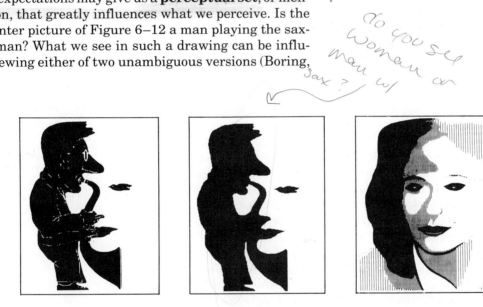

Figure 6–12 Which do you see in the center picture: the male saxophonist or the woman? Glancing first at one of the two unambiguous versions of the picture would likely influence your interpretation. (From Shepard, 1990.)

Knowing this much, see if you can explain the results of another experiment. A slightly blurred picture was identified correctly by 73 percent of first-time viewers, but by only 25 percent of those who had previously been shown a *badly* blurred version of the same picture (Bruner & Potter, 1964). Why do you suppose the second group had such trouble perceiving the image?

It's because people cannot resist imposing a pattern on unpatterned stimuli. Shown a hopelessly blurred picture, people automatically form a preliminary hunch (perceptual set), which then interferes with their later perceptions. Thus, it is much harder to recognize a photo coming into focus than to "hang on" to the same photo going out of focus. Once we have formed a wrong idea about reality, we have more difficulty seeing the truth. Even scientists, striving for objectivity, perceive reality through the lenses of their theories. When first viewing the "canals" on Mars through telescopes, some astronomers and writers perceived them as the product of intelligent life. They were—but the intelligence was on the viewing end of the telescope.

Everyday examples of perceptual set abound. In 1972, a British newspaper published genuine, unretouched photographs of a "monster" in Scotland's Loch Ness—"the most amazing pictures ever taken," stated the paper. If this information creates the same

"The temptation to form premature theories upon insufficient data is the bane of our profession."
Sherlock Holmes, in Arthur Conan Doyle's
The Valley of Fear, 1914

Figure 6-13 Is this the Loch Ness monster or a log? We often see what we expect to see.

perceptual set in you as it did in most of the paper's readers, you, too, will see the monster in the photo reproduced in Figure 6–13. But when Steuart Campbell (1986) approached the photos with a different perceptual set, he saw a curved tree trunk—very likely the same tree trunk others had seen in the lake the day the photo was shot. Moreover, with this different perceptual set, you may now notice that the object is floating motionless, without any water disturbance or wake around it—hardly what we would expect of a lively monster.

Our perceptual set can influence what we hear as well as what we see. Witness the kindly airline pilot who, on a takeoff run, looked over at his depressed co-pilot and said, "Cheer up." The co-pilot heard the usual "Gear up" and promptly raised the wheels—before they had left the ground (Reason & Mycielska, 1982). When viewing a liquor ad or listening to rock music played backward, people often perceive a sexual image or evil message *if* specifically told what to look for or listen to (Vokey & Read, 1985).

What determines our perceptual set? Through experience we form concepts, or *schemas*, which organize and interpret unfamiliar information. Our preexisting schemas for male saxophonists and women, for monsters and tree trunks, for airplane lights and UFOs, all help us interpret ambiguous sensations. Confronted with an ambiguous moving object in the sky, different people may therefore apply different schemas: "It's a bird." "It's a plane." "It's Superman!"

Children's drawings allow us to glimpse their developing perceptual schemas. A preschooler can draw circles and angled lines but cannot combine them to create an elaborate human figure. Why not? The child's problem is not clumsiness. A right-handed adult asked to draw with the left hand will create an awkward drawing, but it will be unlike the child's drawing in Figure 6–14. Part of the difference lies in children's difficulty representing visually what they see. The main difference, however, lies in the child's simplified schema for essential human characteristics. To a 3-year-old, a face is a more essential human feature than a body. From ages 3 to 8, children's schemas for bodies become more elaborate, and so do their drawings.

Our schemas for faces prime us to see facial patterns in cartoonists' caricatures, and even in random configurations such as the lunar landscape. Peter Thompson (1980) at the University of York discovered that our face recognition is especially attuned to the expressive eyes and mouth. Thus, we have trouble imagining what former Prime Minister Margaret Thatcher's inverted eyes and mouth will look like when we turn her face upright (Figure 6–15).

Figure 6-14 Children's drawings reflect their schemas of reality, as well as their abilities to represent what they see. This drawing by a 3-year-old illustrates that the face has far greater importance than the body in young children's schemas of essential human characteristics.

Figure 6-15 Look at Margaret Thatcher's reconstructed face (left) and try to imagine what her face will look like when you turn it upright.

Context Effects A given stimulus may trigger radically different perceptions, partly because of our differing schemas, but also because of the immediate context. Some quick examples:

Did the speaker say "cults and sects" or "cults and sex"? We must discern from the surrounding words.

Does the pursuing monster in Figure 6–7a on page 172 look aggressive? Does the pursued one seem frightened? If so, you are experiencing a context effect. The two monsters are the same.

Is the "Magician's Cabinet" in Figure 6–16 sitting on the floor or hanging from the ceiling? How we perceive it depends on the context defined by the bunnies.

Figure 6–16 Is the box in the far left frame lying on the floor or hanging from the ceiling? The context defined by the inquisitive bunnies guides our perceptions. (From Shepard, 1990.)

Shown various scenes, people more quickly recognize things in their expected context (a fire hydrant on the street) than in a novel context (a hydrant on top of a mailbox) (Biederman, 1981). On campus, you instantly recognize a fellow student. Out of the usual context — at the beach — the student may seem no more than vaguely familiar.

Soviet film director Lew Kulechov believed that skilled directors create audience emotion by defining a context in which viewers interpret an actor's expressions. He once produced three short films, each depicting one of three contexts, followed by identical clips of an actor with a neutral expression (Wallbott, 1988). Shown a dead woman, viewers were struck by the actor's sadness. Shown a dish of soup, viewers judged the actor thoughtful. Shown a playing child, viewers said the actor appeared happy.

Context effects. What is above the woman's head? In this experiment, nearly all the participants from East Africa thought she was balancing a metal box or can on her head and that the family was sitting under a tree. Westerners, to whom corners and boxlike architecture are more common, were more likely to perceive the family as being indoors, with the woman sitting under a window. (Adapted from Gregory & Gombrich, 1973.)

Close-Up   *The Human Factor in Operating Machines*

I love our VCR, though I still haven't figured out how to make it "express record." Our stove is wonderful, except for the moments I spend puzzling over which control works which burner. The push-bar doors on our campus buildings are safe and easy, though occasionally frustrating when I push the wrong end. The extra buttons on my computer-linked phone are handy, though when transferring a call I still must look up which button to press.

Human factors psychologists help to design appliances, machines, and work settings that harness rather than confound our natural perceptions. Psychologist Donald Norman (1988) suggests how simple design changes could reduce some of our frustrations. For example, by exploiting "natural mapping," we could design controls that require no labels.

Understanding "human factors" can do more than design for reduced frustration; it can help avoid disaster. After beginning commercial flights in the late 1960s, the Boeing 727 was involved in several landing accidents caused by pilot error. Psychologist Conrad Kraft (1978) noted a common feature of these accidents: All took place at night and involved landing short of the runway after crossing a dark stretch of water or

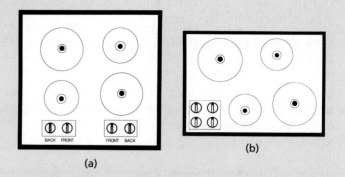

(a) Common stove controls require labeling. (b) By using a natural map, we needn't read labels.

unilluminated ground. By recreating these conditions in flight simulations, Kraft discovered that the lack of monocular cues, such as texture gradient, deceived pilots into thinking they were flying higher than they were (Figure 6–17). Aided by Kraft's finding, the airlines began corrective measures (such as requiring the co-pilot to monitor the altimeter and call out altitudes) and the accidents ceased.

Figure 6–17 Lacking distance cues when approaching a runway from over a dark surface, pilots simulating a night landing tended to underestimate their altitude. (From Kraft, 1978.)

In the hospital where I was once an orderly, we occasionally faced the task of transporting a dead body through crowded hallways without alarming the patients or their visitors. Our solution was to exploit the "Kulechov effect" by creating a context that matched people's schemas for sleeping and sedated patients: With the body's face uncovered and the sheet turned down in normal fashion, we could wheel an apparently "sleeping" body past the unsuspecting.

Amidst conflict, the effect of context can be tragic. During a 1988 military skirmish with Iran's navy, crew members of the U.S. naval destroyer *Vincennes* interpreted radar signals as those from an attacking fighter plane. Actually, they were those of an Iranian airliner flying on course to its scheduled destination. The tragic result of this context effect: the deaths of the 291 people on board.

In everyday life, perceptual sets—for example, stereotypes about gender or culture—can color the context. Without the obvious clues of pink or blue, people will struggle over whether to call the new baby a "he" or a "she." But told an infant is "David," people (especially children) may perceive "him" as bigger and stronger than if the same infant is called "Diana" (Stern & Karraker, 1989). Some apparent gender differences, it seems, exist merely in the eyes of their beholders.

The effects of perceptual sets and context show how experience helps us construct perception. "We hear and apprehend only what we already half know," said Thoreau. To return to our original question—Is perception innate or learned?—we can answer simply: It's both.

Is There Perception Without Sensation?

Can we perceive only what we sense? Or, beyond sensory input, are we capable of **extrasensory perception (ESP)**? Half of Americans say they believe in ESP and another quarter aren't sure (Gallup & Newport, 1991). The media overflow with reports of psychic wonders: crimes solved, dreams come true, futures foretold. Are there people who can read minds, see through walls, or foretell the future?

In laboratory experiments, **parapsychologists**—those who study paranormal (literally, beyond the normal) happenings—have sometimes been astonished at psychics who seem capable of discerning the contents of sealed envelopes, influencing the roll of a die, or drawing a picture of what someone else is viewing at an unknown remote location. But other research psychologists and scientists are skeptical (McClenon, 1982). If ESP is real, we would need to overturn the scientific understanding that we are creatures whose minds are tied to our physical brains and whose perceptual experiences of the world are built of sensations. Sometimes new evidence does overturn our scientific preconceptions. So let's look at some claims for ESP, and then see why scientists remain dubious.

Claims of ESP

Claims of paranormal phenomena include astrological predictions, psychic healing, reincarnation, communication with the dead, and out-of-body travel. Of these, the most respectable, testable, and—for a chapter on perception—relevant claims are for three varieties of ESP:

Telepathy, or mind-to-mind communication—one person sending thoughts to another or perceiving another's thoughts.

Clairvoyance, or perceiving remote events, such as sensing that a friend's house is on fire.

Precognition, or perceiving future events, such as a political leader's death or a sporting event's outcome.

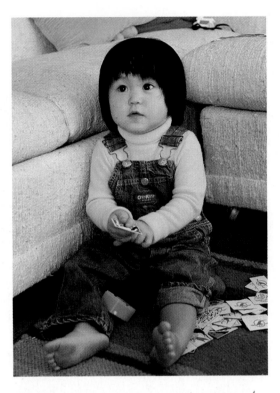

Is this 7-month-old a boy or a girl? (See page 183.) During infancy, boy-girl differences are minimal, but once we know the child's sex we may perceive behavior accordingly.

The Quigmans by Buddy Hickerson; © 1990, Los Angeles Times Syndicate. Reprinted with permission.

Closely linked with these are claims of *psychokinesis*, or "mind over matter," such as levitating a table or influencing the roll of a die.

On stage, the "psychic" controls what the audience sees and hears. In the laboratory, the experimenter controls what the psychic sees and hears. Consider one such experiment conducted by Bruce Layton and Bill Turnbull (1975) at the University of North Carolina. Layton and Turnbull had a computer generate a randomized 100-item list of the digits 1, 2, 3, 4, and 5 for each of their 179 student participants. They gave each student such a list in a sealed envelope and asked the student to guess which number was in each of the 100 positions.

By chance, 1 guess in 5, or 20 guesses out of the 100, should be correct. When told beforehand that ESP was beneficial, subjects averaged 20.66 correct out of 100. When told that ESP was harmful, they averaged only 19.49 correct. The difference might seem insignificant. Indeed, you would never notice so small an effect while observing an experiment. But a statistical analysis revealed that a difference that large among so many participants would seldom occur by chance. So Layton and Turnbull concluded that an ESP effect had occurred.

Bolstered by such experiments, believers in ESP accuse research psychologists of the same sort of skepticism that led eighteenth-century scientists to scoff at the idea that meteorites came from outer space. Novelist Arthur Koestler, who in 1983 left more than $700,000 to fund a British professorship in parapsychology, once complained that today's skeptical scientists resemble the Italian philosophers who refused to look at Jupiter's moons through Galileo's telescope — because they "knew" that such moons did not exist. Skepticism sometimes blinds people to the truth.

Skepticism About ESP

The skeptics reply that an uncritical mind is a gullible mind. Time and again, they point out, so-called psychics have exploited unquestioning audiences with amazing performances in which they *appeared* to communicate with the spirits of the dead, read minds, or levitate objects — only to have it revealed that their acts were a hoax, nothing more than the illusions of stage magicians. Indeed, many psychic deceptions have been exposed by magicians, who resent the exploitation of their arts in the name of psychic powers.

Even scientists get hoodwinked. A notable case involved two teenage magicians, Steve Shaw and Michael Edwards (Randi, 1983a,b). In 1979, this young pair approached Washington University's new parapsychology laboratory, offering to demonstrate their "psychic powers." Over the next 3 years, the two pretended to defy the laws of nature. They appeared to project mental images onto film, cause clocks to slide across a table, effortlessly bend metal objects, and move objects in sealed jars. Although forewarned against trickery by the youngsters' magician-adviser, James Randi, the laboratory director ignored the warnings and for a time proclaimed that "these two kids are the most reliable of the people that we've studied" ("Psychic Abscam," 1983).

This parapsychologist's gullibility illustrates how tempting it is to label phenomena *we* don't understand as beyond explanation: "What other explanation could there possibly be but ESP?" the awestruck observer asks. Thus, before bats' echolocation ability was

"A man does not attain the status of Galileo merely because he is persecuted; he must also be right."
Stephen Jay Gould
Ever Since Darwin, 1973

"A psychic is an actor playing the role of a psychic."
Psychologist-magician Daryl Bem (1984)

"The most eminent scientist, untrained in magic, is putty in the hands of a clever charlatan."
Martin Gardner (1983)

discovered, many people attributed bats' ability to avoid wires in complete darkness to clairvoyance (Gibson, 1979). When the bats were blinded, when their noses were sealed, when their wings were coated with varnish, they still could navigate, so what other explanation could there be but ESP? "Whatever you are *totally* ignorant of, assert to be the explanation of everything else," said William James (1890a, p. 347).

Premonitions or Pretensions? Can psychics see into the future? The tallied forecasts of "leading psychics" reveal meager accuracy. Between 1978 and 1985, the New Year's predictions of the *National Enquirer*'s favorite psychics yielded 2 accurate predictions out of 486 (Strentz, 1986). During these years, the psychics foresaw none of the significant unexpected events—that a woman would run for Vice President of the United States, that famine would devastate Ethiopia, that terrorism would plague Europe.

Checks on psychic visions offered to police departments reveal that these, too, are no more accurate than guesses made by others (Reiser, 1982). Psychics working with the police do, however, generate dozens or even hundreds of predictions; this increases the odds of an occasional correct guess, which psychics can then report to the media. Moreover, vague predictions can later be interpreted to match events, which provide a perceptual set for interpreting them. Nostradamus, a sixteenth-century French psychic, explained in an unguarded moment that his ambiguous prophecies "could not possibly be understood till they were interpreted after the event and by it."

Are the spontaneous "visions" of ordinary people any more accurate? Consider our dreams. Do they foretell the future, as about half of university students believe (Messner & Griggs, 1989)? Or do they only seem to because we are more likely to recall or reconstruct dreams that seem to have come true? More than 50 years ago, two Harvard psychologists (Murray & Wheeler, 1937) tested the prophetic power of dreams. After aviator Charles Lindbergh's baby son was kidnapped and murdered but before the body was discovered, the researchers invited the public to report their dreams about the child. Of the 1300 dream reports submitted, how many accurately envisioned the child dead? A mere 5 percent. And how many also correctly anticipated the body's location—buried among trees? Only 4 of the 1300. Although this number was surely no better than chance, to those four dreamers the accuracy of their *apparent* precognitions must have seemed uncanny.

Every day each of us imagines many events. Occasionally an unlikely imagined event is bound to occur and to astonish us when it does. If you tell everyone in a group of 100 people to think "heads" before each tosses six coins, someone is likely to get all heads (whether thinking heads or not) and to feel eerie afterwards. Given the billions of events that occur in the world each day, and given enough days, some stunning coincidences are sure to occur. As Stephen Jay Gould (1980) noted, "Time converts the improbable to the inevitable."

Finally, consider this, say the skeptics: After tens of thousands of experiments, *there has never been discovered a reproducible ESP phenomenon, nor any individual who can convincingly demonstrate psychic ability* (Marks, 1986). As British psychologist Mark Hansel (1980, p. 314) put it, "After a hundred years of research, not a sin-

Another view of the impossible doghouse in Figure 6–3 (page 167) reveals the secrets of this illusion. From the photo angle in Figure 6–3, the grouping principle of closure leads us to perceive the boards as continuous.

Reprinted from GAMES Magazine (810 Seventh Avenue, New York, NY 10019). Copyright © 1983 PSC Games Limited Partnership.

More recent experiments in which people attempted to send mental images to dreamers produced some intriguing initial results, but these could not be replicated even with the same subjects. Dream telepathy experiments have therefore been discontinued (Hyman, 1986).

The infant in the photo on page 181 is a girl.

gle individual has been found who can demonstrate ESP to the satisfaction of independent investigators," and, thus, "Today ESP is no nearer to being established than it was a hundred years ago" (1985, p. 124). A recent National Research Council investigation of ESP similarly concludes that "the best available evidence does not support the contention that these phenomena exist" (Druckman & Swets, 1988).

One skeptic, magician James Randi, has offered $10,000 to anyone who can demonstrate "*any* paranormal ability" before a group of competent experts. Other similar offers total more than a third of a million dollars (Jones, 1985–1986). To anyone whose claims could be authenticated, the scientific seal of approval would be worth far more. Randi's offer has been publicized for well over two decades, and dozens of people have been tested, sometimes under the scrutiny of an independent panel of judges. To refute those who say there is no ESP, one need only produce a single person who can demonstrate a single reproducible ESP phenomenon. As yet, no one has exhibited any such power.

The Mystique of ESP In times past, there have been all kinds of crazy ideas—that bumps on the head reveal character traits, that bloodletting is a cure-all, that each sperm cell contains a miniature person inside. When faced with such claims—or with claims of mind reading or out-of-body travel or mind-over-matter—how can we separate crazy ideas from those that sound crazy but are true? At the heart of science we find a simple answer: Test them to see if they work. If they do, so much the worse for our skepticism. If they don't, so much the worse for the ideas.

This scientific attitude appears in the agreement of believers and skeptics that what parapsychology needs to give it credibility is a reproducible phenomenon and a theory to explain it. Could the Layton and Turnbull clairvoyance experiment (in which students beat chance in guessing numbers in sealed envelopes) provide such a reproducible phenomenon? The skeptical editor of the *Journal of Experimental Social Psychology*, to which Layton and Turnbull submitted their results for publication, wondered. So he and the authors reached an unusual agreement: The researchers would repeat their experiment, and the journal would then publish the results of both, regardless of the new outcome. (As this illustrates, both ESP researchers and skeptics genuinely seek truth.) The result of the second experiment? Layton and Turnbull summarized honestly and succinctly: "No [statistically] significant effects were present."

Knowing how easily people are deceived, and lacking reproducible results, most research psychologists remain skeptical. Indeed, they are dismayed by all the shows, books, and magazines on paranormal topics. Should we share their skepticism and dismay?

A personal answer: We, too, can be skeptical, but without closing ourselves to all unprovable claims. We can be open to new ideas without being gullible, discerning without being cynical. We can be critical thinkers; yet, knowing that our understanding of nature is incomplete, we can agree with Shakespeare's Hamlet that "there are more things in heaven and earth, Horatio, than are dreamt of in your philosophy."

Some things that we assume to be true—the reality of another's love, the existence or nonexistence of God, the finality of death

"There comes a point where one has to accept the message of the data, that absence of evidence is evidence of absence."
    Frank Close
    Too Hot to Handle: The Race for Cold Fusion, 1991

"At the heart of science is an essential tension between two seemingly contradictory attitudes—an openness to new ideas, no matter how bizarre or counter intuitive they may be, and the most ruthless skeptical scrutiny of all ideas, old and new."
    Carl Sagan (1987)

Even parapsychology advocate Charles Tart (1983) acknowledges that "ESP in the laboratory generally shows up weakly or inconsistently, so it has been hard to study its nature."

or the reality of life after death—are beyond science. That is one reason why, after clearing the decks of tested and rejected pseudo-mysteries, we can retain a humble sense of wonder regarding life's untestable mysteries.

Why are so many people predisposed to believe that ESP exists? In part, such beliefs may stem from understandable misperceptions, misinterpretations, and selective recall. But for some people there also exists an unsatisfied hunger for wonderment, an itch to experience the magical. In Britain and the United States, the founders of parapsychology were mostly people who, having lost their religious faith, were searching for a scientific basis for believing in the meaningfulness of life and the possibility of life after death (Alcock, 1985; Beloff, 1985).

To be awestruck and to gain a deep reverence for life, we need look no further than our own perceptual system and its capacity for organizing formless nerve impulses into colorful sights, vivid sounds, and evocative smells. Within our ordinary perceptual experiences lies much that is truly extraordinary—surely much more than has so far been dreamt of in our psychology. A century of research has revealed many of the secrets of sensation and perception, but for future generations of researchers there remain profound and genuine mysteries.

"I have uttered what I did not understand, things too wonderful for me. . . ."
Job 42:3

We have now examined the first steps in our processing of information, from receiving sensory input to constructing meaningful perceptions. But our skull's information processor does much more: Under the influence of sleep, hypnosis, or drugs, it will construct unreal images (Chapter 7, States of Consciousness). It learns from our experiences, recalling them long afterward (Chapters 8, Learning, and 9, Memory). It uses perceptions when thinking and planning (Chapters 10, Thinking and Language, and 11, Intelligence). Between our receiving sensory information and acting intelligently on it lies an unimaginably complex information system that, more than ever, beckons explorers of our mind's inner space.

Summing Up

From a top-down perspective, we see how, aided by knowledge and expectations, we transform sensory information into meaningful perceptions.

Perceptual Illusions

Visual and auditory illusions were fascinating scientists even as psychology emerged. Explaining illusions required an understanding of how we transform sensations into meaningful perceptions, so the study of perception became one of psychology's first concerns. Conflict between visual and other sensory information is usually resolved with the mind accepting the visual data, a tendency known as visual capture.

Perceptual Organization

The early Gestalt psychologists were impressed with the seemingly innate way in which we organize fragmentary sensory data into whole perceptions. Our minds structure the information that comes to us in several demonstrable ways:

Form Perception To recognize an object, we must first perceive it (see it as a figure) as distinct from surrounding stimuli (the ground). We must also organize the figure into a meaningful form. Several Gestalt principles—proximity, similarity, continuity, closure, and connectedness—describe this process.

Depth Perception Research on the visual cliff reveals that many species perceive the world in three dimensions at, or very soon after, birth. We transform two-dimensional retinal images into three-dimensional perceptions by using binocular cues, such as retinal disparity, and monocular cues, such as the relative sizes of objects.

Perceptual Constancy Having perceived an object as a coherent figure and located it in space, how do we recognize it—despite the varying images that it may cast on our retinas? Size, shape, and brightness constancies describe how objects appear to have unchanging characteristics regardless of their distance, shape, or motion. These constancies explain several of the well-known visual illusions. For example, familiarity with the size-distance relationships in a carpentered world of rectangular shapes makes people more susceptible to the Müller-Lyer illusion.

Interpretation

The most direct tests of the nature-nurture issue come from experiments that modify human perceptions.

Sensory Restriction and Restored Vision For many species, infancy is a critical period during which experience must activate the brain's innate visual mechanisms. If cataract removal restores eyesight to adults who were blind from birth, they remain unable to perceive the world normally. Gener-

ally, they can distinguish figure from ground and perceive colors, but they are unable to distinguish shapes and forms. In controlled experiments, infant kittens and monkeys have been reared with severely restricted visual input. When their visual exposure is returned to normal, they, too, suffer enduring visual handicaps.

Perceptual Adaptation Human vision is remarkably adaptable. Given glasses that shift the world slightly to the left or right, or even turn it upside down, people manage to adapt their movements and, with practice, to move about with ease.

Perceptual Set Clear evidence that perception is influenced by our experience—our learned assumptions and beliefs—as well as by sensory input comes from the many demonstrations of perceptual set and context effects. The schemas we have learned help us to interpret otherwise ambiguous stimuli, a fact that helps explain why some of us "see" monsters, faces, and UFOs that others do not.

Is There Perception Without Sensation?

Many people believe in or claim to experience extrasensory perception. Parapsychologists have tried to document several forms of ESP—telepathy, clairvoyance, and precognition. But for several reasons, especially the lack of a reproducible ESP effect, most research psychologists remain skeptical.

Terms and Concepts to Remember

visual capture The tendency for vision to dominate the other senses; we perceive filmed voices as coming from the screen we see rather than from the projector behind us.

gestalt An organized whole. Gestalt psychologists emphasize our tendency to integrate pieces of information into meaningful wholes.

figure-ground The organization of the visual field into objects (the figures) that stand out from their surroundings (the ground).

grouping The tendency to organize stimuli into coherent groups.

proximity A perceptual tendency to group together visual and auditory events that are near each other.

similarity A perceptual tendency to group together similar elements.

continuity A perceptual tendency to group stimuli into smooth, continuous patterns.

closure The perceptual tendency to fill in gaps, thus enabling one to perceive disconnected parts as a whole object.

connectedness The perceptual tendency to perceive features, such as dots, as a single unit when uniform and linked.

depth perception The ability to see objects in three dimensions although the images that strike the retina are two-dimensional; allows us to judge distance.

visual cliff A laboratory device for testing depth perception in infants and young animals.

binocular cues Depth cues, such as retinal disparity and convergence, that depend on the use of two eyes.

monocular cues Distance cues, such as aerial and linear perspective and overlap, available to either eye alone.

retinal disparity A binocular cue for perceiving depth; the greater the disparity (difference) between the two images the retina receives of an object, the closer the object is to us.

convergence A binocular cue for perceiving depth; the extent to which the eyes converge inward when looking at an object.

relative size A monocular cue for perceiving distance; when we assume two objects are the same size, the one that produces the smaller image appears more distant.

overlap A monocular cue for perceiving distance; nearby objects partially block our view of more distant objects.

aerial perspective A monocular cue for perceiving distance; hazier objects appear more distant than nearby objects.

texture gradient A monocular cue for perceiving distance; a gradual change to a less distinct texture suggests increasing distance.

relative height A monocular cue for perceiving distance; we perceive higher objects as farther away.

relative motion A monocular cue for perceiving distance; when we move, objects at different distances change their relative positions in our visual image, with those closest moving most.

linear perspective A monocular cue for perceiving distance; we perceive the converging of what we know to be parallel lines as indicating increasing distance.

relative brightness A monocular cue for perceiving distance; dimmer objects seem more distant.

perceptual constancy Perceiving objects as unchanging (having consistent brightness, color, shape, and size) even as illumination and retinal images change.

perceptual adaptation In vision, the ability to adjust to an artificially displaced or even inverted visual field.

perceptual set A mental predisposition to perceive one thing and not another.

extrasensory perception (ESP) The controversial claim that perception can occur apart from sensory input. Said to include telepathy, clairvoyance, and precognition.

parapsychology The study of paranormal phenomena including ESP and psychokinesis.

For Further Reading

Perception

Fineman, M. (1981). *The inquisitive eye.* New York: Oxford University Press.

Written for students in psychology, art, design, and photography, this entertaining book discusses and demonstrates many perceptual phenomena.

Rock, I. (1984). *Perception.* New York: Scientific American Books.

A beautifully illustrated treatment of many of the classic concerns of perception.

Shepard, R. N. (1990). *Mind sights.* New York: Freeman.

A delightful collection of original visual illusions and ambiguities, with commentary on how the mind perceives.

ESP

Alcock, J. E. (1990). *Science and supernature: A critical appraisal of parapsychology.* Buffalo, NY: Prometheus Books.

A research psychologist's critique of parapsychology.

The Skeptical Inquirer

An entertaining quarterly periodical that analyzes ongoing paranormal claims, from astrology and ESP to UFOs and psychic healers.

Wolman, B. B., Dale, L. A., Schmeidler, G. R., & Ullman, M. (Eds.). (1985). *Handbook of parapsychology.* New York: Van Nostrand Reinhold.

Parapsychologists summarize their field's research.

States of Consciousness

Chapter 7

In every science there are concepts so fundamental that they are nearly impossible to define. Biologists agree on what is alive, but not on precisely what life is. In physics, matter and energy elude simple definition. To psychologists, consciousness is similarly a fundamental yet slippery concept. Louis Armstrong's remark about jazz could also be said of consciousness: "Unless you know what it is, I ain't never going to be able to explain it to you."

Studying Consciousness

At its beginning, psychology was sometimes defined as "the description and explanation of states of consciousness" (Ladd, 1887). But the difficulty of scientifically studying consciousness led many psychologists during the first half of this century to turn to direct observations of behavior—an approach favored by an emerging school of psychology called *behaviorism* (page 228). By midcentury, psychology was no longer defined as the study of consciousness or "mental life," but rather as the science of behavior. Psychology had nearly lost consciousness.

By 1960, mental concepts began to reenter psychology. Advances in neuroscience made it possible to relate brain activity to various mental states—waking, sleeping, dreaming. Researchers were beginning to study altered states of consciousness induced by hypnosis and drugs. Psychologists of all persuasions were affirming the importance of mental processes (cognition). Psychology was regaining consciousness.

For most psychologists today, **consciousness** involves awareness and intention. We can define it as *selective attention to ongoing perceptions, thoughts, and feelings*. When learning a complex concept or behavior—say, learning to drive—consciousness focuses our attention on the car and the traffic. With practice, driving becomes automatic and largely unconscious, freeing our consciousness to focus on other tasks.

Selective Attention

Perceptions come to us moment by moment, one perception vanishing as the next appears. When you were looking at the Necker cube and figure-ground demonstrations in Chapter 6, you could

"Psychology must discard all reference to consciousness."
Behaviorist John B. Watson (1913)

With experience, many tasks, such as driving, become mostly automatic, freeing our conscious attention for other matters.

know that two interpretations were possible, yet at any moment you consciously experienced only one of them. This illustrates an important principle: Our conscious attention is *selective*. **Selective attention** means that at any moment awareness focuses on only a limited aspect of all that we are capable of experiencing. Until reading this sentence, you have been unaware that your shoes are pressing against your feet or that your nose is in your line of vision. Now, suddenly, your feet feel encased, your nose stubbornly intrudes on the page before you. While attending to these words, you've also been blocking from awareness information coming from your peripheral vision. But you can change that. While staring at the X below, notice what surrounds the book (the edges of the page, your desk top, and so forth).

X

Another example of selective attention is the *cocktail party effect*—the ability to attend selectively to only one voice among many. Imagine hearing two conversations over a headset, one in each ear. When you pay attention to what's being said in your left ear, you don't perceive what is said in your right ear. At the level of conscious awareness, whatever has your attention has your undivided attention.

It's true of other senses, too. Among the immense array of visual stimuli that are constantly before us, we select only a few for consciousness. Ulric Neisser (1979) and Robert Becklen and Daniel Cervone (1983) demonstrated this dramatically. They showed people a 1-minute videotape in which the images of three men in black shirts passing a basketball were superimposed over the images of three men in white shirts doing the same thing. They asked the viewers to press a key every time the black-shirted players passed the ball. Midway through the tape, a young woman carrying an umbrella sauntered across the screen (Figure 7–1). Most of the viewers focused their attention so completely on the black-shirted players that they failed to notice the woman. When the researcher replayed the tape for them, they were astonished to see her.

Our ability to attend to only one conversation at a time enables us to converse coherently in the midst of auditory chaos.

Figure 7–1 In this experiment on selective attention, viewers who were attending to basketball tosses among the black-shirted players usually failed to notice the woman with an umbrella sauntering through. (From Neisser, 1979.)

Can unnoticed stimuli affect us? Indeed yes. In one experiment, women students listened through headphones as a prose passage played in one ear. Their task was to repeat its words out loud and to check them against a written transcript (Wilson, 1979). Meanwhile, some simple, novel tunes played in the other ear. The tunes were not subliminal—the women could hear them easily. But with their attention selectively focused on the passage, the women were no more aware of the tunes than you normally are of your shoes. Thus, when they later heard these tunes interspersed among new ones, they could not recognize them (just as people cannot recall a conversation to which they paid no attention). Nevertheless, when asked to rate their fondness for each tune, they *preferred* the ones previously played. Their preferences revealed what their conscious memories could not. So, perception requires attention, but even unattended stimuli sometimes have subtle effects.

States of Consciousness

Many past and future chapters (Perception, Learning, Memory, Thinking and Language, Emotion) involve the study of normal waking consciousness. Research in each of these areas reveals that we process much information outside of awareness. We register and react to stimuli we do not consciously perceive. We type without paying attention to where the letters are on the keyboard. We change our attitudes and reconstruct our memories with no awareness of doing so.

So far as our information processing is concerned, consciousness is but the tip of the iceberg. It is the part we are aware of, the part that enables us to exert voluntary control and to communicate our mental states to others (Kihlstrom, 1987). Unlike *unconscious* information processing (which occurs simultaneously on several parallel tracks, without our awareness), *conscious* processing takes place in sequence (serially), is relatively slow, and has limited capacity. Unconscious processing, like a good team of assistants, takes care of routine business so that consciousness, like a chief executive, can focus on decision making and public relations.

For a recap of serial and parallel processing, see pages 142–143.

Psychologists may be unsure exactly what consciousness is, but they recognize that it occurs in varied states. Thus, we have not only normal seeing and hearing, reasoning and remembering, but also the altered (distorted or out-of-the-ordinary) consciousness of sleep dreams and daydreams, meditative and hypnotic states, chemically induced hallucinations and near-death visions.

Sleep and Dreams

Sleep—sweet, renewing, mysterious sleep. Sleep—the irresistible tempter to whom we must all succumb. What is it? Why must we have it? Why do we spend a third of our lives—some 25 years, on average—sleeping?

Such questions have intrigued humans for centuries. Now, some of sleep's age-old mysteries are being solved. In laboratories throughout the world, thousands have slept attached to modern gadgetry while others observed. By recording sleepers' brain waves and muscle movements, by observing and awakening them from time to time, the sleep-watchers glimpse things that a thousand years of common sense never told us. Perhaps you can anticipate some of their discoveries. Are the following statements true or false?

1. When people dream of performing some activity, their limbs often move in concert with the dream (pages 193–194).

2. Older adults sleep more than young adults (pages 195–196 and Figure 7–6).

In this sleep laboratory at Technicon Medical School in Israel, a researcher electronically monitors the sleeping subject's physiological state. This information, together with observations made of the sleeper's behavior, provides clues to the mysteries of sleep.

3. After 2 or 3 sleepless days, a person's performance on a brief but demanding intellectual task suffers (page 195).

4. Sleepwalkers are acting out their dreams (pages 193–194).

5. Sleep experts recommend an occasional sleeping pill to break a pattern of insomnia (page 196).

6. The dreams we have before awakening in the morning are similar to those we have soon after falling asleep (page 198).

7. Some people dream every night; others seldom dream at all (page 194).

All these statements (adapted from Palladino & Carducci, 1983) are false. Let's see why.

The Rhythm of Sleep

The rhythm of the day parallels the rhythm of life—from our waking to a new day's birth to our nightly return to what Shakespeare called "death's counterfeit." Our bodies synchronize with the 24-hour cycle of day and night through a biological clock called the **circadian rhythm** (from the Latin *circa*, "about," and *dies*, "day"). Our body temperature, for example, rises as morning approaches, peaks during the day, and then begins to drop before we go to sleep. A transcontinental flight disrupts our circadian rhythm and we experience jet lag, mainly because we are awake when our biological clock cries, "Sleep!"

Researchers are experimenting with drugs and with bright lights during evening hours, hoping to develop methods for reducing jet lag by allowing us to reset our biological clocks (Czeisler & others, 1986, 1989; Turek & Losee-Olson, 1986). Their advice: Speed the resetting of your biological clock after a long flight by spending a day outdoors.

Radically altering your sleeping schedule from weekdays to weekends, as shift workers or college students often do, can also throw off your biological clock. As it begins to reset itself to the weekend sleep schedule, a new work (or school) week begins. The result may be "Sunday night insomnia" and "Monday morning blues."

Mysteriously, people isolated without clocks or daylight typically adopt a 25-hour day. This helps explain why most people find it easier to jet west, with an extended day, than east; why rotating shift workers adapt better to progressively later shifts than to earlier shifts; why we often must discipline ourselves to get to bed on time and force ourselves to get up. When placed in a time-free environment under constant illumination, most animals, too, exceed a 24-hour day.

There is also a biological rhythm during our sleep—we pass through a cycle of five distinct sleep stages several times during the night. This fact was unknown until 8-year-old Armond Aserinsky went to bed one night in 1952. His father, Eugene, a University of Chicago graduate student, needed to test an electroencephalograph he had been repairing during the day (Aserinsky, 1988; Seligman & Yellen, 1987). He placed electrodes near Armond's eyes to record the electric current produced by the rolling eye movements believed to occur during sleep. Before long, the machine went wild, tracing deep zigzags on the graph paper. Aserinsky thought the machine

If our natural circadian rhythm was attuned to a 23-hour cycle, would we instead need to discipline ourselves to stay up later at night and sleep in longer in the morning?

was still broken. But as the night proceeded, the activity periodically recurred, indicating, Aserinsky finally realized, fast, jerky eye movements accompanied by energetic brain activity. When he awakened Armond during one such episode of *rapid eye movement* sleep (**REM sleep**), the boy reported he was having a dream.

To find out if similar cycles occur during adult sleep, Nathaniel Kleitman (1960) and Aserinsky pioneered procedures that have now been used with thousands of volunteers. To appreciate both their methods and findings, imagine yourself as a subject. When you are ready for bed, the researcher tapes electrodes to your scalp (to measure your brain waves) and to the corners of your eyes (to detect eye movements) (Figure 7–2). Other devices allow the researcher to record your heart rate, your respiration rate, your muscle tension, and even the degree of your genital arousal.

Figure 7–2 Sleep researchers measure brain-wave activity, eye movements, and muscle tension by taping electrodes to various parts of the head. (From Dement, 1978.)

When you are in bed with your eyes closed, the researcher in the next room sees on the EEG the relatively slow **alpha waves** of your awake but relaxed state (Figure 7–3). As you adapt to all this gadgetry and grow tired, your breathing rate slows and your brain waves slow further and show the irregular waves of Stage 1 sleep. During this light sleep, which lasts about 2 minutes, you may experience fantastic images, which are like **hallucinations**— sensory experiences that occur without a sensory stimulus. You may have a sensation of falling (at which moment your body may suddenly jerk) or of floating weightlessly.

Soon, you relax more deeply and begin about 20 minutes of Stage 2 sleep, characterized by the periodic appearance of *sleep spindles*—bursts of brain-wave activity. Although you can still be awakened without too much difficulty during this phase, you are now clearly asleep.

Then for the next few minutes you go through the transitional Stage 3 to the deep sleep of Stage 4. Starting in Stage 3 and increasingly in Stage 4, your brain emits large, slow **delta waves**. These stages together are therefore called *delta sleep*. They last for about 30 minutes, during which you are hard to awaken. Curiously, it is during the deep sleep of Stage 4 that we may talk or walk in our sleep, or (as young children) wet the bed. Moreover, even when

Figure 7–3 Brain waves and sleep stages. The regular alpha waves of an awake, relaxed state are quite different from the slower, larger delta waves of deep Stage 4 sleep. The more rapid REM sleep waves resemble the near-waking Stage 1 sleep. (From Dement, 1978.)

we are deeply asleep, our brains somehow process the meaning of certain stimuli. We move around on our beds, but we manage not to fall out of them. The occasional roar of passing vehicles may leave deep sleep undisturbed, but the cry from a baby's nursery quickly interrupts it.

About an hour after you first fall asleep, a strange thing happens. Rather than continuing in deep slumber, you go back up the sleep ladder. Returning through Stages 3 and 2, you enter the most intriguing sleep phase of all—REM sleep (Figure 7–4). For about 10 minutes, your brain waves become more rapid, like those of the nearly awake Stage 1 sleep. But unlike Stage 1 sleep, your heart rate rises, your breathing becomes more rapid and irregular, and every half minute or so your eyes dart around in a momentary burst of activity behind closed lids. Because anyone watching a sleeper's eyes can notice these REM bursts, it is amazing that science was ignorant of REM sleep until 1952.

During REM sleep, your genitals usually show signs of arousal (either an erection or increased vaginal lubrication). The common "morning erection" stems from the night's last REM period, often just before waking. Except during very scary dreams, genital arousal always occurs, regardless of whether the dream's content is sexual (Karacan & others, 1966). In young men, sleep-related erections outlast REM periods, lasting 30 to 45 minutes on average (Karacan & others, 1983; Schiavi & Schreiner-Engel, 1988). A typical 25-year-old man therefore has an erection during nearly half his night's sleep, a 65-year-old man for one-quarter. Many men troubled by "erectile disorder" (impotence) have morning erections, which suggests that their disorder is not physically based.

Although your brain's motor cortex is active during REM sleep, few of its neural messages reach your muscles, which are therefore very relaxed—so relaxed, in fact, that except for an occasional finger or facial twitch, you are essentially paralyzed. Moreover, you cannot easily be awakened. Thus, REM sleep is sometimes called *paradoxical sleep* because internally the body is aroused but externally it appears calm.

Even more intriguing than the paradoxical nature of REM sleep is what the rapid eye movements announce: the beginning of a dream. Even those who claim they never dream will, more than 80 percent of the time, recall a dream after being awakened during REM sleep. Unlike the fleeting images of Stage 1 sleep, REM sleep dreams are often emotional and usually storylike. (People occasionally recall dreams when awakened from stages other than REM sleep, but these dreams usually involve a single incident, such as, "I was asking George if I could borrow his hammer.")

Are the eye movements linked to a dream's visual aspects? Is the dreamer "watching" the dream as if it were a private movie? Most researchers believe not: The darting eyes, like the occasional twitching of muscles, may merely reflect the overflow of the dreamer's active nervous system (Chase & Morales, 1983).

As the night wears on, this sleep cycle repeats itself about every 90 minutes, with the deep Stage 4 sleep getting briefer and then disappearing and the REM sleep period getting progressively longer. By morning, 20 to 25 percent of our average night's sleep— some 100 minutes—has been REM sleep. This means that those who say, "I never dream" actually spend about 600 hours a year experiencing some 1500 dreams.

Figure 7–4 The stages in a typical night's sleep. Most people pass through a cycle of the five sleep stages several times, with the periods of Stage 4 sleep and then Stage 3 sleep diminishing and REM sleep periods increasing in duration. (From Cartwright, 1978.)

This piglet, like her companion, needs REM sleep. Deprived of it, she will replenish this deficiency if allowed to sleep undisturbed.

People rarely snore during dreams. When REM starts, snoring stops.

Why Do We Sleep?

Sleep commands roughly one-third of our lives. Deprived of it, we begin to feel terrible; our bodies yearn for it. You can know you are sleep-deprived—as many college students are (Levine & others, 1988)—if most of the following are true: You need an alarm clock to shorten your natural sleep pattern; you feel sleepy while sitting in class or you lack vigor needed for peak performance; you collapse into sleep almost immediately after your head hits the pillow.

Obviously, we need sleep. But why? It seems an easy question to answer: Just keep people awake for several days and note how they deteriorate. If you were a subject in such an experiment, how do you think it would affect your body and mind?

Of course, you would become terribly drowsy at times—especially during the hours when your biological clock programs you to sleep. But could lack of sleep physically damage you? Would it noticeably alter your biochemistry or body organs? Would you become emotionally disturbed? intellectually disoriented?

The major effect, as some fatigued college students know, is sleepiness. Given the fatigue and general malaise that accompany sleepiness (Mikulincer & others, 1989), that's no small consequence. And, owing to modern light bulbs, TV sets, shift work, and social diversions, people today more than ever suffer from sleep patterns that thwart their having an energized feeling of well-being. As sleep researcher William Dement (1990) laments, "The national sleep debt is larger and more important than the national debt."

Other effects are more subtle: impaired creativity and concentration, diminished immunity to disease, slight hand tremors, irritability, occasional misperceptions on monotonous tasks (Horne, 1989; Webb, 1982a). With some tasks, such as truck driving and controlling air traffic, these effects can be devastating. The *Exxon Valdez* oil spill, the Three Mile Island nuclear accident, and Union Carbide's Bhopal, India, disaster all occurred after midnight when operators were likely to be drowsiest.

On short, highly motivating tasks, however, sleep deprivation has little effect. When 17-year-old Randy Gardner made his way into the *Guinness Book of World Records* by staying awake for 11 days, he at times had to keep moving to stay awake. Nevertheless, during his final night of sleeplessness, Gardner managed to beat researcher Dement 100 straight times in a pinball game. He then slept 15 hours and awoke feeling fine (Gulevich & others, 1966).

In rare cases, brain-diseased people have lost their ability to sleep, with disastrous results. One 52-year-old man gradually lost his ability to sleep and became severely fatigued, shaky, disoriented, and incontinent (Lugaresi & others, 1986). He would lapse into a dreamlike stupor from time to time, but without exhibiting the brain waves of sleep. Nine months after the sleep difficulty began, he died.

Why, then, must we sleep? We have few answers, but sleep probably helps restore body tissues, especially those of the brain. In one study of runners in a 92-kilometer (57-mile) ultramarathon, the competitors averaged 7 hours of sleep during nights before the race and 8½ hours during the two nights after the race. The night after the run, deep Stage 4 sleep doubled (Shapiro & others, 1981).

Sleep may also play a role in the growth process. During deep sleep, the pituitary gland releases a growth hormone. As adults

A few of the unanswered questions about sleep: Why do we sleep more when we are young? Why do some animals sleep most of the day, others not at all? Why, when REM sleep paralyzes our muscles, do we twitch and jerk? Most important, what is sleep's function?
  Adapted from UCLA Brain
  Research Institute, 1989

The current record holder, Robert ("Ramblin Rob") McDonald, reportedly stayed awake for 18 days, 22 hours in a 1986 rocking chair marathon.

"Sleep faster, we need the pillows."
  Yiddish proverb

grow older, they release less of this hormone, and they spend less time in deep sleep (Pekkanen, 1982). In addition, the sleeper's lower body temperature conserves energy for the daytime hours. These physiological discoveries are only beginning to solve the ongoing riddle of sleep. As Dement (1978, p. 83) deadpanned, "we have miles to go before we sleep."

Sleep Disorders

The idea that "everyone needs 8 hours of sleep" is untrue. Newborns spend nearly two-thirds of their day asleep, adults barely more than one-fourth. Age-related differences in average time spent sleeping are rivaled by differences in the normal amount of sleep among individuals at any age. Some people thrive with fewer than 6 hours of sleep per night; others regularly sleep 9 hours or more. (Among various mammals, the need for sleep varies more widely: Horses and cows sleep only 3 to 4 hours per day; rats and cats, 14 to 15 hours [Webb, 1982b].) Human sleep differences are not accompanied by striking personality differences (Webb, 1979). But sleep patterns may be genetically influenced. When Wilse Webb and Scott Campbell (1983) checked the pattern and duration of sleep among fraternal and identical twins, only the identical twins were strikingly similar.

Whatever their normal need for sleep, some 10 to 15 percent of adults complain of **insomnia**—*recurring* problems in falling or staying asleep. True insomnia is not the occasional inability to sleep that we experience when anxious or excited. When stressed, alertness is a natural and adaptive response. We commonly underestimate the amount of sleep we get on restless nights. Even if we've been awake only an hour, we may *think* we've had insomnia much of the night, because that's the part we remember.

The most common quick fixes for true insomnia, sleeping pills and alcohol, can aggravate the problem. Both reduce REM sleep. When the drugs are discontinued, the insomnia may worsen. Sleep experts offer other alternatives:

1. Relax before bedtime.

2. Avoid caffeine (this means chocolate, too) after late afternoon and avoid rich foods before bedtime. A glass of milk may help. (Milk provides raw materials for the manufacture of serotonin, a neurotransmitter that facilitates sleep.)

3. Sleep on a regular schedule (rise at the same time even after a restless night) and avoid naps.

4. Exercise regularly, but not in the late evening.

5. Reassure yourself that the temporary loss of sleep causes no great harm.

6. If nothing else works, aim for less sleep; go to bed later or get up earlier.

Rarer but more severe than insomnia are the sleep disorders narcolepsy and sleep apnea. People with **narcolepsy** suffer periodic, overwhelming sleepiness, sometimes at the most inopportune times—perhaps just after taking a terrific swing at a softball or when laughing loudly or shouting angrily (Dement, 1978). The person collapses directly into a brief period of REM sleep, with its ac-

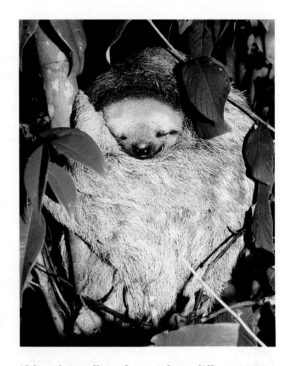

Although we all need some sleep, different animals have different sleep needs. The slothful sloth, for example, spends 18 hours a day soundly asleep.

"The lion and the lamb shall lie down together, but the lamb will not be very sleepy."
  Woody Allen in the movie
  Love and Death, 1975

"Only about one-third of lost sleep is made up. This recovery sleep contains much of the missing Stage 4 sleep and about half of the missing REM sleep."
  James Horne
  Why We Sleep, 1988

companying loss of muscular tension. The estimated 100,000 or more Americans who suffer from narcolepsy must live with extra caution. As a traffic menace, "snoozing is second only to boozing," says the American Sleep Disorders Association, and those with narcolepsy are especially at risk (Aldrich, 1989).

Those who suffer from **sleep apnea** (mostly overweight men) intermittently stop breathing during sleep (*apnea* means "stopping respiration"). After an airless minute or so, decreased blood oxygen arouses the sleeper to snort in air for a few seconds. The process repeats hundreds of times during a night's sleep. Apart from sleepiness during the day—and their mates' complaints about their loud "snoring"—apnea sufferers are often unaware of their disorder.

A monitor connected to this sleep apnea sufferer sounds an alarm each time he stops breathing. By better understanding this disorder, researchers hope to help those afflicted.

Still other sleepers, mostly children, experience **night terrors**. The person might sit up or walk around, talk incoherently, experience a doubling of heart and breathing rates, and appear terrified (Hartmann, 1981). The night-terror sufferer very seldom awakens fully and recalls little or nothing the next morning—at most a fleeting, frightening image. Night terrors are not nightmares, which typically occur during early morning REM sleep. Like sleepwalking, night terrors usually occur during the first few hours of sleep and during Stage 4 sleep (Figure 7–5).

Dreams

Discovering the link between REM sleep and dreaming opened a new era in dream research. Instead of relying on someone's hazy recall of a dream hours afterward, it became possible to catch dreams as they happen. Researchers could awaken their subjects during a REM sleep period, or within 5 minutes afterward, and get a vivid account of the dream.

What Do We Dream? Compared to daydreams, REM dreams are more vivid, more emotional, more bizarre. Several times a night, you are the creator and producer of a surrealistic mental movie, in which events frequently occur in a jumbled sequence, scenes change suddenly, people appear and disappear, and physical laws, such as gravity, may be violated. Yet dreams are so vivid that we may con-

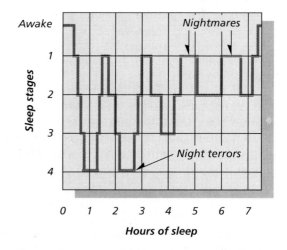

Figure 7–5 Night terrors and nightmares in the sleep laboratory. Night terrors occur within 2 or 3 hours of falling asleep, during Stage 4 sleep. Nightmares occur toward morning, during REM sleep. (From Hartmann, 1984.)

fuse them with reality. Occasionally, we may be sufficiently aware during a dream to wonder whether we are, in fact, dreaming. When experiencing such "lucid dreams," some people are able to test their state of consciousness. If they can perform some absurd act, such as floating in the air, then they know they are dreaming.

Although we are more likely to be awakened by and to remember our most emotional dreams, many dreams are rather ordinary. When awakened during REM sleep, people report dreams with sexual imagery less often than you might think. In one study, only 1 in 10 dreams among young men and 1 in 30 among young women had sexual overtones (Hall & Van de Castle, 1966). (Recall that genital arousal typically accompanies REM sleep, so it is usually *not* caused by sexual dreams.) More commonly, we dream of daily life events, such as a meeting at work or taking an exam. Six years of our life we spend dreaming, most of which is anything but sweet: People commonly dream of repeatedly failing in an attempt to do something; of being attacked, pursued, or rejected; or of experiencing misfortune (Hall & others, 1982).

Across the world, people of all ages show a curious sex difference in dream content. Women dream of males and females equally often, whereas 65 percent of the characters in men's dreams are males. No one is sure why. (Is a tendency to dream of one's sex compromised by our greater consciousness, even during sleep, of those with social power?) Whatever its significance, dream researcher Calvin Hall (1984) believed we could add this fact to the short list of universal sex differences (page 598).

The story line of our dreams — what Sigmund Freud called their **manifest content**— often incorporates experiences and preoccupations from the day's events, especially in our first dreams of the night. The sensory stimuli of our sleeping environment may also intrude. A particular odor or the telephone's ringing may be instantly and ingeniously woven into the dream story. In one experiment, William Dement and Edward Wolpert (1958) lightly sprayed cold water on dreamers' faces. Compared to sleepers who did not get the cold water treatment, these subjects were more likely to dream about water — about waterfalls, leaky roofs, or even about being sprayed by someone.

We do not, however, remember taped information played while we are soundly asleep (Eich, 1990). In fact, experiences that occur during the 5 minutes just before falling asleep are typically lost from memory (Roth & others, 1988). This helps explain why dreams that momentarily awaken us are mostly forgotten by morning. To remember a dream, get up and stay awake for a while.

Why Do We Dream? In his landmark book *The Interpretation of Dreams*, published in 1900, Freud argued that a dream is a psychic safety valve that harmlessly discharges otherwise unacceptable feelings. According to Freud, a dream's manifest content is but a censored, symbolic version of its **latent content**, which consists of drives and wishes that would be threatening if expressed directly. Although most dreams do not have overt sexual imagery, Freud nevertheless believed that most adult dreams can be "traced back by analysis to *erotic wishes.*" In Freud's view, a gun, for example, might be a disguised representation of a penis.

Although Freud considered dreams the key to understanding our inner conflicts, his critics say that dream interpretation leads down a blind alley. Some contend that even if dreams are symbol-

Nocturnal mysteries: Francisco de Goya's "The Sleep Reason Produces Monsters."

"For what one has dwelt on by day, these things are seen in visions of the night."
  Menander of Athens, 342–292 B.C.
  Fragments

"Puuuuut the caaaaat ouuuuuuuut ...
Puuuuut the caaaaat ouuuuuuut ..."

ic, they can be interpreted almost any way one wishes. Others maintain there is nothing hidden in dreams. A dream about a gun, they say, is a dream about a gun. Even Freud, who loved to smoke cigars, acknowledged that "sometimes, a cigar is just a cigar."

Freud's theory of dreams is giving way to newer theories. One of these sees dreams as *information processing*: Dreams may help sift, sort, and fix in memory our day's experiences. Following stressful experiences or intense learning periods, REM sleep increases (Palumbo, 1978). What is more, there is "consistent and compelling evidence" that REM sleep facilitates memory for unusual or anxiety-arousing material (McGrath & Cohen, 1978). In one experiment, people heard unusual phrases before bedtime and then were given a memory test the next morning. If awakened every time they began REM sleep, they remembered less than if awakened during other sleep stages (Empson & Clarke, 1970). A night of solid sleep (and dreaming) does, it seems, have a justifiable place in a student's life.

Another explanation of dreams proposes that they may also serve a physiological function. Perhaps dreams—or the associated brain activity of REM sleep—provide the sleeping brain with periodic stimulation. As you may recall from Chapter 3, stimulating experiences develop and preserve the brain's neural pathways. This theory makes sense from a developmental point of view. Infants, whose neural networks are just developing, spend a great deal of time in REM sleep (Figure 7–6).

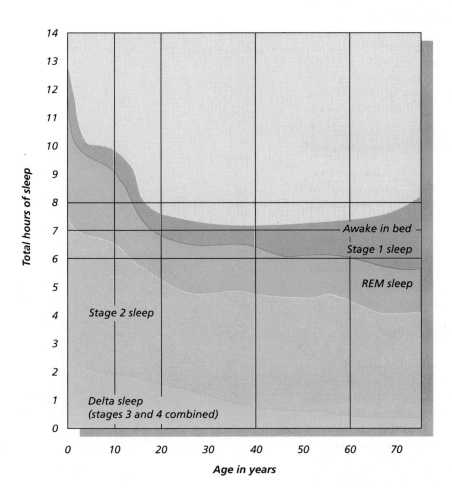

Figure 7–6 As we age, our sleep patterns change. During our first few months, we spend progressively less time in REM sleep. During our first 20 years, we spend progressively less time asleep. From middle age on, sleep is seldom uninterrupted. Occasional awakenings become the norm, not something to fret over or treat with medication. (Adapted from Williams & others, 1974.)

Still other physiological theories propose that dreams erupt from neural activity that spreads upward from the brainstem. According to one version, this neural activity is random, and dreams are the brain's attempt to make sense out of it (Hobson, 1988). Psychologists Martin Seligman and Amy Yellen (1987) note that the seconds-long bursts of rapid eye movements during REM sleep coincide with bursts of activity in the visual cortex. If awakened during one of these bursts of brain activity, people report vivid experiences, usually dramatic hallucinations.

Given these visual scenes, how does our cognitive machinery react? It does what it usually does with meaningless stimuli—it imposes meaning. (Recall from Chapter 2 how split-brain patients instantly "explain" puzzling actions commanded by their right hemisphere. And recall from Chapter 6 how readily we can "see" the man in the moon and monsters in tree trunks.) Thus, say Seligman and Yellen, our ever-active brain weaves a story line from whatever is available—residues from the day's experiences, the alarm clock ringing, or the brief visual hallucinations triggered by the brainstem. Mix in the emotional tone provided by the limbic system (which becomes active during REM sleep) and—voila!—we dream.

The theory, then, is that dreams spring from the mind's relentless effort to make sense of unrelated visual bursts, which are given their emotional setting by the limbic system. This helps explain many of our dream experiences, such as the sudden and bizarre changes in scene (triggered by a new visual burst). Dream reports by Seligman's University of Pennsylvania students confirm that the most vivid dream images are the surprising, discontinuous aspects of the dream; other, less vivid images we presumably conjure up to string the visual bursts together.

The function of dreams provokes vigorous debate, but the disputants all agree that we *need* REM sleep. Deprived of it by repeated awakenings, people return more and more quickly to the REM stage after falling back to sleep. When finally allowed to sleep undisturbed, they literally sleep like babies, with increased REM sleep—a phenomenon called **REM rebound**. The withdrawal of REM-suppressing sleeping medications also increases REM sleep, but with accompanying nightmares. Most other mammals also experience REM sleep and REM rebound. Animals' need for REM sleep suggests that its causes and functions are deeply biological. That REM sleep occurs in mammals (and not in animals such as fish, whose behavior is less influenced by learning) also fits the information-processing theory of dreams. All of which serves to remind us once again of a basic lesson: Biological and psychological explanations of behavior are partners, not competitors.

Daydreams, Fantasies, and Meditation

In James Thurber's classic story "The Secret Life of Walter Mitty," the bland existence of mild-mannered Walter Mitty is spiced with gratifying fantasies. As he drives past a hospital, Mitty imagines himself as Dr. Mitty, rushing to an operating room where two renowned specialists plead for his help. Again and again, the bumbling Walter Mitty relieves the tedium of his life by imagining himself as the triumphant Walter Mitty—now the world's greatest target shooter, now a heroic pilot.

Thurber's story became a classic because most of us can identify with Walter Mitty. From interview and questionnaire studies with hundreds of adults, clinical psychologist Jerome L. Singer (1975) reported that nearly everyone has daydreams or waking fantasies every day—on the job, in the classroom, walking down the street—in fact, almost anywhere at any time. Compared to older adults, young adults spend more time daydreaming and admit to more sexual fantasies (Cameron & Biber, 1973; Giambra, 1974).

Not all daydreaming is as overtly escapist or dramatic as Walter Mitty's. Mostly it involves the familiar details of our lives—perhaps imagining an alternative approach to a task we are performing, or picturing ourselves explaining to an instructor why a paper will be late, or replaying in our minds personal encounters that we relish or wish had gone differently.

Some individuals—perhaps 4 percent of the population—fantasize so vividly they are called **fantasy-prone personalities**. One study of 26 such women found that as children they had enjoyed unusually intense make-believe play with their dolls, stuffed animals, or imaginary companions (Wilson & Barber, 1983). As adults, they reported spending more than half their time fantasizing. They would relive experiences or imagine scenes so vividly that occasionally they later had trouble sorting out their remembered fantasies from their memories of actual events. When watching or imagining violent or scary scenes, they sometimes felt ill. Many reported profound mystical or religious experiences. Three-fourths had experienced orgasms solely by sexual fantasy.

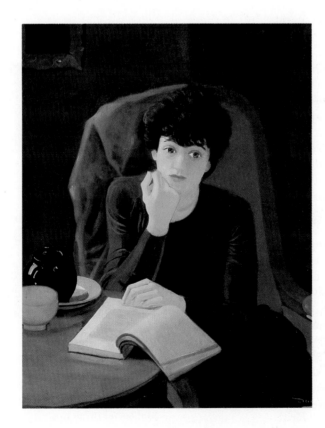

André Derain's (1880–1954) painting *La Tasse de Thé* captures a reflective moment of quiet. The pleasure and relaxation afforded by such moments are part of the adaptive value of daydreams.

Are the hours we spend in fantasy merely a way of escaping rather than facing reality? At times, they are. But daydreaming can also be adaptive. Some daydreams help us prepare for future events by keeping us aware of unfinished business and serving as mental rehearsals. Playful fantasies enhance the creativity of scientists, artists, and writers. For children, daydreaming in the form of imaginative play is important to social and cognitive development—a fact that makes the diversion of television watching a matter of concern to some child psychologists (Singer, 1986).

Daydreams may also substitute for impulsive behavior. People prone to delinquency and violence or who seek the artificial highs of dangerous drugs have fewer vivid fantasies (Singer, 1976). Perhaps Walter Mitty's imaginative reveries not only rescued him from boredom but also allowed him to indulge his impulses within the safety of his inner world.

A more focused, yet fully conscious state of awareness comes through *meditation*. Meditators assume a comfortable position in a quiet environment and adopt a receptive, serene attitude. Then they focus on their breathing, on a word (in Eastern meditation, a mantra such as *Om*), or on a phrase (in Christianity, perhaps a short prayer). Experienced meditators exhibit blood pressure, heart rate, brain wave, and metabolism levels like those of deeply relaxed people (Alexander & others, 1987; Holmes, 1984; Wallace & Benson, 1972). Like relaxation, or even more so, meditation can help relieve pain, anxiety, and stress-related illnesses (Eppley & others, 1989). One astonishing recent study assigned 73 residents of homes for the elderly either to daily meditation or to no treatment. After 3 years, one-fourth of the nonmeditators had died, while all the meditators were still alive (Alexander & others, 1989).

Hypnosis

Imagine you are about to be hypnotized. The hypnotist invites you to sit back, fix your gaze on a spot high on the wall, and relax. In a quiet, low voice the hypnotist suggests, "Your eyes are growing tired. . . . Your eyelids are becoming heavy . . . now heavier and heavier. . . . They are beginning to close. . . . You are becoming more deeply relaxed. . . . Your breathing is now deep and regular. . . . Your muscles are becoming more and more relaxed. Your whole body is beginning to feel like lead."

After a few minutes of this hypnotic induction, your eyes are probably closed and you may undergo **hypnosis**—an apparently heightened suggestibility that enables a hypnotist's coaxings and directions to trigger specific behaviors, perceptions, and perhaps even memories. When the hypnotist suggests, "Your eyelids are shutting so tight that you cannot open them even if you try," your eyelids may seem beyond your control and may remain closed. Told to forget the number 6, you may be puzzled when you count 11 fingers on your hands. Invited to smell a sensuous perfume that is actually ammonia, you may linger delightedly over its pungent odor. Asked to describe a nonexistent picture the hypnotist claims to be holding, you may talk about it in detail. Told that you cannot see a certain object, such as a chair, you may indeed report that it is not there, although, curiously, you may manage to avoid the chair when walking around.

"When I examined myself, and my methods of thought, I came to the conclusion that the gift of fantasy has meant more to me than my talent for absorbing positive knowledge."
  Albert Einstein, 1879–1955

"The art of living requires us to steer a course between the two extremes of external and internal stimulation."
  Psychologist Jerome L. Singer (1976)

"Sit down alone and in silence. Lower your head, shut your eyes, breathe out gently, and imagine yourself looking into your own heart. . . . As you breathe out, say 'Lord Jesus Christ, have mercy on me.'. . . Try to put all other thoughts aside. Be calm, be patient and repeat the process very frequently."
  Gregory of Sinai, died 1346

Despite its exploitation by stage performers, hypnosis has become a topic of serious investigation. Researchers disagree, however, whether hypnosis is a unique psychological state or merely an extension of normal processes of cognition and social influence.

And if instructed to forget all these happenings once you are out of the hypnotic state, you may later report **posthypnotic amnesia**, a temporary memory loss rather like being unable to recall a familiar name. The "forgotten" material is nevertheless "in there," for it can affect later behavior and be recalled at a prearranged signal (Kihlstrom, 1985; Spanos & others, 1985). So, although people *say* they don't remember, subtle tests lead skeptics to doubt their reported amnesia (Coe, 1989a). A critical issue, then, is whether people are genuinely *unable* to recall the "forgotten" material, or whether people distract themselves or withhold information to meet the hypnotist's expectations.

Hypnotic techniques have been used since antiquity, but credit for their modern popularity goes to an Austrian physician, Anton Mesmer (1734–1815), who mistakenly thought he had discovered an "animal magnetism." With great flourish, Mesmer passed magnets over the bodies of ailing people, some of whom would lapse into a trancelike ("mesmerized") state and awaken much improved. A French commission chaired by Benjamin Franklin found no evidence of animal magnetism and attributed Mesmer's "cures" to "mere imagination." Thus, hypnosis—or mesmerism, as it was then called—became linked with quackery.

Also working against the respectability of hypnosis were the grand claims made by its practitioners. Supposedly, mesmerized people could see with the backs of their heads, perceive others' internal organs, and communicate with the dead. Researchers now agree that hypnotized persons can perform no such feats (Figure 7–7). For example, hypnotized subjects can extend their arms for about 6 minutes—but so can unhypnotized subjects.

Before weighing the debate over whether the hypnotic state is actually an altered state of consciousness, let's first consider some areas of general agreement. Then, with the facts of hypnosis in mind, we can ponder two perplexing questions: What is hypnosis? What does hypnosis tell us about human consciousness?

Figure 7–7 The "amazing" hypnotized "human plank." Actually, nonhypnotized people can also perform this feat.

Facts and Falsehoods

Can Hypnosis Work for Anyone? Those who study hypnosis agree that its power resides not in the hypnotist but in the subject's openness to suggestion (Bowers, 1984). To some extent, nearly everyone is suggestible. When people standing upright with their eyes closed are told repeatedly that they are swaying back and forth, most will indeed sway a little. In fact, postural sway is one of the items on the Stanford Hypnotic Susceptibility Scale that assesses a person's hypnotizability. During the assessment, a hypnotist gives a brief hypnotic induction and then presents a series of suggested experiences that range from easy (one's outstretched arms will move together) to difficult (with eyes open one will see a nonexistent person).

Those who are highly hypnotizable—say, the 20 percent who can carry out a suggestion not to smell or react to a bottle of ammonia held under the nose—are still likely to be the most hypnotizable 25 years later (Piccione & others, 1989). These hypnotically susceptible people, like the fantasy-prone people described earlier, frequently become deeply absorbed in imaginative activities (Lynn & Rhue, 1986; Nadon & others, 1991). Typically, they have rich fantasy lives and easily become absorbed in the imaginary events of a novel or movie. Many researchers therefore refer to hypnotic "susceptibility" as hypnotic *ability*, giving it a label with more positive connotations. Few of us would care to be "susceptible" to hypnosis, but most of us would be glad to have the "ability" to focus our attention totally on a task, to become imaginatively absorbed in it, to entertain fanciful possibilities. And that is what fantasy-prone people with hypnotic ability can do.

Actually, anyone can experience hypnotic responsiveness, if led to *expect* it. To convince even skeptical University of Connecticut students that they were hypnotizable, Cynthia Wickless and Irving Kirsch (1989) played a clever stunt on them. After a standard hypnotic induction, they suggested to the students that they would see red, then see green, hear music, and so forth. After each suggestion, the experimenters surreptitiously projected appropriate stimuli—a very faint red or green light, or faint eerie music. Fooled by this weird experience of seeing and hearing what the hypnotist suggested, there were no doubters left. Thus, unlike those in control conditions not similarly persuaded, most scored as *highly* hypnotizable when later given the suggestions of the Stanford Hypnotic Susceptibility Scale; virtually none scored low.

Any real-life hypnotist does much the same in suggesting that "your eyes are growing tired . . . your eyelids are becoming heavy" after having people strain their eyes by staring at a high spot. Anyone's eyes would get tired. But if the hypnotist is successful, the subject will attribute the heavy eyelids to the hypnotist's powers.

Can Hypnosis Enhance Recall of Forgotten Events?

Can hypnotic procedures enable people to relive earlier experiences? To recall kindergarten classmates? To retrieve forgotten or suppressed details of a crime? Should testimony obtained under hypnosis be admissible in court?

Most people believe that our experiences are all "in there," that everything that happens to us gets recorded in our brains and can be recalled if only we can break through our own defenses (Loftus, 1980). Testimonies to this come from **age regression** demonstrations, in which subjects supposedly relive experiences from their childhood. But 60 years of research disputes claims of age regression: Hypnotized people are *not* more genuinely childlike than unhypnotized people who are asked to feign childlike behavior (Nash, 1987). Age-regressed people act as they *believe* children would, but typically miss the mark by outperforming real children of the specified age (Silverman & Retzlaff, 1986). Age-regressed people may, for example, *feel* childlike and may print much as they know a 6-year-old would, but they sometimes do so with perfect spelling and typically without any change in their adult brain waves, reflexes, and perceptions.

On rare occasions, the relaxed, focused state of hypnosis has enabled witnesses to produce leads in criminal investigations. In 1977, 26 children and their bus driver, Ed Ray, were kidnapped and forced into an abandoned trailer truck buried 6 feet underground. After their rescue, Ray, under hypnosis, recalled all but one digit of the kidnapper's license plate. With this crucial information, police tracked down the abductors. This anecdote is atypical and it is not clear whether hypnosis was a critical aspect of the memory retrieval. Nevertheless, many researchers believe that hypnotic pro-

In response to suggestion, this hypnotized subject is outwardly unresponsive to the smell of ammonia.

cedures may have value—or at least do little harm—when used as an investigative tool.

The problem comes in putting on the witness stand someone whose memories are "hypnotically refreshed." Because researchers have found that hypnotically refreshed memories combine fact with fiction, a growing list of state courts ban testimony from witnesses who have been hypnotized. Hypnosis typically either fails to boost recall or, worse, contaminates memory (Dywan & Bowers, 1983; Orne & others, 1984; Smith, 1983). When pressed, following hypnotic procedures, to recall details, perhaps to "zoom in on your visual memory screen," people use their imaginations to construct their memories. Without either person being aware of what is going on, the hypnotist's hints—"Did you hear loud noises?"—can become the subject's memory. Thus, previously hypnotized witnesses may end up testifying confidently to events they never experienced (Laurence & Perry, 1988). "Hypnosis is not a psychological truth serum," reports researcher Kenneth Bowers (1987), "and to regard it as such has been a source of considerable mischief."

Can Hypnosis Force People to Act Against Their Will? Researchers Martin Orne and Frederick Evans (1965) demonstrated that hypnotized subjects *could* be induced to perform an apparently dangerous act. For example, they followed a request to dip a hand briefly in fuming acid and then throw the "acid" in a research assistant's face. When interviewed a day later, they exhibited no memory of their acts and emphatically denied they would follow orders to commit such actions.

Had hypnosis given the hypnotist a special power to control these people against their will? To find out, Orne and Evans unleashed that enemy of so many illusory beliefs—the control group: Orne asked some additional subjects to *pretend* they had been hypnotized. The laboratory experimenter, unaware that these control subjects had not been hypnotized, treated all subjects in the same manner. The result? All the *un*hypnotized subjects performed the same acts as the hypnotized ones. Similarly, most hypnotized subjects can be induced to cut up an American flag or deface a Bible, and a few will even cooperate in stealing an exam or selling illegal drugs. But people asked to simulate hypnosis are no less likely to perform the same acts (Levitt, 1986).

This illustrates a principle that Chapter 18, Social Psychology, emphasizes: An authoritative person in a legitimate context can induce people—hypnotized or not—to perform some unlikely acts. Hypnosis researcher Spanos (1982) puts it simply: "The overt behaviors of hypnotic subjects are well within normal limits."

Can Hypnosis Be Therapeutic? The clinical use of hypnosis is mushrooming. Hypnotherapists do nothing magical. Rather, they try to help patients harness their own healing powers (Baker, 1987). **Posthypnotic suggestions** (suggestions to be carried out after the hypnosis session has ended) have helped alleviate headaches, asthma, warts, and psychophysiological skin disorders. One woman, who suffered open sores all over her body for more than 20 years, was asked to imagine herself swimming in shimmering, sunlit liquids that would cleanse her skin and to experience her skin as smooth and unblemished. Within 3 months her sores had disappeared (Bowers, 1984).

Close-Up   *A True Story*

Remembrances of Christmases Past?

What shall we make of a clever study by Robert True (1949)? He regressed hypnotized volunteers back to their Christmases and birthday parties at ages 10, 7, and 4. In each case, he asked them what day of the week it was. Without hypnosis, the odds that a person could name offhand the day of a long-ago date are but 1 in 7. Remarkably, the hypnotized subjects' answers were 82 percent correct.

Other investigators were unable to replicate True's results. When Martin Orne (1982) asked Dr. True why, he replied that *Science*, the journal that published his article, had shortened his key question to "What day is this?" Actually, he had asked his age-regressed subjects, "Is it Monday? Is it Tuesday?" and so forth until the subject stopped him with a yes. When Orne asked True if he knew the actual day of the week while posing the questions, True granted that he did but was puzzled that Orne would ask.

Can you see why? True's experiment appears to be a beautiful example of how hypnotists can subtly influence the memories of their subjects (and, more generally, of how experimenters can subtly communicate their expectations to their subjects). "Given the eagerness of the hypnotized subject to fulfill the demands placed upon him," surmised Orne, it takes only the slightest change of inflection (in asking "Is it Wednesday?") for the subject to respond, "Yes."

The final blow to True's experiment came when Orne simply asked 10 4-year-olds what day of the week it was. To his surprise, none knew. If 4-year-olds typically do not know the day of the week, then True's adults were reporting information they likely didn't know when they were 4.

Drawing by M. Stevens; © 1987 The New Yorker Magazine, Inc.

Remembrances of Lives Past?

If people's hypnotic regressions to childhood are partly imagined, then how believable are claims of "regression to past lives"? Nicholas Spanos (1987–1988) reports that when hypnotized, fantasy-prone people who believe in reincarnation will offer vivid details of "past lives." But they nearly always report being their same race—unless the researcher has informed them that different races are common. They often report being someone famous rather than one of the countless "nobodies," and some contradict one another by claiming to have been the same person, such as King Henry VIII (Reveen, 1987–1988). Moreover, they typically do not know things that any person of that historical time would have known. One subject who "regressed" to a "previous life" as a Japanese fighter pilot in 1940 could not name the emperor of Japan and did not know that Japan was already at war. Hypnotic regressions to past lives thus offer no credible evidence of reincarnation.

Some psychologists believe that whether hypnosis is therapeutic depends on whether the disorder is voluntary. In studies that apply hypnosis to problems of self-control, such as nail biting or smoking, it has been equally helpful to those who could be deeply hypnotized and to those who couldn't. This suggests that the treatment benefits may be due to something other than hypnotic suggestion. With problems unrelated to willpower, such as hypersensitive allergic reactions, the greatest relief *is* sometimes experienced by the most hypnotizable people (Bowers & LeBaron, 1986).

But even in cases of involuntary problems, for which hypnotizable subjects experience greater benefits, is hypnosis the therapeutic agent? Another way to find out is to ask whether hypnosis does a better job than other ways of encouraging people to relax and form positive images. For example, hypnosis speeds the disappearance of warts. But in controlled studies, so do the same positive suggestions given without hypnosis (Spanos & others, 1988). So the actual therapeutic value of hypnosis remains in doubt.

Can Hypnosis Alleviate Pain? Yes, hypnosis can relieve pain (Kihlstrom, 1985). When unhypnotized subjects put their arms in an ice bath, they feel intense pain within 25 seconds. When hypnotizable subjects do the same after being given suggestions to feel no pain, they indeed report feeling little pain. Even light hypnosis can reduce fear, and thus hypersensitivity to the pain of, say, dental treatment. And some 10 percent of us can become so deeply hypnotized that even surgery can be performed without anesthesia.

How can this be? One theory of hypnotic pain relief involves **dissociation**, a split between different levels of consciousness that allows some mental processes to occur simultaneously. Hypnosis, it suggests, dissociates the sensation of the pain stimulus (of which the subject is still aware) from the emotional suffering that defines our pain experience. The ice water therefore feels very cold, but not painful.

Another theory proposes that hypnotic pain relief is due to selective attention, as when an injured athlete, caught up in the heat of competition, feels little or no pain until the game ends. Support for this view comes from several studies showing that hypnosis relieves pain no better than relaxing and distracting people without hypnosis (Chaves, 1989). With their attention distracted during hypnosis, for example, some women can experience childbirth with minimal pain; but so can some women without hypnosis, especially if given childbirth training (D'Eon, 1989).

Both views of pain assume that at some level a hypnotized person does experience the pain stimulus. Indeed, people who report feeling no pain will nevertheless perspire with pounding heart in response to electric shock or a surgeon's knife. Likewise, following a suggestion of deafness, hypnotized people will deny being able to hear their own voices, but will respond as do unhypnotized people when hearing their voice over a headset with a half-second delay: The delayed feedback disrupts their ability to speak fluently. If told they are color blind, hypnotized people will respond to tests of color blindness differently than do people with actual color-deficient vision.

Although the subjects report perceiving no pain, sound, or color, the stimuli have quite obviously registered within their sensory systems. Similarly, when told to forget having heard certain words, deeply hypnotized subjects will deny any memory of them. Their behavior tells a different story, however, for the "forgotten" words influence their later thoughts and perceptions (Kihlstrom, 1990). Moreover, when highly hypnotizable people are told that a piece of paper (with a large number on it) is blank, they will sometimes insist that they see nothing. But when told that genuinely hypnotized people, unlike fakers, briefly see the number before it gradually disappears, they will accurately reveal what the number was (Spanos & others, 1989).

The Lamaze method of childbirth uses several techniques in common with hypnosis, such as relaxation, controlled breathing, eye fixation, and suggestion. Women for whom the Lamaze method effectively lessens pain tend also to have high hypnotic ability (Venn, 1986).

So, researchers debate what hypnosis is, but all agree that it does *not*, as hypnotized subjects and their audiences may think, block sensory input. What people *say* they experience doesn't jibe with their behavior. The unanswered question of how hypnosis relieves pain—by dissociating the pain sensation from conscious awareness, or merely by focusing attention on other things—brings us to the basic issue: Is hypnosis a unique psychological state?

Is Hypnosis an Altered State of Consciousness?

We have seen that hypnosis involves heightened suggestibility. We have also seen that hypnotic procedures do not endow a person with special powers. But they can sometimes enhance recall of real (and unreal) past events, aid in overcoming psychosomatic ailments, and help alleviate pain. So, just what is hypnosis? Does it qualify as an altered—out-of-the-ordinary—state of consciousness?

Hypnosis as a Social Phenomenon   Skeptics note that hypnosis is not a unique physiological state. Moreover, behaviors produced through hypnotic procedures can also be produced without them. This suggests that hypnotic phenomena may be nothing more than the workings of normal consciousness (Spanos, 1986a).

In Chapter 6 we saw how powerfully our interpretations influence ordinary perceptions. Especially in the case of pain, for which the effects of hypnosis seem most dramatic, our perceptions depend on where our attention is. We have also seen that imaginative people can manufacture vivid perceptions without hypnosis. Perhaps, then, "hypnotized" people are merely acting the role of "good hypnotic subjects" and allowing the hypnotist to direct their fantasies.

It's not that people are consciously faking hypnosis. Rather, they're doing and reporting what's expected of them. And like actors who get caught up in their roles, they may begin to feel and behave in ways appropriate to the hypnotic role. Sure enough, the more people like and trust the hypnotist and feel motivated to demonstrate hypnotic behavior, the more they do so (Gfeller & others, 1987). If an experimenter eliminates the motivation for acting hypnotized—by telling subjects that hypnosis reveals "gullibility"—they become unresponsive. If told later to scratch their ear when they hear the word *psychology*, subjects will likely do so only if they think the experiment is still under way (and scratching is therefore expected). Based on such findings, advocates of the social influence theory contend that hypnotic phenomena are *not* unique to hypnosis. Like other supposed altered states, such as multiple personality (page 456) and spirit or demon possession (Spanos, 1989), hypnotic phenomena are instead an extension of everyday social behavior.

Hypnosis as Divided Consciousness   Most hypnosis researchers grant that normal social and cognitive processes play a part in hypnosis, but they believe that hypnosis is more than imaginative acting. For one thing, hypnotized subjects will *sometimes* carry out suggested behaviors on cue, even when they believe no one is watching. Their doing so shows that more may be at work than merely trying to be a "good subject." Moreover, many practitioners remain convinced that certain phenomena *are* unique to hypnosis, and that a special state of consciousness explains hypnotic experiences such as the reduction of pain, the compelling hallucinations, and the relief from allergic reactions and other physical problems (Bowers, 1989). Skeptics say, of course, that hypnotists' livelihoods depend on maintaining the aura of mysterious power that many clients associate with hypnosis (Coe, 1989b).

To veteran hypnosis researcher Ernest Hilgard (1986), dissociation is at work. Hilgard considers the dissociation that occurs during hypnosis to be a more extreme form of the everyday dissociations that occur in our information processing. Putting a child to bed, we might read *Cinderella* for the fourteenth time while mentally organizing a busy schedule for the next day. Under the influence of my dentist's nitrous oxide—a real gas—I hear her ask me to "open wide." As my conscious self contemplates her request, my mouth, much to my surprise, immediately obeys. "Turn toward me," she says. Again, as if controlled by some strange force, my head instantly complies. With practice, it is even possible to read and comprehend a short story while copying dictated words, much as you can doodle while listening to a lecture or much as a skilled pianist can converse while playing a familiar piece (Hirst & others, 1978). Thus, when hypnotized subjects write answers to questions about one topic while talking or reading about a different topic, they display an accentuated form of normal cognitive dissociation.

Hilgard's discovery of hypnotic dissociation occurred dramatically. During a class demonstration of hypnosis, he induced deafness in a subject and then set about showing the class that the person was now utterly unresponsive to questions, taunts, and even sudden loud sounds. When a student asked whether some part of the subject might still be able to hear, Hilgard decided to show that the answer was no. He quietly asked the subject to raise his right index finger if some part of him could still hear. To everyone's surprise—including Hilgard's and the subject's—the finger rose. When the subject's hearing was restored, he explained that "it was a little boring just sitting here . . . when I suddenly felt my finger lift; that is what I want you to explain to me."

This phenomenon spurred further inquiry. Hypnotized subjects, as we noted earlier, report far less pain than others when they place their arms in ice water. But when asked to press a key if "some part" of them does feel the pain, they invariably press the key. To Hilgard, this suggests that a dissociated consciousness, a **hidden observer**, is passively aware of what is happening.

The divided-consciousness theory of hypnosis is controversial, because what the "hidden observer" reports varies with what the experimenter seems to want. But this much seems clear: You and I process much information without conscious awareness. We have seen examples of unconscious information processing in the chapters on sensation and perception, and we will see more in later chapters on learning, memory, and thinking. Without doubt, there is more to thinking than we are aware of.

Then again, there is little doubt that social influences do play an important role in hypnosis. So, might the two views—social influence and divided consciousness—be bridged? Researchers John Kihlstrom and Kevin McConkey (1990) believe there is no contradiction between the two approaches, which may eventually converge into a "unified account of hypnosis." Until then, they suggest, we can understand hypnosis as an extension *both* of normal principles of social influence *and* of everyday splits in consciousness.

"The total possible consciousness may be split into parts which co-exist but mutually ignore each other."
William James
Principles of Psychology, 1890

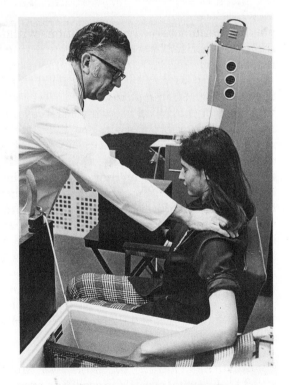

A hypnotized subject being tested by Ernest Hilgard exhibits no pain response when her arm is placed in an ice bath. But when asked to press a key if some part of her feels the pain, she does so. To Hilgard, this suggests that hypnosis divides consciousness into one part that is unaware of the pain and another "hidden observer" part that is aware.

Drugs and Consciousness

If there is controversy about whether hypnosis alters consciousness, there is little dispute that drugs do. **Psychoactive drugs** are chemicals that change perceptions and moods. An imaginary drug user's day dramatizes the widespread use of legal psychoactive drugs: It begins with a wake-up cup of strong coffee. By midday, several cigarettes and a prescription tranquilizer have calmed the nerves. Leaving work early, a happy-hour cocktail provides a relaxing and sociable prelude to a dental appointment, where nitrous oxide makes an otherwise painful experience mildly pleasurable. A diet pill before dinner helps stem the appetite, and its stimulating effects can later be partially offset with a sleeping pill. Before drifting off into REM-depressed sleep, our hypothetical drug user is dismayed by a news report of "rising drug abuse."

Continued use of a psychoactive drug produces **tolerance**: The user requires larger and larger doses to experience the drug's effect. A person who rarely drinks alcohol might get tipsy on one can of beer, but an experienced drinker might not get tipsy until the second six-pack. Don't be misled by the word "tolerance": Alcoholics may have a high tolerance for alcohol, but their brains, hearts, and livers suffer enormous damage from the excessive doses of alcohol they are "tolerating."

Users who stop taking psychoactive drugs may experience the undesirable side effects of **withdrawal**. As the body responds to the drug's absence, the user may feel physical pain and intense cravings for a dose. This indicates a **physical dependence** on the drug. People can also develop **psychological dependence**, particularly for drugs used to relieve stress. Although the drug may not be physically addictive, it nevertheless becomes an important part of the user's life, often as a way of relieving negative emotions. With either physical addiction or psychological dependence, the user's primary focus becomes obtaining and using the drug.

There are three types of psychoactive drugs: **depressants**, or "downers," which calm neural activity and slow down body functions; **stimulants**, or "uppers," which temporarily excite neural activity and arouse body functions; and **hallucinogens**, which distort perception and evoke sensory images without sensory input. Drugs in all three categories do their work at the brain's synapses, by stimulating, inhibiting, or mimicking the activity of neurotransmitters, the brain's chemical messengers.

Depressants

Let's look first at drugs such as alcohol, tranquilizers, and opiates, which slow down body functions.

Alcohol True or false? In large amounts, alcohol is a depressant; in small amounts, it is a stimulant.

False. Small doses of "spirits" may, indeed, enliven a drinker, but they do so by slowing activity in brain centers that control judgment and inhibitions. Alcohol facilitates urges that the individual might otherwise resist by focusing attention on the immediate situation and away from future consequences (Steele & Josephs, 1990). If provoked, people under alcohol's influence respond more aggressively than usual. If asked to help, people under alcohol's influence

"Just tell me where you kids got the idea to take so many drugs."

© 1992 by Sidney Harris.

respond more helpfully than usual. In everyday life, alcohol *disinhibits* both harmful tendencies, as when sexually coercive college men try to disinhibit their dates by getting them to drink (Mosher & Anderson, 1986), and helpful tendencies, as when restaurant patrons tip more when tipsy (M. Lynn, 1988). Thus, alcohol makes us more aggressive or helpful—or self-disclosing or sexually daring—when such tendencies are present. Whatever urges you feel when sober, you are more likely to act upon if intoxicated.

Low doses of alcohol relax the drinker by slowing sympathetic nervous system activity. With larger doses, alcohol can become a staggering problem: Reactions slow, speech slurs, and skilled performance deteriorates. These physical effects, combined with the lowering of inhibitions, contribute to alcohol's worst consequences—in America, the more than 100,000 lives claimed annually in alcohol-related car accidents and violent crime (Lord, 1987).

Alcohol has an intriguing effect on memory. It impairs neither short-term recall for what just happened nor existing long-term memories. Rather, it disrupts the *processing* of recent experiences into long-term memories. Thus, the day after being intoxicated, heavy drinkers may not recall whom they met or what they said or did the night before. This memory blackout stems partly from an inability to transfer memories from the intoxicated to the sober state (Eich, 1980). Blackouts after drinking may also result from alcohol's suppression of REM sleep. (Recall that people deprived of REM sleep have difficulty fixing their day's experiences into permanent memories.)

A University of Illinois campus survey showed that before sexual assaults, 80 percent of the male assailants and 70 percent of the female victims had been drinking (Camper, 1990).

With billboards like this one, Mothers Against Drunk Driving (MADD) has vigorously promoted more awareness of the problems of driving under the influence of alcohol and stiffer penalties for drunk drivers.

Alcohol has another intriguing effect on consciousness: It reduces self-awareness (Hull & others, 1986). Compared with people who feel good about themselves, those who want to suppress their awareness of failures or shortcomings are more likely to drink. The Nazi doctors who selected "unfit" inmates for the gas chambers often did so while drunk, or got drunk afterwards (Lifton, 1986).

As with other psychoactive drugs, alcohol's behavioral effects stem not only from its alteration of brain chemistry but also from the user's expectations. Many studies have found that when people *believe* that alcohol affects social behavior in certain ways, and *believe*, rightly or wrongly, that they have been drinking alcohol, they will behave accordingly (Leigh, 1989). For example, alcohol per se has some effect on sexual arousal, by decreasing cognitive inhibitions (Crowe & George, 1989). But people become even more responsive to sexual stimuli if they believe alcohol promotes arousal and believe they have been drinking. From their review of research, Jay Hull and Charles Bond (1986) concluded that for some people alcohol serves "as an excuse to become sexually aroused."

Consider one such experiment by David Abrams and Terence Wilson (1983). They gave Rutgers University men who volunteered for a study on "alcohol and sexual stimulation" either an alcoholic or a nonalcoholic drink. (Both drinks had a strong taste that masked any alcohol.) In each group, half the subjects thought they were drinking alcohol and half thought they were not. Regardless of what they drank, after being shown an erotic movie clip, the men who *thought* they had consumed alcohol were more likely to report having strong sexual fantasies and feeling guilt-free. Thus, being able to *attribute* their sexual responses to alcohol released their inhibitions—whether they actually had drunk alcohol or not. This illustrates an important principle: A drug's psychological effects are powerfully influenced by the user's psychological state.

Barbiturates The **barbiturate** drugs, or *tranquilizers,* have effects similar to those of alcohol. Because they depress sympathetic nervous system activity, barbiturates such as Nembutal and Seconal are sometimes prescribed to induce sleep or reduce anxiety. In larger doses, they can lead to impaired memory and judgment. In combination with alcohol—as when people take a sleeping pill after an evening of drinking—the total depressive effect on body functions can be lethal. With sufficient doses, barbiturates by themselves can also cause death, which make them the drugs often chosen by those attempting suicide.

Opiates The **opiates**—opium and its derivatives, morphine and heroin—also depress neural functioning. The pupils constrict, the breathing slows, and the user becomes lethargic. For a few hours, pain and anxiety are replaced by blissful pleasure. But for pleasure one pays a price, which for the heroin user is the gnawing craving for another fix, the need for progressively larger doses, the weeklong physical anguish of withdrawal—and for some the ultimate price, death by overdose.

The pathway to addiction is treacherous. When repeatedly flooded with artificial opiates, the brain eventually stops producing its own opiates, the endorphins (Chapter 2, pages 31–32). Then, when the drug is withdrawn, the brain lacks the normal level of these painkilling neurotransmitters. The result is the agony of withdrawal.

Stimulants

The most widely used stimulants are caffeine, nicotine, the powerful **amphetamines**, and the even more powerful cocaine. Stimulants speed up body functions, hence the nickname "speed" for amphetamines. Strong stimulants increase heart and breathing rates; the pupils dilate; appetite diminishes (because blood sugar rises); and energy and self-confidence rise. For these reasons, people use stimulants to stay awake, lose weight, or boost mood or athletic performance. As with other drugs, the "benefits" of stimulants come

Fact: College students drink more alcohol than their noncollege peers (Atwell, 1986).

Fact: 10 percent of drinkers account for half of the alcohol consumed (Centers for Disease Control, 1989).

Fact: Most drug-dependent people use more than one drug. Most alcoholics smoke cigarettes. Most heroin users abuse alcohol.

Fact: Alcoholism plagues more men than women. In Asia and North America, roughly 1 in 10 men, but no more than 1 in 50 women, are problem drinkers (Helzer & others, 1990).

Fact: Because women produce less of an enzyme that breaks down alcohol in the stomach, more gets into their bloodstream—producing a greater effect than in men (Frezza & others, 1990).

Fact: Binge drinking—defined as the consumption of five or more drinks on some occasion during the last month—is reported by 22 percent of American adults. The highest rate of binge drinking—52 percent—is among 18- to 24-year-old males (Centers for Disease Control, 1983).

Fact: Anheuser-Busch Brewery's annual advertising budget has been seven times the budget of the National Institute on Alcohol Abuse and Alcoholism (McCarthy, 1988).

Fact: Alcohol kills more people than all illegal drugs combined. So does tobacco (Siegel, 1990).

with a price. When drug stimulation ends, the user experiences a compensating slowdown and may "crash" into tiredness, headaches, irritability, and depression. Like the depressants, stimulants can be addictive. (For information on nicotine addiction, see page 535.)

In a 1990 national survey, 5 percent of American high school seniors reported having tried cocaine during the past year and 2 percent said they had smoked crack, a potent form of cocaine (Johnston & others, 1991). (These figures may be *under*estimates, for high school dropouts were not included in this survey.) When animals and people chew coca leaves, small amounts of cocaine enter the bloodstream gradually, without seeming ill effects (Siegel, 1990). But when extracted cocaine is sniffed ("snorted"), and especially when smoked ("free-based") or injected, it enters the bloodstream quickly, producing a rush of euphoria that lasts 15 to 30 minutes. Because the "rush" has depleted the brain's supply of the neurotransmitters dopamine and norepinephrine, a "crash" of agitated depression occurs as the drug's effect wears off (Figure 7–8). Crack works even faster and produces a briefer but more intense high, a more intense crash, and a craving for more crack, which wanes after several hours and then returns several days later (Gawin, 1991).

The recipe for Coca-Cola originally included an extract of the coca plant, creating a cocaine tonic for tired elderly people. Between 1896 and 1905, Coke was indeed "the real thing."

Figure 7–8 Cocaine euphoria and crash. After neurotransmitters carry a message across a synapse, the sending nerve cell normally reabsorbs excess neurotransmitters. Cocaine blocks this reuptake of three neurotransmitters: dopamine, norepinephrine, and serotonin (Ray & Ksir, 1990). The extra neurotransmitter molecules therefore remain in the synapse, intensifying their normal mood-altering effects and producing a euphoric rush. When the cocaine is metabolized out of the body, the absence of these neurotransmitters produces a crash. Amphetamines act differently—by stimulating the release of excess norepinephrine (Julien, 1988). (Left, adapted from *The New York Times*, June 25, 1988.)

Regular cocaine users become addicted—monkeys so strongly addicted that they have pressed a lever more than 12,000 times to gain each cocaine injection (Siegel, 1990). Human and animal cocaine users may experience emotional disturbance, suspiciousness, convulsions, cardiac arrest, or respiratory failure. As with all psychoactive drugs, cocaine's psychological effects depend not only on the dosage and form in which one takes the drug but also on one's expectations, one's personality, and the situation—a mix of factors. Given a placebo, cocaine users who *think* they are taking cocaine often have a cocainelike experience (Van Dyke & Byck, 1982). In situations that often trigger aggression, ingesting cocaine may increase aggressive reactions. Caged rats fight when given foot shocks, and fight even more when given foot shocks and cocaine (Siegel, 1990).

Close-Up **Misconceptions About Addiction**

An *addiction* has traditionally meant a craving for a substance, with physical withdrawal symptoms such as aches, nausea, and distress when suddenly discontinued. In recent pop psychology, the supposedly irresistible seduction of addiction has been extended to cover many behaviors formerly considered bad habits, or even sins. Has the concept been stretched too far? Are addictions as irresistible as commonly believed? Many drug researchers believe the following three myths about addiction are false:

1. Addictive drugs quickly corrupt. For example, morphine taken to control pain is powerfully addictive, and often leads to heroin abuse. After taking a psychoactive drug, some people—perhaps 10 percent—do indeed have a hard time using it in moderation or stopping altogether. However, there are many more controlled, occasional users than addicts of drugs such as alcohol, marijuana, and cocaine (Gazzaniga, 1988; Siegel, 1990). The crazed user, who will do anything to get more of the drug, is more the exception than the rule. Moreover, people typically don't become addicted when using drugs medically. Those given morphine to control pain rarely develop the cravings of the addict who uses morphine as a mood-altering drug (Melzack, 1990). Thus, taking a psychoactive drug is necessary, but for most people not by itself sufficient, to cause addiction.

2. Addictions can't be overcome voluntarily; therapy is a must. The thriving addiction-treatment business promotes the notion that we're helpless without them. True, some addicts do benefit from treatment programs. Alcoholics Anonymous, for example, has supported many people in overcoming their alcohol dependence. But, say critics, the recovery rates of treated and untreated groups differ less than you might suppose. Moreover, viewing addiction as a disease, as diabetes is a disease, can undermine self-confidence and the will to change cravings that, without treatment, "one can't fight." And that, critics say, would be unfor-

tunate, for many people do voluntarily stop using addictive drugs, without treatment. Some 70 percent of smokers who seek treatment for their addiction later return to smoking, while most of America's 41 million ex-smokers kicked the habit on their own (page 536). Half of the American soldiers in Vietnam tried heroin or opium, and 20 percent became regular users. Worried about an influx of returning addicts, the Defense Department commissioned a research team led by Lee Robins (1974) to follow nearly 500 men whose urine revealed narcotic use upon their departure from Vietnam. Back home, one-third of this group did try narcotics again. Yet, removed from the war's stressful setting and all the stimulus cues associated with their drug use (the place, the friends, the circumstances), only 7 percent of the 500 became readdicted. The rest—all but the relatively few hard-core addicts—left their dependence behind.

3. We can extend the concept of addiction to cover not just drug dependencies, but a whole spectrum of repetitive, pleasure-seeking behaviors. We can, and we have, but should we? How far should we stretch the concept of addiction?

The addiction-as-disease-needing-treatment idea has been extended to cover a host of driven behaviors, including overeating, shopping, exercise, gambling, and sex. Initially, we may use the term metaphorically. "I'm a ski addict" is just a way of saying, "I love skiing." But when people begin taking the metaphor as reality, addiction becomes an all-purpose excuse. Those who embezzle to feed their "gambling addiction" or abuse or betray to indulge their "sex addiction" can protest that "I can't help it" and seek sympathy and treatment rather than judgment and jail.

If the addiction-as-disease-needing-treatment model is controversial even with drug dependencies, it is doubly controversial when extended to other excessive behaviors.

Hallucinogens

Hallucinogens are psychoactive drugs that distort perceptions and evoke vivid images without sensory input (which is why they are also called *psychedelics*, meaning "mind-manifesting"). Some hallucinogens are natural substances, such as marijuana, which is sometimes classified as a mild hallucinogen. Others are synthetic. Of the synthetics, the two best known are PCP ("angel dust"), a potent and illegal pain killer that has highly unpredictable and sometimes devastating psychological effects, and LSD.

LSD The first "acid trip" was taken in 1943 by chemist Albert Hofmann, the creator of **LSD (lysergic acid diethylamide)**. After accidentally ingesting some of the chemical, Hofmann reported that he "perceived an uninterrupted stream of fantastic pictures, extraordinary shapes with intense, kaleidoscopic play of colors" (Siegel, 1984). LSD and other powerful hallucinogens are chemically similar to, and therefore block the actions of, a subtype of the neurotransmitter serotonin (Jacobs, 1987). The emotions that accompany an LSD trip vary from euphoria to detachment to panic.

As with all drug use, a person's current mood and expectations color the LSD experience. Despite emotional variations, the resulting perceptual distortions and hallucinations have commonalities. Psychologist Ronald Siegel (1982) reports that whether you provoke your brain to hallucinate by loss of oxygen, sensory deprivation, or drugs, "it will hallucinate in basically the same way." The experience typically begins with simple geometric forms, such as a lattice, a cobweb, or a spiral (Figure 7–9). The next phase consists of more meaningful images; some may be superimposed on a tunnel or funnel, others may involve the replay of past emotional experiences. When the hallucinogenic experience peaks, people frequently feel separated from their bodies and experience dreamlike scenes as if they were real—so real that users may become panic-stricken or may harm themselves.

Marijuana Marijuana consists of the leaves and flowers of the hemp plant, which for 5000 years has been cultivated for its fiber. Marijuana's major active ingredient is **THC,** the everyday name of the complex organic molecule delta-9-tetrahydrocannabinol. The recent discovery of brain receptors for this molecule hints that the brain produces a similar chemical (Matsuda & others, 1990). Whether smoked or eaten in such foods as brownies, THC produces a mixture of effects that makes the drug difficult to classify. (Smoking gets the drug into the brain in about 7 seconds; this produces a greater effect than does eating the drug, which causes its peak concentration to be reached at a slower, unpredictable rate.) Like alcohol, marijuana relaxes, disinhibits, and may produce a euphoric high. But marijuana also acts as a mild hallucinogen by amplifying sensitivity to colors, sounds, tastes, and smells.

As with other drugs, the marijuana user's experience varies, depending on the situation in which it is taken. If the person feels anxious or depressed, taking the drug may intensify these feelings. In other situations, using marijuana can be not only pleasurable but therapeutic. For those who suffer the pain of glaucoma (caused by pressure within the eyeball) or the nausea that sometimes accompanies cancer chemotherapy, marijuana may spell relief. In acknowledging such benefits, a review of marijuana research published by the National Academy of Sciences (1982) also identified some not-so-pleasant consequences. Like alcohol, marijuana impairs the motor coordination, perceptual skills, and reaction time necessary for safe driving and machine operation. "THC causes animals to misjudge events," reports Ronald Siegel (1990, p. 163); "pigeons wait too long to respond to buzzers or lights that tell them food is available for brief periods; and rats turn the wrong way in mazes." Marijuana also disrupts memory formation and interferes with immediate recall of information learned only a few minutes before. Clearly, being stoned is not conducive to learning.

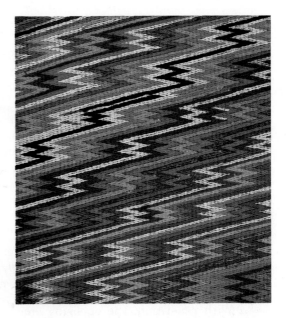

Figure 7–9 Geometric forms, such as those experienced by drug users during drug-induced hallucinations, can be seen in the embroidery of the Huichol, Mexican Indians who use peyote, from which the hallucinogen mescaline derives.

Unlike alcohol, which the body eliminates within hours, THC and its by-products linger in the body for a month or more. Thus, contrary to the usual tolerance phenomenon, regular users may achieve a high with less drug than do occasional users.

Uncertainty persists about marijuana's physical effects, but medical research suggests that long-term marijuana use may depress male sex hormone and sperm levels and damage the lungs more than cigarette smoking (Wu & others, 1988). Large doses hasten the loss of brain cells (Landfield & others, 1988). Although marijuana is not as addictive as cocaine or nicotine, one study that followed 654 junior high students into their early twenties found that adolescents who heavily used marijuana developed more health and family problems than did nonusers (Newcomb & Bentler, 1988).

Despite their differences, the psychoactive drugs summarized in Table 7–1 share a common effect: They trigger negative aftereffects that offset their immediate positive effects. The aftereffects illustrate the more general principle that emotions tend to produce opposing emotions, which linger after the original emotions disappear. With repetition, the opposing emotions get stronger (page 400). This emotions-trigger-opposing-emotions principle parallels that of drug-induced pleasures; the pleasures wane as the drug exacts its compensatory price. And that helps explain tolerance and withdrawal. Because the opposing, negative aftereffects are getting stronger, it takes larger and larger doses to produce the desired high, causing the aftereffects to worsen in the drug's absence. This in turn creates a need to switch off the ensuing withdrawal symptoms by taking yet more of the drug.

"How strange would appear to be this thing that men call pleasure! And how curiously it is related to what is thought to be its opposite, pain! . . . Wherever the one is found, the other follows up behind."
Plato
Phaedo, Fourth century B.C.

Table 7–1	**A Guide to Selected Psychoactive Drugs**			
Type	**Drug**	**Pleasurable effects**		**Adverse effects**
Depressant	Alcohol	Initial high followed by relaxation and disinhibition		Depression, memory loss, organic damage, impaired reactions
	Heroin	Rush of euphoria, relief from pain		Depressed physiology, agonizing withdrawal
Stimulant	Cocaine	Rush of euphoria, confidence, energy		Cardiovascular stress, suspiciousness, depressive crash
	Nicotine	Arouses and relaxes, sense of well-being		Heart disease, cancer (from tars)
Mild hallucinogen	Marijuana	Enhances sensation, relieves pain, distorts time, relaxed high		Lowered sex hormones, disrupted memory, lung damage

Influences on Drug Use

Drug use by North American youth increased during the 1970s and declined during the 1980s. In the University of Michigan's annual survey of 16,000 high school seniors, the proportion who believed there is "great risk" in regular marijuana use rose from 35 percent in 1978 to 78 percent in 1990 (Johnston & others, 1991). Marijuana use by this age group peaked in 1979 and has since declined (Figure 7–10). The American Council on Education's annual survey of new college students similarly reveals that between 1977 and 1990 support for the legalization of marijuana dropped from 53 percent to 19 percent (Astin & others, 1987, 1991). Similar attitude and usage changes appear in surveys of Canadian teens (Smart & Adlaf, 1989).

Other studies reveal a changing national attitude toward alcohol. More than at any time since prohibition, health- and safety-conscious Americans see alcohol less as a cheerful beverage than as a drug to be shunned along with others. Gallup surveys show the number of abstainers steadily rising—from 29 percent in 1978 to 43 percent in 1990 (Gallup & Newport, 1990). Likewise, the number of new collegians who reported abstinence from beer during the past year increased from 25 percent in 1981 to 42 percent in 1990. In the United States, hard liquor sales from 1980 to 1987 dropped 23 percent (Bureau of the Census, 1990). When the alcohol industry starts substituting wine coolers for wine and nonalcoholic beer for alcoholic, you know attitudes are changing.

Cigarette smoking, though addictive, has similarly plummeted, as described in Chapter 17, Health. This is especially so among highly educated people, the vast majority of whom have never started or have stopped. Effectively inform people about the health hazards of using alcohol, cocaine, marijuana, or tobacco and—without therapy, support groups, or medicines—many will simply stop.

Why, then, do some people continue to use psychoactive drugs? Why, for example, did one-third of American high school seniors report having tried an illicit drug during the past year (Johnston & others, 1991)? For those adolescents whose focus is on having fun in the here-and-now, occasional drug use may represent thrill-seeking. Such experimentation is not linked with maladjustment (Shedler & Block, 1990). Others, though, become regular drug users. Why?

Some people may be biologically vulnerable. For example, evidence accumulates that heredity influences alcoholic tendencies. Consider:

Adopted individuals are more susceptible to alcoholism if one or both of their biological parents is alcoholic (Mirin & Weiss, 1989).

Having an alcoholic identical twin also puts one at increased risk (Heath & others, 1989).

Compared to children of nonalcoholics, children of alcoholics appear more sensitive to alcohol's intoxicating effect (Newlin & Thomson, 1990).

Researchers have bred rats that prefer alcoholic drinks to water (Holden, 1991).

Such findings have fueled the search for a better understanding of genetic and biochemical influences on addiction. The biggest study yet—a $25 million, 5-year analysis of 600 U.S. alcoholics and their relatives—was underway in 1991. If biological markers of addiction-proneness can be found, then perhaps young people at risk for specific addictions can be identified and counseled.

Figure 7–10 The percentage of high school seniors who report having used alcohol, marijuana, or cocaine during the past 30 days has declined since the late 1970s. (From Johnston & others, 1991.)

"Outlawing drugs in order to solve drug problems is much like outlawing sex in order to win the war against AIDS."
Ronald Siegel
Intoxication, 1990

But psychological and social factors also have an influence. In their studies of New Jersey and California youth and young adults, Michael Newcomb and L. L. Harlow (1986) found that one psychological factor is the feeling that one's life is meaningless and directionless, a common feeling among school dropouts who subsist without job skills, without privilege, without hope.

Other studies reveal that heavy users of alcohol, marijuana, and cocaine often have experienced significant stress or failure and are depressed. As we noted earlier, alcohol temporarily dulls the pain of self-awareness, which can make it a way to avoid having to cope with depression, anger, anxiety, or insomnia. The relief may be temporary, but as Chapter 8, Learning, explains, behavior is often more controlled by its immediate than by its later consequences.

Especially for teenagers, drug use also has social roots. Peers influence attitudes about drugs; they also provide the drugs and establish the social context for their use. If an adolescent's friends use drugs, the odds are that he or she will, too. If the friends don't, the temptation may not even arise. Indeed, the peer factor is so powerful that other predictors of adolescent drug use, such as family strength, religiousness, and school adjustment, seem to operate through their effects on peer associations. Those who do use drugs are more likely to stop if indeed their drug use was peer influenced (Kandel & Raveis, 1989). When the friends stop or the social network changes, usage typically ceases. Teenagers who come from happy families and do well in school seldom use drugs, in large part because they rarely associate with those who do (Oetting & Beauvais, 1987, 1990).

These findings suggest three channels of influence for drug prevention and treatment programs: (1) education about the long-term costs of a drug's temporary pleasures, (2) efforts to boost people's self-esteem and purpose in life, and (3) attempts to modify peer associations or to "inoculate" youth against peer pressures. Said differently, people are *very* unlikely to abuse drugs if they understand the physical and psychological costs, feel good about themselves and where their lives are heading, and are in a peer group that disapproves of drug use.

Some warning signs of alcoholism:
* *drinking binges*
* *regretting things done or said when drunk*
* *feeling low or guilty after drinking*
* *failing to honor a resolve to drink less*
* *drinking to alleviate depression or anxiety*
* *avoiding family or friends when drinking*

In the real world, alcohol accounts for one-sixth or less of beverage use. In television's world, alcohol drinking occurs more often than the combined drinking of coffee, tea, soft drinks, and water (Gerbner, 1990).

Near-Death Experiences

A man . . . hears himself pronounced dead by his doctor. He begins to hear an uncomfortable noise, a loud ringing or buzzing, and at the same time feels himself moving very rapidly through a long dark tunnel. After this, he suddenly finds himself outside of his own physical body . . . and sees his own body from a distance, as though he is a spectator. . . . Soon other things begin to happen. Others come to meet and to help him. He glimpses the spirits of relatives and friends who have already died, and a loving, warm spirit of a kind he has never encountered before—a being of light—appears before him. . . . He is overwhelmed by intense feelings of joy, love, and peace. Despite his attitude, though, he somehow reunites with his physical body and lives. (Moody, 1976, pp. 23, 24)

This passage from Raymond Moody's best-selling book, *Life After Life*, is a composite description of a **near-death experience**. Because reports of these experiences are nearly always positive,

Snow White and Sleeping Beauty Have Tea

Drawing by Frascino; © 1990 The New Yorker Magazine, Inc.

they are devoured by those eager for "proof" that there is happiness after death. (Upon being revived, people seldom recall having teetered on the brink of hell.)

What should we make of these reports? Do they prove that we can look forward to bliss on the other side of death? Do they confirm Plato's doctrine that mind—or soul—is separable from body? Do such flights of mind reliably occur to those who face death?

Near-death experiences are more common than you might suspect. Several investigators each interviewed a hundred or more people who had come close to death through such physical traumas as cardiac arrest. In every one of these studies, 30 to 40 percent of those interviewed recalled some sort of near-death experience (Ring, 1980; Schnaper, 1980). When George Gallup, Jr. (1982; Gallup & O'Connell, 1986) interviewed a national sample of Americans, 15 percent reported having experienced a close brush with death. One-third of these people—representing some 8 million people by Gallup's estimate—reported an accompanying mystical experience. Some of these people claim to recall things said while they lay unconscious and near death (but then, some anesthetized patients undergoing major surgery later display similar recall of operating room conversation [Hilgard, 1986]).

Did Moody's description of the "complete" near-death experience sound familiar? The parallels between it and Ronald Siegel's (1977) descriptions of the typical hallucinogenic experience are striking: replay of old memories, out-of-body sensations, and visions of tunnels or funnels and bright lights or beings of light (Figure 7–11). In short, the content of the near-death experience is just what one would expect from a knowledge of hallucinations. Moreover, oxygen deprivation and other insults to the brain are known to produce hallucinations.

Perhaps, then, the brain under stress manufactures the near-death experience. Patients who experience temporal lobe seizures often report similarly profound mystical experiences, as have solitary sailors and polar explorers while enduring monotony, isolation, and cold (Suedfeld & Mocellin, 1987). Even the twilight state between waking and sleeping may produce sensations of floating up off the bed. Fantasy-prone persons are especially susceptible—or should we say *open*—to near-death and other out-of-body experiences (Wilson & Barber, 1983).

Siegel (1980) concludes that the near-death experience is best understood "as a dissociative hallucinatory activity of the brain": When external input dims, the brain's own interior activity becomes perceptible. He illustrates with an analogy: When gazing out a window at dusk, we begin to see the reflected interior of the room as if it were outside, either because the light from outside is dimming (as in the near-death experience) or because the inside light is being amplified (as with LSD). When projected on our perceptual window, says Siegel, our mind's internal images appear real. Those having a near-death experience, like those on an LSD trip, explore "the beyond within."

Some investigators of near-death experiences object. People who have experienced both hallucinations and the near-death phenomenon often deny their similarity. Moreover, a near-death experience often changes people in ways that a drug trip doesn't. They become kinder, more spiritual, more believing in life after death. Skeptics reply that these effects stem from the death-related context of the experience.

Although some of these people were thought "dead," none had suffered true brain death. If they had, they would not have survived to recall their experience—hence the label "near-death."

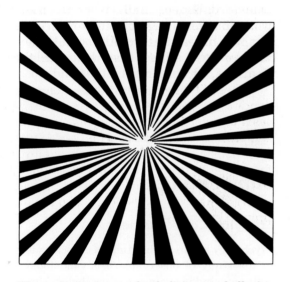

Figure 7–11 A near-death vision or a hallucination? Psychologist Ronald Siegel (1977) reports that under the influence of hallucinogenic drugs, people often see "a bright light in the center of the field of vision. . . . The location of this point of light create[s] a tunnel-like perspective." (From "Hallucinations" by R.K. Siegel. Copyright © 1977 Scientific American, Inc. All rights reserved.)

*"**Joan [of Arc]:** I hear voices telling me what to do. They come from God.*
*"**Robert:** They come from your imagination.*
*"**Joan:** Of course. That is how the messages of God come to us."*
George Bernard Shaw
Saint Joan, 1924

The controversy over interpreting near-death experiences raises a basic mind-body issue: Is the mind immaterial? Can it exist separate from the body? **Dualists** answer yes. They believe that the mind and body are two distinct entities—the mind nonphysical, the body physical—that somehow interact with each other. As Socrates says in Plato's *Phaedo*, "Does not death mean that the body comes to exist by itself, separated from the soul, and that the soul exists by herself, separated from the body? What is death but that?" For Socrates, as for those today who believe that near-death experiences are proof of immortality, death is not really the death of the person. Death is merely a person's liberation from the bodily prison, an occasion for rejoicing. (Carried to its extreme, this dualist view has given rise to glorifications of the afterlife trip under such titles as "The Thrill of Dying" and "The Wonderful World of Death.")

Monists answer no to the separation of mind and body. They contend that mind and body are different aspects of the same thing. Whether they are scientists who assume the inseparability of mind and brain or theologians who hold to an afterlife that involves some form of bodily resurrection, monists generally believe that death is real and that without bodies we truly are nobodies.

As debates over the significance of dreams, fantasy, hypnotic states, drug-induced hallucinations, and near-death experiences illustrate, science informs our wondering about human consciousness and human nature. Although there remain questions that it cannot answer, science nevertheless helps fashion our image of who we are, of our human potentials and our human limits.

"The mind seems to act independently of the brain in the same sense that a programmer acts independently of his computer."
Wilder Penfield (1975)

"Everything in science to date seems to indicate that conscious awareness is a property of the living functioning brain and inseparable from it."
Roger W. Sperry (1985)

Summing Up

Studying Consciousness

Psychology began as the study of consciousness, then turned to the study of observable behavior. Today, investigating states of mind is again one of psychology's pursuits.

Selective Attention At any moment we are conscious of a very limited amount of all that we are capable of experiencing. One example is the cocktail party effect—attending to only one voice among many.

States of Consciousness Consciousness can be experienced in various states, all of which involve a focused awareness of perceptions, thoughts, and feelings as they occur. This chapter considers several alternatives to normal waking consciousness.

Sleep and Dreams

The Rhythm of Sleep Our daily schedule of waking and sleeping is timed by a body clock known as circadian rhythm. Each night's sleep also has a rhythm of its own, running from transitional Stage 1 sleep to deep Stage 4 sleep and back up to the more internally active REM sleep stage. This cycle repeats several times during a normal night's sleep, with periods of Stage 4 sleep progressively shortening and of REM sleep lengthening.

Why Do We Sleep? Depriving people of sleep has failed to reveal why, physiologically, we need sleep. Recent research reveals that sleep is linked with the release of pituitary growth hormone and that it may help to restore exhausted tissues.

Sleep Disorders The disorders of sleep include insomnia (recurring wakefulness), narcolepsy (uncontrollable lapsing into REM sleep), and sleep apnea (the stopping of breathing while sleeping).

Dreams Although conscious thoughts can occur during any sleep stage, awakening people during REM sleep yields predictable "dreamlike" reports; awakening during other sleep stages only occasionally yields a fleeting image. Our dreams are mostly of ordinary events; they often relate to everyday experiences and more frequently involve anxiety or misfortune than triumphant achievements.

Freud believed that a dream's manifest content is a censored version of its latent content, which gratifies our unconscious wishes. Newer explanations of why we dream suggest that dreams (a) help process information from the day and fix it in memory, (b) serve a physiological function, and/or (c) are the brain's efforts to string periodic hallucinations (from activity bursts in the visual cortex) into a story line. Despite their differences, most theorists agree that REM sleep and its associated dreams serve an important function, as shown by the REM rebound that occurs following REM deprivation.

Daydreams, Fantasies, and Meditation

Virtually everyone daydreams, especially fantasy-prone people and especially in times when attention can be freed from the tasks at hand. Daydreaming can be adaptive; it can help us prepare for future events and may substitute for impulsive behavior. Meditation, like deep relaxation, can help relieve stress-related symptoms and illnesses.

Hypnosis

Facts and Falsehoods Although hypnosis was historically linked with quackery, it has more recently become the subject of serious research. Psychologists now agree that hypnosis is a state of heightened suggestibility to which people are subject to varying degrees; that although hypnotic procedures may help someone to recall something, the hypnotist's beliefs frequently work their way into the subject's recollections; that hypnotized people cannot be made to act against their will any more than nonhypnotized people can; that hypnosis can be at least temporarily therapeutic; and that hypnotizable people can enjoy significant pain relief.

Is Hypnosis an Altered State of Consciousness? There is debate, however, on whether hypnosis is a by-product of normal social and cognitive processes or whether it is an altered state of consciousness, perhaps involving a dissociation between levels of consciousness.

Drugs and Consciousness

Psychoactive drugs, including depressants, stimulants, and hallucinogens, also alter consciousness. Drugs often trigger negative aftereffects that oppose and offset their temporary pleasure.

Depressants Alcohol, barbiturates, and the opiates act by depressing neural functioning. Each offers its pleasures, but at the cost of impaired memory and self-awareness or other physical consequences.

Stimulants Caffeine, nicotine, the amphetamines, and cocaine act by stimulating neural functioning. As with nearly all psychoactive drugs, they act at the synapses by influencing the brain's neurotransmitters, and their effects depend on dosage and the user's personality and expectations.

Hallucinogens LSD and marijuana can distort the user's judgments of time and, depending on the setting, can alter sensations and perceptions.

Influences on Drug Use Drug use among teenagers and young adults declined during the 1980's, as attitudes changed. Nevertheless, psychological factors (such as stress, depression, and hopelessness) and social factors (such as peer pressure) combine to lead many people to experiment with—and become dependent on—drugs. Some people also appear to have a greater biological susceptibility to dependence on drugs such as alcohol.

Near-Death Experiences

About one-third of those who have survived a brush with death, such as through cardiac arrest, later recall visionary near-death experiences. Dualists interpret these experiences as evidence of human immortality, while monists point out that reports of such experiences closely parallel reports of hallucinations.

Terms and Concepts to Remember

consciousness Selective attention to ongoing perceptions, thoughts, and feelings.

selective attention The focusing of conscious awareness on a particular stimulus, as in the cocktail party effect.

circadian rhythm [ser-KEY-dee-an] The biological clock; regular bodily rhythms (for example, of temperature and wakefulness) that occur on a 24-hour cycle.

REM sleep Rapid eye movement sleep, a recurring sleep stage during which vivid dreams commonly occur. Also known as *paradoxical sleep*, because the muscles are relaxed (except for minor twitches) but other body systems are active.

alpha waves The relatively slow brain waves of a relaxed, awake state.

hallucinations False sensory experiences, such as seeing something without any external visual stimulus.

delta waves The large, slow brain waves associated with deep sleep.

insomnia A sleep disorder involving recurring problems in falling or staying asleep.

narcolepsy A sleep disorder characterized by uncontrollable sleep attacks in which the sufferer lapses directly into REM sleep, often at inopportune times.

sleep apnea A sleep disorder characterized by temporary cessations of breathing during sleep and consequent momentary reawakenings.

night terrors A sleep disorder characterized by high arousal and an appearance of being terrified; unlike nightmares, night terrors occur during Stage 4 sleep, within 2 or 3 hours of falling asleep, and are seldom remembered.

manifest content According to Freud, the remembered story line of a dream (as distinct from its latent content).

latent content According to Freud, the underlying but censored meaning of a dream (as distinct from its manifest content). Freud believed that a dream's latent content functions as a safety valve.

REM rebound The tendency for REM sleep to increase following REM sleep deprivation (created by repeated awakenings during REM sleep).

fantasy-prone personality Someone who imagines and recalls experiences with lifelike vividness and who spends considerable time fantasizing.

hypnosis An apparently heightened suggestibility in which some people narrow their focus of attention and claim to experience imaginary happenings as if they were real.

posthypnotic amnesia Supposed inability to recall what one experienced during hypnosis, induced by the hypnotist's suggestion.

age regression In hypnosis, the supposed reliving of earlier experiences, such as in early childhood; greatly susceptible to false recollections.

posthypnotic suggestion A suggestion, made during a hypnosis session, to be carried out after the subject is no longer hypnotized; used by some clinicians to help control undesired symptoms and behaviors.

dissociation A split in consciousness, which allows some thoughts and behaviors to occur simultaneously with others.

hidden observer Hilgard's term describing a hypnotized subject's awareness of experiences, such as pain, that go unreported during hypnosis.

psychoactive drug A chemical substance that alters mood and perceptions.

tolerance The diminishing of a drug's effect with regular use of the same dose, requiring the user to take larger and larger doses before experiencing the drug's effect.

withdrawal The discomfort and distress that follow the discontinued use of addictive drugs.

physical dependence A physiological need for a drug, with unpleasant withdrawal symptoms when discontinued.

psychological dependence A psychological need to use a drug, such as to relieve negative emotions.

depressants Drugs (such as alcohol, barbiturates, and opiates) that reduce neural activity and slow body functions.

stimulants Drugs (such as caffeine, nicotine, and the more powerful amphetamines and cocaine) that excite neural activity and speed up body functions.

hallucinogens Psychedelic ("mind-manifesting") drugs, such as LSD, that distort perceptions and evoke sensory images in the absence of sensory input.

barbiturates Drugs that depress the activity of the central nervous system, reducing anxiety, but impairing memory and judgment.

opiates Opium and its derivatives, such as morphine and heroin; they depress neural activity, temporarily lessening pain and anxiety.

amphetamines Drugs that stimulate neural activity, causing speeded-up body functions and associated energy and mood changes.

LSD (lysergic acid diethylamide) A powerful hallucinogenic drug; also known as *acid*.

THC The major active ingredient in marijuana; triggers a variety of effects, including mild hallucinations.

near-death experience An altered state of consciousness reported after a close brush with death (such as through cardiac arrest); often similar to drug-induced hallucinations.

dualism The presumption that mind and body are two distinct entities that interact.

monism The presumption that mind and body are different aspects of the same thing.

For Further Information

You can find further information in this text regarding drugs on the following pages:

Addiction, explained, p. 400

Alcohol and aggression, p. 569

Alcohol and memory, p. 269

Alcoholism treatment, pp. 232, 489

Drugs and the fetus, p. 65

Drug therapies, pp. 502–504

Smoking (nicotine), pp. 534–537

For Further Reading

Consciousness

Wallace, B., & Fisher, L. E. (1991). *Consciousness and behavior* (3rd ed.). Boston: Allyn & Bacon.

A useful, in-depth overview of the psychology of consciousness and its altered states.

Sleep and Dreams

Coleman, R. (1987). *Wide awake at 3 A.M.* New York: Freeman.

The latest applications of sleep research in business, industry, and even in the Olympics, with practical hints on identifying sleep disorders, coping with jet lag, and simply getting a better night's sleep.

Dement, W. C. (1978). *Some must watch while some must sleep.* New York: Norton.

A highly readable paperback that surveys sleep disorders as well as normal sleeping and dreaming.

Hobson, J. A. (1988). *The dreaming brain.* New York: Basic Books.

A provocative analysis of dreaming, drawing on both psychology and neurobiology.

Horne, J. (1988). *Why we sleep: The functions of sleep in humans and other mammals.* Oxford: Oxford University Press.

An insightful overview of what we know about sleep.

Hypnosis

Spanos, N. P., & Chaves, J. F. (1989). *Hypnosis: The cognitive-behavioral perspective.* Buffalo: Prometheus Books.

A survey of ingenious testing procedures for getting at the truth about what hypnosis is and how it affects people.

Zilbergeld, B., Edelstien, M. G., & Araoz, D. L. (1986). *Hypnosis: Questions and answers.* New York: Norton.

Here 85 experts answer 78 questions, from "Are stage hypnotists really doing hypnosis?" to "Can hypnosis enhance athletic performance?"

Drugs

Ray, O. (1986). *Drugs, society, and human behavior* (4th ed.). St. Louis: Mosby.

A thorough textbook introduction to the physical and psychological effects of psychoactive drugs.

Siegel, R. K. (1990). *Intoxication.* New York: Pocket Books.

A guide to intoxicants, how animals and people use them, and with what effects.

Snyder, S. H. (1986). *Drugs and the brain.* New York: Scientific American Library.

An authoritative and beautifully illustrated summary of how psychoactive drugs, both therapeutic and illicit, affect the brain.

Part Four

Learning and Thinking

A central focus in psychology is how we learn, retain, and use information. Chapter 8, Learning, describes three fundamental types of learning and suggests how they influence our emotions and behavior and how we can use them to our benefit. Chapter 9, Memory, examines the process by which we take in, store, and retrieve information, and the factors that sometimes cause us to forget. Chapter 10, Thinking and Language, points out the efficient (though some-times error-prone) ways in which we make judgments and decisions, and discusses how we use language to communicate. Chapter 11, Intelligence, recounts the history of attempts to define and assess intelligence, and tackles head on a controversial issue: What role do genes and environment play in determining dif-ferences in intelligence scores between individuals and between racial groups?

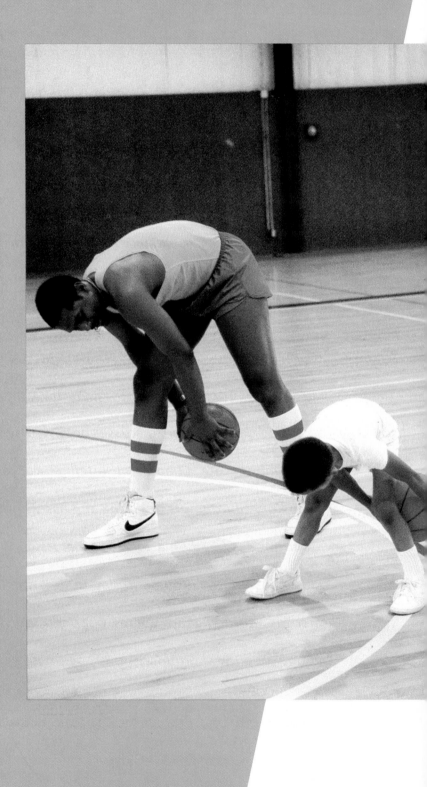

Learning

When a chinook salmon first emerges from its egg in the gravel bed of a stream, its genes provide many of the behavioral instructions it needs for life. It instinctively knows how and where to swim, what to eat, and how to protect itself from predators. Following this built-in plan, the young salmon soon begins a trek to the sea. After some 4 years in the ocean, instinct drives the mature salmon back to its birthplace. It navigates hundreds of miles to the mouth of its home river and then, guided by the scent of its home stream, begins an upstream odyssey to its ancestral spawning ground. Once there, the salmon seeks out the exact conditions of temperature, gravel, and water flow that will maximize the success of its breeding, and then mates.

Unlike the salmon, we are not born with a genetic blueprint for life. Much of what we do we must learn from experience. Although we must struggle to find the life direction a salmon is born with, our learning gives us vastly more flexibility. We can learn how to build igloos or grass huts or underwater air chambers and thereby adapt to almost any environment. Indeed, nature's most important gift to us may be our *adaptability*— our capacity to learn new behaviors that enable us to cope with ever-changing circumstances.

No topic is closer to the heart of psychology than **learning**, *a relatively permanent change in an organism's behavior due to experience*. In earlier chapters we considered the learning of moral ideas, of self-concept, of visual perceptions. In later chapters we will consider how learning shapes our thought and language, our motivations and emotions, our personalities and attitudes.

Learning in all such realms breeds hope. What is learnable we can potentially teach—a fact that encourages parents, educators, athletic coaches, and animal trainers. What has been learned we can potentially change by new learning—an assumption that underlies counseling, psychotherapy, and rehabilitation. No matter how unhappy, unsuccessful, or unloving we are, that need not be the end of our story. Of all the world's creatures, we humans are the most capable of changing our behavior through learning.

By definition, experience is key to learning. More than 200 years ago, philosophers such as John Locke and David Hume echoed Aristotle's conclusion from 2000 years earlier: We learn by association. Our minds naturally connect events that occur in sequence:

"Actually, sex just isn't that important to me."
© 1984 by Sidney Harris; American Scientist Magazine.

"Learning is the eye of the mind."
Thomas Drake
Bibliotheca Scholastica
Instructissima, 1633

We *associate* them. If, after seeing and smelling freshly baked bread, you eat some and find it satisfying, then the next time you see and smell fresh bread, your experience will lead you to expect that eating some will be satisfying again. And if you associate a sound with a frightening consequence, then your fear may be aroused by the sound itself. As one 4-year-old exclaimed after watching a TV character get mugged, "If I had heard that music, I wouldn't have gone around the corner!" (Wells, 1981).

Simple animals can learn simple associations. If disturbed by a squirt of water, the sea snail *Aplysia* will protectively withdraw its gill. If the squirts continue, as happens naturally in choppy water, the withdrawal response diminishes. (The snail "habituates.") But if the sea snail repeatedly receives a shock just after being squirted, its withdrawal response to the squirt alone becomes stronger. Somehow the animal learns to associate the squirt with the impending shock. More complex animals can learn more complex associations, especially those that bring favorable consequences. Sea lions in an aquarium will repeat behaviors, such as slapping and barking, that prompt people to toss them food. Very complex animals, such as chimpanzees, can learn behaviors by merely observing others perform them. We humans can learn in all these ways, and through language we can learn things we have neither experienced nor observed.

All these ways of learning enable us to adapt to our environments. As this chapter will explain, we learn to expect and prepare for significant events such as food or pain— a basic type of learning called *classical conditioning*. We also learn to repeat acts that bring good results and to avoid acts that bring bad results — a type of learning called *operant conditioning*. And by watching others, we gain new behaviors indirectly– a phenomenon called *observational learning*.

Discovering the laws underlying such learning became one of psychology's early goals. A century ago, studies focused on people's subjective, introspective reports of their inner mental processes. Early in this century, psychologist John B. Watson (1913) urged psychologists to discard reference to inner thoughts, feelings, and motives. Forget the mind, said Watson. Psychology should instead study how organisms respond to stimuli in their environments. "Its theoretical goal is the prediction and control of behavior. Introspection forms no essential part of its methods." Simply said, psychology should be an objective science of *behavior*. This view, called **behaviorism**, influenced American psychology during the first half of this century. American academic culture, with its concerns for scientific objectivity and for the created equality of all, proved fertile soil for the new behaviorism.

This boy is experiencing classically conditioned apprehension. Because of previous negative experiences in the dentist chair, he has learned to expect discomfort there.

Psychology's "factual and theoretical developments in this century—which have changed the study of mind and behavior as radically as genetics changed the study of heredity—have all been the product of objective analysis—that is to say, behavioristic analysis."
Psychologist D. O. Hebb (1980)

Classical Conditioning

Although the idea of learning by association generated much discussion, it was not until the twentieth century that it was verified by some of psychology's most famous research. For many people, the name Ivan Pavlov rings a bell. His experiments are classics, and the phenomenon he explored we justly call **classical** (or *Pavlovian*) **conditioning**.

Pavlov's Experiments

Pavlov was driven by a lifelong passion for research. After receiving a medical degree at age 33, he spent the next two decades studying the digestive system, work that earned him Russia's first Nobel prize in 1904. But it was the novel work to which he devoted the last three decades of his life, up to his death at age 86, that earned this feisty scientist his place in history.

Pavlov's new direction came when his creative mind seized on an incidental finding. After studying salivary secretion in dogs, he knew that when he put food in a dog's mouth the animal would invariably salivate. He also noticed that when he worked with the same dog repeatedly, the dog salivated to food-related stimuli— to the mere sight of the food, to the food dish, to the person who regularly brought the food, or even to the sound of that person's approaching footsteps. Because these "psychic secretions" interfered with his experiments on digestion, Pavlov considered them an annoyance—until he realized they pointed to a simple but important form of learning. From that time on, Pavlov studied learning, which he hoped might enable him to understand better the workings of the brain.

At first, Pavlov and his assistants tried to imagine what the dog was thinking and feeling as it drooled in anticipation of the food. This only got them into fruitless debates. So to attack the phenomenon more objectively, they experimented. They paired various neutral stimuli with food in the mouth to see if the dog would begin salivating to the neutral stimuli alone. To eliminate the possible influence of extraneous stimuli, they isolated the dog in a small room, secured it in a harness, and attached a device that diverted its saliva to a measuring instrument (Figure 8–1). From an adjacent room they could present food— at first by sliding in a food bowl, later by blowing meat powder into the dog's mouth at a precise moment. If a neutral stimulus— something the dog could see or hear— now regularly signaled the arrival of food, would the dog eventually begin salivating to the neutral stimulus alone?

The answer proved to be yes. Just before placing food in the dog's mouth to produce salivation, Pavlov would sound a tone. After several pairings of tone and food, the dogs began salivating to the tone alone in anticipation of the meat powder. Using this procedure, Pavlov conditioned a dog to salivate to other stimuli—a buzzer, a light, a touch on the leg, even the sight of a circle.

Now for some necessary terminology: Pavlov called the salivation in response to food in the mouth an **unconditioned response (UCR)** because the response is not conditional upon the dog's previous experience (Figure 8–2, page 230). Food in the mouth automatically, unconditionally, triggers a dog's salivary reflex. It is an innate, or *unlearned*, response. Because food always has this effect, Pavlov called it an **unconditioned stimulus (UCS)**.

Salivation in response to the tone is conditional upon the dog's learning the association between the tone and the food. This learned response we therefore call the **conditioned response (CR)**. The previously neutral tone stimulus that now triggers the conditional salivation is called the **conditioned stimulus (CS)**. You can distinguish between these two kinds of stimuli and responses by remembering that *conditioned* = learned, and *unconditioned* = *un*learned.

Ivan Pavlov (1927): "Experimental investigation . . . should lay a solid foundation for a future true science of psychology."

Figure 8–1 Pavlov's device for recording salivation. The isolated dog's saliva was collected drop by drop in a tube. Food was delivered by remote control, and, through a window, the experimenter observed the dog. (Adapted from Goodwin, 1990.)

Remember:
UCS = UnConditioned Stimulus
UCR = UnConditioned Response
CS = Conditioned Stimulus
CR = Conditioned Response

BEFORE CONDITIONING

UCS (food in mouth) → UCR (salivation)

Neutral stimulus (tone) → No salivation

An unconditioned stimulus (UCS) produces an unconditioned response (UCR). A neutral stimulus produces no response.

DURING CONDITIONING

Neutral stimulus (tone) + UCS (food in mouth) → UCR (salivation)

The unconditioned stimulus is presented just after a neutral stimulus. The unconditioned stimulus continues to produce an unconditioned response.

AFTER CONDITIONING

CS (tone) → CR (salivation)

The neutral stimulus now produces a conditioned response (CR), thereby becoming a conditioned stimulus (CS).

If the experiment was so simple, what did Pavlov do for the next three decades? He and his associates explored the causes and effects of classical conditioning. Their research identified five major conditioning processes: acquisition, extinction, spontaneous recovery, generalization, and discrimination.

Acquisition Regarding the **acquisition**, or initial learning, of the response, there was first a question of timing: How much time should elapse between presenting the neutral stimulus (the tone, the light, the touch, or whatever) and the unconditioned stimulus? Not much. With many species and procedures, half a second works well. This finding fits the presumption that classical conditioning is biologically adaptive: It helps organisms *prepare* for good or bad events that are about to occur. Because there is no need to prepare for events that have already occurred, acquisition typically does not occur when the neutral stimulus comes after the UCS. When, however, the neutral stimulus comes first, signaling a significant event — say, when the sound of a snapping twig repeatedly precedes danger for a deer — it becomes a CS, and the deer flees more and more rapidly in anticipation of what often follows.

Michael Domjan and his colleagues (1986) showed how this works with male Japanese quail. The researchers turned on a red light before presenting an approachable female. Over time, the quail developed a liking for their cage's red light district. Moreover, when the red light heralded a female's impending arrival, the excited male quail began copulating with her more quickly.

In humans, too, objects, smells, and sights associated with sexual pleasure become conditioned stimuli for sexual arousal (page 368). Psychologist Michael Tirrell (1990) recalls: "My first girlfriend loved onions, so I came to associate onion breath with kissing. Before long, onion breath sent tingles up and down my spine. Oh what a feeling!" (Question: What is the unconditioned stimulus here?)

Figure 8–2 Pavlov's classic experiment. By presenting a neutral stimulus — the sound of a tone — just before an unconditioned stimulus (UCS) — food in mouth — the neutral stimulus became a conditioned stimulus (CS). The CS now triggers a conditioned response (CR) — salivation.

Check yourself: If the aroma of brownies baking sets your mouth to watering, what is the UCS? the CS? the CR? (See page 233.)

UCS (female in heat) → UCR (sexual arousal)

CS (red light) → CR (sexual arousal)

The quail's sexual conditioning. As in Figure 8–2, the top row indicates *before* conditioning, and the bottom row *during* conditioning.

Extinction and Spontaneous Recovery After conditioning, what happens if the CS occurs repeatedly without the UCS? Will the CS continue to elicit the CR? Pavlov found that when he sounded the tone again and again without presenting food, the dogs salivated less and less. This decline of a CR in the absence of a UCS is called **extinction**. However, Pavlov also found that if he allowed several hours to elapse before sounding the tone again, the CR (salivation) to the tone would reappear (Figure 8–3). This **spontaneous recovery**—the reappearance of a (weakened) CR after a rest pause—suggested to Pavlov that extinction was suppressing the CR rather than eliminating it.

Figure 8–3 Idealized curve of acquisition, extinction, and spontaneous recovery. The rising curve shows that the CR rapidly grows stronger as the CS and UCS are repeatedly paired (acquisition), then wanes as the CS is presented alone (extinction), but reappears after a rest pause (spontaneous recovery).

| Acquisition trials (CS paired with UCS) | Extinction trials (CS alone) | Pause | More extinction trials (CS alone) |

After breaking up with his fire-breathing heartthrob, Tirrell experienced extinction and spontaneous recovery. He recalls that "the smell of onion breath, no longer paired with the unconditioned stimulus (kissing), lost its ability to shiver my timbers. Occasionally, though, after not sensing the aroma for a long while, smelling onion breath awakens a small version of the emotional response I once felt."

Generalization Pavlov and his students noticed that a dog conditioned to the sound of one tone also responded somewhat to the sound of a different tone or even to a buzzer never paired with food. Likewise, a dog conditioned to salivate when rubbed would also salivate some when scratched (Windholz, 1989), or when stimulated on a different body part (Figure 8–4). This tendency to respond to stimuli similar to the CS is called **generalization**. Generalization can be adaptive, as when toddlers taught to fear moving cars in the street respond similarly to trucks and motorcycles.

Because of generalization, stimuli that are similar to naturally disgusting or appealing objects will, by association, evoke some disgust or liking. Normally desirable foods, such as fudge, are unappealing when presented in a disgusting form, as when shaped to resemble dog feces (Rozin & others, 1986). We perceive adults with childlike facial features (round face, large forehead, small chin, large eyes) as having childlike warmth, submissiveness, and naiveté (Berry & McArthur, 1986). In both cases, people's emotional reactions to one stimulus generalize to similar stimuli.

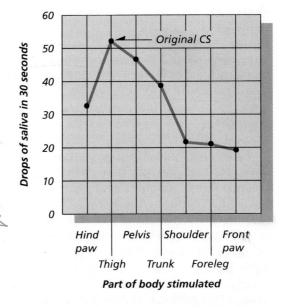

Figure 8–4 Generalization. Pavlov demonstrated generalization after attaching miniature vibrators to various parts of a dog's body. After conditioning salivation to stimulation of the thigh, he stimulated other body areas. The closer they were to the original site of stimulation, the stronger the conditioned response. (Data from Pavlov, 1927.)

Discrimination Pavlov's dogs also learned to respond to the sound of a particular tone and *not* to other tones. This learned ability to *distinguish* between conditioned stimuli and similar but irrelevant stimuli is **discrimination**. Like generalization, discrimination has survival value. Slightly different stimuli are at times followed by vastly different consequences. Being able to recognize these differences is adaptive. Confronted by a pit bull, your heart may race; confronted by a cocker spaniel, it does not.

Updating Pavlov's Understanding

Pavlov and Watson's disdain for "mentalistic" concepts such as consciousness has given way to a growing realization that they underestimated the importance of cognitive processes (thoughts, perceptions, expectations) and of biological constraints on an organism's capacity for learning.

Cognitive Processes The early behaviorists believed that the learned behaviors of various organisms could be reduced to universal stimulus-response mechanisms. As recently as 30 years ago, the idea that rats and dogs exhibit important cognitive appraisals struck many psychologists as silly, but no longer. Classical conditioning experiments by Robert Rescorla and Allan Wagner (1972) revealed that animals act as if they mentally associate one event with another, especially if the second event is significant and if the first event *predicts* it. What matters is not how *often* an electric shock, say, follows a tone, but how predictably. The more predictable the association, the stronger the conditioned response.

It's as if the animal learns an *expectancy*, an awareness of how likely it is that the UCS will follow the CS. Rescorla (1988) surmises that classical conditioning "is not a stupid process by which the organism willy-nilly forms associations between any two stimuli that happen to occur." Rather, the organism is an information seeker, using relations among events to form its own adaptive representation of the world. Indeed, says Rescorla, a simple rule of thumb summarizes a host of facts about classical conditioning: Conditioning occurs best when the CS and UCS have just the sort of relationship that would lead a scientist to conclude that the CS *causes* the UCS.

This analysis helps to explain why classical conditioning treatments that ignore cognitive appraisals are often not completely successful. When, for therapeutic purposes, alcoholics are given alcohol spiked with a nauseating drug, will they always associate alcohol with sickness? If classical conditioning were merely a matter of "stamping in" stimulus-response associations, we might hope so. To some extent, this does occur (as we will see on page 489). However, alcoholics are aware that they can blame their nausea on the drug rather than the alcohol. This cognition often weakens the association between alcohol and sickness. So, even in classical conditioning, it is not only the simple stimulus-response association but also the thought that counts.

Biological Predispositions Ever since Darwin, most scientists have assumed that animals share a common evolutionary history, as well as the resulting commonalities in their make-up and functioning. Pavlov and Watson, for example, believed the basic laws of learning were essentially similar in all animals. So it should make little difference whether one studied rats, pigeons, or people.

Moreover, it seemed that any natural response could be conditioned to any neutral stimulus. As learning researcher Gregory Kimble proclaimed in 1956, "just about any activity of which the organism is capable can be conditioned and . . . these responses can be conditioned to any stimulus that the organism can perceive" (p. 195).

Twenty-five years later, Kimble (1981) humbly acknowledged that "half a thousand" scientific reports had proven him wrong. More than the early behaviorists realized, an animal's capacity for conditioning is constrained by its biology. The biological predispositions of each species dispose it to learn the particular associations that enhance its survival.

The person most responsible for challenging the prevailing behaviorist view was John Garcia. While researching the effects of radiation on laboratory animals, Garcia and Robert Koelling (1966) noticed that rats began to avoid drinking water from the plastic bottles in the radiation chambers. They wondered whether classical conditioning might be the culprit. Might the rats have linked the plastic-tasting water (a CS) to the sickness (UCR) induced by the radiation (UCS)?

To test their hunch, Garcia and Koelling gave the rats a particular taste, sight, or sound and later nauseated them with radiation or drugs. Two startling findings emerged: First, even if sickened as late as several hours after tasting a particular flavor, the rats thereafter avoided that flavor. This violated the notion that for conditioning to occur, the UCS must follow the CS immediately.

Second, the sickened rats developed aversions to the tastes but not to the sights or sounds. This contradicted the behaviorists' idea that any perceivable stimulus could serve as a CS. But it made adaptive sense, because for rats taste is a more valuable cue than sight. Birds, which hunt by sight, are biologically primed to develop aversions to the *sight* of tainted food (Nicolaus & others, 1983). Humans, too, are biologically prepared to learn some things rather than others. We more readily learn to fear snakes and spiders than to fear flowers (Cook & others, 1986). It makes sense: Such animals harm us more frequently than do flowers. We learn an aversion to alcohol better by associating its taste with nausea than with something unrelated to consumption such as electric shock. All these cases support Darwin's principle that natural selection favors traits that aid survival. Nature prepares each species to learn those things crucial to its survival.

The philosopher Schopenhauer once said that important ideas are first ridiculed, then attacked, and finally taken for granted. So it was with Garcia's findings on taste aversion. At first, the leading journals refused to publish his work. The findings were impossible, said some critics. But as often happens in science, Garcia's provocative findings stimulated new research, which in this case confirmed and extended his surprising findings to other species. For example, when coyotes are tempted into eating sheep carcasses laced with a sickening poison, they will develop an aversion to sheep meat (Gustavson & others, 1974). Research on taste aversion suggests ways other than extermination for controlling predators and agricultural pests. (This is but one instance in which psychological research that began with the discomfort of some laboratory animals enhanced the welfare of many more animals —in this case, saving both the sheep from the coyotes and the coyotes from angry ranchers and farmers, who, with their livestock no longer endangered, were less adamant about destroying the coyotes.)

Answer to questions on page 230: Brownies (and their taste) are the UCS. The associated aroma is the CS. Salivation to the aroma is the CR.

Saving coyotes by making them sick. When coyotes were fed poisoned lamb meat, the poison (UCS) made them sick (UCR). As a result, they developed an aversion (CR) to the lamb (CS) and returned to feeding on their natural prey.

Have such results compelled researchers to abandon the search for universal principles of learning that generalize across species? No, biological predispositions affirm a deeper principle: *Learning enables animals to adapt to their environments*. Adaptation shows us why animals would be responsive to stimuli that announce significant events, such as food or pain. Animals are predisposed to associate a CS with a UCS that follows predictably and immediately, for causes often immediately precede effects.

Adaptation also helps explain exceptions such as the taste-aversion finding. In this case, cause need not precede effect immediately—bad food usually causes sickness quite a while after it has been consumed. Similarly, cancer patients who suffer nausea and vomiting beginning more than an hour following chemotherapy often develop classically conditioned nausea to stimuli associated with taking the drug. Merely returning to the clinic or seeing the nurses can provoke sick feelings (Burish & Carey, 1986).

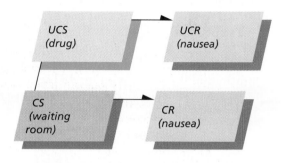

Nausea conditioning.

Pavlov's Legacy

What, then, remains of Pavlov's ideas about conditioning? A great deal. All the researchers we have met so far in this chapter agree that classical conditioning, though constrained by cognitive processes and biological predispositions, is an important kind of learning. Judged by today's knowledge, Pavlov's ideas were incomplete. But if we see further than Pavlov did, it is in large measure because we stand on his shoulders.

Why is Pavlov's work so important? Had he taught us only that old dogs can learn new tricks, his experiments would have long ago been forgotten. Why should anyone care that a dog can be conditioned to drool at the sound of a tone? The importance lies first in this fact: Many other responses to many other stimuli can be classically conditioned in many other organisms—in fact, in every species tested, from worms to fish to dogs to monkeys to people (Schwartz, 1984). Thus, classical conditioning is one way that virtually all organisms learn to adapt to their environment.

Second, Pavlov showed us how a significant internal process such as learning can be studied objectively. Pavlov was proud that his methods involved virtually no subjective judgments or guesses about what went on in the dogs' minds. The salivary response is an overt behavior measurable as so many drops or cubic centimeters of saliva. Pavlov's success therefore suggested a scientific model for how the young discipline of psychology might proceed—by isolating the elementary building blocks of complex behaviors and studying them with objective laboratory procedures.

Applications of Classical Conditioning In later chapters on motivation, emotion, psychological disorders, therapy, and health we will see how Pavlov's principles of classical conditioning apply to human health and well-being. For example, former crack users often feel a craving when they again encounter cues (people, places) associated with previous highs. Thus, drug addicts are advised to steer clear of settings associated with the euphoria of previous drug use. And alcoholics are given experiences that reverse their associations with alcohol (page 489). Classical conditioning even works upon the body's disease-fighting immune system. When, say, a par-

John B. Watson (1924): "Give me a dozen healthy infants, well-formed, and my own specified world to bring them up in and I'll guarantee to take any one at random and train him to become any type of specialist I might select—doctor, lawyer, artist, merchant-chief and, yes, even beggar-man and thief, regardless of his talents, penchants, tendencies, abilities, vocations, and race of his ancestors."

Close-Up   *Rape as Fear Conditioning*

"A burnt child dreads the fire," says a medieval proverb. Experiments with dogs reveal that, indeed, if a painful stimulus is sufficiently powerful, a single event is sometimes enough to traumatize the animal when it again faces the situation. The human counterparts to these experiments can be tragic, as illustrated by one young woman's experience of being attacked and raped, and thereby conditioned to a life of fear. Her fear (CR) is most powerfully associated with particular locations and people (CS), but it generalizes to other places and people. Note, too, how her traumatic experience has robbed her of the normally relaxing associations with such stimuli as home and bed.

Four months ago I was raped. In the middle of the night I awoke to the sound of someone outside my bedroom. Thinking my housemate was coming home, I called out her name. Someone began walking slowly toward me, and then I realized. I screamed and fought, but there were two of them. One held my legs, while the other put a hand over my mouth and a knife to my throat and *said, "Shut up, bitch, or we'll kill you." Never have I been so terrified and helpless. They both raped me, one brutally. As they then searched my room for money and valuables, my housemate came home. They brought her into my room, raped her, and left us both tied up on my bed.*

We never slept another night in that apartment. We were too terrified. Still, when I go to bed at night—always with the bedroom light left on—the memory of them entering my room repeats itself endlessly. I was an independent person who had lived alone or with other young women for four years; now I can't even think about spending a night alone. When I drive by our old apartment, or when I have to go into an empty house, my heart pounds and I sweat. I am afraid of strangers, especially men, and the more they resemble my attackers the more I fear them. My housemate shares many of my fears, and is frightened when entering our new apartment. I'm afraid to stay in the same town, I'm afraid it will happen again, I'm afraid to go to bed. I dread falling asleep.

ticular taste accompanies a drug that influences immune responses, the taste by itself may come to produce an immune response (page 523).

Pavlov's work provided a basis for John Watson's idea that human behavior, though biologically influenced, is also a bundle of conditioned responses. In one famous though ethically troublesome study, Watson and Rosalie Rayner (1920; Harris, 1979) showed how specific fears might be conditioned. Their subject was an 11-month-old infant named Albert. "Little Albert," like most infants, feared loud noises, but not white rats. So Watson and Rayner presented him with a white rat and, as he reached to touch it, struck a hammer against a steel bar just behind his head. After seven repetitions of seeing the rat and then hearing the frightening noise, Albert burst into tears at the mere sight of the rat. What is more, 5 days later Albert showed generalization of his conditioned response by reacting with fear when presented with a rabbit, a dog, and a sealskin coat, but not to dissimilar objects such as toys.

Although some psychologists had difficulty repeating these findings with other children, Watson and Rayner's work with Little Albert has had legendary significance for many psychologists. Some have wondered if each of us might not be a walking repository of conditioned emotions. Might our less adaptive emotions be controlled by the application of extinction procedures or by conditioning new responses to emotion-arousing stimuli? In Chapter 16, Therapy, we will see how psychologists use behavioral techniques to treat emotional disorders.

Psychologist Gregory Razran (1940) found that associating political slogans (a CS) with the eating of food (a UCS) made people more approving of them. Similarly, advertisers like to associate their products with naturally pleasing images, such as sexually appealing models.

Little Albert's conditioning.

Operant Conditioning

Classical conditioning links neutral stimuli with simple, involuntary responses. How then do we learn complex, voluntary behaviors? It's one thing to teach an animal to salivate at the sound of a tone or a child to fear cars in the street, and quite another to teach an elephant to walk on its hind legs or a child to learn arithmetic. Another type of conditioning explains — and trains — such behaviors. Through **operant conditioning** a subject becomes more likely to repeat rewarded (reinforced) behaviors and less likely to repeat punished behaviors.

Through operant conditioning, these pigs have learned that their running around the racetrack will be rewarded with cookies.

   Classical and operant conditioning both involve acquisition, extinction, spontaneous recovery, generalization, and discrimination. Yet their difference is straightforward: Classical conditioning involves **respondent behavior**—reflexive behavior that occurs as an automatic *response* to some stimulus (such as Pavlov's meat powder and tone). Operant conditioning involves voluntary (nonreflexive) action, called **operant behavior** because the act *operates* on the environment to produce rewarding or punishing stimuli.

   We can therefore distinguish classical from operant conditioning by asking: Does the controlling stimulus come before or after the response? In classical conditioning, it comes before, no matter what the organism is doing, as when the tone elicits salivation. In operant conditioning, the controlling stimulus, a reinforcer or punisher, comes after. This consequence is *contingent* on the animal's behavior, as when a dog performs a trick and obtains food.

Respondent behavior responds *to stimuli.*
Operant behavior operates *to produce stimuli.*

~~Skinner~~'s Experiments

B. F. ~~Skinner~~ (1904–1990) was a college English major and aspiring writer who, seeking a new direction, entered graduate school in psychology and went on to become modern behaviorism's most influential and controversial figure. Skinner's work elaborated a simple fact of life that turn-of-the-century psychologist Edward L. Thorndike called the *law of effect*: Rewarded behavior is likely to recur. Using Thorndike's law of effect as a starting point, Skinner developed a "behavioral technology" that enabled him to teach pigeons such unpigeonlike behaviors as walking in a figure 8, playing Ping-Pong, and keeping a "guided missile" on course by pecking at a moving target displayed on a screen.

For his pioneering studies with rats and later with pigeons, Skinner designed the now famous **Skinner box** (Figure 8–5). The "box" is typically a soundproof chamber with a bar or key that an animal presses or pecks to release a food or water reward, and with a device that records these responses. Experiments by Skinner and other operant researchers did far more than teach us how to pull habits out of a rat. They explored the precise conditions that foster efficient and enduring learning.

Shaping In his experiments, Skinner used **shaping**, a procedure in which rewards, such as food, guide an animal's natural behavior toward a desired behavior. Imagine that you wanted to condition a rat to press a bar. After observing how the animal naturally behaves before training, you would build on its existing behaviors. You might, for example, give the rat a food reward each time it approaches the bar. Once the rat is approaching regularly, you would require it to move closer before rewarding it; then closer still, and finally to touch the bar before giving it the food. With this method of *successive approximations*, you reward responses that are ever-closer to the final desired behavior and ignore all other responses. In this same way, researchers and animal trainers gradually shape complex behaviors. By shaping nonverbal organisms to discriminate between stimuli, a psychologist can also determine what they perceive. Can a dog distinguish colors? Can a baby discriminate sounds? If we can shape them to respond to one stimulus and not to another, then obviously they can perceive the difference. Experiments show that some animals are remarkably capable of forming concepts, by discriminating between classes of events or objects (Hackenberg & Hineline, 1990). If an experimenter reinforces a pigeon for pecking after seeing a human face, but not after seeing a non-face, the pigeon will learn to recognize faces (Herrnstein & Loveland, 1964). With similar training, pigeons have even been taught to discriminate Bach from Stravinsky selections (Porter & Neuringer, 1984).

Parents may use rewards to shape good table manners by praising eating behavior that is more and more adultlike. This sounds simple. But let's compare the essential features of shaping to what often happens at home and at school. In the shaping procedure, the trainer builds on the individual's existing behaviors by immediately rewarding successively closer approximations of a desired behavior. In everyday life, too, we continually reward and shape the behavior of others, said Skinner, but often unintentionally. Sometimes we even reward offensive behavior. Billy's parents, for example, are annoyed and mystified by his loud whining. But look at how they typically deal with Billy—by rewarding the very behavior they find so annoying:

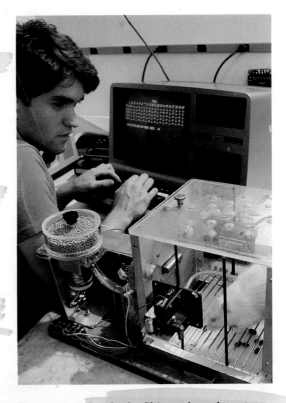

Figure 8–5 Inside the Skinner box, the rat presses a bar for a food reward. Outside, a measuring device records the animal's accumulated responses.

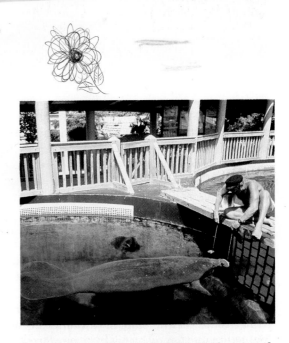

Can a manatee distinguish different shapes and colors? University of Windsor psychologist Dale Woodyard is training this manatee to discriminate between objects of different shapes, colors, and sizes for a food reward. The manatee remembers such lessons for as long as a year.

Billy: *"Could you tie my shoes?"*

Father: *(Continues reading paper.)*

Billy: *"Dad, I need my shoes tied."*

Father: *"Uh, yeah, just a minute."*

Billy: *"DAAAAD! TIE MY SHOES!"*

Father: *"How many times have I told you not to whine? Now, which shoe do we do first?"*

Or compare the way learning psychologists shape behavior—by rewarding small improvements—to the way some teachers use rewards. On a wall chart, the teacher pastes gold stars after the names of children scoring 100 percent on spelling tests. All children take the same tests. As everyone can then see, some children, the academic all-stars, easily get 100 percent. The others, no matter how hard they try or how much they improve, get no reward. Better if the teacher would reward poor spellers for gradual improvement (successive approximations toward their potential) or for doing their best.

Principles of Reinforcement So far, we have referred rather loosely to the power of "rewards." This idea gains a more precise meaning in Skinner's concept of the **reinforcer**, any event that increases the frequency of a response it follows. A reinforcer may be a tangible reward. It may be praise or attention. It may even, noted David Premack (1965), be a preferred activity. Children who prefer operating a pinball machine to eating candy will eat more candy, he found, when reinforced for doing so by a chance to play pinball. Those who'd rather eat candy will play more pinball if such play leads to eating candy. **Premack's principle**—that any activity can be reinforced by a more preferred activity—is used by parents who reinforce teenagers' doing homework by letting them use the car.

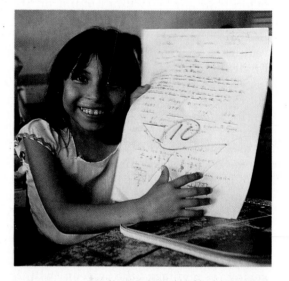

A good score has reinforced this girl for her hard work. She may be reinforced again when she brings this score home to her parents.

Positive and Negative Reinforcers Although most people think of reinforcers as rewards, there actually are two kinds of reinforcers: positive and negative. Positive and negative reinforcers have the same effect; they strengthen behavior.

So, how do they differ? A **positive reinforcer** strengthens a response by presenting a positive stimulus after a response. Food is a positive reinforcer for animals; attention, approval, and money are positive reinforcers for most people. A **negative reinforcer** strengthens a response by reducing or removing an aversive (unpleasant) stimulus. To an animal in an electrified Skinner box, switching off a foot shock is a rewarding event (a negative reinforcer). When someone stops nagging or whining, that, too, is a negative reinforcer.

So imagine that whenever a child throws a tantrum, the parent gives in for the sake of peace and quiet. The child's tantrums will be strengthened by positive reinforcement (the parent gives in). The parent's behavior will be strengthened by negative reinforcement (the child stops screaming). Or imagine a worried student who, after goofing off and getting a bad exam grade, studies harder for the next exam. The student may be negatively reinforced by reduced anxiety and positively reinforced by a better grade. *Remember*: Whether it works by giving something positive or reducing something negative, *a reinforcer always strengthens behavior*.

Note that "positive" means onset—presenting a stimulus. "Negative" means offset—withdrawing a stimulus. All reinforcers strengthen behavior. Thus, the removal of an aversive stimulus (such as nagging) is a reinforcer—a negative reinforcer.

Primary and Secondary Reinforcers **Primary reinforcers**—getting the food or being relieved of the shock—are innately satisfying. We need not learn to like them. **Secondary reinforcers** are learned. They get their power through association with primary reinforcers. If a rat in a ~~Skinner~~ box learns that the sound of a buzzer reliably signals that food is coming, the rat will work to turn on the buzzer. The buzzer has become a secondary reinforcer associated with food. Our lives are filled with secondary reinforcers—money, good grades, a pleasant tone of voice, a word of praise—each of which has been linked with more basic rewards. Secondary reinforcers greatly enhance our ability to influence one another.

Immediate and Delayed Reinforcers Consider a typical shaping experiment. Before performing a "wanted" behavior such as pressing the bar, an animal will engage in a sequence of "unwanted" behaviors—scratching, sniffing, and moving around. Whichever of these behaviors immediately precedes the reinforcer becomes more likely to occur again. If we delay the reinforcer for bar pressing for as long as 30 seconds, allowing other behaviors to intervene and be reinforced, virtually no learning of the bar pressing occurs.

Humans learn to respond to reinforcers that are greatly delayed: the paycheck at the end of the week, the grade at the end of the semester, the trophy at the end of the season. Indeed, to function effectively we *must* learn to postpone immediate rewards for greater long-term rewards. Four-year-old children who in laboratory testing show an ability to delay gratification—who'd sooner have a big reward tomorrow than a small one right now—become more socially competent and high achieving as adolescents (Mischel & others, 1989).

The immediacy of reinforcement does influence many of our behaviors, however. Smokers, alcoholics, and other drug users may know that their immediate pleasure—the kick that often comes within seconds—is more than offset by future punishments and dangers. Still, immediate reinforcement prevails. Likewise, the hour-long enjoyment of staying up to watch another TV show may seem to outweigh the prospect of tomorrow's day-long sluggishness. Unfortunately, we must conclude, immediate reinforcement is often more effective than delayed reinforcement.

Reinforcement Schedules So far, most of our examples assume **continuous reinforcement**: The desired response gets reinforced every time it occurs. Under such conditions, learning occurs rapidly. But when the reinforcement stops—when we disconnect the food delivery chute—extinction also occurs rapidly. The rat soon stops pressing the bar. If a normally dependable candy machine fails to deliver a candy bar twice in a row, we stop putting money into it (although a week later we may exhibit spontaneous recovery by trying again).

In real life, continuous reinforcement is rare. A salesperson does not make a sale with every pitch, nor does an angler get a bite with every cast. But they persist because their efforts have occasionally been rewarded. Researchers have explored several **partial** (or **intermittent**) **reinforcement** schedules in which responses are sometimes reinforced, sometimes not (Nevin, 1988). Initial learning is typically slower with partial reinforcement, which makes continuous reinforcement preferable until a behavior is mastered. But partial reinforcement produces greater persistence—a *resistance to extinction*—than found with continuous reinforce-

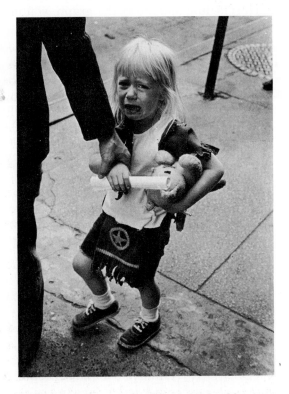

Seneca (4 B.C.–A.D. 65): "The child should gain no request by anger; when he is quiet let him be offered what was refused when he wept."

"The charm of fishing is that it is the pursuit of what is elusive but attainable, a perpetual series of occasions for hope."
Scottish author John Buchan, 1875–1940

ment. Imagine a pigeon that has learned to peck a key to obtain food. When the delivery of food has gradually faded out until it occurred only rarely and unpredictably, pigeons have pecked over 150,000 times without a reward (Skinner, 1953). With partial reinforcement, hope springs eternal.

Corresponding human examples come readily to mind. Slot machines reward gamblers occasionally and unpredictably, and this partial reinforcement affects them much as it affects pigeons: They keep trying, sometimes interminably. There is also a valuable lesson here for parents. *Occasionally* giving in to children's tantrums for the sake of peace and quiet puts the child on a partial reinforcement schedule. That's the very best procedure for making a behavior persist.

Skinner (1961) and his collaborators compared four schedules of partial reinforcement. Some are rigidly fixed, some unpredictably variable. Some are linked to time intervals, some to ratios of response-to-reinforcement. Skinner found that each schedule produces a typical pattern, as seen in Figure 8–6. As you read about each schedule and study the graph, you may be surprised by how familiar you are with its effects.

Fixed-ratio schedules reinforce behavior after a set number of responses. Like people paid on a piecework basis — say, for every 30 pieces — laboratory animals may be reinforced on a fixed ratio of, say, one reinforcer for every 30 responses. Typically, the animal will pause only briefly after a reinforcer and will then return to a high rate of responding. Resting while on a fixed-ratio schedule reduces rewards, and employees often find such arrangements tiring. Unions have therefore pressured employers to replace piecework pay with hourly wage schedules.

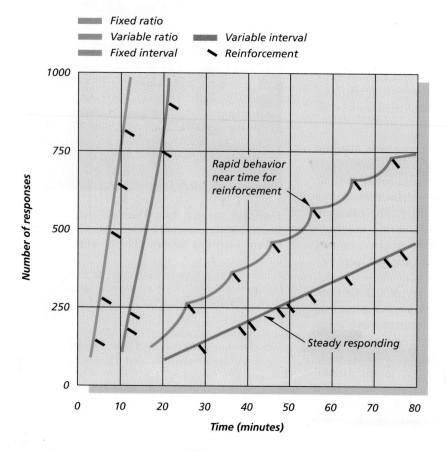

Figure 8–6 Partial reinforcement schedules. Skinner's laboratory pigeons produced these response patterns to each of four reinforcement schedules. For people as for pigeons, reinforcers (hash marks on the graph) linked to responses produce higher response rates. Reinforcers linked to time intervals produce lower response rates than reinforcers linked to either fixed or variable ratio of responses. Fixed schedules produce higher response rates than the related variable schedules. (Adapted from "Teaching Machines" by B. F. Skinner. Copyright © 1961 Scientific American, Inc. All rights reserved.)

Variable-ratio schedules provide reinforcers after an unpredictable number of responses. This is what gamblers experience—reinforcement after an unpredictable number of bets—and what makes gambling behavior so hard to extinguish. Like the fixed-ratio schedule, it produces high rates of responding, because reinforcers increase as the responding increases.

Fixed-interval schedules feature an equal pause after each reinforcer. During this time no reinforcers are available. When the fixed interval ends, the next response is reinforced. Like people checking more frequently for the mail as the delivery time approaches, pigeons on a fixed-interval schedule peck a key more frequently as the anticipated time for reward draws near, producing a choppy start-stop pattern.

Variable-interval schedules reinforce the first response after *varying* time intervals. Like the unpredictable pop quiz that reinforces studying or the "hello" that finally rewards persistence in calling back a busy phone number, variable-interval schedules tend to produce slow, steady responding. This makes sense, because there is no knowing when the waiting will be over. Should the pop quiz become predictable, students will begin the stop-start work pattern that characterizes fixed-interval schedules.

Animal behaviors differ, yet Skinner (1956) contended that these reinforcement principles of operant conditioning are universal. It matters little, he said, what response, what reinforcer, or what species you use. The effect of a given reinforcement schedule is pretty much the same: "Pigeon, rat, monkey, which is which? It doesn't matter. . . . Behavior shows astonishingly similar properties."

Punishment **Punishment** has the opposite effect of reinforcement: A punisher is any consequence that *decreases* the frequency of a behavior that it follows. Swift, strong, and consistent punishers can powerfully restrain unwanted behavior. If punishers are swift and sure, the rat that is shocked after touching the forbidden object and the child who loses a treat after running into the street will learn more quickly not to repeat the behavior.

Nevertheless, punishment has drawbacks. As powerful as punishment can be, punished behavior is not forgotten; it is suppressed. This temporary effect may reinforce the people who administer the punishment. But if the punishment is avoidable, the punished behavior may reappear in safe settings. The child who learns through spankings not to swear around the house may swear elsewhere. The driver who is hit with a couple of tickets for speeding may buy a radar detector and continue to speed freely when no radar patrol is in the area.

Opponents of punishment also say that it increases aggressiveness, by demonstrating aggression as a way to cope with problems. This helps explain why so many aggressive delinquents and abusive parents come from abusive families (Straus & Gelles, 1980). Moreover, punishment can create fear; the person receiving the punishment may associate the fear not only with the undesirable behavior but also with the person who administers it or the situation in which it occurs. Thus, a child may come to fear the punitive teacher and want to avoid school. Worse, when punishments are unpredictable and inescapable, both animals and people may develop the sense that events are beyond their control. As a result, they may come to feel helpless and depressed. (More on "learned helplessness" in later chapters.)

Question: Airline frequent-flyer programs that offer a free flight after every 20,000 miles of travel use which reinforcement schedule? (See page 242.)

Note: **Punishment** *decreases a behavior by delivering an aversive stimulus, or withdrawing a positive stimulus.* **Negative reinforcement** *is rewarding, not punishing. It strengthens behavior by removing an aversive stimulus. Thus, the delivery of shock after a response is a punisher; the termination of shock after a response is a negative reinforcer. Negative reinforcement is perhaps psychology's most often misunderstood concept. Check yourself: Which of the following illustrates negative reinforcement? (See page 245.)*

1. Matt roughs up his football opponent and draws a penalty.

2. To alleviate the discomfort of nicotine deprivation after a flight, Wilma lights up a cigarette.

3. After Hector makes a big sale, his boss takes him out to lunch.

Even when punishment suppresses unwanted behavior, it often does not guide one toward more desirable behavior. Punishment tells you what *not* to do; reinforcement tells you what *to* do. (Children more easily understand positive instructions than negative ones — see page 73.) Thus, punishment combined with positive reinforcement is usually more effective than punishment alone. Emotionally disabled children who bite themselves or bang their heads may be mildly punished (say, with a squirt of water in the face) whenever they bite themselves, while also rewarded with positive attention and food when behaving well. The teacher whose feedback on a paper says, "No, but try this . . . " and "Yes, that's it!" reduces unwanted behavior by reinforcing alternative behaviors.

To sum up, swift and sure punishment can be effective, and may on occasion cause less pain than does the self-destructive behavior it suppresses. However, punished behavior may reappear if the threatened punishment can be avoided. (What punishment often teaches, said Skinner, is how to avoid it.) Punishment can also have undesirable side effects, such as creating fear and teaching aggression, and it often fails to teach how to act positively. Thus, most psychologists join Skinner in favoring an emphasis on reinforcement rather than punishment. Catch people doing something right and affirm them for it.

When you stop to think about it, many threats of punishment are just as forceful, and perhaps more effective, if rephrased positively: "Johnny, if you don't clean your room, you may not go outside" could become "Johnny, when you clean your room you may go outside." Likewise, "Maria, if you don't get your homework done, there'll be no TV" could become. . . .

Updating ~~Skinner~~'s Understanding

Although ~~Skinner~~ granted both the existence of mental processes and the biological underpinnings of behavior, many psychologists criticized him for discounting their importance in his theory.

Cognition and Operant Conditioning A mere 8 days before dying of leukemia, ~~Skinner~~ (1990) stood before the American Psychological Association convention for one final blast at "cognitive science," which he viewed as a throwback to turn-of-the-century introspectionism. ~~Skinner~~ died resisting the growing belief that cognitive processes — thoughts, perceptions, expectations — have a necessary place in the science of psychology, and even in our understanding of conditioning. Yet we have seen several hints that cognitive processes are at work in operant learning. For example, animals on a fixed-interval reinforcement schedule respond more and more frequently as the time approaches when a response will produce a reinforcer. The animals behave as if they expect that repeating the response will soon produce the reward.

Latent Learning Other evidence of cognitive processes comes from studies of rats in mazes. Rats exploring a maze, with no obvious reward, are like people driving around a new town. The rats develop a **cognitive map,** a mental representation of the maze. This occurs even if the rats are carried passively through the maze in a wire basket. When an experimenter then places a reward in the maze's goal box, the rats immediately perform as well as rats that have

Punishment is most effective when strong, immediate, and consistent, but it can also have undesirable side effects. This teenager's anger at his mother's scolding might, if this were to become their principal mode of communication, translate into a resistance to listening to her.

Reinforcement: The process by which consequences increase behaviors.

Positive reinforcement: Increasing behaviors by presenting positive stimuli (such as food).

Negative reinforcement: Increasing behaviors by stopping negative stimuli (such as shock).

Punishment: The process by which aversive consequences decrease behaviors.

Answer to question on page 241: Frequent-flyer programs use a fixed-ratio schedule.

been reinforced with food for running the maze (Figure 8–7). During their explorations, the rats seemingly experience **latent learning**— learning that becomes apparent only when there is some incentive to demonstrate it. The unavoidable conclusion: Learning can occur without reinforcement. As the cognitive mapping experiments suggest, there is more to learning than associating a response with a tangible consequence. There is also cognition. In Chapter 10, Thinking and Language, we will encounter striking evidence of animals' cognitive abilities in solving problems and using aspects of language.

Drawing by Nurit; ©1985 The New Yorker Magazine, Inc.

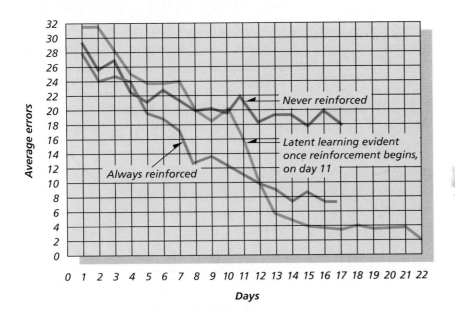

Figure 8–7 Latent learning. Animals, like people, can learn from experience, with or without reinforcement. After exploring a maze for 10 days, rats received a food reward at the end of the maze. They quickly demonstrated their prior learning of the maze — by immediately doing as well as (and even better than) rats that had been reinforced for running the maze. (From Tolman & Honzik, 1930.)

Overjustification The cognitive perspective has also led to an important qualification concerning the power of rewards: Unnecessary rewards carry hidden costs. Most people think that offering tangible rewards will boost anyone's interest in a task (Boggiano & others, 1987). Actually, promising people a reward for a task they already enjoy can backfire. People who begin to see the *reward* as their motive for performing the task may lose their intrinsic interest in it. This phenomenon is called the **overjustification effect**, because an already justifiable activity becomes *over*justified by the promise of added reward.

In experiments, children promised a payoff for playing with an interesting puzzle or toy later exhibit less interest in it than do children who are not paid to play (Deci, 1980; Lepper & Greene, 1979; Newman & Layton, 1984). It is as if the children think, "If I have to be bribed into doing this, then it must not be worth doing for its own sake."

Wendy Grolnick and Richard Ryan (1987) showed how overjustification can affect teaching and learning. They invited fifth graders to read a passage from a social studies book. Some they instructed in a controlling way: "I'll be grading you on the test to see if you're learning enough." Others, treated in a less controlling manner ("You won't be graded on [the questions]—I'm just interested in what children can remember"), learned as much *and found the passage more interesting.* Interest also survives when rewards

When the first-grade teacher offers candy each day to children who do their homework, how might this affect their natural eagerness to do schoolwork?

Have you ever thought you'd enjoy learning more if you didn't have to do it for a grade?

are used not to bribe or to control but to signal a job well done (Boggiano & others, 1985). If, after doing good work, a reward boosts your feeling of competence, your liking of the task may increase.

Biological Predispositions As with classical conditioning, an animal's natural predispositions constrain its capacity for operant conditioning. When reinforced with food, you can easily condition the golden hamster to dig or to rear up, because these actions are among the animal's natural behaviors when searching for food. But it's much harder to use food reinforcers to shape hamster behaviors, such as face washing, not normally associated with food or hunger (Shettleworth, 1973). Pigeons easily learn to flap their wings to avoid shock and to peck to obtain food, because they naturally flee with their wings and eat with their beaks. But they have a hard time learning to peck to avoid shock or to flap to obtain food. Such constraints predispose organisms to learn associations that are naturally adaptive.

Skinner's former associates, Keller Breland and Marian Breland (1961), came to appreciate biological predispositions while using operant procedures to train animals for circuses, TV shows, and movies — procedures that most trained animal shows now apply (Bailey & Bailey, 1980). The Brelands had originally assumed that operant principles would work on almost any response that any animal could make. But after training 6000 animals of 38 different species, from chickens to whales, they concluded that biological predispositions were more important than they had supposed. In one act, they trained pigs to pick up large wooden "dollars" and deposit them in a piggy bank. After learning this behavior, however, the animals began to drift back to their natural ways. They would drop the coin, push it with their snouts as pigs are prone to do, pick it up again, and then repeat the sequence — delaying their food reinforcer. As this "instinctive drift" illustrates, "misbehaviors" occurred when the animals reverted to their biologically predisposed patterns.

Animals can most easily learn and retain behaviors that draw on their biological predispositions, such as a raccoon's natural tendency to use its paws.

Skinner's Legacy

B. F. Skinner was one of the most controversial intellectual figures of our time. He stirred a hornet's nest by repeatedly insisting that external influences, not internal thoughts and feelings, shape behavior and by urging the use of operant principles to control people's behavior at school, work, and home. To help or manage people effectively, Skinner said, we should worry less about their illusions of freedom and dignity. Recognizing that behavior is shaped by its consequences, we should administer rewards in ways that promote more desirable behavior.

Skinner's critics objected: He dehumanized people, they said, by neglecting their personal freedom and by seeking to control their actions. Skinner's reply: People's behavior is already controlled by external reinforcers, so why not manipulate those controls for human betterment? In place of the widespread use of punishment in homes, schools, and prisons, would not *positive* reinforcers be more humanitarian? And if it is humbling to think that we are shaped by our histories, this very idea also creates the hope that we may actively shape our future.

B. F. Skinner (1983): "I am sometimes asked, 'Do you think of yourself as you think of the organisms you study?' The answer is yes. So far as I know, my behavior at any given moment has been nothing more than the product of my genetic endowment, my personal history, and the current setting."

Applications of Operant Conditioning We have already seen many everyday applications of operant conditioning principles, and in later chapters we will see how psychologists apply these principles to problems ranging from high blood pressure to social withdrawal. Reinforcement technologies are also at work in schools, businesses, and homes.

At School A generation ago, Skinner and others advocated teaching machines and textbooks that would shape learning in small steps and provide immediate reinforcement for correct responses. These machines and texts, they said, would revolutionize education and free teachers to concentrate on their students' special needs.

To envision Skinner's dream, imagine two mathematics teachers. Faced with a class of academically diverse students, Teacher *A* gives the whole class the same math lesson. The teacher knows that some students already understand the concepts and that others will be frustrated by their inability to comprehend. But with so many different children, how can one teacher guide them individually? When test time comes, the whiz kids breeze through unchallenged, and the slower learners once again experience failure. Faced with a similar class, Teacher *B* paces the material according to each student's rate of learning and provides prompt feedback with positive reinforcement to slow and fast learners. Does the individualized instruction of Teacher *B* sound like an impossible ideal?

Although the predicted revolution has not occurred, to the end of his life Skinner (1986, 1988, 1989) believed the ideal achievable. "Good instruction demands two things," he said. "Students must be told immediately whether what they do is right or wrong and, when right, they must be directed to the step to be taken next." To do this, and to free teachers for uniquely human tasks, computers were his final hope. For reading and math drills, the computer could be Teacher *B*: engaging the student actively, pacing material according to the student's rate of learning, quizzing the student to find gaps in understanding, providing immediate feedback, and keeping flawless records for the supervising teacher.

Experiments comparing computer-assisted instruction (CAI) to traditional classroom instruction suggest that, for some drill and practice tasks, the computer can indeed be more effective (Kulik & others, 1980, 1985). As microcomputers have become more widely available, so too have new techniques of CAI. A computer can effectively train students to type or play the piano, while tracking progress and providing positive reinforcements. Educational games and simulations can also entice students to explore and discover principles on their own.

At Work Believing that reinforcers influence productivity, business managers have capitalized on psychological research. For example, Ed Pedalino and Victor Gamboa (1974) showed how reinforcement could decrease absenteeism. In one manufacturing plant, they invited all workers who showed up on time to pick a card from a poker deck each day. At the end of each week, the worker in each department with the best poker hand won $20. Immediately, absenteeism dropped 18 percent and remained low—for as long as the incentive was offered.

Positive reinforcement for jobs well done boosts productivity especially when the desired performance is *well-defined and achievable*. Reward specific behaviors, not vaguely defined merit.

Answer to "check yourself" on page 241: Wilma's smoking provides negative reinforcement.

"You mene I've bin spending this whol term with a defektiv reeding machin?"

© 1992 by Sidney Harris.

Criticism, too, triggers the least resentment and the greatest performance boost when specific as well as considerate (Baron, 1988).

It's also a good idea to make the reinforcement *immediate*. Thomas Watson, who led IBM during its tremendous growth, would write out a check on the spot for achievements he observed (Peters & Waterman, 1982). But the rewards need not be material, nor so big that they become political and a source of discouragement to those who don't receive them. The effective manager might simply walk the floor and praise people for good work, or write unexpected notes of appreciation for a completed project. As Skinner said, "How much richer would the whole world be if the reinforcers in daily life were more effectively contingent on productive work?"

Animals, too, can be trained to perform useful work. Imagine a self-propelled marine vehicle with a sonar system and on-board computer suitable for detecting, classifying, and manipulating targets. That pretty well describes how the U.S. Navy has viewed its dolphins and sea lions, which at various times have been trained to perform salvage duties, serve as watch dogs around a Trident submarine base, or seek out explosive mines in the Persian Gulf. All such training reportedly uses food reinforcements to shape the animals toward ever-closer approximations of the desired behavior (Holing, 1988; Morrison, 1988).

At Home   Many economists and psychologists view people's spending behavior as controlled by its consequences (what economists call its costs and benefits). Compared with people who rent apartments in buildings where energy costs are paid by the landlord, those who live in comparable buildings but pay their own energy costs (therefore reaping the rewards of their own energy savings) use about 20 percent less energy. Similarly, home electricity users on an "energy diet" are helped by frequent feedback that shows their current usage compared with their past consumption (Darley & others, 1979). In homes, as elsewhere, immediate consequences most effectively influence behavior.

We can also use operant conditioning on ourselves, by reinforcing our most desired behaviors and extinguishing those undesired. To take charge of your own behavior, psychologists suggest these step-by-step procedures:

1. State your goal—say, to stop smoking, lose weight, or study or exercise more—in measurable terms, and make it public. You might, for example, aim to boost your study time by an hour a day. Announce your goal to friends.

2. Record how often you engage in the behavior you wish to promote and note how this behavior is being reinforced. You might log your current study time, noting under what conditions you do and don't study. (When I began writing textbooks, I logged my time and was astonished to discover how much time I was wasting.)

3. Begin systematically to reinforce the desired behavior. To increase your study time, allow yourself a snack (or some other reinforcing activity) only after specified periods of study. Agree with your friends that you will join them for weekend activities *only* if you have met your weekly studying goal.

4. As your new behaviors become more habitual, gradually reduce the incentives.

Drawing by Ziegler; © 1989 The New Yorker Magazine, Inc.

Table 8–1	*Comparison of Classical and Operant Conditioning*	
	Classical conditioning	**Operant conditioning**
Behavior	Involuntary (reflexive), including emotions	Voluntary (nonreflexive), goal-seeking
Acquisition	Association of events; conditioned stimulus announces unconditioned stimulus	Association of response with a subsequent consequence (reinforcer or punisher)
Extinction	CR decreases when CS is repeatedly presented alone	Responding decreases, especially when consistent reinforcement stops
Biological predispositions	Natural predispositions constrain what stimuli and responses can easily be associated	Organisms best learn behaviors similar to their natural behaviors; unnatural behaviors instinctively drift back toward natural ones
Cognitive processes	Subjects develop an expectation that the CS signals the arrival of the UCS	Subjects develop an expectation that a response will be reinforced or punished; they also exhibit latent learning

Contrasting Conditioning Techniques

The last two decades of research have changed our views of both classical and operant conditioning (summarized in Table 8–1). Biological predispositions make certain types of learning easier than others. Animals exhibit more sophisticated mental representations of their worlds than once seemed likely. And rewarding people to do what they already enjoy may undermine their interest.

Learning by Observation

From drooling dogs, running rats, and pecking pigeons we have learned much about the basic processes of learning. But conditioning principles alone do not tell us the whole story. Among higher animals, especially humans, learning need not occur through direct experience. **Observational learning**, in which we observe and imitate others' behaviors, also plays a big part. The process of observing and imitating a specific behavior is often called **modeling.** By observing and imitating models we learn all kinds of social behaviors. By 9 months of age, infants will imitate novel play behaviors, and by age 14 months will imitate acts modeled on television (Meltzoff, 1988a,b,c). To persuade children to smoke, expose them to parents and older youth who smoke. To encourage children to read, read to them and surround them with books and people who read them. To increase the odds of your children practicing your religion, worship and attend other religious activities with them.

Bandura's Experiments

Picture this scene from a famous experiment devised by Albert Bandura, the pioneering researcher of observational learning (Bandura & others, 1961). A nursery school child is at work on a picture. An adult in another part of the room is working with some Tinker Toys. The adult then gets up and for nearly 10 minutes

Albert Bandura (1977): "Learning would be exceedingly laborious, not to mention hazardous, if people had to rely solely on the effects of their own actions to inform them what to do."

pounds, kicks, and throws a large inflated Bobo doll around the room, while yelling such remarks as, "Sock him in the nose. . . . Hit him down. . . . Kick him."

After observing this outburst, the child is taken to another room where there are many appealing toys. Soon the experimenter interrupts the child's play and explains that she has decided to save these good toys "for the other children." She now takes the frustrated child to an adjacent room containing a few toys, including a Bobo doll. Left alone, what does the child do?

Compared to children not exposed to the adult model, children who observed the aggressive outburst were much more likely to lash out at the doll. Apparently, observing the adult model beating up the doll lowered their inhibitions. But something more than lowered inhibitions is at work, for the children also imitated the very acts and used the identical words that they had observed.

Applications of Observational Learning

The bad news from such studies is that antisocial models —in one's family, neighborhood, or on TV—may have antisocial effects (pages 569–574). This helps us understand how abusive parents might have aggressive children and why men who batter their wives often had wife-battering fathers. The lessons that we learn as children are not easily unlearned as adults, and are sometimes visited on future generations.

The good news is that **prosocial** (positive, helpful) models can have prosocial effects. People who exemplify nonviolent, helpful behavior can prompt similar behavior in others. Mahatma Gandhi and Martin Luther King, Jr., both drew on the power of modeling, making nonviolent action a powerful force for social change. Parents are powerful models. European Christians who risked their lives to rescue Jews from the Nazis and civil rights activists of a generation ago usually had a close relationship with at least one parent who modeled a strong moral or humanitarian concern (London, 1970; Oliner & Oliner, 1988).

Models are most effective when their actions and words are consistent. Sometimes, however, models say one thing and do another. Many parents seem to operate according to the principle "Do as I *say*, not as I do." Experiments suggest that children learn to do both (Rice & Grusec, 1975; Rushton, 1975). When exposed to a hypocrite, they tend to imitate the hypocrisy by doing what the model did and saying what the model said.

What determines whether we will imitate a model? Bandura believes part of the answer is reinforcements and punishments — those received by the model as well as by the imitator. We look and we learn. By looking, we learn to anticipate a behavior's consequences in situations like those we are observing. By watching TV programs, for example, children may "learn" that physical intimidation is an effective way to control others, that free and easy sex brings pleasure without the misery of unwanted pregnancy or disease, or that men are supposed to be tough and women gentle. We are especially likely to imitate those we respect and admire, those we perceive as similar to ourselves, and those we perceive as successful.

Although our knowledge of learning principles comes from the work of thousands of investigators, this chapter has focused on the

Children learn a great deal by observing adult models. This 14-month-old boy in Andrew Meltzoff's laboratory is imitating from TV. In (a) the adult pulls apart a novel toy. The infant leans forward and carefully studies the adult's action. In (b) the infant is given the toy. In (c) the baby pulls the toy apart, imitating what he has seen the adult do.

This boy is learning how to cook by observing his grandmother. As the sixteenth-century proverb stated, "Example is better than precept."

ideas of a few pioneers —Pavlov, Watson, Skinner, and Bandura. They illustrate the impact that can result from single-minded devotion to a few well-defined problems and ideas. They defined the issues and impressed on us the importance of learning. As their legacy demonstrates, intellectual history is often made by people who, at the risk of overstatement, pursue ideas to their limits.

Summing Up

All animals, especially humans, adapt to their environments aided by learning. Through classical conditioning, we learn to anticipate events such as being fed or experiencing pain. Through operant conditioning, we learn to repeat acts that bring desired results and avoid acts that bring punishment. Through observational learning, we learn from the experience and example of others.

Classical Conditioning

Pavlov's Experiments Although learning by association had been discussed for centuries, it remained for Ivan Pavlov to capture the phenomenon in his classic experiments on conditioning. Pavlov would repeatedly present a neutral stimulus (such as a tone) just before an unconditioned stimulus (food) triggered an unconditioned response (salivation). After several repetitions, the tone alone (now the conditioned stimulus, CS) began triggering a conditioned response (CR, salivation). Further experiments on acquisition revealed that classical conditioning was usually greatest when the CS was presented just before the UCS, thus preparing the organism for what was coming. Other experiments explored the phenomena of extinction, spontaneous recovery, generalization, and discrimination.

Updating Pavlov's Understanding Pavlov's work laid a foundation for John B. Watson's emerging belief that, to be an objective science, psychology should study only overt behavior, without considering unobservable mental activity. Watson called this position behaviorism. The behaviorists' optimism that learning principles would generalize from one response to another and from one species to another has been tempered. Conditioning principles, we now know, are cognitively and biologically constrained. In classical conditioning, animals learn when to "expect" an unconditioned stimulus. Moreover, rats are biologically prepared to learn associations between a peculiar taste and a sickness-producing drink, which they will then avoid. But they don't learn to avoid a sickening drink announced by a noise.

Pavlov's Legacy Pavlov taught us that principles of learning apply across species, that significant psychological phenomena can be studied objectively, and that conditioning principles have important practical applications.

Operant Conditioning

Classical (Pavlovian) conditioning works with involuntary (reflexive) behaviors. Operant conditioning works with voluntary behaviors that actively operate on the environment. Behaviors followed by positive or negative reinforcers increase; those followed by punishment decrease.

Skinner's Experiments When placed in a Skinner box, rats or pigeons can be shaped to display successively closer approximations of a desired behavior. Researchers have also studied the effects of positive and negative reinforcers, primary and secondary reinforcers, and immediate and delayed reinforcers. Partial reinforcement schedules (fixed-ratio, variable-ratio, fixed-interval, and variable-interval) produce slower acquisition of the target behavior than does continuous reinforcement, but more resistance to extinction. Punishment is most effective when strong, immediate, and consistent. However, it can have undesirable side effects.

Updating Skinner's Understanding Skinner's emphasis on external control of behavior made him an influential but controversial figure. Many psychologists criticized Skinner as they did Pavlov, for underestimating the importance of cognitive and biological constraints. For example, research on latent learning and overjustification further indicates the importance of cognition in learning.

Skinner's Legacy Skinner stimulated vigorous intellectual debate regarding the nature of human freedom and strategies and ethics of managing people. Nevertheless, his operant principles are being applied in schools, businesses, and homes. For example, computer-assisted instruction can embody the operant ideal of individualized shaping and immediate positive reinforcement.

Learning by Observation

An important type of learning among higher animals, including humans, is what Albert Bandura and others call observational learning. In experiments, children tend to imitate both what a model does and says, whether the behavior is prosocial or antisocial. Such experiments have stimulated research on social modeling, in the home, on television, and within peer groups.

Terms and Concepts to Remember

learning A relatively permanent change in an organism's behavior due to experience.

behaviorism The view that (1) psychology should be an objective science that (2) studies only overt behavior without reference to mental processes. Most research psychologists today agree with (1) but not (2).

classical conditioning A type of learning in which an organism comes to associate different events. A neutral stimulus that signals an unconditioned stimulus (UCS) begins to produce a response that anticipates and prepares for the unconditioned stimulus. (Also known as *Pavlovian conditioning*.)

unconditioned response (UCR) In classical conditioning, the unlearned, automatic response to the unconditioned stimulus, such as salivation when food is in the mouth.

unconditioned stimulus (UCS) In classical conditioning, a stimulus that unconditionally—naturally and automatically—triggers a response without conditioning.

conditioned response (CR) In classical conditioning, the learned response to a conditioned stimulus (CS).

conditioned stimulus (CS) In classical conditioning, an originally neutral stimulus that, after association with an unconditioned stimulus (UCS), comes to trigger a conditioned response.

acquisition The initial stage of learning, during which a response is established and gradually strengthened. In classical conditioning, the phase in which a stimulus comes to evoke a conditioned response. In operant conditioning, the strengthening of a reinforced response.

extinction The diminishing of a response when, in classical conditioning, an unconditioned stimulus (UCS) does not follow a conditioned stimulus (CS); or when, in operant conditioning, a response is no longer reinforced.

spontaneous recovery The reappearance, after a rest period, of an extinguished conditioned response.

generalization The tendency, once a response has been conditioned, for stimuli similar to the conditioned stimulus to evoke similar responses.

discrimination In classical conditioning, the ability to distinguish between a conditioned stimulus and similar stimuli that do not signal an unconditioned stimulus. In operant conditioning, responding differently to stimuli that signal that behavior will be reinforced or nonreinforced.

operant conditioning A type of learning in which behavior is strengthened if followed by reinforcement, or diminished if followed by punishment.

respondent behavior Behavior that occurs as an automatic response to some stimulus; Skinner's term for behavior learned through classical conditioning.

operant behavior Behavior that operates on the environment, producing consequences.

Skinner box A chamber containing a bar or key that an animal can manipulate to obtain a food or water reinforcer, and devices to record the animal's rate of bar pressing or key pecking. Used in operant conditioning research.

shaping An operant conditioning procedure in which reinforcers guide behavior toward closer and closer approximations of a desired goal.

reinforcer In operant conditioning, any event that *strengthens* the behavior it follows.

Premack's principle The principle that a preferred (more frequently engaged in) activity can serve as a reinforcer for a less probable activity.

positive reinforcement Increasing behaviors by presenting positive stimuli, such as food. A positive reinforcer is any stimulus that, when presented after a response, strengthens the response.

negative reinforcement Strengthening behavior by stopping or reducing negative stimuli, such as a shock. (Note: Negative reinforcement is *not* punishment.)

primary reinforcer An innately reinforcing stimulus, such as one that satisfies a biological need.

secondary reinforcer A conditioned reinforcer; a stimulus that gains its reinforcing power by association with a primary reinforcer.

continuous reinforcement Reinforcing the desired response every time it occurs.

partial (or **intermittent**) **reinforcement** Reinforcing a response only part of the time; results in slower acquisition of response but much greater resistance to extinction than does continuous reinforcement.

intermittent reinforcement See *partial reinforcement*.

fixed-ratio schedule In operant conditioning, a schedule of reinforcement that reinforces a response only after a specified number of responses.

variable-ratio schedule In operant conditioning, a schedule of reinforcement that reinforces a response after an unpredictable number of responses.

fixed-interval schedule In operant conditioning, a schedule of reinforcement that reinforces a response only after a specified time has elapsed.

variable-interval schedule In operant conditioning, a schedule of reinforcement that reinforces a response at unpredictable time intervals.

punishment Any event that *decreases* the behavior that it follows.

cognitive map A mental representation of the layout of one's environment. For example, after exploring a maze, rats act as if they learned a cognitive map of it.

latent learning Learning that occurs but is not apparent until there is an incentive to demonstrate it.

overjustification effect The effect of promising a reward for doing what one already likes to do. The person may now see the reward, rather than intrinsic interest, as the motivation for performing the task.

observational learning Learning by observing and imitating the behavior of others.

modeling The process by which a behavior is observed and imitated.

prosocial behavior Positive, constructive, helpful behavior. The opposite of antisocial behavior.

For Further Reading

Pryor, K. (1984). *Don't shoot the dog!: How to improve yourself and others through behavioral training.* New York: Simon & Schuster (Bantam Books paperback, 1985).

A practical guide to applying reinforcement principles to various everyday problems, from training animals, managing employees, and dealing with messy roommates, to reforming your own bad habits.

Skinner, B. F. (1948). *Walden two.* New York: Macmillan.

A controversial novel by the noted behavioral psychologist, presenting his view of a utopian world guided by an intelligent application of the principles of operant learning.

Williams, R. L., & Long, J. D. (1991). *Manage your life* (4th ed.). Boston: Houghton Mifflin.

This book suggests how learning principles can be applied to managing one's own health, social relations, and academic and vocational pursuits.

MIGHTY STREAM

MARTIN LUTHER

Memory

Imagine your life without memory. There would be no savoring the remembrances of joyful moments, no guilt or misery over painful recollections. Each moment would be a fresh experience. But each person would be a stranger, each task—dressing, cooking, biking—a novel challenge, every language foreign.

Your memory is your mind's storehouse, the reservoir of your accumulated learning. To Cicero, memory was "the treasury and guardian of all things." To a psychologist, **memory** is any indication that learning has persisted over time.

The Phenomenon of Memory

The range of human memory is evident in some fascinating cases:

Conversing with John, you are impressed by his wit, his intelligence (he might tell you the title of his master's thesis in physics), and his skill at tasks such as typing. It might be some time before you notice that John suffers a tragic defect, caused by a brain injury suffered in a motorcycle accident. John cannot form new memories. Although he remembers his life before the accident, John otherwise lives in an eternal present. Each morning when his rehabilitation therapist greets him she must reintroduce herself. She must listen patiently as over and over he retells anecdotes from his preaccident life. Each time the need arises, he inquires, "Where is the bathroom?" and is told anew.

At the other extreme are some special people who would be medal winners in a memory Olympics. One woman, whom psychologist Ulric Neisser (1982) calls MZ, would be the envy of every student. Until suffering a severe illness at age 29, MZ could recall anything her teachers wrote on the board and whole sections from her textbooks. When she worked as a biology technician, her employer began each day by giving her detailed instructions on the exact order in which to mount some 150 insects, which MZ then did without writing anything down.

The gold medalist of our memory Olympics would probably be a Russian, Shereshevskii, or S as the distinguished Soviet psychologist Alexander Luria (1968) called him. S's memory earned him a place in virtually every modern book on memory. You and I can repeat back a string of about seven digits—almost surely no more than nine. S could repeat up to 70 digits or words, provided they were read about 3 seconds apart in an otherwise silent room.

Moreover, he could recall them as easily backward as forward. His accuracy was unerring, even when asked to recall a list as much as 15 years later, after having memorized hundreds of other lists. "Yes, yes," he might recall. "This was a series you gave me once when we were in your apartment. . . . You were sitting at the table and I in the rocking chair. . . . You were wearing a gray suit and you looked at me like this. . . ."

Do these memory feats make your own memory seem feeble? If so, consider your capacity for remembering countless voices, sounds, and songs; tastes, smells, and textures; faces, places, and happenings. Imagine viewing more than 2500 slides of faces and places, for only 10 seconds each, and later seeing 280 of these slides one at a time, paired with a previously unseen slide. If you are like the subjects in an experiment by Ralph Haber (1970), you would recognize 90 percent of those you saw before.

Or consider the vividness of your memories of unique and highly emotional moments in your past—perhaps a car accident, your first romantic kiss, your first day as an immigrant in a new country, or where you were when you heard some tragic news. One such memory of mine is of my only hit in an entire season of Little League baseball. Most Americans over 45 feel sure of exactly what they were doing when they heard the news of President Kennedy's assassination (Brown & Kulik, 1982). Few San Francisco Bay area residents will hesitate in recalling exactly where they were when the 1989 earthquake struck. You perhaps remember where you were when you learned that the space shuttle *Challenger* had exploded. This clarity for our memories of surprising, significant events leads some psychologists to call them **flashbulb memories,** because it's as if the brain commands, "Print this!"

How do we accomplish such memory feats? How can we remember things we have not thought about for years, yet forget the name of someone we met a minute ago? How are memories stored in our brains? Why can even our flashbulb memories sometimes prove dead wrong? (People who hours after the *Challenger* explosion recalled where they heard the news were sometimes wildly inaccurate when again recalling their whereabouts 1 to 3 years later [McCloskey & others, 1988; Neisser & Harsch, 1992].) Does what we know about memory give us clues to how we can improve our memories? These will be among our questions as we review insights gleaned from a century of research on memory.

Forming Memories: An Example

History is sometimes determined by what people can remember about events. On June 17, 1972, police caught five men trying to tap the telephones of the Democratic National Committee in the Washington, DC, Watergate Office Building. In 1973, when President Nixon's legal counselor, John Dean, testified before a U.S. Senate committee investigating White House involvement in what came to be called "the Watergate scandal," his recall of conversations with the President was so impressive that some writers called him "the human tape recorder." Ironically, it was later revealed that a secret taping system had actually recorded the conversations that Dean recounted, providing a rare opportunity to compare an eyewitness's recollections with the actual event. Dean's recollection of the essentials proved correct. The highest ranking members of the

MR. TOTAL RECALL

Drawing by Miller; ©1987 The New Yorker Magazine, Inc.

Which is more important—your experiences, or your memories of them?

"The memory is sometimes so retentive, so serviceable, so obedient; at others, so bewildered and so weak; and at others again, so tyrannic, so beyond control! We are, to be sure, a miracle every way; but our powers of recollecting and forgetting do seem peculiarly past finding out."
Jane Austen
Mansfield Park, 1814

White House staff went to prison for doing what John Dean said they did, and President Nixon was forced to resign.

However, when Ulric Neisser (1981) compared the details in the tapes to the testimony, he discovered that John Dean was far from a human tape recorder. For example, Dean recalled that entering a September 15 meeting,

> [I] found Haldeman and the President. The President asked me to sit down. Both men appeared to be in very good spirits and my reception was very warm and cordial. The President then told me that Bob — referring to Haldeman—had kept him posted on my handling of the Watergate case. The President told me I had done a good job and he appreciated how difficult a task it had been and the President was pleased that the case had stopped with [his reelection committee's attorney] Liddy.

But almost every detail Dean recalled was wrong. The tape of the meeting revealed that the President did not ask Dean to sit down. He did not say Dean had done a good job. He did not say anything about Liddy or the indictments.

Dean's memory was better for a March 15 conversation during which he delivered a well-prepared report to the President on the unraveling of the White House cover-up. The tape caught Dean actually saying, "We have a cancer within, close to the presidency, that is growing. It is growing daily . . . because (1) we are being blackmailed, (2) people are going to start perjuring themselves...." In his later congressional testimony, Dean *recalled* "telling the President that there was a cancer growing on the presidency and . . . that it was important that this cancer be removed immediately because it was growing more deadly every day."

How could John Dean have been so right in his basic understanding of the Watergate discussions, yet, except for the March 15 conversation, so wrong in recalling the details of most conversations? Why are you likely to misrecall a sentence such as, "The angry rioter threw the rock at the window?" To understand Dean's memory (and our own), we need a model for organizing the many aspects of memory.

John Dean testifying before the Senate Watergate Committee. When compared to the White House tapes, John Dean's memory was found to be accurate for the substance of most conversations but not for the details.

Memory as Information Processing

One helpful model of human memory is that of a computer-like information-processing system. To remember any event requires that we *get information into our brain, retain it,* and later *get it back out.* These three steps—**encoding**, **storage**, and **retrieval**—apply not only to human memory but also to other information-processing systems: A library, for example, must have some way of acquiring and cataloging information (encoding), retaining it (storage), and making it available to users (retrieval). For our purposes, though, the computer provides a handy model of how our memory system works.

Consider how a computer encodes, stores, and retrieves information. First, the computer translates input (via keystrokes, for example) into an electronic language, much like the brain encodes sensory information into a neural language. The computer then permanently stores vast amounts of information on a disk. From this information storehouse it can retrieve a file or document into a short-term or "working" memory, which also receives new information from the keyboard. Part of this working memory is visible on the screen.

Likewise, we store vast amounts of information in **long-term memory**. From our memory storehouse we can retrieve information into a limited-capacity **short-term memory**, our "working" memory, which also receives information from our current experience. Part of this short-term working memory is displayed on the mental screen we call consciousness. Our short-term memory typically stores but seven or so chunks of information (give or take two), a recall capacity that has been enshrined in psychology as "the Magical Number Seven, plus or minus two" (Miller, 1956). Actually, people's short-term memory spans—the quantity of information they can immediately recall correctly 50 percent of the time—vary. Short-term recall is slightly better for random digits (such as those of a phone number) than for random letters, which sometimes have similar sounds. It is slightly better for information we hear rather than see. Adults have greater memory spans than children (Chi, 1976). Still, the basic principle holds true: At any given moment, we can process only a very limited amount of information.

What controls each system? With the computer, the operator retrieves or adds information into working memory. With our memory system, novel stimuli have a way of intruding into consciousness. (Chapter 5, Sensation, shows how changing sounds and sights, not constant stimulation, grab our attention.) Like orchestra conductors, we can't focus on everything at once. So we shine the flashlight beam of attention on certain incoming stimuli and on experiences that we retrieve from long-term memory (Cowan, 1988) (Figure 9–1).

Figure 9–1 A simplified model of human memory. Sensory memory registers incoming information, and short-term (working) memory processes selected bits into long-term memory. We also retrieve information from long-term memory into short-term memory.

Novel stimuli and selective attention

External events → Sensory memory → *encoding* → Short-term memory → *storage* → Long-term memory → *retrieval*

Sensory Memory

Consider what one intriguing memory experiment revealed about our **sensory memory**—the initial recording of sensory information in the memory system. As part of his doctoral research, George Sperling (1960) showed people three rows of three letters each for only 1/20th of a second (Figure 9–2). It was like trying to read by the flashes of a lightning storm. After the nine letters disappeared from the screen, the subjects could recall only about half of them.

Why? Was it because they had insufficient time to glimpse them? No, Sperling cleverly demonstrated that even at such lightning-flash speed, people actually *can* see and recall all the letters, but only momentarily. Rather than ask them to recall all nine letters at once, Sperling would sound a high, medium, or low tone immediately *after* flashing the nine letters. This cue directed the subject to report only the letters of the top, middle, or bottom row, respectively. Now the subjects rarely missed a letter, showing that all nine letters were momentarily available for recall.

K	Z	R
Q	B	T
S	G	N

Figure 9–2 Momentary photographic memory. When George Sperling flashed a group of letters similar to this for 1/20th of a second, people could recall only about half of the letters. But when signaled to recall a particular row *immediately* after the letters had disappeared, they could do so with near-perfect accuracy.

Sperling's experiment revealed that we have a fleeting photographic memory called **iconic memory**. For an instant, the eyes register an exact representation of a scene and we can recall any part of it in amazing detail. But only for a few tenths of a second. If Sperling delayed the tone signal by as much as a second, the iconic memory was gone and the subjects once again recalled only about half of the letters. The visual screen clears quickly, as it must, lest new images be superimposed over old ones. The auditory sensory image, called **echoic memory**, also lasts less than a second (Cowan, 1988). But a partially interpreted auditory echo disappears more slowly. The last few words spoken seem to linger for 3 or 4 seconds. Sometimes, just as you ask, "What did you say?" you can hear in your mind the echo of what was said.

How We Encode Information

How does sensory information, once registered, get encoded and transferred into the memory system? As you read this sentence, how do its words get encoded? Did you encode the *image* of the words, a process called **visual encoding**? Did you encode the *sound* of the words, a process called **acoustic encoding**? Or was the sentence coded by its *meaning*, a process called **semantic encoding**?

To some extent, encoding occurs automatically, freeing your conscious attention for processing information that requires effort. Thus, your memory for the route you walked to class yesterday can be handled by **automatic processing**. Your learning this chapter's concepts requires **effortful processing**.

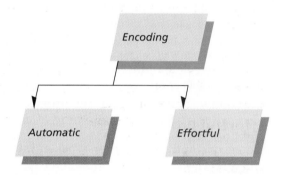

We process information either automatically or effortfully.

Automatic Processing

With little or no effort, you encode an enormous amount of information about *space, time,* and *frequency*: During an exam, you may recall the place on the textbook page where the forgotten material appears. You can recreate a sequence of the day's events in order to guess where you left your coat. You may realize that "this is the third time I've run into you this afternoon." Memories like these form almost automatically. In fact, not only can automatic processing occur effortlessly, but it is also difficult to shut off. When you hear or read a word in your native language, it is virtually impossible not to register its meaning automatically.

Other kinds of processing, such as the encoding of word meanings, are not built into our automatic systems. We must *learn* them first. Then their encoding becomes automatic. For example, learning to read reversed sentences at first requires effort:

.citamotua emoceb nac gnissecorp luftroffE

After practice, it begins to be easier, much as reading from right to left becomes easy for students of Hebrew (Kolers, 1975).

Automatic processing occurs with little or no effort, without our awareness, and without interfering with our thinking about other things. If such processing requires no special attention, then asking people to pay special attention to information they encode automatically, such as judging the frequency of words presented during an experiment, should be of little benefit. That is just what Lynn Hasher and Rose Zacks (1979, 1984) report is often the case.

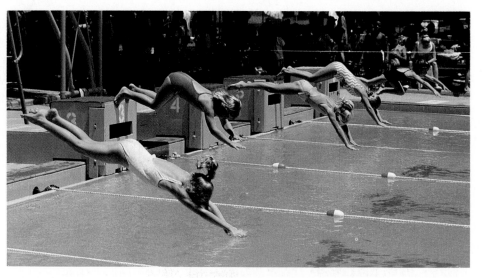

With practice, effortful activities can become automatic.

Although memory for such material may be modestly boosted by effort (Naveh-Benjamin, 1990), our encoding is mostly automatic: We cannot switch it on and off at will.

Effortful Processing

We encode and retain other types of information only with effort and attention. During your finger's trip from the phone book to the phone, your memory of a telephone number will disappear unless you work to maintain it in consciousness. To find out how quickly it will disappear, Lloyd Peterson and Margaret Peterson (1959) asked people to remember three consonants, such as CHJ. To prevent rehearsal of the letters, they asked the subjects to begin immediately counting aloud backward by threes from some number. With the help of a friend, you can demonstrate the result shown in Figure 9–3. After 3 seconds people recalled the letters only about half the time; after 12 seconds they seldom recalled them at all.

The importance of **rehearsal**, or conscious repetition, was shown long ago by the pioneering researcher of verbal memory, German philosopher Hermann Ebbinghaus (1850–1909). Ebbinghaus did for the study of memory what Ivan Pavlov did for the study of conditioning. Impatient with philosophical speculations about memory, Ebbinghaus wanted to study it scientifically. To do so, he decided to study his own learning and forgetting of novel verbal materials.

Where could Ebbinghaus find verbal material that was not familiar? His solution was to form a list of all possible nonsense syllables created by sandwiching a vowel between two consonants. Then, for a particular experiment, he would randomly select a sample of the syllables. To get a feel for how Ebbinghaus tested himself, rapidly read aloud, eight times over, the following list. Then recall the items (from Baddeley, 1982):

JIH, BAZ, FUB, YOX, SUJ, XIR, DAX, LEQ, VUM, PID, KEL, WAV, TUV, ZOF, GEK, HIW.

After learning such a list, Ebbinghaus could recall few of the syllables the following day. But were they entirely forgotten? As Figure

Figure 9–3 Verbal information may be quickly forgotten unless rehearsed. (From Peterson & Peterson, 1959.)

9–4 portrays, the more frequently he repeated the list aloud on day 1, the fewer repetitions he required to relearn the list on day 2. Here, then, was a simple beginning principle: *The amount remembered depends on the time spent learning.* Even after we learn material, additional rehearsal (*overlearning*) increases retention. Thus, John Dean almost perfectly recalled his "cancer on the presidency" remarks, which he had written out and rehearsed several times before uttering them to President Nixon.

Harry Bahrick (1984a) confirmed Ebbinghaus's principle. He found that teachers at Ohio Wesleyan University soon forgot the names and faces of most of their former students, whom they saw for only one term. In contrast, these classmates saw each other repeatedly for 4 years, and this overlearning enabled them a quarter-century later to recognize each other's names and yearbook pictures.

Classmates' names were not only overlearned through rehearsal, they also were learned over time. Experiments (Dempster, 1988) confirm the added benefit of a **spacing effect**: Distributed study often yields better long-term retention than cramming. The benefits of overlearning and spacing are apparent in a new study of adults' memory of their high school algebra. Bahrick and Lynda Hall (1991) found that students who did reasonably well in algebra, but who went no further in math after high school, forgot virtually everything over the next 50 years. Others, who did no better in high school but rehearsed their knowledge of algebra while taking college courses in calculus or beyond, showed minimal forgetting of basic algebra over the ensuing half-century—especially if their college math was spaced over several semesters rather than massed into 1 year. Bahrick and Hall see a practical implication: Restudying material for comprehensive final exams, capstone review courses, and senior examinations will enhance lifelong retention. Spreading out learning—say, over a semester or a year rather than over shorter terms—should also help. As the Roman philosopher Seneca noted in the first century, "The mind is slow in unlearning what it has been long in learning."

A phenomenon that you have surely experienced further illustrates the benefits of rehearsal. Experimenters have shown people a list of items (words, names, dates) and then immediately asked them to recall the items in any order. As people struggle to recall the list, they often demonstrate the **serial position effect**: They often remember the last and first items better than the middle items (Figure 9–5). Perhaps because they are still in working memory, the last items are briefly recalled especially well. But after a delay, recall is best for the first items. As an everyday parallel, imagine that as you are being introduced to several people, you repeat (rehearse) all their names from the beginning as you meet each one. By the end, you will have spent more time rehearsing the earlier names than the later names; thus, the next day you will probably recall the earlier names better.

Rehearsal will not encode all information equally well. Sometimes merely repeating information, such as the new phone number we are about to dial, is not enough to store it for later recall (Craik & Watkins, 1973; Greene, 1987). How, then, do we process information into long-term memory? Processing our sensory input is like sorting through the day's mail: We instantly discard some items and open, read, and retain others. We process information in three key ways—by encoding meaning, by visualizing the information, and by mentally organizing it.

Number of repetitions of list on day 1

Figure 9–4 Ebbinghaus's retention curve. Ebbinghaus found that the more times he practiced a list of nonsense syllables on day 1, the fewer repetitions he required to relearn it on day 2. Said simply, the more time we spend learning novel information, the more we retain. (From Baddeley, 1982.)

Position of word in list

Figure 9–5 The serial position effect. After being presented with a list of words, people immediately recall the last and first items most accurately. But later they recall only the first items most accurately—even if they had repeated the last items for a few moments to keep them in their consciousness. (From Craik & Watkins, 1973.)

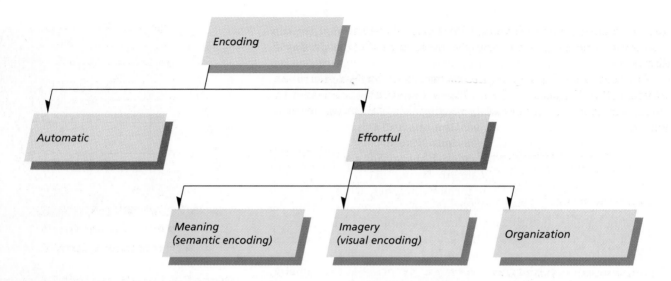

Semantic Encoding: The Processing of Meaning Do you recall (from page 255) the sentence about the rioter? Can you complete the sentence: "The angry rioter threw . . ."?

When processing verbal information for storage, we usually encode its meaning. For example, we associate it with what we already know or imagine. Whether we hear "eye-screem" as "ice cream" or "I scream" depends on how the context and our experience guide us to interpret the sounds.

Perhaps, then, like the subjects in an experiment by William Brewer (1977), you recalled the rioter sentence as the meaning you encoded when you read it (for example, "The angry rioter threw the rock through the window") and not as written ("The angry rioter threw the rock *at* the window"). As such recall indicates, we tend not to remember things exactly as they were. Rather, we remember what we encoded. Studying for an exam, you may remember your lecture notes rather than the lecture itself. Likewise, as we hear or read about a situation, our minds construct a model of it. Gordon Bower and Daniel Morrow (1990) liken our minds to theater directors who, given a raw script, imagine a finished stage production. Later, when asked to recall what we heard or read, we recall not the literal text but the mental model we constructed from it. This helps us understand John Dean's misrecollections of precisely what President Nixon said and did, and Dean's better recall of the *meaning* that he encoded from his conversations with the President.

To see whether semantic encoding (the processing of meaning) yields better memory of verbal information than acoustic or visual processing, Fergus Craik and Endel Tulving (1975) flashed a word at people. Then they asked a question that required the people to process the words either (1) visually (the appearance of the letters), (2) acoustically (the sound of the words), or (3) semantically (the meaning of the word). To experience the task, rapidly answer the following questions:

	Word flashed	Yes	No
1. Is the word in capital letters?	chair	___	___
2. Does the word rhyme with train?	BRAIN	___	___
3. Would the word fit in this sentence: The girl put the _____ on the table.	gun	___	___

Which type of processing would best prepare you to recognize the

When effortfully processing information, we encode it by meaning, imagery, or organization.

words at a later time? In Craik and Tulving's experiment, the deeper, semantic encoding—question 3—yielded much better memory (Figure 9–6).

To experience the importance of meaning for verbal memory, put yourself in the place of the students whom John Bransford and Marcia Johnson (1972) asked to remember the following recorded passage:

> The procedure is actually quite simple. First you arrange things into different groups. Of course, one pile may be sufficient depending on how much there is to do. . . . After the procedure is completed one arranges the materials into different groups again. Then they can be put into their appropriate places. Eventually they will be used once more and the whole cycle will then have to be repeated. However, that is part of life.

When the students heard the paragraph you have just read, without a meaningful context, they remembered little of it. When told that the paragraph was about washing clothes (something meaningful to them), they remembered much more of it—as you probably could now after rereading it.

Such research suggests the futility of trying to remember words we do not understand and the benefits of rephrasing what we read and hear into meaningful terms. From his experiments on himself, Ebbinghaus estimated that, compared to nonsense material, learning meaningful material required but one-tenth the effort. Further, as memory researcher Wayne Wickelgren (1977, p. 346) noted, "The time you spend thinking about material you are reading and relating it to previously stored material is about the most useful thing you can do in learning any new subject matter."

We have excellent recall for information that we relate to ourselves. If asked to rate how well certain adjectives describe themselves, people remember the adjectives well; if asked how well the adjectives describe another person, people are more likely to forget them (Kuiper & Rogers, 1979). Thus, students profit from taking time to find personal meaning in what they are studying. Information deemed "relevant to me" is more likely to be thought about and to be accessible in memory.

Imagery We struggle to memorize formulas, definitions, and dates, yet we can easily picture where we were yesterday, who was with us, where we sat, and what we wore. Your earliest memories— probably of something that happened at around age 3 or 4—almost surely involve visual **imagery**, or mental pictures.

In a variety of experiments, researchers have documented the benefits of mental images. For one thing, people who form the most vivid visual images of strangers also remember them best (Swann & Miller, 1982). For another, we remember words that lend themselves to picture images better than abstract, low-imagery words. (When I quiz you later—and I will—which three of the following words will you most likely recall: *typewriter, void, cigarette, inherent, fire, process*?) Similarly, you probably still recall the sentence about the rock-throwing rioter, not only because of the meaning you encoded, but also because the sentence lent itself to a visual image. As the example suggests and some memory experts believe (Marschark & others, 1987; Paivio, 1986), memory for concrete nouns is aided by encoding them *both* semantically and visually. Two codes are better than one.

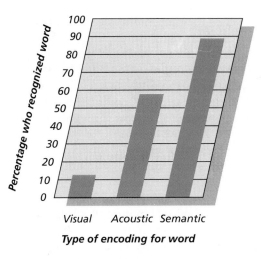

Figure 9–6 Processing a word by its meaning (semantic encoding) produces better recognition of it than does processing it according to its visual or acoustic features. (From Craik & Tulving, 1975.)

How many Fs are in the following sentence?
FINISHED FILES ARE THE RESULTS
OF YEARS OF SCIENTIFIC STUDY COMBINED WITH THE EXPERIENCE OF YEARS.
(See page 263.)

"A thing when heard, remember, strikes less keen on the spectator's mind than when 'tis seen."
Horace
Ars Poetica, 8 B.C.

The imagery principle—that people have excellent memory for pictures and picture-evoking words—applies to teaching, preaching, and writing. Abstract principles become memorable when tied to vivid examples. Consider how difficult it is to remember the statistics of the nuclear age: The approximately 9100-megaton destructive capacity of Soviet and American nuclear weapons is 3000 times greater than the 3 megatons of firepower exploded in all of World War II (*Bulletin of the Atomic Scientists*, 1990, 1991). Tomorrow you will probably have trouble recalling these statistics, but I suspect you will remember their visual representation in Figure 9–7.

Imagery is at the heart of many memory aids. **Mnemonic** (nih-MON-ik) devices (so named after the Greek word for memory) were developed by ancient Greek scholars and orators as aids to remembering lengthy passages and speeches. Using the "method of loci," they imagined themselves moving through a familiar series of locations, associating each place with a visual representation of the to-be-remembered topic. Then, when speaking, the orator would mentally revisit each location and retrieve the associated image.

A variation on this method uses vivid stories to organize words to be memorized. Gordon Bower and Michael Clark (1969) used lists of unrelated nouns, asking one group simply to study the lists and another group to invent stories using the nouns. (A sample made-up story: "A LUMBERJACK DARTed out of a forest, SKATEd around a HEDGE past a COLONY of DUCKs. He tripped on some FURNITURE, tearing his STOCKING while hastening toward the PILLOW where his MISTRESS lay.") After working through 12 lists of 10 words each, the group that merely studied each list struggled to recall 13 percent of the words; the group that invented vivid stories recalled an astounding 93 percent. Other mnemonic devices involve both acoustic and visual codes. For example, the "peg-word" system requires that you first memorize a jingle:

> One is a bun; two is a shoe;
> Three is a tree; four is a door;
> Five is a hive; six is sticks;
> Seven is heaven; eight is a gate;
> Nine is swine; ten is a hen.

Without much effort, you will soon be able to count by peg-words instead of numbers: bun, shoe, tree. . . . Then you can visually associate the peg-words with to-be-remembered items. Now you are ready to challenge anyone to give you a grocery list to remember. Carrots? Imagine them stuck into a bun. Milk? Fill the shoe with it. Paper towels? Drape them over the tree branch. Think "bun, shoe, tree" and you see their associated images: carrots, milk, paper towels. With few errors (Bugelski & others, 1968), you will be able to recall the items in any order and to name any given item. Such mnemonic systems are often the secret behind the feats of memory experts who repeat long lists of names and objects.

Organizing Information Glance for a few seconds at row 1 of Figure 9–8, then look away and try to reproduce what you saw. It's nearly impossible. But you can easily reproduce the second row, which is no less complex. Similarly, row 4 is much easier to remember than row 3, although both contain the same letters. And the sixth cluster is more easily remembered than the fifth, although both contain the same words.

Figure 9–7 Pictures often convey ideas far better than words. The dot in the center square represents all the firepower of World War II. The other dots represent the number of World War II equivalents that exist today in nuclear weapons. Just two squares represent enough firepower to destroy all the large and medium-size cities on earth: 300 megatons.

1.	⊲ ⊃ ⅁ ⋈ ⊥ Ͷ
2.	K L C I S N E

| 3. | KLCISNE NVESE YNA NI CSTTIH TNDO |
| 4. | NICKELS SEVEN ANY IN STITCH DONT |

| 5. | NICKELS SEVEN ANY IN STITCH DONT SAVES AGO A SCORE TIME AND NINE WOODEN FOUR YEARS TAKE |
| 6. | DONT TAKE ANY WOODEN NICKELS FOUR SCORE AND SEVEN YEARS AGO A STITCH IN TIME SAVES NINE |

Figure 9–8 Effects of chunking on memory. When we organize information into meaningful units, such as letters, words, and phrases, we recall it more easily. (From *The Psychology of Learning and Memory* by Douglas L. Hintzman. Copyright 1978 W. H. Freeman and Company. Reprinted with permission.)

Chunking As this demonstrates, we organize easily remembered information into meaningful units, or chunks. **Chunking** information into meaningful units occurs so naturally that we take it for granted. Consider your ability to reproduce perfectly the 150 or so line segments that make up the sixth cluster of phrases. Surely it would astonish an illiterate person, or someone unfamiliar with the English alphabet.

You or I might feel similar admiration for the ability of someone literate in Chinese to glance at the ideographs in Figure 9–9 and then to reproduce all the strokes; or for chess masters who, after a 5-second look at the board during a game, can recall the exact positions of most of the pieces (Chase & Simon, 1973); or for varsity basketball players who, given a 4-second glance at a basketball play, can recall the positions of the players (Allard & Burnett, 1985). Like the experienced chess masters and athletes, we all remember information best when we can organize it into personally meaningful arrangements.

Chunking can also aid our recall of unfamiliar material. One mnemonic technique organizes it into a more familiar form by creating words (called acronyms) or sentences from the first letters of words to be remembered. Should you ever need to recall the names of the five Great Lakes, just remember HOMES (*H*uron, *O*ntario, *M*ichigan, *E*rie, *S*uperior). Want to remember the colors of the rainbow in order of wavelength? Think of ROY G. BIV (*r*ed, *o*range, *y*ellow, *g*reen, *b*lue, *i*ndigo, *v*iolet).

With chunking, you can increase your recall of digits, too. An impossible string of 16 numbers—1-4-9-2-1-7-7-6-1-8-1-2-1-9-4-1—becomes easy when chunked into 1492, 1776, 1812, 1941. After more than 200 hours of practice in the laboratory of Anders Ericsson and William Chase (1982), two Carnegie-Mellon University students even managed to increase their memory span from the typical seven digits to more than 80. In one testing session, Dario Donatelli heard the researcher read one digit per second in a monotonous voice: "1518593765502157841665850612094885686772731418186105462974801294974965928." Motionless while learning the numbers, Donatelli then sprang alive. He whispered numbers, rubbed his chin, tapped his feet, counted on his fingers, and ran his hands through his hair. "Okay," he announced almost 2 minutes later. "The first set is 1518. Then 5937. . . ." He repeated all 73 digits, in groups of three and four.

How did he do it? By increasing the capacity of his short-term memory? No. When asked to remember letters, Donatelli fell back to about a seven-item capacity. Rather, he had developed a sophisticated strategy for number chunking. "First set was a three-mile time," reported Donatelli, an All-American cross-country runner. "Second set was a ten-mile time. Then a mile. Half-mile. Two-mile time. An age. . . . Two mile. Age. Age. Age. Two-mile. . . ." (Wells, 1983).

Hierarchies For Donatelli to reach his peak—106 digits—he retrieved the chunks of numbers by clustering them as a hierarchy (Waldrop, 1987). First came "three groups of four," he might think, and so forth. When people develop expertise in an area, they similarly process information not only in chunks but also in hierarchies composed of a few broad concepts divided into lesser concepts and facts, which are divided into still more specific categories. By organizing their knowledge in such ways, experts can retrieve informa-

Figure 9–9 After looking at these ideographs, can you reproduce them exactly? If so, you are almost certainly literate in Chinese.

Answer to question on page 261: Partly because your initial processing of the letters was primarily acoustic rather than visual, you probably missed some of the six Fs, especially those that sound like a V rather than an F.

tion efficiently. This chapter therefore aims not only to teach you the elementary facts of memory but also to help you organize these facts around broad principles, such as encoding; subprinciples, such as automatic and effortful processing; and still more specific concepts, such as meaning, imagery, and organization (Figure 9–10).

Gordon Bower and his colleagues (1969) demonstrated the benefits of hierarchical organization by presenting words either randomly or grouped into categories. When the information was hierarchically organized, recall was two to three times better. Such results show the benefits of organizing what you study—of giving special attention to chapter outlines, headings, topic sentences, and summary paragraphs. If you can master a chapter's concepts with its overall organization, the odds are that your recall will be good at test time. Taking lecture and text notes in outline format—a type of hierarchical organization—may also prove effective.

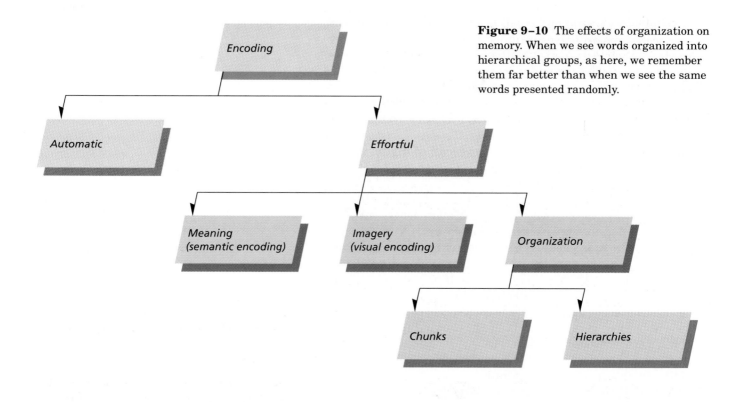

Figure 9–10 The effects of organization on memory. When we see words organized into hierarchical groups, as here, we remember them far better than when we see the same words presented randomly.

Forgetting as Encoding Failure

Amidst all the applause for memory—all the efforts to understand it, all the books on how to improve it—have any voices been heard in praise of forgetting? William James (1890, p. 680) was such a voice: "If we remembered everything, we should on most occasions be as ill off as if we remembered nothing." To discard the clutter of useless or out-of-date information—where we parked the car yesterday, a friend's old phone number, restaurant orders already cooked and served—is surely a blessing (Bjork, 1978). The Russian memory whiz S, whom we met at the beginning of the chapter, was haunted by his junk heap of memories, which continually dominated his consciousness. He found it more difficult than others to think abstractly—to generalize, to organize, to evaluate. A good memory is helpful, but so is the ability to forget.

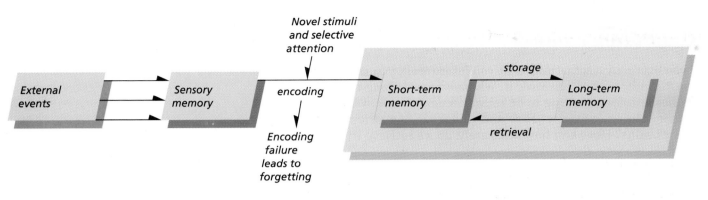

What causes forgetting? One answer is that we failed to encode the information. Thus, it never entered the memory system. The English novelist-critic C. S. Lewis (1967, p. 107) vividly described why we remember "next to nothing":

> Each of us finds that in his own life every moment of time is completely filled. He is bombarded every second by sensations, emotions, thoughts, which he cannot attend to for multitude, and nine-tenths of which he must simply ignore. . . . The past . . . was a roaring cataract of billions upon billions of such moments: any one of them too complex to grasp in its entirety, and the aggregate beyond all imagination. . . . At every tick of the clock, in every inhabited part of the world, an unimaginable richness and variety of "history" falls off the world into total oblivion.

Indeed, much of what we sense we never notice. If you live in the United States, you have probably looked at thousands of pennies in your lifetime. Can you recall what the side with Lincoln's head looks like? If not, let's make the memory test easier: Can you *recognize* the real thing in Figure 9–11? Raymond Nickerson and Marilyn Adams (1979) found that most people cannot. The details of a penny are not very meaningful—nor are they essential for distinguishing pennies from other coins—and few of us have made the effort to encode them. As we noted earlier, we encode some information automatically; other types of information require effortful processing. Without effort, the memory decays into oblivion.

Forgetting can occur as a result of encoding failure.

How many of the six quiz words on page 261 can you now recall? Of these, how many are high-imagery words? How many are low-imagery?

Figure 9–11 Which one of these pennies is the real thing? (From Nickerson & Adams, 1979.) (See page 268.)

Long-Term Memory

If you experience something that you later recall, you must, somehow, have stored and retrieved it. What is stored in long-term memory lies dormant, waiting to be reawakened by a cue. What is our memory storage capacity? How and where are memories recorded in our brains? How, and how accurately, do we retrieve them?

Storage

Memory Storage Capacity and Duration In Arthur Conan Doyle's *A Study in Scarlet*, Sherlock Holmes offers a popular theory of memory capacity:

> I consider that a man's brain originally is like a little empty attic, and you have to stock it with such furniture as you choose. . . . It is a mistake to think that that little room has elastic walls and can distend to any extent. Depend upon it, there comes a time when for every addition of knowledge you forget something that you knew before.

Contrary to Sherlock Holmes's supposition, our capacity for storing long-term memories is essentially limitless. By one careful estimate, the average adult has about a billion bits of information in memory. Allowing for all the brain must do to encode, store, retrieve, and manipulate this information, its storage capacity is probably a thousand to a million times greater (Landauer, 1986). So our brains are *not* like attics, which once filled can only store more by discarding old items.

Indeed, the more expertise we have, and therefore the better we can organize and form meaningful associations with new information, the easier it is to learn and remember. The point is vividly illustrated by those whose efforts and expertise have enabled phenomenal memory feats. Beginning at age 60, Stephen Van Nest Powelson, a 71-year-old business executive, had (at last report) memorized the first 22 books of Homer's 24-book, 600-page *Iliad* (Stone, 1989). Rajan Mahadevan, a Kansas State University graduate student from India, has correctly recited the first 31,811 digits of pi—a world record recently surpassed when Hideaki Tomoyori of Japan recalled the first 40,000 digits in a 17-hour, 21-minute recitation (Thompson & others, 1991).

But how precise and durable are our everyday stored memories? Ebbinghaus (1885) learned lists of nonsense syllables, and measured how much he retained when relearning each list, from 20 minutes to 30 days later. His famous "forgetting curve" (Figure 9–12) indicates that much of what we learn we may quickly forget.

Harry Bahrick (1984b), a modern-day descendant of the Ebbinghaus tradition, examined the forgetting curve for Spanish learned in school. By using the cross-sectional method (page 114), he compared the knowledge of Spanish among people who had just taken Spanish with the Spanish knowledge of those who had studied it up to 50 years before. Compared with those just completing a high school or college Spanish course, those who had been out of school for 3 years had forgotten much of what they had learned (Figure 9–13). However, after roughly 3 years, forgetting leveled off; what people remembered then, they still remembered 25 years later, even if they had not used their Spanish at all.

Is the forgotten Spanish gone—lost from storage—or merely inaccessible? If we could somehow uncover them, would we find our

Figure 9–12 Ebbinghaus's forgetting curve. After learning lists of nonsense syllables, Ebbinghaus studied how much he retained from 20 minutes to 30 days later. He found that memory for novel information fades quickly, then levels out. (Adapted from Ebbinghaus, 1885.)

Figure 9–13 The forgetting curve for Spanish vocabulary. Compared with people just completing a Spanish course, those 3 years out of the course remembered much less. Compared with the 3-year group, however, those who studied Spanish even longer ago did not forget much more. (Adapted from Bahrick, 1984b.)

past experiences intact, like long-lost books in a dusty attic? Sigmund Freud thought so. If only we could recover and resolve the painful repressed memories of our childhoods, he thought, emotional healing would follow. When "age-regressed" under hypnosis, some people do offer detailed reports of childhood experiences. But as we noted in Chapter 7, such reports are unreliable and typically contain fabricated material.

Memory's Physical Storage For a time, it was thought that brain stimulation during surgery provided evidence that our past is "in there," in complete detail, just waiting to be relived. As you may recall from page 43, to predict possible side effects of surgery, brain surgeon Wilder Penfield helped map the brain's motor cortex by electrically stimulating wide-awake patients. Occasionally, Penfield's patients would report hearing things, such as "a mother calling her little boy." Penfield (1969) assumed that he was activating long-lost experiences etched permanently on the brain.

On closer scrutiny, memory researchers Elizabeth Loftus and Geoffrey Loftus (1980) discovered that these flashbacks were extremely rare, occurring in only a handful of Penfield's 1100 stimulated patients. Moreover, the content of these few recollections suggested that the experiences were not being relived but invented. As if they had been dreaming, people would recall being in locations they had never actually visited. So, although the brain's storage capacity may be essentially unlimited, the evidence does *not* suggest that we store most information with the exactness of a tape recorder. A more likely explanation for the forgetting curves is that new experiences interfere with our retrieval (page 278) and that the physical memory trace gradually decays.

But what exactly is the "memory trace"? Since the 1970s, new clues to the physical basis of memory have surfaced rapidly. While cognitive psychologists study our memory "software," neuropsychologists are gaining new insights into our memory "hardware"—how and where we physically store information in our brains.

For several decades, neuropsychologists have searched the brain for physical evidence of memory. The search has at times been exasperating. One psychologist, Karl Lashley (1950), trained rats to solve a maze, then cut out pieces of the rats' cortexes and tested their memory of the maze. Eventually, he hoped to locate where memory of the maze was stored. Alas, no matter what part of the cortex he removed, the rats retained at least a partial memory of how to solve the maze. Lashley's conclusion: Memories do not reside in single, specific spots.

Are memories instead rooted in the brain's ongoing electrical activity? If so, then temporarily shutting down that activity should eliminate them, much as a power failure eliminates the settings on an electronic clock. To test this, Ralph Gerard (1953) trained hamsters to turn right or left to get food. Then he lowered their body temperature until the brain's electrical activity ceased. When the hamsters were revived and their brains were active again, would they remember which way to turn? Yes. Their long-term memories survived the electrical blackout.

Synaptic Changes Other neuroscientists are analyzing memory on a finer scale, by exploring changes within and between single neurons. Memories begin as impulses whizzing through brain circuits but then somehow consolidate into permanent neural changes. Although passing an electric current through the brain won't disrupt existing memories, not-yet-consolidated memories will be wiped out. Such is the experience both of laboratory animals and of depressed people given electroconvulsive therapy (page 505). A blow to the head can do the same. When football players who have been dazed or momentarily knocked unconscious are interviewed a few minutes later, they typically cannot recall the name of the play during which the incident occurred (Yarnell & Lynch, 1970). Likewise, a boxer knocked out in round 2 may have no memory of round 1. The information in short-term memory before the blow just didn't have time to consolidate into long-term memory.

Where does the neural change occur that makes memories permanent? The available clues point to the synapses—the sites where nerve cells communicate with one another through their neurotransmitter messengers (Lynch & Baudry, 1984). Chapter 3 notes how experience modifies the brain's neural networks. In response to increased activity in a particular pathway, neural interconnections form or strengthen. Cutting these neural pathways, as

Answer to question on page 265: The first penny (a) is the real penny.

neuropsychologist Richard Thompson (1985) did with some conditioned reflex pathways through animals' cerebellums, destroys the learned response.

To reveal precisely how neural pathways get strengthened, Daniel Alkon (1989), Gary Lynch (1990), and their colleagues observed molecular changes in animals' dendrite receptors after conditioning—changes making the receiving neurons more sensitive. Eric Kandel and James Schwartz (1982) also observed changes in the sending neurons. Their subjects were among the simplest of animals, the California sea snail, *Aplysia*. Its mere 20,000 or so nerve cells are unusually large and accessible, enabling the researchers to observe synaptic changes during learning.

Chapter 8 notes how the sea snail can be classically conditioned (with electric shock) to reflexively withdraw its gills when squirted with water. By observing the snail's neural connections before and after conditioning, the researchers pinpointed changes. When learning occurs, the snail releases more of the neurotransmitter serotonin at certain synapses, and these synapses become more efficient at transmitting signals. When drugs block neurotransmitters, information storage is disrupted (Squire, 1987). Likewise, Alzheimer's disease disrupts memory by destroying brain tissue that secretes important neurotransmitters.

Alcohol disrupts serotonin's messenger activity, which helps explain why alcohol impairs the formation of memories (Weingartner & others, 1983). The morning after a night of heavy drinking, a person may have trouble remembering the previous evening. In general, depressants impede memory formation. The naturally stimulating hormones that humans and animals produce when excited or stressed have an opposite effect: They boost learning and retention. When a rat receives an arousing hormone and then a mild foot shock, it forms an indelible memory—like the one it forms when an intense foot shock naturally triggers release of the same hormone (Gold, 1987; McGaugh, 1990). Such hormones make more glucose energy available to fuel brain activities. Emotion-triggered hormonal changes help explain why we long remember exciting or shocking events, such as our first kiss, a political assassination, or an earthquake. (Another reason for the durability of these memories is our reliving and rehearsing them.)

Types of Memories After a memory-to-be enters the cortex through the senses, it winds its way into the depths of the brain. Where it goes depends on the type of information, as strikingly illustrated in the special cases of amnesic patients similar to John, whom we met at the beginning of this chapter.

Neurologist Oliver Sacks (1985, pp. 26–27) describes another such patient. Jimmie, a brain-damaged man, had no memories—thus, no sense of elapsed time—beyond 1945. Asked who is President, he replied, "FDR's dead. Truman's at the helm."

When Jimmie gave his age as 19, Sacks thrust a mirror at him: "Look in the mirror and tell me what you see. Is that a nineteen-year-old looking out from the mirror?"

Jimmie turned ashen, gripped the sides of the chair, cursed, then became frantic: "What's going on? What's happened to me? Is this a nightmare? Am I crazy? Is this a joke?" When his attention was diverted to some children playing baseball, his panic ended, the dreadful mirror swiftly forgotten.

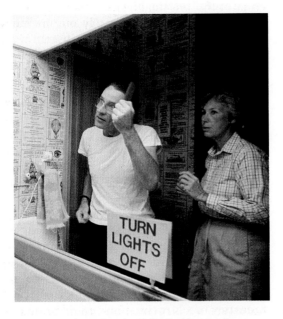

Understanding the physiological basis of memory is of more than academic interest. Discovering the neural and chemical mechanisms of memory may help this man and the many others like him suffering from Alzheimer's disease.

Flipping through a *National Geographic*, Sacks showed Jimmie a photo. "What is this?" he asked.

"It's the moon," Jimmie replied.

"No, it's not," Sacks answered. "It's a picture of the earth taken from the moon."

"Doc, you're kidding? Someone would've had to get a camera up there!"

"Naturally."

"Hell! You're joking—how the hell would you do that?" Jimmie's wonder was that of a bright young man from 40 years ago reacting with amazement to his travel back to the future.

Careful testing of these unique people reveals something even stranger: Although incapable of recalling new facts or anything they have recently done, John (whom we met earlier in the chapter), Jimmie, and other similarly amnesic people can learn. They can be classically conditioned, and with practice they can learn to read mirror-image writing or do a jigsaw puzzle (Squire, 1987). They do all these things with absolutely no memory of having learned them. Or consider what happens when such patients have learned to solve a Tower of Hanoi puzzle, which requires moving rings from one pole to another until they are stacked in order of size. Amnesia victims will deny having seen the puzzle before, insist it is silly for them to try, and then proceed to solve it like a practiced expert.

These curious findings make it hard to argue that memory is a single, unified system. They instead suggest two types of memory. For whatever has destroyed the amnesics' conscious recall has not destroyed their unconscious capacity for learning. They can learn *how* to do something—**implicit memory** (*nondeclarative memory*)—without knowing and declaring *that* they know—**explicit memory** (*declarative memory*). Having read a story once, they will read it faster a second time through, although they cannot recall having seen the story before. Having played golf on a new course, they will forget it completely, yet their game will improve with experience on the course. If repeatedly shown the word PERFUME, they wouldn't recall having seen it. But if asked the first word that comes to mind in response to the letters PER, they surprise themselves by readily displaying their learning. Strangely, they retain their past but do not explicitly recall it (Figure 9–14).

This reinforces an important principle introduced in Chapter 5's description of "parallel processing": Mental feats such as vision, thinking, and memory may seem to be single abilities, but they are not. Rather, we decompose information into different components for separate and simultaneous processing.

Figure 9–14 Researchers Larry Squire (1990) and Daniel Schacter (1987) classify long-term memories into explicit and implicit memories.

Brain scans and autopsies reveal that amnesic patients usually have suffered damage to the **hippocampus**, a limbic system structure that plays a vital role in the gradual processing of our explicit memories for names, images, and events into long-term memory (Figure 9–15). When monkeys lose their hippocampus to surgery, they lose most of their recall for things learned during the preceding 8 weeks (Squire, 1990). Chickadees and other birds can store food in hundreds of places and return to these unmarked caches months later, but not if their hippocampus has been removed (Sherry & Vaccarino, 1990). Older memories remain intact, suggesting that the hippocampus is not the permanent storehouse, but a way station that feeds new information to other brain circuits for permanent storage (Mishkin & Appenzeller, 1987). Implicit memories for skills and conditioned associations still form after damage to the hippocampus and seem to be processed in the brain's even more ancient regions.

This dual explicit-implicit memory system helps explain infantile amnesia. Behaviorally, the reactions and skills we learned during infancy reach far into our future. Yet as adults we recall nothing of our first 2 years. Our conscious minds are blank, not only because we index so much of our explicit memory by words that nonspeaking children have not learned, but also because the hippocampus is one of the last brain structures to mature fully.

Hippocampus

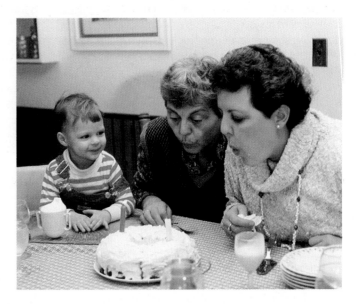

Figure 9–15 The hippocampus processes explicit memories for facts and episodes. This boy's hippocampus is not yet fully mature. Despite his obvious pleasure at his second birthday celebration, he won't remember this event later in life, except through pictures and stories.

Although clues to the physical basis of memory are accumulating, many answers remain uncertain. Are memories stored at specific synaptic locations, as Kandel and Schwartz's work with sea snails implies? Or are the memories dispersed as Lashley's inability to cut them out suggests? Or is it both? And precisely how do we store explicit and implicit memories? In some as yet unknown way, the interaction between the whole memory system and its dispersed subsystems and networks enables us to store residues of a lifetime of experiences with their associated smells, sights, and sounds. Clearly, most of what there is to be known about the physical basis of memory has yet to be discovered.

Retrieval

To most people, memory is **recall,** the ability to retrieve information not in conscious awareness. To a psychologist, memory is any sign that something learned has been retained. So *recognizing* or more quickly *relearning* information also indicates memory.

An example: Long after you cannot recall most of the people in your high school graduating class, you may still recognize their yearbook pictures from a photographic lineup and pick their names out from a list of names. Harry Bahrick and his colleagues (1975) reported that people who graduated 25 years earlier could not *recall* many of their classmates, but they could *recognize* 90 percent of their old classmates' pictures and names. And if you once learned something and then forgot it, you will probably relearn it more quickly than when you learned it originally. When studying for a final exam or when resurrecting a language used in early childhood, the relearning is easier. Tests of **recognition** and of time spent **relearning** reveal that we remember more than we can recall.

Multiple-choice questions test:
(a) recall
(b) recognition
(c) relearning.

Fill-in-the-blank questions test _____.
(See page 275.)

Madonna Ciccone
Adams High School 1976
Rochester, Mich.
Thespian Society.

Paul Newman
Shaker High School 1943
Shaker Heights, Ohio
Travel Club 2, 3; Booster 3, 4.

Even if Madonna and Paul Newman had not become famous, their high school classmates would likely still recognize their yearbook photos.

Retrieval Cues To retrieve a fact from a library of stored information, you need a way to gain access to it. In recognition tests, retrieval cues (such as photographs) provide reminders of information (classmates' names) we could not otherwise recall. Retrieval cues also guide us where to look. If you want to know what the pyramid on the back of a dollar bill signifies, you might look in *Collier's Encyclopedia* under "dollar," "currency," or "money." But your efforts would be futile. To get the information you want, you would have to look under "Great Seal of the United States" (Hayes, 1981). Like information stored in encyclopedias, memories are inaccessible unless we have cues for retrieving them. The more and better learned the retrieval cues, the more accessible the memory.

You can think of a memory as held in storage by a web of associations (J. R. Anderson, 1983). To retrieve a specific memory, you first need to identify one of the strands that leads to it, a process called **priming** (Bower, 1986). Philosopher-psychologist William

| Seeing or hearing the word *rabbit* | → | Activates concept | → | Primes spelling the spoken word *hair/hare* as *h-a-r-e* |

Figure 9–16 Priming—another type of implicit memory. The spreading of associations can unconsciously activate related associations. After seeing or hearing *rabbit*, we are later more likely to spell the spoken word *hair* as *h-a-r-e*. (Adapted from Bower, 1986.)

James referred to priming as the "wakening of associations." Often our associations are activated, or primed, without our awareness. Hearing or seeing the word *rabbit* can unconsciously prime people to spell the spoken word *hair* as *h-a-r-e*. As Figure 9–16 indicates, *rabbit* primes associations with *hare* even though we may not recall having heard *rabbit*. (Recall from Chapter 5 that even subliminal stimuli can sometimes prime responses to later stimuli.)

Can we remember better if we activate retrieval cues within our web of associations? Definitely. Mnemonic devices provide us with handy retrieval cues: ROY G. BIV; HOMES; bun, shoe, tree. We can also expose ourselves to cues that prime our memories for earlier experiences. Before the Watergate hearings, John Dean refreshed his memory "by going through every single newspaper article outlining what had happened and then placing myself in what I had done in a given sequence in time" (Neisser, 1981).

Context Effects   It does help to put yourself back in the context where you experienced something. Duncan Godden and Alan Baddeley (1975) discovered this by having scuba divers listen to a list of words in two different settings, either 10 feet underwater or sitting on the beach. As Figure 9–17 illustrates, the divers recalled more words when they were retested in the same place.

You have probably experienced similar context effects. Returning to where you once lived or the school you once attended, you may have been flooded with retrieval cues, and then with memories. Taking an exam in the same room where you are taught may help a little. In several experiments, Carolyn Rovee-Collier (1989) found that a familiar context activates memories even in 3-month-olds. After learning that kicking would move a crib mobile (via a connecting ribbon from the ankle), the infants retrieved this learning much better when again tested in the same crib with the same bumper (Figure 9–18).

Figure 9–17 The effects of context on memory. Words heard underwater are best recalled underwater; words heard on land are best recalled on land. (Adapted from Godden & Baddeley, 1975.)

Figure 9–18 Infants learned to move a mobile by kicking. Later, this learning was reactivated most strongly when retesting the infants in the same rather than a different context. (From Butler & Rovee-Collier, 1989.)

Sometimes, being in a context similar to one we've been in before may trigger the experience of **déjà vu**—that eerie sense that "I've been in this exact situation before." People who pose the question as, "How could I recognize a situation that I'm experiencing for the first time?" may suppose that something paranormal is occurring. Could it be reincarnation ("I must have experienced this in a previous life") or precognition ("I viewed this scene in my mind before experiencing it")? If we pose the question differently ("Why do I feel as if I recognize this situation?"), we can see how our memory system might produce the déjà vu feeling (Alcock, 1981). If we have previously been in a similar situation, although we can't recall what it was, the current situation may be loaded with cues that unconsciously help us to retrieve the earlier experience. Thus, if you see a stranger who looks and walks like one of your friends, the similarity may give rise to a feeling of recognition. Because the feeling conflicts with your knowing that the person is a stranger, you may think, "I've seen that person before."

Moods and Memories Associated words, events, and contexts are not the only retrieval cues. Events in the past may have aroused a specific emotion, which can later prime us to recall its associated events. Cognitive psychologist Gordon Bower (1983) explains: "A specific emotional state is like a specific room in a library into which the subject places memory records, and he can most easily retrieve those records by returning to that same room or emotional state." The things we learn in one state—be it joyful or sad, drunk or sober—are more easily recalled when we are again in the same state, a phenomenon called **state-dependent memory**. What is learned when drunk, high, or depressed is not recalled well in *any* state (drugs and depression interfere with encoding); but it's recalled slightly better when again drunk, high, or depressed. Someone who hides money when drunk may forget where, until drunk again.

Even more striking is a mood's effect on emotionally tinged memories (Ellis & Ashbrook, 1989; Ucros, 1989). A debated explanation is that we associate good or bad events with their accompanying emotions. Thus, when again feeling good or bad, we more easily recall associated good or bad times. Some examples: If people are put in a buoyant mood—whether under hypnosis or just by the day's events (a World Cup soccer victory for the German subjects of one study)—they commonly recall the world through rose-colored glasses (Forgas & others, 1984; Schwarz & others, 1987). They judge themselves to be competent and effective, other people to be benevolent, life in general to be wonderful. Put in a bad mood by negative events, the very same people suddenly recall everything more negatively.

So it shouldn't surprise us that *currently* depressed people recall their parents as having been rejecting, punitive, and guilt-promoting, whereas *formerly* depressed people describe their parents as do those who have never suffered severe depression (Lewinsohn & Rosenbaum, 1987). Their memories are "mood-congruent." Being depressed sours memories by priming negative associations. You and I may nod our heads knowingly. Yet, curiously, when in a good or bad mood, we persist in attributing our changing judgments and memories to reality rather than to our temporary moods.

Sometimes we counteract the effect by retrieving ego-boosting memories after receiving a jolt of bad news, such as a poor exam

"When a feeling was there, they felt as if it would never go; when it was gone, they felt as if it had never been; when it returned, they felt as if it had never gone."
George MacDonald
What's Mine's Mine, 1886

grade (Parrott & Sabini, 1990). Nevertheless, ongoing moods color our retrieval of past experiences and, even more powerfully, affect our encoding of new experiences (Johnson & Magaro, 1987; Mayer & Salovey, 1987). Happy people are more receptive to positive feedback, depressed people to negative feedback (Esses, 1989). Bad moods also predispose us to notice and interpret other people's behavior in negative ways. When we're in a good mood, the same actions create a more positive impression. It's true that your mood depends on the world around you. But it's also true that how you perceive the world depends on your mood. Passions exaggerate.

Your mood's effect on encoding and retrieval helps explain why moods persist. When happy, you recall happy events, which helps prolong the good mood. When depressed, you recall depressing events, which in turn feeds depressing interpretations of current events. As we will see in Chapter 15, this process maintains depression's vicious cycle.

Memory Construction Picture yourself having the following pleasant experience:

> You decide to go to your favorite restaurant for dinner. You enter the restaurant and are seated at a table with a white tablecloth. You study the menu. You tell the waiter that you want prime rib, medium rare, a baked potato with sour cream, and a salad with blue cheese dressing. You also order some red wine from the wine list. A few minutes later the waiter returns with your salad. Later he brings the rest of the meal, which you enjoy, except that the prime rib is a bit overdone.

Were I immediately to quiz you on this paragraph (from Hyde, 1983), you could surely retrieve considerable detail. For example, without looking back, answer the following questions:

1. What kind of salad dressing did you order?
2. Was the tablecloth red checked?
3. What did you order to drink?
4. Did the waiter give you a menu?

Answers to questions on page 272: Multiple-choice questions test recognition. Fill-in-the-blank questions test recall.

You were probably able to recall exactly what you ordered, and maybe even the color of the tablecloth. Does retrieval therefore consist merely of "reading" the information stored in our brain's library? We do have an enormous capacity for storing and reproducing the incidental details of our daily experience. But as we have seen, we often construct our memories as we encode them, and we may also alter our memories as we withdraw them from the memory bank. Like a scientist who infers a dinosaur's appearance from its remains, we infer our past from stored information plus what we now assume. Did the waiter give you a menu? Not in the paragraph given. Nevertheless, many people answer yes. Why? Their schemas for restaurants direct their memory construction, by filtering information and filling in missing pieces.

Elizabeth Loftus has repeatedly shown how eyewitnesses similarly construct their reports when asked to recall incidents. In one experiment with John Palmer, Loftus showed a film of a traffic accident and then quizzed the viewers about what they saw (Loftus & Palmer, 1973). Those asked, "How fast were the cars going when they *smashed* into each other?" gave higher speed estimates than those asked, "How fast were the cars going when they *hit* each other?" A week later, the researchers asked the viewers if they recalled seeing any broken glass. Compared to those who had been asked the question with "hit," those asked the question with "smashed" were more than twice as likely to recall broken glass (Figure 9–19). In fact, there was no broken glass.

In many follow-up experiments around the world, people have witnessed an event, received or not received misleading information about it, and then taken a memory test. The repeated result is a **misinformation effect**: After exposure to subtle misinformation, many people misremember. They have misrecalled a yield sign as a stop sign, hammers as screwdrivers, Coke cans as peanut cans, *Vogue* magazine as *Mademoiselle*, "Dr. Henderson" as "Dr. Davidson," breakfast cereal as eggs, and a clean-shaven man as having a mustache (Loftus & others, 1989).

So unwitting is the effect that people later find it nearly impossible to discriminate between their memories of real and suggested events (Schooler & others, 1986). This difficulty was strikingly true among those who 3 years later misrecalled their whereabouts upon hearing of the space shuttle *Challenger's* explosion (Neisser & Harsch, 1989). When shown their own handwritten accounts from the day after, many were surprised. Some were so sure of their made-up memories that they insisted their original version must have been flawed. Similarly, the psychologist Jean Piaget was startled as an adult to learn that his vivid, detailed memory of his nursemaid thwarting his kidnapping was utterly false. Piaget apparently constructed the memory from the many retellings of the story he had heard (later confessed by the nursemaid to have been false).

The moral: You can't be sure whether a memory is real by how real it feels. Unreal memories feel like real memories. In experiments on eyewitness testimony, researchers have repeatedly found that the most confident eyewitnesses are the most persuasive, but often not the most accurate. On average, eyewitnesses express roughly similar self-assurance, whether right or wrong (Bothwell & others, 1987; Cutler & Penrod, 1989; Wells & Murray, 1984).

Recognizing that the misinformation effect can occur as police and attorneys ask questions framed by their own understandings of an event, Ronald Fisher, Edward Geiselman, and their colleagues (1987, 1989) train police interviewers to ask less suggestive, more effective questions. To activate retrieval cues, the detective first asks witnesses to visualize the scene—the weather, time of day, lighting, sounds, smells, positions of objects, and their mood. Then the witness tells in detail, and without interruption, every point recalled, no matter how trivial. Only then does the detective ask evocative follow-up questions: "Was there anything unusual about the person's appearance or clothing?" Using this "cognitive interview" technique, Fisher and Geiselman report that accurate recall increases by some 50 percent.

Memory construction helps explain why John Dean's recollections of the Watergate conversations were a mixture of real and imagined events. It explains why "hypnotically refreshed" memories of crimes so easily incorporate errors, some of which originate with the hypnotist's leading questions ("Did you hear loud noises?"). It explains why patients with memory loss, such as those suffering from Alzheimer's disease, so readily invent sensible-sounding accounts of their activities. Memory construction explains why dating partners who fall in love *over*estimate their first impressions of

Accident

Leading question:

"About how fast were the cars going when they *smashed* into each other?"

Memory construction

Figure 9–19 Memory construction. When people who saw the film of a car accident were asked a leading question, they recalled a more serious accident than they had witnessed. (From Loftus, 1979.)

4 I witness accounts are not very reliable

one another, while those who break up *under*estimate their earlier liking (McFarland & Ross, 1987). And it explains why people's confident answers to survey questions—"When you were growing up, how frequently did your father attend religious services?"—often contain inaccuracies (Bradburn & others, 1987).

Knowing What We Know Sometimes we know more than we are aware. Other times—perhaps when taking an exam—we discover that we do not know as much as we thought. The difficulties of knowing what you know are striking in the amnesic patients who implicitly know *how* to do things without explicitly knowing *that* they know.

How accurate are we at assessing what we know? John Shaughnessy and Eugene Zechmeister (1991) explored this question in an experiment with two groups of students. Group 1 repeatedly reread dozens of factual statements, then judged the likelihood that they would later remember each fact, and then were tested on their recall. Students in this group felt fairly confident of their knowledge, even on the questions they later missed. Students in group 2 read the statements, but then spent the rest of the time responding to practice tests requiring them to retrieve the facts. Compared to the "reread" group, group 2 students did just as well on the final recall test. What is more, this practice-test group could better discriminate what they did and didn't know. Thus, self-testing enhances recall and can help you to know what you know—and thus to focus your study time on what you don't yet know. As the British Prime Minister Benjamin Disraeli once said, "To be conscious that you are ignorant is a great step to knowledge."

Forgetting as Retrieval Failure

We have seen that forgetting occurs when we fail to encode information and when our stored memories decay. Forgotten events are like books you can't find in your library—some because you never acquired them, others because you discarded them from storage.

"Memory is a great betrayer."
Anaïs Nin
The Diary of Anaïs Nin, 1974

Drawing by Cheney; ©1983 *Omni* Magazine, Penthouse Enterprises, Inc.

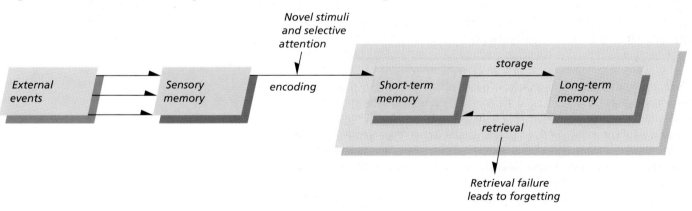

Forgetting can occur as a result of retrieval failure.

There is a third possibility: Even if the book is stored and available, it may be inaccessible. Perhaps you don't have the information needed to look it up and retrieve it. Likewise, information sometimes gets into our brain and, though we know it is there, we cannot get it out. A person's name may lie poised on the tip of the tongue, waiting to be retrieved. When people who cannot recall information get retrieval cues ("It begins with an *m*"), they will often remember what they could not recall. Retrieval problems help explain the occasional memory failures of older adults. (Chapter 4 notes how older people tend to recall less than do younger adults, but they usually remember as well if given reminders or a recognition test.)

Interference   Learning some items may interfere with retrieving others, especially when the items are similar. If someone gives you a phone number to remember, you may be able to recall it later. But if two more people give you their numbers, each successive number will be more difficult to recall. Such **proactive interference** refers to the disruptive effect of previous learning on the recall of new information. As you collect more and more information, your mental attic never fills, but it certainly gets cluttered.

Proactive means forward-acting.

For example, after buying a new combination lock or receiving a new phone number, the old one may interfere. Benton Underwood (1957) explored this phenomenon. He found that people who learn different lists of words on successive days have more and more difficulty remembering each new list the next day. This proactive interference explains why Ebbinghaus, after memorizing countless lists of nonsense syllables during his career, could remember only about one-fourth of a new list of syllables on the day after he learned it—far fewer than you as a novice could remember after learning a single list.

Retroactive interference refers to the disruptive effect of new information on the recall of previous information. For example, the learning of new students' names typically interferes with a professor's recall of names learned in previous classes. Table 9–1 illustrates both types of interference.

Retroactive means backward-acting.

Table 9-1	*Proactive and Retroactive Interference*		
Time 1	**Time 2**	**Test**	**Interference**
Study French	Study Spanish	Recall Spanish	French proactively interferes
Study French	Study Spanish	Recall French	Spanish retroactively interferes

You can minimize retroactive interference by reducing the number of interfering events—say, by going to sleep shortly after learning new information. This is what John Jenkins and Karl Dallenbach (1924) found in a classic experiment. Day after day, two people each learned some nonsense syllables, then tried to recall them after up to 8 hours of being awake or asleep. As Figure 9–20 shows, forgetting occurred more rapidly after being awake and involved with other activities. The investigators surmised that "forgetting is not so much a matter of the decay of old impressions and associations as it is a matter of interference, inhibition, or obliteration of the old by the new" (p. 612). Later experiments confirm that the hour before sleep is a good time to commit information to memory (Fowler & others, 1973).

Although interference is an important cause of forgetting, we should not overstate the point. Sometimes old information facilitates our learning of new information. Knowledge of Latin may aid

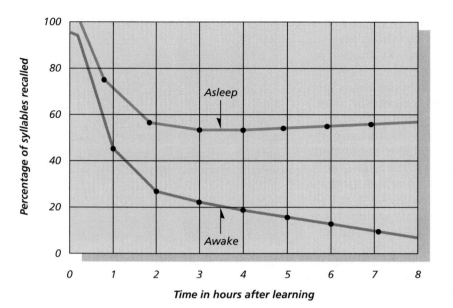

Figure 9-20 Retroactive interference. More forgetting occurs when a person stays awake and learns other new material. (From Jenkins & Dallenbach, 1924.)

Time in hours after learning

one's learning of French—a phenomenon called "positive transfer." It's when the old and new information compete with each other that interference occurs.

Motivated Forgetting The huge cookie jar in our kitchen was jammed with freshly baked chocolate chip cookies. Still more spread across the cooling racks on the counter. Twenty-four hours later, not a crumb was left. Who had taken them? My wife, three children, and I were the only people in the house during that time. So while memories were still fresh, I immediately undertook a little memory test. Andy acknowledged wolfing down as many as 20. Peter admitted eating 15. Laura guessed that she had stuffed her then 6-year-old body with 15 cookies. My wife, Carol, recalled eating 6, and I remembered consuming 15 and taking 18 more to the office. Collectively, our memories sheepishly accepted responsibility for 89 cookies. Still, we had not come close; 160 cookies had been baked.

Why did our memories fail us? Why did we not encode, store, and retrieve almost half the instances of our cookie-eating? As noted earlier, we encode information about frequency fairly automatically. So was it a storage problem? Might our memories of cookies, like Ebbinghaus's memory of nonsense syllables, have vanished almost as fast as the cookies themselves? Or might the information still be intact, but irretrievable because it would be embarrassing to remember?

With his concept of **repression**, Sigmund Freud proposed that our memory systems are indeed self-censoring. To protect our self-concepts and to minimize anxiety, we may repress painful memories. But the submerged memory still lingers, said Freud, and with patience and effort may be retrieved during therapy or by some later cue. One such case involved a woman with an intense, unexplained fear of running water. An aunt solved the mystery one day by whispering, "I have never told." The words cued the woman's memory of an incident when, as a disobedient young child, she wandered away from a family picnic and became trapped under a waterfall—until being rescued by her aunt, who promised not to tell her parents (Kihlstrom, 1990).

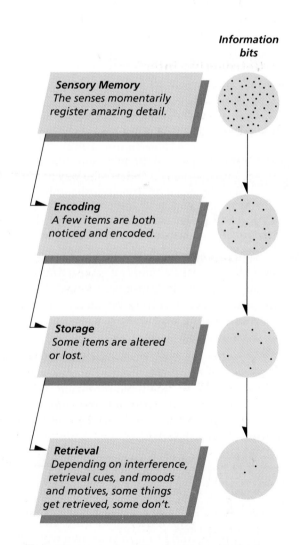

Information bits

Sensory Memory
The senses momentarily register amazing detail.

Encoding
A few items are both noticed and encoded.

Storage
Some items are altered or lost.

Retrieval
Depending on interference, retrieval cues, and moods and motives, some things get retrieved, some don't.

Forgetting can occur at any memory stage. As we process information, we filter, alter, or lose much of it.

Evidence of repression comes from torture or war victims who cannot remember their horror-filled moments. The closest laboratory counterpart to repression (and an alternative explanation of it) is the phenomenon of state-dependent memory (page 274): What we learn in one emotional or physiological state we sometimes forget in a radically different state. Thus, what we experience when embarrassed or horror-struck may be forgotten when relaxed.

In experiments that more closely parallel the cookie-memory phenomenon, Michael Ross and his colleagues (1981) found that people unknowingly revise their own histories. After Ross persuaded a group of people that frequent toothbrushing is desirable, they (more than other people) recalled having frequently brushed their teeth in the last 2 weeks. Having taken a highly touted study skills course, students later inflated their estimates of self-improvement. By *de*flating their evaluations of their previous study habits they convinced themselves that they had really benefitted (Conway & Ross, 1984). To remember our past is often to revise it. By recalling events in a desired manner we protect and enhance our self-images.

After 20 years of repressing the memory, a number of small cues triggered Eileen Franklin-Lipsker's coming forward to claim herself the only witness to her father's molestation and murder of her childhood girlfriend.

Improving Memory *essay*

Now and then we are dismayed at our forgetfulness—at our embarrassing inability to recall someone's name, at forgetting to bring up a point in conversation, at forgetting to bring along something important, at finding ourselves standing in a room unable to recall why we are there (Herrmann, 1982). What can we do to minimize such lapses? Much as biology benefits medicine and botany benefits agriculture, so can the psychology of memory benefit education. Sprinkled throughout this chapter and summarized here for easy reference are concrete suggestions for improving memory. The SQ3R—Study, Question, Read, Recite, Review—study technique introduced in Chapter 1 incorporates several of these strategies.

Study repeatedly to boost long-term recall. Overlearn. To learn a name, say it to yourself after being introduced; wait a few seconds and say it again; wait longer and say it again. To provide many separate study sessions, make use of life's little intervals—riding on the bus, walking across campus, waiting for class to start.

Spend more time rehearsing or actively practicing the material. Speed-reading (skimming) complex material—with minimal rehearsal—yields little retention. Rehearsal helps more. "The act of retrieving an item from memory facilitates subsequent retrieval," advises memory researcher Robert Bjork (1988). It pays to study actively!

Make the material personally meaningful. To build a network of retrieval cues, take thorough text and class notes in your own words. Mindlessly repeating information is relatively ineffective. Better to form images, understand and organize information, relate the material to what you already know or have experienced, and put it in your own words. Without such cues, you may be stuck when a question uses different phrasing than you memorized. To increase retrieval cues, form as many associations as possible.

"Knit each new thing on to some acquisition already there."
William James
Principles of Psychology, 1890

- *Use mnemonic devices to remember a list of unfamiliar items.* Associate items with peg-words. Make up a story that incorporates vivid images of the items. Chunk information into acronyms.

- *Refresh your memory by activating retrieval cues.* Mentally recreate the situation and the mood in which the original learning occurred. Return to the same location. Jog your memory by allowing one thought to cue the next.

Recall events while they are fresh, before you encounter possible misinformation. If you are an eyewitness to an important event, record your memory before allowing others to suggest what may have occurred.

Test your own knowledge, both to rehearse it and to help you determine what you do not yet know. If you must later *recall* information, do not be lulled into overconfidence by your ability to *recognize* it. Test your recall. Outline sections on a blank page. Define concepts before reading their end-of-chapter definitions. Take practice tests; the study guides that accompany many texts, including this one, can help.

- *Minimize interference.* Study right before sleeping. Don't study topics in close proximity that are likely to interfere with each other, such as Spanish and French.

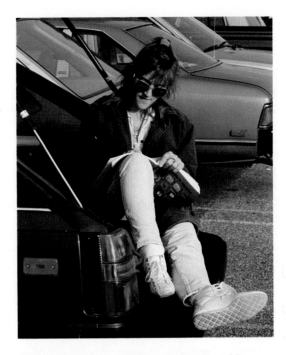

Repeated study—a little and often—yields more lasting memory than massed study.

Summing Up

The Phenomenon of Memory

Memory as Information Processing Memory is the persistence of learning over time. The computer is a convenient model for thinking about human memory. Both systems must encode, store, and retrieve information.

Sensory Memory Information first enters the memory system through the senses. We register visual images via iconic memory and sound via echoic memory.

How We Encode Information

We encode information visually, acoustically, and semantically, and remember better if we have encoded in more than one way.

Automatic and Effortful Processing Some types of information, notably concerning space, time, and frequency, we encode mostly automatically. Other types of information, including much of our processing of meaning, imagery, and organization, require effort. Mnemonic devices depend on the memorability of visual images and of information that is organized into chunks. Organizing information into hierarchies also aids memory.

Forgetting as Encoding Failure One explanation of forgetting is that we fail to encode information for entry into our memory system. Without effortful processing, much of what we sense we never notice or process.

Long-Term Memory

Storage In the short run, our memory span for information just presented is very limited—up to about seven or eight items, depending on the information and how it is presented. Our capacity for storing information permanently is essentially unlimited, but how and where we store it is uncertain. The search for the physical basis of memory has recently focused on the synapses and their neurotransmitters and on brain circuits, such as those running through the hippocampus. Studies of brain-damaged patients reveal two types of memory—explicit (declarative) memories that are processed by the hippocampus, and implicit (nondeclarative) memories processed by even more ancient brain regions.

Retrieval To be remembered, information that is "in there" must be retrieved, with the aid of associations (cues) that serve as primers. Retrieval is sometimes aided by returning to the original context. Mood affects memory, too. While in a good or bad mood, we often retrieve memories congruent with that mood. Memories are not stored as exact copies, and they certainly are not retrieved as such. Rather, we construct our memories, using both stored and new information. Thus, when eyewitnesses are subtly exposed to misinformation after an event, they often believe they *saw* the misleading details as part of the event.

Forgetting as Retrieval Failure Retrieval failures may be caused by proactive or retroactive interference or even by motivated forgetting.

Improving Memory

The psychology of memory suggests concrete strategies for improving memory. These include spaced study; active rehearsal; encoding of well-organized, vivid, meaningful associations; mnemonic techniques; the return to contexts and moods that are rich with associations; self-testing and rehearsal; and minimizing interference.

Terms and Concepts to Remember

memory The persistence of learning over time.

flashbulb memory A clear memory of an emotionally significant moment or event.

encoding The processing of information into the memory system, for example by extracting meaning.

storage The maintenance of encoded information over time.

retrieval The process of getting information out of memory storage.

long-term memory The relatively permanent and limitless storehouse of the memory system.

short-term memory "Working memory" that holds a few items briefly, such as the seven digits of a phone number while dialing, before the information is stored or forgotten.

sensory memory The immediate, initial recording of sensory information in the memory system.

iconic memory A momentary sensory memory of visual stimuli; a photographic or picture-image memory lasting no more than a second or so.

echoic memory A momentary sensory memory of auditory stimuli; if attention is elsewhere, sounds and words can still be recalled within 3 or 4 seconds.

visual encoding The encoding of picture images.

acoustic encoding The encoding of sound, especially the sound of words.

semantic encoding The encoding of meaning, including the meaning of words.

automatic processing Unconscious encoding of incidental information, such as space, time, and frequency, and of well-learned information, such as word meanings.

effortful processing Encoding that requires attention and conscious effort.

rehearsal The conscious repetition of information, either to maintain it in consciousness or to encode it for storage.

spacing effect The tendency for distributed study or practice to yield better long-term retention than massed study or practice.

serial position effect Our tendency to recall best the last and first items in a list.

imagery Mental pictures. A powerful aid to effortful processing, especially when combined with semantic encoding.

mnemonics [nih-MON-iks] Memory aids, especially those techniques that use vivid imagery and organizational devices.

chunking Organizing items into familiar, manageable units; often done automatically.

implicit memory Retention without conscious recollection (of skills, preferences, and dispositions). (Also called *nondeclarative memory*.)

explicit memory Memory of facts and experiences that one can consciously know and "declare." (Also called *declarative memory*.)

hippocampus A neural center in the limbic system that helps process explicit memories for storage.

recall A measure of memory in which the person must retrieve information learned earlier, as on a fill-in-the-blank test.

recognition A measure of memory in which the person need only identify items previously learned, as on a multiple-choice test.

relearning A memory measure that assesses the amount of time saved when relearning previously learned information.

priming The implicit (unconscious) activation of particular associations in memory.

déjà vu (From French, literally meaning "already seen.") That eerie sense that "I've experienced this before." Cues from the current situation may subconsciously trigger retrieval of an earlier experience.

state-dependent memory The tendency to recall information best in the same emotional or physiological state as when the information was learned.

misinformation effect After witnessing an event and receiving misleading information about it, incorporating the "misinformation" into one's memory of the event.

proactive interference The disruptive effect of prior learning on the recall of new information.

retroactive interference The disruptive effect of new learning on the recall of old information.

repression The blocking from consciousness of painful memories and unacceptable impulses.

For Further Reading

Allport, S. (1986). *Explorers of the black box: The search for the cellular basis of memory.* New York: Norton.

The story of the race to find the memory trace, and of the motives and emotions of the scientists involved.

Ashcroft, M. H. (1989). *Human memory and cognition.* Glenview, IL: Scott, Foresman.

A delightfully written textbook introduction to human information processing.

Baddeley, A. (1990). *Human memory.* Boston: Allyn and Bacon.

One of the world's leading researchers offers a new and comprehensive review of memory research.

Brown, A. S. (1987). *Maximizing memory power: Using recall to your advantage in business.* New York: Wiley.

A practical guide to applying memory principles in everyday work.

Higbee, K. L. (1988). *Your memory: How it works and how to improve it* (2nd ed.). Englewood Cliffs, NJ: Prentice-Hall.

A practical guide that shows how to use memory principles to remember names, faces, and appointments, and to cope with aging.

Loftus, E., & Ketcham, K. (1991). *Witness for the defense: The accused, the eyewitness, and the expert who puts memory on trial.* New York: St. Martin's Press.

Memory researcher and frequent expert witness Elizabeth Loftus shows how the imperfections of human memory can produce persuasive but flawed eyewitness reports, by adults and especially by children.

Thinking and Language   *Chapter 10*

Throughout history, we humans have lamented the depths of our foolishness and celebrated the heights of our wisdom. In a moment of humility the psalmist wondered, "What is man that thou art mindful of him?" but in the next breath rhapsodized that human beings were "little less than God." The poet T. S. Eliot was struck by "the hollow men . . . Headpiece filled with straw." But Shakespeare's Hamlet extolled the human species as "noble in reason! . . . infinite in faculties! . . . in apprehension how like a god!" In the preceding chapters, we, too, have sometimes marveled at our capabilities, sometimes at our propensity to err.

We have studied the human brain—a mere 3 pounds of tissue containing circuitry more complex than all the planet's telephone networks. We have marveled at the competence of newborn infants. We have appreciated the human sensory system, which disassembles visual stimuli into millions of nerve impulses, distributes them for parallel processing, and then reassembles them into clear and colorful perceived images. We have acknowledged the seemingly limitless capacity of human memory and the ease with which we process information, consciously and unconsciously. Little wonder, then, that our species has the genius to invent the camera, the car, and the computer; to unlock the atom and crack the genetic code; to travel into space and probe the ocean depths.

At the same time, we have seen that our species is kin to the other animals, influenced by the same principles of learning as rats and pigeons. We have noted that we assimilate reality into our preconceptions and succumb to perceptual illusions and distortions. We have seen how easily we deceive ourselves about hypnotic regressions, pseudopsychic claims, and constructed memories. Little wonder, then, that we sometimes imagine we can read minds and travel outside our bodies; that we form distorted images of other ethnic, age, and gender groups; that we are subject to the same biological impulses as "lesser" creatures.

In this chapter, we encounter further instances of these two images of the human condition—the rational and the irrational. Consider some of the questions we will explore in the pages ahead:

What are concepts? How do we form them?

How do we solve problems?

How reasonable are our judgments and decisions? How can we improve them?

To what extent can computers simulate human thought?

What are the elements of language? How do they develop?

Are humans the only species capable of language?

How do language and thinking affect each other?

The answers to these questions tell us much about the human condition and allow us to contemplate further how deserving we are of our name, *Homo sapiens* — wise human.

Thinking

Previous chapters explain how we receive, perceive, store, and retrieve information. Now we consider how our cognitive system uses this information. **Thinking**, or *cognition,* is the mental activity associated with understanding, processing, and communicating knowledge. **Cognitive psychologists** study these mental activities. We begin this chapter by considering the logical and sometimes illogical ways in which we create concepts, solve problems, make decisions, and form judgments. First, let's consider the building blocks of thinking: concepts.

Concepts

To think about the countless events, objects, and people in our world, we simplify things. We organize them into mental groupings called **concepts**. The concept *chair* sums up a variety of items — a baby's high chair, a wing chair, the chairs around a dining room table, and folding chairs. Most share common features: They have legs, a back, and can be sat on.

Imagine life without concepts. We would need a different name for every object and idea. We could not ask a child to "throw the ball" because there would be no concept of ball. Instead of saying, "He was angry," we would have to describe facial expression, vocal intensity, gestures, and words. Concepts such as *ball* and *angry* provide much information with a minimum of cognitive effort. That is why concepts are the basic building blocks of thought.

To simplify things further, we organize concepts into hierarchies. The earliest naturalists simplified and ordered the overwhelming complexity of some 5 million living species by clustering them into two basic categories — the plant kingdom and the animal kingdom. Then they divided these basic categories into smaller and smaller subcategories — vertebrates, fish, and sharks, for instance, in order of increasing specificity.

The urge to classify the world reflects our human tendency to order our environment into hierarchies of concepts. Doing so makes for cognitive efficiency. Using basic physical concepts, physicists speedily classify and solve physics problems. Cab drivers organize their cities into geographical sectors, which subdivide into neighborhoods and again into blocks. Chess masters conceptually organize chess games in ways that help them see the significance of various game positions (Bransford & others, 1986; Chi & others, 1988).

"Attention everyone! I'd like to introduce the newest member of our family."

Drawing by Kaufman; ©1977 The New Yorker Magazine, Inc.

We form some concepts by definition. Told the rule that a triangle has three sides, we thereafter classify all three-sided geometric forms as triangles. By definition, a bird is an animal that has wings, feathers, and hatches from an egg. More often, we form our concepts by developing **prototypes**—a best example of a particular category (Rosch, 1978). The more closely objects match our prototype of a concept, the more readily we recognize them as examples of the concept. A robin and a goose both satisfy our rule for *bird*. Yet people agree more quickly with the statement, "A robin is a bird" than with the statement, "A goose is a bird." For most of us, the robin is the birdier bird; it more closely resembles our prototype of a bird. This quick and easy way of deciding what belongs to a specific concept is not as logical as the rule-bound method, but it is certainly more efficient. Likewise, "maternal love" and "self-love" both qualify as love. But people more instantly agree that "maternal love is a type of love," because it better matches their prototype (Fehr & Russell, 1991).

If something fails to match our prototype, we may have trouble classifying it. Thus, we might be slow to recognize nonflying penguins and kiwis as birds. We are much quicker to perceive an illness when our symptoms fit one of our disease prototypes (Bishop, 1991). People whose heart attack symptoms don't precisely match their prototype of a heart attack are therefore slow to seek help.

Solving Problems

One tribute to our rationality is our ability to form and use concepts. Another is our skill at solving problems—at coping with novel situations for which we have no well-established response. When arriving home without a key and finding the front door locked, ingenuity often triumphs through a series of steps. First, define the problem: You have no key to unlock the front door. Next, develop a specific strategy: Try the back door; if it's locked, find an unlocked window. Now, carry out the strategy and see if it works.

We solve some problems through trial and error. Thomas Edison tried thousands of light bulb filaments before stumbling upon one that worked. For other problems, we may follow a step-by-step procedure, called an **algorithm**. Told to find another word using all the letters in CINERAMA, we could systematically try each letter in each position—but generating and examining the 20,160 resulting combinations would take too long. Because algorithms can be laborious, we often solve problems with simple rule-of-thumb strategies, called **heuristics**. Thus, in rearranging the letters of CINERAMA, we might exclude letter combinations such as two *a*'s together or words starting with two consonants, such as *mc* or *nm*. By using rules of thumb and then applying trial and error, many people can come up with the answer (page 288).

Sometimes we are unaware of using any problem-solving strategy; the answer just comes to us. We can all recall occasions when we puzzled over a problem for some time and then, suddenly, the pieces fell together and we perceived the solution. This facility for sudden flashes of inspiration we call **insight**.

We humans aren't the only creatures who display insight. German psychologist Wolfgang Köhler (1925) observed insight

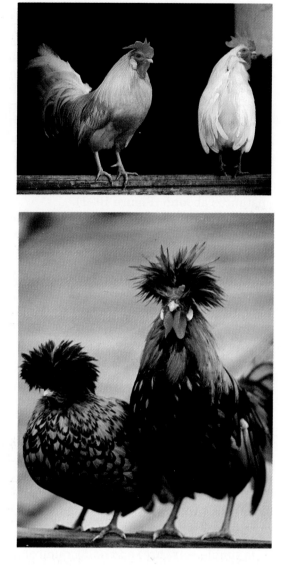

Some chickens match our chicken prototype better than others.

To search for horseradish in a supermarket you could search every aisle (an algorithm) or check the mustard, spice, and gourmet sections (heuristics).

while studying chimpanzees placed on an island off the coast of Africa. In one experiment with a chimp named Sultan, Köhler placed a piece of fruit and a long stick outside the chimp's cage, well beyond reach, and placed a short stick inside the cage. Spying the short stick, Sultan grabbed it and tried to reach the fruit with it. But the stick, by design, was too short. After several unsuccessful attempts, the chimp dropped the stick and paused to survey the whole situation. Then suddenly, as if thinking, "Aha!" Sultan jumped up, seized the short stick again, and this time used it to pull in the longer stick—which he then used to reach the fruit. Sultan's actions displayed animal cognition, claimed Köhler, and showed that there is more to learning than conditioning. Other apparent instances abound (Figure 10–1).

In human experience, insight is common. Köhler described it as the sense of satisfaction that accompanies a flash of inspiration. After solving a difficult problem or discovering how to resolve a conflict, we feel happy. The joy of a joke may similarly lie in our capacity for insight—in our sudden comprehension of an unexpected ending or a double meaning, as in the story of Professor Smith, who complained to his colleagues that student interruptions had become a problem. "The minute I get up to speak," he explained, "some fool begins to talk."

Figure 10–1 Chimpanzee inventiveness. After learning that he could see himself on TV, Austin apparently wanted to see his throat better. So he picked up a flashlight and shined it in his throat, facing the camera. (Based on illustration by Vichai Makilul modified by Richard Swartz in Rumbaugh & Savage-Rumbaugh, 1986.)

Obstacles to Problem Solving Inventive as we can be in solving problems, two cognitive tendencies—*confirmation bias* and *fixation*—often interfere.

Confirmation Bias A major obstacle to problem solving is our eagerness to search for information that confirms our ideas, a phenomenon known as **confirmation bias**. In an experiment with British university students, P. C. Wason (1960) demonstrated our reluctance to seek information that might disprove our beliefs. Wason gave students the three-number sequence, 2-4-6, and asked them to guess the rule he had used to devise the series. (The rule was simple: any three ascending numbers.) Before submitting their answers, the students generated their own sets of three numbers, and each time Wason told them whether or not their sets conformed to his rule. Once they had done enough testing to feel *certain* they had the rule, they were to announce it.

The result? Seldom right but never in doubt: Most people convinced themselves of a wrong rule. Typically, they formed an erroneous idea ("Maybe it's counting by twos") and then searched only for confirming evidence (by testing 6-8-10, 100-102-104, and so forth). Such experiments reveal that we more eagerly seek evidence that will verify our ideas than evidence that might refute them (Klayman & Ha, 1987; Skov & Sherman, 1986). Business managers, for example, are more likely to follow the successful careers of those they've hired than of those they've rejected, which helps them confirm their perceived hiring ability.

In other experiments Wason (1981) found that once people have a wrong idea they often will not budge from their illogic. "This incorrigible conviction that they are right when they are, in fact, wrong has analogies to real-life crises of belief. . . . Ordinary people evade facts, become inconsistent, or systematically defend themselves against the threat of new information relevant to the issue."

"The human understanding, when any proposition has been once laid down . . . forces everything else to add fresh support and confirmation."
Francis Bacon
Novum Organum, 1620

Answer to CINERAMA anagram on page 287: AMERICAN.

Fixation Try your hand at some brainteasers drawn from classic experiments.

Arrange the six matches shown in Figure 10–2 so they form four equilateral triangles.

Suppose that you have a 21-cup jug, a 127-cup jug, and a 3-cup jug. Drawing and discarding as much water as you like, how will you measure out exactly 100 cups of water? This problem is the first of seven presented in Figure 10–3. Solve the remaining problems, too.

Figure 10–2 How would you arrange six matches to form four equilateral triangles? (From "Problem solving" by M. Scheerer. Copyright 1963 by Scientific American, Inc. All rights reserved.)

Problem	Given jugs of these sizes:			Measure out this much water:
	A	B	C	
1	21	127	3	100
2	14	46	5	22
3	18	43	10	5
4	7	42	6	23
5	20	57	4	29
6	23	49	3	20
7	15	39	3	18

Figure 10–3 Using jugs *A*, *B*, and *C* with the capacities shown in the table, how would you measure out the volumes indicated in the right-hand column? (From Luchins, 1946.)

I ♡ Brad

How can you use the box of matches, thumbtacks, and candle shown in Figure 10–4 to mount the candle on a bulletin board?

(It will pay you to read on only after trying all these problems.)

Figure 10–4 Using these materials, how would you mount the candle on a bulletin board? (From Duncker, 1945.)

A major obstacle to problem solving is **fixation**—the inability to see a problem from a fresh perspective. Once we incorrectly represent the problem, it's hard to restructure how we approach it. If your attempts to solve the match problem were fixated on two-dimensional solutions, then the three-dimensional solution shown in Figure 10–5 will have eluded you.

We become fixated on certain solutions for good reason: Solutions that worked in the past often work on new problems. Consider one more brainteaser:

Given the sequence O-T-T-F-?-?-?, what are the final three letters?

Most people have difficulty recognizing that the three final letters are F(ive), S(ix), and S(even). But solving this problem may make the next one easier:

Given the sequence J-F-M-A-?-?-?, what are the final three letters?

(If you had difficulty with this one, too, you might ask yourself what month it is.)

Although past success can help solve present problems, it may also interfere with our taking a fresh approach when faced with problems that demand an entirely new solution. This tendency to repeat solutions that have worked in the past is a type of fixation called **mental set**. The match problem is one example of mental set. You likely ran into it again in the water jug problems. For the first jug problem, you probably developed the following formula:

B - A - $2C$ = desired amount of water.

This same formula works for all seven problems. Once you developed this mental set, you probably solved the later problems much faster than you did the first. But how did you solve problems 6 and 7? Did the mental set cause you to miss the much simpler solutions (A - C for 6; A + C for 7) shown in Figure 10–6?

Figure 10–5 Solving the matchstick problem requires breaking a fixation, that of limiting your considerations to two-dimensional solutions. (From "Problem Solving" by M. Scheerer. Copyright 1963 by Scientific American, Inc. All rights reserved.)

A mental set is like a perceptual set (page 177), except it affects problem solving rather than perception.

Figure 10–6 (a) The solution to all the three-jug problems is: B - A - $2C$ = desired volume of water. (b) But simpler solutions exist for problems 6 and 7, such as A - C for problem 6. Did your mental set cause you to miss it? (From Luchins, 1946.)

Flexible, rational thinking becomes more difficult in times of stress and tension (Janis, 1989). During international crises, for example, views of an enemy become fixed in simplified good-versus-bad terms. During personal crises, too, thinking often becomes rigid. During the Korean War, a paratrooper readying for a mission was given the last parachute—a left-handed one. "It's the same as the others," explained the ordnance sergeant, "but the rip cord hangs on the left side of the harness." At 8000 feet, the soldiers jumped one by one, and all went well—except for this one man who fell straight to his death. Investigators discovered that under the stress of the jump the man had become fixated on the familiar way to open a chute. The right side of his uniform, where normally he found the rip cord, was completely torn off. Even his chest flesh had been gouged by his bloody right hand. Inches to the left was the rip cord, apparently untouched (Csikszentmihalyi, 1990).

Another type of fixation goes by the awkward but appropriate label, **functional fixedness**. This is our tendency to perceive the functions of objects as fixed and unchanging. A person may ransack the house for a screwdriver when a dime would have done the job. Perhaps you fell victim to functional fixedness when you tried to solve the candle-mounting problem. If you thought of the matchbox as having only the function of holding matches, you may have overlooked its potential for serving as a platform for the candle, as shown in Figure 10–7. Perceiving and relating familiar things in new ways is an important aspect of creativity, which we will consider in Chapter 11, Intelligence.

Figure 10–7 Solving the candle-mounting problem requires recognizing that a box need not always serve as a container. (From Duncker, 1945.)

Making Decisions and Forming Judgments

When making each day's hundreds of tiny judgments and decisions—Is it worth the bother to take an umbrella? Can I trust this person? Should I shoot the basketball or pass to the player who's hot?—we seldom take the time and effort to reason systematically (see Close-Up: Making Sound Decisions). Usually, we follow our intuition. After interviewing policymakers in government, business, and education, social psychologist Irving Janis (1986) concluded that they "often do not use a reflective problem-solving approach. How do they usually arrive at their decisions? If you ask, they are likely to tell you ... they do it mostly by the *seat of their pants*."

Using and Misusing Heuristics Those mental shortcuts we call heuristics often help us make reasonable seat-of-the-pants judgments. But the price we pay for their efficiency can sometimes be costly bad judgments. To gain an idea of how heuristics determine our intuitive judgments—and how they can lead us astray—consider two heuristics identified by cognitive psychologists Amos Tversky and Daniel Kahneman (1974): *representativeness* and *availability*.

The Representativeness Heuristic To judge the likelihood of things in terms of how well they represent particular prototypes is to use the **representativeness heuristic**. To illustrate, consider:

> A stranger tells you about a person who is short, slim, and likes to read poetry, and then asks you to guess whether this person is more likely to be a professor of classics at an Ivy League university or a truck driver. Which would be the better guess? (Adapted from Nisbett & Ross, 1980.)

If you are like most people, you answered a professor because the description seems more *representative* of Ivy League scholars than of truck drivers. The representativeness heuristic enabled you to make a snap judgment. But it also led you to ignore other relevant information, such as the total number of classics professors versus truck drivers. When I help people think through this question, their own reasoning usually leads them to an answer that contradicts their immediate intuition. The typical conversation goes something like this:

"The information-processing shortcuts—called heuristics—which are normally both highly efficient and immensely time-saving in day-to-day situations, work systematically against us in the marketplace. . . . The tendency to underestimate or altogether ignore past probabilities in making a decision is undoubtedly the most significant problem of intuitive predictions."
David Dreman
*Contrarian Investment Strategy:
The Psychology of Stock Market Success*, 1979

Question: *First, let's figure out how many professors fit the description. How many Ivy League universities do you suppose there are?*

Answer: *Oh, about 10, I suppose.*

Question: *How many classics professors would you guess there are at each?*

Answer: *Maybe four.*

Question: *Okay, that's 40 Ivy League classics professors. What fraction of these are short and slim?*

Answer: *Let's say half.*

Question: *And, of these 20, how many like to read poetry?*

Answer: *I'd say half—10 professors.*

Question: *Okay, now let's figure how many truck drivers fit the description. How many truck drivers do you suppose there are?*

Answer: *Maybe 400,000.*

Question: *What fraction are short and slim?*

Answer: *Not many—perhaps 1 in 8.*

Question: *Of these 50,000, what percentage like to read poetry?*

Answer: *Truck drivers who like poetry? Maybe 1 in 100—oh, oh, I can see where this is going—that leaves me with 500 short, slim, poetry-reading truck drivers.*

Question: *Yup. So, although the person I described may be much more representative of classics professors than of truck drivers, this person is still (even accepting your stereotypes) 50 times more likely to be a truck driver.*

The power of the representativeness heuristic is illustrated in the "conjunction fallacy" (Tversky & Kahneman, 1983). They told college students that "Bill is 34 years old. He is intelligent but unimaginative, compulsive, and generally lifeless. In school, he was strong in mathematics but weak in social studies and humanities." Based on this description, students judged there was little chance that "Bill plays jazz for a hobby." But 87 percent thought there was a better chance that "Bill is an accountant who plays jazz for a hobby" (because Bill seemed more representative of accountants). If you agree, think about it: Is there a better chance that Bill *both* plays jazz *and* is an accountant than that he plays jazz alone? (The conjunction of two events can't be more likely than either event alone.)

These examples all point to the power of the representativeness heuristic. To judge the likelihood of something, we intuitively compare it to our mental representation of that category—of, say, what truck drivers or accountants are like. If the two match, then that fact usually overrides other considerations of statistics or logic.

The Availability Heuristic The **availability heuristic** operates when we base our judgments on the availability of information in our memories. If instances of an event are easily available—if they come to mind readily—we presume such events are common. Usually they are—but not always. To see this, make a guess: Does the letter *k* appear more often as the first or third letter in English words?

Because words beginning with *k* come to mind more easily than words having *k* as their third letter, most people guess that *k* occurs more frequently as the first letter. Actually, *k* is three times more likely to appear as the third letter. So far in this chapter, words such as *know*, *kingdoms*, and *kin* are outnumbered more than 2 to 1 by words such as *make*, *likely*, *asked*, and *acknowledged*.

Close-Up
Making Sound Decisions

Benefits	Costs
1. Gains for self:	1. Losses for self:
2. Gains for others:	2. Losses for others:
3. Self-approval:	3. Self-disapproval:
4. Social approval:	4. Social disapproval:

"In creating these problems, we didn't set out to fool people. All our problems fooled us, too."
Amos Tversky (1985)

After studying how people arrive at good and bad decisions, psychologists Daniel Wheeler and Irving Janis (1980) devised a system for making wise decisions. They recommend five steps to people faced with a challenge:

1. *Accept the challenge.* If the opportunity or the problem is genuine, do not ignore it. Do not rationalize ("It can't happen to me"). Do not procrastinate ("I'll deal with it later"). Do not shuck responsibility ("Let George handle it"). And do not panic.

2. *Search for alternatives.* Specify your goals and think up ways to achieve them.

3. *Evaluate the alternatives.* For each reasonable alternative, fill out a balance sheet, such as the one in the figure at left. List positive and negative considerations in several categories. Wheeler and Janis reported that people who do so later express fewer regrets and remain more strongly committed to their choice.

4. *Make a commitment.* Choose the alternative that gives you maximum benefits at minimum costs.

5. *Stick to your decision.* Anticipate likely difficulties and prepare to deal with them. Assess the consequences and begin the next decision cycle, by accepting the challenge of new problems and opportunities.

The judgmental errors influenced by the availability heuristic are frequently harmless, but not always. Many important decisions involve judgments of risk. Whether we favor using nuclear power or coal to produce energy depends partly on our judgments of the risks to health and environment. Our efforts to prevent various deadly diseases depend on our judgments of the likelihood of their occurrence. Our choice to spend or not to spend money on state lotteries (which return in prizes only about half of each dollar bet) depends on our hunch of the odds of striking it rich. Based on the roughly 10 million to 1 odds against a bet winning a state Lotto jackpot, the chances are not much better than the odds of being struck by lightning.

Those who sell life, health, and theft insurance sometimes exploit our tendency to believe that events are more likely if we can picture them readily (Cialdini & Carpenter, 1981). By having people imagine their families in mourning or their possessions stolen, sellers of insurance may cause the images of these disasters to linger, making them seem more likely to occur and, therefore, to be worth insuring against. In one experiment, Larry Gregory and his colleagues (1982) gave Arizona residents promotional information about cable TV, and asked others to picture themselves enjoying movies on cable instead of spending money on babysitters and gas. The latter group, having readily available images of themselves as subscribers, were more than twice as likely to subscribe.

The availability heuristic also affects our social judgments. Ruth Hamill and her co-workers (1980) presented people with a single, vivid case of welfare misuse. The case involved a long-term welfare recipient who had several unruly children fathered by different men. The statistical fact is that this case is exceptional: Most Americans who receive welfare do so for 4 years or less (Duncan & others, 1988). Yet when the statistical reality was pitted against the single vivid case, the memorable case proved more persuasive when people later gave their opinions about welfare recipients. A graphic anecdote, it seems, is worth a thousand factual statistics.

"The human understanding is most excited by that which strikes and enters the mind at once and suddenly, and by which the imagination is immediately filled and inflated. It then begins almost imperceptibly to conceive and suppose that everything is similar to the few objects which have taken possession of the mind."
Francis Bacon
Novum Organum, 1620

Close-Up   *Perceiving Risk–When Statistics Clash with Heuristics*

Because vivid events are more available to memory, they seem more common than they are.

"Most people reason dramatically, not quantitatively," said Oliver Wendell Holmes. With horrific television and magazine images of air crashes in mind, many people, petrified of air travel, prefer the safety of their own cars. Of those who did fly during 1989, 44 percent reported feeling fearful (*Gallup Report*, 1989).

Ironically, the statistical reality is that, mile for mile, U.S. travelers during the 1980s were 26 times more likely to die in a car crash than on a commercial flight (National Safety Council, 1991). During 1986 and 1987,

for example, 5 scheduled flights out of 13 million—that's 1 flight in every 2.6 million—involved an accident that caused anyone's death (Hebert, 1988).

Still, when overall statistics vie with vivid images of helpless crash victims, many people find the memorable instances more persuasive. It's like judging the likelihood of shark attacks after watching *Jaws*: Regardless of statistics, memorable images have a way of heightening swimmers' feelings of risk. Or like judging, from seeing the faces of missing children on milk cartons, your child's risk of being abducted by a stranger—which the U.S. Justice Department reports actually happens no more than 300 times a year nationwide (Bonner, 1990). In fact, virtually all child snatchings are family related.

In 1988, a terrorist bomb exploded on Pan Am Flight 103 over Scotland, causing many would-be international vacationers to stay home and brave the more dangerous highways. The same fearful public continues to drive without seatbelts, smoke billions of cigarettes a year, guzzle alcohol, and devour foods that put people at risk for the greatest of killers—heart disease. All because people's *perceptions* of risk are virtually unrelated to actual risk (Slovic, 1987)—a phenomenon due partly to our greater fear of things we cannot control and partly to our overestimating the likelihood of dreaded, publicized, and cognitively available events.

And that is why, whether making travel plans or diet decisions, defining safety standards or evaluating environmental hazards, rational people will define risks based not on mentally available media images but on statistical reality.

Overconfidence Our use of intuitive heuristics when forming judgments, our eagerness to confirm the beliefs we already hold, and our facility for explaining away failures combine to create **overconfidence,** a tendency to overestimate the accuracy of our knowledge and judgments.

Kahneman and Tversky (1979) asked people to estimate the answers to little-known factual questions, by making their answers cover a wide enough range to surely include the actual answer. For example, "I feel 98 percent certain that the number of nuclear power plants operating in the world in 1980 was more than _____ but fewer than _____." Nearly one-third of the time, people's estimates made with 98 percent confidence failed to include the correct answer (189 nuclear power plants, in this instance). Although very sure of themselves, people were often wrong.

Similarly, people are more confident than correct when answering such questions as, "Is absinthe a liqueur or a precious stone?" On questions where people's answers are only 60 percent correct, they typically feel 75 percent confident. Even when people feel 100 percent certain of their answers to such questions, they err about 15 percent of the time (Fischhoff & others, 1977). (In case you are wondering, absinthe is a licorice-flavored liqueur.)

Overconfidence plagues decision making outside the laboratory, too. Stockbrokers and investment managers market their services with confidence that they can outperform the market average in picking stocks, despite overwhelming evidence to the contrary (Malkiel, 1985). (A purchase of stock *X*, recommended by a broker who judges this to be the time to buy, is balanced by a seller who judges this to be the time to sell. Despite their confidence, they can't both be right.)

To check people's confidence in making social judgments, David Dunning and his colleagues (1990) asked Stanford University students to guess a stranger's answers to 20 two-choice questions. Topics included whether the person would pocket $5 found in a restaurant or turn it in, whether the person studies for exams alone or with others, and whether the person's lecture notes are neat or messy. Knowing the type of questions (but not the actual questions), the subjects were first given a chance to interview the target person about academic interests, hobbies, family background, aspirations, strengths and weaknesses, astrological sign, and anything else they thought might prove helpful. Then the target person answered the 20 questions while the interviewer predicted the target's answers.

The result? The interviewers were "markedly overconfident." Although they guessed right on 63 percent of their predictions, they felt, on average, 75 percent sure. When guessing their own roommates' responses to the 20 questions, subjects were somewhat more accurate—68 percent. But, again, their 78 percent confidence exceeded their accuracy. And the most confident people were the most *over*confident.

Would people better predict their *own* future actions? To find out, Robert Vallone and his associates (1990) had students predict at the beginning of the school year whether they would drop a course, vote in the November election, call their parents more than twice a month, and so forth. On average, the students felt 84 percent confident in making these self-predictions. Quizzed later about their actual behavior, however, their predictions were correct only 71 percent of the time. Even when 100 percent sure of themselves, their self-predictions erred 15 percent of the time.

Or consider the confidence of new collegians about their college future: As they begin college, only 2 percent of American students say there is a very good chance they will drop out permanently or temporarily (Astin, 1991). But the optimism of the other 98 percent is unrealistic. Nearly half of students entering a 4-year college or university do not earn a degree within 5 years.

As do other cognitive limitations, overconfidence has adaptive value. Failing to appreciate one's potential for error when making military, economic, or political judgments can have devastating consequences, but so can *lack* of self-confidence. People who err on the side of overconfidence live more happily and find it easier to make tough decisions (Baumeister, 1989; Taylor, 1989). Moreover, when given prompt and clear feedback on the accuracy of their judg-

'What do you mean 'Your guess is as good as mine'? My guess is a hell of a lot better than your guess!'

Drawing by Ross; ©1983 The New Yorker Magazine, Inc.

"We don't like their sound. Groups of guitars are on their way out."
    Decca Records, in turning down a recording contract with the Beatles

ments—as weather forecasters are after each day's predictions—people soon learn to assess their accuracy more realistically (Fischhoff, 1982). The wisdom to know when we know a thing and when we do not is born of experience.

Framing Decisions   A further test of rationality is whether the same issue, presented in two different but logically equivalent ways, will elicit the same answer. For example, whether a surgeon tells someone that 10 percent die during a particular surgery or that 90 percent survive, the information is the same. But the effect is not. The risk seems greater to people who hear that 10 percent will die (Marteau, 1989). This effect of the way we present an issue is called the **framing** effect.

Kahneman and Tversky (1984) studied the effect of framing by setting up situations such as the following:

> Imagine that the United States is preparing for the outbreak of a rare flu that is expected to kill 600 people. Two alternative programs to combat the disease have been proposed.

Those given the following two choices overwhelmingly favored Program *A*:

> If Program *A* is adopted, 200 people will be saved.
> If Program *B* is adopted, there is ⅓ probability that all 600 people will be saved, and ⅔ probability that no people will be saved.

Others, given the same choices in different words, overwhelmingly favored Program *B*:

> If Program *A* is adopted, 400 people will die.
> If Program *B* is adopted, there is ⅓ probability that nobody will die, and ⅔ probability that all 600 people will die.

Similarly, consumers respond more positively to ground beef described as "75 percent lean" rather than "25 percent fat" (Levin & Gaeth, 1988). A new medical treatment strikes people as more successful and recommendable if framed as having a "50 percent success rate" rather than a "50 percent failure rate" (Levin & others, 1988).

And consider the framing effect on economic and business decisions. Many people find a 7 percent pay cut when there is no inflation much more objectionable than a 5 percent pay raise when inflation is 12 percent—though the effect is basically the same (Kahneman & others, 1986). If your dentist offers a 5 percent discount for immediate cash payment, you may not feel particularly unhappy if you have to pay the full fee when making a late payment. But you would probably be irritated if the same fee were framed differently—say, if the basic fee were lowered 5 percent with an equivalent surcharge for late payment. Somehow, a 5 percent surcharge is more irritating than a forfeited 5 percent discount, although they add up to the same thing. And people who say they would drive to another store to save $5 on a pocket calculator typically say they would *not* do so to save $5 on a $200 stereo. Thus, the way a $5 saving is framed affects how we react.

That people's judgments flip-flop so dramatically is startling. It suggests that our judgments and decisions may not be well reasoned, and that those who understand the power of framing can use it to influence important decisions—for example, by framing survey questions to support or reject a particular viewpoint.

"When you know a thing, to hold that you know it; and when you do not know a thing, to allow that you do not know it; this is knowledge."
Confucius, 551–479 B.C.
Analects

"This CD player costs less than players selling for twice as much."
Drawing by Weber; © 1989 The New Yorker Magazine, Inc.

Belief Bias

We have seen that part of psychology's new thinking about thinking emphasizes that we are prone to bias—from seeking confirmation for our hunches, to reliance on efficient but fallible heuristics, to overconfidence and the effects of framing. Through brute logic, can we escape the bias inflicted by our beliefs?

Logic helps, but we still find it easier to accept conclusions that agree with our opinions. Consider the logical argument:

Premise 1: Some communists are golfers.
Premise 2: All golfers are Marxists.
Conclusion: Some communists are Marxists.

In experiments, nearly everyone correctly recognized that the conclusion logically follows from the premises (Oakhill & others, 1989). But consider:

Premise 1: Some communists are golfers.
Premise 2: All golfers are capitalists.
Conclusion: Some communists are capitalists.

Many people had a harder time seeing that, given the premises, this conclusion is equally valid. (Given changing economic policies in some communist countries, people today find the conclusion easier to accept.) Judge this next conclusion for yourself (adapted from Hunt, 1982):

Premise 1: People who believe in democracy believe in free speech.
Premise 2: Dictators do not believe in democracy.
Conclusion: Dictators do not believe in free speech.

If that conclusion seems logical, you are experiencing **belief bias**—the tendency for our beliefs to distort logical reasoning (Oakhill & others, 1990). Consider another set of statements *with identical form and logic* and note how much easier it feels to refute the conclusion:

Premise 1: Robins have feathers.
Premise 2: Chickens are not robins.
Conclusion: Chickens do not have feathers.

Thus, belief bias: We more easily see the illogic of conclusions that run counter to our beliefs ("Chickens do not have feathers") than those that agree with our beliefs ("Dictators do not believe in free speech").

The Belief Perseverance Phenomenon An additional source of irrationality is our tendency, called **belief perseverance**, to cling to our beliefs in the face of contrary evidence. Belief perseverance often fuels social conflict. Charles Lord and his colleagues (1979) revealed how this happens when they studied two groups of students. One favored capital punishment, the other opposed it. People on both sides studied two supposedly new research findings, one supporting and the other refuting the claim that the death penalty deters crime. Each side was more impressed by the study that supported its beliefs, and readily disputed the other study. Thus, showing the pro- and anti-capital punishment groups the *same* mixed evidence actually *increased* their disagreement.

For those who wish to rein in the belief perseverance phenomenon, a simple remedy exists: *Consider the opposite.* When Lord

"Once you have a belief, it influences how you perceive all other relevant information. Once you see a country as hostile, you are likely to interpret ambiguous actions on their part as signifying their hostility."
Political scientist Robert Jervis (1985)

and his colleagues (1984) repeated the capital punishment study, they asked some of their subjects to be "as *objective* and *unbiased* as possible." The plea did nothing to reduce the biased evaluation of evidence. They asked another group, however, to consider the opposite—to ask themselves "whether you would have made the same high or low evaluations had exactly the same study produced results on the *other* side of the issue." Having imagined and pondered opposite findings, these people were much less biased in their evaluations of the evidence.

If ambiguous evidence gets interpreted as supporting a person's preexisting belief, would the belief be demolished by information that clearly discredits its premises? Not necessarily. In some provocative experiments, Craig Anderson and Lee Ross discovered that it can be surprisingly difficult to change a false belief once a person has in mind ideas that support it. In one such study with Mark Lepper (1980), they asked subjects to consider whether risk-prone people or cautious people are better fire fighters. Then they told half of the subjects about a risk-taker who was an excellent fire fighter and a cautious person who was a poor fire fighter. From these cases, the subjects surmised that risk-prone people tend to be better fire fighters. Asked to explain their belief, a typical response was, "Risk-takers are braver." The researchers gave the other subjects two cases suggesting the opposite conclusion, that cautious people are better fire fighters. Subjects typically reasoned, "Cautious people think before they act. They're less likely to make foolish mistakes."

The researchers then discredited the foundation for the beliefs of both groups by truthfully informing them that the cases were simply made up for the experiment. Did discrediting the evidence undermine the subjects' newly formed beliefs? Not by much, because the subjects held on to their explanations for *why* these new beliefs made sense. Although the evidence was gone, their theory survived.

Paradoxically, the more we come to appreciate why our beliefs *might* be true, the more tightly we cling to them. Once people have explained to themselves why they believe that a child is "gifted" or "learning disabled," that presidential candidate X or Y will be more likely to preserve peace or start a war, or that women are naturally superior or inferior, they tend to ignore evidence that undermines that belief.

Belief perseverance applies even to our beliefs about ourselves. Lepper and Ross (with Richard Lau, 1986) encountered it after showing California high school students either an effective or a confusing instructional film. Each film demonstrated how to solve some reasoning problems. Those shown the effective film did well on a later test, felt successful, and surmised that they were good at such problem solving. Those shown the useless film did poorly, felt like failures, and surmised that they weren't very competent on such problems. Even when the researchers then explained that the *film* was responsible for their success or failure and showed them the other film as evidence, the students persisted in seeing themselves as either good or incompetent at that type of reasoning problem.

And that, say the researchers, helps explain why early school failures can be so damaging. Even clearly demonstrating to children that their poor school performance "may well have been the consequence of an inept or biased teacher, a substandard school, or even prior social, cultural, or economic disadvantages" may fail to

Do risk-prone or cautious people make better fire fighters? Once persuaded to have an opinion on such a question, with reasons for our view, we are often reluctant to change it—even if shown that the information on which we formed the opinion is invalid.

"To begin with, it was only tentatively that I put forward the views I have developed . . . but in the course of time they have gained such a hold upon me that I can no longer think in any other way."
Sigmund Freud
Civilization and Its Discontents, 1930

To prevent subjects from leaving the experiment feeling incompetent, the researchers extensively debriefed and reassured them.

dent their feelings of incompetence. Once the belief forms that "I'm not very smart," it tends to persist.

The belief perseverance phenomenon does not rule out people's changing their beliefs. It's just that once beliefs form and get justified, it takes more compelling evidence to change them than it did to create them.

We have seen how our irrational thinking can plague our efforts to solve problems, make wise decisions, form valid judgments, and reason logically. For this we might be tempted to conclude that our heads are indeed filled with straw. All in all, the findings we have reviewed—and many more that we have not—suggest "bleak implications for human rationality" (Nisbett & Borgida, 1975). Still, let us not forget that our cognition is effective and efficient: It enables our survival and our inventive genius.

One reason we function as well as we do is that in many real-life situations flawed reasoning may nevertheless lead to correct conclusions (Funder, 1987). Physicians, for example, recognize the similarity between a patient's symptoms and those typical of a particular disease and then proceed to check out the hunch. In effect, their reasoning goes like this (Hunt, 1982):

"I'm happy to say that my final judgment of a case is almost always consistent with my prejudgment of the case."

Drawing by Fradon; ©1973 The New Yorker Magazine, Inc.

> Symptoms *A*, *B*, and *C* indicate disease *X*.
> This patient has symptoms *A*, *B*, and *C*.
> Therefore, I presume this patient has disease *X*.

The physician's conclusion is not logically necessary. (Other diseases may also have symptoms *A*, *B*, and *C*.) Yet it is efficient and plausible, perhaps even probable. We reason, then, not so much by formal logic as by simplified, speedy heuristics, such as, "This situation reminds me of situations I have faced before, so what was true in those situations should be true here." Experts in fields other than medicine—even avid racetrack bettors who intuitively calculate the odds on horses (Ceci & Liker, 1986)—are similarly shrewd without necessarily knowing exactly how they reason.

Still, we should not underestimate the worth of sound reasoning. When deriving scientific hypotheses, playing chess, or debating political issues, it helps to have the powers of reason at our disposal. This is why many college courses, including this one, aim to enhance logical and critical thinking. This is also why psychologists study obstacles to problem solving and biases in reasoning. By learning about our irrational tendencies, we hope to discover how we might learn to reason more logically. You solve arithmetic problems efficiently *and* rationally because you were taught to do so. Perhaps we could also teach people how to think through other sorts of problems more efficiently *and* rationally. This is one of my goals in the Appendix, which suggests remedies for common flaws in people's statistical reasoning.

Artificial Intelligence

A tribute to human cognition comes from attempts to simulate human thinking on computers. **Artificial intelligence (AI)** is the science of designing computer systems to perform operations that mimic human thinking and do "intelligent" things. AI systems rely on massive amounts of stored information and on explicit rules for retrieving it. A hybrid of cognitive psychology and computer science, AI has two facets, one practical, the other theoretical.

The practical side of AI has given us industrial robots that can "sense" their environment; "expert systems" that can carry out chemical analyses, offer tax planning advice, forecast weather, and help physicians diagnose their patients' diseases; and chess programs that can now beat all but a handful of masters and are close to defeating the world chess champion (Hsu & others, 1990). The theoretical side of AI, pioneered by psychologist Herbert Simon, studies how humans think by trying to design computer systems that mimic or rival human thought processes. The goal is a "unified theory of cognition" embodied in a computer system that can process information, solve problems, learn from experience, and remember much as humans do (Waldrop, 1988).

Can computers mimic our thinking powers? In those areas where humans seem to have the most difficulty—manipulating huge amounts of numerical data, retrieving detailed information from memory, making decisions using specified rules—the computer shines. Indeed, its proficiency makes the computer indispensable to banks, libraries, and the space program. But even the most sophisticated computers are dwarfed by the most ordinary of human mental abilities—recognizing a face, distinguishing a cat from a dog, knowing whether the word *line* refers to a rope or a fragment of poetry or a social come-on, and exercising common sense. Notes Donald Griffin (1984), "Human minds do more than process information; they think and feel. We experience beliefs, desires, fears, expectations, and many other subjective mental states."

Compare computer operations with the brain's. Electricity races through the computer's microcircuits millions of times faster than neural impulses travel through our systems. Yet most computers process information serially—one step at a time in sequence. Serial processing resembles a parade, where row after row passes by the reviewing stand, one at a time. By contrast, the human brain more closely resembles New York City's Grand Central Station at rush hour, processing millions of unrelated bits of information simultaneously. One part of the brain analyzes speech while other parts recognize pictures, detect smells, or plan action. As Chapter 5, Sensation, explains, the visual system splits information about color, depth, movement, and form into separate channels, processes each channel simultaneously, and reassembles the information into a recognized image. Through this capacity for simultaneous, or "parallel," processing, the brain outclasses the serial computer. Computer processing exceeds our thinking at tasks that use its unique strengths—vast memory and precise logic and retrieval. But computers have not duplicated the wide-ranging intelligence of a human mind, a mind that can *all at once* converse naturally, perceive the environment, use common sense, experience emotion, and consciously reflect on its own existence.

As enthusiasm for traditional artificial intelligence moderates, excitement grows over **neural networks**—computer systems designed to mimic the brain's interconnected neural units (McClelland & Rumelhart, 1988). As the brain has billions of neurons, each connected to thousands of others, so each computer processing unit can be connected to many others. The computer's electronic "neural network" can be programmed to execute rules that mimic how the brain's neurons communicate, with positive (excitatory) or negative (inhibitory) messages that fire when the signal strength reaches a certain threshold. As in the brain, the "neural"

Imagine a relatively simple task—instructing a computer to discern the difference between these two ads (from Schnitzer, 1984):

1. *Car for sale. A classic! Lemon yellow coupe. Exterior is completely rustproof. Can be delivered upon request. No engine runs better. If the sun is out, you can remove the roof for the feel of the wind in your hair. Go ahead and kick the tires.*
2. *Car for sale. A classic lemon. Yellow coupe exterior is completely rust. Proof can be delivered upon request! No engine. Runs better if the sun is out. You can remove the roof. For the feel of the wind in your hair, go ahead and kick the tires.*

"The things that distinguish us from monkeys— playing chess, for example—are easy for computers to do. But when it comes to doing things we share with the animal kingdom, computers are awful. In computing vision or movement, for example, no computer comes even close to matching the abilities of a fly."
Brain researcher Christof Koch (1988)

connections are programmed to gain strength with experience. The computer system's complex interaction is mind-boggling, but the basic idea is that simple.

The most exciting feature of artificial neural networks is their capacity to learn from experience as some interconnections strengthen and others weaken. This feature, together with their capacity for parallel processing, enables neural network computers to learn to recognize particular shapes, sounds, and smells, which conventional computers find extremely difficult. The hoped-for payoffs go two ways. Neural network systems provide neuroscientists with new ways to test models of how living neural systems process sensations and memories. And they provide computer scientists with new insights into how to mimic the brain's thinking power. The dream is that someday we may better understand how our own brains function—*and* benefit from tools such as robots that can learn and telephone systems that can understand and translate speech, allowing, say, an English- and a Spanish-speaking person to converse directly (Waldrop, 1988). More and more, the brain provides a model of how, in the future, computers might work.

This neural network, used for robot vision, is loosely modeled on the human retina. Its central area (fovea) has 102 photo cells, and its peripheral area consists of 30 concentric circles, each with 64 photo cells.

Language

The most tangible indication of our thinking power is **language**—our spoken, written, or gestured words and how we combine them as we think and communicate. Humans have long and proudly proclaimed that language sets us above all other animals. "When we study human language," asserted linguist Noam Chomsky (1972), "we are approaching what some might call the 'human essence,' the distinctive qualities of mind that are, so far as we know, unique" to humans. To cognitive scientist Steven Pinker (1990), language is "the jewel in the crown of cognition." When the human vocal tract evolved the capacity to utter the commonest vowels (which chimps cannot), our capacity for language exploded. Complex vocalization boosted our ancestors' ability to communicate information, catapulting our species in a great leap forward (Diamond, 1989).

Language enables us to transmit knowledge and lore from generation to generation.

Whether spoken, written, or signed, language enables us to communicate complex ideas from person to person and to transmit civilization's accumulated knowledge from generation to generation.

Language Structure

Consider how we might go about inventing a language. For a spoken language, we would need three building blocks. First, we would need a set of basic sounds, which linguists call **phonemes**. To say *bat* we utter the phoneme sounds *b, a,* and *t. Chat* has three phonemes—*ch, a,* and *t.* Different languages have different numbers of phonemes. English has about 40; other languages have anywhere from half to twice that many.

Changes in phonemes produce changes in meaning. For example, variations in the vowel sound between a *b* and a *t* can create 12 different meanings: *bait, bat, beat/beet, bet, bit, bite, boat, boot, bought, bout,* and *but* (Fromkin & Rodman, 1983). Generally, though, consonant phonemes carry more information than do vowel phonemes. The treth ef thes stetement shed be evedent frem thes bref demenstretien.

People who grow up learning one set of phonemes usually have difficulty pronouncing the phonemes of another language. The native English speaker may smile at the native German speaker's difficulties with the *th* sound, which often makes *this* sound like *dis.* But the German speaker can smile at the problems English speakers have rolling the German *r* or pronouncing the breathy *ch* in *Ich,* the German word for *I.*

The next building block of our language is the **morpheme**, the smallest unit of language that carries meaning. In English, a few morphemes are also phonemes—the personal pronoun *I* and the article *a,* for instance. But most are combinations of two or more phonemes. Some morphemes, like *bat,* are words, but others are only parts of words. Morphemes include prefixes and suffixes, such as the *pre* in *preview* or the *-ed* that shows past tense. *Undesirables* has four morphemes—*un, desire, able,* and *s*—each of which adds to the word's total meaning.

Finally, our new language must have a **grammar**, a system of rules that enables us to speak to and understand others. Two important aspects of grammar are *semantics* and *syntax.* **Semantics** refers to the rules we use to derive meaning from morphemes, words, and even sentences. A semantic rule tells us that adding *-ed* to *laugh* means that it happened in the past. **Syntax** refers to the rules we use to order words into sentences. One rule of English syntax says that adjectives usually come before nouns, so we say *white house.* Spanish adjectives usually come after nouns, so a Spanish speaker says *casa blanca.* The English rules of syntax tell us that the sentence *They are hunting dogs* is proper. Given the context in which the sentence was written, semantics tells us whether it refers to people looking for dogs or dogs looking for animals.

Note that language becomes more complex at each succeeding level. In English, the relatively small number of 40 or so phonemes can be combined to form more than 100,000 morphemes, which alone or in combination produce the 616,500 word forms in the *Oxford English Dictionary* (including 290,500 main entries, such as *meat* and 326,000 subentries such as *meat-eater*). We can then use these words to create an almost infinite number of sentences, most of which, like this one, are original. Like the brain that conceives it, language is complexity built of simplicity.

How many morphemes are in the word cats*? (See page 307.)*

"Let me get this straight now. Is what you want to build a jean factory or a gene factory?"
From the *Wall Street Journal*—permission Cartoon Features Syndicate.

Same phonemes but different morphemes.

Language Development

Make a quick guess: How many words did you learn in one average day during the years between your first birthday and your high school graduation?

The average North American high school graduate knows some 80,000 words (Miller & Gildea, 1987). That averages (after age 1) to nearly 5000 words learned a year, or 13 a day! How you did it—how the 5000 words a year you learned could so far outnumber the roughly 200 words a year that your schoolteachers consciously taught you—is one of the great wonders of human development. Before children can add 2 + 2, they are creating their own original and grammatically appropriate sentences. Most parents would have trouble stating the rules of syntax. Yet their preschoolers comprehend and speak with a facility that puts to shame a college student struggling to learn a foreign language or a scientist struggling to simulate natural language on a computer. How does our astonishing facility for language unfold, and how can we explain it?

Although you probably know more than 100,000 words, you use only 150 words for about half of what you say.

Acquiring Language Children's language development mirrors language structure—by moving from simplicity to complexity. By 4 months of age, babies can read lips and discriminate speech sounds. They prefer to look at a face that matches a sound, so we know they can recognize that *ah* comes from wide open lips and *ee* from a mouth with corners pulled back (Kuhl & Meltzoff, 1982). At about this age, babies enter a **babbling stage** in which they spontaneously utter a variety of sounds such as *ah-goo*. Babbling is not the imitation of adult speech, for it includes sounds from various languages, even sounds that do not occur in the household's language. From this early babbling, a listener could not identify an infant as being, say, French, Korean, or Ethiopian. Deaf infants babble (repeat syllable-like gestures), too, and they obviously are not imitating speech (Petitto & Marentette, 1991). It seems, then, that before nurture molds our speech, nature provides a range of possible phoneme sounds.

Babbling eventually comes to resemble the characteristic sounds and intonations of the household language. By about age 10 months, a trained ear can identify the language of the household by listening to an infant's babbling (deBoysson-Bardies & others, 1989). Phoneme sounds outside the infant's native tongue are disappearing. And infants gradually lose their ability to discriminate sounds that they never hear. An untrained Japanese adult cannot distinguish between the English *ra* and *la* because Japanese uses a single phoneme intermediate between these two. Clever experiments by Janet Werker (1989) reveal that 6-month old infants can perceive phoneme differences from any language, but by 12 months they cannot (Figure 10–8, page 304).

Around the first birthday (the exact age varies from child to child), most children enter the **one-word stage**. Having already learned that sounds carry meanings, they begin to use sounds to communicate meaning. Their first words usually contain but one syllable—*ma* or *da*, for instance—and may be barely recognizable. But family members quickly learn to understand the infant's language, and gradually it conforms more and more to the family's language.

Most of the child's first words refer to things that move or can be played with—things such as a dog or a ball, rather than the table or crib that just sits there (Nelson, 1973). At this one-word stage,

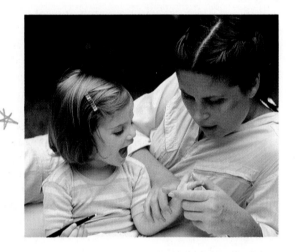

Preschoolers have an astonishing capacity to soak up new words and combine them in grammatically sensible sentences.

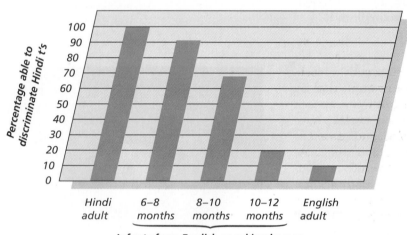

Infants from English-speaking homes

Figure 10–8 We are all born with the ability to recognize speech sounds from all the world's languages. In Janet Werker's lab, an infant is reinforced with applause and by activating toy animals when he looks to the right after hearing a changed sound (as in ba, ba, ba, ba, da, da). Hindi adults and young infants from English-speaking homes can easily discriminate two Hindi *t* sounds not spoken in English. By age 1 and beyond, however, English-speaking listeners rarely perceive the sound difference. (Adapted from Werker, 1989.)

an inflected word may equal a sentence. "Doggy!" may mean "Look at the dog out there!"

Children typically use more and more single words during the second year and, by about their second birthday, start uttering two-word sentences (Table 10–1). This **two-word stage** exemplifies **telegraphic speech**: Like telegrams (TERMS ACCEPTED. SEND MONEY.), it contains mostly nouns and verbs (*Want juice*). Also like telegrams, there is already syntax; the words are in a sensible order. The English-speaking child typically says adjectives before nouns—*big doggy* rather than *doggy big*.

There seems to be no "three-word stage." Once children move out of the two-word stage, they quickly begin uttering longer phrases (Fromkin & Rodman, 1983). Although the sentences may still sound like a Western Union message, they continue to follow the rules of syntax (*Mommy get ball*). By early elementary school, the child understands complex sentences and begins to enjoy the humor conveyed by double meanings: "You never starve in the desert because of all the sand-which-is there."

Table 10–1	*Summary of Language Development*
Approximate month	**Stage**
4	Babbling discriminates speech sounds
10	Babbling reveals household language
12	One-word stage
24	Two-word, telegraphic speech
24+	Language develops rapidly into complete sentences

Explaining Language Development   Those who study language acquisition inevitably wonder how we do it. Attempts to answer this question have sparked a spirited intellectual controversy. The controversy parallels the debate we noted in Chapter 8, Learning, over the behaviorist view of the malleable organism versus the view that each organism comes biologically prepared to learn certain associations. The nature-nurture debate surfaces again, and here, as elsewhere, appreciation for innate predisposition has grown.

Behaviorist B. F. Skinner (1957) believed we can explain language development with familiar learning principles, such as association (of the sights of things with the sounds of words); imitation (of the words and syntax modeled by others); and reinforcement (with success, smiles, and hugs when the child says something right). Thus, Skinner argued, babies learn to talk in many of the same ways that animals learn to peck keys and press bars. "Verbal behavior evidently came into existence when, through a critical step in the evolution of the human species, the vocal musculature became susceptible to operant conditioning," Skinner (1985) surmised.

Linguist Noam Chomsky (1959, 1987) sees Skinner's view of learning language as naive. Surely, says Chomsky, a Martian scientist observing children in a single-language community would conclude that language is almost entirely inborn. It isn't, because children do learn the language used in their environment. But the rate at which they acquire words and grammar without being taught is too extraordinary to be explained solely by learning principles. Children create all sorts of sentences they have never heard and, therefore, could not be imitating. They begin using morphemes in a predictable order. They begin adding *-ing* to words. Then they start using the prepositions *in* and *on*. Then come *a* and *the*, followed by *is* (Brown, 1973). Moreover, many of their errors result from the application of logical grammatical rules. For example, children overgeneralize the rule about adding *-ed* to a verb to form the past tense (from de Cuevas, 1990):

Child: *My teacher holded the baby rabbits and we petted them.*

Mother: *Did you say your teacher held the baby rabbits?*

Child: *Yes.*

Mother: *What did you say she did?*

Child: *She holded the baby rabbits and we petted them.*

Mother: *Did you say she held them tightly?*

Child: *No, she holded them loosely.*

"No, Timmy, not 'I sawed the chair.' It's 'I saw the chair' or 'I have seen the chair.'"

Drawing by Glenn Bernhardt.

Chomsky (1987) likens the behaviorist view of how language develops to filling a bottle with water, and his own view to "helping a flower to grow in its own way." Language development, he believes, is akin to sexual maturation—given adequate nurture, it just "happens to the child." Thanks to their inborn "universal grammar," children readily learn the grammar of whatever language they hear. Other worlds may have languages that, for us humans, are unlearnable, but not our world. Chomsky maintains that our language acquisition capacity is like a box—a "language acquisition device"—in which grammar switches are thrown as children experience their language. Thus, English-speaking children learn to put the object of a sentence last ("She ate an apple"). Japanese-speaking children put the object before the verb ("She an apple ate").

Those who learn a second language as adults usually speak it with the accent of their first language. Do they more easily master the foreign grammar? To find out, Jacqueline Johnson and Elissa Newport (1989) gave Korean and Chinese immigrants to the United States a grammar test, requiring them to identify each of 276 sentences ("Yesterday the hunter shoots a deer") as grammatically correct or incorrect. Some subjects had immigrated in early childhood, others as adults. Regardless of their age at immigration, the participants had each been in the United States for approximately 10 years. If anything, this gave the adult immigrants—most of whom were professors, researchers, or graduate students—an edge in years of learning English, because they had all studied it in their native country as well. Nevertheless, as Figure 10–9 reveals, those who learned their second language early learned it best. Chomsky would say that once the grammar switches are thrown during a child's developing years, mastering another grammar becomes more difficult.

As a flower's growth is stunted without nourishment, so, too, are children linguistically stunted when isolated from language during the critical period for its acquisition. Consider Genie, who spent most of her early years tied to a chair without being spoken to. When discovered by Los Angeles authorities, she was mute and uncomprehending (Curtiss, 1977, 1981). In the years that followed, Genie has learned some individual words but not how to construct grammatically correct sentences.

The impact of early experience is also evident among the deaf. Hearing children of hearing-speaking parents, and deaf children of deaf-signing parents, share much in common. Both groups experience language in infancy and develop their early vocabularies at roughly comparable rates (Meier, 1991). But consider the 90+ percent of deaf children born to hearing-nonsigning parents. These children typically do not experience language during their early years. Compared to deaf children exposed to sign language from birth, those who learn signing as teens or adults are like immigrants who learn English after childhood. They can master the basic words and how to order them, but they never become as fluent as native signers in producing and comprehending subtle grammatical differences (Newport, 1990).

To summarize, children are biologically prepared to learn language as they interact with their caregivers. Skinner's emphasis on learning helps explain why infants acquire the language they hear

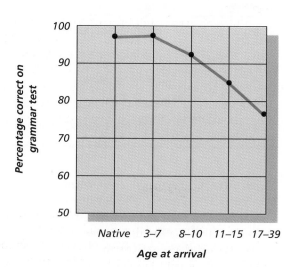

Figure 10–9 Children have a readiness to learn language. Ten years after coming to the United States, Asian immigrants took a grammar test. Those who arrived at or before age 5 understood grammar as well as native speakers. Those who arrived later did not. (From Johnson & Newport, 1989.)

Deaf children of deaf-signing parents develop language skills at about the same rate as hearing children of hearing-speaking parents. This girl is expressing "not" in her native language— ASL (American Sign Language).

and how they add new words to their vocabularies. Chomsky's emphasis on our built-in readiness to learn grammar rules helps explain why preschoolers acquire language so readily and use grammar so well. Once again, we see biology and experience working together.

Returning to our debate about humanity's thinking powers, let's pause to issue a report card. On decision making and judgment, our error-prone species might rate a *C+*. On problem solving, where humans are inventive yet vulnerable to fixation, we would probably receive better marks, perhaps a *B+*. On cognitive efficiency, our fallible but quick heuristics earn us an *A*. And when it comes to learning and using language, the awestruck experts would surely award the human species an *A+*.

Animal Language

If in our use of language we humans are, as the psalmist rhapsodized, "little less than God," where do other animals fit in the scheme of things? Are they "little less than human"? In part, the answer lies in the extent to which animals share our capacity for language. Without doubt, animals communicate. But can they use language?

The Case of the Honeybee   More than 2000 years ago, the Greek philosopher Aristotle observed that once a lone honeybee discovers a source of nectar, other bees soon leave the hive and go straight to the newfound food source. Aristotle surmised that the original explorer must return to the hive and lead other bees back to the food. He was wrong. In 1901, a clever German researcher followed the explorer bee back to the hive and trapped it as it left to return to the food source. Although deprived of their guide, the new recruits still flew straight to the nectar.

How did the bees know where to go? Intrigued, Austrian biologist Karl von Frisch (1950) undertook experiments for which he later shared the Nobel prize. The experiments revealed that the explorer bee communicates with the other worker bees by means of an intricate dance. The direction and duration of the dance, Frisch discovered, informs other bees of the direction and distance of the food source (Figure 10–10).

Impressive as it is, the honeybee's dance hardly challenges the complexity, flexibility, and power of human language. The honeybee communicates, but not with the elements of language.

The Case of the Apes   A greater challenge to humanity's claim to be the only language-using species has come from reports of apes that "talk" with people. Knowing that chimpanzees could not vocalize more than a few words, University of Nevada researchers Allen and Beatrice Gardner (1969) tried to teach sign language to a chimp named Washoe, as though she were a deaf human child. After 4 years, Washoe could use 132 signs. The Gardners' announcement of the success of their efforts aroused enormous scientific and public interest. One *New York Times* reporter, who had learned sign language from his deaf parents, visited Washoe and exclaimed, "Suddenly I realized I was conversing with a member of another species in my native tongue."

Answer to question on page 302: Two—cat and -s.

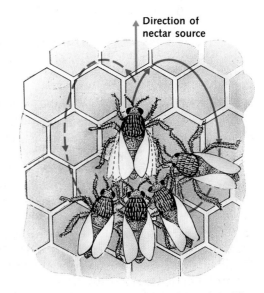

Figure 10–10 The dance of the honeybee. The straight-line part of the dance points in the direction of a nectar source relative to the sun, and its duration indicates the distance. The other bees, who cannot see the dance in the dark hive, huddle close to feel what is going on. (From von Frisch, 1974.)

Washoe, the first sign-language-trained chimpanzee, aroused new interest in the possibility of animal language.

During the 1970s, further evidence of "ape language" surfaced. Not only could apes sign, they could string signs together to form intelligible sentences. Washoe signed, "You me go out, please." Apes even appeared to combine words creatively. Washoe designated a swan as a "water bird." Koko, a gorilla trained by Francine Patterson (1978) in California, reportedly described a long-nosed Pinocchio doll as an "elephant baby." Lana, a chimpanzee that "talks" by punching buttons wired to a computer that translates her punchings into English, wanted her trainer's orange one day. She had no word for *orange*, but she did know her colors and the word for *apple*, so she improvised: "? Tim give apple which-is orange" (Rumbaugh, 1977).

As ape language reports accumulated, it seemed that apes might indeed be "little less than human." Although their vocabularies and sentences were simple compared to ours — corresponding roughly to the capacities of a typical 2-year-old child — apes did seem to share what we humans have considered our unique ability.

Lana, another chimpanzee, has learned to "speak" by punching word symbols on a computer console in a coherent order.

But Can Apes Really Talk? By the late 1970s, the claims of "talking apes" raised a question: Were the chimps language champs or were the researchers chumps? The ape language researchers were making monkeys out of themselves, said the skeptics. Consider some of their arguments:

> Apes gain their limited vocabularies only with great difficulty. They are hardly like speaking or signing children, who effortlessly soak up dozens of new words each week. Saying that apes can learn language because they can sign words is like saying humans can fly because they can jump.

> Chimps can make signs or push buttons in sequence to get a reward, but so can pigeons — by pecking a sequence of keys to get grain (Straub & others, 1979) — and no one says that the pigeon is "talking."

Apes can certainly use symbols meaningfully, but the evidence is far from convincing that they can equal even a 3-year-old's ability to order words with proper syntax. To the child, "you tickle" and "tickle you" communicate different ideas, but a chimp might sign the phrases interchangeably.

After training a chimp whom he named Nim Chimpsky, Herbert Terrace (1979) concluded that much of chimpanzees' signing is nothing more than their imitating their trainers' signs.

Presented with ambiguous information, people tend to see what they want or expect to see. (Recall the demonstrations of perceptual set in Chapter 6.) Interpreting chimpanzee signs as language may be little more than wishful thinking on the part of their trainers, claims Terrace. (When Washoe signed "water bird," she perhaps was separately naming "water" and "bird.")

Seeing a doll floating in her water, Washoe signed, "Baby in my drink."

"Although humans make sounds with their mouths and occasionally look at each other, there is no solid evidence that they actually communicate with each other."

© 1979 by Sidney Harris; American Scientist Magazine.

In science as in politics, controversy stimulates progress. The provocative claim that "apes share our capacity for language" and the skeptical rejoinder that "apes no use language" (as Washoe might have put it) have moved psychologists toward a greater appreciation of apes' remarkable capabilities and of our own genius at using words. Everyone agrees that humans alone possess language, if by the term we mean verbal or signed expression of complex grammar. If we mean, more simply, the ability to communicate through a meaningful sequence of symbols, then apes do have a capacity for language.

On reflection, one of chimpanzee Lana's trainers, Duane Rumbaugh (1985, 1987), believes that it is too simplistic to ask, "Do the apes have a capacity for human language—or don't they?" Language "is very complex with many, many dimensions and facets. Our nearest living relatives have some, but not all, of those parts." So, rather than thinking of language, like pregnancy, as all or none, we might better view it as a continuum of skills, some of which apes possess.

Although chimpanzees do not have our facility for language, their thinking and communicating abilities continue to impress their trainers. Loulis, a foster son of Washoe, picked up 68 signs simply by observing Washoe and three other language-trained chimps. Moreover, Washoe, Loulis, and the others now sign spontaneously, as when asking one another to *chase, tickle, hug, come,* or *groom.* People who sign can eavesdrop on these chimp-to-chimp conversations with near-perfect agreement about what the chimps are saying, 90 percent of which pertains to social interaction, reassurance, or play (Fouts & Bodamer, 1987). Moreover, the chimps are modestly bilingual; they can translate spoken English words into signs (Shaw, 1989–1990).

Lana's instructors have trained two other chimps, Sherman and Austin, to use computer keyboards to communicate with each other. The chimps ask one another for a specific food (as shown in Figure 10–11) or even for a tool they can use to get food (Rumbaugh & Savage-Rumbaugh, 1986). Also impressive is Savage-Rumbaugh's (1987, 1990) discovery that pygmy chimpanzees can learn to comprehend the semantic nuances of spoken English. Kanzi, one such chimp, behaves intelligently whether asked, "Can you show me the light?" or "Can you bring me the light [a flashlight]?" or "Can you turn the light on?" Kanzi also knows the spoken words *snake, bite,* and *dog.* Given stuffed animals and asked, for the first time, to "make the dog bite the snake," he put the snake to the dog's mouth.

> *"[Our] egocentric view that [we are] unique from all other forms of animal life is being jarred to the core."*
> Duane Rumbaugh and Sue Savage-Rumbaugh (1978)

So, trained apes' language capabilities are modest by human standards. Yet their impressive cognitive powers seem indeed to make them "little less than human."

Figure 10–11 Chimpanzees using computer-mediated language. After reading Austin's computer-signaled request for bread, Sherman selects the correct food from a tray (left). He then feeds Austin (center) and licks his fingers (right).

Thinking and Language

Thinking and language intricately intertwine. Asking which comes first is one of psychology's chicken-and-egg questions. Do our ideas come first and wait for words to name them? Or are our thoughts conceived in words and unthinkable without them?

Linguistic Influences on Thinking

Linguist Benjamin Lee Whorf contended that language determines the way we think. According to Whorf's (1956) **linguistic relativity hypothesis**, different languages impose different conceptions of reality: "Language itself shapes a man's basic ideas."

> *"All words are pegs to hang ideas on."*
> Henry Ward Beecher
> *Proverbs from Plymouth Pulpit,* 1887

Whorf's idea seldom occurs to people who speak but one language. To them, language seems only a vehicle for thought. But to those who speak two dissimilar languages, such as English and Japanese, it seems obvious that one thinks differently in different languages (Brown, 1986). For example, the several Japanese words for *give* support important cultural distinctions. Which *give* one uses depends on whether the giver is of higher or lower status and whether or not the giver is a friend or family member.

Another example: In English, there is one word for *snow*. The Eskimo language has many. This, said Whorf, allows Eskimos to *perceive* differences in snow that would go unnoticed by people who speak another language. The language-thought link also occurs at the level of grammar. The Hopi Indians have no past tense for their verbs. Therefore, Whorf contended, the Hopi cannot so readily *think* about the past.

Critics of the language-determines-thought idea claim that words *reflect* rather than create the way we think. The Eskimos' very lives depend on their ability to recognize different conditions of snow and ice, so they need different words for these conditions (Skiers likewise describe the slopes with such terms as *sticky snow* or *powder*.) You lack the Eskimos' rich vocabulary for describing snow, but that does not mean you are incapable of perceiving these differences. Likewise, a New Guinean without our words for shapes and colors nevertheless perceives them much as we do (Rosch, 1974).

So, although it is too strong to say that language *determines* the *way* we think, our words certainly can *influence what* we think (Hoffman & others, 1986). We therefore do well to choose our words carefully. When people refer to women as *girls*—as in "the girls at the office"—it perpetuates a view of women's lower status, does it not? Or consider the generic use of the pronoun *he*. Does it make any difference whether I write "A child learns language as *he* interacts with *his* caregivers" or "Children learn language as *they* interact with *their* caregivers"? Some argue that it makes no difference because every reader knows that "the masculine gender shall be deemed and taken to include females" (as the British Parliament declared in 1850).

But is the generic *he* always taken to include females? Twenty studies have consistently found that it is not (Henley, 1989). For example, Janet Hyde (1984) asked children to finish stories for which she gave them a first line such as, "When a kid goes to school, _____ often feels excited on the first day." When Hyde used *he* in the blank, the children's stories were nearly always about males. *He or she* in the blank resulted in female characters about one-third of the time. Studies with adolescents and adults in North America and New Zealand have found similar effects of the generic *he* (Hamilton, 1988; Martyna, 1978; Ng, 1990). Sentences about "the artist and his work" tend to conjure up images of a man.

Consider, too, that people use generic pronouns selectively, as in "the doctor . . . he" and "the secretary . . . she" (MacKay, 1983). If *he* and *his* were truly gender-free, we shouldn't skip a beat when hearing that "a nurse must answer his calls" or that "man, like other mammals, nurses his young." That we are startled indicates that the *his* carries a gender connotation that clashes with our idea of *nurse*.

The power of language to influence thought makes vocabulary building a crucial part of education. To expand language is to ex-

"To call forth a concept, a word is needed."
Antoine Lavoisier
Elements of Chemistry, 1789

pand the ability to think. David Premack (1983) reported that even among chimpanzees, language training enhances the ability to think abstractly and to reason by analogy. Shown a cylinder half filled with water, a chimp not trained in language had difficulty recognizing that half an apple was more like the half-filled cylinder than was three-fourths of an apple. But language-trained chimps could more readily grasp the analogy. In young children, too, thinking develops hand in hand with language (Gopnik & Meltzoff, 1986). What is true for chimpanzees and preschoolers is true for everyone: *It pays to increase your word power.* That is why most textbooks, including this one, introduce new words—to teach new ideas and new ways of thinking.

Thinking Without Language

When you are alone, do you talk to yourself? Is "thinking" simply conversing with yourself? Without a doubt, words convey ideas. But are there not times when ideas precede words? To turn on the cold water in your bathroom, in which direction do you turn the handle?

To answer this question, you probably thought not in words but with a mental picture. Indeed, we often think in images. Artists think in images. So do composers, poets, mathematicians, athletes, and scientists. Albert Einstein reported that he achieved some of his greatest insights through visual images and only later put them into words.

One American prisoner of war returned home from North Vietnam 80 pounds lighter after several years in a jungle camp. One of his first desires was to play golf. To the astonishment of his fellow officers, given his time away from the game and his emaciated condition, he played superbly. They wondered how. The pilot replied that every day of his imprisonment he imagined himself playing 18 holes, carefully choosing his clubs and playing the ball under varying conditions (Csikszentmihalyi, 1990).

Many successful athletes prepare for contests by imagining themselves performing their events (Suinn, 1986; Mahoney, 1989).

This girl's efforts to increase her word power will expand her capacity to think.

Drawing by Maslin; © 1984 The New Yorker Magazine, Inc.

Georgia Nigro demonstrated the wisdom of this technique in a laboratory test of mental practice (Neisser, 1984). She had subjects make 24 actual dart throws at a target. She then had half the subjects throw 24 darts mentally. Finally, she had all the subjects again make 24 throws. Only those who had mentally practiced showed any improvement. A National Research Council committee of psychologists investigated claims of performance-enhancement techniques for the U.S. Army and concluded that most (including ESP and "neurolinguistic programming") were of no value (Druckman & Swets, 1988). Based on experiments such as Nigro's, however, they deemed the mental practice of motor skills useful.

What, then, should we say about the relationship between thinking and language? We have seen that language influences thinking. But if thinking did not also affect language, there would never be any new words. New words express new ideas. The basketball term *slam dunk* was coined after the act itself had become fairly common. So, let us simply say that *thinking affects our language, which then affects our thought.*

Psychological research on thinking and language mirrors the mixed reviews given our species in literature and religion. The human mind is simultaneously capable of striking intellectual failures and of vast intellectual power. In an age when misjudgments can have disastrous consequences, we do well to appreciate our capacity for error. Yet our heuristics often serve us well, and they certainly are efficient. Moreover, our ingenuity at problem solving and our extraordinary power of language surely, among the animals, rank humankind as almost "infinite in faculties."

Summing Up

Our cognitive system receives, perceives, and retrieves information, which we then use to think and communicate, sometimes wisely, sometimes foolishly. This chapter explored how we form concepts, solve problems, make judgments and decisions, and use language.

Thinking

Concepts The building blocks of thinking, our concepts simplify and order the world by organizing it into a hierarchy of categories. Concepts often form around prototypes, or best examples of a category.

Solving Problems When faced with a novel situation for which no well-learned response will do, we may use any of several strategies, such as trial and error, algorithms, and rule-of-thumb heuristics. Sometimes the solution comes in a flash of insight. We do, however, face obstacles to successful problem solving. The confirmation bias predisposes us to verify rather than challenge our hypotheses. And fixations, such as mental set and functional fixedness, may prevent our taking a needed fresh perspective on a problem.

Making Decisions and Forming Judgments Our use of heuristics, such as representativeness and availability, provide highly efficient but occasionally misleading guides for making quick decisions and forming intuitive judgments. Our tendencies to seek confirmation of our hypotheses and to use quick and easy heuristics can blind us to our vulnerability to error, a phenomenon known as overconfidence. And the way a question is posed, or framed, can significantly affect our responses.

Belief Bias People show a belief bias in their reasoning, accepting as more logical those conclusions that agree with their beliefs. We also exhibit belief perseverance, clinging to our ideas after their basis has been discredited because the explanation we accepted as valid lingers in our minds. Yet despite our capacity for error and our susceptibility to bias, human cognition is remarkably efficient and adaptive. As we gain expertise in a field, we grow adept at making quick, shrewd judgments.

Artificial Intelligence Today, experimental computers and robots perform operations that mimic human thinking. The most notable AI successes focus computer capacities for memory and precise logic on specific tasks, such as playing chess or diagnosing illnesses. For now, the brain's capacity for processing unrelated information simultaneously and the wide range of its abilities dwarf those of the most sophisticated computer. But hopes grow that a new generation of computer neural networks, mimicking the brain's neural networks, will produce more humanlike capabilities.

Language

Language—our words and how we combine them to communicate meaning—facilitates and expresses our thoughts.

Language Structure Spoken language is built of basic speech sounds, called phonemes; elementary units of meaning, called morphemes; words; and the semantics (meaning) and syntax (rules for word order) that make up grammar.

Language Development Among the marvels of nature is a child's ability to acquire language. The ease with which children progress from the babbling stage through the one-word stage to the telegraphic speech of the two-word stage and beyond has sparked a lively debate concerning how they do it.

Behaviorist Skinner explains that we learn language by the familiar principles of association, imitation, and reinforcement. Challenging this claim is the fact that children are biologically prepared to learn words and use grammar.

Animal Language Another vigorously debated issue is whether language is uniquely human. Animals obviously communicate. Bees, for example, communicate the location of food through an intricate dance. And several teams of psychologists have taught various species of apes, including a number of chimpanzees, to communicate with humans by signing or by pushing buttons wired to a computer. Apes have developed considerable vocabularies. They string words together to express meaning and to make and follow requests. Skeptics point out important differences between apes' and humans' facilities with language, especially in their respective abilities to order words using proper syntax. Nevertheless, these studies reveal that apes have considerable cognitive ability.

Thinking and Language

We consider thinking and language in the same chapter, for they are hard to separate.

Linguistic Influences on Thinking There is no disputing that words convey ideas and that different languages can embody different ways of thinking. Although the linguistic relativity hypothesis suggests that language *determines* thought, it is more accurate to say that language *influences* thought. Studies of the effects of the generic pronoun *he* and the ability of vocabulary enrichment to enhance thinking reveal the influence of words.

Thinking Without Language Some ideas, such as the ability to perceive and remember different colors, do not depend on language. We sometimes think in images rather than in words, and we invent new words to describe new ideas. So we might say that our thinking affects our language, which then affects our thought.

Terms and Concepts to Remember

thinking (or *cognition*) Mental activity associated with understanding, processing, and communicating knowledge.

cognitive psychology The field of psychology that studies mental representations and the processing of information. Topics include the mental activities that underlie problem solving, judgments, decision making, and language.

concept A mental grouping of similar objects, events, or people.

prototype The best example of a category; matching new items to the prototype provides a quick and easy method for including items in a category (as when comparing feathered creatures to a prototypical bird, such as a robin).

algorithm A methodical, logical rule or procedure for solving a particular problem. May be contrasted with the usually speedier, but also more error-prone use of *heuristics*.

heuristic A rule-of-thumb strategy that often allows us to make judgments and solve problems efficiently; usually speedier, but more error-prone than *algorithms*.

insight A sudden and often novel realization of the solution to a problem; it contrasts with strategy-based solutions.

confirmation bias A tendency to search for information that confirms one's preconceptions.

fixation The inability to see a problem from a new perspective; an impediment to problem solving.

mental set A tendency to approach a problem in a particular way, especially a way that has been successful in the past but may or may not be helpful in solving a new problem.

functional fixedness The tendency to think of things only in terms of their usual functions; an impediment to problem solving.

representativeness heuristic A rule of thumb for judging the likelihood of things in terms of how well they seem to represent, or match, particular prototypes; may lead one to ignore other relevant information.

availability heuristic A rule of thumb for estimating the likelihood of events based on their availability in memory; if instances come readily to mind (perhaps because of their vividness), we presume such events are likely.

overconfidence The tendency to be more confident than correct—to overestimate the accuracy of one's beliefs and judgments.

framing The way an issue is posed. How an issue is framed can significantly affect decisions and judgments.

(10) **belief bias** The tendency for one's preexisting beliefs to distort logical reasoning, sometimes by making invalid conclusions seem valid or valid conclusions seem invalid.

belief perseverance Clinging to one's initial conceptions after the basis on which they were formed has been discredited.

(12) **artificial intelligence (AI)** The science of designing and programming computer systems to do intelligent things and to simulate human thought processes such as intuitive reasoning, learning, and understanding language. Includes practical applications (chess playing, industrial robots, expert systems) and efforts to model human thinking inspired by our current understanding of how the brain works.

neural networks Computer circuits that mimic the brain's interconnected neural cells, performing tasks such as learning to recognize visual patterns and smells.

language Our spoken, written, or gestured words and how we combine them to communicate meaning.

phonemes The smallest distinctive sound units in a spoken language.

morphemes In a language, the smallest units that carry meaning; may be words or parts of words (such as a prefix).

grammar A system of rules in a language that enables us to communicate with and understand others.

semantics Meaning (or the study of meaning), as derived from morphemes, words, and sentences.

syntax Rules for combining words into grammatically sensible sentences.

babbling stage Beginning at 3 to 4 months, the stage of speech development in which the infant spontaneously utters various sounds at first unrelated to the household language.

one-word stage The stage in speech development from about age 1 to 2 years during which a child speaks mostly in single words.

two-word stage Beginning about age 2, the stage in speech development during which a child speaks mostly two-word statements.

telegraphic speech Early speech stage in which the child speaks like a telegram—using mostly nouns and verbs and omitting "auxiliary" words.

linguistic relativity Whorf's hypothesis that language determines the way we think.

For Further Reading

Gilovich, T. (1991). *How we know what isn't so: The fallibility of human reasoning in everyday life.* New York: Free Press.

A provocative analysis of pitfalls in everyday reasoning, and how to avoid them.

Halpern, D. F. (1989). *Thought and knowledge: An introduction to critical thinking* (2nd ed.). Hillsdale, NJ: Erlbaum.

A marvelous book that shows how the findings of psychology research can help us think more rationally and critically.

Hunt, M. (1982). *The universe within: A new science explores the human mind.* New York: Simon & Schuster.

Science journalist Morton Hunt offers an engaging and informative report of the new thinking about thinking. Hunt draws on interviews with scores of researchers in presenting his well-documented summary of recent discoveries.

Janis, I. L. (1988). *Crucial decisions: Leadership in policy-making and crisis management.* New York: Free Press.

Analyzes reasons for poor, ill-fated decisions and suggests four steps to reduce errors and produce better decisions.

Intelligence

Scott, an energetic kindergartner, acts bored and restless in class. Concerned that he might have a learning disability, Scott's teacher asks the school psychologist to evaluate him. The psychologist's testing reveals that Scott is actually an extraordinarily capable boy who can read like a third grader and add numbers like a second grader. Little wonder that he acts bored; Scott needs activities better suited to his intellectual abilities.

After testing Larry and six other California children, all of whom were African American, school officials assigned them to special education classes for the mentally retarded. Their parents and the San Francisco Bay Area Black Psychology Association were unconvinced by the psychologists' judgments. They suspected the tests were biased. In 1979, Federal District Court Judge Robert Peckham agreed. Intelligence tests, he ruled, are "racially and culturally biased, have a discriminatory impact on Black children, and have not been validated for the purpose of [putting] Black children into educationally dead-end, isolated, and stigmatizing classes" (Opton, 1979). In 1986, Judge Peckham reiterated his complete prohibition against using IQ tests in California "as part of an assessment . . . placing Black pupils in special education" (Landers, 1986).

Maria and Jennifer have been close friends throughout high school. Both have grade averages near the top of the class, and both hope to study premedicine at the same college. Early in their senior year, they spend a morning taking the Scholastic Aptitude Test. Maria does very well, and the school she and Jennifer have chosen admits her. Jennifer does less well, and, despite her excellent high school record, is rejected. "How awful!" they moan. "After three years of making *A*s in the same classes, a 150-minute test separates us!"

Of all psychology's controversies, the most heated has been provoked by the idea that in each person there exists a general mental capacity (intelligence) and that we can measure and quantify this capacity as a number (an IQ score). School boards, courts, and scientists debate the usefulness and fairness of **intelligence tests**—tests for assessing a person's mental abilities and comparing them to others, using numerical scores. Should we use such tests to rank people and admit them to a particular college or hire them for a particular job? If so, how might we assess intelligence? What *is* intelligence? To what extent does it result from nature (heredity) rather than nurture (environment)? What do test score differences among individuals and groups really mean? Is intelligence testing a positive way to guide people toward suitable opportunities? Or is it a potent, discriminatory weapon camouflaged as science? This chapter aims to provide a base from which you can form answers to these hotly debated questions.

Assessing Intelligence

To understand intelligence as a psychological concept, it helps first to know the origins and purposes of intelligence testing. The story of the testing movement once again illustrates an important lesson: Although science strives for objectivity, scientists can be influenced by their biases.

The Origins of Intelligence Tests

Some societies concern themselves less with promoting individual opportunity and uniqueness than with the welfare of the family, community, and society. Other societies emphasize the individual over the group. In this individualist tradition, Plato wrote more than 2000 years ago in the *Republic* that "no two persons are born exactly alike; but each differs from the other in natural endowments, one being suited for one occupation and the other for another." As heirs to Plato's individualism, people in Western societies ponder how and why individuals differ. About a century ago, Western attempts to assess individual differences in mental ability began in earnest.

Sir Francis Galton: Quantifying Superiority In the history of the testing movement, no one measured and ranked people with greater enthusiasm than the brilliant English scientist Sir Francis Galton (1822–1911). While a student at Cambridge University, Galton's letters home revealed a constant interest in how examinations ranked him relative to his fellow students (Fancher, 1979). In time, his fascination with quantification led him to invent methods for measuring boredom, even-temperedness, the beauty of British women, the effects of prayer, and much more.

When his cousin Charles Darwin proposed that nature selects successful traits through the "survival of the fittest," Galton concluded that he could scientifically apply the principle. Why not measure human traits, he reasoned, and then selectively breed superior people? Those with the greatest "natural ability" could be encouraged to mate with each other, and those not so well endowed could be discouraged or prevented from reproducing. To promote his plan for human betterment, Galton founded the "eugenics" movement (taking its name from the Greek word *eugenes*, which means "well-born").

Galton assumed that human traits are inherited. He supported this assumption by noting that, like height, social prominence tended to run in families. Not surprisingly, Galton himself was an eminent child of a well-known upper-class family, and he married a "suitable" woman (though, ironically, his marriage was childless). Furthermore, although he popularized the phrase "nature and nurture," he was oblivious to the cultural and environmental advan-

Sir Francis Galton (1892): "I have no patience with the hypothesis occasionally expressed, and often implied, especially in tales written to teach children to be good, that babies are born pretty much alike, and that the sole agencies in creating differences between boy and boy, and man and man, are steady application and moral effort. It is in the most unqualified manner that I object to pretensions of natural equality."

tages enjoyed by the upper class in Victorian England (Fancher, 1979). As a British male, he believed in the natural superiority of White men.

With his commitment to quantifying human "superiority" and his belief in heredity, Galton set about trying to measure innate mental capacity. In his 1869 book, *Hereditary Genius*, he toyed with the idea of assessing intelligence by measuring head size, and over the next few years he developed various measures of what he presumed were the biological underpinnings of genius. Galton put his ideas to the test at London's 1884 International Exposition. Over 10,000 exposition visitors paid to receive his assessment of their "intellectual strengths," based on such things as reaction time, sensory acuity, muscular power, and body proportions.

How did the tests turn out? Did "superior" individuals (eminent adults and excellent students) outscore those supposedly not so bright? Did they, for instance, process information more swiftly on the tests of reaction time? They did not. Nor did the various measures correlate with one another. Nor did men consistently outscore women.

Although Galton failed in his efforts to invent simple measures of general mental ability, he was an innovative researcher who created some statistical techniques that we still use. Galton was the first proponent of an idea that survives to this day—that we can quantitatively measure people's mental abilities.

Alfred Binet: Predicting School Achievement   The modern intelligence testing movement began when the pioneering French psychologist Alfred Binet (1857–1911) successfully applied Galton's idea of measuring intellectual abilities. When the French government passed a law requiring that all children attend school, teachers soon received a wider range of individual differences than they could handle. Some of the children seemed incapable of benefitting from the regular school curriculum and appeared to need special classes. But how could the schools objectively identify children with these special needs?

The government was justifiably reluctant to trust teachers' subjective judgments of children's learning potential. Academic slowness might merely reflect inadequate prior education. Also, teachers might tend to prejudge children on the basis of their social backgrounds. To minimize bias, the Minister of Public Education in 1904 commissioned Binet to develop an objective test that would identify those children who were likely to have difficulty in the regular classes.

Binet and his collaborator, Théodore Simon, began by assuming that all children follow the same course of intellectual development but that some develop more rapidly than others. "Dull" children, they presumed, were merely "retarded" in their development. On tests, therefore, a dull child should perform like a normal child of a younger age. A "bright" child should perform like a typical older child.

Binet and Simon's task was to measure what came to be called a child's **mental age**, the chronological age that typically corresponds to a given level of performance. The average 9-year-old, then, has a mental age of 9. But some 9-year-olds have mental ages below or above 9. Children below average, such as 9-year-olds who perform like the typical 7-year-old, would struggle with normal schoolwork for their age.

Alfred Binet (Binet & Simon, 1905): "The scale, properly speaking, does not permit the measure of intelligence, because intellectual qualities . . . cannot be measured as linear surfaces are measured."

In devising a method for measuring mental age, Binet and Simon theorized that mental aptitude, like athletic aptitude, is a general capacity that shows up in various ways. They therefore set about developing various reasoning and problem-solving questions that might predict school achievement. By testing "bright" and "backward" Parisian schoolchildren on these questions, Binet and Simon succeeded in identifying items that did indeed predict how successfully the children handled age-appropriate schoolwork.

Note that Binet and Simon made no assumptions concerning *why* a particular child was slow, average, or precocious. Binet personally leaned toward an environmental explanation. To raise the capacities of children who had low scores, he recommended "mental orthopedics" that would train such children to develop their attention span and self-discipline. He refused to speculate what the test was actually measuring, but he insisted that it did not measure inborn intelligence as a yardstick measures height. Rather, it had a single practical purpose: to identify schoolchildren needing special attention in the Paris school system of the early 1900s. Binet hoped that his test would be used to improve children's education, but he feared that it would be used to label children and limit their opportunities (Gould, 1981).

Lewis Terman: The Innate IQ What Binet viewed as merely a practical guide for identifying slow learners who needed special help was soon seen by others to be what Galton sought: a numerical measure of inherited intelligence. After Binet's death in 1911, Stanford University professor Lewis Terman (1877–1956) decided to use Binet's test. He soon found, however, that the Paris-developed age norms worked poorly with California schoolchildren. So Terman revised the test. He adapted some of Binet's original items, added others, established new age norms, and extended the upper end of the test's range from teenagers to "superior adults." Terman gave his revision the name that it retains today—the **Stanford-Binet**.

For such tests, German psychologist William Stern derived the famous **intelligence quotient**, or **IQ**. The IQ was simply a person's mental age divided by chronological age and multiplied by 100 to get rid of the decimal point:

$$IQ = \frac{\text{mental age}}{\text{chronological age}} \times 100$$

Thus, an average child, with the same mental and chronological age, has an IQ of 100. But an 8-year-old who answers questions like a typical 10-year-old has an IQ of 125.

Most current intelligence tests, including the Stanford-Binet itself, no longer compute an IQ. The original IQ formula works fairly well for children, but not for adults. Consider: Should a 40-year-old who does as well on the test as the average 20-year-old be assigned an IQ of only 50? Obviously, something is out of whack. Today's intelligence tests therefore produce a mental ability score based on the test-taker's performance relative to the average performance of others the same age. As on the original Stanford-Binet, they define this score to make 100 average, with about two-thirds of all people scoring between 85 and 115. Although there is no longer any intelligence *quotient*, the term "IQ" still lingers in everyday vocabulary as a shorthand expression for "intelligence test score."

"The IQ test was invented to predict academic performance, nothing else. If we wanted something that would predict life success, we'd have to invent another test completely."
Social psychologist Robert Zajonc (1984b)

It was not until World War II that the IQ test became fashionable in France—under the name of Terman, not Binet!

"You did very well on your IQ test. You're a man of 49 with the intelligence of a man of 53."
© 1982 by Sidney Harris; American Scientist magazine.

Terman shared Galton's belief that intelligence was measurable and promoted the widespread use of intelligence testing. His motive was to "take account of the inequalities of children in original endowment" by assessing their "vocational fitness" (Terman, 1916). In sympathy with the eugenics movement, Terman (1916, pp. 91–92) lamented what he believed was the "dullness" and "unusually prolific breeding" of certain ethnic groups. He envisioned that the use of intelligence tests would "ultimately result in curtailing the reproduction of feeble-mindedness and in the elimination of an enormous amount of crime, pauperism, and industrial inefficiency" (p. 7).

During the same era, the U.S. government used adaptations of Binet's and Terman's tests to evaluate World War I army recruits and newly arriving immigrants. Some psychologists misinterpreted the results as documenting the inferiority of people who did not share their Anglo-Saxon heritage. For instance, following his 1913 study of European immigrants arriving at Ellis Island, psychologist Henry Goddard claimed that 83 percent of the Jewish immigrants, 80 percent of the Hungarians, 79 percent of the Italians, and 87 percent of the Russians were "feeble-minded" (Eysenck & Kamin, 1981).

That adaptations of his tests were being used to draw such conclusions would surely have horrified Binet. Indeed, such sweeping judgments eventually became an embarrassment to most of those who championed testing. Terman, for instance, came to appreciate that test scores reflect not only people's innate mental abilities but also their education and their familiarity with the culture assumed by the test. Nevertheless, abuses of the early intelligence tests serve to remind us that science can be value-laden. Behind the screen of scientific objectivity, ideology sometimes hides.

Modern Tests of Mental Abilities

By this point in your life, you've faced dozens of different tests of your mental abilities: elementary school tests of basic reading and math skills, course examinations, intelligence tests, driver's license examinations, and college entrance examinations, to mention just a few. Psychologists classify such tests as either **aptitude tests**, intended to *predict* your ability to learn a new skill, or **achievement tests**, intended to *reflect* what you have learned. Thus, a college entrance exam, which seeks to predict your ability to do college work, is an aptitude test. A final exam covering what you have learned in this course would be an achievement test.

The actual differences between aptitude tests and achievement tests are not so clear-cut. Your achieved vocabulary influences your score on most aptitude tests. Similarly, your aptitudes for learning and test-taking influence your grades on tests of your course achievement. Most tests, whether labeled aptitude or achievement, assess both ability and its development. Distinguishing aptitude and achievement is mainly a matter of practicality: We use aptitude tests to predict future performance and achievement tests to assess current performance.

To get a better feel for modern intelligence-related tests and some of the differences among them, let's look at two widely used tests. We can then refer to these examples as we consider what makes an effective test and how people might use and abuse test scores.

Lewis Terman (1916): "The children of successful and cultured parents test higher than children from wretched and ignorant homes for the simple reason that their heredity is better."

"Science must be understood as a social phenomenon, a gutsy, human enterprise, not the work of robots programmed to collect pure information."
Stephen Jay Gould (1981)

The Most Widely Used Intelligence Test: The WAIS   Among the supposedly feeble-minded Eastern European immigrants of the early 1900s was a 6-year-old Romanian boy, David Wechsler. Ironically, three decades later psychologist David Wechsler created today's most widely used intelligence test, now known as the **Wechsler Adult Intelligence Scale—Revised (WAIS-R)**. Later he developed a similar test for school-age children called the Wechsler Intelligence Scale for Children (WISC), and still later a test for preschool children. The WAIS consists of 11 subtests, as illustrated in Figure 11–1. It yields not only an overall intelligence score, as does the Stanford-Binet, but also separate "verbal" and "performance" (nonverbal) scores. Striking differences between the two scores alert the examiner to possible learning problems. For example, a much lower verbal than performance score might indicate a reading or language disability. The tests also give a trained examiner clues to cognitive strengths that a teacher or employer might build upon.

College Aptitude Tests: The SAT   Large-scale group testing is now efficiently accomplished through multiple-choice tests, such as the well-known Scholastic Aptitude Test (SAT), which is taken annually by 1.6 million people seeking college admission. Like the original Binet test, the SAT attempts to predict academic performance. Unlike the Stanford-Binet and Wechsler tests, however, the SAT yields no overall intelligence score. Rather, it assesses verbal and mathematical aptitudes separately.

As you can see from the sample items in Figure 11–2, the SAT is a good example of an aptitude test that also assumes some prior achievement. More than half of its 60 mathematical questions, for example, presume a basic knowledge of either algebra or geometry. The American College Testing (ACT) exam, taken annually by a million college-bound high school students, is even more of an achievement test. On the ACT, the average high school student today would probably outscore Aristotle and other geniuses of the distant past, because the test measures students' "educational development" in English usage, mathematics, social studies, and natural science.

Principles of Test Construction

To be widely accepted, psychological tests must meet three criteria: They must be *standardized, reliable,* and *valid.* The Stanford-Binet, Wechsler tests, and SAT meet these requirements.

Standardization   Knowing how many questions you got right on an intelligence test would tell us almost nothing. To evaluate your performance, we need a basis for comparing it with others' performance. To enable meaningful comparisons, test makers first give the test to a representative sample of people. When other individuals take the test, we can then compare their scores with the standards defined by this group. This process of defining meaningful scores relative to a pretested group is called **standardization**.

Recall that when Terman realized that the test Binet created in France did not work so well with California schoolchildren, he revised the test and standardized the new version by testing 2300 native-born, White Americans of differing socioeconomic levels. These people defined the performance yardstick for evaluating later test-takers.

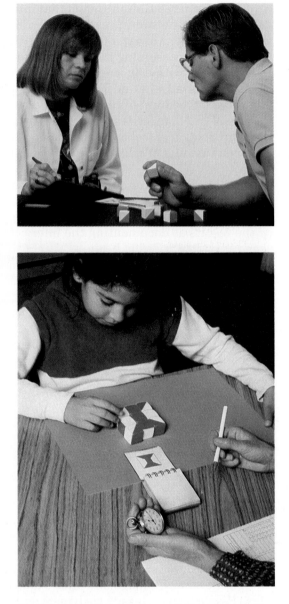

The individually administered Wechsler intelligence test comes in forms suited for adults (WAIS-R) and for children (WISC).

Terman and his colleagues recognized that a scale standardized on Parisians did not provide a satisfactory standard for evaluating Americans. Ironically, they proceeded to evaluate non-White and immigrant groups based on the native-born White American standard (Van Leeuwen, 1982).

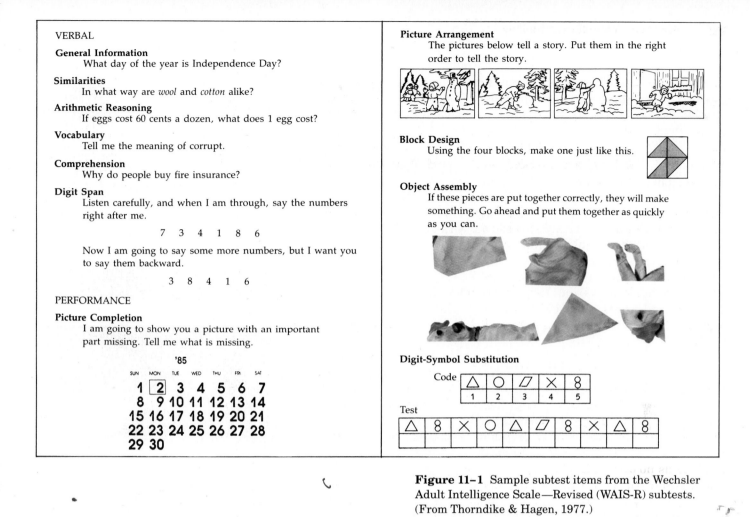

VERBAL

General Information
What day of the year is Independence Day?

Similarities
In what way are *wool* and *cotton* alike?

Arithmetic Reasoning
If eggs cost 60 cents a dozen, what does 1 egg cost?

Vocabulary
Tell me the meaning of corrupt.

Comprehension
Why do people buy fire insurance?

Digit Span
Listen carefully, and when I am through, say the numbers right after me.

7 3 4 1 8 6

Now I am going to say some more numbers, but I want you to say them backward.

3 8 4 1 6

PERFORMANCE

Picture Completion
I am going to show you a picture with an important part missing. Tell me what is missing.

'85

SUN	MON	TUE	WED	THU	FRI	SAT
1	2	3	4	5	6	7
8	9	10	11	12	13	14
15	16	17	18	19	20	21
22	23	24	25	26	27	28
29	30					

Picture Arrangement
The pictures below tell a story. Put them in the right order to tell the story.

Block Design
Using the four blocks, make one just like this.

Object Assembly
If these pieces are put together correctly, they will make something. Go ahead and put them together as quickly as you can.

Digit-Symbol Substitution

Code

△	○	⟋	×	8
1	2	3	4	5

Test

△	8	×	○	△	⟋	8	×	△	8

Figure 11–1 Sample subtest items from the Wechsler Adult Intelligence Scale—Revised (WAIS-R) subtests. (From Thorndike & Hagen, 1977.)

VERBAL

Choose the word or phrase that is most nearly *opposite* in meaning to the word in capital letters.

WILT: (A) prevent (B) drain (C) expose (D) revive (E) stick

(93 percent correctly answered D)

GARNER: (A) disfigure (B) hedge (C) connect (D) forget (E) disperse

(26 percent correctly answered E)

Each question below consists of a related pair of words or phrases, followed by five lettered pairs of words or phrases. Select the lettered pair that <u>best</u> expresses a relationship similar to that expressed in the original pair.

PAINTING: CANVAS (A) drawing: lottery (B) fishing: pond (C) writing: paper (D) shading: crayon (E) sculpting: design

(92 percent correctly answered C)

SCOFF: DERISION (A) soothe: mollification (B) slander: repression (C) swear: precision (D) stimulate: appearance (E) startle: speediness

(21 percent correctly answered A)

MATHEMATICAL

If $x^3 + y = x^3 + 5$, then $y =$
(A) -5 (B) $-\sqrt[3]{5}$ (C) $\sqrt[3]{5}$ (D) 5 (E) 5^3
(93 percent correctly answered D)

In a race, if Bob's running speed was 4/5 Alice's and Chris's speed was 3/4 Bob's, then Alice's speed was how many times the average (arithmetic mean) of the other two runners' speeds?
(A) 3/5 (B) 7/10 (C) 40/31 (D) 10/7 (E) 5/3
(10 percent correctly answered D)

FOR THE NEW (1994) MATH TEST:

Martin and Alice buy newspapers for $0.20 each and sell them for $0.25 each. If, at the end of one week, Martin made a profit of $12.60 and Alice made a profit of $18.75, how many more papers did Alice sell than Martin?

(Fill in answer at right.)

Figure 11–2 Sample items from the Scholastic Aptitude Test (SAT). Beginning in 1994, the test will also include questions that require students to generate their own answers. (From College Entrance Examination Board, 1983, 1990.)

A random group of test results typically forms a **normal distribution**, a bell-shaped pattern of scores that forms the **normal curve** (Figure 11–3). Whether we are measuring people's heights, weights, or mental aptitudes, most values tend to cluster around the average. On an intelligence test, we call this average "100." As we move out from the average (toward either extreme) we find fewer and fewer values. Within each age group, the Stanford-Binet and the Wechsler tests assign any person a score according to how much that person's performance "deviates" above or below the average. As Figure 11–3 shows, a raw score higher than 98 percent of all scores earns an intelligence score of 130. A raw score that is comparably *below* 98 percent of all the scores earns an intelligence score of 70.

Any person's score can be expressed in terms of its deviation from the average. The Appendix describes the statistical measures of this deviation (called "standard deviation").

Wechsler intelligence score

Initially, researchers standardized the SAT using a group of 10,654 students who took the test in April 1941 (Carroll, 1982). They arbitrarily assigned the average performance of these students on each portion of the SAT (verbal and mathematical) a score of "500" (rather than 100 as on most intelligence tests). The points above and below the average that included 68 percent of all the raw scores were assigned SAT scores of 600 and 400, respectively (Figure 11–4). All the students in the SAT standardization sample were college-bound and were thus a select group, especially back in 1941. So this yardstick sample differs from the broader population samples used in standardizing the Stanford-Binet and Wechsler tests. A person who scores 500 on each part of the SAT would probably score well above 100 on an intelligence test.

Figure 11–3 The normal curve. Scores on aptitude tests tend to form a normal, or bell-shaped, curve. For example, the Wechsler scale calls the average score 100. It defines other scores to make about 68 percent of them fall within 15 points above or below 100. About 95 percent fall within 30 points above and below 100.

Figure 11–4 When the SAT test was standardized in 1941, the average score for each part was assigned a value of 500. The other SAT scores were defined to make 68 percent of them fall within about 100 points above and below 500. A score of 115 on the WAIS is therefore at the same relative position as a score of 600 on the SAT. Yet the two scores are not equivalent, because the academic ability of the groups on which the tests were standardized was not the same.

Math or verbal SAT score

If you took the SAT in the past year or so—some 50 years after those first 10,654 students set the standard—you answered different questions than they did. However, the items on the test you took had been statistically equated to those on all previous versions of the test. (To equate the difficulty of past, present, and future items, each year's test-takers respond not only to the current test but also to items being developed for use in future tests.) Thus, your performance was measured with the 1941 yardstick.

Because of this comparability, the SAT has become a sort of educational barometer. Between 1963 and 1980, scores dropped steadily (Figure 11–5). In 1981, only those scoring in the upper 30 percent did better than the average test-taker in 1963. How can we explain this decline? Does it expose, as many believe, a failure of American public education?

Let's look at history. During the 1960s, the number of aspiring college students taking the test grew to include a broader range of people, including those with relatively modest academic achievements (Astin & Garber, 1982). With more and more people taking the test, SAT averages began to drop.

But what might explain the decline during the 1970s, when the range of students taking the SAT had stabilized? The displacement of reading by the spread of television? A combination of grade inflation, nonacademic electives, simplified textbooks, and reduced homework (Turnbull, 1986)? Decreased adult influence and attention associated with increased family size during the 1950s? All these factors seem to have contributed to the score decline.

Unlike the SAT, the Stanford-Binet and the Wechsler scales are periodically restandardized to keep the average score near 100. If you took the revised WAIS-R today, your performance would be compared with a standardization sample of Americans who took the test between 1976 and 1980, not to David Wechsler's initial 1930s standardization sample. When we compare the performance of the most recent standardization sample with that of the 1930s sample, do you suppose we find rising or declining test performance? Amazingly—given the decline in SAT scores—intelligence test performance has *improved* (Flynn, 1987). A raw score that would earn you a 100 today would have earned you a 114 in the 1930s! This is not just an American phenomenon; similar rising performance has occurred in other developed nations.

What an intriguing puzzle: Are aptitudes decreasing, as some have inferred from the decline in SAT scores, or are they rising, as the WAIS-R data suggest? First, remember that the SAT decline is due partly to the greater academic diversity of the students who began taking the test during the 1960s. Conversely, the broadly representative group of people taking the WAIS has always been more diverse than the college-bound SAT-takers. People in general—and therefore the intelligence test standardization groups—have become more literate and better educated since the 1930s. Remember, too, that the SAT assesses a mix of aptitude and academic achievement, which have not improved as have the basic problem-solving skills tested by intelligence tests. These facts help explain why performance on the more complex SAT dropped while performance rose on the basic skills tested by the WAIS-R.

Reliability A good test must yield dependably consistent scores; in a word, it must have **reliability**. To check a test's reliability, researchers will retest people using the same test or another form of

Figure 11–5 Between 1963 and 1980, average SAT scores dropped significantly, with a slight recovery until recent years. (Data from The College Board.)

it. If the two scores generally agree, or *correlate*, the test is reliable. Alternatively, the researcher may split a test in half and see whether scores derived from odd and even questions agree.

The higher the correlation between the *test-retest* or the *split-half* scores, the higher the test's reliability. The lowest correlation, -1.0, represents perfect disagreement between two sets of scores— as the first score goes up, the second goes down. A correlation of 0 represents no consistency. The highest correlation, +1.0, represents perfect consistency—as the first score goes up, so does the second. The tests we have considered so far—the Stanford-Binet, the WAIS-R and WISC, and the SAT and ACT—all have reliabilities of about +0.9, which is very high. When retested, people's scores tend to match their first score closely.

For further information on correlation, see the Appendix.

Validity High reliability does not ensure a test's **validity**—that it actually measures what it is supposed to measure or predicts what it is supposed to predict. If you use a shrunken tape measure to measure people's heights, your data would have high reliability (consistency) but low validity. How, then, can we determine whether a test is valid? For some tests, it is enough that they have **content validity**, which means that they do indeed tap the behavior they were designed to assess. The road test for a driver's license has content validity because it samples those tasks a driver routinely faces. Your course exams have content validity if they accurately assess your mastery of a representative sample of course material.

Other tests are evaluated in terms of how well they agree with some **criterion**, an independent measure of what the test aims to assess. For some tests, the criterion is future performance. For example, aptitude tests must have **predictive validity**, which means they predict future achievement.

Is the predictive validity of general aptitude tests as high as their reliability? As critics are fond of noting, the answer is plainly no. The predictive power of aptitude tests is fairly strong in the early grades, but later it weakens. Academic aptitude test scores are reasonably good predictors of achievement in elementary school, where the correlation between intelligence score and grades is about +0.60 (Jensen, 1980). The SAT is less successful in predicting the grades of college freshmen; here, the correlation is only about +0.40 (Linn, 1982). By the time we get to the Graduate Record Examination (GRE) (an aptitude test similar to the SAT but for those applying to graduate school), the correlation with graduate school grades is an even more modest +0.30 (GRE, 1990). Why does the predictive power of aptitude scores diminish as students move up the educational ladder?

Consider a parallel situation: Among all football linemen, body weight correlates with success. A 270-pound player tends to overwhelm a 190-pound opponent. But within the narrow 250- to 290-pound range typically found at the professional level, the correlation between weight and success becomes negligible (Figure 11–6). The narrower the *range* of weights, the lower the predictive power of body weight becomes.

A similar narrowing of range explains why the GRE is only a modest predictor of graduate school grades. If a graduate school takes in only students whose aptitude scores fall within a narrow range—say, students with high scores—it should not surprise us that their aptitude scores will not closely predict their grades. This will be true even if the test has excellent predictive validity with a

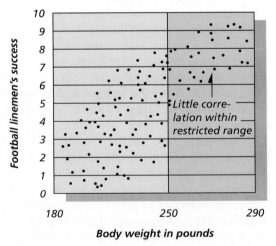

Figure 11–6 Let's imagine a correlation between football linemen's body weight and their success on the field. Note how insignificant the relationship becomes when we narrow the range of weights to 250–290 pounds. As the range of data under consideration narrows, its predictive power diminishes.

Close-Up   *Coaching Effects*

"I'm studying for my IQ test."

© 1992 by Sidney Harris.

Suppose that after taking the SAT, the Law School Aptitude Test (LSAT), the Medical College Admission Test (MCAT), or the Graduate Record Examination (GRE), you were disappointed by your score. By enrolling in one of the widely advertised test-preparation courses, could you count on increasing your score when retaking the test? Or is your score on the test likely to be stable?

Being familiar with a test and knowing how to pace yourself on it does help. But this much you can get from spending an evening with the sample test that is available to anyone who registers for one of these tests. Beyond this, does it pay to sign up for a crash test-preparation course? These courses help people brush up on their academic knowledge, especially in mathematics. They may also provide a few useful tips about how to take the test. For instance, on the first questions in a section, which 80 percent or more people get right, the most obvious answer is usually correct; on the final questions, which more than 75 percent typically get wrong, the "obvious" answer is often wrong.

Despite the test-relevant teaching and the test-taking clues that SAT-preparation courses provide, and contrary to advertised claims, three separate research reviews have concluded that the courses increased math and verbal scores by an average of only about 15 points each on the 200- to 800-point scale (DerSimonian & Laird, 1983; Kulik & others, 1984; Messick & Jungeblut, 1981). This small boost is greatest on test items that have complex and possibly confusing formats (Powers, 1986). So, for the SAT at least, the best advice is to study hard during your academic courses, brush up on algebra and geometry, and familiarize yourself with the test. Having done that, you needn't feel intimidated by those who have also taken a test-preparation course.

more diverse sample of students. So, when we validate a test using a wide range of people but then use it with a restricted range of people, it loses much of its predictive validity. A narrowed range of grades—as in graduate school departments that award mostly *A*s and *B*s—similarly reduces predictive validity.

What Is Intelligence?

So far in this chapter we have used the term *intelligence* as though we all agree on what it means. We don't. Psychologists debate whether we should define intelligence as an inherent brain capacity, an achieved level of intellectual functioning, or an ascribed quality that, like beauty, is in the eye of the beholder. Reading all the conflicting ideas about intelligence can leave you feeling like Lewis Carroll's Alice in Wonderland after reading "Jabberwocky": "Somehow it seems to fill my head with ideas—only I don't exactly know what they are."

The best predictor of future grades is past grades, which reflect both aptitude and motivation. More generally, the best predictor of future behavior is a large sample of past behaviors of the same sort. So there is good reason to suppose that Maria and Jennifer (page 317) would perform comparably if attending the same college.

Intelligence experts agree on this much: Intelligence is not a "thing." When we refer to someone's "IQ" as if it were a fixed and objectively real trait like height, we commit a reasoning error called — *reification*—viewing an abstract, immaterial concept as if it were a real, concrete thing. To reify is to invent a concept, give it a name, and then convince ourselves that such a thing objectively exists in the world. When someone says, "She has an IQ of 120," they are reifying IQ; they are imagining IQ to be a thing one *has*, rather than a score once obtained on a particular test.

Intelligence is a concept intended to explain why some people perform better than others on cognitive tasks. In the *Handbook of Human Intelligence*, Robert Sternberg and William Salter (1982, p. 3) reported that most experts view **intelligence** as a person's capacity for "goal-directed adaptive behavior." Intelligent behavior reflects a capacity to adapt, by learning from experience, solving problems, and reasoning clearly. Those behaving intelligently meet challenges and achieve their goals.

"Intelligence is the particular facility a person has to cope with any given situation."
M. S. Michel
Sweet Murder, 1943

Despite this general agreement about the concept, three controversies remain. First, should we consider intelligence as defined by one's culture or as a culture-free ability to solve problems? Second, is intelligence a single overall ability or several specific abilities? Third, can we, after all, measure intelligence as the brain's information-processing speed?

Is Intelligence Culturally Defined? Or Is It a Culture-Free Problem-Solving Ability?

According to one view, intelligent behavior varies with the situation. For Binet and the later intelligence testers, intelligence meant children's adapting successfully to academic demands. For islanders in the South Pacific, it might mean the ability to excel at fishing and navigating. For a manager or salesperson in our society, it might mean social skills. For an inner city resident, it might mean street smarts.

Those who view intelligence as people's successful adaptation to their environment are skeptical about the prospects for a "culture-free" test of intelligence—a test uninfluenced by one's culture. They believe that those who hope for such a test fail to understand that "intelligence" is whatever abilities your culture deems important. It might make sense to talk about a "culture-free" measure of height, but not of intelligence. As intelligence researcher Howard Gardner noted, basketball superstar Larry Bird may not have been considered exceptionally intelligent when in school, but in a society of keen-eyed hunters and spear-throwing warriors he would be the gifted one.

Others view intelligence as basic cognitive abilities that help people solve problems and succeed in *any* environment (Baron, 1985). The abstract and novel questions asked on intelligence tests evaluate our abilities to solve various problems effectively, regardless of our cultural backgrounds. The assumption is that people who on the WAIS can recite a string of eight digits in reverse order, or who can find the missing element in a picture, will likely have an edge at solving other problems, be they taking tests in school, navigating the sea, or growing corn. (As we will see, the support for this assumption is modest. There is only a slight tendency for people who do well on academic aptitude tests also to do well on practical and vocational tasks outside of school.)

"I've never gotten the hang of hunting. Luckily, we're invited out a lot."

Drawing by Weber; ©1988 The New Yorker Magazine, Inc.

Is Intelligence One General Ability? Or Several Specific Abilities?

We all know some people talented in mathematics, others in creative writing, and still others in art, music, or dance. We may therefore wonder whether people's mental abilities are too diverse to justify the single label "intelligence" or to quantify them with a single number. Should we think of intelligence not as one general ability but as a collection of specific abilities?

The Factor Analysis Approach Virtually everyone agrees: There *are* specific mental abilities. Recall that the WAIS distinguishes verbal and performance intelligence, and that the SAT distinguishes verbal and mathematical skills. In your own experience, you may know a talented artist who is dumbfounded by the simplest mathematical problems or a brilliant math student who has little aptitude for literary discussion.

But might there not be a general ability factor that runs through our specific mental abilities? To find out, psychologists study how various abilities relate.

A statistical method called **factor analysis** allows researchers to identify clusters of test items that measure a common ability. For example, people who do well on vocabulary items often do well on paragraph comprehension. This cluster helps define a verbal intelligence factor. Psychologists have identified several such clusters, including a spatial ability factor and a reasoning ability factor.

Charles Spearman (1863–1945), who helped develop factor analysis, believed there is also a **general intelligence**, or **g**, factor that underlies the specific factors. People often have special abilities that stand out, Spearman allowed. But those who score high on one factor, such as verbal intelligence, typically score higher than average on other factors, such as spatial or reasoning ability. So there is at least a small tendency for different abilities to come in the same package. Spearman believed that this commonality, the g factor, underlies all of our intelligent behavior, from excelling in school to navigating the sea.

This idea of a general mental capacity expressed by a single intelligence score was controversial in Spearman's day, and it remains so in our own. Opposing Spearman, L. L. Thurstone (1887–1955) gave 56 different tests to people. By analyzing the results mathematically, he identified eight clusters of "primary mental abilities," such as word fluency, memory, and reasoning. Thurstone did not rank his subjects on a single scale of general aptitude. But when other investigators studied the profiles of his subjects, they detected a small tendency for those who excelled in one of the eight clusters to score well on the others. So, they concluded, there was still some evidence of a g factor.

We might, then, liken mental abilities to physical abilities. Athleticism is not one thing but many. The ability to run fast is distinct from brute strength, which is distinct from the eye-hand coordination required to throw a ball on target. A champion weight lifter therefore rarely has the potential to be a skilled ice skater. Yet there remains some tendency for good things to come packaged together—for running speed and throwing accuracy to correlate, thanks to general athletic ability. Likewise, intelligence involves several distinct abilities, which cluster together in the same individual often enough to define a small general intelligence factor.

Contemporary Theories of Multiple Intelligences More recently, psychologist Howard Gardner (1983) reaffirmed and expanded Thurstone's view. Rather than doing the sort of mathematical analysis that Thurstone performed, Gardner assembled other evidence that intelligence comes in different packages. He noted that brain damage may diminish one type of ability but not others. He analyzed the importance of different abilities in different eras and cultures, from hunting societies to Japanese work groups to North American schoolrooms. He studied reports of people with exceptional abilities, including those who excel in only one. People with **savant syndrome**, for example, score at the low end on intelligence tests but possess incredible specific abilities, such as in computation, drawing, or musical memory (Figure 11–7). These people may have virtually no language ability, yet may be able to compute numbers as quickly and accurately as an electronic calculator or be capable of identifying almost instantly the day of the week that corresponds to any given date in history.

Using such evidence, Gardner argued that we do not have *an* intelligence, but *multiple* intelligences, each independent of the others. In addition to the verbal and mathematical aptitudes assessed by the standard tests, Gardner identified distinct aptitudes for musical accomplishment, for spatially analyzing the visual world, for mastering movement skills, such as those characteristic of dance, and for insightfully understanding ourselves and others. According to Gardner, the computer programmer, the poet, the street-smart adolescent who becomes a crafty executive, and the point guard on the basketball team are all exhibiting different kinds of intelligence.

Wouldn't it be wonderful if the world were so just, responds intelligence researcher Sandra Scarr (1989), that being weak in any area was likely to be compensated by genius in some other area? Alas, the world is not just, for there remains some tendency for different skills to correlate. Because mentally disadvantaged people often have lesser physical abilities as well, we hold Special Olympics to give them a chance to experience winning.

Moreover, Gardner's critics question, does it really make sense to lump all sorts of abilities under the concept of intelligence? Are not some, such as verbal and reasoning skills, really more crucial than others? Intelligence is *mental* ability. Abilities that we can manage without, such as in music and athletics, are better considered *talents* than intelligences. If people lack physical talent, do we consider them as lacking an intelligence?

Robert Sternberg and Richard Wagner (1986, 1987) distinguish more simply among three intelligences: the *academic* problem-solving skills assessed by intelligence tests, the *practical* intelligence often required for everyday tasks, and the *creative* intelligence demonstrated in reacting to novel situations. Intelligence tests predict school grades reasonably well but predict vocational success less well. Success in managerial work, for example, depends less on the abilities assessed by an intelligence score (assuming the score is average or above) than on having know-how in managing oneself, one's tasks, and other people. Business executives who score high on Sternberg and Wagner's test of practical managerial intelligence (by knowing how to write effective memos, how to motivate people, when to delegate tasks and responsibilities, how to read people, and how to promote their own careers) earn higher salaries and

Figure 11–7 Although lacking in language ability, a severely subnormal English girl named Nadia could draw scenes she had witnessed with remarkable skill and accuracy. Nadia drew this horse and rider at age 5.

receive better performance ratings than do those who score low. Likewise, Stephen Ceci and Jeffrey Liker (1986) report that race-track fans' expertise in handicapping the horses—a practical but complex cognitive task—is unrelated to their intelligence scores.

Nancy Cantor and John Kihlstrom (1987) similarly distinguish between academic intelligence and social intelligence—the know-how involved in comprehending social situations and managing oneself successfully. Consistent with their distinction between academic and social intelligence is the repeated finding that college grades only modestly predict later work achievement (Bretz, 1989; Dye & Reck, 1989). And James Flynn (1987) finds it curious that while performance on intelligence tests has improved dramatically during the last generation, rates of inventiveness and scientific discovery seem not to have increased comparably.

Some researchers note that intelligence scores *do* predict both occupational attainment and performance in mentally demanding jobs (Austin & Hanisch, 1990; Gottfredson, 1985). Nevertheless, Sternberg, Wagner, and others insist on distinguishing academic, practical, and creative intelligences. Seymour Epstein and Petra Meier (1989), for example, note that if academic aptitude equals personal competence, then why are high-aptitude people "not, by a wide margin, more effective . . . in achieving better marriages, in successfully raising their children, and in achieving better mental and physical well-being?"

On balance, it seems that the academic aptitude tapped by intelligence and other aptitude tests is indeed central to our lives. Yet personal competence in everyday living requires much that traditional intelligence tests do not measure.

"You're wise, but you lack tree smarts."

Drawing by Reilly; ©1988 The New Yorker Magazine, Inc.

Is Intelligence Speedy Information Processing?

A different approach to intelligence has emerged. It asks, if the mind is what the brain does, then shouldn't intelligence differences be detectable as some sort of measurable brain difference? Might we trace differences in people's performance on intelligence tests to differences in their basic capacities for processing information?

As a pioneer of this new approach, Robert Sternberg wasted no time getting his career under way (Dorsey, 1987). His first studies of intelligence began as a seventh grader, when he gave intelligence tests to his classmates and did a science project on achievement testing. His senior yearbook quoted him as saying, "Intelligence is the most misunderstood personality trait." A decade and more later, he was stalking the roots of intelligence by identifying the information-processing procedures people use when taking intelligence tests.

To find out what goes on in people's heads, Sternberg had subjects signal as soon as they understood the question portions of multiple-choice analogies, such as, "Lawyer is to client as doctor is to _____." Then he showed them the answer choices, such as (a) patient or (b) medicine, and measured how speedily they responded. Those scoring as highly intelligent spend *more* time analyzing the questions than do those who score lower, but they then recognize the correct answer faster. Sternberg (1984, 1985) and fellow researcher James Pellegrino (1985) noted that their research findings put a qualification on the common-sense maxim that "smart is fast." High scorers are "quick-witted" *after* they comprehend a problem.

Examining a more elementary level of cognitive processing, Earl Hunt (1983) and his colleagues found that verbal intelligence scores are predictable from the speed with which people retrieve information from memory. For example, those who recognize quickly that *SINK* and *wink* are different words, or that *A* and *a* share the same name, tend to score high in verbal ability. Brilliant 12- to 14-year-old college students are especially quick in responding to such tasks (Jensen, 1989).

Philip Vernon (1987) and Hans Eysenck (1982) confirmed that people with high intelligence scores react faster than low-scoring people on various tests that measure their speed of processing simple information. Intelligence test items, such as "In what way are *wool* and *cotton* alike?" might seem a long way from a measure of mental reaction time or of how quickly a flash of light registers in someone's brain. But Vernon (1983) speculated that "faster cognitive processing may allow more information to be acquired." Perhaps people who more quickly process information accumulate more information—about wool, cotton, and a million other things.

Do Vernon's and Eysenck's attempts to link intelligence scores to information-processing speed sound familiar? A century after Galton's futile attempts to gauge intelligence in terms of people's reaction times and sensory abilities, his ideas still live. Will the new efforts be more successful? Will they achieve Galton's aim of reducing what we now call the g factor to simple measures of underlying brain activity? Or are these efforts totally wrongheaded because what we call intelligence is not a single general trait but several culturally defined adaptive skills? The controversies surrounding the nature of intelligence are a long way from resolution.

The Dynamics of Intelligence

We now know enough about aptitude test scores to answer some age-old questions about the dynamics of human intelligence—about its stability over the life span, about the extremes of intelligence, and about that special ability called creativity.

Stability or Change?

If we retested people periodically throughout their lives, would their intelligence scores be stable? Chapter 4 explores the stability of intelligence in later life. What about the stability of intelligence scores early in life?

The search for indicators of infants' later intelligence has left few stones unturned. Unable to talk with infants, developmental researchers have assessed what they can observe—everything from birth weight to head circumference to whether the third toe was longer than the second to age of sitting up alone. None of these measures provide any useful prediction of intelligence scores at much later ages (Bell & Waldrop, 1989; Broman, 1989). Perhaps, reflected developmental psychologist Nancy Bayley (1949), "we have not yet found the right tests." Maybe someday, she thought, we may yet find "some infant behaviors which are characteristic of underlying intellectual functions" and that will predict later intelligence.

To the surprise of many of us, such a test has been found.

Studies by Joseph Fagan (Fagan & Montie, 1988), Marc Bornstein (1989), and others reveal that 2- to 6-month-old babies who grow quickly bored with a picture—who, given a choice, prefer to look at a new one—score higher on intelligence tests several years later. Although the prediction is crude, the tests can help identify children likely to be extremely below or above average.

So, can everyday observation or intelligence test scores now predict preschoolers' future performance and educational needs? The question is especially interesting to new parents wondering about their baby's intelligence and to educators wanting to identify children with special needs early on. Those anxious about comparing their baby with others can relax. Except for extremely retarded or precocious children, casual observation and intelligence tests before age 3 minimally predict children's future aptitudes (Humphreys & Davey, 1988).

By age 3, however, children's performances on intelligence tests begin to predict their adolescent and adult scores. Although there are anecdotal reports to the contrary—Einstein, for instance, was slow in learning to talk (Quasha, 1980)—precocious adolescents tend to have been precocious preschoolers. One study surveyed the parents of 187 seventh and eighth graders who had taken the SAT as part of a seven-state talent search and had scored considerably higher than most high school seniors. If their parents' memories can be trusted, more than half of this precocious group of adolescents began reading by age 4 and more than 80 percent were reading by age 5 (Van Tassel-Baska, 1983). Thus, intelligence tests given in kindergarten can predict school achievement (Tramontana & others, 1988).

After about age 7, though certainly not fixed, intelligence scores become even more stable (Bloom, 1964). So, the consistency of scores over time increases with the age of the child. The remarkable stability of aptitude scores by late adolescence is seen in a recent Educational Testing Service study of 23,000 students who took the SAT and then later took its more advanced counterpart, the GRE (Angoff, 1988). On either test, verbal scores correlate only modestly with math scores—revealing that these two aptitudes are distinct. Yet scores on the SAT verbal test correlated +0.86 with GRE verbal scores 4 to 5 years later. An equally astonishing +0.86 correlation occurred between the two math tests. The aptitudes the SAT assesses are reliably assessed by the GRE as well.

Infants' preference for novel stimuli is a moderate predictor of future intelligence. While briefly showing this infant a previously seen picture alongside a new picture, this developmental psychologist in Joseph Fagan's laboratory records how many seconds the infant looks at each.

Ironically, the SAT and GRE correlate better with each other than either does with its intended criterion, school achievement. Thus, their reliability far exceeds their predictive validity.

Extremes of Intelligence

One way to glimpse the validity and significance of any test is to compare people who score at the two extremes of the normal curve. The two groups should differ noticeably, and they do.

The "Challenged" At one extreme are people whose intelligence scores fall below 70. To be labeled **mentally retarded** a child must have both a low test score *and* difficulty adapting to the normal demands of living independently. Only about 1 percent of the population meets both criteria, with males outnumbering females by 50 percent (American Psychiatric Association, 1987). As Table 11–1 (page 334) indicates, most such mentally challenged individuals can, with support, live in the mainstream society.

Table 11–1	*Degrees of Mental Retardation*		
Level	Typical intelligence scores	Percent of the retarded	Adaptation to demands of life
Mild	50–70	85%	May learn academic skills up to sixth-grade level. Adults may, with assistance, achieve self-supporting social and vocational skills.
Moderate	35–49	10%	May progress to second-grade level academically. Adults may contribute to their own support by labor in sheltered workshops.
Severe	20–34	4%	May learn to talk and to perform simple work tasks under close supervision, but are generally unable to profit from vocational training.
Profound	Below 20	Less than 1%	Require constant aid and supervision.

Source   Adapted from the American Psychiatric Association (1987, pp. 32–33).

Severe mental retardation, characteristic of only 4 percent of the retarded, usually results from known physical causes, such as **Down syndrome**, a disorder attributed to an extra chromosome in the person's genetic makeup.

During the last two centuries the pendulum of opinion about how best to care for the retarded has made a complete swing. Until the mid-nineteenth century, the mentally challenged were cared for at home. The most severely disabled often died, but the mildly retarded found a place in a farm-based society. Then, in the United States, residential schools for slow learners were established. By the twentieth century, many of these institutions had become warehouses providing residents no privacy, little attention, and no hope. Parents were often told to separate themselves permanently from a retarded child before they became attached.

Now, in the last half of this century, the pendulum has swung back to normalization—allowing mentally impaired people to live in their own communities as normally as their functioning permits. We educate mildly retarded children in less restrictive environments and we integrate, or *mainstream*, many into regular classrooms. Most grow up with their own families until moving into a protected living arrangement, such as a group home. The hope, and often the reality, is a happier and more dignified life.

The "Gifted"   In one famous project begun in 1921, Lewis Terman studied more than 1500 California school children with IQ scores over 135. Contrary to the popular myth that intellectually "gifted" children are frequently maladjusted because they are "in a different world" from their nongifted peers, Terman's high-scoring children were unusually healthy, well adjusted, and academically successful. When restudied over the next six decades (Goleman, 1980), most of these people had attained high levels of education. Their vocational success varied, yet the group included many doctors, lawyers, professors, scientists, and writers.

Thus, critics question many of the assumptions of currently popular "gifted child" programs, such as that only some 3 to 5 per-

Thanks to medical advances and being mainstreamed within society rather than outcast from it, mentally retarded people are not only living more productive and satisfying lives, they are also living longer. Jane, who has Down Syndrome, was not expected to live to her current age of 37.

cent of children are gifted, and that it pays to identify and label these special few—to segregate them from the "nongifted" and give them academic enrichment not available to the masses. Most research studies conclude that students grouped by aptitude have academic achievement scores no higher than similar students not grouped, and that this "ability tracking" actually tends to lower all students' self-concepts (Noland, 1986; Oakes, 1989).

A report of the Carnegie Council on Adolescent Development (1989) therefore condemned academic tracking as "one of the most divisive and damaging school practices in existence." Denying "low-ability" students opportunities for enriched education serves to widen the achievement gap between the two groups and to increase their social isolation from one another, one reason why there is no tracking in the elementary schools of Japan and China (Stevenson & Lee, 1990). Because minority youth are more often placed in lower academic groups, tracking can also promote racial segregation and prejudice—hardly healthy preparation for working and living in a multicultural society.

Sorting children into gifted and nongifted groups often presumes that giftedness is a single trait—measured by an intelligence test—rather than any one of many potentials. Newspaper and magazine articles advise parents on how to spot "the signs of giftedness" in their children, as if giftedness were an objective quality, like blue eyes, that a child either has or lacks. This reifies giftedness—by creating the concept and then presuming that it has a concrete reality. It ignores the fact that we, not nature, are deciding the criteria of giftedness.

Creativity and Intelligence

Creativity is the ability to produce ideas that are both novel and valuable. The outlets for creativity vary by culture. Samoan culture encourages creativity in dance, Balinese culture in music, the African Ashanti culture in wood carvings (Lubart, 1990). In each, creativity means expressing familiar themes in novel ways.

Results from tests of intelligence and creativity suggest that a certain level of aptitude is necessary but not sufficient for creativity. In general, people with high intelligence scores do well on creativity tests ("How many uses can you think of for a brick?"). But beyond a certain level—a score of about 120—the correlation between intelligence scores and creativity disappears. Exceptionally creative architects, mathematicians, scientists, and engineers usually score no higher on intelligence tests than their less creative peers (MacKinnon & Hall, 1972). So there is clearly more to creativity than intelligence test scores.

Studies of creative people suggest four other components (Sternberg, 1988; Sternberg & Lubart, 1990). The first is *expertise*—a well-developed base of knowledge. "Chance favors only the prepared mind," observed Louis Pasteur. The second is *imaginative thinking skills*—an ability to see things in new ways, to recognize patterns, to make connections. To be creative you must first master the basic elements of a problem, then redefine the problem in a new way. Copernicus first developed expertise regarding the solar system's sun and planets, then defined the system as revolving around the sun, not the earth.

At age 10, Lenny Ng became the youngest child to score a perfect 800 on the SAT math test. Contrary to the myth that such precocious children suffer socially, high-aptitude children are typically well adjusted.

"Alpha children wear grey. They work much harder than we do, because they're so frightfully clever. I'm really awfully glad I'm a Beta, because I don't work so hard. And then we are much better than the Gammas and Deltas. Gammas are stupid."
Aldous Huxley
Brave New World, 1932

On his way home from picking up a Nobel prize in Stockholm, physicist Richard Feynman stopped in Queens, New York, to look at his high school record. "My grades were not as good as I remembered," he reported, "and my IQ was [a good, though unexceptional] 124" (Faber, 1987).

Creativity's third ingredient is a *venturesome personality*—one that tolerates ambiguity and risk, perseveres in overcoming obstacles, and seeks new experiences rather than following the pack. Inventors, for example, have a knack for persisting after failures, as Thomas Edison did in trying countless substances for his light bulb filament.

The fourth component is what psychologist Teresa Amabile calls the *intrinsic motivation* principle of creativity: "People will be most creative when they feel motivated primarily by the interest, enjoyment, satisfaction, and challenge of the work itself—and not by external pressures" (Amabile & Hennessey, 1988). Creative people focus not so much on extrinsic motivators—meeting deadlines, impressing people, or making money—as on the intrinsic pleasure and challenge of their work.

Amabile's (1983, 1987) experiments show how freeing people from concern about social approval enhances creativity. In one experiment, she asked college students to make paper collages, telling half beforehand that experts would evaluate their work. Those unaware their work would be evaluated produced collages that judges later rated as more creative. Unworried about being evaluated, they felt freer to be creative.

At work, managers who wish to foster innovation should keep the intrinsic motivation principle in mind, notes Amabile (1988). They should set employees to work on activities that naturally interest them. And they can emulate managers who have successfully nurtured creativity—by providing their subordinates with time, freedom, and support to attain set goals.

More on intrinsic motivation in the next chapter.

Genetic and Environmental Determinants of Intelligence

Having considered the nature and the dynamics of intelligence, we need to ask: What determines intelligence, genes or environment? As Sir Francis Galton recognized, intelligence seems to run in families. But why? Are intellectual abilities inherited? Or are they molded by one's environment? To understand why these questions stir up stormy debate, consider how people with differing views sometimes use "nature" and "nurture" to further their social agenda.

If, on the one hand, we mainly inherit our differing mental abilities, and if success reflects those abilities (especially in societies where social position depends mostly on individual merit), then people's socioeconomic standings will correspond to their inborn differences. Thus, those on top may believe their innate mental superiority justifies their social positions. They may even remind us that it was Thomas Jefferson, not God, who insisted that all people are created equal.

If, on the other hand, mental abilities are primarily nurtured by the environments that raise and school us, then children from disadvantaged environments will often lead disadvantaged lives. Their abilities will not have fully developed. In this case, people's socioeconomic standings will result from unequal opportunities, a situation that many regard as basically unjust. Setting aside such political implications as best we can, let's examine the evidence.

"I am, somehow, less interested in the weight and convolutions of Einstein's brain than in the near certainty that people of equal talent have lived and died in cotton fields and sweatshops."
Stephen J. Gould
The Panda's Thumb, 1980

Genetic Determinants

Virtually everyone now acknowledges that both genes and the environment influence intelligence. The unresolved question for each is, "How much?"

Twin Studies Do people who share the same genes also share comparable mental abilities? As you can see from Figure 11–8, which summarizes the accumulated data, the answer is clearly yes.

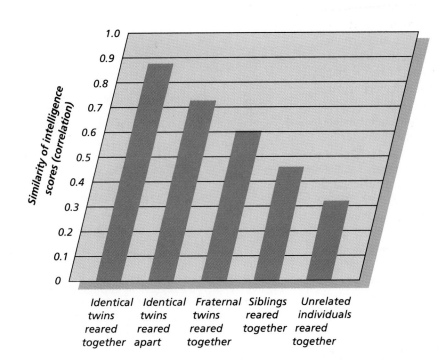

Figure 11–8 Intelligence: Nature or nurture? How similar are the intelligence scores of identical twins? of fraternal twins? of nontwin brothers and sisters? The most genetically similar people have the most similar intelligence scores. But the correlations also reveal an effect of environment: Identical twins reared apart test somewhat less alike than those reared together. Remember: 1.0 indicates a perfect correlation; 0.0 indicates no correlation at all. (From Bouchard, 1982.)

For example, the intelligence scores of identical twins reared together are more similar than those of fraternal twins. What shall we make of these results? Let's eavesdrop on an imaginary conversation between two psychologists—one who believes that heredity powerfully influences intelligence test performance, and one who does not.

Hereditarian: *Intelligence scores of genetically identical twins are almost as similar as those of the same person taking the test twice. Fraternal twins, who share only half their genes, are much less similar in intelligence score.*

Environmentalist: *Ah, but the identical twins are similar because they were treated similarly. Look at the data again and you'll see that fraternal twins, who are genetically no more alike than any other siblings, nevertheless score more alike. John Loehlin and Robert Nichols (1976) studied hundreds of twins and found that identical twins are more likely than fraternal twins to be dressed alike, to sleep in the same room, to have the same friends and teachers, and so forth. So their greater similarity in test scores may be environmental.*

Hereditarian: *But Loehlin and Nichols also found that identical twins whose parents do not dress or treat them alike are virtual carbon copies of one another in intelligence score. Much the same is true for identical twins who have been reared separately (Bouchard & others, 1990). Having the same genes has more effect than having the same environment.*

Environmentalist: *After analyzing the older studies of separated identical twins, Leon Kamin (1974) reported that the separated twins often were selectively placed in similar environments. Storks don't deliver these babies at random, you know. Moreover, as new data accumulate, behavior geneticists are dropping their estimates of the extent to which variation in intelligence scores can be attributed to heredity—from earlier estimates of around 80 percent to newer estimates of between 50 percent (Loehlin, 1989; Plomin & Rende, 1991) and 60 percent (Bouchard & Segal, 1988). Certainly, studies of the genetic determinants of behavior can tell us as much about the importance of environment as about the importance of genes.*

Adoption Studies Psychologists struggle to disentangle the effects of genes and environment. In addition to twin studies, several researchers have therefore asked whether adopted children have intelligence scores more like those of their biological parents, from whom they receive their genes, or those of their adoptive parents, who provide their home environment. As Figure 11–9 illustrates, adopted children's intelligence scores are more like their biological parents' scores than their adoptive parents'. Moreover, the older the children are, the more they score like their *biological* parents (Fulker & others, 1988; Loehlin & others, 1989). Being reared "together in the same adoptive home does not make you intellectually similar to your brothers and sisters," notes Sandra Scarr (1989); "being genetically related by half of your genes does."

Heritability To say that the **heritability** of intelligence—the variation in intelligence scores attributable to genetic factors—is roughly 50 to 60 percent does *not* mean that your genes are responsible for 50 to 60 percent of your intelligence and your environment for the rest. (Likewise, saying that the heritability of height is 90 percent does not mean that a 60-inch-tall woman can credit her genes for 54 inches and her environment for the other 6 inches.) Rather, it means that we can attribute to heredity 50 to 60 percent *of the variation in intelligence within a group of people.* This point is so often misunderstood that I repeat: We can never say what percent of an *individual's* intelligence is inherited. Heritability refers instead to the extent to which *differences among people* are attributable to genes.

Even this conclusion must be qualified. First, heritability can vary from study to study. To see why, imagine two researchers separately investigating how genes and life experience influence intelligence. One researcher gives intelligence tests to two groups of adopted children: one group the biological offspring of retarded parents, the other of Nobel prize winners. Her conclusion: Differences in the children's intelligence are mostly attributable to the intelligence they inherited from their biological parents, not to their home environments. Meanwhile, another researcher compares the biological offspring of parents with average intelligence scores to the offspring of parents with slightly above-average scores. Half of each group of children are in loving homes, the other half in an impoverished orphanage. This researcher finds a bigger effect of environment. Meeting at a convention, the first researcher reports that in her study intelligence differences were primarily genetic; the second researcher reports that in his study they were primarily environmental. Who is right?

They both are—for the specific groups they studied. Let's generalize the point: Compare people with very different heredities

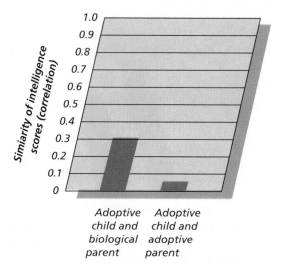

Figure 11–9 The correlations of intelligence scores between 245 adopted Colorado children and their adoptive and biological parents. By age 7, the adopted children had intelligence test scores more like those of their biological parents. (From Fulker & others, 1988.)

from basically similar environments, and heritability—differences due to genes—will be high. Compare people with not-so-different heredities in drastically different environments and heritability will be low. If everyone had the same heredity, heritability would be zero.

Second, remember that genes and environment intertwine. Given the dissimilarities among children who grow up in the same families, researchers infer that our most important experiences are personal. Our genetically unique traits affect our experience: They make others react in ways that encourage us to develop our natural gifts, and they lead us to select congenial environments. Students with a natural aptitude for mathematics are more likely to select math courses in high school, and later to score well on the SAT math test—thanks *both* to their natural math aptitude *and* their math experience. Thus, our genes shape the experiences that shape us.

Environmental Determinants

We have seen that our genes make a difference. Were we all raised in the same intellectually stimulating environment, we would not have the same aptitudes. But we have also seen that heredity doesn't tell the whole story. Within the limits dictated by our genes, our life experiences shape us. As Chapter 3 notes, experience literally leaves its mark on the brain: Rats reared in impoverished environments develop lighter and thinner brain cortexes than normal. And as Chapter 9 notes, particular learning experiences have detectable effects on their brains' neural connections.

Human environments are rarely so impoverished as the dark and barren cages inhabited by deprived rats. Yet life experiences also leave marks on a person's mental abilities, as psychologist J. McVicker Hunt (1982) observed in an Iranian orphanage in Tehran. The typical child could not sit up unassisted at age 2 or walk at age 4. What care the infants received was not in response to their crying, cooing, or other behaviors. The infants were therefore not developing any sense of personal control over their environment, and so were becoming passive "glum lumps." Extreme deprivation was bludgeoning native intelligence.

Aware of the benefits of responsive caregiving, Hunt began a program of "tutored human enrichment." For instance, he trained caregivers to play vocal games with the infants. First, they imitated the babies' babbling. Then they led the babies in vocal follow-the-leader by shifting from one familiar sound to another. Then they began to teach sounds from the Persian language.

The results were dramatic. All 11 infants who received these language-fostering experiences could name more than 50 objects and parts of the body by 22 months. So charming had the infants become that most were adopted—an unprecedented success for the orphanage.

Hunt's findings testify to the importance of environment. But do they indicate how to "give your child a superior intellect"? Some popular books claim this is possible, but many experts are doubtful. Sandra Scarr (1984) agrees that neglectful upbringing can have grave long-term consequences. However, she also believes that "as long as an infant has normal human contact and normal exposure to sights, sounds, human speech and so forth, the baby will thrive."

As for future intelligence, she maintains: "Parents who are very concerned about providing special educational lessons for their babies are wasting their time." Parents of children with high intelligence scores may be more likely to hang mobiles over their cribs, take them to the theater, or whatever. But do such experiences have any effect? We don't know, says Scarr (1986). Parents supply their children with both genes and environments. So even if the environments of children with high intelligence scores are noticeably different from those with low scores, we can't be sure how much difference their environments make.

Hunt would probably agree with Scarr that extra instruction has little effect on the intellectual development of children from stimulating environments. But he was optimistic when it came to children from disadvantaged environments. Indeed, his 1961 book, *Intelligence and Experience*, helped launch Project Head Start in 1965.

Head Start is a U.S. government-funded preschool program serving 450,000 children, 90 percent of whom come from families below the poverty level (Horn, 1990). It aims to enhance children's chances for success in school and beyond by boosting their cognitive and social skills. Psychologist Edward Zigler, the program's first director, recalls that the program began with the hope that early childhood was a critical period during which intervention would have "indelible effects on the child" (Holden, 1990).

Does it? Researchers have studied Head Start and other preschool programs by comparing equivalent groups of children who do versus don't experience the intervention. Their findings indicate that high-quality programs for disadvantaged children produce at least short-term cognitive gains, even on intelligence tests (Haskins, 1989). Quality programs also increase school readiness, decreasing the likelihood of a child repeating a grade or being placed in special education. On a less encouraging note, the benefits dissipate over time, reminding us that life experiences *after* Head Start matter, too.

Are there *any* long-term benefits? If Head Start doesn't make children fundamentally smarter, does it steer them onto a pathway toward success? Although the scientific jury is still out, studies of model programs give hope that ultimate graduation and employment rates can be increased. Zigler (1990), for one, believes it is now "abundantly clear that high-quality preschool programs do indeed generate long-term effects." Although other researchers are less

"There is a large body of evidence indicating that there is little if anything to be gained by exposing middle-class children to early education."
Developmental psychologist
Edward F. Zigler (1987)

Intelligence experts dispute claims that special lessons (left) can give preschoolers superior minds. But Project Head Start does help educationally disadvantaged children adjust to school.

sure, all look forward to the results of an intensive new Comprehensive Child Development Program under way at 24 centers (Gall, 1990).

Group Differences in Intelligence Test Scores

Scholars could debate the issue of hereditary versus environmental determinants of intelligence dispassionately if there were no aptitude score differences among various groups. But there are:

On the SAT, males in 1990 scored 45 points higher than females on the math test and a nominal 10 points higher on the verbal test. (For more on gender and aptitude, see Chapter 19.)

Japanese children score slightly higher than American children on nonverbal items from the WISC-R (Lynn, 1982, 1983) and significantly higher on math achievement tests (Stevenson & Lee, 1990). During the 1980s, Asian-Americans constituted less than 3 percent of the U.S. population and won about 25 percent of the Westinghouse Science Talent Search awards (Goleman, 1990).

African Americans average about 15 points lower than White Americans on intelligence tests and a comparable 100 points lower on the SAT verbal and math aptitude tests (Jacobson, 1986; Jensen, 1985; Loehlin & others, 1975). Similar score differences exist between privileged and disadvantaged groups around the world—between European and native Maori New Zealanders; between Israeli Jews and Arabs; between Israeli Jews of Middle-Eastern descent and those of European descent; and between a stigmatized Japanese minority, the Burakumin, and other ethnic Japanese (Steele, 1990a; Zeidner, 1990).

Bear in mind that *group* differences don't tell us about specific *individuals*. Women outlive men by about 6 years, but knowing an individual's sex doesn't tell us how long that person is going to live. Similarly, knowledge of your race tells us very little about your likely performance on a mental aptitude test.

On the other hand, argues sociologist Linda Gottfredson (1986), "Ignoring or denying the importance of group IQ differences does nothing to blunt their impact on society." We can all wish it were otherwise, but the fact is that the racial test score gap persists and that high-scoring people are more likely than low-scoring people to attain high levels of education and pay. The hard truth: Using academic aptitude tests to select people for scholarships, school admissions, athletic eligibility, or jobs tends to exclude certain ethnic minorities. Racial-group gaps in test scores therefore raise a potent issue: Do they reflect racial gaps in inherent mental aptitude?

Let's start with a basic question: If heredity contributes to individual differences in intelligence, does it also contribute to group differences? Not necessarily. Consider the following hypothetical case. Suppose that we were to study math aptitude in an American school and in a Japanese school. Suppose further that we were somehow able to determine that the differences among the children *within* each school were entirely due to heredity. If we then found that the Japanese children had higher scores than the American children, could we also attribute the differences *between* the two groups to heredity?

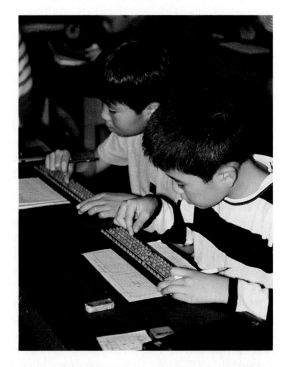

On mathematics tests, Japanese schoolchildren outperform their American counterparts. What, if anything, does this tell us about the math aptitude of youngsters in the United States relative to those in Japan?

Might test scores predict job attainment because such scores are used to admit or exclude people from educational opportunities?

Figure 11–10 Even if the variation within a group reflects genetic differences (differences between seeds), the average difference between groups may be wholly due to the environment. (From Lewontin, 1976.)

The answer to this question is plainly no, and geneticist Richard Lewontin (1976) shows why. If a mixture of seeds is sown on poor soil, the differing heights of the resulting plants will be the result of genetic differences among them. If seeds from the same mixture are sown on fertile soil, the differing heights of these plants will again be the result of genetic differences. But, as Figure 11–10 illustrates, the average height difference *between* the two groups of plants will be due to environmental soil differences. Thus, even if the heritability of a trait is extremely high *within* a particular group, differences in that trait *between* groups may nevertheless have environmental causes.

This point is so important, and so widely misunderstood, that it demands repeating. Consider: If each identical twin were exactly as tall as his or her co-twin, heritability would be 100 percent. Imagine that we then separated some young twins and gave only half of them a nutritious diet, and that the well-nourished twins all grew to be exactly 3 inches taller than their counterparts—an environmental effect comparable to that actually observed in Britain and America where adolescents are several inches taller than they were half a century ago (Angoff, 1987; Lynn, 1987). What would the heritability of height be now for our well-nourished twins? Still 100 percent, because the variation in height within the group would remain entirely predictable from the heights of their malnourished identical siblings. So even perfect heritability within groups would not eliminate the possibility of a strong environmental impact on the group differences.

This is reflected in the belief of most expert psychologists that racial gaps in test scores are in large measure environmental (Snyderman & Rothman, 1987). To see why, consider the following findings:

1. The impact of environment is evident in the mathematical achievement of Asian and American children. When psychologist Harold Stevenson and his co-workers (1986, 1990) studied randomly selected elementary schoolchildren in three comparable cities—Sendai in Japan, Minneapolis in the United States, and Taipei in Taiwan—they found that by fifth grade the Asian children scored one standard deviation higher than the American children (Figure 11–11). In fact, in fifth grade the best of the 20 American classes studied fell below the lowest of the Japanese classes. Among the top 100 students, 1 was American; among the lowest 100, 67 were American.

Compared to elementary school students in Minneapolis, those in Sendai and Taipei are nurtured in a more fertile academic soil. They attend school 30 percent more days per year, spend much more of their school day studying math, do much more homework, labor under great parental pressure and support, and more strongly believe that "any student can be good at math if he/she works hard

Recall that intelligence test differences of 15 points can occur over generations of the same national group—clearly not a genetic effect. Surely equivalent differences among racial groups might also not be genetic.

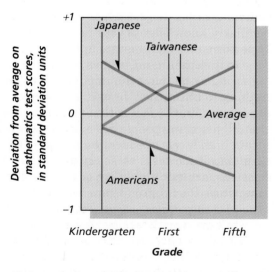

Figure 11–11 Children's mathematics performance in Minneapolis, Sendai, and Taipei. With time in school, math test scores by Minneapolis children fell further and further below the three-city average. (Adapted from Stevenson & others, 1986.)

enough." These differences extend to high school, where U.S. students average 4 hours of homework per week and Japanese students average 19 hours (Juster & Stafford, 1991). Similarly, the current academic success rate of Asian-Americans is generally attributed not to heredity but to the values their culture places on hard work, family cohesiveness, and educational achievement as an escape from limits imposed by discrimination (Sue & Okazaki, 1990).

2. The average American of European descent has grown up and been educated in a somewhat different culture than the average African American. One attempt at equalizing educational opportunities, desegregation, had only slight effects on the school achievements of African American children during its first 30 years. However, the benefits have been notable where desegregation began by first grade and extended over a number of years (Cook, 1984). As educational opportunities moved toward more equality between 1979 and 1990, the Black-White difference in combined SAT scores (verbal + math) scores shrank by 49 points. Motivate children with rewards for correct answers on intelligence tests and the racial difference shrinks even more (Bradley-Johnson & others, 1984). Create "learning environments that affirm the potential, value and prospects of Black students," thereby raising their academic self-esteem, and grades and graduation rates also rise (Steele, 1990a). Martin Luther King, Jr., anticipated this (Gardner, 1988). After hearing an address on education titled, "First, Teach Them to Read," he leaned over to a friend and said, "First, teach them to believe in themselves."

3. Further evidence of environmental impact on intelligence test scores comes from adoption studies. Consider: If African American children were reared in privileged, White middle-class homes, would their average intelligence score be closer to the average middle-class score? Sandra Scarr and Richard Weinberg (1976) studied 99 such children in Minneapolis. The average intelligence score of these children was 110, which is comparable to the average score of White children adopted into similarly advantaged families. Follow-up tests a decade later revealed "persisting beneficial effects of being reared in the culture of the school and tests" (Weinberg & others, 1990).

4. Scarr and her colleagues (1977) also found that having more or less African ancestry bears no relation to scores on cognitive tests within the African American population. If racial group differences in intelligence scores are due to racial differences per se, then people of uniform racial heritage should exhibit the racial difference more strongly. But in this study they didn't. Moreover, German children whose mothers were German and whose fathers were American servicemen stationed in Germany after World War II had nearly identical average intelligence scores, regardless of whether their fathers were Black or White (Mackenzie, 1984).

5. At different times in history, different ethnic groups have experienced "golden ages," periods of remarkable achievement. Twenty-five hundred years ago it was the Greeks and the Egyptians, then the Romans; in the eighth and ninth centuries genius seemed to reside in the Arab world; 500 years ago it was the Aztec Indians and the peoples of northern Europe. Cultures rise and fall over centuries; genes do not. That fact makes it difficult to attribute to any race a "natural" superiority.

Despite all the evidence supporting environmental explanations, suppose that genetic differences *do* contribute to race and sex differences not only in physical traits and susceptibility to certain diseases, but also in test scores. Would it, should it, matter? Not to individuals, for whom what matters is their own potential. Not to potential employers, for knowing a person's race or sex does not reveal the individual applicant's potential. And not to social policy, for the impact of environmental disadvantages and cultural differences would unquestionably remain significant.

Finally, we must remember that *intelligence scores reflect only one aspect of personal competence*. Other attributes—motivation, character, social skills, artistic talent, athletic ability, sensitivity, emotional maturity—matter. In other words, the competence that intelligence tests sample is important, but far from all-inclusive. The spatial ability of the carpenter differs from the logical ability of the computer programmer, which differs from the verbal ability of the poet. Differences are not deficits. Because there are many ways of being successful, our personal and cultural differences— regardless of their origins—are valuable variations on the human theme of adaptability. Like ice cream, human traits and gifts come in many flavors.

"Almost all the joyful things of life are outside the measure of IQ tests."
Madeleine L'Engle
A Circle of Quiet, 1972

The Question of Bias

Are intelligence tests biased? How we answer depends on what we mean by *bias*. One meaning is that the tests detect not only innate differences in intelligence but also differences caused by cultural experiences. In this sense, everyone agrees that intelligence tests are biased. No one claims that heritability is 100 percent responsible for any test score. An intelligence test measures a person's developed abilities at a particular time. These abilities necessarily reflect that person's experiences and environment. If people's experiences and backgrounds are unequal, the test's results will reflect those inequalities.

You may have read examples of intelligence test items that make middle-class assumptions (for example, that a cup goes with a saucer, or, as in one of the sample test items from the WAIS [page 323], that people buy fire insurance to protect the value of their homes and possessions). Do such items bias the test against those who do not use saucers and whose meager possessions hardly warrant the cost of fire insurance? Could such questions explain the racial differences in test performance? If so, are tests a discriminatory vehicle, consigning potentially capable children to dead-end classes and jobs (as the judge argued in the case of Larry and the six other children noted at the beginning of this chapter)?

The defenders of aptitude testing respond that racial group differences occur on nonverbal items, such as counting digits backward, as well as on verbal items, such as vocabulary knowledge (Jensen, 1983). Moreover, they say that to blame the test for a group's lower scores is like blaming a messenger for bad news. Why blame the tests for exposing unequal experiences and opportunities? If, because of malnutrition, people were to suffer stunted growth, would one blame the measuring stick that reveals it? If unequal past experiences predict unequal future achievements, a valid aptitude test will detect such inequalities.

Another meaning of *bias* hinges on whether a test is less valid for some groups than for others. If the SAT accurately predicts the college achievement of one race but not another, then the test would be biased. The near consensus among psychologists, as summarized by the National Research Council's Committee on Ability Testing (Wigdor & Garner, 1982), is that the major aptitude tests are *not* biased in this meaning of the term. The predictive validity of the SAT, for example, is roughly the same for Blacks and Whites. Likewise, the question, "Name three parks in Manhattan" would put Texans at a disadvantage compared to New Yorkers. But on a test for selecting Manhattan cab drivers, such a question might nevertheless be a valid predictor of job success—for both Texans and New Yorkers (Angoff, 1988).

So, it is possible for aptitude tests to be biased in one sense and not in another. Imagine a college—perhaps your own—where courses and teachers share a particular vocabulary and set of assumptions that make it difficult for people from a foreign culture to excel there. Test scores that predict success in such a school will be influenced by a person's cultural background. The test would therefore be culturally biased, because it mirrors the school's cultural bias. Yet the test might be an equally valid predictor of performance for all who take it, and in this sense be unbiased.

Are tests discriminatory? Again, the answer can be yes or no. In one sense, yes, their purpose is to discriminate—to distinguish among individuals. In another sense, their purpose is to reduce discrimination by reducing reliance on the subjective criteria that were once more crucial for school and job placement—criteria such as who you know, what you look like, or how much the interviewer happens to like "your kind of person." Banning aptitude tests would force the people who decide on admissions and jobs to rely more on other considerations, such as their personal opinions. Civil service tests, for example, discriminate among individuals, but were devised to do so more fairly and objectively, by reducing the political, racial, and ethnic discrimination that preceded their use. So perhaps our aim should be to realize the benefits that Alfred Binet foresaw for intelligence tests—to enable schools to recognize who might best benefit from early intervention—while being wary of Binet's fear that test scores might be misinterpreted as literal measures of a person's worth and fixed potential.

Tests assess developed ability, which is influenced by life experience. A child's test scores benefit from growing up in a stimulating environment with interested caregivers.

Summing Up

Among the most controversial issues in psychology is the debate over intelligence testing: whether or not tests can measure and quantify a person's abilities and how widely the results can be used fairly.

Assessing Intelligence

The Origins of Intelligence Tests More than a century ago in Great Britain, Sir Francis Galton sought to measure individual mental abilities. Although Galton failed to develop simple, quantifiable measures of mental ability, Alfred Binet picked up the idea of assessing intellectual aptitude. Binet developed questions that helped predict children's future progress in the Paris school system. Like Galton, Lewis

Terman of Stanford University believed intelligence was inherited. Like Binet, he believed his test (the Stanford-Binet) could help guide people toward appropriate opportunities. During the early part of this century, intelligence tests were sometimes used in ways that, in hindsight, even their designers regretted—to "document" a presumed innate inferiority of certain ethnic and immigrant groups.

Modern Tests of Mental Abilities Tests are commonly classified as either aptitude tests (designed to predict learning ability, as the Wechsler and SAT) or achievement tests (designed to assess current competence).

Principles of Test Construction A good test must be *standardized*, so that any person's performance can be meaningfully compared to others'; *reliable*, so it yields dependably consistent scores; and *valid*, so it measures what it is supposed to measure. Test scores usually fall into a bell-shaped distribution, the normal curve. The average score is assigned an arbitrary number (such as 100 on an intelligence test). Aptitude tests tend to be highly reliable, but they are weak predictors of success in life. Their predictive validity for academic success is fairly strong in the early grades, however. Test validity weakens for predicting grades in college and even more so in graduate school, as the range of student abilities becomes more restricted.

What Is Intelligence?

It is misleading to reify concepts such as "intelligence" and "giftedness"—to regard these abstract concepts as if they were real, concrete things. To most psychologists, intelligence is the capacity for goal-directed and adaptive behavior.

Is Intelligence Culturally Defined? Or Is It a Culture-Free Problem-Solving Ability? Some psychologists argue that intelligent behavior (say, a person's ability to adapt successfully to the demands of school or work) is culturally relative; others contend that intelligence is a culture-free ability to solve all sorts of problems.

Is Intelligence One General Ability? Or Several Specific Abilities? Psychologists agree that people have specific abilities, such as verbal and mathematical aptitudes. However, they debate whether a general intelligence (g) factor runs through them all. Factor analysis and studies of special conditions, such as savant syndrome, have identified clusters of mental aptitudes.

Is Intelligence Speedy Information Processing? Recently, psychologists have linked people's intelligence to their basic capacities for processing information. Some psychologists are studying the components that make up problem-solving skill, others the speed with which people's brains can process information. There does seem to be at least a modest tendency for highly intelligent people to have quick-witted reactions.

The Dynamics of Intelligence

Stability or Change? The stability of intelligence test scores increases with age, with practical predictive value beginning by age 3 and scores becoming fairly stable by age 7. Among infants, those who become quickly bored with a picture, preferring to look at a new one, tend to score well on later intelligence tests.

Extremes of Intelligence Comparing those who score extremely low (the "challenged" or mentally retarded) versus high (the "gifted") magnifies a test's apparent validity.

Creativity and Intelligence Intelligence correlates weakly with creativity. Increases in intelligence beyond a necessary threshold level are not linked with increased creativity.

Genetic and Environmental Determinants of Intelligence

Because of its political and racial overtones, the debate over the nature and nurture of intelligence is an ongoing controversy.

Genetic Determinants Studies of twins, family members, and adopted children together point to a significant hereditary contribution to intelligence scores.

Environmental Determinants These same studies, plus others that compare children reared in extremely neglectful or enriched environments or in different cultures, indicate that life experiences also significantly influence intelligence test performance.

Group Differences in Intelligence Test Scores Like individuals, groups vary in intelligence scores. Hereditary variation *within* a group need not signify a hereditary explanation of *between*-group differences. In the case of the racial gaps in test scores, the evidence suggests that environmental differences are largely, perhaps entirely, responsible.

The Question of Bias Aptitude tests predict how well a test-taker will perform in a given situation. So they are necessarily "biased" in the sense that they are sensitive to performance differences caused by cultural experience. But if biased means what psychologists commonly mean by the term—that a biased test predicts less accurately for one group than for another—then the major tests we have considered seem unbiased.

Terms and Concepts to Remember

intelligence test A method for assessing an individual's mental aptitudes and comparing them to others using numerical scores.

mental age A measure of intelligence test performance devised by Binet; the chronological age that most typically corresponds to a given level of performance. Thus, a child who does as well as the average 8-year-old is said to have a mental age of 8.

Stanford-Binet The widely used American revision (by Terman at Stanford University) of Binet's original intelligence test.

intelligence quotient (IQ) Defined originally as the ratio of mental age to chronological age multiplied by 100 (thus, $IQ = ma/ca \times 100$). On contemporary intelligence tests, the average performance for a given age is assigned a score of 100.

aptitude tests Tests designed to predict a person's future performance; aptitude is the capacity to learn.

achievement tests Tests designed to assess what a person has learned.

Wechsler Adult Intelligence Scale (WAIS) The current revision (WAIS-R) is the most widely used intelligence test; contains verbal and performance (nonverbal) subtests.

standardization Defining meaningful scores by comparison with the performance of a pretested "standardization group."

normal curve (or normal distribution) The symmetrical bell-shaped curve that describes the distribution of many physical and psychological attributes. Most scores fall near the average, and fewer and fewer scores lie near the extremes.

reliability The extent to which a test yields consistent results, as assessed by the consistency of scores on two halves of the test, on alternate forms of the test, or on retesting.

validity The extent to which a test measures or predicts what it is supposed to. (See also *content validity* and *predictive validity*.)

content validity The extent to which a test samples the behavior that is of interest (such as a driving test that samples driving tasks).

criterion The behavior (such as college grades) that a test (such as the SAT) is designed to predict; thus, the measure used in defining whether the test has predictive validity.

predictive validity The success with which a test predicts the behavior it is designed to predict; it is assessed by computing the correlation between test scores and the criterion behavior.

intelligence The capacity for goal-directed and adaptive behavior. Involves the abilities to profit from experience, solve problems, reason, and successfully meet challenges and achieve goals.

factor analysis A statistical procedure that identifies clusters of related items (called factors) on a test; used to identify different dimensions of performance that underlie one's total score.

general intelligence (g) A general underlying intelligence factor believed by Spearman and others to be measured by every task on an intelligence test.

savant syndrome A condition in which a person otherwise limited in mental ability has an amazing specific skill, such as in computation or drawing.

mental retardation A condition of limited mental ability, as indicated by an intelligence score below 70, that produces difficulty in adapting to the demands of life; varies from mild to profound.

Down syndrome A condition of retardation and associated physical disorders caused by an extra chromosome in one's genetic makeup.

creativity The ability to produce novel and valuable ideas.

heritability The extent to which we can attribute individuals' differences in a trait to genes. The heritability of a trait may vary, depending on the range of populations and environments studied.

For Further Reading

Fancher, R. E. (1985). *The intelligence men.* New York: Norton.

An account of past and current controversies about the nature of intelligence and the people who set out to measure it.

Gould, S. J. (1981). *The mismeasure of man.* New York: Norton.

Offers a provocative, engaging, and sharply critical look at the history of the intelligence testing movement and its abuses.

Stevenson, H. W. (1992). *Cultural lessons: A new look at the education of American children.* New York: Simon & Schuster.

The leading researcher of Asian versus American academic achievements and values reflects on the implications of his studies.

Wigdor, A. K., & Garner, W. R. (1982). *Ability testing: Uses, consequences, and controversies.* Washington, DC: National Academic Press.

A blue-ribbon panel of the U.S. National Research Council offers its analysis of ability testing. An authoritative source of prevailing professional opinion on the major issues.

Part Five

Motivation and Emotion

A mix of motives and emotions energize and direct our behavior. In Chapter 12, Motivation, we consider the nature of motivation by looking closely at the workings of three motives—hunger, sex, and the need to achieve. Chapter 13, Emotion, examines feelings such as fear, anger, and happiness that add color to our lives, and shows how each combines physiological arousal, expressive behaviors, and conscious experiences.

Motivation

Chapter 12

In everyday conversation, the question "What motivated you to do that?" is a way of asking "What *caused* you to do that? *Why* did you act that way?" To psychologists, a **motivation** is a need or desire that serves to *energize* behavior and to *direct* it toward a goal. Like intelligence, motivation is a hypothetical concept. We infer motivation from behaviors we observe, as in the following examples:

The yearning for food—

> In the Nazi concentration camps . . . we would get up early, about 4 or 4:30 in the morning, and stand in line. They would give us a hot tea or a coffee which was hot water boiled with some kind of grassy substance. There was no sugar or anything else to put in it. It was just something hot. We downed it and that was our breakfast. . . .
>
> I was so glad I wasn't with my father or brother during this time. You have no idea how a father and son would fight over a piece of bread. Like dogs.
>
> One man in my barracks was about 45. He was dignified in spite of his emaciated state. He had a son about 20 who also lived in the barracks.
>
> One evening the son ate his own bread while the father placed his under a piece of cloth he used as a pillow. The next morning I heard the father scream—his bread was gone. His son had eaten it during the night.
>
> The father went into a deep depression. He kept asking how his son could do such a thing to him. I guess the father lost his will to live, because the next day he was dead. . . .
>
> Hunger does something to you that's hard to describe. I can't believe it myself today, so how can I expect anyone else to understand it?

David Mandel (1983)

The longing for sexual intimacy—

> I am sick with love.
>
> O that his left hand were under my head, and that his right hand embraced me! . . .
>
> By night on my bed I sought him whom my soul loves: I sought him but I found him not.
>
> I will rise now, and go about the city in the streets, and in the broad ways I will seek him whom my soul loves: I sought him but I found him not.

How fair and pleasant you are, O loved one, delectable maiden!

You are stately as a palm tree, and your breasts are like its clusters.

I say I will climb the palm tree and lay hold of its branches.

Oh, may your breasts be like clusters of the vine, and the scent of your breath like apples,

And your kisses like the best wine that goes down smoothly, gliding over lips and teeth. . . .

Song of Solomon (Old Testament)

The need to achieve—

Alfredo Gonzales, winner of his community's "man of the year" award and three-time chairperson of Michigan's Commission on the Spanish-Speaking, is a graduate school-educated college administrator.

Although born in the United States, Alfredo as a 14-year-old would have been found where he had spent all but the first year of his life—working on his grandparents' farm in Mexico. Later that year, after Alfredo rejoined his parents in Texas, a school truant officer discovered him picking fruit and ordered him off to the local junior high school. There, for the first time in his life, he saw the inside of a school classroom and heard English. "I walked into a room filled mostly with other Mexican-Americans," recalls Gonzales, "all of whom were prohibited from speaking Spanish. Several times I was caught trying to ask a question in Spanish—for which the 'cure' was being beaten with a paddle."

Although placed at the lowest skill level by his schools and discouraged from high aspirations, he began to sense, as he still does, that "I could do better. I don't know as much as I could know." So, while working as a city human relations officer after his release from the army, he completed his college education part-time. Later he became director of a college Upward Bound program, and then a dean. His aim, he says, is to motivate youth by giving them what he developed in himself—"an awareness of their own potential and a desire to achieve it."

In this chapter, we will explore motivation by focusing on these three motives—hunger, sex, and achievement. Although other identifiable motives exist (thirst, curiosity, need for approval, and so forth), a close look at these three reveals the interplay between nature (the biological "push") and nurture (the cognitive and cultural "pulls") that underlies all motivated behavior. Along the way, we will discover answers to some intriguing questions:

What is the source of gnawing hunger or ardent sexual desire?

Why is the arousal provided by these motives directed toward some targets rather than others—say, toward a person of one sex rather than the other?

What motivates us to achieve—is it more an inner quest to excel, or a desire for rewards such as social recognition?

Concepts of Motivation

Early in this century, as the influence of Charles Darwin's evolutionary theory grew, it became fashionable to classify all sorts of behaviors as instincts. If people criticized themselves, it was because of their "self-abasement instinct." If they boasted, it reflected their "self-assertion instinct." After scanning 500 books, one sociologist compiled a list of 5759 supposed human instincts! Before long, the instinct-naming fad collapsed under its own weight. For rather than *explaining* human behaviors, the early instinct theorists were simply *naming* them.

There is an important lesson here. What the early instinct theorists did we still find tempting—fooling ourselves into thinking we are explaining a behavior by giving it a name. The result is circular reasoning:

> "Why do we spend $3 billion per *day* for arms and armies, while hundreds of millions of people must subsist without adequate food and shelter?"
>
> "It's because of our aggression instinct."
>
> "How do you know we have an aggression instinct?"
>
> "Just look at how much world governments spend on preparing for war—$200 per year for every person on earth, millions of whom will never receive $200 in a year!"

While we might agree that these priorities are tragic, this circular argument offers no explanation at all. It is like "explaining" a bright child's low grades by saying he or she is an "underachiever." To name a behavior is *not* to explain it.

To qualify as an **instinct**, a behavior must have a fixed pattern and be unlearned (Tinbergen, 1951). Such behaviors are common in other species (recall the return of salmon to their birthplace to spawn, and imprinting in birds). *Ethologists*—psychologists and biologists who study animal behavior in natural settings—have revived interest in fixed behavior patterns, by studying feeding, mating, nest building, and other behaviors that characterize a species. Because ethologists now use the term *instinct* to describe rather than explain such behaviors, other scientists are working to identify the precise mechanisms that drive animals to feed, mate, and care for their young.

Human behavior, too, exhibits certain innate tendencies, including simple fixed patterns such as an infant's rooting and sucking. Most psychologists, though, view human behavior as directed by biological needs and psychological wants. To most psychologists a *need* is a deprivation, such as a lack of food, that *pushes* us to meet the need. Psychological wants (sometimes also loosely called needs, as in the "need for achievement") are fueled by *incentives* that *pull* or lure us.

Biological Needs: The Internal Pushes

When the instinct theory of motivation collapsed, it was replaced by *drive theory*—the idea that a biological need creates an aroused state, or **drive**, which motivates an organism to satisfy the need. The drive prompts the organism to reduce the need by, say, eating or drinking. When a biological need increases, its psychological consequence, a drive, usually increases, too.

The physiological aim of drive reduction is **homeostasis**—the maintenance of a balanced or constant internal state. An example of homeostasis (which literally means "staying the same") is the body's temperature-regulation system, which works much as a thermostat works to keep room temperature constant. Both systems operate through feedback loops, with adjustments based on information continually fed back into the system. Sensors detect the

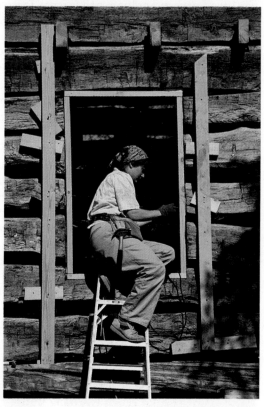

The more complex the nervous system, the more adaptable the organism. The weaver bird's construction skills are instinctual; the human's are learned.

temperature of the room or body and feed this information to a control device. If the room temperature cools, the control device notes this deviation from the desired state and switches on the furnace. If body temperature cools, blood vessels constrict to conserve warmth, and we feel driven to put on more clothes or seek a warmer environment. If the water level in our cells drops, sensors detect our need for water and we feel thirsty.

Learning and Culture: The External Pulls ✶

There are, however, motives that do not satisfy any obvious biological need. Monkeys will monkey around trying to figure out how to unlock a latch that opens nothing or how to open a window that allows them to see outside their room (Butler, 1954). The 9-month-old infant who investigates every accessible corner of the house, the scientists whose work this text discusses, and the voyagers who first ventured across and beneath oceans were all motivated to explore. Asked why he wanted to climb Mt. Everest, George Mallory answered, "Because it is there."

Recall, too, the experiments on sensory restriction described in Chapter 5. The peace and quiet of sensory monotony sensitized the subjects to any available stimulation. Despite having all our biological needs satisfied, we feel driven to experience stimulation. Without it, we feel bored and look for a way to increase stimulation to some optimum level.

Not only are we pushed by our "need" for optimum stimulation, we are also pulled by incentives. This is where our individual learning histories influence our motives, because an **incentive** is any stimulus that has positive or negative value in motivating our behavior. Depending on our learning, the aroma of fresh roasted peanuts (or toasted ants), the sight of someone we find attractive, and the threat of disapproval can all motivate our behavior. Our internal needs energize and direct our behavior, but so do these external incentives. When there is both a need and an incentive, we feel driven. The food-deprived person who smells bread baking hungers for it. For each motive, we can therefore ask, how is it pushed by our inborn biological needs and pulled by incentives in the environment?

Curiosity. The activities of young monkeys and children demonstrate the early presence of an insatiable urge to explore—one of several motives that does not fulfill any obvious physiological need.

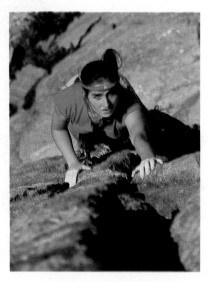

For people who crave the stimulation of ever-increasing tests of their courage or mastery, mental and physical challenges are powerful incentives. According to one theory, some thrill-seeking people become daring inventors, entrepreneurs, or artists, while other thrill-seekers become reckless drivers, drug users, or criminals (Farley, 1986).

A Hierarchy of Motives

Some needs take priority over others. At this moment, your needs for air and water are probably satisfied, so other motives—such as your desire to achieve a good grade—energize and direct your behavior. If your need for water goes unsatisfied, your thirst will preoccupy you. Deprived of air, your thirst will disappear.

These examples illustrate how the particular needs that motivate our behavior depend on which needs are unmet and, among those, which are the more fundamental. Abraham Maslow (1970) proposed one such **hierarchy of needs** (Figure 12–1). At the base are our physiological needs, such as for food, water, and shelter. Only if these needs are met are we prompted to meet our need for safety, and then to meet the uniquely human needs to give and receive love, and to enjoy self-esteem. Beyond this, said Maslow (1971), lies the highest of human needs: to actualize one's full potential. (More on self-esteem and self-actualization in Chapter 14, Personality.)

Maslow's hierarchy is somewhat arbitrary. Moreover, the order of such needs is not universally fixed. People have starved themselves to make a political statement. Nevertheless, the simple idea that some motives are more compelling than others—until they are satisfied—provides a framework for thinking about motivation. Let's now consider three representative motives, beginning at the basic, physiological level with hunger and working up through sexual motivation to a higher-level motive, achievement. At each level, we will see how psychological factors interact with what is biologically given.

Hunger

A vivid demonstration of the supremacy of physiological needs followed reports of starvation in World War II prison camps and occupied areas. To learn more about the results of semistarvation, scientist Ancel Keys and his colleagues (1950) solicited volunteers for an experiment. From among the more than 100 conscientious objectors to the war who applied, they selected 36 men. First, they fed the men just enough to maintain their initial weight. Then, for 6 months, they cut this food level in half.

The effects soon became visible. Without thinking about it, the men began conserving energy; they appeared listless and apathetic. Their body weights dropped rapidly, eventually stabilizing at about 25 percent below their starting weights. The psychological effects were even more dramatic. Consistent with Maslow's idea of a need hierarchy, the men became obsessed with food. They talked food. They daydreamed food. They collected recipes, read cookbooks, and feasted their eyes on delectable forbidden foods. Meanwhile, they lost their former interests in sex and social activities. They became preoccupied with their unfulfilled needs. As one subject reported, "If we see a show, the most interesting part of it is contained in scenes where people are eating. I couldn't laugh at the funniest picture in the world, and love scenes are completely dull."

What caused this gnawing hunger? For that matter, what drives us to eat periodically?

Self-actualization needs
Need to live up to one's fullest and unique potential

Esteem needs
Need for self-esteem, achievement, competence, and independence; need for recognition and respect from others

Belongingness and love needs
Need to love and be loved, to belong and be accepted; need to avoid loneliness and alienation

Safety needs
Need to feel that the world is organized and predictable; need to feel safe, secure, and stable

Physiological needs
Need to satisfy hunger and thirst

Figure 12–1 Maslow's hierarchy of needs. Once our lower-level needs are met, we are prompted to satisfy our higher-level needs. (From Maslow, 1970.)

During Keys' semistarvation experiment, his conscientious objector subjects became obsessed with food.

The Physiology of Hunger

The hunger of Keys' semistarved subjects was the response of a homeostatic system designed to maintain normal body weight and an adequate supply of nutrients. But precisely what is it that triggers hunger? Is it the pangs of an empty stomach? So it feels, and so it seemed after A. L. Washburn, working with Walter Cannon (Cannon & Washburn, 1912), intentionally swallowed a balloon. When inflated in his stomach, the balloon transmitted his stomach contractions to a recording device (Figure 12–2). While his stomach was being monitored, Washburn pressed a key each time he felt hungry. This, too, was transmitted to the recording device, which revealed that Washburn was having stomach contractions whenever he felt hungry. (Some diet aids reduce this empty stomach feeling by filling the stomach with indigestible fibers that swell as they absorb water.)

Alas, there is more to hunger than the pangs of an empty stomach. Researchers discovered this a quarter-century later when they removed some rats' stomachs and attached their esophagi to their small intestines (Tsang, 1938). Without stomach pangs, did hunger persist? Did the rats continue to eat regularly? Indeed they did. Hunger persists similarly in humans whose ulcerated or cancerous stomachs have been removed. In fact, one can feel hungry even on a full stomach. Animals that fill their stomachs by eating low-calorie food will eat more than animals that consume a less filling, high-calorie diet (McHugh & Moran, 1978). If the pangs of an empty stomach are not the only source of our hunger, what else is involved?

Body Chemistry Changes in body chemistry also affect hunger. That people and other animals automatically regulate their caloric intake to maintain a stable body weight suggests that the body is somehow, somewhere keeping tabs on its available resources. One such resource is blood **glucose** (a type of sugar). Injecting large doses of the hormone **insulin** diminishes blood glucose, partly by converting it to stored fat, thus causing hunger to increase.

As food is absorbed and hunger diminishes, eating behavior changes. Eliot Stellar (1985) discovered this after outfitting people with a special dental retainer engineered to record each chew and swallow. The device answers questions about "the microstructure of human eating" that you may never have thought to ask. During a meal of sandwich snacks, how often does the average person swallow? Every 14 seconds. How many chews on average per swallow? 19. How fast do people chew? 1.8 chews per second. As the meal progresses and both hunger and food tastiness decrease, people chew more. Ironically, the better a food tastes, the less time people leave it in their mouths.

Our taste preference for sweet and salty are genetic and universal. Other tastes are conditioned, as when people given highly salted foods develop a liking for excess salt (Beauchamp, 1987) or when people develop an aversion to a food eaten before becoming violently ill (recall page 234). (The frequency of children's illnesses provides many chances for them to learn food aversions.)

Cultural conditioning affects taste, too. Bedouins enjoy eating the eye of a camel, which most North Americans would find repulsive. Similarly, North Americans shun dog, rat, and horse meat, all of which are prized elsewhere, but welcome beef, which Hindus wouldn't think of eating.

Figure 12–2 The procedure by which Washburn showed that stomach contractions (transmitted by the stomach balloon) accompany our feelings of hunger (indicated by a key press). (From Cannon, 1929.)

Culture and taste preferences. Pizza and cola are popular cuisine in the United States, but other cultures not yet introduced to this combination may find it unappetizing.

Body chemistry also influences taste preferences. When feeling tense or depressed, do you crave sweet or starchy carbohydrate-laden foods? Carbohydrates help boost levels of the neurotransmitter serotonin, which has calming effects. Given a drug that similarly increases serotonin, carbohydrate cravers lose their cravings. This suggests that stress-related cravings might be treatable by providing food substitutes that mimic carbohydrates' biochemical effects (Hall, 1987).

The Brain and Set Point Low blood glucose is a source of hunger. But you do not consciously feel your blood chemistry. Rather, the brain monitors information on your body's internal state. Signals from the stomach, the intestines, and the liver (indicating whether glucose is being deposited or withdrawn) all signal the brain to motivate eating or not. But where in the brain are these messages integrated? During the 1940s and 1950s, researchers located hunger controls within the hypothalamus, a small but complex neural traffic intersection buried deep in the brain (Figure 12–3).

Actually, there are two distinct hypothalamic centers that control eating. Activity in the side areas of the hypothalamus, known as the *lateral hypothalamus,* or *LH,* brings on hunger. When electrically stimulated there, a well-fed animal will begin to eat; when the area is destroyed, even a starving animal has no interest in food. Activity in an area near the bottom and middle of the hypothalamus, known as the *ventromedial hypothalamus,* or *VMH,* depresses hunger. Stimulate this area and an animal will stop eating; destroy it and the animal's stomach and intestines will process food more rapidly, causing it to eat more often and to become grossly fat (Duggan & Booth, 1986; Hoebel & Teitelbaum, 1966).

How do these complementary areas of the hypothalamus work? One theory is that manipulating these two areas of the hypothalamus alters the body's "weight thermostat," which predisposes us to keep our body at a particular weight level, called its **set point** (Keesey & Corbett, 1983). When semistarved rats fall below their normal weight, biological pressures act to restore the lost weight: Hunger increases and energy expenditure decreases. If body weight rises—as happens when rats are force-fed—hunger decreases and energy expenditure increases. Even VMH-lesioned rats will stop overeating, once fat enough. This stable weight toward which semistarved and overstuffed rats return is their set point. (Some researchers believe that slow, sustained changes in body weight can, however, alter one's set point.)

Another theory discounts the idea that a ventromedial lesion damages a direct "off switch" for feeding. The effect may instead be indirect, by increasing the conversion of glucose into fat even when an animal is fed a normal amount. If too much glucose is being stored by the miserly body, not enough may be available to fuel everyday needs. Thus, the animal is hungry.

Regardless of the precise method of regulation, this much is clear: Despite the day-to-day variations in our eating, our bodies are astonishingly good at regulating our weight, much better than we could be through conscious efforts to control food intake precisely. If today you weigh within a pound of what you weighed a year ago, you kept your average energy intake and expenditure within 10 calories a day of one another. Keep all else equal and add a single carrot per day to caloric input, and within a decade you will gain 30 pounds!

Figure 12–3 As we saw in Chapter 2, the hypothalamus performs various body maintenance functions, including control of hunger. Blood vessels supply the hypothalamus, enabling it to respond to our current blood chemistry as well as to incoming neural information about the body's state.

Hypothalamus

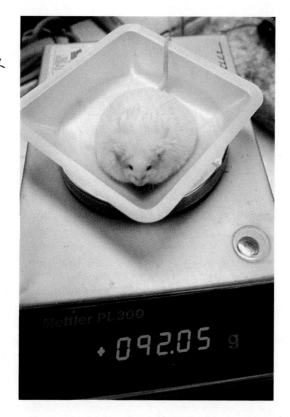

Lesioning the ventromedial hypothalamus (VMH) raised this rodent's set point, causing its weight to triple.

Our bodies regulate weight much as rats' bodies do—through the control of food intake and energy output. If our body weight rises above our set point, we tend not to feel so hungry; if our weight drops below, we tend to eat more. To maintain its set-point weight, the body also adjusts its **metabolic rate**—its base rate of energy expenditure. By the end of their 24 weeks of semistarvation, the subjects in the World War II experiment had stabilized at three-quarters of their normal weight—while eating half what they previously did. The stabilization resulted from reduced energy expenditure, achieved partly by physical lethargy and partly by a 29 percent drop in their resting metabolic rate.

External Incentives

Our eagerness to eat is both pushed by our physical state—our body chemistry and hypothalamic activity—and pulled by external stimuli. Like Pavlov's dogs, people learn to salivate in anticipation of appealing foods. When food is abundant, those who are especially responsive to external food stimuli tend to gain the most weight.

Consider the 9- to 15-year-old girls studied by Judith Rodin and Joyce Slochower (1976) at an 8-week summer camp. During the first week of camp, some girls could not resist munching readily visible M&Ms even after a full meal. Such people, whose eating is triggered more by the presence of food than by internal factors, are called *externals*. In the 7 weeks that followed, the "external" girls gained the most weight.

In a delicious demonstration of how internal and external factors interact, Rodin (1984) invited people to her laboratory for lunch after they went 18 hours without food. While blood samples were being taken, a large, juicy steak was wheeled in, crackling as it finished grilling. As the hungry subjects sat watching, hearing, and smelling the soon-to-be-eaten steak, Rodin noted their rising blood insulin levels and their accompanying feelings of hunger. When stimulated by the sight, sound, and aroma of the steak, "externals" had the greatest insulin/hunger response. This illustrates how our psychological experience of an external incentive (the steak) can affect our internal physiological state.

Drawing by Charles Schulz; ©1989 United Feature Syndicate, Inc. Reprinted by permission of UFS, Inc.

Eating Disorders

Psychological influences on eating behavior are strikingly evident in those who suffer eating disorders. Consider two cases:

Mary is a 5' 3" 15-year-old who, having reached 100 pounds, decided she needed to lose weight to enhance her attractiveness. After gradually reducing her food intake to a few vegetables a day and then adding a vigorous exercise program, she now weighs a mere 80 pounds. Yet she still feels "fat" and plans to continue dieting. Mary has been having difficulty sleeping, has at times been depressed, and no longer has regular menstrual periods. She is socially inactive and seldom dates, but she is very successful academically. Mary does not regard herself as ill or needing treatment.

Alice is a 5' 9", 160-pound 17-year-old who says she has always been a little chubby. For the last 5 years, she has often eaten in binges followed by vomiting. She will eat a quart of ice cream or an entire pie and then, to control her weight, make herself vomit in secret. Alice wants to date, but doesn't because she is ashamed of her looks. She has at times taken diet pills to try to lose weight.

Mary is diagnosed as having **anorexia nervosa**—a disorder in which a person becomes significantly underweight (typically, 15 percent or more) yet feels fat and fears becoming obese. Even when emaciated, the person continues to limit food intake. The disorder usually develops in adolescence, 9 times out of 10 in females.

Alice's condition, which is more common, is **bulimia nervosa**— a disorder characterized by repeated "binge-purge" episodes of overeating followed by vomiting or using a laxative. Bulimia patients eat as some alcoholics drink—not steadily and in moderation, but in spurts, sometimes under the influence of friends who also are binging (Crandall, 1988). Most binge-purge eaters are women in their late teens or twenties. Like those with anorexia, they are preoccupied with food, fearful of becoming overweight, and depressed or anxious (Hinz & Williamson, 1987). The depression and shame are felt most keenly during and following binges. About half of those with anorexia also display the binge-purge-depression symptoms of bulimia. But most bulimics fluctuate within or above normal weight ranges, which makes the condition easy to hide.

Researchers report that the families of bulimia patients have a higher than usual incidence of alcoholism, obesity, and depression. Anorexia patients often come from families that are high-achieving and protective (Yates, 1989, 1990). Biology also may influence susceptibility to eating disorders. When one twin has bulimia, the chances are much greater that the other twin will share the disorder if they are identical rather than fraternal twins (Fichter & Noegel, 1990). People with eating disorders may also have abnormal neurotransmitter supplies that put them at risk for anxiety or depression (Fava & others, 1989).

There is, however, a cultural explanation for the fact that anorexia and bulimia occur mostly in women and mostly in weight-conscious cultures. Anorexia nervosa always begins as a weight-loss diet, and the self-induced vomiting of bulimics nearly always begins after a dieter has broken diet restrictions and gorged. Although ideals of beauty have varied over the centuries, women in every era have struggled to make their bodies conform to the ideal of their day. Thus, the "sickness" of today's eating disorders lies not just within the victims but also within their weight-obsessed culture—a culture that says, in countless ways, "Fat is bad," that motivates millions of women to be "always dieting," and that encourages eating binges by pressuring women to live in a constant state of semistarvation. As obesity researchers Susan Wooley and Orland Wooley (1983) noted, "an increasingly stringent cultural standard of thinness for women has been accompanied by a steadily increasing incidence of serious eating disorders in women."

Consistent with this explanation, the extremely thin women pictured in fashion magazines and advertisements distort women's perceptions of what men find attractive. In one study of nearly 500 University of Pennsylvania students, April Fallon and Paul Rozin (1985) found that women's ideal body weight was less than their current weight. Moreover, the weight they thought men preferred was less than the weight men actually preferred (Figure 12–4, page 360). The researchers found no such discrepancies in the men's self-ratings. The men more often judged their current weight, their ideal weight, and the weight they thought women preferred as all quite

Singer Karen Carpenter's death of cardiac arrest at age 32 was believed related to her long struggle with anorexia nervosa.

In recent years, the average weight of American women has increased. Simultaneously—to judge from the decreasing measurements of Miss America contestants, Playboy *centerfolds, and female magazine models—the cultural ideal has become thinner (Striegel-Moore & others, 1986).*

Figure 12-4 Many American women students tend to idealize, and misperceive men as idealizing, a body shape considerably thinner than their own. (From Fallon & Rozin, 1985.) In India, women students rate their ideals as close to their current shape (From Fallon, 1990.)

Thinnest — Women's ideal — What women believed men preferred — What men actually preferred — Women's current body image — Fattest

similar. Women's greater self-dissatisfaction stems from their perceiving their cheeks, waist, and hips as looking larger than they do (Thompson, 1986). Women with low self-esteem are particularly likely to have a negative body image and are especially vulnerable to eating disorders (Mintz & Betz, 1986; Striegel-Moore & others, 1986).

Sexual Motivation

Sexual motivation is part of life. Had this not been so for all your ancestors, you would not be reading this book. Sexual motivation is nature's clever way of making people procreate, thus enabling our species' survival. When two people feel attracted, they hardly stop to think of themselves as guided by their invisible genetic code. As the pleasure we take in eating is nature's inventive method of getting our body nourishment, so the pleasure of sex is our genes' way of preserving and spreading themselves.

"I lose my respect for the man who can make the mystery of sex the subject of a coarse jest, yet, when you speak earnestly and seriously on the subject, is silent."
  Henry David Thoreau
  Journal, 1852

Describing Sexual Behavior

Before looking at what energizes and directs sexual arousal, let's consider the behavior patterns that a theory of sexual motivation must explain.

Unable to answer his students' questions about people's sexual practices, Indiana University biologist Alfred Kinsey and his colleagues (1948, 1953) set out to find some answers. Kinsey's confidential interviews with more than 5000 men and nearly 6000 women made history. Social scientists were quick to point out what Kinsey readily acknowledged—that his nonrandom sample contained an overrepresentation of well-educated, White, urban residents of Indiana, Illinois, and several Eastern states. Nevertheless, his statistics-laden volumes became best sellers. Here readers learned the then surprising news that, among Kinsey's sample at least, most men and nearly half of the women reported having had premarital sexual intercourse, that a majority of women and virtually all men reported they masturbated, and that women who reported masturbating to orgasm before marriage seldom had difficulties experiencing orgasm after marriage. One could also find evidence that sexual behavior is enormously varied. Kinsey found some men and women who said they had never had an orgasm, and others who said they had four or more a day. For those who evalu-

Kinsey, shown here giving one of many interviews, did not begin his interviews with sexually explicit questions. Rather, he first helped people feel at ease by asking less threatening questions about family background, health, and education.

ate themselves by comparisons with others, Kinsey's findings—and others showing wide variations in "normal" sexual behavior around the world—are reassuring. Given the range of sex drives and the variety of sexual behaviors, your own sexual interests probably fall well within the range of "normal."

Because we do not know whether Kinsey's sample accurately represented the nation's sexual practices in the 1940s, let alone those of today, it can be misleading to report his precise findings. But Kinsey's surveys were surely less misleading than some of the haphazard sexual surveys that have been reported more recently in the popular press. Recall from Chapter 1 that when popular "sex reports" begin with a biased sample of people (such as subscribers to selected magazines) and receive replies from only 3 percent of this nonrandom sample of people, there is good reason to doubt the generality of their findings.

Better information is now becoming available. In the United States, for example, two new surveys of randomly sampled adults counter the media image of rampant marital infidelity—an image reinforced by media psychologist Joyce Brothers' (1990) pronouncement that two-thirds of married men and half of married women have affairs. Actually, in a recent Gallup survey 9 in 10 married adults claimed to have had sex only with their spouse during their present marriage (Greeley, 1991). When the National Opinion Research Center added an anonymous, self-administered, return envelope sex questionnaire to their annual survey, they found that during the past year only "1.5 percent of married people [had] a sex partner other than their spouse" (Smith, 1991). Faithful attractions greatly outnumbered fatal attractions. And disapproval of extramarital sex, at 91 percent, runs as high as ever among adult Americans (Greeley, 1991).

Eager to understand why the AIDS (Acquired Immune Deficiency Syndrome) virus has spread more among some groups than others, researchers undertook new sex surveys at the beginning of this decade. One survey is interviewing a random sample of 20,000 people in Britain (Holden, 1989). The World Health Organization will be conducting the first-ever global survey of human sexuality, based on interviews with some 2000 people in each of 20 countries (Carballo & others, 1989). Researchers hope that results from such surveys, including perhaps a much-debated, government-sponsored U.S. sex survey, will help us better understand the behaviors that spread sexually transmitted diseases.

"The psychologist-asker averages up all the lies . . . and everybody in America feels inferior."
Psychologist Sol Gordon (1923–)

The Physiology of Sex

Like hunger, sexual arousal depends on the interplay of internal and external stimuli. To understand sexual motivation, we must consider both.

The Sexual Response Cycle The headlines created by Kinsey's 1940s surveys reappeared after some 1960s studies in which scientists recorded the physiological responses of volunteers who masturbated or had intercourse. With the help of 382 female and 312 male volunteers—a somewhat atypical sample, consisting only of people able and willing to display arousal and orgasm while being observed in a laboratory—gynecologist-obstetrician William Masters and his collaborator Virginia Johnson (1966) monitored or filmed more than 10,000 sexual "cycles."

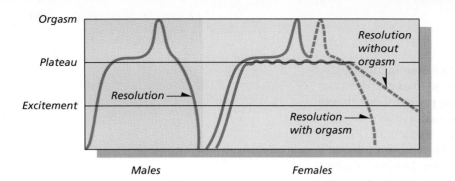

Figure 12–5 The sexual response cycle in men and in women. (Adapted from Masters & Johnson, 1966.)

skip

Their description of the **sexual response cycle** identified four stages, similar in men and women (Figure 12–5). During the initial *excitement phase*, the genital areas become engorged with blood, causing the man's penis to become partially erect and the woman's clitoris to swell and the inner lips covering her vagina to open up. Her vagina also expands and secretes lubricant, and her breasts and nipples may enlarge.

In the *plateau phase*, excitement peaks as breathing, pulse, and blood pressure rates continue to increase. The penis becomes fully engorged and some fluid (frequently containing enough live sperm to enable conception to occur) may appear at the tip of the penis. Vaginal secretion continues to increase, the clitoris retracts, and orgasm feels imminent.

During the *orgasm phase*, Masters and Johnson observed muscle contractions all over the body and further increases in breathing, pulse, and blood pressure rates. In the excitement of the moment, men and women are hardly aware of all this, but are more aware of their rhythmic genital contractions that create a pleasurable feeling of sexual release. The feeling apparently is much the same for both sexes. In one study, a panel of experts could not reliably distinguish between descriptions of orgasm written by men and those written by women (Vance & Wagner, 1976).

After orgasm, the body gradually returns to its unaroused state as the engorged genital blood vessels release their accumulated blood—relatively quickly if orgasm has occurred, relatively slowly otherwise. (It is like the nasal tickle that goes away rapidly if you have sneezed, slowly otherwise.) During this *resolution phase*, a male enters a **refractory period**, lasting from a few minutes to a day or more, during which he is incapable of another orgasm. A female does not have so lengthy a refractory period, which may make it possible for her to have another orgasm if restimulated during or soon after resolution.

Hormones and Sexual Behavior Sex hormones have two effects: They direct the development of male and female sex characteristics, and (especially in nonhuman animals) they activate sexual behavior. In most mammals, nature neatly synchronizes sex with fertility. The female becomes sexually receptive ("in heat") if and only if production of the female hormone **estrogen** has peaked, which occurs at ovulation. (In experiments, researchers simulate this by injecting females with estrogen.) Male hormone levels are more constant, and researchers cannot so easily manipulate the sexual behavior of male animals by hormone treatments (Feder, 1984). Nevertheless, castrated male rats—having lost their testes, which manufacture the male hormone **testosterone**—gradually lose much of their interest in receptive females, and gradually regain it if injected with testosterone.

Hormones don't so neatly control human sexual behavior. Natural daily and monthly hormone fluctuations do not greatly affect sexual desire. Women's sexual desire is only slightly higher at ovulation (Harvey, 1987) and is actually more responsive to testosterone than to estrogen (Kaplan, 1979; Meyer-Bahlburg, 1980). Normal fluctuations in men's testosterone levels, from man to man and hour to hour, have little effect on their sexual drives (Byrne, 1982). Indeed, such fluctuations are partly a response to sexual stimulation. When James Dabbs and his colleagues (1987) had male collegians converse separately with a male and a female student, the men's testosterone levels rose with the social arousal, but especially after talking with the female. Like the effect of the crackling steak on insulin level, sexual arousal can be a cause as well as a consequence of increased testosterone levels.

Although normal short-term hormonal changes have little effect on desire, large hormone shifts have a bigger effect over the life span. A person's interest in dating and sexual stimulation usually increases with the pubertal surge in sex hormones. If the hormonal surge is precluded—as happened with prepubertal boys who were castrated during the 1700s and 1800s to preserve their soprano voices for Italian opera—the normal development of sex characteristics and sexual desire does not occur (Peschel & Peschel, 1987). Among adult men who suffer castration, sex drive typically falls along with declining testosterone levels (Hucker & Bain, 1990). Likewise, male sex offenders lose much of their sexual urge when voluntarily taking Depo-Provera, a drug that reduces testosterone levels to that of a prepubertal boy (Money & others, 1983). And in later life, the typical frequency of intercourse declines as sex hormone levels decline.

Hormones influence sexual arousal via the hypothalamus, which both monitors variations in blood hormone levels and activates the neural circuits involved in arousal. In rats, destroying a key area of the hypothalamus may end sexual activity; stimulating this area, either electrically or by directly inserting minute quantities of hormones, may activate sexual behavior.

To summarize, we might compare human sex hormones, especially testosterone, to the fuel in a car. Lacking fuel, the car will not run. But if the fuel level is minimally adequate, adding more fuel to the gas tank won't change how the car runs. The analogy is imperfect, because the interaction between hormones and sexual motivation is two-way. However, the analogy correctly suggests that biology is a necessary but not sufficient explanation of human sexual behavior. The biological fuel is essential, but so are the psychological stimuli that turn on the engine and shift it into high gear.

The Psychology of Sex

We have seen similarities between hunger and sexual motivation. Both are motivated by internal biological factors, but also influenced by external stimuli.

External Stimuli In many species, the members of one sex are aroused automatically by odors emitted by the other sex. Are humans, also? Despite the millions of dollars spent on advertising scents that supposedly attract sexual interest, attempts to detect unlearned human sexual responses to particular odors have not been very successful (Morris & Udry, 1978). The only unlearned

"Ours is a society which stimulates interest in sex by constant titillation. . . . Cinema, television, and all the formidable array of our marketing technology project our very effective forms of titillation and our prejudices about man as a sexy animal into every corner of every hovel in the world."
Germaine Greer (1984)

stimulus for human sexual arousal appears to be touch—the pleasurable genital caresses that are part of foreplay worldwide (Byrne, 1982).

Many studies reveal that men become aroused when they see, hear, or read erotic material. More surprising to many people (because sexually explicit materials are sold mostly to men) is that most women—at least the less inhibited women who volunteer to participate in such studies (Morokoff, 1986)—report similar arousal to the same stimuli (Harrell & Stolp, 1985).

In one such study, psychologist Julia Heiman (1975) attached instruments that detected arousal (changes in the penis circumference or in vaginal color) to sexually experienced university volunteers. Then the students listened to either a sexually explicit erotic tape, a romantic tape (of a couple expressing love without physical contact), a combined erotic-romantic tape, or a neutral control tape. Which do you suppose the men were most aroused by? And the women? Both the men and the women found the tape of explicit sex most arousing, especially when a woman initiated the sex and when the depiction centered on her responses.

People may find such arousal either pleasing or disturbing. (Those who find it disturbing often limit their exposure to such materials, just as those wishing to control hunger limit their exposure to tempting cues.) Some explicit materials can have additional effects that are not so harmless. First, those depicting women being sexually coerced—and enjoying it—tend to increase viewers' acceptance of the false idea that women enjoy rape, and tend to increase male viewers' willingness to hurt women (pages 572–573). Second, images of sexually attractive people may lead people to devalue their partners and relationships. Several studies (Gutierres & others, 1985; Kenrick & Gutierres, 1980; Weaver & others, 1984) found that after male collegians view TV or magazine depictions of sexually attractive women, they suddenly find an average woman, or their own girlfriends or wives, less attractive. Viewing X-rated sex films similarly tends to diminish people's satisfaction with their sexual partner (Zillmann, 1989). Some sex researchers fear that reading or viewing erotica may create expectations that few men and women can hope to live up to.

Imaginative Stimuli   Sexual arousal and desire arise from the interplay of biology and environment. But the stimuli inside our heads—our imaginations—also influence our sexual motivation (Figure 12–6). The brain, it has been said, is our most significant sex organ. People who, because of a spinal cord injury, have no genital sensation, can still feel sexual desire (Willmuth, 1987). Consider, too, the erotic potential of dreams. As noted on page 194, genital arousal accompanies all types of dreams, including the majority of dreams, which have no sexual content. But in nearly all men and some 40 percent of women (Wells, 1986), dreams sometimes do contain sexual imagery that leads to orgasm. In men, these nocturnal emissions ("wet dreams") are more likely when orgasm has not occurred recently.

Wide-awake people become sexually aroused not only by memories of prior sexual activities but also by fantasies. Fantasies need not correspond to actual behavior. In one survey of masturbation-related fantasies (Hunt, 1974), 19 percent of women and 10 percent of men reported imagining someone forcing them to have sex. Fantasy is not reality, however. To paraphrase Susan Brownmiller

Figure 12–6 Sexual motivation results from the interplay of biology, environment, and imagination. (From Byrne, 1982.)

(1975), for women there's a big difference between fantasizing that Eddie Murphy or Tom Cruise just won't take no for an answer and having a stranger actually force himself on you at knife point. (See also page 572 for a discussion of the "rape myth.")

"There is no difference between being raped and being run over by a truck except that afterward men ask if you enjoyed it."
Marge Piercy
Rape Poem, 1976

Sexual Dysfunctions and Therapy

Masters and Johnson sought not only to describe the normal sexual response cycle, but to understand and treat the inability to complete it. **Sexual dysfunctions** are problems that consistently impair sexual functioning. Some of these dysfunctions are problems in sexual motivation, especially in one's sexual energy and arousability. Men, for example, may experience *premature ejaculation* (before they or their partners wish) or *impotence* (the inability to have or maintain an erection). Women more often than men experience low sexual desire or *orgasmic dysfunction* (infrequently or never experiencing orgasm).

What causes such problems? The idea that personality disorders are to blame has been largely discounted. Men who experience premature ejaculation are similar, even in their sexual arousal patterns, to men who do not; they simply ejaculate at lower levels of sexual arousal—something that often occurs with young men who have had long periods of sexual abstinence (Spiess & others, 1984).

When Barbara Anderson (1983) reviewed research on the diagnosis and treatment of orgasmic dysfunction in women, she, too, could find no associated personality traits. Furthermore, she reported that treating orgasmic dysfunction through traditional psychotherapy (as though it were a disorder of personality) has been unsuccessful. On the other hand, she reported a nearly 100 percent success rate with a treatment that trains women to enjoy their bodies and to give themselves orgasms, with a vibrator if necessary. Some of these women can then generalize their new sexual responsiveness to interactions with their mates (LoPiccolo & Stock, 1986; Wakefield, 1987). Success has also been reported in training men to control their premature ejaculations by repeatedly stimulating the penis and then stopping stimulation (or even firmly squeezing the head of the penis) when the urge to ejaculate arises.

Sexual Orientation

To motivate is to energize and direct behavior. So far, we have considered the energizing of sexual motivation but not its direction. We express the direction of our sexual interest in our **sexual orientation**—our enduring sexual attraction toward members of a particular sex. As far as we know, virtually all cultures in all times have been predominantly heterosexual (Bullough, 1990), although they vary in their attitude toward homosexuality. Yet whether a culture condemns and punishes homosexuality or views it as an acceptable alternative, homosexuality survives and heterosexuality prevails.

Although most homosexual people report that they first became aware of same-gender sexual feelings during or shortly after puberty, they typically do not think of themselves as gay or lesbian until nearer to or after age 20 (Garnets & Kimmel, 1990). How many people are exclusively homosexual? In both Europe and the United States, studies suggest about 4 percent of men and 1 percent of women (Ellis & Ames, 1987). Because a homosexuality rate of 10 percent is so often mentioned in the popular press, let's pause to sample the recent evidence. A 1970 national survey sponsored by the Kinsey Institute found that 1.4 percent of men reported having had homosexual sex "fairly often," and another 1.9 percent "occasionally" (Fay & others, 1989). Some 2 percent had such contact within the previous year. In 1985, ABC News and the *Washington Post* put this question to a random sample of men:

> I have only one more question. You may consider it somewhat personal to answer but most people have been willing to answer it once we remind them that this is a totally confidential survey. We reached you on the phone simply by chance and don't know your identity. Here's the question: Would you say that you are sexually attracted to members of the opposite sex or members of your own sex?

In reply, 2.4 percent indicated they were homosexual, 0.8 percent indicated they were bisexual (Harry, 1990). Among sexually active Americans responding to the National Opinion Research Center's confidential survey, 1.6 percent of sexually active people reported having had homosexual contact during the past year (Smith, 1990). If we adjust this figure upward to include homosexuals who are sexually inactive, it roughly concurs with the other findings of at least a 2 to 3 percent homosexuality rate (combining men and women).

Some consider themselves bisexual, but a study of 173 male bisexuals in San Francisco found their behavior to be mostly homosexual: 68 percent reported having had no female sex partners over a 6-month period, while only 14 percent had no male partners during that time (Winkelstein & others, 1987). Nevertheless, many adults—perhaps 20 to 25 percent of men and 15 percent of women—report having had a homosexual experience. And most people have had occasional homosexual fantasies.

Although health experts find it helpful to know the statistics of sexual behavior patterns, the actual numbers of homosexual and heterosexual people does not decide the issue of any individual's human rights. Similarly, it's helpful in manufacturing school desks to know what percent of people are left-handed. But whether left-handers—or red-heads or bald-heads—are 3 percent or 10 percent of the population doesn't answer the moral question of whether such minorities should enjoy equal rights.

What does it feel like to be homosexual in a heterosexual culture? One way for heterosexual people to understand is to imagine how they would feel if they were to be ostracized or fired for openly admitting or displaying their feelings toward someone of the other sex; if they were to overhear people making crude jokes about heterosexual people; if every movie, TV show, and advertisement portrayed (or implied) homosexuality; and if their family members were pleading with them to change their heterosexual lifestyle and to enter into a homosexual marriage.

Facing such reactions, homosexual people often struggle with their sexual motivation. At first, they may try to ignore or deny their desires, hoping they will go away; but they don't. Then they may try to change them, through psychotherapy, willpower, or prayer. But the feelings typically persist, as do those of heterosexual people—who, similarly, are incapable of becoming homosexual. Eventually, homosexuals may accept their orientation—by electing celibacy (as do some heterosexuals); by engaging in promiscuous sex (a choice more commonly made by men than women); or by entering into a committed, long-term love relationship (a choice more often made by women than men) (Peplau, 1982; Weinberg &

Like heterosexuals, homosexual couples face joys and challenges as their relationship deepens.

The AIDS threat has prompted safer sex. Gay men, especially, report fewer sexual partners (Joseph & others, 1987; Winkelstein & others, 1987). Yet there remains a streak of unrealistic optimism, which explains why so many homosexual men still seldom use condoms (Baumann & Siegel, 1987; Fineberg, 1988). Noting that "AIDS is the kind of problem that causes a lot of people to look the other way," Grand Rapids, Michigan, artist Mark Heckman created a billboard—pasted with 2000 condoms—that people could not ignore.

Williams, 1974). Compared to the years preceding the AIDS threat, gay men are now reporting fewer partners. One study of 5000 gay men found that between 1984 and 1986 the number saying they were celibate or monogamous rose from 14 to 39 percent (Fineberg, 1988).

There is a growing agreement that sexual orientation is neither willfully chosen nor willfully changed. Sexual orientation in some ways is like handedness: Most people are one way, some the other. Few are equally ambidextrous. Regardless, the way one is endures. Nor is sexual orientation linked with psychological disorder or sexual crime, such as being a child molester. Some homosexuals do abuse children, but most child molesters are heterosexual males (Gonsiorek, 1982). These facts led the American Psychiatric Association in 1973 to drop homosexuality from its list of "mental illnesses."

Understanding Sexual Orientation If our sexual orientation is something we do not choose and cannot change, then where do these preferences come from? How do we move toward either a heterosexual or homosexual orientation? See if you can anticipate the consensus that has emerged from hundreds of research studies by responding yes or no to the following questions:

1. Is homosexuality linked with problems in a child's relationships with parents, such as with a domineering mother and an ineffectual father, or a possessive mother and a hostile father? *no*

2. Does homosexuality involve a fear or hatred of the other sex that leads people to direct their sexual desires toward members of their own sex? *no*

3. Is sexual orientation linked with levels of sex hormones currently in the blood? *no*

4. As children, were many homosexuals molested or seduced by an adult homosexual, or otherwise sexually victimized? *no*

Contrary to widely held ideas about homosexuality, the answer to all these questions is no (Storms, 1983). Consider the findings of lengthy Kinsey Institute interviews with nearly 1000 homosexuals and 500 heterosexuals (Bell & others, 1981; Hammersmith, 1982). The investigators assessed nearly every imaginable psychological cause of homosexuality—parental relationships, childhood sexual experiences, peer relationships, dating experiences, even number of brothers and sisters. Their findings: Apart from homosexuals' somewhat greater nonconformity, the reported backgrounds of homosexuals and heterosexuals were similar.

Michael Storms (1981) has proposed the controversial theory that sexual orientation is determined at puberty, as sexual desire emerges. We know that objects, smells, and sights associated with early experiences of sexual pleasure can become conditioned cues for arousal. In laboratory experiments, even a geometric figure can become sexually arousing if repeatedly associated with an erotic stimulus (Byrne, 1982). (Note that in this case the geometric figure is a conditioned stimulus, which gains its power to arouse by repeated pairing with a naturally erotic stimulus.) Perhaps, then, the time when the sex drive matures is a critical period for developing erotic associations with homosexual or heterosexual cues. Seventh-grade boys are still associating almost exclusively with other boys. So perhaps a boy who matures early is more likely to associate his developing feelings with other boys, an association that can become a lifelong preference.

It is a simple and logical idea. But the Kinsey researchers doubt it. They found that sexual orientation was unrelated to sexual precocity. Moreover, their homosexual sample usually recalled having homosexual feelings *before* engaging in any homosexual behavior. And homosexual behavior seems not to make people homosexual. Growing up among the Sambia of New Guinea, who expect homosexual behavior of all boys before marriage, fails to impede males' later heterosexual behavior (Money, 1988).

An alternative theory is very nearly the opposite of Storms' theory of erotic attachment. Alan Bell (1982) believes that people develop romantic attachments to those who are *different* from, and thus more fascinating than, the sex they have mostly associated with while growing up. He speculates that boys who have grown up in a male peer group will find it "virtually impossible" to be fascinated by other males when they reach adolescence. The bottom line of these conflicting theories is that after 100 years of research, the determinants of sexual orientation remain, for now, a mystery.

New research hints that the mystery's eventual solution may be at least partly biological. We know there is no *simple* biological explanation, because sex hormone levels do not predict sexual orientation and because hormone injections do not alter sexual orientation. But in animals and some exceptional human cases, sexual orientation has been altered by abnormal prenatal hormone conditions. Female sheep, for example, will show homosexual behavior if their pregnant mothers were injected with testosterone during a critical gestation period (Money, 1987). With humans, a critical period for the brain's neural-hormonal control system may exist between the middle of the second and fifth month after conception (Ellis & Ames, 1987). It seems that exposure to the hormone levels typically experienced by females during this time may predispose the person (whether female or male) to become attracted to males.

Should this critical period theory prove correct, it would explain why sexual orientation is so difficult to change. It might also lead to changed attitudes toward homosexuals. Most people hesitate to judge someone for atypical behaviors attributed to causes beyond the person's control. As we might expect, those who believe that sexual orientation is uncontrollable express fewer negative attitudes toward homosexuals (Whitley, 1990). Such beliefs are common among homosexual people, many of whom assume their sexual orientation to be genetically influenced (Furnham & Taylor, 1990).

Other types of learned associations with pleasure may also facilitate arousal. Infant male rats that suckle females whose nipples and vagina have been painted with a lemon scent will, as adults, ejaculate more quickly with a female whose vagina has been similarly scented (Fillion & Blass, 1986.)

"Were it not for delicately balanced combinations of genetic, neurological, hormonal, and environmental factors, largely occurring prior to birth, each and every one of us would be homosexual."
Lee Ellis and M. Ashley Ames (1987)

Sex and Human Values ✗

Questions of how we should act, what choices we should make, and what ends are desirable are questions of human values. Recognizing that values are both personal and cultural, most sex researchers and educators strive to keep their writings on sexuality value-free. As scientists and teachers, they aim for objectivity as they help us understand sexual behavior and what motivates it.

Can the study of sex be free of values? Should it be? Critics think not. First, they note that the words we use to describe behavior often reflect our personal values. When sex researchers label sexually restrained individuals as "erotophobic" and as having "high sex guilt," they express their values. Whether we label sexual acts we do not practice as "perversions," "deviations," or as part of an "alternative sexual life-style" depends on our attitudes toward the behaviors. Labels both describe and evaluate.

Second, critics suspect that when sexual information is separated from the context of human values, some students get the idea that sexual intercourse is merely recreational activity, or a biological act that is nothing more than "the depositing of seminal fluid, like squirting jam in a doughnut" (Greer, 1984). Diana Baumrind (1982), a University of California child-rearing expert, suspects that adolescents interpret sex education that pretends to be "value-free" as meaning that adults are neutral about adolescent sexual activity. She feels that such an implication is unfortunate, because "promiscuous recreational sex poses certain psychological, social, health, and moral problems that must be faced realistically."

On the other hand, researchers have found that teenagers who have had formal sex education are no more likely to engage in premarital sex than those who have not (Furstenberg & others, 1985; Zelnik & Kim, 1982). Moreover, consider the benefits of sex research and education. We enrich our lives by knowing ourselves, by realizing that others share our feelings, by understanding what is likely to please or displease our loved one. Witness the gradual crumbling of falsehoods about homosexuality. Witness the growing realization that some types of sexually explicit material can lead people to devalue or hurt others.

Perhaps we can agree that the knowledge provided by sex research is preferable to ignorance, yet also agree that researchers' values should be stated openly, enabling us to debate them and to reflect on our own values. We might also remember that although scientific research on sexual motivation has answered important questions, it does not aim to define the personal meaning of sex in our lives. One can know every available fact about sex—that the initial spasms of male and female orgasm come at 0.8-second intervals, that the female nipples expand 10 millimeters at the peak of sexual arousal, that systolic blood pressure rises some 60 points and the respiration rate to 40 breaths per minute—but fail to understand the human significance of sexual intimacy.

Surely one significance of sexual intimacy is its expression of our deeply social nature. Sex is a social as well as a biological act. Men and women can achieve orgasm alone. Yet most people find greater satisfaction in embracing their loved one. As philosopher Bertrand Russell noted in *Marriage and Morals* (1929), "People cannot fully satisfy their sexual instinct without love." Although the yearning for closeness was not part of our description of sexual motivation, sexual experience is life-uniting and love-renewing.

For most adults, sexual intimacy is not only a biological motive but also an emotional one—a sharing of love.

"Let us say with all possible emphasis that human sexuality is a very good thing. . . . It is tied in with and expressive of the urgent desire to love."
Norman Pittenger
Making Sexuality Human, 1970

Close-Up *Do Trial Marriages Reduce Divorce?*

The number of cohabiting unmarried couples in the United States tripled during the 1970s and doubled again during the 1980s (Bennett & others, 1988; Bumpass & Sweet, 1989). Similar trends have occurred since 1960 in Scandinavia and throughout much of Western Europe. Many see premarital cohabitation as a trial marriage that serves to weed out unsuccessful unions before marriage occurs. In a 1989 survey of nearly 300,000 first-year American college students, 51 percent agreed that "a couple should live together before marriage" (Astin & others, 1989). Might those who are sexually experienced and thoroughly familiar with the living habits of their partner indeed be less likely to stumble into an ill-fated marriage?

It seems not. Eight recent studies concur that, compared to couples who don't cohabit with their spouses-to-be, those who do have *higher* divorce rates. Three national surveys illustrate: A U.S. survey of 13,000 adults found that couples who lived together before marriage were one-third more likely to separate or divorce within a decade (Bumpass & Sweet, 1989). (A 1990 Gallup survey of still-married Americans also found that 21 percent of those who had not cohabited before marrying, and 40 percent of those who had, said they might divorce [Greeley, 1991].) A Canadian national survey of 5300 women found that those who cohabited were 54 percent more likely to divorce within 15 years

U.S. rates of cohabitation and marriage by age 25. From the U.S. National Survey of Families and Households. (From Bumpass & Sweet, 1989.)

(Balakrishan & others, 1987). And a Swedish study of 4300 women found cohabitation linked with an 80 percent greater risk of divorce (Bennett & others, 1988).

We can only speculate why. Perhaps people who cohabit are more likely later to engage in extramarital sex, which tends to disrupt a marriage. Or perhaps people who cohabit are simply less committed to the institution of marriage. Regardless, successful trial marriages do *not* predict a successful marriage.

Achievement Motivation

— learned Behavior

We have seen that the biological perspective on motivation—the idea that biological needs drive us to satisfy those needs—provides only a partial explanation of what energizes and directs our behavior. There also are motives that, unlike hunger and sex, seem not to satisfy any biological need. Millionaires may be motivated to make ever more money, movie stars to become ever more famous, politicians to achieve ever more power, daredevils to seek ever greater thrills. Such motives seem not to diminish when they are fed. The more we achieve, the more we may need to achieve.

Identifying Achievement Motivation

Think of two friends, one who strives to succeed by excelling at any task where evaluation is possible, and one who is less disciplined and driven. Psychologist Henry Murray (1938) defined the first person's high need for achievement, or **achievement motivation**, as a desire for significant accomplishment, for mastering skills or ideas, for control, and for rapidly attaining a high standard.

Not content with her Emmy Award-winning talk show and estimated $38 million in 1990 earnings, Oprah Winfrey is seeking new ways to excel through her film-TV company. "I've been blessed—but I create the blessings," she said.

To study this motive, we first need a way to measure it. But how? Recall from the semistarvation studies that people driven by hunger begin to fantasize about food. Our sexual orientation is similarly reflected in our sexual fantasies. Do these examples suggest a way to assess a person's need to achieve?

Murray and investigators David McClelland and John Atkinson presumed that people's fantasies would reflect their achievement concerns. So they asked subjects to invent stories about ambiguous pictures. If, when shown the daydreaming boy in Figure 12–7, a subject commented that the boy was preoccupied with his pursuit of a goal, that he imagined himself performing a heroic act, or that he was feeling pride in some success, the story was scored as indicating achievement concerns. McClelland and Atkinson regarded people whose stories consistently included such themes as having a high need for achievement.

Would you expect people whose stories express a high need for achievement to prefer tasks that are easy, moderately challenging, or very difficult? People whose stories suggest a low need for achievement tend to choose either very easy or very difficult tasks, where failure is either unlikely or unembarrassing (Geen, 1984). Those whose stories express a high need for achievement tend to prefer moderately difficult tasks, where success is attainable yet attributable to their own skill and effort. In a ring toss game, for instance, they often stand at an intermediate distance from the stake; this allows them some successes, yet provides a suitable challenge. People with a strong need to achieve also are more likely to persist on a task when things get difficult (Cooper, 1983).

As you might expect from their persistence and eagerness for realistic challenge, people with high needs for achievement do achieve more. Compared with children of equal ability, they are more successful. One study of outstanding athletes, scholars, and artists found that all were highly motivated and self-disciplined, willing to dedicate hours every day to the pursuit of their goals (Bloom, 1985). These superstar achievers were distinguished not so much by their extraordinary natural talent as by their extraordinary daily discipline.

When achievement motivation increases, so does achievement. By training the businessmen of a village in India to think, talk, and act like achievement-motivated people, McClelland (1978) and his colleagues were able to boost the villagers' business successes. Compared with other businessmen from a comparable nearby town, those trained in achievement motivation started more new businesses and employed over twice as many new people during the ensuing 2 years.

Figure 12–7 What is this boy daydreaming about? By analyzing responses to ambiguous photos like this, motivation researchers seek clues to people's levels of achievement motivation.

What is your greatest achievement to date? What is your greatest future ambition—to attain fame? fortune? creative accomplishment? security? love? power? wisdom? spiritual wholeness?

Sources of Achievement Motivation

Why, despite similar potentials, does one person become more motivated to achieve than another? Highly motivated children often have parents who encourage their independence from an early age and praise and reward them for their successes (Teevan & McGhee, 1972). Such parents encourage their children to dress and feed themselves and to do well in school, and they express their delight when their children achieve. Theorists speculate that the high achievement motivation displayed by such children has *emotional* roots, as children learn to associate achievement with positive emotions. There may also be *cognitive* roots, as children learn to attribute their achievements to their own competence and effort and so to develop higher expectations (Dweck & Elliott, 1983).

These parental influences also help explain a fascinating finding—that birth order correlates with achievement. First-born and only children do slightly better in school and on intelligence tests and are more likely to achieve admission to prestigious colleges than are their later-born brothers and sisters (Falbo & Polit, 1986). This may partly reflect the generally higher socioeconomic status of small families, which contribute fewer later-born children (Blake, 1989). However, in separate studies of eminent people from two-child families, 64 percent of "distinguished Americans" were first-born, as were 61 percent of the Rhodes Scholars, 66 percent of the National Merit Scholars, and 64 percent of those in *Who's Who*. Among the *Who's Who* designates and National Merit Scholars who came from three-child families, 52 percent of both groups were first-born (Altus, 1966).

It is fun to speculate about differences between the experiences of first-born and later-born children. One difference might be the greater parental attention given the first-born during their years as solo children. Perhaps parents are more invested in a first-born child. They may take more pictures of their first child and provide that child with more encouragement and higher expectations. On the other hand, the later-born often have noteworthy social strengths. They tend to be more socially relaxed and popular. Having less power than one's older siblings—less size, strength, verbal facility, and experience—apparently fosters more effective social skills (Miller & Maruyama, 1976).

Moreover, throughout history later-born scientists have been more supportive of new ideas. Copernicus, who proposed the earth's orbiting around the sun, was the second of four children; Tycho Brahe, who defended the traditional view, was raised as an only child. Charles Darwin, the fifth of six children, found his new ideas supported by most later-born scientists but rejected by his first-born peers (Figure 12–8). In fact, science historian Frank Sulloway (1990) reports that 23 of 28 such scientific revolutions were led by later-borns. Among the 2784 scientists who participated in these controversies, 34 percent of the first-borns and 64 percent of the later-borns were supportive of the new ideas. The same was true of

"They can because they think they can."
Virgil
Aeneid, 19 B.C.

Remember the two people you chose, one who consistently strives to succeed, the other who is less concerned with achievement? Is either a first-born (or only) child?

■ First-born ■ Later-born

Percentage supporting new ideas

80 70 60 50 40 30 20 10 0

Copernican revolution   Darwinian revolution   Indeterminacy in physics   Mesmerism

Figure 12–8 Acceptance of new ideas by first-born and later-born scientists. (Data from Sulloway, 1990.)

the Protestant Reformation, which later-born religious and political leaders were more likely to support. First-borns, it seems, identify more closely with the views of their parents and of tradition. Of course, sometimes tradition is right. In cases such as phrenology (discerning traits by the shape of one's skull) and mesmerism (healing by restoring proper "magnetism" to one's body), the first-borns were less deceived by these new ideas later shown to be false. So, first-borns' eagerness to achieve often gets expressed in conventional ways. First-borns, it seems, tend to be more conscientious, later-borns to be freewheeling.

Intrinsic Motivation and Achievement

In the classroom, at the workplace, and on the athletic field, two types of achievement motivation operate. **Intrinsic motivation** is the desire to be effective and to perform a behavior for its own sake. **Extrinsic motivation** is seeking external rewards and avoiding punishments.

To sense the difference between extrinsic and intrinsic motivation, you might reflect on your own current experience. Are you feeling pressured to get this reading finished before a deadline? Worried about your course grade? Eager for rewards that depend on your doing well? If your answers are yes, then you are extrinsically motivated (as, to some extent, almost all students are). Are you also finding the course material interesting? Does learning it enable you to feel more competent? If there were no grade at stake, might you be curious enough to want to learn the material for its own sake? If your answers are yes, intrinsic motivation also fuels your efforts.

After studying the motivations and achievements of thousands of college students, scientists, pilots, business people, and athletes, Janet Spence and Robert Helmreich (1983) concluded that intrinsic motivation produces high achievement, and that extrinsic motivation (such as the desire for a high-paying career) often does not. Spence and Helmreich identified and assessed three facets of intrinsic motivation: people's quests for *mastery* (as shown for example, by their strongly agreeing that "If I am not good at something, I would rather keep struggling to master it than move on to something I may be good at"); their drive to *work* ("I like to work hard"); and their *competitiveness* ("I really enjoy working in situations involving skill and competition").

Despite similar abilities, people oriented toward mastery and hard work typically achieve more. If students, they get better grades; if MBA graduates, they earn more money; if scientists, their work is more often cited by other scientists. No surprise there. But, surprisingly, in Spence and Helmreich's studies those who were *most* competitive (which is a more extrinsic orientation) often achieved *less*.

Figure 12–9 illustrates: People driven by a desire for mastery and work achieved more if they were *not* highly competitive. Lacking these drives, a competitive spirit did boost achievement. These results illustrate an **interaction effect**: Two factors interact if *the effect of one factor depends on the other*. In this case, the effect of competitiveness depends on the degree of combined work/mastery orientation. Among people who don't intrinsically enjoy mastery and hard work, it pays to be highly competitive; among those driven to master and work hard, it pays to be less competitive.

The Reverend Jesse Jackson's high intrinsic need for achievement drives him to seek new and more difficult challenges. A phrase from his speech at the 1983 civil rights march on Washington sums it up: "If my mind can conceive it and my heart can believe it, I know I can achieve it."

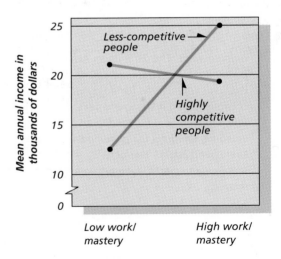

Figure 12–9 Among MBA graduates with a low work/mastery orientation, highly competitive people achieved the highest earnings. Among the high work/mastery group, the less competitive did better. The effect of competitiveness thus depends on ("interacts with") the effect of work and mastery. (From *Achievement and Achievement Motives* by Janet T. Spence. Copyright 1983 W. H. Freeman and Company. Reprinted with permission.)

Close-Up   *Intrinsic Motivation and Sports*

In sports, as in other activities, excessive external pressures and incentives can undermine intrinsic enjoyment. This boy's enjoyment of soccer will increase if his coach emphasizes mastery of the game and decrease if he is feeling excessive pressure to win.

For most people, participation in sports activities is its own reward. The 20 million American youngsters who participate in organized sports do so not so much for extrinsic rewards as for enjoyment and the sense of accomplishment it brings. In fact, motivation researchers Edward Deci and Richard Ryan (1985) reported that rewarding children for participating in physical activities can "overjustify" the activity. This makes the children less likely to participate again after the rewards are removed.

Another researcher, Dean Ryan (1980), studied football players. He found that those on athletic scholarships (who were, in a sense, playing for pay) enjoyed their play less than did nonscholarship players. Apparently, pay and pressure turn play into work. However, rewards can increase intrinsic motivation if their effect is to inform the players of their athletic competence (as with a "most improved player" award).

Researchers have also found that sports enjoyment is greatest when the activity is neither too easy (and therefore boring) nor too demanding (causing us to worry about our performance). When the challenge optimally suits our skills, we experience *flow*: Without feeling anxious or self-conscious, we become totally involved in the challenge (Csikszentmihalyi, 1990). This absorption in a game is similar to the flow experienced by dancers, chess players, surgeons, and writers as they become caught up in the task at hand.

Does a competitive orientation enhance or diminish the intrinsic love of sports activities? It all depends, say Deci and Ryan (1985). Like other extrinsic incentives, the lure of victory can be very motivating. Moreover, winning makes us feel competent. As long as we are winning, we are likely to enjoy the activity. Yet in the long run, especially if we begin losing, a competitive orientation may undermine our love of the activity for its own sake.

So, should coaches emphasize extrinsic pressures, rewards, and competition? It depends on the goal, report Deci and Ryan. If, as professional football coach Vince Lombardi once said, "Winning isn't everything; it's the only thing," then it may pay to control the players with pressures and rewards for winning. But what if the goal is—as it should be for most programs of physical education, fitness, and amateur sports—the promotion of an enduring interest and participation in physical activity? Then, say Deci and Ryan, "external pressures, competitive emphasis, and evaluative feedback are in contradiction to this goal." Thus, if Little League coaches want their players to continue playing baseball after Little League, they should focus not on the urgency of winning, but on the joy of playing well.

Motivating People

The growing field of industrial/organizational psychology studies how managers might best:

    screen and select motivated, well-suited personnel;

    match people with suitable work assignments;

    create work environments that boost morale and output and minimize absenteeism and turnover;

    evaluate performance and create incentives for excellence;

    promote teamwork and group achievement.

What every manager wants to know is: How can I manage in ways that ensure motivated, productive, satisfied employees? Among the factors known to affect a manager's effectiveness are the following four.

Cultivate Intrinsic Motivation If intrinsic motivation stimulates achievement, especially in situations where people work independently (as students, executives, and scientists often do), then how might we encourage it? The consistent answers, from hundreds of studies: First, provide tasks that challenge and trigger curiosity (Malone & Lepper, 1986). Second, avoid snuffing out people's sense of self-determination with an overuse of extrinsic rewards (Deci & Ryan, 1987).

Note that we can use extrinsic rewards in two ways: to *control* ("If you clean up your room, you can have some ice cream") or to *inform* someone of successes ("That was outstanding—we congratulate you"). Attempts to *control* people's behaviors through rewards and surveillance may be successful as long as these controls are present; but if taken away, interest in the activity often drops. Ironically, teachers who try hardest to boost their students' achievement on competency tests tend to be most controlling, thus undermining their students' intrinsic interest. This is similar to the finding that children whose parents don't encourage independence tend to have lower achievement motivation. And recall from Chapter 8, Learning, the principle that unnecessary or excessive rewards can undermine intrinsic interest by "overjustifying" an activity.

On the other hand, rewards that *inform* people they are doing well can boost their feelings of competence and intrinsic motivation. In one experiment, Thane Pittman and his colleagues (1980) asked college students to work on puzzles. Those given informative compliments ("Compared to most of my subjects, you're doing really well") usually continued playing with the puzzles when left alone. Those given either no praise or a controlling form of praise ("If you keep it up, I'll be able to use your data") were less likely to continue on their own. So, depending on whether we use rewards to control or inform, they can either lower or raise intrinsic motivation.

There is an important practical principle here. Because the controlling use of rewards undermines intrinsic motivation (and creativity—see page 336), parents, teachers, and managers should take care not to be overcontrolling. It is important to expect, support, challenge, and inform; but if you want to encourage internally motivated, self-directed achievements, do not overly control.

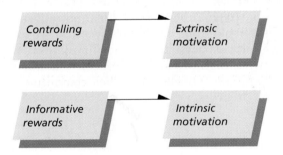

The type of reward affects intrinsic motivation.

Keep an Eye on People's Motives What managerial style is effective varies with the people managed. To motivate people, Martin Maehr and Larry Braskamp (1986; Braskamp, 1987) advise managers to assess their people's motives and adjust their managerial style accordingly. Challenge employees who value *accomplishment* to try new things and to exhibit excellence. Give those who value *recognition* the attention they desire. Place those who value *affiliation* in a unit that has a trustful family feeling and that shares decision making. Motivate those who value *power* with competition and opportunities for triumphant success. Different strokes for different folks, but for each a way to energize and direct—in a word, to motivate—behavior.

What workers value—and the management style to which they respond best—also varies from culture to culture. In cultures where work is less intrinsically valued than in, say, Japan, personal relationships are often a key to motivating workers (England & Misumi, 1986). As we noted in Chapter 3's discussion of culture and child-rearing (page 86), human societies differ in whether they socialize children primarily toward social harmony and loyalty or to think and achieve for themselves. The greater individualism of Europe and North America, compared to the communalism of Asian values, surfaced in surveys of work-related attitudes among 116,000 people in 40 countries (all working for the same multinational corporation). Individualism—for example, people's valuing their private lives outside of the company and wanting to adopt their own approach to their job—was highest in the United States, Australia, Britain, and Canada, somewhat lower in Scandinavia, and much lower in Asia and South America (Hofstede, 1980). Such cultural differences have implications for multicultural business ventures. A study for the Dutch Ministry of Economic Affairs, for example, found that Norwegian and Swedish business people shared the same cluster of values as the Dutch. Thus, their management styles have worked better in the Netherlands than have those of American managers (Hofstede, 1980).

Set Specific, Challenging Goals In study after study, challenging goals have motivated higher achievement, especially when combined with progress reports (Locke & Latham, 1990; Mento & others, 1987; Tubbs, 1986). Clear objectives, such as those you might set in planning your course work, serve to direct attention, promote effort and persistence, and stimulate creative strategies. So, to motivate high productivity, effective managers work with employees to define explicit goals, elicit commitments, and provide feedback on progress.

Choose an Appropriate Leadership Style Whether a directive/autocratic or participative/democratic leadership style works best depends on the situation and the manager. The best leadership style for leading a discussion is not the best style for leading the troops on a charge (Fiedler, 1981). Moreover, different managers are better suited to different leadership styles. Some excel at **task leadership**—setting standards, organizing work, and focusing attention on goals. Being goal-oriented, task leaders are good at keeping a group centered on its mission. Typically, they have a directive style, which can work well if the leader is bright enough to give good orders (Fiedler, 1987).

Other managers excel at **social leadership**—building team-

"Good leaders don't ask more than their constituents can give, but they often ask—and get—more than their constituents intended to give or thought it was possible to give."
John W. Gardner
Excellence, 1984

work, mediating conflicts, and supporting their work force. Social leaders often have a democratic style: They delegate authority and welcome the participation of team members. Many experiments show that social leadership is good for morale. Subordinates usually feel more satisfied when they can participate in decision making (Spector, 1986). Given some control over their tasks, they also are more motivated to achieve (Burger, 1987). Women more often excel at social leadership, men at task leadership (Eagly & Karau, 1991).

Because effective leadership styles vary with the situation and the person, the once-popular "great person theory of leadership"—that all great leaders share certain traits—fell out of favor. However, Peter Smith and Monir Tayeb (1989) report from recent studies in India, Taiwan, and Iran that effective managers in coal mines, banks, and government offices often exhibit a high degree of *both* task and social leadership. As achievement-minded people, they care about how work is progressing, yet they are sensitive to their subordinates' needs. Effective leaders of laboratory groups, work teams, and large corporations also tend to exude a self-confident "charisma" (Bennis, 1984; House & Singh, 1987). Their charisma involves a *vision* of some goal, an ability to *communicate* this clearly and simply, and enough optimism and faith in their group to *inspire* others to follow.

Drawing by Anthony; ©1988 The New Yorker Magazine, Inc.

Whether managers favor a directive/autocratic or a participative/democratic approach depends on their assumptions about human motivation. Douglas McGregor (1960) identified two contrasting views. **Theory X** managers assume that workers are basically lazy, error-prone, and extrinsically motivated by money. Thus, they need simple tasks, close monitoring, and incentives to work harder. **Theory Y** managers make opposite assumptions—that people are intrinsically motivated to work for reasons beyond money—for example, to promote self-esteem, enjoy satisfying relations with others, and fulfill their potential. Thus, given enough freedom and challenge, employees will strive to demonstrate their competence and creativity. Theory Y managers are more likely to give employees control over work procedures, to welcome employee participation in decision making, and to have creative and satisfied subordinates (Deci & others, 1989).

Theory Y is one guiding force behind the contemporary move by many businesses toward employee involvement and management, a management style common in Sweden and Japan (Naylor, 1990; Sundstrom & others, 1990). Ironically, a major influence on the "Japanese-style participative management" now increasingly popular in the United States was M.I.T. social psychologist Kurt Lewin. Lewin and his students demonstrated the effects of worker participation on productivity in laboratory and factory experiments. Shortly before World War II, Lewin visited Japan and explained his findings to industrial and academic leaders (Nisbett & Ross, 1991).

Back in the United States, several companies quietly began implementing Lewin's participative management. One of these pioneer companies was Michigan's Herman Miller, Inc., now the world's second largest manufacturer of office furniture and one of America's 10 most admired companies in *Fortune* magazine's survey of 8000 executives (Davenport, 1989). Its chair, Max DePree (1987), believes that workers want to be effective and productive, to feel they are making a meaningful contribution, to have control over their own destinies, and to be appreciated. When workers share in corporate profits and become part owners, they become invested in their company's success. When workers participate in decision making and know that they and their managers are mutually accountable, a shared commitment to corporate and personal goals replaces labor versus management hostility. When workers feel respected, cared about, and involved, they find work more satisfying and, thanks to their productivity, their company benefits. Every dollar of Herman Miller stock purchased when the company went public in 1970 was worth $27 by 1991.

In this chapter we have seen that identifiable physiological mechanisms drive some motives, such as hunger, though external incentives and learned tastes matter, too. Other motives, such as achievement, are more obviously driven by psychological factors such as an intrinsic quest for mastery and the external rewards of recognition. What unifies all such motives is their common effect: the energizing and directing of behavior. Without motivation—without hunger, thirst, sex, curiosity, a need to achieve, and so forth—life would be dull and aimless. With motivation, our lives are instead animated and, in some sense at least, purposeful.

Participative management. At General Motors' new Saturn plant in Tennessee, there are 165 10-member "teams" of employees. Each work team helps decide such things as new hires for their team and how to run their own area. Part of their salary depends on resulting car quality and company profits.

Summing Up

Motivation is the energizing and directing of behavior, the force behind our yearning for food, our longing for sexual intimacy, and our desire to achieve.

Concepts of Motivation

Under Darwin's influence, early theorists came to view behavior as controlled by biological forces, such as instincts. But when it became clear that people were naming, not explaining, various behaviors by calling them instincts, psychologists turned to a drive theory of motivation.

Biological Needs: The Internal Pushes Most physiological needs create psychological drives that motivate need satisfaction. The aim of drive reduction is internal stability, or homeostasis. Thus, drive reduction motivates survival behaviors, such as eating and drinking, but seems not so applicable to motives such as curiosity and achievement, that seek increasing stimulation, spurred by external incentives.

Learning and Culture: The External Pulls Not only are we pushed by our internal drives, we are also pulled by external incentives. Depending on our personal and cultural experiences, some stimuli (for example, certain foods or erotic images) will arouse our desires.

A Hierarchy of Motives Maslow's hierarchy of needs expresses the idea that, until satisfied, some motives are more compelling than others.

Hunger

The Physiology of Hunger Hunger's inner push originates not primarily from the stomach's pangs, but from variations in body chemistry. For example, we are likely to feel hungry when our glucose levels are low and our insulin levels are high. This information is monitored by the hypothalamus, which regulates the body's weight by influencing our feelings of hunger and satiety. To maintain a set-point weight, the body also adjusts its metabolic rate of energy expenditure.

External Incentives Especially in "external" people, the sight and smell of food can trigger hunger and eating, partly by stimulating a rise in insulin level.

Eating Disorders The impact of psychological factors, such as challenging family settings and weight-obsessed societal pressures, on eating behavior is dramatic in people with anorexia nervosa, who keep themselves on near-starvation rations, and those with bulimia nervosa, who binge and purge in secret.

Sexual Motivation

Describing Sexual Behavior Sexual behaviors vary across both place and time. The range of "normal" sexual interests and behaviors remains broad.

The Physiology of Sex Biologically, the human sexual response cycle normally follows a pattern of excitement, plateau, orgasm, and resolution, followed in males by a refractory period, during which renewed arousal and orgasm are not possible. Sex hormones help our bodies develop and function as either male or female. In nonhuman animals, hormones also help stimulate sexual activity. In humans, they influence sexual behavior more loosely, especially once sufficient hormone levels are present.

The Psychology of Sex External stimuli can trigger sexual arousal in both men and women. Sexually explicit materials may also lead people to perceive their partners as comparatively less appealing and to devalue their relationships. In combination with the internal hormonal push and the external pull of sexual stimuli, fantasies (imagined stimuli) influence sexual arousal.

Sexual Dysfunctions and Therapy Sexual dysfunctions, such as premature ejaculation and orgasmic dysfunction, are being successfully treated by new methods, which assume that people learn and can modify their sexual responses.

Sexual Orientation One's heterosexual or homosexual orientation seems neither willfully chosen nor willfully changed. Although it is beginning to look as though biological factors are involved, we are still unsure why one person becomes heterosexual and another homosexual.

Sex and Human Values Sex research and education are not value-free. Sex-related values should therefore be openly acknowledged, recognizing the emotional significance of sexual expression.

Achievement Motivation

Some human behaviors are energized and directed without satisfying any obvious biological need. Achieving personal goals, for example, may be motivated by a person's need for competence and self-determination.

Identifying Achievement Motivation People with a high need to achieve tend to prefer moderately challenging tasks and to persist in accomplishing them.

Sources of Achievement Motivation Many achievement-oriented children have parents and teachers who encourage and affirm independent achievement rather than overly controlling them with rewards and threats. First-born children tend to be higher achievers, but later-borns tend to have greater social skills and to be more accepting of new ideas.

Intrinsic Motivation and Achievement Intrinsic motivation is the desire to be effective and to perform a behavior for its own sake.

Motivating People Industrial/organizational psychologists explore how best to create a motivated, productive, and satisfied workforce. Rewards may increase intrinsic motivation if used not to control people but to boost their sense of competence or to inform them of improvement. It also helps to adjust one's managerial style in response to workers' motives; to set specific, challenging goals; and to combine goal-oriented task leadership with group-oriented social leadership.

Terms and Concepts to Remember

motivation The forces that energize and direct behavior.

instinct A behavior that is rigidly patterned and unlearned.

drive An aroused state that typically arises from an underlying need.

homeostasis A tendency to maintain a balanced or constant internal state; refers especially to the body's tendency to maintain an optimum internal state for functioning.

incentives Positive or negative environmental stimuli that motivate behavior.

hierarchy of needs Maslow's pyramid of human needs, beginning at the base with physiological needs that must first be satisfied before higher level safety needs and then psychological needs become active.

glucose The form of sugar that circulates in the blood and provides the major source of energy for body tissues. When its level is low, we feel hunger.

insulin A hormone that, among its effects, helps body tissues convert blood glucose into stored fat. When its level in the body is high, we feel hunger.

set point The point at which an individual's "weight thermostat" is set. When the body falls below this weight, an increase in hunger and a lowered metabolic rate act to restore the lost weight.

metabolic rate The body's base rate of energy expenditure.

anorexia nervosa An eating disorder in which a normal-weight person (usually an adolescent female) diets to become significantly (15 percent or more) underweight, yet, still feeling fat, continues to starve.

bulimia nervosa An eating disorder characterized by private, "binge-purge" episodes of overeating, usually of highly caloric foods, followed by vomiting or laxative use.

sexual response cycle The four stages of sexual responding described by Masters and Johnson—excitement, plateau, orgasm, and resolution.

refractory period A resting period after orgasm during which a man cannot achieve another orgasm.

estrogen A sex hormone, secreted in greater amounts by females than males. In nonhuman female mammals, estrogen levels peak during ovulation, promoting sexual receptivity.

testosterone The most important of the male sex hormones. Although both males and females have it, the additional testosterone in males stimulates the growth of male sex characteristics and, especially in nonhuman animals, influences sexual arousal.

sexual dysfunction A problem that consistently impairs sexual arousal or functioning.

sexual orientation An enduring sexual attraction toward members of either one's own sex (homosexual orientation) or the other sex (heterosexual orientation).

achievement motivation A desire for significant accomplishment: for mastery of things, people, or ideas; for attaining a high standard.

intrinsic motivation A desire to perform a behavior for its own sake and to be effective.

extrinsic motivation A desire to perform a behavior due to promised rewards or threats of punishment.

interaction effect A result in which the effect of one factor depends on the level of another.

task leadership Goal-oriented leadership that sets standards, organizes work, and focuses attention on goals.

social leadership Group-oriented leadership that builds teamwork, mediates conflict, and offers support.

theory X Assumes that workers are basically lazy, error-prone, and extrinsically motivated by money and thus should be directed from above.

theory Y Assumes that, given challenge and freedom, workers are motivated to achieve self-esteem and to demonstrate their competence and creativity.

For Further Information

You can find further information in this text regarding industrial/organizational psychology on the following pages:

For Further Reading

Hunger

Logue, A. W. (1986). *The psychology of eating and drinking.* New York: Freeman.

Why do some foods taste better to you than others? Why do people develop problems related to eating and drinking? Logue provides authoritative and readable answers to these and other questions about hunger and thirst.

Sexuality

Hyde, J. S. (1990). *Understanding human sexuality* (4th ed.). New York: McGraw-Hill.

A comprehensive overview of every aspect of human sexuality, including sexual orientation and sexual disorders.

Reinisch, J. M. (1990). *The Kinsey Institute new report on sex.* New York: St. Martin's.

Informative answers to people's most frequently asked questions about sexuality.

Achievement

Mook, D. G. (1987). *Motivation: The organization of action.* New York: Norton.

Provides a lucid and up-to-date overview of the major topics in motivation.

Steers, R. M., & Porter, L. W. (1987). *Motivation and work behavior.* New York: McGraw-Hill.

Reviews research on maximizing worker motivation and minimizing absenteeism and turnover.

Emotion   *Chapter 13*

Feelings—powerful, spontaneous, sometimes unforgettable. Where do feelings come from? Of all the species, we humans seem the most emotional (Hebb, 1980). More often than any other creature, we express fear, anger, sadness, joy, and love. No one needs to tell you that emotions add color to your life, that in times of stress they can disrupt your life or save it. But what are the ingredients of emotion?

Consider a young basketball player. Thanks to her last-second basket, her team has just defeated its archrival. As she leaves the gymnasium to board the team bus, she feels elated. Basking in the congratulations of her teammates, she cannot stop smiling. Seldom has she felt more alive, stronger, more confident.

Approaching the bus, she notices a cluster of young men nearby making loud comments intended for her ears. One questions her team's ability, while another snidely impugns her femininity. As she strides past the taunters, she feels a surge of anger. Her heart pounding, her teeth and fists clenched, her face flushed, she controls her impulse to respond in kind. Once aboard, she throws herself into a seat and seethes: "Those creeps! Where do they get their sick ideas about women athletes?" As the rest of the team boards the bus, hollering and whooping it up, her attention returns to the thrill of victory, and her intense feelings are rechanneled into celebration.

As this basketball player's experience illustrates, **emotions** involve a mixture of (1) physiological arousal (heart pounding), (2) expressive behavior (teeth clenched), and (3) conscious experience (interpretations of the men's behavior, and angry feelings). The puzzle is how these three pieces fit together. Did the athlete first notice her pounding heart, her clenched jaw, and *then* feel anger toward the men? Or did the sense of anger come first, stirring her heart and facial muscles to respond? These are difficult questions to answer. Before assembling the emotions puzzle, let's study its individual pieces—its physiology, expression, and conscious experience.

The Physiology of Emotion

Arousal

When emotionally aroused, you are physically aroused. Some physical responses are so obvious that you easily notice them. Imagine that while walking down a deserted street late at night, a motorcyclist begins stalking you. Hearing the rumble of the bike's engine behind you, your heart begins to race, your muscles tense, your stomach develops butterflies, your mouth becomes dry.

Your body also mobilizes for action in less noticeable ways. To provide energy, your liver pours extra sugar into your bloodstream. To help burn the sugar, your respiration rate increases to supply the needed extra oxygen. Your digestion slows, diverting blood from your internal organs to your muscles. Your pupils dilate, letting in more light. To cool your stirred-up body, you perspire more. If wounded, your blood clots more quickly. Think of this after your next emergency: Without any conscious effort, your body's response to danger was wonderfully coordinated and adaptive—preparing you to fight or flee.

As we note in Chapter 2, the sympathetic nervous system (page 33) activates these responses. It directs the adrenal glands on top of the kidneys to release the hormones epinephrine (adrenaline) and norepinephrine (noradrenaline). The surge in epinephrine and norepinephrine triggers increased heart rate, blood pressure, and blood sugar levels. When the emergency passes, the parasympathetic neural centers become active, calming the body. Even after the parasympathetic nervous system inhibits further hormone release, the hormones already in the bloodstream linger awhile, so arousal diminishes gradually.

Prolonged arousal, produced by sustained stress, taxes the body (more on this in Chapter 17, Stress and Health). Yet in many situations arousal is adaptive. In fact, both too little arousal (say, being sleepy) and extremely high levels of arousal can be disruptive. When taking an exam, it pays to be moderately aroused—alert but not trembling with nervousness.

Although performance is usually best when arousal is moderate, the level of arousal for optimal performance varies for different tasks. With easy or well-learned tasks, peak performance comes with relatively high arousal, which enhances the dominant, usual-

"Fear lends wings to his feet."
Virgil
Aeneid, 19 B.C.

One explanation of sudden death caused by a voodoo "curse" is that the terrified person's parasympathetic nervous system, which calms the body, overreacts to the extreme arousal by slowing the heart to a stop (Seligman, 1974).

Although one is terrified and the other thrilled by this roller coaster, both riders are experiencing the physiological symptoms of an activated sympathetic nervous system: increased perspiration, racing heart, tense muscles.

ly correct, response⌐With more difficult or unrehearsed tasks, the optimal arousal is somewhat less. Thus, runners, who perform a well-learned task, usually achieve their peak performances when highly aroused by competition. With less routine skills—say, basketball players shooting free throws—performance declines slightly when a packed fieldhouse makes players hyper-aroused (Sokoll & Mynatt, 1984). Likewise, students who feel great anxiety during exams perform more poorly than equally able but more confident students. ⌐Training anxious students how to relax before an exam often enables them to perform better (Hembree, 1988).⌐

Physiological States Accompanying Specific Emotions

Imagine conducting an experiment exploring the physiological indicators of arousal. In each of four rooms, you have someone watching a movie: In the first, there's a horror show; in the second, an anger-provoking film; in the third, a sexually arousing film; in the fourth, an utterly boring film. From the control center you monitor each person's physiological responses. By examining the perspiration, breathing, and heart rates of the viewers, could you tell who was frightened, who was angry, who was sexually aroused, and who was bored?

With training, you could probably pick out the bored viewer from the other three. Discerning physiological differences among fear, anger, and sexual arousal is much harder (Zillmann, 1986). Apart from the breathing disruption caused by laughter, experts even have difficulty distinguishing viewers' physiological responses to sad versus funny movies (Averill, 1969).

Fear, anger, sexual arousal, and sadness certainly *feel* different (and, as we will see, cognitively they *are* different). A terrified person may feel a clutching, sinking sensation in the chest and a knot in the stomach. An angry person may feel "hot under the collar" and will probably experience a pressing, inner tension. The sexually stimulated person will experience a genital response. The sad person may be choked up and have an empty, drained feeling (Epstein, 1984). Moreover, frightened, angered, and saddened people often *look* different—"paralyzed with fear," "ready to explode," or "down in the dumps." Knowing this, can we pinpoint some distinct physiological indicators of each emotion?

Fear and rage are accompanied by differing finger temperatures and hormone secretions (Ax, 1953). Scientists increasingly agree that different brain regions and distinct patterns of brain activity also underlie different emotions (Panksepp, 1982). As we saw on page 39, stimulate one area of a cat's limbic system and it will pull back in terror at the sight of a mouse. Stimulate another limbic area and the cat will become enraged—pupils dilated, fur and tail erect, claws out, hissing furiously. As people experience negative emotions, such as disgust, the right hemisphere becomes more electrically active. The left hemisphere activates when processing positive emotions (Davidson & others, 1990, 1991). For some infants and adults, the left frontal lobe shows more activity than the right. These individuals are typically more cheerful and less readily threatened or depressed than those with more active right front lobes. "It may be that those people with more left frontal activity are better able to turn off upsetting feelings," speculates researcher Richard Davidson (1991).

"No one ever told me that grief felt so much like fear. I am not afraid, but the sensation is like being afraid. The same fluttering in the stomach, the same restlessness, the yawning. I keep on swallowing."
   C. S. Lewis
   A Grief Observed, 1961

In 1966, a young man named Charles Whitman, after developing what an autopsy later revealed was a tumor in his limbic system, killed his wife and mother and then climbed to the top of a tower at the University of Texas and shot 38 people.

So, although emotions as varied as fear and anger involve a similar general autonomic arousal (thanks to the sympathetic nervous system), there are real, if subtle, physiological differences that help explain why we experience them so differently. Moreover, the physical accompaniments of emotion appear innate and universal— the same in a Sumatran village as in North America (Levenson & others, 1991).

Lie Detection

Given the physical indicators of emotion, might we, like Pinocchio, give some telltale sign whenever we lie? The "lie detector," or **polygraph**, was once used mainly in law enforcement work and national security matters. By the mid-1980s, 2 million Americans annually were reportedly being tested, usually by corporations trying to screen applicants for honesty or to uncover employee theft (Holden, 1986a). In 1983, President Reagan signed a directive requiring government employees, if requested, to take lie detector tests during investigations of leaks of classified information (Biddle, 1986).

Just what does the polygraph do? It does not literally detect lies. Rather, it measures several of the physiological responses that accompany emotion, such as changes in breathing, pulse rate, blood pressure, and perspiration.

Before testing you, an examiner would try first to convince you that the instrument is highly accurate (to make you fearful of lying). The examiner might, for example, unerringly identify (secretly marked) cards that you choose. While you try to relax, the examiner measures your physiological responses as you answer questions. Some of these, called control questions, are designed to make anyone a little nervous. If asked, "In the last 20 years, have you ever taken something that didn't belong to you?" many people will tell a little white lie and say no, but the polygraph may detect slight physiological changes. If your physiological reactions to the critical questions ("Did you ever steal anything from your previous employer?") are weaker than to the control questions, the examiner infers you are telling the truth. The assumption is that only a thief becomes agitated when denying a theft (Figure 13–1).

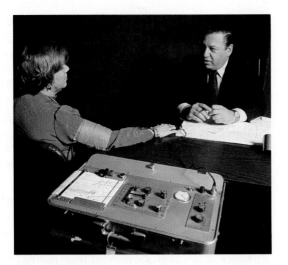

The polygraph test.

Figure 13–1 Physiological responses to a lie detector test. (a) This is the record of a witness who supported an accused murderer's alibi. She reacted more strongly when answering no to a control question, "Up to age 18, did you ever deceive anyone?" than when answering yes to the relevant question, "Was [the accused] at another location at the time of the murder?" As a result, the examiner concluded she was telling the truth. (b) This is the record of an accused murderer judged to be lying when he pleaded self-defense. He reacted less strongly in answering no to the control question, "Up to age 18, did you ever physically harm anyone?" than when answering yes to the relevant question, "Did [the deceased] threaten to harm you in any way?" (From Raskin, 1982.)

(a)   (b)

How well does the polygraph work? That depends on whether liars exhibit anxiety while lying. An innocent person might respond with heightened tension to the accusations implied by the relevant questions. A practiced liar, trained spy, or hardened criminal might stay relaxed while lying or know how to beat the test, such as by biting the tongue to display arousal in response to control questions. From 1977 to 1987, Fidel Castro's agents reportedly duped the CIA's polygraph testers into certifying them as truth-tellers. This enabled the Cuban double agents to convince the CIA of a stream of misinformation regarding the Cuban, Soviet, and Nicaraguan military (Safire, 1989).

A major adversary of the commercial use of lie detector tests is University of Minnesota psychologist David Lykken (1983). He notes that because physiological arousal is much the same from one emotion to another, the polygraph cannot distinguish among anxiety, irritation, and guilt. They all appear as arousal. Thus, these tests err about one-third of the time. They more often label the innocent guilty — when the relevant question upsets the scrupulously honest person — than the guilty innocent (Figure 13–2). Good advice, then, would be never to take a lie detector test if you are innocent. Those who are believed guilty, and are guilty, can welcome the test, because it may exonerate them.

Though more accurate than a 50-50 coin toss, polygraph tests have been deemed too inaccurate for most U.S. state courts. Moreover, a report by the Congressional Office of Technology Assessment (U.S. Congress, 1983, p. 4) warned that "the available research evidence does not establish the scientific validity of the polygraph test for personnel security screening." The American Psychological Association (1986) similarly "has great reservations about the use of polygraph tests to detect deception," as does the British Psychological Society (1986).

Indeed, injustices are inevitable in this sort of screening. Imagine that you were an executive of a government agency in which 5 percent of the 1000 employees are guilty of misconduct. You hire a polygraph examiner to help identify these guilty people. After all your employees take the test, how many of the 50 guilty persons will be correctly identified? If this imaginary polygraph examiner is right 70 percent of the time, 35 of the 50 guilty people will be correctly identified. So far, so good. But because the examiner errs 30 percent of the time, 30 percent of the 950 innocent employees — 285 people — will be accused wrongly. Thus, 8 out of 9 employees labeled "guilty" would be falsely accused. If 1 in every 1000 employees of a government and its defense contractors were a spy, hundreds of loyal employees would probably fail the polygraph clearance procedures for every spy caught. This, in itself, would be "a victory for the nation's enemies," says Lykken (1987).

The polygraph functions more appropriately as a tool in criminal investigation. Police sometimes use the polygraph to induce confessions by criminals whom they scare into thinking that any lies will be transparent. A more honest approach uses the *guilty knowledge test*, which assesses a suspect's physiological responses to details of a crime known only to the police and the guilty person. If a camera and money were stolen, the polygraph examiner could see whether the suspect reacts strongly to such details as the specific brand name of the camera and the dollar amounts. Presumably, only a guilty person would. Given enough such specific probes, an innocent person will seldom be wrongly accused. Nevertheless, crit-

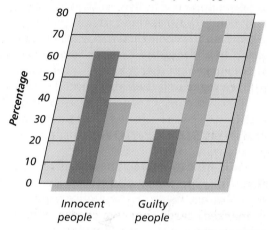

Figure 13–2 How often do lie detectors lie? Benjamin Kleinmuntz and Julian Szucko (1984) had polygraph experts study the polygraph data of 50 theft suspects who later confessed to being guilty and 50 suspects whose innocence was later established by someone's confession. Had the polygraph experts been the judges, more than one-third of the innocent would have been declared guilty, and almost one-fourth of the guilty would have been declared innocent.

"If you hang them all, you will get the guilty."
Folksinger Tom T. Hall

ics and advocates alike disapprove widespread commercial use of the polygraph. The truth is that lie detectors sometimes lie. The U.S. Congress recognized this when it passed the Employee Polygraph Protection Act of 1988, prohibiting most nongovernmental polygraph testing.

Given these polygraph restrictions, businesses are seeking new ways to protect themselves, and entrepreneurs are offering new methods. More than a million people a year are now taking "integrity tests." These paper-and-pencil tests ask people about their past behavior and their opinions about the commonality of employee theft and how severely it should be punished. Once again, the Congressional Office of Technology Assessment (1990), after scrutinizing the available evidence, is skeptical. Research to date is inconclusive. But even if the tests are better than a mere toss of the coin, they exclude more honest people than thieves. An American Psychological Association committee discerned some validity to a few of the honesty tests (Goldberg & others, 1990). But it also urged greater openness and honesty from honesty-test publishers regarding their evidence.

Expressing Emotion

Even if we cannot decipher people's emotions by measuring their body arousal, we can, and often do, use a simpler method: We "read" their bodies, listen to their voices, and look at their faces.

Nonverbal Communication

All of us communicate nonverbally as well as verbally. If irritated, we may tense our bodies, press our lips together, and gesture with our eyebrows. With a gaze, an averted glance, or a stare we can communicate intimacy, submission, or dominance (Kleinke, 1986).

Most of us are good enough at reading nonverbal cues to decipher the emotions in an old silent film. We are especially good at detecting nonverbal threats. In a crowd of faces, a single angry face will "pop out" faster than a single happy one (Hansen & Hansen, 1988). Some of us are more sensitive to these cues than others. Robert Rosenthal, Judith Hall, and their colleagues (1979) discov-

Through the silent language of nonverbal expression, the body communicates emotion. Without a word from either one, we know these two spelling bee finalists are anguished.

ered this by showing hundreds of people brief film clips of portions of a person's emotionally expressive face or body, sometimes with a garbled voice added. For example, after a 2-second scene revealing only the face of an upset woman, the researchers would ask whether the woman was expressing anger or discussing a divorce. Rosenthal and Hall reported that some people are much better emotion detectors than others, and that women are better at it than men.

Among couples passionately in love, eye-gazing is typically prolonged and mutual (Rubin, 1970). Would intimate gazes similarly stir feelings between strangers? To find out, Joan Kellerman, James Lewis, and James Laird (1989) asked unacquainted male-female pairs to gaze intently for 2 minutes either at one another's hands or into one another's eyes. After separating, the eye-gazers reported feeling a greater tingle of attraction and affection.

Armed with high-tech equipment, psychologists are now linking various emotions with specific facial muscles (Figure 13–3).

(a)

(b)

(c)

(d)

Hard-to-control facial muscles reveal signs of emotions you may be trying to conceal. Lifting just the inner part of your eyebrows, which few people do consciously, reveals distress or worry. Eyebrows raised and pulled together signal fear. A feigned smile, such as one we make for a photographer, gets switched on and off more abruptly than a genuine smile (Bugental, 1986) and often continues for more than 4 or 5 seconds, by which time most authentic expressions fade. These subtle facial indicators of emotion may someday enable a new behavioral approach to lie detection. For example, given mild emotional stimuli, electrodes attached to your facial muscles can now detect your hidden reactions (Cacioppo & others, 1988). Your face might not look any different, but voltage changes on the skin reveal micromuscular smiles or frowns underneath.

The growing awareness that we communicate through the body's silent language has led to studies of how job applicants and interviewers communicate (or miscommunicate) nonverbally, and to popular guidebooks on how to interpret nonverbal signals. Whether negotiating a business deal, selling a product, or flirting with someone, it pays to be able to read feelings that "leak through" via subtle facial expressions, body movements, and postures. Fidgeting, for example, may reveal anxiety or boredom. More specific interpretations of postures and gestures are risky. Different expressions may convey the same emotion: Either a cold stare or the avoidance of eye-contact may signify hostility. And a given expression can convey very different emotions: Folded arms, for example, can signify irritation or relaxation.

Figure 13–3 Paul Ekman's system for classifying a particular smile consists of a specific code for each of the 80 facial muscles used to create it. Notice how different these smiles are: (a) a smile that masks anger (the woman has just been told she is being dismissed); (b) an overly polite smile (the man is telling a patient to enjoy her hospital stay); (c) a smile softening verbal criticism ("I'd appreciate it if you wouldn't come to rehearsal drunk"); and (d) a reluctant, compliant smile ("I guess I don't have any choice, so OK").

Culture and Emotional Expression

The meaning of gestures varies with the culture. Some years ago, psychologist Otto Klineberg (1938) observed that in Chinese literature people clapped their hands to express worry or disappointment, laughed a great "ho-ho" to express anger, and stuck out their tongues to show surprise. Similarly, the "thumbs up" and "A-OK" signs of North American culture would be interpreted as insults in certain other cultures.

Do facial expressions also mean something different in different cultures? To find out, two investigative teams—one led by Paul Ekman and Wallace Friesen (1975, 1987), the other by Carroll Izard (1977)—showed photographs of different facial expressions to people in different parts of the world and asked them to guess the emotion. You can try this yourself. Match the six emotions with the six faces of Figure 13–4.

Paul Ekman (Ekman & Friesen, 1975): "Emotions are shown primarily in the face, not in the body. There is no specific body movement pattern that always signals anger or fear, but there are facial patterns specific to each emotion."

Figure 13–4 Which face expresses disgust? anger? fear? happiness? sadness? surprise? The answers are on page 393.

You probably did pretty well. How do you suppose people from Brazil or Japan did when judging these pictures? About the same as Americans, it turns out. A smile's a smile the world around. Ditto for the other basic expressions.

Do people from different cultures make and interpret facial expressions similarly because they experience similar influences, such as American movies and CNN? Apparently not. Ekman and his team went to an isolated New Guinea people and asked them to display various emotions by saying, for example, "Pretend your child has died." When they showed videotapes of the New Guineans' facial reactions to American collegians, the Americans could easily read them. People in various cultures also agree on how to convey a given emotion most intensely and on which combinations of two emotions an expression conveys (Ekman & others, 1987). Children's facial expressions—even those of blind children who have never seen a face—are also universal (Eibl-Eibesfeldt, 1971). The world

While weightless, astronauts' fluids move toward their upper body and their faces become puffy. This makes nonverbal communication more difficult, increasing the risks of misunderstanding, especially among multinational crews (Gelman, 1989).

over, children cry when distressed, shake their heads when defiant, and smile when happy.

The discovery that the facial muscles speak a universal language would come as no surprise to Charles Darwin. He speculated that in prehistoric times, before our ancestors communicated in words, their ability to convey threats, greetings, and submission with facial expressions helped them to survive. That shared heritage, he believed, is why all humans express the basic emotions by similar facial expressions. A sneer, for example, retains elements of an animal's teeth-baring snarl. Smiles, too, are social communications, not just emotional reflexes. Bowlers don't smile when they score a strike — they smile when they turn to face their companions (Jones & others, 1991; Kraut & Johnston, 1979).

Although cultures share a universal nonverbal language, they differ in how, and how much, they use it. In cultures that encourage individuality, as in Western Europe, Australia, New Zealand, and North America, emotional displays often are intense and prolonged. People focus on their own goals and attitudes and express themselves accordingly. In Asian and Third World cultures that emphasize social connections and interdependence, emotions such as sympathy, respect, and shame are more common than in the West. Moreover, people in such cultures more rarely and briefly display self-aggrandizing or negative emotions that might disrupt communal feeling within closely knit groups (Markus & Kitayama, 1991; Matsumoto & others, 1988).

The Effects of Facial Expressions

Expressions not only communicate emotion, they also amplify and regulate it. In his 1872 book, *The Expression of the Emotions in Man and Animals*, Darwin contended that "the free expression by outward signs of an emotion intensifies it. . . . He who gives way to violent gestures will increase his rage."

Was Darwin right? I was driving in my car one day when the song "Put On a Happy Face" came on the radio. "How phony," I thought. But I tested Darwin's hypothesis anyway, as you can, too: Fake a big grin. Now scowl. Can you feel the difference?

The subjects in dozens of experiments could feel a difference. When James Laird and his colleagues (1974, 1984, 1989) subtly induced students to make a frowning expression — by asking them to "contract these muscles," "pull your brows together," and the like while he attached electrodes to their faces — the students reported feeling a little angry. Compared with the frowners, students whom he similarly induced to smile felt happier, found cartoons more humorous, and recalled happier memories. People instructed to express other basic emotions react similarly. People report feeling more fear than anger, disgust, or sadness when made to construct an expression of fear: "Raise your eyebrows. And open your eyes wide. Move your whole head back, so that your chin is tucked in a little bit, and let your mouth relax and hang open a little" (Duclos & others, 1989). Going through the motions awakens the emotions.

The effect is subtle, yet detectable in the absence of competing emotions. Just activating one of the smiling muscles by holding a pen in the teeth (rather than with the lips, which activates a frowning muscle) is enough to make cartoons seem more amusing (Strack

& others, 1988). A heartier smile, made not just with the mouth but with raised cheeks as well, works even better (Ekman & others, 1990). Smile warmly on the outside and you feel better on the inside. Scowl and the whole world seems to scowl back.

Why might this be so? Paul Ekman and his colleagues (1983) designed an experiment to find out. Their subjects were professional actors trained in the Stanislavsky method, in which they physically (and psychologically) "become" the characters they are playing. The actors would assume an expression and then hold it for 10 seconds while the researchers measured changes in their heart rates and finger temperatures. When they made a fearful expression, their heart rate increased some eight beats per minute and finger temperature was steady. When making an angry expression, both heart rate and finger temperature increased as though the actor were indeed "hot-headed." Our facial expressions, it seems, send signals to our autonomic nervous system, which then responds accordingly.

⌐This experiment shows how ⌐"facial feedback"⌐ affects our emotions, and it provides further evidence that different emotions accompany subtly different body states⌐ Sara Snodgrass and her associates (1986) observed the same phenomenon with walking behavior. You can duplicate her subjects' experience: Walk for a few minutes while taking short, shuffling steps, keeping your eyes downcast. Now walk around taking long strides, with your arms swinging and your eyes looking straight ahead. Does your mood perceptibly brighten when you shift gaits?

If assuming an emotional expression triggers a feeling, then imitating others' expressions should help us feel what they are feeling. Again, the laboratory evidence is supportive. Kathleen Burns Vaughn and John Lanzetta (1981) asked some students but not others to make a pained expression whenever an electric shock was apparently delivered to someone they were watching. With each apparent shock, the observers perspired more and had a faster heart rate if grimacing than if not. So one small way to become more empathic — to feel what others feel — is to let your own face mimic the other person's expression. Acting as another acts helps us feel what another feels.

Experiencing Emotion

The ingredients of emotion include not only physiological arousal and expressive behavior, but also our conscious experience. Our feelings are "obscure and confused," noted Benjamin Constant de Rebecque in 1816. To cut through the obscurity, psychologists have asked people to report their experience of different emotions. Estonians, Poles, Greeks, Chinese, and Canadians all seem to place emotions along two dimensions—pleasant versus unpleasant and intensely aroused versus sleepy (Russell & others, 1989). On the intensity scale, for example, terrified is more frightening than afraid, enraged is angrier than angry, delighted is happier than happy. To these two dimensions, we might add a third: duration. Among Americans and Japanese, at least, the emotions of joy and sadness typically endure longer than anger and guilt, which outlast fear and disgust (Matsumoto & others, 1988).

Other psychologists have sought to identify emotions that are biologically, facially, and experientially distinct. Carroll Izard

"Refuse to express a passion and it dies. . . . If we wish to conquer undesirable emotional tendencies in ourselves, we must . . . go through the outward movements of those contrary dispositions which we prefer to cultivate."
William James
Principles of Psychology, 1890

Carroll Izard (1990): "Patterns of expressive behavior can be effectively used in the management of emotion. . . . Such methods can be tailored for use by parents and teachers, and they can be combined with established behavioral and cognitive techniques for an integrated approach to therapy."

(a)   (b)   (c)   (d)   (e)

(f)   (g)   (h)

Figure 13–5 Infants' naturally occurring emotions. To identify the emotions present from birth, Carroll Izard analyzed the facial expressions of very young infants. Shown here are (a) joy (mouth forming smile, cheeks lifted, twinkle in eye); (b) anger (brows drawn together and downward, eyes fixed, mouth squarish); (c) interest (brows raised or knitted, mouth softly rounded, lips may be pursed); (d) disgust (nose wrinkled, upper lip raised, tongue pushed outward); (e) surprise (brows raised, eyes widened, mouth rounded in oval shape); (f) distress (eyes tightly closed; mouth, as in anger, squared); (g) sadness (brows' inner corners raised, mouth corners drawn down); and (h) fear (brows level, drawn in and up, eyelids lifted, mouth corners retracted).

(1977) believes there are 10 such basic emotions (joy, interest-excitement, surprise, sadness, anger, disgust, contempt, fear, shame, and guilt), most of which are present in infancy (Figure 13–5). Other emotions, he says, are combinations of these. Love, for instance, is a mixture of joy and interest-excitement.

Let's now examine three of the basic emotions: fear, anger, and happiness. What functions do these emotions serve? And what influences our experience of them?

Fear

Fear can be a poisonous emotion. It can torment us, rob us of sleep, and preoccupy our thinking. People can be literally scared to death. Fear can also be contagious. In 1903, someone yelled "Fire!" as a fire broke out in Chicago's Iroquois Theater. Eddie Foy, the comedian on stage at the time, tried to reassure the crowd by calling out, "Don't get excited. There's no danger. Take it easy!" Alas, the crowd panicked. During the 10 minutes it took the fire department to arrive and quickly extinguish the flames, more than 500 people perished, most of them trampled or smothered in a stampede. Bodies were piled 7 or 8 feet deep in the stairways, and many of the faces bore heel marks (Brown, 1965).

More often, fear is an adaptive response. Fear prepares our bodies to flee danger. Fear of real or imagined enemies binds people together as families, tribes, and nations. Fear of injury protects us from harm. Fear of punishment or retaliation constrains us from harming one another.

People can be afraid of almost anything—"afraid of truth, afraid of fortune, afraid of death, and afraid of each other," observed Ralph Waldo Emerson. Why so many fears? Psychologists note that we can learn to fear almost anything. Recall from Chapter 8, Learning, that dogs learn to fear neutral stimuli associated with shock, that infants come to fear furry objects associated with frightening noises, and that adults can become terrified of incidental stimuli linked with traumatic experiences such as rape. Through such condition-

Answers to the question in Figure 13–4: From left to right: top row—happiness, anger, sadness; bottom row—surprise, disgust, fear.

"He who fears all snares falls into none."
Publilius Syrus
Sententiae, 43 B.C.

ing, the short list of naturally painful and frightening events multiplies into a long list of human fears—fear of driving or flying, fear of mice or cockroaches, fear of closed or open spaces, fear of failure, fear of another race or nation.

Learning by observation extends the list. Susan Mineka (1985) wondered why nearly all monkeys reared in the wild fear snakes, yet lab-reared monkeys do not. Surely, most wild monkeys do not actually suffer snake bites. Might they learn their fear through observation? To find out, Mineka experimented with six wild-reared monkeys (all strongly fearful of snakes) and their lab-reared offspring (virtually none of which feared snakes). After repeatedly observing their parents or peers refusing to reach for food in the presence of a snake, the younger monkeys developed a similar strong fear of snakes. When retested 3 months later, their learned fear persisted. This suggests that our fears reflect not only our own past traumas but also the fears of our parents and friends.

Moreover, we may be biologically prepared to learn some fears more quickly than others. We humans quickly learn to fear snakes, spiders, and cliffs—fears that probably helped our ancestors survive. We are less predisposed to fear cars, electricity, bombs, and environmental warming, which in modern society are far more dangerous (Lumsden & Wilson, 1983; McNally, 1987). Stone Age fears leave us unprepared for high-tech dangers.

Some biologically predisposed fears develop with little or no learning. Donald Hebb (1980) was astonished at what happened when he showed a clay model of a chimpanzee head to adult chimpanzees. The animals panicked. "Some of them screamed, defecated, fled from their outer cages to the inner rooms where they were not within sight of the clay model; those that remained in sight stood at the back of the cage, their gaze fixed on the model held in my hand" (p. 60). The animals' terror parallels most people's horror the first time they see a dead or dismembered human body.

Of course, some people's fears of specific things, such as spiders, are greater than others'. For a few people, intense fears of specific objects or situations disrupt their ability to cope. Furthermore, some people are very fearful of threatening or embarrassing situations. Others—courageous heroes and remorseless criminals—are less fearful. Astronauts and adventurers who have "the right stuff"—who can keep their wits and function coolly and effectively in moments of severe stress—seem to thrive on risk. So, too, do con artists and killers who charm their intended victims without a hint of nervousness, and who in laboratory tests exhibit little fear of a tone that predictably precedes a painful electric shock. Experience helps shape such fearfulness or fearlessness, but so do our genes. Even among identical twins reared separately, one twin's level of fearfulness is similar to the other's (Lykken, 1982).

✳ Anger

Anger is said by the sages to be "a short madness" (Horace, 65–8 B.C.) that "carries the mind away" (Virgil, 70–19 B.C.) and can be "many times more hurtful than the injury that caused it" (Thomas Fuller, 1654–1734). But other sages say "noble anger" (William Shakespeare, 1564–1616) "makes any coward brave" (Cato, 234–149 B.C.) and "brings back his strength" (Virgil).

Chapters 15 and 16 discuss how such phobias develop and are treated.

Although a horse encounter may be traumatic for this boy, his fear of large animals is certainly an adaptive response.

What makes us angry? To find out, James Averill (1983) asked many people to recall or keep careful records of their experiences with anger. Most reported becoming at least mildly angry several times a week; some became angry several times a day. Often the anger was a response to a friend or loved one's perceived misdeed. Anger was especially common when another person's act seemed willful, unjustified, and avoidable. But blameless annoyances—foul odors, high temperatures, aches and pains—also have the power to make us angry (Berkowitz, 1990).

What do people do with their anger? What *should* they do with it? When anger fuels physically or verbally aggressive acts that are later regretted, it is maladaptive. But Averill's subjects recalled that when they were angry they often reacted assertively rather than hurtfully. Their anger frequently led them to talk things over with the offending person and so to lessen the aggravation. Such controlled expressions of anger are more adaptive than either hostile outbursts or just keeping the angry feelings inside. The poet William Blake (1757–1827) had the idea:

> I was angry with my foe,
> I told it not, my wrath did grow,
> I was angry with my friend,
> I told my wrath, my wrath did end.

Popular books and articles on aggression sometimes advise that even hostile outbursts can be better than keeping anger pent up. If the Roman statesman Seneca was right—"It is hidden anger that harms"—then, when irritated, should we go ahead and curse, tell a person off, or retaliate? Was Ann Landers (1969) right to assert that "youngsters should be taught to vent their anger"?

Such advice is typical of individualized cultures, but would seldom be heard in cultures where people's identity is more group-centered. People who keenly sense their interdependence see anger as a threat to group harmony (Markus & Kitayama, 1991). In Tahiti, for instance, people learn to be considerate and gentle. From infancy on in Japan, expressions of anger are less common than in America.

The "vent your anger" advice presumes that emotional expression provides emotional release, or **catharsis**. The catharsis hypothesis maintains that we reduce anger after releasing it through aggressive action or fantasy. Experimenters report that this sometimes occurs. When people retaliate against someone who has provoked them, they may indeed calm down—*if* their counterattack is directly against the provoker, *if* their retaliation seems justifiable, and *if* their target is not intimidating (Geen & Quanty, 1977; Hokanson & Edelman, 1966). In short, expressing anger can be *temporarily* calming *if* it does not leave us feeling guilty or anxious.

But expressing anger can also breed more anger. For one thing, it may provoke retaliation, thus escalating a minor conflict into a major confrontation. For another, expressing anger can magnify anger. (Recall Darwin's suggestion that making violent gestures can increase anger.) Ebbe Ebbesen and his colleagues (1975) saw this when they interviewed 100 frustrated engineers and technicians just laid off by an aerospace company. Some were asked questions that released hostility, such as, "What instances can you think of where the company has not been fair with you?" When these people later filled out a questionnaire that assessed their attitudes toward the company, did this opportunity to "drain off"

One problem with chronic hostility is its link with heart disease (page 520).

"Anger will never disappear so long as thoughts of resentment are cherished in the mind."
Buddha, 500 B.C.

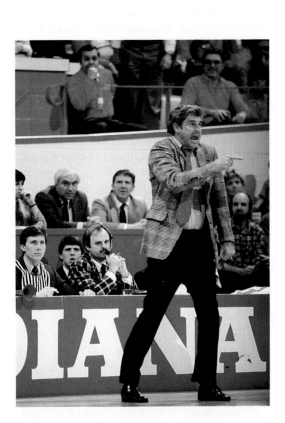

Indiana University basketball coach Bobby Knight's angry outbursts may be temporarily cathartic. If so, they may also be reinforcing.

their hostility reduce it? Quite the contrary. Compared with those who had not vented their anger, those who had done so exhibited more hostility.

Thus, although "blowing off steam" may temporarily calm an angry person, it may also amplify underlying hostility. When angry outbursts do calm us, they may be reinforcing and therefore habit forming. If by berating referees, basketball coaches can drain off some of their tension, then the next time they feel tense with irritation they may be more likely to explode again. Similarly, the next time you are angry you are likely to do whatever has relieved your anger in the past.

What's the best way to handle anger? Anger experts offer several suggestions. First, bring down the physiological arousal of anger by waiting. "It is true of the body as of arrows," notes Carol Tavris (1982), "what goes up must come down. Any emotional arousal will simmer down if you just wait long enough." Second, deal with anger in a way that involves neither being chronically angry over every little annoyance nor passively sulking, which is merely rehearsing one's reasons for anger. Don't be like those who, stifling their feelings over a series of provocations, finally overreact to a single incident (Baumeister & others, 1991). Vent the anger by playing an instrument, exercising, or confiding one's feelings to a friend or in a diary.

As we noted earlier, anger can benefit relationships when it expresses a grievance in ways that promote reconciliation rather than retaliation. Civility means not only keeping silent about trivial irritations but also communicating important ones clearly and assertively. A nonaccusing statement of feeling—perhaps letting one's partner know that "I get irritated when you leave your dirty dishes for me to clean up"— can help resolve the conflicts that cause anger.

Happiness

"How to gain, how to keep, how to recover happiness is in fact for most men at all times the secret motive for all they do," observed William James (1902, p. 76). Understandably so, for one's state of happiness or unhappiness colors everything else. People who are happy perceive the world as safer (Johnson & Tversky, 1983), make decisions more easily (Isen & Means, 1983), rate job applicants more favorably (Baron, 1987), and report greater satisfaction with their whole lives (Schwarz & Clore, 1983). When your mood is gloomy, life as a whole seems depressing; let your mood brighten, and suddenly your relationships, your self-image, and your hopes for the future all seem more promising.

Moreover — and this is one of psychology's most consistent findings — when we feel happy we are more willing to help others. In study after study, people given a mood-boosting experience, such as finding money, succeeding on a challenging task, or recalling a happy event, are more likely to give money, pick up someone's dropped papers, volunteer time, and so forth. It's called the "feel-good, do-good" phenomenon (Salovey, 1990).

In search of the roots of happiness, psychologists have studied influences upon both our temporary moods and our long-term life satisfaction. Studying people's reports of daily moods confirms that stressful events — an argument with someone, a sick child, a car problem — trigger bad moods. No surprise there. But by the next day, the gloom nearly always lifts. If anything, people tend to rebound from bad days to a *better*-than-usual good mood the day following (Bolger & others, 1989; Stone & Neale, 1984). Have you noticed this effect in your own life? When in a bad mood, can you usually depend on rebounding within a day or two? Are your times of elation similarly hard to sustain?

Apart from prolonged grief over the loss of a loved one or lingering anxiety after a personal trauma, such as child abuse, rape, or the terrors of war, even tragedy is not permanently depressing. The finding is surprising but reliable. People who become blind or paralyzed usually recover near-normal levels of day-to-day happiness. For example, able-bodied University of Illinois students described themselves as happy 50 percent of the time, unhappy 22 percent of the time, and neutral 29 percent of the time. To within 1 percentage point, disabled students rated their emotions identically (Chwalisz & others, 1988). Moreover, students perceive their disabled friends as just as happy as their nondisabled friends (Allman, 1989). The effect of dramatically positive events is similarly temporary. Once their rush of euphoria wears off, state lottery winners typically find their overall happiness unchanged (Brickman & others, 1978).

Other research confirms that there is much more to well-being than being well-off. Many people (including most new collegians, as Figure 13–6 hints) believe they would be happier if they had more money. They probably would be — temporarily. In the long run, increased affluence hardly affects happiness. Those with lots of money are not much happier than those with only enough money to afford life's necessities. Within a given country there is a slight tendency for the wealthy to be happier than the poor. But people in wealthier countries hardly report feeling more satisfied with their lives than do those in poorer countries. Interviews with more than 160,000 Europeans since the mid-1970s reveal that the Danes, Swiss, Irish, and Dutch have been much more likely than the French, Greeks, Italians, and West Germans to report themselves happy and satisfied with life. These puzzling national differences do not closely mirror differences in standards of living (Inglehart, 1990). West Germans, for example, had double the incomes of the Irish; but, year after year, the Irish were happier.

We can also ask whether, over time, our happiness grows with our paychecks. The American experience illustrates the answer: It

"Weeping may tarry for the night, but joy comes with the morning."
Psalms 30:5

Note that the capacity of people in poor nations to be happy no more justifies poverty than does slaves' capacity to be happy justify slavery.

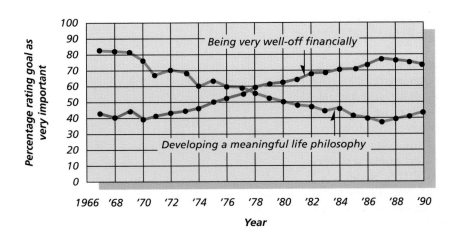

Figure 13–6 Are today's collegians increasingly materialistic? From 1970 through most of the 1980s, annual surveys of more than 200,000 entering American college students revealed an increasing desire for wealth. (From Dey & others, 1991.)

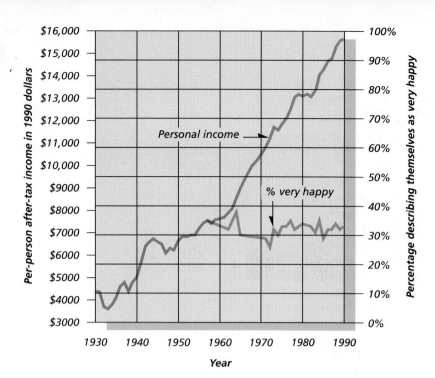

Figure 13–7 Does money buy happiness? It surely helps us to avoid certain types of pain. Yet, though buying power has doubled since the 1950s, self-reported happiness has remained almost unchanged. (Happiness data from Niemi, 1989, and T. Smith, 1990; income data from *Historical Statistics of the U.S.* and *Economic Indicators.*)

does not. During the last three decades, Americans' buying power doubled. Their 1957 per person income, expressed in 1990 dollars, was $7500; by 1990 it was over $15,000. With so much more of what money buys—twice as many cars per capita, and color TVs, VCRs, home computers, microwave ovens, and answering machines galore—did their increased wealth buy more happiness? As Figure 13–7 shows, the average American is now twice as rich, but no happier. In 1957, and still in 1990, only one in three said they were "very happy." Indeed, judging by increased rates of depression (page 458), Americans are more often miserable. It's shocking, and contradicts popular materialism, but how can we deny it: An affluent society's economic growth does not improve its morale.

Two psychological principles explain why more money buys no more than a temporary surge of happiness, and why our emotions seem attached to elastic bands that pull us back from highs or lows. Each principle, in its own way, suggests that happiness is relative.

The Adaptation-Level Principle: Happiness Is Relative to Our Prior Experience The **adaptation-level phenomenon** describes our tendency to judge various stimuli relative to what we have previously experienced. We adjust our "neutral" levels—the points at which sounds seem neither loud nor soft, lights neither bright nor dim, events neither pleasant nor unpleasant—based on our experience. We then notice and react to variations up or down from these levels.

Thus, if our income, grade-point average, or social prestige increases, we feel an initial surge of pleasure. We then adapt to this new level of achievement, come to see it as normal, and require something better yet to give us another surge of happiness. From my childhood, I can recall the thrill of watching my family's first 12-inch, black-and-white television set. Now, if the color goes out on our 25-inch TV, I feel deprived. Having adapted upward, I perceive as negative what I once experienced as positive. Yesterday's luxury has become today's necessity. **The moral:** Satisfaction and dissatisfaction, success and failure—all are relative to our recent experience.

"No happiness lasts for long."
Seneca
Agamemnon, A.D. 60

"Continued pleasures wear off. . . . Pleasure is always contingent upon change and disappears with continuous satisfaction."
Nico Frijda (1988)

Skip

Calvin and Hobbes © 1991 Universal Press Syndicate. Reprinted with permission. All rights reserved.

It follows that we will never create a social paradise on earth (Campbell, 1975). If you woke up tomorrow to your utopia—perhaps a world with no bills, no ills, all *A*s, someone who loves you unreservedly—you would soon recalibrate your adaptation level. Before long you would again sometimes feel gratified (when achievements surpass expectations), sometimes deprived (when they fall below), and sometimes neutral. That helps explain why, despite the realities of triumph and tragedy, million-dollar lottery winners and paraplegics report similar levels of happiness. It also explains why material wants can be insatiable—why many a child "needs" just one more Nintendo game. Or why Imelda Marcos, surrounded by poverty while living in splendor as wife of the Philippines' president, bought 2700 pairs of shoes, more than she could ever wear in her lifetime. When the victor belongs to the spoils and the possessor is possessed by possessions, adaptation level has run amuck.

Seeking happiness through material achievement requires an ever-increasing abundance of things. At the end of his *Chronicles of Narnia*, writer C. S. Lewis depicts heaven as a place where good things *do* continually increase, where life is a never-ending story "in which every chapter is better than the one before." Here on earth the unavoidable ups and downs of real life preclude a perpetual high.

"I have also learned why people work so hard to succeed: It is because they envy the things their neighbors have. But it is useless. It is like chasing the wind. . . . It is better to have only a little, with peace of mind, than be busy all the time with both hands, trying to catch the wind."
　Ecclesiastes 4: 4

Because of our capacity to adapt to past events, our emotional ups and downs tend to reflect current happenings, such as a frightening visit with Santa or a joyful inauguration day for Gallaudet University President I. King Jordan.

Close-Up: Opponent-Process Theory of Emotion

The adaptation-level principle helps explain why, in the long run, our emotional ups and downs tend to balance. University of Pennsylvania psychologist Richard Solomon (1980) believes that emotions balance in the short run as well, and he has developed a theory to explain why. Solomon was intrigued by the emotional price tag that so often follows pleasure, and the emotional dividends that can compensate for past suffering. For the pleasure of a drug high, one pays the price of discomfort when the drug wears off. For the pain of hard exercise or a hot sauna bath, one afterward receives the dividend of a pleasurable feeling of well-being.

Solomon proposes, with support from laboratory studies of human and animal emotions, that *every emotion triggers an opposing emotion*. He calls this the opponent-process theory. Imagine that you are about to take your first parachute jump. Solomon would say that the primary emotion you experience before the jump— fear—triggers an opposing emotion—elation—as you land. Once the opposing emotion activates, perhaps to keep the initial emotion under control, you experience a diminishing of the initial emotion's intensity. As the initial emotion subsides, the opposing emotion lingers awhile (Figure 13–8a). After parachutists survive their first free-fall, which for many is a terrifying experience, the fear switches off and they typically feel elated. For some women, the pain of labor and childbirth may enhance a euphoric feeling afterward.

Repetitions of the emotion-arousing event strengthen the opposing emotion. Thus, the emotional experi-ence, such as the high from drug use or the fear aroused by parachuting, diminishes with repetition. This helps explain drug tolerance (with repetition, the initial pleasure lessens).

With repetition, the after reaction, such as the pain of drug withdrawal or the euphoria after childbirth, remains strong or becomes stronger (Figure 13–8b). This helps explain both drug hangovers (the opponent feelings that "knock down" the initial pleasure and linger afterward), and drug addiction (the craving for more of the drug to switch off the pain of withdrawal).

As Solomon wisely notes, opponent-process theory and the research that supports it are good news for puritans and bad news for hedonists: Those who seek pleasure pay for it later, and with repetition their pleasure will lose much of its intensity. With every kick comes a kickback. An old Spanish saying anticipated opponent-process theory: "'Take what you want,' said God. 'Take it, and pay for it.'" On the other hand, those who suffer will receive their reward. With most pain comes a gain.

Looking over the whole of psychology, we can see a deep principle emerging: Human nature is a battle-field of opposing tendencies. Our sympathetic and parasympathetic nervous systems, our neural balance between excitation and inhibition, our endorphin responses to pain, our opponent neural processes that create color and negative afterimages, our regulation of hunger and satiety, and our experiences of pleasure and misery all involve carefully negotiated truces between opposing forces.

First experience
(a)

After repeated experiences
(b)

Figure 13–8 Opponent processes in emotion. (a) A primary emotional response to a stimulus triggers an opposing emotion. What we experience is the primary emotion minus the opposing emotion. (b) With repeated stimula-tion, the opponent emotion becomes stronger, weakening the experience of the primary emotion and lingering on. (From Solomon, 1980.)

The Relative Deprivation Principle: Happiness Is Relative to Others' Attainments To explain the frustration expressed by U.S. Air Corps soldiers during World War II, researchers formulated the concept of **relative deprivation** (the sense that we are worse off than others with whom we compare ourselves). Despite a relatively rapid promotion rate, many soldiers were frustrated about their promotion rates (Merton & Kitt, 1950). Apparently, seeing so many others being promoted inflated the soldiers' expectations. And when expectations soar above attainments, the result is frustration. When the Oakland Athletics signed outfielder Jose Canseco to a $4.7 million annual salary, his fellow outfielder Rickey Henderson became openly dissatisfied with his $3 million salary. Refusing to show up on time to spring training, he complained, "I don't think my contract is fair" (King, 1991).

Such comparisons help us understand why the middle- and upper-income people in a given country tend to be slightly more satisfied with life than the relatively poor, with whom the better-off can compare themselves (Diener, 1984). Nevertheless, once a person reaches a moderate income level, further increases do little to increase happiness. Why? Because as people climb the ladder of success they mostly compare themselves with those who are at or above their current level (Gruder, 1977; Suls & Tesch, 1978). For Rickey Henderson, Jose Canseco was the standard of comparison. As Bertrand Russell (1930, pp. 68–69) observed, "Napoleon envied Caesar, Caesar envied Alexander, and Alexander, I daresay, envied Hercules, who never existed. You cannot, therefore, get away from envy by means of success alone, for there will always be in history or legend some person even more successful than you are."

By "counting our blessings" when we compare ourselves with those less fortunate, we can, however, increase our satisfaction. As comparing ourselves with those better-off creates envy, so comparing ourselves with those less well-off boosts contentment. Marshall Dermer and his colleagues (1979) demonstrated this by asking University of Wisconsin-Milwaukee women to study others' deprivation and suffering. After viewing vivid depictions of how grim life was in Milwaukee in 1900, or after imagining and then writing about various personal tragedies, such as being burned and disfigured, the women expressed greater satisfaction with their own lives. Similarly, when mildly depressed people read about someone who is even more depressed, they feel somewhat better (Gibbons, 1986).

Predictors of Happiness If, as the adaptation-level principle implies, our emotions tend to balance around normal, then why do some people seem so filled with joy and others so gloomy day after day? What makes one person normally happy and another depressed? In reviewing research on people's feelings of general happiness and well-being, Ed Diener (1984) spotted several predictors of life satisfaction. Remember, though, that knowing that two variables correlate does not tell us whether one causes the other. For example, many studies indicate that religiously active and committed people tend to report greater happiness and life satisfaction (Myers, 1992). Is happiness conducive to religiousness? Or, by providing meaning, inner peace, and a sense of ultimate acceptance, does religious faith enhance happiness ?

Whether at work or leisure, most of us derive greatest enjoyment from engaging, challenging activities. Mihaly Csikszentmihalyi (1990; pronounced chick-SENT-me-hi) and his colleagues dis-

The effect of comparison with others helps us understand why students of a given level of academic ability tend to have a higher academic self-concept if they attend a school where most other students are not exceptionally able (Marsh & Parker, 1984). If you were near the top of your class in high school, you might feel inferior upon entering a college where everyone was near the top of their class.

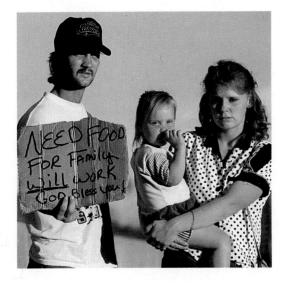

Comparing with those worse off can prompt us to count our blessings, as some people surely did when passing Mike and Jean Richardson and their son, who were lured from Houston to Dallas by a promised job that didn't materialize.

Table 13–1	*Happiness Is . . .*
Researchers have found that happy people tend to:	**However, other factors that seem unrelated to happiness include:**
Have high self-esteem	Age
Have a satisfying marriage or other love relationship	Race
Have a meaningful religious faith	Gender (women are more often depressed but also more often joyful)
Be optimistic and outgoing	Educational level
Sleep well	Intelligence
Exercise	Parenthood (having or not having children)
Be employed	

Source   Summarized from Diener (1984) and Myers (1992).

covered this after interrupting volunteers several times a day with an electronic paging device. When beeped, the people would note what they were doing and how they were feeling. Usually, they felt happier if mentally engaged by work or active leisure than if passively vegetating. Ironically, the less expensive (and usually more involving) a leisure activity, the more absorbed and happier people are while doing it. People are happier gardening than sitting on a power boat. They're happier talking to friends than watching TV. Indeed, happy are those whose work and leisure absorb them, enabling them unself-consciously to "flow" in focused activity.

Theories of Emotion

We have seen that emotions are built from the interplay of physiological arousal, expressive behavior, and conscious experiences. But there is controversy over this interplay. One debate concerns the connection between what we *think* and how we *feel*: Do emotions always grow from thoughts? Is the heart always subject to our mind's appraisal of a situation? Before considering this question, let's consider an older debate: Does your heart pound because you are afraid, or are you afraid because you feel your heart pounding?

The James-Lange and Cannon-Bard Theories

Common sense tells most of us that we cry because we are sad, lash out because we are angry, tremble because we are afraid. However, to pioneering psychologist William James the common-sense view of emotion was 180 degrees out of line. According to James, "we feel sorry because we cry, angry because we strike, afraid because we tremble" (1890, p. 1066). If an oncoming car is in your lane, you will swerve sharply to avoid it; *then* you will notice your racing heart and feel shaken with fright. Your feeling of fear follows your body's response (Figure 13–9).

James's idea, which was independently proposed by Danish physiologist Carl Lange and is therefore called the **James-Lange theory**, struck American physiologist Walter Cannon as implausible. For one thing, Cannon thought the body's responses were not distinct enough to evoke the different emotions. Does a racing heart

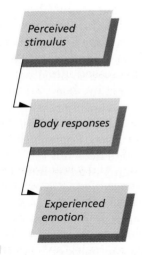

Figure 13–9 The James-Lange theory of emotion.

signal fear, anger, or love? For another, changes in heart rate, perspiration, and body temperature seemed to occur too slowly to trigger sudden emotion. Cannon, and later another American physiologist, Philip Bard, concluded that body arousal and the emotional experience occur simultaneously: The emotion-arousing stimulus is routed simultaneously to the cortex, causing the subjective awareness of emotion, and to the sympathetic nervous system, causing the body's responses. Thus, this **Cannon-Bard theory** implies that your heart begins pounding as you experience fear, but one does not cause the other (Figure 13–10).

As long as the evidence suggested that the arousal of one emotion is much the same as another, the James-Lange assumption that we experience our emotions through differing body states seemed improbable. With new evidence showing subtle physiological distinctions among the emotions, the James-Lange theory has become more plausible. As James struggled with his own feelings of depression and grief, he came to believe that we can control emotions by going "through the outward motions" of whatever emotion one wants to experience. "To feel cheerful," he advised, "sit up cheerfully, look around cheerfully, and act as if cheerfulness were already there." The new findings concerning emotional effects of facial expressions (page 391) are precisely what James might have predicted.

Let's check your understanding of the James-Lange and Cannon-Bard theories. Imagine that your brain could not sense your heart pounding or your stomach churning. According to each theory, how would this affect your experiencing of emotions?

Cannon and Bard would have expected you to experience emotions normally, because they believe emotions occur separately from (though simultaneously with) the body's responses. James and Lange would expect greatly diminished emotions because they believed that to feel emotion you must perceive your body responses.

The imagined situation actually exists in people with severed spinal cords. Psychologist George Hohmann (1966) interviewed 25 soldiers who received such injuries in World War II. He asked them to recall emotion-arousing incidents that occurred before and after their spinal injuries. Those with injuries in the lower part of the spine, who had lost sensation only in their legs, reported little change in their emotions. Those who could feel nothing below the neck reported a considerable decrease in emotional intensity (as James and Lange would have expected). These soldiers said they might act much the same as before in emotion-arousing situations, but as one confessed about his anger, "It just doesn't have the heat to it that it used to. It's a mental kind of anger." On the other hand, emotions expressed mostly in body areas above the neck are felt more intensely by those with spinal cord injury. Virtually all the men Hohmann interviewed reported increases in weeping, lumps in the throat, and getting choked up when saying good-bye, worshipping, or watching a touching movie.

Although such evidence has breathed new life into the James-Lange theory, many researchers agree with Cannon and Bard that our experience of emotions also involves cognitive activity in the cortex. Whether or not we fear the character in the dark alley depends entirely on whether we interpret his actions as hostile or friendly. So with James and Lange we can say that our body responses are an important ingredient of emotion. And with Cannon and Bard we can say that there is more to the experience of emotion than reading our physiology.

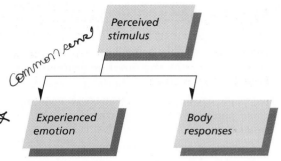

Common sense

Figure 13–10 The Cannon-Bard theory of emotion.

important

"Whenever I feel afraid
I hold my head up high
And whistle a happy tune."
  Richard Rodgers and Oscar Hammerstein
  The King and I

Cognition and Emotion

Now, the new controversy: Put simply, what is the connection between what we *think* and how we *feel*?

We know that our emotions affect our thinking. When we *feel* like singing "Oh, what a beautiful morning!" we *see* the world and the people around us as wonderful; if the following day we feel crabby, we perceive the same world and the same people as less than wonderful.

Can we experience emotion apart from thinking? This issue has practical implications for self-improvement. To change our emotions, must we change our thinking? Or can we modify our emotions by changing our behavior?

Schachter's Two-Factor Theory of Emotion Most psychologists today believe that our cognitions — our perceptions, memories, and interpretations — are an essential ingredient of emotion. One such theorist is Stanley Schachter, whose **two-factor theory** proposes that emotions have two ingredients: physical arousal and a cognitive label (Figure 13–11). Like James and Lange, Schachter presumed that our experience of emotion grows from our awareness of our body's arousal. But he also believed, like Cannon and Bard, that emotions are physiologically similar, so he argued that an emotional experience requires a conscious interpretation of the arousal.

It is often hard to disentangle our arousal response to an event from our interpretation of the event. Imagine that you are aroused and are not sure why, or that you attribute some of your arousal to the wrong source. Perhaps after an invigorating run you arrive home to find a message that you got the longed-for job. Would you feel more elated (because your lingering arousal from running spills into your emotion) than if you received the same news after awakening from a nap?

To find out, Schachter and Jerome Singer (1962) aroused college men with injections of the stimulating hormone, epinephrine. Picture yourself as one of their subjects: After receiving the injection, you go to a waiting room, where you find yourself with another person (actually an accomplice of the experimenters) who is acting either euphoric or irritated. As you observe this person, you begin to feel your heart race, your body flush, and your breathing becoming more rapid. If told to expect these effects from the injection, what would you feel? Schachter and Singer's subjects felt little emotion — because they attributed their arousal to the drug. But if told the injection would produce no effects, what would you feel? Perhaps you would react, as another group of subjects did, by "catching" the apparent emotion of the person you are with — becoming happy if the accomplice is acting euphoric and testy if the accomplice is acting irritated.

This discovery — that a stirred-up state can be experienced as one emotion or another very different one, depending on how we interpret and label it — has been replicated in dozens of experiments. Although emotional arousal is not as undifferentiated as Schachter believed, arousal can intensify just about any emotion (Reisenzein, 1983). Insult people who have just been aroused by pedaling an exercise bike or watching a rock concert film and they will find it easy to misattribute their arousal to the provocation. Like the excited basketball player at the beginning of this chapter, they will feel angrier than do similarly provoked people not previously aroused.

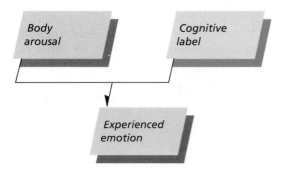

Figure 13–11 A summary of Schachter's two-factor theory of emotion. To experience emotion, we must be aroused and must cognitively label the arousal.

Thus, arousal from emotions as diverse as anger, fear, and sexual excitement can indeed spill from one emotion to another (Zillmann, 1986a). In anger-provoking situations, sexually aroused people react with more hostility. Similarly, the arousal that lingers after an intense argument or a frightening experience may intensify sexual passion (Palace & Gorzalka, 1990).

Must Cognition Precede Emotion? So, to have an emotion must we label our arousal? Robert Zajonc (pronounced ZI-yence) (1980, 1984a) contends the answer is no. He argues that our emotional reactions are sometimes quicker than our interpretations of a situation; we therefore feel some emotions *before* we think. (Can you recall immediately liking something or someone without at first knowing why?)

Figure 13–12 The brain's short-cut for emotions. Sensory input may be routed both to the cortex and directly to the amygdala for a more instant emotional reaction.

In earlier chapters, we noted that when people repeatedly view stimuli flashed too briefly for them to perceive and recall, they nevertheless come to prefer these stimuli. Without being consciously aware of having seen the stimuli, they rather like them. Moreover, some neural pathways involved in emotion bypass the cortical areas involved in thinking. One such pathway runs from the eye via the thalamus to one of the brain's emotional control centers, the amygdala (LeDoux, 1986). This enables a quick, automatic emotional response, which may then be modified after the cortex has further interpreted a threat (Figure 13–12). Such evidence convinces Zajonc that *some* of our emotional reactions involve no deliberate thinking. Cognition, he believes, is not necessary for emotion. The heart is not always subject to the mind.

Emotion researcher Richard Lazarus (1984, 1991) disagrees. He concedes that our brains process and react to vast amounts of information without our conscious awareness, and he willingly grants that some emotional responses do not require *conscious* thinking. Nevertheless, he says, even instantaneously felt emotions require some sort of quick cognitive appraisal of the situation; otherwise, how do we *know* what we are reacting to? The appraisal may be effortless and we may not be conscious of it, but it is still a function of the mind (Figure 13–13).

Figure 13–13 Emotion and cognition feed each other. But which is the chicken and which the egg? Lazarus believes that, although emotions influence thinking, our cognitive appraisal of a situation always precedes emotion. Zajonc contends that some of our emotional reactions precede cognitive processing.

The more important emotions, such as anger, guilt, happiness, and love, clearly arise from our conscious interpretations, memories, and inferences. Highly emotional people are intense partly because of their interpretations. They *personalize* events as being somehow directed at them and *generalize* their experiences by blowing single incidents out of proportion (Larsen & others, 1987). How we explain good and bad events affects both our emotions and our motivation. Whether we attribute a low grade to an unfair exam, bad luck, or our own inability or laziness determines whether we feel irritated or depressed (Weiner, 1985). Attributing failure to our own inability erodes motivation. If I just don't have it, why try?

For us, the important conclusion concerns what Lazarus and Zajonc agree on: Some emotional responses—especially simple likes, dislikes, and fears—involve no conscious thinking. We may fear the spider, even if we "know" it is harmless. After conditioning, Little Albert was afraid of furry objects. Such responses are hard to alter by changing our thinking.

Other emotions—including moods such as depression and complex feelings such as hatred and love—are greatly affected by our interpretations, memories, and expectations. For these emotions, as we will see in Chapter 16, learning to *think* more positively about ourselves and the world around us makes us *feel* better.

Summing Up

Emotions are psychological responses that involve an interplay among (1) physiological arousal, (2) expressive behaviors, and (3) conscious experience.

The Physiology of Emotion

Arousal Our performance on a task is usually best when arousal is moderate, though this varies with the difficulty of the task.

Physiological States Accompanying Specific Emotions The physical arousal that occurs with one emotion is, in most ways, indistinguishable from arousal that occurs with another. However, scientists have discovered subtle differences in the brain pathways and hormones associated with different emotions.

Lie Detection The polygraph measures several physiological indicators of emotion. Can it therefore detect lies by revealing the tension that one might feel while lying? The polygraph does better than chance, but not nearly well enough to justify its widespread use in business and government.

Expressing Emotion

Nonverbal Communication Much of our communication is through the body's silent language.

Culture and Emotional Expression Is nonverbal language universal? Although some gestures are culturally determined, facial expressions, such as those of happiness and fear, are common the world over. In communal cultures that value interdependence, intense displays of potentially disruptive emotions are infrequent.

The Effects of Facial Expressions Expressions not only communicate emotion, but they also amplify the felt emotion and signal the body to respond accordingly.

Experiencing Emotion

Among various human emotions, we looked closely at how we experience three: fear, anger, and happiness.

Fear Fear is an adaptive emotion, but it can be traumatic. Although we seem biologically predisposed to acquire some fears, what we learn through experience best explains the variety of human fears.

Anger Anger is most often aroused by events that are not only frustrating or insulting but also interpreted as willful and unjustified. Other negative emotions, such as depression, can also feed anger. Although blowing off steam may be temporarily calming, it does not, in the long run, reduce anger. Expressing anger can actually arouse more anger.

Happiness A good mood boosts people's perceptions of the world and their willingness to help others. The moods triggered by the day's good or bad events seldom last beyond that day. Even significant good events, such as a substantial raise in income, seldom increase happiness for long. We can explain the relativity of happiness with the adaptation-level and relative-deprivation principles. Nevertheless, some people are usually happier than others, and researchers have identified factors that predict such happiness.

Theories of Emotion

The James-Lange and Cannon-Bard Theories One of the oldest theoretical controversies regarding emotion is whether we feel emotion *after* we notice our body responses (as James and Lange proposed) or *when* our bodies respond (as Cannon and Bard believed).

Cognition and Emotion A more recent controversy among emotion researchers concerns whether we can experience human emotions apart from cognition. Can we feel before we think? Stanley Schachter's two-factor theory of emotion contends that the cognitive labels we put on our states of arousal are an essential ingredient of emotion. Richard Lazarus agrees that cognition is essential: Many important emotions arise from our interpretations or inferences. Robert Zajonc, however, believes that some simple emotional responses occur instantly, not only outside of conscious awareness but before any cognitive processing occurs. The issue has practical implications: To the degree that emotions are rooted in thinking, we can hope to change them by changing our thinking.

Terms and Concepts to Remember

① emotion A response of the whole organism, involving (1) physical arousal, (2) expressive behaviors, and (3) conscious experience.

polygraph A machine, commonly used in attempts to detect lies, that measures several of the physiological responses accompanying emotion (such as perspiration, heart rate, and breathing changes).

catharsis Emotional release. In psychology, the catharsis hypothesis maintains that "releasing" aggressive energy (through action or fantasy) relieves aggressive urges.

adaptation-level phenomenon The tendency for our judgments (of sounds, of lights, of income) to be relative to a "neutral" level defined by our experience.

relative deprivation The perception that one is worse off relative to those with whom one compares oneself.

② James-Lange theory The theory that our experience of emotion is our awareness of our physiological responses to emotion-arousing stimuli.

③ Cannon-Bard theory The theory that an emotion-arousing stimulus simultaneously triggers (1) physiological responses and (2) the subjective experience of emotion.

④ two-factor theory Schachter's theory that to experience emotion one must (1) be physically aroused and (2) cognitively label the arousal.

For Further Reading

Carlson, J. G., & Hatfield, E. (1989). *Psychology of emotion*. Belmont, CA: Wadsworth.

A delightfully down-to-earth account of the biology and psychology of emotion, from anger to depression to joy.

Darwin, C. (1872/1965). *The expression of the emotions in man and animals*. Chicago: University of Chicago Press.

The classic description of emotional expressions and their adaptive functions.

Ekman, P. (1985). *Telling lies: Clues to deceit in the marketplace, politics, and marriage*. New York: Norton.

A fascinating book about how our faces and gestures communicate emotion and betray actual feelings.

Myers, D. G. (1992). *Searching for joy: Who is happy—and why*. New York: William Morrow.

A look at the things that do and don't predict happiness, and how you can use this knowledge to enhance your own well-being.

Tavris, C. (1984). *Anger: The misunderstood emotion*. New York: Simon & Schuster.

A provocative, beautifully written summary of research that points to the dangers of unrestrained expression of anger.

Part Six

Personality, Disorder, and Well-Being

Each of us is unique. In Chapter 14, Personality, we explore four influential perspectives on how we come to have our own unique personalities and how we can best understand and describe human personality. In Chapter 15, Psychological Disorders, we delve into how and why people are labeled "disordered," and we consider the symptoms and causes of major disorders such as depression and schizophrenia. In Chapter 16, Therapy, we review the major approaches to treating psychological disorders and take a hard look at their effectiveness. Finally, in Chapter 17, Stress and Health, we describe new research on how our behavior and emotions affect our health and how we can promote our own health and well-being.

Personality

Chapter 14

Novelist William Faulkner was a master at creating characters with vivid personalities.[1] One of his creations, Ike McCaslin, appears at various ages in more than a dozen novels and short stories. Ike is highly principled, and consistently so. At age 10 he feels a deep reverence for the wilderness and its creatures. At 21 he forfeits a "tainted" inheritance. In his late seventies he counsels his nephew to use his land responsibly. Ike the adult is an extension of Ike the child.

Another Faulkner character, Jason Compson, is a selfish, whining 4-year-old in the opening section of *The Sound and the Fury*, and a selfish, screaming 34-year-old as the novel closes. As head of the Compson household, he verbally abuses family members and household servants. Lying, threatening, conniving, he is a self-centered child who has become a self-centered adult.

Faulkner's characters, as they appear and reappear throughout his fiction, exhibit the distinctiveness and consistency that define personality. Having emphasized in the preceding chapters how we are similar—how we develop, perceive, learn, remember, think, and feel—we now acknowledge that each of us has an individual personality. Your **personality** is your characteristic pattern of thinking, feeling, and acting. If your behavior pattern is unusually distinctive and consistent—if, say, you are strikingly outgoing, whether at a party or in a classroom—people are likely to say that you have a "strong" personality.

Actually, much of this book deals with personality. We have considered biological influences on personality, personality development across the life span, and personality-related aspects of learning, motivation, and emotion. In later chapters we will study disorders of personality, personal and physical well-being, and social influences on personality.

In this chapter we explore and evaluate four major perspectives that seek to explain personality:

Sigmund Freud's *psychoanalytic* theory emphasizes childhood sexuality and unconscious motivations as possible causes of personality.

Trait researchers identify specific dimensions of our personality.

---

[1] Faulkner scholar Nancy Taylor assisted with these examples.

The *humanistic* approach focuses on our inner capacities for growth and self-fulfillment.

Social-cognitive psychologists emphasize how we shape and are shaped by interaction with our environment.

Each perspective offers a distinct view of personality that provides valuable insights and increases our understanding.

The Psychoanalytic Perspective

Well before entering the University of Vienna in 1873, the youthful Sigmund Freud showed signs of the independence and brilliance that often mark people of eminence. He had a prodigious memory. He so loved serious reading that he once ran up a bookstore debt beyond his means, feeding his insatiable interest in playwrights, poets, and philosophers—Goethe, Shakespeare, Kant, Hegel, and Nietzsche among them. As a teen he often took his evening meal in his tiny bedroom, to lose no time from his studies.

After medical school, Freud began a private practice, specializing in nervous disorders. Before long, however, he faced patients whose disorders made no neurological sense. A patient might have lost all feeling in her hand—yet there is no sensory nerve that when damaged would numb the entire hand and nothing else. Noting that hypnosis could also produce such symptoms, Freud wondered whether they might be psychologically rather than physiologically caused. His wonderings set his mind running in a direction that was destined to change human self-understanding.

Freud wrote about his views, which evolved as he treated patients and analyzed himself, in 24 volumes published between 1888 and 1939. Although his first solo book, *The Interpretation of Dreams* (1900), sold but 600 copies in its first 8 years, his ideas gradually began to attract many followers—and intense criticism. For now, let us reserve judgment on Freud's theory and try to see things as he did. It is difficult to summarize 24 volumes in a few pages, but we will highlight Freud's psychoanalytic theory—the first comprehensive theory of personality.

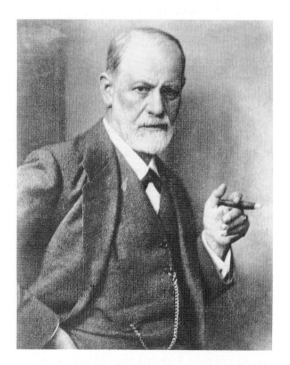

Sigmund Freud (1856–1939): "I was the only worker in a new field."

Exploring the Unconscious

To explore the possible psychological roots of nervous disorders, Freud spent several months in Paris studying with Jean Charcot, a French neurologist who was using hypnosis to treat patients suffering from these disorders. On returning to Vienna, Freud began to hypnotize his patients, encouraging them while hypnotized to talk freely about themselves and the circumstances surrounding the onset of their symptoms. Often the patients responded openly, at times becoming quite agitated during the hypnotic experience. Sometimes their symptoms diminished or even disappeared.

It was in this way that Freud "discovered" the unconscious. Piecing together his patients' accounts of their lives, he decided that the loss of feeling in one's hand might be caused by, say, the fear of touching one's genitals; that blindness or deafness might be caused by not wanting to see or hear something that aroused intense anxiety. In time, Freud began to see patients with a variety of symptoms. Given patients' uneven capacity for hypnosis, he turned to **free association**—in which he merely told the patient to relax and say whatever came to mind, no matter how embarrassing or trivial. Freud believed that free association produced a chain of thought leading into the patient's unconscious, thereby retrieving and releasing painful unconscious memories, often from childhood. Freud called the process **psychoanalysis**.

Underlying Freud's psychoanalytic conception of personality was his belief that the mind is like an iceberg—mostly hidden. Our conscious awareness is the part of the iceberg that floats above the surface. Below the surface is a much larger, **unconscious** region containing thoughts, wishes, feelings, and memories, of which we are largely unaware. Some of these thoughts we store temporarily in a **preconscious** area, from which we can retrieve them at will into conscious awareness. Of greater interest to Freud was the mass of unacceptable passions and thoughts that we *repress*—forcibly block from our consciousness because they would be so painful to acknowledge. Although we are not consciously aware of these troublesome feelings and ideas, Freud believed they powerfully influence us. In his view, our unacknowledged impulses express themselves in disguised forms—the work we choose, the beliefs we hold, our daily habits, our troubling symptoms. In such ways, the unconscious seeps into our thoughts and actions.

Freud believed he glimpsed the unconscious not only in people's free associations, beliefs, habits, and symptoms but also in their dreams and slips of the tongue and pen. Slips while reading, writing, and speaking suggested to Freud that what we say and do may reflect the workings of our unconscious minds. Consider his example of a financially stressed patient who, not wanting any large pills, said, "Please do not give me any bills, because I cannot swallow them." Jokes, too, he viewed as a way to express repressed sexual and aggressive tendencies. For Freud the determinist, nothing was ever accidental.

Dreams, he contended, are a major outlet for people's unconscious wishes. The remembered content of dreams (their "manifest content"—see page 198) he believed to be a censored expression of those wishes (the dream's "latent content"). For Freud, dreams were the "royal road to the unconscious." By analyzing people's dreams, Freud believed he could reveal the nature of their inner conflicts and release their inner tensions.

Personality Structure For Freud, human personality—its emotions, strivings, and ideas—arises from a conflict between our aggressive, pleasure-seeking biological impulses and the social restraints against them. In his view, personality results from our efforts to resolve this basic conflict—to express these impulses in ways that bring satisfaction without also bringing guilt or punishment.

Freud theorized that the conflict centers on three interacting systems, id, ego, and superego. Like intelligence and memory, these are abstract psychological concepts (Figure 14–1). They are, said Freud, "useful aids to understanding" that he proposed to help explain the mind's dynamics.

The **id** is a reservoir of unconscious psychic energy that constantly strives to satisfy basic drives to survive, reproduce, and aggress. The id operates on the **pleasure principle**: If unconstrained by reality, it seeks immediate gratification. Think of newborn infants, who, governed by the id, cry out for satisfaction the moment they feel a need, caring nothing for the outside world's conditions and demands.

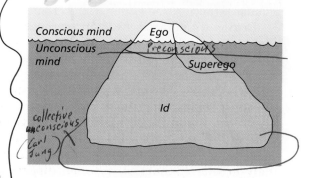

"*Good morning, beheaded—uh, I mean beloved.*"
Drawing by Fradon; ©1983 The New Yorker Magazine, Inc.

Figure 14–1 Freud's idea of the mind's structure. Consciousness is like an iceberg's visible tip. Note that the id is totally unconscious, but ego and superego operate both consciously and unconsciously. (Adapted from Freud, 1933, p. 111.)

As the **ego** develops, the young child learns to cope with the real world. The ego operates on the **reality principle**, which seeks to gratify the id's impulses in realistic ways that will bring long-term pleasure rather than pain or destruction. Imagine what would happen if, lacking an ego, we expressed our unrestrained sexual or aggressive impulses whenever we felt them. The ego, which contains our partly conscious perceptions, thoughts, judgments, and memories, is the personality "executive." It decides on our actions as it intervenes among the impulsive demands of the id, the restraining demands of the superego, and the real-life demands of the external world.

Beginning around age 4 or 5, a child's ego recognizes the demands of the newly emerging **superego**. The superego is a voice of conscience that forces the ego to consider not only the real but the ideal. Its sole focus is on how one *ought* to behave. The superego develops as we internalize the morals and values of parents and culture, thereby providing both our sense of right and wrong and our ideals. It strives for perfection and judges our actions, producing positive feelings of pride or negative feelings of guilt. Someone with an exceptionally strong superego may be continually upright yet ironically guilt-ridden; another with a weak superego may be wantonly self-indulgent and remorseless. Because the superego's demands often oppose the id's, the ego struggles to reconcile the two. The chaste student who is sexually attracted to someone and joins a volunteer organization to work alongside the desired person, satisfies both id and superego.

Personality Development Analysis of his patients' histories convinced Freud that personality forms during life's first few years. Again and again his patients' symptoms seemed rooted in unresolved conflicts from early childhood. He concluded that children pass through a series of **psychosexual stages** during which the id's pleasure-seeking energies focus on distinct pleasure-sensitive areas of the body called "erogenous zones" (Table 14–1).

During the **oral stage**, which lasts throughout the first 18 months, the infant's sensual pleasures focus on sucking, biting, and chewing.

During the **anal stage**, from about 18 months to 3 years, the sphincter muscles become sensitive and controllable, and bowel and bladder retention and elimination become a source of gratification.

During the **phallic stage**, from roughly ages 3 to 6 years, the pleasure zone shifts to the genitals. Freud believed that during this stage boys seek genital stimulation and develop both unconscious sexual desires for their mother and jealousy and hatred for their father, whom they consider a rival. Boys also were said to feel guilt and a lurking fear that their father would punish them, such as by castration. Freud called this collection of feelings the **Oedipus complex** after the Greek legend of Oedipus, who unknowingly killed his father and married his mother. Although some psychoanalysts believed that girls experience a parallel "Electra complex," Freud (1931, p. 229) said no: "It is only in the male child that we find the fateful combination of love for the one parent and simultaneous hatred for the other as a rival."

Children eventually cope with these threatening feelings by repressing them and by identifying with (trying to become like) the rival parent. It's as if something inside the child decides, "If you can't beat 'em (the parent of the same sex), join 'em." Through this

"Fifty is plenty."

"Hundred and fifty."

Drawing by Woodman; © 1987 The New Yorker Magazine, Inc.

Table 14–1	*Freud's Psychosexual Stages*
Stage	**Focus**
Oral (0–18 months)	Pleasure centers on the mouth—sucking, biting, chewing
Anal (18–36 months)	Pleasure focuses on bowel/bladder elimination; coping with demands for control
Phallic (3–6 years)	Pleasure zone is the genitals; coping with incestuous sexual feelings
Latency (6 to puberty)	Repressed sexual feelings
Genital (puberty on)	Maturation of sexual interests

identification process children's superegos gain strength as they incorporate many of their parents' values. Freud believed that identification with the same-sex parent provides our **gender identity** —our sense of being male or female.

With their sexual feelings repressed and redirected, children enter a **latency stage**. Freud maintained that during latency, extending from around age 6 to puberty, sexuality is dormant and children play mostly with peers of the same sex.

At puberty, latency gives way to the final stage, the **genital stage**, as youths begin to experience sexual feelings toward others.

In Freud's view, maladaptive behavior in the adult results from conflicts unresolved during earlier psychosexual stages. At any point in the oral, anal, or phallic stage, strong conflict can lock, or **fixate**, the person's pleasure-seeking energies in that stage. Thus, people who were either orally overindulged or deprived (perhaps by abrupt, early weaning) might fixate at the oral stage. Orally fixated adults are said to exhibit either passive dependence (like that of a nursing infant) or an exaggerated denial of this dependence—perhaps by acting tough and uttering biting sarcasm. They might also continue to seek oral gratification through excessive smoking and eating. Those who never quite resolve the anal conflict, between the desire to eliminate at will and the demands of toilet training, may be either messy and disorganized ("anal expulsive") or highly controlled and compulsively neat ("anal retentive"). In such ways, believed Freud, the twig of personality is bent at an early age.

Defense Mechanisms To live in social groups, we cannot act out our sexual and aggressive impulses willy-nilly. We must control them. When the ego fears losing control of the inner war between the demands of the id and the superego, the result is anxiety. Anxiety, said Freud, is the price we pay for civilization.

Unlike specific fears, the dark cloud of anxiety is unfocused. Anxiety is therefore hard to cope with, as when we feel unsettled but are not sure why. Freud proposed that the ego protects itself against anxiety with ego **defense mechanisms**. Defense mechanisms reduce or redirect anxiety in various ways, but always by distorting reality. Some examples:

Repression banishes anxiety-arousing thoughts and feelings from consciousness. According to Freud, repression underlies the other defense mechanisms, all of which disguise threatening impulses and keep them from reaching consciousness. Freud believed that repression explains why we do not remember our childhood lust for our parent of the other sex. However, he also believed that repression is often incomplete, with the repressed urges seeping out in dream symbols and slips of the tongue.

We also cope with anxiety through **regression**—retreating to an earlier, more infantile stage of development where some of our psychic energies still fixate. Thus, when facing the anxious first days of school, a child may regress to the oral comfort of thumb sucking or nail biting. Juvenile monkeys, when anxious, retreat to infantile clinging to their mothers or to one another (Suomi, 1987). Even homesick new college students may long for the security and comfort of home.

In **reaction formation**, the ego unconsciously makes unacceptable impulses look like their opposites. En route to consciousness, the unacceptable proposition "I hate him" becomes "I love him." Timidity becomes daring. Feelings of inadequacy become

Faced with a mild stress, anxious children and monkeys will regress, by retreating to the comfort of earlier behaviors.

bravado. According to the principle behind this defense mechanism, vehement social crusaders, such as those who urgently campaign against gay rights, may be motivated by the very sexual desires against which they are crusading.

Projection disguises threatening impulses by attributing them to others. Thus, "He hates me" may be a projection of the actual feeling "I hate him" or "I hate myself." According to Freudian theory, racial prejudice may be the result of projecting one's own unacceptable impulses or characteristics onto members of another group. (As you can imagine, reaction formation and projection have sometimes provided a handy way to ridicule other people's motives.)

The familiar mechanism of **rationalization** lets us unconsciously generate self-justifying explanations so we can hide from ourselves the real reasons for our actions. Thus, habitual drinkers may say they drink with their friends "just to be sociable." Students who fail to study may rationalize, "All work and no play makes Jack [or Jill] a dull person."

Displacement diverts one's sexual or aggressive impulses toward a more psychologically acceptable object than the one that aroused them. Children who can't express anger against their parents may displace their anger onto the family pet. Students upset over an exam may snap at their roommate.

Sublimation is the transformation of unacceptable impulses into socially valued motivations. Sublimation is therefore socially adaptive and may even be a wellspring for great cultural and artistic achievements. Freud suggested that Leonardo da Vinci's paintings of Madonnas were a sublimation of his longing for intimacy with his mother, who was separated from him at an early age.

Note again that all these defense mechanisms function indirectly and unconsciously. They reduce anxiety by disguising our threatening impulses. We never say, "I'm feeling anxious; I'd better project my sexual or hostile feelings onto someone else." Defense mechanisms would not work if we recognized them. As the body unconsciously defends itself against disease, so, believed Freud, the ego unconsciously defends itself against anxiety.

Freud's Descendants and Dissenters Although Freud was known to change his mind, he was deeply committed to his ideas and principles, even in the face of harsh criticism. Although controversial, his writings soon attracted followers, mostly young, ambitious physicians who formed an inner circle around their strong-minded leader. From time to time sparks flew, and one member or another would leave or be outcast. Even the ideas of the outcasts, however, reflected Freud's influence.

These pioneering psychoanalysts and others, whom we now call "neo-Freudians," accepted Freud's basic ideas: the personality structures of id, ego, and superego; the importance of the unconscious; the shaping of personality in childhood; and the dynamics of anxiety and the defense mechanisms. But they differed with Freud in two important ways. First, they placed more emphasis on the role of the conscious mind in interpreting experience and coping with the environment. What's more, they doubted that sex and aggression were all-consuming motivations. Instead, they placed more emphasis on loftier motives and on social interaction, as the following examples illustrate.

"The lady doth protest too much, methinks."
William Shakespeare
Hamlet, 1600

Alfred Adler (*Problems of Neurosis*, 1964): "The individual feels at home in life and feels his existence to be worthwhile just so far as he is useful to others and is overcoming feelings of inferiority."

Karen Horney (*Feminine Psychology*, 1923–1937): "The view that women are infantile and emotional creatures, and as such, incapable of responsibility and independence is the work of the masculine tendency to lower women's self-respect."

Alfred Adler and Karen Horney agreed with Freud that childhood is important. But they believed that childhood *social*, not sexual, tensions are crucial for personality formation. Adler, who himself struggled to overcome childhood illnesses and accidents, said that much of our behavior is driven by an effort to conquer childhood feelings of inferiority, feelings that trigger strivings for superiority and power. (It was Adler who proposed the still-popular idea of the "inferiority complex.") Horney said that childhood anxiety, caused by the dependent child's sense of helplessness, triggers the desire for love and security. In countering Freud's assumptions that women have weak superegos and suffer "penis envy," Horney sought to balance the bias she detected in this masculine view of psychology.

Erich Fromm and other "ego psychologists" agreed with Freud that the ego is important. But in deemphasizing sexual and aggressive impulses, they viewed the ego as more than a mediator between id and superego. The ego, they said, strives for unity and love, for truth and freedom; such conscious strivings are not merely a sublimation of baser motives.

Erik Erikson agreed with Freud that development proceeds through a series of critical stages. But he believed these are psycho*social*, not psycho*sexual*, stages. As we noted in Chapters 3 and 4, Erikson also argued that life's developmental stages encompass the whole life span. He maintained that infancy is a time for establishing basic trust, adolescence for establishing an identity. In adulthood, he contended, people strive first for intimacy with another; then for generativity (a feeling of productivity through family and work); and finally for integrity (a sense that their lives have been meaningful).

Unlike these other neo-Freudians, Carl Jung—Freud's disciple-turned-dissenter—placed less emphasis on social factors and agreed with Freud that the unconscious exerts a powerful influence. But to Jung, the unconscious contains more than a person's repressed thoughts and feelings. There is also a **collective unconscious**, he believed, a common reservoir of images derived from our early ancestors' universal experiences. Jung said that the collective unconscious explains why, for many people, spiritual concerns are deep-rooted and why people in different cultures share certain myths and images, such as that of mother as a symbol of nurturance.

"The female . . . acknowledges the fact of her castration, and with it, too, the superiority of the male and her own inferiority; but she rebels against this unwelcome state of affairs."
Sigmund Freud
Female Sexuality, 1931

Carl Jung (*Symbols of Transformation*, 1912): "We can keep from a child all knowledge of earlier myths, but we cannot take from him the need for mythology."

Assessing the Unconscious

Those who study personality or provide therapy need ways to evaluate personality characteristics. Different personality theories imply different methods of assessment.

Freud's theory maintains that the significant influences on our personalities arise from the unconscious, which contains residues from early childhood experiences. Psychoanalysts therefore dismiss objective assessment tools, such as agree-disagree or true-false questionnaires, as merely tapping the conscious surface. Needed is a sort of psychological x-ray—a test that can see through our surface pretensions and reveal our hidden conflicts and impulses.

Projective tests aim to provide such a view, by providing people with an ambiguous stimulus and then asking them to describe it or tell a story about it. The stimulus has no inherent meaning, so whatever meaning people read into it presumably reflects their interests and conflicts. Henry Murray (1933) demonstrated a possible basis for such a test at a house party hosted by his 11-year-old daughter. Murray got the children to play a frightening game called "Murder." When shown some photographs after the game, the children perceived the photos as more malicious than they had before the game.

These children, it seemed to Murray, had *projected* their inner feelings into the pictures. A few years later, Murray introduced the **Thematic Apperception Test (TAT)**—ambiguous pictures about which people make up stories. As you may recall from page 371, one use of the TAT has been to assess achievement motivation. Shown a daydreaming boy, those who imagine him fantasizing an achievement are presumed to be projecting their own concerns.

There are now a variety of projective tests. These tests ask subjects to draw a person, to complete sentences ("My mother . . ."), or to provide the first word that comes to mind after the examiner says a test word. Most widely used is the famous **Rorschach inkblot test**, introduced in 1921 by Swiss psychiatrist Hermann Rorschach. The test assumes that what we see in its 10 inkblots reflects our inner feelings and conflicts. If we see fierce animals or weapons, the examiner may infer that we have aggressive tendencies.

Is this a reasonable assumption? If so, can a psychologist use the Rorschach to understand one's personality and diagnose an

"The forward thrust of the antlers shows a determined personality, yet the small sun indicates a lack of self-confidence. . . ."

© 1983 by Sidney Harris; American Scientist Magazine.

This psychologist presumes that the hopes, fears, and interests expressed in this boy's descriptions of a series of ambiguous pictures in the Thematic Apperception Test (TAT) are projections of his inner feelings.

emotional disorder? Recall from our discussion of the intelligence tests the two primary criteria of a good test: reliability and validity. On those criteria, how good is the Rorschach?

Most researchers have considered it not very good (Peterson, 1978). There is no one accepted system for scoring and interpreting the test, so unless two raters have been trained in the same scoring system, their agreement on the results of any given test may be minimal. Nor is the test very successful at predicting behavior or at discriminating between groups (for example, identifying who is suicidal and who is not).

Although not as popular as it once was, the Rorschach remains one of the most widely used psychological instruments (Lubin & others, 1984; Piotrowski & Keller, 1989). Some clinicians continue to be confident of the test's validity—not as a device that by itself can provide a diagnosis, but as a source of suggestive leads that supplement other information. Other clinicians believe that even if the Rorschach scoring systems have little validity, the test is still an icebreaker and a revealing interview technique. Promising new research-based, computer-aided scoring and interpretation tools are improving agreement among raters and enhancing the test's validity (Exner, 1986; Parker & others, 1988). But Freud himself would probably have been uncomfortable with trying to assign each patient a test score and more interested in the therapist-patient interactions that take place during the test.

This woman is taking the most familiar projective test, the Rorschach. Although its reliability and validity are questionable, the Rorschach test is still widely used. Some researchers are working to make its scoring and interpretation more objective.

Evaluating the Psychoanalytic Perspective

Knowing what you do about Freud's ideas, listen now to his critics. Bear in mind that we critique Freud from the perspective of the late twentieth century, a perspective that is itself subject to revision. Freud died in 1939 without the benefit of all that we have since learned about human development, thinking, and emotion and without today's research tools. To criticize Freud's theories by comparing them with current concepts is like comparing Henry Ford's Model T with today's Escort.

⌐*Freud's Ideas in Light of Modern Research*⌐Recent theories and research contradict many of Freud's specific ideas. Research indicates that human development is lifelong, not fixed in childhood. Developmental psychologists also question Freud's idea that conscience and gender identity form as the child resolves the Oedipus complex at age 5 or 6. Children gain their gender identity earlier. They become strongly masculine or feminine even without a same-sex parent present (Frieze & others, 1978). Freud's ideas about childhood sexuality arose from his rejection of stories of childhood sexual abuse told by his female patients—stories he thought were an expression of their own childhood sexual wishes and conflicts. Today we take reports of sexual abuse seriously. Freud's ideas about the natural superiority of men are widely discounted and considered sexist.

As we saw in Chapter 7, new ideas about why we dream dispute Freud's belief that dreams disguise and fulfill wishes. His belief that repression causes forgetting gains support from reports of memory loss among victims of war trauma and sexual abuse, but other mechanisms of forgetting account for most memory loss (pages 277–279). Even slips of the tongue can be explained as competition between similar verbal choices in our memory network (page 273). Researchers find little support for Freud's idea that people protect themselves against painful self-knowledge by projecting their own unrecognized negative impulses onto others (Holmes, 1978, 1981). And Jerome Kagan (1989) notes that history has been equally unkind to Freud's idea that sexual repression causes psychological disorder. From Freud's time to ours, sexual repression has diminished, but psychological disorders have not.

History has been kinder to Freud's "iceberg" view of the mind, at least in part. We now know that we indeed have limited access to all that goes on in our minds (Erdelyi, 1985, 1988; Kihlstrom, 1990). However, the "iceberg" notion held by today's research psychologists differs from Freud's. As we saw in earlier chapters, many researchers think of the unconscious not as seething passions and repressive censoring but as information processing that occurs without our awareness. To them, the unconscious involves the schemas that automatically control our perceptions and interpretations; the processing of stimuli to which we have not consciously attended; the right hemisphere activity that enables the split-brain patient's left hand to carry out an instruction the patient cannot verbalize; the simultaneous parallel processing of different aspects of vision and thinking; the implicit memories that operate without need for conscious recall; the conditioned emotions that activate instantly. This understanding of unconscious information processing is more like the pre-Freudian view of the unconscious—from which, for example, spontaneous creative ideas surfaced from an underground stream of thought.

Freud's Ideas as Scientific Theory Psychologists also criticize Freud's theory for its scientific shortcomings. As we noted in Chapter 1, good scientific theories explain observations and offer testable hypotheses. Freud's theory, say the critics, rests on few objective observations and offers few hypotheses to verify or reject. (For Freud, his own recollections and interpretations of patients' free associations, dreams, and slips were evidence enough.)

The most serious problem with Freud's theory, according to critics, is that it offers after-the-fact explanations of any characteristic (of one person's smoking, another's fear of horses, another's sexual orientation), yet fails to *predict* such behavior and traits. If you feel angry at your mother's death, you support the theory because "your unresolved childhood dependency needs are threatened." If you do not feel angry, you again support the theory because "you are repressing your anger." That, said Calvin Hall and Gardner Lindzey (1978, p. 68), "is like betting on a horse after the race has been run." After-the-fact interpretation is perfectly appropriate for historical and literary scholarship, which helps explain Freud's currently greater influence on literary criticism than on psychological research. But in science a good theory makes testable predictions.

Such criticisms of Freud's specific concepts and after-the-fact interpretations have led some modern critics to scorn his theory. Peter Medawar (1982, pp. 71–72) compared it to "a dinosaur . . . one of the saddest and strangest of all landmarks in the history of twentieth-century thought." Perhaps we can evaluate Freud less harshly, for three reasons:

1. To criticize Freudian theory for not making testable predictions is like criticizing baseball for not being aerobic exercise. Is it fair to fault something for not being what it was never intended to be? Freud never claimed that psychoanalysis was predic-

"We are arguing like a man who should say, 'If there were an invisible cat in that chair, the chair would look empty; but the chair does look empty; therefore there is an invisible cat in it.'"
C. S. Lewis
Four Loves, 1958

Freud's consulting room was rich with antiquities from around the world, including artwork related to his ideas about our unconscous motives. His famous couch, piled high with pillows, placed patients in a comfortable, reclining position.

tive science. He merely claimed that, looking back, psychoanalysts could find meaning in our state of mind (Rieff, 1979).

2. Some of Freud's ideas are enduring. It was Freud who drew our attention to the unconscious and the irrational, to anxiety and our struggle to cope with it, to the importance of human sexuality, and to the tension between our biological impulses and our social well-being. It was Freud who challenged our self-righteousness, punctured our pretensions, and reminded us of our potential for evil. Few dispute that Freud's ideas were creative, courageous, and comprehensive.

3. Correctly, or incorrectly, Freud influenced our view of human nature. Rightly or wrongly, some ideas that many of us assume to be true—that childhood experiences mold personality, that many behaviors have disguised motives, that dreams have symbolic meaning—are Freud's legacy, which lives on in our own ideas. As Peter Drucker (1982) remarked, "[Many] psychologists have no use for Freud, and I have some grave doubts about him, but he is the only one who created vision and insight and changed our view of ourselves and of the world." For that, Sigmund Freud continues to rank as one of modern history's towering intellectual figures.

The Trait Perspective

Psychoanalytic theory explains personality in terms of the dynamics that underlie behavior. It peers beneath the surface in search of hidden motives. In 1919, Gordon Allport, a curious 22-year-old psychology student, interviewed Freud in Vienna and discovered just how preoccupied the founder of psychoanalysis was with finding hidden motives.

> Soon after I had entered the famous red burlap room with pictures of dreams on the wall, he summoned me to his inner office. He did not speak to me but sat in expectant silence, for me to state my mission. I was not prepared for silence and had to think fast to find a suitable conversational gambit. I told him of an episode on the tram car on my way to his office. A small boy about four years of age had displayed a conspicuous dirt phobia. He kept saying to his mother, "I don't want to sit there . . . don't let that dirty man sit beside me." To him everything was *schmutzig* (filthy). His mother was a well-starched *Hausfrau*, so dominant and purposive looking that I thought the cause and effect apparent.
>
> When I finished my story Freud fixed his kindly therapeutic eyes upon me and said, "And was that little boy you?" Flabbergasted and

feeling a bit guilty, I contrived to change the subject. While Freud's misunderstanding of my motivation was amusing, it also started a deep train of thought (1967, pp. 7–8).

That train of thought ultimately led Allport to do what Freud did not do—to describe personality in terms of fundamental **traits**—people's characteristic behaviors and conscious motives (such as the professional curiosity that actually motivated Allport to see Freud). Meeting Freud, said Allport, "taught me that [psychoanalysis], for all its merits, may plunge too deep, and that psychologists would do well to give full recognition to manifest motives before probing the unconscious." Allport therefore defined personality in terms of identifiable behavior patterns. He was less concerned with *explaining* and more concerned with *describing* individual traits.

How do psychologists describe and classify personalities? An analogy may help. Imagine that you want to describe and classify apples. Someone might correctly say that every apple is unique. Still, you might find it useful to begin by classifying apples as distinct *types*—Delicious, Granny Smith, McIntosh, and so forth. That is how the ancient Greeks described personality—by classifying people according to four types. Depending on which of one's bodily "humors," or fluids, they believed to predominate, they declared people either melancholic (depressed), sanguine (cheerful), phlegmatic (unemotional), or choleric (irritable).

Although this classification system indeed seems humorous, recent ideas of personality types have met with greater success. Based on children's physiological and psychological reactivity, Jerome Kagan (1989b) classifies children's temperaments—as either shy-inhibited or fearless-uninhibited types. Some health psychologists find it useful to classify people as intense, "Type A," or as laid back, "Type B" personalities (pages 519–520).

Psychologist William Sheldon (1954) classified people by body type. Santa Claus typifies the plump "endomorph": relaxed and jolly. Superman typifies the muscular "mesomorph": bold and physically active. Sherlock Holmes typifies the thin "ectomorph": high strung and solitary. Are different body types actually associated with different personalities? When researchers assess people's body types and personalities separately, there is a linkage, but it is modest. The stereotypes of the chubby, happy-go-lucky person and of the muscular, confident person turn out to be just that—stereotypes that exaggerate a kernel of truth (Tucker, 1983).

More popular today, especially in business and career counseling, is an effort to classify people according to Carl Jung's personality types, based on their responses to 126 questions written by Isabel Briggs Myers (1987) and her mother, Kathleen Briggs. The "Myers-Briggs Type Indicator" is quite simple. It gives choices to its 2 million annual takers, such as, "Do you usually value sentiment more than logic, or value logic more than sentiment?" Then it counts their preferences, labels them as indicating, say, a "feeling" or "thinking" type, and describes each type in complimentary terms. Feeling types, for example, are told they are sensitive to values and "sympathetic, appreciative, and tactful"; thinking types are told they "prefer an objective standard of truth" and are "good at analyzing." Most people therefore readily embrace their announced type profile—which mirrors their declared preferences—and may accept it as a basis for being matched with work partners and tasks that supposedly suit their temperaments.

Personality traits can be fundamental to job performance. The outgoing temperament so vital to being a standup comedian would probably not be necessary for a stone carver.

Exploring Traits

If classifying people as one distinct personality type or another fails to fully capture their individuality, how else can we describe their personalities? We can perceive hundreds of thousands of colors with just three color dimensions (hue, saturation, and brightness). To return to our apple analogy, we might describe an apple along several trait dimensions—as relatively large or small, red or yellow, sweet or sour. By placing people on several trait dimensions simultaneously, psychologists similarly describe countless individual personality variations.

What trait dimensions describe personality? Allport and his associate H. S. Odbert (1936) literally counted all the words in an unabridged dictionary with which one could describe people. The list numbered almost 18,000 words! How, then, could psychologists condense the list to a manageable number of basic traits?

One way has been to propose traits, such as anxiety, that some theory regards as basic. A newer technique is *factor analysis*, the statistical procedure described in Chapter 11 to identify clusters of test items that tap basic components of intelligence (such as spatial ability, reasoning ability, or verbal skill). Imagine that people who describe themselves as outgoing also tend to say they like excitement and practical jokes, and that they do not like quiet reading. Such a statistically correlated cluster of behaviors reflects a basic trait, or factor. In this particular case, the identified items are part of a cluster that make up a trait called [*extraversion.*]

British psychologists Hans and Sybil Eysenck believe that we can reduce many of our normal individual variations to two genetically influenced dimensions: *extraversion-introversion* and *emotional stability-instability* (Figure 14–2). The Eysenck Personality Questionnaire has been given to people in 35 countries around the world, from China to Uganda to the USSR. When people's answers are analyzed, the extraversion and emotionality factors inevitably emerge as basic personality dimensions (Eysenck, 1990). Extraverts, they contend, seek stimulation because their normal levels of brain arousal are relatively low. Emotionally stable people react calmly because their autonomic nervous systems are not so reactive as those of unstable people.

Many other trait theorists, too, view personality traits as biologically rooted. Like Eysenck, Jerome Kagan (page 422) attributes differences in children's shyness and inhibition to their autonomic reactivity. Twin and adoption studies of genetic influences on personality traits (pages 87–90) further testify to biology's influence, while reminding us that behavior patterns form as a person's genetic endowment interacts with a particular environment.

Most researchers believe the Eysencks' dimensions are important, but don't tell the whole story of someone's personality. They offer a slightly expanded set of factors—dubbed the "Big Five" (Goldberg, 1990; John, 1990). If a test specifies where you are on the five dimensions of Table 14–2 (page 424), it has said much of what there is to say about your personality. Moreover, whether describing others or themselves, people's natural language reflects these five dimensions (Dingman, 1990; Watson, 1989). In different languages and cultures, people notice and name slightly varying traits (Church & Katigbak, 1989; Yang & Bond, 1990). Yet around the world people describe others in terms roughly consistent with the Big Five—how agreeable they are, how extraverted they are,

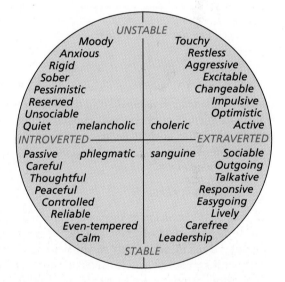

Figure 14-2 In this chart, various combinations of the Eysencks' two primary personality factors—extraversion-introversion and stability-instability—are used to define other, more specific traits. Note that the four basic combinations of the two factors resemble the personality types proposed by the ancient Greeks, which are noted in the center of the chart. (From Eysenck & Eysenck, 1963.)

Table 14–2	*The "Big Five" Personality Factors*

Trait dimension	Description
Emotional stability	Calm versus anxious Secure versus insecure Self-satisfied versus self-pitying
Extraversion	Sociable versus retiring Fun-loving versus sober Affectionate versus reserved
Openness	Imaginative versus practical Preference for variety versus preference for routine Independent versus conforming
Agreeableness	Soft-hearted versus ruthless Trusting versus suspicious Helpful versus uncooperative
Conscientiousness	Organized versus disorganized Careful versus careless Disciplined versus impulsive

Source Adapted from "Clinical assessment can benefit from recent advances in personality psychology" by R. McCrae & P. T. Costa, Jr., 1986, *American Psychologist, 41*, p. 1002.

and so forth. The Big Five may not be the last word. Other theorists wonder whether we should add dimensions not covered under these five categories, such as self-consciousness and masculinity/femininity. But, for now, it seems our best approximation of the basic trait dimensions.

Assessing Traits

Assessment techniques derived from trait concepts aim simply to profile a person's behavior patterns, not to reveal the hidden personality dynamics (which is the intent of projective tests). Many trait scales provide quick assessments of a single trait, such as extraversion, anxiety, or self-esteem. Such measures are commonly used in studies of personality and behavior. Alternatively, psychologists can assess several traits at once by administering **personality inventories**—longer questionnaires on which people respond to items designed to gauge a wide range of feelings and behaviors.

The personality inventory that psychologists have most extensively researched and widely used is the **Minnesota Multiphasic Personality Inventory (MMPI)**. Although it assesses psychological disorders rather than "normal" personality traits, the MMPI illustrates a good way to develop a personality inventory. One of its creators, Starke Hathaway (1960), compared his effort to that of Alfred Binet. Binet, as you may recall, developed the first intelligence test by selecting items that successfully discriminated children who were and were not progressing in Paris schools. The MMPI items, too, were **empirically derived.** That is, from a large pool of items Hathaway and his colleagues selected those that discriminated particular groups.

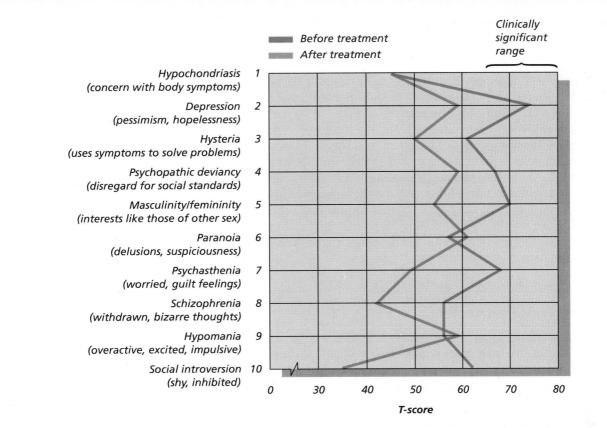

Before treatment
After treatment

Clinically significant range

Hypochondriasis (concern with body symptoms)	1	
Depression (pessimism, hopelessness)	2	
Hysteria (uses symptoms to solve problems)	3	
Psychopathic deviancy (disregard for social standards)	4	
Masculinity/femininity (interests like those of other sex)	5	
Paranoia (delusions, suspiciousness)	6	
Psychasthenia (worried, guilt feelings)	7	
Schizophrenia (withdrawn, bizarre thoughts)	8	
Hypomania (overactive, excited, impulsive)	9	
Social introversion (shy, inhibited)	10	

0   30   40   50   60   70   80

T-score

Figure 14–3 Minnesota Multiphasic Personality Inventory (MMPI-2) test profile of Ed, a depressed and anxious young man, before and after psychotherapy. About two-thirds of people taking the MMPI-2 have a T-score between 40 and 60 on any scale. (Adapted from Butcher, 1990.)

They initially gave hundreds of true-false statements ("No one seems to understand me," "I get all the sympathy I should," "I like poetry") to groups of psychologically disordered patients and to "normal" people. Those items that a patient group answered differently from the normal group they retained, no matter how silly they sounded. "Nothing in the newspaper interests me except the comics" may seem senseless, but it just so happened that depressed people were more likely to answer "true." (Nevertheless, humorists have had fun spoofing the MMPI with their own mock items, such as: "Weeping brings tears to my eyes." "As a child I often suffered from bubonic plague." "I think oatmeal is erotic." "Frantic screams make me nervous." "I stay in the bathtub until I look like a raisin" [Frankel & others, 1983].)

Today's new "MMPI-2," renormed on a full cross-section of Americans and containing revised items, still contains 10 "clinical scales" (Figure 14–3). It also retains several "validity scales," including a "lie scale" that assesses the extent to which a person is faking a good impression (by responding "false" to statements such as "I get angry sometimes"). And it has 15 "content scales" assessing, for instance, work attitudes, family problems, and anger.

In contrast to the subjectivity of projective tests, personality inventories are scored objectively—so objectively a computer can administer and score them. (The computer can also provide descriptions of people who previously responded similarly.) Objectivity does not, however, guarantee validity. Sophisticated test-takers can fake a good impression if taking the MMPI for employment purposes (by answering in socially desirable ways, except on those items for which nearly anyone would admit to being imperfect). Moreover, the ease of computerized testing tempts untrained administrators—including many personnel officers, educational admissions officers, and physicians—to use the test in ways for which it has not been validated (Matarazzo, 1983).

Nevertheless, for better or worse, the objectivity of the MMPI contributes to its rising popularity (Piotrowski & Keller, 1989), and to its translation into more than 100 languages.

Although such self-report personality tests are the most widely used method of assessing traits, psychologist David Funder (1991) believes that peer reports provide more trustworthy information. Friends who have observed you repeatedly in everyday situations provide the acid test for judging, say, how extraverted you are. By and large, self-reports and peer reports agree. But when they disagree, Funder would put his money on peer reports. If everyone who knows you agrees you are outgoing, then, regardless of what you think, you *are*.

Evaluating the Trait Perspective

Are our personality traits stable and enduring? Or does our behavior depend on where we are and whom we're with? William Faulkner strove to mirror reality in fiction by creating characters, like the self-centered Jason Compson, whose personal traits were consistent across various times and places. The Italian playwright Luigi Pirandello had a different view. For him, personality was ever-changing, tailored to the particular role or situation. In one of Pirandello's plays, Lamberto Laudisi describes himself to Signora Sirelli: "I am really what you take me to be; though, my dear madam, that does not prevent me from also being really what your husband, my sister, my niece, and Signora Cini take me to be — because they also are absolutely right!" To which she responds, "In other words you are a different person for each of us."

Who best represents human personality, Faulkner's consistent Jason Compson or Pirandello's inconsistent Laudisi? Most of us agree that this is not strictly an either/or question: Our behavior is influenced by the interaction of our inner disposition with our environment. Still, the question lingers: Which is *more* important? Are we *more* as Faulkner or as Pirandello imagined us to be? Forced to choose, most people would probably side with Faulkner. Until recently, most psychologists would have, too. Isn't it obvious that some people are dependably conscientious and others unreliable, some cheerful and others dour, some outgoing and others shy?

Remember, to be a genuine personality trait a characteristic must *both* persist over time and across situations. If friendliness is a trait, friendly people must act friendly at different times and places. Do they? In Chapter 4, we considered research that has followed lives through time. We noted that some scholars are impressed with personality change (especially those who study infants); others are struck by personality stability from adolescence through adulthood. If people's personalities are assessed in young adulthood and then assessed again several decades later, their characteristics persist. Faulkner would not have been surprised.

The consistency of specific behaviors from one situation to the next is another matter. As Walter Mischel (1968, 1984) points out, people do not act with predictable consistency. In one of the first studies to reveal this, Hugh Hartshorne and Mark May (1928b) gave thousands of children opportunities to lie, cheat, and steal while at home, at play, and in the classroom. Were some children consistently honest, others dishonest? Generally not. "Most children will deceive in certain situations and not in others," the re-

"There is as much difference between us and ourselves, as between us and others."
Michel de Montaigne
Essays, 1588

Roughly speaking, the temporary, external influences on behavior are the focus of social psychology, and the enduring, inner influences are the focus of personality psychology. In actuality, behavior always depends on the interaction of persons with situations (page 435).

"Mr. Coughlin over there was the founder of one of the first motorcycle gangs."
Drawing by Miller; © 1984 The New Yorker Magazine, Inc.

searchers reported. A child's "lying, cheating, and stealing as measured by the test situations used in these studies are only very loosely related" (p. 411). More than a half-century later, Mischel's studies of college students' conscientiousness revealed a similar finding. There was virtually no relation between a student's being conscientious on one occasion (say, showing up for class on time) and being similarly conscientious on another occasion (say, turning in assignments on time). Pirandello would not have been surprised.

Mischel also points out that people's scores on personality tests only mildly predict their behaviors. For example, people's scores on an extraversion test do not neatly predict how sociable they actually will be on any given occasion. If we remember such results, says Mischel, we will be more cautious about labeling and pigeonholing individuals. We will be more restrained when asked to predict if someone is likely to violate parole, commit suicide, or be an effective employee. Years in advance, science can tell us the phase of the moon for any given date, but we're a long way from being able to predict how you will feel and act tomorrow.

In defense of the trait perspective, personality psychologist Seymour Epstein (1983a,b) maintains that trying to predict a specific act on the basis of a personality test is like trying to predict your answer to a single test question on the basis of an intelligence test. Your answer to any given question is unpredictable because it depends on so many variables (your reading of the question, your understanding of the topic, your concentration level at the moment, luck). Your *average* accuracy over many questions on several tests is more predictable. Similarly, says Epstein, people's *average* outgoingness, happiness, or carelessness over *many* situations is predictable. When rating someone's shyness or agreeableness, this consistency enables people who know someone well to agree (Kenrick & Funder, 1988). As our best friends will verify, we *do* have personality traits.

In unfamiliar, formal situations—perhaps at a dinner party in a strange home—our traits may remain hidden as we attend carefully to social cues. In familiar, informal situations—just hanging out with friends—we feel less constrained, allowing our traits to emerge (Buss, 1989). In given situations, our expressive styles are impressively consistent—so much so that we often form lasting impressions within a few moments of seeing someone on TV, or of meeting someone and noting the person's animation, manner of speaking, and gestures. Nalini Ambady and Robert Rosenthal (1991, 1992) videotaped 13 Harvard University graduate students while they taught undergraduate courses. Observers then viewed three thin slices of each teacher's behavior—mere 10-second clips from the beginning, middle, and end of a class—and rated each teachers' confidence, enthusiasm, warmth, and so forth. These behavior ratings, based on *30 seconds* of teaching from an entire semester, predicted amazingly well the teachers' average student ratings at the semester's end.

To sum up, we can say that at any moment the immediate situation powerfully influences a person's behavior, especially when the situation makes clear demands. We can better predict drivers' behavior at traffic lights from knowing the color of the lights than from knowing their personalities. Thus, professors may perceive a student as subdued, but friends may perceive her as rather wild. However, averaging people's behavior across many occasions suggests that each of us does have a consistent personality.

The Humanistic Perspective

By 1960, some prominent personality psychologists became discontented with Freud's negativity, with trait psychology's objectivity, and with what they mocked as behaviorist "rat psychology's" seeming irrelevance. In contrast to Freud's study of the baser motives of "sick" people, these "humanistic psychologists" focused on the strivings of "healthy" people for self-determination and self-realization. In contrast to trait psychologists' profiles, they viewed whole persons as beyond encapsulation as so many test scores. In contrast to behaviorism's mechanistic analysis, which downplayed subjective experience and tied human behavior to conditioned responses, they urged study of personal experiences of sorrow and joy, alienation and intimacy, frustration and fulfillment. Two pioneering theorists illustrate these emphases on human potential and seeing the world through the person's (not the experimenter's) eyes: Abraham Maslow (1908–1970) and Carl Rogers (1902–1987).

Exploring the Self

Abraham Maslow's Self-Actualizing Person Maslow proposed that we are motivated by a hierarchy of needs (page 355). If our physiological needs are met, we become concerned with personal safety; if we achieve a sense of security, we then seek to love, to be loved, and to love ourselves. Given self-esteem, we ultimately seek **self-actualization**, the process of fulfilling our potential.

Unlike many theorists before him, Maslow (1970) developed his ideas by studying healthy, creative people rather than troubled clinical cases. He based his description of self-actualization on a study of acquaintances and Western cultural figures who seemed notable for their rich and productive lives—Abraham Lincoln, Thomas Jefferson, and Eleanor Roosevelt among them. These people shared certain characteristics. Maslow reported they were self-aware and self-accepting, open and spontaneous, loving and caring, and not paralyzed by others' opinions. Secure in their sense of who they were, their interests were problem-centered rather than self-centered. Often they focused their energies on a particular task, which they regarded as their mission in life. Most enjoyed a few deep relationships rather than many superficial ones. Many had been moved by spiritual or ecstatic "peak experiences" that surpassed ordinary consciousness.

These are mature adult qualities, said Maslow, ones found in those who have learned enough about life to be compassionate, to have outgrown their mixed feelings toward their parents, to have found their calling, to have "acquired enough courage to be unpopular, to be unashamed about being openly virtuous, etc." Maslow's work with college students led him to speculate that those likely to become self-actualizing adults were likable, caring, "privately affectionate to those of their elders who deserve it," and "secretly uneasy about the cruelty, meanness, and mob spirit so often found in young people."

Carl Rogers' Person-Centered Perspective Fellow humanistic psychologist Carl Rogers agreed with much of Maslow's thinking. Rogers believed that people are basically good and endowed with actualizing tendencies. Each of us is like an acorn, containing the

Abraham Maslow (*Motivation and Personality*, 1970): "Any theory of motivation that is worthy of attention must deal with the highest capacities of the healthy and strong person as well as with the defensive maneuvers of crippled spirits."

potential for growth and fulfillment, unless thwarted by an environment that inhibits growth. Rogers (1980) surmised that a "growth-promoting" climate required three conditions—genuineness, acceptance, and empathy.

According to Rogers, people nurture others' growth by being *genuine*—by being open with their own feelings, by dropping their facades, by being transparent and self-disclosing.

People also nurture growth by being *accepting*—by offering us what Rogers called **unconditional positive regard**. This is an attitude of grace, an attitude that values us, even knowing our failings. Have you ever experienced the relief of having dropped your pretenses, confessed your worst feelings, and discovered that you were still accepted? This gratifying experience we sometimes enjoy in a good marriage, a close family, or an intimate friendship, where we no longer feel the need to explain ourselves, where we are free to be spontaneous without fear of losing others' esteem.

Finally, people nurture growth by being *empathic*—by nonjudgmentally reflecting our feelings and meanings. "Rarely do we listen with real understanding, true empathy," said Rogers. "Yet listening, of this very special kind, is one of the most potent forces for change that I know."

Genuineness, acceptance, and empathy are the water, sun, and nutrients that enable people to grow like vigorous oak trees. For "as persons are accepted and prized," Rogers (1980, p. 116) continued, "they tend to develop a more caring attitude toward themselves." As persons are empathically heard, "it becomes possible for them to listen more accurately to the flow of inner experiencings." Rogers would have been pleased by a finding published shortly after his death: Preschool children whose parents exhibit such attitudes usually become creative adolescents (Harrington & others, 1987).

For Maslow, and even more for Rogers, a central feature of personality is one's **self-concept**—all the thoughts and feelings we have in response to the question, "Who am I?" If our self-concept is positive, we tend to act and perceive the world positively. If it is negative—if in our own eyes we fall far short of our "ideal self"—said Rogers, we feel dissatisfied and unhappy. A worthwhile goal for parents, teachers, and friends is, therefore, to help others know, accept, and be true to themselves.

Research on the Self Psychology's concern with people's sense of self dates back at least to William James, who spent more than 100 pages on it in his 1890 *Principles of Psychology*. By 1943, Gordon Allport lamented that the self had become "lost to view." Although humanistic psychology's emphasis on the self did not instigate much scientific research, it did help renew the concept of self and keep it alive. Now, a century after James, the self is one of psychology's most vigorously researched topics. Every year new studies galore appear on "self-esteem," "self-disclosure," "self-awareness," "self-schemas," "self-monitoring," and so forth.

One example of the new thinking about self is the concept of "possible selves" put forth by Hazel Markus and her University of Michigan colleagues (Inglehart & others, 1989; Markus & Nurius, 1986). Your possible selves include your visions of the self you dream of becoming—the rich self, the thin self, the loved and admired self. They also include the self you fear becoming—the unemployed self, the alcoholic self, the academically failed self. Such possible selves motivate us by laying out specific goals to pursue and the energy to

Being open and sharing confidences is easier when you have empathic listeners.

Rogers believed that genuineness, acceptance, and empathy nurture growth not only in the relationship between therapist and client but between parent and child, leader and group, teacher and student, administrator and staff member—in fact, any two human beings.

Skip

work toward them. Olympian Carl Lewis concentrated on the achievements of Olympic hero Jesse Owens to give form to his aspirations. Similarly, University of Michigan students in a combined undergraduate/medical school program earn higher grades if they undergo the program with a clear vision of themselves as successful doctors. Those who dream most, achieve most.

Underlying this research is an assumption (shared by humanistic psychologists) that the self, as organizer of our thoughts, feelings, and actions, is a pivotal center of personality (Markus & Wurf, 1987). We even remember information better if we encode it in terms of ourselves. Asked whether specific words such as *friendly* describe us, we later recall those words better than if asked whether they describe someone else (Higgins & Bargh, 1987).

How we *feel* about ourselves is also important. Research studies reveal the benefits of positive self-esteem and the hazards of self-righteous pride.

What possible future selves do you envision? To what extent do these imagined selves motivate you now?

The Benefits of Self-Esteem High **self-esteem**—a feeling of self-worth—pays dividends. People who feel good about themselves have fewer ulcers, fewer sleepless nights, succumb less to pressures to conform, are less likely to use drugs, are more persistent at difficult tasks, and are just plain happier (Brockner & Hulton, 1978; Brown, 1991).

Low self-esteem exacts costs. People who feel they are falling short of their *hopes* are vulnerable to depression. Those whose self-image falls short of what they think they *ought* to be are vulnerable to anxiety (Higgins, 1987). Psychotherapy researcher Hans Strupp (1982, pp. 64–65) reflected, "As soon as one listens to a patient's story, one encounters unhappiness, frustration, and despair. . . . Basic to all these difficulties are impairments in self-acceptance and self-esteem."

These correlational links between low self-esteem and life problems have other possible interpretations (maybe life problems cause low self-esteem). However, an effect of low self-esteem occurs in experiments. Temporarily deflate people's self-image (say, by telling them they did poorly on an aptitude test or by disparaging their personality) and they will be more likely to disparage other people or to express heightened racial prejudice. People who are negative about themselves also tend to be thin-skinned and judgmental (Baumgardner & others, 1989; Crocker & Schwartz, 1985). In experiments, those made to feel insecure often become excessively critical, as if to impress others with their own brilliance (Amabile, 1983). Although some "love their neighbors as themselves," others loathe their neighbors as themselves. Such findings are consistent with Maslow's and Rogers' presumptions that a "healthy" self-image pays dividends. Accept yourself and you'll find it easier to accept others.

Seneca (*Ad Lucilium*, A.D. 64): "What you think of yourself is much more important than what others think of you."

The Pervasiveness of Self-Serving Bias Carl Rogers (1958) once objected to the religious doctrine that humanity's problems arise from excessive self-love, or pride. He noted that most people he had known "despise themselves, regard themselves as worthless and unlovable." Mark Twain had the idea: "No man, deep down in the privacy of his heart, has any considerable respect for himself."

Actually, most of us have a good reputation with ourselves. In studies of self-esteem, even low-scoring people respond in the midrange of possible scores (Baumeister & others, 1989). (A "low" self-esteem person responds to statements such as "I have good ideas"

"To love oneself is the beginning of a life-long romance."
Oscar Wilde
An Ideal Husband, 1895

with qualifying adjectives such as "somewhat" or "sometimes.") Moreover, one of psychology's most provocative yet firmly established recent conclusions concerns our potent **self-serving bias**— our readiness to perceive ourselves favorably (Brown, 1991; Headey & Wearing, 1988; Myers, 1990). Consider:

In experiments, *people accept more responsibility for good deeds than bad, and for successes than failures*. Athletes often privately credit their victories to their own prowess, their losses to bad breaks, lousy officiating, or the other team's exceptional performance. After receiving poor exam grades, students in a half dozen studies criticized the exam *if* led to believe they had done poorly. On insurance forms, drivers have explained accidents in such words as: "An invisible car came out of nowhere, struck my car and vanished." "As I reached an intersection, a hedge sprang up, obscuring my vision, and I did not see the other car." "A pedestrian hit me and went under my car." The question "What have I done to deserve this?" is one we ask of our troubles, not our successes. Success we assume we deserve.

On nearly any subjective and socially desirable dimension, *most people see themselves as better than average*. In national surveys, most business executives say they are more ethical than their average counterpart. In several studies, 90 percent of business managers and over 90 percent of college professors rated their performance as superior to their average peer. In Australia, 86 percent of people rate their job performance as above average, 1 percent as below average. And in the United States, most high school seniors rate themselves in the top 10 percent of their age mates in their "ability to get along with others." Although the phenomenon is less striking in Asia, self-serving biases have been observed worldwide: with Dutch, Australian, and Chinese students; Japanese drivers; Indian Hindus; and French people of all ages. The world, it seems, is like Garrison Keillor's Lake Wobegon—a place where "all the women are strong, all the men are good-looking, and all the children are above average."

Self-serving bias flies in the face of today's pop psychology. "All of us have inferiority complexes," insists John Powell (1989, p. 15). "Those who seem not to have such a complex are only pretending." But additional streams of evidence remove any doubts: We remember and justify our past actions in self-enhancing ways. We exhibit an inflated confidence in the accuracy of our beliefs and judgments. We overestimate how desirably *we* would act in situations where most people behave less than admirably. We are quicker to believe flattering descriptions of ourselves than unflattering ones, and we are impressed with psychological tests that flatter us. We shore up our self-image by overestimating how much others support our opinions and share our foibles and by *under*estimating the commonality of our strengths. We exhibit group pride—a tendency to see our group (our school, our country, our race) as superior.

Moreover, pride does often go before a fall. The self-serving perceptions that underlie conflicts range from other-blaming marital discord to self-promoting ethnic snobbery. It was "Aryan pride" that fueled Nazi atrocities. It was national self-righteousness that led both the Americans and Soviets during the arms race to say, "Your weapons threaten us—ours are only for defense." No wonder reli-

"It is only our bad temper that we put down to being tired or worried or hungry. We put our good temper down to ourselves."
C. S. Lewis (1898–1963)

"The [self-]portraits that we actually believe, when we are given freedom to voice them, are dramatically more positive than reality can sustain."
Shelley Taylor
Positive Illusions, 1989

gion and literature so often warn against the perils of excessive pride.

Still, people object. They think of those who do seem to despise themselves, who feel worthless and unlovable. If self-serving bias prevails, why do so many people disparage themselves? For at least two reasons. Sometimes people's self-directed put downs are subtly strategic: They elicit reassuring strokes. Usually, a remark such as "No one likes me" will at least elicit a "But not everyone has met you!" At other times, self-disparaging comments, such as before a game or an exam, prepare for possible failure. The coach who extols the superior strength of the upcoming opponent makes a loss understandable, a victory noteworthy.

Even so, it's true: All of us some of the time, and some of us much of the time, *do* feel inferior — especially when comparing ourselves with those who are a step or two higher on the ladder of status, grades, looks, income, or agility. The deeper and more frequently we have such feelings, the more unhappy, even depressed, we are.

We can therefore affirm what humanistic psychologists rightly emphasize: For the individual, self-affirming thinking is generally adaptive. To a point, even our positive illusions are beneficial. They maintain our self-confidence, protect against anxiety and depression, and sustain our sense of well-being. "Life is the art of being well-deceived," observed the English essayist William Hazlitt.

Recognizing both the perils of self-righteousness and the dividends of positive self-esteem, psychologists Roy Baumeister (1989), Jonathan Brown (1991), and Shelley Taylor (1989) all suggest that humans function best with modest self-enhancing illusions. We are like the new Japanese and European magnetic levitation trains, says Brown: We function optimally when riding high, just off the rails — not so high that we gyrate and crash, yet not so in touch that we grind to a halt.

"If you compare yourself with others, you may become vain and bitter; for always there will be greater and lesser persons than yourself."
Desiderata
Found in Old St. Paul's Church, London, 1692

Assessing the Self

Humanistic psychologists sometimes assess personality with questionnaires that evaluate people's self-concepts. One questionnaire, inspired by Carl Rogers, asks people to describe themselves both as they ideally would like to be and as they actually are. When the ideal and the actual self are nearly alike, said Rogers, the self-concept is positive. Thus, he looked for successively closer ratings of actual and ideal self as a way to assess his clients' personal growth during therapy.

Other humanistic psychologists believe that any standardized assessment of personality is depersonalizing. Even a questionnaire detaches the psychologist from the living human. Rather than forcing the person to respond to narrow categories, these humanistic psychologists believe that interviews and intimate conversation enable a better understanding of each person's unique experiences.

Evaluating the Humanistic Perspective

One thing said of Freud can also be said of the humanistic psychologists: Their impact has been pervasive. Their ideas have influenced counseling, education, child-rearing, and management. They have also influenced — sometimes in ways they did not intend — much of today's popular psychology.

Mini Debate

*Are People Basically Good?
Two Humanistic
Psychologists Debate*

Carl Rogers: YES

Though I am very well aware of the incredible amount of destructive, cruel, malevolent behavior in today's world—from the threats of war to the senseless violence in the streets—I do not find that this evil is inherent in human nature. In a psychological climate which is nurturant of growth and choice, I have never known an individual to choose the cruel or destructive path. Choice always seems to be in the direction of greater socialization, improved relationships with others. So my experience leads me to believe that it is cultural influences which are the major factor in our evil behaviors. The rough manner of childbirth; the infant's mixed experience with the parents; the constricting, destructive influence of our educational system; the injustice of our distribution of wealth; our cultivated prejudices against individuals who are different—all these elements and many others warp the human organism in directions which are antisocial. So I see members of the human species, like members of other species, as essentially constructive in their fundamental nature, but damaged by their experience.

(From Rogers, 1981. Reprinted with permission.)

Rollo May: NO

Culture admittedly has powerful effects upon us. But it could not have these effects were these tendencies not already present in us. Who makes up the culture except persons like you and me? The culture is evil as well as good because we, the human beings who constitute it, are evil as well as good. We are bundles of both evil and good potentialities.

Some people who join and lead the humanistic movement do so in order to find a haven, a port in the storm, a community of like-minded persons who also are playing possum to the evils about us. Life, to me, is not a requirement to live out a preordained pattern of goodness, but a challenge coming down through the centuries out of the fact that each of us can throw the lever toward good or evil. This seems to me to require the age-old religious truths of mercy and forgiveness and it leaves no place for self-righteousness.

(Excerpted from May, 1982. Reprinted with permission.)

It is through popular psychology that many of us absorb some of what Maslow and Rogers so effectively taught—that a positive self-concept is key to happiness and success, that acceptance and empathy help nurture positive feelings about oneself, and that people are basically good and capable of self-improvement. The National Opinion Research Center (1985) reports that by a 4 to 1 margin, Americans now believe "human nature is basically good" rather than "fundamentally perverse and corrupt." Humanistic psychologists can also take satisfaction in the dramatically different responses today from those of 50 years ago to one of the MMPI statements (Holden, 1986c): Among those in the 1930s normal standardization sample, only 9 percent agreed that "I am an important person." In the mid-1980s, more than half of the new sample agreed with the statement. And responding to a 1989 Gallup Poll, 85 percent of Americans rated "having a good self-image or self-respect" as *very* important; 0 percent rated it unimportant. Humanistic psychology's message has been heard.

The prominence of the humanistic perspective set off a backlash of criticism. First, said the critics, its concepts are vague and subjective. Consider the description of self-actualizing people as open, spontaneous, loving, self-accepting, and productive. Is this really a scientific description? Or is it merely a description of Maslow's personal values and ideals? What Maslow did, noted M. Brewster Smith (1978), was offer impressions of his own personal heroes. Imagine another theorist who began with a different set of heroes— perhaps Napoleon, Alexander the Great, and John D. Rockefeller, Sr. This theorist would likely describe self-actualizing people as "undeterred by the needs of others," "motivated to achieve," and "obsessed with power."

Second, some critics object to the idea that, as Carl Rogers put it, "The only question which matters is, 'Am I living in a way which is deeply satisfying to me, and which truly expresses me?'" (quoted by Wallach & Wallach, 1985). They fear that the individualism encouraged by humanistic psychology—trusting and acting on one's feelings, being true to oneself, fulfilling oneself—promotes self-indulgence, selfishness, and an erosion of moral restraints (Campbell & Specht, 1985; Wallach & Wallach, 1983). Indeed it is those who focus not on themselves but beyond themselves who are most likely to experience social support, to enjoy life, and to cope effectively with stress (Crandall, 1984).

Humanistic psychologists rebut such objections. They counter that belligerence, hostility, and insensitivity are often traceable to a poor self-concept. Moreover, they argue, self-love is actually the first step toward loving others.

Finally, the humanistic psychologists have been accused of failing to appreciate the reality of our human capacity for evil. Faced with assaults on the environment, overpopulation, and threats of nuclear war, two rationalizations can promote apathy. One is a naive optimism that denies the threat ("People are basically good; everything will work out"). The other is a dark despair ("It's hopeless; why try?"). Action requires enough realism to fuel concern and enough optimism to provide hope. Humanistic psychology, say the critics, encourages the needed hope, but not the equally necessary realism.

"We do pretty well when you stop to think that people are basically good."

Drawing by Fradon; ©1979 The New Yorker Magazine, Inc.

The Social-Cognitive Perspective

Our fourth major perspective on personality derives from psychological principles of learning, cognition, and social behavior. Called the social-cognitive perspective by psychologist Albert Bandura (1986), its proponents emphasize the importance of external events. Like learning theorists, they believe that we learn many of our behaviors either by conditioning or by observing others and modeling our behavior after them. Like cognitive and social psychological theorists, they emphasize the importance of mental processes:

How we think and feel about the situations we find ourselves in affects our behavior. So instead of focusing solely on how our environment controls us (behaviorism), social-cognitive theorists focus on how we and our environment interact: How do we interpret and respond to external events? How do our schemas, our memories, and our expectations influence our behavior patterns?

This interactive, reciprocal perspective has inspired researchers to study how the environment shapes personal factors, such as self-control and self-concept, and how these in turn influence behavior. Unlike some humanistic psychologists, social-cognitive theorists do not assume that one's "self" is innate, waiting to be "discovered" or "actualized." Rather, they assume that our environment shapes our self-understanding.

Exploring Behavior in Situations

Reciprocal Influences Bandura (1986) calls the process of interacting with our environment **reciprocal determinism.** "Behavior, internal personal factors, and environmental influences," he says, "all operate as interlocking determinants of each other" (Figure 14–4). For example, children's TV viewing habits (past behavior) influence their viewing preferences (internal personal factor), which influence how television (environmental factor) affects their current behavior. The influences are mutual. As we noted earlier, persons and environments interact.

Consider three specific ways in which persons and environments interact:

1. *Different people choose different environments.* The college you attend, the reading you do, the television you watch, the music you listen to, the friends you associate with—all are an environment you have chosen, based partly on your dispositions. You choose it and it shapes you.

2. *Our personalities shape how we interpret and react to events.* Anxious people are more likely to be attuned to potentially threatening events than are nonanxious people (Eysenck & others, 1987). Thus, anxious people perceive the world as more threatening, and react accordingly.

3. *Our personalities help create situations to which we react.* Many experiments reveal that how we view and treat our families, roommates, and friends influences how they in turn treat us. If we expect someone to be angry with us, we may give the person a cold shoulder, touching off the very behavior we expect.

We are both the products and the architects of our environments. If all this has a familiar ring, it may be because it parallels and reinforces a pervasive theme in psychology and in this book: Behavior emerges from the interplay of external and internal influences. Boiling water turns an egg hard and a potato soft. A threatening environment turns one person into a hero, another into a scoundrel. *At every moment,* our behavior is determined by our experiences *and* our genes, our environments *and* our personalities.

Personal Control One important aspect of personality is our sense of **personal control**—whether we learn to see ourselves as controlling, or as controlled by, our environments. Studies of people's sense of personal control demonstrate that behavior is affected by whether people perceive the control of their lives as internal (in themselves) or external (at the mercy of the outside world).

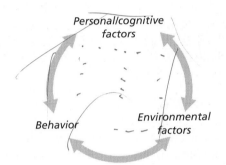

Figure 14–4 Reciprocal determinism. The social-cognitive perspective proposes that our personalities are shaped by the interaction of our situations, our thoughts and feelings, and our behaviors.

Unbearable crisis or exhilarating challenge? Our individual personalities are expressed in the distinctive ways we perceive and react to situations.

Psychologists have two basic ways to study the effect of personal control (or any personality factor). One: *Correlate* people's feelings of control with their behaviors and achievements. Two: *Experiment*, by raising or lowering people's sense of control and noting the effects.

Locus of Control   Consider your own feelings of control. Do you feel that your life is beyond your control? That the world is run by a few powerful people? That getting a good job depends mainly on being in the right place at the right time? Or do you more strongly believe that what happens to you is your own doing? That the average person can influence government decisions? That being a success is a matter of hard work, not luck?

Hundreds of studies have compared people who perceive what psychologist Julian Rotter calls an **external locus of control**— that chance or outside forces determine their fate— with those who perceive an **internal locus of control**—that to a great extent they control their own destinies. In study after study, "internals" have achieved more in school (Findley & Cooper, 1983), are more independent, and are less depressed (Benassi & others, 1988; Lefcourt, 1982). Moreover, they are better able to delay gratification and cope with various stresses, including marital problems (Miller & others, 1986).

Learned Helplessness Versus Personal Control   Helpless, oppressed people often perceive that control is external, and this perception may deepen their feelings of resignation. This is precisely what researcher Martin Seligman (1975, 1991) and others found in experiments with both animals and people. When dogs are strapped in a harness and given repeated shocks, with no opportunity to avoid them, they learn a sense of helplessness. When later placed in another situation where they *could* escape the punishment by merely leaping a hurdle, they cower without hope. Faced with repeated traumatic events over which they have no control, people, too, come to feel helpless, hopeless, and depressed. This passive resignation is called **learned helplessness** (Figure 14–5). In contrast, animals that escape shocks in the first situation learn personal control and easily escape shocks in the new situation.

Figure 14–5 Learned helplessness.

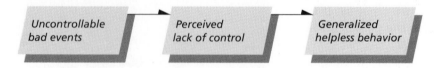

| Uncontrollable bad events | Perceived lack of control | Generalized helpless behavior |

In concentration camps, in prisons, even in factories, colleges, and well-meaning nursing homes, people given little control experience a similar lowering of morale and increased stress. Increasing control— allowing prisoners to move chairs and control room lights and the TV, workers to participate in decision making, and nursing home patients to make choices about their environment—noticeably improves health and morale (Miller & Monge, 1986; Ruback & others, 1986; Wener & others, 1987). In one famous study of nursing home patients, 93 percent of those encouraged to exert more control became more alert, active, and happy (Rodin, 1986). As researcher Ellen Langer (1983, p. 291) concluded, "Perceived control is basic to human functioning." Thus, "for the young and old alike," we should create environments that enhance a sense of control and personal efficacy.

To those who worry that the behavioral sciences might undermine traditional values, the verdict of these studies is reassuring: People thrive under conditions of democracy, personal freedom, and empowerment. Small wonder that the citizens of stable democracies report higher levels of happiness (Inglehart, 1990). Shortly before the democratic revolution in East Germany, psychologists Gabriele Oettingen and Martin Seligman (1990) compared the telltale body language of working class men in East and West Berlin bars. Compared to their counterparts on the other side of the Wall, the empowered West Berliners much more often sat upright rather than slumped, had upward- rather than downward-turned mouths, and smiled and laughed. To paraphrase the Roman philosopher Seneca, happy are those who choose their own business.

Optimism   One measure of how helpless or effective you feel is where you stand on the trait dimension of optimism/pessimism. How do you characteristically explain negative and positive events? Perhaps you have known students who blame poor grades on situations beyond their control—their lack of ability ("I can't do this") or "bad" teachers, textbooks, or exam questions. Such students are more likely to persist in getting low grades than are students who adopt the more hopeful attitude that effort, good study habits, and self-discipline can make a difference (Noel & others, 1987; Peterson & Barrett, 1987). Similarly, Seligman and Peter Schulman (1986) compared new life insurance representatives who were more or less optimistic in their outlooks. Those who put an optimistic spin on setbacks—by seeing them as flukes or as suggesting a new approach rather than as signs of incompetence—sold more policies during their first year and were half as likely to quit. Seligman's finding came to life for him when one of the optimistic recruits who began selling for Metropolitan Life after taking Seligman's optimism test later dialed him up and sold him a policy.

If positive thinking in the face of adversity pays dividends, so, too, can a realistic dash of pessimism. Unrealistic optimists sometimes fail to take sensible precautions. One wonders about America's college administrators. Because of a temporary decline in the 18- to 22-year-old population, the U.S. Department of Education projects declining college enrollments from 1991 to 1995. Nevertheless, when surveyed by the American Council on Education in 1990, only 5 percent of senior administrators projected declining enrollment during the next 5 years on *their* campus; 83 percent foresaw increasing enrollment (*Chronicle of Higher Education*, 1990). This clash between reality and hope neatly illustrates the dilemma of illusory optimism. Colleges that thrive in a declining market will likely be led by optimistic, positive-thinking administrators, but many equally optimistic and positive-thinking administrators are cruising toward disappointment.

Anxiety over contemplated failure can actually fuel energetic efforts to avoid the dreaded fate (Cantor & Norem, 1989; Goodhart, 1986; Showers & Ruben, 1987). Overconfident students often perform less well than their equally able peers who, fearing they are going to bomb the upcoming exam, proceed to study furiously and get fabulous grades. Success, it indeed seems, requires enough optimism to provide hope, but also enough pessimism to prevent complacency.

Nursing home patients who take an active part in their own care and pursue their own interests are more alert and happy than those who do not.

"O God, give us grace to accept with serenity the things that cannot be changed, courage to change the things which should be changed, and the wisdom to distinguish the one from the other."
  Reinhold Niebuhr
  The Serenity Prayer, 1943

Close-Up   *Pseudo-Assessment: How to Be a "Successful" Astrologer or Palm Reader*

Some personality assessment techniques have no validity, though you wouldn't know it by talking to their devotees. Ray Hyman (1981), palm reader turned research psychologist, helps us to see why people get suckered, by revealing the methods of astrologers, palm readers, and crystal-ball gazers.

Their first technique, the "stock spiel," builds on the truth of the observation that each of us is in some ways like no one else and in other ways like everyone. That some things are true of us all enables the "seer" to offer statements that seem impressively accurate: "I sense that you're nursing a grudge against someone; you really ought to let that go." "You worry about things more than you let on, even to your best friends." "You are adaptable to social situations and your interests are wide-ranging."

Such generally true statements can be combined into a personality description. Imagine that you take a personality test and then receive the following character sketch:

> You have a strong need for other people to like and to admire you. You have a tendency to be critical of yourself. . . . You pride yourself on being an independent thinker and do not accept other opinions without satisfactory proof. You have found it unwise to be too frank in revealing yourself to others. At times you are extraverted, affable, sociable; at other times you are introverted, wary, and reserved. Some of your aspirations tend to be pretty unrealistic (Forer, 1949).

In experiments, college students have received stock assessments like the one above. When they thought the bogus feedback was prepared just for them and when it was generally favorable, they nearly always rated the description as either "good" or "excellent." Peter Glick and his co-workers (1989) found that even skeptics of astrology, when given a flattering description attributed to an astrologer, begin to think that "maybe there's something to this astrology business after all."

French psychologist Michael Gauguelin placed an ad in a Paris newspaper offering a free personal horoscope. Ninety-four percent of those receiving the horoscope later praised the description as accurate. Actually, all had received the horoscope of France's Dr. Petiot, a notorious mass murderer (Kurtz, 1983).

This acceptance is called the Barnum effect, named in honor of master showman P. T. Barnum's dictum,

"There's a sucker born every minute." So powerful is the Barnum effect that, given a choice between this stock spiel and an individualized personality description actually based on a real test, most people choose the phony description as being more accurate. Astrologers and palm readers sprinkle their assessments with stock statements, as in the description just quoted, which was drawn from statements in a newsstand astrology book.

Another technique is to "read" the person's clothing, physical features, nonverbal gestures, and reactions to what you are saying. Imagine yourself as the character reader who was visited by a young woman in her late twenties or early thirties. Hyman describes the woman as "wearing expensive jewelry, a wedding band, and a black dress of cheap material. The observant reader noted that she was wearing shoes which were advertised for people with foot trouble." Do these clues suggest anything?

Drawing on these observations, the character reader proceeded to amaze his client with his insights. He assumed that the woman had come to see him, as did most of his female customers, because of a love or financial problem. The black dress and the wedding band led him to reason that her husband had died recently. The expensive jewelry suggested that she had been financially comfortable during marriage, but the cheap dress suggested that her husband's death had left her impoverished. The therapeutic shoes signified that she was now standing on her feet more than she was used to, implying that she has been working to support herself since her husband's death.

If you are not as shrewd as this character reader (who correctly guessed that the woman was wondering if she should remarry in hope of ending her economic hardship), no matter, says Hyman. Just tell people what they want to hear. Memorize some Barnum statements from astrology and fortune-telling manuals and use them liberally. Tell people it is their responsibility to cooperate by relating your message to their specific experiences, and later they will recall that you predicted the specifics. Phrase statements as questions, and when you detect a positive response assert the statement strongly. Be a good listener, and later, in different words, reveal to people what they earlier revealed to you.

Better yet, beware of fortune-tellers, who, by exploiting people with these techniques, become fortune-takers.

Assessing Behavior in Situations

Social-cognitive researchers explore the effect of differing situations on people's behavior patterns and attitudes. They study, for example, how viewing aggressive or nonaggressive models affects behavior. They assess the impact of dehumanizing situations on people's attitudes. And they examine the consistency of people's personalities in varying circumstances.

An ambitious example that predates social-cognitive theory is the U.S. Army's World War II strategy for assessing candidates for spy missions. Rather than use paper-and-pencil tests, army psychologists subjected the candidates to simulated undercover conditions. They tested their ability to handle stress, solve problems, maintain leadership, and withstand intense interrogation without blowing their covers. Although time-consuming and expensive, the assessment of behavior in a realistic situation helped predict later success on real spy missions (OSS Assessment Staff, 1948).

Business, military, and educational organizations are continuing this strategy in their evaluations of several hundred thousand persons each year. The American Telephone and Telegraph Company observes prospective managers doing simulated managerial work (Bray, 1982). Many colleges assess potential faculty members' teaching abilities by observing them teach. The army assesses its soldiers by observing them during military exercises.

These procedures exploit the principle that the best way to predict people's future behavior is to observe their past behavior patterns in similar situations (Mischel, 1981). So long as the situation as well as the person remain much the same, the best predictor of future job performance is past job performance; the best predictor of future grades is past grades; the best predictor of future aggressiveness is past aggressiveness; the best predictor of drug use in young adulthood is high school drug use. If you can't check the person's past behavior, the next best thing is to create an assessment situation that simulates the task demands so you can see how the person handles them.

Evaluating the Social-Cognitive Perspective

The social-cognitive perspective on personality sensitizes researchers to how situations affect, and are affected by, individuals. More than the other perspectives, we can also credit it with building on psychological research on learning and cognition.

One criticism is that the theory works *too* well, after the fact. In hindsight, we can "explain" anything as a product of cognition and the social environment. Another criticism is that the theory focuses so much on the situation that it fails to appreciate the person's inner traits. Where is the *person* in this view of personality, ask the dissenters (Carlson, 1984). And where are human emotions? Granted, the situation guides our behavior. But in many instances our unconscious motives, our emotions, and our pervasive traits shine through, say the critics. And so do genetic influences. Twin and adoption studies show that heredity influences personality traits such as extraversion, aggressiveness, and even helpfulness (Chapter 3).

And that brings us back to the thought with which we began our review of the major personality theories: Each of the perspectives summarized in Table 14–3 can teach us something. The psychoanalytic perspective draws our attention to the unconscious and irrational aspects of human existence. The trait perspective systematically describes and classifies important personality components. The humanistic perspective reminds us of the pivotal importance of our sense of self and of our healthy potential. The social-cognitive perspective applies psychology's basic concepts of learning and thinking and teaches us that we always act in the context of situations that we help to create.

Seldom in life does a single perspective on any issue give us the complete picture. The kaleidoscope of human personality is mysterious and complex, yet it reveals its different aspects when we view it from different perspectives. Each perspective enlarges our vision of the whole.

"Nature is always more subtle, more intricate, more elegant than what we are able to imagine."
Carl Sagan
"Science—Who Cares?" 1991

Table 14–3	*The Four Perspectives on Personality*		
Perspective	**Behavior springs from . . .**	**Assessment techniques**	**Evaluation**
Psychoanalytic	Processing unconscious conflicts between pleasure-seeking impulses and social restraints	Projective tests aim to reveal unconscious motivations	A speculative, hard-to-confirm theory with enormous cultural impact
Trait	Expressing biologically influenced dispositions, such as extraversion or introversion	Personality inventories assess the strength of different traits; peers rate behavior patterns	A descriptive approach criticized as sometimes underestimating the variability of behavior from situation to situation
Humanistic	Processing conscious feelings about oneself in light of one's experiences	(a) Questionnaire assessments of self-concept (b) Empathic understandings of people's unique experiences	A humane theory that reinvigorated contemporary interest in the self; criticized as subjective and sometimes naively self-centered and optimistic
Social-cognitive	Reciprocal influences between people and their situations, colored by perceptions of control	(a) Questionnaire assessments of people's feelings of control (b) Observations of people's behavior in particular situations	An interactive theory that integrates research on learning, cognition, and social behavior; criticized as underestimating the importance of the unconscious, of emotions, and of enduring traits

Summing Up

Like intelligence, personality is an abstract concept that cannot be seen, touched, or directly measured. To psychologists, personality is one's relatively distinctive and consistent pattern of thinking, feeling, and acting. We have examined four major perspectives on personality, each valuable for the light it sheds on our complex workings.

The Psychoanalytic Perspective

Exploring the Unconscious Sigmund Freud's treatment of emotional disorders led him to believe that they sprang from unconscious dynamics, which he sought to analyze through his own and his patients' free associations and dreams. Freud saw personality as composed of pleasure-seeking psychic impulses (the id), a reality-oriented executive (the ego), and an internalized set of ideals (the superego).

Freud believed that children develop through psychosexual stages, which he labeled the oral, anal, phallic, latency, and genital stages. He suggested that people's later personalities are influenced by how they resolve conflicts associated with these stages and whether they remain fixated at any stage.

Tensions between demands of the id and superego cause anxiety. The ego copes by using defense mechanisms, of which repression is the most basic.

Neo-Freudians Alfred Adler, Karen Horney, Erich Fromm, and Erik Erikson accepted many of Freud's ideas, as did Carl Jung. But they also argued that we have more positive motives than sex and aggression and that the ego's conscious control is greater than Freud supposed.

Assessing the Unconscious Psychoanalytic assessment aims to reveal unconscious aspects of personality. Although some criticize projective tests, such as the Rorschach inkblots, because they have only modest reliability and validity, the Rorschach continues to be used by many clinicians.

Evaluating the Psychoanalytic Perspective Critics say many of Freud's specific ideas are implausible, unvalidated, or contradicted by new research, and that his theory offers only after-the-fact explanations. Nevertheless, Freud drew psychology's attention to the unconscious, to the struggle to cope with anxiety and sexuality, and to the conflict between biological impulses and social restraints. His cultural impact has been enormous.

The Trait Perspective

Exploring Traits Rather than explain the hidden aspects of personality, trait researchers describe the predispositions that underlie our actions. For example, through factor analysis, researchers have isolated five distinct dimensions of personality. Most such traits are biologically influenced by genetic predispositions and perhaps by autonomic reactivity.

Assessing Traits To assess traits, psychologists have devised self-report inventories, such as the empirically derived MMPI-2. Peer reports may provide even more trustworthy clues to a person's behavioral traits.

Evaluating the Trait Perspective Critics of traits question the consistency with which they are expressed. Although people's traits do seem to persist over time, human behavior varies widely from situation to situation. Despite these variations, a person's *average* behavior across different situations is fairly consistent.

The Humanistic Perspective

Humanistic psychologists have sought to turn psychology's attention from baser motives and environmental conditioning to the growth potential of healthy people, as seen through the individual's own experiences.

Exploring the Self Abraham Maslow believed that if basic human needs are fulfilled and self-esteem is achieved, people will strive to actualize their highest potential. To describe self-actualization, he studied some exemplary personalities and summarized his impressions of their qualities. To nurture growth in others, Carl Rogers advised being genuine, accepting, and empathic. In such a climate, people can develop a deeper self-awareness and a more realistic and positive self-concept. Research on the self documents the importance of high self-esteem and the potency of self-serving bias.

Assessing the Self Humanistic psychologists assess personality through questionnaires on which people report their self-concept and by seeking to understand others' subjective personal experiences in therapy.

Evaluating the Humanistic Perspective Humanistic psychology's critics complain that its concepts are vague and subjective, its values individualistic and self-centered, and its assumptions naively optimistic. Nevertheless, humanistic psychology helped to renew psychology's interest in the self.

The Social-Cognitive Perspective

Exploring Behavior in Situations The social-cognitive perspective applies principles of learning, cognition, and social behavior to personality, with particular emphasis on the ways in which our personalities influence and are influenced by our interaction with the environment. It assumes reciprocal determinism—that personal-cognitive factors combine with the environment to influence people's behavior. By studying variations among people in their perceived locus of control and in their experiences of learned helplessness, researchers have found that an inner locus of control helps people to cope with life.

Assessing Behavior in Situations Social-cognitive researchers observe how people's behaviors and beliefs both affect and are affected by their situations. They have found that the best way to predict someone's behavior in a given situation is to observe that person's behavior pattern in similar situations.

Evaluating the Social-Cognitive Perspective Although faulted for slighting the importance of unconscious dynamics and inner traits, the social-cognitive perspective builds on psychology's well-established concepts of learning and cognition and reminds us of the power of social situations.

Terms and Concepts to Remember

personality An individual's characteristic pattern of thinking, feeling, and acting.

free association A psychoanalytic method of exploring the unconscious in which the person relaxes and says whatever comes to mind, no matter how trivial or embarrassing.

psychoanalysis The technique of treating psychological disorders by seeking to expose and interpret unconscious tensions. Freud's psychoanalytic theory of personality sought to explain what he observed during psychoanalysis.

unconscious According to Freud, a reservoir of mostly unacceptable thoughts, wishes, feelings, and memories. According to contemporary research psychologists, a level of information processing of which we are unaware.

preconscious Information that is not conscious, but is retrievable into conscious awareness.

id A reservoir of unconscious psychic energy that, according to Freud, strives to satisfy basic sexual and aggressive drives.

pleasure principle The id's demand for immediate gratification.

ego The largely conscious, "executive" part of personality that, according to Freud, mediates among the demands of the id, superego and reality.

reality principle The ego's tendency to satisfy the id's desires in ways that will realistically bring pleasure rather than pain.

superego The part of personality that, according to Freud, represents internalized ideals and provides standards for judgment (the conscience) and for future aspirations.

psychosexual stages The childhood stages of development (oral, anal, phallic, latency, genital) during which, according to Freud, the id's pleasure-seeking energies focus on distinct erogenous zones.

oral stage The first of Freud's psychosexual stages, from birth to about 18 months, during which sensual pleasure centers on the mouth via sucking, biting, and chewing.

anal stage The second of Freud's psychosexual stages, from about 18 months to 3 years, during which pleasure focuses on bowel and bladder elimination, retention, and control.

phallic stage The third of Freud's psychosexual stages, from about ages 3 to 6, during which the pleasure zone is the genitals and sexual feelings arise toward the parent of the other sex.

Oedipus [ED-uh-puss] **complex** According to Freud, a boy's sexual desires toward his mother and feelings of jealousy and hatred for his father.

identification The process by which, according to Freud, children incorporate their parents' values into their developing superegos.

gender identity One's sense of being male or female.

latency stage The fourth of Freud's psychosexual stages, from about age 6 to puberty, during which sexual impulses are repressed.

genital stage The last of Freud's psychosexual stages, beginning in puberty, during which sexuality matures and the person seeks pleasure through sexual contact with others.

fixation According to Freud, a lingering focus of pleasure-seeking energies at an earlier psychosexual stage, where conflicts were unresolved.

defense mechanisms In psychoanalytic theory, the ego's protective methods of reducing anxiety by unconsciously distorting reality.

repression In psychoanalytic theory, the basic defense mechanism that banishes anxiety-arousing thoughts and feelings from consciousness.

regression In psychoanalytic theory, an individual's retreat, when faced with anxiety, to a more infantile psychosexual stage where some psychic energy remains fixated.

reaction formation In psychoanalytic theory, a defense mechanism by which the ego unconsciously switches unacceptable impulses into their opposites. Thus, people may express feelings that are the opposite of their anxiety-arousing unconscious feelings.

projection In psychoanalytic theory, the defense mechanism by which people disguise their own threatening impulses by attributing them to others.

rationalization In psychoanalytic theory, a defense mechanism that offers self-justifying explanations in place of the real, more threatening, unconscious reasons for one's actions.

displacement In psychoanalytic theory, the defense mechanism that shifts sexual or aggressive impulses toward a more acceptable or less threatening object or person, as when redirecting anger toward a safer outlet.

sublimation In psychoanalytic theory, the defense mechanism by which people rechannel their unacceptable impulses into socially approved activities.

collective unconscious Carl Jung's concept of a shared, inherited reservoir of memory traces from our species' history.

projective tests Personality tests, such as the Rorschach and TAT, for which subjects interpret ambiguous stimuli designed to trigger projection of one's inner dynamics.

Thematic Apperception Test (TAT) A projective test in which people express their inner hopes, fears, and interests through the stories they make up about ambiguous scenes.

Rorschach inkblot test The most widely used projective test, designed by Hermann Rorschach; seeks to identify people's projected feelings by analyzing their interpretation of a set of 10 inkblots.

trait A characteristic pattern of behavior or conscious motive; assessed by self-report inventories and peer reports.

personality inventory A questionnaire (often with true-false or agree-disagree items) on which people respond to items designed to gauge a wide range of feelings and behaviors; used to assess selected personality traits.

Minnesota Multiphasic Personality Inventory-2 (MMPI-2) The most widely researched and clinically used of all personality tests. Originally developed to identify the traits of emotionally troubled people (still considered its most appropriate use), this test is now also used for other screening purposes.

empirically derived test A test (such as the MMPI-2) developed by testing a pool of items and then selecting those that discriminate groups of interest.

self-actualization According to Maslow, the ultimate psychological need that arises after basic physical and psychological needs are met and self-esteem is achieved; the motivation to fulfill one's potential.

unconditional positive regard According to Rogers, an attitude of total acceptance toward another person.

self-concept All our thoughts and feelings about ourselves in answer to the question, "Who am I?"

self-esteem One's feelings of high or low self-worth.

self-serving bias A readiness to perceive oneself favorably.

reciprocal determinism The interacting influences between personality and environmental factors.

personal control Our sense of being in control of our environment rather than feeling helpless.

external locus of control The perception that chance or outside forces beyond one's personal control determine one's fate.

internal locus of control The perception that one controls one's own fate.

learned helplessness The hopelessness and passive resignation learned when an animal or human is unable to avoid repeated aversive events.

For Further Reading

Freud, S. (1933). *Introductory lectures on psychoanalysis.* In J. Strachey (Ed. & trans.), *The standard edition of the complete psychological works of Sigmund Freud.* London: Hogarth, 1963.

One of Freud's most popular works, introducing his ideas about human motivation, dream interpretation, slips of the tongue, and psychoanalytic therapy.

Goleman, D. (1985). *Vital lies, simple truths: The psychology of self-deception and shared illusions.* New York: Simon & Schuster.

An engaging account of how self-deception helps us avoid anxiety, but not without costs.

Rogers, C. R. (1961). *On becoming a person.* Boston: Houghton Mifflin.

A warm and readable introduction to Carl Rogers' view of the person and of how to nurture personal growth.

Ross, L., & Nisbett, R. E. (1991). *The person and the situation: Perspectives of social psychology.* New York: McGraw-Hill.

A stimulating analysis of how personality and social environment jointly influence behavior.

Seligman, M. (1991). *Learned optimism.* New York: Knopf.

A leading researcher describes his research on learned helplessness and optimism, showing why optimism is important and how to acquire it.

Storr, A. (1989) *Freud.* New York: Oxford.

A concise overview and evaluation of Freud—the man and his ideas.

Psychological Disorders

Chapter 15

Most people are fascinated by the exceptional, the unusual, and the abnormal. "The sun shines and warms and lights us and we have no curiosity to know why this is so," observed Ralph Waldo Emerson, "but we ask the reason of all evil, of pain, and hunger, and mosquitoes and silly people."

Why this fascination with disturbed people? Perhaps in them we often see something of ourselves. At various moments, all of us feel, think, or act as disturbed people do much of the time. We, too, may be anxious, depressed, withdrawn, suspicious, deluded, or antisocial, although less intensely and enduringly. Studying psychological disorders may therefore at times evoke an eerie sense of self-recognition that illuminates our own personality dynamics. "To study the abnormal is the best way of understanding the normal," proposed William James.

Another reason for our curiosity is that so many of us have felt, either personally or through friends or family members, the bewilderment and pain of a psychological disorder. In all likelihood, you or someone you care about has been disabled by unexplained physical symptoms, overwhelmed by irrational fears, or paralyzed by the feeling that life is not worth living. Each year there are nearly 1.7 million inpatient admissions to U.S. mental hospitals and psychiatric units (Rosenstein & others, 1989). Some 2.4 million others, often troubled but not disabled, seek help as outpatients from mental health organizations and clinics. Many more—15 percent of Americans, according to one government study—are judged to need such help (Robins & Regier, 1991). Nor are such problems peculiar to the United States. So far as we know, no human culture is free of the two terrible maladies this chapter examines in depth—depression and schizophrenia (Draguns, 1990a,b). As members of the human family, few of us go through life unacquainted with the reality of psychological disturbance.

> *"We are all mad at some time or another."*
> Battista Mantuanus
> *Eclogues*, 1500

Perspectives on Psychological Disorders

Most people would agree that someone who is too depressed to get out of bed for weeks at a time suffers a psychological disorder. But what about those who, having experienced a loss, are unable to resume their usual social activities? Where should we draw the line between normality and abnormality? How should we *define* psychological disorders? Equally important, how should we *understand* disorders—as sicknesses that need to be diagnosed and cured, or as natural responses to a troubling environment? Finally, how might we *classify* disordered personalities? Can we do so in a way that allows us to help disturbed people and not merely stigmatize them with labels?

Defining Psychological Disorders

James Oliver Huberty had been hearing voices. He "talked with God," his wife reported. Although he had never been to Vietnam, he strode into a San Ysidro, California, McDonald's restaurant one summer day in 1984 screaming, "I've killed a thousand in Vietnam and I'll kill a thousand more." In the next few minutes, before police gunned him down, Huberty gunned down 21 people.

At the end of World War II, James Forrestal, the first U.S. Secretary of Defense, became convinced that Israeli secret agents were following him. His suspiciousness struck his physicians as bizarre. They diagnosed him as mentally ill and confined him to an upper floor of Walter Reed Army Hospital. From there he plunged to his death. Although Forrestal had problems, it was later discovered that he was, in fact, being followed by Israeli agents, who feared he might secretly negotiate with representatives of Arab nations (Sagan, 1979b). As Woody Allen once said, even paranoids can have enemies.

Both the voices that Huberty heard and the degree of anxiety and depression that Forrestal experienced were deviations from the normal. These were "*ab*normal" (atypical) perceptions. Being different from most other people is *part* of what it takes to define a psychological disorder. As the reclusive poet Emily Dickinson observed in 1862,

> Assent—and you are sane—
> Demur—you're straightaway dangerous—
> and handled with a Chain.

Clearly, there is more to a disorder than being atypical. Olympic gold medalists are abnormal in their physical capabilities, and they are heroes. To be considered disordered, other people must find the atypical behavior *disturbing*. Certainly the atypical behavior of a James Oliver Huberty is disturbing.

But standards of acceptability for behaviors vary. In some cultures, people routinely behave in ways (such as going about naked) that in other cultures would get them arrested. In at least one cultural context—wartime—even mass killing may be viewed as heroic. One person's homicidal "terrorist" is another person's "freedom fighter." Standards of acceptability vary not only from culture to culture but also from time to time. Two decades ago, the American Psychiatric Association dropped homosexuality as a disorder (because it is now believed unconnected with psychological problems) (page 367). Later it added tobacco dependence (because it deemed smoking both addictive and self-destructive).

Atypical and disturbing behaviors are more likely to be considered disordered when judged as harmful. Indeed, many clinicians define disorders as behaviors that are *maladaptive*—as when a smoker's nicotine dependence produces physical damage. Accord-

Although street cleaner Snowy Farr's eccentric behavior may indeed be *atypical,* clinicians would not label it disordered because it is not particularly *disturbing* nor is it *maladaptive* or *unjustifiable*.

ingly, even typical behaviors, such as the occasional despondency that many college students feel, may signal a psychological disorder if they become disabling.

Finally, abnormal behavior is most likely to be considered disordered when others find it rationally *unjustifiable*. Doctors attributed Forrestal's suspicions to his imagination—and declared him disordered. Had he managed to convince others of his suspicions, he might have been helped, not merely labeled. James Oliver Huberty claimed to hear voices and to talk with God, and we presume he was deranged. But Shirley MacLaine can wear a crystal on her neck and say, "See the outer bubble of white light watching you. It is part of you," and she is not considered disordered because enough people take her seriously (Friedrich, 1987). It is acceptable to be different from others if both you and they can justify or are undisturbed by the difference.

So, mental health workers label behavior **psychologically disordered** when they judge it *atypical, disturbing, maladaptive,* and *unjustifiable*. Huberty's behavior met these criteria, so we have few doubts in judging him a disordered man.

Understanding Psychological Disorders

Imagine yourself living hundreds or thousands of years ago. How might you have accounted for the behavior of a James Oliver Huberty? To explain puzzling behavior, our ancestors often presumed that strange forces—the movements of the stars, godlike powers, or evil spirits—were at work. "The devil made him do it," you might have said. The cure might have been to get rid of the evil force—by exorcising the demon or even by chipping a hole in the skull to allow the evil spirit to escape (Figure 15–1). Until the last two centuries, "mad" people were sometimes caged under zoolike conditions or given "therapies" appropriate to a demon. Disordered people have been beaten, burned, and castrated. They have had teeth pulled, lengths of intestines removed, and the clitoris cauterized. They have had their own blood removed and replaced with transfusions of animal blood (Farina, 1982).

The Medical Perspective In response to such brutal treatment, reformers such as Philippe Pinel (1745–1826) in France insisted that madness was not demon possession but a disease that, like other diseases, we could treat and cure. For Pinel, treatment meant boosting patients' morale by talking with them and by providing humane living conditions. When it was later discovered that an infectious brain disease, syphilis, produced a particular psychological disorder, people came to believe in physical causes for disorders and to search for medical treatments.

Today, Pinel's medical perspective is familiar to us in the medical terminology of the mental *health* movement: A mental *illness* (also called a psycho*pathology*) needs to be *diagnosed* on the basis of its *symptoms* and *cured* through *therapy*, which may include *treatment* in a psychiatric *hospital*. In the 1800s, the assumption of this **medical model**—that psychological disorders are sicknesses—provided the impetus for much needed reforms. The "sick" were unchained and hospitals replaced asylums.

"If a man is in a minority of one, we lock him up."
Oliver Wendell Holmes, 1841–1935

Figure 15–1 A skull found in Peru, showing a hole chipped through the cranium to allow evil spirits to escape. One wonders whether the patient survived the cure.

Equating psychological disorders with sickness does, however, have its critics, among them psychiatrist Thomas Szasz. Szasz believes that mental "illnesses" are socially, not medically, defined. When, for many years, Soviet psychiatrists diagnosed dissident citizens as "psychotic," they were using medical metaphors to disguise their contempt for these people's political ideas. Szasz (1984, 1987) concludes that in North America, too, mental health practitioners have too much authority in today's society. When they demean people with the label "mentally ill," their patients may begin to view themselves as "sick" and therefore give up taking responsibility for coping with their problems. As we noted in the earlier discussion of drug abuse (page 217), many critics respond similarly to the idea that alcohol abuse, overeating, gambling, and sexual promiscuity are addictive diseases—purely uncontrollable compulsions that require sympathy and treatment. As we will see, labels can be self-fulfilling fables.

Despite such criticisms, the medical perspective survives and even gains renewed credibility from recent discoveries. Genetically influenced disorders in brain biochemistry have been linked with two of the most troubling psychological disorders, depression and schizophrenia, both of which are often treated medically.

Those who accept Freud's psychoanalytic perspective agree that psychological disorders are sicknesses that have diagnosable and treatable causes. However, they insist that these causes may include psychological factors. We see such factors in the lingering emotional aftereffects of traumatic stress, such as that caused by rape (page 235) and combat (page 515).

Alternative Perspectives Psychologists who reject the "sickness" idea typically contend that *all* behavior, whether called normal or disordered, arises from the interaction of nature (genetic and physiological factors) and nurture (past and present experiences). To presume that a person is "mentally ill" attributes the condition solely to an internal problem—to a "sickness" that must be found and cured. Maybe there *is* no deep, internal problem. Maybe there is instead a growth-blocking difficulty in the person's environment, in the person's current interpretations of events, or in the person's bad habits and poor social skills.

When Native Americans were banished from their ancestral lands, forced onto reservations to live in poverty and unemployment, and deprived of personal control, the result was a rate of alcoholism more than five times that of other Americans (May, 1986). Because only some Native Americans become alcoholic, the medical model would attribute such alcoholism to individual "sickness." A psychological perspective would emphasize the interaction between an individual's vulnerability and a particular environment.

Evidence of environmental effects comes from links between disorder and culture. Although major disorders such as depression and schizophrenia are universal, others are culture-bound (Carson & others, 1988). Different cultures have different stresses and produce different ways of coping. Anorexia nervosa, for example, is mostly a disorder of Western cultures (page 359).

Most mental health workers today assume that disorders are indeed influenced by genetic predispositions and physiological states. And by inner psychological dynamics. And by social circumstances. To get the whole picture, we need an interdisciplinary "bio-psycho-social" perspective.

"According to official data, nearly 5 million people are listed on the psychiatric register in the Soviet Union. During the next two years, the authorities intend to take up to 2 million of them off the register. . . . To be on it officially permits a healthy person to be placed in a psychiatric prison at any time and to be deprived of all rights."
  Sergei Grigoryants, chief editor of
  Glasnost magazine, February 23, 1988

"It's no measure of health to be well adjusted to a profoundly sick society."
  Krishnamurti, 1895–1986

Close-Up *The Insanity Defense on Trial*

A posed self-portrait of John W. Hinckley, Jr., former President Reagan's would-be assassin.

In defining psychological disorders, I have not mentioned insanity. That is because sane and insane are *legal*, not psychological, terms, ones judged either/or. You can be a little depressed or greatly depressed; you cannot be a little insane.

The British created the insanity defense in 1843 after a deluded Scotsman, Daniel M'Naghten, tried to shoot the Prime Minister (who he thought was persecuting him) and killed the Prime Minister's secretary by mistake. A furor erupted after M'Naghten was acquitted as insane and sent to a mental hospital rather than to prison. When the M'Naghten verdict was upheld, an insanity rule emerged. It limited the insanity defense to cases where persons were judged not to have known what they were doing or not to have known that it was wrong. Shakespeare's Hamlet anticipated the defense. If I wrong someone when not myself, he explains, "then Hamlet does it not, Hamlet denies it. Who does it then? His madness."

By the time John Hinckley, Jr., came to trial in 1982 for shooting President Reagan and his press secretary, the insanity defense had been broadened. The prosecution had to prove that Hinckley was sane. Under the Model Penal Code this meant his having "a substantial capacity" not merely to "know" his act was wrong but to "appreciate" its wrongfulness and to act accordingly.

The prosecution was unable to prove sanity to the jurors' satisfaction. So Hinckley, like M'Naghten, was sent to a mental hospital. As in the first insanity case, the public was outraged. One newspaper headlined

"Hinckley Insane, Public Mad." The outrage was partly because Hinckley, like others declared not guilty by reason of insanity, will be released when declared sane and no longer dangerous—conceivably earlier, though quite possibly later, than would have been his release from a prison.

Some news commentators complained that the heinousness of a crime had become the very basis for evading responsibility for it, "like the person who kills his parents and demands mercy because he is an orphan." Are "sick crimes" necessarily the products of sick minds that need treatment, not punishment? Are the genuinely bad truly mad? If so, said one commentator, then modern society has become like Aldous Huxley's nightmarish *Brave New World*, in which when someone commits a crime the correct response is, "I did not know he was ill."

In defense of the insanity plea, psychologist David Rosenhan (1983a,b) noted that, actually, such a plea is entered only about 2 times in every 1000 felony cases. In 85 percent of those cases, all parties—mental health experts, prosecutor, and defense attorney—agree that the deranged person was not responsible. In fact, the most important issues that involve psychology and law are not the rare disputes over insanity. They are instead the far more frequent cases concerning child custody (judging who will be the better parent), involuntary commitment to mental hospitals, and predictions about a criminal's future behavior made at the time of sentencing or parole. (When psychiatrists and psychologists use their clinical judgment to predict violence, they are more often wrong than right [Faust & Ziskin, 1988; Monahan, 1988].)

In Canada, and now in the United States under a 1984 law, the insanity defense survives in a restricted format that shifts the burden of proving insanity to the defense. Now defendants must show that they did not understand the wrongfulness of their acts.

By 1987, 13 states instituted a verdict of "guilty but mentally ill." This verdict recognizes a need for treatment but holds people responsible and sends them to prison if they are judged recovered before their sentence is over (Rosenfeld, 1987). Jurors find the verdict a viable option. In mock trials, defendants who otherwise would have been judged either innocent or not guilty by reason of insanity are often judged guilty but mentally ill (Savitsky & Lindblom, 1986).

Classifying Psychological Disorders

In biology and the other sciences, classification creates order. To classify an animal as a mammal says a great deal—that it is warm-blooded, has hair or fur, and nourishes its young with milk. In psychiatry and psychology, too, classification orders and describes clusters of symptoms. To classify a person's disorder as "schizophrenia" suggests that the person talks incoherently, hallucinates or has delusions (bizarre beliefs), shows either little emotion or inappropriate emotion, or is socially withdrawn. Thus, the diagnostic term provides a handy shorthand for describing a complex disorder.

In psychiatry and psychology, diagnostic classification ideally aims to describe a disorder, to predict its future course, to imply appropriate treatment, and to stimulate research into its causes. Indeed, to study a disorder we must first name and describe it. The current authoritative scheme for classifying psychological disorders is the American Psychiatric Association's *Diagnostic and Statistical Manual of Mental Disorders (Third Edition—Revised)*, nicknamed **DSM-III-R**. This 1987 volume and the book of case illustrations that accompanies it provide the basis for much of the material in this chapter.

Although the task force that prepared DSM-III-R included not only psychiatrists (who are medical doctors) but clinical psychologists as well, DSM-III-R assumes the medical model. The very idea of "diagnosing" people's problems in terms of their "symptoms" presumes a mental "illness." Some practitioners are not enthralled with this medical terminology, but most find DSM-III-R a helpful and practical tool. And a necessary one: Most North American health insurance companies require a DSM-III-R diagnosis before paying for therapy.

The DSM was revised to describe disorders and their prevalence without presuming to explain their causes. Thus, the once popular term *neurosis* is no longer a diagnostic category—because neurosis was Freud's idea of the process by which unconscious conflicts create anxiety. DSM-III-R does mention **neurotic disorders**—psychological disorders that, although distressing, still allow one to think rationally and function socially. But even this term is so vague that psychologists now use it minimally, usually as a contrast to the more bizarre and debilitating **psychotic disorders**, marked by irrationality.

Instead of emphasizing the old neurotic/psychotic distinction, DSM-III-R groups some 230 psychological disorders and conditions into 17 major categories of "mental disorder." There are diagnoses for almost every conceivable complaint. In fact, some critics fault DSM-III-R for bringing "almost any kind of behavior within the compass of psychiatry" (Eysenck & others, 1983)—from irrational fear of humiliation and embarrassment (social phobia) to persistently breaking rules at home or school (conduct disorder).

Before establishing the validity of the DSM-III-R categories, we must first confirm their reliability. If one psychiatrist or psychologist diagnoses someone as having, say, a "catatonic schizophrenia disorder," what are the chances that another mental health worker will independently give the same diagnosis? With the DSM-III-R's diagnostic guidelines, the chances are good. The guidelines work by asking clinicians a series of objective questions about observable behaviors, such as, "Is the person afraid to leave home?" In one study, 16 psychologists used this structured interview pro-

Due out by the mid-1990s are new editions of both DSM (DSM-IV) and the World Health Organization's international classification of mental disorders.

"I'm always like this, and my family was wondering if you could prescribe a mild depressant."

© 1992 by Sidney Harris.

cedure to diagnose 75 psychiatric patients as suffering either (1) depression, (2) generalized anxiety, or (3) some other disorder (Riskind & others, 1987). Without knowing the first psychologist's diagnosis, another psychologist viewed a videotape of each interview and offered a second opinion. For 83 percent of the patients, the two opinions agreed.

Let us now consider a few of the most prevalent and perplexing disorders, remembering that the people we will meet are not sideshow curiosities but real people—troubled people whose loved ones are troubled for them.

Anxiety Disorders

When speaking in front of a class, when peering down from a ledge, when waiting for a big game to begin, any one of us might feel anxious. At one time or another, most of us feel enough anxiety in some social situation that we fail to make eye contact or we avoid talking to someone—"shyness" we call it. But for some people, two-thirds of whom are women, anxiety becomes so distressing and persistent that they suffer an **anxiety disorder**.

Anxiety is part of our everyday experience. Fortunately for most of us, our occasional uneasiness does not entail the intense suffering endured by those with anxiety disorders. There are three important types: **generalized anxiety disorder**, in which a person feels unexplainably tense and uneasy; **phobic disorder**, in which a person feels irrationally afraid of a specific object or situation; and **obsessive-compulsive disorder**, in which a person is troubled by repetitive thoughts or actions.

Generalized Anxiety Disorder

Tom, a 27-year-old electrician, seeks help, complaining of dizziness, sweating palms, heart palpitations, and ringing in the ears. He feels edgy and sometimes finds himself shaking. With reasonable success he hides his symptoms from his family and co-workers. Nevertheless, he has had few social contacts since the symptoms began 2 years ago. Worse, he occasionally has to leave work. His family doctor and neurologist can find no physical problem, and a special diet for those with low blood sugar has not helped.

Tom's unfocused, out-of-control, threatened feelings suggest a generalized anxiety disorder. The symptoms of this disorder are commonplace; their persistence is not. The sufferers are continually tense and jittery, apprehensive about bad things that might happen, and experiencing all the symptoms of autonomic nervous system arousal (racing heart, clammy hands, stomach butterflies). The tension and apprehension may leak out through furrowed brows, twitching eyelids, or fidgeting.

One of the worst characteristics of a generalized anxiety disorder is that the person cannot identify, and therefore cannot avoid, its cause. To use Freud's term, the anxiety is "free-floating." Indeed, for no apparent reason the anxiety may at times suddenly escalate into a terrifying **panic attack**—an episode of intense dread, usually lasting several minutes. Chest pain, choking or smothering sensations, trembling, dizziness, or fainting typically accompany the panic. The experience is unpredictable and so frightening that the sufferer may then avoid situations where attacks have occurred.

Phobic Disorders

Phobic anxiety focuses on some specific object, activity, or situation. (See Figure 15–2 for a ranking of some common fears.) Phobias—irrational fears—are a common psychological disorder that people often accept and live with. Some phobic disorders are incapacitating, however. Marilyn, a 28-year-old homemaker, so fears thunderstorms that she feels anxious as soon as a weather forecaster mentions possible storms later in the week. If her husband is away and a storm is forecast, she sometimes stays with a close relative. During a storm, she hides from windows and buries her head to avoid seeing the lightning. She is otherwise healthy and happy.

Figure 15–2 This national survey ranks the relative fear levels of Americans to some common sources of anxiety. A fear becomes a phobia if it provokes a compelling but irrational desire to avoid the dreaded object or situation. (From *Public Opinion*, 1984.)

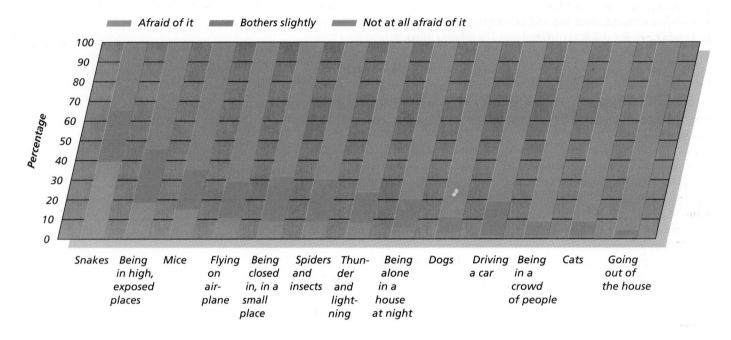

Afraid of it Bothers slightly Not at all afraid of it

Snakes | Being in high, exposed places | Mice | Flying on airplane | Being closed in, in a small place | Spiders and insects | Thunder and lightning | Being alone in a house at night | Dogs | Driving a car | Being in a crowd of people | Cats | Going out of the house

Other people with phobic disorders suffer from irrational fears of specific animals or of airplanes or elevators or even public places such as department stores. Sometimes it is possible to avoid the fear-arousing stimulus: One can hide during thunderstorms or avoid air travel. With other phobias, such as an intense fear of being scrutinized by others ("social phobia"), avoiding fear-arousing situations may dictate never leaving home. Compared to the other disorders discussed in this chapter, phobias have an earlier onset—often by the early teens (Burke & others, 1990).

Obsessive-Compulsive Disorder

As with the generalized anxiety and phobic disorders, we can see aspects of ourselves in the obsessive-compulsive disorder. We may at times be obsessed with senseless or offensive thoughts that will not go away. Or we may engage in compulsive, rigid behavior—rechecking the locked door, stepping over cracks in the sidewalk, or lining up our books and pencils "just so" before studying.

Obsessive thoughts and compulsive behaviors cross the fine line between normality and disorder when they become so persistent that they interfere with the way we live or when they cause dis-

"He always times '60 Minutes.'"

Drawing by Richter; © 1983 The New Yorker Magazine, Inc.

tress. Checking to see that the door is locked is normal; checking the door 10 times is not. Hand washing is normal; hand washing so often that one's skin becomes raw is not. (See Table 15–1 for more examples.) At some time during their lives, often during their late teens or in their twenties, 2 to 3 percent cross that line from normal preoccupations and fussiness to debilitating disorder (Karno & others, 1988).

One such person was billionaire Howard Hughes. Hughes would compulsively dictate the same phrases over and over again. Under stress, he developed an obsessive fear of germs. He became reclusive and insisted that his assistants carry out elaborate hand-washing rituals and wear white gloves when handling documents he would later touch. He ordered tape around doors and windows and forbade his staff to touch or even look at him. "Everybody carries germs around with them," he explained. "I want to live longer than my parents, so I avoid germs" (Fowler, 1986).

Explaining Anxiety Disorders

In seeking to understand anxiety disorders, psychologists have emphasized three familiar perspectives—the psychoanalytic, learning, and biological.

The Psychoanalytic Perspective Psychoanalytic theory assumes that, beginning in childhood, intolerable impulses, ideas, and feelings get repressed. This submerged mental energy nevertheless influences our actions and emotions, sometimes producing feelings of anxiety, depression, or other maladaptive symptoms that mystify even the sufferer.

One of Freud's classic cases concerned a 5-year-old boy known as Little Hans, whose phobia of horses prevented (in those days before cars) his going outdoors. Freud's controversial speculation was that Little Hans's fear of horses expressed his underlying fear of his father, whom Hans viewed as a rival for his mother's affections.

Alternatively, the forbidden impulses may break through as thinly disguised thoughts, which may provoke acts aimed at suppressing the associated anxiety. The result: obsessions and compulsions. Repetitive hand washing, for instance, may help suppress anxiety over one's "dirty" urges.

The Learning Perspective Learning researchers link general anxiety with learned helplessness (page 436). In the laboratory, researchers can create chronically anxious, ulcer-prone rats by giving them unpredictable electric shocks (Schwartz, 1984). Like the rape victim who reported feeling anxious when entering her old neighborhood (page 235), the animals are apprehensive in their lab environment. For many victims of "post-traumatic stress disorder" (page 515), anxiety swells with any reminder of their trauma.

When the shocks become predictable—when preceded by a particular conditioned stimulus—the animals' fear focuses on *that* stimulus and they relax in its absence. So it can happen with human fears. Recently, my car was struck by another whose driver did not see a stop sign. For months afterward, I felt a twinge of unease with the approach of any car from a side street. Perhaps Marilyn's phobia was similarly conditioned during a terrifying or painful experience associated with a thunderstorm.

Table 15–1	*Common Obsessions and Compulsions*

Seventy children and adolescents suffering obsessive-compulsive disorder reported their symptoms.

Obsessions	Reporting symptom
Concern with dirt, germs, or toxins	40%
Something terrible happening (fire, death, illness)	24%
Symmetry, order, or exactness	17%

Compulsions	
Excessive hand washing, bathing, tooth brushing, or grooming	85%
Repeating rituals (in/out of a door, up/down from a chair)	51%
Checking doors, locks, appliances, car brake, homework	46%

Source   Adapted from Rapoport, 1989.

Conditioned fears may remain long after we have forgotten the experiences that produced them (Jacobs & Nadel, 1985). Moreover, some fears arise from stimulus generalization. A person who fears heights after a fall may be afraid of airplanes without ever having flown. Someone might also learn such a fear through observational learning—by observing others' fears. As we saw in Chapter 13, Emotion, wild monkeys transmit their fear of snakes to their offspring, and human parents transmit their fears to their children. Avoiding or escaping the feared situation reduces anxiety, thus reinforcing the phobic behavior. Compulsive behaviors similarly reduce anxiety. If washing your hands relieves your feelings of unease, you will likely wash your hands again when the feelings return.

The Biological Perspective Biologically oriented researchers explain our anxiety-proneness in evolutionary, genetic, and physiological terms.

As we noted on page 394, we humans seem biologically prepared to develop fears of heights, storms, snakes, and insects—dangers that our ancestors faced. Compulsive acts typically exaggerate behaviors that contributed to our species' survival. Grooming gone wild becomes hair pulling. Washing up becomes ritual hand washing. Checking territorial boundaries becomes checking and rechecking a door known to be locked (Rapoport, 1989).

Some people more than others seem genetically predisposed to particular fears and high anxiety. Identical twins often develop similar phobias, in some cases even when raised separately (Carey, 1990; Eckert & others, 1981). One pair of 35-year-old identical female twins independently developed claustrophobia. They also become so fearful of water that each would gingerly wade backward into the ocean, only up to the knees. Among monkeys, fearfulness runs in families. Individual monkeys react more strongly to stress if their close relatives are anxiously reactive (Suomi, 1986).

The biology of general anxiety disorder, panic, and even obsessions and compulsions is measurable as overarousal (Baxter & others, 1987; Buchsbaum & others, 1987; Reiman & others, 1989). For example, PET scans of persons with obsessive-compulsive disorder reveal unusually high activity in an area of the frontal lobes just above the eyes (Figure 15–3) and in a more primitive area deep in the brain. Some antidepressant drugs control obsessive-compulsive behavior by dampening this activity, through affecting the availability of the neurotransmitter serotonin (Rapoport, 1989).

Somatoform Disorders

Ellen becomes dizzy and nauseated in the late afternoon—shortly before she expects her husband home. Her doctor and a neurologist cannot identify a physical cause. They suspect the symptoms have an unconscious psychological origin, possibly triggered by her mixed feelings about her husband. In **somatoform disorders**, such as Ellen's, the distressing symptoms take a somatic (bodily) form, without apparent physical causes. One person may have a variety of complaints—vomiting, dizziness, blurred vision, difficulty in swallowing. Another may experience severe and prolonged pain.

In China, where people less often express the emotional aspects of distress, bodily complaints are common (Draguns, 1990a). Be-

Although we humans seem biologically predisposed to fear heights—certainly an adaptive response—this construction worker seems fearless. Weeks of uneventful existence in his aerial office, and perhaps even an exhilarating moment or two, may have reinforced his comfortable feeling.

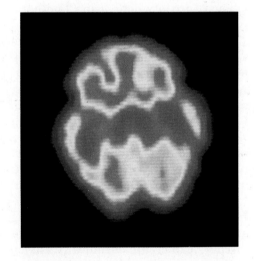

Figure 15–3 A PET scan of a person with obsessive-compulsive disorder reveals abnormally high metabolic activity in the frontal lobes. This is visible in a region of the left hemisphere's frontal lobe involved in directing attention.

cause psychological explanations of anxiety and depression are less socially approved, the Chinese appear more sensitive to and willing to report the bodily symptoms of their distress. Mr. Wu, a 36-year-old technician in Hunan, illustrates one of China's most common psychological disorders (Spitzer & others, 1989). He finds work difficult because of his insomnia, fatigue, weakness, and headaches. Chinese herbs and Western medicines provide no relief. To his Chinese clinician, he seems not so much depressed as exhausted. Similar, generalized bodily complaints have often been observed in African cultures (Binitie, 1975).

Even to people in the West, somatic symptoms are familiar. To a lesser extent, we have all experienced inexplicable physical symptoms under stress. It is little comfort to be told that the problem is "all in your head." Although the symptoms may be psychological in origin, they are nevertheless genuinely felt.

One type of somatoform disorder, more common in Freud's day than ours, is **conversion disorder**, so called because anxiety presumably is converted into a physical symptom. (As we noted in Chapter 14, Freud's effort to treat and understand psychological disorders stemmed from his puzzlement over ailments that had no physiological basis.) A patient with a conversion disorder might, for example, lose sensation in a way that makes no neurological sense. Yet the physical symptoms are real; one could stick pins in the affected area and get no response. Others experience unexplained paralysis, blindness, or an inability to swallow, and are strangely indifferent to their problems.

As you can imagine, somatoform disorders send people not to a psychologist or psychiatrist but to a physician. This is especially true of those who experience **hypochondriasis**. In this relatively common somatoform disorder, people interpret normal sensations (a stomach cramp today, a headache tomorrow) as symptoms of a dreaded disease. Sympathy or temporary relief from everyday demands may reinforce such complaints. No amount of reassurance by any physician convinces the patient not to worry. So the patient moves on to another physician, seeking and receiving more medical attention—but failing to confront the disorder's psychological root.

"He was a dreadful hypochondriac."

Punch/Rothco

Dissociative Disorders

Among the most intriguing disorders are the rare **dissociative disorders**, in which a person experiences a sudden loss of memory or change in identity. Under extreme stress, conscious awareness becomes *dissociated*, or separated, from previous memories, thoughts, and feelings. Certain symptoms of dissociation are not so rare. Now and then, many people may have a sense of being unreal, of being separated from one's body, of watching oneself as in a movie. Facing trauma, such detachment may actually protect a person from being overwhelmed by emotion. Only when such experiences are severe and prolonged do they suggest a dissociative disorder.

Amnesia

Amnesia, the failure to recall events, can be caused by head injuries or alcoholic intoxication. But psychogenic amnesia—a dissociative disorder—usually begins as a response to intolerable psychological stress. One 18-year-old victim was rescued from his sail-boat by the Coast Guard and brought to a hospital. He knew he had gone sailing with friends and that he was a college student, but could not recall what happened to his friends. Moreover, he kept forgetting that he was in the hospital; each reminder surprised him. Later, aided by a drug that relaxed him, he remembered: A ferocious storm had washed his companions overboard.

As this case illustrates, the forgetfulness of amnesia is selective: The young man forgot what was intolerably painful. Those with amnesia may be somewhat disoriented and may forget who they are, but they will remember how to drive, count, and talk. Typically, the amnesia vanishes as abruptly as it began and rarely recurs.

Fugue

Like amnesia, **fugue** (pronounced *fewg*, meaning "flight") involves forgetting, but it also involves fleeing one's home and identity for days, months, or years. Gene Saunders, a mid-level manager, had been passed over for promotion, faulted by his supervisor, and rejected by his 18-year-old son, who during a violent argument called him a "failure." Two days later, Saunders disappeared. A month later and 200 miles away, police brought a man who said he was "Burt Tate" to the emergency room. Tate had been hurt in a fight at a diner, where he had been working as a short-order cook since drifting into town a month earlier. He claimed not to recall where he had lived or worked before that. He admitted that was strange but did not seem upset by it. After a missing person's check, Mrs. Saunders confirmed that Burt Tate was Gene Saunders. Though noticeably anxious when faced with his wife, he denied recognizing her. When "awakening" from a fugue state, people such as Gene Saunders remember their old identities but typically deny remembering what occurred during the fugue.

Multiple Personality

Even more mysterious and controversial is the massive dissociation of self from ordinary consciousness in those with **multiple personality disorder**. These people have two or more distinct personalities. The first is usually restrained and dull, the second more impulsive and uninhibited. The person may be prim and proper one moment and loud and flirtatious the next. Each personality has its own voice and mannerisms, and the original one typically denies awareness of the other(s).

Although people diagnosed as having multiple personality disorder are usually not violent, there have been cases in which the person reportedly became dissociated into a "good" and a "bad" or aggressive personality—a modest version of the Dr. Jekyll/Mr. Hyde split immortalized in Robert Louis Stevenson's story. Freud would say that, rid of the original "good" personality's awareness, the wanton second personality is free to discharge forbidden impulses. One unusual case that for a time seemed to support this interpretation involved Kenneth Bianchi, who was convicted of the "Hillside Strangler" rapes and murders of 10 California women. During a hypnosis session with Bianchi, psychologist John Watkins (1984) "called forth" a hidden personality:

Watkins: *I've talked a bit to Ken, but I think that perhaps there might be another part of Ken that I haven't talked to, another part that maybe feels somewhat differently from the part that I've talked to. . . . Would you talk with me, Part, by saying, "I'm here"?*

Bianchi answered "yes" and engaged in the following interchange:

Watkins: *Part, are you the same thing as Ken, or are you different in any way?*

Bianchi: *I'm not him.*

Watkins: *You're not him? Who are you? Do you have a name?*

Bianchi: *Steve. You can call me Steve.*

When speaking as Steve, Bianchi stated that he hated Ken because Ken was nice and that he (Steve), aided by a cousin, had murdered women. He also claimed that Ken knew nothing about his existence and that Ken was innocent of the murders.

Was Bianchi's second personality a ruse, simply a way of disavowing responsibility for his actions? The psychologist who diagnosed Bianchi believed he was a genuine case of multiple personality. Others doubted it. Perhaps Bianchi, a consistent rule-breaker and liar since childhood, was consciously faking it to save his own skin (Orne, 1984). Or perhaps to dissociate himself from his impulses and actions he unconsciously created the multiple personality during the hypnotic session (Allison, 1984).

Might normal people, for strategic reasons, act as if they had a multiple personality? To find out, one skeptic, Nicolas Spanos (1986b), asked college students to pretend they were accused murderers being examined by a psychiatrist. When given the same hypnotic treatment that Bianchi received, most spontaneously expressed a second personality. Spanos wonders (as he does about similar claims of dissociation during hypnosis): Are clinicians who discover multiple personalities merely triggering people to enact a role? If so, can such people then convince themselves of the authenticity of their own role enactments?

Those who accept multiple personality as a genuine disorder find support in the distinct brain and body states often associated with differing personalities. In one study, ophthalmologists detected shifting visual acuity and eye-muscle balance as patients switched personalities. Such changes did not occur among control subjects trying to simulate multiple personality (Miller & others, 1991).

Skeptics nevertheless find it suspicious that the disorder has just recently become rather popular. There have been at least three times more cases of the disorder reported since 1970 than in the previous 150 years (Orne & others, 1984)—just what one might expect now that the role of multiple personality has been well publicized in books and films, such as *The Three Faces of Eve* and *Sybil*. Moreover, most clinicians have never encountered a multiple personality, and outside North America the disorder is almost nonexistent (Aldridge-Morris, 1989). Yet, strangely, a few North American clinicians claim to encounter them regularly (Levitt, 1988).

With the dissociative disorders as with the anxiety and somatoform disorders, the psychoanalytic and learning perspectives view the symptoms as ways of dealing with anxiety. Psychoanalysts see them as defenses against the anxiety caused by the eruption of unacceptable impulses. Learning theorists see them as behaviors reinforced by anxiety reduction.

"Hillside Strangler" Kenneth Bianchi at his trial.

"Pretense may become reality."
Chinese proverb

Others view dissociative disorders as hypnotic-like states into which people lapse as a protective response to traumatic childhood experiences. Most people diagnosed as multiple personality are women, many of whom suffered physical, sexual, or emotional abuse as children (Coon & others, 1988; Kluft, 1987). Perhaps, then, multiple personalities are the desperate efforts of the traumatized to flee inward. Maladaptive as they may be, such psychological disorders are expressions of our human struggle to cope with and survive the stresses of life.

"Though this be madness, yet there is method in 't."
William Shakespeare
Hamlet, 1600

Mood Disorders

The emotional extremes of **mood disorders** come in two principal forms: (1) **major depression**, in which the person experiences the hopelessness and lethargy of prolonged depression until eventually rebounding to normalcy; and (2) **bipolar disorder**, in which the person alternates between depression and *mania*, an overexcited, hyperactive state.

Major Depression

Perhaps you know what depression feels like. If you are like most of the college students studied by Aaron Beck and Jeffrey Young (1978), at some time during this year—more likely the dark months of winter than during summer—you will probably experience a few of the symptoms of depression. You may feel deeply discouraged about the future, dissatisfied with your life, or isolated from others. You may lack the energy to get things done or even to force yourself out of bed; be unable to concentrate, eat, or sleep normally; or even wonder if you would be better off dead. Perhaps academic success came easily to you in high school, and now you find that disappointing grades jeopardize your goals. Maybe conflicting parental and peer pressures seem intolerable. Perhaps social difficulties, such as loneliness or the breakup of a romance, have plunged you into despair. And maybe your brooding has at times only worsened your self-torment.

If so, you are not alone. Depression is a "common cold" of psychological disorders—an expression that well states its pervasiveness but not its seriousness. Among Americans born since World War II, depression has increased dramatically—tenfold, reports Martin Seligman (1988). Similar trends are evident in Canada, Sweden, Germany, and New Zealand (Klerman & Weissman, 1989). Young adults and women are especially vulnerable.

The line between life's normal "downs" and major depression is difficult to define. Joy, contentment, sadness, and despair are different points on a continuum, points at which any of us may be found at any given moment. Depression can be an appropriate response to profoundly sad events, such as a significant loss or bereavement. To feel bad in reaction to painful events is to be in touch with reality. Major depression occurs when signs of depression (poor appetite; insomnia; lethargy; feelings of worthlessness; or loss of interest in family, friends, and activities) last 2 weeks or more without any notable cause. The difference between a blue mood after bad news and a mood disorder is like the difference between gasping for breath after exercising and being chronically short of breath.

For some people, recurring depression during winter's dark months constitutes a "seasonal affective disorder."

"My life had come to a sudden stop. I was able to breathe, to eat, to drink, to sleep. I could not, indeed, help doing so; but there was no real life in me."
Leo Tolstoy
My Confession, 1887

Bipolar Disorder

After a few weeks or months, depressive episodes usually end with or without therapy. Depressed people typically rebound—usually by returning to their previous behavior patterns. However, some people rebound to or from the opposite emotional extreme—a euphoric, hyperactive, wildly optimistic state of **mania**. If depression is living in slow motion, mania is fast forward. Alternating between depression and mania signals *bipolar disorder*. During the manic phase of a bipolar disorder, the person is typically overtalkative, overactive, elated (though easily irritated if crossed), has little need for sleep, and shows fewer sexual inhibitions. Speech is loud, flighty, and hard to interrupt.

One of mania's maladaptive symptoms is grandiose optimism and self-esteem, which may lead to reckless spending and investment sprees. Although people in a manic state find advice irritating, they need protection from their own poor judgment. In milder forms, however, the energy and free-flowing thinking of mania can fuel creativity. Poets, artists, and playwrights are especially prone to bipolar disorder (DeAngelis, 1989; Jamison, 1989). Handel composed his nearly 4-hour-long Messiah during 3 weeks of intense, creative energy.

It is as true of emotions as all else: What goes up comes down. Before long, the mood either returns to normal or plunges into a brief depression. Though equally maladaptive as major depression, bipolar disorder is much less common, occurring in about 1 percent of the U.S. population. Unlike major depression, it afflicts as many men as women.

Explaining Mood Disorders

Because depression profoundly affects many people, it has been the subject of thousands of studies. Psychologists are working to develop a theory of mood disorders that will suggest ways to treat or prevent them. Researcher Peter Lewinsohn and his colleagues (1985) summarized the facts that any theory of depression must explain. Among them are:

1. Many behavioral and cognitive changes accompany depression. Depressed people are inactive and unmotivated. They also are sensitive to negative happenings. They expect negative outcomes. And they are more likely to recall negative information. When the depression lifts, these behavioral and cognitive accompaniments disappear.

2. Depression is widespread. Its commonality suggests that its causes, too, must be common.

3. Compared to men, women are doubly vulnerable to major depression, even more so if they have been depressed before. Curiously, the gender difference in depression rates does *not* exist in college students or among bereaved persons (Nolen-Hoeksema, 1990).

4. Most depressive episodes last less than 3 months. Although therapy can speed recovery, most people suffering major depression return to normal without professional help.

5. Stressful events related to work, marriage, and close relationships often precede depression. A family member's death, a

Actress Patty Duke spent years suffering with bipolar disorder before she was finally diagnosed and treated. Now she spends her free time educating others about mental illness in thanks "for having been saved from that pit." CBS correspondent Mike Wallace became debilitated by severe depression during a tough libel trial. "Depression is palpable," he says. "You begin to feel like a fake and a fraud. You second-guess everything about everything."

About 50 percent of those who recover from depression will suffer another episode within 2 years. Recovery is more likely to be enduring the longer patients stay well, the fewer their previous episodes, the less stress they experience, and the more social support they have (Belsher & Costello, 1988).

Close-Up **Suicide**

"But life, being weary of these worldly bars,
Never lacks power to dismiss itself."
William Shakespeare
Julius Caesar, 1599

Each year in the United States, more than 25,000 wearied, despairing people will say no to life by electing a permanent solution to what may be a temporary problem. In retrospect, their families and friends may recall signs they now believe should have forewarned them—the suicidal talk, the giving away of possessions, or the withdrawal and preoccupation with death. One-third of those who kill themselves have tried suicide before.

Few of those who talk suicide or think suicidal thoughts (a number that includes one-third of all adolescents and college students) actually attempt suicide, and few of these succeed in killing themselves (Centers for Disease Control, 1989; Westefeld & Furr, 1987). Still, most individuals who do commit suicide have talked of it. And any who do talk suicide are at least sending a signal of their desperate or despondent feelings.

To find out who commits suicide, researchers have compared the suicide rates of different groups.

National differences are puzzling: The suicide rates of Britain, Italy, and Spain are half that in the United States; those of Austria, Denmark, and Switzerland are nearly double (Bureau of the Census, 1990).

Racial differences are intriguing: In the United States, Whites are twice as likely as Blacks to kill themselves (Figure 15–4).

Group differences are suggestive: Suicide rates are higher among the rich, the nonreligious, and the unmarried—including the widowed and divorced (Gartner & others, 1991; Stengel, 1981).

Gender differences are dramatic: Women are much more likely than men to attempt suicide. Depending on

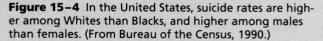

Figure 15–4 In the United States, suicide rates are higher among Whites than Blacks, and higher among males than females. (From Bureau of the Census, 1990.)

wage cut, or a physical assault increase one's risk of depression (Shrout & others, 1989). National samples of Israelis, whose tiny nation is a living stress laboratory, revealed greater feelings of depression after the outbreak of the 1982 Israel-Lebanon war (Hobfull & others, 1989).

As you might expect, researchers understand and interpret these facts in ways that reflect their different perspectives.

The Psychoanalytic Perspective Psychoanalytic theory applies Freud's ideas about the importance of early childhood experiences and unconscious impulses to depression. It suggests that depression occurs when significant losses evoke feelings associated with losses experienced in childhood. Loss of a romantic relationship or job might evoke feelings associated with the loss of the intimate relationship with one's mother. Unresolved anger toward one's parents is also a factor, Freud believed. Some losses, such as a loved the country, however, men are two to three times more likely to succeed. (Men are more likely to use foolproof methods, such as putting a bullet into the brain.)

Age differences have vanished: Due partly to improved reporting (Gist & Welch, 1989), the known suicide rate among 15- to 19-year-olds has more than doubled since 1950 and now nearly equals the traditionally higher suicide rate among adults (Figure 15–5).

Suicide often occurs not when the person is in the depths of depression, when energy and initiative are lacking, but when the person begins to rebound and becomes capable of following through. Teenage suicides may follow a traumatic event, such as a romantic breakup or a guilt-provoking antisocial act, and are often linked with drug and alcohol abuse (Fowler & others, 1986; Kolata, 1986). Compared to people who suffer no disorder, alcoholics are roughly 100 times more likely to commit suicide, as some 3 percent of them do (Murphy & Wetzel, 1990). Even among those who have attempted suicide, alcoholics are five times more likely than nonalcoholics eventually to kill themselves (Beck & Steer, 1989). Among the elderly, suicide is sometimes chosen as an alternative to future suffering. In people of all ages, suicide is not necessarily an act of hostility or revenge, as many people think, but may be a way of switching off unendurable pain (Shneidman, 1987).

Social suggestion may trigger the final act. Following highly publicized suicides and TV programs featuring suicide, known suicides increase. So do fatal auto "accidents" and private airplane crashes (page 558).

Contrary to popular opinion, there are fewer suicides on holidays such as Christmas than at other times of the year (Phillips & Wills, 1987).

Figure 15–5 Teen and young adult suicide has soared since 1950. (From National Center for Health Statistics, 1990; Wilentz, 1987.) In both the United States and Australia, the teen suicide surge is almost entirely among males (Hassan & Carr, 1989).

one's death, may evoke the anger once felt toward parents who were similarly "abandoning" or "rejecting." This anger is unacceptable to the superego, so the emotion turns inward against the self. Combined with the sense of loss, this internalized anger is said to produce depression.

The Biological Perspective Most of the U.S. government's mental health research dollars of late have funded biological explorations of mood disorders. Depression is clearly a whole-body disorder, involving genetic predispositions, biochemical imbalances, melancholy mood, and negative thoughts.

Genetic Influences We have long known that mood disorders run in families. The risk of major depression increases if you have a parent or sibling who became depressed before age 30 (Weissman & others, 1986). If an identical twin has bipolar disorder, the chances are 7 in 10 that the other twin will at some point be diagnosed similarly. If diagnosed as suffering major depression, the chances are about 1 in 2 that at some time the other twin will be, too. Among fraternal twins, the corresponding odds are just under 1 in 5 (Tsuang & Faraone, 1990). Moreover, adopted people who suffer a mood disorder often have close biological relatives who suffer mood disorders, become alcoholic, or commit suicide (Wender & others, 1986).

Biochemical Influences Genes act by directing biochemical events that, down the line, influence behavior. Through what biochemical processes might genes predispose mood disorders? Neurotransmitters, those messenger molecules that shuttle signals between nerve cells, influence depression. Norepinephrine, a neurotransmitter that increases arousal and boosts mood, is overabundant during mania and scarce during depression. A second neurotransmitter, serotonin, sometimes appears scarce during depression. Drugs that alleviate mania reduce norepinephrine; drugs that relieve depression tend to increase norepinephrine or serotonin supplies by blocking either their uptake or chemical breakdown.

Researchers continue to explore the role of these and other neurotransmitters. They hope eventually to identify people who are vulnerable to mood disorders and to prevent their symptoms by counteracting the disorder's biological and psychological underpinnings.

The Social-Cognitive Perspective Biological factors do not operate in a vacuum: As Figure 15–6 suggests, they accompany psychological reactions to experience. Negative interpretations, created by the mind, somehow influence biochemical events that in a vicious cycle amplify the depressing thoughts.

Recent research reveals the precise sorts of *self-defeating beliefs* that feed the vicious cycle. Depressed people view life through dark glasses. Their intensely negative assumptions about themselves, their situations, and their futures lead them to magnify bad experiences and minimize good ones. As one occasionally depressed young woman put it (Burns, 1980, pp. 28–29):

> My thoughts become negative and pessimistic. As I look into the past, I become convinced that everything that I've ever done is worthless. Any happy period seems like an illusion. My accomplishments appear as genuine as the false facade of a Western movie. I become convinced that the real me is worthless and inadequate. I can't move forward with my work because I become frozen with doubt.

Self-defeating beliefs may arise from *learned helplessness*. As we saw in Chapter 14, both dogs and humans act depressed, passive, and withdrawn after experiencing uncontrollable painful events. Women more often than men have been abused or made to feel helpless, which helps explain why women have been twice as vulnerable to depression as men (Nolen-Hoeksema, 1990, and see page 472). (Another explanation is that men more often repress their depressed feelings or drown them in alcohol.)

Maladaptive Explanations Feed Depression Why do life's unavoidable failures lead some people, but not others, to become depressed? The difference lies partly with people's *attributions* of blame. We have some choice of whom or what to blame for our failures. If you fail a test and blame yourself, you may feel stupid and depressed. If you externalize the blame—if you attribute your failure to an unfair test—you are more likely to feel angry.

Figure 15–6 Depression—an ailing mind in an ailing body. Altering any component of the chemistry-cognition-mood circuit can alter the others.

"I have learned to accept my mistakes by referring them to a personal history which was not of my making."
B. F. Skinner (1983)

In more than 100 studies involving some 15,000 subjects (Sweeney & others, 1986), depressed people have tended to explain bad events in terms that are *stable* ("It's going to last forever"), *global* ("It's going to affect everything I do"), and *internal* ("It's all my fault"). Lyn Abramson, Gerald Metalsky, and Lauren Alloy (1989) theorize that the result of these pessimistic, overgeneralized, self-blaming attributions is a depressing sense of hopelessness.

Martin Seligman (1988) argues that depression is now common among young Americans because of epidemic hopelessness, which stems from the rise of individualism and the decline of commitment to religion and family. When facing failure or rejection, contends Seligman, the self-focused individual takes on personal responsibility for problems and has nothing to fall back on for hope. In non-Western cultures, where close-knit relationships and cooperation are more common, major depression is less common and less tied to guilt and self-blame over perceived failure. In Japan, for example, depressed people instead tend to report feeling shame over letting down their family or co-workers (Draguns, 1990a).

Negative Moods Feed Negative Thoughts and Actions There is, however, a chicken-and-egg problem with the cognitive explanation of depression. Self-defeating beliefs, self-blame, and negative attributions surely do support depression, but do they cause it? Peter Barnett and Ian Gotlib (1988) note that such cognitions are better *indicators* than predictors of depression. Depressing thoughts *coincide* with a depressed mood. But before or after being depressed, people's thoughts are less negative. Perhaps this is because, as we noted in our discussion of state-dependent memory (page 274), a depressed mood triggers negative thoughts. If you temporarily put people in a bad or sad mood, their memories, judgments, and expectations are suddenly more pessimistic.

Joseph Forgas and his associates (1984) provide a striking demonstration of the mood effect. Subjects put in a good or bad mood via hypnosis watched a videotape of themselves talking with someone the day before. The happy subjects detected in themselves more instances of positive than negative behavior; the unhappy subjects more often saw themselves behaving negatively (Figure 15–7). Thus, even when viewing themselves on videotape, people judge themselves more negatively when feeling depressed.

Depression's Vicious Cycle Depression is often brought on by stressful experiences—losing a job, being criticized or rejected, physical trauma—anything that disrupts your sense of who you are and why you are a worthy human being (Dohrenwend & others, 1987; Oatley & Bolton, 1985). But bad events per se don't cause depression, for such events don't depress everyone. Depressed people, though, respond to such events in a more self-focused, self-blaming way (Pyszczynski & others, 1991; Wood & others, 1990a,b). This brooding amplifies negative feelings, which in turn trigger depression's other cognitive and behavioral symptoms.

New evidence suggests that there is two-way traffic between depressed mood and negative thinking. Depression causes self-focused negative thinking, and a self-focused, self-blaming style of explaining events puts one at risk for depression when bad events strike. If you tend to see bad grades, social rejection, and work problems as inevitable and your own fault, and if you ruminate about such things, then when bad events happen you will experience a bad case of the blues. For example, Susan Nolen-Hoeksema and

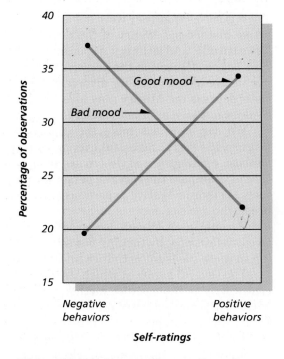

Figure 15–7 A happy or depressed mood strongly influences people's rating of their own behavior. In this experiment, those in a hypnotically induced good mood detected many more positive than negative behaviors. The reverse was true for those in a bad mood. (From Forgas & others, 1984.)

Jannay Morrow (1991) assessed Stanford University students' moods and ruminations 2 weeks before the 1989 earthquake devastated much of their area. Those identified as prone to brood over negative events showed more symptoms of depression both 10 days and 7 weeks after the earthquake. If you have an optimistic way of interpreting events, a failure or stress is unlikely to provoke depression (Seligman, 1991). Even if you do get depressed, you are more likely to recover soon when events brighten (Needles & Abramson, 1990).

Drawings by Charles Shultz; © 1956 United Feature Syndicate, Inc.

Another source of depression's vicious cycle is its social consequences. Being withdrawn, self-focused, and complaining elicits rejection (Coyne & others, 1991). In one study, researchers Stephen Strack and James Coyne (1983) noted that "depressed persons induced hostility, depression, and anxiety in others and got rejected. Their guesses that they were not accepted were not a matter of cognitive distortion." Weary of the depressed person's fatigue, hopeless attitude, and lethargy, a spouse may threaten to leave or a boss may begin to question the person's competence. Indeed, depressed people are at high risk for divorce and job loss, thus compounding their depression. Misery may love another's company, but company does not love another's misery.

We can now assemble the pieces of the depression puzzle (Figure 15–8): (1) Stressful events interpreted through (2) a pessimistic explanatory style create (3) a hopeless, depressed state that (4) hampers the way the person thinks and acts. This, in turn, fuels (1) more negative experiences. On the brighter side, one can break the cycle of depression at any of these points—by moving to a different environment, by reversing one's self-blame and negative attributions, by turning one's attention outward, or by engaging in more pleasant activities and more competent behavior.

The several points at which the cycle can be broken enable several different therapeutic methods (Chapter 16, Therapy). Even without therapy, depression will usually end on its own. Winston Churchill called depression a "black dog" that periodically hounded him. Poet Emily Dickinson was so afraid of bursting into tears in public that she spent much of her adult life in seclusion (Patterson, 1951). Abraham Lincoln was so withdrawn and brooding as a young man that his friends feared he might take his own life (Kline, 1974). As each of these lives reminds us, people can and do struggle through depression. Most regain their capacity to love, to work, and even to succeed at the highest levels.

"Man never reasons so much and becomes so introspective as when he suffers, since he is anxious to get at the cause of his sufferings."
Luigi Pirandello
Six Characters in Search of an Author, 1922

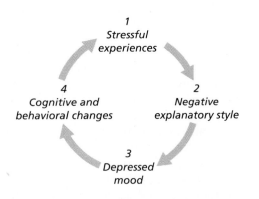

Figure 15–8 The vicious cycle of depression can be broken at any point. The next chapter describes some therapeutic techniques. (Adapted from Lewinsohn & others, 1985.)

Close-Up *Loneliness*

Drawing by Cheney; © 1989 The New Yorker Magazine, Inc.

Loneliness—the painful awareness that one's social relationships are deficient—is both a contributor to depression and a problem in itself. The deficiency stems from a mismatch between one's actual and desired social contacts. One person may feel lonely when isolated and another may feel lonely in a crowd (Peplau & Perlman, 1982). Yet people who are alone—unmarried, unattached, and often young (Figure 15–9)—are more likely to feel lonely. Dutch psychologist Jenny de Jong-

Gierveld (1987) therefore speculates that the modern emphasis on individual fulfillment and the downgrading of stable relationships and commitment to others are "loneliness-provoking factors."

People commonly experience one or more of four types of loneliness (Beck & Young, 1978). To be lonely is to feel *excluded* from a group you would like to belong to; to feel *unloved* and uncared about by those around you; to feel *constricted* and unable to share your private concerns with anyone; or to feel *alienated*, or different from, those in your community. Like depressed people, lonely people tend to blame themselves, attributing their deficient social relationships to their own inadequacies (Snodgrass, 1987). There may be a basis for this self-blame: Chronically lonely people tend to be shy, self-conscious, and lacking in self-esteem (Check & Melchior, 1990; Vaux, 1988). They often find it hard to introduce themselves, make phone calls, and participate in groups (Rook, 1984; Spitzberg & Hurt, 1987). In addition, their belief in their social unworthiness restricts their noticing and remembering positive feedback and from taking steps that would reduce their loneliness (Frankel & Prentice-Dunn, 1990). Thus, factors that work to create and maintain the cycle of depression can also produce a cycle of loneliness.

Figure 15–9 Age differences in loneliness. A statistical digest of 14 data sets involving 25,000 people reveals that loneliness is most common among young adults. (From Perlman, 1991.)

Schizophrenic Disorders

About 1 in 100 people will develop schizophrenia, joining the millions who have suffered one of humanity's most dreaded disorders. Schizophrenia is a psychotic disorder in which a person loses contact with reality by experiencing grossly irrational ideas and distorted perceptions. Schizophrenia typically first strikes during adolescence or young adulthood; it knows no national boundaries and it affects the two sexes about equally.

Symptoms of Schizophrenia

Schizophrenia literally translated means "split mind." It refers not to a multiple-personality split, but rather a *split from reality* that shows itself in disorganized thinking, disturbed perceptions, and inappropriate emotions and actions.

Disorganized Thinking Imagine trying to communicate with Sylvia Frumkin, a young woman whose thoughts spill out in no logical order. Her biographer, Susan Sheehan (1982, p. 25), observed her saying aloud to no one in particular,

> "This morning, when I was at Hillside [Hospital], I was making a movie. I was surrounded by movie stars. The X-ray technician was Peter Lawford. The security guard was Don Knotts. That Indian doctor in Building 40 was Lou Costello. I'm Mary Poppins. Is this room painted blue to get me upset? My grandmother died four weeks after my eighteenth birthday." Miss Frumkin laughed.

As this strange monologue illustrates, the schizophrenia patient's thinking is fragmented, bizarre, and distorted by false beliefs, called **delusions** ("I'm Mary Poppins"). Jumping from one idea to another may even occur within sentences, creating a sort of "word salad." One young man begged for "a little more allegro in the treatment," and suggested that "liberationary movement with a view to the widening of the horizon" will "ergo extort some wit in lectures."

Many psychologists believe disorganized thoughts result from a breakdown in selective attention. As we noted on page 190, we normally have a remarkable capacity for selective attention—for, say, giving our undivided attention to one voice at a party while filtering out competing sensory stimuli. Schizophrenia sufferers have impaired attention (Gjerde, 1983). Thus, an irrelevant stimulus or an extraneous part of the preceding thought easily distracts them. As one former schizophrenia patient recalled, "What had happened to me . . . was a breakdown in the filter, and a hodge-podge of unrelated stimuli were distracting me from things which should have had my undivided attention" (MacDonald, 1960, p. 218).

Disturbed Perceptions The schizophrenia victim experiences an altered world. Minute stimuli, such as the grooves on a brick or the inflections of a voice, may distract attention from the whole scene or from the speaker's meaning. Worse, the person may perceive things that are not there.

Such *hallucinations* (sensory experiences without sensory stimulation) are usually auditory. The person may hear voices that seem to come from outside the head and that make insulting statements or give orders. The voices may tell the patient that she is bad or

Commenting on artwork by schizophrenia patients, as shown here, poet John Ashbery wrote: "The lure of the work is strong, but so is the terror of the unanswerable riddles it proposes."

that he must burn himself with a cigarette lighter or even commit murder. Less commonly, people see, feel, taste, or smell things that are nonexistent. Such hallucinations have been compared to dreams breaking into waking consciousness. When the unreal seems real, the resulting perceptions are at best bizarre and at worst terrifying.

Inappropriate Emotions and Actions The emotions of schizophrenia are often utterly inappropriate. Sylvia Frumkin's emotions seemed split off from reality. She laughed after recalling her grandmother's death. On occasion, she became angry for no apparent reason or cried when others laughed. Other victims of schizophrenia sometimes lapse into "flat affect," a zombielike state of apparent apathy.

Motor behavior also may be inappropriate. The person may perform senseless, compulsive acts, such as continually rocking or rubbing an arm. Those who exhibit "catatonia" may remain motionless for hours on end, and then become agitated.

As you can imagine, disorganized thinking, disturbed perceptions, and inappropriate emotions and actions disrupt social relationships. During their most severe periods, schizophrenia sufferers live in a private inner world, preoccupied with illogical ideas and unreal images. Although most people suffer from schizophrenia only intermittently, others remain socially withdrawn and isolated throughout much of their lives. Rarely is there a one-time episode that is "cured," never to return.

Types of Schizophrenia

We have described schizophrenia as if it were a single disorder. Actually, it is a cluster of disorders that have common features but also some distinguishing symptoms. Schizophrenia patients with *positive symptoms* are conspicuously disorganized and deluded in their talk or prone to inappropriate laughter, tears, or rage. Schizophrenia patients with *negative symptoms* have toneless voices, expressionless faces, or mute and rigid bodies. Thus, schizophrenia is not a single disorder for which there could be but one set of causes.

Sometimes, as in the case of Sylvia Frumkin, schizophrenia develops gradually, emerging from a long history of social inadequacy (which partially explains why those predisposed to schizophrenia often end up in the lower socioeconomic levels, or even as homeless people). Other times it appears suddenly, seemingly as a reaction to stress. There is a rule that holds true around the world (World Health Organization, 1979): When the schizophrenia is a slow-developing process (called *chronic*, or *process*, schizophrenia), recovery is doubtful. When, in reaction to particular life stresses, a previously well-adjusted person develops schizophrenia rapidly (*acute*, or *reactive*, schizophrenia), recovery is much more likely.

Understanding Schizophrenia

Schizophrenia is not only the most dreaded psychological disorder but also one of the most heavily researched. Some important new discoveries link schizophrenia with biological factors, such as brain abnormalities and genetic predispositions.

Brain Abnormalities The idea that imbalances in brain chemistry might underlie schizophrenia has long intrigued scientists. Strange behaviors, they knew, can have strange chemical causes. The saying "Mad as a hatter" refers to the psychological deterioration of British hatmakers whose brains, it was later discovered, were slowly poisoned as they moistened the brims of mercury-laden felt hats with their lips (Smith, 1983). As we saw on page 215, scientists are beginning to understand the mechanism by which chemicals such as LSD produce hallucinations. These discoveries fuel hope that a biochemical key to schizophrenia might be found.

One chemical key to schizophrenia involves the neurotransmitter dopamine. When researchers examined patients' brains after death, they found an excess of receptors for dopamine (Wong & others, 1986). What is more, drugs that block dopamine receptors often lessen schizophrenia symptoms. Drugs that increase dopamine levels, such as amphetamine and cocaine, sometimes intensify schizophrenia symptoms (Swerdlow & Koob, 1987). Such dopamine overactivity may be what makes schizophrenia victims overreactive to irrelevant external and internal stimuli.

Modern brain scanning techniques reveal that many chronic schizophrenia patients have a detectable brain abnormality. Some have abnormally low brain activity in the frontal lobes (Cohen & others, 1988). Others, most often men, have enlarged, fluid-filled areas and a corresponding shrinkage of cerebral tissue (Andreasen & others, 1990a,b; Raz & Raz, 1990).

Genetic Factors Naturally, scientists wonder whether people inherit a predisposition to these brain abnormalities. The evidence strongly suggests that some do. The 100-to-1 odds against any person's being diagnosed with schizophrenia become 10-to-1 among those who have an afflicted sibling or parent, and close to 50-50 among those who have an afflicted identical twin (Figure 15–10). Although there are only a dozen such known cases, it appears that an identical twin of a schizophrenia victim retains that 50-50 chance whether they are reared together or apart.

Adoption studies confirm a genetic link (Gottesman, 1991). Children adopted by someone who develops schizophrenia are unlikely to "catch" the disorder. But adopted children do have an elevated risk if a biological parent is diagnosed with schizophrenia.

People who suffer from schizophrenia often withdraw into an inner world of bizarre thoughts and disturbed perceptions.

When twins differ, only the one afflicted with schizophrenia typically has enlarged, fluid-filled cranial cavities (Suddath & others, 1990). The difference between the twins implies some non-genetic factor is also at work.

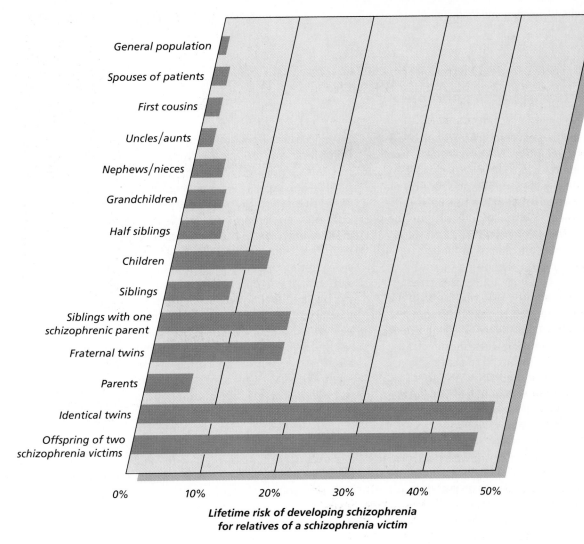

General population

Spouses of patients

First cousins

Uncles/aunts

Nephews/nieces

Grandchildren

Half siblings

Children

Siblings

Siblings with one
schizophrenic parent

Fraternal twins

Parents

Identical twins

Offspring of two
schizophrenia victims

0%   10%   20%   30%   40%   50%

**Lifetime risk of developing schizophrenia
for relatives of a schizophrenia victim**

Figure 15–10 The lifetime risks of suffering from schizophrenia vary with one's genetic relatedness to someone having this disorder. (From Irving Gottesman, 1991, from family and twin studies conducted between 1920 and 1987 in Europe.)

The genetic contribution to schizophrenia is beyond question. But the genetic role is not so straightforward as the inheritance of eye color. After all, about half the twins who share identical genes with a schizophrenia victim do *not* develop the disorder. Thus, behavior geneticists Susan Nicol and Irving Gottesman (1983) conclude that some people "have a genetic predisposition to the disorder but that this predisposition by itself is not sufficient for the development of schizophrenia."

Psychological Factors If, by themselves, genetically predisposed physiological abnormalities do not cause schizophrenia, neither do psychological factors alone. As Nicol and Gottesman report, "no environmental causes have been discovered that will invariably, or even with moderate probability, produce schizophrenia in persons who are not related to a schizophrenic."

Nevertheless, if genes predispose some people to *react* to particular experiences by developing schizophrenia, then there must be identifiable triggering experiences. Researchers have asked: Can stress trigger schizophrenia? Can difficulties in family communications be a contributing factor?

The answer to each question is a strong, clear maybe. The psychological triggers of schizophrenia have proved elusive, partly because they may vary with the type of schizophrenia and whether it is a slow-developing, chronic schizophrenia, or a sudden, acute reaction to stress. It is true that young people with schizophrenia tend to have unusually disturbed communications with their parents.

Does a full moon trigger "madness" in some people? James Rotton and I. W. Kelly (1985) examined data from 37 studies that related lunar phase to crime, homicides, crisis calls, and mental hospital admissions. Their conclusion: There is virtually no evidence of "moon madness." Nor does lunar phase correlate with suicides, assaults, emergency room visits, or traffic disasters (Kelly & others, 1990).

Close-Up **Experiencing Schizophrenia**

These recollections by a recovered schizophrenia patient illustrate the delusions of persecution and grandeur and the hallucinations often experienced by those suffering the positive symptoms of schizophrenia.

One night I was invited to listen to a talk by a worker in the foreign service. I was suspicious of him and thought he thought I was a Communist spy. I didn't say anything. I just leaned over and stared at him.

I thought the Government was spying on my room with a telescope in a building across the street. I thought people were loading down my food in the cafeteria with salt. In criminology class I thought the professor and the other students were laughing about me. I thought they were directing the poisoning of my food in the cafeteria. When I went to the cafeteria my hand shook as the waitress poured what I thought was poisonous coffee into my cup. I thought everyone in the cafeteria knew I was going to die. They all thought it was too bad but I was so evil it was necessary.

On a Saturday I drank lemonade to try to neutralize the poison. Then I would take showers to try to sweat the poison out. I was so nervous I could hardly think. I thought I might only have hours left to live. I thought of taking a bus home to my parents. But no, I thought, it was too late for that.

One day when my strange behavior landed me in a jail cell, the walls began to buzz like bees. I felt there were thousands of bees in the walls buzzing. The buzzing went on and on. There was no relief. It was maddening. Finally, I felt my father's hand rest on my head and I felt peace. Then voices, like the roar of a crowd came. I felt like Jesus; I was being crucified. Night settled in. It was dark. I just continued to huddle under the blanket, feeling weak, laid bare and defenseless in a cruel world I could no longer understand.

When someone asks me to explain schizophrenia I tell them, you know how sometimes in your dreams you are in them yourself and some of them feel like real nightmares? My schizophrenia was like I was walking through a dream. But everything around me was real. At times, today's world seems so boring and I wonder if I would like to step back into the schizophrenic dream, but then I remember all the scary and horrifying experiences. (Excerpted with permission from S. Emmons and C. Geiser, *Adventures in Schizophrenia*, unpublished.)

But is this a cause or a result of their disorder? It is true that stressful experiences, biochemical abnormalities, and schizophrenia's symptoms often occur together. But the traffic between brain biochemistry and psychological experiences runs both ways, so cause and effect are difficult to sort out. It is true that schizophrenic withdrawal often occurs in adolescence or early adulthood, coinciding with the stresses of having to become independent, to assert oneself, and to achieve social success and intimacy. So is schizophrenia the maladaptive coping reaction of biologically vulnerable people?

Hoping to identify the psychological causes of schizophrenia, several investigators are now following the development of "high-risk" children, such as those born to a parent with schizophrenia (Asarnow, 1988; King, 1990). By comparing the experiences of high- and low-risk children who do and don't develop schizophrenia, they are seeking the early warning signs of schizophrenia. So far, these warning signs seem to include:

- a mother whose schizophrenia was severe and long-lasting;
- birth complications and low birth weight;
- separation from parents;
- short attention span and poor muscle coordination; and
- disruptive behavior at school.

Most of us can relate more easily to the ups and downs of mood disorders than to the strange thoughts, perceptions, and behaviors

The odds of any four people picked at random all suffering from schizophrenia are 1 in 100 million. But the identical Genain quadruplets (shown here) do. Problems for the sisters began in high school. Since then they have been in and out of hospitals. Of course, these women shared not only identical genes but also a similar environment.

of schizophrenia. Sometimes our thoughts do jump around, but we do not talk nonsensically. Occasionally we feel unjustly suspicious of someone, but we do not fear that the world is plotting against us. Often our perceptions are distorted, but rarely do we see or hear things that are not there. We have felt regret after laughing at someone's misfortune, but we rarely giggle in response to bad news. At times we just want to be alone, but we do not live in social isolation. However, millions of people around the world do talk strangely, suffer delusions, hear nonexistent voices, see things that are not there, laugh or cry at inappropriate times, or withdraw into their private imaginary worlds. Because this is true, the quest to solve the cruel puzzle of schizophrenia continues.

Personality Disorders

Personality disorders—inflexible and enduring patterns of behavior that impair one's social functioning—sometimes coexist with one of the other psychological disorders, but need not involve anxiety, depression, or loss of contact with reality. For example, a person with a "histrionic personality disorder" displays a shallow, attention-getting emotionality. Histrionic individuals go to great lengths to gain others' praise and reassurance. Those with "narcissistic personality disorder" exaggerate their own importance, aided by success fantasies. They find criticism hard to accept, often reacting with rage or shame.

The most frequent of these disorders, and the most troubling to society, is the **antisocial personality** disorder. The person (formerly called a *sociopath* or a *psychopath*) is typically a male whose lack of conscience becomes plain before age 15, as he begins to lie, steal, fight, or display unrestrained sexual behavior. In adulthood, he may be unable to keep a job, be irresponsible as a spouse and parent, and be assaultive or otherwise criminal. When the antisocial personality combines a keen intelligence with amorality, the result may be a charming and clever con artist.

Despite their antisocial behavior, most criminals do not fit the description of antisocial personality disorder. Most criminals show responsible concern for their friends and family members; antisocial personalities feel little and fear little. In extreme cases, the results can be tragic. Henry Lee Lucas reported that at age 13 he strangled a woman who refused to have sex with him. He at one time confessed to having bludgeoned, suffocated, stabbed, shot, or mutilated some 360 women, men, and children during his 32 years of crime. During the last 6 years of his reign of terror, Lucas teamed with Elwood Toole, who slaughtered about 50 people whom he "didn't think was worth living anyhow." It ended when Lucas confessed to stabbing and dismembering his 15-year-old common-law wife, who was Toole's niece.

The antisocial personality expresses little regret over violating others' rights. "Once I've done a crime, I just forget it," said Lucas. Toole was equally matter-of-fact: "I think of killing like smoking a cigarette, like another habit" (Darrach & Norris, 1984).

As with mood disorders and schizophrenia, the antisocial personality disorder is woven of biological as well as psychological strands. The usual twin and adoption studies reveal that biological relatives of certain individuals are at increased risk for criminality (DiLalla & Gottesman, 1991; Mednick & others, 1987). Their ge-

Cult leader Charles Manson, who with his followers brutally killed nine people over a 2-day period in 1969, is perhaps North America's best known antisocial personality.

netic vulnerability surfaces as minimal arousal under stress, which makes for a rather fearless approach to life. When they await aversive events, such as electric shocks or loud noises, they show little autonomic nervous system arousal (Hare, 1975). Even as youngsters, before committing any crime, it takes more to get them excited (Figure 15–11). If channeled in more productive directions, such fearlessness may lead to courageous heroism or adventurism. Lacking a sense of social responsibility, the same disposition produces a cool con artist or killer (Lykken, 1982).

Perhaps a biologically-based fearlessness, as well as early environment, helps explain the reunion of long-separated sisters Joyce Lott, 27, and Mary Jones, 29 — in a South Carolina prison where both were sent on drug charges. After a newspaper story about their reunion, their long-lost half-brother Frank Strickland called. He explained it would be a while before he could come see them — because he, too, was in jail, on drug, burglary, and larceny charges (Shepherd & others, 1990).

The Commonality of Psychological Disorders

How prevalent are the various disorders discussed in this chapter? Who is most vulnerable to them? At what times of life? To answer such questions, the National Institute of Mental Health undertook during the 1980s a sort of census of psychological disorders in America. In five different regions of the country researchers conducted lengthy, structured interviews with representative samples of people — all told, nearly 20,000 people — and then projected their findings to the entire U.S. population. After asking hundreds of questions that probed for symptoms—"Has there ever been a period of 2 weeks or more when you felt like you wanted to die?"—the researchers estimated both the current and the lifetime prevalence of various disorders.

How many people suffer, or have suffered, a psychological disorder? More than most of us suppose. Sociologist Lee Robins and psychiatrist Darrel Regier (1991, p. 329) report that "one or more of the psychiatric disorders described in this volume had been ex-

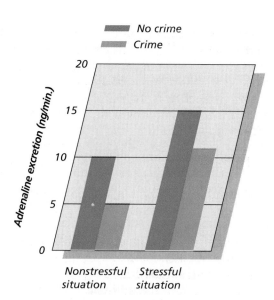

Figure 15–11 Arousability and criminality. Levels of the stress hormone adrenaline were measured in two groups of 13-year-old Swedish boys. In both stressful and nonstressful situations, those who were later convicted of a crime (as 18- to 26-year-olds) showed relatively low reactivity. (From Magnusson, 1990.)

Table 15–2	*Percent of Americans Who Have Ever Experienced Psychological Disorders*					
	Ethnicity			**Sex**		
	White	*Black*	*Hispanic*	*Men*	*Women*	**Total**
Alcohol abuse or dependence	13.6%	13.8%	16.7%	23.8%	4.6%	13.8%
Generalized anxiety	3.4	6.1	3.7	2.4	5.0	3.8
Phobic disorder	9.7	23.4	12.2	10.4	17.7	14.3
Obsessive-compulsive disorder	2.6	2.3	1.8	2.0	3.0	2.6
Mood disorder	8.0	6.3	7.8	5.2	10.2	7.8
Schizophrenic disorders	1.4	2.1	0.8	1.2	1.7	1.5
Antisocial personality	2.6	2.3	3.4	4.5	0.8	2.6

Source   Data from Robins & Regier, 1991.

perienced at some time in their lives by 32% of American adults, and 20% had an active disorder." These surprisingly high rates reflect the inclusion of institutionalized as well as community samples, and surely also reflect how well many people manage to hide disorders such as a phobia, alcohol abuse, or depression. Table 15–2 shows the relative prevalence of most of the disorders we have considered among three ethnic groups and among men and women. As you can see, despite differences in their rates of various psychological disorders, all these groups are vulnerable.

Those who experience a psychological disorder usually do so by early adulthood. "Over 75% of our sample with any disorder had experienced its first symptoms by age 24," report Robins and Regier (p. 331). The symptoms of antisocial personality and of phobic disorder appear earliest, by a median age of 8 and 10, respectively. Symptoms of alcohol abuse, obsessive-compulsive disorder, bipolar disorder, and schizophrenia appear at a median age near 20. Major depression often hits somewhat later, at a median age of 25. Such findings point up the need for research and treatment to help the growing number of people, especially youth and young adults, who suffer the bewilderment and pain of a psychological disorder.

Labeling People: The Power of Preconceptions

As noted earlier, the practice of attaching diagnostic labels to people is controversial. Most clinicians believe that classification helps in describing, treating, and researching the causes of psychological disorders. Critics, however, say that these labels are at best arbitrary and at worst value judgments that, thanks to the medical model, masquerade as science. It is better, they say, to study the roots of specific symptoms, such as delusions or hallucinations, than to study catchall categories, such as schizophrenia (Persons, 1986). Moreover, once we label a person, we view that person differently (Farina, 1982). Labels create preconceptions that can bias our perceptions and interpretations.

In the most controversial demonstration of the biasing power of diagnostic labels, David Rosenhan (1973) and seven of his friends and Stanford University colleagues went to mental hospital admissions offices, complaining of "hearing voices" that were saying "empty," "hollow," and "thud." Apart from this complaint and giving false names and occupations, they truthfully answered all the questions. All eight were diagnosed as psychotic, seven of them as suffering schizophrenia.

That these normal people were misdiagnosed is not surprising. As one psychiatrist noted, if someone swallowed blood, went to an emergency room, and spit it up, would we fault the doctor for diagnosing a bleeding ulcer? What followed was more startling. After admission, the "patients" exhibited no further symptoms. Yet the clinicians were able to "discover" the causes of their disorders after analyzing their (quite normal) life histories. One person was said to be reacting to mixed emotions about his parents. Furthermore, before being released (an average of 19 days later) the "patients'" normal behaviors, such as their note-taking, were often misinterpreted as symptoms.

Other studies confirm that a label can affect how we perceive someone. Ellen Langer and her colleagues (1974, 1980) had people

"One of the unpardonable sins, in the eyes of most people, is for a man to go about unlabelled. The world regards such a person as the police do an unmuzzled dog, not under proper control."
T. H. Huxley
Evolution and Ethics, 1893

rate an interviewee they thought was either normal (a job applicant) or out of the ordinary (a psychiatric or cancer patient). All subjects saw the identical videotape. Yet those who watched unlabeled interviewees perceived them as normal, while those who watched supposed patients perceived them as "different from most people." Therapists (who thought they were evaluating a psychiatric patient) perceived the interviewee as "frightened of his own aggressive impulses," a "passive, dependent type," and so forth. Thus, a label can serve a useful purpose but, as Rosenhan discovered, it can also have "a life and an influence of its own."

Labels can also affect people's self-images and stigmatize them in others' eyes. U.S. Senator Thomas Eagleton experienced this in 1972, when he was dumped as the Democratic party's vice-presidential candidate after it was discovered he had been treated for depression with electroshock therapy. The same stigma surfaced when a female associate of psychologist Stewart Page (1977) called 180 people in Toronto who were advertising furnished rooms for rent. When she merely asked if the room was still available, the answer was nearly always yes. When she said that she was about to be released from a mental hospital, the answer three times out of four was no (as it was when she said she was calling for her brother who was about to be released from jail). When some of those who answered no were called by a second person who simply asked if the room was still available, the advertiser nearly always revealed that it was. Surveys in Western Europe have uncovered similar attitudes toward those labeled mentally ill.

If people form their impressions of psychological disorder from the media, such findings are hardly surprising. Television researcher George Gerbner (1985) reports that 1 in 5 prime-time and daytime programs depicts a psychologically disordered person, and 7 in 10 such programs portray this character as violent or criminal. More than a few schizophrenia-prone people do commit crimes, and some disordered people are amoral and antisocial (Silverton, 1988). However, *most* disordered people are *not* dangerous; instead, they are anxious, depressed, or withdrawn.

Labels not only bias perceptions, they can also change reality. When teachers are told certain students are "gifted," when students expect someone to be "hostile," or when interviewers check to see whether someone is "extraverted," they may act in ways that elicit the very behavior expected (Snyder, 1984). Someone led to think you are nasty may treat you coldly, provoking you to respond as a nasty person would. Labels can serve as self-fulfilling prophecies.

But let us also remember the benefits of diagnostic labels. As Robert Spitzer (1975), the chief author of DSM-III-R, explains:

> There is a purpose to psychiatric diagnosis. It is to enable mental health professionals to (a) communicate with each other about the subject matter of their concern, (b) comprehend the pathological processes involved in psychiatric illness, and (c) control psychiatric outcomes.

We need not dismiss psychological labels in order to be encouraged by the many successful people—including Leonardo da Vinci, Isaac Newton, and Leo Tolstoy—who pursued brilliant careers while enduring psychological difficulties. The bewilderment, fear, and sorrow caused by psychological disorders are real. But, as the next chapter shows, hope is also real.

Summing Up

Psychological disorders fascinate us, partly because most of us will at some time experience or witness them close at hand.

Perspectives on Psychological Disorders

Defining Psychological Disorders Between normality and abnormality there is not a gulf, but a fine and somewhat arbitrary line. Where we draw the line depends on how atypical, disturbing, maladaptive, and unjustifiable a person's behavior is.

Understanding Psychological Disorders The medical model's assumption that psychological disorders are mental illnesses has displaced earlier views that demons and evil spirits were to blame. However, critics question the medical model's labeling of psychological disorders as sicknesses. They argue that the disorders are socially defined and that the labels may be self-fulfilling.

Classifying Psychological Disorders Many psychiatrists and psychologists believe that a system for naming and describing psychological disorders facilitates treatment and research. The current edition of the *Diagnostic and Statistical Manual of Mental Disorders* (DSM-III-R) provides an authoritative classification scheme.

Anxiety Disorders

Those who suffer an anxiety disorder may for no clear reason feel uncontrollably tense and uneasy (generalized anxiety disorder), an anxiety that can escalate into a panic attack. They may be irrationally afraid of a specific object or situation (phobic disorder). Or they may be troubled by repetitive thoughts and actions (obsessive-compulsive disorder). The psychoanalytic perspective views anxiety disorders as the discharging of repressed impulses. The learning perspective sees them as a product of learned helplessness or fear conditioning. The biological perspective considers possible evolutionary, genetic, and physiological influences.

Somatoform Disorders

The somatoform disorders involve a somatic (bodily) symptom—a physiologically unexplained but genuinely felt ailment. Freud was particularly fascinated by conversion disorders, in which anxiety seemed converted to a symptom that had no physiological basis. Today, hypochondriasis (interpreting one's normal sensations as symptoms of a dreaded disease) is a more common somatoform disorder.

Dissociative Disorders

Under stress, a person's conscious awareness may become dissociated (separated) from previous memories, thoughts, and feelings. Dissociative amnesia usually involves selective forgetting in response to stress. Fugue involves not only for-

getting one's identity but also fleeing one's home. Most mysterious of all dissociative disorders are cases of multiple personality; the afflicted person is said to have two or more distinct personalities, with the original typically unaware of the other(s).

Mood Disorders

Major Depression In major depression, the person—without apparent reason—descends for weeks or months into deep unhappiness, lethargy, and feelings of worthlessness before rebounding to normality.

Bipolar Disorder In the less common bipolar disorder, the person alternates between the hopelessness and lethargy of depression and the hyperactive, wildly optimistic, impulsive phase of mania.

Explaining Mood Disorders Current research on depression is vigorously exploring (1) genetic predispositions and neurotransmitter abnormalities and (2) cyclic self-defeating beliefs, learned helplessness, negative attributions, and aversive experiences.

Schizophrenic Disorders

Symptoms of Schizophrenia Schizophrenia shows itself in disorganized thinking (nonsensical talk and delusions, which may stem from a breakdown of selective attention); disturbed perceptions (including hallucinations); and inappropriate emotions and actions.

Types of Schizophrenia Schizophrenia is a set of disorders that emerge either gradually from a long history of social inadequacy (in which case the outlook is dim) or suddenly in reaction to stress (in which case the prospects for recovery are brighter).

Understanding Schizophrenia As they have for depression, researchers have linked certain forms of schizophrenia with brain abnormalities, such as enlarged, fluid-filled cerebral cavities or increased receptors for the neurotransmitter dopamine. Twin and adoption studies also point to a genetic predisposition that, in conjunction with environmental factors, may bring about a schizophrenia disorder.

Personality Disorders

Personality disorders are enduring, maladaptive personality traits. For society, the most troubling of these is the remorseless and fearless antisocial personality.

The Commonality of Psychological Disorders

A 1980s National Institute of Mental Health survey of nearly 20,000 institutionalized and community residents revealed that 1 in 3 American adults has experienced a psychological disorder, and that 1 in 5 does so currently. The three most common disorders are phobic disorder and mood disorder (with women outnumbering men 2 to 1) and alcohol abuse or dependence (with men outnumbering women 5 to 1).

Labeling People: The Power of Preconceptions

Diagnostic labels facilitate mental health professionals' communications and research. Critics point out that we pay a price for these benefits. Labels also create preconceptions that bias our perceptions of people's past and present behavior and unfairly stigmatize them.

Terms and Concepts to Remember

psychological disorder A condition in which behavior is judged atypical, disturbing, maladaptive, and unjustifiable.

medical model The concept that diseases have physical causes that can be diagnosed, treated, and, in most cases, cured. When applied to psychological disorders, the medical model assumes that these "mental" illnesses can be diagnosed on the basis of their symptoms and cured through therapy, which may include treatment in a psychiatric hospital.

DSM-III-R The American Psychiatric Association's *Diagnostic and Statistical Manual of Mental Disorders (Third Edition—Revised)*, a widely used system for classifying psychological disorders. It will be replaced by the forthcoming DSM-IV.

neurotic disorders Former term for psychological disorders that are usually distressing, but allow one to think rationally and function socially. Freud saw the neurotic disorders as ways of dealing with anxiety.

psychotic disorders Psychological disorders in which a person loses contact with reality, experiencing irrational ideas and distorted perceptions.

anxiety disorders Psychological disorders characterized by distressing, persistent anxiety or maladaptive behaviors that reduce anxiety. See *generalized anxiety disorder, obsessive-compulsive disorder, panic attack*, and *phobic disorder*.

generalized anxiety disorder An anxiety disorder in which a person is continually tense, apprehensive, and in a state of autonomic nervous system arousal.

phobic disorder An anxiety disorder marked by a persistent, irrational fear of a specific object or situation.

obsessive-compulsive disorder An anxiety disorder characterized by unwanted repetitive thoughts (obsessions) and/or actions (compulsions).

panic attack A minutes-long episode of intense dread in which a person experiences terror and accompanying chest pain, choking, or other frightening sensations.

somatoform disorders Psychological disorders in which the symptoms take a somatic (bodily) form without apparent physical cause. See *conversion disorder* and *hypochondriasis*.

conversion disorder A rare somatoform disorder in which a person experiences very specific genuine physical symptoms for which no physiological basis can be found.

hypochondriasis A somatoform disorder in which a person misinterprets normal physical sensations as symptoms of a disease.

dissociative disorders Disorders in which conscious awareness becomes separated (dissociated) from previous memories, thoughts, and feelings. See *amnesia, fugue*, and *multiple personality*.

amnesia Loss of memory. Psychogenic amnesia, a dissociative disorder, is selective memory loss often brought on by extreme stress.

fugue [fewg] A dissociative disorder in which flight from one's home and identity accompanies amnesia.

multiple personality disorder A rare dissociative disorder in which a person exhibits two or more distinct and alternating personalities.

mood disorders Psychological disorders characterized by emotional extremes. See *bipolar disorder, major depression*, and *mania*.

major depression A mood disorder in which a person, for no apparent reason, experiences 2 or more weeks of depressed moods, feelings of worthlessness, and diminished interest or pleasure in most activities.

bipolar disorder A mood disorder in which the person alternates between the hopelessness and lethargy of depression and the overexcited state of mania.

mania A hyperactive, wildly optimistic state.

schizophrenia A group of severe psychotic disorders characterized by disorganized and deluded thinking, disturbed perceptions, and inappropriate emotions and actions.

delusions False beliefs, often of persecution or grandeur, that may accompany psychotic disorders.

personality disorders Psychological disorders characterized by inflexible and enduring behavior patterns that impair social functioning.

antisocial personality A personality disorder in which the person (usually a man) exhibits a lack of conscience for wrongdoing, even toward friends and family members. May be aggressive and ruthless or a clever con artist.

For Further Information

You can find further information in this text regarding psychological disorders on the following pages:

Alcoholism, pp. 210–212

Alzheimer's disease, p. 112

Amnesia, pp. 253, 268–271

Brain damage, Chapter 2

Color blindness, pp. 143–144

Eating disorders, pp. 358–360

Epilepsy, p. 48

Hearing impairment, pp. 149–150

Illness, Chapter 17

Mental retardation, pp. 333–334

Post-traumatic stress disorder, p. 515

Sexual dysfunction, p. 365

Sleep disorders, pp. 196–197

Substance abuse, pp. 210–218

For Further Reading

Diagnostic and statistical manual of mental disorders (3rd ed., revised, 1987). Washington, DC: American Psychiatric Association.

Provides the most widely accepted definitions and descriptions of the categories of psychological disorder, including those described in this chapter.

Gottesman, I. I. (1991). *Schizophrenia genesis: The origins of madness.* New York: Freeman.

A leading expert reviews the genetic and environmental roots of schizophrenia and provides first-person accounts of the disorder by patients and their families.

Sheehan, S. (1982). *Is there no place on earth for me?* Boston: Houghton Mifflin.

This Pulitzer prize-winning biography chronicles the transformation of "Sylvia Frumkin" from a highly intelligent grade-school student through her 17 years in mental institutions as a schizophrenia patient.

Styron, W. (1990). *Darkness visible: A memoir of madness.* New York: Random House.

A famous writer's poignant description of his descent into depression. Highly recommended for the family members of depressed people—indeed, for anyone wishing to understand depression's anguish and despair.

Torrey, E. F. (1988). *Surviving schizophrenia: A family manual* (rev. ed.). New York: Harper/Collins.

A comprehensive and caring guide to coping with schizophrenia, written for laypeople.

Therapy

The history of treating psychological disorders reveals how mystifying and intractable these problems are. We can now state with certainty the chemical composition of Jupiter's atmosphere. But in understanding and treating what is much closer to home—the psychological disorders described in Chapter 15—we are only beginning to make real progress. Consider: In the 2200 years since Eratosthenes correctly estimated the earth's circumference, we have charted the heavens, explored the solar system, reconstructed the basic history of life on earth, cracked the genetic code, and eliminated or found cures for all sorts of diseases. Meanwhile, we have treated psychological disorders with a bewildering variety of methods, harsh and gentle: by cutting holes in the head and by giving warm baths and massages; by restraining, bleeding, or "beating the devil" out of people and by placing them in sunny, serene environments; by administering drugs and electric shocks and by talking—talking about childhood experiences, about current feelings, about maladaptive thoughts and behaviors.

Today's favored treatment depends on the therapist's viewpoint. Those who believe that psychological disorders are learned tend to favor psychological therapies. Those who view disorders as biologically rooted are likely to advocate medication as well. Those who believe that disorders are responses to social conditions will, in addition, want to reform the "sick" environment.

William Hogarth's (1697–1764) painting (left) of St. Mary of Bethlehem hospital in London (commonly called Bedlam) depicts the treatment of mental disorders in the eighteenth century. Patients were treated like animals. This chair was designed by Benjamin Rush (1746–1813) "for the benefit of maniacal patients." Rush, considered by many the founder of America's movement for more humane treatment of the mentally ill, believed that they required restraint to regain their sensibilities.

We can classify therapies into two main categories: The *psychological therapies* involve structured interaction (usually verbal) between a trained professional and a client with a problem. The *biomedical therapies* directly affect the nervous system.

The Psychological Therapies

Psychological therapy, or **psychotherapy**, is "a planned, emotionally charged, confiding interaction between a trained, socially sanctioned healer and a sufferer" (Frank, 1982). From among the 250 or more types of psychotherapy (Parloff, 1987), we will consider the most influential techniques. These derive from psychology's major personality theories: psychoanalytic, humanistic, behavioral, and cognitive.

Each technique is distinctive, yet common threads run through them. Therapists who view disorders as an interplay of bio-psycho-social influences may welcome a combination of treatments. Indeed, half of all psychotherapists describe themselves as taking an **eclectic approach**—as using a blend of therapies (Beitman & others, 1989; Smith, 1982). Depending on the client and the problem, an eclectic therapist will use a variety of techniques.

Psychoanalysis

Although most of today's therapists do not practice as Sigmund Freud did, his psychoanalytic techniques survive. **Psychoanalysis** is part of our modern vocabulary, and its assumptions influence many other therapies.

Aims As we noted when considering Freud's theory in Chapters 14 and 15, psychoanalysis assumes that many psychological problems are fueled by childhood's residue of repressed impulses and conflicts. Psychoanalysts try to bring these repressed feelings into conscious awareness where the patient can deal with them. By gradually gaining conscious insight into the origins of the disorder—by fulfilling the ancient imperative to "know thyself" in a deep way—the person in analysis "works through" the buried feelings. The theory presumes that healthier, less anxious living becomes possible when patients release the energy previously devoted to id-ego-superego conflicts.

Methods Psychoanalysis is historical reconstruction. It unearths the past in hopes of unmasking the present. But how?

When Freud discarded hypnosis as unreliable, he turned to **free association**. Imagine yourself as a patient using the free association technique. The analyst invites you to relax, perhaps by lying on a couch. He or she will probably sit out of your line of vision, helping you focus attention on your internal thoughts and feelings. Beginning with a childhood memory, a dream, or a recent experience, you say aloud whatever comes to your mind from moment to moment. It sounds easy, but soon you notice how often you edit your thoughts as you speak, by omitting material that seems trivial, irrelevant, or shameful. Even in the safe presence of the analyst, you may pause momentarily before uttering an embarrassing thought. You may make a joking remark or change the subject to something

In this classical Freudian setting, the psychoanalyst minimizes distraction from the inward journey by sitting out of view of the patient on the couch.

less threatening. Sometimes your mind may go blank or you may find yourself unable to remember important details.

To the psychoanalyst, these blocks in the flow of your free associations are **resistances**. They hint that anxiety lurks and that you are repressing sensitive material. The analyst will want to explore these sensitive areas by making you aware of your resistances and by helping you interpret their underlying meaning. The analyst's **interpretations**—suggestions of underlying wishes, feelings, and conflicts—aim to provide rational, nonpsychotic people with *insight*. If offered at the right moment, the analyst's interpretation—of, say, your not wanting to talk about your mother—may illuminate what you are avoiding. You may then discover what your resistances mean and how they fit with other pieces of your psychological puzzle.

Freud believed that another clue to repressed impulses is our dreams' *latent content* (page 198). Thus, after inviting you to report a dream, the analyst may suggest its hidden meaning, thereby adding yet another piece to your developing self-portrait.

Drawing by Miller; © 1983 The New Yorker Magazine, Inc.

During many such sessions you will probably disclose more of yourself to your analyst than you have ever revealed to anyone. Because psychoanalytic theory emphasizes the formative power of childhood experiences, much of what you reveal will pertain to your earliest memories. You will also probably find yourself experiencing strong positive or negative feelings for your analyst. Such feelings may express the dependency or mingled love and anger that you earlier experienced toward family members or other important people in your life. When this happens, Freud would say you are actually "transferring" your strongest feelings from those other relationships to the analyst. Analysts and other therapists believe that this **transference** exposes long-repressed feelings, giving you a belated chance to work through them with your analyst's help. By examining your feelings toward the analyst you may also gain insight into your current relationships.

Critics say that psychoanalysts' interpretations are hard to refute. If, in response to the analyst's suggested interpretation, you say, "Yes! I see now," your acceptance confirms the analyst's interpretation. If you emphatically say, "No! That doesn't ring true," your denial may be taken to reveal more resistance, which would also confirm the interpretation. Psychoanalysts acknowledge that it's hard to prove or disprove their interpretations. But they insist that interpretations often are a great help to patients.

useful

Traditional psychoanalysis is slow and expensive. It requires up to several years of several sessions a week with a highly trained and well-paid analyst. (Three times a week for just two years at $100 per hour equals about $30,000.) Only those with a high income can afford such treatment.

Although there are relatively few traditional psychoanalysts, psychoanalytic assumptions influence many therapists. We can see this influence in any therapist who tries to understand patients' current symptoms by exploring their childhood experiences; who probes for repressed, emotion-laden information; who seeks to help people gain insight into the unconscious roots of problems and work through newly resurrected feelings. Although influenced by psychoanalysis, these therapists may talk to people face-to-face (rather than out of the line of vision), once a week (rather than several times weekly), and for only a few weeks or months (rather than several years).

No brief therapy excerpt can exemplify the lengthy process of probing the past. But we can illustrate psychoanalysts' goal of enabling insight by offering interpretations. In the following interaction, therapist David Malan responds to all that he has heard from a depressed patient by suggesting insights into her problems. Note how Malan interprets the woman's earlier remarks and suggests that her relationship with him reveals a characteristic pattern of behavior (1978, pp. 133–134):

> **Malan:** *I get the feeling that you're the sort of person who needs to keep active. If you don't keep active, then something goes wrong. Is that true?*
>
> **Patient:** *Yes.*
>
> **Malan:** *I get a second feeling about you and that is that you must, underneath all this, have an awful lot of very strong and upsetting feelings. Somehow they're there but you aren't really quite in touch with them. Isn't this right? I feel you've been like that as long as you can remember.*
>
> **Patient:** *For quite a few years, whenever I really sat down and thought about it I got depressed, so I tried not to think about it.*
>
> **Malan:** *You see, you've established a pattern, haven't you? You're even like that here with me, because in spite of the fact that you're in some trouble and you feel that the bottom is falling out of your world, the way you're telling me this is just as if there wasn't anything wrong.*

Humanistic Therapies

As we noted in Chapter 14, the humanistic perspective emphasizes people's inherent potential for self-fulfillment. Not surprisingly, then, humanistic therapists aim to boost self-fulfillment by helping people grow in self-awareness and self-acceptance. Unlike psychoanalytic therapists, humanistic therapists tend to focus on:

- the present instead of the past;

- awareness of feelings as they occur rather than achieving insights into the childhood origins of the feelings;

- conscious rather than unconscious material;

- taking immediate responsibility for one's feelings and actions rather than uncovering hidden determinants; and

- promoting growth and fulfillment instead of curing illness.

Woody Allen, after awakening from suspended animation in Sleeper: *"I haven't seen my analyst in 200 years. He was a strict Freudian. If I'd been going all this time, I'd probably almost be cured by now."*

Although in this therapy session the couch has disappeared, the influence of psychoanalytic theory probably has not, especially if the therapist probes for the origin of the patient's symptoms by analyzing repressed information from his past.

The late Carl Rogers, at right, actively listening to a client during a group therapy session.

Person-Centered Therapy The most widely used humanistic technique is Carl Rogers' (1961, 1980) **person-centered therapy**. Person-centered therapists focus on the client's conscious self-perceptions rather than on their own interpretations as therapists. The therapist listens, without judgment or interpretation, and refrains from directing the client toward certain insights. This strategy has earned person-centered therapy the label *nondirective* therapy.

Believing that most people already have within themselves the resources for growth, Rogers encouraged therapists to exhibit *genuineness, acceptance,* and *empathy*. When therapists drop their facades and genuinely express their true feelings, when they enable their clients to feel unconditionally accepted, and when they empathically sense and reflect their clients' feelings, the clients may increase in self-understanding and self-acceptance. Rogers (1980, p. 10) explained:

> Hearing has consequences. When I truly hear a person and the meanings that are important to him at that moment, hearing not simply his words, but him, and when I let him know that I have heard his own private personal meanings, many things happen. There is first of all a grateful look. He feels released. He wants to tell me more about his world. He surges forth in a new sense of freedom. He becomes more open to the process of change.
>
> I have often noticed that the more deeply I hear the meanings of the person, the more there is that happens. Almost always, when a person realizes he has been deeply heard, his eyes moisten. I think in some real sense he is weeping for joy. It is as though he were saying, "Thank God, somebody heard me. Someone knows what it's like to be me."

"Hearing" refers to Rogers' technique of **active listening**—echoing, restating, and seeking clarification of what the person expresses—verbally or nonverbally—and acknowledging the expressed feelings. Active listening is now an accepted part of therapeutic counseling practices in many schools, colleges, and clinics. The counselor listens attentively and interrupts only to restate and confirm the client's feelings, to accept what the client is expressing, or to seek clarification. In fact, active listening is so easily described (though not so easily practiced) that computer scientist Joseph Weizenbaum developed a delightful computer pro-

"We have two ears and one mouth that we may listen the more and talk the less."
    Zeno, 335–263 B.C.
    Diogenes Laertius

gram named ELIZA that simulates a Rogerian counselor. A few moments ago I (DGM) sat before a computer terminal and had the following "conversation" with ELIZA:

ELIZA: *How do you do. Please state your problem.*

DGM: *Hi, I guess I am feeling just a little nervous.*

ELIZA: *How long have you been feeling a little nervous?*

DGM: *I suppose that when I am writing I am always a little anxious.*

ELIZA: *Can you think of a specific example?*

DGM: *Well, I'm wondering whether students will find this stuff as interesting as I do.*

ELIZA: *Why do you believe it isn't normal to be wondering whether students will find this stuff as interesting as you do?*

DGM: *Maybe it is normal. I guess every author must feel the same. . . .*

ELIZA: *What are your feelings now?*

DGM: *Glad that you are willing to listen.*

ELIZA: *Why would you confide in someone who is willing to listen?*

DGM: *Sometimes it just helps to talk things over.*

ELIZA: *What does that suggest to you?*

DGM: *Perhaps that I should share my feelings more openly.*

ELIZA: *Your feelings more openly.*

DGM: *Yes.*

ELIZA: *I understand, please go on.*

DGM: *Do you understand?*

ELIZA: *Oh, I do understand at times.*

Although ELIZA is infinitely patient and nonjudgmental, she does not understand. She is nothing more than what Weizenbaum programmed—a parody of a nonjudgmental, person-centered therapist. Real interaction requires what the computer lacks—a sensitivity to meaning and nonverbal cues and an ability to clarify by reflecting meanings in *different* words. Compare ELIZA's conversation with me with the interaction between Carl Rogers and a 28-year-old male client (Meador & Rogers, 1984, p. 167):

Client: *I just ain't no good to nobody, never was, and never will be.*

Rogers: *Feeling that now, hm? That you're just no good to yourself, no good to anybody. Never will be any good to anybody. Just that you're completely worthless, huh?—Those really are lousy feelings. Just feel that you're no good at all, hm?*

Client: *Yeah. (Muttering in low, discouraged voice) That's what this guy I went to town with just the other day told me.*

Rogers: *This guy that you went to town with really told you that you were no good? Is that what you're saying? Did I get that right?*

Client: *M-hm.*

Rogers: *I guess the meaning of that if I get it right is that here's somebody that—meant something to you and what does he think of you? Why, he's told you that he thinks you're no good at all. And that just really knocks the props out from under you. (Client weeps quietly.) It just brings the tears. (Silence of 20 seconds)*

Client: *(Rather defiantly) I don't care though.*

Rogers: *You tell yourself you don't care at all, but somehow I guess some part of you cares because some part of you weeps over it.*

As this brief excerpt illustrates, the person-centered counselor seeks to provide a psychological mirror that helps clients see themselves more clearly. But can a therapist be a perfect mirror, without selecting and interpreting what is reflected? Rogers conceded that one cannot be *totally* nondirective. Nevertheless, he believed that the therapist's most important contribution is to accept and understand the client. Given a nonjudgmental, grace-filled environment that provides "unconditional positive regard," people may accept even their worst traits and feel valued and whole.

Gestalt Therapy Another influential humanistic therapy, developed by Fritz Perls (1969), joins the psychoanalytic emphasis on bringing unconscious feelings and conflicts into awareness with the humanistic emphasis on getting in touch with oneself and taking responsibility for oneself in the present. Perls' **Gestalt therapy** aims to make people whole by breaking through their defenses and helping them sense and express their moment-to-moment feelings. "All therapy that has to be done can only be done in the now," said Perls (1970). "Nothing exists except in the now."

Eavesdropping on a Gestalt therapy session, we might hear the therapist using any one of several techniques for getting people to express their real feelings and to "own responsibility" for them. One way is to train people to speak in the first person (Passons, 1975, p. 79):

Client: *When you go skiing you feel healthy and vigorous. You have this sense of excitement.*

Therapist: *Sue, try saying the same thing only substituting the word "I" for "you."*

Client: *Why?*

Therapist: *Because I believe you're saying something about yourself except you're not sounding that way.*

Client: *When I'm skiing I feel healthy and excited.*

Therapist: *Do you hear the difference?*

Client: *Yes. The second one is what I really meant.*

To encourage people to take responsibility for their feelings, the Gestalt therapist might get them to change their verbs—to say, "I want" instead of "I need," "I choose to" instead of "I have to," and "I won't" instead of "I can't" (Passons, 1975, p. 82):

Client: *Every day I just sit there and feel like a stooge. I just can't speak up in that class.*

Therapist: *You say you can't.*

Client: *That's right. I've tried and I know I should, I mean I know the stuff, that's not the problem. I just can't get the words out.*

Therapist: *Try saying "I won't talk" instead of "I can't talk."*

Client: *I won't talk in that class.*

Therapist: *Let yourself feel how you are refusing to talk.*

Client: *I guess I am holding myself back a little.*

Therapist: *What are your objections to speaking up?*

Client: *Well, everyone else in there seems to be talking just to talk. I don't like doing that.*

Gestalt therapists also capitalize on the power of actions to affect thoughts and feelings (see Chapter 18, Social Psychology). The

In this Gestalt therapy session, the client is role-playing by addressing the "empty chair" in an effort to better understand her feelings. She may be addressing a person from her past or present, or herself, or even an important inanimate object.

therapist may ask people to role-play different aspects of their relationships or to act out suppressed feelings. Gestalt therapists encourage people to be true to themselves by becoming more aware and expressive of their feelings.

Group Therapies Most of the therapies we are considering may also occur in therapist-led small groups. Although it does not provide the same degree of therapist involvement with each client, group therapy saves therapists' time and clients' money. More important, the social context allows people to discover that others have problems similar to their own and to try out new ways of behaving. As you have perhaps experienced, it can help to get honest feedback—to be reassured that you look poised even while feeling anxious and self-conscious. And it can be a relief to find that you are not alone—to learn that others, despite their seeming composure, share your problems and your feelings of loneliness, inadequacy, or anger. Such has been the experience of a wide range of people, from cancer patients to dieters to alcoholics (Yalom, 1985).

One popular form of group experience for those not seriously disturbed began as sensitivity training groups (T-groups, for short) in which teachers, executives, and others practiced relating to one another more sensitively and openly. Leaders encouraged groups of 12 to 20 people to be less inhibited and defensive, to "talk straight," and to listen empathically. Before long, Carl Rogers (1970) and others were offering *encounter groups*—groups that confronted emotion-laden experiences openly and honestly. Although encounter groups are not as popular today as they were during the 1970s, they set the stage for the emergence of countless *self-help* and *support groups*—for substance abusers, divorced people, gamblers, the bereaved, and for those simply seeking personal growth. Each year in the United States, some 7 million people participate in such groups (Jacobs & Goodman, 1989).

One special type of group interaction, **family therapy**, assumes that no person is an island. We live and grow in relation to others, especially our families. We struggle to differentiate ourselves from our families but we also need to connect with them emotionally. Some of our problem behaviors arise from the tension between these two tendencies, which often creates family stress.

Carl Rogers

Family therapists therefore work with family groups to heal relationships. Their aim is to help family members discover the role they play within their family's social system. A child's rebellion, for example, affects and is affected by other family tensions. Family

Family therapy often acts as a preventive mental health strategy. The therapist helps family members understand how the ways they relate to each other create problems. The treatment emphasis is not on changing the individuals but rather on changing their relationships and interactions.

therapists also aim — usually with some success, research suggests (Hazelrigg & others, 1987; Shadish, 1992) — to open up communication within the family or to help family members discover new ways of preventing or resolving conflicts.

Behavior Therapies ✗

All the therapies we have considered so far assume that, for nonpsychotic people at least, psychological problems diminish as self-awareness grows. The psychoanalyst expects problems to subside as people gain insight into their unresolved and unconscious tensions. So does the humanistic therapist, as people "get in touch with their feelings." Behavior therapists, however, doubt that self-awareness is the key. They assume that the problem behaviors *are* the problems. You can, for example, become aware of why you are highly anxious during exams and still be anxious. Instead of trying to alleviate distressing behaviors by resolving a presumed underlying problem, **behavior therapy** applies well-established learning principles to eliminate the unwanted behavior. To treat phobias or sexual dysfunctions, behavior therapists do not delve deep below the surface looking for inner causes. Rather, they try to replace problem thoughts and maladaptive behaviors with more constructive ways of thinking and acting.

Classical Conditioning Techniques One cluster of behavior therapies derives from principles developed in Pavlov's conditioning experiments (pages 229–232). As Pavlov and others showed, we learn various behaviors and emotions through classical conditioning. So, are maladaptive symptoms conditioned responses? If, say, a claustrophobic fear of elevators is a learned response to the stimulus of being in an enclosed space, then might one unlearn the fear by applying extinction principles? Even if stimulus associations are only maintaining a maladaptive response, might we countercondition the response? **Counterconditioning** pairs the trigger stimulus with a new response that is incompatible with fear. For example, if we repeatedly pair the enclosed space of the elevator with a relaxed response, the fear response may be displaced. Two such counterconditioning techniques are *systematic desensitization* and *aversive conditioning*.

Systematic Desensitization Picture this scene reported in 1924 by Mary Cover Jones, an associate of the behaviorist John B. Watson: Three-year-old Peter is woefully afraid of rabbits and other furry objects. (Unlike Little Albert's laboratory-conditioned fear of white rats, described in Chapter 8, Peter's fears arose during the course of his life at home and is more intense.) Jones' aim is to replace Peter's fear of rabbits with a conditioned response that is incompatible with fear. Her strategy is to associate a fear-evoking rabbit with the pleasurable, relaxed response associated with eating.

As the hungry child begins eating his mid-afternoon snack, Jones introduces a caged rabbit on the other side of the huge room. Peter hardly notices as he eagerly munches his crackers and milk. On succeeding days, she gradually moves the rabbit closer and closer. Within 2 months, Peter tolerates the rabbit in his lap and strokes it while he eats. Moreover, his fear of other furry objects subsides as well, having been "countered" or replaced by a relaxed state that cannot coexist with fear (Fisher, 1984; Jones, 1924).

Unfortunately for those who might have been helped by her counterconditioning procedures, Jones' story of Peter and the rabbit did not immediately become part of psychology's lore. More than 30 years later, psychiatrist Joseph Wolpe (1958, 1982) refined her technique into what has become the most widely used method of behavior therapy: **systematic desensitization**. Wolpe assumed, as did Jones, that you cannot simultaneously be anxious and relaxed. Therefore, if you can repeatedly relax when faced with anxiety-provoking stimuli, you can gradually eliminate your anxiety. The trick is to proceed gradually.

Let's see how this might work with a common phobia. Imagine yourself afraid of public speaking. A behavior therapist might first ask your help in constructing a hierarchy of anxiety-triggering speaking situations. Your anxiety hierarchy could range from mildly anxiety-provoking situations, such as speaking up in a small group of friends, to panic-provoking situations, such as having to address a large audience.

The therapist would then train you to relax. You learn to relax one muscle group after another, until you achieve a drowsy state of complete relaxation and comfort. Then, with your eyes closed, the therapist asks you to imagine a mildly anxiety-arousing situation: You are having coffee with a group of friends and are deciding whether or not to speak up. If imagining the scene causes you to feel any anxiety, you signal your tension by raising your finger, and the therapist instructs you to switch off the mental image and go back to deep relaxation.

This imagined scene is repeatedly paired with relaxation until you can feel no trace of anxiety while imagining it. The therapist progresses up your anxiety hierarchy with this *progressive relaxation* technique, by using the relaxed state to desensitize you to each imagined situation. After several therapy sessions, you practice the imagined behaviors in actual situations, beginning with relatively easy tasks and gradually moving to more anxiety-filled ones (Figure 16–1). Conquering your anxiety in an actual situation, not just in your imagination, raises your self-confidence (Foa & Kozak, 1986; Williams, 1987). Eventually, you may even become a confident public speaker.

Therapists sometimes combine systematic desensitization with other techniques. With phobias, they may have someone model appropriate behavior in a fear-arousing situation. If you were afraid of snakes, you would first observe someone handling a snake. Then you would be coaxed in gradual steps to approach, touch, and handle it yourself (Bandura & others, 1969). By applying this principle of observational learning, therapists have helped people overcome disruptive fears of snakes, spiders, and dogs.

Notice that the systematic desensitization and modeling procedures make no attempt to help you achieve insight into your fear's underlying cause. If you are afraid of heights, the therapist will not spend much time probing when you first experienced this fear or what may have caused it. Nor do behavior therapists worry that eliminating your fear of heights will leave an underlying problem that may now be expressed as, say, a fear of elevators. On the contrary, they find that overcoming maladaptive behaviors helps people feel better about themselves.

Aversive Conditioning In systematically desensitizing a patient, the therapist seeks to substitute a positive (relaxed) response for a negative (fearful) response to a harmless stimulus. In **aversive**

Professor Gallagher and his controversial technique of simultaneously confronting the fear of heights, snakes and the dark.

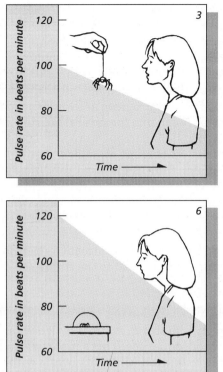

Figure 16-1 Systematic desensitization of a phobia. Beverly, who is terribly afraid of spiders, is gradually able to relax— as shown by her decreasing pulse rate as she spends time in the presence of the aversive object—first at the sight of a spider, then in the presence of a toy spider, a dead spider, and a live one. (From Gilling & Brightwell, 1982.)

conditioning, the therapist tries to replace a positive response to a harmful stimulus with a negative (aversive) response. Thus, aversive conditioning is the reverse of systematic desensitization.

The procedure is simple: It associates unwanted behavior with unpleasant feelings. In treating an alcoholic, aversion therapists offer appealing drinks laced with a drug that produces severe nausea. By linking the drinking of alcohol with violent nausea, the therapist seeks to transform the alcoholic's reaction to alcohol from positive to negative (see Figure 16-2, and recall the taste aversion experiments in Chapter 8). Similarly, by giving child molesters electric shocks as they view photos of nude children, aversion therapists aim to eliminate the molesters' sexual response to children. And by giving withdrawn and self-abusing autistic children harmless "aversives," such as a spray of cold water in the face, therapists hope to suppress self-injury while reinforcing more appropriate behavior. Because this therapy involves an unpleasant experience, it is practiced sparingly and only with the appropriate consent.

Does aversive conditioning work? In the short run it may. But, as we saw in Chapter 8, the problem is that cognition influences conditioning. People know that outside the therapist's office they can drink without fear of nausea or engage in sexually deviant be-

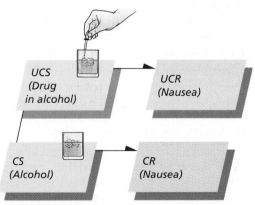

Figure 16-2 Aversion therapy for alcoholics. After repeatedly imbibing an alcoholic drink mixed with a drug that produces severe nausea, some patients develop at least a temporary conditioned aversion to alcohol.

havior without fear of shock. The person's ability to discriminate between the aversive conditioning situation and all other situations can limit the treatment's effectiveness.

Aversive conditioning of alcoholics has, nevertheless, enjoyed renewed popularity. For example, Arthur Wiens and Carol Menustik (1983) studied 685 alcoholic patients who completed an aversion therapy program at a Portland, Oregon, hospital. One year later, after returning for several booster treatments of alcohol-sickness pairings, 63 percent were still successfully abstaining. Three years later, 33 percent remained abstinent.

A milder form of classical conditioning, developed by learning theorist O. H. Mowrer, exists for chronic bedwetters. The child sleeps on a liquid-sensitive pad connected to an alarm. Moisture on the pad triggers the alarm, awakening the child. With repetition, this association of urinary relaxation with awakening stops the bedwetting. Usually, the treatment is permanently effective and the success provides a boost to the child's self-image (Sherman & Levin, 1979).

Operant Conditioning Through Behavior Modification As we saw in Chapter 8, voluntary behaviors are strongly influenced by their consequences. This simple fact enables behavior therapists to reinforce desired behaviors, while withholding reinforcement for undesired behaviors. Using operant conditioning to solve specific behavior problems is called **behavior modification**, a therapy that has raised hopes for some cases thought hopeless. Retarded children have been taught to care for themselves. Autistic children have learned to interact. People with schizophrenia have been helped to behave more rationally on the hospital ward.

In extreme cases, the treatment must be intensive. For 19 withdrawn, uncommunicative, 3-year-old autistic children in one study, it involved a 2-year, 40-hour-a-week shaping program by their parents (Lovaas, 1987). But the combination of positive reinforcement of desired behaviors and the ignoring or punishing of aggressive and self-abusive behaviors worked wonders. By first grade, 9 of the 19 children were functioning successfully in school and exhibiting normal intelligence. Only 1 of 40 comparable children who did not undergo this treatment showed similar improvement.

The rewards used to modify behavior vary. With some people the reinforcing power of attention or praise is sufficient. Others require more concrete rewards, such as food. In institutional settings, therapists may create a **token economy**. When people display appropriate behavior, such as getting out of bed, washing, dressing, eating, talking coherently, cleaning up their rooms, or playing cooperatively, they receive a token or plastic coin (Kazdin, 1982). Later, they can exchange their accumulated tokens for various rewards, such as candy, television watching, trips to town, or better living quarters. Therapists use tokens to shape behavior in the step-by-step manner described on page 237. Token economies have been successfully applied in various settings (classrooms, hospitals, homes for the delinquent) and with various populations (disturbed children, the mentally retarded, schizophrenia patients).

Critics of behavior modification express two concerns. One concern is practical: What happens when the reinforcers stop, as when the person leaves the institution? Might the person have become so dependent on the extrinsic rewards that the appropriate behaviors

The best candidates for alcoholism treatment programs are people with good jobs, stable relationships, and no history of treatment failures (Holden, 1987b).

What might a psychoanalyst say about this therapy for bedwetting? How might a behavior therapist reply?

If this boy completes his work before the timer goes off, the therapist will reward him with a token. He can later exchange the accumulated tokens for special privileges. This form of behavior modification can effectively overcome specific behavior problems.

quickly disappear? If so, how can behavior therapists make the appropriate behaviors durable? First, they may wean patients from the tokens by shifting them toward rewards, such as social approval, more typical of life outside the institution. They may also train patients to behave in ways that are intrinsically rewarding. As a withdrawn person becomes more socially competent, for example, the intrinsic satisfactions of social interaction may help maintain the behavior.

The second concern is ethical: Is it right for one human to control another's behavior? Those who set up token economies typically deprive people of something they desire and then decide which behaviors they will reinforce. To critics, the whole behavior modification process has a totalitarian taint. Advocates reply that control already exists; rewards and punishers are already maintaining destructive behavior patterns. So why not reinforce adaptive behavior instead? What is more, behavior modification increases *self*-control. They argue that treatment with positive rewards is more humane than being institutionalized or punished, and that the right to effective treatment and to an improved life justifies temporary deprivation.

Cognitive Therapies

We have seen how behavior therapists treat specific fears and problem behaviors. But how do they deal with major depression or general anxiety? One can reinforce healthier behaviors and train people to avoid "high risk" situations. Still, when anxiety has no focus, making a hierarchy of anxiety-triggering situations is difficult. The "cognitive revolution" that has so changed psychology during the last three decades has influenced how therapists treat these less clearly defined psychological problems.

The **cognitive therapies** assume that our thinking colors our feelings (Figure 16–3). As we noted in the last chapter's discussion of depression, self-blaming and overgeneralized explanations of bad events are an integral part of the vicious cycle of depression. The depressed person interprets a suggestion as criticism, disagreement as dislike, praise as flattery, friendliness as pity. If such thinking patterns are learned, then surely they can be replaced (Brewin, 1989). Thus, cognitive therapists try in various ways to teach people new, more constructive ways of thinking.

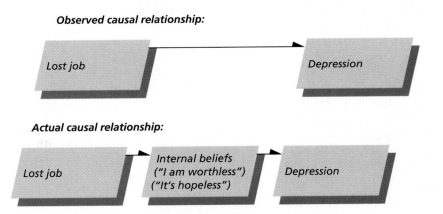

Observed causal relationship:

Lost job → Depression

Actual causal relationship:

Lost job → Internal beliefs ("I am worthless") ("It's hopeless") → Depression

Figure 16–3 A cognitive perspective on psychological disorders. The person's emotional reactions are produced not directly by the event, but by the person's thoughts in response to the event.

Rational-Emotive Therapy According to Albert Ellis (1962, 1987), the creator of **rational-emotive therapy**, many problems arise from irrational thinking. For example, he describes a disturbed woman (1984, p. 198):

> [She] does not merely believe it is *undesirable* if her love partner is rejecting. She tends to believe, also, that (1) it is *awful*; (2) she *cannot stand* it; (3) she *should not*, must not be rejected; (4) she will *never* be accepted by any desirable partner; (5) she is a *worthless person* because one lover has rejected her; and (6) she *deserves to be damned* for being so worthless. Such common covert hypotheses are nonsensical. . . . They can be easily elicited and demolished by any scientist worth his or her salt; and the rational-emotive therapist is exactly that: an exposing and nonsense-annihilating scientist.

Does this sound like the opposite of the warm, caring, reflective acceptance of feelings expressed by Carl Rogers? It very nearly is. Ellis intends to "make mincemeat" of people's illogical ideas—that we must be loved by everyone, that we must be thoroughly competent and successful at everything, that it is a disaster when things do not go as we wish. Change people's thinking by revealing the "absurdity" of their self-defeating ideas, he believes, and you will change their self-defeating feelings and actions. Let's eavesdrop as tart-tongued Ellis exhibits his confrontational style with a 25-year-old female client who suffers feelings of guilt, unworthiness, and depression (1989, p. 219):

> **Ellis:** *The same crap! It's always the same crap. Now if you would look at the crap—instead of "Oh, how stupid I am! He hates me! I think I'll kill myself!"—then you'd get better right away.*
>
> **Client:** *You've been listening! (laughs)*
>
> **Ellis:** *Listening to what?*
>
> **Client:** *(laughs) Those wild statements in my mind, like that, that I make.*
>
> **Ellis:** *That's right! Because I know that you have to make those statements—because I have a good theory. And according to my theory, people couldn't get upset unless they made those nutty statements to themselves. . . . Even if I loved you madly, the next person you talk to is likely to hate you. So I like brown eyes and he likes blue eyes, or something. So you're then dead! Because you really think: "I've got to be accepted! I've got to act intelligently!" Well, why?*
>
> **Client:** *(very soberly and reflectively) True.*
>
> **Ellis:** *You see?*
>
> **Client:** *Yes.*
>
> **Ellis:** *Now, if you will learn that lesson, then you've had a very valuable session. Because you don't have to upset yourself. As I said before: If I thought you were the worst [expletive] who ever existed, well that's my opinion. And I'm entitled to it. But does it make you a turd?*
>
> **Client:** *(reflective silence)*
>
> **Ellis:** *Does it?*
>
> **Client:** *No.*
>
> **Ellis:** *What makes you a turd?*
>
> **Client:** *Thinking that you are.*
>
> **Ellis:** *That's right! Your belief that you are. That's the only thing that could ever do it. And you never have to believe that. See? You control your thinking. I control my thinking—my belief about you. But you don't have to be affected by that. You always control what you think.*

Mini Debate

Values in Psychotherapy

Essentially all therapists aim to enhance their clients' sensitivity, openness, personal responsibility, and sense of purpose (Jensen & Bergin, 1988). But on other matters they may differ from one another and from their clients (Kelly, 1990). That raises an issue: What values prevail in psychotherapy? What values *should* prevail? Psychotherapists Allen Bergin (co-editor of the *Handbook of Psychotherapy and Behavior Change*) and Albert Ellis (rational-emotive therapist) offer sharply contrasting positions. Bergin and Ellis disagree more radically than most therapists regarding what values are healthiest. In so doing, however, they illustrate what they agree on: that values are an inevitable part of psychotherapy and that therapists should acknowledge them more openly.

Allen Bergin

Albert Ellis

The dominant values in psychotherapy can be contrasted with those of a theistic approach that roots values in faith in God. The prevailing clinical-humanistic values assume that (a) because humans are supreme, the individual self should be liberated from external authority, (b) self-expression and self-gratification are to be encouraged, (c) self-worth is defined through relationships with others, and (d) meaning and purpose are derived from one's own reason and intellect. By contrast, theistic values assume that (a) because God is supreme, humility and the acceptance of divine authority are virtues, (b) self-control and committed love and self-sacrifice are to be encouraged, (c) self-worth is defined through a relationship with God, and (d) meaning and purpose are derived from spiritual insight.

Drawing from my own religious values, I offer some testable hypotheses: (1) Religious communities that provide both a belief structure and a network of loving support should manifest lower rates of emotional disorder. (2) Those who endorse high standards of impulse control will suffer lower than average rates of alcoholism, addiction, divorce, and emotional instability. (3) Infidelity to any interpersonal commitment, especially marriage, leads to harmful consequences. (4) Teaching clients love, commitment, service, and sacrifice for others will help heal interpersonal difficulties and reduce intrapsychic distress. (5) Improving male commitment, caring, and responsibility in families will reduce marital and familial conflict and associated psychological disorders.

Source Adapted, with permission, from an exchange in the *Journal of Consulting and Clinical Psychology*, 1980, Vol. 48, pp. 102–103, 635, 637–638.

Bergin does not properly represent the views of nondogmatic atheistic clinicians like myself who tend to believe that human disturbance largely springs from absolutistic thinking—from dogmatism, inflexibility, and devout shoulds, oughts, and musts—and that extreme religiosity is essentially emotional disturbance. I assume that (a) no one and nothing is supreme, (b) relationships with others do not define self-worth (nothing does—self-acceptance can be had for the asking), (c) self-gratification is encouraged with mutually chosen partners, with or without long-term responsibilities, and (d) meaning is derived from personal desire and validated by test and by reason.

I therefore offer the following alternative hypotheses: (1) That devout, orthodox, or dogmatic religion is significantly correlated with emotional disturbance, because devoutly religious persons tend to be inflexible, closed, intolerant, and unchanging. (2) The elegant therapeutic solution to emotional problems is to be quite unreligious and have no degree of dogmatic faith that is unfounded or unfoundable in fact. (3) There is no intrinsic connection between religion and morality, and one can be a highly moral atheist or a distinctly immoral religionist (or vice versa). (4) Unequivocal and eternal fidelity to any interpersonal commitment, especially marriage, leads to harmful consequences. (5) Teaching clients unselective, universal, and unequivocal love, commitment, service, and sacrifice for others will help sabotage interpersonal relations and increase intrapsychic distress.

Cognitive Therapy for Depression Like Ellis, cognitive thera-pist Aaron Beck was originally trained in Freudian techniques. As Beck analyzed his depressed patients' dreams, negative themes of loss, rejection, and abandonment recurred and extended into their waking thoughts. So in his form of cognitive therapy, Beck and his colleagues (1979) seek to reverse clients' catastrophizing beliefs about themselves, their situations, and their futures. Beck shares with Ellis the goal of getting depressed people to take off the dark glasses through which they view life. But his technique is a kinder, gentler questioning that aims to help people discover their irra-tionalities (Beck & others, 1979, pp. 145–146):

Patient: *I agree with the descriptions of me but I guess I don't agree that the way I think makes me depressed.*

Beck: *How do you understand it?*

Patient: *I get depressed when things go wrong. Like when I fail a test.*

Beck: *How can failing a test make you depressed?*

Patient: *Well, if I fail I'll never get into law school.*

Beck: *So failing the test means a lot to you. But if failing a test could drive people into clinical depression, wouldn't you expect everyone who failed the test to have a depression? . . . Did everyone who failed get de-pressed enough to require treatment?*

Patient: *No, but it depends on how important the test was to the per-son.*

Beck: *Right, and who decides the importance?*

Patient: *I do.*

Beck: *And so, what we have to examine is your way of viewing the test (or the way that you think about the test) and how it affects your chances of getting into law school. Do you agree?*

Patient: *Right.*

Beck: *Do you agree that the way you interpret the results of the test will affect you? You might feel depressed, you might have trouble sleep-ing, not feel like eating, and you might even wonder if you should drop out of the course.*

Patient: *I have been thinking that I wasn't going to make it. Yes, I agree.*

Beck: *Now what did failing mean?*

Patient: *(tearful) That I couldn't get into law school.*

Beck: *And what does that mean to you?*

Patient: *That I'm just not smart enough.*

Beck: *Anything else?*

Patient: *That I can never be happy.*

Beck: *And how do these thoughts make you feel?*

Patient: *Very unhappy.*

Beck: *So it is the meaning of failing a test that makes you very un-happy. In fact, believing that you can never be happy is a powerful fac-tor in producing unhappiness. So, you get yourself into a trap—by def-inition, failure to get into law school equals "I can never be happy."*

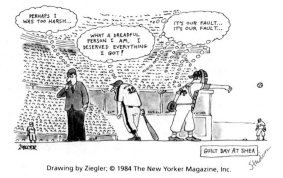

Drawing by Ziegler; © 1984 The New Yorker Magazine, Inc.

A new variety of cognitive therapy builds on the finding that depressed people do not exhibit the self-serving bias common in nondepressed people (page 462). Instead, they often attribute their failures to themselves and their successes to external circumstances. Thus, Adele Rabin and her colleagues (1986) first explained to 235 depressed adults the advantages of interpreting events as nondepressed people do. She then trained them to reform their habitually negative patterns of thinking and labeling. For example, she gave the patients homework assignments that required them to record each day's positive events and to write down how they contributed to each. Compared with depressed people who remained on a waiting list, those who went through the positive thinking exercises became much less depressed (Figure 16–4).

The more people change their negative thinking styles, the more their depression lifts (Seligman, 1989). Cognitive therapists often combine the reversal of self-defeating thinking with efforts to modify behavior. *Cognitive behavior therapy* aims to make people aware of their irrational negative thinking, to replace it with new ways of thinking and talking, *and* to practice the more positive approach in everyday settings.

Because we often think in words, notes Donald Meichenbaum (1977, 1985), getting people to change what they say to themselves is an effective way to change their thinking. Perhaps you can identify with the anxious students who before an exam make matters worse with self-defeating thoughts: "This exam is probably going to be impossible. All these other students seem so relaxed and self-confident. I wish I were better prepared. Anyhow, I'm so nervous I'll forget everything." To change such negative patterns, Meichenbaum trains people to restructure the way they think in stressful situations. Sometimes it may be enough simply to say more positive things to oneself: "Relax. The exam may be hard, but it will be hard for everyone else, too. I studied harder than most people. Besides, I don't need a perfect score to get a good grade."

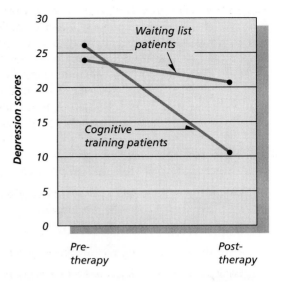

Figure 16–4 Cognitive therapy for depression. After undergoing a program that trained them to think more like nondepressed people—by noticing and taking personal credit for good events and by not taking blame for or overgeneralizing from bad events—patients' depression dropped dramatically. (From Rabin & others, 1986.)

Evaluating Psychotherapies

Advice columnist Ann Landers frequently advises her troubled letter writers to get professional help. One response urged the writer "not to give up. Hang in there until you find [a psychotherapist] who fills the bill. It's worth the effort." She advised the same day's second letter writer, "There are many excellent mental health facilities in your city. I urge you to make an appointment at once" (Farina & Fisher, 1982).

Many people share Ann Landers' confidence in psychotherapy's effectiveness. Between the mid-1950s and the mid-1980s, the percentage of Americans who had ever sought psychological counseling more than doubled, from 13 to almost 30 percent (Meredith, 1986). The National Institute of Mental Health estimates that 15.5 million Americans undergo psychotherapy each year (Trafford, 1988).

Before 1950, the main mental health providers were psychiatrists. Since then the demand has outgrown the psychiatric profession, so most psychotherapy is now done by clinical and counseling psychologists; clinical social workers; pastoral, marital, abuse, and school counselors; and psychiatric nurses (Table 16–1, page 496). Is the faith that Ann Landers and millions of other Americans have placed in these therapists justified?

Table 16–1	*A Consumer's Guide to Psychotherapists*

If you are looking for a therapist, you may wish to shop around by having a preliminary consultation with two or three therapists, during which you can describe your problem, gather information about their treatment approaches, credentials, and fees, and assess your feelings about each.

Type	Description	Number practicing in U.S.	Approximate average hourly fee in U.S. $
Psychiatrists	Physicians who specialize in the treatment of psychological disorders. Not all psychiatrists have had extensive training in psychotherapy, but as M.D.s they can prescribe medications. Thus, they tend to see those with the most serious problems. Many have a private practice.	38,000	$100
Clinical psychologists	Most are Ph.D. psychologists with expertise in research, assessment, and therapy, usually supplemented by a supervised internship. About half work in agencies and institutions, half in private practice.	90,000	$80
Clinical or psychiatric social workers	A 2-year Master of Social Work graduate program plus postgraduate supervision prepares some social workers to offer psychotherapy, mostly to people with everyday personal and family problems. About half have earned the National Association of Social Workers designation of clinical social worker.	80,000	$65
Other therapists	Marriage and family counselors specialize in problems arising from family relations. Pastoral counselors, some certified by the American Association of Pastoral Counselors, provide counseling to countless people. Abuse counselors work with substance abusers, spouse and child abusers, and their victims.	55,000+	0–$70

Note   Numbers and fees from Hunt (1987), Gates (1989), and *Psychiatric News* (1989). Fees adjusted for inflation.

Is Psychotherapy Effective? The question, though simply put, is not simply answered. For one thing, measuring therapy's effectiveness is not like taking your body's temperature. If you and I were to undergo psychotherapy, how would we gauge its effectiveness? By how we feel about our progress? how our therapist feels about it? how our friends and family feel about it? how our behavior has changed?

Clients' Perceptions If clients' testimonials were the only yardstick, we could strongly affirm the effectiveness of psychotherapy. Three out of four clients report themselves satisfied, and one in two say they are "very satisfied" (Lebow, 1982). We have their word for it — and who should know better?

We should not dismiss these testimonials lightly. People enter therapy because they are suffering, and most leave feeling better about themselves. But there are several reasons why client testimonials do not persuade psychotherapy's skeptics:

> People often enter therapy in crisis. When, with the normal ebb and flow of events, the crisis passes, they may attribute their improvement to the therapy.

> Clients may need to believe the therapy was worth the effort.

To admit investing time and money in something ineffective is like admitting to having one's car serviced repeatedly by a mechanic who never fixed it. Self-justification is a powerful human motive.

Clients generally like their therapists and speak kindly of them. Even if the clients' problems remain, say the therapy critics, "they work hard to find something positive to say. The therapist had been very understanding, the client had gained a new perspective, he learned to communicate better, his mind was eased, anything at all so as not to have to say treatment was a failure" (Zilbergeld, 1983, p. 117).

Such testimonials can be misleading. As earlier chapters document, we are prone to selective and biased recall and to making judgments that confirm our beliefs. Consider a massive experiment with over 500 Massachusetts boys, aged 5 to 13 years, many of whom seemed bound for delinquency. By the toss of a coin, half the boys were assigned to a 5-year treatment program. Counselors visited them twice a month. They were involved in community programs such as the Boy Scouts. And, as the need arose, they received academic tutoring, medical attention, and family assistance. Some 30 years after the end of the program, Joan McCord (1978, 1979) located 97 percent of the participants. To assess the treatment's impact she sent them questionnaires and checked public records from courts, mental hospitals, and other sources.

Assessing the treatment program with client testimonials yielded encouraging results. Many of the men offered glowing reports. Some noted that had it not been for their counselors, "I would probably be in jail," "My life would have gone the other way," or "I think I would have ended up in a life of crime." The court records offered apparent support for these testimonials. Even among the "difficult" boys in the program, 66 percent had no official juvenile crime record.

But recall that psychology's most powerful weapon for sorting reality from wishful thinking is the *control group.* For every boy who was counseled there was a similar boy in a control group who was not. McCord tracked down these untreated people and found that among the predelinquent boys in the control group, *70* percent had no juvenile record. Moreover, on some measures, such as a record of having committed a second crime, alcoholic tendencies, death rate, and job satisfaction, the untreated men exhibited slightly *fewer* problems. The glowing testimonials of those treated had been deceiving. Perhaps, McCord speculated, the intervention had created a dependency. Or maybe it generated such high expectations that the boys later experienced greater frustration. Or perhaps it led the boys to view themselves as requiring help.

Clinicians' Perceptions If clinicians' perceptions accurately reflected their own therapeutic effectiveness, we would have even more reason to celebrate. Case studies of successful treatment abound. Furthermore, every therapist treasures compliments from clients as they say goodbye or later express their gratitude. The problem is that clients justify entering psychotherapy by emphasizing their woes, justify leaving therapy by emphasizing their well-being, and stay in touch only if satisfied. Therapists are aware of failures—mostly the failures of *other* therapists, those whose clients, having experienced only temporary relief, are now seeking

Although many suicide-prone people have turned to suicide-prevention centers for help, such centers have not been found to affect community suicide rates (Dew & others, 1987).

↑ People who go to therapy tend to get through the problem faster & w/ more insight.

a new therapist for their recurring problems. Thus, the same person with the same recurring difficulty—the same old weight problem, depression, or marital difficulty—may represent "success" stories in several therapists' files.

Outcome Research   How, then, can we objectively measure the effectiveness of psychotherapy? What types of people and problems are best helped, and by what type of psychotherapy? The questions have both academic and personal relevance. If you or someone you care about feels anxious or depressed, or suffers some psychological disorder, how likely is it that psychotherapy will help?

In hopes of better assessing psychotherapy's effectiveness, psychologists have turned to controlled research studies. Similar research in the 1800s transformed medicine from concocted treatments (bleeding, purging, infusions of plant and metal substances) into a science. The transformation occurred when skeptical physicians began to realize that many patients got better on their own, that most of the fashionable treatments were doing no good, and that sorting sense from nonsense required closely following illnesses—with and without a particular treatment.

In psychology, the opening volley in what became a spirited debate over such research was fired by British psychologist Hans Eysenck (1952). He concluded that studies show that after undergoing eclectic psychotherapy, two-thirds of those suffering nonpsychotic disorders improve markedly. To this day, no one disputes that optimistic estimate.

So why are we still debating psychotherapy's effectiveness? Because Eysenck also reported similar improvement among *untreated* persons, such as those who were on waiting lists. With or without psychotherapy, he said, roughly two-thirds improved noticeably.

The avalanche of criticism prompted by Eysenck's conclusions revealed shortcomings in his analyses. Also, in 1952 Eysenck could find only 24 studies of psychotherapy outcomes to analyze. Today, there are hundreds. The best of these studies randomly assign people on a waiting list to alternative treatments or to no treatment. Afterward, researchers evaluate everyone using tests and the reports of friends and family or of psychologists who don't know whether therapy was given. The results of such studies are then digested by a technique called **meta-analysis**, a procedure for statistically combining the results of many different studies as if they came from one huge study with thousands of participants.

In the first reported meta-analysis of psychotherapy outcome studies, Mary Lee Smith and her colleagues (1980) combined the results of 475 investigations. For psychotherapists, the welcome result was that "the evidence overwhelmingly supports the efficacy of psychotherapy" (p. 183). Figure 16–5 depicts their finding—that the average therapy client ends up better off than 80 percent of the untreated individuals on waiting lists. The claim is more modest than it first appears—by definition, about 50 percent of untreated people also are better off than the average untreated person. Nevertheless, Smith and her collaborators concluded that "psychotherapy benefits people of all ages as reliably as schooling educates them, medicine cures them, or business turns a profit" (p. 183).

Newer research summaries confirm this optimism (McLean & Carr, 1989; Robinson & others, 1990). The most ambitious of the new psychotherapy studies is a National Institute of Mental Health evaluation of three depression treatments: cognitive therapy, in-

"Fortunately, [psycho]analysis is not the only way to resolve inner conflicts. Life itself still remains a very effective therapist."
Karen Horney
Our Inner Conflicts, 1945

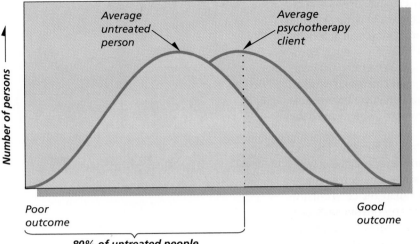

Figure 16–5 The two normal distribution curves based on data from 475 studies show the improvement of untreated people and psychotherapy clients. The outcome for the average therapy client surpasses that for 80 percent of the untreated people. (Adapted from Smith & others, 1980.)

terpersonal therapy (which focuses on social relations), and a standard drug therapy. Twenty-eight experienced therapists at research sites in Norman, Oklahoma, Washington, DC, and Pittsburgh were trained in one of the three methods and randomly assigned their share of the 239 depressed patients who participated. Patients in all three groups improved more than did those in a control condition who received merely an inert medication and supportive attention, encouragement, and advice. Among patients who completed a full 16-week treatment program, the depression had lifted for slightly more than half of those in each treatment group—but only for 29 percent of those in the control group (Elkin & others, 1989). This verdict echoes the results of the earlier outcome studies: *Those not undergoing therapy improved, but those undergoing therapy improved more.*

So, while extravagant expectations that psychotherapy will transform your life and personality seem unwarranted, Eysenck's pessimism also seems unwarranted. On the average, psychotherapy is somewhat effective—and is also cost-effective compared with the greater costs of physician care for underlying psychological ailments (Turkington, 1987). The annual cost of psychological disorders and substance abuse is staggering—in the United States, $273 billion annually in crime, accidents, and lost productivity, says the Alcohol, Drug Abuse, and Mental Health Administration (1990). Thus, as an investment in prenatal and well-baby care *reduces* long-term costs, so will an investment in almost any effective treatment for psychological problems. Anything that boosts employees' psychological well-being will reduce medical costs, improve work efficiency, and diminish absenteeism.

But note that "on the average" refers to no one therapy in particular. It is like saying "surgery is somewhat effective," or like reassuring lung cancer patients that "on the average" medical treatment of health problems is effective. What people want to know is not the effectiveness of therapy in general but the effectiveness of particular treatments for their particular problems.

In general, therapy is most effective when the problem is clear-cut and specific (Singer, 1981). Those who suffer phobias, who are unassertive, or who are frustrated by sexual performance problems can hope for improvement. Those who suffer chronic schizophrenia or who wish to change their whole personality are unlikely to benefit from psychotherapy alone (Zilbergeld, 1983).

SKiP

The Relative Effectiveness of Different Therapies People considering therapy also want to know *which* psychotherapy will be most effective for their problem. The meta-analysis conducted by Mary Lee Smith and her colleagues (1977, 1980) allowed a comparison of the effectiveness of different therapies. What do you suppose they found? Did one therapeutic technique get the best results? Did people benefit more from group or individual therapy? from sustained or short-term therapy? from therapy with experienced or novice therapists?

Despite claims of superiority by advocates of different types of therapy, Smith's comparison of the therapies revealed no clear winner. No one type of therapy proved consistently superior. Moreover— and more astonishing—it made no discernible difference whether the therapy was group or individual, whether many or few sessions were offered, or how well trained and experienced the therapist was.

Some therapies are, however, well suited to particular disorders. With specific behavior problems such as phobias, compulsions, or sexual dysfunctions, behavioral conditioning therapies achieve especially favorable results (Bowers & Clum, 1988; Giles, 1983). With depression, the cognitive therapies prove most successful (Dobson, 1989; Shapiro & Shapiro, 1982). Just as physicians offer particular treatments for specific problems rather than treating every complaint with the same drug or surgical procedure, so psychotherapists increasingly offer particular treatments for specific problems (Stiles & others, 1986).

Given the roughly 230 psychological disorders defined in the DSM-III-R, the research questions are almost limitless: *What specific therapeutic techniques are helpful with what problems for what types of people under what conditions?* As answers become available, it is becoming possible to integrate different therapies and to guide people toward those likely to be most effective for them.

Commonalities Among Psychotherapies Some clinicians suggest a reason why no one therapeutic method proves generally superior or inferior to another. Despite their differences, each therapy's effectiveness may derive from underlying commonalities. Jerome Frank (1982), Marvin Goldfried (Goldfried & Padawer, 1982), and Hans Strupp (1986) studied common ingredients of various therapies and suggested that they all offer at least three benefits: hope for demoralized people; a new perspective on oneself and the world; and an empathic, trusting, caring relationship. These "nonspecific" factors aren't all that therapy offers (Barker & others, 1988; Jones & others, 1988), but they are important aspects. They also are part of what the growing numbers of mutual help and support groups offer their members.

Hope for Demoralized People People who seek therapy typically are anxious, depressed, lacking in self-esteem, and feeling incapable of turning things around. What any therapy offers is the expectation that, with commitment from the patient, things can and will get better. Apart from the particular therapeutic technique, this belief may itself promote improved morale, new feelings of self-efficacy, and diminished symptoms (Prioleau & others, 1983). This benefit of a person's belief in a treatment is the *placebo effect*. As we saw in Chapter 1, a placebo is an inert treatment often used as a control treatment in drug experiments. The placebo has no effect apart from a person's belief in it. In psychotherapy experiments, the placebo treatment may be listening to inspirational tapes, attending group discussions, or taking a fake pill.

The finding that placebo-treated people improve more than do untreated people, although not as much as those receiving actual psychotherapy, suggests that one reason therapies help is the hope they offer. In their individual ways, each therapy may harness the person's own healing powers. And that, says psychiatrist Jerome Frank, helps us understand why all sorts of treatments—including some folk healing rites known to be powerless apart from the patient's belief—may in their own time and place produce cures. Until the 1800s, most medicines and the healers who prescribed them owed their good reputations to placebo effects. (In the next chapter we will explore the power and the limits of this mind-over-body factor.)

A New Perspective on Oneself and the World Every therapy offers people a plausible explanation of their symptoms and an alternative way of looking at themselves or responding to their worlds. Therapy also offers new experiences that help people change their views of themselves and their behaviors. Armed with a believable fresh perspective, they may approach life with a new attitude.

An Empathic, Trusting, Caring Relationship To say that all therapies are about equally effective is not to say all *therapists* are equally effective. Regardless of their therapeutic technique, effective therapists are empathic people who seek to understand another's experience; whose care and concern the client feels; and whose respectful listening, reassurance, and advice earn the client's trust and respect. Indeed, some believe that warmth and empathy are hallmarks of healers everywhere, whether psychiatrists, witch doctors, or shamans (Torrey, 1986).

The notion that all therapies offer *hope* through the *fresh perspective* offered by a *caring person* gains support from a meta-analysis of 39 studies. Each study compared treatment offered by professional therapists with treatment offered by laypeople. These

Effective therapists form a bond of trust with their clients.

laypeople included friendly professors, people given a few hours' training in empathic listening skills, and college students supervised by a professional clinician. The result? The "paraprofessionals," as we call these briefly trained people, typically proved as effective as the professionals (Berman & Norton, 1985; Hattie & others, 1984). Most of the problems they treated were mild. In these studies, however, trained paraprofessionals were—believe it or not—as effective as professionals, even when dealing with more disturbed adults, such as those diagnosed as seriously depressed.

To sum up, people who seek help usually improve. So do many of those who do not undergo psychotherapy, and that is a tribute to our human resourcefulness and to our capacity to care for one another. Nevertheless, though it appears not to matter much which type of therapy is practiced, how much is received, or how experienced the therapist, those who receive some psychotherapy usually improve more than those who do not. Mature, articulate people with specific emotional or behavior problems often improve the most.

Part of what all therapies offer is hope, a fresh way of looking at life, and an empathic, caring relationship. That may explain why the empathy and friendly counsel of paraprofessionals are so often as helpful as professional psychotherapy. And that may also explain why those who feel supported by close relationships—who enjoy the fellowship and friendship of caring people—are less likely to need or seek therapy (Frank, 1982; O'Connor & Brown, 1984).

The Biomedical Therapies

Psychotherapy is one way to treat psychological disorders. The other is to alter the brain's functioning—by altering its electrochemical transmissions with drugs, by overloading its circuits with electroconvulsive shock, or by disconnecting its circuits through psychosurgery.

Drug Therapies

By far the most widely used biomedical treatments today are the drug therapies. When introduced in the 1950s, drug therapy greatly reduced the need for psychosurgery or hospitalization. Discoveries in **psychopharmacology** (the study of drug effects on mind and behavior) revolutionized the treatment of severely disordered people, liberating hundreds of thousands from confinement in mental hospitals. Thanks to drug therapy—and to political and legal efforts to minimize involuntary hospitalization and to return hospitalized people to their communities—the resident population of state and county mental hospitals in the United States today is but 20 percent of what it was 30 years ago (Torrey, 1988) (Figure 16–6).

For those still unable to care for themselves, however, release from hospitals has meant not liberation but homelessness. Studies suggest that about one-third of the homeless suffer disabling psychological disorders (Levine & Rog, 1990; Rossi, 1990). Unlike the homeless on yesterday's skid rows in major cities, 3 percent of whom were female, 25 percent of today's homeless are female.

"The mentally ill were out of the hospital, but in many cases they were simply out on the streets, less agitated but lost, still disabled but now uncared for."
Lewis Thomas
Late Night Thoughts on Listening to Mahler's Ninth Symphony, 1983

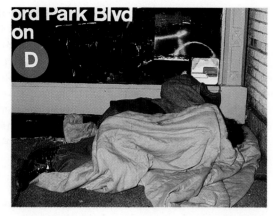

Figure 16–6 The emptying of America's mental hospitals. After the widespread introduction of antipsychotic drugs, starting in about 1955, the number of residents in state and county mental hospitals declined sharply. But the rush to "deinstitutionalize" the mentally ill left many people who are ill-equipped to care for themselves homeless on city streets. (Data from NIMH.)

With almost any new treatment, including drug therapy, there is a first wave of enthusiasm as many people apparently improve. But that enthusiasm often diminishes after researchers subtract the rate of (1) normal recovery among untreated persons, and (2) recovery due to the placebo effect, which arises from the positive expectations of patients and staff alike. So, to evaluate the effectiveness of any new drug, researchers use the double-blind technique. Half the patients receive the drug, the other half a similar-appearing placebo. Neither the staff nor the patients know who gets which. In double-blind studies, several types of drugs have proved useful in treating psychological disorders.

Antipsychotic Drugs The revolution in drug therapy for psychological disorders began when it was accidentally discovered that certain drugs, used for other medical purposes, also calmed psychotic patients. These antipsychotic drugs, such as chlorpromazine (sold as Thorazine), provide most help to people experiencing the positive symptoms of auditory hallucinations and paranoia, by dampening their responsiveness to irrelevant stimuli (Lenzenweger & others, 1989). Schizophrenia patients with the negative symptoms of apathy and withdrawal often do not respond well to these antipsychotic drugs. A new drug, clozapine (marketed as Clozaril), does help reanimate such people and has been effectively used in Europe. But the high cost of weekly blood tests required in the United States to monitor dosage have initially made it prohibitively expensive for most patients.

The molecules of the Thorazine-like antipsychotic drugs are similar enough to molecules of the neurotransmitter dopamine to occupy its receptor sites and block its activity (Pickar & others, 1984). This finding—that most antipsychotic drugs block dopamine receptors—reinforces the idea that, as psychopharmacologist Soloman Snyder (1984) put it, "dopamine systems in the brain are closely related to whatever is fundamentally abnormal in schizophrenic brains—either an excess of dopamine formation or perhaps a supersensitivity of dopamine receptors."

Antipsychotics such as Thorazine are powerful drugs that can produce sluggishness, tremors, and muscular coordination problems similar to those of Parkinson's disease (Kaplan & Saddock, 1989). What is an effective dose for some people may be an overdose for others. Asians, for example, seem to require lower doses than Caucasians (Holden, 1991). By carefully monitoring the dosage and its effects, therapist and patient tread the fine line between relieving the symptoms and causing some extremely unpleasant side effects. In this way, and with the help of supportive people, hundreds of thousands of schizophrenia patients who had been consigned to the back wards of mental hospitals have returned to jobs and to near-normal lives.

Antianxiety Drugs Among the most heavily prescribed and abused drugs are the antianxiety agents, such as Valium and Librium. Like alcohol, these drugs depress central nervous system activity. Because they reduce tension and anxiety without causing excessive sleepiness, they have been prescribed even for minor emotional stresses. Used in combination with other therapy, an antianxiety drug sometimes helps a person learn to cope successfully with frightening situations. Calmed with the help of a drug, the person may learn to deal with fear-triggering stimuli.

The criticism sometimes made of the behavior therapies—that they reduce symptoms without resolving underlying problems—is also made of antianxiety drugs. Unlike the behavior therapies, they may even be used as a continuing treatment. Routinely "popping a Valium" at the first sign of tension can produce psychological dependence on the drug. When heavy users stop taking the drug, they may experience increased anxiety and insomnia, driving them back to the drug for relief.

Antidepressant Drugs If the antianxiety drugs calm anxious people down, the antidepressants aim to lift depressed people up. Most of these drugs increase the availability of the neurotransmitters norepinephrine and serotonin, which appear scarce during depression. For example, the popular new antidepressant fluoxetine (marketed as Prozac) blocks the reabsorption and removal of serotonin from the synapse. Patients who begin taking antidepressants do not wake up the next day singing "Oh, what a beautiful morning!" The full effect often requires 3 or 4 weeks, sometimes aided by cognitive therapy to help the patient reverse a now-habitual negative thinking style.

For those suffering the manic-depressive mood swings of a bipolar disorder, the simple salt **lithium** is often an effective mood stabilizer. An Australian physician, John Cade, discovered this in the 1940s when he administered lithium to a severely manic patient. Although his reason for doing so was misguided—he thought lithium had calmed excitable guinea pigs when actually it made them sick—Cade found that in less than a week the patient became perfectly well (Snyder, 1986b). With continued lithium use, the emotional highs and lows typically level. After suffering mood swings for years, many people find relief with a daily dose of a cheap salt.

Electroconvulsive Therapy

A more controversial brain manipulation occurs through shock treatment, or **electroconvulsive therapy (ECT)**. When ECT was first introduced in 1938, the wide-awake patient was strapped to a table and jolted with roughly 100 volts of electricity to the brain, producing racking convulsions and momentary unconsciousness. ECT therefore gained a barbaric image that lingers to the present. Today, however, the patient first receives a general anesthetic and a muscle relaxant to prevent injury from convulsions. Then a psychiatrist electrically shocks the unconscious patient's brain for a fraction of a second. Within 30 minutes the patient awakens and remembers nothing of the treatment or of the hours preceding.

Psychiatrists give ECT to severely depressed patients. (It is usually ineffective in treating other psychological disorders.) After three such treatments a week for 2 to 4 weeks, 80 percent or more of depressed people improve markedly and without discernible brain damage (Bergsholm & others, 1989; Coffey & Weiner, 1990). "A miracle had happened in two weeks," reported noted research psychologist Norman Endler (1982) after ECT alleviated his deep depression. A 1985 panel of the National Institutes of Health reported that for many others, too, ECT is an effective treatment for severe depression that has not responded to drug therapy (Consensus Conference, 1985). Thus, ECT has regained respectability as a "major treatment" for depression, according to the American Psychiatric Association (1990).

How does ECT work? After more than 50 years, no one knows for sure. Perhaps electrical shock increases the release of norepinephrine, the neurotransmitter that elevates arousal and mood and seems in short supply during depression. Or perhaps the shock-induced seizures cause the brain to react by calming neural centers where overactivity produces depression (Sackeim, 1988).

Although ECT is credited with saving many from suicide and is now used on some 100,000 Americans a year (S. Squire, 1987), its Frankenstein-like image continues. No matter how impressive the results, the idea of electrically shocking people into convulsions still strikes many as barbaric, especially given our ignorance about why ECT works. Moreover, ECT-treated patients, like other formerly depressed patients, are vulnerable to relapse. Nevertheless, electroconvulsive therapy is, in the minds of many psychiatrists and patients, a godsend—or at least a lesser evil than depression's misery, anguish, and risk of suicide.

Psychosurgery

Because its effects are irreversible, **psychosurgery**—surgery that removes or destroys brain tissue to change behavior—is the most drastic and the least-used biomedical intervention. In the 1930s, Portuguese physician Egas Moniz developed what became the best known psychosurgical operation: the **lobotomy**. Moniz found that cutting the nerves connecting the frontal lobes with the emotion-controlling centers of the inner brain calmed uncontrollably emotional and violent patients. During the 1940s and 1950s, tens of thousands of severely disturbed people were "lobotomized," and Moniz was honored with a Nobel prize (Valenstein, 1986).

Although the intention was simply to disconnect emotion from thought, the effect was often more drastic: The lobotomy produced a permanently lethargic, immature, impulsive personality. During the 1950s, when calming drugs became available, psychosurgery was largely abandoned. Today, lobotomies are very rarely performed. Other psychosurgery is used only in extreme cases. For example, if a patient suffers uncontrollable seizures, surgeons can de-

The medical use of electricity is an ancient practice. Physicians treated the Roman Emperor Claudius (10 B.C.–A.D. 54) for headaches by pressing electric eels to his temples.

Electroconvulsive therapy remains a controversial treatment that can provide relief from serious depression.

activate the specific nerve clusters that cause or transmit the convulsions. Because such beneficial operations are irreversible, however, neurosurgeons perform them only as a last resort.

The effectiveness of the biomedical therapies reminds us of a fundamental lesson: We find it convenient to talk of separate psychological and biological influences, but everything psychological *is* biological. Every thought and feeling depends on the functioning brain. Every creative idea, every moment of joy or anger, every period of depression emerges from the electrochemical activity of the brain.

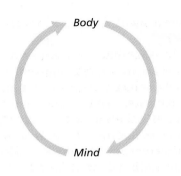

The biomedical therapies assume that mind and body are a unit: Affect one and you will affect the other.

Preventing Psychological Disorders

Psychotherapies and biomedical therapies tend to locate the cause of psychological disorders within the disordered person. We infer that people who act cruelly must be cruel and that people who act "crazy" must be "sick." We attach labels to such people, thereby distinguishing them from "normal" folks. It follows, then, that we try to treat "abnormal" people by giving them insight into their problems, by changing their thinking, or by controlling them with drugs.

There is another way to view many psychological disorders: as an understandable response to a disturbed and stressful society. According to this view, it is not just the person who needs treatment, but also the person's social context. Better to prevent a problem by reforming a sick situation than to wait for a problem to arise and then treat it.

A story about the rescue of a drowning person from a rushing river illustrates the need for prevention. Having successfully administered first aid, the rescuer spots another struggling person and pulls her out, too. After a half dozen repetitions, the rescuer suddenly turns and starts running away while the river sweeps yet another floundering person into view. "Aren't you going to rescue that fellow?" asks a bystander. "Heck no," the rescuer replies. "I'm going upstream to find out what's pushing all these people in."

Preventive mental health is upstream work. It seeks to prevent psychological casualties by identifying and alleviating the conditions that cause them. George Albee (1986), a past president of the American Psychological Association, believes there is abundant evidence that poverty, meaningless work, constant criticism, unemployment, racism, and sexism undermine people's sense of competence, personal control, and self-esteem. Such stresses increase their risk of depression, alcoholism, and suicide.

Albee contends that those who care about preventing psychological casualties should therefore support programs that alleviate poverty, discrimination, and other demoralizing situations. We eliminated smallpox not by treating the afflicted but by inoculating the unafflicted. We conquered yellow fever by controlling mosquitos. Prevention of psychological problems means empowering those who have learned an attitude of helplessness, changing environments that breed loneliness, and bolstering parents' and teachers' skills at nurturing children's self-esteem. Indeed, "everything aimed at improving the human condition, at making life more fulfilling and meaningful, may be considered part of primary prevention of mental or emotional disturbance" (Kessler & Albee, 1975, p. 557).

Albee reminds us again of one of this book's themes: A human being is an integrated bio-psycho-social system. For years we have trusted our bodies to physicians and our minds to psychiatrists and psychologists. That neat separation no longer seems valid. Chemical imbalances can produce schizophrenia and depression. And anger, depression, and stress, as the next chapter shows, can threaten our physical health. "*Mens sana in corpore sano*," says an ancient Latin adage: A healthy mind in a healthy body. ⟳

"Mental disorders arise from physical ones, and likewise physical disorders arise from mental ones."
The Mahabharata, c. 200 A.D.

Summing Up

Treatment for psychological disorders encompasses both the psychological therapies, involving structured interactions, and the biomedical therapies, which alter neural functions.

The Psychological Therapies

The major psychotherapies derive from the familiar psychoanalytic, humanistic, behavioral, and cognitive perspectives on psychology.

Psychoanalysis Psychoanalysts aim to help people gain insight into the unconscious origins of their disorders and to work through the accompanying feelings. To do so, an analyst draws on techniques such as free association and the interpretation of patients' dreams, resistances, and their transference to the therapist of long-repressed feelings. Like psychoanalytic theory, psychoanalysis is criticized for after-the-fact interpretations and for being time-consuming and costly. Although traditional psychoanalysis is not practiced widely, its influence can be seen in therapists who explore childhood experiences, who assume that defense mechanisms repress emotion-laden information, and who seek to help their (nonpsychotic) clients achieve insight into the root of their problems.

Humanistic Therapies Unlike psychoanalysts, humanistic therapists focus on clients' current conscious feelings and on their taking responsibility for their own growth. Carl Rogers, in his person-centered therapy, used active listening to express genuineness, acceptance, and empathy. With Gestalt therapy, Fritz Perls sought to break down people's defenses and to make them accept responsibility for their feelings. Many therapeutic techniques can also be applied in group therapy. One special form is family therapy, which treats the family as an interactive system, from which problems may arise.

Behavior Therapies Behavior therapists worry less about promoting self-awareness and more about directly modifying problem behaviors. Thus, they may countercondition behaviors through systematic desensitization or aversive conditioning. Or they may apply operant conditioning principles with behavior modification techniques such as token economies.

Cognitive Therapies The newer cognitive therapies, such as Ellis's rational-emotive therapy and Beck's cognitive therapy for depression, aim to change self-defeating thinking by training people to look at themselves in new, more positive ways.

Evaluating Psychotherapies Because the positive testimonials of clients and therapists cannot prove that therapy is actually effective, psychologists have conducted hundreds of studies of psychotherapy's outcomes. Meta-analyses of these studies reveal that (1) people who remain untreated often improve; (2) those who receive psychotherapy are more likely to improve, regardless of what kind of therapy they receive and for how long; (3) mature, articulate people with specific behavior problems often receive the greatest benefits from therapy; but (4) placebo treatments or the sympathy and friendly counsel of paraprofessionals also tend to produce more improvement than occurs with untreated people.

The Biomedical Therapies

Drug Therapies The most widely used of biomedical therapies are the antipsychotic, antianxiety, and antidepressant drugs.

Electroconvulsive Therapy Although controversial, ECT is an effective treatment for many severely depressed people who do not respond to drug therapy.

Psychosurgery Neurosurgeons rarely perform brain surgery to alleviate specific problems, because the effects of radical psychosurgical procedures such as lobotomy are irreversible and potentially drastic.

Preventing Psychological Disorders

Preventive mental health experts argue that many psychological disorders could be prevented. Their aim is to change oppressive, esteem-destroying environments into more benevolent, nurturing environments that foster individual growth and self-confidence.

Terms and Concepts to Remember

psychotherapy An emotionally charged, confiding interaction between a trained therapist and someone who suffers a psychological difficulty.

eclectic approach An approach to psychotherapy that takes advantage of techniques from the various forms of therapy, depending on the client's problems.

psychoanalysis Sigmund Freud's therapeutic technique, in which the patient's free associations, resistances, dreams, and transferences—and the therapist's interpretations of them—release previously repressed feelings, allowing the patient to gain self-insight.

free association In psychoanalysis, the patient's uncensored reporting of everything that comes to mind as one thought leads to the next.

resistance In psychoanalysis, the blocking from consciousness of anxiety-laden material.

interpretation In psychoanalysis, the analyst's assisting the patient to note and understand resistances and other significant behaviors in order to promote insight.

transference In psychoanalysis, the patient's transfer to the analyst of emotions linked with other relationships (such as love or hatred for a parent).

person-centered therapy A humanistic therapy, developed by Carl Rogers, in which the therapist uses techniques such as active listening within a genuine, accepting, empathic environment to facilitate clients' growth.

active listening Empathic listening in which the listener echoes, restates, and clarifies. A feature of Rogers' person-centered therapy.

Gestalt therapy Developed by Fritz Perls to combine the psychoanalytic emphasis on bringing unconscious feelings to awareness and the humanistic emphasis on getting "in touch with oneself"; aims to help people become more aware of and able to express their feelings, and to take responsibility for their feelings and actions.

family therapy Therapy that treats the family as a system. Views an individual's unwanted behaviors as influenced by or directed at other family members; encourages family members toward positive relationships and improved communication.

behavior therapy Therapy that applies learning principles to the elimination of unwanted behaviors.

counterconditioning A behavior therapy procedure that conditions new responses to stimuli that trigger unwanted behaviors; based on classical conditioning. See also *systematic desensitization* and *aversive conditioning*.

systematic desensitization A type of counterconditioning that associates a pleasant, relaxed state with gradually increasing anxiety-triggering stimuli. Commonly used to treat phobias.

aversive conditioning A type of counterconditioning that associates an unpleasant state (such as nausea) with an unwanted behavior (such as drinking alcohol).

behavior modification The application of operant conditioning principles to the modification of human behavior.

token economy An operant conditioning procedure that rewards desired behavior. A patient exchanges a token of some sort, earned for exhibiting the desired behavior, for various privileges or treats.

cognitive therapy Therapy that teaches people new, more adaptive ways of thinking and acting; based on the assumption that thoughts intervene between events and our emotional reactions.

rational-emotive therapy A confrontational cognitive therapy, developed by Albert Ellis, that vigorously challenges people's illogical, self-defeating attitudes and assumptions.

meta-analysis A procedure for statistically combining the results of many different research studies.

psychopharmacology The study of the effects of drugs on mind and behavior.

lithium A chemical that provides an effective drug therapy for the mood swings of bipolar (manic-depressive) disorders.

electroconvulsive therapy (ECT) Shock treatment. A biomedical therapy for severely depressed patients in which a brief electric current is sent through the brain of an anesthetized patient.

psychosurgery Surgery that removes or destroys brain tissue in an effort to change behavior.

lobotomy A now-rare psychosurgical procedure once used to calm uncontrollably emotional or violent patients. In this procedure the nerves that connect the frontal lobes to the emotion-controlling centers of the inner brain are cut.

For Further Reading

Burns, D. D. (1989). *The feeling good handbook*. New York: William Morrow.

Cognitive therapist David Burns suggests practical strategies for overcoming depression, conquering anxiety and fears, and building better relationships.

Corsini, R. J., & contributors (1991). *Five therapists and one client*. Itasca, IL: Peacock.

Therapists taking five distinct approaches describe their assumptions and techniques and show how they might work in therapy with the same fictitious client.

Endler, N. S. (1982). *Holiday of darkness*. New York: Wiley.

A psychologist's account of his own struggle with depression. Discusses various attempts at treatment, including electroconvulsive therapy.

Garfield, S. L., & Bergin, A. E. (Eds.). (1986). *Handbook of psychotherapy and behavior change* (3rd ed.). New York: Wiley.

An authoritative source of research information. Contains expertly written chapters on every major therapeutic approach and on scientific issues regarding psychotherapy.

Kaplan, H. I., & Saddock, B. J. (Eds.). (1989) *Comprehensive textbook of psychiatry, V.* Baltimore, MD: Williams and Wilkins.

Experts offer state-of-the-art summaries of psychological disorders and treatment possibilities. Not bedtime reading, but an authoritative resource for answering questions.

Zilbergeld, B. (1983). *The shrinking of America: Myths of psychological change*. Boston: Little, Brown.

One clinical psychologist's analysis of psychotherapy and its limitations. Challenges myths about the need for and practicality of personal change and reassures readers about accepting their own uniqueness.

Stress and Health

Chapter 17

No one needs to be told that psychological states cause physical reactions. Nervous about an important exam, we feel stomach butterflies. Anxious over a public speaking assignment, we frequent the bathroom. Smoldering over a conflict with a family member, we develop a splitting headache. If such psychological stress endures, it may also bring on (in those physiologically predisposed) skin rashes, asthma attacks, or ulcers.

Many people are less aware of how behavior can kill. Our behaviors influence whether we will become victims of one of today's four leading causes of serious illness and death: heart disease, cancer, stroke, and accidents (Figure 17–1). In fact, the National Academy of Sciences' Institute of Medicine (1982) traces half the mortality from the *10* leading causes of death in the United States to people's behavior—to cigarette smoking, alcohol abuse, maladaptive responses to stress, ignoring doctors' orders, insufficient exercise, use of illicit drugs, and poor nutrition. If we could understand and modify the behavioral sources of illness, we might lessen people's suffering and increase their life expectancy and quality of life. To pursue these goals, psychologists and physicians created the interdisciplinary field of **behavioral medicine**, integrating behavioral and medical knowledge.

Research psychologists Mary Jasnoski and Gary Schwartz (1985) contrast traditional efforts to link specific diseases to single causes (genes, germs, or emotions) with behavioral medicine's *systems theory* perspective. Every level of our existence is composed of subsystems and is itself a subcomponent of a larger system. Thus, to understand health we must consider how these biological, psychological, and social systems interact. Your body organs, for example, form larger systems for digestion, circulation, and information processing, which are part of an even larger system — you. You are a part of your family, your community, your culture, and so forth. Your internal organs, in turn, are composed of subsystems — cells — which are composed of biochemicals. At every level, our existence is both part of a larger system and a combination of smaller systems. Instead of assuming that illness has *either* a physical *or* a psychological cause, systems theorists presume that illness results from the interaction of all these interdependent systems (as studied by physiologists, psychologists, sociologists, and others). As integrated systems, we function like mobiles: Touch us at one level and everything else changes, too.

Figure 17–1 The four leading causes of death in the United States in 1900 and 1988. With the conquering of the major infectious diseases, behavior—consumption patterns, reactions to stress, and other health-related behaviors—has emerged as a more important determinant of serious illness and death. (From National Center for Health Statistics, 1990.)

511

Health psychology is a fast-growing subfield that provides psychology's contribution to behavioral medicine. Health psychology's key issues are this chapter's key questions:

> How do our emotions and responses to stress influence our risk of disease?

> How do people decide they are sick and when do they seek and follow treatment?

> What attitudes and behaviors help prevent illness and promote health and well-being?

> How can we reduce or control stress?

"Health has its science as well as disease."
Elizabeth Blackwell
Medicine as a Profession for Women, 1860

Stress and Illness

Walking along the path toward her Rocky Mountain campsite, Karen hears a rustle at her feet. As she glimpses a rattlesnake, her body mobilizes for fight or flight: Her muscles tense, her adrenaline flows, her heart pounds. Flee she does, racing to the security of camp. Once there, Karen's muscles gradually relax and her heart rate and breathing ease.

Karl leaves his suburban apartment one morning and, delayed by road construction, arrives at the parking lot of the commuter train station just in time to see the 8:05 pull away. Catching the next train, he arrives in the city late and elbows his way through crowds of rush-hour pedestrians. Once at his bank office, he apologizes to his first client, who wonders where Karl has been and why his quarterly investment report is not ready. Karl does his best to mollify the client. Afterward, Karl notices his pent-up emotion—his tense muscles, clenched teeth, and churning stomach.

Karen's response to stress saved her life; Karl's, if chronic, could increase his risk of heart disease, high blood pressure, and other stress-linked health problems. Moreover, feeling under pressure, he might sleep and exercise less and smoke and drink more, further endangering his long-term health.

According to the American Academy of Family Physicians, symptoms related to stress prompt two-thirds of office visits to family doctors (Wallis, 1983).

Stress and Stressors

Stress is a slippery concept. It sometimes describes threats or challenges ("Karl faced considerable stress") and sometimes describes our responses to them ("When Karen saw the rattler, she experienced acute stress"). To encompass both these meanings, we can define **stress** as the whole process by which we appraise and respond to events, called *stressors*, that threaten or challenge us. Stressors can have positive effects by arousing and motivating us to conquer problems. Championship athletes, successful entertainers, and great teachers and leaders all thrive and excel when aroused by a challenge. But more often stressors threaten our resources—our status and security on the job, our loved ones' health or well-being, our deeply held beliefs, our self-image (Hobfoll, 1989). And when such stress is severe or prolonged, it may also cause mental or physiological harm.

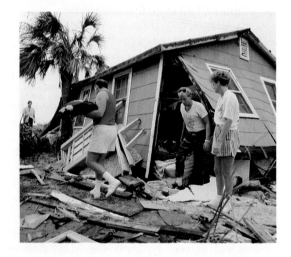

Tragedies, like the destruction of this family's home by a hurricane, cause stress. But so, too, can an accumulation of everyday hassles.

The Stress Response System Although medical interest in stress dates back to Hippocrates (460–377 B.C.), it was not until the 1920s that physiologist Walter Cannon (1929) confirmed that the stress response is part of a unified mind-body system. He observed that a variety of stressors—extreme cold, lack of oxygen, emotion-arousing incidents—trigger an outpouring of epinephrine and norepinephrine (commonly known as *adrenaline* and *noradrenaline*). These stress hormones enter the bloodstream from sympathetic nerve endings in the inner part of the adrenal glands. As we saw in Chapter 13's discussion of emotional arousal, this is but one part of the sympathetic nervous system's response. When alerted by any of a number of brain pathways, the sympathetic nervous system increases heart rate and respiration, diverts blood to skeletal muscles, and releases fat from the body's stores—all to prepare the body for what Cannon called "fight or flight." All in all, this response struck Cannon as a wonderfully adaptive system. Physiologists have also identified a second stress response system (Figure 17–2). On orders from the cerebral cortex, the outer (cortex) part of the adrenal gland secretes the stress hormone cortisol.

Canadian scientist Hans Selye's (1936, 1976) 40 years of research on stress extended Cannon's findings and helped make stress a major concept in both psychology and medicine. The story of how Selye arrived at his concept of the stress response is one worth remembering in times of intellectual discouragement. Hoping to discover a new sex hormone, Selye injected rats with ovarian hormone extract. He detected three effects: enlargement of the adrenal cortex, shrinkage of the thymus gland (which contains disease-fighting white blood cells), and bleeding ulcers. Because no known hormone had ever produced such symptoms, Selye was elated. "At the age of 28, I seemed to be already on the track of a new hormone."

Before long, Selye's elation became disappointment. When he injected the rats with other fluids, he observed the same adrenal enlargement, thymus shrinkage, and bleeding ulcers. Alas, Selye concluded that the effects were *not* due to a new hormone:

> All my dreams of discovering a new hormone were shattered. All the time and all the materials that went into this long study were wasted. . . . I became so depressed that for a few days I could not do any work at all. I just sat in my laboratory, brooding. . . . The ensuing period of introverted contemplation turned out to be the decisive factor in my whole career; it pointed the way for all my subsequent work. . . . As I repetitiously continued to go over my ill-fated experiments and their possible interpretation, it suddenly struck me that one could look at them from an entirely different angle. If there was such a thing as a single nonspecific reaction of the body to damage of any kind, . . . the general medical implications of the syndrome would be enormous! (1976, pp. 24–26)

To verify his hunch, Selye studied animals' reactions to various other stressors, such as electric shock, surgical trauma, and immobilizing restraint. He discovered that these, too, had similar physiological effects. In fact, the body's adaptive response to stress seemed so general—like a single burglar alarm that would sound no matter what intruded—that he called it the **general adaptation syndrome (GAS)**.

Figure 17–2 The adrenal glands (atop the kidneys) release stress hormones on orders received through a dual-track system.

Selye saw the GAS as having three phases (Figure 17–3). Let's say you suffer a physical or emotional trauma. In Phase 1, you experience an *alarm reaction* due to the sudden activation of your sympathetic nervous system. Your heart rate zooms, blood is diverted to your skeletal muscles, and you feel the faintness of shock. With your resources mobilized you are now ready to fight the challenge during Phase 2, *resistance*. Your temperature, blood pressure, and respiration remain high, and there is a sudden outpouring of hormones. If persistent, the stress may eventually deplete your body's reserves during Phase 3, *exhaustion*. With exhaustion, you are more vulnerable to illness or even, in extreme cases, collapse and death.

Figure 17–3　Selye's general adaptation syndrome.

Newer research reveals subtle differences in the body's reactions to different stressors. Nevertheless, few medical experts today quarrel with Selye's basic point: Prolonged stress can produce physical deterioration. This leads to the practical concerns of today's health psychologists: What causes stress? What are the effects of stress? And how can we alleviate those effects?

Stressful Life Events　The level of stress we experience depends on how we appraise the events of our lives. One person alone in a house dismisses its creaking sounds and experiences no stress; someone else suspects an intruder and becomes alarmed. Research has focused on the health consequences of three types of stressors: catastrophes, significant life changes, and daily hassles.

Catastrophes　Catastrophes are unpredictable, large-scale events such as war and natural disasters. Although people often provide one another with aid and comfort after such events, the health consequences can be significant. Paul and Gerald Adams (1984) documented this by studying the aftermath of the 1980 Mount Saint Helens eruption and ash fall. Compared with the same period during the previous year, emergency room visits in the nearby town of Othello, Washington, rose 34 percent during the 7 months following the eruption (Figure 17–4). Stress-related physical illness complaints at the local mental health clinic doubled and deaths rose 19 percent.

Do community disasters usually produce effects this great? After digesting data from 52 such studies of catastrophic floods, hurricanes, and fires, Anthony Rubonis and Leonard Bickman (1991) found the typical effect more modest but nonetheless genuine. In disaster's wake, rates of psychological disorders, such as depression and anxiety, rose an average 17 percent. Refugees fleeing their homeland also suffer increased rates of psychological disorder. Their stress stems from the trauma of uprooting and family separation and from the challenges of adjusting to a foreign culture, with its differing language, ethnicity, climate, and social norms (Williams & Berry, 1991).

Figure 17–4　Health consequences of a cataclysmic event. During the 7 months following the May 18, 1980, eruption of Mount Saint Helens, emergency room visits in nearby Othello, Washington, rose 34 percent compared to the same 7-month period during the previous year. (From Adams & Adams, 1984.)

Close-Up   *The Wounds of War: Post-Traumatic Stress Disorder*

During the fighting in Vietnam, Jack's platoon was repeatedly under fire. In one ambush, his closest friend was killed while standing a few feet away. Jack himself killed a young Vietcong soldier by bludgeoning him with a rifle butt. Years later, images of these events intrude as flashbacks and nightmares. He still jumps at the sound of a cap gun or the backfire of a car. When annoyed by family or friends, he lashes out in ways he seldom did before Vietnam. To calm his continuing anxiety, he drinks more than he should.

Such has been the experience of Vietnam combat veterans, Holocaust survivors, and sexual assault victims who suffer from *post-traumatic stress disorder*, symptoms of which include haunting memories and nightmares, social withdrawal, and anxiety or depression (Kaylor & others, 1987; Nadler & Ben-Shushan, 1989; Wilson & others, 1988). To pin down the frequency of such problems, the Centers for Disease Control (1988) compared 7000 Vietnam combat veterans with 7000 noncombat veterans who served during the same years. Combat stress more than doubled a veteran's risk of suffering alcohol abuse, depression, or anxiety.

Studies of Israeli and American soldiers reveal that the more terrifying and prolonged the battle experience, the greater the psychological casualties (King & King, 1991; Solomon, 1990). Among Vietnam veterans, the roughly 15 percent rate of post-traumatic stress symptoms was halved among those who never saw combat and tripled among those who experienced heavy combat. For example, more than a decade after the war, one study located 2095 identical twins among Vietnam-era veterans (Goldberg & others, 1990). Compared to co-twins who served noncombat roles in Vietnam, those who experienced heavy combat were 5.4 times more likely to be suffering post-traumatic stress disorder. Although most of these combat-stressed veterans are living productive lives, many still experience nightmares, have trouble sleeping and concentrating, and find themselves easily startled. This is especially so for those exposed to savage mutilation, torture, or the sight of a friend's death.

Most calculations of the costs of war count fatalities, injuries, and expenditures. There are also emotional costs of fighting. On February 28, 1991, the shooting in the Persian Gulf war stopped. But for many, especially among battle-stressed Iraqi soldiers and citizens and victimized Kuwaitis, the psychological wounds of war had only begun.

Significant Life Changes The second type of life event stressor is personal life changes—the death of a loved one, the loss of a job, a marriage or divorce. Some psychologists study the health effects of life changes by following people over time to see if such events precede illnesses. Others compare the life changes recalled by those who have or have not suffered a specific health problem such as a heart attack. A review of these studies commissioned by the National Academy of Sciences revealed that people recently widowed, fired, or divorced are more vulnerable to disease (Dohrenwend & others, 1982). A Finnish study of 96,000 widowed people confirmed the phenomenon: Their risk of death doubled in the week following their partner's death (Kaprio & others, 1987). Experiencing a cluster of crises puts one even more at risk.

Many recent magazine articles on stress offer a scale for scoring your life-change "stress points." Stress scores above a certain level are said to put one at risk for illness, but researchers find that such scales actually are not good predictors of future health problems (Depue & Monroe, 1986; Maddi & others, 1987). For one thing, positive life stressors, such as getting married, are less harmful than negative changes, such as being fired (Anderson & Arnoult, 1989; Brown & McGill, 1989). Moreover, life's major crises are fairly infrequent. When they occur, it's how we appraise them that matters. Retirement may increase stress for one person and reduce it for another. Having an abortion creates stress for women who

Close-Up   *The Perceived-Stress Scale*

How much stress do you feel in your life? With the help of pollster Louis Harris, researchers Sheldon Cohen and Gail Williamson (1988) asked the following questions of a cross-section of adult Americans.

In the last month, how often have you felt:

a. unable to control the important things in your life?
   0. Never
   1. Almost never
   2. Sometimes
   3. Fairly often
   4. Very often

b. confident about your ability to handle your personal problems?
   0. Very often
   1. Fairly often
   2. Sometimes
   3. Almost never
   4. Never

c. that things were going your way?
   0. Very often
   1. Fairly often
   2. Sometimes
   3. Almost never
   4. Never

d. that difficulties were piling up so high that you could not overcome them?
   0. Never
   1. Almost never
   2. Sometimes
   3. Fairly often
   4. Very often

Your score (from adding the points indicated) provides a crude but quick index to your experienced stress level. In Cohen and Williamson's national study, an average score was 4.7 points for women and 4.2 for men. People with low stress scores were slightly more likely to report themselves in good health and to be practicing good health habits (exercising, not smoking, etc.).

---

morally oppose abortion and who lack their partner's or parents' support. Yet most women do not experience severe distress after an abortion (Adler & others, 1990; Major & others, 1990). Thus, notes biologist Robert Sapolsky (1990), "the psychological filters through which external events are perceived can alter physiology at least as profoundly as the external events themselves."

Daily Hassles As a famous Peanuts book says, *"Happiness is . . . an A on your spelling test . . . finding someone you like at the front door . . . an invitation to a party . . . your first kiss in the rain."* As we noted in Chapter 13, today's happiness stems less from enduring good fortune than from daily events—a longed-for date, a gratifying letter, your team's winning the big game.

The principle works for negative events, too. Everyday annoyances may be the most significant sources of stress (Lazarus, 1990; Weinberger & others, 1987). These daily hassles include rush-hour traffic, aggravating housemates, long lines at the bank or store, and getting caught in the rain without an umbrella. Although some people can simply shrug them off, others are "driven up the wall" by such inconveniences. Thus, 6 in 10 Americans say they feel "great stress" at least once a week (Harris, 1987; see also Close-Up: The Perceived-Stress Scale).

Over time, these little stressors can add up and take a toll on health and well-being. Hypertension (high blood pressure) is common among the residents of America's urban ghettos, who endure the daily stresses that accompany poverty, unemployment, single parenting, crime, and overcrowding. There is a correspondingly low rate of heart attacks among those who live the relatively peaceful, monastic life (Henry & Stephens, 1977).

"It's not the large things that send a man to the madhouse . . . no, it's the continuing series of small tragedies . . . not the death of his love but the shoelace that snaps with no time left.'"
   Charles Bukowski (cited by Lazarus in Wallis, 1983)

Persistent on-the-job hassles can lead to a condition of mental, physical, and emotional exhaustion called **burnout** (Maslach, 1982). Teachers, nurses, social workers, and police officers—indeed, anyone facing persistent work hassles—may become worn down by the never-ending stress of their job. The result may be a sharp drop in performance caused by the fatigue of physical exhaustion, the depression and hopelessness of emotional exhaustion, and the cynicism of mental exhaustion.

Another source of everyday stress comes from the conflicts we face between our different motives. Least stressful are the *approach-approach* conflicts, in which two attractive but incompatible goals pull us—to go to a sporting event or out for pizza, to take sociology or anthropology, to wear the green or the beige sweater.

Other times we face an *avoidance-avoidance* conflict between two undesirable alternatives. Do you avoid studying a disliked subject or do you avoid failure by opening the book? Do you suffer someone's wrath for admitting the truth or feelings of guilt for having told a fib?

In times of *approach-avoidance* conflict we feel simultaneously attracted and repelled. Some things you may adore about a person you are dating, other things you dislike. Compared to the approach tendency, the avoidance tendency grows more rapidly as you approach the goal (Figure 17–5). Thus, you vacillate. From a distance, the goal—a happy relationship—looks pretty good. Up close, you feel an urge to escape. Stepping back, the negative aspects fade and you again feel attracted. Stress multiplies when we face several approach-avoidance conflicts simultaneously—regarding whom to date, which school to attend, which job to accept.

Perceived Control Catastrophes, important life changes, and daily hassles and conflicts are especially stressful when we appraise them as both negative *and* uncontrollable. If two rats receive simultaneous shocks, but one of them can turn a wheel to stop the shocks, the helpless rat becomes most susceptible to ulcers and lowered immunity to disease (Laudenslager & Reite, 1984) (Figure 17–6).

Figure 17–5 Approach-avoidance conflict. As people approach the goal, their avoidance tendency often rises faster than their approach tendency, causing them to vacillate. This Australian youth's fear is keeping him from diving into the pool.

"Executive" rat   "Subordinate" rat   Control rat

To shock control   To shock source   No connection to shock source

Figure 17–6 The health consequences of a loss of control. The "executive" rat at the left can switch off the tail shock by turning the wheel. Because it has control over the shock, it is no more likely to develop ulcers than the unshocked control rat on the right. The "subordinate" rat in the center receives the same shocks as the executive rat. But because it has no control over the shocks, the subordinate rat is more likely to develop ulcers. (From Weiss, 1977.)

So it goes in humans: Perceiving a loss of control, we are vulnerable to ill health. As we noted in Chapter 14, elderly nursing home patients who have little control over their activities tend to decline faster and die sooner than do those given more control over their activities (Rodin, 1986).

Another factor that influences our stress vulnerability is optimism. Psychologists Michael Scheier and Charles Carver (1991) report that optimists—people who agree with statements such as, "In uncertain times, I usually expect the best"—cope more successfully with stressful events and enjoy better health. During the last month of a semester, students previously identified as optimistic report less fatigue and fewer coughs, aches, and pains. Optimists also respond to stress with smaller increases in blood pressure and recover faster from heart bypass surgery.

Why do perceived lack of control and a pessimistic outlook contribute to health problems? Animal studies show—and human studies confirm—that losing control provokes an outpouring of stress hormones. When rats cannot control shock or when humans feel unable to control their environment, cortisol levels rise and immune responses drop (Rodin, 1986). Captive animals therefore experience more stress and are more vulnerable to disease than wild animals (Roberts, 1988). The crowding that occurs in high-density neighborhoods, prisons, and college dorms is another source of diminished control—and of increased levels of stress hormones and blood pressure (Fleming & others, 1987; Ostfeld & others, 1987).

Stress and Heart Disease

Although infrequent before this century, **coronary heart disease**—the narrowing of the vessels that nourish the heart muscle—became by the 1950s North America's leading cause of death. In the United States alone, more than half a million people die annually from heart attacks. Why this dramatic increase in coronary deaths? Clearly, people live longer now, and older people are more vulnerable to heart attacks. (Everyone dies. Thus, eliminating some causes of death, such as diphtheria, boosts the frequency of others.) But changing longevity does not explain why more younger adults are dying of heart disease (Chesney, 1984).

Many factors increase the risk of heart disease—smoking, obesity, family history of the disease, high-fat diet, physical inactivity, elevated blood pressure, and elevated cholesterol level. But even taking all these factors together still leaves many instances of heart disease unexplained. Many inactive, overweight smokers do not suffer the disease and many who do suffer heart attacks are active, slender nonsmokers.

So what else might be involved? In 1956, cardiologists Meyer Friedman, Ray Rosenman, and their colleagues stumbled upon an idea (Friedman & Ulmer, 1984). While studying the eating behavior of White, San Francisco Junior League women and their husbands, Friedman and Rosenman discovered that the women consumed as much cholesterol and fat as their husbands, yet were far less susceptible to heart disease. Was it because of their female sex hormones? No, the researchers surmised, because African-American women with the same sex hormones but facing more stress are as prone to heart disease as their husbands.

The Junior League president thought she knew the answer. "If you really want to know what is going to give our husbands heart attacks, I'll tell you. It's stress," she said sadly, "the stress they have to face in their businesses, day in, day out. Why, when my husband comes home at night, it takes at least one martini just to unclench his jaws."

Although the medical textbooks of the day never hinted that stress might be a killer, Friedman and Rosenman were already wondering whether stress affected the heart. They sent out questionnaires to hundreds of industrialists and physicians, asking them what they thought had caused their friends' or patients' heart attacks. Both groups suspected that the stresses of meeting deadlines and competing for success had contributed.

To test the idea that stress increases heart disease, Friedman and Rosenman measured the blood cholesterol level and clotting speed of 40 U.S. tax accountants. From January through March, both of these coronary warning indicators were completely normal. Then, as the accountants began scrambling to finish their clients' tax returns before the April 15th filing deadline, their cholesterol and clotting measures rose to dangerous levels. In May and June, with the deadline past, the measures returned to normal. The researchers' hunch had paid off: Stress predicted heart attack risk.

The stage was set for what was to become Friedman and Rosenman's classic 9-year study of more than 3000 healthy men aged 35 to 59. At the start of the study, they interviewed each man for 15 minutes about his work and eating habits. During the interview, they noted the man's manner of talking and other behavioral patterns. Those who seemed the most reactive, competitive, hard-driving, impatient, time-conscious, super motivated, verbally aggressive, and easily angered they called **Type A**. A roughly equal number who were more easygoing they called **Type B**. Which group do you suppose turned out to be the most coronary-prone? By the time the study was complete, 257 of the men had suffered heart attacks, 69 percent of whom were Type A. Thus, compared to the Type B men, the Type As were more than twice as vulnerable. Moreover, not one of the "pure" Type Bs—the most mellow and laid back of their group—had suffered a heart attack.

As often happens in science, this exciting discovery provoked enormous public interest: Millions of people have by now analyzed and labeled themselves and their friends using newspaper and magazine checklists, such as the one in Figure 17–7. But after the honeymoon period, in which the finding seemed definitive and revolutionary, other researchers began the necessary labor of replicating and refining the conclusions.

Why may Type A people be more prone to heart disease? There are at least two possibilities: First, such individuals smoke more, sleep less, and drink less milk and more caffeinated drinks (Hicks & others, 1982, 1983a,b), all of which contribute to coronary risk. Second, their temperament may contribute directly to heart disease. In relaxed situations, the arousal of Type As and Type Bs is no different. But when harassed, given a difficult challenge, or threatened with a loss of freedom and control, Type A individuals are more physiologically reactive. Their hormonal secretions, pulse rate, and blood pressure soar, while those of Type Bs remain moderate (Krantz & others, 1988). For example, when Redford Williams (1989) asked Duke University men to do simple math problems (with a prize for the fastest), the Type A students' stress hormone levels rose to more than double those of their Type B classmates. These hormones accelerate the buildup of plaques (scarlike mass-

Self-evaluation:
Which type are you?

Type A	Type B
1. Very competitive	1. Noncompetitive
2. Always on the go, in a hurry	2. Relaxed, in control
3. Hard-driving	3. Easygoing
4. Demands perfection	4. Understanding, forgiving
5. Ambitious, wants quick promotions	5. Confident and happy in job
6. Is a "workaholic" —even at play	6. Enjoys leisure and weekends

Figure 17–7 One of the many questionnaires found in the popular press for evaluating whether your behavior patterns are more those of a Type A or Type B personality. (From "How to Cope Better with Stress," *Reader's Digest,* March 1984.)

es formed by cholesterol deposits) on the artery walls, producing atherosclerosis, or "hardening" of the arteries. Atherosclerosis also makes reactive people vulnerable to high blood pressure, a risk factor for strokes and heart attacks (Schneiderman & others, 1989).

These findings suggest that reactive Type A individuals are more often "combat ready." When harassed or challenged, their active sympathetic nervous system redistributes blood flow to the muscles and away from the internal organs—including the liver, which removes cholesterol and fat from the blood. Thus, their blood may contain excess cholesterol and fat that later get deposited around the heart. Further stress may then trigger the altered heart rhythms that, especially in those with weakened hearts, cause sudden death (Kamarck & Jennings, 1991). In such ways, the hearts and minds of people interact.

Can we say, then, that Type A behavior leads to heart attacks? No, because some follow-up studies reveal little relation between Type A personality and later heart disease. Type A people are not only reactive, they also seek out challenge, value productivity and success, and like to know how well they are doing (Smith & Anderson, 1986; Strube, 1987). (These very qualities motivate Type A people to change their life-style after a first heart attack, reducing the likelihood of a second attack [Glass, 1989].) So, does some particular aspect of the Type A personality better predict coronary risk? Perhaps time urgency? Competitiveness? Irritability?

Newer research reveals that Type A's toxic core is negative emotions, especially the anger associated with an aggressively reactive temperament (Friedman & Booth-Kewley, 1988; Matthews, 1988). The effect of an anger-prone personality appears mostly in studies in which interviewers assess verbal assertiveness and intensity. (If you pause in the middle of a sentence, an anger-prone person may jump in and finish it for you.) Among young and middle-aged adults, those who react with anger over little things are the most coronary-prone. One study followed Duke University law students over 25 years. Those inclined to be hostile and cynical were five times more likely than their gentler, trusting classmates to die by middle age (Williams, 1989). As Charles Spielberger and Perry London (1982) put it, rage "seems to lash back and strike us in the heart muscle."

Not on Test

Stress and Resistance to Disease

Not so long ago, the term *psychosomatic* described psychologically caused physical symptoms. To laypeople, the term implied that the symptoms were unreal—they were "merely" psychosomatic. To avoid such connotations and to describe better the genuine physiological effects of psychological states, most experts today refer instead to **psychophysiological** ("mind-body") **illnesses**. These illnesses, which include certain forms of hypertension, ulcers, and headaches, are not caused by known physical disorders. Instead, the culprit is stress. In people with reactive temperaments, chronic stress produces various changes. In one person, prolonged resentment, anger, or anxiety may stimulate an excess of digestive acids that eats away parts of the lining of the stomach or small intestine, creating ulcers. Another person under stress may retain excess sodium and fluids, which, together with constriction of the arteries' muscle walls, contributes to increased blood pressure (Light & others, 1983).

"At ten-thirty, you have an appointment to get even with Ward Ingram. At twelve, you're going to get even with Holus Wentworth at lunch. At three, you're getting even with the Pro-Tech Company at their annual meeting. And at five you're going to get even with Fred Benton over drinks."

Drawing by Fradon; © 1985 The New Yorker Magazine, Inc.

In both India and America, Type A bus drivers are literally hard-driving; they brake, pass, and honk their horns more often than their more easygoing Type B colleagues (Evans & others, 1987).

"The fire you kindle for your enemy often burns you more than him."
Chinese proverb

Stress and the Immune System Evidence that psychophysiological ailments are real comes from hundreds of new experiments that reveal the nervous and endocrine systems' influence on the immune system. The immune system is a complex surveillance system that defends the body by isolating and destroying bacteria, viruses, and other foreign substances. It includes two types of white blood cells, called **lymphocytes**. B lymphocytes form in the *b*one marrow and release antibodies that fight bacterial infections. T lymphocytes form in the *t*hymus and other lymphatic tissue and attack cancer cells, viruses, and foreign substances—even "good" ones, such as transplanted organs. Another agent of the immune system is the *macrophage* ("big eater"), which identifies, pursues, and ingests harmful invaders. Age, nutrition, genetics, body temperature, and—we now know—stress all influence the immune system's activity.

The immune system can err in two directions. Responding too strongly, it may attack the body's own tissues, causing arthritis or an allergic attack. Other times, it underreacts, allowing, say, a dormant herpes virus to erupt or cancer cells to multiply.

The immune system is not a headless horseman. Rather, it exchanges information with the brain and the hormone-secreting endocrine system. The brain regulates the secretion of stress hormones, which in turn suppress the disease-fighting lymphocytes (Institute of Medicine, 1989). Thus, when animals are physically restrained, given unavoidable electric shocks, or subjected to noise or crowding, they become more susceptible to disease (Jemmott & Locke, 1984).

To explore the link between stress and cancer, experimenters have also given rodents tumor cells or cancer-producing substances. Those rodents also exposed to uncontrollable stress, such as inescapable shocks, are more prone to cancer (Sklar & Anisman, 1981). With their immune systems weakened by stress, their tumors develop sooner and grow larger.

Does stress similarly depress the immune system of humans? Yes Consider:

Accumulating evidence shows that stress lowers the body's resistance to upper respiratory infections and herpes (Cohen & Williamson, 1991).

The U.S. National Academy of Sciences (1984) reports that the grief and depression that follow the death of a spouse decrease immune defenses and increase the risk of having a heart attack or stroke.

In three separate Skylab missions, the immune systems of the astronauts showed reduced effectiveness immediately after the stress of reentry and splashdown (Kimzey, 1975; Kimzey & others, 1976).

Other studies show that students' disease-fighting mechanisms are weaker during high-stress times, such as exam weeks, and on days when they are upset (Jemmott & Magloire, 1988; Stone & others, 1987). In one experiment, a stressful experience increased the severity of symptoms experienced by volunteers who were knowingly infected with a cold virus (Dixon, 1986).

Can stress depress the immune system? Indeed yes.

Stress and Cancer Even more provocative are controversial findings that link stress and other negative emotions to cancer. Several

"Each patient carries his own doctor inside him."
Albert Schweitzer, 1875–1965
↳ macrophage

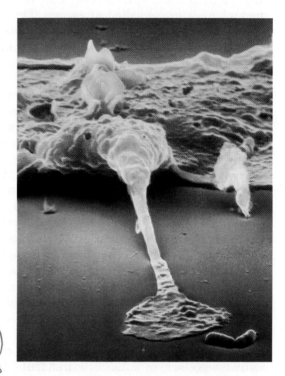

A large macrophage (at top) about to trap and ingest a tiny bacterium (lower right). Macrophages constantly patrol the body in their search for invaders, such as this *Escherichia coli* bacterium, and for debris, such as worn-out red blood cells.

investigators report that people are at risk for cancer a year or so after experiencing depression, helplessness, or bereavement. For example, cancer occurs more often than usual among those widowed, divorced, or separated. One study of the husbands of women with terminal breast cancer pinpointed a possible reason: During the first 2 months after their wives' deaths, the bereaved men's lymphocyte responses dropped (Schleifer & others, 1979). Another study gave the MMPI personality test to 2018 middle-aged men employed by the Western Electric Company in 1958. During the next 20 years, 7 percent of those not depressed and 12 percent of those somewhat depressed died of cancer. This difference was not attributable to differences in age, smoking, drinking, or physical characteristics (Persky & others, 1987). Similar findings come from studies in Yugoslavia and Germany (Eysenck & Grossarth-Maticek, 1991).

What is more, cancer patients who bottle up their negative emotions may have less chance of survival than those who express them (O'Leary, 1990). A UCLA survey of 649 cancer specialists, who had treated more than 100,000 cancer patients, supported the idea that patients' attitudes matter. Four in five of the physicians rated "a positive approach to the challenge of the illness" and a "strong will to live" as important contributors to longevity (Cousins, 1989).

"A cheerful heart is a good medicine, but a downcast spirit dries up the bones."
Proverbs 17:22

In the first weeks after receiving their diagnosis, cancer patients are understandably anxious and depressed (Andersen, 1989). Might promoting their fighting spirit and sense of hope aid their survival? Can beliefs boost biology, by alleviating negative emotions that suppress the cancer-fighting immune system? Several studies offer hope. Compared to UCLA cancer patients in a control condition, those who participated in support groups and received morale-boosting reeducation became more upbeat, with an accompanying increase in certain immune cells (Cousins, 1989). A similar training program with cancer-prone (stressed but emotionally restrained) German subjects found that 90 percent were alive 13 years later, compared to 38 percent in an untrained control group (Eysenck & Grossarth-Maticek, 1991). And a study of 86 women undergoing breast cancer therapy at Stanford University Medical School found that those who participated in weekly group therapy survived an average of 37 months, double the 19-month average survival rate among the nonparticipants (Spiegel & others, 1989). If such findings prove reliable—a replication of the Stanford study is under way with 100 new patients (Adler, 1991)—they will sure-

This "Sharing Group" is part of California's Wellness Community program, which promotes stress reduction and optimism as possible boosts for its cancer-patient participants.

ly reinforce efforts to train physicians to communicate with patients in ways that minimize resignation and sustain hope.

In noting the link between emotions and cancer, we must be careful not to overstep the thin fringe between cutting-edge science and wishful thinking. Researcher Alan Justice (1985) notes that stress does not *create* cancer cells; rather, it affects their growth by weakening the body's natural defenses against a few proliferating, malignant cells. A relaxed, hopeful state may enhance these defenses. Mastectomy patients who display a determination to conquer their breast cancer more often survive than do those who are stoic or feel hopeless (Hall & Goldstein, 1986; Pettingale & others, 1985).

One danger in publicizing such reports is that they may lead some patients to blame themselves for their cancer—"If only I had been more expressive, relaxed, and hopeful." A corollary danger is a "wellness macho" among the healthy, who credit their health to their healthy character and lay a guilt trip on the ill: "She has cancer? Tough darts. That's what you get for holding your feelings in and being so nice." Dying thus becomes "the ultimate failure."

Actually, the biological processes at work in advanced cancer are *not* likely to be derailed by a relaxed but determined spirit. We can do some things to control our experiences of stress, but our emotional reactivity is partly inherited (recall pages 77–78). As theologian Reinhold Niebuhr recognized in his "serenity prayer" (page 437), we therefore do well to accept those things about ourselves that we cannot change, to change those things that we can, and to seek wisdom to discern the difference. By studying the interplay among emotions, the brain, and the immune system, health psychologists seek the wisdom needed to distinguish between pseudo-scientific hocus-pocus and the genuine effects of emotions on health.

Conditioning the Immune System A hay fever sufferer sees the flower on the restaurant table and, not realizing it is plastic, begins to sneeze. Such experiences hint that stress is not the sole psychological influence on the body's ailments. Simple classical conditioning may be an added influence. This raises an intriguing question: If conditioning affects the body's overt physiological responses, might it affect the immune system as well?

Psychologist Robert Ader together with immunologist Nicholas Cohen (1985) discovered that the answer is yes. Ader came upon this discovery while researching taste aversion in rats. He paired the rats' drinking of saccharin-sweetened water with injections of a drug that causes stomachaches. Not surprisingly, the rats developed a taste aversion for sweetened water, an aversion the experimenter could extinguish only by force-feeding the rats sweetened water without the drug for several days. About 40 days after the experiment, some of the animals unexpectedly died. Ader later learned that the stomachache drug also suppresses immune functioning. "It dawned on me that at the same time we were conditioning an aversion to saccharin, we might be inadvertently conditioning a suppression of immune response" (quoted by Anderson, 1982). Further experiments confirmed the phenomenon. After repeated pairings, sweetened water alone triggers immune suppression as if the drug had been given (Figure 17–8).

Many questions about the role of the immune system and how to harness its healing potential remain unanswered. If it is possible to condition the immune system's suppression, should it not also

When organic causes of illness are unknown, it is tempting to invent psychological explanations. Before the germ that causes tuberculosis was discovered, personality explanations of TB were popular (Sontag, 1978).

"I didn't give myself cancer."
  Mayor Barbara Boggs Sigmund, 1939–1990
  Princeton, New Jersey

Figure 17–8 The conditioning of immune suppression. After Ader and Cohen associated sweetened water with a drug that causes immune suppression, the inert substance alone triggered the immune response.

be possible to condition its enhancement? Might this be one way in which placebos—treatments that have no actual effect—promote healing? Can a placebo sometimes elicit the same healthful state produced by an actual drug? Research now under way may soon answer such questions.

For now, we can view the toll that stress sometimes takes on our resistance to disease as a price we pay for the adaptive benefits of stress (Figure 17–9). Stress, as we noted earlier, invigorates our lives by arousing and motivating us. An unstressed life would hardly be challenging or productive. Spending our resources in fighting or fleeing an external challenge aids our immediate survival. But it does so at the cost of diminished resources for fighting internal challenges to our body's health. When the stress is momentary, the cost is negligible. When uncontrollable aggravations persist, however, the cost may become considerable.

On the up side, we can celebrate the self-healing powers of people who maintain a sense of control and a positive approach to life. "Hardy" people actually thrive on moderate challenge (Kobasa, 1982; Maddi & others, 1987). Facing surmountable challenges and striving for realistic goals may at first be fatiguing. But in the long run, it's not avoiding challenges but conquering them that enhances our self-confidence, stability, and future stress resistance (Friedman, 1991). *Stress is going to be a part of life and should not be avoided*

Figure 17–9 Negative emotions caused by stressful life events can have a variety of health-related consequences. This is especially so when experienced by "disease-prone" angry, depressed, or anxious persons.

Reactions to Illness

Health psychologists study not only the links between stress and illness but also how we cope with illness. In a perfect world, people would behave rationally when deciding whether to seek and follow medical treatment as shown in Figure 17–10. First, they would notice and realistically evaluate the seriousness of their aches and pains. Second, they would seek medical care when needed. Third, they would follow the prescribed treatment. But most people do not do this. To find out why, health psychologists are studying people's behaviors at each of the three steps.

Figure 17–10 Three steps in the decision scheme for seeking and complying with medical treatment. (From Safer & others, 1979.)

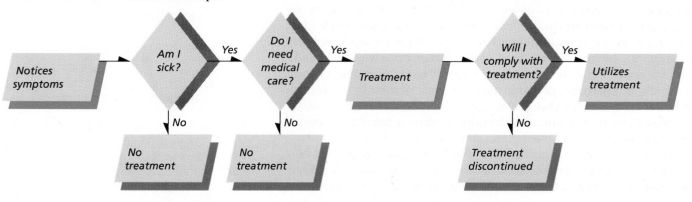

Am I Sick?

College students' typical physical complaints include headache, stomachache, nasal congestion, sore muscles, ringing in the ears, excess perspiration, cold hands, racing heart, dizziness, stiff joints, and diarrhea or constipation. Chances are you have recently experienced one or more of these symptoms (Pennebaker, 1982). Such symptoms require your interpretation. Are they meaningless? Or are you coming down with the flu or a cold? Hardly a week goes by without our playing doctor by self-diagnosing the significance of some symptom.

With more serious aches and pains, the questions become more specific—and serious. Is your stubbed toe bruised or broken? Is your abdominal pain caused by indigestion or a ruptured appendix? Is the chest pain a muscle spasm or a heart attack? Is the small lump a meaningless cyst or a tumor? What factors influence whether we notice and how we explain such symptoms?

Noticing Symptoms Noticing and interpreting our body's signals is like noticing and interpreting how our car is running. Unless the signals are loud and clear, we often miss them. Most of us cannot tell whether our car needs an oil change merely by listening to its engine. Similarly, most of us are not astute judges of our heart rate, blood-sugar level, or blood pressure. People guess their blood pressure based on how they feel, which often is unrelated to their actual blood pressure (Baumann & Leventhal, 1985). Furthermore, the early signs of many illnesses, including cancer and heart disease, are subtle and easy to miss. Half or more of heart attack victims die before seeking and receiving medical help (Friedman & DiMatteo, 1989).

Explaining Symptoms Once we notice symptoms, we interpret them according to familiar disease schemas. In medical schools, this can have amusing results. As part of their training, medical students learn the symptoms associated with various diseases. They also experience various symptoms. Understandably, medical students sometimes attribute their symptoms to recently learned disease schemas ("Maybe this wheeze is the beginning of pneumonia"). As you may have already discovered, psychology students are prone to this same effect as they read about psychological disorders.

Once people form the idea that their symptoms match those of a particular disease, they often attribute negative feelings to it. And that, researchers Pamela Kato and Diane Ruble (1992) maintain, helps explain why many women believe they are more depressed, tense, and irritable during the 2 or 3 days before menstruation. As we saw in Chapter 10, people tend to notice and remember instances that confirm their beliefs and not to notice instances that contradict them. Thus, a woman who feels tense the day before her period is due may attribute the tension to her being premenstrual. But if the woman feels similarly tense a week later or does not feel tense the day her next period is about to start, she may be less likely to notice and remember these disconfirming instances.

Many researchers now believe that some women do indeed experience not only menstrual discomfort but also premenstrual tension (Haemmerlie & Montgomery, 1987; McMillan & Pihl, 1987; Richardson, 1990). Nevertheless, anxiety and depression seem not as strongly related to the premenstrual phase as many people be-

"When a man can't explain a woman's actions, the first thing he thinks about is the condition of her uterus."
Clare Boothe Luce
Slam the Door Softly, 1970

lieve (Brooks-Gunn & Ruble, 1986). Moreover, although many women *recall* feeling out of sorts just before their last period, their own day-to-day self-reports reveal little emotional fluctuation across the menstrual cycle (McFarlane & others, 1988) (Figure 17–11). In one study of 65 women, those who reported severe premenstrual symptoms differed only slightly from other women in actual day-to-day reports throughout their menstrual cycles (Gallant & others, 1991). And contrary to the presumptions of some employers, women's physical and mental skills do not fluctuate noticeably with their menstrual cycles (Sommer, 1991).

Seeking Treatment Once people notice a symptom and interpret it as possibly serious, several factors influence their decision to seek medical care. People more often seek treatment if they believe their symptoms have a physical rather than a psychological cause (Bishop, 1987). However, they may delay seeking help if they feel embarrassed about their ailment, if they think the likely benefits of medical attention or counseling won't justify the cost and inconvenience, or if they want to avoid a possibly devastating diagnosis.

The U.S. National Center for Health Statistics reports a gender difference in decisions to seek medical treatment: Women report more symptoms, use more prescription and nonprescription drugs, and visit physicians 40 percent more often. Are women more often sick? In fact, men may be more disease-prone. Among other problems, men have higher rates of hypertension, ulcers, and cancer as well as shorter life expectancies. So why are women more likely to see a doctor? Perhaps women are more attentive to their internal state. Perhaps they are less reluctant to admit "weakness" and seek help (Bishop, 1984). Or perhaps women not employed full-time simply feel freer to make time for a doctor's appointment (Marcus & Siegel, 1982).

The Patient Role

As she approaches the hospital, Mrs. Hernandez anxiously wonders whether a woman in her seventies should really be having heart surgery. After filling out the admission forms, she puts on the standard hospital gown and sits in a bare, white-walled room with three other patients. From time to time—she can never predict when—nurses or technicians come in to stick her with a needle or cart her off for another unexplained test. Many of the staff talk strangely to her, as if she were a child. "Climb up on this table, dear," the x-ray technician orders, "so we can have a little look inside your tummy." With visits by friends and family members prohibited during some hours and occurring unpredictably during others, Mrs. Hernandez feels no more control over her social contacts than over her hospital regimen.

Mrs. Hernandez's experience certainly does not describe that of all hospital patients. Such treatment is typical enough, however, to draw psychologists' attention to people's reactions to their loss of control in hospital settings. We know that having no control over what happens to you can make unpleasant events profoundly stressful. In hospitals, people who adopt what psychologist Shelley Taylor (1979) called the *good-patient role*—being cooperative, undemanding, and unquestioning—experience the greatest loss of control. Thus, "good" behavior can be bad for the docile patient who feels helpless, anxious, and depressed. Because most people are rea-

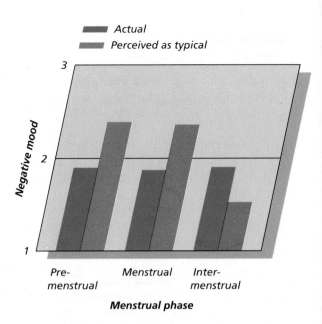

Figure 17–11 Menstruation, actual mood, and perceived mood. Cathy McFarland and her colleagues (1989) found that Ontario women's daily mood reports did not vary across their menstrual cycle. Yet they *perceived* that their moods were generally worse just before and after menstruation and better at other times of the cycle.

sonably good patients, their doctors underestimate their desire for information (Krupat, 1986).

Those who adopt the more uncooperative, complaining, demanding *bad-patient role* may not be much better off, because another familiar lesson is that anger and hostility exact a price. Moreover, medical staff may avoid disagreeable patients or subdue them with medication. On a more positive note, the stress experienced by both the helpless "good" patient and the angry "bad" patient can be lessened when patients actively participate by helping to decide which course of treatment to pursue and then monitoring their own progress (Pomerleau & Rodin, 1986).

Can anything else be done to reduce the stress caused by medical procedures? Imagine that you have just been admitted to the hospital and that tomorrow you will undergo surgery. Should the doctor give you kindhearted reassurances that "it really won't be so bad"? Or should the doctor candidly divulge what you can expect afterward so that you can prepare yourself for any pain? Several studies reveal that realistic information about what one can expect before, during, and after a medical procedure, together with coping suggestions, reduces later distress (Suls & Wan, 1989). When patients know that things are going according to plan, they are less anxious. And when they are less anxious, they are better able to cope with discomfort (Figure 17–12). As a patient in one study explained, "I knew there might be some bad pains, so when my side started to ache, I told myself that this didn't mean anything had gone wrong" (Janis, 1969, p. 98).

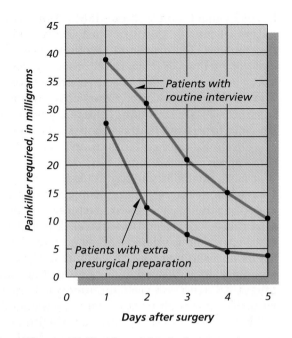

Figure 17–12 After abdominal surgery, informed patients required less painkilling morphine than unforewarned patients. (From Egbert & others, 1964.)

Realistic information about medical procedures helps patients prepare for and cope with the stress and discomfort of hospitalization and its aftermath.

Adhering to Treatment For years, it was widely assumed that the doctor ordered and the patient dutifully obeyed. Then, between 1974 and 1977, some 250 research studies revealed that as many as half of all patients fail to follow their doctor's recommendations (Adler & Stone, 1984). Patients stop taking their prescribed medications, ignore suggestions for adopting more healthful life-styles, and fail to report recurrences of symptoms. Of people with dangerously high blood pressure who seek treatment, only about half adhere to the prescribed treatment regimen (Leventhal & others, 1984). Even among women who have had breast cancer, fewer than half follow their doctors' recommendation of breast self-examination (Taylor & others, 1984).

Why don't more patients follow their doctor's orders? To some extent, it may be good that patients do not mindlessly follow doctors' edicts. Yet surprising numbers of patients do not *understand* the instructions. Told to take prescribed medication "as needed for water retention," they may take this to mean "take the pill when you need to retain water" (Mazullo & others, 1974). And sometimes instructions *are* confusing. Does "Take one pill every 6 hours" apply only to waking hours—that is, three pills a day?

Often, though, patients understand perfectly well what behaviors are health-enhancing. Nevertheless, when the delayed rewards of a more healthful life-style compete with the immediate discomfort or inconvenience of exercising, flossing their teeth, or giving up smoking, the immediate consequences often win out. Recall from Chapter 8, Learning, that immediate reinforcements are more effective than delayed ones. We can *know* that in the long run smoking is harmful and hardly worth the pleasure it provides, yet continue to smoke. We can *know* that high blood pressure is dangerous and still ignore the problem, especially if our hypertension medication has immediate side effects, such as sexual impotence. Thus, to be effective, strategies for increasing patients' compliance need to stress immediate rewards for compliant behavior.

Health care providers' communication skills influence patients' decisions to comply with treatment regimens. The boy learning about his diabetes from his nurse will be more likely to follow clearly explained instructions.

Promoting Health

Traditionally, people have sought out medical doctors for the diagnosis and treatment of disease. That, say the advocates of behavioral medicine, is like ignoring your car's maintenance and going to a mechanic only when the car breaks down. Now that we realize that our attitudes and behaviors affect our health, attention is focusing more and more on health maintenance—on ways of coping with stress, preventing illness, and promoting well-being.

Coping with Stress

Coping with stress can mean confronting or escaping the problem and taking steps to prevent its recurrence. Yet stress is an unavoidable ingredient of modern life. This fact, coupled with the growing awareness that recurring stress correlates with heart disease, lowered immunity, and other bodily ailments, gives us a clear message. If the stress cannot be eliminated by changing or ignoring the situation, we had best learn to manage it. Stress management includes aerobic exercise, biofeedback, relaxation, and social support networks.

Aerobic Exercise Many studies suggest that **aerobic exercise**—sustained exercise, such as jogging, that increases heart and lung fitness—can reduce stress, depression, and anxiety. People who exercise regularly cope with stressful events better, exhibit more self-confidence, and are less depressed than those who don't (Brown, 1991; Hogan, 1989). But when stated the other way around—stressed and depressed people exercise less—cause and effect become unclear.

Experiments resolve the ambiguity by randomly assigning stressed, depressed, or anxious people either to aerobic exercise

Studies of stress, anxiety, and depression reveal that aerobic exercise strengthens the spirit as well as the body.

treatments or to other treatments. In one such experiment, Lisa McCann and David Holmes (1984) assigned one third of a group of mildly depressed female college students to a program of aerobic exercise and another third to a treatment of relaxation exercises; the remaining third received no treatment and served as controls. As Figure 17–13 shows, 10 weeks later the women in the aerobic exercise program reported the greatest decrease in depression.

Other research confirms that exercise benefits our emotions. Shipboard sailors report less stress if assigned to an exercise routine (Pavett & others, 1987). Repeated surveys, some by government health agencies, reveal that Canadians and Americans are more self-confident, self-disciplined, and psychologically resilient if physically fit (Stephens, 1988). Even a 10-minute walk stimulates two hours of increased well-being, by raising energy levels and lowering tension (Thayer, 1987).

Still other studies show that exercise also benefits health. One 16-year study of 17,000 middle-aged Harvard alumni found that those who exercised regularly were likely to live longer (Paffenbarger & others, 1986). Another study of 15,000 Control Data Corporation employees found that those who exercised had 25 percent fewer hospital days than those who didn't (Anderson & Jose, 1987). And a digest of data from 43 studies revealed that, compared to inactive adults, people who exercise vigorously suffer half as many heart attacks (Powell & others, 1987). The "movement movement" is reaping dividends. Off your duffs, couch potatoes!

Researchers are now wondering *why* aerobic exercise alleviates the effects of stress and negative emotions. They know that exercise strengthens the heart and lowers both blood pressure and the blood pressure reaction to stress (Perkins & others, 1986; Roviario & others, 1984). Does exercise increase production of mood-boosting neurotransmitters, such as the endorphins? Are the emotional benefits of exercise a side effect of increased body warmth or of the muscle relaxation and sounder sleep that occur afterward? Does a sense of accomplishment and an improved physique enhance one's emotional state? Such effects help explain why exercise relieves stress and boosts well-being (Martinsen, 1987).

Biofeedback When a few psychologists started experimenting with ways to train people to bring their heart rate and blood pressure under conscious control, many of their colleagues thought them foolish. These functions are, after all, controlled by the autonomic ("involuntary") nervous system. Then, in the late 1960s, ingenious experiments by respected psychologists began to make the doubters wonder. Neal Miller, for one, found that rats could modify their heartbeat if given pleasurable brain stimulation when their heartbeat increased or decreased. Later research revealed that some paralyzed humans (who cannot use their skeletal muscles) could also learn to control their blood pressure (Miller & Brucker, 1979).

Miller was experimenting with **biofeedback**, a system of electronically recording, amplifying, and feeding back information about subtle physiological responses. Biofeedback instruments have been likened to a mirror (Norris, 1986). The instruments no more control the body than does a mirror comb one's hair. Rather, they reflect the results of a person's own efforts. This allows one to assess which techniques are most effective in controlling a particular physiological response.

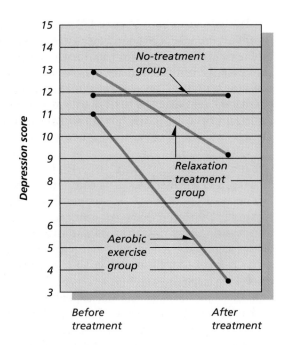

Figure 17–13 Aerobic exercise and depression. Mildly depressed college women who participated in an aerobic exercise program showed markedly reduced depression compared to those who participated in a treatment of relaxation exercises or received no treatment. (From McCann & Holmes, 1984.)

In the example in Figure 17–14, a sensor records tension in the forehead muscle of a headache sufferer. A computer processes this biological information and instantly feeds it back to the person in some easily understood image. As a person relaxes the forehead muscle, a pointer on a screen may go lower or a light may grow brighter. The patient's task is to learn to control the pointer or the light and thereby learn how to control the tension in the forehead muscle and the accompanying headaches.

Figure 17–14 Biofeedback systems such as this one, which records tension in the forehead muscle of a headache sufferer, allow people to monitor their subtle physiological responses.

Initially, biofeedback researchers and practitioners reported that people could learn to increase their production of alpha brain waves, warm their hands, and lower their blood pressure—all signs of a more relaxed state. A decade later, when researchers stepped back to assess the results of hundreds of experiments, the initial claims for biofeedback were found to have been overblown and oversold (Miller, 1985). During biofeedback training, people do enjoy a relaxing tranquility. But this comes about mostly from accompanying factors, such as restricted sensory input (Plotkin, 1979). Biofeedback does enable some people to influence their finger temperature and forehead-muscle tension, and it can help somewhat in reducing the intensity of migraine headaches and chronic pain (King & Montgomery, 1980; Qualls & Sheehan, 1981; Turk & others, 1979). But other, simpler methods of relaxation, which require no expensive equipment, produce many of the same benefits.

Relaxation If relaxation is an important part of biofeedback, then might relaxation exercises alone be a natural antidote to stress? Cardiologist Herbert Benson (1976 to 1987) became intrigued with this possibility when he found that experienced meditators could decrease their blood pressure, heart rate, and oxygen consumption and raise their fingertip temperature. You can experience the essence of this "relaxation response," as Benson called it, right now: Assume a comfortable position, close your eyes, breathe deeply, and relax your muscles from foot to face. Now, concentrate on a single phrase—a word, such as *one*, or perhaps a prayer, such as "Lord, have mercy." Let other thoughts drift away when they intrude as you repeat this phrase continually for 10 to 20 minutes. Simply by setting aside a quiet time or two each day, many people report enjoying a greater sense of tranquility. In experiments, people who practice relaxation also commonly exhibit lowered blood pressure and strengthened immune defenses (Hyman & others, 1989; Jasnoski & others, 1986).

Relaxation training is a component of many stress-reduction programs. At New England Deaconess hospital, hypertension patients practice deep relaxation.

If Type A heart attack victims could be taught to relax, might their risk of another attack be reduced? Could the better management of one's emotions do as much as controlled exercise and an altered diet to prevent heart attacks? To find out, Meyer Friedman and his colleagues randomly assigned hundreds of middle-aged heart attack survivors in San Francisco to one of two groups. The first group received standard advice from cardiologists concerning medications, diet, and exercise habits. The second group received similar advice plus continuing support and counseling on how to slow down and relax—by walking, talking, and eating more slowly; smiling at others and laughing at themselves; admitting mistakes; taking time to enjoy life; and renewing their religious faith. As Figure 17–15 indicates, during the ensuing 3 years the second group experienced half as many repeat heart attacks as the first group. This, wrote the exuberant Friedman, is "a spectacular reduction in their cardiac recurrence rate. No drug, food, or exercise program ever devised, not even a coronary bypass surgical program, could match the protection against recurrent heart attacks" (Friedman & Ulmer, 1984, p. 141). A smaller-scale British study similarly divided heart attack-prone people into control and lifestyle modification groups (Eysenck & Grossarth-Maticek, 1991). During the next 13 years, it too found a 50 percent reduction in death rate among those trained to alter their thinking and life-style.

Type Z behavior

Drawing by Reilly; © 1987 The New Yorker Magazine, Inc.

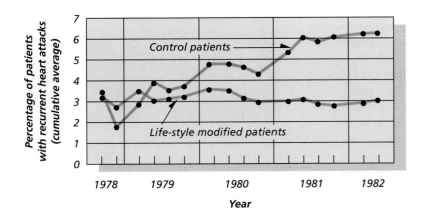

Figure 17–15 The San Francisco Recurrent Coronary Prevention Project. Heart attack survivors guided in modifying their Type A behavior suffered fewer repeat heart attacks than those in a control group who received only counseling from a cardiologist. (From Friedman & Ulmer, 1984.)

It remains for other researchers to do the painstaking work of identifying which of Friedman's dozens of stress reduction drills are beneficial. Even while Friedman was collecting his data, other investigators were studying specific stress buffers. For example, laughter seems to work in ways similar to exercise—it arouses us, massages muscles, and then leaves us feeling relaxed (Robinson, 1984). This may help explain findings that stressful life events are less disturbing to good-humored people (Lefcourt & Davidson-Katz, 1991; Nezu & others, 1988). Although it would probably be an overstatement to suggest that "laughter is the best medicine," there is reason to suspect that he or she who laughs, lasts.

Social Support Linda and Emily had much in common. When interviewed for a study conducted by UCLA social psychologist Shelley Taylor (1989), both Los Angeles women had married, raised three children, suffered comparable breast tumors, and recovered from surgery and 6 months of chemotherapy. But there was a difference. Linda, a widow in her early fifties, was living alone, her children scattered in Atlanta, Boston, and Europe. "She had become odd in ways that people sometimes do when they are isolated," reported Taylor. "Having no one with whom to share her thoughts on a daily basis, she unloaded them somewhat inappropriately with strangers, including our interviewer."

Interviewing Emily was difficult in a different way. Phone calls interrupted. Her children, all living nearby, were in and out of the house, dropping things off with a quick kiss. Her husband called from his office for a brief chat. Two dogs roamed the house, greeting visitors enthusiastically. All in all, Emily "seemed a serene and contented person, basking in the warmth of her family."

Three years later the researchers tried to reinterview the women. Linda, they learned, had died 2 years before. Emily was still lovingly supported by her family and friends, and as happy as ever.

Because no two cancers are identical, we can't be certain that different situations led to Linda and Emily's fates. But they do illustrate a conclusion drawn from several large studies: Social support—feeling liked, affirmed, and encouraged by intimate friends and family—promotes happiness and health.

At the same time we can, however, easily imagine why close relationships could contribute to illness. Relationships are often fraught with stress, especially in crowded living conditions lacking privacy (Evans & others, 1989). "Hell is others," wrote Jean-Paul Sartre. Peter Warr and Roy Payne (1982) at the University of Sheffield asked a representative sample of British adults what, if anything, had emotionally strained them the day before. "Family" was their most frequent answer. Even when well-meaning, family intrusions can be stressful. And stress, as we have seen, contributes to coronary heart disease, hypertension, and a suppressed immune system.

On balance, however, close relationships more often contribute to health and happiness than to illness. Asked what prompted yesterday's times of pleasure, the same British sample, by an even larger margin, again answered "family." For most of us, family relationships provide not only our greatest heartaches, but also our greatest comfort and joy.

Moreover, six massive investigations, each following thousands of people for several years, reveal that close relationships affect

"There ain't much fun in medicine, but there's a heck of a lot of medicine in fun."
Josh Billings, 1818–1885

Humans aren't the only source of stress-buffering comfort. After stressful events, Medicare patients who have a dog or other companionable pet are less likely to visit their doctor (Siegel, 1990).

Friendships are good medicine. Several long-term studies of thousands of people have found that people with close supportive relationships are less likely to die prematurely.

health. Compared to those with few social ties, people are less likely to die prematurely if supported by close relationships with friends, family, or fellow members of church, work, or other support groups (Cohen, 1988; House & others, 1988; Nelson, 1988). Friendships somehow buffer life's major stresses.

There are several possible reasons for the link between health and social support. Perhaps people with strong social ties eat better, exercise more, and smoke and drink less. Perhaps such relationships help us evaluate and overcome stressful events, such as social rejection. Perhaps they help bolster our self-esteem. When wounded by someone's dislike or the loss of a job, a friend's advice, assistance, and reassurance may be good medicine (Cutrona, 1986; Rook, 1987). Given lots of social support, spouses of cancer patients exhibit stronger immune functioning (Baron & others, 1990).

Close relationships also provide the opportunity to confide painful feelings. In one study, health psychologists James Pennebaker and Robin O'Heeron (1984) contacted the surviving spouses of people who had committed suicide or died in car accidents. Those who bore their grief alone had more health problems than those who openly expressed it. Talking about our troubles can be therapeutic. In a simulated confessional, Pennebaker asked volunteers to share with a hidden experimenter some upsetting events that had been preying on their minds. He asked some of the volunteers to describe a trivial event before they divulged the troubling one. Physiological measures revealed that their bodies remained tense the whole time they talked about the trivial event; they relaxed only when they later confided the cause of their turmoil. Even writing about personal traumas in a diary can help. When volunteers in other experiments did this, they had fewer health problems during the ensuing 4 to 6 months (Pennebaker, 1990). As one subject explained, "Although I have not talked with anyone about what I wrote, I was finally able to deal with it, work through the pain instead of trying to block it out. Now it doesn't hurt to think about it."

Suppressed traumas sometimes eat away at us for months or years and affect our physical health. When Pennebaker surveyed more than 700 undergraduate women, he found that about 1 in 12 reported a traumatic sexual experience in childhood. Compared with women who had experienced nonsexual traumas, such as parental death or divorce, the sexually abused women—especially those who had kept their secret to themselves—reported more headaches and stomach ailments. Pennebaker and his colleagues (1989) also invited 33 Holocaust survivors to spend 2 hours recalling their experiences. Many did so in intimate detail never before disclosed, and most watched and showed family and friends a videotape of their recollections in the weeks following. Again, those who were most self-disclosing had the most improved health 14 months later. Confession is good for the soul.

Summing up, stressful events can be debilitating, but the level of stress depends on the person and the environment. Because nothing is stressful until we appraise it as such, our personalities influence how we react when stressful things happen. Moreover, the negative impacts of stressful events can be buffered by a relaxed, healthy life-style and by the comfort and aid provided by supportive friends and family (Figure 17–16).

"I get by with a little help from my friends."
John Lennon and Paul McCartney
Sgt. Pepper's Lonely Hearts Club Band, 1967

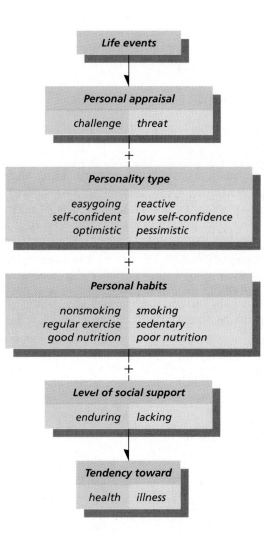

Figure 17–16 Coping with stress. Life events can be debilitating or not, depending on how we appraise them and whether the stresses are buffered by a stress-resistant disposition, healthy habits, and enduring social support.

Modifying Illness-Related Behaviors

Researchers are only beginning to compute the cost-effectiveness of various health-promotion programs (Kaplan, 1984; Taylor, 1987). But most are optimistic that creating programs to prevent disease by modifying people's personal habits will cost far less than it now costs to treat their diseases. With North America's annual health care expenditures now at more than $600 billion—in the United States, 11 percent of the Gross National Product—even modestly successful health-promotion programs could prove cost-effective. The economic costs of alcohol abuse, for example, exceed $100 billion annually, counting everything from medical bills to lost workdays (Desmond, 1987). Any program that reduces alcohol use would surely save more money than its abuse now costs.

In the United States, where businesses pay half the nation's health care costs, two-thirds of organizations with more than 50 employees now offer some sort of health-promoting program, most of which began during the 1980s (Gebhardt & Crump, 1990; Roberts & Harris, 1989). Such programs commonly provide health assessments and support fitness training, quitting smoking, and stress management. The workplace is an ideal location for the promotion of health and vitality because most employees are there regularly. In addition, employers can actively encourage healthy behaviors by providing social support, arranging for competition among work groups, and awarding bonuses or days off for sticking to an exercise or smoking cessation regimen (Cataldo & Coates, 1986).

Are such programs effective? Several careful evaluations reveal that they can be. At Prudential Insurance Company, for example, a fitness program reduced sick days by 20 percent and major medical costs by 46 percent. Thus, the company saved $1.93 for every dollar spent operating the program (Bowne & others, 1984). At work sites where Control Data Corporation implemented its Stay Well health program, smoking dropped 20 percent compared to other work sites, the number of overweight employees dropped 25 percent, and the number not exercising dropped 32 percent—with corresponding reductions in health care claims and sick leave (Anderson & Jose, 1987).

How might such programs modify health-related behaviors such as smoking and eating habits? Let's see.

Smoking In 1980, the U.S. Public Health Service announced that smoking is "clearly the largest preventable cause of illness and premature death." By 1988, the U.S. Surgeon General declared that tobacco products are as addictive as heroin and cocaine. According to a 1989 Surgeon General's report, the tobacco industry each year kills nearly 400,000 of its best customers. Indirectly, these customers in turn kill another 50,000 people who die of passive smoking—inhaling smokers' toxic fumes (Altman, 1990). Thus, the elimination of smoking would do more to increase life expectancy than any other preventive measure. Smoking's destructiveness has prompted psychologists to study why people start smoking, why they keep smoking, and how we might prevent smoking or help people to quit.

Smokers repay society for the health, disability, and fire risk costs of their habit by dying earlier, saving Social Security and retirement pension payments (Manning & others, 1989).

When and Why Do People Start Smoking? Smoking usually begins during early adolescence and is especially common among those whose friends, parents, and siblings smoke (Chassin & others, 1987). If you are still a nonsmoker, the odds are overwhelming that you will forever remain so.

Aware that virtually all smokers start as teenagers, cigarette companies often target their ads at a young audience. By portraying tough, appealing, socially adept smokers, they entice teens to imitate such models.

We can understand adolescents' vulnerability to the allure of smoking with the help of social-cognitive theory, which explains how we learn behaviors through the models we imitate and the social rewards we receive (page 247). Teens who start smoking typically have friends who model smoking, pressure them to start, and offer cigarettes (Evans & others, 1988). Moreover, many teens perceive teenage smokers as tough, precocious, and sociable (Barton & others, 1982). Self-conscious adolescents, who think the world is watching their every move, may begin smoking to imitate those cool models, to receive the social reward of being accepted by them, and to project a mature image (Covington & Omelich, 1988).

Why Do People Continue Smoking? Three out of four smokers have tried to stop (Niemi & others, 1989). However, once addicted to nicotine it is hard to quit. The smoking habit is tough to break because the craving, hunger, and irritability that accompany nicotine withdrawal are aversive states that a cigarette relieves. After an hour or a day without smoking, the habitual smoker finds a cigarette powerfully reinforcing. Given low-nicotine cigarettes, the smoker will smoke more of them to maintain a roughly constant level of nicotine in the blood.

Smoking not only serves as a negative reinforcer—by terminating the aversive craving—but also as a pleasurable positive reinforcer. Nicotine triggers the release of epinephrine and norepinephrine, which in turn diminish appetite and boost alertness and mental efficiency. More important, nicotine also stimulates the central nervous system to release neurotransmitters that calm anxiety and reduce pain sensitivity (Pomerleau & Pomerleau, 1984). These rewards of smoking, combined with the relief smoking provides from the unpleasantness of withdrawal, keep people smoking even when they wish they could stop—indeed, even when they know that they are committing slow-motion suicide.

How Effective Are Programs to Stop Smoking? Efforts to help people stop smoking include public health warnings, counseling, drug treatments, hypnosis, aversive conditioning (for example, having people sicken themselves by rapidly smoking cigarette after cigarette), operant conditioning, cognitive therapy, and support groups. These treatments are often effective in the short run. But

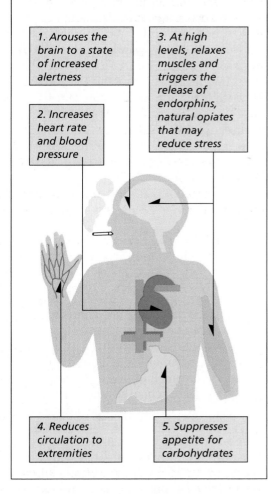

WHERE THERE'S SMOKE . . .
Nicotine reaches the brain within seven seconds, twice as fast as intravenous heroin. Within minutes, the amount in the blood soars. Nicotine stimulates neurons by mimicking the action of the neurotransmitter acetylcholine and produces these effects:

1. Arouses the brain to a state of increased alertness

2. Increases heart rate and blood pressure

3. At high levels, relaxes muscles and triggers the release of endorphins, natural opiates that may reduce stress

4. Reduces circulation to extremities

5. Suppresses appetite for carbohydrates

The physiological effects of nicotine.

the bad news is that all but one-fifth of the participants eventually succumb to the habit again (Cohen & others, 1989).

Better news comes from a 1990 report by the Centers for Disease Control, that half of Americans who have ever smoked have quit. More than 90 percent did so on their own, often after repeated attempts. The overall teen smoking rate, 1 in 4 in 1959, dropped to 1 in 10 by 1988, though by age 18 1 in 5 are smokers (Gallup, 1988; Johnston & others, 1991). Because so many people have stopped or not started smoking, the percentage of Americans who smoke is declining (Figure 17–17). Time was when public places were aswirl with tobacco smoke. Among those of lower socioeconomic levels, smoking rates remain higher. But among college students and graduates, smoking has become gauche rather than cool. The drop has been most pronounced in the male smoking rate, which now barely exceeds women's smoking rate. Thanks in part to such trends, the death rate due to coronary heart disease has declined by about 30 percent since the mid-1960s.

Figure 17–17 The Gallup Organization's periodic survey of smoking behavior revealed that in 1989 smoking was at its lowest level in a half century. (From the Gallup Organization, 1989.)

How Can We Prevent Smoking? It is vastly easier never to begin smoking than to stop once addicted. Drawing on social psychological analyses of why youngsters start smoking, several research teams have devised strategies for interrupting the behavior pattern that leads to smoking (Evans & others, 1984; Murray & others, 1984). In one such study, a research team led by Alfred McAlister (1980) had high school students "inoculate" seventh graders against peer pressure to smoke. The older peers taught the youngsters to respond to ads implying that liberated women smoke by saying, "She's not really liberated if she is hooked on tobacco." They also role-played calling someone a "chicken" for not trying a cigarette and responding with statements like, "I'd be a real chicken if I smoked just to impress you." After several sessions during the seventh and eighth grades, these students were only half as likely to begin smoking as those in a control group at a neighboring junior high school, even though the parents of both sets of students had the same smoking rate (Figure 17–18).

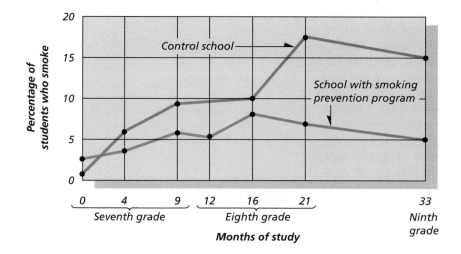

Figure 17–18 After participating in a smoking prevention program that prepared them to cope with smoking ads and peer pressure, junior high school students were much less likely to begin smoking than were students at a matched control school. (Data from McAlister & others, 1980.)

This experiment and others like it have generated curricular programs that teachers can implement easily and inexpensively. According to a National Cancer Institute panel, the key ingredients of such programs are information about the effects of smoking; information about peer, parent, and media influences; and training in refusal skills, through modeling and role playing. To be permanently effective, such programs may require follow-up booster sessions in later years (Murray & others, 1989). Nevertheless, the plummeting rate of smoking suggests that smoking prevention programs are succeeding.

Nutrition Is the way you feel and act affected by what you eat? The discovery that specific neurotransmitters affect emotion and behavior fueled speculation: Might eating foods that provide the biochemical building blocks for those neurotransmitters affect mood and behavior? For example, the body synthesizes the neurotransmitter serotonin from the amino acid tryptophan. Several studies have found that high-carbohydrate foods (such as bread, potatoes, and pasta) increase the relative amount of tryptophan reaching the brain. That, in turn, raises the level of serotonin, which makes us feel relaxed, sleepy, and less sensitive to pain (Spring, 1988). When we desire food for thought, a low-carbohydrate, high-protein meal improves concentration and alertness. If deprived of adequate protein, malnourished young children may suffer enduring cognitive deficits (Lozoff, 1989).

Other nutritional issues are now the subject of vigorous research and debate. Are children and prisoners hyped by a diet high in sugar and calmed by one that is low in sugar? Researchers now doubt this folk wisdom (Spring & others, 1987). Do diets high in cholesterol literally eat your heart out? Researchers are still debating this, although men with high cholesterol levels who take a cholesterol-reducing drug and go on a low cholesterol diet are less likely to suffer heart disease (Roberts, 1987). What are the links between diet and high blood pressure? Hypertensive people tend to have higher than normal salt intake and lower than normal calcium intake (Feinleib & others, 1984; McCarron & others, 1984).

Even clearer are the links between diet and cancer. Throughout most of its history, our species existed on a low fat, high fiber diet, a diet still common in today's remaining hunter-gatherer societies. For the rest of us, our Stone Age physiology now contends with a more sedentary way of life and a diet high in fat and low in fiber. According to a 1988 report of the Surgeon General, dietary fat accounts for an unhealthy 37 percent of Americans' caloric intake. Such a diet contains more of the biochemicals that promote the growth of cancerous cells and less of the dietary elements, such as those found in broccoli, cabbage, and cauliflower, that inhibit such growth (Cohen, 1987).

One of the results of a high fat diet can be seen in Figure 17–19, which displays the strong positive correlation between different nations' fat consumption and their death rates from breast cancer. These correlational data are strengthened by laboratory experiments. Mice on a high fat diet are twice as likely as other mice to develop mammary tumors. Diet is surely one reason why members of the Seventh Day Adventists denomination—who eat well-balanced, low fat diets and who rarely smoke or drink—live longer and have lower rates of all forms of cancer (Ilola, 1990).

Figure 17–19 Diet and cancer. As a nation's fat intake increases, so also does its rate of breast cancer deaths. (From "Diet and Cancer" by L. A. Cohen. Copyright © 1987 by Scientific American, Inc. All rights reserved.)

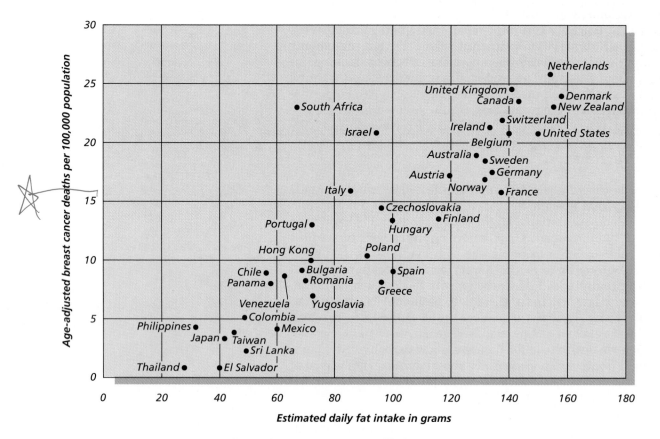

Estimated daily fat intake in grams

Obesity and Weight Control A heightened cancer rate is not the only result of a high fat diet. Another result can be obesity. But there is more to obesity than caloric intake—otherwise, why do some people gain while others who eat the same amount remain slim? Why do so few overweight people win the battle of the bulge? And what hope is there for the one-quarter of Americans who, according to the National Center for Health Statistics (1985), are **obese**—with surplus body fat causing them to be 20 percent or more over their optimum body weight?

One can weigh more than normal—due to an athletic muscle and bone mass—and not be even slightly obese.

Let's preview the current understanding of obesity with a quiz: Are the following statements true or false?

1. Compared to other body tissues, we maintain fat tissue with fewer calories.

2. Once we acquire fat cells, we never lose them, no matter how severely we diet.

3. If two equally active people of identical height eat the same food, it is possible for one to become overweight and the other to stay thin.

4. To maintain a significant weight loss, formerly overweight people usually must remain on an exercise program and continue to restrict their eating.

5. Most researchers today discount the idea that people are obese because they lack normal willpower or turn to food as a substitute for other satisfactions.

See if you can spot the truth or falsity of these statements in what follows.

First, the good news about fat. Fat is an ideal form of stored energy that provides the body with a high caloric fuel reserve to carry it through periods when food is scarce — a common occurrence in the feast-or-famine existence of our prehistoric ancestors. Eating three meals every day is a relatively recent phenomenon and a luxury many hundreds of millions of people still do not enjoy. In circumstances of alternating feast and famine, overeating and storing the excess as fat is adaptive; it prepares the body to withstand periods of starvation. This may explain why in most developing societies today, as in Europe in earlier centuries, obesity is a sign of affluence and status (Sobal & Stunkard, 1989).

The bad news is that in those parts of the world where food and sweets are now abundantly available, the adaptive tendency to store fat has become maladaptive. Being slightly overweight poses no health risks. But the National Institutes of Health reports that genuine obesity increases the risk of diabetes, high blood pressure and heart disease, gallstones, arthritis, and certain types of cancer (Kolata, 1985). This is more true for apple-shaped people who carry their weight in pot bellies than for pear-shaped people with ample hips and thighs (Greenwood, 1989).

Obesity is not just a threat to physical health. Being obese can affect how you are treated and how you feel about yourself. Many people think fat people are gluttons. They see obesity as a matter of choice or as a reflection of a personality problem (a maladjusted way of reducing anxiety, dealing with guilt, or gratifying an "oral fixation"). If being obese signifies either a lack of self-discipline or a personality problem, then who would want to hire, date, or associate with such people? And if obese people believe such things about themselves, how could they feel anything but unworthy and undesirable?

The Physiology of Obesity The arithmetic of obesity is simple: People get fat by consuming more calories than they expend, and the energy equivalent of a pound of fat is 3500 calories. Therefore, dieters have been told for years that they will lose a pound for every 3500-calorie reduction in their diet. Surprise: This conclusion turns out to be false. To see why, we must assemble the pieces of the obesity puzzle.

Fat cells The immediate determinants of our body fat are the size and number of our fat cells. A typical adult has about 30 billion of these miniature fuel tanks, about half of which lie near the skin's surface. A fat cell can vary from relatively empty, like a deflated balloon, to overly full. In the obese, fat cells may swell to two or three times their normal size and then divide. Once the number of fat cells increases—due to genetic predisposition, early childhood eating patterns, or adult overeating—it never decreases. On a diet, fat cells may shrink, but they do not disappear (Sjöstrum, 1980).

The unyielding nature of our fat cells is but one way in which, once we become fat, our bodies maintain fat. Another way is that fat tissue has a low metabolic (energy expenditure) rate. Compared to other tissue, fat takes less food energy to maintain. Thus, once we become fat, we require less food to maintain our weight than we did to attain it.

Body chemistry For the would-be dieter there are more reasons why being fat works to keep a person fat. In Chapter 12, we noted that insulin is a short-term hunger trigger that helps convert blood sugar to fat and is secreted in response to tempting food stimuli, particularly in people who are most responsive to external food cues. Because they are often dieting, obese people become more responsive to external food cues (Herman & others, 1983). For a dieter, a waitress's appetizing description of a dessert evokes a bigger physiological response, felt as a stronger craving.

Set points and metabolism Many scientists believe there is another reason why most fat people find it so difficult to become and stay thin. Their bodies' weight "thermostats" are set to maintain a higher than average set-point weight. When weight drops below the set point, hunger increases and metabolism decreases.

As many a dieter can testify, the drop in resting metabolic rate can be particularly frustrating. After the rapid weight losses that occur during the initial 3 weeks or so of a rigorous diet, further weight loss comes slowly. In one experiment (Bray, 1969), obese patients whose daily food intake was reduced from 3500 to 450 calories lost only 6 percent of their weight—partly because their metabolic rates dropped 15 percent (Figure 17–20). Thus, the body adapts to starvation by burning off fewer calories, and to extra calories by burning off more. That is why reducing your food intake by

Figure 17–20 The effects of a severe diet on obese patients' body weight and metabolism. After 7 days on a 3500-calorie diet, six obese patients were given only 450 calories a day for the next 24 days. Body weight declined only 6 percent and then leveled off, because metabolism dropped 15 percent. (From Bray, 1969.)

3500 calories may not reduce your weight by 1 pound. And that is why when a diet ends and the body is still conserving energy, amounts of food that only maintained weight before the diet may now be fattening.

Individual differences in resting metabolism explain why—contrary to the stereotype of the overweight glutton—it is possible for two people of the same height, age, and activity level to maintain the same weight, even if one of them eats *twice* what the other does. Or why it is possible for a person to eat less than another similarly active person, yet weigh more (Rose & Williams, 1961).

The genetic factor Studies of adoptees and twins reveal a genetic influence. The fatness of adopted people correlates with that of their biological parents, not with that of their adoptive parents (Price, 1987). Brought together in a laboratory and fed an extra 1000 calories a day for 14 weeks, some identical twin pairs gained considerable weight and others didn't (C. Bouchard & others, 1990). If one of a twin pair gained extra fat, the other twin responded similarly. Moreover, identical twins have closely similar weights, even if reared apart (Eckert & others, 1987). Being overweight is therefore *not* simply a matter of scarfing too many hot fudge sundaes. And losing weight is not simply a matter of mind over platter.

Genes aren't the whole story, however. Gender and culture play a role in obesity, as well. Weight resemblance is somewhat less among identical twin women than men. And diet or exercise rather than genes must explain why obesity is six times more common among lower-class than upper-class women, more common among Americans than Japanese and Europeans, and more common among Americans in 1988 than in 1900. Ironically, the growing pudginess of Americans coincides with an idealization of thinness. Most models and actresses have hardly more than half the 22 to 26 percent body fat of a normal woman (Brownell, 1991).

Losing Weight Perhaps you shake your head in sympathy with obese people: "Slim chance they (or we) have of becoming and staying thin. If they lose weight on a diet, their metabolism slows and their hungry fat cells cry out 'Feed me!'" Indeed, the condition of an overweight body reduced to normal weight is much like that of a semistarved body. Held under normal set point, each body "thinks"

The female ideal of 1637 was a rounded contrast to today's thin fashion models. There was biological wisdom in this: A plump woman stored more of the energy and nutrients needed to nourish a fetus and nurse an infant through a famine. However, to many people today, thinness connotes fitness, vitality, and self-control.

it is starving. Having lost weight, formerly obese people look normal, but their fat cells may be abnormally small, their caloric expenditure falls, and, like the semistarved subjects we met in Chapter 12, their minds are obsessed with food.

All this explains why most people who succeed on a weight loss program eventually gain it nearly all back (Wing & Jeffery, 1979). One study followed 207 obese patients who had lost large amounts of weight during a 2-month hospital fast (Johnson & Drenick, 1977). Half gained back all the lost weight within 3 years, and virtually all were again obese within 9 years. Programs that modify life-style and ongoing eating behavior have better carryover to post-diet weight management. Yet participants in these programs, too, typically regain much of their lost weight (Figure 17–21). When cultural ideals of slimness collide with one's physiological pressures, physiology usually wins. So, most commercial weight loss programs can justifiably proclaim that they help people lose weight, *temporarily*. For most people, however, the only long-term result is a thinner wallet.

Dieting failure rates become poignant when viewed on a personal level. Consider Ray Goldsmith, a 5' 6½" man who dropped from 300 to 170 pounds:

> When I lost the weight, I was just obsessed about the fact of not putting it back on. So I literally did just about everything: I went into behavior modification, I tried slowing down my eating patterns, and that kind of thing. And then, at one point, where I saw myself still binging and still eating, I actually fasted a couple days a week, just to try to keep it off. I would sit there and eat six apples to try to . . . make it work. I mean I got really fanatic and very scared about putting the weight back on. I was very, very nervous about that, but I also found that I was not in control. . . . I even went to a hypnotist to try to stop eating and that worked for 3 days.
>
> It took me about a year and a half to put the 130 pounds back on. I mean, I fought it. I tried to fight it like a son of a gun. . . . I did it. I lost 130 pounds. I was able to do it. So clearly, it can be done. And I probably could have kept it off somehow, but I never found out the way to. (WGBH, 1983)

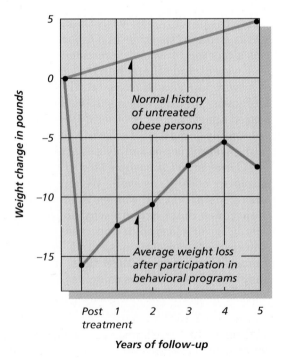

Figure 17–21 Weight change with and without participation in behavior management weight loss programs. (From Brownell & Jeffery, 1987.)

The battle of the bulge rages more intensely than ever, especially in North America, where weight concern and dieting are a greater preoccupation than in, say, Australia or Third World countries (Rothblum, 1990; Tiggemann & Rothblum, 1988). Americans spend $33 billion a year trying to lose weight (Scanlan, 1990). In 1986, the National Center for Health Statistics reported that 27 percent of men and 46 percent of women said they were trying to lose weight. The gender difference is even larger for teenagers: 23 percent of boys and 56 percent of girls have dieted (Gallup Organization, 1988). With fat cells, blood chemistry, set points, metabolism, and genetic factors all tirelessly conspiring to make losing weight a big problem, what advice can we offer to those who wish to shed excess pounds?

We should first advise assessing the costs. Maintaining weight loss will be difficult. And some researchers believe that the more weight fluctuates from going on and off a diet, the more quickly the body switches on its energy-saving metabolic slowdown with each new diet. Kelly Brownell and his associates (1986) confirmed this effect of yo-yo dieting by making rats obese, putting them on a diet, and then repeating the cycle of weight gain and loss. On the first diet, the rats lost their excess weight in 21 days and took 46 days to regain it. The second time, eating precisely the same amount of food, they took 46 days to lose the weight and 24 days to regain it.

It's as if the body learns from previous diets how to defend its set-point weight, thereby protecting itself from what it interprets as the threat of starvation. So rather than following the principle of "If at first you don't succeed, try, try again," a dieter's motto should be, "Get it right the first time." Begin a diet only if you feel motivated and self-disciplined enough to restrict your eating permanently. For most people, permanent weight loss requires a lifelong change in eating habits combined with increased exercise (see Close-Up: Helpful Hints for Dieters).

Although preserving weight loss is a constant challenge, Stanley Schachter (1982) is not as pessimistic as most obesity researchers about the likelihood of doing it successfully. He recognizes the overwhelming rate of failure among people in structured weight loss programs. But he also notes that these are a special group of people, probably people who have been unable to help themselves. Moreover, the failure rates recorded for these programs are based on single attempts at weight loss. Perhaps when people try repeatedly to lose weight, more eventually succeed, despite the negative effects of repeated dieting. When Schachter interviewed a haphazard sample of people, he found that one-fourth of them had at one time been significantly overweight and had tried to slim down. Of these, 6 out of 10 had *succeeded*, by weighing at least 10 percent less than their maximum pre-diet weight (average loss = 35 pounds) and being no longer obese.

Two other studies reveal less encouraging results: Fewer than a third of formerly overweight people were no longer overweight (Jeffery & Wing, 1983; Rzewnicki & Forgays, 1987). But the findings do hint that prospects for losing weight may be somewhat brighter than the dismal conclusions we draw from following patients who undergo a single weight loss program. If all this has a familiar ring, recall that stop-smoking programs tend to be (1) effective in the short run and (2) ineffective in the long run, but that (3) many people are former smokers.

Janet Polivy and Peter Herman (1987) believe that widespread, chronic dieting among basically normal-weight girls and women represents the seeds of eating disorder on a massive scale.

Close-Up *Helpful Hints for Dieters*

For those determined to lose weight, research on hunger and obesity suggests some helpful hints:

Minimize exposure to tempting food cues. For all of us to some extent, and some of us to a great extent, tempting food cues accentuate hunger. So keep tempting foods out of the house, or at least stored out of sight. Go to the supermarket only on a full stomach.

Take steps to boost your metabolism. Remember, the only way to lose weight is to burn more calories than you take in. One way to do this is by exercising. Sustained exercise, such as brisk walking, running, and swimming, not only empties fat cells, builds muscle, and makes you feel better, it can also temporarily speed up metabolism (Kolata, 1987; Thompson & others, 1982). Thus, sustained exercise can be a weapon against the body's normal metabolic slowdown when dieting and inactive (Figure 17–22). Exercise during and after dieting is one of the few predictors of successful long-term weight loss (Brownell, 1989).

Modify both your hunger and your metabolic rate by changing the food you eat. Findings suggest that carbohydrates increase metabolism and are less readily converted to body fat than the same calories eaten as fats (Rodin, 1979, 1985). Among the fats, saturated fats (those, like animal fat, that turn hard when left standing) are the worst culprits. Also, some foods, such as glucose (as in pancake syrup) and sucrose (table sugar), boost insulin levels, causing hunger to return sooner and stronger. Fructose (in fruits) and complex carbohydrates, such as in potatoes and rice, produce less of the hunger-producing insulin jump. So how hungry you are by lunchtime depends not just on how much but also on what you had for breakfast.

Figure 17–22 A correlational study of TV watching and obesity. In one study of 6671 12- to 17-year-olds, obesity was more common among those who watched the most television. Of course, overweight people may avoid activity, preferring to sit and watch TV. But the association between TV watching and obesity remained when many other factors were controlled, suggesting that the inactivity of TV watching contributes to obesity. (From Dietz & Gortmaker, 1985.)

There is, however, another option for overweight people, the one chosen by 13 percent of the people Schachter interviewed—simply to accept one's weight. We all do well to note what researchers have *not* identified as causes of obesity: guilt, hostility, oral fixation, or any similar personality maladjustment. Nor is obesity simply a matter of a lack of willpower. If obese people are more likely to binge when under stress or after breaking their diets, this may be more a consequence of their constant dieting than a cause of their obesity. "Fat is not a four-letter word," proclaims the National Association to Aid Fat Americans. Although this motto disregards the health risks linked with significant obesity, it does convey a valid point: It may be better to accept oneself as a little chubby than to diet and binge and feel continually out of control and guilty. America loved Oprah Winfrey before she lost 67 pounds, and it still loved her after she put some of them back on.

Don't starve all day and eat one big meal at night. This eating pattern, common among overweight people, slows metabolism. With regular meals we maintain our metabolism and thus burn more calories.

Beware of the binge. Among people who consciously restrain their eating, drinking alcohol or feeling anxious or depressed can unleash the urge to eat (Herman & Polivy, 1980). Stress can also break down one's normal restraints. Temporarily going off a diet, by eating just a little of a forbidden food, can do the same. In several "taste testing" experiments, Peter Herman, Janet Polivy, and their colleagues (Herman & Mack, 1975; Polivy & others, 1986) asked Northwestern University students to drink zero, one, or two milkshakes. Then they had the students taste-test ice cream, helping themselves to as much as they wished. Those who normally restrained their eating ate *more* ice cream than normally unrestrained eaters if their restraint was first broken with the milkshakes (Figure 17–23). Thus, dieting—now the "normal" eating behavior for nearly half of North American women—is often self-defeating. Once the diet is broken, binging often follows (Polivy & Herman, 1985, 1987). A lapse becomes a collapse.

Set realistic goals. As we noted on page 376, goal setting can motivate achievement, especially when combined with feedback on progress. Targeting an ambitiously low weight usually dooms a dieter to eventual defeat. However, a realistic objective—such as losing a pound a week—can promote effort and persistence.

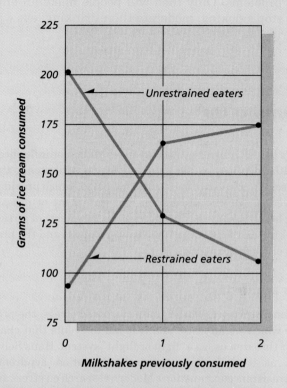

Figure 17–23 A laboratory eating binge. Normally unrestrained eaters (nondieters) ate less ice cream if they first consumed one or two milkshakes. Restrained eaters (dieters) ate *more* ice cream after having their restraint broken with a milkshake or two, a tendency dubbed the "what-the-hell phenomenon." (From Herman & Mack, 1975.)

While working to clarify the precise relation among diet, behavior, and health, health psychologists continue their efforts to persuade people to adopt healthier life-styles. Doing so is quite a challenge, however. Happy people tend to see themselves as relatively invulnerable to health problems, especially those that might arise from their own actions (Salovey & Birnbaum, 1989; Weinstein, 1987). They also typically believe their own life-style is healthier than other people's—that they drink less alcohol, consume less fat and cholesterol, and get more exercise. Often they are fooling themselves. Furthermore, many individuals who admit to behaviors known to increase health risks will deny that the behaviors actually make them personally more vulnerable to illness or injury. Unlike people told they have normal blood pressure, those told they have high blood pressure tend to dismiss its seriousness (Croyle & Ditto, 1990). Smokers may delude themselves by saying that their exercising counteracts the negative effects of smoking.

The statements in the obesity quiz on page 539 are all true.

Because of people's optimistic denials of health risks, the first hurdle that health promotion programs must surmount is to get people to realize their vulnerability to stress- and behavior-related health problems. Only then will people make an effort to control stress, stop smoking, moderate their drinking, eat wisely, exercise regularly, and even buckle their seat belts.

Summing Up

People's behaviors and stress responses are major influences on health and disease. Health psychology contributes to the interdisciplinary field of behavioral medicine, which provides new avenues for the prevention and treatment of illness. Among health psychology's concerns are the effects of stress, the seeking and following of medical treatment, and the promotion of healthier living.

Stress and Illness

Stress and Stressors Walter Cannon viewed stress, the process by which we appraise and respond to events that challenge or threaten us, as a "fight or flight" system. Hans Selye saw it as a three-stage, general adaptation syndrome (alarm/resistance/exhaustion). Modern research on stress assesses the health consequences of cataclysmic events, significant life changes, and daily hassles. Events are stressful when perceived as both negative and uncontrollable.

Stress and Heart Disease Coronary heart disease, North America's number one cause of death, has been linked with the competitive, hard-driving, impatient, and (especially) anger-prone Type A personality. Under stress, the body of the reactive, Type A person secretes more of the hormones that accelerate the buildup of plaques on the heart's artery walls.

Stress and Resistance to Disease Stress can suppress the immune system, making a person more vulnerable to infections and malignancy. New experiments show that conditioning also influences the immune system's responses.

Reactions to Illness

Am I Sick? Our body provides us with a variety of ambiguous signals. If they catch our attention, we often interpret them according to familiar disease schemas. If the symptoms fit one of our disease schemas, we must decide whether anticipated costs and benefits warrant our seeking diagnosis and treatment.

The Patient Role When given realistic information before stressful medical procedures and advice on how to cope, patients endure medical trauma more effectively. Feelings of loss of control—a common experience of those who adopt the good-patient role—can trigger an outpouring of stress hormones, as does hostility for those who adopt the bad-patient role. The realization that patients often ignore doctors' instructions prompted social psychologists to study ways to increase patients' compliance. How and what the physician communicates and the immediate incentives for adhering to treatment regimens influence the patient's behavior.

Promoting Health

Rather than treating problems after they occur, it is far better to prevent illness and promote health through stress management and behavior change.

Coping with Stress Among the components of stress management programs are training in aerobic exercise, biofeedback, and relaxation. Although the degree of mind control over the body that can be gained through biofeedback has fallen short of early expectations, it sometimes helps people control tension headaches and high blood pressure. Simple relaxation exercises offer some of the same benefits. Counseling Type A heart attack survivors to slow down and relax has helped them lower their rate of recurring attacks. Social support also helps people cope, partly by buffering the impact of stress.

Modifying Illness-Related Behaviors The largest preventable cause of death in North America is cigarette smoking, a fact that motivates psychologists to study the social influences that motivate adolescents to start smoking, the negative and positive reinforcers that maintain the habit, and possible ways to stop and prevent smoking.

Researchers are now exploring how certain foods, by providing the building blocks for specific neurotransmitters, affect mood and behavior.

Fat is a concentrated fuel reserve stored in fat cells. The number and size of these cells determine one's body fat. Obese people find it difficult to lose weight permanently because the number of fat cells is not reduced by a diet, because the energy expenditure necessary for tissue maintenance is lower in fat than in other tissues, and because the overall metabolic rate decreases when body weight drops below the set point. Those who nevertheless wish to diet should minimize exposure to food cues, boost energy expenditure through exercise, and make a lifelong change in eating patterns.

Terms and Concepts to Remember

behavioral medicine An interdisciplinary field that integrates and applies behavioral and medical knowledge to health and disease.

health psychology A subfield of psychology that provides psychology's contribution to behavioral medicine.

stress The whole process by which we perceive and respond to certain events, called *stressors*, that we appraise as threatening or challenging.

general adaptation syndrome (GAS) Selye's concept of the body's adaptive response to stress as composed of three stages—alarm, resistance, exhaustion.

burnout Physical, emotional, and mental exhaustion brought on by persistent job-related stress.

coronary heart disease The clogging of the vessels that nourish the heart muscle; the leading cause of death in the United States.

Type A Friedman and Rosenman's term for competitive, hard-driving, impatient, verbally aggressive, and anger-prone people.

Type B Friedman and Rosenman's term for easygoing, relaxed people.

psychophysiological illness Literally, "mind-body" illness; any physical illness not caused by a known physical disorder. For example, stress can produce hypertension, ulcers, and headaches. Note: This is distinct from *hypochondriasis*—misinterpreting normal physical sensations as symptoms of a disease.

lymphocytes The two types of white blood cells that are part of the body's immune system: B lymphocytes form in the *b*one marrow and release antibodies that fight bacterial infections; T lymphocytes form in the *t*hymus and, among other duties, attack cancer cells, viruses, and foreign substances.

aerobic exercise Sustained exercise that increases heart and lung fitness; may also alleviate depression and anxiety.

biofeedback A system for electronically recording, amplifying, and feeding back information regarding a subtle physiological state, such as blood pressure or muscle tension.

obesity A surplus of body fat that causes one to be 20 percent or more overweight.

For Further Reading

Friedman, H. S. (1991). *The self-healing personality: Why some people achieve health and others succumb to illness.* New York: Holt.

Health psychologist Howard Friedman offers a lucid, state-of-the-art analysis of how our genes, habits, and emotions make us disease-prone or health-prone.

Ornstein, R., & Sobel, D. (1987). *The healing brain.* New York: Simon & Schuster.

A nontechnical summary of the new discoveries about how the brain normally works to keep us healthy.

Pennebaker, J. (1990). *Opening up: The healing power of confiding in others.* New York: William Morrow.

Researcher James Pennebaker explains why disclosing oneself to others is good for the body as well as the soul.

Polivy, J., & Herman, C. P. (1983; paperback, 1985). *Breaking the diet habit: The natural weight alternative.* New York: Basic Books.

Two psychologists who are obesity researchers question the practice of dieting and instead recommend realizing one's "natural weight" with an "undiet" that meets needs and discourages eating when hunger is satisfied.

Rodin, J. (1992). *Body traps.* New York: William Morrow.

A leading obesity researcher examines our obsession with weight and appearance—how we form our body image, how it affects our self-esteem, and how we can free ourselves from dieting-related "body traps" that provoke needless anguish and shame.

Part Seven

Social Behavior

Social psychologists study interpersonal behavior—

how we relate to one another. They investigate the

origins and consequences of attitudes and beliefs,

conformity and independence, love and hate. Chapter

18, Social Psychology, examines the social forces that

affect how we think about, influence, and relate to

one another. Chapter 19, Social Diversity, explores

important dimensions of multicultural and gender

diversity, and how people can and do deal with

differences.

Social Psychology

"We cannot live for ourselves alone," remarked the novelist Herman Melville, for "our lives are connected by a thousand invisible threads." **Social psychologists** explore these connections by scientifically studying how we *think about, influence,* and *relate* to one another.

Social thinking: How do we explain people's behavior? How do we form our beliefs and attitudes? What is the relationship between what we think and what we do?

Social influence: What invisible social threads pull us? How strong are they? How do they operate?

Social relations: What makes us harm or help or fall in love? What can we do to transform the closed fists of aggression into the open arms of compassion?

Social Thinking

Especially when something unexpected occurs, we analyze and discuss why people act as they do. Does her warmth reflect romantic interest in me, or is that how she relates to everyone? Does his absenteeism signify laziness or an oppressive work atmosphere?

Attributing Behavior to Persons or to Situations

As a way to analyze how we answer such questions, Fritz Heider (1958) proposed **attribution theory**—a theory of how people explain someone's behavior. Heider noted that people often attribute others' behavior either to their *dispositions* (internal causes, such as their personality) or to their *situations* (external causes, such as their environment). A teacher may wonder whether a child's hostility reflects an aggressive personality (a "dispositional attribution") or whether the child is reacting to stress or abuse (a "situational attribution").

Consider how we typically make attributions. In class, we notice that Julie doesn't say much; over coffee, Jack talks nonstop. Attributing their behaviors to their personal dispositions, we decide that Julie is shy and Jack is outgoing. Because people do have enduring personality traits, such attributions are sometimes valid. However, we often overestimate the influence of personality and underestimate the impact of the situation. In class, Jack may be as quiet as Julie. Catch Julie at a party and you may hardly recognize your quiet classmate. Underestimating situational influences is known as the **fundamental attribution error.**

An experiment by David Napolitan and George Goethals (1979) illustrates this. The researchers had Williams College students talk, one at a time, with a young woman who acted either aloof and critical or warm and friendly. Beforehand, they told half the students the woman's behavior would be spontaneous. They told the other half the truth—that she had been instructed to *act* friendly (or unfriendly). What effect do you suppose this information had?

None. The students disregarded the information. If the woman acted friendly, they inferred she really was a warm person. If she acted unfriendly, they inferred she really was a cold person. In other words, they attributed her behavior to her personal disposition, *even when told that her behavior was situational,* that she was merely acting that way for purposes of the experiment.

Knowing about the fundamental attribution error is helpful—yet committing it is almost irresistible. In a high school play I attended recently, a talented 16-year-old girl convincingly played the part of a bitter old woman—so convincingly that, although I reminded myself of the fundamental attribution error, I still assumed that the young actress was typecast because she was well-suited for the part. Meeting her later at a cast party, I discovered she actually has a very pleasant disposition. I then remembered that several months earlier I had seen her play the part of a charming 10-year-old in *The Sound of Music*. Leonard Nimoy of *Star Trek* fame would not have been surprised by my error. He titled one of his books *I Am Not Spock*.

You, too, have surely committed the fundamental attribution error. In judging, say, whether your psychology instructor is shy or outgoing, you perhaps inferred from your class experience that he or she has an outgoing personality. But you know your instructor only from the classroom, a situation that demands outgoing behavior. Catch the instructor in a different situation and you might be surprised (as some of my students are when confronting me in a pick-up basketball game). Outside of their assigned roles, professors seem less professorial, presidents less presidential, servants less servile.

The instructor, on the other hand, observes his or her own behavior in many different situations—in the classroom, in meetings, at home, and the like—and so might say, "Me, outgoing? It all depends on the situation. In class or with good friends, yes, I'm outgoing. But at conventions I'm really rather shy."

So, when explaining *our own* behavior, we are sensitive to how our behavior changes with the situations we encounter. However, when explaining others' behavior, particularly after observing them in only one type of situation, we often commit the fundamental attribution error. We disregard the situation and leap to unwarranted conclusions about their personality traits. We do so partly because our attention focuses on the person more than on the situational context. To use the language of perception, the person is a "figure" that stands out from the situational "ground." Meanwhile, the person's own attention focuses more on the situation to which he or she is reacting.

So, what do you suppose happens when we reverse the perspectives of actor and observer—by having each view a videotape

Recall from Chapter 14 that personality psychologists study the enduring, inner determinants of behavior that help to explain why different people act differently in a given situation. Social psychologists study the social influences that help explain why a person will act differently in different situations.

replay of the situation from the other's perspective? As the focus-of-attention explanation predicts, this reverses the attributions (Lassiter & Irvine, 1986; Storms, 1973). By seeing the world from the actor's perspective, the observers better appreciate the situation. Given an observer's point of view, the actors better appreciate their own initiative and personal style.

The Effects of Attribution In everyday life we often struggle to explain why others act as they do. A jury must decide whether a shooting was malicious or in self-defense. An unhappy wife and husband each ponders why the other behaves so selfishly. An interviewer must judge whether the applicant's geniality is genuine. When making such judgments, our attributions—either to the person or to the situation—have important consequences (Bradbury & Fincham, 1990; Fletcher & others, 1990). Happily married couples attribute their spouse's tart-tongued remark to a temporary situation ("She must have had a bad day at work"). Unhappily married persons attribute the same remark to a mean disposition ("Geesh—what a cold and hostile person").

Or consider the political effects of attribution: How do you explain poverty or unemployment? Researchers in Britain, India, Australia, and the United States (Furnham, 1982; Pandey & others, 1982; Wagstaff, 1982) report that political conservatives tend to attribute these and other social problems to the personal dispositions of the poor and unemployed themselves: "People generally get what they deserve. Those who don't work are often lazy freeloaders. People who take initiative can still get ahead." Political liberals are more likely to blame past and present situations: "If you or I had to live with the same poor education, lack of meaningful opportunity, and outright discrimination, would we be any better off?"

And how do you explain homelessness? Some people—45 percent in one survey (Lee & others, 1990)—attribute homelessness to society's failure to provide adequate jobs and housing. Others—33 percent—blame the homeless themselves. President Reagan (1988), for example, believed that many homeless people "make it their own choice" not to seek shelter. Clearly, there are political implications to whether we attribute people's behavior to social conditions or to their own choices and shortcomings.

In evaluating employees, managers must also make attributions. They are likely to attribute the poor performance of workers to personal factors such as low ability or lack of motivation. Workers who are doing poorly on a job recognize situational influences: inadequate supplies, poor working conditions, difficult co-workers, impossible or ambiguous demands (Rice, 1985).

The point to remember: Our attributions—to individuals' dispositions or to their situations—have practical consequences.

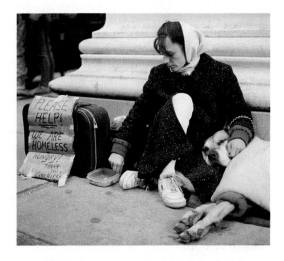

"Judge not" may be our ideal, but most of us cannot resist judging. Is this woman's homelessness likely attributable to her own disposition and choices or to her situation? What attributions might political conservatives and liberals suggest?

Attitudes and Actions

Social psychology's single most important concept has been that of *attitudes*. **Attitudes** are beliefs and feelings that predispose our reactions to objects, people, and events. If we *believe* that someone is mean, we may *feel* dislike for the person and *act* unfriendly. "Change the way people think," said South African civil rights martyr Steve Biko, "and things will never be the same."

Do Our Attitudes Guide Our Actions? Although most persuasive appeals assume that changed attitudes can indeed change behavior, dozens of studies during the 1960s challenged this idea (Wicker, 1971). Moreover, studies of people's attitudes and behaviors regarding cheating, the church, and racial minorities revealed that folks often talk and act a different game. "Thinking is easy," said the German poet Goethe (1749–1832), "acting difficult, and to put one's thoughts into action, the most difficult thing in the world."

But the seeming hypocrisy did startle social psychologists, most of whom shared Steve Biko's belief that there is a close connection between private words and public deeds, character and conduct, thought and action. So they conducted many follow-up studies during the 1970s and 1980s (Kraus, 1991). These studies reveal that our attitudes *will* guide our actions if:

Outside influences on what we say and do are minimal. Social pressures may blur the underlying connection between our attitudes and actions by affecting either what we say or what we do (Figure 18–1). In 1990, 4 weeks before a congressional election, President Bush and political leaders from both parties asked members of the U.S. House of Representatives to pass a compromise deficit-reducing budget. Privately, most members of Congress agreed that the painful cuts and tax increases were essential to the nation's health: Among those retiring or unopposed for reelection and thus facing little external pressure, 86 percent voted for the bill. For others, voting their privately held attitudes was more difficult. Among the 36 representatives who were about to face angry voters in close races back home, there were no profiles in courage: All 36 voted against it.

The attitude is specifically relevant to the behavior. People readily profess *general* attitudes that are inconsistent with their behavior. They proclaim love while practicing hate, cherish honesty while cheating on their income tax returns, and value good health while smoking and not exercising. Attitudes about the specific act do, however, guide action. Attitudes toward exercise predict exercising behavior.

We are keenly aware of our attitudes. When we mindlessly follow habit or social expectations, our attitudes lie dormant. If

"I do not understand my own actions. For I do not do what I want, but I do the very thing I hate."
St. Paul
Romans 7:15

Figure 18–1 Our behavior is affected by our inner attitudes and by external social influences.

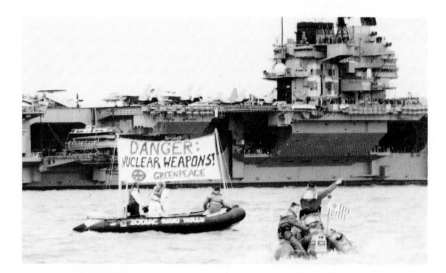

The attitudes of Greenpeace members toward the environment predict their environmentalist actions.

something makes us self-conscious or reminds us of how we feel, we are truer to our convictions. For example, Martha Powell and Russell Fazio (1984) had people rate their attitudes about gun control and about the Equal Rights Amendment. They found that repeating an attitude makes it come more quickly to mind. And attitudes that come quickly to mind are more likely to guide our behavior (Fazio, 1990). When we know what we believe and are conscious of its implications for our actions, we probably will be true to ourselves.

Do Our Actions Affect Our Attitudes? So, under certain conditions people will stand up for what they believe. Now consider a less obvious but equally valid principle: People also come to believe in what they have stood up for. Many streams of evidence confirm that *attitudes follow behavior*. Consider two.

The Foot-in-the-Door Phenomenon   During the Korean War, many captured American soldiers were imprisoned in war camps run by Chinese communists. Without using brutality, the captors secured their prisoners' collaboration in ways ranging from running errands and accepting favors, to making radio appeals and false confessions, to informing on fellow prisoners and divulging military information. When the war ended, 21 prisoners chose to stay with the communists. Many others returned home "brainwashed"—convinced that communism was a good thing for Asia.

A key ingredient of the Chinese "thought-control" program was their effective use of the **foot-in-the-door phenomenon**—a tendency for people who agree to a small request to comply later with a larger one. The Chinese harnessed this phenomenon by gradually escalating their demands on the prisoners, beginning with harmless requests (Schein, 1956). Having "trained" the prisoners to speak or write trivial statements, the communists then asked them to copy or create something more important, noting, perhaps, the flaws of American capitalism. The prisoners then participated in group discussions, wrote self-criticisms, or uttered public confessions. Once they did so, perhaps to gain privileges, the prisoners then often adjusted their beliefs toward consistency with their public acts.

Research studies show that the foot-in-the-door tactic also helps boost charitable contributions, blood donations, and product sales. In one experiment, researchers posing as safety-drive volunteers asked Californians to permit the installation of a large, poorly lettered "Drive Carefully" sign in their front yards. Only 17 percent consented. Others were first approached with a small request: Would they display a 3-inch "Be a Safe Driver" sign? Nearly all readily agreed. When reapproached 2 weeks later to allow the large, ugly sign in their front yards, 76 percent consented (Freedman & Fraser, 1966).

The moral is simple, says Robert Cialdini (1988): To get people to agree to something big, "start small and build." And be wary of those who would exploit you with the tactic. This chicken-and-egg spiraling of actions feeding attitudes feeding actions enables behavior to escalate. A trifling act makes the next act easier. Succumb to a temptation and the next temptation will be harder to resist.

Dozens of experiments have simulated part of the war prisoners' experience, by coaxing people into acting against their attitudes or violating their moral standards. The nearly inevitable result:

Most subjects begin to rationalize their behavior by persuading themselves that they were justified in saying or doing what they did. If induced to speak or write on behalf of a point of view they have doubts about, they begin to believe their own words. Saying becomes believing. Similarly, subjects induced to harm an innocent victim—by making cutting comments or by delivering electric shocks—typically begin to disparage their victim.

Fortunately, the attitudes-follow-behavior principle works as well for good deeds as for bad. In the years immediately following the introduction of school desegregation and the passage of the U.S. Civil Rights Act of 1964, White Americans expressed diminishing racial prejudice. And as Americans in different regions came to act more alike—thanks to more uniform national standards against discrimination—they began to think more alike. Similarly, experiments reveal that moral action has positive effects on the actor, and that doing favors for another person often leads to greater liking of the person. We love people for the good we do them as well as for the good they do us. Evil acts shape the self, but so do moral acts.

"If the King destroys a man, that's proof to the King it must have been a bad man."
Thomas Cromwell in Robert Bolt's
A Man for All Seasons, 1960

Role Playing Affects Attitudes In psychology, as in the theater, a **role** refers to a cluster of prescribed actions—the behaviors we expect of those who occupy a particular social position. When you adopt a new role—when you become a college student, marry, or begin a new job—you strive to follow the social prescriptions. At first, the behaviors may feel phony, because you are *acting* the role. The first weeks in the military feel artificial—as if one is pretending to be a soldier. The first weeks of a marriage may feel like "playing house." Before long, however, your behavior no longer feels forced. What began as play-acting in the theater of life becomes you.

Researchers have confirmed this effect by assessing people's attitudes before and after they adopt a new role. Sometimes this occurs in laboratory situations, sometimes in everyday situations, such as before and after taking a job. In one laboratory study, college students volunteered to spend time in a simulated prison devised by psychologist Philip Zimbardo (1972). Some he randomly designated as guards; he gave them uniforms, billy clubs, and whistles and instructed them to enforce certain rules. The remainder became prisoners; they were locked in barren cells and forced to wear humiliating outfits. After a day or two of self-consciously "playing" their roles, the simulation became real—too real. The guards devised cruel and degrading routines, and one by one the prisoners either broke down, rebelled, or passively resigned, causing Zimbardo to call the study off after only 6 days.

Meanwhile, in real life, the military junta then in power in Greece was training another group of men to become torturers (Staub, 1989). The men's indoctrination into their roles occurred in small steps. First, the trainee stood guard outside the interrogation cells—the "foot in the door." Next, he stood guard inside. Only then was he ready to become actively involved in the questioning and torture. As the nineteenth-century writer Nathaniel Hawthorne noted, "No man, for any considerable period, can wear one face to himself and another to the multitude without finally getting bewildered as to which may be true." Behavior affects attitudes. What we do we gradually become.

Why Do Our Actions Affect Our Attitudes? Without doubt, then, actions can affect attitudes, sometimes turning prisoners into collaborators, doubters into believers, or mere acquaintances into friends.

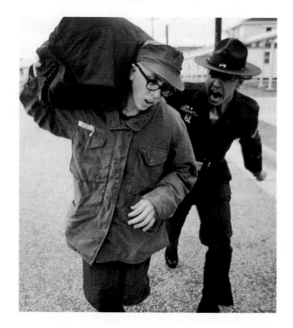

Both the obedient recruit and the abusive sergeant may have begun by consciously adopting the behavior expected of them in these roles, but they often end up becoming the characters they are playing.

But why? One explanation is that we feel motivated to justify our actions. When aware that our thoughts and actions don't coincide, we experience tension, called *cognitive dissonance*. To relieve this tension, according to the **cognitive dissonance theory** proposed by Leon Festinger, people will bring their attitudes into line with their actions. It's as if people rationalize, "If I chose to do it (or say it), I must believe in it." The less coerced and more responsible we feel for a troubling act, the more dissonance we feel. The more dissonance we feel, the more our attitudes change to justify the act.

The attitudes-follow-behavior principle has heartening implications. Although we cannot directly control all our feelings, we can influence them by altering our behavior. If we are unloving, we can become more loving by behaving as if we were so—by doing thoughtful things, expressing affection, giving affirmation. If we are down in the dumps, we can do as cognitive therapists advise and talk in more positive, self-accepting ways with fewer self put-downs. **The moral:** We can as easily act ourselves into a way of thinking as think ourselves into a way of acting.

Social Influence

Social psychology's great lesson—the enormous power of social influence on our attitudes, beliefs, decisions, and actions—can be seen in our conformity, compliance, and group behavior. Suicides, bomb threats, airplane hijackings, and UFO sightings all have a curious tendency to come in waves. Armed with principles of social influence, advertisers and salespeople aim to sway our decisions to buy, to donate, to vote. Isolated with others who share their grievances, dissenters may gradually become rebels and rebels may become terrorists. Let's examine these potent social forces.

Conformity and Obedience

How powerful are the social strings that pull us? How do they operate? To find out, social psychologists often create laboratory simulations of everyday social situations. In the miniature social world of the experiment, researchers hold constant all the factors that might influence our behavior, except for one or two. These they vary, to pinpoint how changes in them affect us. Let's see how social psychologists work.

Suggestibility You've often witnessed the contagiousness of some behaviors. One person giggles, coughs, or yawns, and others in the group are soon doing the same. A cluster of people stands gazing upward, and passersby pause to do likewise. Laughter, even canned laughter, can be infectious. Bartenders and street musicians know to "seed" their tip cups with money that suggests that others have given. The suggestibility apparent in these examples is a form of **conformity**, adjusting our thinking or behavior to bring it into line with some group standard.

Muzafer Sherif (1937) designed a simple social situation to study people's suggestibility. Shown a stationary point of light in a dark room, people misperceive it as moving. Some might see it as moving about 8 inches, others just an inch or two. When such people then participate together, hearing one another's estimates of how far the light moved, their estimates gradually converge. And

"Sit all day in a moping posture, sigh, and reply to everything with a dismal voice, and your melancholy lingers. . . . If we wish to conquer undesirable emotional tendencies in ourselves, we must . . . go through the outward movements of those contrary dispositions which we prefer to cultivate."
William James
Principles of Psychology, 1890

"The person we have to thank is Arthur here. He's the one with the infectious grin."
Drawing by Handelsman; © 1984 The New Yorker Magazine, Inc.

when later retested individually, they still maintain their revised judgments.

In real life, the effects of suggestibility are sometimes devastating. Sociologist David Phillips and his colleagues (1985, 1989) found that known suicides increase following a highly publicized suicide (Figure 18–2). So do fatal auto accidents and private airplane crashes (some of which disguise suicides). These increases occur only in areas where the suicide is publicized; deaths increase with the amount of media coverage; and the victims tend to be near the age of the publicized suicide victim. Following film star Marilyn Monroe's suicide on August 6, 1962, there were 200 more August suicides in the United States than normal. In Germany and the United States, escalated suicide rates have also followed fictional suicides on soap operas, and even on well-intentioned dramas dealing with the issue (Gould & Shaffer, 1986; Hafner & Schmidtke, 1989; Phillips, 1982). Such outbreaks of copycat suicides help explain the clusters of teenage suicides that occasionally occur in some communities.

> *"I often marvel that while each man loves himself more than anyone else, he sets less value on his own estimate than on the opinions of others."*
> Marcus Aurelius, A.D. 121–180
> *Meditations*

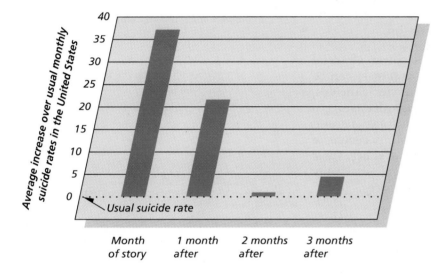

Figure 18–2 Imitative suicides? During the 2 months following each of 35 highly publicized suicides between 1947 and 1968, an average of 58 more people than usual killed themselves. (From Phillips, 1974.)

Group Pressure and Conformity Suggestibility is a subtle type of conformity, one in which the influence isn't blatant. Faced with the "moving" light, Sherif's subjects were unsure of the truth, so it is easy to understand why they adjusted their responses toward one another. But what would happen if people could easily judge the truth for themselves? Would they conform to a clearly incorrect group standard? Solomon Asch (1955) thought not. To test his assumption and to examine factors he thought might affect conformity, Asch devised a simple test.

As one of his subjects, you arrive at the experiment location in time to take a seat at the end of a row where four people are already seated. The experimenter asks which of the three comparison lines in Figure 18–3 is identical to the standard line. You see clearly that the answer is line 2 and await your turn to say so after the others. Your boredom with this experiment begins to show when the next set of lines proves equally easy.

Now comes the third trial, and the correct answer seems just as clear-cut, but the first person gives what strikes you as a wrong answer: "line 3." When the second person and then the third give

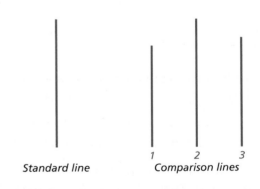

Figure 18–3 An example of the perceptual judgments made in Asch's conformity experiments. Which of the three comparison lines is equal to the standard line? What do you suppose most people would say after hearing four others say "line 3"?

In this photo from the Asch experiment, the subject (center) shows the severe discomfort that comes from disagreeing with the responses of other group members.

the same wrong answer, you sit straight up and squint. When the fourth person agrees with the first three, you feel your heart begin to pound. The experimenter then looks to you for your answer. Torn between the unanimity of your four fellow subjects and the evidence of your own eyes, you feel tense and much less sure of yourself than you were moments ago. You hesitate before answering, wondering whether you should suffer the discomfort of being viewed as an oddball. What answer do you give?

In the experiments conducted by Asch and others after him, thousands of college students have experienced this conflict. Answering such questions alone, they erred less than 1 percent of the time. But it was a different story when several others—who were actually confederates working for the experimenter—answered incorrectly. Asch reports that his "intelligent and well-meaning" college subjects were then "willing to call white black" more than one-third of the time by going along with the group.

Conditions That Strengthen Conformity   Asch's procedure became the model for later investigations. Although experiments have not always found such a high degree of blind conformity, they reveal that conformity increases when:

We are made to feel incompetent or insecure.

The group has at least three people. (Further increases in the group size yield smaller increases in conformity.)

The group is unanimous. (The support of a single fellow dissident greatly increases our social courage.)

We admire the group's status and attractiveness.

We have made no prior commitment to any response.

Others in the group observe our behavior.

Our culture strongly encourages respect for social standards.

Thus, we might predict the behavior of Joe, an eager but insecure new member of a prestigious fraternity: Noting that the 40 other members appear unanimous in their plans for an upcoming fundraiser, Joe is unlikely to voice his dissent.

Reasons for Conforming   Why do people comply with social pressure? Why do we clap when others clap, eat as others eat, believe what others believe, even see what others see? Frequently, it is to avoid rejection or to gain social approval. In such cases, we are responding to what social psychologists call **normative social**

"It is too easy to go over to the majority."
Seneca
Ad Lucilium Epistula, A.D. 63–65

influence. We are sensitive to social **norms**—understood rules for accepted and expected behavior—because the price we pay for being different may be severe. Marco Lokar knows. During the 1991 Persian Gulf War, Lokar, an Italian, was the only Seton Hall University basketball player who chose not to display an American flag on his uniform. When, as the team travelled about, the fan abuse over his nonconforming behavior became unbearable, he quit the team and returned to Italy.

But there is another reason: The group can provide valuable information. When we accept others' opinions about reality, we are responding to **informational social influence**. As a subject in Sherif's experiment—feeling very unsure about how far the light had moved—would it not have seemed reasonable to be open to others' judgments? "Those who never retract their opinions love themselves more than they love truth," observed Joseph Joubert, an eighteenth-century French essayist.

As these reasons for conformity suggest, social influence can be either constructive or destructive. When influence supports what we approve, then we applaud those who are "open-minded" and "sensitive" enough to be "responsive." When influence supports what we disapprove, then we scorn the "submissive conformity" of those who comply with others' wishes. As we will see in Chapter 19, Social Diversity, cultures vary in the value they place on independence versus responsiveness to others. Europeans and those in most English-speaking countries tend to prize independence more than conformity and obedience.

Obedience Social psychologist Stanley Milgram (1974) knew that people often comply with social pressures. But how would they respond to outright commands? To find out, he undertook what have become social psychology's most famous and controversial experiments. Imagine yourself as one of the nearly 1000 participants in Milgram's 20 experiments.

Responding to an advertisement, you come to Yale University's psychology department to participate in an experiment. Professor Milgram's assistant explains that the study concerns the effect of punishment on learning. You and another subject draw slips out of a hat to see who will be the "teacher" (which your slip says) and who will be the "learner." The learner is then led to an adjoining room and strapped into a chair that is wired through the wall to an electric shock machine. You sit down in front of the machine, which has switches labeled with voltages. Your task: to teach and then test the learner on a list of word pairs. You are to punish the learner for wrong answers by delivering brief electric shocks, beginning with a switch labeled "15 Volts—Slight Shock." After each error by the learner you are to move up to the next higher voltage. With each flick of a switch, lights flash, relay switches click on, and an electric buzzing fills the air.

If you comply with the experimenter's instructions, you hear the learner grunt when you flick the third, fourth, and fifth switches. After you activate the eighth switch (labeled "120 Volts"), the learner shouts that the shocks are painful. After the tenth switch ("150 Volts—Strong Shock"), he cries, "Experimenter, get me out of here! I won't be in the experiment anymore! I refuse to go on!" You draw back when you hear these pleas, but the experimenter prods you: "Please continue—the experiment requires that you continue." If you still resist, he insists, "It is absolutely essential that you continue," or "You have no other choice, you *must* go on."

"'The way to get along,' I was told when I entered Congress, 'is to go along.'"
John F. Kennedy
Profiles in Courage, 1956

Stanley Milgram (1933–1984), whose obedience experiments now "belong to the self-understanding of literate people in our age" (Sabini, 1986).

If you obey, you hear the learner's protests escalate to shrieks of agony as you continue to raise the shock level with each succeeding error. After the 330-volt level, the learner refuses to answer and soon falls silent. Still, the experimenter pushes you toward the final, 450-volt switch, ordering you to ask the questions and, if a correct answer is not given, to administer the next shock level.

How far do you think you would follow the experimenter's commands? When Milgram surveyed people before conducting the experiment, most declared they would stop playing such a sadistic role soon after the learner first indicates pain and certainly before he shrieks in agony. This also was the prediction made by each of 40 psychiatrists whom Milgram asked to guess the outcome. When Milgram actually conducted the experiment with men aged 20 to 50, he was astonished to find that 63 percent complied fully—right up to the last switch.

Did the teachers figure out the hoax—that no shock was being delivered? Did they guess that the learner was a confederate who only pretended to feel the shocks? Did they realize that the experiment was really testing their willingness to comply with commands to inflict punishment? No, the teachers typically displayed genuine agony: They sweated, trembled, laughed nervously, and bit their lips. In defense of his use of deception, Milgram pointed out that, after learning of the deception and actual research purposes, virtually none regretted participating. When 40 of the subjects who had agonized most were later interviewed by a psychiatrist, none appeared to be suffering emotional aftereffects.

Perhaps the subjects obeyed because the learners' protests were not convincing. To preclude this possibility, Milgram repeated the experiment. This time his confederate mentioned a "slight heart condition" while being strapped into the chair and then complained and screamed more intensely as the shocks became more punishing. Still, when 40 new teachers were tested, 65 percent complied fully (Figure 18–4).

Standing up for democracy. Some individuals— roughly one in three in Milgram's experiments— resist social coercion, as did this unarmed man in Beijing, by single-handedly challenging an advancing line of tanks the day after the 1989 Tiananmen Square uprising was crushed.

Figure 18–4 In Milgram's follow-up obedience experiment, 65 percent of the adult male subjects fully obeyed the experimenter's commands to continue. This was despite the victim's "heart condition" and despite hearing cries of protest after 150 volts and agonized protests after 330 volts. (Data from Milgram, 1974.)

In later experiments, Milgram discovered that when he varied the social conditions, the proportion of fully compliant subjects varied from 0 to 93 percent. Obedience was highest when:

The one giving the orders was close at hand and perceived as a legitimate authority figure.

The authority figure was supported by a prestigious institution. (Milgram got somewhat less compliance when he dissociated his experiments from Yale University.)

The victim was depersonalized or at a distance, even in another room. (Similarly, in combat with an enemy they can see, many soldiers will either not fire their rifles or not aim them properly. Such refusals to kill are rare among those who operate the more distant weapons of artillery or aircraft [Padgett, 1989].)

There were no role models for defiance; that is, there were no other subjects seen disobeying the experimenter.

Lessons from the Conformity and Obedience Studies What do these experiments teach us about ourselves? How does guessing the movement of a point of light, judging a line length, or flicking a shock switch relate to everyday social behavior? Recall from Chapter 1 that psychological experiments aim not to recreate the literal behaviors of everyday life but to capture and explore the underlying processes that shape those behaviors. Sherif, Asch, and Milgram devised experiments in which the subjects had to choose between holding to their own standards and being responsive to others, a dilemma we all face frequently.

In Milgram's experiments, subjects were also torn between what they should respond to—the pleas of the victim or the orders of the experimenter. Their moral sense warned them not to harm another, but it also prompted them to obey the experimenter and to be a good subject. With kindness and obedience on a collision course, obedience usually won.

These experiments demonstrate that social influences can be strong enough to make people conform to falsehoods or capitulate to cruelty. "The most fundamental lesson of our study," Milgram noted, is that "ordinary people, simply doing their jobs, and without any particular hostility on their part, can become agents in a terrible destructive process" (1974, p. 6). Milgram entrapped his subjects not by asking them first to zap someone with enough electricity to stand their hair on end. Rather, he exploited the foot-in-the-door effect, beginning with a little tickle of electricity and escalating step by step. In the subjects' minds, the little action became justified, making the next act tolerable.

So it happens when people succumb, gradually, to evil. In any society, great evils sometimes grow out of people's compliance with apparently innocuous little evils. The Nazi leaders suspected that most German civil servants would resist shooting or gassing Jews directly, but found them surprisingly willing to handle the paperwork of the Holocaust (Silver & Geller, 1978). Likewise, when Milgram asked 40 men to administer the learning test while someone else did the shocking, 93 percent complied.

Group Influence

How do groups affect our behavior? To find out, social psychologists study the various influences that operate in the simplest of groups—one person in the presence of another—and those that operate in more complex groups, such as families, teams, and committees.

"*Drive off the cliff, James, I want to commit suicide.*"

Drawing by Mel Yauk.

"*I was only following orders.*"
    Adolf Eichmann, Director of Nazi deportation of Jews to concentration camps

"*. . . the Milgram experiment is really a valuable attack on the denial and indifference of all of us. Whatever upset follows facing the truth, we must eventually face up to the fact that so many of us are, in fact, available to be genociders or their assistants.*"
    Israel W. Charny (1982, p. 16)
    Executive Director, International Conference on the Holocaust and Genocide

Individual Behavior in the Presence of Others Appropriately, social psychology's first experiments focused on the simplest of all questions about social behavior: How are we influenced by the mere presence of others—by people watching us or joining us as we engage in various activities?

Social Facilitation Having noticed that cyclists' racing times were faster when they competed against each other rather than competing with a clock, Norman Triplett (1898) guessed that the presence of others boosts performance. To test his hypothesis, Triplett had adolescents wind a fishing reel as rapidly as possible. He discovered that they wound faster in the presence of a **co-actor**, someone who works simultaneously on the same task. This stronger performance in the presence of others is known as **social facilitation**. For example, after a light turns green, drivers take about 15 percent less time to travel the first 100 yards when another car is beside them at the intersection than when they are alone (Towler, 1986).

For a while, social facilitation seemed a universal principle, an effect that occurred in varying circumstances. Researchers were therefore mystified when they began to find the opposite effect: On tasks such as learning nonsense syllables or solving complex multiplication problems, people performed less well when there were observers or co-actors. Some 300 studies and 25,000 subjects later (Guerin, 1986), the mystery of why the presence of others sometimes helps and sometimes hurts task performance has been solved. The Sherlock Holmes in this scientific detective story was social psychologist Robert Zajonc (1965). Zajonc recalled an effect of arousal on performance (page 384): Arousal facilitates the most likely response—the correct one on an easy task, an incorrect one on a difficult task. If performing tasks in the presence of others causes people to become aroused, reasoned Zajonc, then easy tasks should become easier and difficult tasks should become harder.

Sure enough, when observed by others, people do become aroused (Geen & Gange, 1983; Moore & Baron, 1983). And with arousal, they do perform well-learned tasks more quickly and accurately and unmastered tasks less quickly and accurately. James Michaels and his associates (1982) found that expert pool players who made 71 percent of their shots when alone made 80 percent when four people came up to watch them. Poor shooters, who made 36 percent of their shots when alone, made only 25 percent when watched. The moral: What you do well, you are likely to do even better in front of an audience; what you normally find difficult may seem impossible when others are watching.

Social facilitation also helps explain a funny effect of crowding: Comedy records that are mildly amusing to people in an uncrowded room seem funnier to people in a densely packed room (Aiello & others, 1983; Freedman & Perlick, 1979). As comedians and actors know, a "good house" is a full one. The arousal triggered by crowding amplifies other reactions, too. If sitting close, experimental subjects like a friendly person more, an unfriendly person less (Schiffenbauer & Schiavo, 1976; Storms & Thomas, 1977).

Social Loafing The social facilitation experiments test people's *individual* efforts in tasks ranging from winding fishing reels to shooting pool. But what happens in situations that require a *team* effort to achieve a common goal? In a team tug-of-war, do you suppose people would individually exert more, less, or the same effort as they would in a one-on-one tug-of-war?

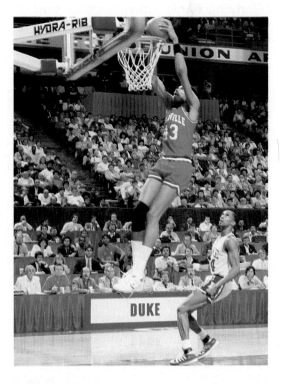

Performers often find they are "on" before an audience. An audience inspires them to excel, illustrating the principle that emotional arousal leads to better performance on well-learned tasks.

To find out, Alan Ingham and his fellow researchers (1974) asked blindfolded University of Massachusetts students to "pull as hard as you can" on a rope. When Ingham fooled the students into believing three others were also pulling behind them, they exerted only 82 percent as much effort as when they knew they were pulling alone.

To describe the diminished effort by those submerged in a group, Bibb Latané and his colleagues (1981; Jackson & Williams, 1988) coined the term **social loafing**. In more than four dozen experiments conducted in the United States, India, Thailand, Japan, and Taiwan, social loafing occurred on various tasks (Gabrenya & others, 1983). For example, blindfolded subjects seated in a group have clapped or shouted as loud as they could while listening through headphones to the sound of loud clapping or shouting. When told they were doing it with the others, the subjects produced about one-third less noise than when they thought their individual efforts were identifiable.

Why? First, people acting as part of a group feel less accountable and therefore worry less about what others think. Second, they may view their contribution as dispensable (Harkins & Szymanski, 1989; Kerr & Bruun, 1983). As many leaders of organizations know, if group members share equally in the group's benefits regardless of how much they contribute, they may slack off and "free-ride" on the other group members' efforts.

Deindividuation We have seen that the presence of others can arouse people (as in the social facilitation experiments) or can diminish their feelings of responsibility (as in the social loafing experiments). Sometimes the presence of others both arouses people *and* diminishes their sense of responsibility. The result can be uninhibited behavior ranging from a food fight in the dining hall or screaming at a basketball referee to vandalism or rioting. Abandoning normal restraints to the power of the group is termed **deindividuation**. To be deindividuated is to be unself-conscious and unrestrained in a group situation.

Deindividuation often occurs when group participation makes people feel aroused and anonymous. In one experiment, New York University women dressed in depersonalizing Ku Klux Klan-style hoods delivered twice as much electric shock to a victim as did identifiable women (Zimbardo, 1970). (As in all such experiments, the "victim" did not actually receive the shocks.) Similarly, tribal warriors who depersonalize themselves with face paints or masks are more likely than those with exposed faces to kill, torture, or mutilate captured enemies (Watson, 1973). Whether in a mob, at a rock concert, at a dance, or at worship, to lose one's self-consciousness (to become deindividuated) is to become more responsive to the group experience and—for better or for worse—to give up some self-control.

Deindividuation. Whether in experiments or in real-life situations, like this rock concert, people made anonymous act on their impulses with less restraint.

Effects of Group Interaction We have examined the conditions under which the presence of others can fuel mob violence and enhance humor, make easy tasks easier and difficult tasks harder, tempt people to free-ride on the efforts of others and motivate them to jog faster. Research shows how group interaction, too, can have both bad and good effects.

Group Polarization Educational researchers have noted that, over time, initial differences between groups of college students often grow. If the first-year students at College *X* are more intellectually oriented than those at College *Y*, chances are their difference will be amplified by the time they are seniors. Similarly, if the political conservatism of students who join fraternities and sororities is greater than that of students who do not, the gap in the political attitudes of the two groups will probably widen as they progress through college (Wilson & others, 1975).

This enhancement of a group's prevailing tendencies—called **group polarization**—occurs when people within a group discuss attitudes that most of them favor or oppose. For example, George Bishop and I discovered that when prejudiced high school students discussed racial issues, their attitudes became more prejudiced. When low-prejudice students discussed the same issues, they became more tolerant (Figure 18–5).

Figure 18–5 If a group is like-minded, discussion strengthens its prevailing opinions. Talking over racial issues increased prejudice in a high-prejudice group of high school students and decreased it in a low-prejudice group. (Data from Myers & Bishop, 1970.)

Group polarization can have beneficial results, as when it strengthens the resolve of those in a self-help group. But it can also have dire consequences. From their analysis of terrorist organizations around the world, psychologists Clark McCauley and Mary Segal (1987) note that the terrorist mentality does not erupt suddenly. Rather, it arises among people who have come together because of a grievance and who become more and more extreme as they interact in isolation from moderating influences.

Groupthink Does the polarization that often occurs when like-minded people discuss their concerns ever distort important group decisions? Social psychologist Irving Janis thought so when he first read historian Arthur M. Schlesinger, Jr.'s, account of how President John F. Kennedy and his advisers blundered into an ill-fated plan to invade Cuba with 1400 CIA-trained Cuban exiles. When the invaders were easily captured and soon linked to the American government, Kennedy wondered aloud, "How could we have been so stupid?"

To find out, Janis (1982) studied the decision-making procedures that led to the fiasco. He discovered that the high morale of the recently elected President and his advisers fostered a sense that the plan would succeed. To preserve the good group feeling, dissenting views were suppressed or self-censored, especially after the President voiced his enthusiasm for the scheme. Since no one spoke sharply against the idea, everyone assumed there was consensus support for it. To describe this harmonious but unrealistic group thinking, Janis coined the term **groupthink**.

"One's impulse to blow the whistle on this nonsense was simply undone by the circumstances of the discussion."
Arthur M. Schlesinger, Jr. (1965, p. 255)

Janis and others then examined other historical fiascos—the failure to anticipate the Pearl Harbor attack, the escalation of the Vietnam war, the Watergate cover-up, the Chernobyl reactor accident (Reason, 1987), and the space shuttle *Challenger* explosion (Esser & Lindoerfer, 1989). They discovered that in these cases, too, groupthink was fed by overconfidence, conformity, self-justification, and group polarization. Buoyed by a string of successful space shuttle launches, the NASA management team approached the 1985 *Challenger* mission brimming with confidence but frustrated by launch delays. When the rocket booster's engineers opposed the launch because of dangers posed by freezing temperatures, group pressures to go ahead effectively silenced their warnings. Unless the engineers could *prove* that the rocket seals would not hold, the management group would not agree to another delay. Moreover, managers shielded the NASA executive who made the final "go" decision from information about the warnings. Wrongly assuming that support was unanimous, he launched the *Challenger* on its one-way flight to annihilation.

Despite such fiascos and tragedies, Janis also knew that, with some types of problems, two heads are better than one. So he also studied instances in which American presidents and their advisers collectively made good decisions. Examples were the Truman administration's formulation of the Marshall Plan for getting Europe back on its feet after World War II and the Kennedy administration's actions to keep the Soviets from installing missiles in Cuba. In such instances—and in the business world, too, Janis believed—groupthink is prevented by a leader who welcomes various opinions, invites experts' critiques of developing plans, or even assigns people to identify possible problems. As the suppression of dissent bends a group toward bad decisions, so open debate often shapes good decisions.

In affirming the power of social influence, we must not overlook our power as individuals. As we noted in Chapter 14, Personality, *social control* (the power of the situation) and *personal control* (the power of the individual) interact. For example, many of the situations that influence us are ones we choose or help create. If we expect people to be uncooperative and hostile, we may treat them in ways that elicit such behavior. Thus, our expectations may be self-fulfilling. In one experiment, men talked more charmingly by phone to women they believed to be beautiful. This led the women to respond more warmly—confirming the men's idea that attractive people are likable (Snyder & others, 1977). Moreover, people aren't billiard balls. When feeling coerced but not intimidated, we may react by doing the opposite, thereby reasserting our sense of freedom (Brehm & Brehm, 1981).

Minority Influence The powers of individuals also appear in their influence over their groups. Social history is often made by a minority that sways the majority. Were this not so, women would still not have the right to vote in the United States, communism would be an obscure theory, and Christianity would be a small Middle Eastern sect. Technological history, too, is often made by innovative minorities who overcome the majority's resistance to change. To many folks, the railroad was a nonsensical idea; some farmers feared that train noise would prevent hens from laying eggs. People derided Robert Fulton's steamboat as "Fulton's Folly." As Fulton later said, "Never did a single encouraging remark, a bright hope,

"There was a serious flaw in the decision-making process."
Report of the Presidential Commission on the Space Shuttle Challenger *Accident, 1986*

a warm wish, cross my path." Much the same reaction greeted the printing press, the telegraph, the incandescent lamp, and the typewriter (Cantril & Bumstead, 1960).

To understand better how minorities can sway majorities, social psychologists in Europe have investigated groups in which an individual or two consistently expresses a controversial attitude or an unusual perceptual judgment. They have repeatedly found that a minority that unswervingly holds to its position is far more successful in swaying the majority than is a minority that waffles. Holding consistently to a minority opinion will not make you popular, but it may make you influential. This is especially so if your self-confidence stimulates others to consider why you react as you do. Although people often follow the majority view publicly, they may privately develop sympathy for the minority view. Even when a minority's influence is not yet visible, it may be persuading some members of the majority to rethink their views (Maass & Clark, 1984; Nemeth, 1986).

Thus, the combined powers of social thinking and social influence are enormous. But so are the powers of the individual. Many of the situations that influence us are ones we choose or help create. When threatened but not intimidated, we also reassert our sense of freedom and uniqueness. And minority opinions can move empires.

We do well to remember that explaining *why* someone adopts a particular belief says nothing about the belief's truth or falsity. To know why someone does or doesn't believe that running benefits health does not tell us whether running is, in fact, beneficial. To know why one person is a theist and another is an atheist does not tell us whether God exists. So let no one say to you and do not say to anyone, "Your convictions are silly. You believe them because of social influence." The second statement may be true, but it doesn't justify the first.

As the life of Mahatma Gandhi (1869–1948) powerfully testifies, a consistent and persistent minority voice can sometimes sway the majority. Gandhi was often vilified and imprisoned. But his nonviolent appeals and fasts eventually won independence for India.

Social Relations

Having sampled how we *think* about and *influence* one another, we come finally to social psychology's third focus—how we *relate* to one another. We will consider the bad and the good: aggression, helpfulness, and attraction.

Aggression

In psychology, aggression has a more precise meaning than it does in everyday usage. The assertive, persistent salesperson is not aggressive. Nor is the dentist who makes you wince with pain. But the person who passes along a vicious rumor about you and the attacker who mugs you are. **Aggression** is any physical or verbal behavior intended to hurt or destroy, whether done out of hostility or as a calculated means to an end. Some of the 23,438 murders and 1,054,863 assaults recorded in the United States during 1990 were cool, calculated acts, but more were hostile outbursts.

Time and again, we have seen that behavior emerges from the interaction of nature and nurture. Research on aggression reinforces that theme. For a gun to fire, the trigger must be pulled; with some people, as with hair-trigger guns, it doesn't take much to trip an explosion. Let us look first at biological factors that influence our thresholds for aggressive behavior. Then we will examine the psychological factors that pull the trigger.

The Biology of Aggression According to one view, argued by Sigmund Freud and animal behavior theorist Konrad Lorenz, our species has a volcanic potential to erupt in aggression. Freud thought that, along with positive survival instincts, we harbor a self-destructive "death instinct" that we usually displace toward others as aggression or release in socially approved activities such as painting or sports. Lorenz believed that aggressive energy wells up instinctively from within until released by appropriate stimuli or inhibited by gestures of submission.

Although aggression varies too widely from culture to culture and person to person to be considered an unlearned instinct, biology does influence aggression. Stimuli that trigger aggressive behavior operate through our biological system. We can look for physiological influences at three levels—the genetic, the neural, and the biochemical. Our genes engineer our individual nervous systems, which operate electrochemically.

Genetic Influences Animals have been bred for aggressiveness, sometimes for sport, sometimes for research. Finnish psychologist Kirsti Lagerspetz (1979) took a group of normal mice and bred the most aggressive with one another and the least aggressive with one another. After repeating this selective breeding for another 25 generations, she had a group of vicious mice that would attack immediately when put together and a group of docile mice that, no matter what she did to them, refused to fight. Twin studies suggest that genes influence human aggression as well (Rushton & others, 1986). If one identical twin admits to "having a violent temper," the other twin will often independently admit the same. Fraternal twins are much more likely to respond differently.

Neural Influences Animal and human brains have neural systems that, when stimulated, produce aggressive behavior (Moyer, 1983). Some findings:

> A cat lives harmoniously with a rat until one day an implanted electrode stimulates a specific spot in its hypothalamus. Immediately, the cat attacks its cagemate and kills it as would a wild cat, by biting through its spinal cord at the neck.

> A mild-mannered woman has an electrode implanted deep in her brain's limbic system (in the amygdala) by neurosurgeons seeking to diagnose a disorder. Because the brain has no sensory receptors, she cannot feel any stimulation. But at the flick of a switch she snarls, "Take my blood pressure. Take it now," and then stands up and begins to strike the doctor.

> The domineering leader of a caged monkey colony has a radio-controlled electrode implanted in a brain area that, when stimulated, inhibits aggression. When researchers place the button that activates the electrode in the colony's cage, one small monkey learns to push it every time the boss becomes threatening.

> Intensive evaluation of 15 death-row inmates reveals that all 15 have suffered severe head injury. Researcher Dorothy Lewis and her colleagues (1986) infer that many condemned criminals suffer unrecognized neurological disorders.

A 1985 riot at a soccer game in Brussels left 38 dead and 437 injured. Aroused by the competition and loaded with alcohol, English fans lost all restraint when provoked by Italian fans. They attacked the Italians, who retreated and were then crushed against a wall.

Biochemical Influences Hormones and other substances in the blood influence the neural systems that activate and inhibit aggression. A raging bull will become a gentle Ferdinand when castration reduces its testosterone level. The same is true of castrated mice. And when injected with testosterone, the castrated mice again become aggressive.

Although humans are less sensitive to hormonal changes, violent criminals tend to be muscular young males with lower than average intelligence scores and higher than average testosterone levels (Dabbs & others, 1987; Wilson & Herrnstein, 1985). Drugs that sharply reduce their testosterone levels subdue their aggressive tendencies. Among the normal range of teenage boys and adult men, high testosterone levels correlate with delinquency, hard drug use, and aggressive, bullying responses to provocation (Archer, 1991; Dabbs & Morris, 1990; Olweus & others, 1988).

For both biological and psychological reasons (pages 210–212), alcohol unleashes aggressive responses to provocation (Bushman & Cooper, 1990; Taylor & Leonard, 1983). Police data and prison surveys reinforce conclusions from experiments on alcohol and aggression. Intoxicated people commit 65 percent of murders, 88 percent of knifings, 65 percent of spouse beatings, and 55 percent of physical child abuse (Steele, 1990).

Without disputing genetic, neural, and biochemical influences on aggression, social scientists worry that many people see aggression as so biologically intrinsic to human nature that peace is unattainable. To counter such pessimism, the American Psychological Association and the International Council of Psychologists endorsed a "Statement on Violence" drafted by scientists from a dozen nations (Adams & others, 1987). The statement declares it "scientifically incorrect" to say that genes or instinct program humans for violence or war.

The Psychology of Aggression Biological factors influence the ease with which psychological aggravations pull the aggression trigger. But what psychological factors lead to aggression? And what role does learning play?

Aversive Events Although suffering sometimes builds character, it may also bring out the worst in us. Studies in which animals or humans have unpleasant experiences reveal that those made miserable often make others miserable (Berkowitz, 1983, 1989).

The traffic between hormones and behavior is two-way. Testosterone heightens dominance and aggressiveness, but dominating or defeating also boosts testosterone levels (Gladue & others, 1989).

"He that is naturally addicted to Anger, let him Abstain from Wine; for it is but adding Fire to Fire."
Seneca
De Ira, A.D. 49

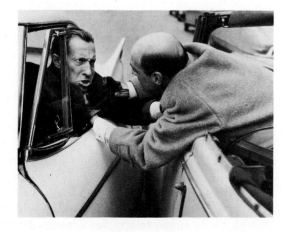

Aversive events can trigger aggression, especially when blamed on another.

Murders and rapes per day

Temperature in degrees Fahrenheit

Figure 18–6 Uncomfortably hot weather can elicit and heighten aggressive reactions. More violent crime and spouse abuse occurs in summer than in winter, in hot years than in cooler years, in hot cities than in cooler cities, and on hotter days than on colder days (Anderson 1989). For example, between 1980 and 1982 in Houston, murders and rapes were more common on days over 91° F. This finding is consistent with those from laboratory experiments in which people working in a hot room react to provocations with greater hostility. (From Anderson & Anderson, 1984.)

Being unable to achieve a goal increases people's readiness to behave aggressively. This phenomenon has led to the **frustration-aggression principle**: Frustration creates anger, which may generate aggression. When social psychologists realized that events such as physical pain and personal insults also trigger aggression, they saw that frustrations are instances of aversive events. Foul odors, hot temperatures, cigarette smoke, and a host of other aversive stimuli can also evoke hostility (Figure 18–6).

Learning to Express and Inhibit Aggression Aggression may be a natural response to aversive events, but learning can alter natural reactions. Animals naturally eat when they are hungry. But if appropriately rewarded or punished, they can be taught either to overeat or to starve.

Aggressive reactions, too, are more likely in situations where experience has taught us that aggression pays. Children whose aggression successfully intimidates other children may become more aggressive. Violent demonstrations that provide demonstrators with desired attention may recur.

Aggressive behavior can be learned through direct rewards, as when animals that have fought successfully to get food or mates become increasingly ferocious. It can also be learned through observation (Chapter 8, Learning). Children who grow up observing aggressive models often imitate the behaviors they see. Parents of delinquent youngsters typically rely on spankings and beatings for discipline. This models the use of aggression as a method of dealing with problems (Patterson & others, 1982). Once established, aggressive behavior patterns are difficult to change. To foster a kinder, gentler world we had best model and reward sensitivity and cooperation from an early age, perhaps by training parents how to discipline without modeling violence.

Television Watching and Aggression Parents aren't the only ones who model aggression. Consider: During their first 18 years, most children spend more time watching television than they spend in school. In urban homes across the world, including those of South America and Asia, television is now commonplace. In Beijing, for example, the percentage of homes with television skyrocketed from 32 percent in 1980 to 95 percent by the end of the '80s (Lull, 1988). Prime-time U.S. programs offer about 6 violent acts per hour; children's weekend programs about 26 (Gerbner & Signorielli, 1990). During their impressionable elementary and junior high school years, children therefore view some 13,000 TV murders among more than 100,000 acts of violence. This is life as rendered by a rather peculiar storyteller, one who reflects the culture's mythology but not its reality. In action-oriented crime shows, TV cops fire

"The problem with television is that the people must sit and keep their eyes glued to a screen: the average American family hasn't time for it. Therefore the showmen are convinced that . . . television will never be a serious competitor of [radio] broadcasting."
   The New York Times, 1939

their guns in almost every episode; in Chicago, the average police officer fires a gun once every 27 years (Radecki, 1989).

Does viewing aggression influence some people to commit aggression? To find out, researchers have conducted correlational and experimental studies (Hearold, 1986; Wood & others, 1991).

Correlational studies reveal a link between young boys' violence-viewing and their combativeness as teenagers and young adults (Eron, 1987; Turner & others, 1986). In the United States and Canada, a doubling of homicide rates between 1957 and 1974 coincided with the introduction and spread of violent television. Moreover, census regions that acquired television late showed the homicide jump correspondingly later. Amongst White South Africans, who were first introduced to television in 1975, a similar near-doubling of the homicide rate did not begin until after 1975 (Centerwall, 1989).

Critics respond that these correlational studies do not prove that viewing violence *causes* aggression (Freedman, 1988; McGuire, 1986). Maybe aggressive children prefer violent programs. Maybe children of neglectful or abusive parents are both more aggressive and more often left in front of the TV. And maybe television merely reflects violent trends.

To pin down causation, experimenters have exposed some viewers to violence and others to entertaining nonviolence and then observed their reactions. Does viewing murder and mayhem make people react more cruelly when irritated? "The consensus among most of the research community," reported the National Institute of Mental Health (1982), "is that violence on television does lead to aggressive behavior by children and teenagers who watch the programs." Statements by the American Psychological Association, American Medical Association, and American Pediatric Association concur. The violence effect stems from a combination of factors—from *arousal* by the violent excitement, from the triggering of violence-related *ideas*, from the erosion of one's *inhibitions*, and from *imitation* (Geen & Thomas, 1986).

Television's unreal world, in which acts of assault greatly outnumber acts of affection, can also affect our thinking about the real world. Those who watch a great deal of prime-time crime regard the world as more dangerous (Gerbner & Signorielli, 1990; Heath & Petraitis, 1987; Singer & Singer, 1986). Prolonged exposure to violence also desensitizes viewers; they become more indifferent to it when later viewing a brawl, whether on TV or in real life (Rule & Ferguson, 1986). Indeed, suggest Edward Donnerstein and his co-researchers (1987), an evil psychologist could hardly imagine a better way to make people indifferent to brutality than to expose them to a graded series of scenes, from fights to killings to the mutilations of slasher movies.

Sexual Aggression and the Media   Over the last 25 years, America's known rape rate has tripled. Recent surveys of both women and men reveal that unreported rapes, most committed by dates or acquaintances, greatly outnumber those reported. In surveys among a nationwide sample of 6200 college students and 2200 Ohio working women, Mary Koss and her colleagues (1987, 1988, 1990) found that 27.5 percent of the women reported an experience that met the legal definition of rape or attempted rape (although just one-fourth of them labeled it as such). Only 1 of 4 victims of stranger rape and 1 of 30 victims of acquaintance rape reported the incident to the police. In eight different surveys, about two-thirds of young males say there is no circumstance under which they would rape, even if un-

In the days before television

Drawing by Gary Larson: "The Far Side" cartoon is reprinted by permission of Chronicle Features, San Francisco.

TV's greatest effect may stem from what it displaces. Children and adults who spend 4 hours a day watching television spend 4 fewer hours in active pursuits—talking, studying, playing, reading, or socializing with friends. What would you have done with your extra time if you had never watched television?

Stayskal/Tampa Tribune

In other surveys, about half of women report some form of unwanted sexual coercion and most report experiencing verbal sexual harassment (Craig & others, 1989; Koss & Burkhart, 1989; Sandberg & others, 1985).

punished (Stille & others, 1987)—which means that one-third admit to the possibility. And in Koss's national sample of college men, almost 1 in 10 acknowledged past behavior that met the definition of rape.

Accompanying the apparent increase in sexual aggression has been, thanks partly to the home video business, easier access to R-rated "slasher films" and X-rated films. Content analyses reveal that X-rated films mostly depict quick, casual sex between strangers, but that scenes of rape and sexual exploitation of women by men are also common (Cowan & others, 1988; NCTV, 1987; Yang & Linz, 1990). Rape scenes often portray the victim at first fleeing and resisting her attacker, then becoming aroused and finally driven to ecstasy. In less graphic form, the same unrealistic, women-enjoy-being-taken myth is commonplace on TV programs and in romance novels. The woman who first pushes the insistent man away ends up passionately kissing him.

Do such films and other similar materials influence sexual aggression? When interviewed, Canadian and American sex offenders (rapists, child molesters, and serial killers) do report a greater-than-usual appetite for sexually explicit and sexually violent materials—materials typically labeled as "pornography" (Marshall, 1989; Ressler & others, 1988). But are the sexual offenders merely, as sex researcher John Money (1988) believes, using pornography "as an alibi to explain to themselves and their captors what otherwise is inexplicable"?

Correlational studies reveal that in times and places where sexual materials are freely available, rates of sexual violence are indeed higher (Court, 1984). In Hawaii, the number of reported rapes rose by 900 percent between 1964 and 1974, dropped when pornography restraints were temporarily imposed, then rose again when the restraints were lifted. Alaska and Nevada, which have the highest sales rates of sexually explicit magazines, also have had the highest rape rates—even after controlling for other factors, such as the population's proportion of young males (Baron & Straus, 1984, 1986). But there are exceptions, such as in Japan, where violent pornography is readily available but rape reports are infrequent. Moreover, as we all know well by now, a correlation never proves cause and effect.

Laboratory experiments, which do pin down cause and effect, reveal that repeated viewing of X-rated films (even if nonviolent) makes one's own partner seem less attractive (page 364) and makes sexual aggression seem less serious. In one such experiment, Dolf Zillmann and Jennings Bryant (1984) showed undergraduates six brief, sexually explicit films a week for 6 weeks. A control group viewed nonerotic films during the same 6-week period. Three weeks later, both groups read a newspaper report about a man convicted but not yet sentenced for raping a hitchhiker. When asked to suggest an appropriate prison term, those who had viewed sexually explicit films recommended sentences half as long as the control group's.

In search of possible effects of films on men's willingness to aggress against women, experimenters examined, first, the effect of film viewing on men's acceptance of the "rape myth" (the idea that some women would enjoy being raped). Neil Malamuth and James Check (1981) compared University of Manitoba men who were shown either two nonsexual movies or two movies depicting a man sexually overpowering a woman. A week later, when surveyed by a different experimenter, those who had seen the films with mild

Pornography means different things to different people. Along with Webster's dictionary, some define pornography as erotic depictions intended to excite sexual arousal. Others define it as sexual materials that exploit, degrade, or subordinate women.

In follow-up studies, Zillmann (1989) found that after massive exposure to X-rated sexual films, men and women became more accepting of extramarital sex, of women's sexual submission to men, and of a man's seducing a 12-year-old girl. As people heavily exposed to televised crime perceive the world as more dangerous, so people heavily exposed to pornography see the world as more sexual, as a place where, say, extramarital and group sex are commonplace.

sexual violence were more accepting of violence against women. Further experiments showed that viewing slasher movies, such as *The Texas Chainsaw Massacre,* can also produce a trivialization of rape.

Experiments have also explored the effect of violent versus nonviolent films on men's willingness to deliver supposed electric shocks to women who earlier provoked them. (Although such experiments cannot study actual sexual violence, they can assess a man's willingness to hurt a woman.) These experiments suggest that it's not eroticism but depictions of sexual *violence,* whether in R-rated slasher films or X-rated films, that most affect men's acceptance and performance of aggression against women. A 1986 conference of 21 social scientists, including many of the researchers who conducted these experiments, produced a consensus that "pornography that portrays sexual aggression as pleasurable for the victim increases the acceptance of the use of coercion in sexual relations." Moreover, "in laboratory studies measuring short-term effects, exposure to violent pornography increases punitive behavior toward women" (Surgeon General, 1986).

TV Violence, Pornography, and Society   We must be careful not to oversimplify the complex causes of violent crime. Murders and assaults were common before television. Rape predated pornographic books and movies, which surely reflect as well as shape cultural sexual attitudes. There is a principle here worth remembering: Because virtually every significant behavior has many determinants, any single explanation is probably an oversimplification. In summarizing the known environmental contributors to sexual aggression (Figure 18–7), researcher Neil Malamuth (1989) emphasizes that every factor, by itself, exerts only a small influence. People

Figure 18–7 Environmental influences on sexual aggression. (Adapted from Malamuth, 1989.)

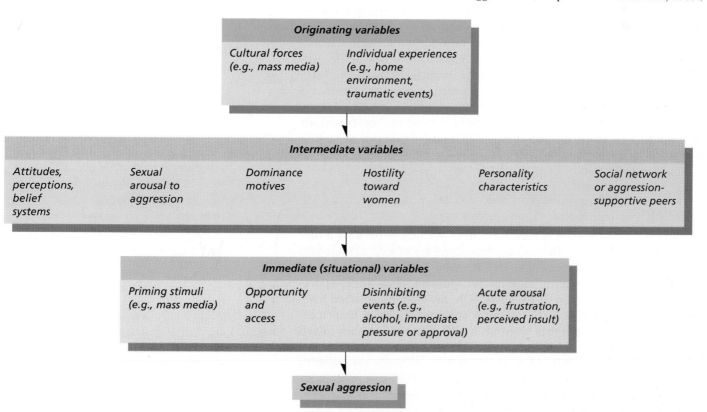

who study, say, the effects of asbestos exposure on cancer rates remind us that a single factor may warrant study, yet by itself be only one cause among many. Likewise, media influences, Malamuth believes, are only one factor influencing thought patterns that may lead to sexual aggression.

Still, if media depictions of violence can disinhibit and desensitize, if viewing sexual violence fosters attitudes and behaviors that degrade women, and if viewing pornography can lead viewers to trivialize rape and devalue their partners, then the issue of violence in the media is not a minor one.

The American Psychological Association advises parents not only to limit their children's TV watching but also to watch and discuss programs with their children (Murray & Lonnborg, 1985). Some researchers advocate "media awareness training." Doubting that the TV networks would ever "face the facts and change their programming," Leonard Eron and Rowell Huesmann (1984) taught Chicago-area children that TV portrays an unreal world, that aggression is less common and effective than TV makes it seem, and that violence is wrong. When restudied 2 years later, viewing violence had less influence on these children than on untrained children.

To promote critical viewing skills, pornography researchers debrief, resensitize, and educate their subjects about pornography's images of women (Intons-Peterson & others, 1989; Linz & Donnerstein, 1989). When surveyed later, these subjects are *less* likely than most people to agree that "being roughed up is sexually stimulating to many women." "Our utopian and perhaps naive hope," say Edward Donnerstein, Daniel Linz, and Steven Penrod (1987, p. 196), "is that in the end the truth revealed through good science will prevail and the public will be convinced that these images not only demean those portrayed but also those who view them."

Might public consciousness be raised by making people aware of the information you have just been reading? In the 1940s, movies often depicted African-Americans as childlike, superstitious buffoons. Today, such images are offensive. In the 1960s and 1970s, entertainment from Beatles' music to movies such as *Easy Rider* glamorized drug use. No longer. Responding to a tidal change in cultural attitudes, entertainment now portrays drugs as dangerous. Is it too much to hope that, without violating artistic freedom, society might soon look back with similar embarrassment on the days when movies "entertained" people with scenes of torture, mutilation, and sexual coercion?

Altruism

Altruism—an unselfish regard for others' welfare—became a major concern of social psychologists after a vile act of sexual violence. A knife-wielding stalker repeatedly stabbed Kitty Genovese, then raped her as she lay dying outside her Queens, New York, apartment at 3:30 A.M. on March 13, 1964. "Oh, my God, he stabbed me!" she screamed into the early-morning stillness. "Please help me!" Windows opened and lights went on as 38 of her neighbors heard her screams. One couple pulled chairs up to the window and turned out the light to see better. Her attacker fled and then returned to stab her eight more times and rape her again. Not until he departed for good did anyone so much as call the police, at 3:50 A.M.

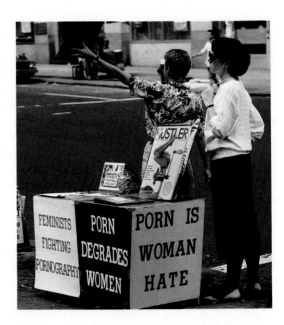

Experiments on the effects of viewing violent pornography raise concerns about society's acceptance of its degradation of women.

"What we're trying to do is raise the level of awareness of violence against women and pornography to at least the level of awareness of racist and Ku Klux Klan literature."
Gloria Steinem (1988)

"Probably no single incident has caused social psychologists to pay as much attention to an aspect of social behavior as Kitty Genovese's murder."
R. Lance Shotland (1984)

Bystander Intervention Reflecting on the Genovese murder and other such incidents, most commentators lamented the bystanders' "apathy" and "indifference." Rather than blaming them, social psychologists John Darley and Bibb Latané (1968b) attributed onlooker inaction to an important situational factor—the presence of others. Given the right circumstances, they suspected, most of us might behave similarly.

After staging emergencies under various conditions, Darley and Latané assembled their findings into a decision scheme: We will help if and only if the situation enables us first to *notice* the incident, then to *interpret* it as an emergency, and finally to *assume responsibility* for helping (Figure 18–8).

Figure 18–8 The decision-making process for bystander intervention. (From Darley & Latané, 1968b.)

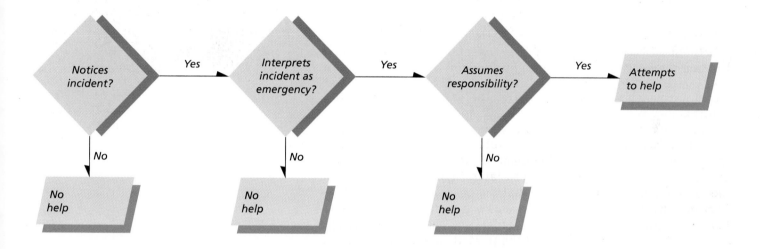

At each step, the presence of other bystanders turns people away from the path that leads to helping. In laboratory experiments and in street situations, people in groups of strangers are more likely than solitary individuals to keep their eyes on what they are doing or where they are going. If they notice an unusual situation, they may infer from the blasé reactions of the other passersby that the situation is not an emergency. "The person lying on the sidewalk must be drunk," they think, and move on.

But sometimes, as with the Genovese murder, the emergency is unambiguous and people still fail to help. The witnesses looking out through their windows noticed the incident, correctly interpreted the emergency, yet failed to assume responsibility. To find out why, Darley and Latané (1968a) simulated a physical emergency in their laboratory. University students participated in a discussion over an intercom. Each student was in a separate cubicle, and only the person whose microphone was switched on could be heard. One of the students was an accomplice of the experimenters. When his turn came, he called for help and made sounds as though he were having an epileptic seizure.

How did the other students react? As Figure 18–9 shows, those who believed they were the only one who could hear the victim—and therefore thought they bore total responsibility for helping—usually went to his aid. Those who thought others could also hear were more likely to react as did Kitty Genovese's neighbors. The more people shared the responsibility for helping, the less likely any single listener was to help.

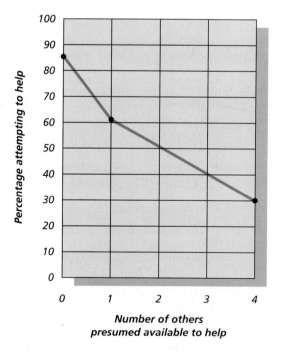

Figure 18–9 When people thought they alone heard an epileptic seizure victim calling for help, they usually helped. But when they thought four others were hearing it, too, fewer than a third responded. (From Darley & Latané, 1968a.)

When passing people slumped on city streets, we may wonder, "Is this person sick? How will the person react if I offer help? What can I do anyway?" Yet sometimes we do offer help. What circumstances prompt our doing so?

In hundreds of additional experiments, psychologists have studied the factors that influence bystanders' willingness to relay an emergency phone call, aid a stranded motorist, donate blood, pick up dropped books, contribute money, and give time to someone. For example, Latané, James Dabbs (1975), and 145 collaborators took 1497 elevator rides in three American cities and "accidentally" dropped coins or pencils in front of 4813 fellow passengers. The women coin-droppers were more likely to receive help than the men—a gender difference often reported by other researchers (Eagly & Crowley, 1986). But the major finding was the **bystander effect**—any particular bystander was less likely to give aid with other bystanders present. When one other person was on the elevator, those who dropped the coins were helped 40 percent of the time. When there were six passengers, help came less than 20 percent of the time.

From their observations of behavior in tens of thousands of such "emergencies," altruism researchers have discerned some additional patterns. The odds of our helping someone are best when:

we have just observed someone else being helpful;

we are not in a hurry;

the victim appears to need and deserve help;

the victim is in some way similar to ourselves;

we are in a small town or rural area;

we are feeling guilty;

we are focused on others and not preoccupied; and

we are in a good mood.

This last result, that happy people are helpful people, is one of the most consistent findings in all psychology. No matter how people are cheered—whether by having been made to feel successful and intelligent, by thinking happy thoughts, by finding money, or even by receiving a posthypnotic suggestion—they become more generous and more eager to help (Carlson & others, 1988).

"Oh, make us happy and you make us good!"
Robert Browning
The Ring and the Book, 1868

The Psychology of Helping Why do we help? One widely held view is that self-interest underlies all human interactions, that our constant goal is to maximize rewards and minimize costs. Accountants call it cost-benefit analysis. Philosophers call it utilitarianism. Social psychologists call it **social exchange theory**. If you are pondering whether to donate blood, you may weigh the costs of doing so (time, discomfort, and anxiety) against the benefits (reduced guilt, social approval, good feelings). If the anticipated rewards of helping exceed the anticipated costs, you help.

Social exchange theory helps explain why we help those whose approval we seek or who can reciprocate favors in the future. But perhaps you are wondering, "Doesn't social exchange theory suggest that helping is not truly altruistic but is rather a disguised form of selfishness?" If we helped merely to feel good, the answer might be yes. But to gain pleasure from helping others is surely more a virtue than a vice. Moreover, from babyhood onward many people exhibit a natural **empathy** for others—they feel distress when they see someone in distress and relief when suffering is alleviated (Batson, 1987).

Social norms also influence helping. They prescribe how we ought to behave, often to our mutual benefit. Through socialization, we learn the "reciprocity norm," the expectation that we should return help, not harm, to those who have helped us. In our relations with others of similar status, the reciprocity norm compels us to give (in favors, gifts, or social invitations) about as much as we receive. With young children, the disabled, and others who cannot give as much as they receive, we also learn to apply a "social responsibility norm"—that we should help those who need our help, even if the costs outweigh the benefits. Cultures vary in the strength of their social responsibility norms. For example, faced with a non-life-threatening need, people in India feel more keenly than do Americans a moral obligation to offer help (Miller & others, 1990).

The Evolutionary Psychology of Helping Culture matters, but don't all humans share inherent altruistic tendencies? **Sociobiology**—the study of how natural selection influences social behavior—suggests that our genes predispose us to act in ways that enhance their chance of surviving and spreading. Sociobiologists are fond of quoting novelist Samuel Butler's century-old remark that "a hen is only an egg's way of making another egg." Genes that don't drive their own perpetuation disappear. Genes that do will live on in biological relatives.

Nature's selection of behavior tendencies that equip organisms to survive and reproduce does not favor altruistic self-sacrifice. Those who sacrifice their lives leave fewer descendants to perpetuate their "heroic" genes. Those who fight and run away may live to fight another day—and to reproduce and nurture offspring.

Sociobiologists remind us, however, that some forms of altruism help to perpetuate our genes. The most obvious example is devotion to our children—the carriers of our genes. Natural selection favors parents who care deeply about their children's survival and welfare. People usually feel empathy toward other relatives, too, in proportion to their genetic closeness. In experiments, people also give more empathy and help to a stranger who looks, acts, and thinks like themselves—someone whose genetic similarities they detect, a sociobiologist would say (Rushton, 1989).

A genetic bias to help our kin and similar strangers (to protect and promote the genes we share with them) is a mixed blessing, notes sociobiologist E. O. Wilson (1978, p. 167): "Altruism based on kin selection is the enemy of civilization. If human beings are to a large extent guided . . . to favor their own relatives and tribe, only a limited amount of global harmony is possible."

Empathy is feeling what another feels. Witnessing distress, many people feel distress.

Social psychologist Daniel Batson (1983) believes that religious images that broaden our concept of family-linked altruism enhance concern for the global human community. And there is evidence that devotion to religious concepts of "brotherly and sisterly love" toward fellow "children of God" in the great "human family" correlates with altruism. Among Americans whom George Gallup (1984) classified as "highly spiritually committed," 46 percent said they were working among the poor, the infirm, or the elderly—significantly more than the 22 percent of "highly uncommitted" people.

For some heroic people, a sense of human kinship entails the risk of self-sacrifice. The Holocaust memorial in Jerusalem honors 8000 "Righteous Gentiles"—those whose identities are known among the many more Europeans who gave refuge to Jews during World War II. These people knew that if the Nazis learned of their subterfuge, they might suffer a common fate with their guest, as many did. For decades afterward, social scientists interviewed rescuers, searching for the patterns of personality and belief that predict why these heroes acted as so few did.

Where did these people gain the compassion to care and the courage to defy power and authority? Among the predictors were having caring parental models, close-knit families, allegiance to religious or humanitarian convictions, and friendships with Jews who confronted them with the need for help (London, 1970; Oliner & Oliner, 1988). Long after the war, rescuers more than bystanders were caring in new ways—feeding the sick and aged, supporting groups and causes, leading recreational activities, offering counsel. Their lives remind us that some attributes of character shine through differing situations.

Volunteers are motivated to help if the rewards, whether psychological or social, are greater than the costs. This volunteer finds satisfaction in time spent comforting "boarder babies"—infants born to crack-addicted mothers who cannot care for them.

Attraction

Pause a moment and think about your relationships with two people—a close friend, and someone who has stirred in you feelings of romantic love. What factors lead to friendship and romance? What factors help us sustain these relationships?

We endlessly wonder how we can win others' affection and what makes our own affections flourish or fade. Do birds of a feather flock together, or do opposites attract? Does familiarity breed contempt or liking? Does absence make the heart grow fonder, or is out of sight out of mind? Social psychology suggests some answers.

The Psychology of Attraction What is the psychological chemistry that binds two people together in that special sort of friendship that helps one cope with all other relationships? In short, what factors predict whether two people will become close friends or lovers?

Proximity Before friendships become close, they must begin. Proximity—geographic nearness—is perhaps the most powerful predictor of friendship. Of course, proximity also provides opportunities for hostility and assault. But much more often it instigates liking. Study after study reveals that people are most likely to like, and even to marry, those who live in the same neighborhood, who sit nearby in class, who work in the same office, who share the same parking lot. Look around.

Why is proximity so conducive to liking? Obviously, part of the answer is the greater availability of those we often meet. But there

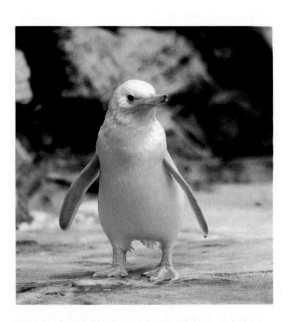

Familiarity breeds acceptance. When this rare white penguin was born in Sydney, Australia's zoo, his tuxedoed peers ostracized him. To gain his acceptance, zookeepers thought they would need to dye him black. But after 3 weeks of contact, the other penguins came to accept him.

is more to it than that. For one thing, repeated exposure to novel stimuli—be they nonsense syllables, musical selections, geometric figures, Chinese characters, human faces, or the letters of our own name—increases our liking for them (Moreland & Zajonc, 1982; Nuttin, 1987). This phenomenon is known as the **mere exposure effect**. Within certain limits (Bornstein, 1989), familiarity breeds fondness.

Physical Attractiveness Once proximity affords you contact, what most affects your first impressions: the person's sincerity? intelligence? personality? Hundreds of experiments reveal that it is likely something more superficial: appearance.

For people taught that "beauty is only skin deep" and that "appearances can be deceiving," the power of physical attractiveness is unnerving. In one early study, Elaine Hatfield and her co-workers (Walster & others, 1966) randomly matched new University of Minnesota students for a "Welcome Week" dance. Before the dance, all took a battery of personality and aptitude tests. On the night of the blind date, the couples danced and talked for more than 2 hours and then took a brief intermission to rate their dates. What determined whether they liked each other? So far as the researchers could determine, only one thing mattered: physical attractiveness (which had been rated by the researchers beforehand). Both the men and the women liked good-looking dates best. Later research confirms that, although women are more likely than men to *say* that another's looks don't affect them, a man's looks do affect women's behavior (Feingold, 1990; Sprecher, 1989; Woll, 1986).

Later studies also reveal that people's physical attractiveness predicts their dating frequency, their feelings of popularity, and others' initial impressions of their personalities. We perceive attractive people, even children and those of our own sex, to be happier, more sensitive, more successful, and more socially skilled, though not more honest or compassionate (Dion, 1986; Eagly & others, 1991; Hatfield & Sprecher, 1986). Attractive and well-dressed people are also more likely to make a favorable impression on potential employers (Cash & Janda, 1984; Solomon, 1987). To judge from their gazing times, even babies prefer attractive over unattractive faces (Langlois & others, 1987).

If looks matter so much, who dates and marries those less attractive? Although people might prefer someone superattractive, they tend not to approach those who are "out of their league." Thus, less attractive people often match up with people who are about as attractive as they are (Murstein, 1986). When partners are noticeably unequal in attractiveness, the less physically attractive person often has compensating assets, such as greater wealth, status, or social competence. This helps explain why beautiful young women sometimes marry older men whose social or financial status is higher than their own (Elder, 1969).

That looks are important may seem unfair and unenlightened. Two thousand years ago the Roman statesman Cicero felt the same way: "The final good and the supreme duty of the wise person is to resist appearance." Cicero might be reassured by two other findings about attractiveness.

First, people's attractiveness is surprisingly unrelated to their self-esteem (Major & others, 1984). One reason may be that few people view themselves as unattractive. (Thanks, perhaps, to the mere exposure effect, most of us become accustomed to our own faces.)

The mere exposure effect applies even to ourselves. Have you ever noticed that you never look quite right in photographs? Most of us prefer our familiar mirror-image look to our photo. Most of our friends prefer an actual photo over its mirror-image (Mita & others, 1977). The Prime Minister Robert Hawke whom Australians know is at the left. But, if asked, Hawke would probably prefer the self at the right, the one he sees in the mirror each morning.

Couples tend to be matched in attractiveness. If unmatched, the less attractive member often has compensating assets.

Another reason is that strikingly attractive people are sometimes suspicious that praise may be simply a reaction to their looks. When less attractive people are praised for their work, they are more likely to accept it as sincere. Attraction researcher Ellen Berscheid (1981) reported that those who improve their appearance by cosmetic surgery are often disturbed to discover from people's reactions that looks matter even more than they had supposed.

Cicero might also find comfort in knowing that judgments about attractiveness are relative. They depend first on the accepted standards of beauty in one's place and time. Hoping to look attractive, people in different places have pierced their noses, lengthened their necks, bound their feet, dyed their skin and hair, eaten to achieve a full figure, and liposuctioned fat to achieve a slim one. (The standards by which judges crown "Miss Universe" hardly even apply to the whole planet.) In North America, the ultra-thin ideal of the Roaring Twenties gave way to the soft, voluptuous Marilyn Monroe ideal of the '50s, to be replaced by the lean, athletic ideal of the '80s.

Some aspects of attractiveness, however, cross place and time. It comes as no surprise to sociobiologists that men in 37 cultures, from Australia to Zambia, judge women as more attractive if they have a youthful appearance (Buss, 1989; Cunningham, 1986). Sociobiologists say that men drawn to healthy, fertile-appearing women have stood a better chance of sending their genes into the future. To women, men seem more attractive if they appear mature and dominant. This connotes, say the sociobiologists, a capacity to support and protect (Sadalla & others, 1987).

People also seem to prefer physical features—noses, legs, physiques—that are neither unusually large or small. In one clever demonstration of this, Judith Langlois and Lori Roggman (1990) digitized the faces of up to 32 college students and used a computer to average them. Students judged the averaged, composite faces as more attractive than 96 percent of the individual faces. To be average is to be beautiful.

Cultural differences and similarities aside, attractiveness also depends on our feelings about the person. In a Rodgers and Hammerstein musical, Prince Charming asks Cinderella, "Do I love you because you're beautiful, or are you beautiful because I love you?" Chances are it is both. As we discover someone's similarities to us, see them again and again, and come to like them, their phys-

"Personal beauty is a greater recommendation than any letter of introduction."
Aristotle
Apothegems, 330 B.C.

"The thin, narrow-shouldered ectomorph who was yesterday's spinster librarian is today's high fashion model; the plump and buxom endomorph who was a Victorian romantic ideal today is eating cottage cheese and grapefruit, and weighing in every Tuesday at Weight Watchers."
Phyllis Bronstein-Burrows (1981)

"Love is a dirty trick played on us to achieve the continuation of the species."
Novelist W. Somerset Maugham (1874–1965)

Conceptions of attractiveness vary by culture as well as by time. What may be attractive in one culture may seem strange or unattractive in another, and each of these cultures' concepts of beauty—in Kenya, Morocco, and the United States—may well change in the future.

ical imperfections grow less noticeable and their attractiveness grows more apparent (Beaman & Klentz, 1983; Gross & Crofton, 1977). As Shakespeare put it in *A Midsummer Night's Dream*, "Love looks not with the eyes, but with the mind." E.T. is as ugly as Darth Vader, until you get to know him.

Similarity Let's say that proximity has brought you into contact with someone and that your appearance has made a favorable first impression. What now influences whether acquaintances develop into friends? For example, as you get to know someone better, is liking more probable if you are opposites, or if you are alike?

It makes a good story—extremely different types living in harmonious union: Rat, Mole, and Badger in *The Wind in the Willows*, Frog and Toad in Arnold Lobel's books. The stories delight us by expressing what we seldom experience, for we tend to dislike dissimilar people (Rosenbaum, 1986). In real life, birds that flock together are usually of a feather. Friends and couples are far more likely than randomly paired people to share common attitudes, beliefs, and interests (and, for that matter, age, religion, race, education, intelligence, smoking behavior, and economic status). Moreover, the greater their likeness, the more their liking will endure (Byrne, 1971). Similarity breeds content.

Proximity, attractiveness, and similarity are not the only determinants of attraction. We also like those who like us, especially when our self-image is low. When we believe someone likes us, we respond to them more warmly, which leads them to like us even more (Curtis & Miller, 1986). To be liked is powerfully rewarding. Indeed, a simple reward theory of attraction—that we will like those whose behavior is rewarding to us and that we will continue relationships that offer more rewards than costs—can explain all the findings we have considered so far. When a person lives or works in close proximity with someone else, it costs less time and effort to develop the friendship and enjoy its benefits. Attractive people are aesthetically pleasing, and associating with them can be socially rewarding. Those with similar views reward us by validating our own.

Romantic Love Occasionally, people progress from initial impressions to friendship to the more intense, complex, and mysterious state of romantic love. Elaine Hatfield (1988) distinguishes two types of love: temporary passionate love, and the more enduring "companionate" love.

Passionate Love Noting that emotional arousal is a key ingredient of **passionate love**, Hatfield suggests that the two-factor theory of emotion (page 404) can help us understand this intense positive absorption in another. The theory assumes that emotions have two ingredients—physical arousal plus a cognitive label—and that arousal from any source can enhance one emotion or another, depending on how we interpret and label the arousal.

In tests of this theory, college men have been aroused by fright, by running in place, by viewing erotic materials, or by listening to humorous or repulsive monologues. They are then introduced to an attractive woman and asked to rate her, or are simply asked to rate their girlfriends. Unlike unaroused men, those who are stirred up attribute some of their arousal to the woman or girlfriend and feel more attracted toward her (Carducci & others, 1978; Dermer & Pyszczynski, 1978; White & others, 1981; White & Kight, 1984).

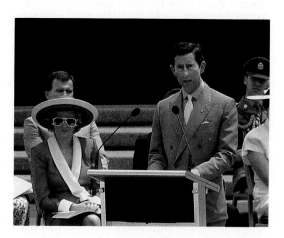

Prince Charles loves opera, art museums, and vacations in Scotland; Princess Diana, 13 years younger, loves rock concerts, nightclubs, and London. Royalty watchers worry: Can a marriage flourish between two people so different in age and interests?

Outside the laboratory, Donald Dutton and Arthur Aron (1974, 1989) went to two bridges across British Columbia's rocky Capilano River. One was a swaying footbridge 230 feet above the rocks; the other was a low, solid bridge. An attractive young female accomplice intercepted men coming off each bridge, sought their help in filling out a short questionnaire, and then offered her phone number in case they wanted to hear more about her project. Far more of those who had just crossed the high bridge—which left their hearts pounding—accepted the number and later called the woman. To be revved up and to associate some of that arousal with a desirable person is to feel the pull of passion. As lovers who take a thrilling roller coaster ride together know, adrenaline makes the heart grow fonder.

Companionate Love Inevitably, the passion of romantic love subsides. The intense absorption in the other, the thrill of the romance, the giddy "floating on a cloud" feeling fades. "Just Married" becomes just married, the magic lost. So, are the French correct in saying that "love makes the time pass and time makes love pass"?

Hatfield notes that as love matures it becomes a warmer, steadier **companionate love**—a deep, affectionate attachment. There may be adaptive wisdom to this change from passion to affection. Passionate love often bears children, whose survival is aided by the parents' waning obsession with one another. Social psychologist Ellen Berscheid and her colleagues (1984) note that the failure to appreciate passionate love's limited half-life can doom a relationship: "If the inevitable odds against eternal passionate love in a relationship were better understood, more people might choose to be satisfied with the quieter feelings of satisfaction and contentment."

One key to a gratifying and enduring relationship is **equity**: Both partners receive in proportion to what they give. When equity exists—when both partners freely give and receive, when they share decision making—their chances for sustained and satisfying companionate love are good (Gray-Little & Burks, 1983; Van Yperen & Buunk, 1990). Mutually sharing self and possessions, giving and getting emotional support, promoting and caring about one another's welfare, are at the core of every type of loving relationship, whether between lovers, parent and child, or intimate friends (Sternberg & Grajek, 1984).

Another vital ingredient of loving relationships is intimacy (Sternberg, 1986). A strong friendship or marriage permits **self-disclosure**, a revealing of intimate details about ourselves—our

"When two people are under the influence of the most violent, most insane, most delusive, and most transient of passions, they are required to swear that they will remain in that excited, abnormal, and exhausting condition continuously until death do them part."
  George Bernard Shaw
  Man and Superman, 1903

"When a match has equal partners then I fear not."
  Aeschylus
  Prometheus Bound, 478 B.C

The quality of love changes as a relationship matures from passionate absorption to affectionate attachment.

likes and dislikes, our dreams and worries, our proud and shameful moments. "When I am with my friend," noted the Roman statesman Seneca, "me thinks I am alone, and as much at liberty to speak anything as to think it. . . ." Self-disclosure grows as a relationship deepens. As one person reveals a little, the other reciprocates, the first person reveals more, and on and on, as friends or lovers move to deeper intimacy. Given self-disclosing intimacy plus mutually supportive equality, the odds favor enduring companionate love.

Summing Up

Social psychology is the study of how people think about, influence, and relate to one another.

Social Thinking

Attributing Behavior to Persons or to Situations We generally explain people's behavior by attributing it either to internal dispositions or to external situations. In accounting for others' actions, we often underestimate the influence of the situation, thus committing the fundamental attribution error. When we explain our own behavior, however, we more often point to the situation and not to ourselves.

Attitudes and Actions Attitudes predict behavior only under certain conditions, as when other influences are minimized, when the attitude is specific to the behavior, and when people are aware of their attitudes. Studies of the foot-in-the-door phenomenon and of role playing reveal that our actions can also modify our attitudes, especially when we feel responsible for those actions. Cognitive dissonance theorists explain that behavior shapes attitudes because people feel discomfort when their actions go against their feelings and beliefs; they reduce the discomfort by bringing their attitudes more into line with what they have done.

Social Influence

Conformity and Obedience As suggestibility studies demonstrate, when we are unsure about our judgments, we are likely to adjust them toward the group standard. Solomon Asch found that under certain conditions people will conform to a group's judgment even when it is clearly incorrect. We may conform either to gain social approval (normative social influence) or because we welcome the information that others provide (informational social influence). In Milgram's famous experiments, people torn between obeying an experimenter and responding to another's pleas usually chose to obey orders, even though obedience supposedly meant harming the other person. Such is the potency of social influence.

Group Influence Experiments on social facilitation reveal that the presence of either observers or co-actors can arouse individuals, boosting their performance on easy tasks but hindering it on difficult ones. When people pool their efforts toward a group goal, social loafing may occur as individuals free-ride on others' efforts. When a group experience arouses people and makes them anonymous, they may become less self-aware and self-restrained, a psychological state known as deindividuation.

Within groups, discussions among like-minded members often produce group polarization, an enhancement of the group's prevailing attitudes. This is one cause of groupthink, the tendency for harmony-seeking groups to make unrealistic decisions after suppressing unwelcome information.

The power of the group is great, but so is the power of the person. Even a small minority sometimes sways a group, especially when expressing its views consistently.

Social Relations

Aggression Aggressive behavior, like all behavior, is a product of nature and nurture. Although psychologists dismiss the idea that aggression is instinctual, aggressiveness *is* genetically influenced. Moreover, certain areas of the brain, when stimulated, activate or inhibit aggression, and these neural areas are biochemically influenced.

A variety of psychological factors also influence aggression. Aversive events heighten people's hostility. Such stimuli are especially likely to trigger aggression in those rewarded for their own aggression or those who have learned aggression from role models or observed violent media portrayals of aggressive models. Such factors desensitize people to cruelty and prime them to behave aggressively when provoked.

Altruism In response to incidents of bystander nonintervention in emergencies, social psychologists undertook experiments that revealed a bystander effect: Any given bystander is less likely to help if others are present. The bystander effect is most likely to occur when the presence of others inhibits one's (1) noticing the event, (2) interpreting it as an emergency, or (3) assuming responsibility for helping. Many factors, including mood, also influence willingness to help someone in distress.

Both psychological and biological explanations have been offered for why we help others. Social exchange theory proposes that our social behaviors—even our helpful acts—maximize our benefits (which may include our own good feelings) and minimize our costs. Our desire to help is also affected by social norms, which prescribe reciprocating the help we receive and being socially responsible toward those in need. Sociobiologists believe that a genetic predisposition to preserve our genes, through devotion to those with whom we share them, underlies altruism.

Attraction Three factors are known to influence our liking for one another. Geographical proximity is conducive to attraction, partly because mere exposure to novel stimuli enhances liking. Physical attractiveness influences social opportunities and the way one is perceived. As acquaintanceship moves toward friendship, similarity of attitudes and interests greatly increases liking.

We can view passionate love as an aroused state that we cognitively label as love. The strong affection of companionate love, which often emerges as a relationship matures, is enhanced by an equitable relationship and by intimate self-disclosure.

Terms and Concepts to Remember

social psychology The scientific study of how we think about, influence, and relate to one another.

attribution theory The theory that we tend to give a causal explanation for someone's behavior, often by crediting either the situation or the person's disposition.

fundamental attribution error The tendency for observers, when analyzing another's behavior, to underestimate the impact of the situation and to overestimate the impact of personal disposition.

attitude A belief and feeling that predisposes one to respond in a particular way to objects, people, and events.

foot-in-the-door phenomenon The tendency for people who have first agreed to a small request to comply later with a larger request.

role A set of expectations about a social position, defining how those in the position ought to behave.

cognitive dissonance theory The theory that we act to reduce the discomfort (dissonance) we feel when two of our thoughts (cognitions) are inconsistent — as when we respond to our having acted contrary to our attitudes by changing our attitude.

conformity Adjusting one's behavior or thinking to coincide with a group standard.

normative social influence Influence resulting from a person's desire to gain approval or avoid disapproval.

norms Understood rules for accepted and expected behavior. Norms prescribe "proper" behavior.

informational social influence Influence resulting from one's willingness to accept others' opinions about reality.

co-actors People who are simultaneously at work on the same noncompetitive task.

social facilitation Improved performance of tasks in the presence of others; occurs with simple or well-learned tasks but not with tasks that are difficult or not yet mastered.

social loafing The tendency for people in a group to exert less effort when pooling their efforts toward attaining a common goal than when individually accountable.

deindividuation The loss of self-awareness and self-restraint occurring in group situations that foster arousal and anonymity.

group polarization The enhancement of a group's prevailing attitudes through discussion.

groupthink The mode of thinking that occurs when the desire for harmony in a decision-making group overrides a realistic appraisal of alternatives.

aggression Any physical or verbal behavior intended to hurt or destroy.

frustration-aggression principle The principle that frustration—the blocking of an attempt to achieve some goal—creates anger, which can generate aggression.

altruism Unselfish regard for the welfare of others.

bystander effect The tendency for any given bystander to be less likely to give aid if other bystanders are present.

social exchange theory The theory that our social behavior is an exchange process, the aim of which is to maximize benefits and minimize costs.

empathy The ability to understand and feel what another feels, to put oneself in someone else's shoes.

sociobiology The study of the evolution of social behavior using the principles of natural selection; it assumes that nat-ural selection favors genetically influenced social behaviors that contribute to the preservation and spread of one's genes.

mere exposure effect The phenomenon that repeated exposure to novel stimuli increases liking of them.

passionate love An aroused state of intense positive absorption in another, usually present at the beginning of a love relationship.

companionate love The deep affectionate attachment we feel for those with whom our lives are intertwined.

equity A condition in which people receive from a relationship in proportion to what they give to it.

self-disclosure Revealing intimate aspects of oneself to others.

For Further Reading

Cialdini, R. B. (1988). *Influence: Science and practice* (2nd ed.). Glenview, IL: Scott, Foresman.

A delightful, captivating introduction to six "weapons of influence." Robert Cialdini brings to life the lessons from social-psychological research on persuasion, with riveting everyday examples of influence—from Tupperware parties to cult indoctrination programs.

Hunt, M. (1990). *The compassionate beast: What science is discovering about the humane side of humankind.* New York: William Morrow.

An intimate look at the new altruism researchers and their discoveries about why and when people help.

Janis, I. L. (1982). *Groupthink: Psychological studies of policy decisions and fiascos.* Boston: Houghton Mifflin.

A provocative, readable analysis of the group decision making that led to several historical fiascos, from the failure to anticipate the Pearl Harbor attack to the Watergate cover-up. Janis beautifully interweaves basic concepts in social psychology with recent American history, explains how groupthink occurs, and suggests how to avoid it.

Milgram, S. (1974). *Obedience to authority.* New York: Harper & Row.

The full description of Milgram's controversial research on obedience, complete with reflections on the dilemmas of obedience and the ethics of such research.

Ross, L., & Nisbett, R. E. (1991). *The person and the situation: Perspectives of social psychology.* New York: McGraw-Hill.

A stimulating exploration of how big ideas from the new research on personal and situational influences relate to social, political, and philosophical issues.

Staub, E. (1989). *The roots of evil: The psychological and cultural sources of genocide.* New York: Cambridge University Press.

How can human beings kill, brutalize, and torture other human beings? By analyzing genocide during the Holocaust and in countries around the world, Staub exposes the roots and evolution of mass killing and cruelty.

Sternberg, R., with C. Whitney (1991). *Love the way you want it: Using your head in matters of heart.* New York: Bantam.

A fresh, research-based look at how unattainable expectations sabotage love, and how to build satisfying, long-lasting relationships.

Social Diversity

Chapter 19

Some 100,000 years ago, we humans were members of one African race. Anticipating the ancient injunction to "be fruitful and multiply, and fill the earth," many of our ancestors moved out of Africa, displacing their humanlike cousins elsewhere, such as the Neanderthals in Europe (Simons, 1989; Stringer, 1990). In adapting to their new environments, our forebears developed differences that, measured on anthropological scales, are relatively recent and superficial. Those who went far north of the equator, for example, evolved lighter skins capable of synthesizing vitamin D in less direct sunlight. Still, historically, we all are Africans.

As descendants of common ancestors, we in the human family share not only a common biological heritage but also common behavior tendencies. Our shared brain architecture predisposes us to sense the world, develop language, and feel hunger through identical mechanisms. Coming from opposite sides of the globe, we know how to read one another's smiles and frowns. Whether our last name is Wong, Nkomo, Gonzales, or Smith, we fear strangers beginning at about 8 months of age and as adults prefer the company of individuals whose attitudes and attributes are similar to our own. Regardless of our culture or gender, we regard female features that signify youth and health—and reproductive potential—as attractive. Whether we live in the Arctic or the tropics, we prefer sweet tastes to sour, shiver when cold, and feel drawn to behaviors that produce and protect offspring. As members of one species, we affiliate, conform, and organize hierarchies of status. A visitor from outer space could drop in anywhere and find humans playing sports and games, dancing and feasting, singing and worshipping, living in families and forming groups. To be human is to be more alike than different. Taken together, such universal behavior tendencies define human nature.

Among our similarities, the most important—the behavioral hallmark of our species—is our enormous capacity to learn and adapt. Ironically, this fundamental likeness enables human diversity. Go barefoot for a summer and you will develop toughened, calloused feet—a biologically disposed adaptation to friction. Meanwhile, your shoed neighbor will remain a tenderfoot. Is the difference between the two of you an effect of environment? Yes, of course. Is it also the product of a biological mechanism? Yes again. Our shared biology enables our adaptive diversity (Buss, 1991).

Likewise, depending on their experiences in particular environments, one person may become aggressive, another gentle; one may value freedom, another order and control; one may prize individuality, another the social ties that bind people together.

As citizens in a multicultural world, we need to understand our similarities and our differences. At various points throughout this book we have examined our *individual differences* in traits such as temperament, intelligence, personality, disorder, and health. Time and again we have also glimpsed a second dimension of diversity— our *group differences* in tendencies ranging from expressing anger to concern about weight. Having examined individual diversity in some depth, let us conclude our journey through psychology by exploring our social diversity and how we respond to it. How do culture and gender shape our social identities and behaviors? What leads us to loathe or to love those who are different?

To review cultural similarities and differences mentioned in previous chapters, see page 620.

Cultural Diversity

A **culture** is the composite of the enduring behaviors, ideas, attitudes, and traditions shared by a large group of people and transmitted from one generation to the next (Brislin, 1988). If we all lived as homogeneous ethnic groups in separate regions of the world, as some people still do, our cultural diversity would be largely irrelevant. Riding along with a unified culture is like riding a bike with the wind: As it carries you along, you hardly notice it's there. It's when we try riding *against* it that we feel its force. Face-to-face with a different culture, people become aware of the cultural winds. Visiting Europe, most Americans are struck by the smallness of the cars, the left-handed use of the fork, the uninhibited attire on the beaches. Stationed in Saudi Arabia, European and American soldiers realized the liberality of their home cultures.

A multicultural space station community of 1000 people fairly sampled from today's global village would have 585 Asians, 151 Europeans, 123 Africans, 55 South Americans, 81 North Americans, and 5 Australians and New Zealanders.

Increasingly, cultural diversity surrounds us. More and more we live in a global village, connected to our fellow villagers by satellite communications, jumbo jets, and international trade. Cultural diversity exists within nations, too. As Soviets, Iraqis, and Israelis know well, conflicts stemming from cultural differences are long-standing. But migration and refugee evacuations make this more true today than ever. "East is East and West is West, and never the twain shall meet," wrote nineteenth-century author Rudyard Kipling. But thanks to modern travel and migration, East and West, and North and South, are now meeting all the time. Italy is home to many Albanians, Germany to Turks, England to Pakistanis and West Indians. For Canadians, Americans, and Australians, too, one's country is more and more a mix of cultures. In half the 100 largest U.S. cities, ethnic minorities will together have become the majority by the end of this decade (Jones, 1990). As we work, play, and live with people from diverse cultural backgrounds, it becomes helpful to understand how our cultures influence us and to appreciate important ways in which cultures differ.

Cultural Norms and Roles

All cultural groups, from homogeneous nations to motorcycle gangs, evolve their own social norms—their rules for accepted and expected behavior. Muslims use only the right hand's fingers for eating. The Japanese have norms for taking shoes off, for giving and opening gifts, and for showing respect to one's social superiors. Sometimes social expectations seem oppressive. Westerners wonder: Wouldn't Middle Eastern women prefer to come out from behind their veils and express their individuality? However, norms also grease the social machinery. Prescribed, well-learned behaviors free us from self-preoccupation. Knowing when to clap or bow, which fork to pick up first at the dinner party, and what sorts of

A universal behavior. You know the meaning of each facial expression, and each of these people would understand the same expression on your face.

People in individualist Western cultures sometimes see the Japanese as straitjacketed by their culture's norms. But from the Japanese perspective the same tradition expresses a "serenity that comes to people who know exactly what to expect from each other" (Weisz & others, 1984).

gestures and compliments are appropriate enables us to relax and enjoy one another without fear of embarrassment.

When cultures collide, their differing norms often bemuse or befuddle. If someone invades our **personal space**—the portable buffer zone we like to maintain around our bodies—we feel uncomfortable. North Americans, Scandinavians, and the British prefer more personal space than do Latin Americans, Arabs, and the French (Sommer, 1969). At a social gathering, a Mexican seeking a comfortable conversation distance may waltz around a room with a back-pedaling North American. To the North American, the Mexican may seem a space invader; to the Mexican, the North American may seem cold and standoffish.

Cultures also vary in their expressiveness and pace of life. People whose roots are in northern European culture often perceive people from Mediterranean cultures as warm and charming but inefficient. The Mediterraneans, in turn, see the northern Europeans as efficient, but cold and preoccupied with punctuality (Triandis, 1981). When cultures mix, misunderstandings are commonplace. The British businessperson may feel frustrated by a

Culture influences personal space. In Arabic countries, such as Morocco, people typically require less personal space than do North Americans.

Latin American client who arrives 30 minutes late for lunch. People from time-conscious Japan, where bank clocks keep exact time, pedestrians walk briskly, and post office clerks fill requests speedily, may find themselves growing impatient when visiting Indonesia, where clocks keep less exact time and the pace of life is slower (Levine, 1990). In adjusting to their host countries, American Peace Corps volunteers report that two of their greatest culture shocks, after the language difference, are the slower pace of life and the differing punctuality of the people (Spradley & Phillips, 1972). This next paragraph will mean more to you if you pause now and jot down quickly 10 phrases that complete the sentence "I am . . . ."

Recall from Chapter 18 that when a whole set of norms accompanies a social position, such as parent or professor, we consider that social category a *role*. In some cultures, such as in Japan, meeting the expectations of one's various roles is an overriding life priority. One's behavior and identity shift, depending on whether one is with a supervisor, a colleague, or a spouse. Other societies define roles more loosely. People therefore develop a more stable sense of self and feel freer to express themselves as individuals (de Rivera, 1991). Thus, compared to students in Japan and China, American university students are much more likely to complete the sentence "I am . . ." with personal traits ("I am sincere," "I am confident") and much less likely to declare their social identities ("I am a Keio University student," "I am the third son in my family") (Cousins, 1989; Triandis, 1989a,b). This priority of either individual or collective identity is an important aspect of cultural diversity.

Individualism Versus Collectivism

Some animals, like wolves, are communal. Others, like tigers, are solitary. Although we humans are basically gregarious, our social styles vary from stressing individual control and achievement to emphasizing social intimacy and solidarity. Most industrialized cultures, especially those based on northern European norms and roles, nurture **individualism**. Individualists give priority to personal goals and define their identity mostly in terms of their personal attributes, not their social groups. Western literature, from the *Iliad* and *Odyssey* to *The Adventures of Huckleberry Finn*, celebrates self-reliant individuals who seek their own fulfillment rather than follow others' expectations.

Other cultures—especially those of Asia, Africa, and Central and South America—nurture **collectivism**. Collectivists give priority to the goals of their groups—often their family, clan, or work group—and define their identity accordingly. Like athletes who take more pleasure in their team's victory than in their own performance, collectivists find satisfaction in advancing their group's interests, even at the expense of personal needs. Eastern literature expresses these ideals by celebrating those who do their duty to others, despite temptations to self-indulgence.

To be sure, there are variations among people within every culture. In Asia, as in North America, some people emphasize their connectedness with one another; others—often the young and the educated—maintain their independence. But cross-cultural psychologists, such as Harry Triandis, Richard Brislin, and C. Harry Hui (1988), are especially fascinated by the ramifications of individualism and collectivism. Here is a culture difference that affects our self-concept, our attitudes, and our family relations.

"We must delight in each other, make others' conditions our own, rejoyce together, mourn together, labor and suffer together, always having before our eyes our community as members of the same body."
Puritan leader John Winthrop at Salem Harbor, just before his people set foot on American soil in 1630

Culture and the Self If someone were to rip away your social connections, say, by making you a solitary refugee in a foreign land, how much of your identity would remain intact? For individualists, a great deal—the very core of their being, their sense of "me," their awareness of their personal convictions and values. In many ways, Western psychology reflects the individualism of its cultures. In Chapter 4, we examined Western adolescents' struggle to separate from parents and define their own personal identity. In Chapter 14, we focused on personality—the distinctiveness and consistency that make each of us in some ways unique. We then reviewed research on the benefits of having a sense of personal control. At each of these points, we assumed—and if you are a product of Western culture, you probably did not question the assumption—that the individual is supreme.

This individualist perspective on the self appears in humanistic psychology's emphasis on getting in touch with oneself, accepting oneself, and being true to oneself. Therapist Fritz Perls' (1972, p. 70) "Gestalt credo" expresses this individualism:

> I do my thing, and you do your thing.
> I am not in this world to live up to your expectations.
> And you are not in this world to live up to mine.
> You are you and I am I,
> And if by chance we find each other, it's beautiful.
> If not, it can't be helped.

For the collectivist, one's social network provides one's bearings. Cut off from their family, their groups, and their loyal friends, collectivists would lose the connections that define who they are. Individualist cultures give priority to person identity, by putting the personal name first ("John Brink"). Collectivist cultures give priority to one's family identity ("Hui Harry"). Individualists easily move in and out of social groups. They feel relatively free to switch churches, leave one job for another, or even to leave their extended families and migrate to a new place. Collectivists have fewer but deeper, more stable attachments to their groups and friends. Relationships are long-term. Thus, loyalties run strong between employer and employees. And compared to American students, university students in Hong Kong talk with half as many people during a day, but for longer periods (Wheeler & others, 1989).

Because they value communal solidarity, people in collectivist cultures place a premium on maintaining harmony and allowing others to save face. Direct confrontation and blunt honesty are rare, as are expressions of personal egotism. Elders and superiors command respect. To preserve group spirit, people avoid touchy topics, defer to others' wishes, and display a polite, self-effacing humility (Markus & Kitayama, 1991). People remember those who have done them favors and make reciprocation a social art. The collectivist self is not independent but *inter*dependent. Among collectivists, no person is an island.

In terms of the self, individualism and collectivism each offers benefits—at a cost. People in competitive, individualist cultures have more personal freedom, take more pride in personal achievements, are less geographically bound to their families, and enjoy more privacy. Their less unified cultures offer a smorgasbord of lifestyles. But compared to collectivists, individualists are also loneli-

"No mind can take the same interest in his neighbor's me as in his own. The neighbor's me falls together with all the rest of things in one foreign mass, against which his own me stands out in startling relief."
William James
Principles of Psychology, 1890

"Good morning, folks, this is Captain Holwood from the flight deck. We'll be cruising at thirty-five thousand feet today, and I'll be finally taking control of my life, struggling to satisfy the needs of only one person—me!"
Drawing by Koren; © 1990 The New Yorker Magazine, Inc.

No wonder, says Triandis (1989b), that modern world colonization was led not by Asians, who would be reluctant to cut social and family ties, but by the more individualist Europeans. And no wonder that once-colonized countries, such as Canada, the United States, and Australia, are today among the most individualist.

er, more alienated, more likely to divorce, more homicidal, and more vulnerable to stress-related diseases, such as heart attacks (Triandis & others, 1988). Thus, Martin Seligman (1988) notes that "rampant individualism carries with it two seeds of its own destruction. First, a society that exalts the individual to the extent ours now does will be ridden with depression. . . . Second, and perhaps most important, is meaninglessness [which occurs when there is no] attachment to something larger than you are."

Culture and Social Judgment Culture also affects our readiness to prejudge others. Individualists in northern Europe and the English-speaking countries idealize *not* stereotyping people based on their group memberships. Because Jane is an individual, you shouldn't prejudge her attitudes and beliefs just from knowing her background and affiliations. Collectivists respond that in their culture it *helps* to know a person's group identifications: "If I know Yasumasa's family, work group, and schooling, I know a good deal about Yasumasa."

Unlike the individualist's exaggerated tendency to see causes residing in personal traits ("He is lazy; she needs therapy"), collectivists are somewhat less vulnerable to this fundamental attribution error (Zebrowitz-McArthur, 1988). When told of someone's actions, Hindus in India are less likely than Americans to offer dispositional explanations ("She is sociable") and more likely to propose situational explanations ("Her friends were with her") (Miller, 1984). Because group identifications are important in judging others, personal attributes, such as physical attractiveness, matter less to collectivists (Dion & others, 1990).

Culture and Parent-Child Relations Right from the start, Japanese and Chinese parents foster interdependence. Even after birth, mother and child continue to be joined—sleeping, bathing, and moving about together. The traditional Japanese mother carries her child on her back for much of the first 2 years, a practice that may account for the greater separation stress experienced by Japanese than American infants (Markus & Kitayama, 1991).

In modern individualist cultures, parents want their children to become independent and "have good judgment," and avow less concern for training conformity and submissiveness—or, as a collectivist might say, for communal sensitivity and cooperation (Alwin, 1990). Schools teach children to clarify their own values so they can make good decisions for themselves. Thus, in Western restaurants, parents and children decide their own orders individually. In Western homes, adolescents open their own mail, refuse parental guidance in choosing their own boyfriends and girlfriends, and often seek the privacy of their own rooms. As adults they chart their own goals and separate from their parents, who already live apart from the grandparents. If a child fails, the embarrassed parents will nevertheless be able to discuss the child's problems openly.

All of this seems strange to Asian collectivists, whose parents more actively guide or decide their children's choices and whose schools are less bashful about teaching accepted cultural values (Hui, 1990). So close is the mutual identification of parent and child that the crushed parents of an errant child seldom discuss their feelings of shame.

"Over the years, I learned to choose from the best opinions. Chinese people had Chinese opinions. American people had American opinions. And in almost every case, the American version was much better.

It was only later that I discovered there was a serious flaw with the American version. There were too many choices, so it was easy to get confused and pick the wrong thing."
Amy Tan
The Joy Luck Club, 1989

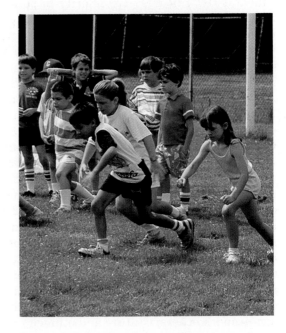

While collectivists teach their children *inter*dependence, children in individualist cultures learn from an early age to be independent and competitive and to take pride in their personal achievements.

Close-Up **Tips for Crossing Cultures**

When people from individualist and collectivist cultures interact, misunderstandings are common. Harry Triandis, Richard Brislin, and C. Harry Hui (1988) offer these tips for cultural voyagers:

Individualists interacting with collectivists should:

1. Pay attention to the other's group memberships and authorities; these define important norms, roles, and attitudes.

2. Seek to persuade by getting the person's superiors to signal approval and show how the other's groups will benefit.

3. Emphasize harmony and cooperation. Help the other save face. Avoid confrontation. Criticize gently and in private, after praising.

4. Patiently cultivate long-term relationships. The other prefers doing business with old friends. Intimacy develops gradually.

5. If the other is East Asian, expect unjustified modesty and self-deprecation. Begin presentations more modestly than you normally would.

6. Let the other know your social position, so the other knows how to relate to you. Expect age to engender respect. Who you are matters more than what you've accomplished.

7. Regard the other's accompanying you and spending time with you as relationship-building, not as an invasion of your privacy.

Collectivists interacting with individualists should:

1. Pay less attention to the other's groups (when outside the group context) than to the other's personal beliefs and attitudes.

2. Expect the other to be less worried about what superiors think and more influenced by peers and spouse than in your culture.

3. Emphasize personal costs and benefits of what you propose. Be aware that lack of criticism may be interpreted as approval.

4. Feel free to get right to business, with few preliminaries. Expect relationships to be good-natured but superficial and short-term.

5. Feel free to present yourself in a positive light but without obvious boasting. It's okay to speak highly of your skills and accomplishments.

6. Expect the other to care less about status differences, such as your age or position. Avoid being bossy to those of lower status or servile toward those of higher status.

7. Do not expect to be accompanied at all times. Individualists are comfortable alone, and show their confidence by leaving you on your own.

Ethnicity

The distinct traditions and styles contributed by different ethnic and racial groups add another dimension to cultural diversity. When groups of people migrate, they do not leave their cultural values behind. Over time and generations, they will absorb many cultural norms from their new homeland. Yet, especially if connected to fellow immigrants, they also will retain much of their original ethnic identity and cultural heritage. Thus, they make their new homeland a more culturally diverse place.

A culture, as we've seen, is a people's shared behaviors, ideas, attitudes, and traditions. **Ethnicity**, an aspect of one's social identity, is defined by the common ancestors and cultural heritage one shares with others. Culture and ethnicity are at times hard to disentangle, but they can be distinguished. A family living in Boston, for example, may be ethnically Italian and culturally eastern, urban Americans who define themselves as Italian-Americans.

Ethnicity and Race In practice, race is socially as well as physically defined. For example, North Americans typically regard those whose ancestors are mostly White, but who retain features that reveal African ancestry, as "Black." Brazilians regard anyone whose features reveal a partial Caucasian ancestry as "White." Thus, studies that purport to compare races often are comparing groups defined socially, not biologically. Moreover, in nearly every trait studied, from blood proteins to intelligence test scores, individual differences within racial groups greatly exceed the small differences between groups. Different "racial groups are much more alike than they are different," concludes Marvin Zuckerman (1990). For these reasons, it is difficult to draw conclusions about biologically based racial differences.

Although we can't really compare groups that differ only on biological race, we *can* explore cultural differences within and between socially defined racial or ethnic groups. In adapting to the geographical and social circumstances of their past, ethnic groups have developed differing styles of communicating and relating. Between East and West, the norms of individualism or collectivism define one such difference. In North America, the language, literature, music, foods, religion, and style of today's White culture incorporate African influences, just as today's Black culture incorporates European influences. *The World They Made Together* is how Mechal Sobel describes the African and European streams that fed the American South. Nevertheless, notes James Jones (1988), partly as a result of its African heritage and partly as an adaptation to the prevailing attitudes of the larger culture, Black American culture has evolved its own style. It tends to be present-oriented, expressive, spiritual, and emotion-driven. White culture is more often future-oriented, reserved, rationalistic, and achievement-driven. Because people so often judge others by their own standards, Jones argues that we are wiser to accept diversity than to pretend such differences don't matter or don't exist. Differing cultures have something to offer each other. In some situations expressiveness is an advantage and in others future-orientation is an advantage. The capacity for each enriches a multicultural society.

Ethnic Self-Awareness Self-concept is a mix of personal identity (self-esteem, outgoingness, appearance) and social identity (identification with certain people and groups). Which aspects we're aware of at any moment depends not only on our culture but also on the immediate context. When invited by researchers to "tell us about yourself," children emphasize their distinctive attributes. Foreign-born children mention their birthplace, redheads their hair color, skinny or obese children their body weight, minority children their ethnicity (McGuire & others, 1978, 1979).

Surely you've noticed. You become conscious of your gender when alone among people of the other sex. You are more racially self-aware when among people of another race but may give no thought to it when everyone around you is the same race. Indeed, notes Jean Phinney (1990), in an ethnically homogeneous society, "ethnic identity is a virtually meaningless concept." The simple principle, say William McGuire and colleagues (1978), is that

> one is conscious of oneself insofar as, and in the ways that, one is different. . . . If I am a Black woman in a group of White women, I tend to think of myself as Black; if I move to a group of Black men, my blackness loses salience and I become more conscious of being a woman.

Self-awareness of our distinctiveness explains why *any* minority group is conscious of itself in contrast with the majority. One way to appreciate the minority experience is to become a minority.

James Jones (1990): "Color makes a difference. Gender makes a difference. Ethnicity makes a difference. Acting as if they don't will create more problems than it will solve."

One doesn't realize how American one is until, as an American Jew, one lives for a time in Israel, or until as an African-American, one sojourns in Africa. Living for a year in Scotland, I was daily conscious of what I hardly noticed at home—the Americanness of my accent, clothing, and personal style. I also wondered how people were reacting to my obvious difference: Is she being extra polite because I am a foreigner? Is he snubbing me because he doesn't like Americans?

In multicultural settings, those who share a minority status may enjoy one another's company. Canadians who have little in common back home in British Columbia will talk like old friends upon discovering one another at a sidewalk cafe in Prague. To the majority culture, the minority may seem peculiarly sensitive or clannish. But that behavior only reflects that unpeculiar tendency for people to be oblivious to their commonalities and conscious of their distinctiveness.

Ethnic Identity and Cultural Identity

In ethnically diverse cultures, how do people balance their ethnic identities and their national identities? "Meet the Press" (1984) interviewer Marvin Kalb asked the question of then presidential candidate Jesse Jackson:

> **Kalb:** *Are you a Black man who happens to be an American running for the presidency, or are you an American who happens to be a Black man running for the Presidency?*
>
> **Jackson:** *Well, I'm both an American and a Black at one and the same time. I'm both of these . . .*
>
> **Kalb:** *What I'm trying to get at is . . . are your priorities deep inside yourself, to the degree that anyone can look inside himself, those of a Black man who happens to be an American or the reverse?*
>
> **Jackson:** *Well, I was born Black in America, I was not born American in Black! You're asking a funny kind of Catch-22 question. My interests are national interests.*

Jackson's response reflects what identity researcher Phinney (1990) calls a bicultural identity, one that identifies both with the ethnic culture and the larger culture. Ethnically conscious Asians living in England may or may not also feel strongly British (Hutnik, 1985). French Canadians who identify with their ethnic roots may or may not also feel strongly Canadian (Driedger, 1975). Hispanic Americans who retain a strong sense of their "Cubanness" (or of their Mexican, Puerto Rican, or Spanish heritage) may or may not feel strongly American (Roger & others, 1991). Other identity orientations noted in Table 19–1 include an ethnicity-blind assimilation into the majority culture, an ethnic pride that rejects and separates from the majority culture, and, on society's margins, those who identify with neither.

Researchers have wondered, as did Marvin Kalb, whether pride in one's ethnic group competes with identification with the larger culture. Does a strong ethnic identification displace other social identities? Social psychologist John Turner (1987) notes that we evaluate ourselves partly in terms of our group memberships. Seeing our own group as superior and deserving helps us feel good about ourselves. A positive ethnic identity can therefore contribute to positive self-esteem. So can a positive mainstream social identity among those who have lost touch with their mixed ethnic roots. "Marginal" people, who have neither an ethnic nor a mainstream

At the moment the man at left may not be conscious of his maleness, but he is probably extremely aware of his Americanness. In a given situation, we tend to be self-conscious of how we are distinct.

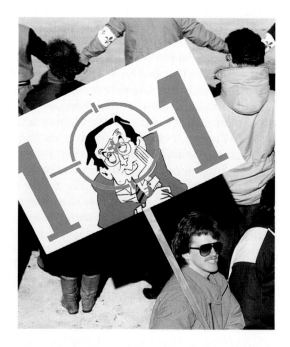

These ethnically conscious French Canadians—supporting Bill 101 "to live in French in Quebec"—may or may not also feel strongly Canadian. As countries become more ethnically diverse, people debate how we can build societies that are both pluralistic and unified.

Table 19–1	*Ethnic and Cultural Identity*	
	Identification with ethnic group	
Identification with majority group	*Strong*	*Weak*
Strong	Bicultural	Assimilated
Weak	Separated	Marginal

identity (Table 19–1), often have low self-esteem. Bicultural people, who affirm both identities, typically have a strongly positive self-concept (Phinney, 1990).

By forging national identities—cultures with unifying ideals—the U.S., Canada, and Australia have suffered less multiethnic divisiveness than have the Soviet Union, India, Yugoslavia, Iraq, and many other countries. Nevertheless, the continuing struggle in the immigrant nations, as elsewhere, is between separation and assimilation, between pride in one's distinct heritage and unity as one nation, between acknowledging the reality of diversity and questing for shared values.

Gender Diversity

As noted in Chapter 10, Thinking and Language, we humans have an urge to organize our complex worlds into simple categories. We categorize people as well as things. Among all the ways we classify people—as tall or short, fair-haired or dark, slim or muscular or rotund, blue-eyed or brown-eyed—two dimensions are especially potent. For people's self-concepts and identities, for selecting friends and mates, and for how others regard and treat them, height and hair color may matter, but ethnicity and sex matter much more. Among the dimensions of diversity, people first attune to another's ethnicity and, especially, to another's sex. When you were born, the first thing people wanted to know about you was, "Is it a boy or a girl?" When your sex was ambiguous—say, when not cued by a pink or blue outfit—people were unsure how to react.

As common ancestry and cultural heritage define our ethnicity, our biological sex dictates our **gender**—the characteristics by which people identify us as male or female. In considering how culture creates social diversity, let's look at the nature and nurture of gender. How different *are* males and females at different life stages? How does our culture's concept of gender affect how we see ourselves? how others see us?

Gender Similarities and Differences

In many traits, the sexes are alike. Whether you are male or female had no bearing on when you sat up, teethed, or walked (Maccoby, 1980). Tell me your sex and you've given me no clues to your vocabulary, intelligence, or happiness. But there are some intriguing differences. Compared to the average man, the average woman has 70 percent more fat, 40 percent less muscle, and is 5 inches short-

Even in physical traits, individual differences among men and among women far exceed the average differences between the sexes. Don Schollander's world-record-setting 4 minutes, 12 seconds in the 400-meter freestyle swim at the 1964 Olympics would have placed him 7th against the women racing in the 1988 Olympics and 8 seconds behind winner Janet Evans.

er. Compared to women, men enter puberty 2 years later, are 20 times more likely to have color-deficient vision, and, depending on the country, die up to 10 years sooner. Unlike women, half of men are balding by age 50. If it's any consolation, men are twice as likely to be capable of wiggling their ears.

In earlier chapters we also noted some intriguing psychological differences. Women are more likely to dream equally of men and women, to become sexually rearoused immediately after orgasm, and to smell faint odors. Women are twice as vulnerable to anxiety disorders and depression, and perhaps 10 times more susceptible to eating disorders. Men are three times more likely to become alcoholic and commit suicide, and far more likely to be diagnosed as hyperactive as children and to display antisocial personalities as adults.

Gender and Cognitive Abilities   In science, as in everyday life, differences, not similarities, excite interest. To some, it is news that there is no gender gap in average verbal ability as assessed by tests of vocabulary, reading comprehension, and solving analogies (Hyde & Linn, 1988). But most people find it more newsworthy that boys outnumber girls at the low extremes. Boys are more often slow to talk. In remedial reading classes, boys outnumber girls three to one (Finucci & Childs, 1981).

In math grades, the average girl typically equals or surpasses the average boy (Kimball, 1989). And on math tests given to more than 3 million representatively sampled people in 100 independent studies, males and females have obtained nearly identical average scores (Hyde & others, 1990). But again—despite much greater diversity within the sexes than between them—group differences make the news. Although females have an edge in math computation, males in various cultures score higher in math problem solving (Benbow, 1988; Lummis & Stevenson, 1990). For example, male high school seniors average 50 points higher on the SAT math aptitude test (which literally means that they average four more correct answers on the 60-question test). The differences are sharpest at the extremes. Among precocious seventh graders scoring above 700 on SAT math, boys outnumber girls 100 to 1 (Benbow, 1988). Even the *average* male-female difference becomes striking at one particular ability—speedily rotating three-dimensional objects in one's mind (Halpern, 1986; Linn & Peterson, 1986; Sanders & Soares, 1986) (Figure 19–1). Such spatial ability helps when fitting suitcases into a car trunk, playing chess, or doing certain types of geometry problems.

More often than others their age, whiz kids such as these also are left-handed, nearsighted, and allergic or asthmatic—traits that some brain scientists attribute to excess testosterone during prenatal development (Geschwind & Behan, 1984).

Which two circles contain a configuration of blocks identical to the one in the circle at the left?

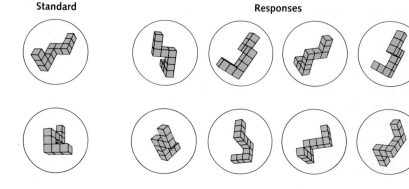

Figure 19–1 A test of spatial abilities: the mental rotation test. Which two responses show a different view of the standard? (See page 600 for answers.)

Do natural sex differences therefore explain why most mathematicians and more than 9 in 10 rated chess players and American architects are men? Before concluding yes, consider how social expectations shape boys' and girls' interests and abilities (Eccles & others, 1990). Many North American parents send their sons to computer camps and give their daughters more encouragement in English. As you might expect, the male edge in math problem solving grows with age, becoming detectable only after elementary school. On the SAT, the male edge arises partly from the smaller, more academically advantaged sample of males who take the test. As more and more girls are encouraged to develop their abilities in math and science, the gender gap is narrowing. Among representative national samples of high school juniors taking the Preliminary Scholastic Aptitude Test (PSAT), the male edge nearly disappeared between 1960 and the mid-1980s (Linn & Hyde, 1991).

Gender and Social Behavior Research on the psychology of women and men evokes concern: Given people's fascination with differences, might studies of male-female differences exaggerate people's gender stereotypes? Reflecting the mood of the 1970s, sociologist Jessie Bernard (1976, p. 13) cautioned that scientific demonstrations of differences between the sexes often serve as "battle weapons against women." When one group has more status and power, group differences often get interpreted as the less powerful group's deficiencies.

During the 1980s, scholars felt freer to search for and affirm gender diversity. Some argued, as did Alice Eagly (1986), that by reducing overblown gender stereotypes "gender-difference research has probably furthered the cause of gender equality." Others asserted that gender differences are not women's deficits. If, for example, women are more socially connected, well, in most cases maybe that is healthy rather than a symptom of an overly supportive ("co-dependent") personality. Whether biologically rooted or socially constructed, such diversity can be accepted, even valued. Let's consider, then, gender comparisons in independence, aggression, social dominance, and sexual initiative.

Independence Versus Interdependence Individual men and women vary from gently nurturant to fiercely competitive. Yet diversity exists between as well as within the sexes. After listening to women's reasoning and concerns, psychologists Nancy Chodorow (1978, 1989), Jean Baker Miller (1986), and Carol Gilligan and her collegues (1982, 1990) concluded that women more than men give priority to relationships. Unlike boys, who must define themselves in separation from their usually female caregiver, girls more easily identify with their mothers and develop an identity based on their social connections. Later experiences reinforce the sense of independent self among men and of interdependent self among women. Women use conversation to explore relationships, men use it to convey solutions. Women emphasize caring and they provide most of the care to the very young and the very old. Although 69 percent of people say they have a close relationship with their father, 90 percent say they're close to their mother (Hugick, 1989). Men, like empowered people generally, emphasize freedom and self-reliance.

Women's social connectedness appears greater not only in the care and support women more often give to their preschoolers and aging parents but also in women's career choices and attitudes. In

As girls feel more comfortable developing their math and science abilities, the gender gap narrows and more women are entering previously male-dominated fields such as engineering.

"There should be no qualms about the forthright study of racial and gender differences; science is in desperate need of good studies that . . . inform us of what we need to do to help under represented people to succeed in this society. Unlike the ostrich, we cannot afford to hide our heads for fear of socially uncomfortable discoveries."
Developmental psychologist Sandra Scarr (1988)

most of the caregiving professions — social worker, teacher, nurse — women outnumber men. Among the 194,000 first-year American college students surveyed in 1991 (Astin & others, 1990), 51 percent of males but 71 percent of females said it was very important to "help others who are in difficulty."

The greater connectedness of females surfaces early, in children's play. Boys typically play in large groups with an activity focus and little intimate discussion. Girls play in smaller groups, often with a single friend. Girls' play is less competitive than boys' and more imitative of social relationships (Lever, 1978). Both in play and in later achievement settings, females are more open and responsive to feedback than are males (Maccoby, 1990; Roberts, 1991). As teens, girls spend more time than do boys with friends and less time alone (Wong & Csikszentmihalyi, 1991).

When surveyed, women also are far more likely than men to describe themselves as having empathy. If you are empathic, you identify with others. You rejoice with those who rejoice and weep with those who weep. You imagine what it must feel like to live with that handicap, what it must be like to try so hard to impress people, what a thrill it must be to win that award. Physiological measures of empathy, such as one's heart rate while seeing another's distress, reveal much less gender gap than reported in surveys (Eisenberg & Lennon, 1983). Nevertheless, females are more likely to *express* empathy—to cry and to report distress when observing someone in distress.

Women *report* more empathy. Do they actually *feel* more empathy? Studies do show that women surpass men at reading others' emotions.

Moreover, studies consistently find females better at reading people's emotional cues (Hall, 1987). Shown a silent, 2-second film clip of an upset woman's face, women are better than men at sensing whether she is angry or discussing a divorce. Women's nonverbal sensitivity helps explain why both men and women report their friendships with women to be more intimate, enjoyable, and nurturing (Rubin, 1985; Sapadin, 1988). When wanting understanding and someone with whom to share worries and hurts, both men and women usually turn to women.

When it comes to relationships, such qualities often prove an asset (Kurdek & Schmitt, 1986; Orlofsky & O'Heron, 1987). In a study of 108 Australian married couples, John Antill (1983) found that when either spouse possessed traditional feminine traits, such as gentleness, sensitivity, or warmth—or better yet, when *both* did—marital satisfaction was higher. Although masculine traits may boost self-esteem, says Antill, "they are apparently not the qualities that hold the key to a happy, long-term relationship."

Answers to the mental rotation test on page 598: For the top standard, the first and fourth alternatives; for the bottom standard, the second and third alternatives.

Given the low value that Western societies place on caregiving (as reflected in the low pay of traditionally female helping occupations, such as preschool teacher or social worker), some psychologists wonder: Doesn't affirming women's connectedness reinforce what should be changed? Should Western women be out of step with their culture's individualism? Better that women stop being dependent on others and become self-reliant individualists. Other psychologists argue that women's approach to life holds the promise of transforming power-oriented, individualist societies into more caring communities. With the growing problems of homelessness, child neglect and abuse, and depression, one doesn't get the impression that too much caring is a massive social problem.

The "new" vision of human connectedness is strikingly similar to the traditional values that predominate in collectivist cultures.

Together, the feminist and cross-cultural scholars are forging what Hazel Markus and Shinobu Kitayama (1991) call a new understanding of dependence. "Being dependent does not invariably mean being helpless, powerless, or without control. It often means being *inter*dependent." It means affecting others and being responsive to them, giving and receiving support, confiding and being confided in. It means defining oneself in relation to others, seeing oneself not as a lone island but as attached to important others.

Aggression In surveys, men admit to considerably more hostility and aggression than do women. In laboratory experiments that assess *physical* aggression, men indeed behave more aggressively, by administering what they think are higher levels of hurtful electric shock (Eagly, 1987; Hyde, 1986a). In every society that keeps crime records, males commit far more physical violence (Kenrick, 1987). In the United States during 1989, the male-to-female arrest ratio was 7.4 to 1 for murder and 10.6 to 1 for robbery. Throughout the world, hunting, fighting, and warring are primarily men's activities.

Social Dominance Around the world, men also are perceived as more dominant. From Finland to France, Peru to Pakistan, Nigeria to New Zealand, people rate men as more dominant, aggressive, and achievement-driven, and women as more deferential, nurturant, and affiliative (Williams & Best, 1990). Indeed, in virtually every society, men *are* socially dominant. When groups are formed, leadership tends to go to males. As leaders, men tend to be directive, even autocratic, and women tend to be more democratic (Eagly & Johnson, 1990). When people interact, men are more likely to utter opinions, women to express support (Aries, 1987; Wood, 1987). In everyday behavior, men are more likely to act as powerful people do—to talk assertively, to interrupt, to initiate touching, to smile less, to stare (J. Hall, 1987; Major & others, 1990).

Such behaviors help maintain the inequities of social power. When political leaders are elected, they usually are men. When salaries are paid, those in traditionally male occupations receive more. When asked what pay they deserve, women often expect less than do similarly qualified men (Major, 1987). In one recent month, only 6 percent of people quoted on the front page of *The New York Times* were women. In self-defense, the paper's executive editor said it wasn't the *Times'* fault that the national and global power players involved in page one issues were mostly men (Leo, 1990).

At last count, 87 percent of the world's legislators were men (Harper's Index, 1989).

Sexual Initiative "With few exceptions anywhere in the world," report cross-cultural psychologist Marshall Segall and his colleagues (1990, p. 244), "males are more likely than females to initiate sexual activity." Susan Hendrick and her colleagues (1985) report a corresponding gender gap in sexual attitudes: Women are "moderately conservative" about casual sex, men "moderately permissive." The annual survey of new American college students illustrates: "If two people really like each other, it's all right for them to have sex even if they've known each other for only a very short time," agreed 66 percent of men but only 38 percent of women (Astin & others, 1991).

Men also have a lower threshold for perceiving someone's warmth as a sexual come-on. Here we find another practical consequence of how we attribute behavior (page 551). In study after study, men more often than women attribute a woman's friendliness to sexual interest (Abbey, 1987; Saal & others, 1989). Such misattribution of a woman's cordiality helps explain men's greater sexual assertiveness (Kenrick & Trost, 1987). The unfortunate results can range from mild sexual harassment to date rape (Kanekar & Nazareth, 1988; Muehlenhard, 1988; Shotland, 1989).

Is Biology Destiny?

What explains our sex-related differences? Are they ordained by biology? By cultural shaping? By the interplay between biology and culture? Let's consider some possibilities. First, do men's and women's hormonal and sexual differences influence their social behavior? The "biosocial" view of gender says yes—perhaps indirectly, via the social consequences of mere physical differences—but yes.

Sex Hormones and Social Behavior Males and females are variations on a single form. Eight weeks after conception, they are anatomically indistinguishable. (For example, both sexes have nipples, although only women will ever nurse.) Then, our genes activate our biological sex. *XY* sex chromosomes direct development of a male; *XX* chromosomes produce a female. After a male embryo's testes form internally, they begin to secrete testosterone, the principal male sex hormone. Testosterone triggers the development of external male sex organs. Otherwise, the embryo continues its course toward the development of female sex organs.

Note to computer geeks: The sex variable has a default value of female.

What, then, do you suppose happens when glandular malfunction or hormone injections expose a female embryo to excess testosterone? Genetically female infants are born with masculine-appearing genitals, which can be corrected surgically. Until puberty, such females typically act in more aggressive "tomboyish" ways than most girls, and dress and play in ways more typical of boys than girls (Ehrhardt, 1987; Money, 1987).

Is their behavior due to the prenatal hormones? Perhaps. (Experiments with many species, from rats to monkeys, confirm that female embryos given male hormones later exhibit more masculine appearance and behavior [Hines, 1982].) But these girls frequently look masculine and are known to be "different," so perhaps people also treat them more like boys. Early exposure to sex hormones thus affects us both directly (physically) and indirectly—by influencing experiences that shape us. Biological appearances have social consequences.

Researchers debate the influence of sex hormones on spatial ability. Melissa Hines (1990) reports that girls whose glands overproduce testosterone have spatial abilities more like those of the average boy. Doreen Kimura (1989) reports that boys whose glands underproduce testosterone (and who therefore fail to undergo normal puberty) have spatial abilities more like those of the average girl. Moreover, there is some tendency—at best a small tendency, say skeptics (Benderly, 1989)—for women's spatial performance to vary with hormonal changes during the menstrual cycle.

Somewhat less controversial is testosterone's influence on aggression. In various animal species, one can increase aggressiveness by administering testosterone. In humans, violent male criminals average higher than normal testosterone levels (Dabbs & others, 1987). National Football League players have higher testosterone levels than ministers (Dabbs & others, 1990). Moreover, the gender difference in aggression appears early in life and across many species of mammals. In humans it wanes as men's testosterone levels decline during adulthood. No one of these findings is conclusive, but the convergence of evidence suggests that male aggressiveness does have biological roots. As we will see, it also has social roots.

Evolution and Sex Differences Working from the perspective of sociobiology, which studies the evolution of social behavior, some psychologists attribute gender diversity to males' and females' differing reproductive strategies (Kenrick & Trost, 1989). Natural selection favors organisms which send their genes into the future, by producing offspring that survive to reproduce. Men, they suggest, are quicker to perceive friendliness as sexual interest and to initiate sexual relations because sperm are cheap. (Males will produce about 2000 new sperm during the time it takes to read this sentence.) Males who compete successfully with other males to fertilize the most females will be winners in the genetic sweepstakes, by producing more offspring who carry their genes and their traits. Thus, nature's mating game favors male sexual initiative toward females and aggressive dominance in competing with other males.

Female reproductive strategy differs radically, say the sociobiologists. A female has relatively few eggs and invests enormous time and energy in carrying and nursing a single offspring. To avoid squandering their few reproductive chances, females are cautiously selective in their choice of mates. They respond to signs of health and strength, and, in our own species, an ability to commit time and resources to protecting and nurturing their young. This helps explain the differing sexual values, mate preferences, and behaviors of women and men, suggests psychologist David Buss (1989). Cultural and individual differences show that genes do not rigidly determine sex differences, he cautions. Yet studies in 37 cultures revealed worldwide similarities in what men find attractive in women (features that suggest fertility) and what women find attractive in men (wealth, power, ambition). And that, says Buss, indicates that our evolutionary heritage matters, too.

Critics question this evolutionary psychology. Granted, our common biology endows us with universal similarities. But when it comes to complex social behaviors, such as fathers' investment in infant care or relations between the sexes, cultural diversity is enormous. Marriage patterns vary from monogamy (one spouse) to serial monogamy (a succession of spouses) to polygamy (several wives) to polyandry (several husbands) to spouse-swapping.

Furthermore, say sociobiology's critics, evolutionary explanations are after the fact. Knowing the sexual double standard, we can imagine how natural selection might predispose men's promiscuous inclinations. But let's also explain the many men who are faithful to one woman. Of course!—the offspring of two invested parents who support each other have better survival chances. Or, imagine that women were the more aggressive sex. But of course, someone might explain, strong and aggressive women more successfully protect their children.

As the new cross-cultural research on mate preferences illustrates, sociobiologists are now seeking to test predictions, not just offer hindsight explanations. What is more, both sides agree on two points. First, sex differences that may have enhanced the survival of our ancestors when hunting animals and gathering roots may no

"There is little doubt that we would all be safer if the world's weapon systems were controlled by average women instead of by average men."
Melvin Konner
The Tangled Wing: Biological Constraints of the Human Spirit, 1982

The average male will produce 8 trillion sperm over his lifetime, and, if living in an industrialized nation, will father two children (Small, 1991).

The male bowerbird of New Guinea and Australia attracts its mates by building an elaborate bower decorated with flowers, fruits, and leaves. Before selecting a mate, the female inspects several of these bowers, which indicate their builder's strength, dexterity, and ability to defend his bower from other males, and, thus, the potential of his genes. Evolutionary psychologists believe that studying such bird behavior helps us better understand human mating and sexual behavior.

longer be adaptive. Evolutionary wisdom is wisdom about what worked in the past, not about what is commendable or inevitable — or even tolerable — today. Second, men and women are the products of their mammalian and human history, *and* of their cultural history. Nature's special gift to humans is our great capacity to learn and adapt. Therein lies a culture's power to create our concept of gender.

The Social Construction of Gender

What biology initiates, environment accentuates. Society assigns us each — even those few whose biological sex is ambiguous at birth — to the social category of male or female. The inevitable result is our strong **gender identity** (our sense of being male or female). To varying extents, we also become **gender-typed**. That is, some boys more than others exhibit traditionally masculine traits and interests, and some girls more than others become distinctly feminine.

Gender-Typing Freud explained gender-typing with his theory that 5- to 6-year-old children resolve tensions linked with their attraction to the other-sex parent by identifying with the same-sex parent and adopting his or her characteristics. But this can't be the entire explanation, because children become gender-typed well before age 6 and even in the absence of a same-sex parent (Frieze & others, 1978; Stevenson & Black, 1988).

Social learning theory assumes that children learn gender-linked behaviors by observing and imitating, and being rewarded or punished. "Susie, you're such a good mommy to your dolls"; "Big boys don't cry, Dick." But this can't be the whole story either, because differences in the way parents rear boys and girls aren't enough to explain gender-typing (Lytton & Romney, 1991). Even when their families discourage traditional gender-typing, children organize themselves into boy worlds and girl worlds, each guided by rules for what boys and girls do.

"The genes sing a prehistoric song that today should sometimes be resisted but which it would be foolish to ignore."
  Thomas J. Bouchard & others (1990)

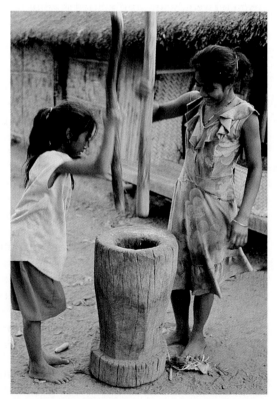

Around the world, from North America to Indonesia, children learn gender-typed behaviors partly by observing and imitating, and being rewarded or punished.

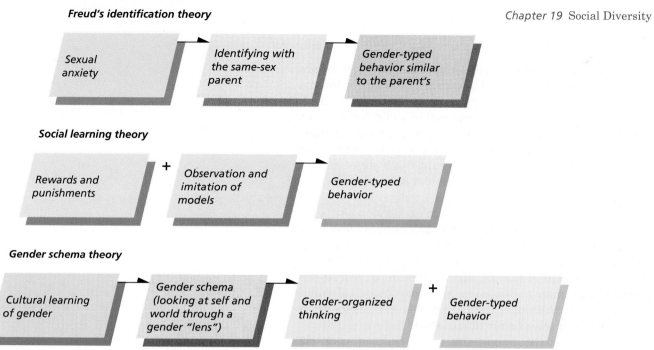

Freud's identification theory

| Sexual anxiety | → | Identifying with the same-sex parent | → | Gender-typed behavior similar to the parent's |

Social learning theory

| Rewards and punishments | + | Observation and imitation of models | → | Gender-typed behavior |

Gender schema theory

| Cultural learning of gender | → | Gender schema (looking at self and world through a gender "lens") | → | Gender-organized thinking | + | Gender-typed behavior |

Figure 19–2 Three theories of gender-typing

Gender schema theory (Figure 19–2) combines cognitive theory with social learning theory: Out of children's struggles to comprehend the world come concepts, or schemas, including a schema for their own gender (Bem, 1987). Gender becomes a lens through which children view their experience. By age 3, they begin organizing their worlds on the basis of gender. Language forces them to. English uses the pronouns he and she. Other languages classify objects as masculine ("*le* train") or feminine ("*la* table"). Through language, dress, toys, and songs, social learning shapes gender schemas. Children then compare themselves to their concept of gender ("I am male—thus, masculine, strong, aggressive" or "I am female—therefore, feminine, sweet, and helpful") and adjust their behavior accordingly.

Gender Roles In becoming gender-typed we learn the social role deemed appropriate to our sex. Traditionally, men initiate dates, drive the car, and pick up the check; women cook the meals, buy the children's clothes, and do the laundry. Such formulas smooth social relations, saving awkward decisions about who does what. But at a cost. When deviating from social convention, as when a woman initiates a formal date with a man, we may feel anxious or be viewed as weird (Green & Sandos, 1983).

Experiments show that many people do act to fulfill **gender-role** expectations. For example, Mark Zanna and Susan Pack (1975) had college women write descriptions of themselves for a tall, unattached, male senior whom they anticipated meeting. Those expecting to meet a man who liked nontraditional women described themselves as relatively nontraditional. Those led to think he favored traditional gender roles described themselves as more traditionally feminine; they also performed more modestly on an aptitude test, solving 15 percent fewer problems. Gender expectations help create a gender difference.

Unlike biological differences, gender roles vary across cultures and over time. Such variations illustrate the social construction of gender.

Gender *The social definition of male and female.*
Gender identity *One's sense of being male or female.*
Gender-typing *The acquisition of a masculine or feminine gender identity and role.*
Gender roles *Expected behaviors for males and females.*

Cultural Variations in Gender Roles Around the world, men predominate in fighting wars and hunting, women in caring for infants. Yet different societies socialize children for varying gender roles. In nomadic societies of food-gathering people, there is little division of labor by sex. Thus, boys and girls receive much the same upbringing. In agricultural societies, women stay close to home, in the fields and with the children; men roam more freely. Such societies typically socialize children into more distinct gender roles (Segall & others, 1990; Van Leeuwen, 1978).

Men and women who assume distinct roles develop skills and attitudes that help explain their differing social behaviors (Eagly & Wood, 1991). In the United States, where women are 3 percent of top executives at Fortune 1000 corporations, 4 percent of the Marine Corps, 97 percent of nurses, and 99 percent of secretaries, the roles enacted by men and women have psychological consequences (Castro, 1990; Williams, 1989). Leadership roles foster assertiveness; caregiving roles foster nurturance.

Roles vary enormously among the industrialized countries (Figure 19–3). In North America, medicine and dentistry are predominantly male occupations; in the Soviet Union, most medical doctors are women, as are most dentists in Denmark. Socialization practices vary just as widely. In countries around the world, girls spend more time than boys helping with housework and child care; boys spend more time in unsupervised play (Edwards, 1991). In rural central India, for example, girls spend two-thirds of their time doing household work, including a daily hour and a half fetching water; boys spend two-thirds of their time in leisure (Sarawathi & Dutta, 1988). In Israel, Arab adolescents favor more distinct gen-

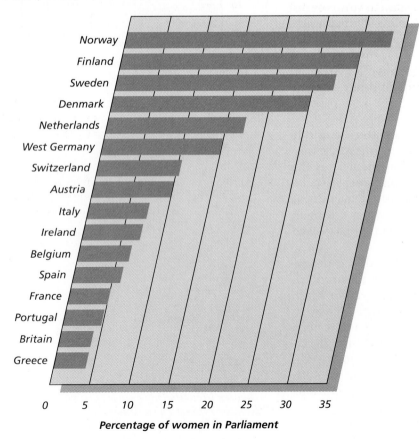

Percentage of women in Parliament

Figure 19–3 In Europe, women's representation in Parliament varies greatly by country. (From *The Economist*, 29 February 1987.)

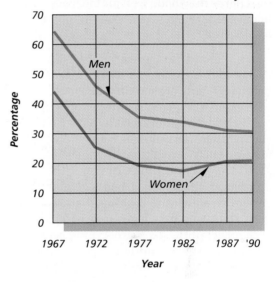

Figure 19–4 Drawing of an ideal man by (a) an American girl, and (b) a Mexican girl (translation: "What is most valued in a man is that he be a chivalrous man and that he give his place to the woman"). (From Stiles & others, 1990.)

der roles than do Jewish adolescents, thus anticipating the adult Arab world's more distinct norms for male and female behavior (Seginer & others, 1990). Similarly, compared to American 14-year-olds, Mexico City youth have more strongly gender-typed ideals (Figure 19–4).

Variations in Gender Roles Over Time Gender roles vary over time as well as across cultures. In 1938, only 1 in 5 Americans approved "of a married woman earning money in business or industry if she has a husband capable of supporting her"; by 1988, 4 in 5 approved (Niemi & others, 1989). In the flick of an apron, the number of American college women hoping to be full-time homemakers plunged during the late '60s and early '70s (Figure 19–5).

The change is behavioral as well. The number of women earning education degrees fell sharply after 1970, while the number of women awarded business degrees rose sharply (Figure 19–6). Moreover, between 1960 and 1990, the proportion of American women in the work force increased from 1 in 3 to nearly 3 in 5. Over the same period, these trends contributed to a 7-fold increase in the number of female doctors and a 24-fold increase in the numbers of female lawyers and engineers (Wallis, 1989).

A more subtle revolution has also been occurring in men's roles. Since 1965, American men have been devoting more and more time

First-year students who agree that "The activities of married women are best confined to home and family"

Figure 19–5 College student endorsement of the traditional view of women's role has declined dramatically. (From Dey & others, 1991.)

Figure 19–6 The shrinking gender gap in American bachelor's degrees awarded in education and business. (From Turner & Bowen, 1990.)

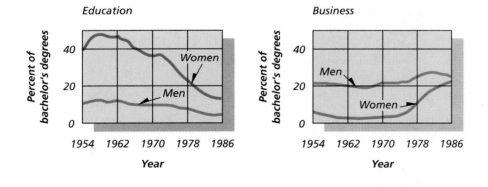

to family work (Figure 19–7). Increasingly, men are found in front of the stove, behind the vacuum cleaner, and over the diaper-changing table. But cultural differences remain huge: The average Japanese husband devotes 3 to 5 hours a week to domestic chores (one-ninth as much as his spouse); Swedish husbands clock 18 domestic hours per week (Juster & Stafford, 1991). Even in countries that have promoted equality, gender distinctions persist. Whether in Russia, China, or Sweden, answers to "Who works in the child care nurseries?" "Who cooks dinner?" and "Who leads the country?" remain the same as in North America.

"Like an ethnic culture in danger of being swallowed up by the culture of the dominant group, the contribution of the traditional homemaker has been devalued first by men and now by more women," reports sociologist Arlie Hochschild (1989, p. 267). "One way to reverse this devaluation is for men to share in that devalued work, and thereby to revalue it." Men's increasing sharing in homemaking chores may bode well for marriage, too. Women in mutually supportive marriages are less likely to consider divorce, reports Hochschild.

Should There Be Gender Roles? Should distinct gender roles be preserved? Psychologist Sandra Bem (1985) answers no: "Human behaviors and personality attributes should no longer be linked with gender." If this requires imposing one's egalitarian values on one's children, then so be it, says Bem. Parents who have deep social, political, or religious convictions need not be timid about transmitting their convictions to their children. If the children don't absorb ideology and values at home, they will absorb them elsewhere. To raise children who are less gender-typed, Bem suggests making gender irrelevant to cooking, dishwashing, and toys. Give boys and girls the same privileges and responsibilities. And teach them to recognize subtle sex stereotyping and discrimination.

Noting the strength and persistence of gender roles worldwide, some psychologists doubt they will ever disappear. Douglas Kenrick (1987) believes that, try as we might to reconstruct our gender concepts, "we cannot change the evolutionary history of our species, and some of the differences between us are undoubtedly a function of that history." True, the sexes share many traits and abilities in common. But each sex also bears special gifts. To distinguish between two wines, composers, or sexes is to appreciate each equally, by discerning their separate virtues. Equality and freedom of individual choice, yes; sameness, no.

Others say that biological differences are socially trivial. Human beings—both women *and* men—should be unshackled from all that constrains their being fully human—assertive *and* nurturant, self-confident *and* tender, independent *and* compassionate. Bem (1987) acknowledges that there may be "biologically based sex differences in behavior." But she believes that the social construction of gender greatly exaggerates them. Thus, she says, if under egalitarian social conditions,

> it turns out that more men than women become engineers or that more women than men decide to stay at home with their children, I'll live happily with those sex differences as well as with any others that emerge. But I am willing to bet that the sex differences that emerge under those conditions will not be nearly as large or as diverse as the ones that currently exist in our society.

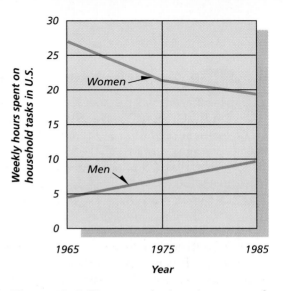

Figure 19–7 Time spent by American men and women on household tasks. (Data from Robinson, 1988.)

The Quigmans by Buddy Hickerson; © 1990, Los Angeles Times Syndicate. Reprinted with permission.

"The finest people marry the two sexes in their own person."
Ralph Waldo Emerson
Journals, 1843

Changing Gender Roles Across the Life Span

Gender differences in connectedness, aggression, dominance, and sexual initiative peak in late adolescence and early adulthood—the very years most commonly studied. Several studies have found that as people age, gender differences diminish. Women become more assertive and self-confident and men more empathic and less domineering (Helson & Moane, 1987; Pratt & others, 1990; Turner, 1982). For example, Florine Livson (1976) followed the evolving gender differences among 80 girls and boys from the teen years to age 50. As teenagers, the girls became progressively less assertive and more flirtatious; the boys became more domineering and unexpressive. But by age 50, these differences had diminished. The men were expressing warmer feelings for others; the women had become more assertive. In another study, M. F. Lowenthal and his colleagues (1975) asked married couples, "Who's the boss in your family?" With increasing age, both spouses were progressively less likely to single out the husband.

Why do gender differences first increase and then decrease as life progresses? Personality theorist Carl Jung (1933) speculated that masculine and feminine tendencies exist in everyone and that, during the second half of life, people develop their previously repressed feminine or masculine aspects. Others speculate that, during courtship and early parenthood, social expectations lead both sexes to downplay traits that interfere with their roles. As long as men are expected to provide and protect, they forgo their more dependent and tender sides (Gutmann, 1977). As long as women are expected to nurture, they forgo their impulses to be assertive and independent. When they graduate from these early adult roles, men and women become freer to develop and express their previously inhibited tendencies.

"In the long years liker must they grow;
The man be more of woman, she of man."
  Alfred, Lord Tennyson
  The Princess, 1847

So, what can we conclude about gender differences? First, gender similarities are impressive, especially during middle and late adulthood. Compared with the huge differences among individuals, differences between the sexes are small. Second, we can appreciate the detectable differences, without using them to judge individuals. Consider: When guessing someone's life expectancy, we seldom pay much attention to sex, preferring to note particulars of this individual—whether the person drinks heavily or smokes, whether the person's parents died young or old, whether the person eats a high fat diet. Because most of the cognitive and social differences are smaller than the life expectancy difference, it makes even more sense to judge people as individuals on these dimensions. Could you become a competent engineer? or child care worker? Knowing that you are a man or a woman tells us little; knowing you as an individual tells us much more.

The overlapping distributions of male and female qualities caused researcher Lauren Harris (1978) to caution against thinking of females and males as *opposite* sexes: "Neither in any physiological nor in any psychological sense are males and females 'contrary or antithetical in nature or tendency, diametrically opposed, or altogether different.'" Instead we might think of our own sex and the *other* sex as like the two halves of an oyster shell—similar but not identical, equally important, and fitting together because they grow together and change around each other.

"This fundamental truth—that women are not just men who can have babies and men are not just women who spike footballs—gives marriage its vitality, its dynamics, its delights, and its divorce."
  Bill Cosby
  Love and Marriage, 1989

Responding to Diversity

As we noted in Chapter 18, similarity promotes attraction. If like-ness leads to liking, do differences foster disliking? If so, how can people of differing cultures or sexes accept, embrace, and enjoy their diversity? In today's world, few questions are more important. Thus, notes Carl Sagan (1980),

> Human history can be viewed as a slowly dawning awareness that we are members of a larger group. Initially our loyalties were to ourselves and our immediate family, next, to bands of wandering hunter-gath-erers, then to tribes, small settlements, city-states, nations. We have broadened the circle of those we love. We have now organized what are modestly described as superpowers, which include groups of people from divergent ethnic and cultural backgrounds working in some sense together—surely a humanizing and character-building experience. If we are to survive, our loyalties must be broadened further, to include the whole human community, the entire planet Earth.

Earth Day celebrations help us to see beyond our own small communities and to identify with the *global* community in all its unity and diversity.

Together we all face the challenges of environmental pollution, global warming, resource depletion, and weapons proliferation. Yet seldom do we identify with our common humanity. Conscious of our diversity, we instead divide the world into "us"—our own nation, culture, creed, ethnic group, and sex—and "them." In a time when ethnic and national loyalties hinder our solving pressing global problems, we need to ask: How can we replace attitudes that lead us to reject diversity with those that promote its acceptance?

"The growing diversity of the American popula-tion makes the quest for unifying ideals and a common culture all the more urgent. In a world savagely rent by ethnic and racial antagonisms, the U.S. must continue as an example of how a highly differentiated society holds itself together."
Historian Arthur Schlesinger
"The Cult of Ethnicity, Good and Bad," 1991

Rejecting Diversity

To what extent does prejudice persist? What causes it? What steps can we take to replace destructive conflict with constructive peace and good will?

Prejudice Prejudice means prejudgment. It is an unjustifiable and usually negative attitude toward a group—typically a differ-ent cultural, ethnic, or gender group. Like all attitudes, **prejudice** is a mixture of beliefs (often overgeneralized and called **stereo-types**), emotions (hostility, envy, or fear), and predispositions to action (to discriminate). To believe that overweight people are gluttonous, to feel unattracted to an overweight person, and to be hesitant to hire or date an overweight person is to be prejudiced.

Like other forms of prejudgment, prejudices are schemas that influence how we notice and interpret events. In one study, most Whites perceived a White man shoving a Black as "horsing around." The same shove by the Black to the White man was more often seen as "violent" (Duncan, 1976). Thus, not only is prejudice nurtured by its social, emotional, and cognitive roots, it also has cognitive effects. Our preconceived ideas about people, sometimes formed by labels put on them, bias our impressions of their behavior. Prejudgments color perceptions.

How prejudiced are people? To find out, we can assess what they say and what they do. To judge by what Americans say, racial and gender attitudes have changed dramatically in the last half century (Figure 19–8). Asked whether they would "have any objection to sending your children to a school where half the children are Black," 9 in 10 White Americans now say no (Gallup & Hugick, 1990). Interviewers no longer ask Americans whether there should be "equal pay for women and men when they are doing the same job" (*Public Opinion*, 1979), because their 16 to 1 "yes" margin long ago revealed a national consensus.

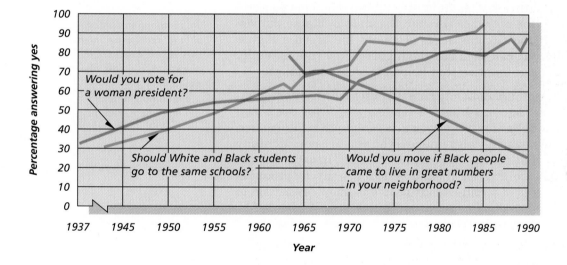

Figure 19–8 Americans today express much less racial and gender prejudice than two and three decades ago. (Responses to the racial questions are from non-Blacks only.) (From Gallup & Hugick, 1990; Niemi & others, 1989; Tom Smith, National Opinion Research Center, personal correspondence.)

Despite these more accepting attitudes, prejudice persists. In socially intimate settings (dating, dancing, marrying), many White people admit they would feel uncomfortable with someone of another race. During the late 1980s, prejudice occasionally resurfaced in public settings as well. American cities and college campuses experienced significant increases in "hate crimes" (slurs, vandalism, and physical violence) against African-Americans and homosexuals (Goleman, 1990; Herek, 1989, 1990; Levine, 1990). In other countries, hate rages even more openly—between Israel's Palestinians and Jews, Northern Ireland's Protestants and Catholics, Yugoslavia's Serbs and Croatians, South Africa's Zulus and African National Congress members.

Around the world, gender prejudice and discrimination persist, too. In the Sudan, women may not leave the country without permission of their husband, father, or brother (Beyer, 1990). In Saudi Arabia, women are forbidden to drive. Nowhere are female infants left out on a hillside to die of exposure, as was the practice in Ancient

Greece. Yet even today boys are often valued more than their sisters. During the 1976–77 famine in Bangladesh, preschool girls were more malnourished than boys, and in many developing countries death rates are higher for girls than boys (Bairagi, 1987). In South Korea, where testing often reveals the sex of an abortable fetus, male births exceed female births by 14 percent. Under China's one-child policy, unmarried men now greatly exceed the number of unmarried women (*Time*, 1990).

Once established, prejudice is maintained both by the inertia of social influence and by emotional and cognitive mechanisms. But why does prejudice arise in the first place?

Social Inequalities When some people have money, power, and prestige and others do not, the "haves" usually develop attitudes that justify things as they are. In the extreme case, slave owners perceived slaves as lazy and irresponsible—as having the very traits that "justified" enslaving them. More commonly, women may be seen as unassertive but sensitive and therefore fit for the tasks they often perform (Hoffman & Hurst, 1990). In short, prejudice rationalizes inequalities.

Discrimination also increases prejudice through the reactions it provokes in its victims. In his classic 1954 book, *The Nature of Prejudice*, Gordon Allport noted that being a victim of discrimination can produce either self-blame or anger. Both reactions may create new grounds for prejudice through the classic "blame the victim" dynamic. If the circumstances of ghetto life breed a higher crime rate, someone can then use the higher crime rate to justify continuing the discrimination that helped to create the ghetto.

Us and Them: Ingroup and Outgroup Group identifications typically promote an **ingroup bias**—a tendency to favor one's own group. The social definition of who you are—your ethnicity, gender, religion, academic major—also implies who you are not. Mentally drawing a circle that defines "us" excludes "them." In experiments, creating even an arbitrary us-them distinction—say, by grouping people with the toss of a coin—leads people to show favoritism to their own group when dividing rewards (Tajfel, 1982; Wilder, 1981).

To Greeks of the classical era, all non-Greeks were "barbarians." Most citizens in the coalition of countries fighting in the 1991 Persian Gulf War felt more pain over the few hundred corpses of their own soldiers than over reports of 100,000 Iraqi corpses. In Africa, where some 700 traditional societies cluster into fewer than 50 nations, people typically like and admire their own group and direct their hostility toward other groups (Segall & others, 1990). Most children believe their school is better than the other schools in town. Even chimpanzees have been seen to wipe themselves clean where touched by a chimp from another group (Goodall, 1986).

Ingroup bias is especially potent in collectivist cultures (Triandis, 1989). Because group identity runs strong, outsiders receive cautious treatment. Ingroup members—friends, colleagues, and extended family—receive favors and other forms of support. Compared to individualist cultures, conflict in collectivist cultures less often occurs within groups (such as families) and more often between groups. Collectivists also feel more awkward relating to outgroup members. In one study, North American students experienced smoother and more intimate interactions with ingroup members (classmates) than with strangers. But this ingroup/outgroup difference was considerably greater among students in collectivist South Korea (Gudykunst & others, 1987).

"Prejudice is never easy unless it can pass itself off for reason."
 William Hazlitt
 On Prejudice, 1839

"It is understandable that the suppressed people should develop an intense hostility toward a culture whose existence they make possible by their work, but in whose wealth they have too small a share."
 Sigmund Freud
 The Future of an Illusion, 1927

"Evil is anyone outside the tribe. Evil works by dehumanizing the Other. A perverse, efficient logic: identifying others as evil justifies all further evil against them."
 Lance Morrow
 "Evil," 1991

Scapegoating Prejudice can spring from the passions of the heart as well as the divisions of society. Prejudice may express anger: When things go wrong, finding someone to blame can provide an outlet. Evidence for this **scapegoat theory** of prejudice comes from high prejudice levels among economically frustrated people and from experiments in which a temporary frustration intensifies prejudice. Nazi leader Hermann Rausching once explained the Nazis' need to scapegoat: "If the Jew did not exist, we should have to invent him" (quoted by Koltz, 1983).

Despised outgroups not only provide a handy emotional outlet for anger, they can also boost self-esteem. In experiments, students who experience failure or are made to feel insecure will often restore their self-esteem by disparaging a rival school or another person (Cialdini & Richardson, 1980; Crocker & others, 1987). To boost our own sense of status, it helps to have others to denigrate. For this reason, a rival's misfortune sometimes provides a twinge of pleasure. To a Chicago Cubs baseball fan, happiness is the Cubs winning—and the Chicago White Sox losing.

Cognitive Roots of Prejudice New research has focused on another source of prejudice. Stereotyped beliefs are a natural by-product of how we cognitively simplify the world.

Categorization One way we simplify our world is to categorize things. A chemist classifies molecules as organic and inorganic. A mental health professional classifies people's psychological disorders by types. In categorizing people into groups we often stereotype them. We overestimate the similarity of people within groups other than our own. "They"—the members of some other group—seem to look and act alike, but "we" are diverse (Bothwell & others, 1989). To us on the outside, the members of fraternity *X* are jocks and those in fraternity *Y* are intellectuals. Members of each fraternity see their own diversity. To those in one ethnic group, those of another often seem more alike in appearance, personality, and attitudes than they are.

Vivid cases As noted in Chapter 10's discussion of the availability heuristic, we often judge the frequency of events by instances that readily come to mind. If asked whether Blacks run faster than Whites, many people may think of Carl Lewis, Leroy Burrell, and Florence Griffith Joyner. From such vivid but exceptional cases they overgeneralize that "yes, Blacks run faster."

In an experiment with University of Oregon students, Myron Rothbart and his colleagues (1978) showed how we overgeneralize from vivid, memorable cases. They divided the students into two groups and showed them information about 50 men. The first group's list included 10 men arrested for nonviolent crimes, such as forgery. The second group's list included 10 men arrested for violent crimes, such as assault. When both groups later recalled how many men on their list had committed any sort of crime, the second group overestimated how many there were. Vivid cases, being readily available to memory, influence our judgments of a group.

The just-world phenomenon We noted earlier that people often justify their prejudice by blaming its victims. Impartial observers may also blame victims, by assuming the world is just and that people get what they deserve. In laboratory experiments, merely observing someone receive painful shocks has led many people to think less of the victim (Lerner, 1980). This **just-world phenomenon** reflects an idea we commonly teach our children—that good is re-

"If the Tiber reaches the walls, if the Nile does not rise to the fields, if the sky doesn't move or the earth does, if there is famine, if there is plague, the cry is at once: 'The Christians to the lion!'"
Tertullian
Apologeticus, A.D. 197

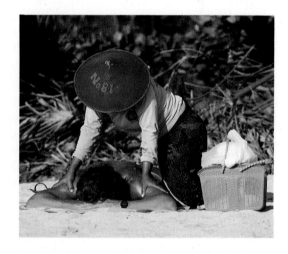

People of another race often seem to look alike. Australian sunbathers on Bali's beaches appreciate the Balinese masseuses wearing numbers, so they can recognize them.

warded and evil is punished. From this it is a short leap to assume that those who succeed must be good and those who suffer must be bad. Such reasoning enables the rich to see their wealth, and the poor's misfortune, as justly deserved. As one German civilian is said to have remarked when visiting the Bergen-Belsen concentration camp shortly after World War II, "What terrible criminals these prisoners must have been to receive such treatment."

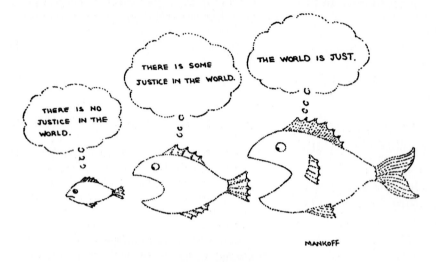

Drawing by Mankoff; © 1981 The New Yorker Magazine, Inc.

Hindsight bias is also at work here (Carli & Leonard, 1989). Have you ever heard people say that rape victims, abused spouses, or people with AIDS got what they deserved? An experiment by Ronnie Janoff-Bulman and her collaborators (1985) illustrates victim-blaming. When given an account of a date that ended with the woman being raped, people perceived the woman as partly to blame. In hindsight, they thought, "She should have known better." (Victim-blaming also reassures people that it couldn't happen to them.) Others who were given the same account, without the rape, did not perceive the woman as inviting rape. Only when she was victimized was she faulted for her behavior.

Conflict We live in surprising times. With astonishing speed, democratic movements have swept away totalitarian rule in Eastern European countries. The hope of a "new world order" has replaced the Cold War chill as Soviet and American leaders cooperate in beating their swords into plowshares and linking their economies. Yet, world spending for arms and armies continues to drain $3 billion per day from spending for housing, nutrition, education, and health. Knowing that, as the UNESCO motto declares, wars begin in human minds, psychologists have wondered what steps might reverse destructive spirals of conflict. How might the perceived threats of social diversity be replaced by a spirit of cooperation?

To a social psychologist, a **conflict** is a seeming incompatibility of actions, goals, or ideas. The elements of conflict are much the same at all levels, from nations in an arms race, to cultural disputes within a society, to individuals in marital strife. In each situation, people become enmeshed in a destructive social process that produces results no one wants. Among these destructive processes are social traps and distorted perceptions.

Social Traps In some situations, we can enhance our collective well-being by pursuing our personal interests. As capitalist Adam Smith

"Every gun that is made, every warship launched, every rocket fired signifies, in the final sense, a theft from those who hunger and are not fed, those who are cold and are not clothed."
President Dwight Eisenhower, in a speech to the American Society of Newspaper Editors, 1953

wrote in *The Wealth of Nations* (1776), "It is not from the benevolence of the butcher, the brewer, or the baker that we expect our dinner, but from their regard to their own interest." In other situations, the parties involved—be they individuals or nations—may become caught up in mutually harmful behavior as they pursue their own ends. Such situations are **social traps**.

Consider the simple game matrix in Figure 19–9, which is similar to those used in experiments with thousands of people. Pretend that you are person 1, and that you and person 2 will each receive the amount of money shown after separately choosing either *A* or *B*. (You might invite someone to look at the matrix with you and take the role of person 2.) Which do you choose—*A* or *B*?

As you ponder the game, you discover that you and person 2 are caught in a dilemma. You both benefit if you both choose *A*, by making 50 cents each, and neither of you benefits if you both choose *B*, for you both make nothing. Nevertheless, on any single trial you serve your own interests if you choose *B*. If you choose *B* you can't lose, and you might make $1. But the same is true for the other person. Hence, the social trap: As long as you both pursue your own immediate best interest and choose *B*, you will both end up with nothing—the typical result—when you could have made 50 cents.

Many real-life situations similarly pit people's individual interests against their communal well-being. Individual whalers reason that the few whales they take don't threaten the species and that if they didn't take them others would anyway. The result: A species of whales becomes endangered. The individual car owner and home owner reasons, "It would cost me comfort or money to buy a more fuel-efficient car and furnace. Besides, the fossil fuels I burn don't noticeably add to the greenhouse gases." When others reason similarly, the collective result threatens disaster—global warming. Political leaders reason that if an antagonist nation is arming, so must their own in order to preserve the capacity to retaliate. But as social psychologist George Levinger (1987) noted, "When multiplied by 2, a national policy of Peace Through Strength leads inevitably to an arms race." In each of these social traps, parties pursuing their self-interest become caught up in mutually destructive behavior.

Social traps challenge us to find ways of reconciling our right to pursue our personal well-being with our responsibility for the well-being of all. Psychologists are therefore exploring ways to convince people to cooperate for their mutual betterment—through agreed-upon regulations, through better communication, and through promoting awareness of our responsibilities toward community, nation, and the whole of humanity (Dawes, 1980; Linder, 1982; Sato, 1987). Under such conditions, people more often cooperate, whether playing laboratory games or playing the game of real life.

Mirror-Image Perceptions Psychologists have noted a curious tendency for those in conflict to form diabolical images of each other. These distorted images are so similar that we call them **mirror-image perceptions**: As we see them—as untrustworthy and evil intentioned—so they see us. Thus, during the early 1980s, the U.S. government viewed the Communist support of guerrillas trying to overthrow the government of El Salvador as evidence of an "evil empire" at work. Meanwhile, the Soviets saw the U.S. support of guerrillas trying to overthrow the government of Nicaragua as the work of "imperialist warmongers." As enemies change, so do perceptions.

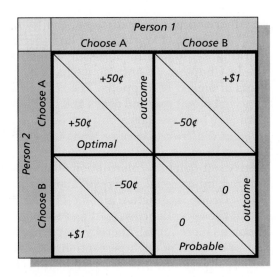

Figure 19–9 By pursuing our self-interest and not trusting others, we can end up losers. To illustrate this, play the game above. The pink triangles show the outcomes for person 1, which depend on the choices made by both persons. If you were person 1, would you choose *A* or *B*? (This game is called a "non-zero-sum game" because the outcomes need not add up to zero; both sides can win or both can lose.)

"Why do you see the speck that is in your brother's eye, but do not notice the log that is in your own eye?"
Jesus
Luke 6:41–42

In American minds and media, the "bloodthirsty, cruel, treacherous," Japanese of World War II later became our "intelligent, hardworking, self-disciplined, resourceful allies" (Gallup, 1972).

In Chapters 18 and 19, we have considered the psychological roots of biased perceptions. The *self-serving bias* leads each party to accept credit for good deeds and to shuck the blame for bad deeds. Although both nations admit to a buildup of military forces, the *fundamental attribution error* leads each to see the other's actions as arising from its aggressive disposition, but its own buildup as necessary self-defense. Information about one another's actions is then filtered, interpreted, and remembered through preconceived *stereotypes*. Group interaction among like-minded policymakers may *polarize* these tendencies, leading to *groupthink* that sees one's own group as more moral, thereby justifying one's retaliation.

The result of such perceptions is a vicious cycle of hostility. If John believes Mary is annoyed at him, he may snub her, causing her to act in ways that justify his perception. As with individuals, so with countries. Perceptions confirm themselves by influencing the other country to react in ways that seem to justify them.

Drawing by Wasserman; © 1990 Los Angeles Times Syndicate. Reprinted with permission.

Accepting Diversity

"Come, my friends,
'Tis not too late to seek
a newer world."
Alfred, Lord Tennyson

How, then, can we transform antagonisms fed by prejudice, social traps, and misperceptions into constructive attitudes that promote peace? Such transformations are most likely in situations characterized by cooperation, communication, and conciliation.

Cooperation Does it help to put two conflicting parties into close contact so they might get to know and like each other? It depends. When the contact is noncompetitive and between parties of equal status, such as fellow store clerks, it may help. Initially prejudiced co-workers of different races have, in such circumstances, usually learned to accept one another (Pettigrew, 1969). However, mere contact is sometimes not enough. In most desegregated junior high schools, Whites and Blacks resegregate themselves in the lunchrooms and on the school grounds (Schofield, 1986).

Mere contact was not enough to defuse intense conflicts instigated by researcher Muzafer Sherif (1966). He placed 22 Oklahoma City boys in two separate areas of a Boy Scout camp. He then put the two groups through a series of competitive activities, with prizes going to the victors. Before long, each group became intensely proud of itself and hostile to the "sneaky," "smart-alecky" "stinkers" in the other group. Food wars broke out during meals. Cabins were ransacked. Fist fights had to be broken up by members of the camp staff. When Sherif brought the two groups together, they avoided one another, except to taunt and threaten.

Nevertheless, within a few days Sherif transformed these young enemies into jovial comrades by giving them **superordinate goals**—shared goals that overrode their differences and required their cooperation. A disruption of the camp water supply necessitated that all 22 boys work together to restore water. Renting a movie required their pooled resources. A truck stalled until all the boys pulled and pushed together to get it moving. Having used iso-

"You cannot shake hands with a clenched fist."
Indira Gandhi, 1971

lation and competition to make strangers into enemies, Sherif used shared predicaments and goals to reconcile the enemies and make them friends. What reduced conflict was not contact itself, but *cooperative* contact.

Extending these findings, Samuel Gaertner and his co-workers (1989) report that cooperation has especially positive effects when it leads people to define a new, inclusive group that dissolves their former subgroups. Seat the members of two groups not on opposite sides, but alternately around the table. Give them a new, shared name. Have them work together. Such experiences change "us and them" into "we." People once perceived as in another group now are part of one's own group.

During the 1970s, several teams of educational researchers simultaneously wondered: If successful, cooperative contacts between members of rival groups encourage positive attitudes, could we apply this principle in multicultural schools? Could we promote interracial friendships by replacing competitive classroom situations with cooperative ones? And could cooperative learning maintain or even enhance student achievement? Many experiments confirm that the answers are yes (Johnson & Johnson, 1987; Slavin, 1989). Members of interracial groups who work together on projects and play together on athletic teams typically come to feel friendly toward those of the other race. So do those who engage in cooperative classroom learning. So encouraging are these results that more than 25,000 teachers have introduced interracial cooperative learning into their classrooms (Kohn, 1987). Working with fellow students in all their diversity sets the stage, declared the Carnegie Council on Adolescent Development (1989), for "adult work life and for citizenship in a multicultural society."

Cooperative efforts to achieve superordinate goals break down social barriers.

The power of cooperative activity to make friends of former enemies has led psychologists to urge increased international exchange and cooperation (Klineberg, 1984). As we engage in mutually beneficial trade, as we work to protect our common destiny on this fragile planet, and as we become more aware that our hopes and fears are shared, we will change misperceptions into a solidarity based on common interests.

Communication In the social trap game matrix we considered earlier, people usually are distrustful and pursue their individual interests as a defense against exploitation. However, when allowed to discuss the dilemma and to negotiate commitment to cooperate, cooperation increases (Jorgenson & Papciak, 1981).

"Great perils have this beauty, that they bring together the fraternity of strangers."
  Victor Hugo
  Les Miserables, 1862

When conflicts become intense, a third-party mediator—a marriage counselor, labor mediator, diplomat, community volunteer—may facilitate communication (Pruitt & Rubin, 1986). Mediators help each party to voice its viewpoint and, in the process, to understand the other's. Such understanding is most needed, yet least likely, in times of crisis (Tetlock, 1988). When conflicts grow intense, images become more stereotyped, communication becomes more difficult, and judgments become more rigid. Iraq's President Saddam Hussein, America's friend while attacking Iran in the 1980s, became to George Bush "another Hitler" after attacking oil-producing Kuwait in 1990. To Hussein, Bush became "Satan in the White House."

Conciliation When tension and suspicion peak, cooperation and communication may become impossible. Each party is likely to threaten, coerce, or retaliate—the very actions that will worsen the conflict. In the weeks before the Persian Gulf War, President Bush threatened, in the full glare of publicity, to "kick Saddam's ass." Saddam Hussein communicated in kind, threatening to make Americans "swim in their own blood."

Under such conditions, is there an alternative to war or surrender? Social psychologist Charles Osgood (1962, 1980) advocates a strategy of "Graduated and Reciprocated Initiatives in Tension-Reduction," nicknamed **GRIT**. In applying GRIT, one side first announces its recognition of mutual interests and its intent to reduce tensions. It then initiates one or more small, conciliatory acts. Without weakening one's retaliatory capability, this modest beginning opens the door for reciprocation by the other party. Should the enemy respond with hostility, one reciprocates in kind. But so, too, with any conciliatory response. Thus, President Kennedy's gesture of stopping atmospheric nuclear tests began a series of reciprocated conciliatory acts that culminated in the atmospheric test-ban treaty.

In laboratory experiments, GRIT is the most effective strategy known for increasing trust and cooperation (Lindskold & others, 1978–1988). Even during intense personal conflict, when communication has been nonexistent, a small conciliatory gesture—a smile, a touch, a word of apology—may work wonders. Conciliations allow both parties to begin edging down the tension ladder to a safer rung where communication and mutual understanding can begin.

And how good that such can happen, for civilization advances not by cultural isolation—maintaining walls around ethnic enclaves—but by tapping the knowledge, the skills, and the arts that are each culture's legacy to the whole human race. Thomas Sowell (1991) notes that, thanks to cultural sharing, every modern society is enriched by a cultural mix. We have China to thank for paper and printing, and for the magnetic compass that opened the great explorations. We have Egypt to thank for trigonometry. We have the Hindus of India and the Islamic world to thank for our Arabic numerals, which, except for numbering Superbowls and Kings and Queens, really are superior to the Roman numerals they replaced. While celebrating and claiming these cultural legacies, we can also welcome the enrichment of today's social diversity. We can view ourselves as individual instruments in a human orchestra. And we can therefore affirm our own culture's heritage while building bridges of communication and understanding across cultural traditions.

"To begin with, I would like to express my sincere thanks and deep appreciation for the opportunity to meet with you. While there are still profound differences between us, I think the very fact of my presence here today is a major breakthrough."

Drawing by W. Miller; © 1983 The New Yorker Magazine, Inc.

Summing Up

As kindred descendants of common ancestors, we humans share all the behavior tendencies that together define our human nature. One such tendency, our capacity to learn and adapt, helps explain our individual diversity, explored in previous chapters, and our social diversity, explored here.

Cultural Diversity

Our shrinking world, with its increasingly multicultural countries, more and more confronts us with our diversity.

Cultural Norms and Roles Cultural rules for accepted and expected behavior vary in ways that befuddle people. Cultures differ, for example, in their requirements for personal space, their expressiveness, their pace of life, and the strength of their role expectations.

Individualism Versus Collectivism Individuals and cultures also vary in whether they emphasize individual self-reliance and control or collective solidarity. This cultural factor affects how people define their self-concepts, make judgments of others, and relate to their families. Industrialized cultures derived from northern Europe are predominantly individualist; those of Asia, Africa, and Central and South America are more collectivist.

Ethnicity Common ancestors and cultural heritage define one's ethnicity. Ethnic groups have developed differing cultural styles. For example, African-Americans tend to be more expressive than European-Americans. Nevertheless, individual differences within ethnic groups greatly exceed differences between the groups.

One's ethnic awareness varies with the situation. In general, we are conscious of our distinctiveness and oblivious to our commonalities. We become especially conscious of our nationality, our sex, or our ethnicity when we are the different ones. And though the phenomenon of ingroup bias leads people to favor the group with which they identify, people who manage to be bicultural typically enjoy a more positive self-esteem than do socially marginal people. As countries become more diverse, we struggle with how to be multicultural yet unified.

Gender Diversity

In considering how culture shapes social diversity we must also consider the nature and nurture of gender.

Gender Similarities and Differences The sexes are in many ways alike, but their differences excite more interest. Although fewer girls than boys have reading and speech disorders, males and females don't noticeably differ in average verbal ability. Males do, however, retain a small edge in the ability to solve math problems and a more significant edge on some spacial tasks. Women and men, like Asians and North Americans, differ in their social connectedness. Boys define themselves apart from their caregivers and playmates, girls through their social ties. As adults, women typically become more caring, supportive, and empathic, and men more independent, self-reliant, and unexpressive. Research studies also reveal male-female diversity in aggressiveness, social dominance, and sexual initiative.

Is Biology Destiny? Hormonal differences, stemming from evolved biological sex differences, help explain certain sex differences. But biology is not destiny. What biology initiates, culture accentuates.

The Social Construction of Gender Cultural socialization explains why some children become more gender-typed than others and why gender roles vary so sharply across cultures and over time.

Changing Gender Roles Across the Life Span The social differences between males and females peak in late adolescence and early adulthood and diminish thereafter, apparently as people graduate from traditional courtship and early parental roles.

Responding to Diversity

Although conscious of our cultural, ethnic, and gender diversity, we also face social and global challenges that require unified answers. What factors impede and promote our sense of human kinship?

Rejecting Diversity Although overt racial and gender animosity have declined, prejudice still surfaces in blatant and subtle ways. Prejudice often arises from social inequalities, social divisions, and emotional scapegoating. New research shows that stereotypes also are a cognitive by-product of our natural ways of simplifying our complex worlds. Conflicts between individuals and cultures often arise from malignant social processes. These include social traps: Each party, by protecting and pursuing its self-interest, creates an outcome that no one wants. The spiral of conflict also feeds and is fed by distorted mirror-image perceptions, in which each party views itself as moral and the other as untrustworthy and evil-intentioned.

Accepting Diversity Enemies sometimes become friends, especially when the circumstances favor cooperation toward superordinate goals, understanding through communication, and reciprocated conciliatory gestures.

Terms and Concepts to Remember

culture The enduring behaviors, ideas, attitudes, and traditions shared by a large group of people and transmitted from one generation to the next.

personal space The buffer zone we like to maintain around our bodies.

individualism Giving priority to one's own goals over group goals, and defining one's identity in terms of personal attributes rather than group identifications.

collectivism Giving priority to the goals of one's groups (often one's extended family or work group) and defining one's identity accordingly.

ethnicity That part of one's social identity defined by the ancestors, heritage, and traits one shares with others.

gender In psychology, the characteristics, whether biologically or socially influenced, by which people define male and female.

gender identity One's sense of being male or female. Note: One's gender identity is distinct from one's sexual orientation (as heterosexual or homosexual) and from the strength of one's gender-typing.

gender-typing The acquisition of a masculine or feminine gender identity and role.

gender schema theory The theory that children learn from their cultures a concept of what it means to be male and female and adjust their behavior accordingly.

gender role A set of expected behaviors for males and for females.

prejudice An unjustifiable (and usually negative) attitude toward a group and its members. Prejudice generally involves stereotyped beliefs, negative feelings, and a predisposition to discriminatory action.

stereotype A generalized (often overgeneralized) belief about a group of people.

ingroup bias The tendency to favor one's own group.

scapegoat theory The theory that prejudice provides an outlet for anger by providing someone to blame.

just-world phenomenon The tendency of people to believe the world is just and that people therefore get what they deserve and deserve what they get.

conflict A perceived incompatibility of actions, goals, or ideas.

social traps Situations in which the conflicting parties, by each rationally pursuing their self-interest, become caught in mutually destructive behavior.

mirror-image perceptions Distinct but similar views of one another often held by parties in conflict; each views itself as moral and peace-loving, the other as evil and aggressive.

superordinate goals Shared goals that override differences among people and require their cooperation.

GRIT Graduated and Reciprocated Initiatives in Tension-Reduction—a strategy designed to decrease international tensions.

For Further Information

For further information in this text on culture and multicultural experience, see:

For further information in this text on the psychology of women and men, see:

For Further Reading

Gilmore, D. D. (1990). *Manhood in the making: Cultural concepts of masculinity.* New Haven: Yale University Press.

An anthropologist's readable and informative analysis of how different cultures construct the masculine role.

Segall, M. H., Dasen, P. R., Berry, J. W., & Poortinga, Y. H. (1990). *Human behavior in global perspective.* New York: Pergamon.

Four leading cross-cultural psychologists, from four different countries, review what their field has learned about the impact of culture.

Tavris, C., Wade, C., & Kimmel, M. (1992). *The longest war: Women and men in perspective* (3rd ed.). San Diego, CA: Harcourt Brace Jovanovich.

An informed and delightfully readable discussion of gender.

Unger, R., & Crawford, M. (1992). *Women and gender.* New York: McGraw-Hill.

A state-of-the-art research review and feminist perspective on how we become gendered, with special attention to women's experiences, achievements, and stresses across the life span.

Wagner, R. V., de Rivera, J., & Watkins, M. (Eds.). (1988). Psychology and the promotion of peace. Special Issue of *Journal of Social Issues, 44,* No. 2.

Psychologists offer research-based strategies for peacemaking and disarmament.

Statistical Reasoning in Everyday Life

Appendix

Science fiction writer H. G. Wells predicted that "statistical thinking will one day be as necessary for efficient citizenship as the ability to read and write." If by statistical thinking Wells meant not a technical knowledge of how to compute statistics but rather an understanding of the principles of statistical reasoning, then that day has arrived. Today's statistics are tools that help us see and interpret what the unaided eye might miss.

My aim in this appendix is not to make you a statistical wizard. Rather, it is to help you use the power of statistical reasoning in your own everyday thinking so that you can:

accurately organize and interpret events;

realistically generalize from instances;

improve your critical thinking skills; and

become a more discerning consumer of research reported in the media.

First, I will introduce you to a few basic statistical concepts and formulas. If you are not mathematically inclined, stay with me, rereading where necessary. You will be amazed at how easy it is to grasp the basics.

Describing Data

Researchers or not, we all make observations or gather data that we must organize and interpret. Let's see how we might effectively do this.

Distributions

Laura is a college admissions officer. Attempting to predict which applicants will likely succeed at her school, she sorts through their high school grades, aptitude scores, biographical statements, and recommendation letters. To discover the past academic performance of her pool of applicants, she could thumb through their files and form some impressions. But there is too much information to remember. Moreover, she knows that impressions are swayed by the information available to memory, often the vivid or extreme instances (see the "availability heuristic," page 292).

So instead of trusting her impressions, she begins by organizing the applicants' high school grade point averages (GPAs) into a **frequency distribution** (Table A–1). To do this, she breaks the entire range of scores into equal intervals and then counts the number of scores that fall in each interval. (Table A–1, in fact, presents a frequency distribution of the actual high school GPAs of 50 randomly selected sophomores at my own college.)

To make the general picture easier to see, Laura displays this frequency distribution in a graph called a **histogram** (Figure A–1). Here she represents the frequency of scores within a particular interval as a bar. This histogram also helps Laura see about where any particular student's score falls relative to the others. She can express any student's ranking as a **percentile rank**, which is simply the percentage of scores that fall below a particular score. A student whose percentile rank is 99 has a GPA that exceeds those of 99 percent of all the students. (You can never have a percentile rank of 100. Your score can never exceed those of 100 percent of the people because you are one of them.)

A note of caution: Take care when reading statistical graphs. Depending on what people want to emphasize, they can design the graph to make the same difference look small or big. For example, Laura can make the difference in the average high school GPAs of male and female students seem small or large depending on the units she chooses for the vertical axis (Figure A–2).

Table A–1	*Frequency Distribution of the High School GPAs of 50 College Students*
Interval	**Number of persons in interval**
3.51–4.00	23
3.01–3.50	6
2.51–3.00	16
2.01–2.50	5

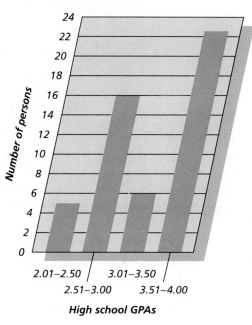

Figure A–1 A histogram of Table A–1's frequency distribution of the high school GPAs of 50 students.

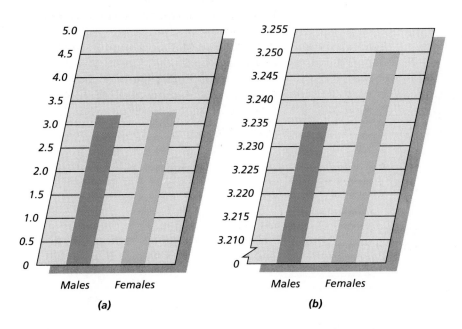

Figure A–2 Two histograms comparing the average high school GPAs of males and females in a sample of 50 students. Notice how a difference in the vertical dimension of the two graphs can make the gap seem either (a) small or (b) large.

The moral: When looking at statistical graphs in books and magazines and on television ads and news broadcasts, always read the labels.

Close-Up   *Florence Nightingale: Pioneer in the Use of Statistics*

Florence Nightingale (1820–1910)

The world remembers Florence Nightingale as a pioneering nurse and hospital reformer. Less well known is her equally pioneering use of statistics. In advocating medical reform, Nightingale also promoted statistical description: She developed a uniform procedure for hospitals to report statistical information. She invented the pie chart, which represents proportions as wedges of a circular diagram. And she struggled to get the study of statistics introduced into higher education.

One of Nightingale's analyses compared the peacetime death rates of British soldiers and civilians. She discovered and showed that the soldiers, who lived in barracks under unhealthy conditions, were twice as likely to die as civilians of the same age and sex (Figure A–3). She then used the soldiers' 2 percent death rate to persuade the Queen and Prime Minister to establish a Royal Commission on the Health of the Army. It is just as criminal, she wrote, for the Army to have a mortality of 20 per 1000 "as it would be to take 1,100 men per annum out upon Salisbury Plain and shoot them."

Bernard Cohen (1984) reports that "Nightingale's commitment to statistics transcended her interest in health care reform, and it was closely tied to her religious convictions. To her, laws governing social phenomena, 'the laws of our moral progress,' were God's laws, to be revealed by statistics."

Figure A–3 Florence Nightingale's histogram comparing peacetime death rates of British soldiers and civilian males illustrates her innovative approach to the presentation of statistics.

Lines
Representing the Relative Mortality of the **Army at Home** and of the **English Male Population** at corresponding Ages.

Ages	Deaths Annually to 1000 living	DEATHS	
20–25	8·4		Englishmen.
	17·0		English Soldiers.
25–30	9·2		Englishmen.
	18·3		English Soldiers.
30–35	10·2		Englishmen.
	18·4		English Soldiers.
35–40	11·6		Englishmen.
	19·3		English Soldiers.

Note.—The Mortality of the English Male Population, at the above ages, is taken from English Life Table (1849–53)

Central Tendencies

Andrew is a government official. To determine the level of poverty in the various small towns in his region, he gathers data about the residents' incomes. To simplify things, he might decide first to calculate the typical income level or *central tendency* for each town. For any distribution of scores (in this case, incomes), there are three commonly used measures of the central tendency. The simplest is the **mode**, the most frequently occurring score. The most commonly reported is the **mean**, or arithmetic average (the total sum of all the scores divided by the number of scores). The **median** is the midmost score — the 50th percentile; if you arrange all the scores in order from the highest to the lowest, half will be above the median and half will be below it.

When the distribution of scores (or incomes) is not symmetrical, the three measures of central tendency tell different stories. Suppose, for instance, that the mean annual family income in the first town Andrew studies is $19,000, whereas mean income in the second town is only $13,000. At first Andrew might assume there are more families living in poverty in the second town. But as Figure A–4 shows, the first town, in which a few wealthy employers and quite a few poorly paid employees live, actually has many families struggling to live on less than $10,000.

The moral: Always take note of the reported measure of central tendency, and consider: Could a few atypical scores be distorting it?

"The poor are getting poorer, but with the rich getting richer it all averages out in the long run."

Drawing by Mirachi; © 1988 The New Yorker Magazine, Inc.

In Brazil, the mean income in 1984 was $1720 and the median income was $808. What does this tell you about the distribution of income in Brazil?

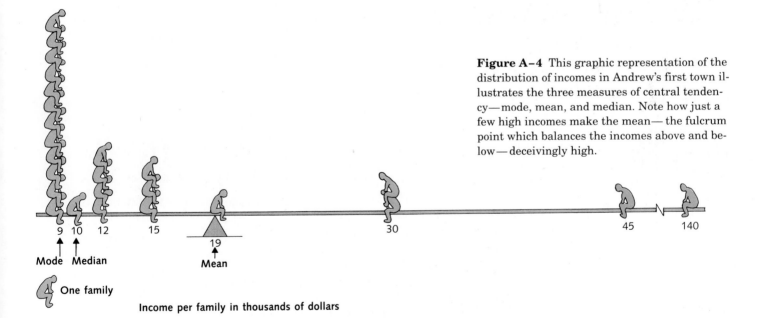

Mode Median

Mean

One family

Income per family in thousands of dollars

Figure A–4 This graphic representation of the distribution of incomes in Andrew's first town illustrates the three measures of central tendency—mode, mean, and median. Note how just a few high incomes make the mean—the fulcrum point which balances the incomes above and below—deceivingly high.

Variation

In any distribution of scores it is often useful to know how much variation there is. Are scores similar or widely spread out? The **range** of scores—the gap between the lowest and highest score—provides only a crude estimate of variation, because just one extreme score in an otherwise uniform group will create a deceptively large range. If, in a small class, all the scores on an exam were between 70 and 80 except for one score of 20, the range of 60 (80 − 20 = 60) would mislead us about the actual amount of variation.

The more standard measure of how much scores deviate from one another is the **standard deviation**. It better gauges whether scores are packed together or dispersed, because it uses information from each score. The standard deviation is important and surprisingly simple to compute: (1) calculate the difference, or deviation, between each score and the mean; (2) square these deviations; (3) find their average; and (4) find the square root of this average.

As an example, consider Peter, the punter on his college football team. To keep track of his progress, he records the distance of each of his punts. He does not trust his gut-level impression of how consistent his punting is. After his first football game, Peter therefore calculates the standard deviation for his four punts (Table A–2).

Table A–2	*Standard Deviation*	
Punting distance	**Deviation from mean (40 yards)**	**Deviation squared**
36	−4	16
38	−2	4
41	+1	1
45	+5	25
Mean = 160/4 = 40		**Sum of (deviations)² = 46**

$$\text{Standard deviation} = \sqrt{\frac{\text{Sum of (deviations)}^2}{\text{Number of scores}}} = \sqrt{\frac{46}{4}} = 3.4 \text{ yards}$$

To grasp the meaning of this statistic, Peter would need to understand how scores tend to be distributed. In nature, large amounts of data—heights, weights, IQ scores, grades, punt distances (though not incomes)—often form a roughly symmetrical, bell-shaped distribution. Most cases fall near the mean and fewer cases fall near either extreme. This bell-shaped distribution is so typical that we call the curve it forms the **normal curve**. As Figure A–5 shows, a useful property of the normal curve is that roughly 68 percent of the cases fall within 1 standard deviation on either side of the mean—in Peter's case, within 3.4 yards of his 40-yard average. Ninety-five percent of cases fall within 2 standard deviations. Thus, Chapter 11, Intelligence, notes that about 68 percent of people taking an intelligence test will score within ±15 IQ points (1 standard deviation) of 100. About 95 percent will score within ±30 points (2 standard deviations).

Correlation

In this book we often ask how much two things relate: How closely do the personality scores of twins relate to one another? How well do IQ scores predict school grades? How often does stress portend disease? To get a feel for whether one set of scores relates to a second set, let's once again begin graphically, with a **scatterplot**.

Figure A–5 The normal curve. Data often form a normal or bell-shaped curve in which 68 percent of the cases fall within 1 standard deviation of the mean and 95 percent fall within 2 standard deviations. For example, on an IQ test such as the WAIS, we assign the mean a value of 100 and 1 standard deviation we call 15 points; therefore 68 percent of the scores fall between 85 and 115, and 95 percent fall between 70 and 130.

Figure A–6 Scatterplots of (a) the relationship between total SAT scores (verbal and mathematical) and first-year college GPAs and (b) the closer relationship between high school and first-year GPAs of 50 college students. Each point represents the data for one student.

Figure A–6a depicts the actual relationship between SAT scores and college first-year GPAs for the 50 college students we met earlier. Each point on the graph represents these two numbers for one student. Figure A–6b is a scatterplot of the relationship between these students' high school and college GPAs.

The **correlation coefficient** is a statistical measure of how strongly related any two sets of scores are. It can range from

+1.00, which means that one set of scores increases in direct proportion to the other

through 0.00, meaning that the scores are unrelated

to –1.00, which means that one set of scores goes up precisely as the other goes down.

Perfect positive correlation (+1.00)

No relationship (0.00)

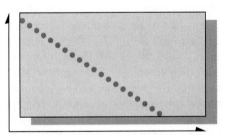
Perfect negative correlation (–1.00)

(Note that a correlation being negative has nothing to do with its strength or weakness; a negative correlation means two things relate inversely. A weak correlation, indicating little or no relationship, is one that has a coefficient near zero.) Now look again at the scatterplots in Figure A–6. Do the correlations look as if they were positive or negative?

In each scatterplot in Figure A–6, the upward slope of the cluster of points as one moves to the right shows that the two sets of scores tend to rise together. This means the correlations are positive: +.64 for the SAT–college GPA relationship shown in Figure A–6a, and a stronger +.80 for the high school GPA–college GPA relationship shown in A–6b. As SAT scores and, especially, high school grades go up, so do college grades. (The GPA–GPA relationship, incidentally, illustrates the common finding that the best predictor of people's future behavior is usually their behavior in similar situations in the past. Still, people can and do change.)

Some examples of positive correlations:
   Child abuse and children's
      aggressiveness
   Education and income
   Achievement motivation and grades

Some examples of negative correlations:
   Self-esteem and depression
   Age and deep sleep
   Stress and health

I said at the beginning that statistics can help us see what the naked eye sometimes misses. To demonstrate this for yourself, try to discern what relationship, if any, exists between two sets of scores not organized into a scatterplot. As an example, Elaine wonders whether men's heights correlate with their temperaments. She measures the heights of 20 men, has someone else independently assess their temperaments (from 0 for extremely calm and placid to 100 for highly reactive), and obtains the data in Table A–3.

With all the relevant data right in front of you, can you tell whether there is (1) a positive correlation between height and reactive temperament, (2) very little or no correlation, or (3) a negative correlation?

Comparing the columns in Table A–3, most people detect very little relationship between height and temperament. In fact, the correlation in this imaginary example is moderately positive, +.57, as you could see if you made a scatterplot of the data. If we fail to see a relationship when data are presented as systematically as in this table, how much less likely are we to notice them in everyday life? To see what is right in front of us, we sometimes need statistical illumination. People can easily see evidence of sex discrimination when given statistically summarized information about job level, seniority, performance, sex, and salary. But they will often see no sex discrimination when the same information dribbles in, case by case (Twiss & others, 1989).

The moral: The correlation coefficient tells us nothing about cause and effect, but it can help us see the world more clearly by revealing the actual extent to which two things relate.

Illusory Correlations We sometimes also "see" relationships that do not exist. A perceived correlation that does not really exist is an **illusory correlation**. When we *believe* there is a relationship between two things, we are likely to *notice* and *recall* instances that confirm our belief (Trolier & Hamilton, 1986). In one experiment, people saw the results of a hypothetical, 50-day experiment (Ward & Jenkins, 1965). For each of the 50 days, the subjects learned whether or not the clouds had been "seeded" to produce rain and whether or not it had rained. The "results" given were actually random; they showed no relationship between cloud seeding and rainfall. Nevertheless, the subjects typically perceived—in keeping with what they expected—a positive relationship between cloud seeding and rainfall.

Because we are sensitive to dramatic or unusual events, we are especially likely to notice and remember the occurrence of two such events in sequence—say, a premonition of an unlikely phone call followed by the call. When the call does not follow the premonition, we are less likely to note and remember the nonevent.

Likewise, instances of positive-thinking people being cured of cancer impress those who believe positive attitudes counter disease. But to assess whether positive thinking actually affects cancer, we need three more types of information. First, we need an estimate of how many positive thinkers *weren't* cured. And among those *not* trying to heal themselves through positive thinking, we need to know how many were and weren't cured. Without these comparison figures, positive examples of a few hope-filled people tell us nothing about the actual correlation between attitudes and disease.

Table A–3	*Height and Temperament of 20 Men*	
Subject	**Height in inches**	**Temperament**
1	80	75
2	63	66
3	61	60
4	79	90
5	74	60
6	69	42
7	62	42
8	75	60
9	77	81
10	60	39
11	64	48
12	76	69
13	71	72
14	66	57
15	73	63
16	70	75
17	63	30
18	71	30
19	68	84
20	70	39

The moral: When we notice and remember vivid, random co-incidences, we may forget that they are random and see them as correlated. Thus, we can easily deceive ourselves by seeing what is not there.

Regression Toward the Mean Illusory correlations feed another illusion—that chance events are subject to our personal control. Gamblers, remembering their lucky rolls, may come to believe they can influence the roll of the dice by again, say, throwing gently for low numbers and hard for high numbers. The illusion that uncontrollable events correlate with our actions is also fed by a statistical phenomenon called **regression toward the mean**. Average results are more typical than extreme results. Thus, after an unusual event, things tend to return toward their average level; that is, extraordinary happenings tend to be followed by more ordinary ones.

Examples are abundant: Basketball players who make or miss all their shots in the first half of the game are likely to "regress" (fall back) to their more usual performance level during the second half. Students who score much lower or higher on an exam than they usually do are likely, when retested, to regress toward their average. Unusual ESP subjects who defy chance when first tested nearly always lose their "psychic powers" when retested (a phenomenon that parapsychologists have called the "decline effect").

The point may seem obvious, yet we regularly miss it. Thus, we may attribute what may be a normal statistical regression (the expected falling back to normal) to something we have done:

> After doing miserably on the first test, we may stop reading the chapter summaries before reading the chapters and then do better on the second test. We may then attribute our improvement to the new study technique.

> After a sudden crime wave, the town council initiates a "stop crime" drive and the crime rate then returns to previous levels. The drive may therefore appear more successful than it was.

> Coaches who yell at their players after an unusually bad first half may feel rewarded for having done so when the team's performance improves (returns to normal) during the second half.

> Scientists who win a Nobel prize often have diminished accomplishments thereafter, leading some to wonder whether winning a Nobel hinders creativity.

> Some people also believe there is a *"Sports Illustrated* jinx"—that athletes whose peak performances get them on the cover of the magazine will then suffer a decline in their performance.

In each of these cases, it is possible that the effect is genuine. It is more likely, however, that these represent the natural tendency for behavior to regress from the unusual to the more usual.

Failure to recognize regression is the source of many superstitions and some ineffective practices as well. When day-to-day behavior has a large element of chance fluctuation, we may notice that others' behavior improves (regresses toward average) after we criticize them for very bad performance, and worsens (regresses toward average) after we warmly praise them for an exceptionally fine performance. Ironically, then, regression toward the average can mislead us into feeling rewarded for having criticized others and punished for having praised them (Tversky & Kahneman, 1974).

The moral: When a fluctuating behavior returns to normal, there is no need to invent fancy explanations for why it does. Regression toward the mean is probably at work.

Generalizing from Instances

So far we have seen how statistical reasoning helps us digest and describe information more accurately. Statistical reasoning also helps in a second important way: to make correct leaps of understanding from our samples of information to what is generally true.

Populations and Samples

A **population** is the whole group we are interested in. For convenience, we often observe just a small sample drawn from a population and then generalize about the whole population. We meet a few students and attend a few classes during a visit to a college and infer from those instances how friendly the campus is and how good the teaching is. We observe the weather during a week-long visit to Seattle and then tell our friends about the climate there. Obviously, we had better be careful when drawing conclusions from specific people or events. Let's take a look at some principles that can guide us when generalizing from instances.

Principle 1: Representative Samples Are Better Than Biased Samples It is often tempting to overgeneralize from highly select samples. For example, we can delude ourselves about the actual difference between two groups when we compare members drawn from their extremes. In the 1988 Olympics, the competitors in the finals of the men's 100-meter dash were predominantly Black. How much would this tell us about the sprinting abilities of the different races? As you can see from the hypothetical illustration in Figure A–7, knowing that any individual is a member of race X or race Y may tell us virtually nothing about the person's sprinting abilities. The same is true when the superstars in some nonathletic pursuit come mostly from a given race, culture, or gender. Though it seems obvious, this principle is often missed in everyday life.

We are particularly prone to overgeneralize when the extremes are vivid cases. Given (a) a statistical summary of the evaluations of all of Professor Zeno's students, and (b) the vivid comments of two irate students, an administrator's impression of the professor may be as much influenced by the two unhappy students as by the favorable evaluations of the many. Driving into Chicago from the south, many people see the miles of tenement houses near the highway and think, "What an ugly city this is." Standing in the checkout line at the supermarket, George sees the woman in front of him pay with food stamps and then drive away in a Cadillac. "What an easy life these welfare cheats have!" he later tells his friends. In each of these situations, the temptation to generalize from a few unrepresentative but vivid cases is nearly irresistible.

The moral: The best basis for generalizing is not from the exceptional cases one finds at the extremes, but from a representative sample of cases.

"Once you become sensitized to it, you see regression everywhere."
Psychologist Daniel Kahneman (1985)

Figure A–7 Hypothetical normal curves for sprinting ability for two races. As you can see, sampling from the extremes is not the best basis for inferring general racial differences.

Principle 2: Random Sequences May Not Look Random As we noted in Chapter 1, we generate a representative sample of any population by gathering a *random* sample—one in which each person in the population has an equal chance of being selected. As chance would have it, though, random sequences often do not look random. If someone flipped a coin six times, would one of the following sequences of heads (H) and tails (T) be more likely than the other two: HHHTTT or HTTHTH or HHHHHH?

Daniel Kahneman and Amos Tversky (1972) found that most people believe HTTHTH would be the most likely random sequence. Actually, all possible sequences are equally likely to occur (or, you might say, equally unlikely). A bridge or poker hand of 10 through Ace, all of hearts, would seem extraordinary; actually, it would be no more or less likely than any other specific hand of cards.

The failure to recognize random occurrences for what they are can predispose people to seek extraordinary explanations for ordinary events. Imagine that on one warm spring day 4000 college students gather for a coin-tossing contest. Their task is to flip heads. On the first toss, 2000 students do so and advance to the second round. As you might expect, about 1000 of these progress to a third round, 500 to a fourth, 250 to a fifth, 125 to a sixth, 62 to a seventh, 31 to an eighth, 15 to a ninth, and 8 amazing individuals, having flipped heads nine times in a row with ever-increasing displays of concentration and effort, advance to the tenth round.

By now, the crowd of losers is in awestruck silence as these expert coin tossers prepare to display their amazing ability yet again. The proceedings are temporarily halted so that a panel of impartial scientists can observe and document the incredible achievement of these gifted individuals. Alas, on succeeding tosses they each flip one or more tails. "But, of course," their admirers say, "coin tossing is a highly sensitive skill. The tense, pressured atmosphere created by the scientific scrutiny has disturbed their fragile gift."

Sometimes, though, events seem so extraordinary that we struggle to conceive an ordinary, chance-related explanation. In such cases, statisticians often are less mystified. When Evelyn Marie Adams won the New Jersey lottery twice, newspapers reported the odds of her feat as 1 in 17 trillion. Bizarre? Actually, 1 in 17 trillion are the odds that a given person who buys a single ticket for two New Jersey lotteries will win both times. But statisticians Stephen Samuels and George McCabe (1989) report that, given the millions of people who buy U.S. state lottery tickets, it was "practically a sure thing" that someday, somewhere, someone would hit a state jackpot twice. Indeed, say fellow statisticians Persi Diaconis and Frederick Mosteller (1989), "With a large enough sample, any outrageous thing is likely to happen." Ron Vachon was astounded during a September, 1990, baseball game in Boston. Oakland A's outfielder Rickey Henderson hit foul balls right to him on successive pitches. That something like that should have happened to Vachon (who dropped them both) was incredibly unlikely. That it sometime would happen to someone was not. In North America, an event that happens to but 1 in 100 million people every day occurs about three times a day, 1000 times a year.

The moral: Whether watching basketball, choosing stocks, or flipping coins (see Close-Up), remember: Random sequences often don't look random. Even when the next outcome cannot be predicted from the preceding ones, streaks will occur.

Your chances of being dealt either of these exact hands is precisely the same: 1 in 2,598,960.

Bizarre-looking, perhaps. But actually no more unlikely than any other number sequence.

© 1990 by Sidney Harris/American Scientist Magazine

Close-Up **When You're Hot You're Hot, Right?**
Random Sequences That Don't Look Random

Every basketball player and fan "knows" that players have hot and cold streaks. Players who have "hot hands" can't seem to miss while those who have "cold" ones can't find the center of the hoop. When Thomas Gilovich, Robert Vallone, and Amos Tversky (1985) interviewed team members of the Philadelphia 76ers, the players estimated they were about 25 percent more likely to make a shot after they had just made one than after a miss. In one survey, 9 in 10 basketball fans agreed that a player "has a better chance of making a shot after having just *made* his last two or three shots than he does after having just *missed* his last two or three shots." Believing in shooting streaks, players will feed a teammate who has just made two or three shots in a row, and many coaches will bench the player who has just missed three in a row.

The only trouble is, it isn't true. When Gilovich and his collaborators studied detailed individual shooting records, they found that the 76ers—and the Boston Celtics, the New Jersey Nets, the New York Knicks, and Cornell University's men's and women's basketball players—were equally likely to score after a miss as after a basket. A typical 50 percent shooter averages 50 percent after just missing three shots, and 50 percent after just making three shots.

Why, then, do players and fans alike believe that players are more likely to score after scoring and miss after missing? In any series of 20 shots by a 50 percent shooter (or 20 flips of a coin), there is a 50-50 chance of four baskets (or heads) in a row, and it is quite possible that 1 person out of 5 will have a streak of five or six. Players and fans notice these random streaks and so form the myth that "when you're hot you're hot" (Figure A–8).

The same misinterpretation of random sequences is common in other settings. Hospital workers sometimes notice streaks of male births or female births. Not realizing that random sequences usually contain such

Statistical intuition goes awry. Detroit Pistons basketball fans perceive Vinnie ("Microwave") Johnson as a premier streak shooter. He and his teammates apparently share this perception. During the 1987–88 season, the likelihood of Johnson *taking* his team's next shot was 20 percent when he missed the Pistons' last shot attempt, and 45 percent when he made it. Although shooting more after scoring increased his chances for a streak of baskets made, he was actually no more likely to make a basket following a make than a miss (Tversky & Gilovich, 1989a,b).

streaks, they may attribute them to mysterious forces, such as phases of the moon.

Likewise, many investors believe that a mutual fund which has had a string of good years will likely outperform one that has had a string of bad years. Based on that assumption, investment magazines report mutual funds' performance. But, as economist Burton Malkiel (1989a) documents, past performances of mutual funds do *not* predict their future performance. When funds have streaks of several good or bad years, we may nevertheless be fooled into thinking that past success predicts future success.

Figure A–8 Who is the chance shooter? Here are 21 consecutive shots, each scoring either a basket or a miss, by two players who each make 50 percent. Within this sample of shots, which player's sequence looks more like what we would expect in a random sequence? (See page 634.) (Adapted from Barry Ross, *Discover*, 1987.)

Principle 3: More Cases Are Better Than Fewer I have seen it happen: An eager high school senior visits two college campuses, each for a day. At the first, the student randomly attends three classes and discovers each instructor to be witty and engaging. At the next campus, the three instructors sampled seem dull and uninspiring. Returning home, the student tells friends what "great teachers" there are at the first school, and what "bores" the faculty are at the second school. Again, we know it but we ignore it: Small samples provide less reliable estimates of the average than do large samples. The proportion of heads in samples of 10 coin tosses varies more than in samples of 100 tosses.

Said differently, *averages based on more cases are more reliable* (less variable) than averages based on only a few cases. Knowing this, maybe you will come up with different answers to a question posed by Christopher Jepson, David Krantz, and Richard Nisbett (1983) to University of Michigan introductory psychology students:

> The registrar's office at the University of Michigan has found that usually about 100 students in Arts and Sciences have a 4.00 GPA at the end of their first term at the University. However, only about 10–15 students graduate with a 4.00 GPA. What do you think is the most likely explanation for the fact that there are more 4.00 GPAs after one term than at graduation?

Most of the students come up with plausible causes for the drop in GPA, such as, "Students tend to work harder at the beginning of their college careers than toward the end." Fewer than a third recognized the statistical phenomenon clearly at work: Averages based on fewer courses are more variable, which guarantees a greater number of extremely low and high GPAs at the end of the first term.

The moral: Don't be overly impressed by a few anecdotes. Generalizations based on only a few cases are unreliable.

Principle 4: Less Variable Observations Are Better Than Highly Variable Observations Averages derived from scores with low variability (such as Peter's punts, which varied by only 9 yards) are more reliable than averages based on scores with high variability. If Peter's four punts in the first game had ranged from 20 to 60 yards, we should be less confident that his 40-yard average would be close to the average of his punts in the next game.

Intuitively, you know this to be the case. You might therefore respond much as did the students in another experiment by Nisbett and his colleagues (1983): Imagine that you are an explorer who has landed on a little-known island in the southeastern Pacific. You encounter three natives, each obese and brown-skinned. What percentage of all the natives on the island would you expect to be obese? brown-skinned? Knowing that body weight is more variable than skin color within a geographical group, the students in the experiment much more often inferred that all the people of the island were brown than that all were obese.

Well and good. The problem comes when we falsely assume groups to be relatively homogeneous. And that is typically what we do with unfamiliar "outgroups." Many experiments show that we perceive groups we don't know as being more homogeneous than groups we know well.

With this in mind, put yourself in the place of the students to whom George Quattrone and Edward Jones (1980) showed a videotape of a subject who chose to sit either alone or with others while awaiting an experiment. Some of these Princeton University students were told the videotaped subject attended Princeton; others were told the subject attended Rutgers. Asked to guess what percentage of the remaining subjects in the experiment similarly chose to wait alone or with others, the viewers were willing to generalize from the single case *if* the supposed subject came from the other school. For example, if the videotaped subject chose to wait with others and was said to be from Rutgers, the Princeton viewers formed an impression of Rutgers students as a sociable group and guessed that most of the Rutgers subjects chose to wait with others. (Rutgers students were similarly more likely to overgeneralize from the behavior of a supposed Princeton student than from the behavior of a supposed Rutgers student.)

The moral: Less variable observations do indeed provide a better basis for generalizing than highly variable observations; nevertheless, we often misperceive people in other groups as being more uniform than they are.

Testing Differences

We have seen that we can have more confidence in the generalizations we make from samples that are (1) representative of the population we wish to study, (2) larger rather than smaller, and (3) less rather than more variable. These principles extend to the inferences we make about differences between groups. So, when can we generalize from a difference we have observed— say, from the male versus female GPA difference in Figure A–2 to the whole campus population of males and females?

Statistical tests help us decide by indicating the reliability of such differences. You needn't understand how they are computed to understand the logic behind them: When *averages* from two samples are each *reliable* measures of their respective populations (as when each is based on many observations that have a small standard deviation), then the difference between the samples is likely to be reliable as well. When the *difference* between the averages for the two samples is *large*, we have even more confidence that the difference between them reflects a real difference in their populations.

In short, when the sample averages are reliable and the difference between them is large, we say the difference has **statistical significance**. This simply means that the difference very likely reflects a real difference and is not due to chance variation between the samples.

When reading about research, you should remember that, given large enough or homogeneous enough samples, a difference between them may be "significant" yet unimportant. For example, when comparing the IQs among several hundred thousand first-born and later-born individuals, there is a highly significant tendency for first-born individuals within a family to have higher average scores than their later-born siblings, but only by a single IQ point or two (Zajonc & Markus, 1975).

The moral: "Statistical significance" does not equal importance; it means the difference is very probably not due to chance.

Answer to Figure A–8 (page 632): Player B, whose outcomes may look more random, actually has fewer streaks than would be expected by chance. For these players, chance shooting, like chance coin tossing, should produce a change in outcome about 50 percent of the time. But 70 percent of the time (14 times out of 20) Player B's outcome changes on successive shots. Player A, on the other hand, is scoring randomly; 10 times out of 20 Player A's next outcome is different.

Using the basic statistical tools discussed in this appendix can help you to think critically—to see more clearly what you might otherwise miss or misinterpret and to generalize more accurately from your observations. People who understand and use the principles of statistics think more rationally (Nisbett & others, 1987). It requires training and practice, but developing the ability to think clearly and critically is part of becoming an educated person. The report of the Project on Redefining the Meaning and Purpose of Baccalaureate Degrees (1985) eloquently asserts why there are few higher priorities in a college education:

> If anything is paid attention to in our colleges and universities, thinking must be it. Unfortunately, thinking can be lazy. It can be sloppy. . . . It can be fooled, misled, bullied. . . . Students possess great untrained and untapped capacities for logical thinking, critical analysis, and inquiry, but these are capacities that are not spontaneous: They grow out of wide instruction, experience, encouragement, correction, and constant use.

Summing Up

To be an educated person today is to be able to apply simple statistical principles to everyday reasoning. One needn't remember complicated formulas to think more clearly and critically about data.

From our consideration of how we can organize and describe data—by constructing distributions and computing measures of central tendency, variation, and correlation—we derived five practical morals for statistical reasoning:

1. When looking at statistical graphs in books and magazines and on TV ads and news broadcasts, always read the labels.

2. Note which measure of central tendency is reported, and consider: Could a few atypical scores be distorting it?

3. The correlation coefficient tells us nothing about cause and effect, but it *can* help us see the world more clearly by revealing the actual extent to which two things relate.

4. When we notice and remember vivid, random events, we may forget that they are random and see them as correlated. Thus, we can easily be deceived into seeing what is not there.

5. When a fluctuating behavior returns to normal, there is no need to invent fancy explanations for why it does. Regression toward the mean is probably at work.

From our consideration of how we can appropriately leap from samples of data to conclusions about what is generally true we derived five more practical morals:

6. The best basis for generalizing is not from the exceptional, memorable cases one finds at the extremes but from a representative sample of cases.

7. Whether watching basketball, choosing stocks, or flipping coins, remember the statistical principle that random sequences often don't look random. Even when the next outcome is unpredictable, streaks can be expected.

8. Don't be overly impressed by a few anecdotes. Generalizations based on only a few cases are unreliable.

9. Less variable observations provide a better basis for generalizing than highly variable observations; nevertheless, we often misperceive people in other groups as being more uniform than they actually are.

10. "Statistical significance" does not equal importance; rather, it means the observed difference is probably not due to chance.

Terms and Concepts to Remember

frequency distribution A listing of the number of individual scores that occur within each equal-sized interval within a distribution.

histogram A bar graph depicting a frequency distribution.

percentile rank The percentage of the scores in a distribution that a given score exceeds.

mode The most frequently occurring score in a distribution.

mean The arithmetic average of a distribution, obtained by adding the scores and then dividing by the number of scores.

median The middle score in a distribution; half the scores are above it and half are below it.

range The difference between the highest and lowest scores in a distribution.

standard deviation A measure of score variability; computed by (1) calculating the deviation of each score from the mean, (2) squaring those deviations, (3) finding their average, and (4) finding the square root of this average.

normal curve (or normal distribution) A symmetrical, bell-shaped curve that describes the distribution of many types of data; most scores fall near the mean (68 percent fall within 1 standard deviation of it) and fewer and fewer near the extremes.

scatterplot A graphed cluster of dots, each of which represents the values of two variables (such as a student's high school and college GPAs). The slope of the points suggests the degree and direction of the relationship between the two variables. (Also called a *scattergram* or *scatter diagram*.)

correlation coefficient A measure of the direction and extent of the relationship between two sets of scores. Scores with a *positive correlation coefficient* go up and down together (as with high school and college GPAs). A *negative correlation coefficient* indicates that one score falls as the other rises (as in the relationship between self-esteem and depression).

illusory correlation The perception of a relationship where none exists.

regression toward the mean The tendency for extreme or unusual scores to fall back (regress) toward the average.

population All the cases in a group, from which samples may be drawn for study.

statistical significance A statistical statement of how likely it is that an obtained result occurred by chance.

For Further Reading

Huff, D. (1954). *How to lie with statistics.* New York: Norton.

An easy-to-read little book on the uses and abuses of statistics. It suggests how to recognize and see through the deceptive ways people use statistics.

Nisbett, R., & Ross, L. (1980). *Human inference: Strategies and shortcomings in social judgments.* Englewood Cliffs, NJ: Prentice-Hall.

This provocative and playful book, written by two prominent social psychologists, reveals the common errors of thinking we can fall into when we fail to use the principles of statistical reasoning. Recommended reading for anyone who wishes to think more clearly and critically.

Paulos, J. A. (1988). *Innumeracy: Mathematical illiteracy and its consequences.* New York: Hill and Wang.

A delightful book filled with humorous examples of how our mathematical intuition fails us, and why we need to become more mathematically and statistically literate.

Shaughnessy, J. J., & Zechmeister, E. B. (1990). *Research methods in psychology* (2nd ed.). New York: McGraw-Hill.

An excellent, gentle introduction to basic statistical methods and procedures used by psychologists; shows how our everyday use of them can sharpen our reasoning.

Stanovich, K. E. (1992). *How to think straight about psychology (3rd ed.).* Glenview, IL: Scott Foresman.

A delightful read for those who want to think straight about many things; alerts us to how popular media mislead, and how we deceive ourselves.

Glossary

absolute threshold The minimum stimulation needed to detect a particular stimulus. (p. 133)

accommodation 1. Adapting one's current understandings (schemas) to incorporate new information. (p. 70) 2. The process by which the eye's lens changes shape to focus the image of near objects on the retina. (p. 138)

acetylcholine [ah-seat-el-KO-leen] **(ACh)** A neurotransmitter that, among its functions, triggers muscle contraction. (p. 31)

achievement motivation A desire for significant accomplishment: for mastery of things, people, or ideas; for attaining a high standard. (p. 370)

achievement tests Tests designed to assess what a person has learned. (p. 321)

acoustic encoding The encoding of sound, especially the sound of words. (p. 257)

acquisition The initial stage of learning, during which a response is established and gradually strengthened. In classical conditioning, the phase in which a stimulus comes to evoke a conditioned response. In operant conditioning, the strengthening of a reinforced response. (p. 230)

active listening Empathic listening in which the listener echoes, restates, and clarifies. A feature of Rogers' person-centered therapy. (p. 483)

adaptation-level phenomenon The tendency for our judgments (of sounds, of lights, of income) to be relative to a "neutral" level defined by our experience. (p. 398)

adolescence The transition period from childhood to adulthood, extending from puberty to independence. (p. 95)

adrenal [ah-DREEN-el] **glands** A pair of endocrine glands just above the kidneys. The adrenals secrete the hormones epinephrine (adrenaline) and norepinephrine (noradrenaline), which help to arouse the body in times of stress. (p. 41)

aerial perspective A monocular cue for perceiving distance; hazier objects appear more distant than nearby objects. (p. 168)

aerobic exercise Sustained exercise that increases heart and lung fitness; may also alleviate depression and anxiety. (p. 528)

age regression In hypnosis, the supposed reliving of earlier experiences, such as in early childhood; greatly susceptible to false recollections. (p. 204)

aggression Any physical or verbal behavior intended to hurt or destroy. (p. 567)

algorithm A methodical, logical rule or procedure for solving a particular problem. May be contrasted with the usually speedier, but also more error-prone use of *heuristics*. (p. 287)

alpha waves The relatively slow brain waves of a relaxed, awake state. (p. 193)

altruism Unselfish regard for the welfare of others. (p. 574)

Alzheimer's disease A progressive and irreversible brain disorder characterized by gradual deterioration of memory, reasoning, language, and, finally, physical functioning. (p. 112)

amnesia Loss of memory. Psychogenic amnesia, a dissociative disorder, is selective memory loss often brought on by extreme stress. (p. 455)

amphetamines Drugs that stimulate neural activity, causing speeded-up body functions and associated energy and mood changes. (p. 212)

amygdala [ah-MIG-dah-la] Two almond-shaped neural centers in the limbic system that are linked to emotion. (p. 39)

anal stage The second of Freud's psychosexual stages, from about 18 months to 3 years, during which pleasure focuses on bowel and bladder elimination, retention, and control. (p. 414)

anorexia nervosa An eating disorder in which a normal-weight person (usually an adolescent female) diets to become significantly (15 percent or more) underweight, yet, still feeling fat, continues to starve. (p. 359)

antisocial personality A personality disorder in which the person (usually a man) exhibits a lack of conscience for wrongdoing, even toward friends and family members. May be aggressive and ruthless or a clever con artist. (p. 471)

anxiety disorders Psychological disorders characterized by distressing, persistent anxiety or maladaptive behaviors that reduce anxiety. See *generalized anxiety disorder, obsessive-compulsive disorder, panic attack*, and *phobic disorder*. (p. 451)

aphasia Impairment of language, usually caused by left hemisphere damage either to Broca's area (impairing speaking) or to Wernicke's area (impairing understanding). (p. 45)

applied research Scientific study that aims to solve practical problems. (p. 8)

aptitude tests Tests designed to predict a person's future performance; aptitude is the capacity to learn. (p. 321)

artificial intelligence (AI) The science of designing and programming computer systems to do intelligent things and to simulate human thought processes such as intuitive reasoning, learning, and understanding language. Includes practical applications (chess playing, industrial robots, expert systems) and efforts to model human thinking inspired by our current understanding of how the brain works. (p. 299)

assimilation Interpreting one's new experience in terms of one's existing schemas. (p. 70)

association areas Areas of the cerebral cortex that are not involved in primary motor or sensory functions; rather, they are involved in higher mental functions such as learning, remembering, thinking, and speaking. (p. 44)

attachment An emotional tie with another person; shown in young children by their seeking closeness to the caregiver and showing distress on separation. (p. 76)

attitude A belief and feeling that predisposes one to respond in a particular way to objects, people, and events. (p. 553)

attribution theory The theory that we tend to give a causal explanation for someone's behavior, often by crediting either the situation or the person's disposition. (p. 551)

audition The sense of hearing. (p. 145)

automatic processing Unconscious encoding of incidental information, such as space, time, and frequency, and of well-learned information, such as word meanings. (p. 257)

autonomic [aw-tuh-NAHM-ik] **nervous system** The part of the peripheral nervous system that controls the glands and the muscles of the internal organs (such as the heart). Its sympathetic division arouses; its parasympathetic division calms. (p. 33)

availability heuristic A rule of thumb for estimating the likelihood of events based on their availability in memory; if instances come readily to mind (perhaps because of their vividness), we presume such events are likely. (p. 292)

aversive conditioning A type of counterconditioning that associates an unpleasant state (such as nausea) with an unwanted behavior (such as drinking alcohol). (p. 488)

axon The extension of a neuron ending in branching terminal fibers through which messages are sent to other neurons or to muscles or glands. (p. 29)

babbling stage Beginning at 3 to 4 months, the stage of speech development in which the infant spontaneously utters various sounds at first unrelated to the household language. (p. 303)

barbiturates Drugs that depress the activity of the central nervous system, reducing anxiety, but impairing memory and judgment. (p. 212)

basic research Pure science; aims to increase the scientific knowledge base. (p. 8)

basic trust According to Erik Erikson, a sense that the world is predictable and trustworthy; said to be formed during infancy by appropriate experiences with responsive caregivers. (p. 80)

behavior modification The application of operant conditioning principles to the modification of human behavior. (p. 490)

behavior therapy Therapy that applies learning principles to the elimination of unwanted behaviors. (p. 487)

behavioral medicine An interdisciplinary field that integrates and applies behavioral and medical knowledge to health and disease. (p. 511)

behavioral perspective Emphasizes environmental influences on observable behaviors. (p. 7)

behaviorism The view that (1) psychology should be an objective science that (2) studies only overt behavior without reference to mental processes. Most research psychologists today agree with (1) but not (2). (p. 228)

belief bias The tendency for one's preexisting beliefs to distort logical reasoning, sometimes by making invalid conclusions seem valid or valid conclusions seem invalid. (p. 297)

belief perseverance Clinging to one's initial conceptions after the basis on which they were formed has been discredited. (p. 297)

binocular cues Depth cues, such as retinal disparity and convergence, that depend on the use of two eyes. (p. 167)

biofeedback A system for electronically recording, amplifying, and feeding back information regarding a subtle physiological state, such as blood pressure or muscle tension. (p. 529)

biological perspective Emphasizes the influences of heredity and physiology upon our behaviors, emotions, memories, and sensory experiences. (p. 7)

biological psychology A branch of psychology concerned with the links between biology and behavior. (Some biological psychologists call themselves *behavioral neuroscientists, neuropsychologists, physiological psychologists*, or *biopsychologists*.) (p. 27)

bipolar disorder A mood disorder in which the person alternates between the hopelessness and lethargy of depression and the overexcited state of mania. (p. 458)

blind spot The point at which the optic nerve leaves the eye, creating a "blind" spot because no receptor cells are located there. (p. 140)

brainstem The central core of the brain, beginning where the spinal cord swells as it enters the skull; it is the oldest part of the brain and is responsible for automatic survival functions. (p. 37)

Broca's area An area of the left frontal lobe that directs the muscle movements involved in speech. (p. 46)

bulimia nervosa An eating disorder characterized by private, "binge-purge" episodes of overeating, usually of highly caloric foods, followed by vomiting or laxative use. (p. 359)

burnout Physical, emotional, and mental exhaustion brought on by persistent job-related stress. (p. 517)

bystander effect The tendency for any given bystander to be less likely to give aid if other bystanders are present. (p. 576)

Cannon-Bard theory The theory that an emotion-arousing stimulus simultaneously triggers (1) physiological responses and (2) the subjective experience of emotion. (p. 403)

case study An observation technique in which one person is studied in depth in the hopes of revealing universal principles. (p. 11)

CAT (computerized axial tomograph) scan A series of x-ray photographs taken from different angles and combined by computer into a composite three-dimensional representation of a slice through the body. (p. 35)

catharsis Emotional release. In psychology, the catharsis hypothesis maintains that "releasing" aggressive energy (through action or fantasy) relieves aggressive urges. (p. 395)

central nervous system (CNS) The brain and spinal cord. (p. 32)

cerebellum [sehr-uh-BELL-um] The "little brain" attached to the rear of the brainstem; it helps coordinate voluntary movement and balance. (p. 38)

cerebral [seh-REE-bruhl] **cortex** The intricate fabric of interconnected neural cells that covers the cerebral hemispheres; the body's ultimate control and information-processing center. (p. 42)

chromosomes Threadlike structures made of DNA molecules that contain the genes. (p. 63)

chunking Organizing items into familiar, manageable units; often done automatically. (p. 263)

circadian rhythm [ser-KAY-dee-an] The biological clock; regular bodily rhythms (for example, of temperature and wakefulness) that occur on a 24-hour cycle. (p. 192)

classical conditioning A type of learning in which an organism comes to associate different events. A neutral stimulus that signals an unconditioned stimulus (UCS) begins to produce a response that anticipates and prepares for the unconditioned stimulus. (Also known as *Pavlovian conditioning*.) (p. 228)

clinical psychology A branch of psychology involving the assessment and treatment of those who suffer psychological disorders. (p. 8)

closure The perceptual tendency to fill in gaps, thus enabling one to perceive disconnected parts as a whole object. (p. 166)

co-actors People who are simultaneously at work on the same noncompetitive task. (p. 563)

cochlea [KOHK-lee-uh] A coiled, bony, fluid-filled tube in the inner ear through which sound waves trigger nerve impulses. (p. 146)

cognition All the mental activities associated with thinking, knowing, and remembering. (p. 69)

cognitive dissonance theory The theory that we act to reduce the discomfort (dissonance) we feel when two of our thoughts (cognitions) are inconsistent— as when we respond to our having acted contrary to our attitudes by changing our attitude. (p. 557)

cognitive map A mental representation of the layout of one's environment. For example, after exploring a maze, rats act as if they learned a cognitive map of it. (p. 242)

cognitive perspective Emphasizes how we process, store, and retrieve information and how we use it to reason and solve problems. (p. 7)

cognitive psychology The field of psychology that studies mental representations and the processing of information. Topics include the mental activities that underlie problem solving, judgments, decision making, and language. (p. 286)

cognitive therapy Therapy that teaches people new, more adaptive ways of thinking and acting; based on the assumption that thoughts intervene between events and our emotional reactions. (p. 491)

collective unconscious Carl Jung's concept of a shared, inherited reservoir of memory traces from our species' history. (p. 417)

collectivism Giving priority to the goals of one's groups (often one's extended family or work group) and defining one's identity accordingly. (p. 591)

color constancy Perceiving familiar objects as having consistent color, even if changing illumination alters the wavelengths reflected by the object. (p. 145)

companionate love The deep affectionate attachment we feel for those with whom our lives are intertwined. (p. 582)

concept A mental grouping of similar objects, events, or people. (p. 286)

concrete operational stage In Piaget's theory, the stage of cognitive development (from about 6 or 7 to 11 years of age) during which children gain the mental operations that enable them to think logically about concrete events. (p. 74)

conditioned response (CR) In classical conditioning, the learned response to a conditioned stimulus (CS). (p. 229)

conditioned stimulus (CS) In classical conditioning, an originally neutral stimulus that, after association with an unconditioned stimulus (UCS), comes to trigger a conditioned response. (p. 229)

conduction deafness Hearing loss caused by damage to the mechanical system that conducts sound waves to the cochlea. (p. 149)

cones Receptor cells concentrated near the center of the retina that function in daylight or in well-lit conditions. The cones detect fine detail and give rise to color sensations. (p. 139)

confirmation bias A tendency to search for information that confirms one's preconceptions. (p. 288)

conflict A perceived incompatibility of actions, goals, or ideas. (p. 614)

conformity Adjusting one's behavior or thinking to coincide with a group standard. (p. 557)

connectedness The perceptual tendency to perceive features, such as dots, as a single unit when uniform and linked. (p. 166)

consciousness Selective attention to ongoing perceptions, thoughts, and feelings. (p. 189)

conservation The principle (which Piaget believed to be a part of concrete operational reasoning) that properties such as mass, volume, and number remain the same despite changes in the forms of objects. (p. 74)

content validity The extent to which a test samples the behavior that is of interest (such as a driving test that samples driving tasks). (p. 326)

continuity A perceptual tendency to group stimuli into smooth, continuous patterns. (p. 166)

continuous reinforcement Reinforcing the desired response every time it occurs. (p. 239)

control condition The condition of an experiment in which the experimental treatment is absent; serves as a comparison for evaluating the effect of the treatment. (p. 15)

convergence A binocular cue for perceiving depth; the extent to which the eyes converge inward when looking at an object. (p. 168)

conversion disorder A rare somatoform disorder in which a person experiences very specific genuine physical symptoms for which no physiological basis can be found. (p. 455)

coronary heart disease The clogging of the vessels that nourish the heart muscle; the leading cause of death in the United States. (p. 518)

corpus callosum [KOR-pus kah-LOW-sum] The largest bundle of neural fibers connecting and carrying messages between the two brain hemispheres. (p. 48)

correlation A statistical measure that indicates the extent to which two factors vary together and thus how well either factor predicts the other. (p. 13)

correlation coefficient A measure of the direction and extent of the relationship between two sets of scores. Scores with a *positive correlation coefficient* go up and down together (as with high school and college GPAs). A *negative correlation coefficient* indicates that one score falls as the other rises (as in the relationship between self-esteem and depression). (p. 627)

counterconditioning A behavior therapy procedure that conditions new responses to stimuli that trigger unwanted behaviors; based on classical conditioning. See also *systematic desensitization* and *aversive conditioning*. (p. 487)

creativity The ability to produce novel and valuable ideas. (p. 335)

criterion The behavior (such as college grades) that a test (such as the SAT) is designed to predict; thus, the measure used in defining whether the test has predictive validity. (p. 326)

critical period An optimal period during which an organism's exposure to certain influences or experiences will produce proper development. (p. 77)

cross-sectional study A study in which people of different ages are tested or observed at one point in time. (p. 114)

crystallized intelligence One's accumulated knowledge and verbal skills; tends to increase with age. (p. 115)

culture The enduring behaviors, ideas, attitudes, and traditions shared by a large group of people and transmitted from one generation to the next. (p. 588)

defense mechanisms In psychoanalytic theory, the ego's protective methods of reducing anxiety by unconsciously distorting reality. (p. 415)

deindividuation The loss of self-awareness and self-restraint occurring in group situations that foster arousal and anonymity. (p. 564)

déjà vu (From French, literally meaning "already seen.") That eerie sense that "I've experienced this before." Cues from the current situation may subconsciously trigger retrieval of an earlier experience. (p. 274)

delta waves The large, slow brain waves associated with deep sleep. (p. 193)

delusions False beliefs, often of persecution or grandeur, that may accompany psychotic disorders. (p. 466)

dendrite The bushy, branching extensions of a neuron that receive messages and conduct impulses toward the cell body. (p. 29)

dependent variable The variable that is being measured; in an experiment, the variable that may change in response to manipulations of the independent variable. (p. 15)

depressants Drugs (such as alcohol, barbiturates, and opiates) that reduce neural activity and slow body functions. (p. 210)

depth perception The ability to see objects in three dimensions although the images that strike the retina are two-dimensional; allows us to judge distance. (p. 167)

developmental psychology A branch of psychology that studies physical, cognitive, and social change throughout the life span. (p. 61)

difference threshold The minimum difference in stimulation that a subject can detect 50 percent of the time. We experience the difference threshold as a just noticeable difference (jnd). (p. 135)

discrimination In classical conditioning, the ability to distinguish between a conditioned stimulus and similar stimuli that do not signal an unconditioned stimulus. In operant conditioning, responding differently to stimuli that signal that behavior will be reinforced or nonreinforced. (p. 232)

displacement In psychoanalytic theory, the defense mechanism that shifts sexual or aggressive impulses toward a more acceptable or less threatening object or person, as when redirecting anger toward a safer outlet. (p. 416)

dissociation A split in consciousness, which allows some thoughts and behaviors to occur simultaneously with others. (p. 207)

dissociative disorders Disorders in which conscious awareness becomes separated (dissociated) from previous memories, thoughts, and feelings. See *amnesia, fugue,* and *multiple personality.* (p. 455)

DNA (deoxyribonucleic acid) A complex molecule containing genetic information that makes up the chromosomes. (p. 64)

double-blind procedure An experimental procedure in which both the subject and the staff are ignorant (blind) about whether the subject has received the treatment or a placebo. Commonly used in drug evaluation studies. (p. 17)

Down syndrome A condition of retardation and associated physical disorders caused by an extra chromosome in one's genetic makeup. (p. 334)

drive An aroused state that typically arises from an underlying need. (p. 353)

DSM-III-R The American Psychiatric Association's *Diagnostic and Statistical Manual of Mental Disorders (Third Edition—Revised)*, a widely used system for classifying psychological disorders. It will be replaced by the forthcoming DSM-IV. (p. 450)

dualism The presumption that mind and body are two distinct entities that interact. (p. 220)

echoic memory A momentary sensory memory of auditory stimuli; if attention is elsewhere, sounds and words can still be recalled within 3 or 4 seconds. (p. 257)

eclectic approach An approach to psychotherapy that takes advantage of techniques from the various forms of therapy, depending on the client's problems. (p. 480)

effortful processing Encoding that requires attention and conscious effort. (p. 257)

ego The largely conscious, "executive" part of personality that, according to Freud, mediates among the demands of the id, superego, and reality. (p. 414)

egocentrism In Piaget's theory, the inability of the preoperational child to take another's point of view. (p. 73)

electroconvulsive therapy (ECT) Shock treatment. A biomedical therapy for severely depressed patients in which a brief electric current is sent through the brain of an anesthetized patient. (p. 504)

electroencephalogram (EEG) An amplified recording of the waves of electrical activity that sweep across the brain's surface. These waves are measured by placing electrodes on the scalp. (p. 35)

embryo The developing human organism from about 2 weeks after fertilization through the second month. (p. 64)

emotion A response of the whole organism, involving (1) physical arousal, (2) expressive behaviors, and (3) conscious experience. (p. 383)

empathy The ability to understand and feel what another feels, to put oneself in someone else's shoes. (p. 577)

empirically derived test A test (such as the MMPI-2) developed by testing a pool of items and then selecting those that discriminate groups of interest. (p. 424)

encoding The processing of information into the memory system, for example by extracting meaning. (p. 255)

endocrine [EN-duh-krin] **system** The body's "slow," chemical communication system; a set of glands that secretes hormones into the bloodstream. (p. 41)

endorphins [en-DOR-fins] "Morphine within"—natural, opiatelike neurotransmitters linked to pain control and to pleasure. (p. 31)

equilibrium The sense of body movement and position, including the sense of balance. (p. 156)

equity A condition in which people receive from a relationship in proportion to what they give to it. (p. 582)

estrogen A sex hormone, secreted in greater amounts by females than males. In nonhuman female mammals, estrogen levels peak during ovulation, promoting sexual receptivity. (p. 362)

ethnicity That part of one's social identity defined by the ancestors, heritage, and traits one shares with others. (p. 594)

experiment A research method in which the investigator manipulates one or more factors (independent variables) to observe their effect on some behavior or mental process (the dependent variable) while controlling other relevant factors. (p. 14)

experimental condition The condition of an experiment that exposes subjects to the treatment, that is, to the independent variable. (p. 15)

explicit memory Memory of facts and experiences that one can consciously know and "declare." (Also called *declarative memory*.) (p. 270)

external locus of control The perception that chance or outside forces beyond one's personal control determine one's fate. (p. 436)

extinction The diminishing of a response when, in classical conditioning, an unconditioned stimulus (UCS) does not follow a conditioned stimulus (CS); or when, in operant conditioning, a response is no longer reinforced. (p. 231)

extrasensory perception (ESP) The controversial claim

that perception can occur apart from sensory input. Said to include telepathy, clairvoyance, and precognition. (p. 181)

extrinsic motivation A desire to perform a behavior due to promised rewards or threats of punishment. (p. 373)

factor analysis A statistical procedure that identifies clusters of related items (called factors) on a test; used to identify different dimensions of performance that underlie one's total score. (p. 329)

family therapy Therapy that treats the family as a system. Views an individual's unwanted behaviors as influenced by or directed at other family members; encourages family members toward positive relationships and improved communication. (p. 486)

fantasy-prone personality Someone who imagines and recalls experiences with lifelike vividness and who spends considerable time fantasizing. (p. 201)

feature detectors Nerve cells in the brain that respond to specific features of the stimulus, such as movement, angle, or shape. (p. 142)

fetal alcohol syndrome Physical and cognitive abnormalities in children caused by a pregnant woman's heavy drinking. In severe cases, symptoms include noticeable facial misproportions. (p. 65)

fetus The developing human organism from 9 weeks after conception to birth. (p. 64)

figure-ground The organization of the visual field into objects (the figures) that stand out from their surroundings (the ground). (p. 166)

fixation 1. The inability to see a problem from a new perspective; an impediment to problem solving. (p. 290) 2. According to Freud, a lingering focus of pleasure-seeking energies at an earlier psychosexual stage, where conflicts were unresolved. (p. 415)

fixed-interval schedule In operant conditioning, a schedule of reinforcement that reinforces a response only after a specified time has elapsed. (p. 241)

fixed-ratio schedule In operant conditioning, a schedule of reinforcement that reinforces a response only after a specified number of responses. (p. 240)

flashbulb memory A clear memory of an emotionally significant moment or event. (p. 254)

fluid intelligence One's ability to reason abstractly; tends to decrease during late adulthood. (p. 115)

foot-in-the-door phenomenon The tendency for people who have first agreed to a small request to comply later with a larger request. (p. 555)

formal operational stage In Piaget's theory, the stage of cognitive development (normally beginning about age 12) during which people begin to think logically about abstract concepts. (p. 75)

fovea The central focal point in the retina, around which the eye's cones cluster. (p. 140)

framing The way an issue is posed. How an issue is framed can significantly affect decisions and judgments. (p. 296)

fraternal twins Twins who develop from separate zygotes (fertilized eggs); genetically no closer than brothers and sisters, but who have shared the fetal environment. (p. 87)

free association 1. A psychoanalytic method of exploring the unconscious in which the person relaxes and says whatever comes to mind, no matter how trivial or embarrassing. (p. 412) 2. In psychoanalysis, the patient's uncensored reporting of everything that comes to mind as one thought leads to the next. (p. 480)

frequency The number of complete wavelengths that pass a point in a given time (for example, per second). (p. 146)

frequency distribution A listing of the number of individual scores that occur within each equal-sized interval within a distribution. (p. 623)

frequency theory In hearing, the theory that the rate of nerve impulses traveling up the auditory nerve matches the frequency of a tone, thus enabling us to sense its pitch. (p. 147)

frontal lobes The portion of the cerebral cortex lying just behind the forehead; involved in speaking and muscle movements and in making plans and judgments. (p. 42)

frustration-aggression principle The principle that frustration—the blocking of an attempt to achieve some goal—creates anger, which can generate aggression. (p. 570)

fugue [fewg] A dissociative disorder in which flight from one's home and identity accompanies amnesia. (p. 456)

functional fixedness The tendency to think of things only in terms of their usual functions; an impediment to problem solving. (p. 291)

fundamental attribution error The tendency for observers, when analyzing another's behavior, to underestimate the impact of the situation and to overestimate the impact of personal disposition. (p. 552)

gate-control theory Melzack and Wall's theory that the spinal cord contains a neurological "gate" that blocks or allows pain signals to pass on to the brain. The "gate" is opened by the activity of pain signals traveling up small nerve fibers and closed by activity in larger fibers or by information coming from the brain. (p. 152)

gender In psychology, the characteristics, whether biologically or socially influenced, by which people define male and female. (p. 597)

gender identity One's sense of being male or female. Note: One's gender identity is distinct from one's sexual orientation (as heterosexual or homosexual) and from the strength of one's gender-typing. (pp. 415, 604)

gender role A set of expected behaviors for males and for females. (p. 605)

gender schema theory The theory that children learn from their cultures a concept of what it means to be male and female and adjust their behavior accordingly. (p. 605)

gender-typing The acquisition of a masculine or feminine gender identity and role. (p. 604)

general adaptation syndrome (GAS) Selye's concept of the body's adaptive response to stress as composed of three stages—alarm, resistance, exhaustion. (p. 513)

general intelligence (g) A general underlying intelligence factor believed by Spearman and others to be measured by every task on an intelligence test. (p. 329)

generalization The tendency, once a response has been conditioned, for stimuli similar to the conditioned stimulus to evoke similar responses. (p. 231)

generalized anxiety disorder An anxiety disorder in which a person is continually tense, apprehensive, and in a state of autonomic nervous system arousal. (p. 451)

genes The biochemical units of heredity that make up the chromosomes; a segment of DNA capable of synthesizing a protein. (p. 62)

genital stage The last of Freud's psychosexual stages, beginning in puberty, during which sexuality matures and the person seeks pleasure through sexual contact with others. (p. 415)

gestalt An organized whole. Gestalt psychologists emphasize our tendency to integrate pieces of information into meaningful wholes. (p. 165)

Gestalt therapy Developed by Fritz Perls to combine the psychoanalytic emphasis on bringing unconscious feelings to awareness and the humanistic emphasis on getting "in touch with oneself"; aims to help people become more aware of and able to express their feelings, and to take responsibility for their feelings and actions. (p. 485)

glucose The form of sugar that circulates in the blood and provides the major source of energy for body tissues. When its level is low, we feel hunger. (p. 356)

grammar A system of rules in a language that enables us to communicate with and understand others. (p. 302)

GRIT Graduated and Reciprocated Initiatives in Tension-Reduction—a strategy designed to decrease international tensions. (p. 618)

group polarization The enhancement of a group's prevailing attitudes through discussion. (p. 565)

grouping The tendency to organize stimuli into coherent groups. (p. 166)

groupthink The mode of thinking that occurs when the desire for harmony in a decision-making group overrides a realistic appraisal of alternatives. (p. 565)

hallucinations False sensory experiences, such as seeing something without any external visual stimulus. (p. 193)

hallucinogens Psychedelic ("mind-manifesting") drugs, such as LSD, that distort perceptions and evoke sensory images in the absence of sensory input. (p. 210)

health psychology A subfield of psychology that provides psychology's contribution to behavioral medicine. (p. 512)

heritability The extent to which we can attribute individuals' differences in a trait to genes. The heritability of a trait may vary, depending on the range of populations and environments studied. (p. 338)

heuristic A rule-of-thumb strategy that often allows us to make judgments and solve problems efficiently; usually speedier, but more error-prone than *algorithms*. (p. 287)

hidden observer Hilgard's term describing a hypnotized subject's awareness of experiences, such as pain, that go unreported during hypnosis. (p. 209)

hierarchy of needs Maslow's pyramid of human needs, beginning at the base with physiological needs that must first be satisfied before higher level safety needs and then psychological needs become active. (p. 355)

hindsight bias The tendency to believe one would have foreseen how something turned out, *after* learning the outcome. (Also known as the *I-knew-it-all-along phenomenon*.) (p. 21)

hippocampus A neural center in the limbic system that helps process explicit memories for storage. (p. 271)

histogram A bar graph depicting a frequency distribution. (p. 623)

homeostasis A tendency to maintain a balanced or constant internal state; refers especially to the body's tendency to maintain an optimum internal state for functioning. (p. 353)

hormones Chemical messengers, such as those manufactured by the endocrine glands, that are produced in one tissue and affect another. (p. 41)

hospice An organization whose largely volunteer staff provides support for dying people and their families either in special facilities or in people's own homes. (p. 123)

hue The dimension of color that is determined by the wavelength of light; what we know as the color names (blue, green, and so forth). (p. 137)

humanistic perspective Emphasizes people's capacities for choice and growth—studies people's subjective experiences. (p. 7)

hypnosis An apparently heightened suggestibility in which some people narrow their focus of attention and claim to experience imaginary happenings as if they were real. (p. 202)

hypochondriasis A somatoform disorder in which a person misinterprets normal physical sensations as symptoms of a disease. (p. 455)

hypothalamus [hi-po-THAL-uh-muss] A neural structure lying below *(hypo)* the thalamus; it directs several maintenance activities (eating, drinking, body temperature), helps govern the endocrine system via the pituitary gland, and is linked to emotion and reward. (p. 40)

hypothesis A testable prediction, often implied by a theory. (p. 10)

iconic memory A momentary sensory memory of visual stimuli; a photographic or picture-image memory lasting no more than a second or so. (p. 257)

id A reservoir of unconscious psychic energy that, according to Freud, strives to satisfy basic sexual and aggressive drives. (p. 413)

identical twins Twins who develop from a single zygote that splits in two, creating two genetic replicas. (p. 87)

identification The process by which, according to Freud, children incorporate their parents' values into their developing superegos. (p. 415)

identity One's sense of self; according to Erikson, the adolescent's task is to solidify a sense of self by testing and integrating various roles. (p. 102)

illusory correlation The perception of a relationship where none exists. (p. 628)

imagery Mental pictures. A powerful aid to effortful processing, especially when combined with semantic encoding. (p. 261)

implicit memory Retention without conscious recollection (of skills, preferences, and dispositions). (Also called *nondeclarative memory*.) (p. 270)

imprinting The process by which certain animals form attachments during a critical period very early in life. (p. 77)

incentives Positive or negative environmental stimuli that motivate behavior. (p. 354)

independent variable The experimental factor that is manipulated; the variable whose effect is being studied. (p. 15)

individualism Giving priority to one's own goals over group goals, and defining one's identity in terms of personal attributes rather than group identifications. (p. 591)

informational social influence Influence resulting from one's willingness to accept others' opinions about reality. (p. 560)

ingroup bias The tendency to favor one's own group. (p. 612)

inner ear The innermost part of the ear, containing the cochlea, semicircular canals, and vestibular sacs. (p. 146)

insight A sudden and often novel realization of the solution to a problem; it contrasts with strategy-based solutions. (p. 287)

insomnia A sleep disorder involving recurring problems in falling or staying asleep. (p. 196)

instinct A behavior that is rigidly patterned and unlearned. (p. 353)

insulin A hormone that, among its effects, helps body tissues convert blood glucose into stored fat. When its level in the body is high, we feel hunger. (p. 356)

intelligence The capacity for goal-directed and adaptive behavior. Involves the abilities to profit from experience, solve problems, reason, and successfully meet challenges and achieve goals. (p. 328)

intelligence quotient (IQ) Defined originally as the ratio of mental age to chronological age multiplied by 100 (thus, IQ = ma/ca 100). On contemporary intelligence tests, the average performance for a given age is assigned a score of 100. (p. 320)

intelligence test A method for assessing an individual's mental aptitudes and comparing them to others using numerical scores. (p. 317)

intensity The amount of energy in a light or sound wave, which we perceive as brightness or loudness, as determined by the wave's amplitude. (p. 137)

interaction effect A result in which the effect of one factor depends on the level of another. (p. 373)

intermittent reinforcement See *partial reinforcement*. (p. 239)

internal locus of control The perception that one controls one's own fate. (p. 436)

interneurons Central nervous system neurons that intervene directly between the sensory inputs and motor outputs. (p. 28)

interpretation In psychoanalysis, the analyst's assisting the patient to note and understand resistances and other significant behaviors in order to promote insight. (p. 481)

intimacy In Erikson's theory, the ability to form close, loving relationships; a primary developmental task in late adolescence and early adulthood. (p. 103)

intrinsic motivation A desire to perform a behavior for its own sake and to be effective. (p. 373)

iris A ring of muscle tissue that forms the colored portion of the eye around the pupil and controls the size of the pupil opening. (p. 138)

James-Lange theory The theory that our experience of emotion is our awareness of our physiological responses to emotion-arousing stimuli. (p. 402)

just noticeable difference (jnd) See *difference threshold*. (p. 135)

just-world phenomenon The tendency of people to believe the world is just and that people therefore get what they deserve and deserve what they get. (p. 613)

kinesthesis [kin-ehs-THEE-sehs] The system for sensing the position and movement of individual body parts. (p. 156)

language Our spoken, written, or gestured words and how we combine them to communicate meaning. (p. 301)

latency stage The fourth of Freud's psychosexual stages, from about age 6 to puberty, during which sexual impulses are repressed. (p. 415)

latent content According to Freud, the underlying but censored meaning of a dream (as distinct from its manifest content). Freud believed that a dream's latent content functions as a safety valve. (p. 198)

latent learning Learning that occurs but is not apparent until there is an incentive to demonstrate it. (p. 243)

learned helplessness The hopelessness and passive resignation learned when an animal or human is unable to avoid repeated aversive events. (p. 436)

learning A relatively permanent change in an organism's behavior due to experience. (p. 227)

lens The transparent structure behind the pupil that changes shape to focus images on the retina. (p. 138)

lesion [LEE-zhuhn] Tissue destruction. A brain lesion is a naturally or experimentally caused destruction of brain tissue. (p. 35)

limbic system A doughnut-shaped system of neural structures at the border of the brainstem and cerebral hemispheres; associated with emotions such as fear and aggression and drives such as those for food and sex. (p. 39)

linear perspective A monocular cue for perceiving distance; we perceive the converging of what we know to be parallel lines as indicating increasing distance. (p. 170)

linguistic relativity Whorf's hypothesis that language determines the way we think. (p. 310)

lithium A chemical that provides an effective drug therapy for the mood swings of bipolar (manic-depressive) disorders. (p. 504)

lobotomy A now-rare psychosurgical procedure once used to calm uncontrollably emotional or violent patients. In this procedure the nerves that connect the frontal lobes to the emotion-controlling centers of the inner brain are cut. (p. 505)

longitudinal study Research in which the same people are restudied over a long time period. (p. 114)

long-term memory The relatively permanent and limitless storehouse of the memory system. (p. 256)

LSD (lysergic acid diethylamide) A powerful hallucinogenic drug; also known as *acid*. (p. 215)

lymphocytes The two types of white blood cells that are part of the body's immune system: B lymphocytes form in the *b*one marrow and release antibodies that fight bacterial infections; T lymphocytes form in the *t*hymus and, among other duties, attack cancer cells, viruses, and foreign substances. (p. 521)

major depression A mood disorder in which a person, for no apparent reason, experiences 2 or more weeks of depressed moods, feelings of worthlessness, and diminished interest or pleasure in most activities. (p. 458)

mania A hyperactive, wildly optimistic state. (p. 459)

manifest content According to Freud, the remembered story line of a dream (as distinct from its latent content). (p. 198)

maturation Biological growth processes that enable orderly changes in behavior, relatively uninfluenced by experience. (p. 62)

mean The arithmetic average of a distribution, obtained by adding the scores and then dividing by the number of scores. (p. 625)

median The middle score in a distribution; half the scores are above it and half are below it. (p. 625)

medical model The concept that diseases have physical causes that can be diagnosed, treated, and, in most cases, cured. When applied to psychological disorders, the medical model assumes that these "mental" illnesses can be diagnosed on the basis of their symptoms and cured through therapy, which may include treatment in a psychiatric hospital. (p. 447)

medulla [muh-DUL-uh] The base of the brainstem; controls heartbeat and breathing. (p. 37)

memory The persistence of learning over time. (p. 253)

menarche [meh-NAR-key] The first menstrual period. (p. 96)

menopause The time of natural cessation of menstruation; also refers to the biological and psychological changes experienced during a woman's years of declining ability to reproduce. (p. 109)

mental age A measure of intelligence test performance devised by Binet; the chronological age that most typically corresponds to a given level of performance. Thus, a child who does as well as the average 8-year-old is said to have a mental age of 8. (p. 319)

mental retardation A condition of limited mental ability, as indicated by an intelligence score below 70, that produces difficulty in adapting to the demands of life; varies from mild to profound. (p. 333)

mental set A tendency to approach a problem in a particular way, especially a way that has been successful in the past but may or may not be helpful in solving a new problem. (p. 290)

mere exposure effect The phenomenon that repeated exposure to novel stimuli increases liking of them. (p. 579)

meta-analysis A procedure for statistically combining the results of many different research studies. (p. 498)

metabolic rate The body's base rate of energy expenditure. (p. 358)

middle ear The chamber between the eardrum and cochlea containing three tiny bones (hammer, anvil, and stirrup) that concentrate the vibrations of the eardrum on the cochlea's oval window. (p. 146)

Minnesota Multiphasic Personality Inventory-2 (MMPI-2) The most widely researched and clinically used of all personality tests. Originally developed to identify the traits of emotionally troubled people (still considered its most appropriate use), this test is now also used for other screening purposes. (p. 424)

mirror-image perceptions Distinct but similar views of one another often held by parties in conflict; each views itself as moral and peace-loving, the other as evil and aggressive. (p. 615)

misinformation effect After witnessing an event and receiving misleading information about it, incorporating the "misinformation" into one's memory of the event. (p. 276)

mnemonics [nih-MON-iks] Memory aids, especially those

techniques that use vivid imagery and organizational devices. (p. 262)

mode The most frequently occurring score in a distribution. (p. 625)

modeling The process by which a behavior is observed and imitated. (p. 247)

monism The presumption that mind and body are different aspects of the same thing. (p. 220)

monocular cues Distance cues, such as aerial and linear perspective and overlap, available to either eye alone. (p. 167)

mood disorders Psychological disorders characterized by emotional extremes. See *bipolar disorder, major depression,* and *mania.* (p. 458)

morphemes In a language, the smallest units that carry meaning; may be words or parts of words (such as a prefix). (p. 302)

motivation The forces that energize and direct behavior. (p. 351)

motor cortex An area at the rear of the frontal lobes that controls voluntary movements. (p. 43)

motor neurons The neurons that carry outgoing information from the central nervous system to the muscles and glands. (p. 28)

MRI (magnetic resonance imaging) A technique that uses magnetic fields and radio waves to produce computer-generated images that distinguish among different types of soft tissue; allows us to see structures within the brain. (p. 36)

multiple personality disorder A rare dissociative disorder in which a person exhibits two or more distinct and alternating personalities. (p. 456)

myelin [MY-uh-lin] **sheath** A layer of fatty cells segmentally encasing the fibers of many neurons; makes possible vastly greater transmission speed of neural impulses. (p. 29)

narcolepsy A sleep disorder characterized by uncontrollable sleep attacks in which the sufferer lapses directly into REM sleep, often at inopportune times. (p. 196)

naturalistic observation Observing and recording behavior in naturally occurring situations without trying to manipulate and control the situation. (p. 12)

nature-nurture issue The longstanding controversy over the relative contributions of genes and experience to the development of psychological traits and behaviors. (p. 6)

near-death experience An altered state of consciousness reported after a close brush with death (such as through cardiac arrest); often similar to drug-induced hallucinations. (p. 218)

negative reinforcement Strengthening behavior by stopping or reducing negative stimuli, such as a shock. (Note: Negative reinforcement is *not* punishment.) (p. 238)

nerve deafness Hearing loss caused by damage to the cochlea's receptor cells or to the auditory nerves. (p. 149)

nervous system The body's speedy, electrochemical communication system, consisting of all the nerve cells of the peripheral and central nervous systems. (p. 27)

neural networks Computer circuits that mimic the brain's interconnected neural cells, performing tasks such as learning to recognize visual patterns and smells. (p. 300)

neuron A nerve cell; the basic building block of the nervous system. (p. 27)

neurotic disorders Former term for psychological disorders that are usually distressing, but allow one to think rationally and function socially. Freud saw the neurotic disorders as ways of dealing with anxiety. (p. 450)

neurotransmitters Chemical messengers that traverse the synaptic gaps between neurons. When released by the sending neuron, neurotransmitters travel across the synapse and bind to receptor sites on the receiving neuron, thereby influencing whether it will generate a neural impulse. (p. 30)

night terrors A sleep disorder characterized by high arousal and an appearance of being terrified; unlike nightmares, night terrors occur during Stage 4 sleep, within 2 or 3 hours of falling asleep, and are seldom remembered. (p. 197)

normal curve (or normal distribution) The symmetrical bell-shaped curve that describes the distribution of many physical and psychological attributes. Most scores fall near the average, and fewer and fewer scores lie near the extremes. (pp. 324, 626)

normative social influence Influence resulting from a person's desire to gain approval or avoid disapproval. (p. 559)

norms Understood rules for accepted and expected behavior. Norms prescribe "proper" behavior. (p. 560)

obesity A surplus of body fat that causes one to be 20 percent or more overweight. (p. 538)

object permanence The awareness that things continue to exist even when not perceived. (p. 72)

observational learning Learning by observing and imitating the behavior of others. (p. 247)

obsessive-compulsive disorder An anxiety disorder characterized by unwanted repetitive thoughts (obsessions) and/or actions (compulsions). (p. 451)

occipital [ahk-SIP-uh-tuhl] **lobes** The portion of the cerebral cortex lying at the back of the head; includes the visual areas, each of which receives visual information from the opposite visual field. (p. 42)

Oedipus [ED-uh-puss] **complex** According to Freud, a boy's sexual desires toward his mother and feelings of jealousy and hatred for his father. (p. 414)

one-word stage The stage in speech development from about age 1 to 2 years during which a child speaks mostly in single words. (p. 303)

operant behavior Behavior that operates on the environment, producing consequences. (p. 236)

operant conditioning A type of learning in which behavior is strengthened if followed by reinforcement, or diminished if followed by punishment. (p. 236)

opiates Opium and its derivatives, such as morphine and heroin; they depress neural activity, temporarily lessening pain and anxiety. (p. 212)

opponent-process theory The theory that opposing retinal processes (red-green, yellow-blue, white-black) enable color vision. For example, some cells are stimulated by green and inhibited by red; others are stimulated by red and inhibited by green. (p. 144)

optic nerve The nerve that carries neural impulses from the eye to the brain. (p. 139)

oral stage The first of Freud's psychosexual stages, from birth to about 18 months, during which sensual pleasure centers on the mouth via sucking, biting, and chewing. (p. 414)

overconfidence The tendency to be more confident than correct—to overestimate the accuracy of one's beliefs and judgments. (p. 294)

overjustification effect The effect of promising a reward for doing what one already likes to do. The person may now see the reward, rather than intrinsic interest, as the motivation for performing the task. (p. 243)

overlap A monocular cue for perceiving distance; nearby objects partially block our view of more distant objects. (p. 168)

ovum The female reproductive cell, or egg. (p. 63)

panic attack A minutes-long episode of intense dread in which a person experiences terror and accompanying chest pain, choking, or other frightening sensations. (p. 451)

parallel processing Information processing in which several aspects of a problem are processed simultaneously. The brain's natural mode of information processing for many functions, including vision; contrasts with the step-by-step (serial) processing of most computers and of conscious problem solving. (p. 142)

parapsychology The study of paranormal phenomena including ESP and psychokinesis. (p. 181)

parasympathetic nervous system The division of the autonomic nervous system that calms the body, conserving its energy. (p. 34)

parietal [puh-RYE-uh-tuhl] **lobes** The portion of the cerebral cortex lying at the top of the head and toward the rear; includes the sensory cortex. (p. 42)

partial (or **intermittent**) **reinforcement** Reinforcing a response only part of the time; results in slower acquisition of response but much greater resistance to extinction than does continuous reinforcement. (p. 239)

passionate love An aroused state of intense positive absorption in another, usually present at the beginning of a love relationship. (p. 581)

percentile rank The percentage of the scores in a distribution that a given score exceeds. (p. 623)

perception The process of organizing and interpreting sensory information, enabling us to recognize meaningful objects and events. (p. 132)

perceptual adaptation In vision, the ability to adjust to an artificially displaced or even inverted visual field. (p. 176)

perceptual constancy Perceiving objects as unchanging (having consistent brightness, color, shape, and size) even as illumination and retinal images change. (p. 171)

perceptual set A mental predisposition to perceive one thing and not another. (p. 177)

peripheral nervous system (PNS) The neurons that connect the central nervous system to the rest of the body. It consists of the sensory neurons, which carry messages to the central nervous system from the body's sense receptors, and the motor neurons, which carry messages from the central nervous system to the muscles and glands. (p. 32)

person-centered therapy A humanistic therapy, developed by Carl Rogers, in which the therapist uses techniques such as active listening within a genuine, accepting, empathic environment to facilitate clients' growth. (p. 483)

personal control Our sense of being in control of our environment rather than feeling helpless. (p. 435)

personal space The buffer zone we like to maintain around our bodies. (p. 590)

personality An individual's characteristic pattern of thinking, feeling, and acting. (p. 411)

personality disorders Psychological disorders characterized by inflexible and enduring behavior patterns that impair social functioning. (p. 471)

personality inventory A questionnaire (often with true-false or agree-disagree items) on which people respond to items designed to gauge a wide range of feelings and behaviors; used to assess selected personality traits. (p. 424)

PET (positron emission tomograph) scan A visual display of brain activity that detects where a radioactive form of glucose goes while the brain performs a given task. (p. 36)

phallic stage The third of Freud's psychosexual stages, from about ages 3 to 6, during which the pleasure zone is the genitals and sexual feelings arise toward the parent of the other sex. (p. 414)

phobic disorder An anxiety disorder marked by a persistent, irrational fear of a specific object or situation. (p. 451)

phonemes The smallest distinctive sound units in a spoken language. (p. 302)

physical dependence A physiological need for a drug, with unpleasant withdrawal symptoms when discontinued. (p. 210)

pitch A tone's highness or lowness; depends on frequency. (p. 146)

pituitary gland The endocrine system's most influential gland. Under the influence of the hypothalamus, the pituitary regulates growth and controls other endocrine glands. (p. 41)

place theory In hearing, the theory that links the pitch we hear with the place where the cochlea's membrane is stimulated. (p. 147)

placebo [pluh-SEE-bo] An inert substance that may be administered instead of a presumed active agent, such as a drug; may trigger the effects believed to characterize the active agent. (p. 17)

plasticity The brain's capacity for modification, as evident in brain reorganization following damage (especially in children) and in experiments on the effects of experience on brain development. (p. 46)

pleasure principle The id's demand for immediate gratification. (p. 413)

polygraph A machine, commonly used in attempts to detect lies, that measures several of the physiological responses accompanying emotion (such as perspiration, heart rate, and breathing changes). (p. 386)

population 1. All the cases or members in a group from which samples may be drawn for study. (p. 11) 2. All the cases in a group, from which samples may be drawn for study. (p. 630)

positive reinforcement Increasing behaviors by presenting positive stimuli, such as food. A positive reinforcer is any stimulus that, when presented after a response, strengthens the response. (p. 238)

posthypnotic amnesia Supposed inability to recall what one experienced during hypnosis, induced by the hypnotist's suggestion. (p. 203)

posthypnotic suggestion A suggestion, made during a hypnosis session, to be carried out after the subject is no longer hypnotized; used by some clinicians to help control undesired symptoms and behaviors. (p. 205)

preconscious Information that is not conscious, but is retrievable into conscious awareness. (p. 413)

predictive validity The success with which a test predicts the behavior it is designed to predict; it is assessed by computing the correlation between test scores and the criterion behavior. (p. 326)

prejudice An unjustifiable (and usually negative) attitude toward a group and its members. Prejudice generally involves stereotyped beliefs, negative feelings, and a predisposition to discriminatory action. (p. 610)

Premack's principle The principle that a preferred (more frequently engaged in) activity can serve as a reinforcer for a less probable activity. (p. 238)

preoperational stage In Piaget's theory, the stage (from about 2 to 6 or 7 years of age) during which a child learns to use language but does not yet comprehend the mental operations of concrete logic. (p. 74)

primary reinforcer An innately reinforcing stimulus, such as one that satisfies a biological need. (p. 239)

primary sex characteristics The body structures (ovaries and testes) that make sexual reproduction possible. (p. 96)

priming The implicit (unconscious) activation of particular associations in memory. (p. 272)

proactive interference The disruptive effect of prior learning on the recall of new information. (p. 278)

projection In psychoanalytic theory, the defense mechanism by which people disguise their own threatening impulses by attributing them to others. (p. 416)

projective tests Personality tests, such as the Rorschach and TAT, for which subjects interpret ambiguous stimuli designed to trigger projection of one's inner dynamics. (p. 418)

prosocial behavior Positive, constructive, helpful behavior. The opposite of antisocial behavior. (p. 248)

prototype The best example of a category; matching new items to the prototype provides a quick and easy method for including items in a category (as when comparing feathered creatures to a prototypical bird, such as a robin). (p. 287)

proximity A perceptual tendency to group together visual and auditory events that are near each other. (p. 166)

psychiatry A branch of medicine dealing with psychological disorders; practiced by physicians and sometimes involving medical (for example, drug) treatments as well as psychological therapy. (p. 8)

psychoactive drug A chemical substance that alters mood and perceptions. (p. 210)

psychoanalysis 1. The technique of treating psychological disorders by seeking to expose and interpret unconscious tensions. Freud's psychoanalytic theory of personality sought to explain what he observed during psychoanalysis. (p. 413) 2. Sigmund Freud's therapeutic technique, in which the patient's free associations, resistances, dreams, and transferences—and the therapist's interpretations of them—release previously repressed feelings, allowing the patient to gain self-insight. (p. 480)

psychoanalytic perspective Emphasizes unconscious drives and conflicts, many of which may stem from childhood experiences. (p. 7)

psychological dependence A psychological need to use a drug, such as to relieve negative emotions. (p. 210)

psychological disorder A condition in which behavior is judged atypical, disturbing, maladaptive, and unjustifiable. (p. 447)

psychology The science of behavior and mental processes. (p. 6)

psychopharmacology The study of the effects of drugs on mind and behavior. (p. 502)

psychophysiological illness Literally, "mind-body" illness; any physical illness not caused by a known physical disorder. For example, stress can produce hypertension, ulcers, and headaches. Note: This is distinct from *hypochondriasis*—

misinterpreting normal physical sensations as symptoms of a disease. (p. 520)

psychosexual stages The childhood stages of development (oral, anal, phallic, latency, genital) during which, according to Freud, the id's pleasure-seeking energies focus on distinct erogenous zones. (p. 414)

psychosurgery Surgery that removes or destroys brain tissue in an effort to change behavior. (p. 505)

psychotherapy An emotionally charged, confiding interaction between a trained therapist and someone who suffers a psychological difficulty. (p. 480)

psychotic disorders Psychological disorders in which a person loses contact with reality, experiencing irrational ideas and distorted perceptions. (p. 450)

puberty The early adolescent period of rapid growth and sexual maturation. (p. 96)

punishment Any event that *decreases* the behavior that it follows. (p. 241)

pupil The adjustable opening in the center of the eye through which light enters. (p. 138)

random assignment Assigning subjects to experimental and control conditions by chance, thus minimizing preexisting differences between those assigned to the different groups. (p. 15)

random sample A sample that fairly represents a population because each member has an equal chance of inclusion. (p. 11)

range The difference between the highest and lowest scores in a distribution. (p. 625)

rational-emotive therapy A confrontational cognitive therapy, developed by Albert Ellis, that vigorously challenges people's illogical, self-defeating attitudes and assumptions. (p. 492)

rationalization In psychoanalytic theory, a defense mechanism that offers self-justifying explanations in place of the real, more threatening, unconscious reasons for one's actions. (p. 416)

reaction formation In psychoanalytic theory, a defense mechanism by which the ego unconsciously switches unacceptable impulses into their opposites. Thus, people may express feelings that are the opposite of their anxiety-arousing unconscious feelings. (p. 415)

reality principle The ego's tendency to satisfy the id's desires in ways that will realistically bring pleasure rather than pain. (p. 414)

recall A measure of memory in which the person must retrieve information learned earlier, as on a fill-in-the-blank test. (p. 272)

reciprocal determinism The interacting influences between personality and environmental factors. (p. 435)

recognition A measure of memory in which the person need only identify items previously learned, as on a multiple-choice test. (p. 272)

reflex A simple, automatic, inborn response to a sensory stimulus, such as the knee-jerk response. (p. 28)

refractory period A resting period after orgasm during which a man cannot achieve another orgasm. (p. 362)

regression In psychoanalytic theory, an individual's retreat, when faced with anxiety, to a more infantile psychosexual stage where some psychic energy remains fixated. (p. 415)

regression toward the mean The tendency for extreme or unusual scores to fall back (regress) toward the average. (p. 629)

rehearsal The conscious repetition of information, either to maintain it in consciousness or to encode it for storage. (p. 258)

reinforcer In operant conditioning, any event that *strengthens* the behavior it follows. (p. 238)

relative brightness A monocular cue for perceiving distance; dimmer objects seem more distant. (p. 170)

relative deprivation The perception that one is worse off relative to those with whom one compares oneself. (p. 401)

relative height A monocular cue for perceiving distance; we perceive higher objects as farther away. (p. 169)

relative motion A monocular cue for perceiving distance; when we move, objects at different distances change their relative positions in our visual image, with those closest moving most. (p. 169)

relative size A monocular cue for perceiving distance; when we assume two objects are the same size, the one that produces the smaller image appears more distant. (p. 168)

relearning A memory measure that assesses the amount of time saved when relearning previously learned information. (p. 272)

reliability The extent to which a test yields consistent results, as assessed by the consistency of scores on two halves of the test, on alternate forms of the test, or on retesting. (p. 325)

REM rebound The tendency for REM sleep to increase following REM sleep deprivation (created by repeated awakenings during REM sleep). (p. 200)

REM sleep Rapid eye movement sleep, a recurring sleep stage during which vivid dreams commonly occur. Also known as *paradoxical sleep*, because the muscles are relaxed (except for minor twitches) but other body systems are active. (p. 193)

replication Repeating the essence of a research study, usually with different subjects in different situations, to see whether the basic finding generalizes to other subjects and circumstances. (p. 10)

representativeness heuristic A rule of thumb for judging the likelihood of things in terms of how well they seem to represent, or match, particular prototypes; may lead one to ignore other relevant information. (p. 291)

repression 1. The blocking from consciousness of painful memories and unacceptable impulses. (p. 279) 2. In psycho-analytic theory, the basic defense mechanism that banishes anxiety-arousing thoughts and feelings from consciousness. (p. 415)

resistance In psychoanalysis, the blocking from consciousness of anxiety-laden material. (p. 481)

respondent behavior Behavior that occurs as an automatic response to some stimulus; Skinner's term for behavior learned through classical conditioning. (p. 236)

reticular formation A nerve network (also called the *reticular activating system*) in the brainstem that plays an important role in controlling arousal and attention. (p. 38)

retina The light-sensitive inner surface of the eye, containing the receptor rods and cones plus layers of neurons that begin the processing of visual information. (p. 138)

retinal disparity A binocular cue for perceiving depth; the greater the disparity (difference) between the two images the retina receives of an object, the closer the object is to us. (p. 168)

retrieval The process of getting information out of memory storage. (p. 255)

retroactive interference The disruptive effect of new learning on the recall of old information. (p. 278)

rods Retinal receptors that detect black, white, and gray; necessary for peripheral and twilight vision, when cones don't respond. (p. 139)

role A set of expectations about a social position, defining how those in the position ought to behave. (p. 556)

rooting reflex A baby's tendency, when touched on the cheek, to open the mouth and search for the nipple. (p. 65)

Rorschach inkblot test The most widely used projective test, designed by Hermann Rorschach; seeks to identify people's projected feelings by analyzing their interpretation of a set of 10 inkblots. (p. 418)

savant syndrome A condition in which a person otherwise limited in mental ability has an amazing specific skill, such as in computation or drawing. (p. 330)

scapegoat theory The theory that prejudice provides an outlet for anger by providing someone to blame. (p. 613)

scatterplot A graphed cluster of dots, each of which represents the values of two variables (such as a student's high school and college GPAs). The slope of the points suggests the degree and direction of the relationship between the two variables. (Also called a *scattergram* or *scatter diagram*.) (p. 626)

schema A concept or framework that organizes and interprets information. (p. 70)

schizophrenia A group of severe psychotic disorders characterized by disorganized and deluded thinking, disturbed perceptions, and inappropriate emotions and actions. (p. 466)

secondary reinforcer A conditioned reinforcer; a stimulus that gains its reinforcing power by association with a primary reinforcer. (p. 239)

secondary sex characteristics Nonreproductive sexual characteristics such as female breasts and hips, male voice quality, and body hair. (p. 96)

selective attention The focusing of conscious awareness on a particular stimulus, as in the cocktail party effect. (p. 190)

self-actualization According to Maslow, the ultimate psychological need that arises after basic physical and psychological needs are met and self-esteem is achieved; the motivation to fulfill one's potential. (p. 428)

self-concept All our thoughts and feelings about ourselves in answer to the question, "Who am I?" (p. 429)

self-disclosure Revealing intimate aspects of oneself to others. (p. 582)

self-esteem One's feelings of high or low self-worth. (p. 430)

self-serving bias A readiness to perceive oneself favorably. (p. 431)

semantic encoding The encoding of meaning, including the meaning of words. (p. 257)

semantics Meaning (or the study of meaning), as derived from morphemes, words, and sentences. (p. 302)

sensation The process by which our sense receptors and nervous system receive and represent stimulus energies from our environment. (p. 132)

sensorimotor stage In Piaget's theory, the stage (from birth to about 2 years of age) during which infants know the world mostly in terms of their sensory impressions and motor activities. (p. 72)

sensory adaptation Diminished sensitivity that is a consequence of constant stimulation. (p. 135)

sensory cortex The area at the front of the parietal lobes that registers and processes body sensations. (p. 44)

sensory interaction The principle that one sense may influence another, as when the smell of food influences its taste. (p. 154)

sensory memory The immediate, initial recording of sensory information in the memory system. (p. 256)

sensory neurons Neurons that carry incoming information from the sense receptors to the central nervous system. (p. 28)

serial position effect Our tendency to recall best the last and first items in a list. (p. 259)

set point The point at which an individual's "weight thermostat" is set. When the body falls below this weight, an increase in hunger and a lowered metabolic rate act to restore the lost weight. (p. 357)

sexual dysfunction A problem that consistently impairs sexual arousal or functioning. (p. 365)

sexual orientation An enduring sexual attraction toward members of either one's own sex (homosexual orientation) or the other sex (heterosexual orientation). (p. 365)

sexual response cycle The four stages of sexual responding described by Masters and Johnson—excitement, plateau, orgasm, and resolution. (p. 362)

shaping An operant conditioning procedure in which reinforcers guide behavior toward closer and closer approximations of a desired goal. (p. 237)

short-term memory "Working memory" that holds a few items briefly, such as the seven digits of a phone number while dialing, before the information is stored or forgotten. (p. 256)

signal detection The task of judging the presence of a faint stimulus ("signal"). Signal detection researchers assume there is no single absolute threshold, because the detection of a weak signal depends partly on a person's experience, expectation, motivation, and level of fatigue. (p. 133)

similarity A perceptual tendency to group together similar elements. (p. 166)

Skinner box A chamber containing a bar or key that an animal can manipulate to obtain a food or water reinforcer, and devices to record the animal's rate of bar pressing or key pecking. Used in operant conditioning research. (p. 237)

sleep apnea A sleep disorder characterized by temporary cessations of breathing during sleep and consequent momentary reawakenings. (p. 197)

social clock The culturally preferred timing of social events such as marriage, parenthood, and retirement. (p. 117)

social-cultural perspective Emphasizes the differences and similarities of thinking and behavior in different social situations and cultures. (p. 7)

social exchange theory The theory that our social behavior is an exchange process, the aim of which is to maximize benefits and minimize costs. (p. 576)

social facilitation Improved performance of tasks in the presence of others; occurs with simple or well-learned tasks but not with tasks that are difficult or not yet mastered. (p. 563)

social leadership Group-oriented leadership that builds teamwork, mediates conflict, and offers support. (p. 376)

social loafing The tendency for people in a group to exert less effort when pooling their efforts toward attaining a common goal than when individually accountable. (p. 564)

social psychology The scientific study of how we think about, influence, and relate to one another. (p. 551)

social traps Situations in which the conflicting parties, by each rationally pursuing their self-interest, become caught in mutually destructive behavior. (p. 615)

sociobiology The study of the evolution of social behavior using the principles of natural selection; it assumes that natural selection favors genetically influenced social behaviors that contribute to the preservation and spread of one's genes. (p. 577)

somatic [so-MAT-ik] **nervous system** The division of the peripheral nervous system that receives information from various sense receptors and controls the skeletal muscles of the body. (p. 33)

somatoform disorders Psychological disorders in which the symptoms take a somatic (bodily) form without apparent physical cause. See *conversion disorder* and *hypochondriasis*. (p. 454)

spacing effect The tendency for distributed study or practice to yield better long-term retention than massed study or practice. (p. 259)

split-brain A condition in which the two hemispheres of the brain are isolated by cutting the connecting fibers between them (mainly those of the corpus callosum). (p. 49)

spontaneous recovery The reappearance, after a rest period, of an extinguished conditioned response. (p. 231)

SQ3R An acronym for *Survey, Question, Read, Rehearse, Review*—a method of study. (p. 23)

standard deviation A measure of score variability; computed by (1) calculating the deviation of each score from the mean, (2) squaring those deviations, (3) finding their average, and (4) finding the square root of this average. (p. 626)

standardization Defining meaningful scores by comparison with the performance of a pretested "standardization group." (p. 322)

Stanford-Binet The widely used American revision (by Terman at Stanford University) of Binet's original intelligence test. (p. 320)

state-dependent memory The tendency to recall information best in the same emotional or physiological state as when the information was learned. (p. 274)

statistical significance A statistical statement of how likely it is that an obtained result occurred by chance. (p. 634)

stereotype A generalized (often overgeneralized) belief about a group of people. (p. 610)

stimulants Drugs (such as caffeine, nicotine, and the more powerful amphetamines and cocaine) that excite neural activity and speed up body functions. (p. 210)

storage The maintenance of encoded information over time. (p. 255)

stranger anxiety The fear of strangers that infants commonly display beginning by about 8 months of age. (p. 72)

stress The whole process by which we perceive and respond to certain events, called *stressors*, that we appraise as threatening or challenging. (p. 512)

sublimation In psychoanalytic theory, the defense mechanism by which people rechannel their unacceptable impulses into socially approved activities. (p. 416)

subliminal Below one's absolute threshold for conscious awareness. (p. 134)

superego The part of personality that, according to Freud, represents internalized ideals and provides standards for judgment (the conscience) and for future aspirations. (p. 414)

superordinate goals Shared goals that override differences among people and require their cooperation. (p. 616)

survey A technique for ascertaining the self-reported attitudes or behaviors of people by questioning a representative, random sample of them. (p. 11)

sympathetic nervous system The division of the autonomic nervous system that arouses the body, mobilizing its energy in stressful situations. (p. 33)

synapse [SIN-aps] The junction between the axon tip of the sending neuron and the dendrite or cell body of the receiving neuron. The tiny gap at this junction is called the *synaptic gap* or *cleft*. (p. 30)

syntax Rules for combining words into grammatically sensible sentences. (p. 302)

systematic desensitization A type of counterconditioning that associates a pleasant, relaxed state with gradually increasing anxiety-triggering stimuli. Commonly used to treat phobias. (p. 488)

task leadership Goal-oriented leadership that sets standards, organizes work, and focuses attention on goals. (p. 376)

telegraphic speech Early speech stage in which the child speaks like a telegram—using mostly nouns and verbs and omitting "auxiliary" words. (p. 304)

temperament A person's characteristic emotional reactivity and intensity. (p. 77)

temporal lobes The portion of the cerebral cortex lying roughly above the ears; includes the auditory areas, each of which receives auditory information primarily from the opposite ear. (p. 42)

teratogens Agents, such as chemicals and viruses, that can reach the embryo or fetus during prenatal development and cause harm. (p. 65)

testosterone 1. The most important of the male sex hormones. Both males and females have it, but the additional testosterone in males stimulates the growth of the male sex organs in the fetus and the development of the male sex characteristics during puberty. (p. 64) 2. The most important of the male sex hormones. Although both males and females have it, the additional testosterone in males stimulates the growth of male sex characteristics and, especially in nonhuman animals, influences sexual arousal. (p. 362)

texture gradient A monocular cue for perceiving distance; a gradual change to a less distinct texture suggests increasing distance. (p. 169)

thalamus [THAL-uh-muss] The brain's sensory switchboard, located on top of the brainstem; directs messages to the sensory receiving areas in the cortex and transmits replies to the cerebellum and medulla. (p. 38)

THC The major active ingredient in marijuana; triggers a variety of effects, including mild hallucinations. (p. 215)

Thematic Apperception Test (TAT) A projective test in which people express their inner hopes, fears, and interests through the stories they make up about ambiguous scenes. (p. 418)

theory An explanation via an integrated set of principles that organizes and predicts observations. (p. 10)

theory X Assumes that workers are basically lazy, error-prone, and extrinsically motivated by money and thus should be directed from above. (p. 377)

theory Y Assumes that, given challenge and freedom, workers are motivated to achieve self-esteem and to demonstrate their competence and creativity. (p. 377)

thinking (or *cognition*) Mental activity associated with understanding, processing, and communicating knowledge. (p. 286)

threshold The level of stimulation required to trigger a neural impulse. (p. 29)

token economy An operant conditioning procedure that rewards desired behavior. A patient exchanges a token of some sort, earned for exhibiting the desired behavior, for various privileges or treats. (p. 490)

tolerance The diminishing of a drug's effect with regular use of the same dose, requiring the user to take larger and larger doses before experiencing the drug's effect. (p. 210)

trait A characteristic pattern of behavior or conscious motive; assessed by self-report inventories and peer reports. (p. 422)

transduction Conversion of one form of energy into another. In sensation, the transforming of stimulus energies into neural impulses. (p. 137)

transference In psychoanalysis, the patient's transfer to the analyst of emotions linked with other relationships (such as love or hatred for a parent). (p. 481)

two-factor theory Schachter's theory that to experience emotion one must (1) be physically aroused and (2) cognitively label the arousal. (p. 404)

two-word stage Beginning about age 2, the stage in speech development during which a child speaks mostly two-word statements. (p. 304)

Type A Friedman and Rosenman's term for competitive, hard-driving, impatient, verbally aggressive, and anger-prone people. (p. 519)

Type B Friedman and Rosenman's term for easygoing, relaxed people. (p. 519)

unconditional positive regard According to Rogers, an attitude of total acceptance toward another person. (p. 429)

unconditioned response (UCR) In classical conditioning, the unlearned, automatic response to the unconditioned stimulus, such as salivation when food is in the mouth. (p. 229)

unconditioned stimulus (UCS) In classical conditioning, a stimulus that unconditionally—naturally and automatically—triggers a response without conditioning. (p. 229)

unconscious According to Freud, a reservoir of mostly unacceptable thoughts, wishes, feelings, and memories. According to contemporary research psychologists, a level of information processing of which we are unaware. (p. 413)

validity The extent to which a test measures or predicts what it is supposed to. (See also *content validity* and *predictive validity*.) (p. 326)

variable-interval schedule In operant conditioning, a schedule of reinforcement that reinforces a response at unpredictable time intervals. (p. 241)

variable-ratio schedule In operant conditioning, a schedule of reinforcement that reinforces a response after an unpredictable number of responses. (p. 241)

visual capture The tendency for vision to dominate the other senses; we perceive filmed voices as coming from the screen we see rather than from the projector behind us. (p. 165)

visual cliff A laboratory device for testing depth perception in infants and young animals. (p. 167)

visual encoding The encoding of picture images. (p. 257)

wavelength The distance from the peak of one light or sound wave to the peak of the next. Electromagnetic wavelengths vary from the long pulses of radio transmission to the short blips of cosmic rays. (p. 137)

Weber's law The principle that, to perceive their difference, two stimuli must differ by a constant minimum percentage (rather than a constant amount). (p. 135)

Wechsler Adult Intelligence Scale (WAIS) The current revision (WAIS-R) is the most widely used intelligence test; contains verbal and performance (nonverbal) subtests. (p. 322)

Wernicke's area An area of the left temporal lobe involved in language comprehension. (p. 46)

withdrawal The discomfort and distress that follow the discontinued use of addictive drugs. (p. 210)

X chromosome The sex chromosome found in both men and women. Females have two *X* chromosomes; males have one. An *X* chromosome from each parent produces a female. (p. 64)

Y chromosome The sex chromosome found only in males. When paired with an *X* sex chromosome from the mother, the result is a male child. (p. 64)

Young-Helmholtz trichromatic (three-color) theory The theory that the retina contains three different color receptors—one most sensitive to red, one to green, one to blue—which combined can produce the perception of any color. (p. 143)

zygote The fertilized egg; it enters a 2-week period of rapid cell division and develops into an embryo. (p. 64)

References

Abbey, A. (1987). Misperceptions of friendly behavior as sexual interest: A survey of naturally occurring incidents. *Psychology of Women Quarterly, 11,* 173–194. (p. 602)

Abrams, D. B., & Wilson, G. T. (1983). Alcohol, sexual arousal, and self-control. *Journal of Personality and Social Psychology, 45,* 188–198. (p. 212)

Abramson, L. Y., Metalsky, G. I., & Alloy, L. B. (1989). Hopelessness depression: A theory-based subtype. *Psychological Review, 96,* 358–372. (p. 463)

Adams, D., & 19 others. (1987). Statement on violence. *Medicine and War, 3,* 191–193. (p. 569)

Adams, P. R., & Adams, G. R. (1984). Mount Saint Helens's ashfall: Evidence for a disaster stress reaction. *American Psychologist, 39,* 252–260. (p. 514)

Adelmann, P. K. (1988). Work and psychological well-being: A meta-analysis. Unpublished manuscript, University of Michigan. (p. 120)

Adelmann, P. K., Antonucci, T. C., Crohan, S. F., & Coleman, L. M. (1989). Empty nest, cohort, and employment in the well-being of midlife women. *Sex Roles, 20,* 173–189. (p. 119)

Ader, R., & Cohen, N. (1985). CNS-immune system interactions: Conditioning phenomena. *Behavioral and Brain Sciences, 8,* 379–394. (p. 523)

Adler, N., & Stone, G. (1984). Psychology and the health system. In J. Ruffini (Ed.), *Advances in medical social science.* New York: Gordon & Breach. (p. 527)

Adler, N. E., David, H. P., Major, B. N., Roth, S. H., Russo, N. F., & Wyatt, G. E. (1990). Psychological responses after abortion. *Science, 248,* 41–44. (p. 516)

Adler, T. (1989, March). FAA establishes unit to study human error. *APA Monitor,* p. 4. (p. 164)

Adler, T. (1991, February). Cancer patients helped by therapy, study finds. *APA Monitor,* p. 9. (p. 522)

Advertising Age (1958, February 10). "Phone now," said CBC subliminally—but nobody did. P. 8. (p. 135)

Aiello, J. R., Thompson, D. D., & Brodzinsky, D. M. (1983). How funny is crowding anyway? Effects of room size, group size, and the introduction of humor. *Basic and Applied Social Psychology, 4,* 193–207. (p. 563)

Ainsworth, M. D. S. (1973). The development of infant-mother attachment. In B. Caldwell & H. Ricciuti (Eds.), *Review of child development research* (Vol. 3). Chicago: University of Chicago Press. (p. 78)

Ainsworth, M. D. S. (1979). Infant-mother attachment. *American Psychologist, 34,* 932–937. (p. 78)

Ainsworth, M. D. S. (1989). Attachments beyond infancy. *American Psychologist, 44,* 709–716. (p. 78)

Akin-Ogundeji, O. (1991). Asserting psychology in Africa. *The Psychologist, 14,* 2–4. (p. 4)

Albee, G. W. (1986). Toward a just society: Lessons from observations on the primary prevention of psychopathology. *American Psychologist, 41,* 891–898. (p. 506)

Alcock, J. E. (1981). *Parapsychology: Science or magic?* Oxford: Pergamon. (p. 274)

Alcock, J. E. (1985, Spring). Parapsychology: The "spiritual" science. *Free Inquiry,* pp. 25–35. (p. 185)

Alcohol, Drug Abuse, and Mental Health Administration. (1990). *Economic costs of alcohol and drug abuse and mental illness: 1985.* Rockville, MD: National Clearinghouse for Alcohol and Drug Information. (p. 499)

Aldrich, M. S. (1989). Automobile accidents in patients with sleep disorders. *Sleep, 12,* 487–494. (p. 197)

Aldridge-Morris, R. (1989). *Multiple personality: An exercise in deception.* Hillsdale, NJ: Erlbaum. (p. 457)

Alexander, C. N., Cranson, R. W., Boyer, R. W., & Orme-Johnson, D. W. (1987). Transcendental consciousness: A fourth state of consciousness beyond sleep, dreaming and waking. In J. Gackenbach (Ed.), *Sleep and dreams: A source-book.* New York: Garland Press. (p. 202)

Alexander, C. N., Langer, E. J., Newman, R. I., Chandler, H. M., & Davies, J. L. (1989). Transcendental meditation, mindfulness, and longevity: An experimental study with the elderly. *Journal of Personality and Social Psychology, 57,* 950–964. (p. 202)

Alkon, D. L. (1989, July). Memory storage and neural systems. *Scientific American,* pp. 42–50. (p. 269)

Allard, F., & Burnett, N. (1985). Skill in sport. *Canadian Journal of Psychology, 39,* 294–312. (p. 263)

Allison, R. B. (1984). Difficulties diagnosing the multiple personality syndrome in a death penalty case. *International Journal of Clinical and Experimental Hypnosis, 32,* 102–117. (p. 457)

Allman, A. L. (1989). Subjective well-being of students with and without disabilities. Paper presented at the Midwestern Psychological Association convention. (p. 397)

Allport, G. W. (1967). Gordon W. Allport. In E. G. Boring & G. Lindzey (Eds.), *A history of psychology in autobiography* (Vol. V). New York: Appleton-Century-Crofts. (p. 421)

Allport, G. W., & Odbert, H. S. (1936). Trait-names: A psycholexical study. *Psychological Monographs, 47*(1). (p. 423)

Altman, L. K. (1990, May 29). The evidence mounts on passive smoking. *The New York Times,* pp. C1, C8. (p. 534)

Altus, W. D. (1966). Birth order and its sequelae. *Science, 151,* 44–49. (p. 372)

Alwin, D. F. (1990). Historical changes in parental orientations to children. In N. Mandell (Ed.), *Sociological studies of child development* (Vol. 3). Greenwich, CT: JAI Press. (pp. 86, 593)

Amabile, T. M. (1983). *The social psychology of creativity.* New York: Springer-Verlag. (pp. 336, 430)

Amabile, T. M. (1987). The motivation to be creative. In S. Isaksen (Ed.), *Frontiers in creativity: Beyond the basics.* Buffalo, NY: Bearly Limited. (p. 336)

Amabile, T. M. (1988). From individual creativity to organizational innovation. In K. Gronhaug & G. Kaufmann (Eds.), *Innovation: A crossdisciplinary perspective.* Oslo: Norwegian University Press. (p. 336)

Amabile, T. M., & Hennessey, B. A. (1988). The motivation for creativity in children. In A. K. Boggiano & T. Pittman (Eds.), *Achievement and motivation: A social-developmental perspective.* New York: Cambridge University Press. (p. 336)

Ambady, N., & Rosenthal, R. (1991). Half a minute: Predicting teacher effectiveness from nonverbal classroom behavior. Unpublished manuscript, Harvard University. (p. 427)

Ambady, N., & Rosenthal, R. (1992). Thin slices of expressive behavior as predictors of interpersonal consequences: A meta-analysis. *Psychological Bulletin,* in press. (p. 427)

American Psychiatric Association. (1987). *Diagnostic and statistic manual of mental disorders (Third Edition—Revised).* Washington, DC: American Psychiatric Association. (p. 333)

American Psychiatric Association. (1990). *The practice of ECT: Recommendations for treatment, training, and privileging.* Washington, DC: American Psychiatric Press. (p. 505)

American Psychological Association. (1986). Council of Representatives statement cited by N. Abeles, Proceedings of the American Psychological Association, Incorporated, for the Year

1985: Minutes of the annual meeting of the Council of Representatives August 22 and 25, 1985, Los Angeles, California, and January 31–February 2, 1986, Washington, DC. *American Psychologist, 41,* 633–663. (p. 387)

Andersen, B. L. (1989). Health psychology's contribution to addressing the cancer problem: Update on accomplishments. *Health Psychology,* 8, 683–703. (p. 522)

Anderson, A. (1982, December). How the mind heals. *Psychology Today,* pp. 51–56. (p. 523)

Anderson, B. L. (1983). Primary orgasmic dysfunction: Diagnostic considerations and review of treatment. *Psychological Bulletin, 93,* 105–136. (p. 365)

Anderson, C. A. (1989). Temperature and aggression: Ubiquitous effects of heat on occurrence of human violence. *Psychological Bulletin, 106,* 74–96. (p. 570)

Anderson, C. A., & Anderson, D. C. (1984). Ambient temperature and violent crime: Tests of the linear and curvilinear hypotheses. *Journal of Personality and Social Psychology, 46,* 91–97. (p. 570)

Anderson, C. A., & Arnoult, L. H. (1989). An examination of perceived control, humor, irrational beliefs, and positive stress as moderators of the relation between negative stress and health. *Basic and Applied Social Psychology, 10,* 101–117. (p. 515)

Anderson, C. A., Lepper, M. R., & Ross, L. (1980). Perseverance of social theories: The role of explanation in the persistence of discredited information. *Journal of Personality and Social Psychology, 39,* 1037–1049. (p. 298)

Anderson, D. R., & Jose, W. S., II. (1987, December). Employee lifestyle and the bottom line: Results from the StayWell evaluation. *Fitness in Business,* pp. 86–91. (pp. 529, 534)

Anderson, J. R. (1983). Retrieval of information from long-term memory. *Science, 220,* 25–30. (p. 272)

Andersson, B. E. (1989). Effects of public daycare: A longitudinal study. *Child Development, 60,* 857–866. (p. 83)

Andreasen, N. C., Ehrhardt, J. C., Swayze, V. W., Alliger, R. J., Yuh, W. T. C., Cohen, G., & Ziebell, S. (1990a). Magnetic resonance imaging of the brain in schizophrenia. *Archives of General Psychiatry, 47,* 35–44. (p. 468)

Andreasen, N. C., Swayze, V. W., Flaum, M., Yates, W. R., Arndt, S., & McChesney, C. (1990b). Ventricular enlargement in schizophrenia evaluated with computed tomographic scanning. *Archives of General Psychiatry, 47,* 1008–1015. (p. 468)

Angoff, W. H. (1987). The nature-nurture debate, aptitudes, and group differences. Presidential address to American Psychological Association Division 5. (p. 342)

Angoff, W. H. (1988, Winter). A philosophical discussion: The issues of test and item bias. *ETS Developments,* pp. 10–11. (pp. 333, 345)

Antaki, C. (1989, May). A brief account of psychology in Nicaragua. *The Psychologist,* pp. 208–209. (p. 4)

Antill, J. K. (1983). Sex role complementarity versus similarity in married couples. *Journal of Personality and Social Psychology, 45,* 145–155. (p. 600)

APS Observer. (1989, September). The number of periodicals in psychology (from Ulrich's International Periodical Directory). P. 21. (p. 4)

Archer, J. (1991). The influence of testosterone on human aggression. *British Journal of Psychology, 82,* 1–28. (p. 569)

Arendt, H. (1963). *Eichmann in Jerusalem: A report on the banality of evil.* New York: Viking Press. (p. 101)

Aries, E. (1987). Gender and communication. In P. Shaver & C. Henrick (Eds.), *Review of Personality and Social Psychology, 7,* 177–200. (p. 601)

Asarnow, J. R. (1988). Children at risk for schizophrenia: Converging lines of evidence. *Schizophrenia Bulletin, 14,* 613–621. (p. 470)

Asch, S. E. (1955). Opinions and social pressure. *Scientific American, 193,* 31–35. (p. 558)

Aserinsky, E. (1988, January 17). Personal communication. (p. 192)

Astin, A. W., Green, K. C., & Korn, W. S. (1987). The American freshman: Twenty year trends. (A report of the Cooperative Institutional Research Program sponsored by the American Council on Education.) Los Angeles, CA: Higher Education Research Institute, Graduate School of Education, UCLA. (pp. 217, 397)

Astin, A. W., Korn, W. S., & Berz, E. R. (1989). *The American freshman: National norms for Fall 1989.* Los Angeles: American Council on Education and UCLA. (pp. 370, 397, 607)

Astin, A. W. & Others (1991). *The American freshman: National norms for Fall 1990.* Los Angeles: American Council on Education and UCLA. (pp. 217, 295, 397, 600–601)

Astin, G. R., & Garber, H. (1982). *The rise and fall of national test scores.* New York: Academic Press. (p. 325)

Atkinson, R. (1988). *The teenage world: Adolescent self-image in ten countries.* New York: Plenum Press. (p. 86)

Atwell, R. H. (1986, July 28). Drugs on campus: A perspective. *Higher Education & National Affairs,* p. 5. (p. 212)

Austin, J. T., & Hanisch, K. A. (1990). Occupational attainment as a function of abilities and interests: A longitudinal analysis using Project TALENT data. *Journal of Applied Psychology, 75,* 77–86. (p. 331)

Averill, J. R. (1969). Autonomic response patterns during sadness and mirth. *Psychophysiology, 5,* 399–414. (p. 385)

Averill, J. R. (1983). Studies on anger and aggression: Implications for theories of emotion. *American Psychologist, 38,* 1145–1160. (p. 395)

Ax, A. F. (1953). The physiological differentiation of fear and anger in humans. *Psychosomatic Medicine, 15,* 433–442. (p. 385)

Bachman, J. G., Johnston, L. D., & O'Malley, P. M. (1987). *Monitoring the future: Questionnaire responses from the nation's high school seniors, 1986.* Ann Arbor, MI: Institute for Social Research, The University of Michigan. (p. 104)

Backus, J. (1977). *The acoustical foundations of music* (2nd ed.). New York: Norton. (p. 148)

Baddeley, A. D. (1982). *Your memory: A user's guide.* New York: Macmillan. (pp. 258–259)

Badenhoop, M. S., & Johansen, M. K. (1980). Do reentry women have special needs? *Psychology of Women Quarterly, 4,* 591–595. (p. 114)

Bahrick, H. P. (1984a). Memory and people. In J. Harris (Ed.), *Everyday memory, actions, and absentmindedness.* Orlando, FL: Academic Press. (p. 259)

Bahrick, H. P. (1984b). Semantic memory content in permastore: 50 years of memory for Spanish learned in school. *Journal of Experimental Psychology: General, 111,* 1–29. (pp. 266–267)

Bahrick, H. P., Bahrick, P. O., & Wittlinger, R. P. (1975). Fifty years of memory for names and faces: A cross-sectional approach. *Journal of Experimental Psychology: General, 104,* 54–75. (p. 272)

Bahrick, H. P., & Hall, L. K. (1991). Lifetime maintenance of high school mathematics content. *Journal of Experimental Psychology: General, 120,* 20–33. (p. 259)

Bailey, R. E., & Bailey, M. B. (1980). A view from outside the Skinner box. *American Psychologist, 35,* 942–946. (p. 244)

Bairagi, R. (1987). Food crises and female children in rural Bangladesh. *Social Science, 72,* 48–51. (p. 612)

Baker, E. L. (1987). The state of the art of clinical hypnosis. *International Journal of Clinical and Experimental Hypnosis, 35,* 203–214. (p. 205)

Balakrishan, T. R., Rao, K. V., Lapierre-Adamcyk, E., & Krotki, K. J. (1987). A hazard model analysis of the covariates of marriage dissolution in Canada. *Demography, 24,* 395–406. (p. 370)

Ball, W., & Tronick, E. (1971). Infant responses to impending collision: Optical and real. *Science, 171,* 818–820. (p. 167)

Baltes, P. B., & Smith, J. (1990). Toward a psychology of wisdom and its ontogenesis. In R. J. Sternberg (Ed.), *Wisdom: Its nature, origins, and development.* New York: Cambridge University Press. (p. 115)

Bandura, A. (1977). *Social learning theory.* Englewood Cliffs, NJ: Prentice-Hall. (p. 247)

Bandura, A. (1982). The psychology of chance encounters and life paths. *American Psychologist, 37,* 747–755. (p. 117)

Bandura, A. (1986). *Social foundations of thought and action: A social-cognitive theory.* Englewood Cliffs, NJ: Prentice-Hall. (pp. 434–435)

Bandura, A., Blanchard, E. B., & Ritter, B. (1969). Relative efficacy of desensitization and modeling approaches for inducing behavioral, affective, and attitudinal changes. *Journal of Personality and Social Psychology, 13,* 173–199. (p. 488)

Bandura, A., Ross, D., & Ross, S. A. (1961). Transmission of aggression through imitation of aggressive models. *Journal of Abnormal and Social Psychology, 63,* 575–582. (p. 247)

Barker, S. L., Funk, S. C., & Houston, B. K. (1988). Psychological treatment versus nonspecific factors: A meta-analysis of conditions that engender comparable expectations for improvement. *Clinical Psychology Review, 8,* 579–594. (p. 500)

Barnes, D. M. (1990, Spring). Silver Spring monkeys yield unexpected data on brain reorganization. *Journal of NIH Research, 2,* 19–20. (p. 47)

Barnett, P. A., & Gotlib, I. H. (1988). Psychosocial functioning and depression: Distinguishing among antecedents, concomitants, and consequences. *Psychological Bulletin, 104,* 97–126. (p. 463)

Baron, J. (1985). *Rationality and intelligence.* New York: Cambridge University Press. (p. 328)

Baron, L., & Straus, M. A. (1984). Sexual stratification, pornography, and rape in the United States. In N. M. Malamuth & E. Donnerstein (Eds.), *Pornography and sexual aggression.* Orlando, FL: Academic Press. (p. 572)

Baron, L., & Straus, M. A. (1986). Rape and its relation to social disorganization, pornography, and sexual inequality in the United States. Unpublished manuscript, Yale University. Cited by E. Donnerstein, D. Linz, & S. Penrod (1987), *The question of pornography.* New York: Free Press. (p. 572)

Baron, R. A. (1987). Interviewer's mood and reaction to job applicants: The influence of affective states on applied social judgments. *Journal of Applied Social Psychology, 17,* 911–926. (p. 396)

Baron, R. A. (1988). Negative effects of destructive criticism: Impact on conflict, self-efficacy, and task performance. *Journal of Applied Psychology, 73,* 199–207. (p. 246)

Baron, R. A. (1990). Environmentally induced positive affect: Its impact on self-efficacy, task performance, negotiation, and conflict. *Journal of Applied Social Psychology, 20,* 368–384. (p. 156)

Baron, R. S., Cutrona, C. E., Hicklin, D., Russell, D. W., & Lubaroff, D. M. (1990). Social support and immune function among spouses of cancer patients. *Journal of Personality and Social Psychology, 59,* 344–352. (p. 533)

Barton, J., Chassin, L., Presson, C. C., & Sherman, S. J. (1982). Social image factors as motivators of smoking initiation in early and middle adolescence. *Child Development, 53,* 1499–1511. (p. 535)

Baruch, G. K., & Barnett, R. (1986). Role quality, multiple role involvement, and psychological well-being in midlife women. *Journal of Personality and Social Psychology, 51,* 578–585. (p. 120)

Bashore, T. R., Osman, A., & Heffley, E. F. (1989). Mental slowing in elderly persons: A cognitive psychophysiological analysis. *Psychology and Aging, 4,* 235–244. (p. 111)

Batson, C. D. (1983). Sociobiology and the role of religion in promoting prosocial behavior: An alternative view. *Journal of Personality and Social Psychology, 45,* 1380–1385. (p. 578)

Batson, C. D. (1987). Prosocial motivation: Is it ever truly altruistic? In L. Berkowitz (Ed.), *Advances in experimental social psychology* (Vol. 20). Orlando, FL: Academic Press. (p. 577)

Baumann, L. J., & Leventhal, H. (1985). "I can tell when my blood pressure is up, can't I?" *Health Psychology, 4,* 203–218. (p. 525)

Baumann, L. J., & Siegel, K. (1987). Misperception among gay men of the risk for AIDS associated with their sexual behavior. *Journal of Applied Social Psychology, 17,* 329–350. (p. 367)

Baumeister, R. F. (1989). The optimal margin of illusion. *Journal of Social and Clinical Psychology, 8,* 176–189. (pp. 295, 432)

Baumeister, R. F., Stillwell, A., & Wotman, S. R. (1991). Victim and perpetrator accounts of interpersonal conflict: Autobiographical narratives about anger. *Journal of Personality and Social Psychology,* in press. (p. 396)

Baumeister, R. F., & Tice, D. M. (1986). How adolescence became the struggle for self: A historical transformation of psychological development. In J. Suls & A. G. Greenwald (Eds.), *Psychological perspectives on the self* (Vol. 3). Hillsdale, NJ: Erlbaum. (p. 95)

Baumeister, R. F., Tice, D. M., & Hutton, D. G. (1989). Self-presentational motivations and personality differences in self-esteem. *Journal of Personality, 57,* 547–579. (p. 430)

Baumgardner, A. H. (1990). To know oneself is to like oneself: Self-certainty and self-affect. *Journal of Personality and Social Psychology, 58,* 1062–1072. (p. 103)

Baumgardner, A. H., Kaufman, C. M., & Levy, P. E. (1989). Regulating affect interpersonally: When low esteem leads to greater enhancement. *Journal of Personality and Social Psychology, 56,* 907–921. (p. 430)

Baumrind, D. (1982). Adolescent sexuality: Comment on Williams' and Silka's comments on Baumrind. *American Psychologist, 37,* 1402–1403. (p. 369)

Baumrind, D. (1983). Rejoinder to Lewis's reinterpretation of parental firm control effects: Are authoritative families really harmonious? *Psychological Bulletin, 94,* 132–142. (p. 85)

Baumrind, D. (1991). Parenting styles and adolescent development. In J. Brooks-Gunn, R. Lerner, & A. C. Petersen (Eds.), *The encyclopedia of adolescence.* New York: Garland, in press. (p. 85)

Baxter, L. R., Jr., Phelps, M. E., Mazziotta, J. C., Guze, B. H., Schwartz, J. M., & Selin, C. E. (1987). Local cerebral glucose metabolic rates in obsessive-compulsive disorder. *Archives of General Psychiatry, 44,* 211–218. (p. 454)

Bayley, N. (1949). Consistency and variability in the growth of intelligence from birth to eighteen years. *Journal of Genetic Psychology, 75,* 165–196. (p. 332)

Beaman, A. L., & Klentz, B. (1983). The supposed physical attractiveness bias against supporters of the women's movement: A meta-analysis. *Personality and Social Psychology Bulletin, 9,* 544–550. (p. 581)

Beauchamp, G. K. (1987). The human preference for excess salt. *American Scientist, 75,* 27–33. (p. 356)

Beck, A. T., Rush, A. J., Shaw, B. F., & Emery, G. (1979). *Cognitive therapy of depression.* New York: Guilford Press. (p. 494)

Beck, A. T., & Steer, R. A. (1989). Clinical predictors of eventual suicide: A 5- to 10-year prospective study of suicide attempters. *Journal of Affective Disorders, 17,* 203–209. (p. 461)

Beck, A. T., & Young, J. E. (1978, September). College blues. *Psychology Today,* pp. 80–92. (pp. 458, 465)

Becklen, R., & Cervone, D. (1983). Selective looking and the noticing of unexpected events. *Memory and Cognition, 11,* 601–608. (p. 190)

Beitman, B. D., Goldfried, M. R., & Norcross, J. C. (1989). The movement toward integrating the psychotherapies: An overview. *American Journal of Psychiatry, 146,* 138–147. (p. 480)

Békésy, G., von. (1957, August). The ear. *Scientific American,* pp. 66–78. (p. 147)

Bell, A. P. (1982, November/December). Sexual preference: A postscript. (SIECUS Report, 11, No. 2) *Church and Society,* pp. 34–37. (p. 368)

Bell, A. P., Weinberg, M. S., & Hammersmith, S. K. (1981). *Sexual preference: Its development in men and women.* Bloomington: Indiana University Press. (p. 367)

Bell, R. Q., & Waldrop, M. F. (1989). Achievement and cognitive correlates of minor physical anomalies in early development. In M. G. Bornstein & N. A. Krasnegor (Eds.), *Stability and continuity in mental development: Behavioral and biological perspectives.* Hillsdale, NJ: Erlbaum. (p. 332)

Bellugi, U., Poizner, H., & Klima, E. S. (1989). Language, modality and the brain. *Trends in Neurosciences, 12,* 380–388. (p. 53)

Beloff, J. (1985, Spring). Science, religion and the paranormal. *Free Inquiry,* pp. 36–41 (p. 185)

Belsher, G., & Costello, C. G. (1988). Relapse after recovery from unipolar depression: A critical review. *Psychological Bulletin, 104,* 84–96. (p. 459)

Belsky, J. (1988). The "effects" of infant day care reconsidered. *Early Childhood Research Quarterly* (Vol. III), 235–272. (p. 83)

Belsky, J. (1990). Parental and nonparental child care and children's socioemotional development: A decade in review. *Journal of Marriage and the Family, 52,* 885–903. (p. 82)

Belsky, J., Lang, M., & Huston, T. L. (1986). Sex typing and division of labor as determinants of marital change across the transition to parenthood. *Journal of Personality and Social Psychology, 50,* 517–522. (p. 118)

Bem, D. J. (1984). Quoted in the *Skeptical Inquirer, 8,* 194. (p. 182)

Bem, S. L. (1985). Androgyny and gender schema theory: A conceptual and empirical integration. *Nebraska Symposium on Motivation, 32,* 179–226. (p. 608)

Bem, S. L. (1987). Masculinity and femininity exist only in the mind of the perceiver. In J. M. Reinisch, L. A. Rosenblum, & S. A. Sanders (Eds.), *Masculinity/femininity: Basic perspectives.* New York: Oxford University Press. (pp. 605, 608)

Benassi, V. A., Sweeney, P. D., & Dufour, C. L. (1988). Is there a relation between locus of control orientation and depression? *Journal of Abnormal Psychology, 97,* 357–367. (p. 436)

Benbow, C. P. (1988). Sex differences in mathematical reasoning ability in intellectually talented preadolescents: Their nature, effects, and possible causes. *Behavioral and Brain Sciences, 11,* 169–182. (pp. 598–599)

Benderly, B. L. (1989, November). Don't believe everything you read: A case study of how the politics of sex-difference research turned a small finding into a major media flap. *Psychology Today,* pp. 67–69. (p. 602)

Bennett, N. G., Blanc, A. K., & Bloom, D. E. (1988). Commitment and the modern union: Assessing the link between premarital cohabitation and subsequent marital stability. *American Sociological Review, 53,* 127–138. (p. 370).

Bennis, W. (1984). Transformative power and leadership. In T. J. Sergiovani & J. E. Corbally (Eds.), *Leadership and organizational culture.* Urbana: University of Illinois Press. (p. 377)

Benson, H., & Klipper, M. Z. (1976). *The relaxation response.* New York: Morrow. (p. 530)

Benson, H., & Proctor, W. (1984). *Beyond the relaxation response: How to harness the healing power of your personal beliefs.* New York: Times Books. (p. 530)

Benson, H., & Proctor, W. (1987). *Your maximum mind.* New York: Times Books/Random House. (p. 530)

Bergsholm, P., Larsen, J. L., Rosendahl, K., & Holsten, F. (1989). Electroconvulsive therapy and cerebral computed tomography. *Acta Psychiatrica Scandinavia, 80,* 566–572. (p. 505)

Berkowitz, L. (1983). Aversively stimulated aggression: Some parallels and differences in research with animals and humans. *American Psychologist, 38,* 1135–1144. (p. 569)

Berkowitz, L. (1989). Frustration-aggression hypothesis: Examination and reformulation. *Psychological Bulletin, 106,* 59–73. (p. 569)

Berkowitz, L. (1990). On the formation and regulation of anger and aggression: A cognitive-neoassociationistic analysis. *American Psychologist, 45,* 494–503. (p. 395)

Berman, J. S., & Norton, N. C. (1985). Does professional training make a therapist more effective? *Psychological Bulletin, 98,* 401–407. (p. 502)

Bernard, J. (1976). *Sex differences: An overview.* New York: MSS Modular Publications. (p. 599)

Berry, D. S., & McArthur, L. Z. (1986). Perceiving character in faces: The impact of age-related craniofacial changes on social perception. *Psychological Bulletin, 100,* 3–18. (p. 231)

Berscheid, E. (1981). An overview of the psychological effects of physical attractiveness and some comments upon the psychological effects of knowledge of the effects of physical attractiveness. In G. W. Lucker, K. Ribbens, & J. A. McNamara (Eds.), *Psychological aspects of facial form* (Craniofacial growth series). Ann Arbor: Center for Human Growth and Development, University of Michigan. (p. 580)

Berscheid, E., Gangestad, S. W., & Kulakowski, D. (1984). Emotion in close relationships: Implications for relationship counseling. In S. D. Brown & R. W. Lent (Eds.), *Handbook of counseling psychology.* New York: Wiley. (p. 582)

Best, J. A., & Suedfeld, P. (1982). Restricted environmental stimulation therapy and behavioral self-management in smoking cessation. *Journal of Applied Social Psychology, 12,* 408–419. (p. 158)

Beyer, L. (1990, Fall issue on women). Life behind the veil. *Time,* p. 37. (p. 611)

Biddle, W. (1986, March). The deception of detection. *Discover,* pp. 24–33. (p. 386)

Biederman, I. (1981). On the semantics of a glance at a scene. In M. Kubovy & J. Pomerantz (Eds.), *Perceptual organization.* Hillsdale, NJ: Erlbaum. (p. 179)

Binet, A., & Simon, T. (1905; reprinted 1916). New methods for the diagnosis of the intellectual level of subnormals. In A. Binet & T. Simon, *The development of intelligence in children.* Baltimore: Williams & Wilkins. (p. 319)

Binitie, A. (1975). A factor-analytical study of depression across cultures (African and European). *British Journal of Psychiatry, 127,* 559–563. (p. 455)

Birren, J. E., & Fisher, L. M. (1990). The elements of wisdom: Overview and integration. In R. J. Sternberg (Ed.), *Wisdom: Its nature, origins, and development.* New York: Cambridge University Press. (p. 115)

Bishop, G. D. (1984). Gender, role, and illness behavior in a military population. *Health Psychology, 3,* 519–534. (p. 526)

Bishop, G. D. (1987). Lay conceptions of physical symptoms. *Journal of Applied Social Psychology, 17,* 127–146. (p. 526)

Bishop, G. D. (1991). Understanding the understanding of illness: Lay disease representations. In J. A. Skelton & R. T. Croyle (Eds.), *Mental representation in health and illness.* New York: Springer-Verlag. (p. 287)

Bjork, R. A. (1978). The updating of human memory. In G. H. Bower (Ed.), *The psychology of learning and motivation* (Vol. 12). New York: Academic Press. (p. 264)

Bjork, R. A. (1988). Retrieval practice and the maintenance of knowledge. In M. M. Bruneberg, P. E. Morris, & R. N. Sykes (Eds.), *Practical aspects of memory: Current research and issues.* New York: Wiley. (p. 280)

Blake, C., & Cohen, H. (1985, May). A meta-analysis of sex differences in moral development. *Resources in Education,* Document ED251749. (p. 101)

Blake, J. (1989). Number of siblings and educational attainment. *Science, 245,* 32–36. (p. 372)

Blakemore, C., & Cooper, G. F. (1970). Development of the brain depends on the visual environment. *Nature, 228,* 477–478. (pp. 175–176)

Blass, E. (1987). Research reported at a National Institute of Child Health and Human Development workshop, June 30 and July 1, 1987; reported by G. Kolata, What babies know, and noises parents make. *Science, 237,* 726. (p. 67)

Block, J. (1981). Some enduring and consequential structures of personality. In A. I. Rabin (Ed.), *Further explorations in personality.* New York: Wiley. (p. 124)

Bloom, B. J. (1964). *Stability and change in human characteristics.* New York: Wiley. (p. 333)

Bloom, B. S. (Ed.). (1985). *Developing talent in young people.* New York: Ballantine. (p. 371)

Boggiano, A. K., Barrett, M., Weiher, A. W., McClelland, G. H., & Lusk, C. M. (1987). Use of the maximal-operant principle to motivate children's intrinsic interest. *Journal of Personality and Social Psychology, 53,* 866–879. (p. 243)

Boggiano, A. K., Harackiewicz, J. M., Bessette, M. M., & Main, D. S. (1985). Increasing children's interest through performance-contingent reward. *Social Cognition, 3,* 400–411. (p. 244)

Bolger, N., DeLongis, A., Kessler, R. C., & Schilling, E. A. (1989). Effects of daily stress on negative mood. *Journal of Personality and Social Psychology, 57,* 808–818. (p. 397)

Bond, M. H. (1988). Finding universal dimensions of individual variation in multi-cultural studies of values: The Rokeach and Chinese values surveys. *Journal of Personality and Social Psychology, 55,* 1009–1015. (p. 86)

Bonner, E. (1990, May 4). Missing-child study: Relative often to blame. *Chicago Tribune.* (p. 294)

Booth, A., & Edwards, J. N. (1989). Transmission of marital and family quality over the generations: The effect of parental divorce on unhappiness. *Journal of Divorce, 12,* 41–58. (p. 81)

Boring, E. G. (1930). A new ambiguous figure. *American Journal of Psychology, 42,* 444–445. (p. 177)

Bornstein, M. H. (1989). Stability in early mental development: From attention and information processing in infancy to language and cognition in childhood. In M. G. Bornstein & N. A. Krasnegor (Eds.), *Stability and continuity in mental development: Behavioral and biological perspectives.* Hillsdale, NJ: Erlbaum. (pp. 77, 333)

Bornstein, R. F. (1989). Exposure and affect: Overview and meta-analysis of research, 1968–1987. *Psychological Bulletin, 106,* 265–289. (p. 579)

Bothwell, R. K., Brigham, J. C., & Malpass, R. S. (1989). Cross-racial identification. *Personality and Social Psychology Bulletin, 15,* 19–25. (p. 613)

Bothwell, R. K., Deffenbacher, K. A., & Brigham, J. C. (1987). Correlation of eyewitness accuracy and confidence: Optimality hypothesis revised. *Journal of Applied Psychology, 72,* 691–695. (p. 276)

Bouchard, C., Tremblay, A., Despres, J-P., Nadeau, A., Lupien, P. J., Theriault, G., Dussault, J., Moorjani, S., Pinault, S., & Fournier, G. (1990). The response to long-term overfeeding in identical twins. *The New England Journal of Medicine, 322,* 1477–1482. (p. 541)

Bouchard, T. (1990). Interview with T. M. Skovholt, Counseling implications of genetic research: A dialogue with Thomas Bouchard. *Journal of Counseling and Development, 68,* 633–636. (p. 90)

Bouchard, T. J., Jr. (1981, December 6). Interview on *Nova: Twins* [program broadcast by the Public Broadcasting Service]. (p. 89)

Bouchard, T. J., Jr. (1982). Twins—Nature's twice told tale. In *1983 Yearbook of science and the future*. Chicago: Encyclopaedia Britannica. (p. 337)

Bouchard, T. J., Jr., & Segal, N. L. (1988). Heredity, environment, and IQ. In *Instructor's Resource Manual* to accompany G. Lindzey, R. Thompson, & B. Spring, *Psychology* (3rd ed.). New York: Worth Publishers. (p. 338)

Bouchard, T. J., Lykken, D. T., McGue, M., Segal, N. L., & Tellegen, A. (1990). Sources of human psychological differences: The Minnesota study of twins reared apart. *Science, 250,* 223–228. (pp. 88, 337, 604)

Bower, G. H. (1983). Affect and cognition. *Philosophical Transaction: Royal Society of London, Series B, 302,* 387–402. (p. 274)

Bower, G. H. (1986). Prime time in cognitive psychology. In P. Eelen (Ed.), *Cognitive research and behavior therapy: Beyond the conditioning paradigm.* Amsterdam: North Holland Publishers. (pp. 272–273)

Bower, G. H., & Clark, M. C. (1969). Narrative stories as mediators for serial learning. *Psychonomic Science, 14,* 181–182. (p. 262)

Bower, G. H., Clark, M. C., Lesgold, A. M., & Winzenz, D. (1969). Hierarchical retrieval schemes in recall of categorized word lists. *Journal of Verbal Learning and Verbal Behavior, 8,* 323–343. (p. 264)

Bower, G. H., & Morrow, D. G. (1990). Mental models in narrative comprehension. *Science, 247,* 44–48. (p. 260)

Bower, T. G. R. (1977). *A primer of infant development.* San Francisco: Freeman. (p. 67)

Bower, T. G. R. (1989). *The rational infant: Learning in infancy.* New York: W. H. Freeman. (p. 66)

Bowers, K. S. (1984). Hypnosis. In N. Endler & J. M. Hunt (Eds.), *Personality and behavioral disorders* (2nd ed.). New York: Wiley. (pp. 203, 205)

Bowers, K. S. (1987, July). Personal correspondence. (p. 205)

Bowers, K. S. (1990). Unconscious influences and hypnosis. In J. E. Singer (Ed.), *Repression and dissociation: Implications for personality theory, psychopathology, and health.* Chicago: University of Chicago Press. (p. 209)

Bowers, K. S., & LeBaron, S. (1986). Hypnosis and hypnotizability: Implications for clinical intervention. *Hospital and Community Psychiatry, 37,* 457–467. (p. 206)

Bowers, T. G., & Clum, G. A. (1988). Relative contribution of specific and nonspecific treatment effects: Meta-analysis of placebo-controlled behavior therapy research. *Psychological Bulletin, 103,* 315–323. (p. 500)

Bowlby, J. (1973). *Separation: Anxiety and anger.* New York: Basic Books. (p. 81)

Bowne, D. W., Russell, M. L., Morgan, M. A., Optenberg, S., & Clarke, A. (1984). Reduced disability and health care costs in an industrial fitness program. *Journal of Occupational Medicine, 26,* 809–816. (p. 534)

Boynton, R. M. (1979). *Human color vision.* New York: Holt, Rinehart & Winston. (p. 144)

Bradburn, N. M., Rips, L. J., & Shevell, S. K. (1987). Answering autobiographical questions: The impact of memory and inference on surveys. *Science, 236,* 157–161. (p. 277)

Bradbury, T. N., & Fincham, F. D. (1990). Attributions in marriage: Review and critique. *Psychological Bulletin, 107,* 3–33. (p. 553)

Bradley, D. R., Dumais, S. T., & Petry, H. M. (1976). Reply to Cavonius. *Nature, 261,* 78. (p. 165)

Bradley-Johnson, S., Johnson, C. M., Shanahan, R. H., Rickert, V. L., & Tardona, D. R. (1984). Effects of token reinforcement on WISC-R performance of black and white, low-socioeconomic second graders. *Behavioral Assessment, 6,* 365–373. (p. 343)

Bransford, J., Sherwood, R., Vye, N., & Rieser, J. (1986). Teaching thinking and problem solving. *American Psychologist, 41,* 1078–1089. (p. 286)

Bransford, J. D., & Johnson, M. K. (1972). Contextual prerequisites for understanding: Some investigations of comprehension and recall. *Journal of Verbal Learning and Verbal Behavior, 11,* 717–726. (p. 261)

Braskamp, L. A. (1987). Spectrum: Utility for educational selection and organizational development. Paper presented at the American Psychological Association convention. (p. 376)

Bray, D. W. (1982). The assessment center and the study of lives. *American Psychologist, 37,* 180–189. (p. 439)

Bray, G. A. (1969). Effect of caloric restriction on energy expenditure in obese patients. *Lancet, 2,* 397–398. (pp. 540–541)

Brehm, S., & Brehm, J. W. (1981). *Psychological reactance: A theory of freedom and control.* New York: Academic Press. (p. 566)

Breland, K., & Breland, M. (1961). The misbehavior of organisms. *American Psychologist, 16,* 661–664. (p. 244)

Bretz, R. D. (1989). College grade point average as a predictor of adult success: A meta-analytic review and some additional evidence. *Public Personnel Management, 18,* 11–22. (p. 331)

Brewer, C. (1990). Personal correspondence. (p. 91)

Brewer, W. F. (1977). Memory for the pragmatic implications of sentences. *Memory & Cognition, 5,* 673–678. (p. 260)

Brewin, C. F. (1989). Cognitive change processes in psychotherapy. *Psychological Review, 96,* 379–394. (p. 491)

Brickman, P., Coates, D., & Janoff-Bulman, R. J. (1978). Lottery winners and accident victims: Is happiness relative? *Journal of Personality and Social Psychology, 36,* 917–927. (p. 397)

Brislin, R. W. (1988). Increasing awareness of class, ethnicity, culture, and race by expanding on students' own experiences. In I. S. Cohen (Ed.), *The G. Stanley Hall Lecture Series* (Vol. 8). Washington, DC: American Psychological Association. (p. 588)

British Psychological Society. (1986). Report of the working group on the use of the polygraph in criminal investigation and personnel screening. *Bulletin of the British Psychological Society, 39,* 81–94. (p. 387)

Broadbent, D. E. (1978). The current state of noise research: Reply to Poulton. *Psychological Bulletin, 85,* 1052–1067. (p. 148)

Brockner, J., & Hulton, A. J. B. (1978). How to reverse the vicious cycle of low self-esteem: The importance of attentional focus. *Journal of Experimental Social Psychology, 14,* 564–578. (p. 430)

Broman, S. H. (1989). Infant physical status and later cognitive development. In M. G. Bornstein & N. A. Krasnegor (Eds.), *Stability and continuity in mental development: Behavioral and biological perspectives.* Hillsdale, NJ: Erlbaum. (p. 332)

Bronstein-Burrows, P. (1981). *Introductory psychology: A course in the psychology of both sexes.* Paper presented at the meeting of the American Psychological Association. (p. 580)

Brooks-Gunn, J. (1989). Adolescents as daughters and as mothers: A developmental perspective. In I. Sigel & G. Brody (Eds.), *Family research.* Hillsdale, NJ: Erlbaum. (p. 97)

Brooks-Gunn, J., & Furstenberg, F. F., Jr. (1989). Adolescent sexual behavior. *American Psychologist, 44,* 249–257. (p. 106)

Brooks-Gunn, J., & Ruble, D. N. (1986). Men's and women's attitudes and beliefs about the menstrual cycle. *Sex Roles, 14,* 287–299. (p. 525)

Brothers, J. (1990, February 18). Why wives have affairs. *Parade,* pp. 4–7. (p. 361)

Brown, E. L., & Deffenbacher, K. (1979). *Perception and the senses.* New York: Oxford University Press. (p. 149)

Brown, J. D. (1991). Accuracy and bias in self-knowledge. In C. R. Snyder & D. F. Forsyth (Eds.), *Handbook of social and clinical psychology: The health perspective.* New York: Pergamon Press. (pp. 430–432)

Brown, J. D. (1991). Staying fit and staying well: Physical fitness as a moderator of life stress. *Journal of Personality and Social Psychology, 60,* 555–561. (p. 528)

Brown, J. D., & McGill, K. L. (1989). The cost of good fortune: When positive life events produce negative health consequences. *Journal of Personality and Social Psychology, 57,* 1103–1110. (p. 515)

Brown, R. (1965). *Social psychology.* New York: Free Press. (p. 393)

Brown, R. (1973). *A first language: The early stages.* Cambridge, MA: Harvard University Press. (p. 305)

Brown, R. (1986). Linguistic relativity. In S. H. Hulse & B. F. Green, Jr. (Eds.), *One hundred years of psychological research in America.* Baltimore: Johns Hopkins University Press. (p. 311)

Brown, R., & Kulik, J. (1982). Flashbulb memories. In U. Neisser (Ed.), *Memory observed.* San Francisco: Freeman. (p. 254)

Browne, A., & Finkelhor, D. (1986). Impact of child sexual abuse: A review of the research. *Psychological Bulletin, 99,* 66–77. (p. 80)

Brownell, K. D. (1989). Weight control and your health. *World Book Encyclopedia,* pp. 369–384. (p. 544)

Brownell, K. D. (1991). Dieting and the search for the perfect body: Where physiology and culture collide. *Behavior Therapy, 22,* 1–12. (p. 541)

Brownell, K. D., Greenwood, M. R. C., Stellar, E., & Shrager, E. E. (1986). The effects of repeated cycles of weight loss and regain in rats. *Physiology and Behavior, 38,* 459–464. (p. 543)

Brownell, K. D., & Jeffery, R. W. (1987). Improving long-term weight loss: Pushing the limits of treatment. *Behavior Therapy, 18,* 353–374. (p. 542)

Brownmiller, S. (1975). *Against our will: Men, women, and rape.* New York: Simon and Schuster. (p. 364)

Bruner, J. S., & Potter, M. C. (1964). Interference in visual recognition. *Science, 144,* 424–425. (p. 177)

Buchsbaum, M. S., Wu, J., Haier, R., Hazlett, E., Ball, R., Katz, M., Sokolski, K., Lagunas-Solar, M., & Langer, D. H. (1987). Positron emission tomography assessment of effects of benzodiazepines on regional glucose metabolic rate in patients with anxiety disorder. *Life Sciences, 40,* 2393–2400. (p. 454)

Buck, L., & Axel, R. (1991). A novel multigene family may encode odorant receptors: A molecular basis for odor recognition. *Cell, 65,* 175–187. (p. 155)

Bugelski, B. R., Kidd, E., & Segmen, J. (1968). Image as a mediator in one-trial paired-associate learning. *Journal of Experimental Psychology, 76,* 69–73. (p. 262)

Bugental, D. B. (1986). Unmasking the "polite smile": Situational and personal determinants of managed affect in adult-child interaction. *Personality and Social Psychology Bulletin, 12,* 7–16. (p. 389)

Bulletin of the Atomic Scientists. (1990, March). Soviet strategic nuclear forces, end of 1989. P. 49. (p. 262)

Bulletin of the Atomic Scientists. (1991, January/February). U.S. strategic nuclear forces, end of 1990. P. 48. (p. 262)

Bullough, V. (1990). The Kinsey scale in historical perspective. In D. P. McWhirter, S. A. Sanders, & J. M. Reinisch (Eds.), *Homosexuality/heterosexuality: Concepts of sexual orientation.* New York: Oxford University Press. (p. 365)

Bumpass, L. L., & Sweet, J. A. (1989). National estimates of cohabitation. *Demography, 26,* 615–625. (p. 370)

Bureau of the Census. (1990). *Statistical abstract of the U.S.* Washington, DC: Superintendent of Documents, U.S. Government Printing Office. (pp. 82, 114, 217, 460)

Burger, J. M. (1987). Increased performance with increased personal control: A self-presentation interpretation. *Journal of Experimental Social Psychology, 23,* 350–360. (p. 377)

Buri, J. R., Louiselle, P. A., Misukanis, T. M., & Mueller, R. A. (1988). Effects of parental authoritarianism and authoritativeness on self-esteem. *Personality and Social Psychology Bulletin, 14,* 271–282. (p. 85)

Burish, T. G., & Carey, M. P. (1986). Conditioned aversive responses in cancer chemotherapy patients: Theoretical and developmental analysis. *Journal of Counseling and Clinical Psychology, 54,* 593–600. (p. 234)

Burke, K. C., Burke, J. D., Regier, D. A., & Rae, D. S. (1990). Age at onset of selected mental disorders in five community populations. *Archives of General Psychiatry, 47*, 511–518. (p. 452)

Burns, D. D. (1980). *Feeling good: The new mood therapy.* New York: Signet. (p. 462)

Burton, S. (1990, May 14). Straight talk on sex in China: Surveys reveal the breadth and depth of the new permissiveness. *Time*, p. 82. (p. 105)

Bushman, B. J., & Cooper, H. M. (1990). Effects of alcohol on human aggression: An integrative research review. *Psychological Bulletin, 107*, 341–354. (p. 569)

Buss, A. H. (1989). Personality as traits. *American Psychologist, 44*, 1378–1388. (p. 427)

Buss, D. M. (1989). Sex differences in human mate preferences: Evolutionary hypotheses tested in 37 cultures. *Behavioral and Brain Sciences, 12*, 1–49. (pp. 105, 580, 603)

Buss, D. M. (1991). Evolutionary personality psychology. *Annual Review of Psychology*, in press. (p. 587)

Butcher, J. N. (1990). *The MMPI-2 in psychological treatment.* New York: Oxford University Press. (p. 425)

Butler, J., & Rovee-Collier, C. (1989). Contextual gating of memory retrieval. *Developmental Psychobiology, 22*, 533–552. (p. 273)

Butler, R. A. (1954, February). Curiosity in monkeys. *Scientific American*, pp. 70–75. (p. 354)

Byrne, D. (1971). *The attraction paradigm.* New York: Academic Press. (p. 581)

Byrne, D. (1982). Predicting human sexual behavior. In A. G. Kraut (Ed.), *The G. Stanley Hall Lecture Series* (Vol. 2). Washington, DC: American Psychological Association. (pp. 363, 364, 368)

Cacioppo, J. T., Martzke, J. S., Petty, R. E., & Tassinary, L. G. (1988). Specific forms of facial EMG response index emotions during an interview: From Darwin to the continuous flow hypothesis of affect-laden information processing. *Journal of Personality and Social Psychology, 54*, 592–604. (p. 389)

Cameron, P., & Biber, H. (1973). Sexual thought throughout the life-span. *Gerontologist, 13*, 144–147. (p. 201)

Campbell, A. (1981). *The sense of well-being in America.* New York: McGraw-Hill. (p. 120)

Campbell, B. A., & Coulter, X. (1976). The ontogenesis of learning and memory. In M. R. Rosenzweig & E. L. Bennet (Eds.), *Neural mechanisms of learning and memory*, pp. 209–235. Cambridge, MA: MIT Press. (p. 67)

Campbell, D. T. (1975). On the conflicts between biological and social evolution and between psychology and moral tradition. *American Psychologist, 30*, 1103–1126. (p. 399)

Campbell, D. T., & Specht, J. C. (1985). Altruism: Biology, culture, and religion. *Journal of Social and Clinical Psychology, 3*(1), 33–42. (p. 434)

Campbell, S. (1986). *The Loch Ness Monster: The evidence.* Willingborough, Northamptonshire, U.K.: Acquarian Press. (p. 178)

Camper, J. (1990, February 7). Drop pompom squad, U. of I. rape study says. *Chicago Tribune*, p. 1. (p. 211)

Cannon, W. B. (1929). *Bodily changes in pain, hunger, fear, and rage.* New York: Branford. (pp. 356, 513)

Cannon, W. B., & Washburn, A. (1912). An explanation of hunger. *American Journal of Physiology, 29*, 441–454. (p. 356)

Cantor, N., & Kihlstrom, J. F. (1987). *Personality and social intelligence.* Englewood Cliffs, NJ: Prentice-Hall. (p. 331)

Cantor, N., & Norem, J. K. (1989). Defensive pessimism and stress and coping. *Social Cognition, 7*, 92–112. (p. 437)

Cantril, H., & Bumstead, C. H. (1960). *Reflections on the human venture.* New York: New York University Press. (p. 567)

Carballo, M., Cleland, J., Carael, M., & Albrecht, G. (1989). A cross national study of patterns of sexual behaviour. Unpublished manuscript, Social and Behavioural Research Unit, Global Programme on AIDS, World Health Organization, 1211 Geneva 27, Switzerland. (p. 361)

Carey, G. (1990). Genes, fears, phobias, and phobic disorders. *Journal of Counseling and Development, 68*, 628–632. (p. 454)

Carli, L. L., & Leonard, J. B. (1989). The effect of hindsight on victim derogation. *Journal of Social and Clinical Psychology, 8*, 331–343. (p. 614)

Carlson, M., Charlin, V., & Miller, N. (1988). Positive mood and helping behavior: A test of six hypotheses. *Journal of Personality and Social Psychology, 55*, 211–229. (p. 576)

Carlson, R. (1984). What's social about social psychology? Where's the person in personality research? *Journal of Personality and Social Psychology, 47*, 1304–1309. (p. 439)

Carlson, S. (1985). A double-blind test of astrology. *Nature, 318*, 419–425. (p. 439)

Carnegie Council on Adolescent Development. (1989, June). *Turning points: Preparing American youth for the 21st century.* (The report of the Task Force on Education of Young Adolescents.) New York: Carnegie Corporation. (pp. 335, 617)

Carr, T. H., Kontowicz, A., & Dagenbach, D. (1987). Subthreshold priming and the cognitive unconscious. Invited paper presented to the Midwestern Psychological Association convention. (p. 134)

Carroll, J. B. (1982). The measurement of intelligence. In R. J. Sternberg (Ed.), *Handbook of human intelligence.* New York: Cambridge University Press. (p. 324)

Carson, R. C., Butcher, J. N., & Coleman, J. C. (1988). *Abnormal psychology and modern life* (8th ed.). Glenview, IL: Scott, Foresman. (p. 448)

Cartwright, R. D. (1978). *A primer on sleep and dreaming.* Reading, MA: Addison-Wesley. (p. 194)

Cash, T., & Janda, L. H. (1984, December). The eye of the beholder. *Psychology Today*, pp. 46–52. (p. 579)

Caspi, A., Elder, G. H., Jr., & Bem, D. J. (1987). Moving against the world: Life-course patterns of explosive children. *Developmental Psychology, 23,* 308–313. (p. 124)

Caspi, A., & Herbener, E. S. (1990). Continuity and change: Assortative marriage and the consistency of personality in adulthood. *Journal of Personality and Social Psychology, 58,* 250–258. (p. 125)

Caspi, A., & Moffitt, T. E. (1991). Individual differences are accentuated during periods of social change: The sample case of girls at puberty. *Journal of Personality and Social Psychology,* in press. (p. 97)

Castro, J. (1990, Fall issue on women). Get set: Here they come. *Time,* pp. 50–52. (p. 606)

Cataldo, M. F., & Coates, T. J. (1986). *Health and industry: A behavioral medicine perspective.* New York: Wiley. (p. 534)

Cattell, R. B. (1963). Theory of fluid and crystallized intelligence: A critical experiment. *Journal of Educational Psychology, 54,* 1–22. (p. 115)

Ceci, S. J., & Liker, J. K. (1986). A day at the races: A study of IQ, expertise, and cognitive complexity. *Journal of Experimental Psychology: General, 115,* 255–266. (pp. 299–331)

Centers for Disease Control. (1983). Behavioral risk factor prevalence surveys–United States. Reported in *Behavior Today Newsletter,* October 29, 1984, p. 7. (p. 212)

Centers for Disease Control. (1989). Results from the national adolescent student health survey. *Morbidity and Mortality Weekly Report, 38*(9), 147–150. (p. 460)

Centers for Disease Control. (1989). Weekly report summarized in *Detroit Free Press,* November 25, p. A1. (p. 212)

Centers for Disease Control. (1991, January 5). Data from the National Survey of Family Growth as reported by Associated Press release. (p. 105)

Centers for Disease Control Vietnam Experience Study. (1988). Health status of Vietnam veterans. *Journal of the American Medical Association, 259,* 2701–2709. (p. 515)

Centerwall, B. S. (1989). Exposure to television as a risk factor for violence. *American Journal of Epidemiology, 129,* 643–652. (p. 571)

Cerella, J. (1985). Information processing rates in the elderly. *Psychological Bulletin, 98,* 67–83. (p. 111)

Charny, I. W. (1982). *How can we commit the unthinkable? Genocide: The human cancer.* Boulder, CO: Westview Press. (p. 562)

Chase, M. H., & Morales, F. R. (1983). Subthreshold excitatory activity and motorneuron discharge during REM periods of active sleep. *Science, 221,* 1195–1198. (p. 194)

Chase, W. G., & Simon, H. A. (1973). Perception in chess. *Cognitive Psychology, 4,* 55–81. (p. 263)

Chassin, L., Presson, C. C., Sherman, S. J., & McGrew, J. (1987). The changing smoking environment for middle and high school students: 1980-1983. *Journal of Behavioral Medicine, 10,* 581–593. (p. 534)

Chaves, J. F. (1989). Hypnotic control of clinical pain. In N. P. Spanos & J. F. Chaves (Eds.), *Hypnosis: The cognitive-behavioral perspective.* Buffalo, NY: Prometheus Books. (p. 207)

Cheek, J. M., & Melchior, L. A. (1990). Shyness, self-esteem, and self-consciousness. In H. Leitenberg (Ed.), *Handbook of social and evaluation anxiety.* New York: Plenum. (pp. 86, 465)

Cherfas, J. (1990). Two bomb attacks on scientists in the U.K. *Science, 248,* 1485. (p. 20)

Cherlin, A. J., Furstenberg, F. F., Jr., Chase-Landale, P. L., Kiernan, K. E., Robins, P. K., Morrison, D. R., & Teitler, J. O. (1991). Longitudinal studies of effects of divorce on children in Great Britain and the United States. *Science, 252,* 1386–1389. (p. 81)

Chesney, M. A. (1984). *Behavioral factors in coronary heart disease separating benign from malignant.* Paper presented at the meeting of the American Psychological Association. (p. 518)

Chess, S., & Thomas, A. (1987). *Know your child: An authoritative guide for today's parents.* New York: Basic Books. (p. 77)

Chi, M. T. H. (1976). Short-term memory limitations in children: Capacity or processing deficits. *Memory & Cognition, 4,* 559–572. (p. 256)

Chi, M. T. H., Glaser, R., & Farr, M. J. (Eds.). (1988). *The nature of expertise.* Hillsdale, NJ: Erlbaum. (p. 286)

Chodorow, N. J. (1978). *The reproduction of mothering: Psychoanalysis and the sociology of gender.* Berkeley, CA: University of California Press. (p. 599)

Chodorow, N. J. (1989). *Feminism and psychoanalytic theory.* New Haven, CT: Yale University Press. (p. 599)

Chomsky, N. (1959). Review of B. F. Skinner's *Verbal behavior. Language, 35,* 26–58. (p. 305)

Chomsky, N. (1972). *Language and mind.* New York: Harcourt Brace Jovanovich. (p. 301)

Chomsky, N. (1987). Language in a psychological setting. Sophia Linguistic Working Papers in Linguistics, No. 22, Sophia University, Tokyo. (pp. 305–306)

Chronicle of Higher Education. (1990, September 5). Administrators' views of enrollment changes in the next five years. P. 5. (p. 437)

Chugani, H. T., & Phelps, M. E. (1986). Maturational changes in cerebral function in infants determined by ^{18}FDG Positron Emission Tomography. *Science, 231,* 840–843. (p. 69)

Church, A. T., & Katigbak, M. S. (1989). Internal, external, and self-report structure of personality in non-Western culture: An investigation of cross-language and cross-cultural generalizability. *Journal of Personality and Social Psychology, 57,* 857–872. (p. 423)

Chwalisz, K., Diener, E., & Gallagher, D. (1988). Autonomic arousal feedback and emotional experience: Evidence from the spinal cord injured. *Journal of Personality and Social Psychology, 54,* 820–828. (p. 397)

Cialdini, R. B. (1988). *Influence: Science and practice* (2nd ed.). Glenview, IL: Scott, Foresman. (p. 555)

Cialdini, R. B., & Carpenter, K. (1981). The availability heuristic: Does imagining make it so? In P. H. Reingen & A. G. Woodside (Eds.), *Buyer-seller interactions: Empirical issues and normative issues.* Chicago: American Marketing Association. (p. 293)

Cialdini, R. B., & Richardson, K. D. (1980). Two indirect tactics of image management: Basking and blasting. *Journal of Personality and Social Psychology, 39,* 406–415. (p. 613)

Clarke-Stewart, K. A. (1989). Infant day care: Maligned or malignant? *American Psychologist, 44,* 266–273. (p. 83)

Coe, W. C. (1989a). Posthypnotic amnesia: Theory and research. In N. P. Spanos & J. F. Chaves (Eds.), *Hypnosis: The cognitive-behavioral perspective.* Buffalo, NY: Prometheus Books. (p. 203)

Coe, W. C. (1989b). Hypnosis: The role of sociopolitical factors in a paradigm clash. In N. P. Spanos & J. F. Chaves (Eds.), *Hypnosis: The cognitive-behavioral perspective.* Buffalo, NY: Prometheus Books. (p. 209)

Coffey, C. E., & Weiner, R. D. (1990). Electroconvulsive therapy: An update. *Hospital and Community Psychiatry, 41,* 515–521. (p. 505)

Cohen, I. B. (1984, March). Florence Nightingale. *Scientific American,* pp. 128–137. (p. 624)

Cohen, L. A. (1987, November). Diet and cancer. *Scientific American,* pp. 42–48. (p. 538)

Cohen, R. M., Semple, W. E., Gross, M., & Nordahl, T. E. (1988). From syndrome to illness: Delineating the pathophysiology of schizophrenia with PET. *Schizophrenia Bulletin, 14,* 169–178. (p. 468)

Cohen, S. (1988). Psychosocial models of the role of social support in the etiology of physical disease. *Health Psychology, 7,* 269–297. (p. 533)

Cohen, S., Evans, G. W., Stokols, D., & Krantz, D. S. (1986). *Behavior, health, and environmental stress.* New York: Plenum. (p. 148)

Cohen, S., Lichtenstein, E., Prochaska, J. O., Rossi, J. S., Gritz, E. R., Carr, C. R., Orleans, C. T., Schoenbach, V. J., Biener, L., Abrams, D., DiClemente, C., Curry, S., Marlatt, G. A., Cummings, K. M., Emont, S. L., Giovino, G., & Ossip-Klein, D. (1989). Debunking myths about self-quitting: Evidence from 10 prospective studies of persons who attempt to quit smoking by themselves. *American Psychologist, 44,* 1355–1365. (p. 536)

Cohen, S., & Williamson, G. M. (1988). Perceived stress in a probability sample of the United States. In S. Spacapan & S. Oskamp (Eds.), *The social psychology of health.* Newbury Park, CA: Sage. (p. 516)

Cohen, S., & Williamson, G. M. (1991). Stress and infectious disease in humans. *Psychological Bulletin, 109,* 5–24. (p. 521)

Coile, D. C., & Miller, N. E. (1984). How radical animal activists try to mislead humane people. *American Psychologist, 39,* 700–701. (pp. 19–20)

Coleman, J. C. (1980). *The nature of adolescence.* London: Methuen. (p. 96)

Coleman, P. D., & Flood, D. G. (1986). Dendritic proliferation in the aging brain as a compensatory repair mechanism. In D. F. Swaab, E. Fliers, M. Mirmiram, W. A. Van Gool, & F. Van Haaren (Eds.), *Progress in brain research* (Vol. 20). New York: Elsevier. (p. 111)

The College Board. (1984). Figure from *The Chronicle of Higher Education, Vol. xxix*(5). (p. 325)

College Entrance Examination Board. (1983, 1990). Sample SAT questions from *10 SATs.* Princeton, NJ: Educational Testing Service. (p. 323)

Colombo, J. (1982). The critical period concept: Research, methodology, and theoretical issues. *Psychological Bulletin, 91,* 260–275. (p. 77)

Conel, J. L. (1939–1963). The postnatal development of the human cerebral cortex (Vols. I–VI). Cambridge, MA: Harvard University Press. (p. 67)

Conley, J. J. (1985). Longitudinal stability of personality traits: A multitrait-multimethod-multioccasion analysis. *Journal of Personality and Social Psychology, 49,* 1266–1282. (p. 124)

Consensus Conference. (1985). Electroconvulsive therapy. *Journal of the American Medical Association, 254,* 2103–2108. (p. 505)

Conway, M., & Ross, M. (1984). Getting what you want by revising what you had. *Journal of Personality and Social Psychology, 47,* 738–748. (p. 280)

Cook, E. W., III, Hodes, R. L., & Lang, P. J. (1986). Preparedness and phobia: Effects of stimulus content on human visceral conditioning. *Journal of Abnormal Psychology, 95,* 195–207. (p. 233)

Cook, S. W. (1984). The 1954 social science statement and school desegregation—A reply to Gerard. *American Psychologist, 39,* 819–832. (p. 343)

Coon, P. M., Bowman, E. S., & Milstein, V. (1988). Multiple personality disorder: A clinical investigation of 50 cases. *Journal of Nervous and Mental Disease, 176,* 519–527. (p. 458)

Cooper, G. D. (1988). Studies in REST: I. Reduced environmental stimulation therapy (REST) and reduced alcohol consumption. *Journal of Substance Abuse Treatment, 5,* 61–68. (p. 158)

Cooper, W. H. (1983). An achievement motivation nomological network. *Journal of Personality and Social Psychology, 44,* 841–861. (p. 371)

Coopersmith, S. (1967). *The antecedents of self-esteem.* San Francisco: Freeman. (p. 85)

Corballis, M. C. (1989). Laterality and human evolution. *Psychological Review, 96,* 492–505. (p. 52)

Coren, S., & Halpern, D. F. (1991). Left-handedness: A marker for decreased survival fitness. *Psychological Bulletin, 109,* 90–106. (p. 52)

Costa, P. T., Jr., & McCrae, R. R. (1988). Personality in adulthood: A six-year longitudinal study of self-reports and spouse ratings on the NEO Personality Inventory. *Journal of Personality and Social Psychology, 54,* 853–863. (p. 124)

Costa, P. T., Jr., & McCrae, R. R. (1989). Personality continuity and the changes of adult life. In M. Storandt & G. R. VandenBos (Eds.), *The adult years: Continuity and change.* Washington, DC: American Psychological Association. (p. 125)

Costa, P. T., Jr., Zonderman, A. B., McCrae, R. R., Cornoni-Huntley, J., Locke, B. Z., & Barbano, H. E. (1987). Longitudinal analyses of psychological well-being in a national sample: Stability of mean levels. *Journal of Gerontology, 42,* 50–55. (p. 121)

Court, J. H. (1984). Sex and violence: A ripple effect. In N. M. Malamuth & E. Donnerstein (Eds.), *Pornography and sexual aggression.* Orlando, FL: Academic Press. (p. 572)

Cousins, N. (1989). *Head first: The biology of hope.* New York: Dutton. (p. 522)

Cousins, S. D. (1989). Culture and self-perception in Japan and the United States. *Journal of Personality and Social Psychology, 56,* 124–131. (p. 591)

Covington, M. V., & Omelich, C. L. (1988). I can resist anything but temptation: Adolescent expectations for smoking cigarettes. *Journal of Applied Social Psychology, 18,* 203–227. (p. 535)

Cowan, G., Lee, C., Levy, D., & Snyder, D. (1988). Dominance and inequality in X-rated videocassettes. *Psychology of Women Quarterly, 12,* 299–311. (p. 572)

Cowan, N. (1988). Evolving conceptions of memory storage, selective attention, and their mutual constraints within the human information-processing system. *Psychological Bulletin, 104,* 163–191. (pp. 256–257)

Cowart, B. J. (1981). Development of taste perception in humans: Sensitivity and preference throughout the life span. *Psychological Bulletin, 90,* 43–73. (p. 154)

Coyne, J. C., Burchill, S. A. L., & Stiles, W. B. (1991). An interactional perspective on depression. In C. R. Snyder & D. O. Forsyth (Eds.), *Handbook of social and clinical psychology: The health perspective.* New York: Pergamon. (p. 464)

Craig, M. E., Kalichman, S. C., & Follingstad, D. R. (1989). Verbal coercive sexual behavior among college students. *Archives of Sexual Behavior, 18,* 421–434. (p. 571)

Craik, F. I. M. (1986). A functional account of age differences in memory. In F. Klix & H. Hagendorf (Eds.), *Human memory and cognitive capabilities.* Amsterdam: Elsevier. (p. 115)

Craik, F. I. M., & Tulving, E. (1975). Depth of processing and the retention of words in episodic memory. *Journal of Experimental Psychology: General, 104,* 268–294. (pp. 260–261)

Craik, F. I. M., & Watkins, M. J. (1973). The role of rehearsal in short-term memory. *Journal of Verbal Learning and Verbal Behavior, 12,* 599–607. (p. 259)

Crandall, C. S. (1988). Social contagion of binge eating. *Journal of Personality and Social Psychology, 55,* 588–598. (p. 359)

Crandall, J. E. (1984). Social interest as a moderator of life stress. *Journal of Personality and Social Psychology, 47,* 164–174. (p. 434)

Crocker, J., & Schwartz, I. (1985). Effects of self-esteem on prejudice and ingroup favoritism in a minimal intergroup situation. *Personality and Social Psychology Bulletin, 11*(4). (p. 430)

Crocker, J., Thompson, L. L., McGraw, K. M., & Ingerman, C. (1987). Downward comparison, prejudice, and evaluation of others: Effects of self-esteem and threat. *Journal of Personality and Social Psychology, 52,* 907–916. (p. 613)

Crombie, A. C. (1964, May). Early concepts of the senses and the mind. *Scientific American,* pp. 108–116. (p. 139)

Crook, T. H., & West, R. L. (1990). Name recall performance across the adult life-span. *British Journal of Psychology, 81,* 335–340. (p. 113)

Crowe, L. C., & George, W. H. (1989). Alcohol and human sexuality: Review and integration. *Psychological Bulletin, 105,* 374–386. (p. 212)

Croyle, R. T., & Ditto, P. H. (1990). Illness cognition and behavior: An experimental approach. *Journal of Behavioral Medicine, 13,* 31–52. (p. 545)

Csikszentmihalyi, M. (1990). *Flow: The psychology of optimal experience.* New York: Harper & Row. (pp. 291, 312, 374, 401)

Csikszentmihalyi, M., & Larson, R. (1984). *Being adolescent: Conflict and growth in the teenage years.* New York: Basic Books. (p. 121)

Cunningham, M. R. (1986). Measuring the physical in physical attractiveness: Quasi-experiments on the sociobiology of female facial beauty. *Journal of Personality and Social Psychology, 50,* 925–935. (p. 580)

Curtis, R. C., & Miller, K. (1986). Believing another likes or dislikes you: Behaviors making the beliefs come true. *Journal of Personality and Social Psychology, 51,* 284–290. (p. 581)

Curtiss, S. (1977). *Genie: A psycholinguistic study of a modern-day "wild child."* New York: Academic Press. (p. 306)

Curtiss, S. (1981). Dissociations between language and cognition: Cases and implications. *Journal of Autism and Developmental Disorders, 11,* 15–30. (p. 306)

Cutler, B. L., & Penrod, S. D. (1989). Forensically relevant moderators of the relation between eyewitness identification accuracy and confidence. *Journal of Applied Psychology, 74,* 650–652. (p. 276)

Cutrona, C. E. (1986). Behavioral manifestations of social support: A microanalytic investigation. *Journal of Personality and Social Psychology, 51,* 201–208. (p. 533)

Czeisler, C. A., Allan, J. S., Strogatz, S. H., Ronda, J. M., Sanchez, R., Rios, C. D., Freitag, W. O., Richardson, G. S., & Kronauer, R. E. (1986). Bright light resets the human circadian pacemaker independent of the timing of the sleep-wake cycle. *Science, 233,* 667–671. (p. 192)

Czeisler, C. A., Kronauer, R. E., Allan, J. S., & Duffy, J. F. (1989). Bright light induction of strong (type O) resetting of the human circadian pacemaker. *Science, 244,* 1328–1333. (p. 192)

Dabbs, J. M., Jr., de La Rue, D., & Williams, P. M. (1990). Testosterone and occupational choice: Actors, ministers, and other men. *Journal of Personality and Social Psychology, 59,* 1261–1265. (p. 602)

Dabbs, J. M., Jr., Frady, R. L., Carr, T. S., & Besch, N. F.

(1987). Saliva testosterone and criminal violence in young adult prison inmates. *Psychosomatic Medicine, 49,* 174–182. (pp. 569, 602)

Dabbs, J. M., Jr., & Morris, R. (1990). Testosterone, social class, and antisocial behavior in a sample of 4,462 men. *Psychological Science, 1,* 209–211. (p. 569)

Dabbs, J. M., Jr., Ruback, R. B., & Besch, N. F. (1987). Male saliva testosterone following conversations with male and female partners. Paper presented at the American Psychological Association convention. (p. 363)

Damon, W., & Hart, D. (1982). The development of self-understanding from infancy through adolescence. *Child Development, 53,* 841–864. (p. 84)

Damon, W., & Hart, D. (1988). *Self-understanding in childhood and adolescence.* Cambridge: Cambridge University Press. (p. 84)

Darley, J. M., & Latané, B. (1968a). Bystander intervention in emergencies: Diffusion of responsibility. *Journal of Personality and Social Psychology, 8,* 377–383. (p. 575)

Darley, J. M., & Latané, B. (1968b, December). When will people help in a crisis? *Psychology Today,* pp. 54–57, 70–71. (p. 575)

Darley, J. M., Seligman, C., & Becker, L. J. (1979, April). The lesson of twin rivers: Feedback works. *Psychology Today,* pp. 16, 23–24. (p. 246)

Darrach, B., & Norris, J. (1984, August). An American tragedy. *Life,* pp. 58–74. (p. 471)

Davenport, C. (1989, January 30). America's most admired corporations. *Fortune,* pp. 68–94. (p. 378)

Davidson, R. J. (1991, February 12). Quoted by Daniel Goleman, Feeling cheerful? Thank brain's left lobe. *The New York Times,* pp. C1, C10. (p. 385)

Davidson, R. J., Ekman, P., Saron, C. D., Senulis, J. A., & Friesen, W. V. (1990). Approach-withdrawal and cerebral asymmetry: Emotional expression and brain physiology I. *Journal of Personality and Social Psychology, 58,* 330–341. (p. 385)

Dawes, R. M. (1980). Social dilemmas. *Annual Review of Psychology, 31,* 169–193. (p. 615)

Dawson, N. V., Arkes, H. R., Siciliano, C., Blinkhorn, R., Lakshmanan, M., & Petrelli, M. (1988). Hindsight bias: An impediment to accurate probability estimation in clinicopathologic conferences. *Medical Decision Making, 8,* 259–264. (p. 22)

Day, R. H. (1984). The nature of perceptual illusions. *Interdisciplinary Science Reviews, 9,* 47–58. (p. 172)

DeAngelis, T. (1988, October). Chinese psychologists focus on the practical. *APA Monitor,* p. 8. (p. 4)

DeAngelis, T. (1989, January). Mania, depression, and genius. *APA Monitor,* pp. 1, 24. (p. 459)

de Boysson-Bardies, B., Halle, P., Sagart, L., & Durand, C. (1989). A cross linguistic investigation of vowel formats in babbling. *Journal of Child Language, 16,* 1–17. (p. 303)

Deci, E. L. (1980). *The psychology of self-determination.*

Lexington, MA: Lexington Books. (p. 243)

Deci, E. L., Connell, J. P., & Ryan, R. M. (1989). Self-determination in a work organization. *Journal of Applied Psychology, 74,* 580–590. (p. 377)

Deci, E. L., & Ryan, R. M. (1985). *Intrinsic motivation and self-determination in human behavior.* New York: Plenum Press. (p. 374)

Deci, E. L., & Ryan, R. M. (1987). The support of autonomy and the control of behavior. *Journal of Personality and Social Psychology, 53,* 1024–1037. (p. 375)

de Cuevas, J. (1990, September–October). "No, she holded them loosely." *Harvard Magazine,* pp. 60–67. (p. 305)

de Jong-Gierveld, J. (1987). Developing and testing a model of loneliness. *Journal of Personality and Social Psychology, 53,* 119–128. (p. 465)

Delgado, J. M. R. (1969). *Physical control of the mind: Toward a psychocivilized society.* New York: Harper & Row. (p. 44)

DeLoache, J. S. (1987). Rapid change in the symbolic functioning of very young children. *Science, 238,* 1556–1557. (p. 74)

Dement, W. (1990). In the PBS film, *Sleep alert.* Quoted by *Behavior Today,* March 12, p. 8. (p. 195)

Dement, W. C. (1978). *Some must watch while some must sleep.* New York: Norton. (pp. 193, 196)

Dement, W. C., & Wolpert, E. A. (1958). The relation of eye movements, body mobility, and external stimuli to dream content. *Journal of Experimental Psychology, 55,* 543–553. (p. 198)

Dempster, F. N. (1988). The spacing effect: A case study in the failure to apply the results of psychological research. *American Psychologist, 43,* 627–634. (p. 259)

Dennis, W. (1940). Does culture appreciably affect patterns of infant behavior? *Journal of Social Psychology, 12,* 305–317. (p. 68)

D'Eon, J. L. (1989). Hypnosis in the control of labor pain. In N. P. Spanos & J. F. Chaves (Eds.), *Hypnosis: The cognitive-behavioral perspective.* Buffalo, NY: Prometheus Books. (p. 207)

De Pree, M. (1987). *Leadership is an art.* East Lansing, MI: Michigan State University Press. (p. 378)

Depue, R. A., & Monroe, S. M. (1986). Conceptualization and measurement of human disorder in life stress research: The problem of chronic disturbance. *Psychological Bulletin, 99,* 36–51. (p. 515)

de Rivera, J. (1989). Comparing experiences across cultures: Shame and guilt in America and Japan. Symposium presentation to the American Psychological Society convention. (p. 591)

Dermer, M., Cohen, S. J., Jacobsen, E., & Anderson, E. A. (1979). Evaluative judgments of aspects of life as a function of vicarious exposure to hedonic extremes. *Journal of Personality and Social Psychology, 37,* 247–260. (p. 401)

Dermer, M., & Pyszczynski, T. A. (1978). Effects of erotica upon men's loving and liking responses for women they love. *Journal of Personality and Social Psychology, 36,* 1302–1309. (p. 581)

DerSimonian, R., & Laird, N. M. (1983). Evaluating the effect of coaching on SAT scores: A meta-analysis. *Harvard Educational Review, 53,* 1–15. (p. 327)

Desmond, E. W. (1987, November 30). Out in the open. *Time,* pp. 80–90. (p. 534)

Deutsch, F. M., Ruble, D. N., Fleming, A., Brooks-Gunn, J., & Stangor, C. (1988). Information-seeking and maternal self-definition during the transition to motherhood. *Journal of Personality and Social Psychology, 55,* 420–431. (p. 118)

Deutsch, J. A. (1972, July). Brain reward: ESP and ecstasy. *Psychology Today,* pp. 46–48. (p. 41)

DeValois, R. L., & DeValois, K. K. (1975). Neural coding of color. In E. C. Carterette & M. P. Friedman (Eds.), *Handbook of perception: Vol. V. Seeing.* New York: Academic Press. (p. 144).

Dew, M. A., Bromet, E. J., Brent, D., & Greenhouse, J. B. (1987). A quantitative literature review of the effectiveness of suicide prevention centers. *Journal of Consulting and Clinical Psychology, 55,* 239–244. (p. 497)

Diaconis, P., & Mosteller, F. (1989). Methods for studying coincidences. *Journal of the American Statistical Association, 84,* 853–861. (p. 631)

Diamond, J. (1986). Variation in human testis size. *Nature, 320,* 488–489. (p. 87)

Diamond, J. (1989, May). The great leap forward. *Discover,* pp. 50–60. (p. 301)

Dickie, J. R. (1987). Interrelationships within the mother-father-infant triad. In P. W. Berman & F. A. Pedersen (Eds.), *Men's transitions to parenthood: Longitudinal studies of early family experience.* Hillsdale, NJ: Erlbaum. (p. 79)

Diener, E. (1984). Subjective well-being. *Psychological Bulletin, 95,* 542–575. (p. 401)

Diener, E., Emmons, R. A., & Sandvik, E. (1986). The dual nature of happiness: Independence of positive and negative moods. Unpublished manuscript, University of Illinois. (p. 121)

Dietz, W. H., Jr., & Gortmaker, S. L. (1985). Do we fatten our children at the television set? Obesity and television viewing in children and adolescents. *Pediatrics, 75,* 807–812. (p. 544)

DiLalla, L. F., & Gottesman, I. I. (1991). Biological and genetic contributors to violence—Widom's untold tale. *Psychological Bulletin, 109,* 125–129. (p. 471)

Dingman, J. M. (1990). Personality structure: The emergence of the five-factor model. *Annual Review of Psychology, 41,* 417–440. (p. 423)

Dion, K. K. (1986). Stereotyping based on physical attractiveness: Issues and conceptual perspectives. In C. P. Herman, M. P. Zanna, & E. T. Higgins (Eds.), *Physical appearance, stigma, and social behavior: The Ontario symposium on personality and social psychology* (Vol. 3). Hillsdale, NJ: Erlbaum. (p. 579)

Dion, K. K., Pak, A. W-P., & Dion, K. L. (1990). Stereotyping physical attractiveness: A sociocultural perspective. *Journal of Cross-Cultural Psychology, 21,* 378–398. (p. 593)

Dixon, B. (1986, April). Dangerous thoughts: How we think and feel can make us sick. *Science, 86,* pp. 63–66. (p. 521)

Dobson, K. S. (1989). A meta-analysis of the efficacy of cogni-

tive therapy for depression. *Journal of Consulting and Clinical Psychology, 57,* 414–419. (p. 500)

Dohrenwend, B. P., Levav, I., Shrout, P. E., Link, B. G., Skodol, A. E., & Martin, J. L. (1987). Life stress and psychopathology: Progress on research begun with Barbara Snell Dohrenwend. *American Journal of Community Psychology, 15,* 677–715. (p. 463)

Dohrenwend, B., Pearlin, L., Clayton, P., Hamburg, B., Dohrenwend, B. P., Riley, M., & Rose, R. (1982). Report on stress and life events. In G. R. Elliott & C. Eisdorfer (Eds.), *Stress and human health: Analysis and implications of research* (A study by the Institute of Medicine/National Academy of Sciences). New York: Springer. (p. 515)

Dolezal, H. (1982). *Living in a world transformed.* New York: Academic Press. (p. 177)

Domjan, M., Lyons, R., North, N. C., & Bruell, J. (1986). Sexual Pavlovian conditioned approach behavior in male Japanese quail (*Coturnix coturnix japonica*). *Journal of Comparative Psychology, 100,* 413–421. (p. 230)

Donaldson, M. (1979, March). The mismatch between school and children's minds. *Human Nature,* pp. 60–67. (p. 74)

Donnerstein, E., Linz, D., & Penrod, S. (1987). *The question of pornography.* New York: Free Press. (pp. 571, 574)

Dorsey, G. (1987, February 8). The love doctor. *Hartford Courant/Northeast,* pp. 12–21, 33–35. (p. 331)

Doty, R. L., Shaman, P., Applebaum, S. L., Giberson, R., Siksorski, L., & Rosenberg, L. (1984). Smell identification ability: Changes with age. *Science, 226,* 1441–1443. (p. 110)

Draguns, J. G. (1990a). Normal and abnormal behavior in cross-cultural perspective: Specifying the nature of their relationship. *Nebraska Symposium on Motivation 1989, 37,* 235–277. (pp. 445, 454, 463)

Draguns, J. G. (1990b). Applications of cross-cultural psychology in the field of mental health. In R. W. Brislin (Ed.), *Applied cross-cultural psychology.* Newbury Park, CA: Sage. (p. 445)

Driedger, L. (1975). In search of cultural identity factors: A comparison of ethnic students. *Canadian Review of Sociology and Anthropology, 12,* 150–161. (p. 596)

Drucker, P. F. (1982, December). A conversation with Peter F. Drucker. *Psychology Today,* pp. 60–67. (p. 421)

Druckman, D., & Swets, J. A. (Eds.). (1988). *Enhancing human performance: Issues, theories, and techniques.* Washington, DC: National Academy Press. (pp. 184, 312)

Duclos, S. E., Laird, J. D., Sexter, M., Stern, L., & Van Lighten, O. (1989). Emotion-specific effects of facial expressions and postures on emotional experience. *Journal of Personality and Social Psychology, 57,* 100–108. (p. 391)

Duggan, J. P., & Booth, D. A. (1986). Obesity, overeating, and rapid gastric emptying in rats with ventromedial hypothalamic lesions. *Science, 231,* 609–611. (p. 357)

Duncan, G. J., Hill, M. S., & Hoffman, S. D. (1988). Welfare dependence within and across generations. *Science, 239,* 467–471. (p. 293)

Duncker, K. (1945). On problem solving. *Psychological*

Monographs, 58 (Whole no. 270). (pp. 289, 291)

Dunnett, S. B. (1989). Neural transplantation: Normal brain function and repair after damage. *The Psychologist, 1*, 4–8. (p. 47)

Dutton, D. G., & Aron, A. (1989). Romantic attraction and generalized liking for others who are sources of conflict-based arousal. *Canadian Journal of Behavioural Sciences, 21*, 246–257. (p. 582)

Dutton, D. G., & Aron, A. P. (1974). Some evidence for heightened sexual attraction under conditions of high anxiety. *Journal of Personality and Social Psychology, 30*, 510–517. (p. 582)

Dweck, C. S., & Elliott, E. S. (1983). Achievement motivation. In P. Mussen & E. M. Hetherington (Eds.), *Handbook of child psychology* (Vol. IV). New York: Wiley. (p. 372)

Dye, D. A., & Reck, M. (1989). College grade point average as a predictor of adult success: A reply. *Public Personnel Management, 18*, 235–241. (p. 331)

Dywan, J., & Bowers, K. (1983). The use of hypnosis to enhance recall. *Science, 222*, 184–185. (p. 205)

Eagly, A. H. (1986). Some meta-analytic approaches to examining the validity of gender-difference research. In J. S. Hyde & M. C. Linn (Eds.), *The psychology of gender: Advances through meta-analysis*. Baltimore: Johns Hopkins University Press. (p. 599)

Eagly, A. H. (1987). *Sex differences in social behavior: A social-role interpretation*. Hillsdale, NJ: Erlbaum. (p. 601)

Eagly, A. H., Ashmore, R. D., Makhijani, M. G., & Kennedy, L. C. (1991). What is beautiful is good, but . . .: A meta-analytic review of research on the physical attractiveness stereotype. *Psychological Bulletin, 110*, 109–128. (p. 179)

Eagly, A. H., & Crowley, M. (1986). Gender and helping behavior: A meta-analytic review of the social psychological literature. *Psychological Bulletin, 100*, 283–308. (p. 576)

Eagly, A. H., & Johnson, B. T. (1990). Gender and leadership style: A meta-analysis. *Psychological Bulletin, 108*, 233–256. (p. 601)

Eagly, A. H., & Karau, S. J. (1991). Gender and the emergence of leaders: A meta-analysis. *Journal of Personality and Social Psychology, 60*, 685–710. (p. 377)

Eagly, A. H., & Wood, W. (1991). Explaining sex differences in social behavior: A meta-analytic perspective. *Personality and Social Psychology Bulletin, 17*, 306–315. (p. 606)

Ebbesen, E. B., Duncan, B., & Konecni, V. J. (1975). Effects of content of verbal aggression on future verbal aggression: A field experiment. *Journal of Experimental Social Psychology, 11*, 192–204. (p. 395)

Ebbinghaus, H. (1885). *Über das Gedächtnis*. Leipzig: Duncker & Humblot. Cited in R. Klatzky (1980), *Human memory: Structures and processes*. San Francisco: Freeman. (pp. 266–267)

Eccles, J. S., Jacobs, J. E., & Harold, R. D. (1990). Gender role stereotypes, expectancy effects, and parents' socialization of gender differences. *Journal of Social Issues, 46*, 183–201. (p. 599)

Eckert, E. D., Bouchard, T. J., Jr., Segal, N. L., Lykken, D. T., & Heston, L. L. (1987). Sex differences in genetic influence on body weight in monozygotic twins reared apart. Unpublished manuscript, University of Minnesota. (p. 541)

Eckert, E. D., Heston, L. L., & Bouchard, T. J., Jr. (1981). MZ twins reared apart: Preliminary findings of psychiatric disturbances and traits. In L. Gedda, P. Paris, & W. D. Nance (Eds.), *Twin research: Vol. 3. Pt. B. Intelligence, personality, and development*. New York: Alan Liss. (p. 454)

Edwards, C. P. (1981). The comparative study of the development of moral judgment and reasoning. In R. H. Munroe, R. L. Munroe, & B. B. Whiting (Eds.), *Handbook of cross-cultural human development*. New York: Garland Press. (p. 100)

Edwards, C. P. (1982). Moral development in comparative cultural perspective. In D. A. Wagner & H. W. Stevenson (Eds.), *Cultural perspectives on child development*. San Francisco: Freeman. (p. 100)

Edwards, C. P. (1991). Behavioral sex differences in children of diverse cultures: The case of nurturance to infants. In M. Pereira & L. Fairbanks (Eds.), *Juveniles: Comparative socioecology*. Oxford: Oxford University Press. (p. 606)

Egbert, L. D., Battit, G. E., Welch, C. E., & Bartlett, M. K. (1964). Reduction of postoperative pain by encouragement and instruction of patients. *New England Journal of Medicine, 270*, 825–827. (p. 527)

Ehrhardt, A. A. (1987). A transactional perspective on the development of gender differences. In J. M. Reinisch, L. A. Rosenblum, & S. A. Sanders (Eds.), *Masculinity/femininity: Basic perspectives*. New York: Oxford University Press. (p. 602)

Ehrlichman, H., & Halpern, J. N. (1988). Affect and memory: Effects of pleasant and unpleasant odors on retrieval of happy and unhappy memories. *Journal of Personality and Social Psychology, 55*, 769–779. (p. 156)

Eibl-Eibesfeldt, I. (1971). *Love and hate: The natural history of behavior patterns*. New York: Holt, Rinehart & Winston. (p. 390)

Eich, E. (1990). Learning during sleep. In R. B. Bootzin, J. F. Kihlstrom, & D. L. Schacter (Eds.), *Sleep and cognition*. Washington, DC: American Psychological Association. (p. 198)

Eich, J. E. (1980). The cue-dependent nature of state-dependent retrieval. *Memory and Cognition, 8*, 157–173. (p. 211)

Einstein, G. O., & McDaniel, M. A. (1990). Normal aging and prospective memory. *Journal of Experimental Psychology: Learning, Memory, and Cognition, 16*, 717–726. (p. 113)

Eisenberg, N., & Lennon, R. (1983). Sex differences in empathy and related capacities. *Psychological Bulletin, 94*, 100–131. (p. 600)

Ekman, P., Davidson, R. J., & Friesen, W. V. (1990). The Duchenne smile: Emotional expression and brain physiology II. *Journal of Personality and Social Psychology, 58*, 342–353. (p. 392)

Ekman, P., & Friesen, W. V. (1975). *Unmasking the face.* Englewood Cliffs, NJ: Prentice-Hall. (p. 390)

Ekman, P., Friesen, W. V., O'Sullivan, M., Chan, A., Diacoyanni-Tarlatzis, I., Heider, K., Krause, R., LeCompte, W. A., Pitcairn, T., Ricci-Bitti, P. E., Scherer, K., Tomita, M., & Tzavaras, A. (1987). Universal and cultural differences in the judgments of facial expressions of emotion. *Journal of Personality and Social Psychology, 53,* 712–717. (p. 390)

Ekman, P., Levenson, R. W., & Friesen, W. V. (1983). Autonomic nervous system activity distinguishes among emotions. *Science, 221,* 1208–1210. (p. 392)

Elder, G. H., Jr. (1969). Appearance and education in marriage mobility. *American Sociological Review, 34,* 519–533. (p. 579)

Elkin, I., Shea, T., Watkins, J. T., Imber, S. D., Sotsky, S. M., Collins, J. F., Glass, D. R., Pilkonis, P. A., Leber, W. R., Docherty, J. P., Fiester, S. J., & Parloff, M. B. (1989). National Institute of Mental Health treatment of depression collaborative research program. *Archives of General Psychiatry, 46,* 971–983. (p. 499)

Elkind, D. (1970). The origins of religion in the child. *Review of Religious Research, 12,* 35–42. (p. 99)

Elkind, D. (1978). *The child's reality: Three developmental themes.* Hillsdale, NJ: Erlbaum. (p. 98)

Ellis, A. (1962). *Reason and emotion in psychotherapy.* Secaucus, NJ: Citadel Press. (p. 492)

Ellis, A. (1984). Rational-emotive therapy. In R. J. Corsini (Ed.), *Current psychotherapies* (3rd ed.). Itasca, IL: Peacock. (p. 492)

Ellis, A. (1987). The impossibility of achieving consistently good mental health. *American Psychologist, 42,* 364–375. (p. 492)

Ellis, A. (1989). Rational-emotive therapy. In R. J. Corsini & D. Wedding (Eds.), *Current psychotherapies* (4th ed.). Itasca, IL: Peacock. (p. 492)

Ellis, H. C., & Ashbrook, P. W. (1989). The "state" of mood and memory research: A selective review. *Journal of Social Behavior and Personality, 4,* 1–21. (p. 274)

Ellis, L., & Ames, M. A. (1987). Neurohormonal functioning and sexual orientation: A theory of homosexuality-heterosexuality. *Psychological Bulletin, 101,* 233–258. (pp. 365, 368)

Empson, J. A. C., & Clarke, P. R. F. (1970). Rapid eye movements and remembering. *Nature, 227,* 287–288. (p. 199)

Endler, N. S. (1982). *Holiday of darkness: A psychologist's personal journey out of his depression.* New York: Wiley. (p. 505)

Engen, T. (1987). Remembering odors and their names. *American Scientist, 75,* 497–503. (p. 156)

England, G. W., & Misumi, J. (1986). Work centrality in Japan and the United States. *Journal of Cross-Cultural Psychology, 17,* 396–416. (p. 376)

Eppley, K. R., Abrams, A. I., & Shear, J. (1989). Differential effects of relaxation techniques on trait anxiety: A meta-analysis. *Journal of Clinical Psychology, 45,* 957–974. (p. 202)

Epstein, S. (1983a). Aggregation and beyond: Some basic issues on the prediction of behavior. *Journal of Personality, 51,* 360–392. (p. 427)

Epstein, S. (1983b). The stability of behavior across time and situations. In R. Zucker, J. Aronoff, & A. I. Rabin (Eds.), *Personality and the prediction of behavior.* San Diego: Academic Press. (p. 427)

Epstein, S. (1984). Controversial issues in emotions. In P. Shaver (Ed.), *Review of Personality and Social Psychology.* Beverly Hills, CA: Sage. (p. 385)

Epstein, S., & Meier, P. (1989). Constructive thinking: A broad coping variable with specific components. *Journal of Personality and Social Psychology, 57,* 332–350. (p. 331)

Erdelyi, M. H. (1985). *Psychoanalysis: Freud's cognitive psychology.* New York: Freeman. (p. 420)

Erdelyi, M. H. (1988). Repression, reconstruction, and defense: History and integration of the psychoanalytic and experimental frameworks. In J. Singer (Ed.), *Repression: Defense mechanism and cognitive style.* Chicago: University of Chicago Press. (p. 420)

Ericsson, K. A., & Chase, W. G. (1982). Exceptional memory. *American Scientist, 70,* 607–615. (p. 263)

Erikson, E. H. (1963). *Childhood and society.* New York: Norton. (p. 102)

Erikson, E. H. (1983, June). A conversation with Erikson (by E. Hall). *Psychology Today,* pp. 22–30. (p. 80)

Eron, L. D. (1987). The development of aggressive behavior from the perspective of a developing behaviorism. *American Psychologist, 42,* 435–442. (pp. 124, 571)

Eron, L. D., & Huesmann, L. R. (1984). The control of aggressive behavior by changes in attitudes, values and the conditions of learning. In R. J. Blanchard & C. Blanchard (Eds.), *Advances in the study of aggression* (Vol. 1). Orlando, FL: Academic Press. (pp. 125, 574)

Esser, J. K., & Lindoerfer, J. S. (1989). Groupthink and the space shuttle *Challenger* accident: Toward a quantitative case analysis. *Journal of Behavioral Decision Making, 2,* 167–177. (p. 566)

Esses, V. M. (1989). Mood as a moderator of acceptance of interpersonal feedback. *Journal of Personality and Social Psychology, 57,* 769–781. (p. 275)

Evans, G. W., Palsane, M. N., & Carrere, S. (1987). Type A behavior and occupational stress: A cross-cultural study of blue-collar workers. *Journal of Personality and Social Psychology, 52,* 1002–1007. (p. 520)

Evans, G. W., Palsane, M. N., Lepore, S. J., & Martin, J. (1989). Residential density and psychological health: The mediating effects of social support. *Journal of Personality and Social Psychology, 57,* 994–999. (p. 532)

Evans, R. I., Dratt, L. M., Raines, B. E., & Rosenberg, S. S. (1988). Social influences on smoking initiation: Importance of distinguishing descriptive versus mediating process variables. *Journal of Applied Social Psychology, 18,* 925–943. (p. 535)

Evans, R. I., Raines, B. E., & Hanselka, L. (1984). Developing data-based communications in social psychological research: Adolescent smoking prevention. *Journal of Applied Social Psychology, 14,* 289–295. (p. 536)

Exner, J. E., Jr. (1986). *The Rorschach: A comprehensive system. Volume 1: Basic Foundations* (2nd ed.). New York: Wiley. (p. 419)

Eysenck, H. J. (1952). The effects of psychotherapy: An evaluation. *Journal of Consulting Psychology, 16,* 319–324. (p. 498)

Eysenck, H. J. (1982). *A model for intelligence.* Berlin: Springer-Verlag. (p. 332)

Eysenck, H. J. (1990, April 30). An improvement on personality inventory. *Current Contents: Social and Behavioral Sciences, 22*(18), 20. (p. 423)

Eysenck, H. J., & Grossarth-Maticek, R. (1991). Creative novation behaviour therapy as a prophylactic treatment for cancer and coronary heart disease: Part II—Effects of treatment. *Behaviour Research and Therapy, 29,* 17–31. (p. 522, 531)

Eysenck, H. J., & Kamin, L. (1981). *The intelligence controversy: H. J. Eysenck vs. Leon Kamin.* New York: Wiley. (p. 321)

Eysenck, H. J., Wakefield, J. A., Jr., & Friedman, A. F. (1983). Diagnosis and clinical assessment: The DSM-III. *Annual Review of Psychology, 34,* 167–193. (p. 450)

Eysenck, M. W., MacLeod, C., & Mathews, A. (1987). Cognitive functioning and anxiety. *Psychological Research, 49,* 189–195. (p. 435)

Eysenck, S. B. G., & Eysenck, H. J. (1963). The validity of questionnaire and rating assessments of extraversion and neuroticism, and their factorial stability. *British Journal of Psychology, 54,* 51–62. (p. 423)

Faber, N. (1987, July). Personal glimpse. *Reader's Digest,* p. 34. (p. 335)

Fagan, J. F., III, & Montie, J. E. (1988). Behavioral assessment of cognitive well-being in the infant. In J. Kavanagh (Ed.), *Understanding mental retardation: Research accomplishments and new frontiers.* Baltimore, MD: Paul H. Brookes. (p. 333)

Falbo, T., & Polit, D. F. (1986). Quantitative review of the only child literature: Research evidence and theory development. *Psychological Bulletin, 100,* 176–189. (p. 372)

Fallon, A. (1990). Culture in the mirror: Sociocultural determinants of body image. In T. F. Cash & T. Pruzinsky (Eds.), *Body images: Development, deviance, and change.* New York: Guilford Press. (p. 360)

Fallon, A. E., & Rozin, P. (1985). Sex differences in perceptions of desirable body shape. *Journal of Abnormal Psychology, 94,* 102–105. (pp. 359–360)

Fancher, R. E. (1979). *Pioneers of psychology.* New York: Norton. (pp. 318–319)

Fantz, R. L. (1961, May). The origin of form perception. *Scientific American,* pp. 66–72. (p. 66)

Farina, A. (1982). The stigma of mental disorders. In A. G. Miller (Ed.), *In the eye of the beholder.* New York: Praeger. (pp. 447, 473)

Farina, A., & Fisher, J. D. (1982). Beliefs about mental disorders: Findings and implications. In G. Weary & H. L. Mirels (Eds.), *Integrations of clinical and social psychology.* New York: Oxford University Press. (p. 495)

Farley, F. (1986, May). The big T in personality. *Psychology Today,* pp. 44–52. (p. 354)

Farrell, P. A., Gates, W. K., Maksud, M. G., & Morgan, W. P. (1982). Increases in plasma beta-endorphin/beta-lipotropin immunoreactivity after treadmill running in humans. *Journal of Applied Physiology, 52,* 1245–1249. (p. 31)

Fava, M., Copeland, P. M., Schweiger, U., & Herzog, D. B. (1989). Neurochemical abnormalities of anorexia nervosa and bulimia nervosa. *American Journal of Psychiatry, 146,* 963–971. (p. 359)

Fay, R. E., Turner, C. F., Klassen, A. D., & Gagnon, J. H. (1989). Prevalence and patterns of same-gender sexual contact among men. *Science, 243,* 338–348. (p. 366)

Fazio, R. H. (1990). Multiple processes by which attitudes guide behavior: The MODE model as an integrative framework. In M. P. Zanna (Ed.), *Advances in experimental social psychology* (Vol. 23). San Diego, CA: Academic Press. (p. 555)

Feder, H. H. (1984). Hormones and sexual behavior. *Annual Review of Psychology, 35,* 165–200. (p. 362)

Feeney, D. M. (1987). Human rights and animal welfare. *American Psychologist, 42,* 593–599. (p. 20)

Feeney, J. A., & Noller, P. (1990). Attachment style as a predictor of adult romantic relationships. *Journal of Personality and Social Psychology, 58,* 281–291. (p. 79)

Fehr, B., & Russell, J. A. (1991). The concept of love viewed from a prototype perspective. *Journal of Personality and Social Psychology, 60,* 425–438. (p. 287)

Feingold, A. (1990). Gender differences in effects of physical attractiveness on romantic attraction: A comparison across five research paradigms. *Journal of Personality and Social Psychology, 59,* 981–993. (p. 579)

Feinleib, M., Lenfant, C., & Miller, S. A. (1984). Hypertension and calcium. *Science, 226,* 384–385. (p. 537)

Fergusson, D. M., Horwood, L. J., & Shannon, F. T. (1987). Breastfeeding and subsequent social adjustment in six- to eight-year-old children. *Journal of Child Psychology & Psychiatry & Allied Disciplines, 28(3),* 379–386. (p. 77)

Fernandez, E., & Turk, D. C. (1989). The utility of cognitive coping strategies for altering pain perception: A meta-analysis. *Pain, 38,* 123–135. (p. 153)

Fichter, M. M., & Noegel, R. (1990). Concordance for bulimia nervosa in twins. *International Journal of Eating Disorders, 9,* 255–263. (p. 359)

Fiedler, F. E. (1981). Leadership effectiveness. *American Behavioral Scientist, 24,* 619–632. (p. 376)

Fiedler, F. E. (1987, September). When to lead, when to stand back. *Psychology Today,* pp. 26–27. (p. 376)

Field, T. (1989). Individual and maturational differences in infant expressivity. In N. Eisenberg (Ed.), *Empathy and related emotional responses.* San Francisco: Jossey-Bass. (p. 66)

Field, T. (1990). Infant daycare has positive effects on grade school behavior and performance. Unpublished manuscript, University of Miami, Florida. (p. 83)

Field, T. M. (1987, May). Baby research comes to age. *Psychology Today*, p. 46. (p. 66)

Field, T. M., Schanberg, S. M., Scafidi, F., Bauer, C. R., Vega-Lahr, N., Garcia, R., Nystrom, J., & Kuhn, C. M. (1986). Tactile/kinesthetic stimulation effects on preterm neonates. *Pediatrics, 77,* 654–658. (p. 68)

Field, T. M., Woodson, R., Greenberg, R., & Cohen, D. (1982). Discrimination and imitation of facial expressions by neonates. *Science, 218,* 179–181. (p. 66)

Fillion, T. J., & Blass, E. M. (1986). Infantile experience with suckling odors determines adult sexual behavior in male rats. *Science, 231,* 729–731. (p. 368)

Findley, M. J., & Cooper, H. M. (1983). Locus of control and academic achievement: A literature review. *Journal of Personality and Social Psychology, 44,* 419–427. (p. 436)

Fineberg, H. V. (1988). Education to prevent AIDS: Prospects and obstacles. *Science, 239,* 592–596. (p. 367)

Finn, S. E. (1986). Stability of personality self-ratings over 30 years: Evidence for an age/cohort interaction. *Journal of Personality and Social Psychology, 50,* 813–818. (p. 125)

Finucci, J. M., & Childs, B. (1981). Are there really more dyslexic boys than girls? In A. Ansara, N. Geschwind, A. Galaburda, M. Albert, & N. Gartrell (Eds.), *Sex differences in dyslexia.* Towson, MD: The Orton Dyslexia Society. (p. 598)

Fischhoff, B. (1982). Debiasing. In D. Kahneman, P. Slovic, & A. Tversky (Eds.), *Judgment under uncertainty: Heuristics and biases.* New York: Cambridge University Press. (p. 296)

Fischhoff, B., Slovic, P., & Lichtenstein, S. (1977). Knowing with certainty: The appropriateness of extreme confidence. *Journal of Experimental Psychology: Human Perception and Performance, 3,* 552–564. (p. 295)

Fischman, J. (1986, June). The wounds of war. *Psychology Today,* pp. 8–9. (p. 48)

Fisher, H. T. (1984). Little Albert and Little Peter. *Bulletin of the British Psychological Society, 37,* 269. (p. 487)

Fisher, R. P., Geiselman, R. E., & Amador, M. (1989). Field test of the cognitive interview: Enhancing the recollection of actual victims and witnesses of crime. *Journal of Applied Psychology, 74,* 722–727. (p. 276)

Fisher, R. P., Geiselman, R. E., & Raymond, D. S. (1987). Critical analysis of police interview techniques. *Journal of Police Science and Administration, 15,* 177–185. (p. 276)

Fitzgerald, R. C. (1970). Reactions to blindness: An exploratory study of adults with recent loss of sight. *Archives of General Psychiatry, 22,* 370–379. (p. 122)

Fleming, I., Baum, A., & Weiss, L. (1987). Social density and perceived control as mediator of crowding stress in high-density residential neighborhoods. *Journal of Personality and Social Psychology, 52,* 899–906. (p. 518)

Fletcher, G. J. O., Fitness, J., & Blampied, N. M. (1990). The link between attributions and happiness in close relationships: The roles of depression and explanatory style. *Journal of Social and Clinical Psychology, 9,* 243–255. (p. 553)

Floderus-Myrhed, B., Pedersen, N., & Rasmuson, I. (1980). Assessment of heritability for personality, based on a shortform of the Eysenck Personality Inventory: A study of 12,898 twin pairs. *Behavior Genetics, 10,* 153–162. (p. 87)

Flynn, J. R. (1987). Massive IQ gains in 14 nations: What IQ tests really measure. *Psychological Bulletin, 101,* 171–191. (pp. 325, 331)

Foa, E. B., & Kozak, M. J. (1986). Emotional processing of fear: Exposure to corrective information. *Psychological Bulletin, 99,* 20–35. (p. 488)

Forer, B. R. (1949). The fallacy of personal validation: A classroom demonstration of gullibility. *Journal of Abnormal and Social Psychology, 44,* 118–123. (p. 438)

Forgas, J. P., Bower, G. H., & Krantz, S. E. (1984). The influence of mood on perceptions of social interactions. *Journal of Experimental Social Psychology, 20,* 497–513. (pp. 274, 463)

Fouts, R. S., & Bodamer, M. (1987). Preliminary report to the National Geographic Society on: "Chimpanzee intrapersonal signing." *Friends of Washoe, 7*(1), 4–12. (p. 310)

Fowler, M. J., Sullivan, M. J., & Ekstrand, B. R. (1973). Sleep and memory. *Science, 179,* 302–304. (p. 278)

Fowler, R. C., Rich, C. L., & Young, D. (1986). San Diego suicide study: II. Substance abuse in young cases. *Archives of General Psychiatry, 43,* 962–965. (p. 461)

Fowler, R. D. (1986, May). Howard Hughes: A psychological autopsy. *Psychology Today,* pp. 22–33. (p. 453)

Fox, J. L. (1984). The brain's dynamic way of keeping in touch. *Science, 225,* 820–821. (p. 44)

Fozard, J. L., & Popkin, S. J. (1978). Optimizing adult development: Ends and means of an applied psychology of aging. *American Psychologist, 33,* 975–989. (p. 110)

Frank, J. D. (1982). Therapeutic components shared by all psychotherapies. In J. H. Harvey & M. M. Parks (Eds.), *The Master Lecture Series: Vol. 1. Psychotherapy research and behavior change.* Washington, DC: American Psychological Association. (pp. 480, 500, 502)

Frank, M. G., & Gilovich, T. (1988). The dark side of self and social perception: Black uniforms and aggression in professional sports. *Journal of Personality and Social Psychology, 54,* 74–85. (pp. 14–15)

Frank, S. J. (1988). Young adults' perceptions of their relationships with their parents: Individual differences in connectedness, competence, and emotional autonomy. *Developmental Psychology, 24,* 729–737. (p. 105)

Frankel, A., Strange, D. R., & Schoonover, R. (1983). CRAP: Consumer rated assessment procedure. In G. H. Scherr & R. Liebmann-Smith (Eds.), *The best of The Journal of Irreproducible Results.* New York: Workman Publishing. (p. 425)

Frankenburg, W. K., & Dodds, J. B. (1967). The Denver developmental screening test. *Journal of Pediatrics, 71*(2), 181–191. (p. 69)

Freedman, D. G. (1979). *Human sociobiology: A holistic approach.* New York: Free Press. (p. 87)

Freedman, J. L. (1978). *Happy people.* San Diego: Harcourt Brace Jovanovich. (p. 120)

Freedman, J. L. (1988). Television violence and aggression: What the evidence shows. In S. Oskamp (Ed.), *Television as a social issue.* Newbury Park, CA: Sage. (p. 571)

Freedman, J. L., & Fraser, S. C. (1966). Compliance without pressure: The foot-in-the-door technique. *Journal of Personality and Social Psychology, 4,* 195–202. (p. 555)

Freedman, J. L., & Perlick, D. (1979). Crowding, contagion, and laughter. *Journal of Experimental Social Psychology, 15,* 295–303. (p. 563)

Freeman, W. J. (1991, February). The physiology of perception. *Scientific American*, pp. 78–85. (p. 143)

Freud, S. (1888–1939; reprinted 1963). In J. Strachey (Ed. & Trans.), *The standard edition of the complete psychological works of Sigmund Freud.* London: Hogarth Press. (p. 412)

Freud, S. (1931; reprinted 1961). Female sexuality. In J. Strachey (Trans.), *The standard edition of the complete psychological works of Sigmund Freud.* London: Hogarth Press. (pp. 414, 417)

Freud, S. (1933). *New introductory lectures on psycho-analysis.* New York: Carlton House. (p. 413)

Freud, S. (1935; reprinted 1960). *A general introduction to psychoanalysis.* New York: Washington Square Press. (p. 118)

Frezza, M., DiPadova, C., Possato, G., Terpin, M., Buraona, E., & Lieber, C. (1990). High blood alcohol levels in women. *New England Journal of Medicine, 322,* 95–99. (p. 212)

Friedman, H. S. (1991). *The self-healing personality: Why some people achieve health and others succumb to illness.* New York: Holt. (p. 524)

Friedman, H. S., & Booth-Kewley, S. (1987). The "disease-prone personality": A meta-analytic view of the construct. *American Psychologist, 42,* 539–555. (p. 524)

Friedman, H. S., & Booth-Kewley, S. (1988). Validity of the Type A construct: A reprise. *Psychological Bulletin, 104,* 381–384. (p. 520)

Friedman, H. S., & DiMatteo, M. R. (1989). *Health psychology.* Englewood Cliffs, NJ: Prentice-Hall. (p. 525)

Friedman, M., & Ulmer, D. (1984). *Treating Type A behavior — and your heart.* New York: Knopf. (pp. 518, 531)

Friedman, W. J., Robinson, A. B., & Friedman, B. L. (1987). Sex differences in moral judgments? A test of Gilligan's theory. *Psychology of Women Quarterly, 11,* 37–46. (p. 101)

Friedrich, O. (1987, December 7). New age harmonies. *Time,* pp. 62–72. (p. 447)

Frieze, I. H., Parsons, J. E., Johnson, P. B., Ruble, D. N., & Zellman, G. L. (1978). *Women and sex roles: A social psychological perspective.* New York: Norton. (pp. 419, 604)

Frijda, N. H. (1988). The laws of emotion. *American Psychologist, 43,* 349–358. (p. 398)

Frisby, J. P. (1980). *Seeing: Illusion, brain and mind.* New York: Oxford University Press. (p. 141)

Fritsch, G., & Hitzig, E. (1870; reprinted 1960). On the electrical excitability of the cerebrum. In G. Von Bonin (Trans.), *Some papers on the cerebral cortex.* Springfield, IL: Charles C. Thomas. (p. 43)

Fromkin, V., & Rodman, R. (1983). *An introduction to language* (3rd ed.). New York: Holt, Rinehart & Winston. (pp. 302, 304)

Fulker, D. W., DeFries, J. C., & Plomin, R. (1988). Genetic influence on general mental ability increases between infancy and middle childhood. *Nature, 336,* 767–769. (p. 338)

Fuller, M. J., & Downs, A. C. (1990). Spermarche is a salient biological marker in men's development. Poster presented at the American Psychological Society convention. (p. 97)

Funder, D. C. (1987). Errors and mistakes: Evaluating the accuracy of social judgment. *Psychological Bulletin, 101,* 75–90. (p. 299)

Funder, D. C. (1991). Global traits: A neo-Allportian approach to personality. *Psychological Science, 2,* 31–39. (p. 426)

Funder, D. C., & Block, J. (1989). The role of ego-control, ego-resiliency, and IQ in delay of gratification in adolescence. *Journal of Personality and Social Psychology, 57,* 1041–1050. (p. 101)

Furnham, A. (1982). Explanations for unemployment in Britain. *European Journal of Social Psychology, 12,* 335–352. (p. 553)

Furnham, A., & Taylor, L. (1990). Lay theories of homosexuality: Aetiology, behaviours, and 'cures.' *British Journal of Social Psychology, 29,* 135–147. (p. 368)

Furstenberg, F. F., Jr., Moore, K. A., & Peterson, J. L. (1985). Sex education and sexual experience among adolescents. *American Journal of Public Health, 75,* 1331–1332. (p. 369)

Gabrenya, W. K., Jr., Latané, B., & Wang, Y-E. (1983). Social loafing in cross-cultural perspective. *Journal of Cross-Cultural Psychology, 14,* 368–384. (p. 564)

Gaertner, S. L., Mann, J., Murrell, A., & Dovidio, J. F. (1989). Reducing intergroup bias: The benefits of recategorization. *Journal of Personality and Social Psychology, 57,* 239–249. (p. 617)

Galanter, E. (1962). Contemporary psychophysics. In R. Brown, E. Galanter, E. H. Hess, & G. Mandler (Eds.), *New directions in psychology.* New York: Holt, Rinehart & Winston. (p. 133)

Gall, M. S. (1990, December 4). Personal correspondence from Assistant Secretary for Human Development Services. (p. 341)

Gallagher, M. (1990). Functional consequences of brain aging: The good news and the bad news. Address to the American Psychological Society convention. (p. 113)

Gallant, S. J., Popiel, D. A., Hoffman, D. H., & Hamilton, J. A. (1991). Daily ratings of premenstrual symptoms: Differentiating women with severe symptoms from women with normal menstrual cycles. Unpublished manuscript, Uniformed Services of the Health Sciences, Bethesda, Maryland. (p. 526)

Gallatin, J. (1980). Political thinking in adolescence. In J. Adelson (Ed.), *Handbook of adolescent psychology.* New York: Wiley. (p. 104)

Gallup, G., Jr., & Hugick, L. (1990, June). Racial tolerance grows, progress on racial equality less evident. *Gallup Poll Monthly*, pp. 23–32. (p. 611)

Gallup, G., Jr., & Newport, F. (1990, December). Americans now drinking less alcohol. *Gallup Poll Monthly*, pp. 2–6. (p. 217)

Gallup, G. G., Jr. (1982). *Adventures in immortality.* New York: McGraw-Hill. (p. 219)

Gallup, G. G., Jr. (1984, March). Religion in America. *The Gallup Report*, No. 222. (p. 578)

Gallup, G. G., Jr., & O'Connell, G. (1986). *Who do Americans say that I am?* Philadelphia, PA: Westminster Press. (p. 219)

Gallup, G. G., Jr., & Suarez, S. D. (1985). Alternatives to the use of animals in psychological research. *American Psychologist, 40,* 1104–1111. (p. 20)

Gallup, G. G., Jr., & Suarez, S. D. (1986). Self-awareness and the emergence of mind in humans and other primates. In J. Suls & A. G. Greenwald (Eds.), *Psychological perspectives on the self* (Vol. 3.). Hillsdale, NJ: Erlbaum. (p. 84)

Gallup, G. H. (1972). *The Gallup poll: Public opinion 1935–1971* (Vol. 3). New York: Random House. (p. 616)

Gallup, G. H., Jr., & Newport, F. (1991, Winter). Belief in paranormal phenomena among adult Americans. *Skeptical Inquirer*, pp. 137–146. (p. 181)

Gallup Organization. (1988). *America's youth 1977–1988.* Princeton, NJ. (pp. 104, 536, 543)

Gallup Organization. (1989, July). Cigarette smoking at 45-year low. *Gallup Poll Monthly*, No. 286, pp. 23–26. (p. 536)

Gallup Report. (1989, March/April). Commercial aviation. Pp. 32–33. (p. 294)

Gallup Report. (1989, March/April). Importance of social values (self-image). P. 42. (p. 434)

Gallup Report. (1989, May). Fifteen percent cite personal knowledge of child abuse cases. Report No. 284. (p. 80)

Galton, F. (1892). *Hereditary genius* (2nd ed.). London: Macmillan. (p. 318)

Garcia, J., & Koelling, R. A. (1966). Relation of cue to consequence in avoidance learning. *Psychonomic Science, 4,* 123–124. (p. 233)

Gardner, H. (1983). *Frames of mind: The theory of multiple intelligences.* New York: Basic Books. (p. 330)

Gardner, J. W. (1984). *Excellence: Can we be equal and excellent too?* New York: Norton. (pp. 120, 376)

Gardner, J. W. (1988, February). *The task of motivating.* Leadership Papers/9. Washington, DC: Independent Sector. (p. 343)

Gardner, M. (1983, Summer). Lessons of a landmark PK hoax. *The Skeptical Inquirer,* pp. 16–19. (p. 182)

Gardner, R. A., & Gardner, B. I. (1969). Teaching sign language to a chimpanzee. *Science, 165,* 664–672. (p. 307)

Garnets, L., & Kimmel, D. (1990). Lesbian and gay dimensions in the psychological study of human diversity. Master lecture, American Psychological Association convention. (p. 365)

Gartner, J., Larson, D. B., Allen, G. D., & Gartner, A. F. (1991). Religious commitment and psychopathology: A review of the empirical literature. *Journal of Psychology and Theology,* in press. (p. 460)

Gash, D. M., Notter, M. F. D., Okawara, S. H., Kraus, A. L., & Joynt, R. J. (1986). Amniotic neuroblastoma cells used for neural implants in monkeys. *Science, 233,* 1420–1421. (p. 47)

Gates, M. (1989, December 10). Psychiatrists not where patients are. *Grand Rapids Press* (Newhouse News Service), p. D8. (p. 496)

Gawin, F. H. (1991). Cocaine addiction: Psychology and neurophysiology. *Science, 251,* 1580–1586. (p. 213)

Gazzaniga, M. S. (1967, August). The split brain in man. *Scientific American,* pp. 24–29. (pp. 48, 50)

Gazzaniga, M. S. (1983). Right hemisphere language following brain bisection: A 20-year perspective. *American Psychologist, 38,* 525–537. (p. 50)

Gazzaniga, M.S. (1985, November). The social brain. *Psychology Today,* 29–38. (p. 51)

Gazzaniga, M. S. (1988). *Mind matters: How mind and brain interact to create our conscious lives.* Boston: Houghton Mifflin. (p. 51)

Gazzaniga, M. S. (1988). Organization of the human brain. *Science, 245,* 947–952. (p. 214)

Gazzaniga, M. S., Steen, D., & Volpe, B. T. (1979). Functional neuroscience. New York: Harper & Row. (p. 40)

Gebhardt, D. L., & Crump, C. E. (1990). Employee fitness and wellness programs in the workplace. *American Psychologist, 45,* 262–272. (p. 534)

Geen, R. G. (1984). Human motivation: New perspectives on old problems. In A. M. Rogers & C. J. Scheirer (Eds.), *The G. Stanley Hall Lecture Series* (Vol. 4). Washington, DC: American Psychological Association. (p. 371)

Geen, R. G., & Gange, J. J. (1983). Social facilitation: Drive theory and beyond. In H. H. Blumberg, A. P. Hare, V. Kent, & M. Davies (Eds.), *Small groups and social interaction* (Vol. 1). New York: Wiley. (p. 563)

Geen, R. G., & Quanty, M. B. (1977). The catharsis of aggression: An evaluation of a hypothesis. In L. Berkowitz (Ed.), *Advances in experimental social psychology* (Vol. 10). New York: Academic Press. (p. 395)

Geen, R. G., & Thomas, S. L. (1986). The immediate effects of media violence on behavior. *Journal of Social Issues, 42*(3), 7–28. (p. 571)

Geiwitz, J. (1980). *Psychology: Looking at ourselves* (2nd ed.). Boston: Little, Brown. (p. 114)

Geldard, F. A. (1972). *The human senses* (2nd ed.). New York: Wiley. (p. 143)

Gelman, D. (1989, May 15). Voyages to the unknown. *Newsweek*, pp. 66–69. (p. 390)

Gelman, D. (1989, December 18). The brain killer. *Newsweek*, pp. 54–56. (p. 112)

Gelman, R. (1979). Preschool thought. *American Psychologist, 34*, 900–905. (p. 74)

Gerard, R. W. (1953, September). What is memory? *Scientific American*, pp. 118–126. (p. 268)

Gerbner, G. (1985). Dreams that hurt: Mental illness in the mass media. Keynote address to the First Rosalynn Carter Symposium on Mental Health Policy, Emory University School of Medicine, Atlanta. (p. 474)

Gerbner, G. (1990). Stories that hurt: Tobacco, alcohol, and other drugs in the mass media. In H. Resnik (Ed.), *Youth and drugs: Society's mixed messages*. Rockville, MD: Office for Substance Abuse Prevention, U.S. Department of Health and Human Services. (p. 218)

Gerbner, G., & Signorielli, N. (1990). Profile 1967 through 1988–89: Enduring patterns. Unpublished report, Annenberg School of Communications, University of Pennsylvania. (pp. 570–571)

Gerrard, M. (1987a). Emotional and cognitive barriers to effective contraception: Are males and females really different. In K. Kelley (Ed.), *Females, males, and sexuality: Theories and research*. Albany: State University of New York Press. (p. 106)

Gerrard, M. (1987b). Sex, sex guilt, and contraceptive use revisited: The 1980s. *Journal of Personality and Social Psychology, 52*, 975–980. (p. 106)

Geschwind, N. (1979, September). Specializations of the human brain. *Scientific American*, pp. 180–199. (p. 46)

Geschwind, N., & Behan, P. O. (1984). Laterality, hormones, and immunity. In N. Geschwind & A. M. Galaburda (Eds.), *Cerebral dominance: The biological foundations*. Cambridge, MA: Harvard University Press. (pp. 52, 598)

Gfeller, J. D., Lynn, S. J., & Pribble, W. E. (1987). Enhancing hypnotic susceptibility: Interpersonal and rapport factors. *Journal of Personality and Social Psychology, 52*, 586–595. (p. 208)

Giambra, L. M. (1974). Daydreaming across the life span: Late adolescent to senior citizen. *Aging and Human Development, 5*, 115–140. (p. 201)

Gibbons, F. X. (1986). Social comparison and depression: Company's effect on misery. *Journal of Personality and Social Psychology, 51*, 140–148. (p. 401)

Gibson, E. J., & Walk, R. D. (1960, April). The "visual cliff." *Scientific American*, pp. 64–71. (p. 167)

Gibson, H. B. (1979). The 'Royal Nonesuch' of parapsychology. *Bulletin of the British Psychological Society, 32*, 65–67. (p. 183)

Giles, T. R. (1983). Probable superiority of behavioral interventions—II: Empirical status of the equivalence of therapies hypothesis. *Journal of Behavior Therapy and Experimental Psychiatry, 14*, 189–196. (p. 500)

Gilligan, C. (1982). *In a different voice: Psychological theory and women's development*. Cambridge, MA: Harvard University Press. (pp. 101, 103, 116, 599)

Gilligan, C., & Attanucci, J. (1988a). Two moral orientations: Gender differences and similarities. *Merrill-Palmer Quarterly, 34*, 223–237. (p. 101)

Gilligan, C., & Attanucci, J. (1988b). Much ado about . . . knowing? Noting? Nothing? A reply to Vasudev concerning sex differences and moral development. *Merrill-Palmer Quarterly, 34*, 451–456. (p. 101)

Gilligan, C., Lyons, N. P., & Hanmer, T. J. (Eds.). (1990). *Making connections: The relational worlds of adolescent girls at Emma Willard School*. Cambridge, MA: Harvard University Press. (pp. 103, 599)

Gilling, D., & Brightwell, R. (1982). *The human brain*. New York: Facts on File. (p. 489)

Gilovich, T., Vallone, R., & Tversky, A. (1985). The hot hand in basketball: On the misperception of random sequences. *Cognitive Psychology, 17*, 295–314. (p. 632)

Gist, R., & Welch, Q. B. (1989). Certification change versus actual behavior change in teenage suicide rates, 1955–1979. *Suicide and Life Threatening Behavior, 19*, 277–288. (p. 461)

Gjerde, P. F. (1983). Attentional capacity dysfunction and arousal in schizophrenia. *Psychological Bulletin, 93*, 57–72. (p. 466)

Gladue, B. A., Boechler, M., & McCaul, K. D. (1989). Hormonal response to competition in human males. *Aggressive Behavior, 15*, 409–422. (p. 569)

Glass, D. C. (1989). Psychology and health: Obstacles and opportunities. *Journal of Applied Social Psychology, 19*, 1145–1163. (p. 520)

Glass, D. C., & Singer, J. E. (1972). *Urban stress*. New York: Academic Press. (p. 148)

Glenn, N. D. (1975). Psychological well-being in the postparental stage: Some evidence from national surveys. *Journal of Marriage and the Family, 37*, 105–110. (p. 119)

Glenn, N. D. (1989). The social and cultural meaning of contemporary marriage. In B. Christensen (Ed.), *The retreat from marriage*. Rockford, IL: The Rockford Institute. (p. 118)

Glenn, N. D., & Weaver, C. N. (1985). The psychological well-being of adult children of divorce. *Journal of Marriage and the Family, 47*, 905–912. (p. 81)

Glenn, N. D., & Weaver, C. N. (1988). The changing relationship of marital status to reported happiness. *Journal of Marriage and the Family, 50,* 317–324. (p. 118)

Glick, P., Gottesman, D., & Jolton, J. (1989). The fault is not in the stars: Susceptibility of skeptics and believers in astrology to the Barnum effect. *Personality and Social Psychology Bulletin, 15,* 572–583. (p. 438)

Godden, D. R., & Baddeley, A. D. (1975). Context-dependent memory in two natural environments: On land and underwater. *British Journal of Psychology, 66,* 325–331. (p. 273)

Gold, M., & Yanof, D. S. (1985). Mothers, daughters, and girlfriends. *Journal of Personality and Social Psychology, 49,* 654–659. (p. 104)

Gold, P. E. (1987). Sweet memories. *American Scientist, 75,* 151–155. (p. 269)

Goldberg, J., True, W. R., Eisen, S. A., & Henderson, W. G. (1990). A twin study of the effects of the Vietnam War on posttraumatic stress disorder. *Journal of the American Medical Association, 263,* 1227–1232. (p. 515)

Goldberg, L. R. (1990). An alternative "description of personality": The big-five factor structure. *Journal of Personality and Social Psychology, 59,* 1216–1229. (p. 423)

Goldberg, L. R., Grenier, J. R., Guion, R. M., Sechrest, L. B., & Wing, H. (1990). Report of the A.P.A. task force on the prediction of dishonesty and theft in employment settings. Washington, DC: American Psychological Association. (p. 388)

Goldberg, S. (1983). Parent-infant bonding: Another look. *Child Development, 54,* 1355–1382. (p. 77)

Goldfried, M. R., & Padawer, W. (1982). Current status and future directions in psychotherapy. In M. R. Goldfried (Ed.), *Converging themes in psychotherapy: Trends in psychodynamic, humanistic, and behavioral practice.* New York: Springer. (p. 500)

Goleman, D. (1980, February). 1,528 little geniuses and how they grew. *Psychology Today,* pp. 28–53. (p. 334)

Goleman, D. (1990, May 29). As bias crime seems to rise, scientists study roots of racism. *The New York Times,* pp. C1, C5. (p. 611)

Goleman, D. (1990, September 16). Asian-Americans using education to escape prejudices. *Grand Rapids Press (The New York Times),* p. F8. (p. 341)

Golub, S. (1983). *Menarche: The transition from girl to woman.* Lexington, MA: Lexington Books. (p. 97)

Gonsiorek, J. C. (1982). Summary and conclusions. In W. Paul, J. D. Weinrich, J. C. Gonsiorek, & M. E. Hotvedt (Eds.), *Homosexuality: Social, psychological, and biological issues.* Beverly Hills, CA: Sage. (p. 367)

Goodall, J. (1968). The behaviour of free-living chimpanzees in the Gombe Stream Reserve. *Animal Behaviour Monographs, 1,* 161–311. (p. 90)

Goodall, J. (1986). *The chimpanzees of Gombe: Patterns of behavior.* Cambridge, MA: Harvard University Press. (p. 612)

Goodchilds, J. (1987). Quoted by Carol Tavris, Old age is not what it used to be. *The New York Times Magazine: Good Health Magazine,* September 27, pp. 24–25, 91–92. (p. 109)

Goodhart, D. E. (1986). The effects of positive and negative thinking on performance in an achievement situation. *Journal of Personality and Social Psychology, 51,* 117–124. (p. 437)

Goodwin, C. J. (1991). Misportraying Pavlov's apparatus. *American Journal of Psychology, 104,* 135–141. (p. 229)

Gopnik, A., & Meltzoff, A. N. (1986). Relations between semantic and cognitive development in the one-word stage: The specificity hypothesis. *Child Development, 57,* 1040–1053. (p. 312)

Gottesman, I. I. (1991). *Schizophrenia genesis: The origins of madness.* New York: Freeman. (p. 468)

Gottfredson, L. (1985). Education as a valid but fallible signal of worker quality: Reorienting an old debate about the functional basis of the occupational hierarchy. In A. C. Kerckhoff (Ed.), *Research in sociology of education and socialization* (Vol. 5). Greenwich, CT: JAI Press. (p. 331)

Gottfredson, L. S. (1986). Intelligence versus training: Job performance and black-white occupational inequality. Paper presented at a symposium on crime and employment: Two non-educational consequences of group IQ differences, American Psychological Association convention. (p. 341)

Gottfried, A. E., & Gottfried, A. W. (Eds.). (1988). *Maternal employment and children's development.* New York: Plenum. (p. 82)

Gould, M. S., & Shaffer, D. (1986). The impact of suicide in television movies: Evidence of imitation. *New England Journal of Medicine, 315,* 690–694. (p. 558)

Gould, S. J. (1981). *The mismeasure of man.* New York: Norton. (pp. 320–321)

Graf, P. (1990). Life-span changes in implicit and explicit memory. *Bulletin of the Psychonomic Society, 28,* 353–358. (p. 113)

Gray-Little, B., & Burks, N. (1983). Power and satisfaction in marriage: A review and critique. *Psychological Bulletin, 93,* 513–538. (p. 582)

GRE. (1990). *GRE guide to the use of the Graduate Record Examinations Program.* Princeton, NJ: Graduate Record Examinations Board, Educational Testing Service. (p. 326)

Greeley, A. M. (1991). *Faithful attraction.* New York: Tor Books. (pp. 12, 361, 370)

Green, S. K., & Sandos, P. (1983). Perceptions of male and female initiators of relationships. *Sex Roles, 9,* 849–852. (p. 605)

Greene, R. L. (1987). Effects of maintenance rehearsal on human memory. *Psychological Bulletin, 102,* 403–413. (p. 259)

Greenough, W. T., Black, J. E., & Wallace, C. S. (1987). Experience and brain development. *Child Development, 58,* 539–559. (p. 68)

Greenwald, A. G., Spangenberg, E. R., Pratkanis, A. R., & Eskenazi, J. (1991). Double-blind tests of subliminal self-help audiotapes. *Psychological Science, 2,* 119–122. (p. 17)

Greenwood, M. R. C. (1989). Sexual dimorphism and obesity. In A. J. Stunkard & A. Baum (Eds.), *Perspectives in behavioral medicine: Eating, sleeping, and sex.* Hillsdale, NJ: Erlbaum. (p. 539)

Greer, G. (1984, April). The uses of chastity and other paths to sexual pleasures. *MS*, pp. 53–60, 96. (pp. 363, 369)

Gregory, R. L. (1968, November). Visual illusions. *Scientific American*, pp. 66–76. (p. 172)

Gregory, R. L. (1978). *Eye and brain: The psychology of seeing* (3rd ed.). New York: McGraw-Hill. (p. 174)

Gregory, R. L., & Gombrich, E. H. (Eds.). (1973). *Illusion in nature and art.* New York: Charles Scribner's Sons. (p. 179)

Gregory, W. L., Cialdini, R. B., & Carpenter, K. M. (1982). Self-relevant scenarios as mediators of likelihood estimates and compliance: Does imagining make it so? *Journal of Personality and Social Psychology, 43,* 89–99. (p. 293)

Greif, E. B., & Ulman, K. J. (1982). The psychological impact of menarche on early adolescent females: A review of the literature. *Child Development, 53,* 1413–1430. (p. 97)

Griffin, D. R. (1984). Animal thinking. *American Scientist, 72,* 456–464. (p. 300)

Grobstein, C. (1979, June). External human fertilization. *Scientific American*, pp. 57–67. (p. 64)

Grolnick, W. S., & Ryan, R. M. (1987). Autonomy in children's learning: An experimental and individual difference investigation. *Journal of Personality and Social Psychology, 52,* 890–898. (p. 243)

Gross, A. E., & Crofton, C. (1977). What is good is beautiful. *Sociometry, 40,* 85–90. (p. 581)

Gruder, C. L. (1977). Choice of comparison persons in evaluating oneself. In J. M. Suls & R. L. Miller (Eds.), *Social comparison processes.* New York: Hemisphere. (p. 401)

Gudykunst, W., Yoon, Y. C., & Nishida, T. (1987). The influence of individualism-collectivism on perceptions of communication in ingroup and outgroup relationships. *Communication Monographs, 54,* 295–306. (p. 612)

Guerin, B. (1986). Mere presence effects in humans: A review. *Journal of Personality and Social Psychology, 22,* 38–77. (p. 563)

Gulevich, G., Dement, W., & Johnson, L. (1966). Psychiatric and EEG observations on a case of prolonged (264 hours) wakefulness. *Archives of General Psychiatry, 15,* 29–35. (p. 195)

Gustavson, C. R., Garcia, J., Hankins, W. G., & Rusiniak, K. W. (1974). Coyote predation control by aversive conditioning. *Science, 184,* 581–583. (p. 233)

Gutierres, S. E., Kenrick, D. T., & Goldberg, L. (1985). *Adverse influence on exposure to popular erotica: Effects on judgments of others and judgments of one's spouse.* Paper presented at the meeting of the Midwestern Psychological Association. (p. 364)

Gutmann, D. (1977). The cross-cultural perspective: Notes toward a comparative psychology of aging. In J. E. Birren & K. Warner Schaie (Eds.), *Handbook of the psychology of aging.* New York: Van Nostrand Reinhold. (p. 609)

Haber, R. N. (1970, May). How we remember what we see. *Scientific American*, pp. 104–112. (p. 254)

Hackenberg, T. D., & Hineline, P. N. (1990). Discrimination, symbolic behavior, and the origins of awareness. Unpublished manuscript, Temple University. (p. 237)

Hafner, H., & Schmidtke, A. (1989). Do televised fictional suicide models produce suicides? In D. R. Pfeffer (Ed.), *Suicide among youth: Perspectives on risk and prevention.* Washington, DC: American Psychiatric Press. (p. 558)

Hahn, W. K. (1987). Cerebral lateralization of function: From infancy through childhood. *Psychological Bulletin, 101,* 376–392. (p. 53)

Hall, C. S. (1984). "A ubiquitous sex difference in dreams" revisited. *Journal of Personality and Social Psychology, 46,* 1109–1117. (p. 198)

Hall, C. S., Dornhoff, W., Blick, K. A., & Weesner, K. E. (1982). The dreams of college men and women in 1950 and 1980: A comparison of dream contents and sex differences. *Sleep, 5,* 188–194. (p. 198)

Hall, C. S., & Lindzey, G. (1978). *Theories of personality* (2nd ed.). New York: Wiley. (p. 420)

Hall, C. S., & Van de Castle, R. L. (1966). *The content analysis of dreams.* New York: Appleton-Century-Crofts. (p. 198)

Hall, G. S. (1904). *Adolescence: Its psychology and its relations to physiology, anthropology, sex, crime, religion and education* (Vol. I). New York: Appleton-Century-Crofts. (p. 96)

Hall, J. A. (1987). On explaining gender differences: The case of nonverbal communication. In P. Shaver & C. Hendrick (Eds.), *Review of Personality and Social Psychology, 7,* 177–200. (pp. 600–601)

Hall, N. R., & Goldstein, A. L. (1986, March/April). Thinking well: The chemical links between emotions and health. *The Sciences*, pp. 34–40. (p. 523)

Hall, T. (1987, September 27). Cravings: Does your body know what it needs? *The New York Times Magazine: Good Health Magazine*, pp. 23, 62–65. (p. 357)

Halpern, D. F. (1986). *Sex differences in cognitive abilities.* Hillsdale, NJ: Erlbaum. (p. 598)

Hamill, R., Wilson, T. D., & Nisbett, R. E. (1980). Insensitivity to sample bias: Generalizing from atypical cases. *Journal of Personality and Social Psychology, 39,* 578–589. (p. 293)

Hamilton, M. C. (1988). Using masculine generics: Does generic "he" increase male bias in the user's imagery? *Sex Roles, 19,* 785–799. (p. 311)

Hammersmith, S. K. (1982, August). *Sexual preference: An empirical study from the Alfred C. Kinsey Institute for Sex Research.* Paper presented at the meeting of the American Psychological Association, Washington, DC. (p. 367)

Hansel, C. E. M. (1980). *ESP and parapsychology: A critical reevaluation.* Buffalo, NY: Prometheus. (p. 183)

Hansel, C. E. M. (1985). The search for a demonstration of ESP. In P. Kurtz (Ed.), *A skeptic's handbook of parapsychology.* Buffalo, NY: Prometheus. (p. 184)

Hansen, C. H., & Hansen, R. D. (1988). Finding the face-in-the-crowd: An anger superiority effect. *Journal of Personality and Social Psychology, 54,* 917–924. (p. 388)

Hare, R. D. (1975). Psychophysiological studies of psychopathy. In D. C. Fowles (Ed.), *Clinical applications of psychophysiology.* New York: Columbia University Press. (p. 472)

Harkins, S. G., & Szymanski, K. (1989). Social loafing and group evaluation. *Journal of Personality and Social Psychology, 56,* 934–941. (p. 564)

Harlow, H. F., Harlow, M. K., & Suomi, S. J. (1971). From thought to therapy: Lessons from a primate laboratory. *American Scientist, 59,* 538–549. (p. 76)

Harper's Index. (1989, November). *Harper's,* p. 15. (p. 601)

Harrell, T. H., & Stolp, R. D. (1985). Effects of erotic guided imagery on female sexual arousal and emotional response. *Journal of Sex Research, 21,* 292–304. (p. 364)

Harrington, D. M., Block, J. H., & Block, J. (1987). Testing aspects of Carl Rogers's theory of creative environments: Child-rearing antecedents of creative potential in young adolescents. *Journal of Personality and Social Psychology, 52,* 851–856. (p. 429)

Harris, B. (1979). Whatever happened to Little Albert? *American Psychologist, 34,* 151–160. (p. 235)

Harris, L. (1987). *Inside America.* New York: Random House. (pp. 11, 512, 516, 539)

Harris, L., & Associates. (1986). American teens speak: Sex, myths, TV, and birth control: The Planned Parenthood Poll. Available from Planned Parenthood, 810 Seventh Avenue, New York, NY 10019. (pp. 105–106)

Harris, L., & Associates. (1988, January 26). Sexual material on American network television during the 1987–88 season. Conducted for Planned Parenthood Federation of America, New York. (p. 107)

Harris, L. J. (1978). Sex differences in spatial ability: Possible environmental, genetic, and neurological factors. In M. Kinsbourne (Ed.), *The asymmetrical function of the brain.* New York: Cambridge University Press. (p. 609)

Harry, J. (1990). A probability sample of gay males. *Journal of Homosexuality, 19,* 89–104. (p. 366)

Hart, D. (1988). The development of personal identity in adolescence: A philosophical dilemma approach. *Merrill-Palmer Quarterly, 34,* 105–114. (p. 103)

Hartmann, E. (1981, April). The strangest sleep disorder. *Psychology Today,* pp. 14, 16, 18. (p. 197)

Hartmann, E. (1984). *The nightmare: The psychology and biology of terrifying dreams.* New York: Basic Books. (p. 197)

Hartshorne, H., & May, M. A. (1928). *Studies in deceit.* New York: Macmillan. (p. 426)

Hartup, W. W. (1989). Social relationships and their developmental significance. *American Psychologist, 44,* 120–126. (p. 79)

Harvey, S. M. (1987). Female sexual behavior: Fluctuations during the menstrual cycle. *Journal of Psychosomatic Research, 31,* 101–110. (p. 363)

Hasher, L., & Zacks, R. T. (1979). Automatic and effortful processes in memory. *Journal of Experimental Psychology: General, 108,* 356–388. (p. 257)

Hasher, L., & Zacks, R. T. (1984). Automatic processing of fundamental information: The case of frequency of occurrence. *American Psychologist, 39,* 1372–1388. (p. 257)

Haskins, R. (1989). Beyond metaphor: The efficacy of early childhood education. *American Psychologist, 44,* 274–282. (p. 340)

Hassan, R., & Carr, J. (1989). Changing patterns of suicide in Australia. *Australian and New Zealand Journal of Psychiatry, 23,* 226–234. (p. 461)

Hatfield, E. (1988). Passionate and companionate love. In R. J. Sternberg & M. L. Barnes (Eds.), *The psychology of love.* New Haven: Yale University Press. (p. 581)

Hatfield, E., & Sprecher, S. (1986). *Mirror, mirror . . . The importance of looks in everyday life.* Albany: State University of New York Press. (p. 579)

Hathaway, S. R. (1960). *An MMPI Handbook* (Vol. 1, Foreword). Minneapolis: University of Minnesota Press. (Revised edition, 1972.) (p. 424)

Hattie, J. A., Sharpley, C. F., & Rogers, H. J. (1984). Comparative effectiveness of professional and paraprofessional helpers. *Psychological Bulletin, 95,* 534–541. (p. 502)

Hayes, J. R. (1981). *The complete problem solver.* Philadelphia: Franklin Institute Press. (p. 272)

Hazan, C., & Shaver, P. R. (1990). Love and work: An attachment-theoretical perspective. *Journal of Personality and Social Psychology, 59,* 270–280. (p. 79)

Hazelrigg, M. D., Cooper, H. M., & Borduin, C. M. (1987). Evaluating the effectiveness of family therapies: An integrative review and analysis. *Psychological Bulletin, 101,* 428–442. (p. 487)

Headey, B., & Wearing, A. (1988). The sense of relative superiority—central to well-being. *Social Indicators Research, 20,* 497–516. (p. 431)

Hearold, S. (1986). A synthesis of 1043 effects of television on social behavior. In G. Comstock (Ed.), *Public communication and behavior.* New York: Academic Press. (p. 571)

Heath, A. C., Eaves, L. J., & Martin, N. G. (1989). The genetic structure of personality: III. Multivariate genetic item analysis of the EPQ scales. *Personality and Individual Differences, 10,* 877–888. (p. 87)

Heath, A. C., Jardine, R., Eaves, L. J., & Martin, N. G. (1989). The genetic structure of personality: II. Genetic item analysis of the EPQ. *Personality and Individual Differences, 10,* 615–624. (p. 87)

Heath, A. C., Jardine, R., & Martin, N. G. (1989). Interactive effects of genotype and social environment on alcohol consumption in female twins. *Journal of Studies on Alcohol, 50,* 38–48. (p. 217)

Heath, L., & Petraitis, J. (1987). Television viewing and fear of crime: Where is the mean world? *Basic and Applied Social Psychology, 8,* 97–123. (p. 571)

Hebb, D. O. (1980). *Essay on mind.* Hillsdale, NJ: Erlbaum. 9–16. (pp. 228, 383, 394)

Hebert, H. J. (1988, January 13). Airlines hit 5-year high in fatalities. *Detroit Free Press*, pp. 1A, 16A. (p. 294)

Heider, F. (1958). *The psychology of interpersonal relations.* New York: Wiley. (p. 551)

Heiman, J. R. (1975, April). The physiology of erotica: Women's sexual arousal. *Psychology Today*, 90–94. (p. 364)

Helson, R., & Moane, G. (1987). Personality change in women from college to midlife. *Journal of Personality and Social Psychology, 53,* 176–186. (p. 609)

Helzer, J. E., Canino, G. J., Eng-Kung, Y., Bland, R. C., Lee, C. K., Hwu, H-G., & Newman, S. (1990). Alcoholism—North America and Asia. *Archives of General Psychiatry, 47,* 313–319. (p. 212)

Hembree, R. (1988). Correlates, causes, effects, and treatment of test anxiety. *Review of Educational Research, 58,* 47–77. (p. 385)

Hendrick, S. S., Hendrick, C., Slapion-Foote, J., & Foote, F. H. (1985). Gender differences in sexual attitudes. *Journal of Personality and Social Psychology, 48,* 1630–1642. (p. 601)

Hendricks, B., Marvel, M. K., & Barrington, B. L. (1990). The dimensions of psychological research. *Teaching of Psychology, 17,* 76–82. (p. 10)

Henley, N. M. (1989). Molehill or mountain? What we know and don't know about sex bias in language. In M. Crawford & M. Gentry (Eds.), *Gender and thought: Psychological perspectives.* New York: Springer-Verlag. (p. 311)

Henry, J. P., & Stephens, P. M. (1977). *Stress, health, and the social environment.* New York: Springer-Verlag. (p. 516)

Hepper, P. G., Shahidullah, S., & White, R. (1990). Origins of fetal handedness. *Nature, 347,* 431. (p. 52)

Herek, G. M. (1989). Hate crimes against lesbians and gay men: Issues for research and policy. *American Psychologist, 44,* 948–955. (p. 611)

Herek, G. M. (1990). The context of anti-gay violence: Notes on cultural and psychological heterosexism. *Journal of Interpersonal Violence, 5,* 316–333. (p. 611)

Herman, C. P., & Mack, D. (1975). Restrained and unrestrained eating. *Journal of Personality, 43,* 647–660. (p. 545)

Herman, C. P., Olmsted, M. P., & Polivy, J. (1983). Obesity, externality, and susceptibility to social influence: An integrated analysis. *Journal of Personality and Social Psychology, 45,* 926–934. (p. 540)

Herman, C. P., & Polivy, J. (1980). Restrained eating. In A. J. Stunkard (Ed.), *Obesity.* Philadelphia: Saunders. (p. 545)

Heron, W. (1957, January). The pathology of boredom. *Scientific American*, pp. 52–56. (p. 157)

Herrmann, D. (1982). Know thy memory: The use of questionnaires to assess and study memory. *Psychological Bulletin, 92,* 434–452. (p. 280)

Herrnstein, R. J., & Loveland, D. H. (1964). Complex visual concept in the pigeon. *Science, 146,* 549–551. (p. 237)

Hershenson, M. (1989). *The moon illusion.* Hillsdale, NJ: Erlbaum. (p. 171)

Hess, E. H. (1956, July). Space perception in the chick. *Scientific American*, pp. 71–80. (p. 176)

Hetherington, E. M. (1979). Divorce: A child's perspective. *American Psychologist, 34,* 851–858. (p. 85)

Hetherington, E. M., & Clingempeel, W. G. (1992). Coping with marital transitions: A family systems perspective. *Society for Research in Child Development Monographs*, in press. (p. 81)

Hetherington, E. M., Stanley-Hagan, M., & Anderson, E. R. (1989). Marital transitions: A child's perspective. *American Psychologist, 44,* 303–312. (p. 81)

Hicks, R. A., & Gaus, W. (1983). Type A-Type B behavior and daily milk consumption in college students. *Bulletin of the Psychonomic Society, 21,* 259. (p. 519)

Hicks, R. A., Kilcourse, J., & Sinnott, M. A. (1983). Type A-B behavior and caffeine use in college students. *Psychological Reports, 52,* 338. (p. 519)

Hicks, R. A., & Pellegrini, R. J. (1982). Sleep problems and Type A-B behavior in college students. *Psychological Reports, 51,* 196. (p. 519)

Higgins, E. T. (1987). Self-discrepancy: A theory relating self and affect. *Psychological Review, 94,* 319–340. (p. 430)

Higgins, E. T., & Bargh, J. A. (1987). Social cognition and social perception. *Annual Review of Psychology, 38,* 369–425. (p. 430)

Hilgard, E. R. (1986). *Divided consciousness: Multiple controls in human thought and action.* New York: Wiley. (pp. 209, 219)

Hines, M. (1982). Prenatal gonadal hormones and sex differences in human behavior. *Psychological Bulletin, 92,* 56–80. (p. 602)

Hines, M. (1990). Gonadal hormones and human cognitive development. In J. Balthazart (Ed.), *Hormones, brain and behaviour in vertebrates, I. Sexual differentiation, neuroanatomical aspects, neurotransmitters and neuropeptides.* Basel: Karger. (p. 602)

Hintzman, D. L. (1978). *The psychology of learning and memory.* San Francisco: Freeman. (p. 262)

Hinz, L. D., & Williamson, D. A. (1987). Bulimia and depression: A review of the affective variant hypothesis. *Psychological Bulletin, 102,* 150–158. (p. 359)

Hirst, W., Neisser, U., & Spelke, E. (1978, June). Divided attention. *Human Nature*, pp. 54–61. (p. 209)

Hobfoll, S. E. (1989). Conservation of resources: A new attempt at conceptualizing stress. *American Psychologist, 44,* 513–524. (p. 512)

Hobfoll, S. E., Lomranz, J., Eyal, N., Bridges, A., & Tzemach, M. (1989). Pulse of a nation: Depressive mood reactions of Israelis to the Israel-Lebanon war. *Journal of Personality and Social Psychology, 56,* 1002–1012. (p. 460)

Hobson, J. A. (1988). *The dreaming brain.* New York: Basic Books. (p. 200)

Hochschild, A. (1989). *The second shift: Working parents and the revolution at home.* New York: Viking. (p. 608)

Hoebel, B. G., & Teitelbaum, P. (1966). Effects of forcefeeding and starvation on food intake and body weight in a rat with ventromedial hypothalamic lesions. *Journal of Comparative and Physiological Psychology, 61,* 189–193. (p. 357)

Hoffman, C., & Hurst, N. (1990). Gender stereotypes: Perception or rationalization? *Journal of Personality and Social Psychology, 58,* 197–208. (p. 612)

Hoffman, C., Lau, I., & Johnson, D. R. (1986). The linguistic relativity of person cognition: An English-Chinese comparison. *Journal of Personality and Social Psychology, 51,* 1097–1105. (p. 311)

Hoffman, L. W. (1989). Effects of maternal employment in the two-parent family. *American Psychologist, 44,* 283–292. (p. 82)

Hofstede, G. (1980). *Culture's consequences: International differences in work-related values.* Beverly Hills: Sage. (p. 376)

Hogan, J. (1989). Personality correlates of physical fitness. *Journal of Personality and Social Psychology, 56,* 284–288. (p. 528)

Hohmann, G. W. (1966). Some effects of spinal cord lesions on experienced emotional feelings. *Psychophysiology, 3,* 143–156. (p. 403)

Hokanson, J. E., & Edelman, R. (1966). Effects of three social responses on vascular processes. *Journal of Personality and Social Psychology, 3,* 442–447. (p. 395)

Holden, C. (1980a). Identical twins reared apart. *Science, 207,* 1323–1325. (p. 88)

Holden, C. (1980b, November). Twins reunited. *Science, 80,* 55–59. (p. 88)

Holden, C. (1986a). Days may be numbered for polygraphs in the private sector. *Science, 232,* 705. (p. 386)

Holden, C. (1986b). Researchers grapple with problems of updating classic psychological test. *Science, 233,* 1249–1251. (p. 434)

Holden, C. (1987). Is alcoholism treatment effective? *Science, 236,* 20–22. (p. 490)

Holden, C. (1989). Private sector to do British sex survey. *Science, 246,* 450. (p. 361)

Holden, C. (1990). Head Start enters adulthood. *Science, 247,* 1400–1402. (p. 340)

Holden, C. (1991). New center to study therapies and ethnicity. *Science, 251,* 748. (pp. 217, 504)

Holing, D. (1988, October). Dolphin defense. *Discover,* pp. 70–74. (p. 246)

Holmes, D. S. (1978). Projection as a defense mechanism. *Psychological Bulletin, 85,* 677–688. (p. 420)

Holmes, D. S. (1981). Existence of classical projection and the stress-reducing function of attributive projection: A reply to Sherwood. *Psychological Bulletin, 90,* 460–466. (p. 420)

Holmes, D. S. (1984). Meditation and somatic arousal reduction: A review of the experimental evidence. *American Psychologist, 39,* 1–10. (p. 202)

Holzman, P. S., & Matthysse, S. (1990). The genetics of schizophrenia: A review. *Psychological Science, 1,* 279–286. (p. 136)

Hooper, J., & Teresi, D. (1986). *The three-pound universe.* New York: Macmillan. (p. 41)

Hooykaas, R. (1972). *Religion and the rise of modern science.* Grand Rapids, MI: Eerdmans. (p. 9)

Horn, J. L. (1982). The aging of human abilities. In J. Wolman (Ed.), *Handbook of developmental psychology.* Englewood Cliffs, NJ: Prentice-Hall. (p. 115)

Horn, W. F. (1990, October). Psychology can help kids get a Head Start. *APA Monitor,* p. 3. (p. 340)

Horne, J. A. (1989). Sleep loss and "divergent" thinking ability. *Sleep, 11,* 528–536. (p. 195)

House, J. S., Landis, K. R., & Umberson, D. (1988). Social relationships and health. *Science, 241,* 540–545. (p. 533)

House, R. J., & Singh, J. V. (1987). Organizational behavior: Some new directions for I/O psychology. *Annual Review of Psychology, 38,* 669–718. (p. 377)

Hsu, F-H., Anantharaman, R., Campbell, M., & Nowatzyk, A. (1990, October). A grandmaster chess machine. *Scientific American,* pp. 44–50. (p. 300)

Hubel, D. H. (1979, September). The brain. *Scientific American,* pp. 45–53. (p. 135)

Hubel, D. H., & Wiesel, T. N. (1979, September). Brain mechanisms of vision. *Scientific American,* pp. 150–162. (pp. 37, 142)

Hucker, S. J., & Bain, J. (1990). Androgenic hormones and sexual assault. In W. Marshall, R. Law, & H. Barbaree (Eds.), *The handbook on sexual assault.* New York: Plenum. (p. 363)

Hugick, L. (1989, July). Women play the leading role in keeping modern families close. *Gallup Report,* No. 286, pp. 27–34. (p. 599)

Hugo, G. (1987). Aging in the third world. *Social Science, 72,* 57–60. (p. 110)

Hui, C. H. (1990). West meets East: Individualism versus collectivism in North America and Asia. Invited address, Hope College. (p. 593)

Hull, J. G., & Bond, C. F., Jr. (1986). Social and behavioral consequences of alcohol consumption and expectancy: A meta-analysis. *Psychological Bulletin, 99,* 347–360. (p. 212)

Hull, J. G., Young, R. D., & Jouriles, E. (1986). Applications of the self-awareness model of alcohol consumption: Predicting patterns of use and abuse. *Journal of Personality and Social Psychology, 51,* 790–796. (p. 211)

Humphreys, L. G., & Davey, T. C. (1988). Continuity in intellectual growth from 12 months to 9 years. *Intelligence, 12,* 183–197. (p. 333)

Hunt, E. (1983). On the nature of intelligence. *Science, 219,* 141–146. (p. 332)

Hunt, J. M. (1982). Toward equalizing the developmental opportunities of infants and preschool children. *Journal of Social Issues, 38*(4), 163–191. (p. 339)

Hunt, M. (1974). *Sexual behavior in the 1970s.* Chicago: Playboy Press. (p. 364)

Hunt, M. (1982). *The universe within.* New York: Simon and Schuster. (pp. 297, 299)

Hunt, M. (1987, August 30). Navigating the therapy maze. *The New York Times Magazine,* pp. 28–49. (p. 496)

Hunter, S., & Sundel, M. (Eds.). (1989). *Midlife myths: Issues, findings, and practice implications.* Newbury Park, CA: Sage. (p. 116)

Hutnik, N. (1985). Aspects of identity in a multi-ethnic society. *New Community, 12,* 298–309. (p. 596)

Hyde, J. S. (1983, November). *Bem's gender schema theory.* Paper presented at GLCA Women's Studies Conference, Rochester, IN. (p. 275)

Hyde, J. S. (1984, July). Children's understanding of sexist language. *Developmental Psychology, 20*(4), 697–706. (p. 311)

Hyde, J. S. (1986). Gender differences in aggression. In J. S. Hyde & M. C. Linn (Eds.), *The psychology of gender: Advances through meta-analysis.* Baltimore: Johns Hopkins University Press. (p. 601)

Hyde, J. S., Fennema, E., & Lamon, S. J. (1990). Gender differences in mathematics performance: A meta-analysis. *Psychological Bulletin, 107,* 139–155. (p. 598)

Hyde, J. S., & Linn, M. C. (1988). Gender differences in verbal ability: A meta-analysis. *Psychological Bulletin, 104,* 53–69. (p. 598)

Hyman, R. (1981). Cold reading: How to convince strangers that you know all about them. In K. Frazier (Ed.), *Paranormal borderlands of science.* Buffalo, NY: Prometheus. (p. 438)

Hyman, R. (1986). Maimonides dream-telepathy experiments. *Skeptical Inquirer, 11,* 91–92. (p. 183)

Hyman, R. B., Feldman, H. R., Harris, R. B., Levin, R. F., & Malloy, G. B. (1989). The effects of relaxation training on clinical symptoms: A meta-analysis. *Nursing Research, 38,* 216–220. (p. 530)

Ilola, L. M. (1990). Culture and health. In R. W. Brislin (Ed.), *Applied cross-cultural psychology.* Newbury Park, CA: Sage. (p. 538)

Ingham, A. G., Levinger, G., Graves, J., & Peckham, V. (1974). The Ringelmann effect: Studies of group size and group performance. *Journal of Experimental Social Psychology, 10,* 371–384. (p. 564)

Inglehart, M. R., Markus, H., & Brown, D. R. (1989). The effects of possible selves on academic achievement — a panel study. In J. P. Forgas & J. M. Innes (Eds.), *Recent advances in social psychology: An international perspective.* North-Holland: Elsevier Science Publishers. (p. 429)

Inglehart, R. (1990). *Culture shift in advanced industrial society.* Princeton, NJ: Princeton University Press. (pp. 118, 121, 397, 437)

Inhelder, B., & Piaget, J. (1958). *The growth of logical thinking.* New York: Basic Books. (p. 98)

Innes, J. M., & Zeitz, H. (1988). The public's view of the impact of the mass media: A test of the 'third person' effect. *European Journal of Social Psychology, 18,* 457–463.

Insel, P. M., & Roth, W. T. (1976). *Health in a changing society.* Palo Alto, CA: Mayfield. (p. 108)

Institute of Medicine. (1989). *Behavioral influences on the endocrine and immune systems.* Washington, DC: National Academy Press. (p. 521)

Intons-Peterson, M. J., Roskos-Ewoldsen, B., Thomas, L., Shirley, M., & Blut, D. (1989). Will educational materials reduce negative effects of exposure to sexual violence? *Journal of Social and Clinical Psychology, 8,* 256–275. (p. 574)

Isen, A. M., & Means, B. (1983). The influence of positive affect on decision-making strategy. *Social Cognition, 2,* 28–31. (p. 396)

Izard, C. E. (1977). *Human emotions.* New York: Plenum Press. (pp. 390, 392)

Izard, C. E. (1990). Facial expressions and the regulation of emotions. *Journal of Personality and Social Psychology, 58,* 487–498. (p. 392)

Jackson, J. M., & Williams, K. D. (1988). Social loafing: A review and theoretical analysis. Unpublished manuscript, Fordham University. (p. 564)

Jacobs, B. L. (1987). How hallucinogenic drugs work. *American Scientist, 75,* 386–392. (p. 215)

Jacobs, M. K., & Goodman, G. (1989). Psychology and self-help groups: Predictions on a partnership. *American Psychologist, 44,* 536–545. (p. 486)

Jacobs, W. J., & Nadel, L. (1985). Stress-induced recovery of fears and phobias. *Psychological Bulletin, 92,* 512–531. (p. 454)

Jacobson, R. L. (1986, September 3). Number of blacks taking SAT drops 5 pct. in 5 years. *Chronicle of Higher Education,* p. 108. (p. 341)

Jacoby, L. L., Woloshyn, V., & Kelley, C. (1989). Becoming famous without being recognized: Unconscious influences of memory produced by dividing attention. *Journal of Experimental Psychology: General, 118,* 115–125.

James, W. (1890). *The principles of psychology* (Vol. 2). New York: Holt. (pp. 28, 151, 183, 209, 264, 280, 392, 402, 557)

James, W. (1902; reprinted 1958). *Varieties of religious experience.* New York: Mentor Books. (p. 396)

Jameson, D. (1985). Opponent-colors theory in light of physiological findings. In D. Ottoson & S. Zeki (Eds.), *Central and peripheral mechanisms of color vision.* New York: Macmillan. (p. 145)

Jamison, K. R. (1989). Mood disorders and patterns of creativity in British writers and artists. *Psychiatry, 52,* 125–134. (p. 459)

Janis, I. L. (1969). *Stress and frustration.* New York: Harcourt Brace Jovanovich. (p. 527)

Janis, I. L. (1982). *Groupthink: Psychological studies of policy decisions and fiascoes.* Boston: Houghton Mifflin. (p. 565)

Janis, I. L. (1986). Problems of international crisis management in the nuclear age. *Journal of Social Issues, 42*(2), 201–220. (p. 291)

Janis, I. L. (1989). *Crucial decisions: Leadership in policymaking and crisis management.* New York: Free Press. (p. 290)

Janoff-Bulman, R., Timko, C., & Carli, L. L. (1985). Cognitive biases in blaming the victim. *Journal of Experimental Social Psychology, 21,* 161–177. (p. 614)

Jarvik, L. F. (1975). Thoughts on the psychobiology of aging. *American Psychologist, 30,* 576–583. (p. 111)

Jasnoski, M. L., Kugler, J., & McClelland, D. C. (1986). Power imagery and relaxation affect psychoneuroimmune indices. Paper presented at the American Psychological Association convention. (p. 530)

Jasnoski, M. L., & Schwartz, G. E. (1985). A synchronous systems model for health. *American Behavioral Scientist, 28,* 468–485. (p. 511)

Jeffrey, R. W., & Wing, R. R. (1983). Recidivism and self-cure of smoking and obesity: Data from population studies. *American Psychologist, 38,* 852. (p. 543)

Jemmott, J. B., III, & Locke, S. E. (1984). Psychosocial factors, immunologic mediation, and human susceptibility to infectious diseases: How much do we know? *Psychological Bulletin, 95,* 78–108. (p. 521)

Jemmott, J. B., III, & Magloire, K. (1988). Academic stress, social support, and secretory immunoglobulin A. *Journal of Personality and Social Psychology, 55,* 803–810. (p. 521)

Jenkins, J. G., & Dallenbach, K. M. (1924). Obliviscence during sleep and waking. *American Journal of Psychology, 35,* 605–612. (pp. 278–279)

Jensen, A. R. (1980). *Bias in mental testing.* New York: The Free Press. (p. 326)

Jensen, A. R. (1983, August). *The nature of the black-white difference on various psychometric tests: Spearman's hypothesis.* Paper presented at the meeting of the American Psychological Association, Anaheim, CA. (p. 344)

Jensen, A. R. (1985). The nature of the black-white difference on various psychometric tests: Spearman's hypothesis. *Behavioral and Brain Sciences, 8,* 193–263. (p. 341)

Jensen, A. R. (1989). New findings on the intellectually gifted. *New Horizons, 30,* 73–80. (p. 332)

Jensen, J. P., & Bergin, A. E. (1988). Mental health values of professional therapists: A national interdisciplinary survey. *Professional Psychology: Research and Practice, 19,* 290–297. (p. 493)

Jepson, C., Krantz, D. H., & Nisbett, R. E. (1983). Inductive reasoning: Competence or skill. *The Behavioral and Brain Sciences, 3,* 494–501. (p. 633)

Jervis, R. (1985, April 2). Quoted by D. Goleman, Political forces come under new scrutiny of psychology. *The New York Times,* pp. C1, C4. (p. 297)

John, O. P. (1990). The "big five" factor taxonomy: Dimensions of personality in the natural language and in questionnaires. In L. A. Pervin (Ed.), *Handbook of personality: Theory and research.* New York: Guilford Press. (p. 423)

Johnson, D. (1990). Animal rights and human lives: Time for scientists to right the balance. *Psychological Science, 1,* 213–214. (p. 20)

Johnson, D., & Drenick, E. J. (1977). Therapeutic fasting in morbid obesity. Long-term follow-up. *Archives of Internal Medicine, 137,* 1381–1382. (p. 542)

Johnson, D. W., & Johnson, R. T. (1987). *Learning together and alone: Cooperative, competitive, and individualistic learning* (2nd ed.). Englewood Cliffs, NJ: Prentice-Hall. (p. 617)

Johnson, E. J., & Tversky, A. (1983). Affect, generalization, and the perception of risk. *Journal of Personality and Social Psychology, 45,* 20–31. (p. 396)

Johnson, J. S., & Newport, E. L. (1989). Critical period effects in second language learning: The influence of maturational state on the acquisition of English as a second language. *Cognitive Psychology, 21,* 60–99. (p. 306)

Johnson, M. H., & Magaro, P. A. (1987). Effects of mood and severity on memory processes in depression and mania. *Psychological Bulletin, 101,* 28–40. (p. 275)

Johnston, L. D., O'Malley, P. M., & Bachman, J. G. (1991). Drug use among American high school seniors, college students and young adults, 1975–1990: Volume 1. [DHHS Pub. No. (ADM) 91-1813.] Washington, DC: GPO. (pp. 213, 216, 217, 536)

Jones, E. E., Cumming, J. D., & Horowitz, M. J. (1988). Another look at the nonspecific hypothesis of therapeutic effectiveness. *Journal of Consulting and Clinical Psychology, 56,* 48–55. (p. 500)

Jones, E. F., Forrest, J. D., Goldman, N., Henshaw, S. K., Lincoln, R., Rosoff, J. I., Westoff, C. F., & Wulf, D. (1985, March/April). Teenage pregnancy in developed countries: Determinants and policy implications. *Family Planning Perspectives, 17,* 53–64. (p. 105)

Jones, J. M. (1988). Piercing the veil: Bi-cultural strategies for coping with prejudice and racism. Invited address, national conference, "Opening doors: An appraisal of race relations in America." University of Alabama. (p. 595)

Jones, J. M. (1990). Promoting diversity in an individualistic society. Keynote address, Great Lakes College Association conference, "Multiculturalism transforming the 21st century." (pp. 589, 595)

Jones, L. (1985–86). CSICOP's international conference in London: Investigation and belief, past lives and prizes. *Skeptical Inquirer, 10,* 98–104. (p. 184)

Jones, M. C. (1924). A laboratory study of fear: The case of Peter. *Journal of Genetic Psychology, 31,* 308–315. (p. 487)

Jones, M. C. (1957). The later careers of boys who were early or late maturing. *Child Development, 28,* 113–128. (p. 97)

Jones, S. S., Collins, K., & Hong, H-W. (1991). An audience effect on smile production in 10-month-old infants. *Psychological Science, 2,* 45–49. (p. 391)

Jones, W. H., Carpenter, B. N., & Quintana, D. (1985). Personality and interpersonal predictors of loneliness in two cultures. *Journal of Personality and Social Psychology, 48,* 1503–1511. (p. 19)

Jorgenson, D. O., & Papciak, A. S. (1981). The effects of communication, resource feedback, and identifiability on behavior in a simulated commons. *Journal of Experimental Social Psychology, 17,* 373–385. (p. 617)

Jorm, A. F., Korten, A. E., & Henderson, A. S. (1987). The prevalence of dementia: A quantitative integration of the literature. *Acta Psychiatrica Scandinavica, 76,* 465–479. (p. 112)

Joseph, J. G., Montgomery, S. B., Emmons, C-A., Kirscht, J. P., Kessler, R. C., Ostrow, D. G., Wortman, C. B., O'Brien, K., Eller, M., & Eshleman, S. (1987). Perceived risk of AIDS: Assessing the behavioral and psychosocial consequences in a cohort of gay men. *Journal of Applied Social Psychology, 17,* 231–250. (p. 367)

Julien, R. M. (1988). *A primer of drug action* (5th ed.). New York: Freeman. (p. 213)

Jung, C. (1933). *Modern man in search of a soul.* New York: Harcourt Brace Jovanovich. (p. 609)

Juster, F. T., & Stafford, F. P. (1991). The allocation of time: Empirical findings, behavioral models, and problems of measurement. *Journal of Economic Literature,* in press. (pp. 343, 608)

Justice, A. (1985). Review of the effects of stress on cancer in laboratory animals: Importance of time of stress application and type of tumor. *Psychological Bulletin, 98,* 108–138. (p. 523)

Kagan, J. (1976). Emergent themes in human development. *American Scientist, 64,* 186–196. (p. 78)

Kagan, J. (1984). *The nature of the child.* New York: Basic Books. (p. 73)

Kagan, J. (1989a). Temperamental contributions to social behavior. *American Psychologist, 44,* 668–674. (p. 78)

Kagan, J. (1989b). *Unstable ideas: Temperament, cognition, and self.* Cambridge, MA: Harvard University Press. (pp. 78, 420, 422)

Kagan, J. (1990). Interview with M. V. Ellis & E. S. Robbins, In Celebration of nature: A dialogue with Jerome Kagan. *Journal of Counseling and Development, 68,* 623–627. (p. 78)

Kahn, S., Zimmerman, G., Csikszentmihalyi, M., & Getzels, J. W. (1985). Relations between identity in young adulthood and intimacy in midlife. *Journal of Personality and Social Psychology, 49,* 1316–1322. (p. 103)

Kahneman, D. (1985, June). Quoted by K. McKean, Decisions, decisions. *Discover,* pp. 22–31. (p. 630)

Kahneman, D., Knetsch, J. L., & Thaler, R. (1986). Fairness as a constraint on profit seeking: Entitlements in the market. *American Economic Review, 76,* 728–741. (p. 296)

Kahneman, D., & Tversky, A. (1972). Subjective probability: A judgment of representativeness. *Cognitive Psychology, 3,* 430–454. (p. 631)

Kahneman, D., & Tversky, A. (1979a). Intuitive prediction: Biases and corrective procedures. *Management Science, 12,* 313–327. (p. 294)

Kahneman, D., & Tversky, A. (1979b). Subjective probability: A judgment of representativeness. *Cognitive Psychology, 3,* 430–454. (p. 294)

Kahneman, D., & Tversky, A. (1984). Choices, values, and frames. *American Psychologist, 39,* 341–350. (p. 296)

Kail, R. (1991). Developmental change in speed of processing during childhood and adolescence. *Psychological Bulletin, 109,* 490–501. (p. 111)

Kamarck, T., & Jennings, J. R. (1991). Biobehavioral factors in sudden cardiac death. *Psychological Bulletin, 109,* 42–75. (p. 520)

Kamin, L. (1974). *The science and politics of IQ.* New York: Wiley. (p. 338)

Kandel, D. B., & Raveis, V. H. (1989). Cessation of illicit drug use in young adulthood. *Archives of General Psychiatry, 46,* 109–116. (p. 218)

Kandel, E. R., & Schwartz, J. H. (1982). Molecular biology of learning: Modulation of transmitter release. *Science, 218,* 433–443. (p. 269)

Kanekar, S., & Nazareth, A. (1988). Attributed rape victim's fault as a function of her attractiveness, physical hurt, and emotional disturbance. *Social Behaviour, 3,* 37–40. (p. 602)

Kaplan, H. I., & Saddock, B. J. (Eds.). (1989). *Comprehensive textbook of psychiatry, V.* Baltimore, MD: Williams and Wilkins. (p. 504)

Kaplan, H. S. (1979). *Disorders of sexual desire.* New York: Brunner/Mazel. (p. 363)

Kaplan, R. M. (1984). The connection between clinical health promotion and health status: A critical overview. *American Psychologist, 39,* 755–765. (p. 534)

Kaprio, J., Koskenvu, M., & Rita, H. (1987). Mortality after bereavement: A prospective study of 95,647 widowed persons. *American Journal of Public Health, 77,* 283–287. (p. 515)

Karacan, I., Aslan, C., & Hirshkowitz, M. (1983). Erectile mechanisms in man. *Science, 220,* 1080–1082. (p. 194)

Karacan, I., Goodenough, D. R., Shapiro, A., & Starker, S. (1966). Erection cycle during sleep in relation to dream anxiety. *Archives of General Psychiatry, 15,* 183–189. (p. 194)

Karno, M., Golding, J. M., Sorenson, S. B., & Burnam, A. (1988). The epidemiology of obsessive-compulsive disorder in five US communities. *Archives of General Psychiatry, 45,* 1094–1099. (p. 453)

Kato, P. S., & Ruble, D. N. (1992). Toward an understanding of women's experience of menstrual cycle symptoms. In V. Adesso, D. Reddy, & R. Fleming (Eds.), *Psychological perspectives on women's health*. Washington, DC: Hemisphere. (p. 525)

Kaufman, A. S., Reynolds, C. R., & McLean, J. E. (1989). Age and WAIS-R intelligence in a national sample of adults in the 20- to 74-year age range: A cross-sectional analysis with educational level controlled. *Intelligence, 13*, 235–253. (p. 115)

Kaufman, J., & Zigler, E. (1987). Do abused children become abusive parents? *American Journal of Orthopsychiatry, 57*, 186–192. (p. 80)

Kaufman, L., & Rock, I. (1962). The moon illusion I. *Science, 136*, 953–961. (p. 172)

Kazdin, A. E. (1982). The token economy: A decade later. *Journal of Applied Behavior Analysis, 15*, 431–445. (p. 490)

Keesey, R. E., & Corbett, S. W. (1983). Metabolic defense of the body weight set-point. In A. J. Stunkard & E. Stellar (Eds.), *Eating and its disorders*. New York: Raven Press. (p. 357)

Kellerman, J., Lewis, J., & Laird, J. D. (1989). Looking and loving: The effects of mutual gaze on feelings of romantic love. *Journal of Research in Personality, 23*, 145–161. (p. 389)

Kelling, S. T., & Halpern, B. P. (1983). Taste flashes: Reaction times, intensity, and quality. *Science, 219*, 412–414. (p. 154)

Kelly, I. W., Laverty, W. H., & Saklofske, D. H. (1990). Geophysical variables and behavior: LXIV. An empirical investigation of the relationship between worldwide automobile traffic disasters and lunar cycles: No relationship. *Psychological Reports, 67*, 987–994. (p. 469)

Kelly, T. A. (1990). The role of values in psychotherapy: A critical review of process and outcome effects. *Clinical Psychology Review, 10*, 171–186. (p. 493)

Kempe, R. S., & Kempe, C. C. (1978). *Child abuse*. Cambridge, MA: Harvard University Press. (p. 80)

Kennedy, S., & Over, R. (1990). Psychophysiological assessment of male sexual arousal following spinal cord injury. *Archives of Sexual Behavior, 19*, 15–27. (p. 29)

Kennell, J. N., & Klaus, M. (1982). *Parent-infant bonding*. St. Louis: C. V. Mosby. (p. 77)

Kenrick, D. T. (1987). Gender, genes, and the social environment. In P. C. Shaver & C. Hendrick (Eds.), *Review of Personality and Social Psychology, 8*, 14–43. (pp. 601, 608)

Kenrick, D. T., & Funder, D. C. (1988). Profiting from controversy: Lessons from the person-situation debate. *American Psychologist, 43*, 23–34. (p. 427)

Kenrick, D. T., & Gutierres, S. E. (1980). Contrast effects and judgments of physical attractiveness: When beauty becomes a social problem. *Journal of Personality and Social Psychology, 38*, 131–140. (p. 364)

Kenrick, D. T., & Trost, M. R. (1987). A biosocial theory of heterosexual relationships. In K. Kelly (Ed.), *Females, males, and sexuality*. Albany: State University of New York Press. (p. 602)

Kenrick, D. T., & Trost, M. R. (1989). Reproductive exchange model of heterosexual relationships: Putting proximate eco-

nomics in ultimate perspective. In C. Hendrick (Ed.), *Review of personality and social psychology* (Vol. 10). Newbury Park, CA: Sage. (p. 603)

Kerr, N. L., & Bruun, S. E. (1983). Dispensability of member effort and group motivation losses: Free-rider effects. *Journal of Personality and Social Psychology, 44*, 78–94. (p. 564)

Kessler, M., & Albee, G. (1975). Primary prevention. *Annual Review of Psychology, 26*, 557–591. (p. 507)

Keys, A., Brozek, J., Henschel, A., Mickelsen, O., & Taylor, H. L. (1950). *The biology of human starvation*. Minneapolis: University of Minnesota Press. (p. 355)

Kihlstrom, J. F. (1985). Hypnosis. *Annual Review of Psychology, 36*, 385–418. (pp. 203, 207)

Kihlstrom, J. F. (1987). The cognitive unconscious. *Science, 237*, 1445–1452. (p. 191)

Kihlstrom, J. F. (1990). Awareness, the psychological unconscious, and the self. Address to the American Psychological Association convention. (p. 207)

Kihlstrom, J. F. (1990). The psychological unconscious. In L. A. Pervin (Ed.), *Handbook of personality: Theory and research*. New York: Guilford Press. (p. 420)

Kihlstrom, J. F., & Harachkiewicz, J. M. (1982). The earliest recollection: A new survey. *Journal of Personality, 50*, 134–148. (p. 67)

Kihlstrom, J. F., & McConkey, K. M. (1990). William James and hypnosis: A centennial reflection. *Psychological Science, 1*, 174–177. (p. 209)

Kimball, M. M. (1989). A new perspective on women's math achievement. *Psychological Bulletin, 105*, 198–214. (p. 598)

Kimble, D. P. (1990). Functional effects of neural grafting in the mammalian central nervous system. *Psychological Bulletin, 108*, 462–479. (p. 47)

Kimble, G. A. (1956). *Principles of general psychology*. New York: Ronald Press. (p. 233)

Kimble, G. A. (1981). *Biological and cognitive constraints on learning*. In L. T. Benjamin, Jr. (Ed.), *The G. Stanley Hall Lecture Series* (Vol. 1). Washington, DC: American Psychological Association. (p. 233)

Kimura, D. (1989, November). How sex hormones boost—or cut—intellectual ability. *Psychology Today*, pp. 62–66. (p. 602)

Kimzey, S. L. (1975). The effects of extended spaceflight on hematologic and immunologic systems. *Journal of the American Medical Women's Association, 30*(5), 218–232. (p. 521)

Kimzey, S. L., Johnson, P. C., Ritzman, S. E., & Mengel, C. E. (1976, April). Hematology and immunology studies: The second manned Skylab mission. *Aviation, Space, and Environmental Medicine*, pp. 383–390. (p. 521)

King, D. W., & King, L. A. (1991). Validity issues in research on Vietnam veteran adjustment. *Psychological Bulletin, 109*, 107–124. (p. 515)

King, N. J., & Montgomery, R. B. (1980). Biofeedback-induced control of human peripheral temperature: A critical review of the literature. *Psychological Bulletin, 88*, 738–752. (p. 530)

King, P. (1991, March 18). Bawl players. *Sports Illustrated*, pp. 14–17. (p. 401)

King, S. (1990). High risk for schizophrenia: From conception to young adulthood. *Journal of Counseling and Development, 69*, 81–84. (p. 470)

Kinsey, A. C., Pomeroy, W., & Martin, C. (1948). *Sexual behavior in the human male*. Philadelphia: Saunders. (p. 360)

Kinsey, A. C., Pomeroy, W., Martin, C., & Gebhard, P. (1953). *Sexual behavior in the human female*. Philadelphia: Saunders. (p. 360)

Kirk, S. A., & Gallagher, J. J. (1989). *Educating exceptional children*. Boston: Houghton Mifflin. (p. 150)

Kisor, H. (1990). *What's that pig outdoors*. New York: Hill and Wang. (p. 150)

Kite, M. E., & Johnson, B. T. (1988). Attitudes toward older and younger adults: A meta-analysis. *Psychology and Aging, 3*, 233–244. (p. 112)

Klayman, J., & Ha, Y-W. (1987). Confirmation, disconfirmation, and information in hypothesis testing. *Psychological Review, 94*, 211–228. (p. 288)

Kleinke, C. L. (1986). Gaze and eye contact: A research review. *Psychological Bulletin, 100*, 78–100. (p. 388)

Kleinmuntz, B., & Szucko, J. J. (1984). A field study of the fallibility of polygraph lie detection. *Nature, 308*, 449–450. (p. 387)

Kleitman, N. (1960, November). Patterns of dreaming. *Scientific American*, pp. 82–88. (p. 193)

Klerman, G. L., & Weissman, M. M. (1989). Increasing rates of depression. *Journal of the American Medical Association, 261*, 2220–2235. (p. 458)

Kline, D., & Schieber, F. (1985). Vision and aging. In J. E. Birren & K. W. Schaie (Eds.), *Handbook of the psychology of aging*. New York: Van Nostrand Reinhold. (p. 110)

Kline, N. S. (1974). *From sad to glad*. New York: Ballantine Books. (p. 464)

Klineberg, O. (1938). Emotional expression in Chinese literature. *Journal of Abnormal and Social Psychology, 33*, 517–520. (p. 390)

Klineberg, O. (1984). Public opinion and nuclear war. *American Psychologist, 39*, 1245–1253. (p. 617)

Kluft, R. P. (1987). An update on multiple personality disorder. *Hospital and Community Psychiatry, 38*, 363–373. (p. 458)

Kluver, H., & Bucy, P. C. (1939). Preliminary analysis of functions of the temporal lobes in monkeys. *Archives of Neurology and Psychiatry, 42*, 979–1000. (p. 39)

Kobasa, S. C. (1982). The hardy personality: Toward a social psychology of stress and health. In G. S. Sanders & J. Suls (Eds.), *Social psychology of health and illness*. Hillsdale, NJ: Erlbaum. (p. 524)

Koch, C. (1988, June 17). Quoted in W. F. Allman, How the brain really works its wonders. *U. S. News & World Report*, pp. 46–54. (p. 300)

Koestner, R., Franz, C., & Weinberger, J. (1990). The family origins of empathic concern: A 26-year longitudinal study. *Journal of Personality and Social Psychology, 58*, 709–717. (p. 79)

Kohlberg, L. (1981). *The philosophy of moral development: Essays on moral development* (Vol. I). San Francisco: Harper & Row. (p. 99)

Kohlberg, L. (1984). *The psychology of moral development: Essays on moral development* (Vol. II). San Francisco: Harper & Row. (p. 99)

Kohler, I. (1962, May). Experiments with goggles. *Scientific American*, pp. 62–72. (p. 177)

Köhler, W. (1925; reprinted 1957). *The mentality of apes*. London: Pelican. (p. 287)

Kohn, A. (1987, October). It's hard to get left out of a pair. *Psychology Today*, pp. 53–57. (p. 617)

Kolata, G. (1985). Obesity declared a disease. *Science, 227*, 1019–1020. (p. 539)

Kolata, G. (1986). Youth suicide: New research focuses on a growing social problem. *Science, 233*, 839–841. (p. 461)

Kolata, G. (1987). Metabolic catch-22 of exercise regimens. *Science, 236*, 146–147. (p. 544)

Kolb, B. (1989). Brain development, plasticity, and behavior. *American Psychologist, 44*, 1203–1212. (p. 47)

Kolers, P. A. (1975). Specificity of operations in sentence recognition. *Cognitive Psychology, 7*, 289–306. (p. 257)

Koltz, C. (1983, December). Scapegoating. *Psychology Today*, pp. 68–69. (p. 613)

Koopman, P., Gubbay, J., Vivian, N., Goodfellow, P., & Lovell-Badge, R. (1991). Male development of chromosomally female mice transgenic for *Sry*. *Nature, 351*, 117–121. (p. 64)

Koss, M. P., & Burkhart, B. R. (1989). A conceptual analysis of rape victimization. *Psychology of Women Quarterly, 13*, 27–40. (p. 571)

Koss, M. P., Dinero, T. E., Seibel, C. A., & Cox, S. L. (1988). Stranger and acquaintance rape: Are there differences in the victim's experience? *Psychology of Women Quarterly, 12*, 1–24. (p. 571)

Koss, M. P., Gidycz, C. A., & Wisniewski, N. (1987). The scope of rape: Incidence and prevalence of sexual aggression and victimization in a national sample of higher education students. *Journal of Consulting and Clinical Psychology, 55*, 162–170. (p. 571)

Koss, M. P., Koss, P., & Woodruff, W. J. (1990). Relation of criminal victimization to health perceptions among women medical patients. *Journal of Consulting and Clinical Psychology, 58*, 147–152. (p. 571)

Kosslyn, S. M. (1987). Seeing and imagining in the cerebral hemispheres: A computational approach. *Psychological Review, 94*, 148–175. (p. 142)

Kotva, H. J., & Schneider, H. G. (1990). Those "talks"–general and sexual communication between mothers and daughters. *Journal of Social Behavior and Personality, 5*, 603–613. (p. 106)

Kraft, C. (1978). A psychophysical approach to air safety: Simulator studies of visual illusions in night approaches. In H. L. Pick, H. W. Leibowitz, J. E. Singer, A. Steinschneider, & H. W. Stevenson (Eds.), *Psychology: From research to practice.* New York: Plenum Press. (p. 180)

Krantz, D. S., Contrada, R. J., Hill, D. R., & Friedler, E. (1988). Environmental stress and biobehavioral antecedents of coronary heart disease. *Journal of Consulting and Clinical Psychology, 56,* 333–341. (p. 519)

Kraus, S. J. (1991). Attitudes and the prediction of behavior. Doctoral dissertation, Harvard University. (p. 554)

Kraut, R. E., & Johnston, R. E. (1979). Social and emotional messages of smiling: An ethological approach. *Journal of Personality and Social Psychology, 37,* 1539–1553. (p. 391)

Krech, D. (1978). Quoted in M. C. Diamond, The aging brain: Some enlightening and optimistic results. *American Scientist, 66,* 66–71. (p. 115)

Krosnick, J. A., & Alwin, D. F. (1989). Aging and susceptibility to attitude change. *Journal of Personality and Social Psychology, 57,* 416–425. (p. 125)

Krosnick, J. A., & Schuman, H. (1988). Attitude intensity, importance, and certainty and susceptibility to response effects. *Journal of Personality and Social Psychology, 54,* 940–952. (p. 11)

Krupat, E. (1986, November). A delicate imbalance. *Psychology Today,* pp. 22–26. (p. 527)

Kübler-Ross, E. (1969). *On death and dying.* New York: Macmillan. (p. 122)

Kuhl, P. K., & Meltzoff, A. N. (1982). The bimodal perception of speech in infancy. *Science, 218,* 1138–1141. (p. 303)

Kuiper, N. A., & Rogers, T. B. (1979). Encoding of personal information: Self-other differences. *Journal of Personality and Social Psychology, 37,* 499–514. (p. 261)

Kulik, J. A., Bangert-Drowns, R. L., & Kulik, C-L. C. (1984). Effectiveness of coaching for aptitude tests. *Psychological Bulletin, 95,* 179–188. (p. 327)

Kulik, J. A., Kulik, C. C., & Bangert-Drowns, R. L. (1985). Effectiveness of computer/based education in elementary schools. *Computers in Human Behavior, 1,* 59–74. (p. 245)

Kulik, J. A., Kulik, C. C., & Cohen, P. A. (1980). Effectiveness of computer-based college teaching: A meta-analysis of findings. *Review of Educational Research, 50,* 525–544. (p. 245)

Kunst-Wilson, W. R., & Zajonc, R. B. (1980). Affective discrimination of stimuli that cannot be recognized. *Science, 207,* 557–558. (p. 134)

Kurdek, L. A., & Schmitt, J. P. (1986). Interaction of sex role self-concept with relationship quality and relationship beliefs in married, heterosexual cohabiting, gay, and lesbian couples. *Journal of Personality and Social Psychology, 51,* 365–370. (p. 600)

Kurtz, P. (1983, Spring). Stars, planets, and people. *The Skeptical Inquirer,* pp. 65–68. (p. 438)

Labbe, R., Firl, A., Jr., Mufson, E. J., & Stein, D. G. (1983). Fetal brain transplants: Reduction of cognitive deficits in rats with frontal cortex lesions. *Science, 221,* 470–472. (p. 47)

Labouvie-Vief, G., & Schell, D. A. (1982). Learning and memory in later life. In B. B. Wolman (Ed.), *Handbook of developmental psychology.* Englewood Cliffs, NJ: Prentice-Hall. (p. 113)

Ladd, G. T. (1887). *Elements of physiological psychology.* New York: Scribner's. (p. 189)

Lagerspetz, K. (1979). Modification of aggressiveness in mice. In S. Feshbach & A. Fraczek (Eds.), *Aggression & behavior change: Biological & social processes.* New York: Praeger. (pp. 87, 568)

Lagerweij, E., Nelis, P. C., van Ree, J. M., & Wiegant, V. M. (1984). The twitch in horses: A variant of acupuncture. *Science, 225,* 1172–1174. (p. 31)

Laird, J. D. (1974). Self-attribution of emotion: The effects of expressive behavior on the quality of emotional experience. *Journal of Personality and Social Psychology, 29,* 475–486. (p. 391)

Laird, J. D. (1984). The real role of facial response in the experience of emotion: A reply to Tourangeau and Ellsworth, and others. *Journal of Personality and Social Psychology, 47,* 909–917. (p. 391)

Laird, J. D., Cuniff, M., Sheehan, K., Shulman, D., & Strum, G. (1989). Emotion specific effects of facial expressions on memory for life events. *Journal of Social Behavior and Personality, 4,* 87–98. (p. 391)

Lamb, M. (1979, June 17). Quoted by G. Collins, A new look at life with father. *The New York Times Magazine,* pp. 30–31, 48–52, 65. (p. 79)

Lamb, M. (1982, April). Second thoughts on first touch. *Psychology Today,* pp. 9–11. (p. 77)

Lamb, M. E. (1987). Predictive implication of individual differences in attachment. *Journal of Consulting and Clinical Psychology, 55,* 817–824. (p. 80)

Lancioni, G. (1980). Infant operant conditioning and its implications for early intervention. *Psychological Bulletin, 88,* 516–534. (p. 67)

Landauer, T. K. (1986). How much do people remember? Some estimates of the quantity of learned information in long-term memory. *Cognitive Science, 10,* 477–493. (p. 266)

Landers, A. (1969, April 8). Syndicated newspaper column. Cited by L. Berkowitz, The case for bottling up rage. *Psychology Today,* September, 1973, pp. 24–31. (p. 395)

Landers, S. (1986, December). Judge reiterates IQ test ban. *APA Monitor,* p. 18. (p. 317)

Landfield, P., Cadwallader, L. B., & Vinsant, S. (1988). Quantitative changes in hippocampal structure following long-term exposure to Delta-9-tetrahydrocannabinol: Possible mediation by glucocorticoid systems. *Brain Research,* Vol. 443, 47–62. (p. 216)

Langer, E. J. (1983). *The psychology of control.* Beverly Hills, CA: Sage. (p. 436)

Langer, E. J., & Abelson, R. P. (1974). A patient by any other name . . . : Clinician group differences in labeling bias. *Journal of Consulting and Clinical Psychology, 42,* 4–9. (p. 473)

Langer, E. J., & Imber, L. (1980). The role of mindlessness in the perception of deviance. *Journal of Personality and Social Psychology, 39,* 360–367. (p. 473)

Langlois, J. H., & Roggman, L. A. (1990). Attractive faces are only average. *Psychological Science, 1,* 115–121. (p. 580)

Langlois, J. H., Roggman, L. A., Casey, R. J., Ritter, J. M., Rieser-Danner, L. A., & Jenkins, V. Y. (1987). Infant preferences for attractive faces: Rudiments of a stereotype? *Developmental Psychology, 23,* 363–369. (p. 579)

Larrance, D. T., & Twentyman, C. T. (1983). Maternal attributions and child abuse. *Journal of Abnormal Psychology, 92,* 449–457. (p. 73)

Larsen, R. J., & Diener, E. (1987). Affect intensity as an individual difference characteristic: A review. *Journal of Research in Personality, 21,* 1–39. (p. 78)

Larsen, R. J., Diener, E., & Cropanzano, R. S. (1987). Cognitive operations associated with individual differences in affect intensity. *Journal of Personality and Social Psychology, 53,* 767–774. (p. 406)

Larson, R. W., & Bradney, N. (1988). Precious moments with family members and friends. In R. M. Milardo (Ed.), *Families and social networks.* Newbury Park, CA: Sage. (p. 104)

Lashley, K. S. (1950). In search of the engram. In *Symposium of the Society for Experimental Biology* (Vol. 4). New York: Cambridge University Press. (p. 268)

Lassiter, G. D., & Irvine, A. A. (1986). Video-taped confessions: The impact of camera point of view on judgments of coercion. *Journal of Personality and Social Psychology, 16,* 268–276. (p. 553)

Latané, B. (1981). The psychology of social impact. *American Psychologist, 36,* 343–356. (p. 564)

Latané, B., & Dabbs, J. M., Jr. (1975). Sex, group size and helping in three cities. *Sociometry, 38,* 180–194. (p. 576)

Laudenslager, M. L., & Reite, M. L. (1984). Losses and separations: Immunological consequences and health implications. *Review of Personality and Social Psychology, 5,* 285–312. (p. 517)

Laurence, J-R., & Perry, C. (1988). *Hypnosis, will and memory: A psycho-legal history.* New York: Guilford. (p. 205)

Layton, B. D., & Turnbull, B. (1975). Belief, evaluation, and performance on an ESP task. *Journal of Experimental Social Psychology, 11,* 166–179. (pp. 182, 184)

Lazarus, R. S. (1984). On the primacy of cognition. *American Psychologist, 39,* 124–129. (p. 405)

Lazarus, R. S. (1990). Theory-based stress measurement. *Psychological Inquiry, 1,* 3–13. (p. 516)

Lazarus, R. S. (1991). Progress on a cognitive-motivational-relational theory of emotion. *American Psychologist,* in press. (p. 405)

Lebow, J. (1982). Consumer satisfaction with mental health treatment. *Psychological Bulletin, 91,* 244–259. (p. 496)

LeDoux, J. E. (1986). Sensory systems and emotions: A model of affective processing. *Integrative Psychiatry, 4,* 237–243. (p. 405)

Lee, B. A., Lewis, D. W., & Jones, S. H. (1990). Blaming the homeless: A test of two theories. Paper presented at the American Psychological Association convention. (p. 553)

Lefcourt, H. M. (1982). *Locus of control: Current trends in theory and research.* Hillsdale, NJ: Erlbaum. (p. 436)

Lefcourt, H. M., & Davidson-Katz, K. (1991). The role of humor and the self. In C. R. Snyder & D. R. Forsyth (Eds.), *Handbook of social and clinical psychology: The health perspective.* New York: Pergamon Press. (p. 532)

Lehman, D. R. Wortman, C. B., & Williams, A. F. (1987). Long-term effects of losing a spouse or child in a motor vehicle crash. *Journal of Personality and Social Psychology, 52,* 218–231. (p. 122)

Leibowitz, H. W. (1985). Grade crossing accidents and human factors engineering. *American Scientist, 73,* 558–562. (p. 170)

Leigh, B. C. (1989). In search of the seven dwarves: Issues of measurement and meaning in alcohol expectancy research. *Psychological Bulletin, 105,* 361–373. (p. 212)

Leikind, B., & McCarthy, W. J. (1985). An investigation of firewalking. *The Skeptical Inquirer, 10,* 23–34. (p. 153)

Leikind, B., & McCarthy, W. J. (1988). Firewalking. *Experientia, 44,* 310–315. (p. 153)

Lenneberg, E. H. (1967). *Biological foundations of language.* New York: Wiley. (p. 67)

Lenzenweger, M. F., Dworkin, R. H., & Wethington, E. (1989). Models of positive and negative symptoms in schizophrenia: An empirical evaluation of latent structures. *Journal of Abnormal Psychology, 98,* 62–70. (p. 503)

Leo, J. (1990, May 14). No, don't give me a number. *U.S. News & World Report,* p. 22. (p. 601)

Lepper, M. R., & Greene, D. (Eds.). (1979). *The hidden costs of reward.* Hillsdale, NJ: Erlbaum. (p. 243)

Lepper, M. R., Ross, L., & Lau, R. R. (1986). Persistence of inaccurate beliefs about the self: Perseverance effects in the classroom. *Journal of Personality and Social Psychology, 50,* 482–491. (p. 298)

Lerner, M. J. (1980). *The belief in a just world: A fundamental delusion.* New York: Plenum Press. (p. 613)

Levenson, R. W., Ekman, P., Heider, K., & Friesen, W. V. (1991). Emotion and autonomic nervous system activity in an Indonesian culture. Unpublished manuscript, University of California, Berkeley. (p. 386)

Leventhal, H., Zimmerman, R., & Gutmann, M. (1984). Compliance: A self-regulation perspective. In D. Gentry (Ed.), *Handbook of behavioral medicine.* New York: Guilford Press. (p. 527)

Lever, J. (1978). Sex differences in the complexity of children's play and games. *American Sociological Review, 43,* 471–483. (p. 600)

Levin, I. P., & Gaeth, G. J. (1988). How consumers are affected by the framing of attribute information before and after consuming the product. *Journal of Consumer Research, 15,* 374–378. (p. 296)

Levin, I. P., Schnittjer, S. K., & Thee, S. L. (1988). Information framing effects in social and personal decisions. *Journal of Experimental Social Psychology, 24,* 520–529. (p. 296)

Levine, A. (1990, May 7). America's youthful bigots. *U.S. News and World Report,* pp. 59–60. (p. 611)

Levine, B., Roehrs, T., Zorick, F., & Roth, T. (1988). Daytime sleepiness in young adults. *Sleep, 11,* 39–46. (p. 195)

Levine, I. S., & Rog, D. J. (1990). Mental health services for homeless mentally ill persons: Federal initiatives and current service trends. *American Psychologist, 45,* 963–968. (p. 502)

Levine, R. V. (1990). The pace of life. *American Scientist, 78,* 450–459. (p. 591)

Levinger, G. (1987). The limits of deterrence: An introduction. *Journal of Social Issues, 43*(4), 1–4. (p. 615)

Levinson, D. J. (1986). A conception of adult development. *American Psychologist, 41,* 3–13. (p. 116)

Levinson, D. J., Darow, C. N., Klein, E. B., Levinson, M. H., & McKee, B. (1978). *The seasons of a man's life.* New York: Knopf. (p. 116)

Levitt, E. E. (1986). Coercion, voluntariness, compliance and resistance: The essence of hypnosis twenty-seven years after Orne. Invited address to the American Psychological Association convention. (p. 205)

Levitt, E. E. (1988). Questions about multiple personality. *Harvard Medical School Mental Health Letter, 4*(10), 8. (p. 457)

Levy, J. (1985, May). Right brain, left brain: Fact and fiction. *Psychology Today,* pp. 38–44. (p. 51)

Lewinsohn, P. M., Hoberman, H., Teri, L., & Hautziner, M. (1985). An integrative theory of depression. In S. Reiss & R. Bootzin (Eds.), *Theoretical issues in behavior therapy.* Orlando, FL: Academic Press. (pp. 459, 464)

Lewinsohn, P. M., & Rosenbaum, M. (1987). Recall of parental behavior by acute depressives, remitted depressives, and nondepressives. *Journal of Personality and Social Psychology, 52,* 611–619. (p. 274)

Lewis, C. C. (1981). The effects of parental firm control: A reinterpretation of findings. *Psychological Bulletin, 90,* 547–563. (p. 85)

Lewis, C. S. (1967). *Christian reflections.* Grand Rapids, MI: Eerdmans. (p. 265)

Lewis, D. O., Pincus, J. H., Bard, B., Richardson, E., Prichep, L. S., Feldman, M., & Yeager, C. (1988). Neuropsychiatric, psychoeducational, and family characteristics of 14 juveniles condemned to death in the United States. *American Journal of Psychiatry, 145,* 584–589. (p. 80)

Lewis, D. O., Pincus, J. H., Feldman, M., Jackson, L., & Bard, B. (1986). Psychiatric, neurological, and psychoeducational characteristics of 15 death row inmates in the United States. *American Journal of Psychiatry, 143,* 838–845. (p. 568)

Lewontin, R. (1976). Race and intelligence. In N. J. Block & G. Dworkin (Eds.), *The IQ controversy: Critical readings.* New York: Pantheon. (p. 342)

Lifton, R. J. (1986). *The Nazi doctors.* New York: Basic Books. (p. 211)

Light, K. C., Koepke, J. P., Obrist, P. A., & Willis, P. W., Jr. (1983). Psychological stress induces sodium and fluid retention in men at high risk for hypertension. *Science, 220,* 429–431. (p. 520)

Linder, D. (1982). Social trap analogs: The tragedy of the commons in the laboratory. In V. J. Derlega & J. Grzelak (Eds.), *Cooperative and helping behavior: Theories and research.* New York: Academic Press. (p. 615)

Lindskold, S. (1978). Trust development, the GRIT proposal, and the effects of conciliatory acts on conflict and cooperation. *Psychological Bulletin, 85,* 772–793. (p. 618)

Lindskold, S. (1986). GRIT: Reducing distrust through carefully introduced conciliation. In S. Worchel & W. G. Austin (Eds.), *Psychology of intergroup relations* (2nd ed.). Chicago: Nelson-Hall. (p. 618)

Lindskold, S., & Han, G. (1988). GRIT as a foundation for integrative bargaining. *Personality and Social Psychology Bulletin, 14,* 335–345. (p. 618)

Lindskold, S., Han, G., & Betz, B. (1986). Repeated persuasion in interpersonal conflict. *Journal of Personality and Social Psychology, 51,* 1183–1188. (p. 618)

Lindskold, S., Walters, P. S., & Koutsourais, H. (1983). Cooperators, competitors, and response to GRIT. *Journal of Conflict Resolution, 27,* 521–532. (p. 618)

Linn, M. C., & Hyde, J. S. (1991). Trends in cognitive and psychosocial gender differences. In R. M. Lerner, A. C. Petersen, & J. Brooks-Gunn (Eds.), *The encyclopedia of adolescence.* New York: Garland Publishing, in press. (p. 599)

Linn, M. C., & Peterson, A. C. (1986). A meta-analysis of gender differences in spatial ability: Implications for mathematics and science achievement. In J. S. Hyde & M. C. Linn (Eds.), *The psychology of gender: Advances through meta-analysis.* Baltimore: Johns Hopkins University Press. (p. 598)

Linn, R. L. (1982). Ability testing: Individual differences, prediction, and differential prediction. In A. K. Wigdor & W. R. Garner (Eds.), *Ability testing: Uses, consequences, and controversies* (Part II). Washington, DC: National Academy Press. (p. 326)

Linville, P. W. (1987). Self-complexity as a cognitive buffer against stress-related illness and depression. *Journal of Personality and Social Psychology, 52,* 663–676. (p. 120)

Linz, D., & Donnerstein, E. (1989). The effects of counter-information on the acceptance of rape myths. In D. Zillmann & J. Bryant (Eds.), *Pornography: Research advances and policy considerations.* Hillsdale, NJ: Lawrence Erlbaum. (p. 574)

Livingstone, M., & Hubel, D. (1988). Segregation of form, color, movement, and depth: Anatomy, physiology, and perception. *Science, 240,* 740–749. (p. 142)

Livson, F. B. (1976, October). Coming together in the middle years: A longitudinal study of sex role convergence. In B. F. Turner (Chair), *The double standard of aging: A question of sex differences.* Symposium conducted at the Annual Scientific Meeting of the Gerontological Society, New York, NY. (p. 609)

Lock, M., Kaufert, P., & Gilbert, P. (1988). Cultural construction of the menopausal syndrome: The Japanese case. *Maturitas, 10,* 317–332. (p. 109)

Locke, E. A., & Latham, G. P. (1990). Work motivation and satisfaction: Light at the end of the tunnel. *Psychological Science, 1,* 240–246. (p. 376)

Loehlin, J. C. (1989). Partitioning environmental and genetic contributions to behavioral development. *American Psychologist, 44,* 1285–1292. (p. 338)

Loehlin, J. C., Horn, J. M., & Willerman, L. (1989). Modeling IQ change: Evidence from the Texas adoption project. *Child Development, 60,* 993–1004. (p. 338)

Loehlin, J. C., Lindzey, G., & Spuhler, J. N. (1975). *Race differences in intelligence.* San Francisco: Freeman. (p. 341)

Loehlin, J. C., & Nichols, R. C. (1976). *Heredity, environment, and personality.* Austin: University of Texas Press. (pp. 88, 337)

Loftus, E. F. (1979). The malleability of human memory. *American Scientist, 67,* 313–320. (p. 276)

Loftus, E. F. (1980). *Memory: Surprising new insights into how we remember and why we forget.* Reading, MA: Addison-Wesley. (p. 204)

Loftus, E. F., Donders, K., Hoffman, H. G., & Schooler, J. W. (1989). Creating new memories that are quickly accessed and confidently held. *Memory and Cognition, 17,* 607–616. (p. 276)

Loftus, E. F., & Loftus, G. R. (1980). On the permanence of stored information in the human brain. *American Psychologist, 35,* 409–420. (p. 267)

Loftus, E. F., & Palmer, J. C. (1973). Reconstruction of automobile destruction: An example of the interaction between language and memory. *Journal of Verbal Learning and Verbal Behavior, 13,* 585–589. (p. 275)

Logothetis, N. K., & Schall, J. D. (1989). Neuronal correlates of subjective visual perception. *Science, 245,* 761–763. (p. 142)

London, P. (1970). The rescuers: Motivational hypotheses about Christians who saved Jews from the Nazis. In J. Macaulay & L. Berkowitz (Eds.), *Altruism and helping behavior.* New York: Academic Press. (pp. 248, 578)

LoPiccolo, J. L., & Stock, W. E. (1986). Treatment of sexual dysfunction. *Journal of Consulting and Clinical Psychology, 54,* 158–167. (p. 365)

Lord, C. G., Lepper, M. R., & Preston, E. (1984). Considering the opposite: A corrective strategy for social judgment. *Journal of Personality and Social Psychology, 47,* 1231–1247. (p. 298)

Lord, C. G., Ross, L., & Lepper, M. (1979). Biased assimilation and attitude polarization: The effects of prior theories on subsequently considered evidence. *Journal of Personality and Social Psychology, 37,* 2098–2109. (p. 297)

Lord, L. J. (1987, November 30). Coming to grips with alcoholism. *U. S. News and World Report,* pp. 56–63. (p. 211)

Lorenz, K. (1937). The companion in the bird's world. *Auk, 54,* 245–273. (p. 77)

Lovaas, O. I. (1987). Behavioral treatment and normal educational and intellectual functioning in young autistic children. *Journal of Consulting and Clinical Psychology, 55,* 3–9. (p. 490)

Lowenthal, M. F., Thurnher, M., Chiriboga, D., Beefon, D., Gigy, L., Lurie, E., Pierce, R., Spence, D., & Weiss, L. (1975). *Four stages of life.* San Francisco: Jossey-Bass. (p. 609)

Lowry, D. T., & Towles, D. E. (1989). Soap opera portrayals of sex, contraception, and sexually transmitted diseases. *Journal of Communication, 39*(2), 76–83. (p. 107)

Lozoff, B. (1989). Nutrition and behavior. *American Psychologist, 44,* 231–236. (p. 537)

Lubart, T. I. (1990). Creativity and cross-cultural variation. *International Journal of Psychology, 25,* 39–59. (p. 335)

Lubin, B., Larsen, R. M., & Matarazzo, J. D. (1984). Patterns of psychological test usage in the United States: 1935–1982. *American Psychologist, 39,* 451–454. (p. 419)

Luchins, A. S. (1946). Classroom experiments on mental set. *American Journal of Psychology, 59,* 295–298. (pp. 289–290)

Lugaresi, E., Medori, R., Montagna, P., Baruzzi, A., Cortelli, P., Lugaresi, A., Tinuper, P., Zucconi, M., & Gambetti, P. (1986). Fatal familial insomnia and dysautonomia with selective degeneration of thalamic nuclei. *New England Journal of Medicine, 315,* 997–1003. (p. 195)

Lull, J. (Ed.). (1988). *World families watch television.* Newbury Park, CA: Sage. (p. 570)

Lummis, M., & Stevenson, H. W. (1990). Gender differences in beliefs and achievement: A cross-cultural study. *Developmental Psychology, 26,* 254–263. (p. 598)

Lumsden, C. J., & Wilson, E. O. (1983). *Promethean fire: Reflections on the origin of mind.* Cambridge, MA: Harvard University Press. (p. 394)

Luria, A. M. (1968). In L. Solotaroff (Trans.), *The mind of a mnemonist.* New York: Basic Books. (p. 253)

Lykken, D. T. (1982, September). Fearlessness: Its carefree charm and deadly risks. *Psychology Today,* pp. 20–28. (pp. 394, 472)

Lykken, D. T. (1983, April). Polygraph prejudice. *APA Monitor,* p. 4. (p. 387)

Lykken, D. T. (1987, Spring). The validity of tests: Caveat emptor. *Jurimetrics Journal,* pp. 263–270. (p. 387)

Lynch, G. (1990). The many shapes of memory and the several forms of synaptic plasticity. Invited address to the American Psychological Society convention. (p. 269)

Lynch, G., & Baudry, M. (1984). The biochemistry of memory: A new and specific hypothesis. *Science, 224,* 1057–1064. (p. 268)

Lynn, M. (1988). The effects of alcohol consumption on restaurant tipping. *Personality and Social Psychology Bulletin, 14,* 87–91. (p. 211)

Lynn, R. (1982). IQ in Japan and the United States shows a growing disparity. *Nature, 297,* 222–223. (p. 341)

Lynn, R. (1983). Lynn replies. *Nature, 306,* 292. (p. 341)

Lynn, R. (1987). Japan: Land of the rising IQ. A reply to Flynn. *Bulletin of the British Psychological Society, 40,* 464–468. (p. 342)

Lynn, S. J., & Rhue, J. W. (1986). The fantasy-prone person: Hypnosis, imagination, and creativity. *Journal of Personality and Social Psychology, 51,* 404–408. (p. 203)

Lytton, H., & Romney, D. M. (1991). Parents' differential socialization of boys and girls: A meta-analysis. *Psychological Bulletin, 109,* 267–296. (p. 604)

Maass A., & Clark, R. D., III. (1984). Hidden impact of minorities: Fifteen years of minority influence research. *Psychological Bulletin, 95,* 428–450. (p. 567)

Maccoby, E. (1980). *Social development: Psychological growth and the parent-child relationship.* New York: Harcourt Brace Jovanovich. (pp. 81, 84, 597)

Maccoby, E. E. (1990). Gender and relationships: A developmental account. *American Psychologist, 45,* 513–520. (p. 600)

MacDonald, N. (1960). Living with schizophrenia. *Canadian Medical Association Journal, 82,* 218–221. (p. 466)

MacFarlane, A. (1978, February). What a baby knows. *Human Nature,* pp. 74–81. (p. 66)

Macfarlane, J. W. (1964). Perspectives on personality consistency and change from the guidance study. *Vita Humana, 7,* 115–126. (pp. 96, 124)

MacKay, D. G. (1983). Prescriptive grammar and the pronoun problem. In B. Thorne, C. Kramarae, & N. Henley (Eds.), *Language, gender and society.* Rowley, MA: Newbury House. (p. 311)

Mackenzie, B. (1984). Explaining race differences in IQ: The logic, the methodology, and the evidence. *American Psychologist, 39,* 1214–1233. (p. 343)

MacKinnon, D. W., & Hall, W. B. (1972). Intelligence and creativity. *Proceedings, XVIIth International Congress of Applied Psychology* (Vol. 2, pp. 1883–1888). Brussels: Editest. (p. 335)

Maddi, S. R., Bartone, P. T., & Puccetti, M. C. (1987). Stressful events are indeed a factor in physical illness: Reply to Schroeder and Costa (1984). *Journal of Personality and Social Psychology, 52,* 833–843. (pp. 515, 524)

Maehr, M. L., & Braskamp, L. A. (1986). *The motivation factor: A theory of personal investment.* Lexington, MA: Lexington Books. (p. 376)

Magno, J. B. (1989, April 15). The Hospice concept of care: Facing the 1990's. Keynote address to the Association for Death Education and Counseling. (p. 123)

Magnusson, D. (1990). Personality research–challenges for the future. *European Journal of Personality, 4,* 1–17. (p. 472)

Magnusson, D., & Bergman, L. R. (1990). A pattern approach to the study of pathways from childhood to adulthood. In L. N. Robins & M. Rutter (Eds.), *Straight and devious pathways from childhood to adulthood.* Cambridge: Cambridge University Press. (p. 124)

Mahoney, M. J. (1989). Sport psychology. In I. S. Cohen (Ed.), *G. Stanley Hall Lecture Series* (Vol. 9). Washington, DC: American Psychological Association. (pp. 63, 312)

Major, B. (1987). Gender, justice, and the psychology of entitlement. In P. Shaver & C. Hendrick (Eds.), *Sex and gender.* Beverly Hills, CA: Sage. (p. 601)

Major, B., Carrington, P. I., & Carnevale, P. J. D. (1984). Physical attractiveness and self-esteem: Attribution for praise from an other-sex evaluator. *Personality and Social Psychology Bulletin, 10,* 43–50. (p. 579)

Major, B., Cozzarelli, C., Sciacchitano, A. M., Cooper, M. L., Testa, M., & Mueller, P. M. (1990). Perceived social support, self-efficacy, and adjustment to abortion. *Journal of Personality and Social Psychology, 59,* 452–463. (p. 516)

Major, B., Schmidlin, A. M., & Williams, L. (1990). Gender patterns in social touch: The impact of setting and age. *Journal of Personality and Social Psychology, 58,* 634–643. (p. 601)

Malamuth, N. M. (1989). Sexually violent media, thought patterns, and antisocial behavior. In G. Comstock (Ed.), *Public communication and behavior* (Vol. 2). San Diego, CA: Academic Press. (p. 573)

Malamuth, N. M., & Check, J. V. P. (1981). The effects of media exposure on acceptance of violence against women: A field experiment. *Journal of Research in Personality, 15,* 436–446. (p. 572)

Malan, D. H. (1978). "The case of the secretary with the violent father." In H. Davanloo (Ed.), *Basic principles and techniques in short-term dynamic psychotherapy.* New York: Spectrum. (p. 482)

Malkiel, B. (1985). *A random walk down Wall Street* (4th ed.). New York: Norton. (p. 295)

Malkiel, B. G. (1989a). Is the stock market efficient? *Science, 243,* 1313–1318. (p. 632)

Malkiel, B. G. (1989b). The efficient market hypothesis. *Science, 244,* 1424–1425. (p. 632)

Malone, T. W., & Lepper, M. R. (1986). Making learning fun: A taxonomy of intrinsic motivations for learning. In R. E. Snow & M. J. Farr (Eds.), *Aptitude, learning, and instruction: III. Cognitive and affective process analysis.* Hillsdale, NJ: Erlbaum. (p. 375)

Mandel, D. (1983, March 13). One man's holocaust: Part II. The story of David Mandel's journey through hell as told to David Kagan. *Wonderland Magazine* (Grand Rapids Press), pp. 2–7. (p. 351)

Mandler, J. M. (1990). A new perspective on cognitive development in infancy. *American Scientist, 78,* 236–243. (p. 73)

Manning, W. G., Keefer, E. B., Newhouse, J. P., Sloss, E. M., & Wasserman, J. (1989). The taxes of sin: Do smokers and drinkers pay their way? *Journal of the American Medical Association, 261,* 1604–1609. (p. 534)

Marcel, A. (1983). Conscious and unconscious perception: Experiments on visual masking and word recognition. *Cognitive Psychology, 15,* 197–237. (p. 134)

Marcus, A. C., & Siegel, J. M. (1982). Sex differences in the use of physician services: A preliminary test of the fixed role hypothesis. *Journal of Health and Social Behavior, 23,* 186–197. (p. 526)

Mark, V., & Ervin, F. (1970). *Violence and the brain.* New York: Harper & Row. (p. 39)

Marks, D. F. (1986). Investigating the paranormal. *Nature, 320,* 119–124. (p. 183)

Markus, H., & Kitayama, S. (1991). Culture and the self: Implications for cognition, emotion, and motivation. *Psychological Review, 98,* 224–253. (pp. 391, 395, 592–593, 601)

Markus, H., & Nurius, P. (1986). Possible selves. *American Psychologist, 41,* 954–969. (p. 429)

Markus, H., & Wurf, E. (1987). The dynamic self-concept: A social psychological perspective. *Annual Review of Psychology, 38,* 299–337. (p. 430)

Marr, D. (1982). *Vision.* San Francisco: W. H. Freeman. (p. 142)

Marschark, M., Richman, C. L., Yuille, J. C., & Hunt, R. R. (1987). The role of imagery in memory: On shared and distinctive information. *Psychological Bulletin, 102,* 28–41. (p. 261)

Marsh, H. W., & Parker, J. W. (1984). Determinants of student self-concept: Is it better to be a relatively large fish in a small pond even if you don't learn to swim as well? *Journal of Personality and Social Psychology, 47,* 213–231. (p. 401)

Marshall, J. C., & Halligan, P. W. (1988). Blindsight and insight in visuo-spatial neglect. *Nature, 336,* 766–767. (p. 143)

Marshall, W. L. (1989). Pornography and sex offenders. In D. Zillmann & J. Bryant (Eds.), *Pornography: Research advances and policy considerations.* Hillsdale, NJ: Erlbaum. (p. 572)

Marteau, T. M. (1989). Framing of information: Its influences upon decisions of doctors and patients. *British Journal of Social Psychology, 28,* 89–94. (p. 296)

Martinsen, E. W. (1987). The role of aerobic exercise in the treatment of depression. *Stress Medicine, 3,* 93–100. (p. 529)

Martyna, W. (1978). What does "he" mean? Use of generic masculine. *Journal of Communication, 28*(1), 131–138. (p. 311)

Marx, J. (1991). Mutation identified as possible cause of Alzheimer's Disease. *Science, 251,* 866–867. (p. 112)

Maslach, C. (1982). *Burnout: The cost of caring.* Englewood Cliffs, NJ: Prentice-Hall. (p. 517)

Maslow, A. H. (1970). *Motivation and personality* (2nd ed.). New York: Harper & Row. (pp. 355, 428)

Maslow, A. H. (1971). *The farther reaches of human nature.* New York: Viking Press. (p. 355)

Masters, W. H., & Johnson, V. E. (1966). *Human sexual response.* Boston: Little, Brown. (pp. 361–362)

Matarazzo, J. D. (1983). Computerized psychological testing. *Science, 221,* 323. (p. 425)

Matheny, A. P., Jr. (1989). Children's behavioral inhibition over age and across situations: Genetic similarity for a trait during change. *Journal of Personality, 57,* 215–235. (p. 87)

Matsuda, L., Lolait, S. J., Brownstein, M. J., Young, A. C., & Bonner, T. I. (1990). Structure of a cannabinoid receptor and functional expression of the cloned CDNA. *Nature, 346,* 561–564. (p. 215)

Matsumoto, D., Kudoh, T., Scherer, K., & Wallbott, H. (1988). Antecedents of and reactions to emotions in the United States and Japan. *Journal of Cross-Cultural Psychology, 19,* 267–286. (pp. 391–392)

Matthews, K. A. (1988). CHD and Type A behaviors: Update on and alternative to the Booth-Kewley and Friedman quantitative review. *Psychological Bulletin, 104,* 373–380. (p. 520)

Maurer, D., & Maurer, C. (1988). *The world of the newborn.* New York: Basic Books. (p. 66)

May, P. A. (1986). Alcohol and drug misuse prevention programs for American Indians: Needs and opportunities. *Journal of Studies on Alcohol, 47,* 187–195. (p. 448)

May, R. (1982). The problem of evil: An open letter to Carl Rogers. *Journal of Humanistic Psychology, 22,* 10–21. (p. 433)

Mayer, J. D., & Salovey, P. (1987). Personality moderates the interaction of mood and cognition. In K. Fiedler & J. Forgas (Eds.), *Affect, cognition, and social behavior.* Toronto: Hogrefe. (p. 275)

Mazullo, J., Lasagna, L., & Grinar, P. (1974). Variations in interpretation of prescription instructions. *Journal of the American Medical Association, 227,* 929–931. (p. 528)

McAlister, A., Perry, C., Killen, J., Slinkard, L. A., & Maccoby, N. (1980). Pilot study of smoking, alcohol and drug abuse prevention. *American Journal of Public Health, 70,* 719–721. (pp. 536–537)

McBurney, D. H., & Collings, V. B. (1984). *Introduction to sensation and perception* (2nd ed.). Englewood Cliffs, NJ: Prentice-Hall. (p. 174)

McBurney, D. H., & Gent, J. F. (1979). On the nature of taste qualities. *Psychological Bulletin, 86,* 151–167. (p. 154)

McCann, I. L., & Holmes, D. S. (1984). Influence of aerobic exercise on depression. *Journal of Personality and Social Psychology, 46,* 1142–1147. (p. 529)

McCarron, D. A., Morris, C. D., Henry, H. J., & Stanton, J. L. (1984). Blood pressure and nutrient intake in the United States. *Science, 225,* 1392–1398. (p. 537)

McCarthy, C. (1988, December 31). Koop versus booze. *Washington Post,* p. A19. (p. 212)

McCarthy, P. (1986, July). Scent: The tie that binds? *Psychology Today,* pp. 6, 10. (p. 154)

McCartney, K., Harris, M. J., & Bernieri, F. (1990). Growing up and growing apart: A developmental meta-analysis of twin studies. *Psychological Bulletin, 107,* 226–237. (p. 89)

McCaul, K. D., & Malott, J. M. (1984). Distraction and coping with pain. *Psychological Bulletin, 95,* 516–533. (p. 153)

McCauley, C. R., & Segal, M. E. (1987). Social psychology of terrorist groups. In C. Hendrick (Ed.), *Group processes and intergroup relations.* Beverly Hills, CA: Sage. (p. 565)

McClanahan, S., & Adams, J. (1989). The effects of children on adults' psychological well-being: 1957–1976. *Social Forces, 68,* 124–146. (p. 120)

McClelland, D. C. (1978). Managing motivation to expand human freedom. *American Psychologist, 33,* 201–210. (p. 371)

McClelland, J. L., & Rumelhart, D. E. (1988). *Explorations in parallel distributed processing: A handbook of models, programs, and exercises.* Cambridge, MA: MIT Press. (p. 300)

McClenon, J. (1982). A survey of elite scientists: Their attitudes toward ESP and parapsychology. *Journal of Parapsychology, 46,* 127–152. (p. 181)

McCloskey, M., Wible, C. G., & Cohen, N. J. (1988). Is there a special flashbulb-memory mechanism? *Journal of Experimental Psychology: General, 117,* 171–181. (p. 254)

McCord, J. (1978). A thirty-year follow-up on treatment effects. *American Psychologist, 33,* 284–289. (p. 497)

McCord, J. (1979). Following up on Cambridge-Somerville. *American Psychologist, 34,* 727. (p. 497)

McCrae, R. R., & Costa, P. T., Jr. (1982). Self-concept and the stability of personality: Cross-sectional comparisons of self-reports and ratings. *Journal of Personality and Social Psychology, 43,* 1282–1292. (p. 124)

McCrae, R. R., & Costa, P. T., Jr. (1986). Clinical assessment can benefit from recent advances in personality psychology. *American Psychologist, 41,* 1001–1003. (p. 424)

McCrae, R. R., & Costa, P. T., Jr. (1988). Psychological resilience among widowed men and women: A 10-year follow-up of a national sample. *Journal of Social Issues, 44,* 129–142. (p. 122)

McCrae, R. R., & Costa, P. T., Jr. (1990). *Personality in adulthood.* New York: Guilford. (p. 117)

McEvoy, G. M., & Cascio, W. F. (1989). Cumulative evidence of the relationship between employee age and job performance. *Journal of Applied Psychology, 74,* 11–17. (p. 116)

McFarland, C., & Ross, M. (1987). The relation between current impressions and memories of self and dating partners. *Psychological Bulletin, 13,* 228–238. (p. 277)

McFarland, C., Ross, M., & DeVourville, N. (1989). Women's theories of menstruation and biases in recall of menstrual symptoms. *Journal of Personality and Social Psychology, 57,* 522–531. (p. 526)

McFarlane, J., Martin, C. L., & Williams, T. M. (1988). Women versus men and menstrual versus other cycles. *Psychology of Women Quarterly, 12,* 201–223. (p. 526)

McGaugh, J. L. (1990). Significance and remembrance: The role of neuromodulatory systems. *Psychological Science, 1,* 15–25. (p. 269)

McGhee, P. E. (1976). Children's appreciation of humor: A test of the cognitive congruency principle. *Child Development, 47,* 420–426. (p. 75)

McGrath, M. J., & Cohen, D. G. (1978). REM sleep facilitation of adaptive waking behavior: A review of the literature. *Psychological Bulletin, 85,* 24–57. (p. 199)

McGregor, D. (1960). *The human side of enterprise.* New York: McGraw-Hill. (p. 377)

McGuire, W. J. (1986). The myth of massive media impact: Savings and salvagings. In G. Comstock (Ed.), *Public communication and behavior.* Orlando, FL: Academic Press. (p. 571)

McGuire, W. J., McGuire, C. V., & Winton, W. (1979). Effects of household sex composition on the salience of one's gender in the spontaneous self-concept. *Journal of Experimental Social Psychology, 15,* 77–90. (p. 595)

McGuire, W. J., & Padawer-Singer, A. (1978). Trait salience in the spontaneous self-concept. *Journal of Personality and Social Psychology, 33,* 743–754. (p. 595)

McHugh, P. R., & Moran, T. H. (1978). Accuracy of the regulation of caloric ingestion in the rhesus monkey. *American Journal of Physiology, 235,* R29–34. (p. 356)

McKinlay, J. B., McKinlay, S. M., & Brambilla, D. (1987b). The relative contributions of endocrine changes and social circumstances to depression in mid-aged women. *Journal of Health and Social Behavior, 28,* 345–363. (p. 109)

McKinlay, J. B., McKinlay, S. M., & Brambilla, D. J. (1987a). Health status and utilization behavior associated with menopause. *American Journal of Epidemiology, 125,* 110–121. (p. 109)

McLean, P. D., & Carr, S. (1989). The psychological treatment of unipolar depression: Progress and limitations. *Canadian Journal of Behavioural Science, 21,* 452–469. (p. 498)

McNally, R. J. (1987). Preparedness and phobias: A review. *Psychological Bulletin, 101,* 283–303. (p. 394)

Meador, B. D., & Rogers, C. R. (1984). Person-centered therapy. In R. J. Corsini (Ed.), *Current psychotherapies* (3rd ed.). Itasca, IL: Peacock. (p. 484)

Meaney, M. J., Aitken, D. H., Van Berkel, C., Bhatnagar, S., & Sapolsky, R. M. (1988). Effect of neonatal handling on age-related impairments associated with the hippocampus. *Science, 239,* 766–768. (p. 68)

Medawar, P. (1982). *Pluto's republic.* New York: Oxford University Press. (p. 420)

Mednick, S. A., Moffitt, T. E., & Stack, S. (1987). *The causes of crime: New biological approaches.* Cambridge: Cambridge University Press. (p. 471)

Meet the Press. (1984, February 13). Quoted by J. M. Jones (1990). Promoting diversity in an individualistic society. Keynote address, Great Lakes College Association conference, Multicultural transforming the 21st century. (p. 596)

Meichenbaum, D. (1977). *Cognitive-behavior modification: An integrative approach.* New York: Plenum Press. (p. 495)

Meichenbaum, D. (1985). *Stress inoculation training.* New York: Pergamon. (p. 495)

Meier, R. P. (1991). Language acquisition by deaf children. *American Scientist, 79,* 60–70. (pp. 150, 306)

Meltzoff, A. N. (1987, May). Baby research comes of age. *Psychology Today,* p. 47. (p. 66)

Meltzoff, A. N. (1988a). Infant imitation and memory: Nine-month-olds in immediate and deferred tests. *Child Development, 59,* 217–225. (pp. 73, 247)

Meltzoff, A. N. (1988b). Infant imitation after a 1-week delay: Long-term memory for novel acts and multiple stimuli. *Developmental Psychology, 24,* 470–476. (p. 247)

Meltzoff, A. N. (1988c). Imitation of televised models by infants. *Child Development, 59,* 1221–1229. (p. 247)

Meltzoff, A. N., & Borton, R. W. (1979). Intermodal matching by human neonates. *Nature, 282,* 403–404. (p. 73)

Meltzoff, A. N., & Moore, M. K. (1983). Newborn infants imitate adult facial gestures. *Child Development, 54,* 702–709. (p. 66)

Meltzoff, A. N., & Moore, M. K. (1985). Cognitive foundations and social functions of imitation and intermodal representation in infancy. In J. Mehler & R. Fox (Eds.), *Neonate cognition: Beyond the blooming, buzzing confusion.* Hillsdale, NJ: Erlbaum. (p. 66)

Meltzoff, A. N., & Moore, M. K. (1989). Imitation in newborn infants: Exploring the range of gestures imitated and the underlying mechanisms. *Developmental Psychology, 25,* 954–962. (p. 66)

Melzack, R. (1984). The myth of painless childbirth. *Pain, 19,* 321–337. (p. 153)

Melzack, R. (1990, February). The tragedy of needless pain. *Scientific American,* pp. 27–33. (p. 214)

Melzack, R., & Wall, P. D. (1965). Pain mechanisms: A new theory. *Science, 150,* 971–979. (p. 152)

Melzack, R., & Wall, P. D. (1983). *The challenge of pain.* New York: Basic Books. (p. 152)

Mento, A. J., Steel, R. P., & Karren, R. J. (1987). A meta-analytic study of the effects of goal setting on task performance: 1966–1984. *Organizational Behavior and Human Decision Processes, 39,* 52–83. (p. 376)

Meredith, N. (1986, June). Testing the talking cure. *Science,* pp. 31–37. (p. 495)

Merikle, P. M., & Reingold, E. M. (1990). Recognition and lexical decision without detection: Unconscious perception? *Journal of Experimental Psychology: Human Perception and Performance, 16,* 574–583. (p. 134)

Merton, R. K. (1938; reprinted 1970). *Science, technology and society in seventeenth-century England.* New York: Fertig. (p. 9)

Merton, R. K., & Kitt, A. S. (1950). Contributions to the theory of reference group behavior. In R. K. Merton & P. F. Lazarsfeld (Eds.), *Continuities in social research: Studies in the scope and method of the American soldier.* Glencoe, IL: Free Press. (p. 401)

Messer, W. S., & Griggs, R. A. (1989). Student belief and involvement in the paranormal and performance in introductory psychology. *Teaching of Psychology, 16,* 187–191. (p. 183)

Messick, S., & Jungeblut, A. (1981). Time and method in coaching for the SAT. *Psychological Bulletin, 89,* 191–216. (p. 327)

Meyer-Bahlburg, H. F. L. (1980). Sexuality in early adolescence. In B. B. Wolman & J. Money (Eds.), *Handbook of human sexuality.* Englewood Cliffs, NJ: Prentice-Hall. (p. 363)

Michaels, J. W., Bloomel, J. M., Brocato, R. M., Linkous, R. A., & Rowe, J. S. (1982). Social facilitation and inhibition in a natural setting. *Replications in Social Psychology, 2,* 21–24. (p. 563)

Michel, G. F. (1981). Right-handedness: A consequence of infant supine head-orientation preference? *Science, 212,* 685–687. (p. 52)

Middlebrooks, J. C., & Green, D. M. (1991). Sound localization by human listeners. *Annual Review of Psychology, 42,* 135–159. (p. 149)

Mikulincer, M., Babkoff, H., Caspy, T., & Sing, H. (1989). The effects of 72 hours of sleep loss on psychological variables. *British Journal of Psychology, 80,* 145–162. (p. 195)

Milan, R. J., Jr., & Kilmann, P. R. (1987). Interpersonal factors in premarital contraception. *Journal of Sex Research, 23,* 289–321. (p. 106)

Milgram, S. (1974). *Obedience to authority.* New York: Harper & Row. (pp. 560–561)

Miller, G. A. (1956). The magical number seven, plus or minus two: Some limits on our capacity for processing information. *Psychological Review, 63,* 81–97. (p. 256)

Miller, G. A., & Gildea, P. M. (1987, September). How children learn words. *Scientific American,* pp. 94–99. (p. 303)

Miller, J. B. (1986). *Toward a new psychology of women* (2nd ed.). Boston, MA: Beacon Press. (p. 599)

Miller, J. G. (1984). Culture and the development of everyday social explanation. *Journal of Personality and Social Psychology, 46,* 961–978. (p. 593)

Miller, J. G., Bersoff, D. M., & Harwood, R. L. (1990). Perceptions of social responsibilities in India and in the United States: Moral imperatives or personal decisions? *Journal of Personality and Social Psychology, 58,* 33–47. (p. 577)

Miller, K. I., & Monge, P. R. (1986). Participation, satisfaction, and productivity: A meta-analytic review. *Academy of Management Journal, 29,* 727–753. (p. 436)

Miller, N., & Maruyama, G. (1976). Ordinal position and peer popularity. *Journal of Personality and Social Psychology, 33,* 123–131. (p. 372)

Miller, N. E. (1983). Value and ethics of research on animals. Paper presented at the meeting of the American Psychological Association. (p. 20)

Miller, N. E. (1985, February). Rx: biofeedback. *Psychology Today,* pp. 54–59. (p. 530)

Miller, N. E., & Brucker, B. S. (1979). A learned visceral response apparently independent of skeletal ones in patients paralyzed by spinal lesions. In N. Birbaumer & H. D. Kimmel (Eds.), *Biofeedback and self-regulation.* Hillsdale, NJ: Erlbaum. (p. 529)

Miller, P. C., Lefcourt, H. M., Holmes, J. G., Ware, E. E., & Saleh, W. E. (1986). Marital locus of control and marital problem solving. *Journal of Personality and Social Psychology, 51,* 161–169. (p. 436)

Miller, S. D., Blackburn, T., Scholes, G., White, G. L., & Mamalis, N. (1991). Optical differences in multiple personality disorder: A second look. *Journal of Nervous and Mental Disease, 179,* 132–135. (p. 457)

Mills, M., & Melhuish, E. (1974). Recognition of mother's voice in early infancy. *Nature, 252,* 123–124. (p. 66)

Mineka, S. (1985). The frightful complexity of the origins of fears. In F. R. Brush & J. B. Overmier (Eds.), *Affect, conditioning and cognition: Essays on the determinants of behavior.* Hillsdale, NJ: Erlbaum. (p. 394)

Mineka, S., & Suomi, S. J. (1978). Social separation in monkeys. *Psychological Bulletin, 85,* 1376–1400. (p. 81)

Mintz, L. B., & Betz, N. E. (1986). Sex differences in the nature, realism, and correlates of body image. *Sex Roles, 15,* 185–195. (p. 360)

Mirin, S. M., & Weiss, R. D. (1989). Genetic factors in the development of alcoholism. *Psychiatric Annals, 19,* 239–242. (p. 217)

Mischel, W. (1968). *Personality and assessment.* New York: Wiley. (p. 426)

Mischel, W. (1981). Current issues and challenges in personality. In L. T. Benjamin, Jr. (Ed.), *The G. Stanley Hall Lecture Series* (Vol. 1). Washington, DC: American Psychological Association. (p. 439)

Mischel, W. (1984). Convergences and challenges in the search for consistency. *American Psychologist, 39,* 351–364. (p. 426)

Mischel, W., Shoda, Y., & Peake, P. K. (1988). The nature of adolescent competencies predicted by preschool delay of gratification. *Journal of Personality and Social Psychology, 54,* 687–696. (p. 101)

Mischel, W., Shoda, Y., & Rodriguez, M. L. (1989). Delay of gratification in children. *Science, 244,* 933–938. (pp. 101, 239)

Mishkin, M. (1986). Physiological psychology and the future: An optimist's view. Paper presented at the American Psychological Association convention. (p. 27)

Mishkin, M., & Appenzeller, T. (1987, June). The anatomy of memory. *Scientific American,* pp. 80–89. (p. 271)

Money, J. (1987). Sin, sickness, or status? Homosexual gender identity and psychoneuroendocrinology. *American Psychologist, 42,* 384–399. (pp. 368, 602)

Money, J. (1988). *Gay, straight, and in-between.* New York: Oxford University Press. (pp. 368, 572)

Money, J., Berlin, F. S., Falck, A., & Stein, M. (1983). *Antiandrogenic and counseling treatment of sex offenders.* Baltimore: Department of Psychiatry and Behavioral Sciences, The Johns Hopkins University School of Medicine. (p. 363)

Moody, R. (1976). *Life after life.* Harrisburg, PA: Stackpole Books. (p. 218)

Mook, D. G. (1983). In defense of external invalidity. *American Psychologist, 38,* 379–387. (p. 18)

Moore, D. L., & Baron, R. S. (1983). Social facilitation: A physiological analysis. In J. T. Cacioppo & R. Petty (Eds.), *Social psychophysiology.* New York: Guilford Press. (p. 563)

Moore, T. E. (1988). The case against subliminal manipulation. *Psychology and Marketing, 5,* 297–316. (p. 135)

Moreland, R. L., & Zajonc, R. B. (1982). Exposure effects in person perception: Familiarity, similarity, and attraction. *Journal of Experimental Social Psychology, 18,* 395–415. (p. 579)

Morokoff, P. J. (1986). Volunteer bias in the psychophysiological study of female sexuality. *Journal of Sex Research, 22,* 35–51. (p. 364)

Morris, N. M., & Udry, J. R. (1978). Pheromonal influences on human sexual behavior: An experimental search. *Journal of Biosocial Science, 10,* 147–157. (p. 363)

Morrison, D. C. (1988). Marine mammals join the Navy. *Science, 242,* 1503–1504. (p. 246)

Morrison, D. M. (1985). Adolescent contraceptive behavior: A review. *Psychological Bulletin, 98,* 538–568. (p. 106)

Moruzzi, G., & Magoun, H. W. (1949). Brain stem reticular formation and activation of the EEG. *Electroencephalography and Clinical Neurophysiology, 1,* 455–473. (p. 38)

Moser, P. W. (1987, May). Are cats smart? Yes, at being cats. *Discover,* pp. 77–88. (p. 140)

Mosher, D. L., & Anderson, R. D. (1986). Macho personality, sexual aggression, and reactions to guided imagery of realistic rape. *Journal of Research in Personality, 20,* 77–94. (p. 211)

Mosher, D. L., & Vonderheide, S. G. (1985). Contributions of sex guilt and masturbation guilt to women's contraceptive attitudes and use. *Journal of Sex Research, 21,* 24–39. (p. 106)

Moss, H. A., & Susman, E. J. (1980). Longitudinal study of personality development. In O. G. Brim, Jr., & J. Kagan (Eds.), *Constancy and change in human development.* Cambridge, MA: Harvard University Press. (p. 125)

Moyer, K. E. (1983). The physiology of motivation: Aggression as a model. In C. J. Scheier & A. M. Rogers (Eds.), *G. Stanley Hall Lecture Series* (Vol. 3). Washington, DC: American Psychological Association. (p. 568)

Muehlenhard, C. L. (1988). Misinterpreted dating behaviors and the risk of date rape. *Journal of Social and Clinical Psychology, 6,* 20–37. (p. 602)

Murphy, G. E., & Wetzel, R. D. (1990). The lifetime risk of suicide in alcoholism. *Archives of General Psychiatry, 47,* 383–392. (p. 461)

Murphy, T. N. (1982). Pain: Its assessment and management. In R. J. Gatchel, A. Baum, & J. E. Singer (Eds.), *Handbook of psychology and health: Vol. I. Clinical psychology and behavioral medicine: Overlapping disciplines.* Hillsdale, NJ: Erlbaum. (p. 152)

Murray, D. M., Johnson, C. A., Luepker, R. V., & Mittelmark, M. B. (1984). The prevention of cigarette smoking in children: A comparison of four strategies. *Journal of Applied Social Psychology, 14,* 274–288. (p. 536)

Murray, D. M., Pirie, P., Luepker, R. V., & Pallonen, U. (1989). Five- and six-year follow-up results from four seventh-grade smoking prevention strategies. *Journal of Behavioral Medicine, 12,* 207–218. (p. 537)

Murray, H. (1938). *Explorations in personality.* New York: Oxford University Press. (p. 370)

Murray, H. A. (1933). The effect of fear upon estimates of the maliciousness of other personalities. *Journal of Social Psychology, 4,* 310–329. (p. 418)

Murray, H. A., & Wheeler, D. R. (1937). A note on the possible clairvoyance of dreams. *Journal of Psychology, 3,* 309–313. (p. 183)

Murray, J. P., & Lonnborg, B. (1985). *Violence on TV: What do children learn? What can parents do?* Washington, DC: American Psychological Association. (p. 574)

Murstein, B. L. (1986). *Paths to marriage.* Newbury Park, CA: Sage. (p. 579)

Myers, B. J. (1987). Mother-infant bonding as a critical period. In M. H. Bornstein (Ed.), *Sensitive periods in development: Interdisciplinary perspectives.* Hillsdale, NJ: Erlbaum. (p. 77)

Myers, D. G. (1990). *Social psychology* (3rd ed.). New York: McGraw-Hill. (p. 431)

Myers, D. G. (1992). *Well-being: Who is happy — and why.* New York: William Morrow. (pp. 105, 401)

Myers, D. G., & Bishop, G. D. (1970). Discussion effects on racial attitudes. *Science, 169,* 778–779. (p. 565)

Myers, I. B. (1987). *Introduction to type: A description of the theory and applications of the Myers-Briggs Type Indicator.* Palo Alto, CA: Consulting Psychologists Press. (p. 422)

Nadler, A., & Ben-Shushan, D. (1989). Forty years later: Long-term consequences of massive traumatization as manifested by Holocaust survivors from the city and the Kibbutz. *Journal of Consulting and Clinical Psychology, 57,* 287–293. (p. 515)

Nadon, R., Hoyt, I. P., Register, P. A., & Kihlstrom, J. F. (1991). Absorption and hypnotizability: Context effects reexamined. *Journal of Personality and Social Psychology, 60,* 144–153. (p. 203)

Napolitan, D. A., & Goethals, G. R. (1979). The attribution of friendliness. *Journal of Experimental Social Psychology, 15,* 105–113. (p. 552)

Nash, M. (1987). What, if anything, is regressed about hypnotic age regression? A review of the empirical literature. *Psychological Bulletin, 102,* 42–52. (p. 204)

National Academy of Science. (1984). *Bereavement: Reactions, consequences, and cure.* Washington, DC: National Academy Press. (p. 521)

National Academy of Sciences, Institute of Medicine. (1982). *Marijuana and health.* Washington, DC: National Academic Press. (pp. 215, 511)

National Center for Health Statistics. (1985). *Health: United States, 1985.* DHHS Pub. No. (PHS) 86–1232. Washington, DC: U.S. Government Printing Office. (p. 538)

National Center for Health Statistics. (1990, November 28). Advance report of final mortality statistics, 1988. *Monthly Vital Statistics Report, 39,* Table 5. (p. 461)

National Center for Health Statistics. (1990). *Health, United States, 1989.* Washington, DC: U.S. Department of Health and Human Services. (p. 511)

National Council on the Aging. (1976). *The myth and reality of aging in America.* Washington, DC. (p. 111)

National Institute of Mental Health. (1982). *Television and behavior: Ten years of scientific progress and implications for the eighties.* Washington, DC: U.S. Government Printing Office. (p. 571)

National Opinion Research Center. (1985, October/November). Images of the world. *Public Opinion,* p. 38. (p. 433)

National Research Council. (1987). *Risking the future: Adolescent sexuality, pregnancy, and childbearing.* Washington, DC: National Academy Press. (p. 106)

National Research Council. (1990). *Human factors research needs for an aging population.* Washington, DC: National Academy Press. (p. 110)

National Safety Council. (1991). *Accident facts.* Chicago: Author. (p. 294)

Naveh-Benjamin, M. (1990). Coding of temporal order information: An automatic process? *Journal of Experimental Psychology: Learning, Memory, and Cognition, 16,* 117–126. (p. 258)

Naylor, T. H. (1990). Redefining corporate motivation, Swedish style. *Christian Century, 107,* 566–570. (p. 378)

NCTV News. (1987, July–August). More research links harmful effects to non-violent porn. National Coalition on Television Violence, p. 12. (p. 572)

Needles, D. J., & Abramson, L. Y. (1990). Positive life events, attributional style, and hopefulness: Testing a model of recovery from depression. *Journal of Abnormal Psychology, 99,* 156–165. (p. 464)

Neisser, U. (1979). The control of information pickup in selective looking. In A. D. Pick (Ed.), *Perception and its development: A tribute to Eleanor J. Gibson.* Hillsdale, NJ: Erlbaum. (p. 190)

Neisser, U. (1981). John Dean's memory: A case study. *Cognition, 9,* 1–22. (pp. 255, 273)

Neisser, U. (1982). Memorists. In U. Neisser (Ed.), *Memory observed: Remembering in natural contexts.* San Francisco: Freeman. (p. 253)

Neisser, U. (1984). The role of invariant structures in the control of movement. In M. Frese & J. Sabini (Eds.), *Goal directed behavior: The concept of action in psychology.* Hillsdale, NJ: Erlbaum. (p. 312)

Neisser, U., & Harsch, N. (1992). Phantom flashbulbs: False recollections of hearing the news about *Challenger.* In E. Winograd & U. Neisser (Eds.), *Affect and accuracy in recall: Studies of "flashbulb" memories.* New York: Cambridge University Press. (pp. 254, 276)

Neitz, J., Geist, T., & Jacobs, G. H. (1989). Color vision in the dog. *Visual Neuroscience, 3,* 119–125. (p. 144)

Nelson, K. (1973). Structure and strategy in learning to talk. *Monographs of the Society for Research in Child Development, 38*(1 & 2, Serial No. 149). (p. 303)

Nelson, N. (1988). *A meta-analysis of the life-event/health paradigm: The influence of social support.* Philadelphia: Temple University Ph.D. dissertation. (p. 533)

Nemeth, C. J. (1986). Differential contributions of majority and minority influence. *Psychological Review, 93,* 23–32. (p. 567)

Neter, E., & Ben-Shakhar, G. (1989). The predictive validity of graphological inferences: A meta-analytic approach. *Personality and Individual Differences, 10,* 737–745. (p. 439)

Neugarten, B. L. (1974). The roles we play. In American Medical Association, *Quality of life: The middle years.* Acton, MA: Publishing Sciences Group. (p. 119)

Neugarten, B. L. (1979). Time, age and the life cycle. *American Journal of Psychiatry, 136,* 887–894. (p. 117)

Neugarten, B. L. (1980, February). Must everything be a midlife crisis? *Prime Time,* pp. 45–48. (pp. 117, 124)

Neugarten, B. L., Wood, V., Kraines, R. J., & Loomis, B. (1963). Women's attitudes toward the menopause. *Vita Humana, 6, 140–151.* (p. 109)

Nevin, J. A. (1988). Behavioral momentum and the partial reinforcement effect. *Psychological Bulletin, 103,* 44–56. (p. 239)

Newcomb, M. D., & Bentler, P. M. (1988). Impact of adolescent drug use and social support on problems of young adults: A longitudinal study. *Journal of Abnormal Psychology, 97,* 64–75. (p. 216)

Newcomb, M. D., & Harlow, L. L. (1986). Life events and substance use among adolescents: Mediating effects of perceived loss of control and meaninglessness in life. *Journal of Personality and Social Psychology, 51,* 564–577. (p. 218)

Newell, A. (1988, March 9). Quoted by D. L. Wheeler, From years of work in psychology and computer science, scientists build theories of thinking and learning. *Chronicle of Higher Education,* pp. A4, A6. (p. 10)

Newlin, D. B., & Thomson, J. B. (1990). Alcohol challenge with sons of alcoholics: A critical review and analysis. *Psychological Bulletin, 108,* 383–402. (p. 217)

Newman, J., & Layton, B. D. (1984). Overjustification: A self-perception perspective. *Personality and Social Psychology Bulletin, 10,* 419–425. (p. 243)

Newport, E. L. (1990). Maturational constraints on language learning. *Cognitive Science, 14,* 11–28. (p. 306)

Nezu, A. M., Nezu, C. M., & Blissett, S. E. (1988). Sense of humor as a moderator of the relation between stressful events and psychological distress: A prospective analysis. *Journal of Personality and Social Psychology, 54,* 520–525. (p. 532)

Ng, S. H. (1990). Androcentric coding of *man* and *his* in memory by language users. *Journal of Experimental Social Psychology, 26,* 455–464. (p. 311)

Nickerson, R. S., & Adams, M. J. (1979). Long-term memory for a common object. *Cognitive Psychology, 11,* 287–307. (p. 265)

Nicol, S. E., & Gottesman, I. I. (1983). Clues to the genetics and neurobiology of schizophrenia. *American Scientist, 71,* 398–404. (p. 469)

Nicolaus, L. K., Cassel, J. F., Carlson, R. B., & Gustavson, C. R. (1983). Taste-aversion conditioning of crows to control predation on eggs. *Science, 220,* 212–214. (p. 233)

Niemi, R. G., Mueller, J., & Smith, T. W. (1989). *Trends in public opinion: A compendium of survey data.* New York: Greenwood Press. (pp. 398, 535, 607, 611)

Nisbett, R., & Ross, L. (1991). *The person and the situation.* New York: McGraw-Hill. (p. 378)

Nisbett, R. E., & Borgida, E. (1975). Attribution and the psychology of prediction. *Journal of Personality and Social Psychology, 32,* 932–943. (p. 299)

Nisbett, R. E., Fong, G. T., Lehman, D. R., & Cheng, P. W. (1987). Teaching reasoning. *Science, 238,* 625–631. (p. 635)

Nisbett, R. E., & Ross, L. (1980). *Human inference: Strategies and shortcomings of social judgment.* Englewood Cliffs, NJ: Prentice-Hall. (p. 291)

Noel, J. G., Forsyth, D. R., & Kelley, K. N. (1987). Improving the performance of failing students by overcoming their self-serving attributional biases. *Basic and Applied Social Psychology, 8,* 151–162. (p. 437)

Noland, T. K. (1986). The effects of ability grouping: A meta-analysis of research findings. *Dissertation Abstracts 46*(10), 2909-A. (p. 335)

Nolen-Hoeksema, S. (1990). *Sex differences in depression.* Stanford, CA: Stanford University Press. (pp. 459, 462)

Nolen-Hoeksema, S., & Morrow, J. (1991). A prospective study of depression and post-traumatic stress symptoms following a natural disaster: The 1989 Loma Prieta earthquake. *Journal of Personality and Social Psychology, 61,* 115–121. (p. 463)

Norman, D. A. (1988). *The psychology of everyday things.* New York: Basic Books. (p. 180)

Norris, P. A. (1986). On the status of biofeedback and clinical practice. *American Psychologist, 41,* 1009–1010. (p. 529)

Nuttin, J. M., Jr. (1987). Affective consequences of mere ownership: The name letter effect in twelve European languages. *European Journal of Social Psychology, 17,* 381–402. (p. 579)

Oakes, J. (1989). Tracking in secondary schools. In R. E. Slavin (Ed.), *School and classroom organization.* Hillsdale, NJ: Erlbaum. (p. 335)

Oakhill, J., Garnham, A., & Johnson-Laird, P. N. (1990). Belief bias effects in syllogistic reasoning. In D. J. Gilhooly, M. T. G. Keane, R. H. Logie, & G. Erdos (Eds.), *Lines of thinking* (Vol. 1). Chichester, England: Wiley. (p. 297)

Oakhill, J. V., Johnson-Laird, P. N., & Garnham, A. (1989). Believability and syllogistic reasoning. *Cognition, 31,* 117–140. (p. 297)

Oatley, K., & Bolton, W. (1985). A social-cognitive theory of depression in reaction to life events. *Psychological Review, 92,* 382–388. (p. 463)

O'Connor, P., & Brown, G. W. (1984). Supportive relationships: Fact or fancy? *Journal of Social and Personal Relationships, 1,* 159–175. (p. 502)

Oetting, E. R., & Beauvais, F. (1987). Peer cluster theory, socialization characteristics, and adolescent drug use: A path analysis. *Journal of Counseling Psychology, 34,* 205–213. (pp. 101, 218)

Oetting, E. R., & Beauvais, F. (1990). Adolescent drug use: Findings of national and local surveys. *Journal of Consulting and Clinical Psychology, 58,* 385–394. (p. 218)

Oettingen, G., & Seligman, M. E. P. (1990). Pessimism and behavioural signs of depression in East versus West Berlin. *European Journal of Social Psychology, 20,* 207–220. (p. 437)

Offer, D., Ostrov, E., Howard, K. I., & Atkinson, R. (1988). *The teenage world: Adolescents' self-image in ten countries.* New York: Plenum. (p. 104)

Office of Technology Assessment. (1990). *Neural grafting: Repairing the brain and spinal cord,* OTA-BA-462, U.S. Congress. Washington, DC: U.S. Government Printing Office. (p. 47)

Office of Technology Assessment. (1990). *The use of integrity tests for pre-employment screening,* OTA-SET-442, U.S. Congress. Washington, DC: U.S. Government Printing Office. (p. 388)

Olds, J. (1958). Self-stimulation of the brain. *Science, 127,* 315–324. (p. 40)

Olds, J. (1975). Mapping the mind onto the brain. In F. G. Worden, J. P. Swazey, & G. Adelman (Eds.), *The neurosciences: Paths of discovery.* Cambridge, MA: MIT Press. (p. 40)

Olds, J., & Milner, P. (1954). Positive reinforcement produced by electrical stimulation of the septal area and other regions of rat brain. *Journal of Comparative and Physiological Psychology, 47,* 419–427. (p. 40)

O'Leary, A. (1990). Stress, emotion, and human immune function. *Psychological Bulletin, 108,* 363–382. (p. 522)

Oliner, S. P., & Oliner, P. M. (1988). *The altruistic personality: Rescuers of Jews in Nazi Europe.* New York: Free Press. (pp. 101, 248, 578)

Olshansky, S. J., Carnes, B. A., & Cassel, C. (1990). In search of Methuselah: Estimating the upper limits to human longevity. *Science, 250,* 634–640. (p. 111)

Olweus, D., Mattsson, A., Schalling, D., & Low, H. (1988). Circulating testosterone levels and aggression in adolescent males: A causal analysis. *Psychosomatic Medicine, 50,* 261–272. (p. 569)

O'Malley, P. M., & Bachman, J. G. (1983). Self-esteem: Change and stability between ages 13 and 23. *Developmental Psychology, 19,* 257–268. (p. 103)

Opton, E., Jr. (1979, December). A psychologist takes a closer look at the recent landmark Larry P. opinion. *American Psychological Association Monitor,* pp. 1, 4. (p. 317)

Orlofsky, J. L., & O'Heron, C. A. (1987). Stereotypic and non-stereotypic sex role trait and behavior orientations: Implications for personal adjustment. *Journal of Personality and Social Psychology, 52,* 1034–1042. (p. 600)

Orne, M. T. (1982, April 28). Affidavit submitted to State of Pennsylvania. (p. 206)

Orne, M. T. (1984). *Compliance, responsibility, and fantasy in hypnotic responding.* Paper presented at the meeting of the American Psychological Association. (p. 457)

Orne, M. T., Dinges, D. F., & Orne, E. C. (1984). On the differential diagnosis of multiple personality in the forensic context. *International Journal of Clinical and Experimental Hypnosis, 32,* 118–169. (p. 457)

Orne, M. T., & Evans, F. J. (1965). Social control in the psychological experiment: Antisocial behavior and hypnosis. *Journal of Personality and Social Psychology, 1,* 189–200. (p. 205)

Orne, M. T., Soskis, D. A., Dinges, D. F., & Orne, E. C. (1984). Hypnotically induced testimony. In G. L. Wells & E. F. Loftus (Eds.), *Eyewitness testimony: Psychological perspectives.* New York: Cambridge University Press. (p. 205)

Orr, D. P., Beiter, M., & Ingersoll, G. (1991). Premature sexual activity as an indicator of psychosocial risk. *Pediatrics, 87,* 141–147. (p. 105)

Osgood, C. E. (1962). *An alternative to war or surrender.* Urbana: University of Illinois Press. (p. 618)

Osgood, C. E. (1980). *GRIT: A strategy for survival in mankind's nuclear age?* Paper presented at the Pugwash Conference on New Directions in Disarmament. (p. 618)

Osherson, D. N., & Markman, E. (1974–1975). Language and the ability to evaluate contradictions and tautologies. *Cognition, 3,* 213–226. (p. 98).

OSS Assessment Staff. (1948). *The assessment of men.* New York: Rinehart. (p. 439)

Ostfeld, A. M., Kasl, S. V., D'Atri, D. A., & Fitzgerald, E. F. (1987). *Stress, crowding, and blood pressure in prison.* Hillsdale, NJ: Erlbaum. (p. 518)

Padgett, V. R. (1989). Predicting organizational violence: An application of 11 powerful principles of obedience. Paper presented to the American Psychological Association convention. (p. 562)

Paffenbarger, R. S., Jr., Hyde, R. T., Wing, A. L., & Hsieh, C-C. (1986). Physical activity, all-cause mortality, and longevity of college alumni. *New England Journal of Medicine, 314,* 605–612. (p. 529)

Page, S. (1977). Effects of the mental illness label in attempts to obtain accommodation. *Canadian Journal of Behavioral Science, 9,* 84–90. (p. 474)

Paivio, A. (1986). *Mental representations: A dual coding approach.* New York: Oxford University Press. (p. 261)

Palace, E. M., & Gorzalka, B. B. (1990). The enhancing effects of anxiety on arousal in sexually dysfunctional and functional women. *Journal of Abnormal Psychology, 99,* 403–411. (p. 405)

Palladino, J. J., & Carducci, B. J. (1983). *"Things that go bump in the night": Students' knowledge of sleep and dreams.* Paper presented at the meeting of the Southeastern Psychological Association. (p. 192)

Palumbo, S. R. (1978). *Dreaming and memory: A new information-processing model.* New York: Basic Books. (p. 199)

Pandey, J., Sinha, Y., Prakash, A., & Tripathi, R. C. (1982). Right-left political ideologies and attribution of the causes of poverty. *European Journal of Social Psychology, 12,* 327–331. (p. 553)

Panksepp, J. (1982). Toward a general psychobiological theory of emotions. *Behavioral and Brain Sciences, 5,* 407–467. (p. 385)

Parke, R. D. (1981). *Fathers.* Cambridge, MA: Harvard University Press. (p. 79)

Parker, K. C., Hanson, R. K., & Hunsley, J. (1988). MMPI, Rorschach, and WAIS: A meta-analytic comparison of reliability, stability, and validity. *Psychological Bulletin, 103,* 367–373. (p. 419)

Parloff, M. B. (1987, February). Psychotherapy: An import from Japan. *Psychology Today,* pp. 74–75. (p. 480)

Parrott, W. G., & Sabini, J. (1990). Mood and memory under natural conditions: Evidence for mood incongruent recall. *Journal of Personality and Social Psychology, 59,* 321–336. (p. 275)

Passons, W. R. (1975). *Gestalt approaches to counseling.* New York: Holt, Rinehart & Winston. (p. 485)

Patterson, F. (1978, October). Conversations with a gorilla. *National Geographic,* pp. 438–465. (p. 308)

Patterson, G. R., Chamberlain, P., & Reid, J. B. (1982). A comparative evaluation of parent training procedures. *Behavior Therapy, 13,* 638–650. (p. 570)

Patterson, R. (1951). *The riddle of Emily Dickinson.* Boston: Houghton Mifflin. (p. 464)

Pavett, C. M., Butler, M., Marcinik, E. J., & Hodgdon, J. A. (1987). Exercise as a buffer against organizational stress. *Stress Medicine, 3,* 87–92. (p. 529)

Pavlov, I. P. (1927). In G. V. Anrep (Trans.), *Conditioned reflexes.* London: Oxford University Press. (pp. 229, 231)

Pedalino, E., & Gamboa, V. U. (1974). Behavior modification and absenteeism. *Journal of Applied Psychology, 59,* 694–698. (p. 245)

Pedersen, N. L., Plomin, R., McClearn, G. E., & Friberg, L. (1988). Neuroticism, extraversion, and related traits in adult twins reared apart and reared together. *Journal of Personality and Social Psychology, 55,* 950–957. (p. 88)

Pekkanen, J. (1982, June). Why do we sleep? *Science, 82,* p. 86. (p. 196)

Pellegrino, J. W. (1985, October). Anatomy of analogy. *Psychology Today,* pp. 49–54. (p. 331)

Penfield, W. (1969). Consciousness, memory, and man's conditioned reflexes. In K. Pigram (Ed.), *On the biology of learning.* New York: Harcourt, Brace & World. (p. 267)

Penfield, W. (1975). *The mystery of the mind.* Princeton: Princeton University Press. (p. 220)

Pennebaker, J. (1990). *Opening up: The healing power of confiding in others.* New York: William Morrow. (p. 533)

Pennebaker, J. W. (1982). *The psychology of physical symptoms.* New York: Springer-Verlag. (p. 525)

Pennebaker, J. W., Barger, S. D., & Tiebout, J. (1989). Disclosure of traumas and health among Holocaust survivors. *Psychosomatic Medicine, 51,* 577–589. (p. 533)

Pennebaker, J. W., & O'Heeron, R. C. (1984). Confiding in others and illness rate among spouses of suicide and accidental death victims. *Journal of Abnormal Psychology, 93,* 473–476. (p. 533)

Peplau, L. A. (1982). Research on homosexual couples: An overview. *Journal of Homosexuality, 8*(2), 3–8. (p. 366)

Peplau, L. A., & Gordon, S. L. (1985). Women and men in love: Gender differences in close heterosexual relationships. In V. E. O'Leary, R. K. Unger, & B. S. Wallston (Eds.), *Women, gender, and social psychology.* Hillsdale, NJ: Erlbaum. (p. 12)

Peplau, L. A., & Perlman, D. (1982). *Loneliness: A sourcebook of current theory, research and therapy.* New York: Wiley. (p. 465)

Perkins, K. A., Dubbert, P. M., Martin, J. E., Faulstich, M. E., & Harris, J. K. (1986). Cardiovascular reactivity to psychological stress in aerobically trained versus untrained mild hypertensives and normotensives. *Health Psychology, 5,* 407–421. (p. 529)

Perlman, D. (1991). Age difference in loneliness: A meta analysis. Vancouver, BC: University of British Columbia. (ERIC Document Reproduction Service No. ED 326767.) (p. 465)

Perlmutter, M. (1983). Learning and memory through adulthood. In M. W. Riley, B. B. Hess, & K. Bond (Eds.), *Aging in society: Selected reviews of recent research.* Hillsdale, NJ: Erlbaum. (p. 113)

Perls, F. S. (1969). *Ego, hunger and aggression: The beginning of Gestalt therapy.* New York: Random House. (p. 485)

Perls, F. S. (1970). Four lectures. In J. Fagan & I. L. Shepherd, *Gestalt therapy now.* Palo Alto, CA: Science and Behavior Books. (p. 485)

Perls, F. S. (1972). Gestalt therapy [interview]. In A. Bry (Ed.), *Inside psychotherapy.* New York: Basic Books. (p. 592)

Perrett, D. I., Harries, M., Misflin, A. J., & Chitty, A. J. (1988). Three stages in the classification of body movements by visual neurons. In H. B. Barlow, C. Blakemore, & M. Weston Smith (Eds.), *Images and understanding.* Cambridge: Cambridge University Press. (p. 142)

Persky, V. W., Kempthorne-Rawson, J., & Shekelle, R. B. (1987). Personality and risk of cancer: 20-year follow-up of the Western Electric study. *Psychosomatic Medicine, 49,* 435–449. (p. 522)

Persons, J. B. (1986). The advantages of studying psychological phenomena rather than psychiatric diagnoses. *American Psychologist, 41,* 1252–1260. (p. 473)

Pert, C. (1986). Quoted in J. Hooper & D. Teresi, *The three-pound universe.* New York: Macmillan. (p. 53)

Pert, C. B., & Snyder, S. H. (1973). Opiate receptor: Demonstration in nervous tissue. *Science, 179,* 1011–1014. (p. 31)

Peschel, E. R., & Peschel, R. E. (1987). Medical insights into the castrati in opera. *American Scientist, 75,* 578–583. (p. 363)

Peters, T. J., & Waterman, R. H., Jr. (1982). *In search of excellence: Lessons from America's best-run companies.* New York: Harper & Row. (p. 246)

Petersen, A. C. (1987, September). Those gangly years. *Psychology Today,* pp. 28–34. (p. 97)

Peterson, C., & Barrett, L. C. (1987). Explanatory style and academic performance among university freshmen. *Journal of Personality and Social Psychology, 53,* 603–607. (p. 437)

Peterson, C., Peterson, J., & Skevington, S. (1986). Heated argument and adolescent development. *Journal of Social and Personal Relationships, 3,* 229–240. (p. 99)

Peterson, L. R., & Peterson, M. J. (1959). Short-term retention of individual verbal items. *Journal of Experimental Psychology, 58,* 193–198. (p. 258)

Peterson, R. (1978). Review of the Rorschach. In O. K. Buros (Ed.), *The eighth mental measurements yearbook* (Vol. I). Highland Park, NJ: Gryphon Press. (p. 419)

Petitto, L. A., & Marentette, P. F. (1991). Babbling in the manual mode: Evidence for the ontogeny of language. *Science, 251,* 1493–1496. (p. 303)

Pettigrew, T. F. (1969). Racially separate or together? *Journal of Social Issues, 25,* 43–69. (p. 616)

Pettingale, K. W., Morris, T., Greer, S., & Haybittle, J. L. (1985, March 30). Mental attitudes to cancer: An additional prognostic factor. *Lancet,* p. 750. (p. 523)

Pfeiffer, E. (1977). Sexual behavior in old age. In E. W. Busse & E. Pfeiffer (Eds.), *Behavior and adaptation in late life* (2nd ed.). Boston: Little, Brown. (p. 111)

Phillips, D. P. (1974). The influence of suggestion on suicide: Substantive and theoretical implications of the Werther effect. *American Sociological Review, 39,* 340–354. (p. 558)

Phillips, D. P. (1982). The impact of fictional television stories on U.S. adult fatalities: New evidence on the effect of the mass media on violence. *American Journal of Sociology, 87,* 1340–1359. (p. 558)

Phillips, D. P. (1985). Natural experiments on the effects of mass media violence on fatal aggression: Strengths and weaknesses of a new approach. In L. Berkowitz (Ed.), *Advances in experimental social psychology* (Vol. 19). Orlando, FL: Academic Press. (p. 558)

Phillips, D. P., Carstensen, L. L., & Paight, D. J. (1989). Effects of mass media news stories on suicide, with new evidence on the role of story content. In D. R. Pfeffer (Ed.), *Suicide among youth: Perspectives on risk and prevention.* Washington, DC: American Psychiatric Press. (p. 558)

Phillips, D. P., & Wills, J. S. (1987). A drop in suicides around major national holidays. *Suicide and Life-Threatening Behavior, 17,* 1–12. (p. 461)

Phillips, J. L. (1969). *Origins of intellect: Piaget's theory.* San Francisco: Freeman. (p. 73)

Phinney, J. S. (1990). Ethnic identity in adolescents and adults: Review of research. *Psychological Bulletin, 108,* 499–514. (pp. 595–597)

Piaget, J. (1930). *The child's conception of physical causality.* London: Routledge & Kegan Paul. (p. 70)

Piaget, J. (1932). *The moral judgment of the child.* New York: Harcourt, Brace & World. (p. 99)

Piaget, J. (1972). Intellectual evolution from adolescence to adulthood. *Human Development, 15,* 1–12. (pp. 98–99)

Piccione, C., Hilgard, E. R., & Zimbardo, P. G. (1989). On the degree of stability of measured hypnotizability over a 25-year period. *Journal of Personality and Social Psychology, 56,* 289–295. (p. 203)

Pickar, D., Labarca, R., Linnoila, M., Roy, A., Hommer, D., Everett, D., & Payl, S. M. (1984). Neuroleptic-induced decrease in plasma homovanillic acid and antipsychotic activity in schizophrenic patients. *Science, 225,* 954–957. (p. 503)

Pinker, S. (1990, September–October). Quoted by J. de Cuevas, "No, she holded them loosely." *Harvard Magazine,* pp. 60–67. (p. 301)

Piotrowski, C., & Keller, J. W. (1989). Psychological testing in outpatient mental health facilities: A national study. *Professional Psychology: Research and Practice, 20,* 423–425. (pp. 419, 426)

Pittman, T. S., Davey, M. E., Alafat, K. A., Vetherill, K. V., & Kramer, N. A. (1980). Informational versus controlling verbal rewards. *Personality and Social Psychology Bulletin, 6,* 228–233. (p. 375)

Planned Parenthood Federation of America. (1986, December 15). Sex education for parents. *USA Today,* p. 11A. (p. 106)

Plomin, R. (1990a). The role of inheritance in behavior. *Science, 248,* 183–188. (p. 89)

Plomin, R. (1990b, June 24). Quoted by M. Gates, Newhouse News Service. See also R. Plomin (1989). Environment and genes: Determinants of behavior. *American Psychologist, 44,* 105–111. (p. 90)

Plomin, R., & Daniels, D. (1987). Why are children in the same family so different from one another? *Behavioral and Brain Sciences, 10,* 1–60. (p. 89)

Plomin, R., McClearn, G. E., Pedersen, N. L., Nesselroade, J. R., & Bergeman, C. S. (1988). Genetic influence on childhood family environment perceived retrospectively from the last half of the life span. *Developmental Psychology, 24,* 37–45. (p. 91)

Plomin, R., & Rende, R. (1991). Human behavioral genetics. *Annual Review of Psychology, 42,* 161–190. (p. 338)

Plotkin, W. B. (1979). The alpha experience revisited: Biofeedback in the transformation of psychological state. *Psychological Bulletin, 86,* 1132–1148. (p. 530)

Polivy, J., & Herman, C. P. (1985). Dieting and binging: A causal analysis. *American Psychologist, 40,* 193–201. (p. 545)

Polivy, J., & Herman, C. P. (1987). Diagnosis and treatment of normal eating. *Journal of Personality and Social Psychology, 55,* 635–644. (pp. 543, 545)

Polivy, J., Herman, C. P., Hackett, C. P., & Kuleshnyk, I. (1986). The effects of self-attention and public attention on eating in restrained and unrestrained subjects. *Journal of Personality and Social Psychology, 50,* 1253–1260. (p. 545)

Pomerleau, O. F., & Pomerleau, C. S. (1984). Neuroregulators and the reinforcement of smoking: Towards a biobehavioral explanation. *Neuroscience and Biobehavioral Reviews, 8,* 503–513. (p. 535)

Pomerleau, O. F., & Rodin, J. (1986). Behavioral medicine and health psychology. In S. L. Garfield & A. E. Bergin (Eds.), *Handbook of psychotherapy and behavior change* (3rd ed.). New York: Wiley. (p. 527)

Poon, L. W. (1987). Myths and truisms: Beyond extant analyses of speed of behavior and age. Address to the Eastern Psychological Association convention. (p. 111)

Porter, D., & Neuringer, A. (1984). Music discriminations by pigeons. *Journal of Experimental Psychology: Animal Behavior Processes, 10,* 138–148. (p. 237)

Powell, J. (1989). *Happiness is an inside job.* Valencia, CA: Tabor. (p. 431)

Powell, J. L. (1988). A test of the knew-it-all-along effect in the 1984 Presidential and statewide elections. *Journal of Applied Social Psychology, 18,* 760–773. (p. 22)

Powell, K. E., Thompson, P. D., Caspersen, C. J., & Kendrick, J. S. (1987). Physical activity and the incidence of coronary heart disease. *Annual Review of Public Health, 8,* 253–287. (p. 529)

Powell, M. C., & Fazio, R. H. (1984). Attitude accessibility as a function of repeated attitudinal expression. *Personality and Social Psychology Bulletin, 10,* 139–148. (p. 555)

Powers, D. E. (1986). Relations of test item characteristics to test preparation/test practice effects: A quantitative summary. *Psychological Bulletin, 100,* 67–77. (p. 327)

Pratkanis, A. R., & Greenwald, A. G. (1988). Recent perspectives on unconscious processing: Still no marketing applications. *Psychology and Marketing, 5,* 337–353. (p. 135)

Pratt, M. W., Pancer, M., Hunsberger, B., & Manchester, J. (1990). Reasoning about the self and relationships in maturity: An integrative complexity analysis of individual differences. *Journal of Personality and Social Psychology, 59,* 575–581. (p. 609)

Premack, D. (1965). Reinforcement theory. *Nebraska Symposium on Motivation.* Lincoln: University of Nebraska Press. (p. 238)

Premack, D. (1983). The codes of man and beasts. *The Behavioral and Brain Sciences, 6,* 125–167. (p. 312)

Price, R. A. (1987). Genetics of human obesity. *Annals of Behavioral Medicine, 9,* 9–14. (p. 541)

Prioleau, L., Murdock, M., & Brody, N. (1983). An analysis of psychotherapy versus placebo studies. *The Behavioral and Brain Sciences, 6,* 275–310. (p. 500)

Pritchard, R. M. (1961, June). Stabilized images on the retina. *Scientific American,* pp. 72–78. (p. 136)

Project on Redefining the Meaning and Purpose of Baccalaureate Degrees. (1985). *Integrity in the college curriculum.* Washington, DC: Association of American Colleges. (p. 635)

Pruitt, D. G., & Rubin, J. Z. (1986). *Social conflict: Escalation, stalemate, and settlement.* New York: Random House. (p. 618)

Psychiatric News. (1989, September 1). Reported by *Behavior Today,* September 25, 1989, pp. 3–4. (p. 496)

Psychic Abscam. (1983, March). *Discover,* p. 10. (p. 182)

Public Opinion. (1979, January/February). NBC News poll, p. 36. (p. 611)

Public Opinion. (1984, August/September). Phears and Phobias, p. 32. (p. 452)

Public Opinion. (1984, August/September). Tradeoffs, p. 36. (p. 11)

Public Opinion. (1985, February/March). Defining woman's place, p. 40. (p. 11)

Public Opinion. (1987, May/June). Teen angels (report of University of Michigan survey), p. 32. (p. 96)

Pyszczynski, T., Hamilton, J. C., Greenberg, J., & Becker, S. E. (1991). Self-awareness and psychological dysfunction. In C. R. Snyder & D. O. Forsyth (Eds.), *Handbook of social and clinical psychology: The health perspective.* New York: Pergamon. (p. 463)

Qualls, P. J., & Sheehan, P. W. (1981). Electromyograph biofeedback as a relaxation technique: A critical appraisal and reassessment. *Psychological Bulletin, 90,* 21–42. (p. 530)

Quasha, S. (1980). *Albert Einstein: An intimate portrait.* New York: Forest. (p. 333)

Quattrone, G. A., & Jones, E. E. (1980). The perception of variability within in-groups and out-groups: Implications for the law of small numbers. *Journal of Personality and Social Psychology, 38,* 141–152. (p. 633)

Rabin, A. S., Kaslow, N. J., & Rehm, L. P. (1986). Aggregate outcome and follow-up results following self-control therapy for depression. Paper presented at the American Psychological Association convention. (p. 495)

Radecki, T. (1989, February–March). On picking good television and film entertainment. *NCTV News, 10*(1–2), p. 5. (p. 571)

Randi, J. (1983a, Summer). The Project Alpha experiment: Part 1. The first two years. *The Skeptical Inquirer,* pp. 24–33. (p. 182)

Randi, J. (1983b, Fall). The Project Alpha experiment: Part 2. Beyond the laboratory. *The Skeptical Inquirer,* pp. 36–45. (p. 182)

Rapoport, J. L. (1989, March). The biology of obsessions and compulsions. *Scientific American,* pp. 83–89. (pp. 453–454)

Raskin, D. C. (1982). University of Utah, as shown in *Science '82,* June, 24–27. (p. 386)

Ray, O., & Ksir, C. (1990). *Drugs, society, and human behavior* (5th ed.). St. Louis: Times Mirror/Mosby. (p. 213)

Raz, S., & Raz, N. (1990). Structural brain abnormalities in the major psychoses: A quantitative review of the evidence from computerized imaging. *Psychological Bulletin, 108,* 93–108. (p. 468)

Razran, G. H. S. (1940). Conditioned response changes in rating and appraising sociopolitical solutions. *Psychological Bulletin, 37,* 481. (p. 235)

Reagan, N., & Libby, B. (1980). *Nancy.* New York: Morrow. (p. 117)

Reagan, R. (1988, December 21). Television interview with David Brinkley, broadcast December 22, and reported by wire services on December 23. (p. 553)

Reason, J. (1987). The Chernobyl errors. *Bulletin of the British Psychological Society, 40,* 201–206. (p. 566)

Reason, J., & Mycielska, K. (1982). *Absent-minded? The psychology of mental lapses and everyday errors.* Englewood Cliffs, NJ: Prentice-Hall. (p. 178)

Regier, D. A., Myers, J. K., Kramer, M., Robins, L. N., Blazer, D. G., Hough, R. L., Eaton, W. W., & Locke, B. Z. (1984, October). The NIMH epidemiologic catchment area program: Historical contact, major objectives, and study population characteristics. *Archives of General Psychiatry, 41*(10), 934–941. (p. 451)

Reiman, E. M., Fusselman, M. J., Fox, P. T., & Raichle, M. E. (1989). Neuroanatomical correlates of anticipatory anxiety. *Science, 243,* 1071–1074. (p. 454)

Reisenzein, R. (1983). The Schachter theory of emotion: Two decades later. *Psychological Bulletin, 94,* 239–264. (p. 404)

Reiser, M. (1982). *Police psychology.* Los Angeles: LEHI. (p. 183)

Remley, A. (1988, October). From obedience to independence. *Psychology Today,* pp. 56–59. (p. 86)

Renner, M. J., & Rosenzweig, M. R. (1987). Enriched and impoverished environments: Effects on brain and behavior. New York: Springer-Verlag. (p. 68)

Rescorla, R. A. (1988). Pavlovian conditioning: It's not what you think it is. *American Psychologist, 43,* 151–160. (p. 232)

Rescorla, R. A., & Wagner, A. R. (1972). A theory of Pavlovian conditioning: Variations in the effectiveness of reinforcement and nonreinforcement. In A. H. Black & W. F. Perokasy (Eds.), *Classical conditioning II: Current theory.* New York: Appleton-Century-Crofts. (p. 232)

Ressler, R. K., Burgess, A. W., & Douglas, J. E. (1988). *Sexual homicide patterns.* Boston: Lexington Books. (p. 572)

Reveen, P. J. (1987-88). Fantasizing under hypnosis: Some experimental evidence. *The Skeptical Inquirer, 12,* 181–183. (p. 206)

Reynolds, D. K. (1982). *The quiet therapies.* Honolulu: University of Hawaii Press. (p. 158)

Reynolds, D. K. (1986). *Even in summer the ice doesn't melt: Japan's Morita Therapy.* New York: Morrow (Quill paperback). (p. 158)

Rheingold, H. L. (1985). Development as the acquisition of familiarity. *Annual Review of Psychology, 36,* 1–17. (p. 77)

Rhodes, S. R. (1983). Age-related differences in work attitudes and behavior: A review and conceptual analysis. *Psychological Bulletin, 93,* 328–367. (p. 111)

Rice, B. (1985, September). Performance review: The job nobody likes. *Psychology Today,* pp. 30–36. (p. 553)

Rice, M. E., & Grusec, J. E. (1975). Saying and doing: Effects on observer performance. *Journal of Personality and Social Psychology, 32,* 584–593. (p. 248)

Richardson, J. T. E. (1990). Questionnaire studies of paramenstrual symptoms. *Psychology of Women Quarterly, 14,* 15–42. (p. 525)

Richardson, J. T. E., & Zucco, G. M. (1989). Cognition and olfaction: A review. *Psychological Bulletin, 105,* 352–360. (p. 155)

Ridenour, M. (1982). Infant walkers: Developmental tool or inherent danger. *Perceptual and Motor Skills, 55,* 1201–1202. (p. 68)

Rieff, P. (1979). *Freud: The mind of a moralist* (3rd ed.). Chicago: University of Chicago Press. (p. 421)

Ring, K. (1980). *Life at death: A scientific investigation of the near-death experience.* New York: Coward, McCann & Geoghegan. (p. 219)

Riskind, J. H., Beck, A. T., Berchick, R. J., Brown, G., & Steer, R. A. (1987). Reliability of DSM-III diagnoses for major depression and generalized anxiety disorder using the structured clinical interview for DSM-III. *Archives of General Psychiatry, 44,* 817–820. (p. 451)

Roberts, L. (1987). Study bolsters case against cholesterol. *Science, 237,* 28–29. (p. 537)

Roberts, L. (1988). Beyond Noah's ark: What do we need to know? *Science, 242,* 1247. (p. 518)

Roberts, M., & Harris, T. G. (1989). Wellness at work. *Psychology Today,* pp. 54–58. (p. 534)

Roberts, T-A. (1991). Gender and the influence of evaluations on self-assessments in achievement settings. *Psychological Bulletin, 109,* 297–308. (p. 600)

Robins, L., & Regier, D. (Eds.). (1991). *Psychiatric disorders in America.* New York: Free Press. (pp. 445, 472, 473)

Robins, L. N., Davis, D. H., & Goodwin, D. W. (1974). Drug use by U.S. Army enlisted men in Vietnam: A follow-up on their return home. *American Journal of Epidemiology, 99,* 235–249. (p. 214)

Robinson, F. P. (1970). *Effective study.* New York: Harper & Row. (p. 23)

Robinson, J. P. (1988, December). Who's doing the housework? *American Demographics,* pp. 24–28, 63. (pp. 120, 608)

Robinson, L. A., Berman, J. S., & Neimeyer, R. A. (1990). Psychotherapy for the treatment of depression: A comprehensive review of controlled outcome research. *Psychological Bulletin, 108,* 30–49. (p. 498)

Robinson, V. M. (1983). Humor and health. In P. E. McGhee & J. H. Goldstein (Eds.), *Handbook of humor research: Vol. II. Applied studies.* New York: Springer-Verlag. (p. 532)

Rock, I., & Palmer, S. (1990, December). The legacy of Gestalt psychology. *Scientific American*, pp. 84–90. (pp. 165–166)

Rodin, J. (1979). *Obesity theory and behavior therapy: An uneasy couple?* Paper presented at the meeting of the Association for the Advancement of Behavior Therapy. (p. 544)

Rodin, J. (1984, December). A sense of control [interview]. *Psychology Today*, pp. 38–45. (p. 358)

Rodin, J. (1985). Insulin levels, hunger and food intake: An example of feedback loops in body weight regulation. *Health Psychology, 4*, 1–18. (p. 544)

Rodin, J. (1986). Aging and health: Effects of the sense of control. *Science, 233*, 1271–1276. (pp. 436, 518)

Rodin, J., & Slochower, J. (1976). Externality in the nonobese: Effects of environmental responsiveness on weight. *Journal of Personality and Social Psychology, 33*, 338–344. (p. 358)

Roger, L. H., Cortes, D. E., & Malgady, R. B. (1991). Acculturation and mental health status among Hispanics: Convergence and new directions for research. *American Psychologist, 46*, 585–597. (p. 596)

Rogers, C. R. (1958). Reinhold Niebuhr's *The self and the dramas of history:* A criticism. *Pastoral Psychology, 9*, 15–17. (p. 430)

Rogers, C. R. (1961). *On becoming a person: A therapist's view of psychotherapy.* Boston: Houghton Mifflin. (p. 483)

Rogers, C. R. (1970). *Carl Rogers on encounter groups.* New York: Harper & Row. (p. 486)

Rogers, C. R. (1980). *A way of being.* Boston: Houghton Mifflin. (pp. 429, 483)

Rogers, C. R. (1981, Summer). Notes on Rollo May. *Perspectives, 2*(1), p. 16. (p. 433)

Roland, A. (1988). *In search of self in India and Japan.* Princeton: Princeton University Press. (p. 86)

Rook, K. S. (1984). Promoting social bonding: Strategies for helping the lonely and socially isolated. *American Psychologist, 39*, 1389–1407. (p. 465)

Rook, K. S. (1987). Social support versus companionship: Effects on life stress, loneliness, and evaluations by others. *Journal of Personality and Social Psychology, 52*, 1132–1147. (p. 533)

Rosch, E. (1974). Linguistic relativity. In A. Silverstein (Ed.), *Human communication: Theoretical perspectives.* New York: Halsted Press. (p. 311)

Rosch, E. (1978). Principles of categorization. In E. Rosch & B. L. Lloyd (Eds.), *Cognition and categorization.* Hillsdale, NJ: Erlbaum. (p. 287)

Rose, G. A., & Williams, R. T. (1961). Metabolic studies on large and small eaters. *British Journal of Nutrition, 1*, 1–9. (p. 541)

Rose, R. J., Koskenvuo, M., Kaprio, J., Sarna, S., & Langinvainio, H. (1988). Shared genes, shared experiences, and similarity of personality: Data from 14,228 adult Finnish co-twins. *Journal of Personality and Social Psychology, 54*, 161–171. (p. 87)

Rose, S. (1983). *The conscious brain.* New York: Alfred A. Knopf. (p. 44)

Rosenbaum, M. (1986). The repulsion hypothesis: On the non-development of relationships. *Journal of Personality and Social Psychology, 51*, 1156–1166. (p. 581)

Rosenfeld, S. P. (1987, March 29). Insanity defense is riskier now and can turn winners to losers. Associated Press release (*Grand Rapids Press*, p. A17). (p. 449)

Rosenhan, D. L. (1973). On being sane in insane places. *Science, 179*, 250–258. (p. 473)

Rosenhan, D. L. (1983a). Psychological abnormality and law. In C. J. Scheirer & B. C. Hammonds (Eds.), *The master lecture series: Vol. 2. Psychology and the law.* Washington, DC: American Psychological Association. (p. 449)

Rosenhan, D. L. (1983b). *Psychological realities and judicial policy.* Paper presented at the meeting of the American Psychological Association. (p. 449)

Rosenstein, M. J., Milazzo-Sayre, L. J., & Manderscheid, R. W. (1989). Care of persons with schizophrenia: A statistical profile. *Schizophrenia Bulletin, 15*, 45–58. (p. 445)

Rosenthal, R., Hall, J. A., Archer, D., DiMatteo, M. R., & Rogers, P. L. (1979). The PONS test: Measuring sensitivity to nonverbal cues. In S. Weitz (Ed.), *Nonverbal communication* (2nd ed.). New York: Oxford University Press. (p. 388)

Rosenzweig, M. R. (1984). Experience, memory, and the brain. *American Psychologist, 39*, 365–376. (p. 68)

Rosenzweig, M. R., Bennett, E. L., & Diamond, M. C. (1972, February). Brain changes in response to experience. *Scientific American*, 22–29. (p. 68)

Ross, H. (1975, June 19). Mist, murk, and visual perception. *New Scientist*, pp. 658–660. (p. 164)

Ross, M., McFarland, C., & Fletcher, G. J. O. (1981). The effect of attitude on the recall of personal histories. *Journal of Personality and Social Psychology, 40*, 627–634. (p. 280)

Rossi, P. H. (1990). The old homeless and the new homelessness in historical perspective. *American Psychologist, 45*, 954–959. (p. 502)

Rossi, P. J. (1968). Adaptation and negative aftereffect to lateral optical displacement in newly hatched chicks. *Science, 160*, 430–432. (p. 176)

Roth, T., Roehrs, T., Zwyghuizen-Doorenbos, A., Stpeanski, E., & Witting, R. (1988). Sleep and memory. In I. Hindmarch & H. Ott (Eds.), *Benzodiazepine receptor ligans, memory and information processing.* New York: Springer-Verlag. (p. 198)

Rothbart, M., Fulero, S., Jensen, C., Howard, J., & Birrell, P. (1978). From individual to group impressions: Availability heuristics in stereotype formation. *Journal of Experimental Social Psychology, 14*, 237–255. (p. 613)

Rothblum, E. D. (1990). Women and weight: Fad and fiction. *Journal of Psychology, 124*, 5–24. (p. 543)

Rothstein, W. G. (1980). The significance of occupations in work careers: An empirical and theoretical review. *Journal of Vocational Behavior, 17*, 328–343. (p. 119)

Rotton, J., & Kelly, I. W. (1985). Much ado about the full moon: A meta-analysis of lunar-lunacy research. *Psychological Bulletin, 97*, 286–306. (p. 469)

Rovee-Collier, C. (1989). The joy of kicking: Memories, motives, and mobiles. In P. R. Solomon, G. R. Goethals, C. M. Kelley, & B. R. Stephens (Eds.), *Memory: Interdisciplinary approaches.* New York: Springer-Verlag. (pp. 67, 273)

Roviaro, S., Holmes, D. S., & Holmsten, R. D. (1984). Influence of a cardiac rehabilitation program on the cardiovascular, psychological, and social functioning of cardiac patients. *Journal of Behavioral Medicine, 7*, 61–81. (p. 529)

Rowe, D. C. (1990). As the twig is bent? The myth of child-rearing influences on personality development. *Journal of Counseling and Development, 68*, 606–611. (p. 89)

Rowe, J. W., & Kahn, R. L. (1987). Human aging: Usual and successful. *Science, 237*, 143–149. (p. 111)

Rozin, P., Millman, L., & Nemeroff, C. (1986). Operation of the laws of sympathetic magic in disgust and other domains. *Journal of Personality and Social Psychology, 50*, 703–712. (p. 231)

Ruback, R. B., Carr, T. S., & Hopper, C. H. (1986). Perceived control in prison: Its relation to reported crowding, stress, and symptoms. *Journal of Applied Social Psychology, 16*, 375–386. (p. 436)

Rubin, L. B. (1979). *Women of a certain age: The midlife search for self.* New York: Harper & Row. (p. 119)

Rubin, L. B. (1985). *Just friends: The role of friendship in our lives.* New York: Harper & Row. (p. 600)

Rubin, Z. (1970). Measurement of romantic love. *Journal of Personality and Social Psychology, 16*, 265–273. (p. 389)

Rubonis, A. V., & Bickman, L. (1991). Psychological impairment in the wake of disaster: The disaster-psychopathology relationship. *Psychological Bulletin, 109*, 384–399. (p. 514)

Rudman, D., Feller, A. G., Nagraj, H. S., Gergans, G. A., Lalitha, P. Y., Goldberg, A. F., Schlenker, R. A., Cohn, L., Rudman, I. W., & Mattson, D. E. (1990). Effects of human growth hormone in men over 60 years old. *New England Journal of Medicine, 323*, 1–6. (p. 41)

Rule, B. G., & Ferguson, T. J. (1986). The effects of media violence on attitudes, emotions, and cognitions. *Journal of Social Issues, 42*(3), 29–50. (p. 571)

Rumbaugh, D. M. (1977). *Language learning by a chimpanzee: The Lana project.* New York: Academic Press. (p. 308)

Rumbaugh, D. M. (1985). Comparative psychology: Patterns in adaptation. In A. M. Rogers & C. J. Scheirer (Eds.), *The G. Stanley Hall Lecture Series* (Vol. 5). Washington, DC: American Psychological Association. (p. 309)

Rumbaugh, D. M. (1987, September 17). Personal communication. (p. 309)

Rumbaugh, D. M., & Savage-Rumbaugh, S. (1978). Chimpanzee language research: Status and potential. *Behavior Research Methods & Instrumentation, 10*, 119–131. (p. 310)

Rumbaugh, D. M., & Savage-Rumbaugh, S. (1986). Reasoning and language in chimpanzees. In R. J. Hoage & L. Goldman (Eds.), *Animal intelligence.* Washington, DC: Smithsonian Institution Press. (pp. 288, 310)

Rushton, J. P. (1975). Generosity in children: Immediate and long-term effects of modeling, preaching, and moral judgment. *Journal of Personality and Social Psychology, 31*, 459–466. (p. 248)

Rushton, J. P. (1989). Genetic similarity, human altruism, and group selection. *Behavioral and Brain Sciences, 12*, 503–559. (p. 577)

Rushton, J. P., Fulker, D. W., Neale, M. C., Nias, D. K. B., & Eysenck, H. J. (1986). Altruism and aggression: The heritability of individual differences. *Journal of Personality and Social Psychology, 50*, 1192–1198. (p. 568)

Russell, B. (1930/1985). *The conquest of happiness.* London: Unwin Paperbacks. (p. 401)

Russell, J. A., Lewicka, M., & Niit, T. (1989). A cross-cultural study of a circumplex model of affect. *Journal of Personality and Social Psychology, 57*, 848–856. (p. 392)

Rutter, M. (1979). Maternal deprivation, 1972–1978: New findings, new concepts, new approaches. *Child Development, 50*, 283–305. (p. 80)

Ryan, E. D. (1980). Attribution, intrinsic motivation, and athletics: A replication and extension. In C. H. Nadeau, W. R. Halliwell, K. M. Newell, & G. C. Roberts (Eds.), *Psychology of motor behavior and sport—1979.* Champaign, IL: Human Kinetics Press. (p. 374)

Rzewnicki, R., & Forgays, D. G. (1987). Recidivism and self-cure of smoking and obesity: An attempt to replicate. *American Psychologist, 42*, 97–100. (p. 543)

Saal, F. E., Johnson, C. B., & Weber, N. (1989). Friendly or sexy? It may depend on whom you ask. *Psychology of Women Quarterly, 13*, 263–276. (p. 602)

Sabini, J. (1986). Stanley Milgram (1933–1984). *American Psychologist, 41*, 1378–1379. (p. 560)

Sackeim, H. A. (1988). Mechanisms of action of electroconvulsive therapy. In A. J. Frances & R. E. Hales (Eds.), *Review of Psychiatry* (Vol. 7). Washington, DC: American Psychiatric Press. (p. 505)

Sacks, O. (1985). *The man who mistook his wife for a hat.* New York: Summit Books. (pp. 49, 269)

Sadalla, E. K., Kenrick, D. T., & Vershure, B. (1987). Dominance and heterosexual attraction. *Journal of Personality and Social Psychology, 52*, 730–738. (p. 580)

Safer, M. A., & others. (1979). Determinants of three stages of delay in seeking care at a medical clinic. *Medical Care, 17*, 11–28. (p. 524)

Safire, W. (1989, February 3). Shultz order on polygraphs a mistake. *The New York Times News Service (Grand Rapids Press).* (p. 387)

Sagan, C. (1979a). *Broca's brain.* New York: Random House. (pp. 9, 34)

Sagan, C. (1979b). *Dragons of Eden.* New York: Random House. (p. 446)

Sagan, C. (1980). *Cosmos.* New York: Random House. (p. 610)

Sagan, C. (1987, February 1). The fine art of baloney detection. *Parade.* (pp. 134, 184)

Salovey, P. (1990, January/February). Interview. *American Scientist,* pp. 25–29. (p. 396)

Salovey, P., & Birnbaum, D. (1989). Influence of mood on health-relevant cognitions. *Journal of Personality and Social Psychology, 57,* 539–551. (p. 545)

Samuels, S., & McCabe, G. (1989). Quoted by P. Diaconis & F. Mosteller, Methods for studying coincidences. *Journal of the American Statistical Association, 84,* 853–861. (p. 631)

Sandberg, G. G., Jackson, T. L., & Petretic-Jackson, P. (1985). *Sexual aggression and courtship violence in dating relationships.* Paper presented at the meeting of the Midwestern Psychological Association. (p. 571)

Sanders, B., & Soares, M. P. (1986). Sexual maturation and spatial ability in college students. *Developmental Psychology, 22,* 199–203. (p. 598)

Sapadin, L. A. (1988). Friendship and gender: Perspectives of professional men and women. *Journal of Social and Personal Relationships, 5,* 387–403. (p. 600)

Sapolsky, R. M. (1990, January). Stress in the wild. *Scientific American,* pp. 116–123. (p. 516)

Sarawathi, T. S., & Dutta, R. (1988). *Invisible boundaries: Grooming for adult roles.* New Delhi: Northern Book Centre. Cited by R. Larson & M. H. Richards (1989). Introduction: The changing life space of early adolescence. *Journal of Youth and Adolescence, 18,* 501–509. (p. 606)

Sato, K. (1987). Distribution of the cost of maintaining common resources. *Journal of Experimental Social Psychology, 23,* 19–31. (p. 615)

Savage-Rumbaugh, S. (1987). Communication, symbolic communication, and language: Reply to Seidenberg and Petitto. *Journal of Experimental Psychology: General, 116,* 288–292. (p. 310)

Savage-Rumbaugh, S. (1990, February 8). Apes, language, math, and minds. Sigma Xi Lecture, Hope College. (p. 310)

Savitsky, J. C., & Lindblom, W. D. (1986). The impact of the guilty but mentally ill verdict on juror decisions: An empirical analysis. *Journal of Applied Social Psychology, 16,* 686–701. (p. 449)

Sayre, R. F. (1979). The parents' last lessons. In D. D. Van Tassel (Ed.), *Aging, death, and the completion of being.* Philadelphia: University of Pennsylvania Press. (p. 112)

Scanlan, C. (1990, March 27). Weight-loss industry diagnosed as unhealthy. *Detroit Free Press,* pp. 1A, 6A. (p. 543)

Scarr, S. (1984, May). What's a parent to do? [Conversation with E. Hall.] *Psychology Today,* pp. 58–63. (p. 339)

Scarr, S. (1986). *Mother care/Other care.* New York: Basic Books. (pp. 82, 340)

Scarr, S. (1988). Race and gender as psychological variables: Social and ethical issues. *American Psychologist, 43,* 56–59. (p. 599)

Scarr, S. (1989). Protecting general intelligence: Constructs and consequences for interventions. In R. J. Linn (Ed.), *Intelligence: Measurement, theory, and public policy.* Champaign: University of Illinois Press. (pp. 330, 338)

Scarr, S. (1990). Back cover comments on J. Dunn & R. Plomin (1990). *Separate lives: Why siblings are so different.* New York: Basic Books. (p. 91)

Scarr, S., & McCartney, K. (1983). How people make their own environments: A theory of genotype → environment effects. *Child Development, 54,* 424–435. (p. 91)

Scarr, S., Pakstis, A. J., Katz, S. H., & Barker, W. B. (1977). The absence of a relationship between degree of white ancestry and intellectual skills within a black population. *Human Genetics, 39,* 69–86. (p. 343)

Scarr, S., Phillips, D., & McCartney, K. (1990). Facts, fantasies and the future of child care in the United States. *Psychological Science, 1,* 26–35. (p. 83)

Scarr, S., Webber, P. L., Weinberg, R. A., & Wittig, M. A. (1981). Personality resemblance among adolescents and their parents in biologically related and adoptive families. *Journal of Personality and Social Psychology, 40,* 885–898. (p. 89)

Scarr, S., & Weinberg, R. A. (1976). IQ test performance of black children adopted by white families. *American Psychologist, 31,* 726–739. (p. 343)

Scarr, S., & Weinberg, R. A. (1986). The early childhood enterprise: Care and education of the young. *American Psychologist, 41,* 1140–1146. (p. 82)

Schab, F. R. (1990). Odors and the remembrance of things past. *Journal of Experimental Psychology: Learning, Memory, and Cognition, 16,* 648–655. (p. 156)

Schab, F. R. (1991). Odor memory: Taking stock. *Psychological Bulletin, 109,* 242–251. (p. 156)

Schachter, S. (1982). Recidivism and self-cure of smoking and obesity. *American Psychologist, 37,* 436–444. (p. 543)

Schachter, S., & Singer, J. E. (1962). Cognitive, social and physiological determinants of emotional state. *Psychological Review, 69,* 379–399. (p. 404)

Schacter, D. L. (1987). Implicit memory: History and current status. *Journal of Experimental Psychology: Learning, Memory, and Cognition, 13,* 501–518. (p. 270)

Schaie, K. W. (1987). Old dogs can learn new tricks: Intellectual decline and its remediation in later adulthood. Address to the Eastern Psychological Association convention. (p. 115)

Schaie, K. W. (1989). Perceptual speed in adulthood: Cross-sectional and longitudinal studies. *Psychology and Aging, 4,* 443–453. (p. 111)

Schaie, K. W., & Geiwitz, J. (1982). *Adult development and aging*. Boston: Little, Brown. (p. 114)

Schaie, K. W., & Strother, C. R. (1968). A cross-sequential study of age changes in cognitive behavior. *Psychological Bulletin, 70,* 671–680. (p. 114)

Scheerer, M. (1963, April). Problem solving. *Scientific American*, pp. 118–128. (pp. 289–290)

Scheier, M. F., & Carver, C. S. (1987). Dispositional optimism and physical well-being: The influence of generalized outcome expectancies on health. *Journal of Personality, 55,* 169–210. (p. 518)

Schein, E. H. (1956). The Chinese indoctrination program for prisoners of war: A study of attempted brainwashing. *Psychiatry, 19,* 149–172. (p. 555)

Schiavi, R. C., & Schreiner-Engel, P. (1988). Nocturnal penile tumescence in healthy aging men. *Journal of Gerontology: Medical Sciences, 43,* M146–150. (p. 194)

Schiffenbauer, A., & Schiavo, R. S. (1976). Physical distance and attraction: An intensification effect. *Journal of Experimental Social Psychology, 12,* 274–282. (p. 563)

Schleifer, S. J., Keller, S. E., McKegney, F. P., & Stein, M. (1979). *The influence of stress and other psychosocial factors on human immunity.* Paper presented at the 36th Annual Meeting of the American Psychosomatic Society. (p. 522)

Schlesinger, A. M., Jr. (1965). *A thousand days*. Boston: Houghton Mifflin. (p. 565)

Schnaper, N. (1980). Comments germane to the paper entitled "The reality of death experiences" by Ernst Rodin. *Journal of Nervous and Mental Disease, 168,* 268–270. (p. 219)

Schneiderman, N., Chesney, M. A., & Krantz, D. S. (1989). Biobehavioral aspects of cardiovascular disease: Progress and prospects. *Health Psychology, 8,* 649–676. (p. 520)

Schnitzer, B. (1984, May). Repunctuated message. *Games*, pp. 57, 62. (p. 300)

Schofield, J. W. (1986). Black-White contact in desegregated schools. In M. Hewstone & R. Brown (Eds.), *Contact and conflict in intergroup encounters.* Oxford: Basil Blackwell Ltd. (p. 616)

Schonfield, D., & Robertson, B. A. (1966). Memory storage and aging. *Canadian Journal of Psychology, 20,* 228–236. (p. 112)

Schooler, J. W., Gerhard, D., & Loftus, E. F. (1986). Qualities of the unreal. *Journal of Experimental Psychology: Learning, Memory, and Cognition, 12,* 171–181. (p. 276)

Schuerger, J. M., Zarrella, K. L., & Hotz, A. S. (1989). Factors that influence the temporal stability of personality by questionnaire. *Journal of Personality and Social Psychology, 56,* 777–783. (p. 125)

Schwartz, B. (1984). *Psychology of learning and behavior* (2nd ed.). New York: Norton. (pp. 234, 453)

Schwarz, N., & Clore, G. L. (1983). Mood, misattribution, and judgments of well-being: Informative and directive functions of affective states. *Journal of Personality and Social Psychology, 45,* 513–523. (p. 396)

Schwarz, N., Strack, F., Kommer, D., & Wagner, D. (1987). Soccer, rooms, and the quality of your life: Mood effects on judgments of satisfaction with life in general and with specific domains. *European Journal of Social Psychology, 17,* 69–79. (p. 274)

Scribner, S. (1977). Modes of thinking and ways of speaking: Culture and logic reconsidered. In P. N. Johnson-Laird & P. C. Wason (Eds.), *Thinking: Readings in cognitive science.* New York: Cambridge University Press. (p. 99)

Segall, M. H., Dasen, P. R., Berry, J. W., & Poortinga, Y. H. (1990). *Human behavior in global perspective: An introduction to cross-cultural psychology.* New York: Pergamon. (pp. 75, 173, 601, 606, 612)

Seginer, R., Karayanni, M., & Mar'i, M. M. (1990). Adolescents' attitudes toward women's roles. *Psychology of Women Quarterly, 14,* 119–133. (p. 607)

Seligman, M. E. P. (1974, May). Submissive death: Giving up on life. *Psychology Today*, pp. 80–85. (p. 384)

Seligman, M. E. P. (1975). *Helplessness: On depression, development and death.* San Francisco: Freeman. (p. 436)

Seligman, M. E. P. (1988, October). Boomer blues. *Psychology Today*, pp. 50–55. (p. 593)

Seligman, M. E. P. (1988). Why is there so much depression today? The waxing of the individual and the waning of the commons. G. Stanley Hall Lecture to the American Psychological Association convention. (pp. 458, 463)

Seligman, M. E. P. (1989). Explanatory style: Predicting depression, achievement, and health. In M. D. Yapko (Ed.), *Brief therapy approaches to treating anxiety and depression.* New York: Brunner/Mazel. (p. 495)

Seligman, M. E. P. (1991). *Learned optimism.* New York: Knopf. (pp. 436, 464)

Seligman, M. E. P., & Schulman, P. (1986). Explanatory style as a predictor of productivity and quitting among life insurance sales agents. *Journal of Personality and Social Psychology, 50,* 832–838. (p. 437)

Seligman, M. E. P., & Yellen, A. (1987). What is a dream? *Behavior Research and Therapy, 25,* 1–24. (pp. 192, 200)

Selye, H. (1936). A syndrome produced by diverse nocuous agents. *Nature, 138,* 32. (p. 513)

Selye, H. (1976). *The stress of life.* New York: McGraw-Hill. (p. 513)

Senden, M., von (1932; reprinted 1960). In P. Heath (Trans.), *Space and sight: The perception of space and shape in the congenitally blind before and after operation.* Glencoe, IL: Free Press. (p. 174)

Shadish, W. R., Jr. (1992). Do family and marital psychotherapies change what people do? A meta-analysis of behavioral outcomes. In T. D. Cook, H. M. Cooper, D. S. Cordray, H. Hartman, L. V. Hedges, R. J. Light, T. A. Louis, & F. Mosteller (Eds.), *Meta-analysis for explanation: A casebook.* New York: Russell Sage, in press.

Shapiro, C. M., Bortz, R., Mitchell, D., Bartel, P., & Jooste, P. (1981). Slow-wave sleep: A recovery period after exercise. *Science, 214,* 1253–1254. (p. 195)

Shapiro, D. A., & Shapiro, D. (1982). Meta-analysis of comparative therapy outcome studies: A replication and refinement. *Psychological Bulletin, 92,* 581–604. (p. 500)

Shaughnessy, J. J., & Zechmeister, E. (1992). Memory monitoring accuracy as influenced by the distribution of retrieval practice. *Bulletin of the Psychonomic Society*, in press. (p. 277)

Shaw, H. L. (1989–90). Comprehension of the spoken word and ASL translation by chimpanzees (Pan troglodytes). *Friends of Washoe, 9*(1/2), 8–19. (p. 310)

Shedler, J., & Block, J. (1990). Adolescent drug use and psychological health: A longitudinal inquiry. *American Psychologist, 45,* 612–630. (p. 217)

Sheehan, S. (1982). *Is there no place on earth for me?* Boston: Houghton Mifflin. (p. 466)

Sheldon, W. H. (1954). *Atlas of man: A guide for somatotyping the adult male of all ages.* New York: Harper & Row. (p. 422)

Shepard, R. N. (1981). Psychophysical complementarity. In M. Kubovy & J. R. Pomerantz (Eds.), *Perceptual organization.* Hillsdale, NJ: Erlbaum. (p. 171)

Shepard, R. N. (1990). *Mind sights.* New York: Freeman. (pp. 166, 172, 179)

Shepherd, C., Kohut, J. J., & Sweet, R. (1990). *More news of the weird.* New York: Penguin/Plume Books. (p. 472)

Sherif, M. (1937). An experimental approach to the study of attitudes. *Sociometry, 1,* 90–98. (p. 557)

Sherif, M. (1966). *In common predicament: Social psychology of intergroup conflict and cooperation.* Boston: Houghton Mifflin. (p. 616)

Sherman, A. R., & Levin, M. P. (1979). *In vivo* therapies for compulsive habits, sexual difficulties, and severe adjustment problems. In A. P. Goldstein & F. H. Kanfer (Eds.), *Maximizing treatment gains: Transfer enhancement in psychotherapy.* New York: Academic Press. (p. 490)

Sherry, D., & Vaccarino, A. L. (1989). Hippocampus and memory for food caches in black-capped chickadees. *Behavioral Neuroscience, 103,* 308–318. (p. 271)

Shettleworth, S. J. (1973). Food reinforcement and the organization of behavior in golden hamsters. In R. A. Hinde & J. Stevenson-Hinde (Eds.), *Constraints on learning.* London: Academic Press. (p. 244)

Shneidman, E. (1987, March). At the point of no return. *Psychology Today,* pp. 54–58. (p. 461)

Shotland, L. (1984, March 12). Quoted by Maureen Dowd, 20 years after the murder of Kitty Genovese, the question remains: Why? *The New York Times,* p. B1. (p. 574)

Shotland, R. L. (1989). A model of the causes of date rape in developing and close relationships. In C. Hendrick (Ed.), *Review of Personality and Social Psychology* (Vol. 10). Newbury Park, CA: Sage. (p. 602)

Showers, C., & Ruben, C. (1987). Distinguishing pessimism from depression: Negative expectations and positive coping mechanisms. Paper presented at the American Psychological Association convention. (p. 437)

Shrout, P. E., Link, B. G., Dohrenwend, B. P., Skodol, A. E., Stueve, A., & Mirotznik, J. (1989). Characterizing life events as risk factors for depression: The role of fateful loss events. *Journal of Abnormal Psychology, 98,* 460–467. (p. 460)

Siegel, J. M. (1990). Stressful life events and use of physician services among the elderly: The moderating role of pet ownership. *Journal of Personality and Social Psychology, 58,* 1081–1086. (p. 532)

Siegel, L. S., & Hodkin, B. (1982). The garden path to the understanding of cognitive development: Has Piaget led us into the poison ivy? In S. Modgil & C. Modgil (Eds.), *Jean Piaget: Consensus and controversy.* New York: Praeger. (p. 74)

Siegel, R. K. (1977, October). Hallucinations. *Scientific American,* pp. 132–140. (p. 219)

Siegel, R. K. (1980). The psychology of life after death. *American Psychologist, 35,* 911–931. (p. 219)

Siegel, R. K. Quoted by J. Hooper (1982, October), Mind tripping. *Omni,* pp. 72–82, 159–160. (p. 215)

Siegel, R. K. (1984, March 15). Personal communication. (p. 215)

Siegel, R. K. (1990). *Intoxication.* New York: Pocket Books. (pp. 212–215, 217)

Silver, M., & Geller, D. (1978). On the irrelevance of evil: The organization and individual action. *Journal of Social Issues, 34,* 125–136. (p. 562)

Silverman, P. S., & Retzlaff, P. D. (1986). Cognitive stage regression through hypnosis: Are earlier cognitive stages retrievable? *International Journal of Clinical and Experimental Hypnosis, 34,* 192–204. (p. 204)

Silverton, L. (1988). Crime and the schizophrenia spectrum: A study of three Danish cohorts. In T. E. Moffitt & S. A. Mednick (Eds.), *Biological contributions to crime causation.* New York: Martinus-Nijhoff. (p. 474)

Simmons, R. G., & Blyth, D. A. (1987). *Moving into adolescence: The impact of pubertal change and school context.* New York: Aldine de Gruyter. (p. 97)

Simons, E. L. (1989). Human origins. *Science, 245,* 1343–1350. (p. 587)

Simonton, D. K. (1988). Age and outstanding achievement: What do we know after a century of research? *Psychological Bulletin, 104,* 251–267. (p. 116)

Simpson, J. A. (1991). The influence of attachment styles on romantic relationships. *Journal of Personality and Social Psychology,* in press. (p. 79)

Singer, J. L. (1975). Navigating the stream of consciousness: Research in daydreaming and related inner experience. *American Psychologist, 30,* 727–738. (p. 201)

Singer, J. L. (1976, July). Fantasy: The foundation of serenity. *Psychology Today,* pp. 32–37. (p. 202)

Singer, J. L. (1981). Clinical intervention: New developments in methods and evaluation. In L. T. Benjamin, Jr. (Ed.), *The G. Stanley Hall Lecture Series* (Vol. 1). Washington, DC: American Psychological Association. (p. 499)

Singer, J. L. (1986). Is television bad for children? *Social Science, 71,* 178–182. (p. 202)

Singer, J. L., & Singer, D. G. (1986). Family experiences and television viewing as predictors of children's imagination, restlessness, and aggression. *Journal of Social Issues, 42*(3), 7–28. (p. 571)

Sjöstrum, L. (1980). Fat cells and body weight. In A. J. Stunkard (Ed.), *Obesity.* Philadelphia: Saunders. (p. 540)

Skinner, B. F. (1953). *Science and human behavior.* New York: Macmillan. (p. 240)

Skinner, B. F. (1956). A case history in scientific method. *American Psychologist, 11,* 221–233. (p. 241)

Skinner, B. F. (1957). *Verbal behavior.* Englewood Cliffs, NJ: Prentice-Hall. (p. 305)

Skinner, B. F. (1961, November). Teaching machines. *Scientific American,* pp. 91–102. (p. 240)

Skinner, B. F. (1983, September). Origins of a behaviorist. *Psychology Today,* pp. 22–33. (pp. 244, 462)

Skinner, B. F. (1985). *Cognitive science and behaviorism.* Unpublished manuscript, Harvard University. (p. 305)

Skinner, B. F. (1986). What is wrong with daily life in the western world? *American Psychologist, 41,* 568–574. (p. 245)

Skinner, B. F. (1988). The school of the future. Address to the American Psychological Association convention. (p. 245)

Skinner, B. F. (1989). Teaching machines. *Science, 243,* 1535. (p. 245)

Skinner, B. F. (1990). Address to the American Psychological Association convention. (p. 242)

Sklar, L. S., & Anisman, H. (1981). Stress and cancer. *Psychological Bulletin, 89,* 369–406. (p. 521)

Skov, R. B., & Sherman, S. J. (1986). Information-gathering processes: Diagnosticity, hypothesis-confirmatory strategies, and perceived hypothesis confirmation. *Journal of Experimental Social Psychology, 22,* 93–121. (p. 288)

Slater, A. (1990). Infant development: The origins of competence. *The Psychologist, 3,* 109–113. (p. 67)

Slavin, R. E. (1989). Cooperative learning and student achievement. In R. E. Slavin (Ed.), *School and classroom organization.* Hillsdale, NJ: Erlbaum. (p. 617)

Slovic, P. (1987). Perception of risk. *Science, 236,* 280–285. (p. 294)

Slovic, P., & Fischhoff, B. (1977). On the psychology of experimental surprises. *Journal of Experimental Psychology: Human Perception and Performance, 3,* 544–551. (p. 21)

Small, M. F. (1991, July). Sperm wars. *Discover,* pp. 48–53. (p. 603)

Smart, R. G., & Adlaf, E. M. (1989). The Ontario student drug use survey: Trends between 1977–1989. 33 Russell Street, Toronto, Ontario M5S: Addiction Research Foundation of Ontario. (p. 217)

Smith, A. (1983). Personal correspondence. (p. 468)

Smith, A. (1987). Personal communication. (p. 47)

Smith, A., & Sugar, O. (1975). Development of above normal language and intelligence 21 years after left hemispherectomy. *Neurology, 25,* 813–818. (p. 47)

Smith, D. (1982). Trends in counseling and psychotherapy. *American Psychologist, 37,* 802–809. (p. 480)

Smith, M. B. (1978). Psychology and values. *Journal of Social Issues, 34,* 181–199. (p. 434)

Smith, M. C. (1983). Hypnotic memory enhancement of witnesses: Does it work? *Psychological Bulletin, 94,* 387–407. (p. 205)

Smith, M. L., & Glass, G. V. (1977). Meta-analysis of psychotherapy outcome studies. *American Psychologist, 32,* 752–760. (p. 500)

Smith, M. L., Glass, G. V., & Miller, R. L. (1980). *The benefits of psychotherapy.* Baltimore: Johns Hopkins Press. (pp. 498–500)

Smith, P. B., & Tayeb, M. (1989). Organizational structure and processes. In M. Bond (Ed.), *The cross-cultural challenge to social psychology.* Newbury Park, CA: Sage. (p. 377)

Smith, T. W. (1990). Adult sexual behavior in 1989: Number of partners, frequency, and risk. General Social Survey Topic Report No. 18, National Opinion Research Center, University of Chicago. (pp. 361, 366, 398)

Smith, T. W., & Anderson, N. B. (1986). Models of personality and disease: An interactional approach to Type A behavior and cardiovascular risk. *Journal of Personality and Social Psychology, 50,* 1166–1173. (p. 520)

Snarey, J. (1987, June). A question of morality. *Psychology Today,* pp. 6–7. (p. 100)

Snarey, J. R. (1985). Cross-cultural universality of social-moral development: A critical review of Kohlbergian research. *Psychological Bulletin, 97,* 202–233. (p. 100)

Snodgrass, M. A. (1987). The relationships of differential loneliness, intimacy and characterological attributional style to duration of loneliness. *Journal of Social Behavior and Personality, 2,* 173–186. (p. 465)

Snodgrass, S. E., Higgins, J. G., & Todisco, L. (1986). The effects of walking behavior on mood. Paper presented at the American Psychological Association convention. (p. 392)

Snowden, R., & Christian, B. (1984). *Patterns and perceptions of menstruation.* New York: St. Martin's Press. (p. 526)

Snyder, M. (1984). When belief creates reality. In L. Berkowitz (Ed.), *Advances in experimental social psychology* (Vol. 18). New York: Academic Press. (p. 474)

Snyder, M., Tanke, E. D., & Berscheid, E. (1977). Social perception and interpersonal behavior: On the self-fulfilling nature of social stereotypes. *Journal of Personality and Social Psychology, 35,* 656–666. (p. 566)

Snyder, S. H. (1984). Neurosciences: An integrative discipline. *Science, 225,* 1255–1257. (pp. 30, 503)

Snyder, S. H. (1986). *Drugs and the brain.* New York: Scientific American Library. (p. 504)

Snyderman, M., & Rothman, S. (1987). Survey of expert opinion on intelligence and aptitude testing. *American Psychologist, 42,* 137–144. (p. 342)

Sobal, J., & Stunkard, A. J. (1989). Socioeconomic status and obesity: A review of the literature. *Psychological Bulletin, 105,* 260–275. (p. 539)

Sokoll, G. R., & Mynatt, C. R. (1984). *Arousal and free throw shooting.* Paper presented at the meeting of the Midwestern Psychological Association. (p. 385)

Solomon, M. (1987, December). Standard issue. *Psychology Today,* pp. 30–31. (p. 579)

Solomon, R. L. (1980). The opponent-process theory of acquired motivation: The costs of pleasure and the benefits of pain. *American Psychologist, 35,* 691–712. (p. 400)

Solomon, Z. (1990). Does the war end when the shooting stops? The psychological toll of war. *Journal of Applied Social Psychology, 20,* 1733–1745. (p. 515)

Sommer, B. (1991). Cognitive performance and the menstrual cycle. In J. T. Richardson (Ed.), *Cognition and the menstrual cycle: Research, theory, and culture.* New York: Springer-Verlag, in press. (p. 526)

Sommer, R. (1969). *Personal space.* Englewood Cliffs, NJ: Prentice-Hall. (p. 590)

Sontag, S. (1978). *Illness as metaphor.* New York: Farrar, Straus, & Giroux. (p. 523)

Sowell, T. (1991, May/June). Cultural diversity: A world view. *American Enterprise,* pp. 44–55. (p. 618)

Spanos, N. P. (1982). A social psychological approach to hypnotic behavior. In G. Weary & H. L. Mirels (Eds.), *Integrations of clinical and social psychology.* New York: Oxford. (p. 205)

Spanos, N. P. (1986a). Hypnotic behavior: A social-psychological interpretation of amnesia, analgesia, and "trance logic." *Brain and Behavioral Sciences, 9,* 449–502. (p. 208)

Spanos, N. P. (1986b). Hypnosis, nonvolitional responding, and multiple personality: A social psychological perspective. *Progress in Experimental Personality Research, 14,* 1–62. (p. 457)

Spanos, N. P. (1987-88). Past-life hypnotic regression: A critical view. *The Skeptical Inquirer, 12,* 174–180. (p. 206)

Spanos, N. P., Flynn, D. M., & Gabora, N. J. (1989). Suggested negative visual hallucinations in hypnotic subjects: When no means yes. *British Journal of Experimental and Clinical Hypnosis, 6,* 63–67. (p. 207)

Spanos, N. P., Radtke, L., & Bertrand, L. D. (1985). Hypnotic amnesia as a strategic enactment: Breaching amnesia in highly susceptible subjects. *Journal of Personality and Social Psychology, 47,* 1155–1169. (p. 203)

Spanos, N. P., Stenstrom, R. J., & Johnson, J. C. (1988). Hypnosis, placebo, and suggestion in the treatment of warts. *Psychosomatic Medicine, 50,* 245–260. (p. 207)

Spector, P. E. (1986). Perceived control by employees: A meta-analysis of studies concerning autonomy and participation at work. *Human Relations, 39,* 1005–1016. (p. 377)

Spence, J. T., & Helmreich, R. L. (1983). Achievement-related motives and behavior. In J. T. Spence (Ed.), *Achievement and achievement motives: Psychological and sociological approaches.* New York: Freeman. (p. 373)

Sperling, G. (1960). The information available in brief visual presentations. *Psychological Monographs, 74* (Whole No. 498). (p. 256)

Sperry, R. W. (1956, May). The eye and the brain. *Scientific American,* pp. 48–52. (p. 176)

Sperry, R. W. (1964). *Problems outstanding in the evolution of brain function.* James Arthur Lecture, American Museum of Natural History, New York. Cited by R. Ornstein (1977), *The psychology of consciousness* (2nd ed.). New York: Harcourt Brace Jovanovich. (p. 51)

Sperry, R. W. (1968). Hemisphere deconnection and unity in conscious awareness. *American Psychologist, 23,* 723–733. (p. 50)

Sperry, R. W. (1982). Some effects of disconnecting the cerebral hemispheres. *Science, 217,* 1223–1226. (p. 51)

Sperry, R. W. (1985). Changed concepts of brain and consciousness: Some value implications. *Zygon, 20,* 41–57. (pp. 143, 220)

Spiegel, D., Bloom, J. R., Kraemer, H. C., & Gottheil, E. (1989, October 14). Effect of psychosocial treatment on survival of patients with metastatic breast cancer. *The Lancet,* pp. 888–891. (p. 522)

Spielberger, C., & London, P. (1982). Rage boomerangs. *American Health, 1,* 52–56. (p. 520)

Spiess, W. F. J., Greer, J. H., & O'Donohue, W. T. (1984). Premature ejaculation: Investigation of factors in ejaculatory latency. *Journal of Abnormal Psychology, 93,* 242–245. (p. 365)

Spitzberg, B. H., & Hurt, H. T. (1987). The relationship of interpersonal competence and skill to reported loneliness across time. *Journal of Social Behavior and Personality, 2,* 157–172. (p. 465)

Spitzer, R. L. (1975). On pseudoscience in science, logic in remission, and psychiatric diagnosis: A critique of Rosenhan's "On being sane in insane places." *Journal of Abnormal Psychology, 84,* 442–452. (p. 474)

Spitzer, R. L., Gibbon, M., Skodol, A. E., Williams, J. B. W., & First, M. B. (1989). *DSM-III-R casebook.* Washington, DC: American Psychiatric Press. (p. 455)

Spradley, J. P., & Phillips, M. (1972). Culture and stress: A quantitative analysis. *American Anthropologist, 74,* 518–529. (p. 591)

Sprecher, S. (1989). The importance to males and females of physical attractiveness, earning potential, and expressiveness in initial attraction. *Sex Roles, 21,* 591–607. (p. 579)

Spring, B. (1988). Foods, brain and behavior: New links. *Harvard Medical School Mental Health Letter, 4*(7), 4–6. (p. 537)

Spring, B., Chiodo, J., & Bowen, D. J. (1987). Carbohydrates, tryptophan, and behavior: A methodological review. *Psychological Bulletin, 102,* 234–256. (p. 537)

Springer, S. P., & Deutsch, G. (1985). *Left brain, right brain.* San Francisco: Freeman. (p. 52)

Squire, L. (1990). Memory and brain systems. Invited address to the American Psychological Society convention. (pp. 270–271)

Squire, L. R. (1987). *Memory and brain.* New York: Oxford University Press. (p. 270)

Squire, S. (1987, November 22). Shock therapy's return to respectability. *The New York Times Magazine,* pp. 78–89. (pp. 269, 505)

Sroufe, L. A., Fox, N. E., & Pancake, V. R. (1983). Attachment and dependency in developmental perspective. *Child Development, 54,* 1615–1627. (p. 80)

Stattin, H., & Magnusson, D. (1990). *Pubertal maturation in female development.* Hillsdale, NJ: Erlbaum. (p. 97)

Staub, E. (1989). *The roots of evil: The psychological and cultural sources of genocide.* New York: Cambridge University Press. (p. 556)

Steele, C. (1990a, May). A conversation with Claude Steele. *APS Observer,* pp. 11–17. (pp. 341, 343)

Steele, C. (1990b). Protecting the self: Implications for social psychological theory and minority achievement. Address to the American Psychological Association meeting. (p. 569)

Steele, C. M., & Josephs, R. A. (1990). Alcohol myopia: Its prized and dangerous effects. *American Psychologist, 45,* 921–933. (p. 210)

Stein, J. A., Newcomb, M. D., & Bentler, P. M. (1986). Stability and change in personality: A longitudinal study from early adolescence to young adulthood. *Journal of Research In Personality, 20,* 276–291. (p. 125)

Steinberg, L. (1987, September). Bound to bicker. *Psychology Today,* pp. 36–39. (p. 104)

Steinem, G. (1988). Six great ideas that television is missing. In G. Comstock (Ed.), *Public communication and behavior.* New York: Academic Press. (p. 574)

Stellar, E. (1985). Hunger in animals and humans. Distinguished lecture to the Eastern Psychological Association convention. (p. 356)

Stengel, E. (1981). Suicide. In *The new encyclopaedia britannica, macropaedia* (Vol. 17, pp. 777–782). Chicago: Encyclopaedia Britannica. (p. 460)

Stephens, T. (1988). Physical activity and mental health in the United States and Canada: Evidence from four population surveys. *Preventive Medicine, 17,* 35–47. (p. 529)

Stern, M., & Karraker, K. H. (1989). Sex stereotyping of infants: A review of gender labeling studies. *Sex Roles, 20,* 501–522. (p. 181)

Sternberg, R. J. (1984). Testing intelligence without IQ tests. *Phi Delta Kappan, 65*(10), 694–698. (p. 331)

Sternberg, R. J. (1985). *Beyond IQ: A triarchic theory of human intelligence.* New York: Cambridge University Press. (p. 331)

Sternberg, R. J. (1986). A triangular theory of love. *Psychological Review, 93,* 119–135. (p. 582)

Sternberg, R. J. (1988). Applying cognitive theory to the testing and teaching of intelligence. *Applied Cognitive Psychology, 2,* 231–255. (p. 335)

Sternberg, R. J., & Grajek, S. (1984). The nature of love. *Journal of Personality and Social Psychology, 47,* 312–329. (p. 582)

Sternberg, R. J., & Lubart, T. I. (1991). An investment theory of creativity and its development. *Human Development, 34,* 1–31. (p. 335)

Sternberg, R. J., & Salter, W. (1982). Conceptions of intelligence. In R. J. Sternberg (Ed.), *Handbook of human intelligence.* New York: Cambridge University Press. (p. 328)

Sternberg, R. J., & Wagner, R. K. (1987). Tacit knowledge: An unspoken key to managerial success. (p. 330)

Sternberg, R. J., & Wagner, R. K. (Eds.). (1986). *Practical intelligence: Origins of competence in the everyday world.* New York: Cambridge University Press. (p. 330)

Stevenson, H. W., & Lee, S-Y. (1990). Contexts of achievement: A study of American, Chinese, and Japanese children. *Monographs of the Society for Research in Child Development, 55* (Serial No. 221, Nos. 1-2). (pp. 335, 341)

Stevenson, H. W., Lee, S. Y., & Stigler, J. W. (1986). Mathematics achievement of Chinese, Japanese, and American children. *Science, 231,* 693–699. (p. 342)

Stevenson, H. W., Lummis, M., Lee, S-Y., Stigler, J. W. (1990). Making the grade in mathematics: Elementary school mathematics in the United States, Taiwan, and Japan. Reston, VA: National Council of Teachers of Mathematics. (p. 342)

Stiles, D. A., Gibbons, J. L., & Schnellmann, J. D. G. (1990). Opposite-sex ideal in the U.S.A. and Mexico as perceived by young adolescents. *Journal of Cross-Cultural Psychology, 21,* 180–199. (p. 607)

Stiles, W. B., Shapiro, D. A., & Elliott, R. (1986). "Are all psychotherapies equivalent?" *American Psychologist, 41,* 165–180. (p. 500)

Stille, R. G., Malamuth, N., & Schallow, J. R. (1987). Prediction of rape proclivity by rape myth attitudes and hostility toward women. Paper presented at the American Psychological Association convention. (p. 572)

Stock, W. A., Okun, M. A., Haring, M. J., & Witter, R. A. (1983). Age and subjective well-being: A meta-analysis. In R. J. Light (Ed.), *Evaluation studies: Review annual* (Vol. 8). Beverly Hills, CA: Sage. (p. 121)

Stone, A. A., Cox, D. S., Valdimarsdottir, H., Jandor, L., & Neale, J. M. (1987). Evidence that secretory IgA antibody is associated with daily mood. *Journal of Personality and Social Psychology, 52,* 988–993. (p. 521)

Stone, A. A., & Neale, J. M. (1984). Effects of severe daily events on mood. *Journal of Personality and Social Psychology, 46,* 137–144. (p. 397)

Stone, J. (1989, September). Homer's greatest hits. *Discover,* pp. 78–84. (p. 266)

Stopes-Roe, M., & Cochrane, R. (1990). The child-rearing values of Asian and British parents and young people: An inter-ethnic and inter-generational comparison in the evaluation of Kohn's 13 qualities. *British Journal of Social Psychology, 29,* 149–160. (p. 86)

Storms, M. D. (1973). Videotape and the attribution process: Reversing actors' and observers' points of view. *Journal of Personality and Social Psychology, 27,* 165–175. (p. 553)

Storms, M. D. (1981). A theory of erotic orientation development. *Psychological Review, 88,* 340–353. (p. 368)

Storms, M. D. (1983). *Development of sexual orientation.* Washington, DC: Office of Social and Ethical Responsibility, American Psychological Association. (p. 367)

Storms, M. D., & Thomas, G. C. (1977). Reactions to physical closeness. *Journal of Personality and Social Psychology, 35,* 412–418. (p. 563)

Strack, F., Martin, L., & Stepper, S. (1988). Inhibiting and facilitating conditions of the human smile: A nonobtrusive test of the facial feedback hypothesis. *Journal of Personality and Social Psychology, 54,* 768–777. (p. 391)

Strack, S., & Coyne, J. C. (1983). Social confirmation of dysphoria: Shared and private reactions to depression. *Journal of Personality and Social Behavior, 44,* 798–806. (p. 464)

Stratton, G. M. (1896). Some preliminary experiments on vision without inversion of the retinal image. *Psychological Review, 3,* 611–617. (p. 176)

Straub, R. O., Seidenberg, M. S., Bever, T. G., & Terrace, H. S. (1979). Serial learning in the pigeon. *Journal of the Experimental Analysis of Behavior, 32,* 137–148. (p. 308)

Straus, M. A., & Gelles, R. J. (1980). *Behind closed doors: Violence in the American family.* New York: Anchor/Doubleday. (p. 241)

Strentz, H. (1986, January 1). Become a psychic and amaze your friends! *Atlanta Journal,* p. 15A. (p. 183)

Striegel-Moore, R. H., Silberstein, L. R., & Rodin, J. (1986). Toward an understanding of risk factors for bulimia. *American Psychologist, 41,* 246–263. (pp. 359–360)

Stringer, C. B. (1990, December). The emergence of modern humans. *Scientific American,* pp. 98–104. (p. 587)

Stroebe, W., Stroebe, M. S., & Domittner, G. (1988). Individual and situational differences in recovery from bereavement: A risk group identified. *Journal of Social Issues, 44,* 143–158. (p. 122)

Strube, M. J. (1987). A self-appraisal model of the Type A behavior pattern. In R. Hogan & W. H. Jones (Eds.), *Perspectives in personality: A research annual* (Vol. 2). Greenwich, CT: JAI Press. (p. 520)

Strupp, H. H. (1982). The outcome problem in psychotherapy: Contemporary perspectives. In J. H. Harvey & M. M. Parks (Eds.), *The master lecture series: Vol. 1. Psychotherapy research and behavior change.* Washington, DC: American Psychological Association. (p. 430)

Strupp, H. H. (1986). Psychotherapy: Research, practice, and public policy (How to avoid dead ends). *American Psychologist, 41,* 120–130. (p. 500)

Suddath, R. L., Christison, G. W., Torrey, E. F., Casanova, M. F., & Weinberger, D. R. (1990). Anatomical abnormalities in the brains of monozygotic twins discordant for schizophrenia. *New England Journal of Medicine, 322,* 789–794. (p. 468)

Sue, S., & Okazaki, S. (1990). Asian-American educational achievements: A phenomenon in search of an explanation. *American Psychologist, 45,* 913–920. (p. 343)

Suedfeld, P. (1980). *Restricted environmental stimulation: Research and clinical applications.* New York: Wiley. (p. 158)

Suedfeld, P., & Kristeller, J. L. (1982). Stimulus reduction as a technique in health psychology. *Health Psychology, 1,* 337–357. (p. 158)

Suedfeld, P., & Mocellin, J. S. P. (1987). The "sensed presence" in unusual environments. *Environment and Behavior, 19,* 33–52. (p. 219)

Suinn, R. M. (1986). *Seven steps to peak performance.* Toronto: Hogrefe. (p. 312)

Sulloway, F. J. (1990). Orthodoxy and innovation in science: The influence of birth order in a multivariate context. Paper delivered at the American Association for the Advancement of Science annual meeting. (p. 372)

Suls, J., & Wan, C. K. (1989). Effects of sensory and procedural information on coping with stressful medical procedures and pain: A meta-analysis. *Journal of Consulting and Clinical Psychology, 57,* 372–379. (p. 527)

Suls, J. M., & Tesch, F. (1978). Students' preferences for information about their test performance: A social comparison study. *Journal of Experimental Social Psychology, 8,* 189–197. (p. 401)

Sundstrom, E., De Meuse, K. P., & Futrell, D. (1990). Work teams: Applications and effectiveness. *American Psychologist, 45,* 120–133. (p. 378)

Suomi, S. J. (1983). Social development in rhesus monkeys: Consideration of individual differences. In A. Oliverio & M. Zappella (Eds.), *The behavior of human infants.* New York: Plenum Press. (p. 78)

Suomi, S. J. (1986). Anxiety-like disorders in young nonhuman primates. In R. Gettleman (Ed.), *Anxiety disorders of childhood.* New York: Guilford Press. (p. 454)

Suomi, S. J. (1987). Genetic and maternal contributions to individual differences in rhesus monkey biobehavioral development. In N. A. Krasnegor & others (Eds.), *Perinatal development: A psychobiological perspective.* Orlando, FL: Academic Press. (pp. 87, 415)

Suppes, P. Quoted by R. H. Ennis (1982). Children's ability to handle Piaget's propositional logic: A conceptual critique. In S. Modgil & C. Modgil (Eds.), *Jean Piaget: Consensus and controversy.* New York: Praeger. (p. 75)

Surgeon General. (1986). *The Surgeon General's workshop on pornography and public health*, June 22-24. Report prepared by E. P. Mulvey & J. L. Haugaard and released by Office of the Surgeon General on August 4, 1986. (p. 573)

Surgeon General. (1988). *The health consequences of smoking: Nicotine addiction*. Rockville, MD: U.S. Department of Health and Human Services. (p. 534)

Surgeon General. (1989). *Reducing the health consequences of smoking: 25 years of progress*. Rockville, MD: U.S. Department of Health and Human Services. (p. 534)

Swann, W. B., Jr., & Miller, L. C. (1982). Why never forgetting a face matters: Visual imagery and social memory. *Journal of Personality and Social Psychology, 43,* 475–480. (p. 261)

Sweeney, P. D., Anderson, K., & Bailey, S. (1986). Attributional style in depression: A meta-analytic review. *Journal of Personality and Social Psychology, 50,* 974–991. (p. 463)

Swerdlow, N. R., & Koob, G. F. (1987). Dopamine, schizophrenia, mania, and depression: Toward a unified hypothesis of cortico-stiato-pallido-thalamic function (with commentary). *Behavioral and Brain Sciences, 10,* 197–246. (p. 468)

Szasz, T. (1984). *The therapeutic state: Psychiatry in the mirror of current events*. Buffalo, NY: Prometheus. (p. 448)

Szasz, T. (1987). *Insanity: The idea and its consequences*. New York: Wiley. (p. 448)

Tajfel, H. (Ed.). (1982). *Social identity and intergroup relations*. New York: Cambridge University Press. (p. 612)

Tanner, J. M. (1978). *Fetus into man: Physical growth from conception to maturity*. Cambridge, MA: Harvard University Press. (p. 96)

Tart, C. T. (1983). *OpenMind, 1*(1), 6. (p. 184)

Tavris, C. (1982, November). Anger defused. *Psychology Today,* pp. 25–35. (p. 396)

Taylor, S. E. (1979). Hospital patient behavior: Reactance, helplessness, or control? *Journal of Social Issues, 35,* 156–184. (p. 526)

Taylor, S. E. (1987). The process and prospects of health psychology: Tasks of a maturing discipline. *Health Psychology, 6,* 73–87. (p. 534)

Taylor, S. E. (1989). *Positive illusions*. New York: Basic Books. (pp. 295, 431–432, 532)

Taylor, S. E., Lichtman, R. R., Wood, J. V., Bluming, A. Z., Dosik, G. M., & Leibowitz, R. L. (1984). Breast self-examination among diagnosed breast cancer patients. *Cancer, 54,* 2528–2532. (p. 527)

Taylor, S. P., & Leonard, K. E. (1983). Alcohol and human physical aggression. In R. Geen & E. Donnerstein (Eds.), *Aggression: Theoretical and empirical reviews* (Vol. 1). New York: Academic Press. (p. 569)

Teevan, R. C., & McGhee, P. E. (1972). Childhood development of fear of failure motivation. *Journal of Personality and Social Psychology, 21,* 345–348. (p. 371)

Terman, L. M. (1916). *The measurement of intelligence*. Boston: Houghton Mifflin. (p. 321)

Terrace, H. S. (1979, November). How Nim Chimpsky changed my mind. *Psychology Today,* pp. 65–76. (p. 309)

Tesser, A., Forehand, R., Brody, G., & Long, N. (1989). Conflict: The role of calm and angry parent-child discussion in adolescent adjustment. *Journal of Social and Clinical Psychology, 8,* 317–330. (p. 104)

Tetlock, P. E. (1988). Monitoring the integrative complexity of American and Soviet policy rhetoric: What can be learned? *Journal of Social Issues, 44,* 101–131. (p. 618)

Thatcher, R. W., Walker, R. A., & Giudice, S. (1987). Human cerebral hemispheres develop at different rates and ages. *Science, 236,* 1110–1113. (pp. 69, 123)

Thayer, R. E. (1987). Energy, tiredness, and tension effects of a sugar snack versus moderate exercise. *Journal of Personality and Social Psychology, 52,* 119–125. (p. 529)

Thoma, S. J. (1986). Estimating gender differences in the comprehension and preference of moral issues. *Developmental Review, 6,* 165–180. (p. 101)

Thomas, A., & Chess, S. (1986). The New York Longitudinal Study: From infancy to early adult life. In R. Plomin & J. Dunn (Eds.), *The study of temperament: Changes, continuities, and challenges*. Hillsdale, NJ: Erlbaum. (p. 124)

Thomas, G. V., & Blackman, D. (1991). Are animal experiments on the way out? *The Psychologist, 14,* 208–212. (p. 20)

Thomas, L. (1974). *The lives of a cell*. New York: Viking Press. (p. 155)

Thompson, C. P., Cowan, T., Frieman, J., Mahadevan, R. S., & Vogl, R. J. (1991). Rajan: A study of a memorist. *Journal of Memory and Language,* in press. (p. 266)

Thompson, J. K. (1986, April). Larger than life. *Psychology Today,* pp. 38–44. (p. 360)

Thompson, J. K., Jarvie, G. J., Lahey, B. B., & Cureton, K. J. (1982). Exercise and obesity: Etiology, physiology, and intervention. *Psychological Bulletin, 91,* 55–79. (p. 544)

Thompson, P. (1980). Margaret Thatcher: A new illusion. *Perception, 9,* 483–484. (p. 178)

Thompson, R. F. (1984). *The brain*. New York: Freeman. (p. 269)

Thorndike, A. L., & Hagen, E. P. (1977). Measurement and evaluation in psychology and education. New York: Macmillan. (p. 323)

Tifft, S. (1985, December 9). The virtue of openness. *Time,* p. 34. (p. 105)

Tiggemann, M., & Rothblum, E. D. (1988). Gender differences in social consequences of perceived overweight in the United States and Australia. *Sex Roles, 18,* 75–86. (p. 543)

Time. (1990, Fall issue on women). Asia: Discarding daughters. P. 40. (p. 612)

Timmer, S. G., Eccles, J., & O'Brien, K. (1985–1986, Winter). How families use time. *ISR Newsletter* (University of Michigan), pp. 3–4. (p. 83)

Tinbergen, N. (1951). *The study of instinct.* Oxford: Clarendon. (p. 353)

Tirrell, M. E. (1990). Personal communication. (p. 230)

Tolman, E. C., & Honzik, C. H. (1930). Introduction and removal of reward, and maze performance in rats. *University of California Publications in Psychology, 4,* 257–275. (p. 243)

Tolstoy, L. (1904). *My confessions.* Boston: Dana Estes. (p. 8)

Torrey, E. F. (1986). *Witchdoctors and psychiatrists.* New York: Harper & Row. (p. 501)

Torrey, E. F. (1988). *Nowhere to go: The tragic odyssey of the homeless mentally ill.* New York: Harper & Row. (p. 502)

Towler, G. (1986). From zero to one hundred: Coaction in a natural setting. *Perceptual and Motor Skills, 62,* 377–378. (p. 563)

Trafford, A. (1988, August 11). Why the beef? Psychotherapy gets bad rap in political campaigns. *Grand Rapids Press* (via *Washington Post*), p. A11. (p. 495)

Tramontana, M. G., Hooper, S. R., & Selzer, S. C. (1988). Research on the preschool prediction of later academic achievement: A review. *Developmental Review, 8,* 89–146. (p. 333)

Treisman, A. (1987). Properties, parts, and objects. In K. R. Boff, L. Kaufman, & J. P. Thomas (Eds.), *Handbook of perception and human performance.* New York: Wiley. (p. 166)

Triandis, H. C. (1981). Some dimensions of intercultural variation and their implications for interpersonal behavior. Paper presented at the American Psychological Association convention. (p. 590)

Triandis, H. C. (1989a). The self and social behavior in differing cultural contexts. *Psychological Review, 96,* 506–520. (pp. 591, 612)

Triandis, H. C. (1989b). Cross-cultural studies of individualism and collectivism. In J. J. Berman (Ed.), *Nebraska symposium on motivation 1989* (Vol. 37). Lincoln: University of Nebraska Press. (pp. 591–592)

Triandis, H. C., Bontempo, R., Villareal, M. J., Asai, M., & Lucca, N. (1988). Individualism and collectivism: Cross-cultural perspectives on self-ingroup relationships. *Journal of Personality and Social Psychology, 54,* 323–338. (p. 86)

Triandis, H. C., Brislin, R., & Hui, C. H. (1988). Cross-cultural training across the individualism-collectivism divide. *International Journal of Intercultural Relations, 12,* 269–289. (pp. 591, 593–594)

Triplett, N. (1898). The dynamogenic factors in pacemaking and competition. *American Journal of Psychology, 9,* 507–533. (p. 563)

Trolier, T. K., & Hamilton, D. L. (1986). Variables influencing judgments of correlational relations. *Journal of Personality and Social Psychology, 50,* 879–888. (p. 628)

Troll, L. E. (1987). Mother-daughter relationships through the life span. In S. Oskamp (Ed.), *Family processes and problems: A social psychological analysis.* Newbury Park, CA: Sage. (p. 101)

True, R. M. (1949). Experimental control in hypnotic age regression states. *Science, 110,* 583–584. (p. 206)

Tsang, Y. C. (1938). Hunger motivation in gastrectomized rats. *Journal of Comparative Psychology, 26,* 1–17. (p. 356)

Tsuang, M. T., & Faraone, S. V. (1990). *The genetics of mood disorders.* Baltimore, MD: Johns Hopkins University Press. (p. 462)

Tubbs, M. E. (1986). Goal setting: A meta-analytic examination of the empirical evidence. *Journal of Applied Psychology, 71,* 474–483. (p. 376)

Tucker, L. A. (1983). Muscular strength and mental health. *Journal of Personality and Social Psychology, 45,* 1355–1360. (p. 422)

Turek, F. W., & Losee-Olson, S. (1986). A benzodiazepine used in the treatment of insomnia phase-shifts in the mammalian circadian clock. *Nature, 321,* 167–168. (p. 192)

Turk, D. C., Meichenbaum, D. H., & Berman, W. H. (1979). Application of biofeedback for the regulation of pain: A critical review. *Psychological Bulletin, 86,* 1322–1338. (p. 530)

Turkington, C. (1987, August). Help for the worried well. *Psychology Today,* pp. 44–48. (p. 499)

Turnbull, C. (1961). *The forest people.* New York: Simon and Schuster. (p. 173)

Turnbull, W. W. (1986). *Student change, program change: Why SAT scores kept falling.* College Board Publications, Box 886, New York City 10101. (p. 325)

Turner, B. F. (1982). Sex-related differences in aging. In B. B. Wolman (Ed.), *Handbook of developmental psychology.* Englewood Cliffs, NJ: Prentice-Hall. (p. 609)

Turner, C. W., Hesse, B. W., & Peterson-Lewis, S. (1986). Naturalistic studies of the long-term effects of television violence. *Journal of Social Issues, 42*(3), 7–28. (p. 571)

Turner, J. C. (1987). *Rediscovering the social group: A self-categorization theory.* New York: Basil Blackwell. (p. 596)

Turner, S. E., & Bowen, W. G. (1990). The flight from the arts and sciences: Trends in degrees conferred. *Science, 250,* 517–521. (p. 607)

Tversky, A. (1985, June). Quoted by K. McKean, Decisions, decisions. *Discover,* pp. 22–31. (p. 292)

Tversky, A., & Gilovich, T. (1989a). The cold facts about the "hot hand" in basketball. *Chance: New Directions for Statistics and Computing, 2*(1), 16–21. (p. 632)

Tversky, A., & Gilovich, T. (1989b). The "hot hand": Statistical reality or cognitive illusion. *Chance: New Directions for Statistics and Computing, 2*(4), 31–34. (p. 632)

Tversky, A., & Kahneman, D. (1974). Judgment under uncertainty: Heuristics and biases. *Science, 185,* 1124–1131. (pp. 291, 630)

Tversky, A., & Kahneman, D. (1983). Extensional versus intuitive reasoning: The conjunction fallacy in probability judgment. *Psychological Review, 90,* 293–315. (p. 292)

Twiss, C., Tabb, S., & Crosby, F. (1989). Affirmative action and aggregate data: The importance of patterns in the perception of discrimination. In F. Blanchard & F. Crosby (Eds.), *Affirmative* *action: Social psychological perspectives.* New York: Springer-Verlag. (p. 628)

Ucros, C. G. (1989). Mood state-dependent memory: A meta-analysis. *Cognition and Emotion, 3,* 139–167. (p. 274)

Uhlenberg, P., & Eggebeen, D. (1986). The declining well-being of adolescents. *Public Interest, 82,* 25–38. (p. 105)

Ulrich, R. S. (1984). View through a window may influence recovery from surgery. *Science, 224,* 420–421. (p. 153)

Underwood, B. J. (1957). Interference and forgetting. *Psychological Review, 64,* 49–60. (p. 278)

United Nations. (1990). *Demographic yearbook.* New York: Department of Economic and Social Affairs, Statistical Office, United Nations. (p. 117)

U.S. Congress, Office of Technology Assessment. (1983, November). *Scientific validity of polygraph testing: A research review and evaluation—A technical memorandum,* p. 4. Washington, DC: U.S. Government Printing Office. (p. 387)

U.S. National Center for Health Statistics. (1990). *Vital and health statistics.* Series 10. (p. 111)

Valenstein, E. S. (1986). *Great and desperate cures: The rise and decline of psychosurgery.* New York: Basic Books. (pp. 39, 505)

Vallone, R. P., Griffin, D. W., Lin, S., & Ross, L. (1990). Overconfident prediction of future actions and outcomes by self and others. *Journal of Personality and Social Psychology, 58,* 582–592. (p. 295)

Vance, E. B., & Wagner, N. N. (1976). Written descriptions of orgasm: A study of sex differences. *Archives of Sexual Behavior, 5,* 87–98. (p. 362)

Van Dyke, C., & Byck, R. (1982, March). Cocaine. *Scientific American,* pp. 128–141. (p. 213)

van IJzendoorn, M. H., & Kroonenberg, P. M. (1988). Cross-cultural patterns of attachment: A meta-analysis of the strange situation. *Child Development, 59,* 147–156. (p. 78)

Van Leeuwen, M. S. (1978). A cross-cultural examination of psychological differentiation in males and females. *International Journal of Psychology, 13,* 87–122. (p. 606)

Van Leeuwen, M. S. (1982). IQism and the just society: Historical background. *Journal of the American Scientific Affiliation, 34,* 193–201. (p. 322)

VanTassel-Baska, J. (1983). Profiles of precocity: The 1982 Midwest Talent Search finalists. *Gifted Child Quarterly, 27,* 139–145. (p. 333)

Van Yperen, N. W., & Buunk, B. P. (1990). A longitudinal study of equity and satisfaction in intimate relationships. *European Journal of Social Psychology, 20,* 287–309. (p. 582)

Vaughn, K. B., & Lanzetta, J. T. (1981). The effect of modification of expressive displays on vicarious emotional arousal. *Journal of Experimental Social Psychology, 17,* 16–30. (p. 392)

Vaux, A. (1988). Social and personal factors in loneliness. *Journal of Social and Clinical Psychology, 6,* 462–471. (p. 465)

Vemer, E., Coleman, M., Ganong, L. H., & Cooper, H. (1989). Marital satisfaction in remarriage: A meta-analysis. *Journal of Marriage and the Family, 51,* 713–725. (p. 118)

Venn, J. (1986). Hypnosis and the Lamaze method: A reply to Wideman and Singer. *American Psychologist, 41,* 475–476. (p. 207)

Vernon, P. A. (1983). Speed of information processing and general intelligence. *Intelligence, 7,* 53–70. (p. 332)

Vernon, P. A. (Ed.). (1987). *Speed of information-processing and intelligence.* Norwood, NJ: Ablex. (p. 332)

Vetter, B. M. (1989, July 7). Manpower data need an overhaul. *AAAS Observer,* p. 10 (presents NSF estimate of 254,000 psychologists and Bureau of Labor Statistics estimate of 165,000). (p. 4)

Vokey, J. R., & Read, J. D. (1985). Subliminal messages: Between the devil and the media. *American Psychologist, 40,* 1231–1239. (p. 178)

von Frisch, K. (1950). *Bees: Their vision, chemical senses, and language.* Ithaca, NY: Cornell University Press. (p. 307)

von Frisch, K. (1974). Decoding the language of the bee. *Science, 185,* 663–668. (p. 307)

Wade, C. (1990). What psychology students need to know about human sexuality. Harry Kirke Wolfe Lecture, American Psychological Association convention. (p. 107)

Wagstaff, G. (1982). Attitudes to rape: The "just world" strikes again? *Bulletin of the British Psychological Society, 13,* 275–283. (p. 553)

Wakefield, J. C. (1987). The semantics of success: Do masturbation exercises lead to partner orgasm? *Journal of Sex and Marital Therapy, 13,* 3–14. (p. 365)

Waldrop, M. M. (1987). The workings of working memory. *Science, 237,* 1564–1567. (p. 263)

Waldrop, M. M. (1988). National Academy looks at computing's future. *Science, 241,* 1436. (pp. 300, 301)

Wallace, R. K., & Benson, H. (1972, February). The physiology of meditation. *Scientific American,* pp. 84–90. (p. 202)

Wallach, M. A., & Wallach, L. (1983). *Psychology's sanction for selfishness: The error of egoism in theory and therapy.* New York: Freeman. (p. 434)

Wallach, M. A., & Wallach, L. (1985, February). How psychology sanctions the cult of the self. *Washington Monthly,* pp. 46–56. (p. 434)

Wallbott, H. G. (1988). In and out of context: Influences of facial expression and context information on emotion attributions. *British Journal of Social Psychology, 27,* 357–369. (p. 179)

Wallis, C. (1983, June 6). Stress: Can we cope? *Time,* pp. 48–54. (pp. 512, 516)

Wallis, C. (1987, October 12). Back off, buddy: A new Hite report stirs up a furor over sex and love in the '80s. *Time*, pp. 68–73. (p. 12)

Wallis, C. (1989, December 4). Onward, women! *Time*, pp. 80–89. (p. 607)

Walster (Hatfield), E., Aronson, V., Abrahams, D., & Rottman, L. (1966). Importance of physical attractiveness in dating behavior. *Journal of Personality and Social Psychology, 4,* 508–516. (p. 579)

Ward, W. C., & Jenkins, H. M. (1965). The display of information and the judgment of contingency. *Canadian Journal of Psychology, 19,* 231–241. (p. 628)

Warm, J. S., & Dember, W. N. (1986, April). Awake at the switch. *Psychology Today*, pp. 46–53. (p. 133)

Warr, P., & Payne, R. (1982). Experiences of strain and pleasure among British adults. *Social Science and Medicine, 16,* 1691–1697. (p. 532)

Wason, P. C. (1960). On the failure to eliminate hypotheses in a conceptual task. *Quarterly Journal of Experimental Psychology, 12,* 129–140. (p. 288)

Wason, P. C. (1981). The importance of cognitive illusions. *The Behavioral and Brain Sciences, 4,* 356. (p. 288)

Wass, H., Christian, M., Myers, J., & Murphey, M. (1978–1979). Similarities and dissimilarities in attitudes toward death in a population of older persons. *Omega, 9,* 337–354. (p. 122)

Waterman, A. S. (1988). Identity status theory and Erikson's theory: Commonalities and differences. *Developmental Review, 8,* 185–208. (p. 103)

Watkins, J. G. (1984). The Bianchi (L. A. Hillside Strangler) case: Sociopath or multiple personality? *International Journal of Clinical and Experimental Hypnosis, 32,* 67–101. (p. 456)

Watson, D. (1989). Strangers' ratings of the five robust personality factors: Evidence of a surprising convergence with self-report. *Journal of Personality and Social Psychology, 57,* 120–128. (p. 423)

Watson, J. B. (1913). Psychology as the behaviorist views it. *Psychological Review, 20,* 158–177. (pp. 189, 228)

Watson, J. B. (1924). *Behaviorism*. New York: Norton. (p. 234)

Watson, J. B., & Rayner, R. (1920). Conditioned emotional reactions. *Journal of Experimental Psychology, 3,* 1–14. (p. 235)

Watson, R. I., Jr. (1973). Investigation into deindividuation using a cross-cultural survey technique. *Journal of Personality and Social Psychology, 25,* 342–345. (p. 564)

Weaver, J. B., Masland, J. L., & Zillmann, D. (1984). Effect of erotica on young men's aesthetic perception of their female sexual partners. *Perceptual and Motor Skills, 58,* 929–930. (p. 364)

Webb, W. B. (1982a). Sleep and biological rhythms. In W. B. Webb (Ed.), *Biological rhythms, sleep, and performance* (pp. 87–110). Chichester, England: Wiley. (p. 195)

Webb, W. B. (1982b). Sleep and dreaming. In *Encyclopedia of Science and Technology* (pp. 470–474). New York: McGraw-Hill. (p. 196)

Webb, W. B., & Campbell, S. S. (1983). Relationships in sleep characteristics of identical and fraternal twins. *Archives of General Psychiatry, 40,* 1093–1095. (p. 196)

Webb, W. G. (1979). Are short and long sleepers different? *Psychological Reports, 44,* 259–264. (p. 196)

Wechsler, D. (1972). "Hold" and "Don't Hold" tests. In S. M. Chown (Ed.), *Human aging*. New York: Penguin. (p. 114)

Weinberg, M. S., & Williams, C. (1974). *Male homosexuals: Their problems and adaptations*. New York: Oxford University Press. (p. 366)

Weinberg, R., Scarr, S., & Waldman, I. (1990). The Minnesota transracial adoption study: A follow-up of IQ test performance at adolescence. Paper presented at the American Psychological Society convention. (p. 343)

Weinberger, M., Hiner, S. L., & Tierney, W. M. (1987). In support of hassles as a measure of stress in predicting health outcomes. *Journal of Behavioral Medicine, 10,* 19–31. (p. 516)

Weiner, B. (1985). An attributional theory of achievement motivation and emotion. *Psychological Review, 92,* 548–573. (p. 406)

Weingartner, H., Rudorfer, M. V., Buchsbaum, M. S., & Linnoila, M. (1983). Effects of serotonin on memory impairments produced by ethanol. *Science, 221,* 472–473. (p. 269)

Weinstein, N. D. (1987). Unrealistic optimism about susceptibility to health problems: Conclusions from a community-wide sample. *Journal of Behavioral Medicine, 10,* 481–500. (p. 545)

Weiss, J. M. (1977). Psychological and behavioral influences on gastrointestinal lesions in animal models. In J. D. Maser & M. E. P. Seligman (Eds.), *Psychopathology: Experimental models*. San Francisco: Freeman. (p. 517)

Weissman, M. M. (1988). The epidemiology of anxiety disorders: Rates, risks and familial patterns. *Journal of Psychiatric Research, 22* (Suppl. 1), 99–114. (p. 451)

Weissman, M. M., Merikangas, K. R., Wickramaratne, P., Kidd, K. K., Prusoff, B. A., Leckman, J. F., & Pauls, D. L. (1986). Understanding the clinical heterogeneity of major depression using family data. *Archives of General Psychiatry, 43,* 430–434. (p. 461)

Weisz, J. R., Rothbaum, F. M., & Blackburn, T. C. (1984). Standing out and standing in: The psychology of control in America and Japan. *American Psychologist, 39,* 955–969. (p. 590)

Wells, B. L. (1986). Predictors of female nocturnal orgasms: A multivariate analysis. *Journal of Sex Research, 22,* 421–437. (p. 364)

Wells, C. (1983, March). Teaching the brain new tricks. *Esquire*, pp. 49–57. (p. 263)

Wells, G., & Murray, D. M. (1984). Eyewitness confidence. In G. L. Wells & E. F. Loftus (Eds.), *Eyewitness testimony: Psychological perspectives*. New York: Cambridge University Press. (p. 276)

Wells, G. L. (1981). Lay analyses of causal forces on behavior. In J. Harvey (Ed.), *Cognition, social behavior and the environment*. Hillsdale, NJ: Erlbaum. (p. 228)

Wender, P. H., Kety, S. S., Rosenthal, D., Schulsinger, F., Ortmann, J., & Lunde, I. (1986). Psychiatric disorders in the biological and adoptive families of adopted individuals with affective disorders. *Archives of General Psychiatry, 43,* 923–929. (p. 462)

Wener, R., Frazier, W., & Farbstein, J. (1987, June). Building better jails. *Psychology Today,* pp. 40–49. (p. 436)

Werker, J. F. (1989). Becoming a native listener. *American Scientist, 77,* 54–59. (pp. 303–304)

West, P. D. B., & Evans, E. F. (1990). Early detection of hearing damage in young listeners resulting from exposure to amplified music. *British Journal of Audiology, 24,* 89–103. (p. 148)

Westefeld, J. S., & Furr, S. R. (1987). Suicide and depression among college students. *Professional Psychology: Research and Practice, 18,* 119–123. (p. 460)

Wever, E. G. (1949). Theories of hearing. New York: Wiley. (p. 149)

WGBH. (1983, March 22). *Fat chance in a thin world.* Transcript of *Nova* PBS program. (Available from WGBH, 125 Western Avenue, Boston, MA 02134). (p. 542)

Wheeler, D. D., & Janis, I. L. (1980). *A practical guide for making decisions.* New York: Free Press. (p. 293)

Wheeler, L. (1986). My year in Hong Kong: Some observations about social behavior. Presidential address to Division 8, American Psychological Association convention. (p. 105)

Wheeler, L., Reis, H. T., & Bond, M. H. (1989). Collectivism-individualism in everyday social life: The middle kingdom and the melting pot. *Journal of Personality and Social Psychology, 57,* 79–86. (p. 592)

White, G. L., Fishbein, S., & Rutsein, J. (1981). Passionate love and the misattribution of arousal. *Journal of Personality and Social Psychology, 41,* 56–62. (p. 581)

White, G. L., & Kight, T. D. (1984). Misattribution of arousal and attraction: Effects of salience of explanations for arousal. *Journal of Experimental Social Psychology, 20,* 55–64. (p. 581)

White, K. M. (1983). Young adults and their parents: Individuation to mutuality. *New Directions for Child Development, 22,* 61–76. (p. 105)

White, L., & Edwards, J. (1990). Emptying the nest and parental well-being: An analysis of national panel data. *American Sociological Review, 55,* 235–242. (p. 119)

Whiten, A., & Byrne, R. W. (1988). Tactical deception in primates. *Behavioral and Brain Sciences, 11,* 233–244, 267–273. (p. 12)

Whiting, B. B., & Edwards, C. P. (1988). *Children of different worlds: The formation of social behavior.* Cambridge, MA: Harvard University Press. (p. 86)

Whitley, B. E., Jr. (1990). The relationships of heterosexuals' attributions for the causes of homosexuality to attitudes toward lesbians and gay men. *Personality and Social Psychology Bulletin, 16,* 369–377. (p. 368)

Whitley, B. E., Jr., & Schofield, J. W. (1986). A meta-analysis of research on adolescent contraceptive use. *Population and Environment, 8,* 173–203. (p. 106)

Whorf, B. L. (1956). Science and linguistics. In J. B. Carroll (Ed.), *Language, thought, and reality: Selected writings of Benjamin Lee Whorf.* Cambridge, MA: MIT Press. (p. 310)

Wickelgren, W. A. (1977). *Learning and memory.* Englewood Cliffs, NJ: Prentice-Hall. (p. 261)

Wicker, A. W. (1971). An examination of the "other variables" explanation of attitude-behavior inconsistency. *Journal of Personality and Social Psychology, 19,* 18–30. (p. 554)

Wickless, C., & Kirsch, I. (1989). Effects of verbal and experiential expectancy manipulations on hypnotic susceptibility. *Journal of Personality and Social Psychology, 57,* 762–768. (p. 204)

Widom, C. S. (1989a). Does violence beget violence? A critical examination of the literature. *Psychological Bulletin, 106,* 3–28. (p. 80)

Widom, C. S. (1989b). The cycle of violence. *Science, 244,* 160–166. (p. 80)

Wiens, A. N., & Menustik, C. E. (1983). Treatment outcome and patient characteristics in an aversion therapy program for alcoholism. *American Psychologist, 38,* 1089–1096. (p. 490)

Wiesel, T. N. (1982). Postnatal development of the visual cortex and the influence of environment. *Nature, 299,* 583–591. (p. 175)

Wigdor, A. K., & Garner, W. R. (1982). *Ability testing: Uses, consequences, and controversies.* Washington, DC: National Academy Press. (p. 345)

Wilder, D. A. (1981). Perceiving persons as a group: Categorization and intergroup relations. In D. L. Hamilton (Ed.), *Cognitive processes in stereotyping and intergroup behavior.* Hillsdale, NJ: Erlbaum. (p. 612)

Wilentz, A. (1987, March 23). Teen suicide: Two death pacts shake the country. *Time,* p. 12. (p. 461)

Will, G. (1989, December 12). Scary to consider horror fixation. *Grand Rapids Press* (Washington Post Writers Group), p. A17. (p. 21)

Williams, C. L. (1989). *Gender differences at work: Women and men in nontraditional occupations.* Berkeley: University of California Press. (p. 606)

Williams, C. L., & Berry, J. W. (1991). Primary prevention of acculturative stress among refugees. *American Psychologist, 46,* 632–641. (p. 514)

Williams, J. E., & Best, D. L. (1990). *Measuring sex stereotypes: A multination study.* Newbury Park, CA: Sage. (p. 601)

Williams, R. (1989). *The trusting heart: Great news about Type A behavior.* New York: Random House. (pp. 519–520)

Williams, R. L., Karacan, I., & Hursch, C. J. (1974). *Electroencephalography (EEG) of human sleep: Clinical applications.* New York: Wiley. (p. 199)

Williams, S. L. (1987). Self-efficacy and mastery-oriented treatment for severe phobias. Paper presented to the American Psychological Association convention. (p. 488).

Willmuth, M. E. (1987). Sexuality after spinal cord injury: A critical review. *Clinical Psychology Review, 7,* 389–412. (p. 364)

Wilson, E. O. (1978). *On human nature.* Cambridge, MA: Harvard University Press. (p. 577)

Wilson, J. P., Harel, Z., & Kahana, B. (1988). *Human adaptation to extreme stress: From the Holocaust to Vietnam.* New York: Plenum Press.

Wilson, J. Q., & Herrnstein, R. J. (1985). *Crime and human nature.* New York: Simon and Schuster. (p. 569)

Wilson, R. C., Gaft, J. G., Dienst, E. R., Wood, L., & Bavry, J. L. (1975). *College professors and their impact on students.* New York: Wiley. (p. 565)

Wilson, R. S. (1978). Synchronies in mental development: An epigenetic perspective. *Science, 202,* 939–948. (p. 69)

Wilson, R. S., & Matheny, A. P., Jr. (1986). Behavior-genetics research in infant temperament: The Louisville twin study. In R. Plomin & J. Dunn (Eds.), *The study of temperament: Changes, continuities, and challenges.* Hillsdale, NJ: Erlbaum. (p. 77)

Wilson, S. C., & Barber, T. X. (1983). The fantasy-prone personality: Implications for understanding imagery, hypnosis, and parapsychological phenomena. In A. A. Sheikh (Ed.), *Imagery: Current theory, research, and applications.* New York: Wiley. (pp. 201, 219)

Wilson, W. R. (1979). Feeling more than we can know: Exposure effects without learning. *Journal of Personality and Social Psychology, 37,* 811–821. (p. 190)

Windholz, G. (1989, April–June). The discovery of the principles of reinforcement, extinction, generalization, and differentiation of conditional reflexes in Pavlov's laboratories. *Pavlovian Journal of Biological Science, 26,* 64–74. (p. 231)

Wing, R. R., & Jeffrey, R. W. (1979). Outpatient treatments of obesity: A comparison of methodology and clinical results. *International Journal of Obesity, 3,* 261–279. (p. 542)

Wingert, P., & Kantrowitz, B. (1990, Winter/Spring). The day care generation. *Newsweek special edition: The 21st century family,* pp. 86–92. (p. 83)

Winkelstein, W., Jr., Samuel, M., Padian, N. S., & Wiley, J. A. (1987). Selected sexual practices of San Francisco heterosexual men and risk of infection by the human immunodeficiency virus. *Journal of the American Medical Association, 257,* 1470. (pp. 366–367)

Witelson, S. F. (1985). The brain connection: The corpus callosum is larger in left-handers. *Science, 229,* 665–667. (p. 52)

Woll, S. (1986). So many to choose from: Decision strategies in videodating. *Journal of Social and Personal Relationships, 3,* 43–52. (p. 579)

Wolpe, J. (1958). *Psychotherapy by reciprocal inhibition.* Stanford, CA: Stanford University Press. (p. 488)

Wolpe, J. (1982). *The practice of behavior therapy.* New York: Pergamon. (p. 488)

Wong, D. F., & associates. (1986). Positron emission tomography reveals elevated D2 dopamine receptors in drug-naive schizophrenics. *Science, 234,* 1588–1563. (p. 468)

Wong, M. M., & Csikszentmihalyi, M. (1991). Affiliation motivation and daily experience: Some issues on gender differences. *Journal of Personality and Social Psychology, 60,* 154–164. (p. 600)

Wood, C. J, & Aggleton, J. P. (1989). Handedness in 'fast ball' sports: Do left-handers have an innate advantage? *British Journal of Psychology, 80,* 227–240. (p. 52)

Wood, G. (1979). The knew-it-all-along effect. *Journal of Experimental Psychology: Human Perception and Performance, 4,* 345–353. (p. 21)

Wood, J. V., Saltzberg, J. A., & Goldsamt, L. A. (1990a). Does affect induce self-focused attention? *Journal of Personality and Social Psychology, 58,* 899–908. (p. 463)

Wood, J. V., Saltzberg, J. A., Neale, J. M., Stone, A. A., & Rachmiel, T. B. (1990b). Self-focused attention, coping responses, and distressed mood in everyday life. *Journal of Personality and Social Psychology, 58,* 1027–1036. (p. 463)

Wood, W. (1987). Meta-analytic review of sex differences in group performance. *Psychological Bulletin, 102,* 53–71. (p. 601)

Wood, W., Wong, F. Y., & Chachere, J. G. (1991). Effects of media violence on viewers' aggression in unconstrained social interaction. *Psychological Bulletin, 109,* 371–383. (p. 571)

Woodruff-Pak, D. S. (1989). Aging and intelligence: Changing perspectives in the twentieth century. *Journal of Aging Studies, 3,* 91–118. (p. 114)

Woods, N. F., Dery, G. K., & Most, A. (1983). Recollections of menarche, current menstrual attitudes, and premenstrual symptoms. In S. Golub (Ed.), *Menarche: The transition from girl to woman.* Lexington, MA: Lexington Books. (p. 97)

Wooley, S., & Wooley, O. (1983). Should obesity be treated at all? *Psychiatric Annals, 13(11),* 884–885, 888. (p. 359)

World Health Organization. (1979). *Schizophrenia: An international follow-up study.* Chichester, England: Wiley. (p. 468)

Worobey, J., & Blajda, V. M. (1989). Temperament ratings at 2 weeks, 2 months, and 1 year: Differential stability of activity and emotionality. *Developmental Psychology, 25,* 257–263. (p. 77)

Worthington, E. L., Jr. (1989). Religious faith across the life span: Implications for counseling and research. *The Counseling Psychologist, 17,* 555–612. (p. 99)

Worthington, E. L., Jr., Martin, G. A., Shumate, M., & Carpenter, J. (1983). The effect of brief Lamaze training and social encouragement on pain endurance in a cold pressor tank. *Journal of Applied Social Psychology, 13,* 223–233. (p. 153)

Wortman, C. B., & Silver, R. C. (1989). The myths of coping with loss. *Journal of Consulting and Clinical Psychology, 57,* 349–357. (p. 122)

Wu, T-C., Tashkin, D. P., Djahed, B., & Rose, J. E. (1988). Pulmonary hazards of smoking marijuana as compared with tobacco. *New England Journal of Medicine, 318,* 347–351. (p. 216)

Wysocki, C. J., & Gilbert, A. N. (1989). National Geographic survey: Effects of age are heterogeneous. *Annals of the New York Academy of Sciences, 561,* 12–28. (p. 155)

Yalom, I. D. (1985). *The theory and practice of group psychotherapy* (3rd ed.). New York: Basic Books. (p. 486)

Yang, K., & Bond, M. H. (1990). Exploring implicit personality theories with indigenous or imported constructs: The Chinese case. *Journal of Personality and Social Psychology, 58,* 1087–1095. (p. 423)

Yang, N., & Linz, D. (1990). Movie ratings and the content of adult videos: The sex-violence ratio. *Journal of Communication, 40*(2), 28–42. (p. 572)

Yarnell, P. R., & Lunch, S. (1970, April 25). Retrograde memory immediately after concussion. *Lancet,* pp. 863–865. (p. 268)

Yarrow, L. J., Goodwin, M. S., Manheimer, H., & Milowe, I. D. (1973). Infancy experience and cognitive and personality development at ten years. In L. J. Stone, H. T. Smith, & L. B. Murphy (Eds.), *The competent infant.* New York: Basic Books. (p. 76)

Yates, A. (1989). Current perspectives on the eating disorders: I. History, psychological and biological aspects. *Journal of the American Academy of Child and Adolescent Psychiatry, 28,* 813–828. (p. 359)

Yates, A. (1990). Current perspectives on the eating disorders: II. Treatment, outcome, and research directions. *Journal of the American Academy of Child and Adolescent Psychiatry, 29,* 1–9. (p. 359)

Zacks, R. T., & Hasher, L. (1988). Capacity theory and the processing of inferences. In L. Light & D. Burke (Eds.), *Language, memory, and aging.* New York: Cambridge University Press. (p. 112)

Zajonc, R. B. (1965). Social facilitation. *Science, 149,* 269–274. (p. 563)

Zajonc, R. B. (1980). Feeling and thinking: Preferences need no inferences. *American Psychologist, 35,* 151–175. (p. 405)

Zajonc, R. B. (1984a). On the primacy of affect. *American Psychologist, 39,* 117–123. (p. 405)

Zajonc, R. B. (1984b, July 22). Quoted by D. Goleman, Rethinking IQ tests and their value. *The New York Times,* p. D22. (p. 320)

Zajonc, R. B., & Markus, G. B. (1975). Birth order and intellectual development. *Psychological Review, 82,* 74–88. (p. 634)

Zanna, M. P., & Pack, S. J. (1975). On the self-fulfilling nature of apparent sex differences in behavior. *Journal of Experimental Social Psychology, 11,* 583–591. (p. 605)

Zebrowitz-McArthur, L. (1988). Person perception in cross-cultural perspective. In M. H. Bond (Ed.), *The cross-cultural challenge to social psychology.* Newbury Park, CA: Sage. (p. 593)

Zeidner, M. (1990). Perceptions of ethnic group modal intelligence: Reflections of cultural stereotypes or intelligence test scores? *Journal of Cross-Cultural Psychology, 21,* 214–231. (p. 341)

Zelnick, M., & Kim, Y. J. (1982). Sex education and its association with teenage sexual activity, pregnancy, and contraceptive use. *Family Planning Perspectives, 14*(3), 117–126. (p. 369)

Zigler, E. F. (1986, February). Quoted in D. Meredith, Day care: The nine-to-five dilemma. *Psychology Today,* pp. 36–39, 42–44. (p. 83)

Zigler, E. F. (1987). Formal schooling for four-year-olds? No. *American Psychologist, 42,* 254–260. (p. 340)

Zigler, E. F. (1990). Letter. *Science, 248,* 1176. (p. 340)

Zigler, E. F., & Frank, M. (1988). *The parental leave crisis: Toward a national policy.* New Haven: Yale University Press. (p. 83)

Zilbergeld, B. (1983). *The shrinking of America: Myths of psychological change.* Boston: Little, Brown. (pp. 497, 499)

Zillmann, D. (1986). Effects of prolonged consumption of pornography. Background paper for *The Surgeon General's workshop on pornography and public health,* June 22–24. Report prepared by E. P. Mulvey & J. L. Haugaard and released by Office of the Surgeon General on August 4, 1986. (pp. 385, 405)

Zillmann, D. (1989). Effects of prolonged consumption of pornography. In D. Zillmann & J. Bryant (Eds.), *Pornography: Research advances and policy considerations.* Hillsdale, NJ: Erlbaum. (pp. 364, 572)

Zillmann, D., & Bryant, J. (1984). Effects of massive exposure to pornography. In N. Malamuth & E. Donnerstein (Eds.), *Pornography and sexual aggression.* Orlando, FL: Academic Press. (p. 572)

Zimbardo, P. G. (1970). The human choice: Individuation, reason, and order versus deindividuation, impulse, and chaos. In W. J. Arnold & D. Levine (Eds.), *Nebraska Symposium on Motivation, 1969.* Lincoln: University of Nebraska Press. (p. 564)

Zimbardo, P. G. (1972, April). Pathology of imprisonment. *Transaction/Society,* pp. 4–8. (p. 557)

Zuckerman, M. (1990). Some dubious premises in research and theory on racial differences: Scientific, social, and ethical issues. *American Psychologist, 45,* 1297–1303. (p. 595)

Illustration Credits

Parenthood Federation of America, Inc.   **Fig. 4–7** Adapted from Insel, P. M., & Roth, W. T. (1976). *Health in a changing society,* p. 98. Mountain View, CA: Mayfield.   **p. 109** © Focus on Sports   **Fig. 4–8** Data from Bureau of the Census (1990). Statistical Abstract of the U. S. Washington, DC: Superintendent of Documents, U. S. Government Printing Office.   **p. 110** Adapted from Doty, R. L., et al. (1984). Smell identification ability: Changes with age.   *Science, 226,* 1441–1443. Copyright © 1984 by the American Association for the Advancement of Science.   **p. 111** © David Wells/The Image Works   **Fig. 4–9** From Jorm, A. F., Korten, A. E., & Henderson, A. S. (1987). The prevalence of dementia: A quantitative integration of the literature. *Acta Psychiatrica Scandinivica, 76,* 465–479.   **Fig. 4–10** From Schonfield, D., & Robertson, B. A. (1966). Memory storage and aging. *Canadian Journal of Psychology, 20,* 228–236. Copyright © 1966 Canadian Psychological Association.   **Fig. 4–11** Data from Crook, P. H., & West, R. L. (1990). Name and recall performance across the adult life-span. *British Journal of Psychology, 81,* 335–349.   **Fig. 4–12** From Geiwitz, J. (1980). *Psychology: Looking at ourselves.* Boston: Little, Brown, & Co. **Fig. 4–13** From Schaie, K. W., & Strother, C. R. (1968). A cross-sequential study of age changes in cognitive behavior. *Psychological Bulletin, 70,* 671–680. Copyright © 1968 by the American Psychological Association. Reprinted by permission of the author.   **Fig. 4–14** Adapted from Kaufman, A. S., Reynolds, C. R. & McLean, J. E. (1989). Age and WAIS-R intelligence in a national sample of adults in the 20- to 74-year age range: A cross-sectional analysis with educational level controlled. *Intelligence, 13,* 235–253.   **p. 116** © Sarah Putnam/NYT Pictures   **Fig. 4–15** From McCrae, R. R., & Costa, P. T., Jr. (1990). *Personality in adulthood.* New York: Guilford.   **p. 117** © Joe McNally   **p. 118** © Greg Smith/Stock Boston   **p. 119** (*left*) © Bob Daemmrich/The Image Works; (*top right*) © Joe McNally; (*bottom right*) © Charles Harbutt/Actuality   **Fig. 4–16** Data from Ingelhart, R. (1990). *Culture shift in advanced industrial society.* Princeton, NJ: Princeton University Press.   **p. 121** © Charles Harbutt/Actuality   **p. 122** AP/Wide World Photos   **Fig. 4–17** Adapted from Eron, L., & Huesman, R. (1984). The control of aggressive behavior by changes in attitudes, values, and the conditions of learning. In R. J. Blanchard & C. Blanchard (Eds.), *Advances in the study of aggression* (Vol. I). Orlando, FL: Academic Press.   **p. 125** © Jim Richardson/WestLight

Chapter 5

Opener © Gerald Brimacombe/The Image Bank   **p. 132** Detail "The Forest Has Eyes" by Bev Doolittle © The Greenwich Workshop, Inc., Trumbull, CT   **p. 133** (*both*) © Thomas Eisner   **p. 135** © Marcia Weinstein   **p. 136** © Jeffrey Cardenas/Sygma   **p. 140** © E. R. Lewis   **Fig. 5–9** Adapted from Frisby, J. P. (1980). *Seeing: Illusion, brain and mind* (p. 157). New York: Oxford University Press. Reprinted by permission of the publisher.   **Fig. 5–10** Fritz Goro, LIFE Magazine © 1971 Time Warner Inc.   **Fig. 5–12** Fritz Goro, LIFE Magazine © 1944 Time Warner, Inc.   **Fig. 5–15** Josef Albers, Interaction of Color. From Albers, J. (1975). *The interaction of color* (revised pocket edition) (Plate VI-3). New Haven: Yale University Press. Photo courtesy of the Josef Albers Foundation   **p. 146** © Lennart Nilsson, from BEHOLD MAN, Little, Brown and Company. Photo courtesy Bonnier Fakta   **p. 148** © Larry Busacca/Retna Ltd.   **p. 149** © Stan Schroeder/Animals Animals   **Fig. 5–18** From Wever, E. G. (1949). *Theory of hearing.* New York: Wiley.   **p. 150** © Jill Levine   **p. 151** © James Carroll   **p. 153** Community News, Christchurch, New Zealand. Photo courtesy *The Skeptical Inquirer.*   **Fig. 5–22** From Wysocki, C. J., & Gilbert, A. N. (1989). In C. Murphy & W. S. Cain (Eds.), *Proceedings of the conference on nutrition and the chemical senses in aging* (Annals of the New York Academy of Sciences). New York: New York Academy of Sciences. **p. 157** (*top*) © Addison Geary/Stock Boston; (*bottom*) © J. Chenet 1989/Woodfin Camp & Associates

Chapter 6

Opener © Jake Rajs/The Image Bank   **p. 164** (*top, both*) Photos by S. Schwartzenberg, © The Exploratorium; (*middle*) © Rick Friedman 1987/Black Star; (*bottom, both*) Photos courtesy Helen E. Ross from

Ross, H. E. (1975), Mist, murk and visual perception. *New Scientist, 66,* 658–660.   **Fig. 6–1** From Bradley, D. R., et al. (1976). Reply to Cavonius. *Nature, 261,* 78. Copyright © 1976 by Macmillan Journals Limited. Reprinted by permission from *Nature.*   **Fig. 6–2** From MIND SIGHTS by Roger N. Shepard. Copyright © 1990 by Roger N. Shepard. Reprinted with permission by W. H. Freeman and Company. **Fig. 6–4** (*left*) © Enrico Ferorelli   **p. 168** (*left*) © Dave Burnett/Photo Researchers; (*right*) © Ron Watts/Black Star   **p. 169** © David de Lossy/The Image Bank   **p. 170** (*top*) © Rainer Grosskopf/Tony Stone/Worldwide/Chicago Ltd.; (*center*) From "Perceiving Shape from Shading" by Vilayanur S. Ramachandran. Copyright © 1988 by Scientific American, Inc., George V. Kelvin. All rights reserved.   **Fig. 6–5** © City Art Gallery, Bristol/ The Bridgeman Art Library, Superstock.   **p. 171** From Shepard, R. N. (1981). Psychophysical. In M. Kubovy & J. R. Pomerantz (Eds.), *Perceptual organization* (pp. 279–341). Hillsdale, NJ: Lawrence Erlbaum. Copyright © 1981 by Lawrence Erlbaum Associates.   **Fig. 6–7**(*a*) From MIND SIGHTS by Roger N. Shepard. Copyright © 1990 by Roger N. Shepard. Reprinted with permission by W. H. Freeman and Company; (*b*) © Alan Choisnet/The Image Bank   **Fig. 6–8** From Day, R. H. (1984). The nature of perceptual illusions. *Interdisciplinary Science Reviews, 9,* 47–58.   **Fig. 6–9** Photo by S. Schwartzenberg © The Exploratorium   **p. 175** © Michael Hayman/Stock Boston   **Fig. 6–11** From Blakemore, C. R., & Cooper, G. F. (1970) Development of the brain depends on the visual environment. *Nature, 228,* 447–448. Copyright © 1970 by Macmillan Journals Limited. Reprinted by permission from *Nature.*   **p. 176** Courtesy Hubert Dolezal   **Fig. 6–12** From MIND SIGHTS by Roger N. Shepard. Copyright © 1990 by Roger N. Shepard. Reprinted with permission by W. H. Freeman and Company.   **Fig. 6–13** © Frank Searle, photo supplied by Steuart Campbell   **Fig. 6–15** Courtesy Dr. Peter Thompson, University of York   **Fig. 6–16** From MIND SIGHTS by Roger N. Shepard. Copyright © 1990 by Roger N. Shepard. Reprinted with permission by W. H. Freeman and Company.   **p. 179** Adapted from Gregory, R. L., & Gombrich, E. H. (Eds.). (1974). *Illusion in nature and art.* New York: Charles Scribner's Sons. Copyright © 1973 by C. Blakemore, J. D. Deregowski, E. H. Gombrich, R. L. Gregory, H. P. Hinton, & R. Primrose. Reprinted by permission of Charles Scribner's Sons.   **p. 180** (*a & b*) From Donald A. Norman, THE PSYCHOLOGY OF EVERYDAY THINGS. Reprinted with permission of Basic Books, Inc., a division of Harper Collins Publishers.   **Fig. 6–18** From Kraft, C. (1978). A psychophysical approach to air safety: Simulator studies of visual illusions in night approaches. In H. L. Pick, H. W. Leibowitz, J. E. Singer, A. Steinschneider, & H. W. Stevenson (Eds.), *Psychology: From research to practice.* New York: Plenum Press.   **p. 181** © Erika Stone

Chapter 7

Opener © Gilles Guittard/The Image Bank   **p. 189** © Will and Deni McIntyre/Photo Researchers   **p. 190** © Ellis Herwig/Stock Boston **Fig. 7–1** From Neisser, U. (1979). The control of information pickup in selective looking. In A. D. Pick (Ed.), *Perception and its development: A tribute to Eleanor J. Gibson.* Hillsdale, NJ: Lawrence Erlbaum. Copyright © 1979 by Lawrence Erlbaum Associates, Inc.   **p. 191** © R. Nowitz/Phototake   **Figs. 7–2 & Fig. 7–3** From Dement, W. (1978). *Some must watch while some must sleep.* Stanford, CA: Portable Stanford Book Series, 1972. Reprinted by permission of the Stanford Alumni Association, Stanford University.   **Fig. 7–4** From Cartwright, R. D. (1978). A primer on sleep and dreaming (Fig. 1–6). Reading, MA: Addison-Wesley. Reprinted by permission.   **p. 194** © Susan Copen Oken   **p. 196** © Janny Sauvanet 1989/Photo Researchers   **p. 197** © Peter Menzel/Stock Boston   **Fig. 7–5** From Hartmann, E. (1984). *The nightmare: The psychology and biology of terrifying dreams.* Copyright © 1984 by Ernest Hartmann. Reprinted by permission of Basic Books, Inc., Publishers.   **p. 198** National Gallery of Art, Washington, Rosenwald Collection   **Fig. 7–6** Adapted from Williams, R. L., Karacan, I., & Hursch, C. J. (1974). *Electroencephalography (EEG) of human sleep: Clinical applications.* New York: Wiley   **p. 201** André Derain, *La Tasse de Thé,* 1935. Musee National d'Art Moderne, Paris.

SEF/Art Resource **p. 202** © Larry Kolvoord/The Image Works **p. 204** © Mimi Forsyth/Monkmeyer Press Photo Service **p. 207** © Joel Gordon 1990 **p. 209** Courtesy News and Publications Service, Stanford University **p. 211** Courtesy MADD, Minnesota State Office **Fig. 7–8** (*left*) From Julien, R, M. (1988). *A primer of drug action* (5th ed.). New York: Freeman; (*right*) © Eugene Richards/Magnum Photos **Fig. 7–9** © Ronald K. Siegel **Fig. 7–10** From Johnston, L. D., O'Malley, P. M., & Bachman, J. G. (1991). Drug use among American high school seniors, college students and young adults, 1975–1990: Volume 1. [Dhhs Pub. No. (ADM) 91-1813.] Washington, DC: GPO.

Chapter 8

Opener © Bob Daemmrich/Stock Boston **p. 228** © Lawrence Migdale 1987/Stock Boston **p. 229** © Sovfoto **Fig. 8–1** Adapted from Goodwin, C. J. (1991). Misportraying Pavlov's apparatus. *American Journal of Psychology, 104,* 135–141. **Fig 8–4** Data from I. P. Pavlov (1927). In G. P. Anrep (Trans.), *Conditioned reflexes* (p. 185). London: Oxford University Press. Reprinted by permission of the publisher. **p. 233** © James Balog/Black Star **p. 234** Brown Brothers **p. 236** AP/Wide World Photos **Fig. 8–5** © Richard Wood/The Picture Cube **p. 237** © Fred Bavendam/Peter Arnold, Inc. **p. 238** © Bob Daemmrich **p. 239** © Jack Prelutsky/Stock Boston **Fig. 8–6** Adapted from "Teaching machines" by B. F. Skinner. Copyright © 1961 Scientific American, Inc. All rights reserved. **p. 242** © Joan Liftin/Actuality **Fig. 8–7** From Tolman, E. C., & Honzik, C. H. (1930). Introduction and removal of reward, and maze performance in rats. *University of California Publications in Psychology, 4,* 257–275. Reprinted by permission of the University of California Press. **p. 244** (*top*) Courtesy Animal Behavior Enterprises; (*bottom*) © Joe McNally **p. 247** Courtesy News and Publications Service, Stanford University **p. 248** (*top*) From Meltzoff, A. N. (1988). Imitation of televised models by infants. *Child Development, 59,* 1221–1229. Photos courtesy A. N. Meltzoff and M. Hanak; (*bottom*) © Bob Daemmrich/The Image Works

Chapter 9

Opener © Mike Clemer/TIME Magazine **p. 255** © Fred Ward/Black Star **p. 258** (*left*) © Erika Stone; (*right*) © Bob Daemmrich/Stock Boston **Fig. 9–3** From Peterson, L. R., & Peterson, M. J. (1959). Short-term retention of individual verbal items. *Journal of Experimental Psychology, 58,* 193–198. Copyright © 1959 by the American Psychological Association. Reprinted by permission of the authors. **Fig. 9–4** Data from H. Ebbinghaus, 1885. Graph from Baddeley, A. D. (1982). *Your memory: A user's guide.* New York: Macmillan. Copyright © 1982 by Macmillan Publishing Co., Inc. Reprinted by permission. **Fig. 9–5** From Craik, F. I. M., & Watkins, M. J. (1973). The role of rehearsal in short-term memory. *Journal of Verbal Learning and Verbal Behavior, 12,* 599–607. **Fig. 9–6** From Craik, F. I. M., & Tulving, E. (1975). Depth of processing and the retention of words in episodic memory. *Journal of Experimental Psychology: General, 104,* 268–294. Copyright © 1975 by the American Psychological Association. Reprinted by permission of the authors. **Fig. 9–7** AP/Wide World Photos **Fig. 9–11** From Nickerson, R. S., & Adams, M. J. (1979). Long-term for a common object. *Cognitive Psychology, 11,* 287–307. **Fig. 9–12** Adapted from Ebbinghaus, E. (1885). Über das Gedächtnis. Leipzig: Dunker. Cited in R. Klatzky (1980). *Human memory: Structures and processes.* Copyright © 1980 by W. H. Freeman and Company. All rights reserved. **Fig. 9–13** Adapted from Bahrick, H. P. (1984). Semantic memory content in permastore: 50 years of memory for Spanish learned in school. *Journal of Experimental Psychology: General, 113,* 1–29. **p. 269** © Lynn Johnson 1986/Black Star **Fig. 9–15** © George Goodwin/Monkmeyer Press Photo Service **p. 272** (*both*) Seth Poppel/Yearbook Archives **Fig. 9–16** Adapted from Bower, G. H. (1986). Prime time in cognitive psychology. In P. Eelen (Ed.), *Cognitive research and behavior therapy: Beyond the conditioning paradigm.* Amsterdam: North Holland Publishers. **Fig. 9–17** Adapted from Godden, D. R., & Baddeley, A. D. (1975). Context-dependent memory in two natural environments: On land and under water. *British Journal of Psychology, 66,* 325–331. **Fig. 9–18** (*both*) Courtesy

Carolyn Rovee-Collier, Rutgers University **Fig. 9–19** From Loftus, E. F. (1979). The malleability of human memory. *American Scientist, 67,* 313–320. Reprinted with permission of *American Scientist,* Journal of Sigma XI. **Fig. 9–20** From Jenkins, J. G., & Dallenbach, K. M. (1924). Obliviscence during sleep and waking. *American Journal of Psychology, 35,* 605–612. Copyright © 1924 by the Board of Trustees and the University of Illinois. **p. 280** © Shahn Kermani/Gamma Liaison **p. 281** © Hugh Rogers/Monkmeyer Press Photo Service

Chapter 10

Opener © Peter Turnley 1990/Black Star **p. 287** (*top*) © Hans Reinhard/Okapia, Photo Researchers; (*bottom*) © Zig Leszczynski/ Animals Animals **Fig. 10–1** Based on illustration by Vichai Makilul modified by Richard Swartz in Rumbaugh, D. M., & Savage-Rumbaugh, S. (1986). Reasoning and language in chimpanzees. In R. J. Hoage & L. Goldman (Eds.), *Animal intelligence.* Washington, DC: Smithsonian Institution Press. **Fig. 10–3** Adapted from Luchins, A. S. (1946). Classroom experiments on mental set. *American Journal of Psychology, 59,* 295–298. Copyright © 1946 by the Board of Trustees of the University of Illinois. Reprinted by permission of the University of Illinois Press. **Fig. 10–4** From Duncker, K. (1945). On problem solving. *Psychological Monographs, 58* (Whole no. 270). (pp. 289–291). **Fig. 10–6** Adapted from Luchins, A. S. (1946). Classroom experiments on mental set. *American Journal of Psychology, 59,* 295–298. Copyright © 1946 by the Board of Trustees of Illinois University. Reprinted by permission of the University of Illinois Press. **Fig. 10–7** From Duncker, K. (1945). On problem solving. *Psychological Monographs, 58* (Whole no. 270). **p. 294** © Chip Peterson/Sygma **p. 298** © Stanley Rowin 1988/The Picture Cube **p. 301** (*top*) Courtesy of IMEC and University of Pennsylvania-EE; (*bottom*) © M. & E. Bernheim/ Woodfin Camp & Associates **p. 303** © Erika Stone **Fig. 10–8** Adapted from Werker, J. F. (1989). Becoming a native listener. *American Scientist, 77,* 54–59. Photos courtesy Professor Peter McLeod, Acadia University. **Fig. 10–9** From Johnson, J. S., & Newport, E. L. (1989). Critical period effects in second language learning: The influence of maturational state on the acquisition of English as a second language. *Cognitive Psychology, 21,* 60–99. **p. 306** © George Ancona 1989 from The Handtalk Zoo, by George Ancona and Mary Beth **Fig. 10–10** From von Frisch, K. (1974). Decoding the language of the bee. *Science, 185,* 663–668. Copyright © The Nobel Foundation 1974. **p. 308** (*top left*) © Paul Fusco/Magnum Photos; (*bottom right*) © Language Research Center, Yerkes Regional Primate Research Center **Fig. 10–11** © Language Research Center, Yerkes Regional Primate Research Center **p. 312** © Elizabeth Crews/The Image Works

Chapter 11

Opener © Bob Daemmrich/Stock Boston **p. 318** National Library of Medicine **p. 319** Brown Brothers **p. 321** News and Publications Service, Stanford University **p. 322** (*top*) © Will and Deni McIntyre/Science Source, Photo Researchers; (*bottom*) © Lew Merrim/Monkmeyer Press Photo Service **Fig. 11–1** From Thorndike, A. L., & Hagen, E. P. (1977). *Measurement and evaluation in psychology and education.* New York: Macmillan. Reprinted with permission of Macmillan Publishing Company. Photo of dog © Russ Kinne/Comstock **Fig. 11–2** From College Entrance Examination Board (1983 and 1990). *Sample SAT questions from 10 SATs.* Copyrights © 1983 and 1990 Educational Testing Service, Princeton, NJ. Reprinted by permission. **Fig. 11–5** Data from The College Board (1984). Figure from *The Chronical of Higher Education,* Vol. XXIX. **Fig. 11–7** From Selfe, L. (1979) *Nadia.* New York: Academic Press. Reprinted by permission. **p. 333** Courtesy Joseph F. Fagen III, Infantest Corporation **p. 334** © Hubert Worley, Jr./NYT Pictures **p. 335** © Michael O'Neill **Fig. 11–8** From Bouchard, T. J., Jr. (1982). Twins—Nature's twice-told tale. In *1983 Yearbook of Science and the Future.* Chicago: Encyclopaedia Britannica. Reprinted with permission from Encyclopaedia Britannica, Inc. **Fig. 11–9** From Fulker, D. W., DeFries, J.C., & Plomin, R. (1988). Genetic influence on general mental ability increases between infancy and middle childhood. *Nature, 336,* 767–769. **p. 340** (*both*) © Jacques

Chenet/Woodfin Camp & Associates   **p. 341** © Fujifotos/The Image Works   **Fig. 11–10** From Lewontin, R. (1976). Race and intelligence. In N. J. Block & D. Dworken (Eds.), The IQ controversy: Critical readings. New York: Pantheon. Copyright © 1976. Reprinted by permission. **Fig. 11–11** Adapted from Stevenson, H. W., et al. (1986). Mathematics achievement in Chinese, Japanese, and American children. *Science, 231,* 639–699. Copyright © 1986 by the American Association for the Advancement of Science   **p. 345** (*top*) © Frank Siteman/Stock Boston; (*bottom*) © Tomas Muscionico/Contact Press Images, Woodfin Camp & Associates

Chapter 12

Opener © François von Sury 1988/Black Star   **p. 353** (*top*) © Tony Brandenburg/Bruce Coleman, Inc.; (*bottom*) © Bob Daemmrich/The Image Works   **p. 354** (*top*) © Harlow Primate Laboratory, University of Wisconsin; (*center*) © Hazel Hankin; (*bottom left*) © Bill Stanton/ Rainbow; (*bottom right*) © David Lokey/Comstock   **Fig. 12–1** From Maslow, A. H. (1970). *Motivation and personality* (2nd ed.). New York: Harper & Row. Copyright © 1970 by Harper & Row, Publishers. Reprinted by permission.   **p. 355** Wallace Kirkland, LIFE Magazine © 1945 Time Warner Inc.   **Fig. 12–2** Adapted from Cannon, W. B. (1929). *Bodily changes in pain, hunger, fear, and rage.* New York: Branford.   **p. 356** © Howard Dratch/The Image Works   **p. 357** © Richard Howard 1980   **p. 358** Drawings by Charles Schulz; © 1989 United Features Syndicate, Inc. Reprinted by permission of UFS, Inc. **p. 359** © Lynn McAfee/Globe Photos   **Fig. 12–4** From Fallon, A. E., & Rozin, P. (1985). Sex differences in perceptions of desirable body shape. *Journal of Abnormal Psychology, 94,* 102–105.   **p. 360** Photo by Dellenbeck. Reprinted by permission of the Kinsey Institute for Research in Sex, Gender and Reproduction, Inc.   **Fig. 12–5** Adapted from Masters, W. H., & Johnson, V. E. (1966). *Human sexual response.* Boston: Little, Brown and Co. Copyright © 1966 by Little, Brown, and Co. Reprinted by permission of the publisher.   **Fig. 12–6** From Byrne, D. (1982). Predicting human sexual behavior. In A. G. Kraut, *The G. Stanley Hall Lecture Series* (Vol. 2). Copyright © 1982 by the American Psychological Association. Reprinted by permission of the author.   **p. 366** (*both*) © Joyce Culver 1990   **p. 367** © David Kryszak/Black Star **p. 369** © Nathaniel Antman/The Image Works   **p. 370** (*top*) From Bumpass, L. L., & Sweet, J. A. (1989). National estimates of combination. *Demography, 26;* 615–625, (*bottom*) © Rob Nelson 1990/Black Star **Fig. 12–7** McClelland, D. C., et al. (1953). *The achievement motive.* New York: Appleton-Century-Crofts. Reprinted with permission of Irvington Publishers, New York.   **Fig. 12–8** From Sulloway, F. J. (1990). Orthodoxy and innovation in science: The influence of birth or- der in a multivatiate context. Paper delivered to the American Association for the Advancement of Science annual meeting.   **p. 373** UPI/Bettmann Archives   **Fig. 12–9** From Spence, J. T., & Helmreich, R. L. (1983). Achievement-related motives and behavior. In J. T. Spence (Ed.), Achievement and achievement motives: Psychological and socio- logical approaches. New York: Freeman. Copyright © 1983 by W. H. Freeman and Company. Reprinted with permission.   **p. 374** © Bob Daemmrich/Stock Boston   **p. 378** © Ted Thai/TIME Magazine

Chapter 13

Opener © Dennis Cook/AP/Wide World Photos   **p. 384** © M. Grecco/Stock Boston   **p. 386** © Bernhard Gottfryd/Woodfin Camp & Associates   **Fig. 13–1** Courtesy David Raskin, University of Utah, as shown in *Science* '82, June, 24–27.   **Fig. 13–2** From Kleinmuntz, B., & Szucko, J. J. (1984). A field study of the fallability of polygraph lie detection. *Nature, 308,* 449–450. Reprinted by permission of *Nature.* Copyright © 1984 Macmillan Journals Limited.   **p. 388** © Craig Ruttle **Fig. 13–3** (*a–d*) Courtesy Dr. Paul Ekman, University of California at San Francisco   **p. 390** © Benjamin E. Boblett   **Fig. 13–4** Courtesy Dr. Paul Ekman from Eckman, P., & Friesen, W. V. (1984). *Unmasking the face* (reprint edition). Palo Alto, CA.: Consulting Psychologists Press **p. 392** Courtesy Carroll Izard, University of Delaware   **Fig. 13–5** (*a–h*) Courtesy Carroll Izard, University of Delaware   **p. 394** © Peter Vandermark/Stock Boston   **p. 395** © Focus on Sports   **Fig. 13–6**

From Dey, E. L., et al. (1991). *The American freshman: Twenty-five year trends.* Los Angeles: Higher Education Research Institute, UCLA. **Fig. 13–7** From Smith, T. W. (1979). Happiness: Time trends, seasonal variations, intersurvey differences, and other mysteries. *Social Psychology Quarterly, 42,* 18–30.   **p. 399** (*bottom left*) © Mimi Forsyth/Monkmeyer Press Photo Service; (*bottom right*) UPI/Bettmann Newsphotos   **Fig. 13–8** Adapted from Solomon, R. L. (1980). The oppo- nent-process theory of acquired motivation: The costs of pleasure and the benefits of pain. *American Psychologist, 35,* 691–712. Copyright © 1980 by the American Psychological Association. Reprinted by permis- sion of the author.   **p. 401** © Shelly Katz 1990/Black Star

Chapter 14

Opener © Robert Frerck/The Stock Market   **p. 412** Culver Pictures **Fig. 14–1** Adapted from Freud, S. (1933). *New introductory lectures on psychoanalysis.* New York: Carlton House (p. 111).   **p. 415** (*top*) © Rick Friedman/Black Star; (*bottom*) © University of Wisconsin Primate Laboratory   **p. 417** (*top, both*) the Bettmann Archive; (*bottom*) © Karsh, Ottawa/Woodfin Camp & Associates   **p. 418** © Sing-Si Schwartz/Betty Dornheim Picture Service   **p. 419** © Will and Deni McIntyre/Photo Researchers   **p. 421** © Edmund Engelman   **p. 422** (*top*) © Arthur Grace/Sygma; (*bottom*) © Rhoda Sidney/The Image Works   **Fig. 14–2** From Eysenck, S. B. G., & Eysenck, H. J. (1963). The validity of questionnaire and rating assessments of extraversion and neuroticism, and their factorial stability. *British Journal of Psychology, 54,* 51–62, Fig. 1.   **Fig 14–3** Adapted from Butcher, J. N. (1990). *The MMPI-2 in psychological treatment.* New York: Oxford University Press.   **p. 428** Ted Polumbaum/LIFE Magazine © 1968 Time Inc.   **p. 429** © Joel Gordon 1990   **p. 430** © Victor Engelbert/Photo Researchers   **p. 433** (*left*) Michael Rougier, LIFE Magazine © Time Warner Inc.; (*right*) Alfred Eisenstaedt, LIFE Magazine © Time Warner Inc.   **Fig. 14–4** Adapted fom Bandura, A. (1978). The self-system in reciprocal determinism. *American Psychologist, 33,* 344–358. Copyright © 1978 by the American Psychological Association. Adapted by permission of the author **p. 435** © Joel Gordon 1985   **p. 437** (*top*) © Joe McNally; (*bottom*) © Bob Daemmrich

Chapter 15

Opener © Joel Gordon 1989   **p. 446** © Tony Ray Jones/Magnum Photos   **Fig. 15–1** J. Otis Wheelock; courtesy Department of Library Services, American Museum of Natural History (neg. no.: 31565) **p. 449** AP/Wide World Photos   **Fig. 15–2** From Roper report 84–3, February 11–25, 1984. *Public Opinion,* August/September, 25. Reprinted with permission of American Enterprise Institute for Public Policy Research.   **Table 15–1** Adapted from Rapoport, J. L. (1989, March). The biology of obsessions and compulsions. *Scientific American,* pp. 83–89.   **p. 454** © Paul Fusco/Magnum Photos   **Fig. 15–3** Baxter, L. R. Archives of General Psychology, 44(3). Copyright © AMA **p. 457** AP/Wide World Photos   **p. 459** (*top*) AP/Wide World Photos; (*bottom*) Stephen P. Allen/Gamma Liaison   **Fig. 15–4** Bureau of the Census (1990). *Statistical abstract of the United States.* Washington, DC: Superintendent of Documents, United States Government Printing Office.   **Fig. 15–5** From National Center for Health Statistics data from Wilentz (1987).   *Time,* p. 457.   **Fig. 15–7** From Forgas, J. P., et al. (1984). The influence of mood on perceptions of social interactions. *Journal of Experimental Social Psychology, 20,* 497–513. Orlando, FL: Academic Press, Journals Division.   **Fig. 15–8** Adapted from Lewinsohn, P. M., et al. (1985). An integrative theory of depression. In S. Reiss and R. Bootzin (Eds.), *Theoretical issues in behavior therapy.* Orlando, FL: Academic Press.   **Fig. 15–9** From Perlman, D. (1990). Age differences in loneliness: A meta-analysis. Paper presented to the American Psychological Association convention.   **p. 467** (*left*) August Natterer, *Witch's Head.* The Prinzhorn Collection, University of Heidelberg; (*right*) Berthold, L., Untitled. The Prinzhorn Collection, University of Heidelberg. Photos: Krannert Museum, University of Illinois at Urbana   **p. 468** © Grunnitus/Monkmeyer Press Photo Service   **Fig. 15–10** Data from Gottesman, I. I. (1991). *Schizophrenia* *genesis: The origins of madness.* New York: Freeman.   **p. 470** Courtesy the Genain Family   **p. 471** © Phil Huber 1988/Black Star   **Fig. 15–11** Adapted from Magnusson, D. (1990). Personality research—challenges for the future. *European Journal of Personality, 4,* 1–17.

Chapter 16

Opener © Stacy Pickerell/TSW Click/Chicago Ltd.   **p. 479** (*left*) The Granger Collection; (*right*) The Bettmann Archive   **p. 481** © Paul Meredith/TSW Click/Chicago, Ltd.   **p. 482** © Nancy Bates/The Picture Cube   **p. 483** Michael Rougier, LIFE Magazine © Time Warner Inc.   **p. 485** © Susan Rosenberg/Photo Researchers   **p. 486** © Stacy Pick/Stock Boston   **Fig. 16–1** From Gilling, D., & Brightwell, R. (1982). *The human brain.* Copyright © 1982 by D. Gilling and R. Brightwell. Reprinted with permission of Facts on File, Inc., New York.   **p. 490** © Sybil Shelton/Monkmeyer Press Photo Service   **p. 493** (*left*) Courtesy University of Oregon; (*right*) Courtesy Institute for Rational-Emotive Therapy   **Fig. 16–4** From Rabin, A. S., et al. (1986). Aggregate outcome and follow-up results following self-control therapy for depression. Paper presented at the American Psychological Association convention.   **Table 16–1** Numbers and fees from Hunt, M. (1987, August 30). Navigating the therapy maze. *The New York Times Magazine,* pp. 28–49, and Gates, M. (1989, December 10). Psychiatrists not where patients are. *Grand Rapids Press* (Newhouse News Service), p. D8, and *Psychiatric News* (1989, September 1). Reported by *Behavior Today,* September 25, 1989, pp. 3–4.   **Fig. 16–5** Adapted from Smith, M. L., et al. (1980). *The benefits of psychotherapy* (p. 88) Baltimore, MD: Johns Hopkins University Press. Reprinted by permission.   **p. 501** © Mark Antman/The Image Works   **Fig. 16–6** Data from NIMH—PSC collaborative study I; (*photo*) © Natsuko Utsumi/Gamma Liaison   **p. 505** © James Wilson/Woodfin Camp & Associates

Chapter 17

Opener © Bob Daemmrich/Stock Boston   **Fig. 17–1** From The National Center for Health Statistics (1990, November 28). Advance report of final mortality statistics, 1988. *Monthly Vital Statistics Report, 39,* Table 5.   **p. 512** © Dennis Capolongo 1989/Black Star   **Fig. 17–4** From Adams, P. R., & Adams, G. R. (1984). Mount St. Helens ashfall: Evidence for a disaster stress reaction. *American Psychologist, 29,* 252–260. Copyright © 1984 by the American Psychological Association. Reprinted by permission of the authors.   **p. 516** © James A. Sugar 1990/Black Star   **p. 517** © Bill Bachman/Photo Researchers   **Fig. 17–6** From Weiss, J. M. (1977). Psychological and behavioral influences on gastrointestinal lesions in animal models. In J. D. Maser & M. E. P. Seigelman (Eds.), *Psychopathology: Experimental models.* Copyright © 1977 by W. H. Freeman and Company. All rights reserved.   **p. 521** Lennart Nilsson © Boehringer Ingelheim International GmbH   **p. 522** © Paul Fusco/Magnum Photos   **Fig. 17–10** Adapted from Safer, M. A., et al. (1979). Determinants of three stages of delay in seeking care at a medical clinic. *Medical Care, 17*(1), 11–28. Reprinted by permission of the publisher   **Fig. 17–11** From McFarland, C., Ross, M., & Decourville, N. (1989). Women's theories of menstruation and the biases in recall of menstrual symptoms. *Journal of Personality and Social Psychology, 57,* 522–531.   **Fig. 17–12** From Egbert, L. D., et al. (1964). Reduction of postoperative pain by encouragement and instruction of patients. *New England Journal of Medicine, 270,* 825–827. Reprinted by permission.   **p. 527** © Susan Lapides 1990/Design Conceptions   **p. 528** (*top*) © Southern Illinois University/Photo Researchers; (*bottom*) © Janeart 1989/The Image Bank   **Fig. 17–13** Adapted from McCann, I. L., & Holmes, D. S. (1984). Influence of aerobic exercise on depression. *Journal of Personality and Social Psychology, 46,* 1142–1147. Copyright © 1984 by the American Psychological Association. Reprinted by permission of the authors.   **Fig. 17–14** © Dan McCoy/Rainbow   **p. 531** © Steve Liss/TIME Magazine   **Fig. 17–15** From Friedman, M., & Ulmer, D. (1984). Treating type A behavior—and your heart. New York: Alfred A. Knopf, Inc. Reprinted by permission.   **p. 532** © Bob Krist 1990/Black Star   **p. 535** (*top*) © Joel Gordon 1991; (*bottom*) Reprinted courtesy of *Time Magazine.*   **Fig 17–17** From The Gallup Poll (1989). Cigarette smoking at 45-year low. *Gallup Report* No. 286, pp. 23–26.

Fig. 17–18 Data from McAlister, A., et al. (1980). Pilot study of smoking, alcohol and drug abuse prevention. *American Journal of Public Health, 70,* 719–721. Data also from Telch, M. J., et. al. (1982). Long-term follow-up of a pilot project on smoking prevention with adolescents. *Journal of Behavioral Medicine, 5,* 1–7.   **p. 539** © Lincoln Russell/Stock Boston   **Fig. 17–20** From Bray, G. A. (1969). Effect of caloric restriction on energy expenditure in obese patients. *Lancet, 2,* 397–398.   **p. 542** (*left*) "The Garden of Love" (detail), Peter Paul Rubens, The Prado, Madrid/The Bridgeman Art Library/ Superstock; (*right*) © J. Baes/Photo Researchers   **Fig. 17–21** From Brownell, K. D., & Jeffery, R. W. (1987). Improving long-term weight loss: Pushing the limits of treatment. *Behavior Therapy, 18,* 353–374.   **Fig. 17–22** From Dietz, W. H., Jr., & Gortmaker, S. L. (1985). Do we fatten our children at the television set? Obesity and television viewing in children and adolescents. *Pediatrics, 75,* 807–812. Reproduced by permission.   **Fig. 17–23** From Herman, C. P., & Mack, D. (1975). Restrained and unrestrained eating. *Journal of Personality, 43*(4), 647–660. Copyright © 1975 Duke University Press.

Chapter 18

Opener © Alexandra Avakian/Woodfin Camp & Associates   **p. 553** © Jeff Dunn/The Picture Cube   **p. 554** AP/Wide World Photos   **p. 556** © Thomas Hopker/Magnum Photos   **Fig. 18–2** From Philips, D. P. (1974). The influence of suggestion on suicide: Substantive and theoretical implications of the Wetther effect. *American Sociological Review, 39,* 340–354. Reprinted by permission of the American Sociological Association.   **p. 559** © William Vanderviert and Scientific American   **p. 560** Courtesy Graduate School and University Center of the City University of New York   **p. 561** AP/Wide World Photos   **Fig. 18–4** Data from Milgram, L. (1974). *Obedience to authority.* Copyright © 1974 by S. Milgram. Reprinted by permission of Harper & Row.   **p. 563** © Focus on Sports   **p. 564** © Keystone Press Agency Inc.   **Fig. 18–5** Data from Myers, D. G., & Bishop, G. D. (1970). Discussion effects on racial attitudes. *Science,* 778–779. Copyright © 1988 by the American Association for the Advancement of Science.   **p. 567** Margaret Bourke-White, LIFE Magazine © 1946 Time Warner Inc.   **p. 569** (*top*) © Presse-Sports; (*bottom*) © Serge de Sazo/Rapho, Photo Researchers   **Fig. 18–6** From Anderson, C. A., & Anderson, D. C. (1984). Ambient temperature and violent crime: Tests on the linear and curvilinear hypotheses. *Journal of Personality and Social Psychology, 46,* 91–97   **Fig. 18–7** Adapted from Malmuth, N. M. (1989). Sexually violent media, thought patterns, and anti-social behavior. In G. Comstock (Ed.), *Public communication and behavior,* Vol. 2. San Diego, CA: Academic Press.   **p. 574** © Joel Gordon   **Fig. 18–8** From Darley, J. M., & Latané, B. (1968b, December). When will people help in a crisis? *Psychology Today,* pp. 54–57, 70–71. Reprinted with permission from *Psychology Today Magazine.* Copyright © 1968 (Sussex Publishers, Inc.).   **Fig. 18–9** From Darley, J. M., & Latané, B. (1968a). Bystander intervention in emergencies: Diffusion of responsibility. *Journal of Personality and Social Psychology, 8,* 377–383.   **p. 576** © Akos Szilvasi/Stock Boston   **p. 577** © Janet Kelly, Reading Eagle/Times   **p. 578** (*top*) © Joel Gordon 1990; (*bottom*) © Rex USA   **p. 579** (*top*) Reuters/Bettmann Newsphotos; (*bottom*) © James Kamp/Black Star   **p. 580** (*left*) © Margaret Gowan/Tony Stone Worldwide; (*center*) © Victor Englebert/Photo Researchers; (*right*) © Nancy Brown/The Image Bank   **p. 581** © Wildlight, Johns/Black Star   **p. 582** (*left*) © Henri Cartier-Bresson/Magnum Photos; (*right*) © Renee Lynn/Photo Researchers

Chapter 19

Opener © David Austen/Stock Boston   **p. 588** (*left*) © Joe Carini/The Image Works; (*center*) © Robert Caputo/Stock Boston; (*right*) © Brett Froomer/The Image Bank   **p. 589** (*top left*) © Willie L. Hill, Jr./Stock Boston; (*top center & right center*) © Sally Cassidy/The Picture Cube; (*top right*) © Lawrence Migdale/Stock Boston; (*bottom right*) © Owen Franken/Stock Boston   **p. 590** (*top*) © Fujifotos/The Image Works; (*bottom*) © Gary Rogers/The Image Bank   **p. 593** © Charles Harbutt/Actuality   **p. 595** Courtesy James Jones   **p. 596** (*top*) © David

Austen/Stock Boston; (*bottom*) © Jonathan Wenk/Black Star   **Fig. 19–1** From Vandenberg, S. G., & Kuse, A. R. (1978). Mental rotations, a group test of three-dimensional spatial visualization. *Perceptual and Motor Skills, 47,* 599–604, Fig. 1. Reprinted with permission of authors and publisher.   **p. 599** © Bob Daemmrich/Stock Boston   **p. 600** © Gale Zucker/Stock Boston   **p. 603** © National Museum of Natural History/Photo Researchers   **p. 604** (*left*) © L. Townshend/The Picture Cube; (*right*) © Lindsay Hebberd/Woodfin Camp & Associates   **Fig. 19–3** From "Women in parliament. Keeping a sense of disproportion." *The Economist* (1987, February 28), *302,* 47–48.   **Fig. 19–4** From Stiles, D. A., Gibbons, J. L., & Schnellmann, J. G. (1990). Opposite-sex ideal in the U.S.A. and Mexico as perceived by young adolescents. *Journal of Cross-Cultural Psychology, 21,* no. 2, 180–199.   **Fig. 19–5** From Dey, E L. (1991). *The American freshman: Twenty-five year trends.* Los Angeles: Higher Education Research Institute, UCLA.   **Fig. 19–6** From Turner, S. E., & Bowen, W. G. (1990). The flight from the arts and sciences: Trends in degrees conferred. *Science, 250,* 517–521.   **Fig. 19–7** From Robinson, J. P. (1988, December). Who's doing the housework? *American Demographics,* pp. 24–28, 63.   **p. 610** © Elsa Peterson/Design Conceptions   **Fig. 19–8** From Gallup, G., Jr., & Hugick, L. (1990, June). Racial tolerance grows, progress on racial equality less evident. *Gallup Poll Monthly,* pp. 23–32, and Niemi, R. G., Moeller, J., & Smith, T. W. (1989). *Trends in public opinion: A compendium of survey data.* New York: Greenwood Press, and Smith, T. W. (1990). Adult sexual behavior in 1989: Number of partners, frequency, and risk. *General Social Survey Topic Report No. 18,* National Opinion Research Center, University of Chicago.   **p. 613** © Michael S. Yamashita 1987/Woodfin Camp & Associates   **p. 617** © Bob Daemmrich/Stock Boston

Appendix

p. 624 (*top*) The Bettmann Archive; (*bottom*) © Tom Pantages, courtesy the Harvard College Library   **p. 632** © Focus on Sports   **Fig. A–8** Adapted from Ross, B. (1987). In K. McKean, The orderly pursuit of pure disorder. *Discover,* January, 72–81.

Name Index

Scribner, S., 99
Sechrest, L. B., 388
Segal, M. E., 565
Segal, N. L., 88, 337–338, 541, 604
Segall, M. H., 75, 173, 601, 606, 612, 621
Seginer, R., 607
Segmen, J., 262
Seibel, C. A., 571
Seidenberg, M. S., 308
Seligman, C., 246
Seligman, M. E. P., 192, 200, 384,
    436–437, 443, 458, 463–464, 495, 593
Selin, C. E., 454
Selye, H., 513–514, 546–547
Selzer, S. C., 333
Semple, W. E., 468
Senden, M., 174
Seneca, 109, 239, 259, 395, 398, 430, 437,
    559, 569, 583
Senulis, J. A., 385
Sexter, M., 391
Shadish, W. R., Jr., 487
Shaffer, D., 558
Shahidullah, S., 52
Shakespeare, W., 184, 192, 285, 394, 412,
    416, 449, 458, 460, 581
Shaman, P., 110
Shanahan, R. H., 343
Shannon, F. T., 77
Shapiro, A., 194
Shapiro, C. M., 195
Shapiro, D., 500
Shapiro, D. A., 500
Sharpley, C. F., 502
Shaughnessy, J. J., 277, 636
Shaver, P. R., 79
Shaw, B. F., 494
Shaw, G. B., 219, 582
Shaw, H. L., 310
Shaw, S., 182
Shea, T., 499
Shear, J., 202
Shedler, J., 217
Sheehan, K., 391
Sheehan, P. W., 530
Sheehan, S., 466, 477
Shekelle, R. B., 522
Sheldon, W. H., 422
Shepard, R. N., 21, 166, 171–172, 179, 187
Shereshevskii, 253
Sherif, M., 557–558, 560, 562, 616–617
Sherman, A. R., 490
Sherman, S. J., 288, 534–535
Sherrington, C., 30
Sherry, D., 271
Sherwood, R., 286
Shettleworth, S. J., 244
Shevell, S. K., 277
Shirley, M., 574
Shneidman, E., 461
Shoda, Y., 101, 239
Shotland, R. L., 574, 602
Showers, C., 437
Shrager, E. E., 543
Shrout, P. E., 460, 463
Shulman, D., 391
Shumate, M., 153
Siciliano, C., 22

Siegel, J. M., 526, 532
Siegel, K., 367
Siegel, L. S., 74
Siegel, R. K., 212–215, 217, 219, 223
Sigmund, B. B., 523
Signorielli, N., 570–571
Siksorski, L., 110
Silberstein, L. R., 359–360
Silver, M., 562
Silver, R. C., 122
Silverman, P. S., 204
Silverstone, B., 127
Silverton, L., 474
Simmons, R. G., 97
Simon, H., 300
Simon, H. A., 263
Simon, T., 5, 319–320
Simons, E. L., 587
Simonton, D. K., 116
Simpson, J. A., 79
Sing, H., 195
Singer, D. G., 571
Singer, J. E., 148, 404
Singer, J. L., 201–202, 499, 571
Singh, J. V., 377
Sinha, Y., 553
Sinnott, M. A., 519
Sjöstrum, L., 540
Skevington, S., 99
Skinner, B. F., 236–238, 240–242,
    244–246, 249–251, 305, 462
Sklar, L. S., 521
Skodol, A. E., 455, 460, 463
Skov, R. B., 288
Slapion-Foote, J., 601
Slater, A., 67
Slavin, R. E., 617
Slinkard, L. A., 536–537
Slochower, J., 358
Sloss, E. M., 534
Slovic, P., 21, 294–295
Smart, R. G., 217
Smith, A., 47, 468, 614
Smith, D., 480
Smith, J., 115
Smith, M. B., 434
Smith, M. C., 205
Smith, M. L., 498–500
Smith, P. B., 377
Smith, T., 611
Smith, T. W., 361, 366, 398, 520, 535, 607,
    611
Snarey, J. R., 100
Snodgrass, M. A., 465
Snodgrass, S. E., 392
Snowden, R., 526
Snyder, D., 572
Snyder, M., 474, 566
Snyder, S. H., 30–31, 223, 503–504
Snyderman, M., 342
Soares, M. P., 598
Sobal, J., 539
Sobel, D., 547
Sobel, M., 595
Socrates, 220
Sokoll, G. R., 385
Sokolski, K., 454
Solomon, M., 579

Solomon, R. L., 400
Solomon, Z., 515
Sommer, B., 526
Sommer, R., 590
Sontag, S., 523
Sophocles, 157
Sorenson, S. B., 453
Soskis, D. A., 205
Sotsky, S. M., 499
Sowell, T., 618
Spangenberg, E. R., 17
Spanos, N. P., 203, 205–208, 223, 457
Spearman, C., 329, 347
Specht, J. C., 434
Spector, P. E., 377
Spelke, E., 209
Spence, D., 609
Spence, J. T., 373
Sperling, G., 256, 257
Sperry, R. W., 48–51, 143, 176, 220
Spiegel, D., 522
Spielberger, C., 520
Spiess, W. F. J., 365
Spitzberg, B. H., 465
Spitzer, R. L., 455, 474
Spradley, J. P., 591
Sprecher, S., 579
Spring, B., 537
Springer, S. P., 52, 57
Spuhler, J. N., 341
Squire, L. R., 270–271
Squire, S., 269, 505
Sroufe, L. A., 80
Stack, S., 471
Stafford, F. P., 343, 608
Stagg, A. A., 115
Stangor, C., 118
Stanley-Hagan, M., 81
Stanovich, K. E., 636
Stanton, J. L., 537
Starker, S., 194
Starr, A., 443
Stattin, H., 97
Staub, E., 556, 585
Steel, R. P., 376
Steele, C., 341, 343, 569
Steele, C. M., 210
Steen, D., 40
Steer, R. A., 451, 461
Steers, R. M., 381
Stein, D. G., 47
Stein, J. A., 125
Stein, M., 363, 522
Steinberg, L., 104
Steinem, G., 574
Stellar, E., 356, 543
Stengel, E., 460
Stenstrom, R. J., 207
Stephens, P. M., 516
Stephens, T., 529
Stepper, S., 391
Stern, L., 391
Stern, M., 181
Stern, W., 320
Sternberg, R. J., 328, 330–331, 335, 582,
    585
Stevenson, H. W., 335, 341–342, 347, 598
Stevenson, M. R., 81, 604

Subject Index